Fodor's 98

Canada

D1280647

The complete guide, thoroughly up-to-date

Packed with details that will make your trip

The must-see sights, off and on the beaten path

What to see, what to skip

Mix-and-match vacation itineraries

City strolls, countryside adventures

Smart lodging and dining options

Transportation tips, distances and directions

Key contacts, savvy travel tips

When to go, what to pack

Clear, accurate, easy-to-use maps

Books to read, videos to watch

Fodor's Travel Publications, Inc.
New York • Toronto • London • Sydney • Auckland
www.fodors.com/

Fodor's Canada

EDITOR: Linda Cabasin

Editorial Contributors: Rosemary Allerston, Robert Andrews, David Brown, Susan Brown, Audra Epstein, Dorothy Guinan, Ed Kirby, Wendy Lindsay, Helga Loverseed, Jens Nielsen, Melissa Rivers, Heidi Sarna, Helayne Schiff, M.T. Schwartzman (Gold Guide editor), Tina Sebert, Dinah Spritzer, Don Thacker, Paul Waters, Julie Watson, Ana Watts, Sara Waxman

Editorial Production: Linda K. Schmidt

Maps: David Lindroth, *cartographer*; Robert Blake, *map editor*

Design: Fabrizio La Rocca, *creative director*; Guido Caroti, *associate art director*; Jolie Novak, *photo editor*

Production/Manufacturing: Rebecca Zeiler

Cover Photograph: Peter Guttman

Copyright

Special Sales

Fodor's Travel Publications are available at special discounts for bulk purchases for sales promotions or premiums. Special editions, including personalized covers, excerpts of existing guides, and corporate imprints, can be created in large quantities for special needs. For more information, contact your local bookseller or write to Special Markets, Fodor's Travel Publications, 201 East 50th Street, New York, NY 10022. Inquiries from Canada should be directed to your local Canadian bookseller or sent to Random House of Canada, Ltd., Marketing Department, 1265 Aerowood Drive, Mississauga, Ontario L4W 1B9. Inquiries from the United Kingdom should be sent to Fodor's Travel Publications, 20 Vauxhall Bridge Road, London, England SW1V 2SA.

PRINTED IN THE UNITED STATES OF AMERICA

10 9 8 7 6 5 4 3 2 1

CONTENTS

ON THE ROAD WITH FODOR'S

WE'RE ALWAYS THRILLED to get letters from readers, especially one like this:

It took us an hour to decide what book to buy and we now know we picked the best one. Your book was wonderful, easy to follow, very accurate, and good on pointing out eating places, informal as well as formal. When we saw other people using your book, we would look at each other and smile.

Our editors and writers are deeply committed to making every Fodor's guide "the best one"—not only accurate but always charming, brimming with sound recommendations and solid ideas, right on the mark in describing restaurants and hotels, and full of fascinating facts that make you view what you've traveled to see in a rich new light.

About Our Writers

Our success in achieving our goals—and in helping to make your trip the best of all possible vacations—is a credit to the hard work of our extraordinary writers.

Travel junkie **Melissa Rivers,** updater of the British Columbia and Vancouver chapters, lives in Texas and travels throughout the Pacific Northwest and the Caribbean on assignments for Fodor's. In updating the Canadian Rockies chapter, Edmonton writer **Don Thacker** traveled 7,000 kilometers (4,300 miles) and managed to escape numerous avalanches. **Jens Nielsen,** a travel writer based in Saskatoon, Saskatchewan, updated the Prairie Provinces chapter. **Wendy Lindsay,** who worked on Ontario and Toronto, is a much-traveled editor, photographer, and travel writer based in Oakville and Guelph, Ontario. She has a fondness for northwestern Ontario after living in Thunder Bay for 10 Years. Columnist and cookbook and restaurant guide author **Sara Waxman** shares insider's knowledge in the Toronto dining section.

Paul Waters, travel editor of *The Gazette* in Montréal, is the expert who handled the Montréal chapter and also wrote the book's new introduction. **Dorothy Guinan,** who updated the Québec City chapter, is a researcher for the Montréal *Gazette* and a freelance writer. She has lived in Québec City since 1985. **Helga Loverseed,** a freelance journalist and photographer based in Magog in the Eastern Townships, shared her insights in the Québec province chapter. She also writes columns for the Montréal *Gazette* and the Chicago *Sun-Times.* Award-winning Fredericton columnist **Ana Watts** updated the chapter on her province, New Brunswick, providing fresh material on new attractions and adventures. **Ed Kirby,** a Newfoundland and Labrador tourism writer who lives in St. John's, carefully combed through his chapter. Food and travel writer **Julie Watson,** who updated Nova Scotia and Prince Edward Island, lives on Prince Edward Island and tours the region researching articles and books such as her latest: *Ship Wrecks and Seafaring Tales of Prince Edward Island* and *A Fine Catch Seafood Cookbook.* Editor of the magazine *Up here, Life in Canada's North* for the past 10 years, Yellowknife resident **Rosemary Allerston,** who updated the Northwest Territories section of the Wilderness Canada chapter, knows what's going on in the region. Award-winning writer and film scout **Tina Sebert,** updater of the Yukon section, lives in Whitehorse. She leads tours of the region and enjoys backpacking and rafting the Yukon River. Writer **Susan Brown,** based in Washington State, updated the Gold Guide material on Canada to make your travels even easier.

New This Year

To give you a feeling for Canada today, Paul Waters has written a new introduction, "A Grand Place," that discusses the dynamics of the country he describes as an "unfinished symphony." His new Pleasures and Pastimes section covers such subjects as dining, the great outdoors, shopping, and Canadian winters. Much of Canada, especially British Columbia, is experiencing a boom in adventure travel. Melissa Rivers has added adventure trips and operators in the Vancouver and British Columbia chapters; she also expanded coverage of the popular Gulf Islands, near

Vancouver Island. In the Québec City chapter, Dorothy Guinan revamped the dining section to reflect the latest options and trends. The New Brunswick chapter reflects the increased number of adventure trips offered in the province, as well as new dining and lodging choices.

And this year, Fodor's joins Rand Mc-Nally, the world's largest commercial mapmaker to bring you a detailed color map of Canada. Just detach it along the perforation and drop it in your tote bag.

We're also proud to announce that the American Society of Travel Agents has endorsed Fodor's as its guidebook of choice. ASTA is the world's largest and most influential travel trade association, operating in more than 170 countries, with 27,000 members pledged to adhere to a strict code of ethics reflecting the Society's motto, "Integrity in Travel." ASTA shares Fodor's devotion to providing smart, honest travel information and advice to travelers, and we've long recommended that our readers consult ASTA member agents for the experience and professionalism they bring to the table.

On the Web, check out Fodor's site (www.fodors.com/) for information on major destinations around the world and travel-savvy interactive features. The Web site also lists the 85-plus stations nationwide that carry the *Fodor's Travel Show,* a live call-in program that airs every weekend. Tune in to hear guests discuss their wonderful adventures—or call in to get answers for your most pressing travel questions.

How to Use This Book

Organization

Up front is the **Gold Guide,** an easy-to-use section divided alphabetically by topic. Under each listing you'll find tips and information that will help you accomplish what you need to in Canada. You'll also find addresses and telephone numbers of organizations and companies that offer destination-related services and detailed information and publications. Here, too, you'll find a books and videos section with recommended pretrip reading and some movies on tape with Canada as a backdrop.

The first chapter in the guide, Destination: Canada helps get you in the mood for your trip. New and Noteworthy cues you in on trends and happenings, What's Where gets you oriented, Pleasures and Pastimes describes the activities and sights that really make Canada unique, Fodor's Choice showcases our top picks, and Festivals and Seasonal Events alerts you to special events you'll want to seek out.

Chapters in *Canada '98* are arranged geographically from west to east. Each city chapter begins with an Exploring section subdivided by neighborhood; each subsection recommends a walking or driving tour and lists sights in alphabetical order. Each regional chapter is divided by geographical area; within each area, towns are covered in logical geographical order, and attractive stretches of road and minor points of interest between them are indicated by the designation *En Route.* Throughout, Off the Beaten Path sights appear after the places from which they are most easily accessible. And within town sections, all restaurants and lodgings are grouped together.

To help you decide what to visit in the time you have, all chapters begin with recommended itineraries; you can mix and match those from several chapters to create a complete vacation. The A-to-Z section that ends all chapters covers getting there and getting around. It also provides helpful contacts and resources.

Icons and Symbols

★	Our special recommendations
✕	Restaurant
🏠	Lodging establishment
✕🏠	Lodging establishment whose restaurant warrants a special trip
🏕	Campgrounds
🦆	Good for kids (rubber duckie)
☞	Sends you to another section of the guide for more information
✉	Address
☎	Telephone number
☉	Opening and closing times
💲	Admission prices (those we give apply to adults; substantially reduced fees are almost always available for children, students, and senior citizens)

Numbers in white and black circles that appear on the maps, in the margins, and within the tours correspond to one another.

Currency

Unless otherwise stated, prices are quoted in Canadian dollars.

Dining and Lodging

The restaurants and lodgings we list are the cream of the crop in each price range. Price charts appear in the Pleasures and Pastimes section that follows each chapter introduction or, in city chapters, with the dining and lodging sections.

Hotel Facilities

We always list the facilities that are available—but we don't specify whether they cost extra: When pricing accommodations, always ask what's included. In addition, assume that all rooms have private baths unless otherwise noted.

Assume that hotels operate on the **European Plan** (EP, with no meals) unless we note that they use the **American Plan** (AP, with all meals), the **Modified American Plan** (MAP, with breakfast and dinner daily), or the **Continental Plan** (CP, with a Continental breakfast daily).

Restaurant Reservations and Dress Codes

Reservations are always a good idea; we note only when they're essential or when they are not accepted. Book as far ahead as you can, and reconfirm when you get to town. Unless otherwise noted, the restaurants listed are open daily for lunch and dinner. We mention dress only when men are required to wear a jacket or a jacket and tie. Look for an overview of local habits in the Pleasures and Pastimes section that follows each chapter introduction or in city chapter dining sections.

Credit Cards

The following abbreviations are used: **AE**, American Express; **D**, Discover; **DC**, Diners Club; **MC**, MasterCard; and **V**, Visa.

Don't Forget to Write

You can use this book in the confidence that all prices and opening times are based on information supplied to us at press time; Fodor's cannot accept responsibility for any errors. Time inevitably brings changes, so always confirm information when it matters—especially if you're making a detour to visit a specific place. In addition, when making reservations be sure to mention if you have a disability or are traveling with children, if you prefer a private bath or a certain type of bed, or if you have specific dietary needs or other concerns.

Were the restaurants we recommended as described? Did our hotel picks exceed your expectations? Did you find a museum we recommended a waste of time? If you have complaints, we'll look into them and revise our entries when the facts warrant it. If you've discovered a special place that we haven't included, we'll pass the information along to our correspondents and have them check it out. So send us your feedback, positive *and* negative: E-mail us at editors@fodors.com (specifying the name of the book on the subject line) or write the Canada editor at Fodor's, 201 East 50th Street, New York, New York 10022. Have a wonderful trip!

Karen Cure
Editorial Director

Canada

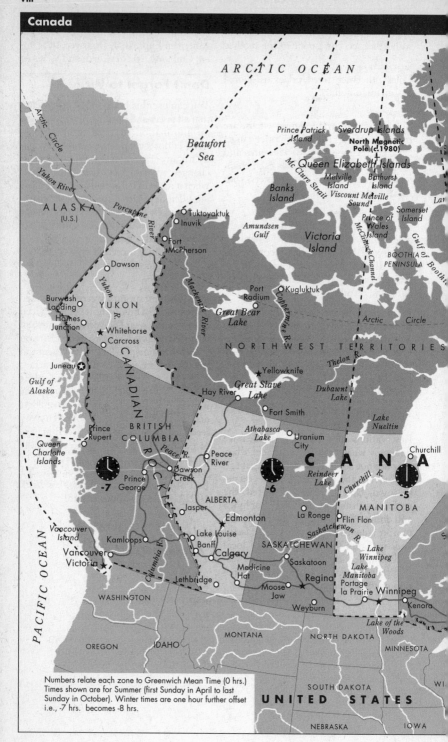

ARCTIC OCEAN

Beaufort Sea

Prince Patrick Island

Sverdrup Islands

North Magnetic Pole (c.1980)

Arctic Circle

Yukon River

ALASKA (U.S.)

Porcupine River

Queen Elizabeth Islands

McClure Strait

Melville Island

Bathurst Island

Viscount Melville Sound

Prince of Wales Island

Somerset Island

Lar

BOOTHIA PENINSULA

Gulf of Boothi

Banks Island

Amundsen Gulf

Victoria Island

McClintock Channel

Tuktoyaktuk

Inuvik

Fort McPherson

Dawson

Yukon R.

YUKON

Mackenzie River

Port Radium

Kugluktuk

Great Bear Lake

Coppermine River

Arctic Circle

Burwash Landing

Haines Junction

★ Whitehorse

Carcross

CANADIAN

Juneau ✪

Gulf of Alaska

Hay River

★ Yellowknife

Great Slave Lake

Fort Smith

N O R T H W E S T   T E R R I T O R I E S

Thelon R.

Dubawnt Lake

Lake Nueltin

Prince Rupert

BRITISH COLUMBIA

ROCKIES

Peace R.

Peace River

Athabasca Lake

Uranium City

C A N A

Churchill

Queen Charlotte Islands

Dawson Creek

Reindeer Lake

Churchill R.

⊘ **-7**

⊘ **-6**

⊘ **-5**

Prince George

Jasper

ALBERTA

Edmonton

La Ronge

Flin Flon

MANITOBA

Saskatchewan R.

Vancouver Island

Kamloops

Lake Louise

Banff

Columbia R.

Calgary

SASKATCHEWAN

Saskatoon

Lake Winnipeg

Lake Manitoba

Vancouver

Victoria ★

PACIFIC OCEAN

Medicine Hat

Lethbridge

Moose Jaw

Regina ★

Portage la Prairie

Winnipeg

Kenora

WASHINGTON

Weyburn

Lake of the Woods

OREGON

IDAHO

MONTANA

NORTH DAKOTA

MINNESOTA

WI

Numbers relate each zone to Greenwich Mean Time (0 hrs.)
Times shown are for Summer (first Sunday in April to last
Sunday in October). Winter times are one hour further offset
i.e., -7 hrs. becomes -8 hrs.

SOUTH DAKOTA

U N I T E D   S T A T E S

NEBRASKA

IOWA

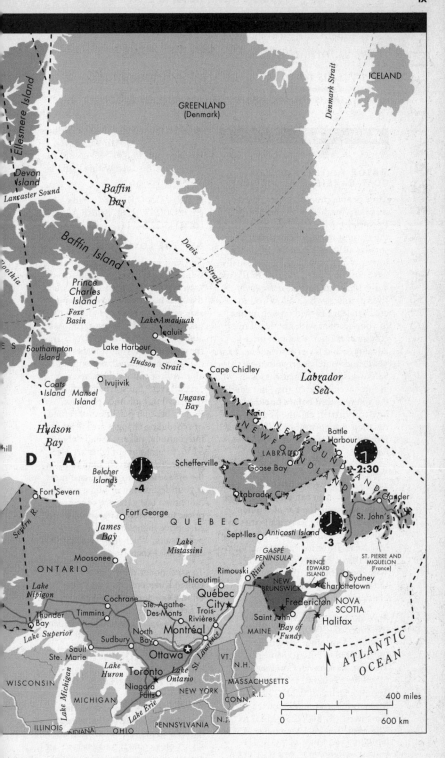

SMART TRAVEL TIPS A TO Z

*Basic Information on Traveling in Canada,
Savvy Tips to Make Your Trip a Breeze, and
Companies and Organizations to Contact*

A

AIR TRAVEL

MAJOR AIRLINE OR LOW-COST CARRIER?

Most people choose a flight based on price. Yet there are other issues to consider. Major airlines offer the greatest number of departures; smaller airlines—including regional, low-cost and no-frill airlines—usually have a more limited number of flights daily. Major airlines have frequent-flyer partners, which allow you to credit mileage earned on one airline to your account with another. Low-cost airlines offer a definite price advantage and fewer restrictions, such as advance-purchase requirements. Safety-wise, low-cost carriers as a group have a good history, but **check the safety record before booking** any low-cost carrier; call the Federal Aviation Administration's Consumer Hotline (☞ Airline Complaints, *below*).

With the liberalizing of bilateral air agreements between the United States and Canada, you can **take advantage of an increased number of regular flights** from many American cities to most major Canadian cities, including Montréal, Toronto, Vancouver, Victoria, Calgary, Edmonton, Regina, Winnipeg, Thunder Bay, London, Ottawa, Québec City, Saint John, Halifax, and Yarmouth.

➤ MAJOR AIRLINES: **Air Canada** (☎ 800/776–3000) to Montréal, Toronto, Vancouver. **American** (☎ 800/433–7300) to Montréal, Toronto, Vancouver. **Continental** (☎ 800/525–0280) to Montréal, Toronto. **Delta** (800/221–1212) to Montréal, Toronto, Vancouver. **Northwest** (☎ 800/225–2525) to Montréal, Toronto, Vancouver. **TWA** (☎ 800/221–2000) to Toronto. **United** (☎ 800/722–5243) to Montréal, Toronto, Vancouver. **US Airways** (☎ 800/428–4322) to Montréal, Toronto.

➤ SMALLER AIRLINES: **Alaska Airlines** (☎ 800/426–0333) to Vancouver. **Horizon Air** (☎ 800/547–9308) to Vancouver. Also *see* Within Canada, *below.*

➤ FROM THE U.K.: **Air Canada** (☎ 0990/247–226). **British Airways** (☎ 0345/222–111).

GET THE LOWEST FARE

The least-expensive airfares to Canada are priced for round-trip travel. Major airlines usually require that you **book far in advance and stay at least seven days** and no more than 30 to get the lowest fares. Ask about "ultrasaver" fares, which are the cheapest; they must be booked 90 days in advance and are nonrefundable. A little more expensive are "supersaver" fares, which require only a 30-day advance purchase. Remember that penalties for refunds or scheduling changes are stiffer for international tickets, usually about $150. International flights are also sensitive to the season: **plan to fly in the off season** for the cheapest fares. If your destination or home city has more than one gateway, **compare prices to and from different airports.** Also price flights scheduled for off-peak hours, which may be significantly less expensive.

To save money on flights from the United Kingdom and back, **look into an APEX or Super-PEX ticket.** APEX tickets must be booked in advance and have certain restrictions. Super-PEX tickets can be purchased at the airport on the day of departure—subject to availability.

DON'T STOP UNLESS YOU MUST

When you book, **look for nonstop flights** and **remember that "direct" flights stop at least once.** International flights on a country's flag carrier are almost always nonstop; U.S. airlines often fly direct. Try to **avoid connecting flights,** which require a change of plane. Two airlines may jointly operate a connecting flight, so ask if your airline operates every segment—you may find that your preferred carrier flies you only part of the way.

USE AN AGENT

Travel agents, especially those who specialize in finding the lowest fares (☞ Discounts & Deals, *below*), can be especially helpful when booking a plane ticket. When you're quoted a price, **ask your agent if the price is likely to get any lower.** Good agents know the seasonal fluctuations of airfares and can usually anticipate a sale or fare war. However, waiting can be risky: The fare could go *up* as seats become scarce, and you may wait so long that your preferred flight sells out. A wait-and-see strategy works best if your plans are flexible, but if you must arrive and depart on certain dates, don't delay.

CHECK WITH CONSOLIDATORS

Consolidators buy tickets for scheduled flights at reduced rates from the airlines then sell them at prices that beat the best fare available directly from the airlines, usually without advance restrictions. Sometimes you can even get your money back if you need to return the ticket. Carefully read the fine print detailing penalties for changes and cancellations, and **confirm your consolidator reservation with the airline.**

➤ CONSOLIDATORS: **United States Air Consolidators Association** (✉ 925 L St., Suite 220, Sacramento, CA 95814, ☎ 916/441–4166, ℻ 916/441–3520).

AVOID GETTING BUMPED

Airlines routinely overbook planes, knowing that not everyone with a ticket will show up, but sometimes everyone does. When that happens, airlines ask for volunteers to give up their seats. In return these volunteers usually get a certificate for a free flight and are rebooked on the next flight out. If there are not enough volunteers the airline must choose who will be denied boarding. The first to get bumped are passengers who checked in late and those flying on discounted tickets, so **get to the gate and check in as early as possible,** especially during peak periods.

Always **bring a photo ID to the airport.** You may be asked to show it before you are allowed to check in.

ENJOY THE FLIGHT

For better service, **fly smaller or regional carriers,** which often have higher passenger-satisfaction ratings. Sometimes you'll find leather seats, more legroom, and better food.

For more legroom, **request an emergency-aisle seat;** don't however, sit in the row in front of the emergency aisle or in front of a bulkhead, where seats may not recline.

If you don't like airline food, **ask for special meals when booking.** These can be vegetarian, low-cholesterol, or kosher, for example.

Some carriers have prohibited smoking throughout their systems; others allow smoking only on certain routes or even certain departures from that route, so **contact your carrier regarding its smoking policy.**

COMPLAIN IF NECESSARY

If your baggage goes astray or your flight goes awry, complain right away. Most carriers require that you file a claim immediately.

➤ AIRLINE COMPLAINTS: U.S. Department of Transportation **Aviation Consumer Protection Division** (✉ C-75, Washington, DC 20590, ☎ 202/366–2220). **Federal Aviation Administration (FAA) Consumer Hotline** (☎ 800/322–7873).

WITHIN CANADA

Regularly scheduled flights to every major city and to most smaller cities are available on Air Canada or Canadian Airlines International, the two major domestic carriers, or the domestic carriers associated with them. The smaller airlines can also be contacted through their parent carrier's (Air Canada or Canadian Airlines) toll-free numbers or at local numbers within each of the many cities they serve.

You should check with the regional tourist agencies for charter companies and with the District Controller of Air Services in the territorial (and provincial) capitals for the locations of air bases that allow private flights and for regulations. Private pilots should obtain information from the Canada Map Office.

➤ AIRLINES: **Air Canada** (☎ 800/776–3000) operates in every province. **Canadian Airlines International** (☎ 800/426–7000). **Air Alliance** (☎ 514/393–3333) and **Inter–Canadien** (☎ 514/847–2211) serve Québec; **Air Atlantic** (☎ 902/427–5500) flies in the Atlantic region; **Air BC** (☎ 604/688–5515) and **Canadian Regional** (☎ 604/279–6611) serve British Columbia and Alberta with extended service out of Portland and Seattle; **Air Nova** (☎ 902/429–7111) serves Atlantic Canada; and **Air Ontario** (☎ 416/925–2311) serves the Ontario region. **Canadian North** (☎ 204/632–1250) and **NWT Air** (☎ 403/423–1222) service communities in the Yukon and Northwest Territories.

➤ INFORMATION FOR PRIVATE PILOTS: The **Canada Map Office**, (✉ 615 Booth St., Ottawa, K1A 0E9, ☎ 800/465–6277) has the "Canada Flight Supplement" (lists of airports with Canada Customs services) as well as aeronautical charts.

AIRPORTS & TRANSFERS

The major gateways to Canada are Montréal's **Dorval International Airport** (for U.S. and domestic flights) and **Mirabel International Airport** (for other international flights), Toronto's **Lester B. Pearson International Airport,** and **Vancouver International Airport** in Vancouver.

Flying time to Montréal is 1½ hours from New York, 2 hours from Chicago, 6 hours from Los Angeles, 6½ hours from London. To Toronto: 1½ hours from New York and Chicago, 4½ hours from Los Angeles. To Vancouver: 6½ hours from Montréal, 4 hours from Chicago, 2½ hours from Los Angeles.

➤ AIRPORT INFORMATION: In Montréal, **Dorval Airport** (☎ 514/633–3105) and **Mirabel International Airport** (☎ 514/476–3010). In Toronto, **Lester B. Pearson International Airport** (☎ 416/247–7678). In Vancouver, **Vancouver International Airport** (☎ 604/276–6101).

B

BOOKS AND VIDEOS

Reading a book or watching a movie about Canada can enhance your travel experience.

FICTION

Mordecai Richler's *St. Urbain's Horseman* and *The Apprenticeship of Duddy Kravitz* (made into a movie starring Richard Dreyfus) are classics about growing up Jewish in Montréal. Margaret Atwood, a prolific poet and novelist, is regarded as a stateswoman of sorts in her native Canada. Her novel *Cat's Eye* is set in northern Canada and Toronto. Alice Munro writes about small-town life in Ontario in *The Progress of Love.* The mordant wit of Robertson Davies lovingly skewers Canadian academic life in works such as *The Deptford Trilogy* and *The Lyre of Orpheus. Northern Lights,* by Howard Norman, focuses on a child's experiences growing up in Manitoba and, later, Toronto. Howard Engel's mystery series follows the adventures of Bennie Cooperman, a Toronto-based detective; *The Suicide Murders* is especially compelling. Jack Hodgin's *Spit Delaney's Island* is peopled with loggers, construction workers, and other rural Canadians. Joy Kogawa's first novel, *Obasan,* tells about the Japanese community of Canada during World War II. *Medicine River* is a collection of short stories by Native American writer Thomas King. For an excellent view of New Brunswick, especially the famed salmon-fishing region called the Miramichi, look for the humorous books *The Americans Are Coming* and *The Last Tasmanian* by local author Herb Curtis. Thomas Raddall's *His Majesty's Yankees* (1994) is a vivid account of a local family's deeply divided loyalties during the American Revolution, when many Nova Scotians sympathized with the rebels. E. Annie Proulx's Pulitzer Prize–winning *The Shipping News* gives a feeling for life in a Newfoundland outport today.

NONFICTION

Stuart McLean's *Welcome Home: Travels in Small-town Canada* profiles seven small towns across the country. *Canada North* is a more recent title by Farley Mowat, whose *Never Cry Wolf* is a humorous account of a naturalist who goes to a remote part of Canada to commune with wolves. Andrew Malcolm gives a cultural and historical overview of the country in *The Canadians*. Stephen Brook's *The Maple Leaf Rag* is a collection of idiosyncratic travel essays. *Why We Act Like Canadians: A Personal Exploration of Our National Character,* is one of Pierre Berton's many popular nonfiction books focusing on Canada's history and culture; another is *Niagara: A History of the Falls. Klondike,* one of Berton's best books, recounts the sensational history of the Klondike Gold Rush. *Short History of Canada,* by Desmond Morton, is a recent historical account of the country. *Local Colour—Writers Discovering Canada,* edited by Carol Marin, is a series of articles about Canadian places by leading travel writers. Thomas King, Cheryl Calver, and Helen Hoy collaborated on *The Native in Literature,* about the literary treatment of Native Americans.

MOVIES

Black Robe (1991) evokes 17th-century Québec in the story of a missionary priest. *Jesus of Montréal* (1989) is a perceptive observation of French Canadian society; it focuses on the conflict between the Church and an actor chosen to play Christ in a religious performance. In the witty *Decline of the American Empire* (1986) intellectuals explore their concepts of gender, sex, and love. The wry comedy *My Uncle Antoine* (1971) focuses on Québec village life.

BUS TRAVEL

WITHIN CANADA

The bus is an essential form of transportation in Canada, especially if you want to visit out-of-the-way towns that do not have airports or rail lines.

➤ BUS COMPANIES: Greyhound (✉ 222 1st Ave. SW, Calgary, Alberta, T2P 0A6, ☎ 403/265–9111 or 800/231–2222) and Voyageur (✉ 505 E. Boulevard Maisonneuve, Montréal, Québec, H2L 1Y4, ☎ 514/843–4231) offer interprovincial service. In the United Kingdom, contact Greyhound International (✉ Sussex House, London Road, E. Grinstead,

East Sussex, RHI9 1LD (☎ 01342/317317).

➤ FROM THE U.S.: Greyhound (☎ 800/231–2222).

BUSINESS HOURS

STORES AND SUPERMARKETS

Stores, shops, and supermarkets are usually open Monday through Saturday from 9 to 6—although in major cities, supermarkets are often open from 7:30 AM until 9 PM. Blue laws are in effect in much of Canada, but a growing number of provinces have stores with limited Sunday hours, usually from noon to 5 (shops in areas highly frequented by tourists are usually open on Sunday). Retail stores are generally open on Thursday and Friday evenings, most shopping malls until 9 PM. Drugstores in major cities are often open until 11 PM, and convenience stores are often open 24 hours a day, seven days a week.

BANKS

Most banks in Canada are open Monday through Thursday from 10 to 3, and from 10 to 5 or 6 on Friday. Some banks are open longer hours and also on Saturday morning. All banks are closed on national holidays.

C

CAMERAS, CAMCORDERS, & COMPUTERS

Always **keep your film, tape, or computer disks out of the sun.** Carry an extra supply of batteries, and **be prepared to turn on your camera, camcorder, or laptop** to prove to security personnel that the device is real. Always **ask for hand inspection of film,** which becomes clouded after successive exposure to airport x-ray machines, and **keep videotapes and computer disks away from metal detectors.**

➤ PHOTO HELP: Kodak Information Center (☎ 800/242–2424). *Kodak Guide to Shooting Great Travel Pictures,* available in bookstores or from Fodor's Travel Publications (☎ 800/533–6478; $16.50 plus $4 shipping).

CUSTOMS

Before departing, **register your foreign-made camera or laptop with U.S.**

Customs (☞ Customs & Duties, *below*). If your equipment is U.S.-made, call the consulate of the country you'll be visiting to find out whether the device should be registered with local customs upon arrival.

CAR RENTAL

Rates in Montréal begin at $14 a day and $75 a week for an economy car with air conditioning, a manual transmission, and 100 free kilometers (62 miles). This does not include tax on car rentals, which is 15%. Rates in Toronto begin at $14 a day and $79 a week. Rates in Vancouver begin at $23 a day and $133 a week. This does not include sales tax on car rentals, which is 15%.

➤ MAJOR AGENCIES: **Alamo** (☎ 800/879–2847 in Canada). **Budget** (☎ 800/527–0700, 0800/181181 in the U.K.). **Dollar** (☎ 800/800–4000; 0990/565656 in the U.K., where it is known as Eurodollar). **Hertz** (☎ 800/654–3001, 800/263–0600 in Canada, 0345/555888 in the U.K.). **National InterRent** (☎ 800/227–3876; 0345/222525 in the U.K., where it is known as Europcar Inter-Rent).

CUT COSTS

To get the best deal, **book through a travel agent who is willing to shop around.**

Also **ask your travel agent about a company's customer-service record.** How has it responded to late plane arrivals and vehicle mishaps? Are there often lines at the rental counter, and, if you're traveling during a holiday period, does a confirmed reservation guarantee you a car?

Be sure to **look into wholesalers,** companies that do not own fleets but rent in bulk from those that do and often offer better rates than traditional car-rental operations. Prices are best during off-peak periods. Rentals booked through wholesalers must be paid for before you leave the United States.

➤ RENTAL WHOLESALERS: **Kemwel Group** (☎ 914/835–5555 or 800/678–0678, ℻ 914/835–5126).

NEED INSURANCE?

When driving a rented car you are generally responsible for any damage to or loss of the vehicle. You also are liable for any property damage or personal injury that you may cause while driving. Before you rent, **see what coverage you already have** under the terms of your personal auto-insurance policy and credit cards.

BEWARE SURCHARGES

Before you pick up a car in one city and leave it in another, **ask about drop-off charges or one-way service fees,** which can be substantial. Note, too, that some rental agencies charge extra if you return the car before the time specified on your contract. To avoid a hefty refueling fee, **fill the tank just before you turn in the car,** but be aware that gas stations near the rental outlet may overcharge.

MEET THE REQUIREMENTS

In Canada your own driver's license is acceptable.

CHILDREN & TRAVEL

CHILDREN IN CANADA

Both Canadian and U.S. Customs and Immigration are cooperating with measures to reduce parental and other kinds of child abduction. Travelers crossing the border with children should **carry identification for them** similar to that required by adults (i.e., passport or birth certificate). Children traveling with one parent or other adult should **bring a letter of permission** from the other parent, parents, or legal guardian. Divorced parents with shared custody rights should **carry legal documents establishing their status.**

Be sure to plan ahead and **involve your youngsters** as you outline your trip. When packing, include things to keep them busy en route. On sightseeing days try to schedule activities of special interest to your children. If you are renting a car don't forget to **arrange for a car seat** when you reserve.

Most hotels in Canada allow children under a certain age to stay in their parents' room at no extra charge, but others charge them as extra adults; be sure to **ask about the cutoff age for children's discounts.**

FLYING

As a general rule, infants under two not occupying a seat fly at greatly reduced fares and occasionally for free. If your children are two or older **ask about children's airfares.**

In general the adult baggage allowance applies to children paying half or more of the adult fare. When booking, **ask about carry-on allowances for those traveling with infants.** In general, for babies charged 10% of the adult fare you are allowed one carry-on bag and a collapsible stroller, which may have to be checked; you may be limited to less if the flight is full.

According to the FAA it's a good idea to use safety seats aloft for children weighing less than 40 pounds. Airlines, however, can set their own policies: U.S. carriers allow FAA-approved models but usually require that you buy a ticket, even if your child would otherwise ride free, since the seats must be strapped into regular seats. Airline rules vary regarding their use, so it's important to **check your airline's policy about using safety seats during takeoff and landing.** Safety seats cannot obstruct any of the other passengers in the row, so get an appropriate seat assignment as early as possible.

When making your reservation, **request children's meals or a free-standing bassinet** if you need them; the latter are available only to those seated at the bulkhead, where there's enough legroom. Remember, however, that bulkhead seats may not have their own overhead bins, and there's no storage space in front of you—a major inconvenience.

CONSUMER PROTECTION

Whenever possible, **pay with a major credit card** so you can cancel payment if there's a problem, provided that you can provide documentation. This is a good practice whether you're buying travel arrangements before your trip or shopping at your destination.

If you're doing business with a particular company for the first time, **contact your local Better Business Bureau and the attorney general's offices** in your state and the company's home state, as well. Have any complaints been filed?

Finally, if you're buying a package or tour, always **consider travel insurance** that includes default coverage (☞ Insurance, *above*).

➤ LOCAL BBBs: **Council of Better Business Bureaus** (✉ 4200 Wilson Blvd., Suite 800, Arlington, VA 22203, ☎ 703/276–0100, FAX 703/525–8277).

CUSTOMS & DUTIES

When shopping, **keep receipts** for all of your purchases. Upon reentering the country, **be ready to show customs officials what you've bought.** If you feel a duty is incorrect, appeal the assessment. If you object to the way your clearance was handled, get the inspector's badge number. In either case, first ask to see a supervisor, then write to the port director at the address listed on your receipt. Send a copy of the receipt and other appropriate documentation. If you still don't get satisfaction you can take your case to customs headquarters in Washington.

ENTERING CANADA

American and British visitors may bring in the following items duty-free: 200 cigarettes, 50 cigars, and 14 ounces of tobacco; 1 bottle (1.1 liters or 40 imperial ounces) of liquor or wine, or 24 355-milliliter (12-ounce) bottles or cans of beer for personal consumption. Any alcohol and tobacco products in excess of these amounts is subject to duty, provincial fees, and taxes. You can also bring in gifts up to the value of $60 (Canadian) per gift. A deposit is sometimes required for trailers (refunded upon return). Cats and dogs must have a certificate issued by a licensed veterinarian that clearly identifies the animal and certifies that it has been vaccinated against rabies during the preceding 36 months. Seeing–eye dogs are allowed into Canada without restriction. Plant material must be declared and inspected. With certain restrictions (some fruits and vegetables), visitors may bring food with them for their own use, providing the quantity is consistent with the duration of the visit.

Canada's firearms laws are significantly stricter than the U.S.'s. All handguns and semi-automatic and fully automatic weapons are prohibited and cannot be brought into the country. Sporting rifles and shotguns may be imported provided they are to be used for sporting, hunting, or competition while in Canada. All firearms must be declared to Canada Customs at the first point of entry. Failure to declare firearms will result in their seizure, and criminal charges may be made.

Legislation has been passed requiring the registration of all firearms in Canada. This will mean that visitors with permitted firearms will also be required to have them registered and temporarily licensed when crossing the border. At press time, details of how this will be done had not been announced.

ENTERING THE U.S.

You may bring home $400 worth of foreign goods duty-free if you've been out of the country for at least 48 hours and haven't already used the $400 allowance or any part of it in the past 30 days.

Travelers 21 and older may bring back 1 liter of alcohol duty-free. In addition, regardless of your age, you are allowed 200 cigarettes and 100 non-Cuban cigars. (At press time, a federal rule restricting tobacco access to persons 18 years and older did not apply to importation.) Antiques, which the U.S. Customs Service defines as objects more than 100 years old, enter duty-free, as do original works of art done entirely by hand, including paintings, drawings, and sculptures.

You may also send packages home duty-free: up to $200 worth of goods for personal use, with a limit of one parcel per addressee per day (and no alcohol or tobacco products or perfume worth more than $5); label the package PERSONAL USE, and attach a list of its contents and their retail value. Do not label the package UNSOLICITED GIFT, or your duty-free exemption will drop to $100. Mailed items do not affect your duty-free allowance on your return.

➤ INFORMATION: **U.S. Customs Service** (Inquiries, ✉ Box 7407, Washington, DC 20044, ☎ 202/927–6724; complaints, ✉ Commissioner's Office, 1301 Constitution Ave. NW, Washington, DC 20229; registration

of equipment, ✉ Resource Management, 1301 Constitution Ave. NW, Washington DC, 20229, ☎ 202/927–0540).

ENTERING THE U.K.

From countries outside the EU, including Canada, you may import, duty-free, 200 cigarettes or 50 cigars; 1 liter of spirits or 2 liters of fortified or sparkling wine or liqueurs; 2 liters of still table wine; 60 milliliters of perfume; 250 milliliters of toilet water; plus £136 worth of other goods, including gifts and souvenirs.

➤ INFORMATION: **HM Customs and Excise** (✉ Dorset House, Stamford St., London SE1 9NG, ☎ 0171/202–4227).

D

DISABILITIES & ACCESSIBILITY

TIPS AND HINTS

When discussing accessibility with an operator or reservationist, **ask hard questions.** Are there any stairs, inside *or* out? Are there grab bars next to the toilet *and* in the shower/tub? How wide is the doorway to the room? To the bathroom? For the most extensive facilities meeting the latest legal specifications, **opt for newer accommodations,** which are more likely to have been designed with access in mind. Older buildings or ships may offer more limited facilities. Be sure to **discuss your needs before booking.**

➤ COMPLAINTS: **Disability Rights Section** (✉ U.S. Department of Justice, Box 66738, Washington, DC 20035–6738, ☎ 202/514–0301 or 800/514–0301, FAX 202/307–1198, TTY 202/514–0383 or 800/514–0383) for general complaints. **Aviation Consumer Protection Division** (☞ Air Travel, *above*) for airline-related problems. **Civil Rights Office** (✉ U.S. Department of Transportation, Departmental Office of Civil Rights, S-30, 400 7th St. SW, Room 10215, Washington, DC, 20590, ☎ 202/366–4648) for problems with surface transportation. Contact the Director, **Accessible Transportation Directorate** (☎ 819/997–6828), to file a complaint about transportation obstacles at Canadian airports (including flights), railroads, or ferries.

TRAVEL AGENCIES & TOUR OPERATORS

The Americans with Disabilities Act requires that travel firms serve the needs of all travelers. That said, you should note that some agencies and operators specialize in making travel arrangements for individuals and groups with disabilities.

➤ TRAVELERS WITH MOBILITY PROBLEMS: **Access Adventures** (✉ 206 Chestnut Ridge Rd., Rochester, NY 14624, ☎ 716/889–9096), run by a former physical-rehabilitation counselor. **CareVacations** (✉ 5019 49th Ave., Suite 102, Leduc, Alberta T9E 6T5, ☎ 403/986–6404, 800/648–1116 in Canada) has group tours and is especially helpful with cruise vacations. **Hinsdale Travel Service** (✉ 201 E. Ogden Ave., Suite 100, Hinsdale, IL 60521, ☎ 630/325–1335), a travel agency that benefits from the advice of wheelchair traveler Janice Perkins. **Wheelchair Journeys** (✉ 16979 Redmond Way, Redmond, WA 98052, ☎ 206/885–2210 or 800/313–4751), for general travel arrangements.

➤ TRAVELERS WITH DEVELOPMENTAL DISABILITIES: **New Directions** (✉ 5276 Hollister Ave., Suite 207, Santa Barbara, CA 93111, ☎ 805/967–2841, FAX 805/964–7344). **Sprout** (✉ 893 Amsterdam Ave., New York, NY 10025, ☎ 212/222–9575 or 888/222–9575, FAX 212/222–9768).

ACCESS IN CANADA

➤ LOCAL RESOURCES: **Canadian Paraplegic Association National Office** (✉ 1101 Prince of Wales Dr., Ottawa, Ontario K2C 3W7, ☎ 613/723–1033) provides information about touring in Canada.

DISCOUNTS & DEALS

Be a smart shopper and **compare all your options before making a choice.** A plane ticket bought with a promotional coupon may not be cheaper than the least expensive fare from a discount ticket agency. For high-price travel purchases, such as packages or tours, keep in mind that what you get is just as important as what you save. Just because something is cheap doesn't mean it's a bargain.

LOOK IN YOUR WALLET

When you use your credit card to make travel purchases you may get free travel-accident insurance, collision-damage insurance, and medical or legal assistance, depending on the card and the bank that issued it. American Express, MasterCard, and Visa provide one or more of these services, so **get a copy of your credit card's travel-benefits policy.** If you are a member of the American Automobile Association (AAA) or an oil-company-sponsored road-assistance plan, always **ask hotel or car-rental reservationists about auto-club discounts.** Some clubs offer additional discounts on tours, cruises, or admission to attractions. And don't forget that auto-club membership entitles you to free maps and trip-planning services.

DIAL FOR DOLLARS

To save money, **look into "1-800" discount reservations services,** which use their buying power to get a better price on hotels, airline tickets, even car rentals. When booking a room, always **call the hotel's local toll-free number** (if one is available) rather than the central reservations number—you'll often get a better price. Always ask about special packages or corporate rates.

When shopping for the best deal on hotels and car rentals **look for guaranteed exchange rates,** which protect you against a falling dollar. With your rate locked in you won't pay more even if the price goes up in the local currency.

➤ AIRLINE TICKETS: ☎ 800/FLY–4–LESS. ☎ 800/FLY–ASAP.

➤ HOTEL ROOMS: **Players Express Vacations** (☎ 800/458–6161). **RMC Travel** (☎ 800/245–5738). **Steigenberger Reservation Service** (☎ 800/223–5652).

SAVE ON COMBOS

Packages and guided tours can both save you money, but don't confuse the two. When you buy a package your travel remains independent, just as though you had planned and booked the trip yourself. Fly/drive packages, which combine airfare and car rental, are often a good deal.

JOIN A CLUB?

Many companies sell discounts in the form of travel clubs and coupon books, but these cost money. You must use participating advertisers to get a deal, and only after you recoup the initial membership cost or book price do you begin to save. If you plan to use the club or coupons frequently you may save considerably. Before signing up, find out what discounts you get for free.

➤ DISCOUNT CLUBS: **Entertainment Travel Editions** (✉ Box 1068, Trumbull, CT 06611, ☎ 800/445–4137; $28–$53, depending on destination). **Great American Traveler** (✉ Box 27965, Salt Lake City, UT 84127, ☎ 800/548–2812; $49.95 per year). **Moment's Notice Discount Travel Club** (✉ 7301 New Utrecht Ave., Brooklyn, NY 11204, ☎ 718/234–6295; $25 per year, single or family). **Privilege Card International** (✉ 201 E. Commerce St., Suite 198, Youngstown, OH 44503, ☎ 330/746–5211 or 800/236–9732; $74.95 per year). **Sears's Mature Outlook** (✉ Box 9390, Des Moines, IA 50306, ☎ 800/336–6330; $14.95 per year). **Travelers Advantage** (✉ CUC Travel Service, 3033 S. Parker Rd., Suite 1000, Aurora, CO 80014, ☎ 800/548–1116 or 800/648–4037; $49 per year, single or family). **Worldwide Discount Travel Club** (✉ 1674 Meridian Ave., Miami Beach, FL 33139, ☎ 305/534–2082; $50 per year family, $40 single).

DRIVING

Canada's highway system is excellent. It includes the Trans-Canada Highway, the longest highway in the world, which runs about 5,000 miles from Victoria, British Columbia, to St. John's, Newfoundland, using ferries to bridge coastal waters at each end. The second-longest Canadian highway, the Yellowhead Highway, follows the old Indian route from the Pacific Coast and over the Rockies to the prairies. North of the population centers, roads become fewer and less developed.

By law, you are required to **wear seat belts** (and use infant seats). Some provinces have a statutory requirement to drive with vehicle headlights on for extended periods after dawn and before sunset. In the Yukon, the law requires that you **drive with your headlights on** when using territory highways. Right turns are permitted on red signals in all provinces except Québec.

Speed limits vary from province to province, but they are usually within the 90–100 kph (50–60 mph) range outside the cities. The price of gasoline costs from 44¢ to 63¢ a liter. (There are 3.8 liters in a U.S. gallon.) Distances are always shown in kilometers, and gasoline is always sold in liters.

AUTO CLUBS

If you're a members of the Automobile Association of America (AAA), **contact the Canadian Automobile Association** (for emergency road service check locally since each regional or provincial affiliated auto club has its own telephone number). Members of the Automobile Association of Great Britain, the Royal Automobile Club, the Royal Scottish Automobile Club, the Royal Irish Automobile Club and the automobile clubs of the Alliance Internationale de Tourisme (AIT) and Fédération Internationale de l'Automobile (FIA) are entitled to all the services of the CAA on presentation of a membership card.

➤ AUTO CLUBS: **Canadian Automobile Association** (✉ 1775 Courtwood Crescent, Ottawa, Ontario K2C 3J2, ☎ 613/226–7631). In the U.S., **American Automobile Association** (☎ 800/564–6222). In the U.K., **Automobile Association** (AA, ☎ 0990/500–600), **Royal Automobile Club** (RAC, membership ☎ 0990/722–722; insurance 0345/121–345).

FROM THE U.S.

Drivers must **carry proper owner registration and proof of insurance coverage,** which is compulsory in Canada. The Canadian Non-Resident Inter-Provincial Motor Vehicle Liability Insurance Card, available from any U.S. insurance company, is accepted as evidence of financial responsibility anywhere in Canada. The minimum liability coverage in Canada is $200,000, except in Québec where the minimum is $50,000. If you are driving a car that is not registered in your name, **carry a letter from the owner that authorizes your use of the vehicle.**

The U.S. Interstate Highway System leads directly into Canada: I–95 from Maine to New Brunswick; I–91 and I–89 from Vermont to Québec; I–87 from New York to Québec; I–81 and a spur off I–90 from New York to Ontario; I–94, I–96, and I–75 from Michigan to Ontario; I–29 from North Dakota to Manitoba; I–15 from Montana to Alberta; and I–5 from Washington state to British Columbia. Most of these connections hook up with the Trans-Canada Highway within a few miles. There are many smaller highway crossings between the two countries as well. From Alaska, take the Alaska Highway (from Fairbanks), the Klondike Highway (from Skagway), and the Top of the World Highway (to Dawson City).

F

FERRIES

Car ferries provide essential transportation on both the east and west coasts of Canada. Ferries also operate between the state of Washington and British Columbia's Vancouver Island.

➤ FERRY COMPANIES: **Marine Atlantic** (✉ Box 250, North Sydney, Nova Scotia B2A 3M3, ☎ 902/794–5700 or 800/341–7981 in the U.S. only) operates ferries between the Atlantic provinces and also between Portland, Maine, and Nova Scotia. On the west coast, the **British Columbia Ferry Corporation** (✉ 1112 Fort St., Victoria, British Columbia V8V 4V2, ☎ 604/669–1211) has 42 ports of call.

G

GAY & LESBIAN TRAVEL

➤ GAY- AND LESBIAN-FRIENDLY TRAVEL AGENCIES: **Advance Damron** (✉ 1 Greenway Plaza, Suite 800, Houston, TX 77046, ☎ 713/682–2002 or 800/695–0880, FAX 713/888–1010). **Club Travel** (✉ 8739 Santa Monica Blvd., West Hollywood, CA 90069, ☎ 310/358–2200 or 800/429–8747, FAX 310/358–2222). **Islanders/Kennedy Travel** (✉ 183 W. 10th St., New York, NY 10014, ☎ 212/242–3222 or 800/988–1181, FAX 212/929–8530). **Now Voyager** (✉ 4406 18th St., San Francisco, CA 94114, ☎ 415/626–1169 or 800/255–6951, FAX 415/626–8626). **Yellowbrick Road** (✉ 1500 W. Balmoral Ave., Chicago,

IL 60640, ☎ 773/561–1800 or 800/642–2488, FAX 773/561–4497). **Skylink Women's Travel** (✉ 3577 Moorland Ave., Santa Rosa, CA 95407, ☎ 707/585–8355 or 800/225–5759, FAX 707/584–5637), serving lesbian travelers.

H

HEALTH

MEDICAL PLANS

No one plans to get sick while traveling, but it happens, so **consider signing up with a medical-assistance company.** Members get doctor referrals, emergency evacuation or repatriation, 24-hour telephone hot lines for medical consultation, cash for emergencies, and other personal and legal assistance. Coverage varies by plan, so **review the benefits carefully.**

➤ MEDICAL-ASSISTANCE COMPANIES: **International SOS Assistance** (✉ Box 11568, Philadelphia, PA 19116, ☎ 215/244–1500 or 800/523–8930; ✉ Box 466, pl. Bonaventure, Montréal, Québec H5A 1C1, ☎ 514/874–7674 or 800/363–0263; ✉ 7 Old Lodge Pl., St. Margarets, Twickenham TW1 1RQ, England, ☎ 0181/744–0033). **MEDEX Assistance Corporation** (✉ Box 5375, Timonium, MD 21094, ☎ 410/453–6300 or 800/537–2029). **Traveler's Emergency Network** (✉ 3100 Tower Blvd., Suite 1000B, Durham, NC 27707, ☎ 919/490–6055 or 800/275–4836, FAX 919/493–8262). **TravMed** (✉ Box 5375, Timonium, MD 21094, ☎ 410/453–6380 or 800/732–5309). **Worldwide Assistance Services** (✉ 1133 15th St. NW, Suite 400, Washington, DC 20005, ☎ 202/331–1609 or 800/821–2828, FAX 202/828–5896).

HOLIDAYS

NATIONAL HOLIDAYS

National holidays for 1998 are: New Year's Day, Good Friday (April 10), Easter Monday (April 13), Victoria Day (May 18), Canada Day (July 1), Labor Day (September 7), Thanksgiving (October 12), Remembrance Day (November 11), Christmas (December 25), and Boxing Day (December 26).

PROVINCIAL HOLIDAYS

Alberta: Family Day (February 16), Heritage Day (August 3). British Columbia: British Columbia Day

(August 3). New Brunswick: New Brunswick Day (August 3). Newfoundland: St. Patrick's Day (March 17), St. George's Day (April 23), Discovery Day (June 27), Memorial Day (July 6). Manitoba, Northwest Territories, Ontario, Saskatchewan, and Nova Scotia: Civic Holiday (August 3). Québec: St. Jean Baptiste Day (June 24). Yukon: Discovery Day (August 17).

I

INSURANCE

Travel insurance is the best way to **protect yourself against financial loss.** The most useful policies are trip-cancellation-and-interruption, default, medical, and comprehensive insurance.

Without insurance you will lose all or most of your money if you cancel your trip, regardless of the reason. It's essential that you **buy trip-cancellation-and-interruption insurance,** particularly if your airline ticket, cruise, or package tour is nonrefundable and cannot be changed. When considering how much coverage you need, look for a policy that will cover the cost of your trip plus the nondiscounted price of a one-way airline ticket, should you need to return home early. Also **consider default or bankruptcy insurance,** which protects you against a supplier's failure to deliver.

Medicare generally does not cover health-care costs outside the United States, nor do many privately issued policies. If your own policy does not cover you outside the United States, **consider buying supplemental medical coverage.** Remember that travel health insurance is different from a medical-assistance plan (☞ Health, *above*).

Citizens of the United Kingdom can **buy an annual travel-insurance policy valid for most vacations** during the year in which it's purchased. If you are pregnant or have a preexisting medical condition, make sure you're covered.

If you have purchased an expensive vacation, particularly one that involves travel abroad, comprehensive insurance is a must. **Look for comprehensive policies that include trip-delay**

insurance, which will protect you in the event that weather problems cause you to miss your flight, tour, or cruise. A few insurers sell waivers for preexisting medical conditions. Companies that offer both features include Access America, Carefree Travel, Travel Insured International, and Travel Guard (☞ *below*).

Always **buy travel insurance directly from the insurance company;** if you buy it from a travel agency or tour operator that goes out of business you probably will not be covered for the agency or operator's default, a major risk. Before you make any purchase, **review your existing health and home-owner's policies** to find out whether they cover expenses incurred while traveling.

➤ TRAVEL INSURERS: In the U.S., **Access America** (⊠ 6600 W. Broad St., Richmond, VA 23230, ☎ 804/285–3300 or 800/284–8300), **Carefree Travel Insurance** (⊠ Box 9366, 100 Garden City Plaza, Garden City, NY 11530, ☎ 516/294–0220 or 800/323–3149), **Near Travel Services** (⊠ Box 1339, Calumet City, IL 60409, ☎ 708/868–6700 or 800/654–6700), **Travel Guard International** (⊠ 1145 Clark St., Stevens Point, WI 54481, ☎ 715/345–0505 or 800/826–1300), **Travel Insured International** (⊠ Box 280568, East Hartford, CT 06128–0568, ☎ 860/528–7663 or 800/243–3174), **Travelex Insurance Services** (⊠ 11717 Burt St., Suite 202, Omaha, NE 68154-1500, ☎ 402/445–8637 or 800/228–9792, FAX 800/867–9531), **Wallach & Company** (⊠ 107 W. Federal St., Box 480, Middleburg, VA 20118, ☎ 540/687–3166 or 800/237–6615). In Canada, **Mutual of Omaha** (⊠ Travel Division, 500 University Ave., Toronto, Ontario M5G 1V8, ☎ 416/598–4083, 800/268–8825 in Canada). In the U.K., **Association of British Insurers** (⊠ 51 Gresham St., London EC2V 7HQ, ☎ 0171/600–3333).

L

LANGUAGE

Canada's two official languages are English and French. Though English is widely spoken, it is useful to **learn a few French phrases** if you plan to travel to the province of Québec or to the French-Canadian communities in the Maritimes (Nova Scotia, New Brunswick, and Prince Edward Island), northern Manitoba, and Ontario. Canadian French has many distinctive words and expressions, but it's no more different from the language of France than North American English is from the language of Great Britain.

LODGING

Aside from the quaint hotels of Québec, Canada's range of accommodations more closely resembles that of the United States than of Europe. In the cities you'll have a choice of luxury hotels, moderately priced modern properties, and smaller older hotels with perhaps fewer conveniences but more charm. Options in smaller towns and in the country include large, full-service resorts; small, privately owned hotels; roadside motels; and bed-and-breakfasts. Even here you'll need to **make reservations at least on the day on which you're planning to pull into town.**

There is no national government rating system for hotels, but many provinces rate their accommodations. For example, in British Columbia and Alberta, a blue Approved Accommodation decal on the window or door of a hotel or motel indicates that it has met provincial hotel association standards for courtesy, comfort, and cleanliness. Ontario's voluntary rating system includes about 1,000 Ontario properties.

Expect accommodations to cost more in summer than in the off-season (except for places such as ski resorts, where winter is high season). When making reservations, **ask about special deals** and packages when reserving. Big city hotels that cater to business travelers often offer weekend packages, and many city hotels offer rooms at up to 50% off in winter. If you're planning to visit a major city or resort area in high season, **book well in advance.** Also be aware of any special events or festivals that may coincide with your visit and fill every room for miles around. For resorts and lodges, consider the winter ski-season high as well and plan accordingly.

APARTMENT AND VILLA RENTALS

If you want a home base that's roomy enough for a family and comes with cooking facilities, **consider a furnished rental.** These can save you money, however some rentals are luxury properties, economical only when your party is large. Home-exchange directories list rentals (often second homes owned by prospective house swappers), and some services search for a house or apartment for you (even a castle if that's your fancy) and handle the paperwork. Some send an illustrated catalog; others send photographs only of specific properties, sometimes at a charge. Up-front registration fees may apply.

➤ RENTAL AGENTS: **Property Rentals International** (✉ 1008 Mansfield Crossing Rd., Richmond, VA 23236, ☎ 804/378–6054 or 800/220–3332, FAX 804/379–2073). **Rent-a-Home International** (✉ 7200 34th Ave. NW, Seattle, WA 98117, ☎ 206/789–9377 or 800/488–7368, FAX 206/789–9379). **Hideaways International** (✉ 767 Islington St., Portsmouth, NH 03801, ☎ 603/430–4433 or 800/843–4433, FAX 603/430–4444) is a travel club whose members arrange rentals among themselves; yearly membership is $99.

B&BS

Bed-and-breakfasts can be found in both the country and the cities. For assistance in booking these, **contact the appropriate provincial tourist board,** which either has a listing of B&Bs or can refer you to an association that will help you secure reservations. Rates vary depending on the property and include a Continental or a full breakfast. Some B&B hosts lock up early; be sure to ask. Room quality varies from house to house as well, so you can **ask to see a room before making a choice.**

DORMS AND HOSTELS

You can **consider a few alternatives to camping if you're on a budget.** Among them are hostels, which are open to young and old, families and singles (☞ Students, *below*), and university campuses, which open their dorms to travelers for overnight stays from May through August.

HOME EXCHANGES

If you would like to exchange your home for someone else's, **join a home-exchange organization,** which will send you its updated listings of available exchanges for a year and will include your own listing in at least one of them. Making the arrangements is up to you.

➤ EXCHANGE CLUBS: **HomeLink International** (✉ Box 650, Key West, FL 33041, ☎ 305/294–7766 or 800/638–3841, FAX 305/294–1148) charges $83 per year.

HOTELS

➤ HOTEL CHAINS: The major hotel chains in Canada include **Best Western International** (☎ 800/528–1234; in the U.K., 0181/541–0033), **Canadian Pacific Hotels & Resorts** (☎ 800/441–1414; in the U.K., 0800/898852), **Choice Hotels International** (☎ 800/424–6423; in the U.K. 0800/444–4444), **Days Inns** (☎ 800/329–7466; in the U.K. 01483/440470), **Delta Hotels** (☎ 800/877–1133; in the U.K., 0171/937–8033), **Four Seasons Hotels** (☎ 800/332–3442; in the U.K., 0800/526648), **Hilton Hotels** (☎ 800/445–8667), **Holiday Inns** (☎ 800/465–4329; in the U.K., 0800/897121), **Hyatt Hotels** (☎ 800/223–1234; in the U.K. 0171/580–8197), **Marriott Hotels and Resorts** (☎ 800/228–9290; in the U.K., 0800/282811), **Novotel Hotels** (☎ 800/668–6835), **Radisson Hotels** (☎ 800/333–3333; in the U.K., 0800/891999), **Ramada** (☎ 800/228–2828; in the U.K., 0181/688–1418), **Relais & Châteaux** (☎ 800/743–8033), **Sheraton** (☎ 800/325–3535; in the U.K., 0800/353535), **Travelodge** (☎ 800/255–3050; in the U.K., 0345/404040), and **Westin Hotels** (☎ 800/228–3000; in the U.K., 0171/408–0636).

M

MAIL

In Canada you can **buy stamps at the post office or from automatic vending machines** in most hotel lobbies, railway stations, airports, bus terminals, many retail outlets, and some newsstands. Within Canada, postcards and letters up to 30 grams cost 45¢; between 31 grams and 50 grams, the cost is 71¢ and between 51 grams and a kilogram the cost is 90¢. Letters and postcards to the United States cost 52¢ for up to 30 grams, 77¢ for between 31 and 50 grams, and $1.17 for up to a kilogram. Prices include GST (Goods and Services Tax).

International mail and postcards run 90¢ for up to 30 grams, and $2.10 for up to 100 grams.

For fast service, **try Telepost, a fast "next day or sooner" service** that combines the CN/CP Telecommunications network with letter-carrier delivery service. Messages may be telephoned to the nearest CN/CP Public Message Centre for delivery anywhere in Canada or the United States. Telepost service is available 24 hours a day, seven days a week, and billing arrangements may be made at the time the message is called in. You can also **consider Intelpost, which allows you to send documents or photographs via satellite** to many Canadian, American, and European destinations. This service is available at main postal facilities in Canada, and is paid for in cash.

RECEIVING MAIL

Visitors may have mail sent to them c/o General Delivery in the town they are visiting, for pickup in person within 15 days, after which it will be returned to the sender.

SENDING MAIL

If you're sending mail to Canada, **be sure to include the postal code** (six digits and letters). Following are postal abbreviations for provinces and territories: Alberta, AB; British Columbia, BC; Saskatchewan, SK; Manitoba, MB; New Brunswick, NB; Newfoundland and Labrador, NF; Northwest Territories, NT; Nova Scotia, NS; Ontario, ON; Prince Edward Island, PE; Québec, PQ; Yukon, YT.

MONEY

American money is accepted in much of Canada (especially in communities near the border). However, to get the most favorable exchange rate, **exchange at least some of your money into Canadian funds at a bank or other financial institution.** Traveler's checks (some are available in Canadian dollars) and major U.S. credit cards are accepted in most areas.

The units of currency in Canada are the Canadian dollar (C$) and the cent, in almost the same denominations as U.S. currency ($5, $10, $20, 1¢, 5¢, 10¢, 25¢, etc.). The $1 and $2 bill are no longer used; they have been replaced by $1 and $2 coins (known as a "loonie," because of the loon that appears on the coin, and a "toonie," respectively). At press time the exchange rate was US$1 to C$1.29 and £1 to C$2.18.

ATMS

Before leaving home, **make sure that your credit cards have been programmed for ATM use in Canada.** Note that Discover is accepted mostly in the United States. Local bank cards often do not work overseas or may access only your checking account; **ask your bank about a MasterCard/Cirrus or Visa debit card,** which works like a bank card but can be used at any ATM displaying a MasterCard/Cirrus or Visa logo. These cards, too, may tap only your checking account; check with your bank about their policy.

➤ ATM LOCATIONS: **Cirrus** (☎ 800/424–7787). **Plus** (☎ 800/843–7587).

COSTS

The following typical prices are for Toronto (prices in other cities and regions are often lower): A soda (pop) costs $1–$1.25; a glass of beer, $3–$6; a sandwich, $3.50–$6; a taxi, as soon as the meter is turned on, $2.20, and $1 for every kilometer; a movie, about $8.

TRAVELER'S CHECKS

Whether or not to buy traveler's checks depends on where you are headed. You should **take cash if your trip includes rural areas** and small towns, traveler's checks if you're visiting cities. If your checks are lost or stolen, they can usually be replaced within 24 hours. To ensure a speedy refund, **buy your checks yourself** (don't ask someone else to make the purchase). When making a claim for stolen or lost checks, the person who bought the checks should make the call.

How you pack will depend on when you go and what you plan to do. In winter, **bring layers,** the best defense against Canada's cold winters; a hat, scarf, and gloves are essential. For summer travel, **select loose-fitting natural-fiber clothes**; bring a wool sweater and light jacket. If you're planning to spend time in Canada's larger cities, pack both casual clothes for day touring and more formal wear for evenings out.

If you plan on camping or hiking in the deep woods during the summer, particularly in northern Canada, **always carry insect repellent,** especially in June, which is blackfly season.

Bring an extra pair of eyeglasses or contact lenses in your carry-on luggage, and if you have a health problem, **pack enough medication** to last the entire trip or have your doctor write you a prescription using the drug's generic name, because brand names vary from country to country. It's important that you **don't put prescription drugs or valuables in luggage to be checked**: it might go astray. To avoid problems with customs officials, carry medications in the original packaging. Also, don't forget the addresses of offices that handle refunds of lost traveler's checks.

LUGGAGE

In general, you are entitled to check two bags on flights within the United States and on international flights leaving the United States. A third piece may be brought on board, but it must fit easily under the seat in front of you or in the overhead compartment.

If you are flying between two foreign destinations, note that baggage allowances may be determined not by piece but by weight—generally 88 pounds (40 kilograms) in first class, 66 pounds (30 kilograms) in business class, and 44 pounds (20 kilograms) in economy. If your flight between two cities abroad *connects* with your transatlantic or transpacific flight, the piece method still applies.

Airline liability for baggage is limited to $1,250 per person on flights within the United States. On international flights it amounts to $9.07 per pound or $20 per kilogram for checked baggage (roughly $640 per 70-pound bag) and $400 per passenger for unchecked baggage. Insurance for losses exceeding these amounts can be bought from the airline at check-in for about $10 per $1,000 of coverage; note that this coverage excludes a rather extensive list of items, which is shown on your airline ticket.

Before departure, **itemize your bags' contents** and their worth, and label the bags with your name, address, and phone number. (If you use your home address, cover it so that potential thieves can't see it readily.) Inside each bag, **pack a copy of your itinerary.** At check-in, **make sure that each bag is correctly tagged** with the destination airport's three-letter code. If your bags arrive damaged or fail to arrive at all, file a written report with the airline before leaving the airport.

PASSPORTS & VISAS

Once your travel plans are confirmed, **get a passport even if you don't need one to enter Canada**—it's always the best form of I.D. It's also a good idea to **make photocopies of the data page**; leave one copy with someone at home and keep another with you, separated from your passport. If you lose your passport, promptly call the nearest embassy or consulate and the local police; having a copy of the data page can speed replacement.

U.S. CITIZENS

Citizens and legal residents of the United States do not need a passport or a visa to enter Canada, but proof of citizenship (a birth certificate or valid passport) and photo identification may be requested. Naturalized U.S. residents should carry their naturalization certificate or "green card." U.S. residents entering Canada from a third country must have a valid passport, naturalization certificate, or "green card."

U.K. CITIZENS

Citizens of the United Kingdom need only a valid passport to enter Canada for stays of up to six months days.

➤ INFORMATION: **London Passport Office** (☎ 0990/21010) for fees and documentation requirements and to request an emergency passport.

S
SENIOR-CITIZEN TRAVEL

To qualify for age-related discounts, **mention your senior-citizen status up front** when booking hotel reservations (not when checking out) and before you're seated in restaurants (not when paying the bill). Note that discounts may be limited to certain menus, days, or hours. When renting a car, **ask about promotional car-rental discounts,** which can be cheaper than senior-citizen rates.

VIA Rail Canada (☞ Train Travel, *below*) offers those 60 and over a 10% discount on basic transportation for travel any time and with no advance-purchase requirement. This 10% discount can also apply to off-peak reduced fares that have advance-purchase requirements.

➤ EDUCATIONAL TRAVEL PROGRAMS: **Elderhostel** (✉ 75 Federal St., 3rd floor, Boston, MA 02110, ☎ 617/426–7788).

SPORTS

BICYCLING

➤ ASSOCIATION: **Canadian Cycling Association** (✉ 1600 James Naismith Dr., Gloucester, Ontario K1B 5N4, ☎ 613/748–5629).

CANOEING AND KAYAKING

Provincial tourist offices can be of assistance, especially in locating an outfitter to suit your needs.

➤ ASSOCIATION: **Canadian Recreational Canoeing Association** (✉ 5–1029 Hyde Park Rd., London, Ontario N0M 1Z0, ☎ 519/473–2109).

CLIMBING/MOUNTAINEERING

➤ ASSOCIATION: **Alpine Club of Canada** (✉ Box 2040, Canmore, Alberta T0L 0M0, ☎ 403/678–3200).

GOLF

➤ ASSOCIATION: **Royal Canadian Golf Association** (✉ 1333 Dorval Dr., Oakville, Ontario L6J 4Z3, ☎ 905/849–9700).

SCUBA DIVING

➤ ASSOCIATION: **Canadian Amateur Diving Association** (✉ 1600 James Naismith Dr., Suite 705, Gloucester, Ontario K1B 5N4, ☎ 613/748-5631).

TENNIS

➤ ASSOCIATION: **Tennis Canada** (✉ 3111 Steeles Ave. W., Downsview, Ontario M3J 3H2, ☎ 416/665-9777).

STUDENTS

Persons under 18 years of age who are not accompanied by their parents should **bring a letter from a parent or guardian** giving them permission to travel to Canada.

To save money, **look into deals available through student-oriented travel agencies.** To qualify you'll need a bona fide student ID card. Members of international student groups are also eligible.

➤ STUDENT IDS AND SERVICES: **Council on International Educational Exchange** (✉ CIEE, 205 E. 42nd St., 14th floor, New York, NY 10017, ☎ 212/822-2600 or 888/268-6245, FAX 212/822-2699), for mail orders only, in the United States. **Travel Cuts** (✉ 171 College St., 2nd Floor, Toronto, Ontario M5T 1P7, ☎ 416/977-5228 or 800/667-2887) in Canada.

➤ HOSTELING: **Hostelling International—American Youth Hostels** (✉ 733 15th St. NW, Suite 840, Washington, DC 20005, ☎ 202/783-6161, FAX 202/783-6171). **Hostelling International—Canada** (✉ 400-205 Catherine St., Ottawa, Ontario K2P 1C3, ☎ 613/237-7884, FAX 613/237-7868). **Youth Hostel Association of England and Wales** (✉ Trevelyan House, 8 St. Stephen's Hill, St. Albans, Hertfordshire AL1 2DY, ☎ 01727/855215 or 01727/845047, FAX 01727/844126). Membership in the U.S., $25; in Canada, C$26.75; in the U.K., £9.30).

➤ STUDENT TOURS: **Contiki Holidays** (✉ 300 Plaza Alicante, Suite 900, Garden Grove, CA 92840, ☎ 714/740-0808 or 800/266-8454, FAX 714/740-0818).

T

TAXES

A goods and services tax of 7% (GST) applies on virtually every transaction in Canada except for the purchase of basic groceries.

SALES

In addition to the GST, all provinces except Alberta, the Northwest Territories, and the Yukon levy a sales tax from 6% to 12% on most items purchased in shops, on restaurant meals, and sometimes on hotel rooms. In Newfoundland, Nova Scotia, and New Brunswick, the single harmonized sales tax (HST) is used. Manitoba and Québec offer a sales-tax rebate system similar to the federal one; **call the provincial toll-free visitor information lines for details** (☞ Visitor Information, *below*). Most provinces do not tax goods shipped directly by the vendor to the visitor's home address.

GST REFUNDS

You can **get a GST refund on purchases taken out of the country and on short-term accommodations** (but not on food, drink, tobacco, car or motorhome rentals, or transportation); rebate forms, which must be submitted within 60 days of leaving Canada, may be obtained from certain retailers, duty-free shops, customs officials, or from Revenue Canada. Instant cash rebates up to a maximum of $500 are provided by some duty-free shops when leaving Canada, and most provinces do not tax goods that are shipped directly by the vendor to the purchaser's home. Always **save your original receipts** from stores and hotels, and **be sure the name and address of the establishment is shown on the receipt.** Original receipts are not returned. The total amount of GST on each receipt must be at least $3.50 and visitors have to claim at least $14 in tax per rebate application form.

➤ INFORMATION: **Revenue Canada** (✉ Visitor Rebate Program, Summerside Tax Centre, Summerside, Prince Edward Island C1N 6C6, ☎ 902/432-5608 or 800/668-4748 in Canada).

THE GOLD GUIDE / SMART TRAVEL TIPS

CALLING HOME

AT&T, MCI, and Sprint long-distance services make calling home relatively convenient and let you avoid hotel surcharges. Typically you dial an 800 number in the United States.

➤ To Obtain Access Codes: AT&T USADirect (☎ 800/874–4000). MCI Call USA (☎ 800/444–4444). Sprint Express (☎ 800/793–1153).

DIRECTORY ASSISTANCE

For directory assistance in Canada, dial the area code followed by 555–1212; dial 1 before the area code if the area code is not the same as the one you are calling from.

TIPPING

Tips and service charges are not usually added to a bill in Canada. In general, **tip 15% of the total bill.** This goes for waiters, waitresses, barbers and hairdressers, taxi drivers, etc. Porters and doormen should get about $1 a bag (or more in a luxury hotel). For maid service, $1 a day is sufficient ($2 in luxury hotels).

TOUR OPERATORS

Buying a prepackaged tour or independent vacation can make your trip to Canada less expensive and more hassle-free. You'll spend less time planning.

Operators that handle several hundred thousand travelers per year can use their power to give you a good price. Their high volume may also indicate financial stability. But some small companies provide more personalized service; because they tend to specialize, they may also be more knowledgeable about a given area.

A GOOD DEAL?

The more your package or tour includes, the better you can predict the ultimate cost of your vacation. Make sure you know exactly what is covered, and **beware of hidden costs.** Are taxes, tips, and service charges included? Transfers and baggage handling? Entertainment and excursions? These can add up.

If the package or tour you are considering is priced lower than in your wildest dreams, **be skeptical.** Also,

make sure your travel agent knows the accommodations and other services. Ask about the hotel's location, room size, beds, and whether it has a pool, room service, or programs for children, if you care about these. Has your agent been there in person or sent others you can contact?

BUYER BEWARE

Each year consumers are stranded or lose their money when tour operators go out of business. So **check out the operator.** Find out how long the company has been in business, and ask several agents about its reputation. **Don't book unless the firm has a consumer-protection program.**

Members of the National Tour Association and United States Tour Operators Association are required to set aside funds to cover your payments and travel arrangements in case the company defaults. Nonmembers may carry insurance instead. Look for the details, and for the name of an underwriter with a solid reputation, in the operator's brochure. Note: **don't trust escrow accounts.** Although there are laws governing charter-flight operators, no governmental body prevents tour operators from raiding the till. For more information, *see* Consumer Protection, *above.*

➤ Tour-Operator Recommendations: **National Tour Association** (✉ NTA, 546 E. Main St., Lexington, KY 40508, ☎ 606/226–4444 or 800/755–8687). **United States Tour Operators Association** (✉ USTOA, 342 Madison Ave., Suite 1522, New York, NY 10173, ☎ 212/599–6599, FAX 212/599–6744).

USING AN AGENT

Travel agents are excellent resources. When shopping for an agent, however, you should **collect brochures from several sources**; some agents' suggestions may be skewed by promotional relationships with tour and package firms that reward them for volume sales. If you have a special interest, **find an agent with expertise in that area** (☞ Travel Agencies, *below*). Don't rely solely on your agent, who may be unaware of small-niche operators. Note that some special-interest travel companies only sell directly to the public and that some large operators only accept bookings made through travel agents.

SINGLE TRAVELERS

Prices for packages and tours are usually quoted per person, based on two sharing a room. If traveling solo, you may be required to pay the full double-occupancy rate. Some operators eliminate this surcharge if you agree to be matched with a roommate of the same sex, even if one is not found by departure time.

GROUP TOURS

Among companies that sell tours to Canada, the following are nationally known, have a proven reputation, and offer plenty of options. The classifications used below represent different price categories, and you'll probably encounter these terms when talking to a travel agent or tour operator. The key difference is usually in accommodations, which run from budget to better, and better-yet to best.

➤ DELUXE: **Globus** (✉ 5301 S. Federal Circle, Littleton, CO 80123-2980, ☎ 303/797–2800 or 800/221–0090, FAX 303/347–2080). **Maupintour** (✉ 1515 St. Andrews Dr., Lawrence, KS 66047, ☎ 913/843–1211 or 800/255–4266, FAX 913/843–8351). **Tauck Tours** (✉ Box 5027, 276 Post Rd. W, Westport, CT 06881-5027, ☎ 203/226–6911 or 800/468–2825, FAX 203/221–6828).

➤ FIRST-CLASS: **Brendan Tours** (✉ 15137 Califa St., Van Nuys, CA 91411, ☎ 818/785–9696 or 800/421–8446, FAX 818/902–9876). **Caravan Tours** (✉ 401 N. Michigan Ave., Chicago, IL 60611, ☎ 312/321–9800 or 800/227–2826, FAX 312/321–9845). **Collette Tours** (✉ 162 Middle St., Pawtucket, RI 02860, ☎ 401/728–3805 or 800/832–4656, FAX 401/728–1380). **Gadabout Tours** (✉ 700 E. Tahquitz Canyon Way, Palm Springs, CA 92262–6767, ☎ 619/325–5556 or 800/952–5068). **Mayflower Tours** (✉ Box 490, 1225 Warren Ave., Downers Grove, IL 60515, ☎ 708/960–3430 or 800/323–7064).

➤ BUDGET: **Cosmos** (☞ Globus, *above*).

PACKAGES

Like group tours, independent vacation packages are available from major tour operators and airlines. The companies listed below offer vacation packages in a broad price range.

➤ AIR/HOTEL: **Air Canada Vacations** (☎ 514/876–4141). **American Airlines Fly AAway Vacations** (☎ 800/321–2121). **Delta Dream Vacations** (☎ 800/872–7786, FAX 954/357–4687). **United Vacations** (☎ 800/328–6877). **US Airways Vacations** (☎ 800/455–0123).

➤ AIR/HOTEL/CAR: **Air Canada Vacations** (☞ Air/Hotel, *above*). **American Airlines Fly AAway Vacations** (☞ Air/Hotel, *above*). **Delta Dream Vacations** (☞ Air/Hotel, *above*).

➤ FLY/DRIVE: **Delta Dream Vacations** (☞ Air/Hotel, *above*). **Budget World-Class Drive** (☎ 800/527–0700, 0800/181181 in the U.K.).

➤ FROM THE U.K.: **Trailfinders** (✉ 42–50 Earls Court Rd., London W8 6FT, ☎ 0171/937–5400). **Travel Cuts** (✉ 295A Regent St., London W1R 7YA, ☎ 0171/637–3161; ☞ Students, *above*). **Flight Express Travel** (✉ 77 New Bond St., London W1Y 9DB, ☎ 0171/409–3311).

THEME TRIPS

The companies listed below provide multiday tours in Canada. More local or regionally based companies that have different-length trips with these themes are listed in each chapter, either with information about the town or in the A to Z section that concludes the chapter.

➤ ADVENTURE: **American Wilderness Experience** (✉ 2820-A Wilderness Pl., Boulder, CO 80301-5454, ☎ 303/444–2622 or 800/444–0099, FAX 303/444–3999). **Canadian Adventure Tours** (✉ Box 929, Whistler, British Columbia VON 1BO, ☎ 604/938–0727, FAX 604/938–0728). **Mountain Travel-Sobek** (✉ 6420 Fairmount Ave., El Cerrito, CA 94530, ☎ 510/527–8100 or 800/227–2384, FAX 510/525–7710). **OARS** (✉ Box 67, Angels Camp, CA 95222, ☎ 209/736–4677 or 800/346–6277, FAX 209/736–2902). **Trek America** (✉ Box 189, Rockaway, NJ 07866, ☎ 201/983–1144 or 800/221-0596, FAX 201/

983–8551). **Wells Gray Park Back-country Chalets** (✉ Box 188, Clearwater, British Columbia V0E 1N0, ☎ 250/587–6444 or 888/754–8735, FAX 250/587–6446).

➤ BICYCLING: **Backroads** (✉ 801 Cedar St., Berkeley, CA 94710-1800, ☎ 510/527–1555 or 800/462–2848, FAX 510/527–1444. **Bicycle Adventures** (✉ Box 11219, Olympia, WA 98508, ☎ 360/786–0989 or 800/443–6060, FAX 360/786–9661). **Bike Riders** (✉ Box 254, Boston, MA 02113, ☎ 617/723–2354 or 800/473–7040, FAX 617/723–2355). **Butterfield & Robinson** (✉ 70 Bond St., Toronto, Ontario M5B 1X3, ☎ 416/864–1354 or 800/678–1147, FAX 416/864–0541). **Classic Adventures** (✉ Box 153, Hamlin, NY 14464-0153, ☎ 716/964–8488 or 800/777–8090, FAX 716/964-7297). **Easy Rider Tours** (✉ Box 228, Newburyport, MA 01950, ☎ 508/463–6955 or 800/488–8332, FAX 508/463–6988). **Rocky Mountain Worldwide Cycle Tours** (✉ 333 Baker St., Nelson, BC, Canada V1L 4H6, ☎ 250/354–1241 or 800/661–2453, FAX 250/354–2058). **Timberline** (✉ 7975 E. Harvard, #J, Denver, CO 80231, ☎ 303/759–3804 or 800/417–2453, FAX 303/368–1651).

➤ CROSS-COUNTRY SKIING: **Backroads** (☞ *Bicycling, above*).

➤ CULTURAL: **Creeway Wilderness Experiences** (✉ Box 347, Moose Factory, Ontario, Canada P0L 1W0, ☎ /FAX 705/658–4390).

➤ CUSTOMIZED SELF-DRIVE ITINERARIES: **Off the Beaten Path** (✉ 27 E. Main St., Bozeman, MT 59715, ☎ 406/586–1311 or 800/445–2995, FAX 406/587–4147).

➤ DUDE RANCHES: **American Wilderness Experience** (☞ *Adventure, above*).

➤ FISHING: **Anglers Travel** (✉ 3100 Mill St., #206, Reno, NV 89502, ☎ /FAX 702/853–9132). **Cutting Loose Expeditions** (✉ Box 447, Winter Park, FL 32790-0447, ☎ 407/629–4700 or 800/533–4746, FAX 407/740–7816). **Fishing International** (✉ Box 2132, Santa Rosa, CA 95405, ☎ 707/539–3366 or 800/950–4242, FAX 707/539–1320). **Rod and Reel Adventures** (✉ 3507 Tully Rd., #B6, Modesto, CA 95356-1052, ☎ 209/524–7775 or 800/356–6982, FAX 209/524–1220).

➤ FOOD AND WINE: **Le Cordon Bleu** (✉ 404 Airport Executive Pk., Nanuet, NY 10954, ☎ 800/457–2433).

➤ GOLF: **ITC Golf Tours** (✉ 4134 Atlantic Ave., #205, Long Beach, CA 90807, ☎ 310/595–6905 or 800/257–4981).

➤ HORSEBACK RIDING: **American Wilderness Experience** (☞ *Adventure, above*). **Equitour FITS Equestrian** (✉ Box 807, Dubois, WY 82513, ☎ 307/455–3363 or 800/545–0019, FAX 307/455–2354).

➤ LEARNING: **Earthwatch** (✉ Box 9104, 680 Mount Auburn St., Watertown, MA 02272, ☎ 617/926–8200 or 800/776–0188, FAX 617/926–8532) for research expeditions. **National Audubon Society** (✉ 700 Broadway, New York, NY 10003, ☎ 212/979–3066, FAX 212/353–0190). **Natural Habitat Adventures** (✉ 2945 Center Green Ct., Boulder, CO 80301, ☎ 303/449–3711 or 800/543–8917, FAX 303/449–3712). **Oceanic Society Expeditions** (✉ Fort Mason Center, Bldg. E, San Francisco, CA 94123-1394, ☎ 415/441–1106 or 800/326–7491, FAX 415/474–3395). **Questers** (✉ 381 Park Ave. S, New York, NY 10016, ☎ 212/251–0444 or 800/468–8668, FAX 212/251–0890). **Smithsonian Study Tours and Seminars** (✉ 1100 Jefferson Dr. SW, Room 3045, MRC 702, Washington, DC 20560, ☎ 202/357–4700, FAX 202/633–9250).

➤ SINGLES AND YOUNG ADULTS: **Contiki Holidays** (✉ 300 Plaza Alicante, #900, Garden Grove, CA 92840, ☎ 714/740–0808 or 800/266–8454, FAX 714/740–0818).

➤ SKIING: **Canadian Mountain Holidays** (✉ Box 1660, Banff, Alberta, Canada T0L 0C0, ☎ 800/661–0252, FAX 403/762–5879). **Mountain Tours** (✉ Box 1409, Golden, British Columbia, Canada V0A 1H0, ☎ 250/344–5016 or 800/663–7080). **Tyax Heli/Skiing** (✉ Box 849, Whistler, British Columbia, Canada V0N 1B0, ☎ 604/932–7007 or 800/663–8126, FAX 604/932–2500).

➤ Spas: **Spa-Finders** (✉ 91 5th Ave., #301, New York, NY 10003-3039, ☎ 212/924–6800 or 800/255–7727).

➤ Sports: **Championship Tennis Tours** (✉ 7350 E. Stetson Dr., #106, Scottsdale, AZ 85251, ☎ 602/990–8760 or 800/468–3664, FAX 602/990–8744).

➤ Walking/Hiking: **Backroads** (☞ Bicycling, *above*). **Country Walkers** (✉ Box 180, Waterbury, VT 05676-0180, ☎ 802/244–1387 or 800/464–9255, FAX 802/244–5661).

➤ Yacht Charters: **Ocean Voyages** (✉ 1709 Bridgeway, Sausalito, CA 94965, ☎ 415/332–4681, FAX 415/332–7460).

Amtrak currently has service from New York to Montréal, New York and Buffalo to Toronto, Chicago to Toronto, and Seattle to Vancouver, providing connections between Amtrak's U.S.-wide network and VIA Rail's Canadian routes.

Transcontinental rail service is provided by VIA Rail Canada. Rocky Mountaineer Railtours operates spectacular two-day, all-daylight rail trips through the Canadian Rockies to the west coast.

➤ Information: **Amtrak** (☎ 800/872–7245). **Rocky Mountaineer Railtours** (☎ 800/665–7245). **VIA Rail Canada** (☎ 800/561–3949). In the U.K., **Long-Haul Leisurail** (✉ Box 113, Peterborough, PE3 8HY, ☎ 01733/335599) represents both VIA Rail and Rocky Mountaineer Railtours.

DISCOUNT PASSES

If you're planning to travel a lot by train, **look into the Canrailpass.** It allows 12 days of coach-class travel within a 30-day period; sleeping cars are available, but they sell out very early and must be reserved at least a month in advance during the high season (mid–May to mid–October), when the pass is C$535 for adults age 25–60, C$482 for travelers under 25 or over 60. Low-season rates (October 16–December 14 and January 6–May 14) are C$365 for adults and C$329 for youths and senior citizens. The pass is not valid during the

Christmas period (December 15–January 5). The Canrailpass must be purchased prior to arrival in Canada; for more information and reservations, contact a travel agent in the U.S. or Long-Haul Leisurail in the United Kingdom (☞ *above*).

A good travel agent puts your needs first. **Look for an agency that specializes in your destination, has been in business at least five years, and emphasizes customer service.** If you're looking for an agency-organized package or tour, your best bet is to choose an agency that's a member of the National Tour Association or the United States Tour Operator's Association (☞ Tour Operators, *above*).

➤ Local Agent Referrals: **American Society of Travel Agents** (✉ ASTA, 1101 King St., Suite 200, Alexandria, VA 22314, ☎ 703/739–2782, FAX 703/684–8319). **Alliance of Canadian Travel Associations** (✉ Suite 201, 1729 Bank St., Ottawa, Ontario K1V 7Z5, ☎ 613/521–0474, FAX 613/521–0805). **Association of British Travel Agents** (✉ 55–57 Newman St., London W1P 4AH, ☎ 0171/637–2444, FAX 0171/637–0713).

Travel catalogs specialize in useful items, such as compact alarm clocks and travel irons, that can **save space when packing.** They also offer dual-voltage appliances, currency converters, and foreign-language phrase books.

➤ Mail-Order Catalogs: **Magellan's** (☎ 800/962–4943, FAX 805/568–5406). **Orvis Travel** (☎ 800/541–3541, FAX 540/343–7053). **TravelSmith** (☎ 800/950–1600, FAX 800/950–1656).

U

The U.S. government can be an excellent source of inexpensive travel information. When planning your trip, **find out what government materials are available.**

➤ Advisories: **U.S. Department of State American Citizens Services Office** (✉ Room 4811, Washington,

DC 20520); enclose a self-addresses, stamped envelope. **Interactive hot line** (☎ 202/647–5225, FAX 202/647–3000). **Computer bulletin board** (☎ 202/647–9225).

➤ PAMPHLETS: **Consumer Information Center** (✉ Consumer Information Catalogue, Pueblo, CO 81009, ☎ 719/948–3334) for a free catalog that includes travel titles.

V
VISITOR INFORMATION

For general information contact these regional tourism bureaus.

➤ PROVINCES AND TERRITORIES: U.S.: In Alberta, **Travel Alberta** (✉ Box 2500, Edmonton, T5J 2Z4, ☎ 800/661–8888); in British Columbia, **Tourism British Columbia** (✉ 802–865 Hornby St., Vancouver, V6Z 2G3, ☎ 604/660–2861 or 800/663–6000); in Manitoba, **Travel Manitoba** (✉ 155 Carlton St., 7th floor, Winnipeg, R3C 3H8, ☎ 800/665–0040); in New Brunswick, **Tourism New Brunswick** (✉ Box 12345, Woodstock, E0J 2B0, ☎ 800/561–0123); in Newfoundland and Labrador, **Newfoundland and Labrador Department of Tourism, Recreation and Culture** (✉ Box 8730, St. John's, A1B 4K2, ☎ 800/563–6353); in the Northwest Territories, **Northwest Territories Tourism** (✉ Box 1320, Yellowknife, X1A 2L9, ☎ 800/661–0788); in Nova Scotia, **Nova Scotia Tourism** (✉ Box 130, Halifax, B3J 2M7, ☎ 800/565–0000); in Ontario, **Travelinx Ontario** (✉ 1 Concord Gate Place, 9th floor, Don Mills, Ontario, ☎ 800/668–2746); in Prince Edward Island, **Prince Edward Island Department of Tourism, Parks and Recreation** (✉ Box 940, Charlottetown, C1A 7M5, ☎ 800/463–4734); in Québec, **Tourisme Québec** (✉ C.P. 979, Montréal, Québec, H3C 2W3, ☎ 800/363–7777); in Saskatchewan, **Tourism Saskatchewan** (✉ 1900 Albert St., Suite 500, Regina S4P 4L9, ☎ 800/667–7191); in the Yukon, **Tourism Yukon** (✉ Box 2703, Whitehorse, Y1A 2C6, ☎ 867/667–5340).

➤ IN THE U.K.: **Visit Canada Center** (✉ 62–65 Trafalgar Sq., London, WC2 5DY, ☎ 0891/715–000). Calls to the Visit Canada Center cost 50p per minute peak rate and 45p per minute cheap rate. **Québec Tourism** (✉ 59 Pall Mall, London SW1Y 5JH, ☎ 0990/561–705).

W
WHEN TO GO

When to visit Canada will depend on your itinerary and your interests. In the maritime provinces of Nova Scotia, New Brunswick, and Prince Edward Island, the weather is relatively mild, though snow can remain on the ground well into spring and fog is common year-round. In Newfoundland and Labrador temperatures vary widely; winter days can be about 32°F (0°C) in St. John's—and as low as −50°F (−45°C) in Labrador and on the west coast. Québec and Ontario have hot, steamy summers and severe winters, with snow lasting from mid-December to mid-March. The whole of eastern Canada enjoys blooming springs and brilliant autumns.

Farther west, in Manitoba, Saskatchewan, and Alberta, summers are short but sunny, and marked by an occasional heavy shower. In winter, snowfall here is light, but temperatures stay low. Southern British Columbia has warmer winters and mild summers. Though the weather fluctuates because of the mountain ranges—the Coast Mountains and the eastern chain of the Rockies—the coastal region has the country's mildest winters, with rainfall almost inevitable. Summers here are fairly sunny, but seldom oppressively hot. The best time to visit northern Canada is during its short but surprisingly warm summer. The area—which includes the northern parts of the provinces of British Columbia, Alberta, Saskatchewan, Manitoba, Ontario, and Québec, as well as the Yukon and Northwest Territories—is like Siberia in winter, with devastating cold and dangerous wind chill.

Climate in Canada

The following are average daily maximum and minimum temperatures for some of Canada's major cities.

CALGARY

Jan.	23F	− 5C	May	61F	16C	Sept.	63F	17C
	2	−17		37	3		39	4
Feb.	29F	− 2C	June	67F	19C	Oct.	54F	12C
	8	−13		44	7		30	− 1
Mar.	34F	1C	July	74F	23C	Nov.	38F	3C
	14	−10		49	9		17	− 8
Apr.	49F	9C	Aug.	72F	22C	Dec.	29F	− 2C
	27	− 3		47	8		8	−13

EDMONTON

Jan.	14F	−10C	May	63F	17C	Sept.	62F	17C
	− 3	−19		41	5		41	5
Feb.	22F	− 6C	June	69F	21C	Oct.	52F	11C
	4	−16		48	9		32	0
Mar.	31F	− 1C	July	74F	23C	Nov.	32F	0C
	13	−11		53	12		17	− 8
Apr.	49F	9C	Aug.	71F	22C	Dec.	21F	− 6C
	29	− 2		50	10		5	−15

HALIFAX

Jan.	33F	1C	May	58F	14C	Sept.	67F	19C
	20	− 7		41	5		53	12
Feb.	33F	1C	June	67F	19C	Oct.	58F	14C
	19	− 7		50	10		44	7
Mar.	39F	4C	July	73F	23C	Nov.	48F	9C
	26	− 3		57	14		36	2
Apr.	48F	9C	Aug.	73F	24C	Dec.	37F	3C
	33	1		58	13		25	4

MONTRÉAL

Jan.	23F	− 5C	May	65F	18C	Sept.	68F	20C
	9	−13		48	9		53	12
Feb.	25F	− 4C	June	74F	23C	Oct.	57F	14C
	12	−11		58	14		43	6
Mar.	36F	2C	July	79F	26C	Nov.	42F	6C
	23	− 5		63	17		32	0
Apr.	52F	11C	Aug.	76F	24C	Dec.	27F	− 3C
	36	2		61	16		16	− 9

OTTAWA

Jan.	20F	− 7C	May	65F	18C	Sept.	68F	20C
	4	−16		44	7		49	9
Feb.	23F	− 5C	June	75F	24C	Oct.	57F	14C
	6	−14		54	12		39	4
Mar.	34F	1C	July	80F	27C	Nov.	41F	5C
	18	− 8		58	14		29	− 2
Apr.	51F	11C	Aug.	77F	25C	Dec.	25F	− 4C
	33	1		56	13		12	−11

QUÉBEC CITY

Jan.	20F	– 7C	**May**	62F	17C	**Sept.**	66F	19C
	6	–14		43	6		49	9
Feb.	23F	– 5C	**June**	72F	22C	**Oct.**	53F	12C
	8	–13		53	12		39	4
Mar.	33F	1C	**July**	78F	26C	**Nov.**	39F	4C
	19	– 7		58	14		28	– 2
Apr.	47F	8C	**Aug.**	75F	24C	**Dec.**	24F	– 4C
	32	0		56	13		12	–11

TORONTO

Jan.	30F	– 1C	**May**	64F	18C	**Sept.**	71F	22C
	18	– 8		47	8		54	12
Feb.	32F	0C	**June**	76F	24C	**Oct.**	60F	16C
	19	– 7		57	14		45	7
Mar.	40F	4C	**July**	80F	27C	**Nov.**	46F	8C
	27	– 3		62	17		35	2
Apr.	53F	12C	**Aug.**	79F	26C	**Dec.**	34F	1C
	38	3		61	16		23	– 5

VANCOUVER

Jan.	42F	6C	**May**	60F	16C	**Sept.**	65F	8C
	33	1		47	8		52	11
Feb.	45F	7C	**June**	65F	18C	**Oct.**	56F	13C
	36	2		52	11		45	7
Mar.	48F	9C	**July**	70F	1C	**Nov.**	48F	9C
	37	3		55	13		39	4
Apr.	54F	12C	**Aug.**	70F	21C	**Dec.**	43F	6C
	41	5		55	13		35	2

➤ FORECASTS: **Weather Channel Connection** (☎ 900/932–8437), 95¢ per minute from a Touch-Tone phone.

1 Destination: Canada

A GRAND PLACE

LET'S FACE IT, Canadians have an image problem. To most people we come across as a bit, well, dull. Nice enough and certainly polite. But boring. Good at driving in snow, perhaps, and excellent at helping little old ladies across the street, but not the kind of people you're likely to run into in a soap opera or a gunfight. Not heroic or sexy and certainly not nasty. Canadians can't even curse each other without adding a faintly interrogatory "eh" at the end, as if seeking approval for the harsh words. As in "Go to hell, eh?"

We also get overlooked a lot. The *Boston Globe* runs a regular quiz in its travel section, and one week it asked which country most foreign visitors to the United States come from. The answer given was Japan. Huh? What about us? We're foreign, too, and on any given night there are more Canadians bedding down in Vermont than there are Japanese in all 50 states.

So, given all this, how do you explain hockey—12 guys on ice with steel blades on their feet and big sticks in their hands, slamming each other around in a wood and Plexiglas box? That's not the sort of thing you'd expect from a polite and diffident people. But it's our national passion—almost a religion in some places. "You don't like hockey," Stuart McLean writes in his delightful *Welcome Home.* "You believe in it." And the reputation we have is dreadful. Russians, the conventional wisdom goes, play with skill. Americans play with heart. Canadians just play dirty.

Mary Henderson sees no contradiction. She's a sweet and tiny lady who runs a day care center in Manitoba and helps raise money for the local hospital. But every Saturday night from September through April, she watches Hockey Night in Canada on CBC television with blood in her eye and heat in her heart. "We're so nice everybody takes us for granted," she says. "In hockey we're allowed to be nasty. We can even break the rules. You can't take us for granted there."

Maybe she's right. It's hard to overlook Stéphane Richer or Eric Lindros on the ice,

no matter whose sweater they're wearing. Or maybe it's just that hockey is one of the main patriotic outlets Canadians allow themselves. The rest of the time we're too busy being diffident to indulge in any kind of showy display. Sometimes this goes to ridiculous extremes. My daughter goes to a French high school for girls in Montréal. One day the school took everyone to Ottawa, the nation's capital, to tour the Parliament Buildings and visit a couple of museums. On the way home, some of the girls, mostly English-speaking ones, wanted to sing "O Canada." The teachers said "non." It might offend the Québec nationalists on the bus. Even if they sang it in French.

Canada's kind of an accident, a big disjointed puzzle spread across the top of a continent, and it's much too large for the people who inhabit it. There are only 30 million Canadians—no more than the population of New York and California combined—scattered across a land bigger than China. They have two official languages, five time zones, and 10 provincial governments. It's a wonder anything gets done. It's true that most Canadians live within 323 km (200 mi) of the American border, and 75% of them live in cities, but even that doesn't create much density. Cole Harris, an editor of the *Canadian Encyclopedia,* described the inhabited part of Canada as "an island archipelago spread over 4,000 east–west miles."

In a particularly unkind moment, Lucien Bouchard, the leader of the separatist Parti Québécois, angered the nation by saying Canada wasn't a real country at all—this from a man who served as the non-country's ambassador to France for several years. But he had something of a point. Canada's not so much a country as a work in progress, an unfinished symphony. And we can be irritatingly undecided about who we are. Take our spelling, for example. We see plays in "theatres" just like the English, but we live in "neighborhoods" just like the Americans.

And then there's our birthday. We celebrate it on July 1 because on that day in 1867, the British Parliament joined the four provinces of Québec, Ontario, Nova Scotia, and New Brunswick into a new and independent federation. Well, sort of independent. The holiday used to be called Dominion Day, because Canada was once officially a dominion, whatever that is. Then for some reason, the name was changed to Canada Day, a lamentable choice. There's no such thing as Greece Day or France Day. And it gives the unfortunate impression that Canada popped out of nowhere in 1867, without history or feeling. And that just isn't true.

THE CONSTITUTIONAL conundrum that is Canada was actually conceived, if not born, in a flash of smoke and passion more than 100 years earlier on a warm September night in 1759 when Major-General James Wolfe scrambled up the 300-ft cliffs outside Québec City and mustered his men on the Plains of Abraham. It's a long, steep climb for any man. It must have been murder for a frail, tubercular general wearing red serge, buckled shoes, and a powdered wig.

His soldiers, of course, had to make the climb as well. But a lot of them had names like Fraser and Murray and were used to steep hills. They were also wearing kilts, which make surprisingly good climbing outfits if you're not worried about modesty.

Wolfe had about 4,500 men on the field that day and so did his French opponent, General the Marquis de Montcalm. A lot of Montcalm's soldiers, however, were militiamen, good at the cat-and-mouse tactics of Indian warfare perhaps, but lacking the stand-and-take-it discipline required to fight a pitched battle in the 18th century. So once Wolfe had lured them out of their fortified position, his hardened regulars took about an hour to drive them from the field. When it was all over, the British crown had a new French-speaking colony to govern, the "Canadiens" had new imperial masters to manipulate, and the undertakers had two dead generals to bury.

It all worked fairly well for a while. As conquerors go, the British were pretty benign, and the French kept their faith, their language, and their seigneurs. Then those pesky Americans to the south rebelled against their British masters. Tory refugees—traitors at home, Loyalists to us—fled north. Presto—biculturalism was born. And so was the struggle that consumes our poetry and our politics.

The province of Québec is the true cradle of Canada. Its population's about 85% French, and it totters on the brink of going it alone, of leaving the federation. Its most popular politicians are separatists and its poets and singers are relentlessly nationalist. Talk of independence is everywhere.

Eric Deschênes is a merry little man who's mayor of Godbout on the North Shore of the Gulf of St. Lawrence. It's a tiny place of austere beauty, but it's Eric's hometown and he loves it dearly. He gave up an academic career to go back there to fish and hunt and to run a little inn. He's cheerfully matter-of-fact about his nationalism. "Why don't you and your family spend the day with us?" he asked one sunny afternoon in late August. "As long as you don't mind the company of a good little separatist."

He took us for a boat ride on his favorite lake and then to his fishing camp on the Rivière Godbout, where we devoured a whole salmon he'd smoked himself. He tried to explain the reluctance of half the province's population to buy the nationalist dream. A lack of self-confidence, he suggested. "People here thought Godbout was finished when the American paper company pulled out," he said. "They were wrong. People have to learn to rely on themselves. And they will."

None of which washes with Malcolm Turner, a peach farmer in British Columbia's warm and lush Okanagan Valley. Quebecers like to paint themselves as oppressed, he told me as we rode a chairlift together at the Big White ski resort. "What a crock. Right now the prime minister is French, the Governor General is French, the chief justice of the Supreme Court is French, and I think the next commander of the armed forces is going to be French. That's an oppressed people? Give me a break."

The odd thing about all this is the civilized way in which this passionate debate is conducted. Rancorous things get said, all right, and spokespeople for both sides can sometimes come off sounding like bigots, but all in all we seldom lose our cool. When separatist leader Bouchard lost his leg and nearly his life to a grue-some disease in 1995, Canadian congre-gations across the country prayed for him in both official languages (and a few un-official ones, as well). When floods wiped out thousands of homes in the notori-ously nationalist Saguenay–Lac-St-Jean region of Québec in summer 1996, Cana-dians raised $28 million in aid and sent the area truckloads of clothing, toys, and food. Even on October 30, 1995, when a Quebec referendum on independence ended in a virtual dead heat, nothing much happened. Tempers were high and patience thin, but there were no riots and no angry demonstrations, just a few scuf-fles outside the various campaign head-quarters. Then everyone went out for a drink.

To MANY CANADIANS, of course, the endless debate and the "neverendums" are irrele-vant, even plain silly. A lot of people have moved to Canada since 1867, people from Italy, Greece, China, Ukraine, Portugal, Ire-land, Iceland, India, Spain, the Caribbean, and most recently, Latin America. They've brought their faiths and their customs, their food and their music, and sometimes even their own quarrels. And they have irre-vocably changed the country: Women in veils drive Montréal buses; Edmonton has an Ethiopian restaurant; and at least one Mountie wears a turban. Toronto is now the most multicultural city on earth; French-speaking Montréal counts smoked meat and bagels among its distinctive dishes; and Vancouver has been strug-gling with ways to accommodate the thou-sands of Hong Kong Chinese who have poured into the city since Britain decided to give its Far East colony back to China. Most of these people have a hard time un-derstanding what the English and the French are fighting about.

"What this country needs is a real prob-lem," a Guatemalan refugee told me. He smiled when he said it, but I could see the pain in his eyes. He was sitting in a church-sponsored legal clinic finding out what he had to do to become a landed immigrant. "There are people who look at Canada from afar. Canada—big, rich, and beau-tiful—and they just can't understand what's happening."

And he, too, has a point. Our economy is shaky, the national debt is high, and our social-safety net has taken a bit of a beat-ing. And we've had some shocks in the last few years. A madman gunned down 14 women at an engineering school in Mont-réal in 1989 and our well-loved peace-keeping soldiers beat a Somali teenager to death in 1992. But all those troubles must seem pretty trivial to someone from Guatemala or India or Vietnam.

For this is still a rich and tolerant land. No one has to go hungry, medical care is free for anyone who needs it, and even the poorest of our poor are affluent beyond the imagining of much of the world. The cities where most of us live are safe and clean, with downtowns that are bright and full of life. People wander freely about at night, strolling from restaurant to cabaret to theater with little thought about personal safety.

And there's always that landscape, that end-less and achingly beautiful landscape. We may be an urban people now, but the wilderness is never far away. I live in Montréal, one of the country's great metropolises, but in two hours I can be skiing on Mont-Tremblant, in four I can be hopelessly lost in the tundra of Charlevoix, and in 12 I can be on the shore of James Bay, celebrating the annual goose hunt with Cree whose lifestyle has changed little over the centuries.

Canadians make much ado about winter. They love to whine about the cold and day-dream about palm trees. But the truth is, winter is part of what makes us Canadian, and many of us revel in it. "*Mon pays, ce n'est pas un pays, c'est l'hiver*," chan-sonier Gilles Vigneault sang in his most famous song. "My country's not a coun-try; it's winter."

I remember a night in late January walk-ing along the shores of Lac Turgeon in the middle of northeastern Québec. The drifts were deep enough to bury me standing up and stiff enough to bear my weight. It was bitterly cold. The snow squeaked as I walked and my sinuses crackled every time I inhaled. But the air smelled sweetly of wood smoke, and the black velvet sky sparkled with the brittle light of a million stars. God, it was beautiful.

And all this landscape and beauty is ours. From the coves of Newfoundland to the mountains of British Columbia, from the Great Lakes to the Arctic desert. It's all ours—the wheat farms of the prairies, the beef ranches of the Rocky Mountain foothills, the Gaelic songs of Cape Breton, the great cathedrals of Québec, the vineyards of the Niagara Peninsula, the clouds of snow geese that fill our sky every spring and fall—ours to hold, ours to pass on to our children and our grandchildren, ours to share with whoever wants to join us.

One July 1, I rode into the Yukon back country with a Tutchone grandfather named Fred Brown. He's a lean wiry whip of a man who owns a modern bungalow with all the conveniences but who prefers to live in the bush. We spent the morning plodding a zigzag course from a hot, dusty valley to the cool uplands of the Ruby Mountains. At noon we stopped and stretched out on lichen-covered rocks to doze in the sun, while our horses rested and snuffled in their bags for oats. In the evening we camped by a lake whose water was so clean and cold we could lie on our stomachs and suck it up the way the horses did. I caught a trout and Fred fried it over an open fire. We drank tea and he told me outrageous stories about how his grandmother used to snare moose and drink animal blood. The stories were funny but might have been true; you could never tell from Fred's deliberately blank face. At midnight it was still bright enough outside to play cards without a lantern. We hadn't said anything about Dominion Day or Canada Day, but just before we turned in, Fred looked at me with a smile and said, "This is a grand place, white man. Be thankful."

And so I am.

— Paul Waters

Paul Waters, a Canadian journalist, was raised and educated on the Atlantic coast and has had the privilege to have lived in all three of Canada's major cities: Montréal, Toronto, and Vancouver. He now lives in Montréal with his family.

NEW AND NOTEWORTHY

You may be planning to visit Canada for any number of reasons—to enjoy the great outdoors in spectacular national parks, to explore the beautiful Atlantic and Pacific coasts, or to savor the pleasures of sophisticated cities. Wherever you're heading, it's good to know that your dollar will go farther in Canada, even with higher Canadian taxes. Following the trend of the past few years, the exchange rate (summer 1997) is about US$1 to C$1.29, and £1 to C$2.18.

BRITISH COLUMBIA➤ Transportation into popular **Vancouver** is improving, with more direct flights (a result of the Open Skies agreement signed by the United States and Canada) and with Amtrak daily train service into Vancouver from Seattle. The Adams River east of Kamloops will be the site of a massive **sockeye salmon run** in 1998; this happens only every four years, and it's an impressive sight.

MONTRÉAL➤ This island city has never let politics get in the way of a good time. Its summer **festivals** of jazz, film, fireworks, and comedy are among the most important in the world. And the Canadiens hockey team moved into a brand-new downtown home, **Centre Molson.**

NEW BRUNSWICK➤ The **Kingsbrae Gardens,** a horticultural garden complete with mazes, is scheduled to open in spring 1998 on a historic estate in St. Andrews.

NEWFOUNDLAND AND LABRADOR➤ A new Marine Interpretation Centre in **Terra Nova National Park** in the Bonavista Bay area of eastern Newfoundland includes touch tanks, displays, and tours. It signals a change in the park's focus from land to sea. The **Ryan Premises National Historic Site** in Cape Bonavista depicts the almost 500-year history of the commercial cod fishery in a restored fish merchant's properties.

ONTARIO➤ The latest hot spot in Niagara Falls is **Casino Niagara,** which occupies an old strip mall opposite the Falls. The 3,000 slot machines and more than 100 gaming tables mean that no one will be left out of the action.

PRAIRIE PROVINCES➤ In Cochrane, west of Calgary, the **Western Heritage Centre** is a new interpretive center dedicated to the history of ranching, farming, and rodeos; and the people who operated the first ranches in Alberta.

PRINCE EDWARD ISLAND➤ Travelers coming to the province via New Brunswick will see the completion of the Island's newest attraction: The 13-km (8-mi) **Confederation Bridge** is the Island's first fixed link to the mainland. You'll be able to get to the Island now in about 12 minutes, instead of waiting for the ferry.

WILDERNESS CANADA➤ A yearlong celebration will mark the **centennial of the Yukon Gold Rush.** Festivals throughout the region will feature dog-sled races, hot-air ballooning, music, and storytelling. The Dawson City International Gold Show in May and Gold-Panning Championships in July promise to be highlights.

WHAT'S WHERE

The sections below correspond to regional chapters in this book; major cities that have their own chapters are indicated below in boldface type.

British Columbia

Canada's westernmost province harbors Pacific beaches, forested islands, year-round skiing, world-class fishing—a wealth of outdoor action and beauty. Its towns and cities, from Anglophile Victoria to the re-created Native American village of 'Ksan reflect the diversity of its inhabitants. Cosmopolitan **Vancouver,** Canada's answer to San Francisco, enjoys a spectacular setting. Tall fir trees stand practically downtown, rock spires tower close by, the ocean is at your doorstep, and people from every corner of the earth create a young and vibrant atmosphere.

Canadian Rockies

The series of ranges that form the Canadian Rockies straddles the British Columbia–Alberta line from the U.S. border in the south to the Yukon in the north. Their beauty has been preserved in provincial and national parks; in these mountains you can fish, ski, hike, mountain climb, boat, and horseback ride, as well as enjoy some of the best resort facilities anywhere.

New Brunswick

New Brunswick is where the great Canadian forest, sliced by sweeping river valleys and modern highways, meets the

Atlantic. To the north and east, the gentle, warm Gulf Stream washes quiet beaches. Besides the seacoast, there are pure inland streams, pretty towns, and historic cities. The province's dual heritage (35% of its population is Acadian French) provides added spice.

Newfoundland and Labrador

Canada's easternmost province, Newfoundland, was a center of the world's cod fishing industry for 400 years until the supply ran out in 1992. In summer, Newfoundland's stark cliffs, bogs, and meadows become a riot of wildflowers and greenery, and the sea is dotted with boats and buoys. St. John's, the capital, is a classic harbor city.

Nova Scotia

This little province on the Atlantic coast, compact and distinctive, has a capital city, Halifax, the same size as Christopher Marlowe's London. The days when Nova Scotians were prosperous shipwrights and merchants trading with the world left Victorian mansions in all the salty little ports that dot the coastline and created a uniquely Nova Scotian outlook: worldly, approachable, and sturdily independent.

Ontario

With shorelines on four of the five Great Lakes, Ontario is Canada's second-largest and most urbanized province, but only 10 million people live in this vast area, and 90% of them are within a narrow strip just north of the U.S. border. A bit north of the strip, Ottawa, Canada's capital, gathers government workers and parliamentarians. **Toronto** thrives on ethnic diversity, filled as it is with Italians, Chinese, Portuguese, and other groups in a vibrant mix of cultures. This cosmopolitan, world-class city, established by Scots who set up banks and built churches, is Canada's center of culture, commerce, and communications.

Prairie Provinces

Between the eastern slopes of the Rockies and the wilds of western Ontario lie Canada's three prairie provinces: Alberta, Saskatchewan, and Manitoba. The northern parts of this region are sparsely populated expanses of lakes, rivers, and forests. The fertile plains of the south support farms and ranches—interspersed with wide river valleys, lakes, rolling hills, badlands, dry hills of sand, and oil wells—as well as five busy cities: Calgary, Edmonton, Saskatoon, Regina, and Winnipeg.

Prince Edward Island

In the Gulf of St. Lawrence north of Nova Scotia and New Brunswick, Prince Edward Island seems too good to be true, with its crisply painted farmhouses, manicured green fields rolling down to sandy beaches, the warmest ocean water north of Florida, lobster boats in trim little harbors, and a vest-pocket capital city, Charlottetown, packed with architectural heritage.

Québec

Québec is set apart by its strong French heritage, a matter not only of language but of customs, religion, and political structure. Defining the land outside the cities are innumerable lakes, streams, and rivers; farmlands and villages; great mountains, such as the Laurentians with their ski resorts, and deep forests; and a rugged coastline along the Gulf of St. Lawrence. **Québec City,** which enjoys one of the most beautiful natural settings in North America, perched on a cliff above a narrow point in the St. Lawrence River, is the capital of, as well as the oldest municipality in, Québec province. **Montréal** is Canada's most romantic metropolis, an island city that seems to favor grace and elegance over order and even prosperity—a city full of music, art, and joie de vivre.

Wilderness Canada

Life above the 60th parallel in the mountainous, river-threaded Yukon and the flat, lake-dotted Northwest Territories is strange and wonderful. The landscape is austere and beautiful in ways unlike anywhere else in North America: tundra plains that reach to the Arctic Ocean, remote ice fields of the St. Elias Mountains, and white-water rivers snaking through mountain ranges and deep canyons. This is also the last region of North America where native peoples have managed to sustain traditional cultures relatively undisturbed.

PLEASURES AND PASTIMES

Dining

Canadian fine dining really began in Québec, where eating out in a good restaurant with a good bottle of wine has long been a traditional part of life. Eating out was slower to catch on in other parts of the country, however, and right up until the early 1970s, Toronto was notorious for its poor food and barbarous drinking laws. But immigrants from places like Italy, Greece, Portugal, Japan, China, and India changed all that. They liked to eat and found the drinking laws incomprehensible. Soon, even the stuffiest Torontonians were eschewing the traditional overdone beef and soggy vegetables and learning how to pronounce things like velouté, *forestière,* tagliolini, manicotti, and *tzatziki.* In Vancouver there's plenty of West Coast flair, a kind of modified California fusion that makes fine use of local specialties from salmon to Pacific halibut and Dungeness crab. The country, of course, is rich in the basic ingredients—native cheeses from Québec and Ontario; lobster, mussels, salmon, and sole from both oceans; fine beef from Alberta; and lots of local delicacies like fiddlehead ferns, wild rice, game meat, and seal-flipper pie.

The Great Outdoors

Most Canadians live in towns and cities within 300 km (200 mi) of the American border, but the country does have a splendid backyard to play in. Even major cities like Montréal and Vancouver are just a few hours drive from a wilderness full of rivers, lakes, and mountains. A network of 34 national parks, from Kluane in Yukon to Cape Breton Highlands in Nova Scotia, is backed by dozens of provincial and regional parks. All this wilderness provides abundant opportunities for bicycling, camping, canoeing, hiking, boating, horseback riding, mountain climbing, skiing, white-water sports, and fishing. The coasts of British Columbia, the Gulf of St. Lawrence, and the Atlantic provinces are also ideal for whale-watching. The chapters in this book and provincial tourism authorities have information on all these activities.

Nightlife and the Arts

Canadians rejoice in their cities, which are clean, safe, and lively. A night on the town still means just that. Dinner, a play or concert, drinks, and maybe even a late show can be squeezed into an evening. And you can walk or take public transport from one event to the next. If you prefer, you can just stroll the brightly lit, crowded streets and do some people-watching. No one will mind. They'll be watching you.

Musically, Canada has managed to hold its own against its giant neighbor to the south. And it has done it on its own terms. Festivals celebrating everything from fiddles to fugues ornament summer schedules across the country and provide showcases for local talent. Names like Teresa Stratas, Anne Murray, k.d. lang, Joni Mitchell, Céline Dion, and Bryan Adams are already familiar south of the border. Less well-known people to look for are the Tragically Hip, perhaps the country's most popular rock band; Cape Breton's Rankin Family, who blend modern rhythms with traditional Gaelic songs; and Ashley MacIsaac, who has made Scottish fiddle music popular among the urban young. In French there are the heartbreaking lyrics of traditional chansonniers like Gilles Vigneault and Felix Leclerc and the carefully crafted pop-rock of Daniel Bélanger. On the classical scene, conductor Charles Dutoît has given the Orchéstre Symphonique de Montréal international lustre, and Toronto's Canadian Opera Company is highly rated.

Toronto has emerged as the third most important center for English-language theater after London and New York. The city has more than four dozen venues staging original plays, new musicals, recycled classics, and touring versions of big hits. Montréal is a center of French-language production, with 10 major companies. Shakespeare's classics are honored along with more modern plays at the Stratford Festival in rural Ontario every summer and the works of George Bernard Shaw anchor another major festival at Niagara-on-the-Lake, Ontario.

Shopping

Distinctively Canadian items include furs from Montréal, fashions from Montréal and Toronto, wood carvings from rural Québec, woven goods and hooked rugs from the Maritimes, quilts from the Men-nonite communities of Ontario, Inuit carvings from the Northwest Territories, native art and prints from the West Coast, native handicrafts from the prairies, and antiques from Montréal, Toronto, and Victoria. The most distinctive Canadian products, of course, come from the maple tree—sugar, syrup, taffy, candy, and even liqueur. Eastern Canada, in fact, produces more than three quarters of the world's supplies of such products.

Sports to Watch

Officially, Canada's national sport is lacrosse, but the nation's dominant passion is hockey. Millions of little boys—and, increasingly, little girls—start learning the sport when they're about five years old. Winter life for many families revolves around early morning rink times and evening telecasts of National Hockey League games. There are only six Canadian teams in the NHL—the Vancouver Canucks, Calgary Flames, Edmonton Oilers, Toronto Maple Leafs, Ottawa Senators, and Montréal Canadiens—but American teams are well stocked with Canadian-born stars. Getting tickets to NHL games is only slightly less difficult than getting a royal audience, so try going to see a Junior A or college game instead. The play is fast, tough, and entertaining.

Canadians also excel at something called curling, a game invented in Scotland. It looks a little like bowling, except that it's played on ice with 40-pound lumps of polished granite. Millions of Canadians participate in local leagues, especially in the prairie provinces, and major competitions, called bonspiels, get national television coverage.

Other sports do have their fans. There are two major-league baseball teams—the Montréal Expos and the Toronto Blue Jays—and two National Basketball Association franchises—the Toronto Raptors and the Vancouver Grizzlies. (Oddly enough, basketball was invented by Canadian James Naismith.) As for football, Canada has its own version of the game played with three downs on a bigger field than the American version. The Canadian Football League, however, is in a constant state of financial crisis, and it's nearly impossible to tell from one year to the next how many teams it will have.

Winter

If asked, most Canadians would probably claim they hate winter. Whining about the cold is a national pastime. But the fact is, the country revels in winter. There are major carnivals celebrating the season in Québec City, Ottawa, Montréal, Winnipeg, and Edmonton. Every town and village has at least a few skating rinks, and everyone has a favorite toboggan hill. In January and February fishermen erect whole villages of little huts on frozen rivers and lakes, and dog teams yap through the forest as soon as the snow is deep enough. There are thousands of miles of cross-country ski trails, and first-rate downhill ski resorts in Québec, Alberta, and British Columbia. Several major ski magazines have rated the Whistler-Blackcomb ski resort, north of Vancouver, the best in the world. One of the fastest-growing sports is snowmobiling. A network of 112,255 km (69,600 mi) of trails with its own restaurants, road signs, and maps crisscrosses much of the country, but the purists head for the backcountry to roar through untracked powder.

FODOR'S CHOICE

No two people will agree on what makes a perfect vacation, but it's fun and helpful to know what others think. We hope you'll have a chance to experience some of Fodor's Choices yourself in Canada. For detailed information about each entry, refer to the appropriate chapter.

Historic Sites

★ **Basilique Notre-Dame-de-Montréal, Montréal.** The enormous (3,800-seat) neo-Gothic church, opened in 1829, has a medieval-style interior with stained-glass windows, a star-studded, vaulted blue ceiling, and pine and walnut carving.

★ **Basilique Ste-Anne-de-Beaupré, outside Québec City.** The monumental church is an important shrine that draws hordes of pilgrims. According to local legend, St. Anne was responsible over the years for saving voyagers from shipwrecks in the harsh waters of the St. Lawrence; she is also believed to have healing powers.

★ **Vieux-Québec, Québec City.** The old town is small and dense, steeped in four centuries of history and French tradition. Immaculately preserved as the only fortified city in North America, it is a UNESCO World Heritage Site.

★ **Plains of Abraham, Québec City.** The site of the famous 1759 battle between the French and the British that decided the fate of New France is now part of a large park overlooking the St. Lawrence River.

★ **Kings Landing Historical Settlement, outside Fredericton, New Brunswick.** This reconstructed village—including homes, an inn, a forge, a store, a church, a school, working farms, and a sawmill—illustrates life in the central Saint John River valley between 1790 and 1900.

★ **Dredge No. 4, Dawson City, the Yukon, Wilderness Canada.** Dredge No. 4 was used to dig up the creek bed during the height of Bonanza Creek's gold-bearing largesse.

Parks and Gardens

★ **Butchart Gardens, Victoria, British Columbia.** This world-class horticultural collection grows more than 700 varieties of flowers and has Italian, Japanese, and English rose gardens.

★ **Pacific Rim National Park, Vancouver Island, British Columbia.** The first national marine park in Canada comprises a hard-packed white-sand beach, a group of islands, and a demanding coastal hiking trail where you'll find panoramic views of the sea, the rain forest, sandstone cliffs, and wildlife.

★ **Banff National Park, Canadian Rockies.** Canada's first national park was officially established in 1887 and includes Lake Louise and part of the Icefields Parkway. Its spectacular mountain peaks, forests, and wildlife remain relatively untouched by human development, protected by strict laws.

★ **Jardin Botanique de Montréal, Montréal.** This botanical garden, with 181 acres of gardens in summer and 10 greenhouses open all year, has one of the best bonsai collections in the West and the largest Ming-style garden outside Asia.

★ **Cape Breton Highlands National Park, Nova Scotia.** A wilderness of wooded valleys, plateau barrens, and steep cliffs, it stretches across the northern peninsula of Nova Scotia's Cape Breton Island.

🟊 **Prince Edward Island National Park, Prince Edward Island.** Along the north shore of the island on the Gulf of St. Lawrence, sky and sea meet red sandstone cliffs, rolling dunes, and long stretches of sand.

🟊 **Nahanni National Park, Wilderness Canada.** Access to this mountainous park in the Northwest Territories is possible only by helicopter or plane; inside the park, canoes and rafts are the principal means of travel.

Views to Remember

🟊 **The view from the Jasper Tramway, Canadian Rockies.** From the steep flank of Whistlers Mountain you can see the summit of Mt. Robson (the Canadian Rockies' highest mountain), the Miette valley to the west, and Athabasca valley to the east.

🟊 **View of Niagara Falls by helicopter, Ontario.** Niagara Helicopters Ltd. takes you over the Giant Whirlpool, up the Niagara Gorge, and past the American Falls and then banks around the curve of the Horseshoe Falls.

🟊 **Peggy's Cove, Nova Scotia.** At the mouth of a bay facing the open Atlantic, the cove, with its houses huddled around the narrow slit in the boulders, has the only Canadian post office in a lighthouse.

🟊 **Signal Hill National Historic Site, St. John's, Newfoundland.** Overlooking the snug, punch-bowl harbor of St. John's and the sea, this hilltop was taken and retaken by opposing forces in the 17th and 18th centuries.

Restaurants

🟊 **Star Anise, Vancouver.** Pacific Rim cuisine with French flair shines in this intimate restaurant on the west side of town. $$$

🟊 **Emerald Lake Lodge, Yoho, Canadian Rockies.** The eclectic menu of this glass-enclosed dining room at the edge of a glacier-fed lake in Yoho National Park joins traditional Canadian and American fare with nouvelle sauces. $$$$

🟊 **Toqué, Montréal.** This is the most fashionable and the most zany restaurant in Montréal. The menu depends on what the two chefs found fresh that day and on which way their ever-creative spirit moved them. $$$

🟊 **North 44, Toronto.** A steel compass highlighting Toronto's latitude embedded in a gorgeous marble floor and textured walls hung with mirrored sconces set the scene for innovative dining. $$$–$$$$

🟊 **L'Eau à la Bouche, Ste-Adèle, Québec.** At this Bavarian-style property you'll find a superb marriage of nouvelle cuisine and traditional Québec cooking in such dishes as roast veal in a cognac and Roquefort sauce. $$$$

Hotels

🟊 **English Bay Inn, Vancouver.** In this 1930s Tudor house a block from the ocean, the guest rooms have wonderful sleigh beds with matching armoires. A small, sunny English country garden brightens the back of the inn. $$

🟊 **Four Seasons Toronto.** The most exclusive property in town, it often tops all the "best hotel" lists. A great location, fine service, afternoon tea—what could be more civilized? $$$$

🟊 **Auberge du Vieux-Port, Montréal.** In an 1880s building in Vieux-Montréal, the inn overlooks the Vieux-Port and has tall windows and massive exposed beams. $$

🟊 **West Point Lighthouse, West Point, Prince Edward Island.** A functioning lighthouse in a provincial park, this small inn sits next to the beach. $$

FESTIVALS AND SEASONAL EVENTS

Contact local or provincial tourist boards for more information about these and other festivals.

WINTER

DECEMBER➤ **British Columbia:** The **Carol Ships,** sailboats full of carolers and decorated with colored lights, ply the waters of the Vancouver harbor.

Newfoundland and Labrador: In St. John's, **New Year's** revelers pour out of downtown pubs to gather on the waterfront to ring in the new year.

Prince Edward Island: The Prince Edward Island Crafts Council **Annual Christmas Craft Fair** brings juried producers to Charlottetown for the largest event of its kind on the Island.

JANUARY➤ **Alberta: Jasper Winter Festival** in Jasper and Marmot Basin presents dog sledding, skating, and ice sculpting.

British Columbia: The **Polar Bear Swim,** on New Year's Day in Vancouver, is said to bring good luck all year. **Skiing competitions** take place at most alpine ski resorts (through February).

Ontario: The **Niagara Falls Festival of Lights** is an extravaganza of colored lights in the parks surrounding the Falls.

FEBRUARY➤ **Alberta: Calgary Winter Festival** is a 10-day celebration of Calgary's Olympic spirit, with winter sports and ice sculpting.

Manitoba: Festival du Voyageur, in St. Boniface, Winnipeg, celebrates the history of the region's early fur traders.

Ontario: Ontario Winter Carnival Bon Soo animates Sault Ste. Marie. Ottawa's **Winterlude** encourages ice sculpting, snowshoe races, and ice boating.

Québec: *La Fête des Neiges* is winter carnival in Montréal. **Winter Carnival** in Québec City is an 11-day festival of winter sports competitions, ice-sculpture contests, and parades. Cross-country skiers race between Lachute and Gatineau in the **Canadian Ski Marathon.**

Yukon: The **Yukon Sourdough Rendezvous,** in Whitehorse, has dog-team races, leg wrestling, log sawing, snowshoe races, and talent contests.

SPRING

MARCH➤ **British Columbia:** The **Pacific Rim Whale Festival** on Vancouver Island's west coast celebrates the spring migration of gray whales with guided tours by whale experts and accompanying music and dancing. The **Vancouver International Wine Festival** is held at this time.

Manitoba: The **Royal Manitoba Winter Fair** takes place in Brandon.

Northwest Territories: The **Caribou Carnival** fills three days with traditional Inuit and Dene northern games, ice sculpting, cultural exhibits, and races in Yellowknife.

APRIL➤ **Alberta: Silver Buckle Rodeo** at Red Deer attracts cowboys from all over North America.

British Columbia: TerrifVic Jazz Party, in Victoria, has top international Dixieland bands.

Ontario: The **Maple Syrup Festival** sweetens Elmira. The distinguished **Shaw Festival** in Niagara-on-the-Lake (through November) presents plays by George Bernard Shaw and his contemporaries.

Québec: Sugaring-off parties celebrate the beginning of the maple syrup season.

MAY➤ **Alberta:** The **International Children's Festival** in Calgary and Edmonton draws musicians, mimes, jugglers, clowns, puppeteers, and singers worldwide. At the **Red Deer Annual Western Spring Quarter Horse Show,** horses from western Canada and the United States compete.

British Columbia: Cloverdale Rodeo in Surrey is rated sixth in the world by the Pro Rodeo Association. **Vancouver Children's Festival** provides free open-air stage performances.

Nova Scotia: In the Annapolis Valley, the **Apple Blossom Festival** includes dancing, parades, and entertainment.

Ontario: The internationally known **Stratford Festival,** in Stratford, presents many of Shakespeare's plays (through early November). **Folk Arts Festival** draws artists to St. Catharines. The **Canadian Tulip Festival,** in Ottawa, celebrates spring with 3 million blossoming tulips.

Saskatchewan: The **International Band and Choral Festival,** in Moose Jaw, attracts 7,000 musicians, 100 bands, and 25 choral groups. **Vesna Festival,** in Saskatoon, is the world's largest Ukrainian cabaret, with traditional Ukrainian food and crafts.

SUMMER

JUNE➤ **Alberta: Jazz City International Festival** in Edmonton has 10 days of jazz concerts, workshops, club dates, and free outdoor events. **Ponoka Annual Stampede** professional rodeo attracts participants from across the continent. **Banff Festival of the Arts** (through August) showcases nearly 1,000 young artists in music, opera, dance, drama, comedy, and visual arts.

British Columbia: Canadian International Dragon Boat Festival, in Vancouver, includes entertainment, exotic foods, and the ancient "awakening the dragons" ritual of long, slender boats decorated with huge dragon heads. **Whistler Summer Festivals,** through September, present daily street entertainment and a

variety of music festivals at the international ski and summer resort.

Manitoba: Winnipeg's **Red River Exhibition** features lumberjack contests, body-building shows, and an international band festival. **Winnipeg International Children's Festival** provides top national and international entertainment and activities.

New Brunswick: St. John's Day commemorates the city's birthday and includes a parade, street dance, concerts, and sporting and cultural events.

Nova Scotia: The **International Blues Festival** draws music lovers to Halifax.

Ontario: Toronto's **Metro International Caravan** is an ethnic fair. **Changing of the Guard** begins at Ottawa's Parliament Buildings (through August).

Prince Edward Island: Charlottetown Festival Theatre offers concerts and musicals (through September). In Summerside the annual **Summerside Highland Gathering** kicks off a summer of concerts and "Come to the Ceilidh" evenings.

Québec: Some of the world's best drivers compete in the **Player's Grand Prix** in Montréal. Québec City hops with the **International Jazz Festival.** Beauport hosts the **International Children's Folklore Festival.**

Saskatchewan: Frontier Days Regional Fair and Rodeo, in Swift Current, is a community fair with parades, a horse show, and a rodeo. **Mosaic,** in

Regina, celebrates cultures from around the world.

Yukon: The **Yukon International Festival of Storytelling,** in Whitehorse, draws storytellers from all over the North.

Northwest Territories: The **Midnight Classic Golf Tournament** in Yellowknife tees off at midnight on the first day of summer.

JULY➤ **Alberta: Ukrainian Pysanka Festival** in Vegreville celebrates with costumes and traditional singing and dancing. **Calgary Exhibition and Stampede** is one of the most popular Canadian events and includes 10 days of Western showmanship, hot-air balloon races, chuck wagon races, agricultural shows, and crafts exhibits. **Edmonton's Klondike Days** celebrate the town's early frontier community with pancake breakfasts, gambling casinos, gold panning, and raft races.

British Columbia: Harrison Festival of the Arts focuses on different ethnic music, dance, and theater, such as African, Caribbean, or Central American. **Vancouver Sea Festival** celebrates the city's nautical heritage with the World Championship Bathtub Race, sailing regattas, and windsurfing races.

Manitoba: At the **Winnipeg Folk Festival,** in Birds Hill Park, 24 km (15 mi) northeast of Winnipeg, country, bluegrass, folk, Acadian music, and jazz can be heard on 10 stages. **Manitoba Stampede and Exhibition** in Morris is an agricultural fair with rodeos and chuck wagon races.

New Brunswick: Loyalist City Festival, in St. John, celebrates the town's founding with parades, dancing, and sidewalk festivities. The **Shediac Lobster Festival** takes place in the town that calls itself the Lobster Capital of the World. There's an **Irish Festival** in Miramichi. The **New Brunswick Highland Games & Scottish Festival** is in Fredericton. In Edmunston the **Foire Brayonne** has music, cultural events, and sports; it's the biggest Francophone festival outside Québec's Winter Carnival.

Newfoundland and Labrador: The **Hangashore Folk Festival** is in Corner Brook, the **Exploits Valley Salmon Festival** in the Grand Falls area, the **Fish, Fun and Folk Festival** in Twillingate, and the **Conception Bay Folk Festival** in Carbonear. **Musicfest** in Stephenville celebrates music, from rock and roll to traditional Newfoundland. **Signal Hill Tattoo** in St. John's (through August) reenacts the final 1762 battle of the Seven Years' War between the British and the French. The **Burin Peninsula Festival of Folk Song and Dance** features traditional Newfoundland entertainment.

Nova Scotia: Antigonish Highland Games, staged annually since 1861, has Scottish music, dance, and such ancient sporting events as the caber toss. Halifax hosts the **Nova Scotia International Tattoo.** The **Atlantic Jazz Festival** is a Halifax highlight.

Ontario: Ottawa celebrates **Canada Day** with entertainment and fireworks. The **Queen's Plate** Thoroughbred horse race takes place in Toronto. There's a **Blueberry Festival** in Sudbury. The **Molson INDY** race roars through Toronto. **Caribana** festival celebrates Toronto's West Indian community. The **Glengarry Highland Games,** in Maxville, is North America's largest Highland gathering.

Prince Edward Island: The **Annual Outdoor Scottish Fiddle and Dance Festival** skirls through Richmond. Rollo Bay hosts a **Fiddle Festival.** Summerside's **Lobster Carnival** is a weeklong feast of lobster. **Canada Day** festivities abound in even the smallest community on the first of the month.

Québec: Festival International de Jazz de Montréal draws more than 2,000 musicians from all over the world for this 11-day series. **Québec International Summer Festival** offers entertainment in the streets and parks of old Québec City. Montréal's **Juste pour Rire** (Just for Laughs) comedy festival features comics from around the world, in French and English. Drummondville **World Folklore Festival** brings troupes from more than 20 countries to perform in the streets and parks. At **Festival Orford** international artists perform in Orford Park's music center (through August). **Matinée Ltd. International** spotlights the best male tennis players in Montréal.

Saskatchewan: *The Trial of Louis Riel,* in Regina, one of Canada's longest-running stage shows, reenacts the events surrounding the Northwest Rebellion of 1885 (late July through August). **Shakespeare on the Saskatchewan Festival,** in Saskatoon, has productions in tents on the banks of the South Saskatchewan River (early July–late August).

Northwest Territories: The **Annual Great Northern Arts Festival** in Inuvik presents displays, workshops, live performances, and artist demonstrations for the region's premiere cultural event.

AUGUST➤ **Alberta:** The **Fringe Theatre Festival,** in Edmonton, is one of the major festivals for alternative theater in North America. The **Golden Walleye Classic** in High Prairie is a three-day fishing tournament, with $90,000 in prizes.

British Columbia: Squamish Days Loggers Sports Festival draws loggers from around the world to compete in a series of incredible logging feats. The **Abbotsford International Airshow** is three days of flight performances and a large-aircraft display. **Pacific National Exhibition** in Vancouver has parades, exhibits, sports, entertainment, and logging contests.

Manitoba: Folklorama, the largest multicultural festival in the world, sets up more than 40 pavilions throughout Winnipeg. The **National Ukrainian Festival,** in Dauphin, offers costumes, artifacts, exhibits, fiddling contests, dancing, and workshops.

The **Icelandic Festival,** in Gimli, gathers the largest Icelandic community outside of Iceland. **Pioneer Days,** in Steinbach, celebrates the heritage of the Mennonites with demonstrations of threshing and baking, a parade, a horse show, a barbecue, and Mennonite foods.

New Brunswick: The **Miramichi Folk Song Festival** features traditional and contemporary folk songs steeped in Maritime lore. **Acadian Festival,** at Caraquet, celebrates the region's Acadian heritage with folk singing and food. The **Chocolate Festival** in St. Stephen includes suppers, displays, and children's events.

Newfoundland and Labrador: Gander's **Festival of Flight** celebrates this town as the aviation "Crossroads of the World," with dances, parades, and a folk festival. *Une Longue Veillée* folk festival, celebrating western Newfoundland's French heritage, brings traditional musicians, singers, and dancers to Cape St. George.

Nova Scotia: There's Lunenburg's **Nova Scotia Fisheries Exhibition and Fishermen's Reunion.** The **Nova Scotia Gaelic Mod** in St. Ann's celebrates Scottish culture on the grounds of the only Gaelic college in North America. The **Halifax International Buskerfest** has daily outdoor shows by street performers, a food festival, and stage entertainment.

Ontario: Brantford's **Six Nations Native Pageant** celebrates Iroquois culture and history. **Royal Canadian Henley Regatta,** in St. Catharines, is the largest rowing regatta in North America.

Prince Edward Island: Eldon's **Highland Games** gathers Scotsmen and women. The **Annual Community Harvest Festival** animates Kensington. **Old Home Week** fills Charlottetown with nostalgia. An **International Hydroplane Regatta** brings speed to the Summerside waterfront.

Québec: Montréal hosts a **World Film Festival.** St-Jean-sur-Richelieu's **Hot Air Balloon Festival** is the largest gathering of hot-air balloons in Canada.

Saskatchewan: Buffalo Days Exhibition, in Regina, features rides, a grandstand show, livestock judging, and horse racing.

AUTUMN

SEPTEMBER➤ **Alberta: Spruce Meadows Masters' Tournament,** in Calgary, is an international horse-jumping competition at one of North America's leading equestrian centers.

British Columbia: Cars speed through downtown Vancouver in the **Molson Indy Formula 1 race.**

Newfoundland and Labrador: Deer Lake hosts the **Humber Valley Agricultural Home and Handicraft Exhibition.**

Ontario: The **Canadian Open Golf Championship** plays through Oakville. Toronto's **International Film Festival** salutes the world of film. St. Catharines toasts the **Niagara Grape and Wine Festival.**

Prince Edward Island: Festival Acadien de la Region Evangeline is an agricultural fair with Acadian music, a parade, and lobster suppers, at Wellington Station.

Québec: Québec International Film Festival screens in Québec City. The **Gatineau Hot Air Balloon Festival** brings together hot air balloons from across Canada, the United States, and Europe.

OCTOBER➤ **British Columbia:** The **Vancouver International Film Festival** is held. **Okanagan Wine Festivals** take place in the Okanagan-Similkameen area.

Nova Scotia: There's the **Shearwater International Air Show.**

Ontario: Kitchener–Waterloo's **Oktoberfest** attracts more than a half-million enthusiasts to its beer halls and tents.

Québec: Festival of Colors celebrates foliage throughout the province.

NOVEMBER➤ **Ontario:** Toronto's **Royal Agricultural Winter Fair** draws exhibitors and contestants to the largest indoor agricultural fair and equestrian competition in the world.

2 Vancouver

The spectacular setting of cosmopolitan Vancouver, Canada's answer to San Francisco, has drawn people from around the world to settle here. The ocean and mountains form a dramatic backdrop to downtown's gleaming towers of commerce and make it easy to pursue all kinds of outdoor pleasures. You can trace the city's history in Gastown and Chinatown, savor the wilderness only blocks from the city center in Stanley Park, or dine on superb ethnic or Pacific Northwest cuisine before you sample the city's vibrant nightlife.

Updated by
Melissa Rivers

VANCOUVER IS A YOUNG CITY, even by North American standards. Although 300 to 400 years of settlement may make cities like Québec and Halifax historically interesting, Vancouver's youthful vigor attracts people to its powerful elements that have not yet been ground down by time. Vancouver is just over 100 years old; it was not yet a town in 1870, when British Columbia became part of the Canadian confederation. The city's history, such as it is, remains visible to the naked eye: Eras are stacked east to west along the waterfront like some century-old archaeological dig—from cobblestone late-Victorian Gastown to shiny postmodern glass cathedrals of commerce.

The Chinese were among the first to recognize the possibilities of Vancouver's setting. They came to British Columbia during the 1850s seeking the gold that inspired them to name the province Gum-shan, or Gold Mountain. As laborers they built the Canadian Pacific Railway, giving Vancouver's original townsite a purpose—one beyond the natural splendor that Royal Navy captain George Vancouver admired during his lunchtime cruise around its harbor on June 13, 1792. The transcontinental railway, along with the city's Great White Fleet of clipper ships, gave Vancouver a full week's edge over the California ports in shipping tea and silk to New York at the dawn of the 20th century.

Vancouver's natural charms are less scattered than those in many other cities. On clear days, the mountains appear close enough to touch. Two 1,000-acre wilderness parks lie within the city limits. The salt water of the Pacific and fresh water direct from the Rocky Mountain Trench form the city's northern and southern boundaries.

Bring a healthy sense of reverence when you visit: Vancouver is a spiritual place. For its original inhabitants, the Coast Salish peoples, it was the sacred spot where the mythical Thunderbird and Killer Whale flung wind and rain all about the heavens during their epic battles—how else to explain the coast's fits of meteorological temper? Devotees of a later religious tradition might worship in the sepulchre of Stanley Park or in the rough-hewn interior of Christ Church Cathedral, the city's oldest church.

Today Vancouver, with a metropolitan area population of 1.7 million people, is booming. A tremendous number of Asians have migrated here, including many from Hong Kong who are drawn to the city because of its supportive business environment and protective banking regulations. The milder climate, exquisite natural scenery, and thriving cultural scene also bring new residents to British Columbia's business center. The number of visitors is increasing, too, because of the city's scenic attractions and its proximity to outdoor activities. Many people get their first glimpse of Vancouver when catching an Alaskan cruise (Vancouver is the major port of embarkation/disembarkation for these cruises, with more ships calling here every year), and almost all return at some point to spend more time here.

Vancouver has a level of nightlife possible only in a place where the finer things in life have never been driven out to the suburbs and where sidewalks have never rolled up at 5 PM. But you can find good theater, accommodations, and dining in many places these days. Vancouver's real culture consists of its tall fir trees practically downtown and its towering rock spires close by, the ocean at your doorstep, and people from every corner of the earth all around you.

Pleasures and Pastimes

Dining

The gastronomical experience here is satisfyingly diverse; restaurants—from the bustling downtown area to trendy beachside neighborhoods—have enticing locales in addition to succulent cuisine. A new wave of Asian immigration and tourism has brought a proliferation of upscale Asian (Chinese, Japanese, Korean, Thai, and Vietnamese) restaurants, serving dishes that would be at home in their own leading cities. Cutting-edge restaurants currently perfecting and defining Pacific Northwest fare—including such homegrown regional favorites as salmon and oysters, accompanied by British Columbia and Washington State wines—have become some of the city's leading attractions.

The Great Outdoors

Mother Nature has truly blessed this city, surrounding it by verdant forests, towering mountains, coves, inlets, rivers, and the wide sea. Biking, hiking, skiing and snowboarding, rafting, and sailing are among the many outdoor activities available within minutes of anywhere in the city. Whether you prefer to relax on a beach by yourself or join a kayaking tour with an outfitter, Vancouver has plenty to offer.

Nightlife and the Arts

Vancouver compares favorably to New York or London (although the scale is smaller) in terms of its range of nightlife and arts venues. The arts are enthusiastically supported, so you'll find everything here, from nationally touring musicals to off-off Broadway shows to film and performing arts festivals to renowned symphonic, opera, and ballet companies. You'll also find the city a hotbed for live music—from jazz and blues to head-bangers' heavy metal and everything in between.

EXPLORING VANCOUVER

Vancouver may be small when compared to New York or even San Francisco, but it still takes time to explore. You can see a lot of the city in two days, but a day or two more will give you time to explore sights in the larger Vancouver area and the surrounding countryside.

Many sights of interest are concentrated in the hemmed-in peninsula of downtown Vancouver. The heart of Vancouver—which includes the downtown area, Stanley Park, and the West End high-rise residential neighborhood—sits on this peninsula bordered by English Bay and the Pacific Ocean to the west; by False Creek, the inlet home to Granville Island, to the south; and by Burrard Inlet, the working port of the city, to the north, past which loom the North Shore mountains. The oldest part of the city—Gastown and Chinatown—lies at the edge of Burrard Inlet, around Main Street, which runs north–south and is roughly the dividing line between the east side and the west side. All the avenues, which are numbered, have east and west designations. One note about printed Vancouver street addresses: Suite numbers often appear *before* the street number, followed by a hyphen.

You'll also find places of interest elsewhere in the city, either on the North Shore across Burrard Inlet or south of downtown in the Kitsilano area across English Bay or in the Granville Island area across False Creek. Then, too, there's Whistler, a renowned winter and summer resort a few hours' drive north of Vancouver.

Numbers in the text correspond to numbers in the margin and on the Vancouver, Downtown Vancouver, Stanley Park, and Granville Island maps.

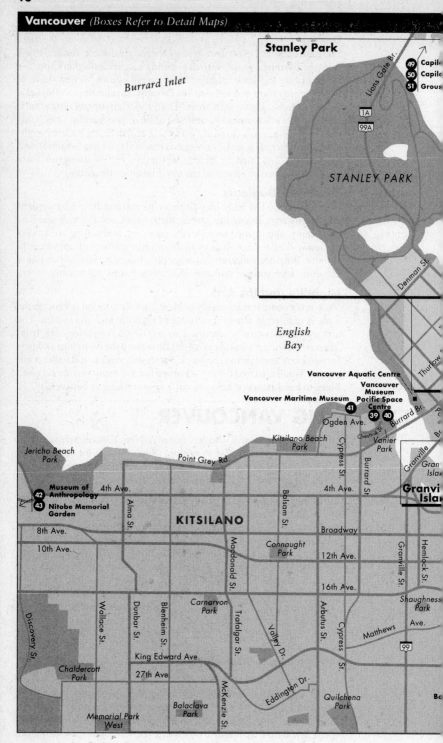

Stanley Park

49 Capil
50 Capil
51 Grous

1A
99A

STANLEY PARK

Denman St.

Burrard Inlet

English Bay

Thurlow

Vancouver Aquatic Centre
Vancouver Maritime Museum
Vancouver Museum
Pacific Space Centre
41
39 40
Ogden Ave.
Chestnut St.
Vanier Park
Kitsilano Beach Park
Cypress St.
Burrard Br.

Granville
Gran Isla
Granvi Isla

Jericho Beach Park
Point Grey Rd.

Museum of Anthropology
42
4th Ave.
4th Ave.
43 Nitobe Memorial Garden
Alma St.
Balsam St.
8th Ave.
KITSILANO
Broadway
10th Ave.
Connaught Park
12th Ave.
Granville St.
Hemlock St.
Macdonald St.
16th Ave.
Carnarvon Park
Shaughnessy Park
Ave.
Wallace St.
Dunbar St.
Blenheim St.
Trafalgar St.
Valley Dr.
Arbutus St.
Cypress St.
Matthews
99
Discovery St.
King Edward Ave.
Chaldercott Park
27th Ave.
McKenzie St.
Eddington Dr.
Quilchena Park
Bo
Memorial Park West
Balaclava Park

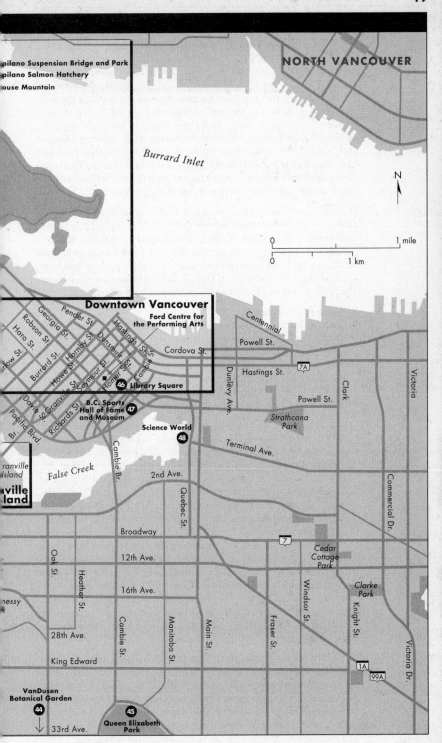

NORTH VANCOUVER

pilano Suspension Bridge and Park
pilano Salmon Hatchery
ouse Mountain

Burrard Inlet

N

0   1 mile

0   1 km

Downtown Vancouver

Ford Centre for
the Performing Arts

Centennial

Powell St.

Pender St.
Georgia St.
Robson St.
Haro St.
Hastings St.
Dunsmuir St.
Cordova St.
Hastings St.
7A
Powell St.
Clark
Victoria

rlow St.
Burrard St.
Hornby St.
Howe St.
Seymour St.
Homer St.
Cambie St.
Dunlevy Ave.

Library Square
46

Dowie St.
Granville St.
Richards St.
Pacific Blvd.
Br.

B.C. Sports
Hall of Fame
and Museum
47

Strathcona
Park

Powell St.

Science World
48

Terminal Ave.

ranville
sland
nville
LAND

False Creek

Cambie Br.

2nd Ave.

Quebec St.

Commercial Dr.

Broadway

7

Cedar
Cottage
Park

12th Ave.

Clarke
Park

16th Ave.

Oak St.
Heather St.
Cambie St.
Manitoba St.
Main St.
Fraser St.
Windsor St.
Knight St.
Victoria Dr.

28th Ave.

King Edward

1A
99A

VanDusen
Botanical Garden
44

45

33rd Ave.

Queen Elizabeth
Park

nessy
k

Great Itineraries

IF YOU HAVE 1–2 DAYS

If you have only one day in Vancouver, start with an early morning drive through Stanley Park to see the Vancouver Aquarium and other park sights such as Second Beach on English Bay. Allow at least two hours to take in the wonderful marine exhibits at the aquarium and another hour or two for a driving tour through the park. In the early afternoon, your tour of the park will conclude in the West End; head northeast on Denman Street to Robson Street to lunch and meander on foot through the trendy shops lining the street between Denman and Burrard, then walk northeast on Burrard Street to view the many buildings of architectural interest. Stops along the way at the Vancouver Art Gallery, the Canadian Craft Museum, and the tiny Sri Lankan Gem Museum will make for a very full day of sightseeing.

Day two can follow a more leisurely paced walking tour of the shops, eateries, and cobblestone streets of Gastown, the original townsite of Vancouver, and Chinatown, the second-largest Chinatown in North America. Take a camera to capture the false-front buildings and the steam-powered clock in Gastown and the brightly painted buildings, Chinese gates, and the classical Dr. Sun Yat-Sen Gardens in Chinatown. There are plenty of places to eat and shop in both districts.

IF YOU HAVE 3–4 DAYS

If you have another day to tour Vancouver following your exploration of Stanley Park, Robson Street, Gastown, and Chinatown in the down-town core, head to the south side of False Creek and English Bay on day three to delve into the many boutiques, dining outlets, theaters, and lively public markets of Granville Island. Buses and ferries provide easy transit, and there is plenty of parking if you prefer to drive; touring Granville Island is best accomplished on foot.

On day four, you'll need a car to tour the far-flung sights south of down-town Vancouver. Museum and history buffs will want to tour the Museum of Anthropology (housing fantastic totem poles, canoes, jewelry, costumes, and other art of Pacific Northwest natives and other aboriginal groups) on the campus of the University of British Columbia, and the Vancouver Museum (showcasing the city's history in cheerful, life-size displays), Pacific Space Centre (a new high-tech museum focusing on outer space), and the Vancouver Maritime Museum (tracing the maritime history of the West Coast), all just south of downtown in the Kitsilano area. Gardening and outdoor enthusiasts may prefer to spend day four touring Nitobe Memorial Garden (a traditional Japanese strolling garden on the campus of the University of British Columbia), VanDusen Botanical Garden (55 ornamental acres showcasing the abundant plant life of the Pacific Northwest), and Queen Elizabeth Park (the highest point in southern Vancouver, with outstanding views of downtown). All are south of downtown in the residential section of Vancouver.

If you still have a couple of daylight hours left, make your way back through downtown Vancouver to the Lions Gate Bridge and follow the signs into the mountains of the North Shore to see the Capilano Suspension Bridge and Park, a park built around a cedar plank suspension footbridge that swings high above the Capilano River, before heading to the peak of Grouse Mountain to enjoy the splendid panorama of Vancouver highlighted by the rich colors of the setting sun.

IF YOU HAVE 5–7 DAYS

If you have another two days to explore and you've already seen Stanley Park, Robson Street, Gastown, Chinatown, Granville Island, and the museums and gardens of Vancouver and parks on the North Shore, don't miss a side trip to beautiful Whistler, in the mountains north of the city. Although it's ranked as one of the top ski destinations in the world, this growing resort has an ever-expanding array of outdoor activities and festivals that make it worth a visit any time of year. The 2½-hour drive there on the scenic Sea to Sky Highway takes you from glorious seaside vistas into the heart of lush alpine country.

Robson to the Waterfront

Museums and buildings of architectural and historical significance are the primary draw in downtown Vancouver. There's also plenty of fine shopping to provide breaks (or to distract, depending on your perspective) along the way. Vancouver is a new city, when compared to others, but still highly rich in culture and diversity.

A Good Walk

If you're a shopaholic, coffee junkie, and/or people-watcher, begin your tour of Vancouver on **Robson Street** ①, also referred to as Vancouver's Rodeo Drive because of the sheer number of see-and-be-seen sidewalk cafés and high-end boutiques, and as Robson Strasse because of its European flavor. Start at the northwest end near the cross streets of Bute or Thurlow and follow Robson southeast to Hornby to reach **Robson Square** ②, a central park area that encompasses landscaped walkways, government office buildings, and the **Vancouver Art Gallery** ③, which houses the city's finest art collection. On the north side of the gallery across Hornby Street sits the **Hotel Vancouver** ④, its copper, château-style roof making it one of the city's best-known landmarks. Cathedral Place, a spectacular office tower, stands across the street on the corner of Hornby and Georgia. Three large sculptures of nurses at the corners of the building are replicas of the statues that ornamented the Art Deco Georgia Medical-Dental Building, the site's previous structure. If you're fascinated by gemstones, pop inside to visit the **Sri Lankan Gem Museum** ⑤. To the left of Cathedral Place is the Gothic-style **Christ Church Cathedral** ⑥, the oldest church in Vancouver. Head east up Burrard and you'll see on your right a restored terra-cotta arch—formerly the front entrance to the medical building—and frieze panels showing scenes of individuals administering care; these decorate the **Canadian Craft Museum** ⑦, one of the first national cultural facilities dedicated to crafts. Farther still up Burrard, on the opposite side of the street, is the **Marine Building** ⑧, its terra-cotta bas-reliefs making it one of Canada's best examples of Art Deco architecture.

Across the street (due east, on the corner of Burrard and Hastings) is the elaborate **Vancouver Club** ⑨, the private haunt of the city's top business movers and shakers. This marks the start of the old financial district, which runs southeast along Hastings, where temple-style banks, investment houses, and businesspeople's clubs survive as evidence of the city's sophisticated architectural advances prior to World War I. Until the period between 1966 and 1972, when the first of the bank towers and underground malls on West Georgia Street were developed, this was Canada's westernmost business terminus. **Sinclair Centre** ⑩, at Hastings and Howe streets, is a magnificently restored complex of government buildings that now houses offices and retail shops. Near Granville Street you'll find the former headquarters of the **Canadian Imperial Bank of Commerce (CIBC)** ⑪. The more Gothic **Royal Bank** ⑫ stands directly across the street.

Head northeast up Seymour toward Burrard Inlet and you'll run into the **Waterfront Station** ⑬, the third and most pretentious of three

Downtown Vancouver

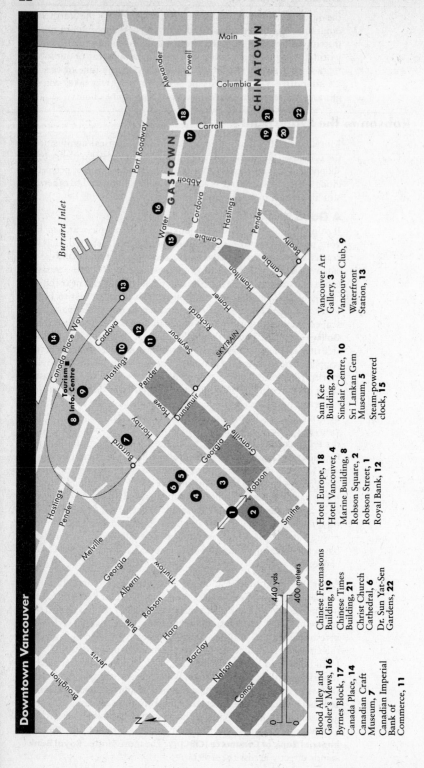

Blood Alley and
Gaoler's Mews, **16**
Byrnes Block, **17**
Canada Place, **14**
Canadian Craft
Museum, **7**
Canadian Imperial
Bank of
Commerce, **11**

Chinese Freemasons
Building, **19**
Chinese Times
Building, **21**
Christ Church
Cathedral, **6**
Dr. Sun Yat-Sen
Gardens, **22**

Hotel Europe, **18**
Hotel Vancouver, **4**
Marine Building, **8**
Robson Square, **2**
Robson Street, **1**
Royal Bank, **12**

Sam Kee
Building, **20**
Sinclair Centre, **10**
Sri Lankan Gem
Museum, **5**
Steam-powered
clock, **15**

Vancouver Art
Gallery, **3**
Vancouver Club, **9**
Waterfront
Station, **13**

Canadian Pacific Railway passenger terminals built in the city. From here, you can either meander through the station and the courtyards to its left or turn north up Cordova, take a right on Howe, and you'll face the soaring canopies of **Canada Place** ⑭, site of Vancouver's primary cruise ship pier, the Trade and Convention Center, and the luxurious Pan Pacific Hotel (☞ Lodging, *below*), with its three-story lobby, waterfall, and totem poles. Here you can stop for a snack in one of the dining outlets on the water or catch a film at the IMAX theater. Stop off at the **Vancouver Tourist Info Centre** across the street (next door to the Waterfront Centre Hotel) to pick up brochures on other Vancouver attractions and events before leaving the area.

TIMING

This walking tour, with time to soak in the intriguing architecture along the route, will take approximately two to three hours if you're not drawn into all the shops along the way. Allow about an hour at the Canadian Craft Museum, and another two to three to see the collections at the Vancouver Art Gallery.

Sights to See

⑭ **Canada Place.** Originally built on an old cargo pier to be the off-site Canadian pavilion in Expo '86, Canada Place was later converted into Vancouver's **Trade and Convention Center.** It is dominated at the shore end by the luxurious **Pan Pacific Hotel** (☞ Lodging, *below*), with its spectacular three-story lobby and waterfall. The fabric roof shaped like 10 sails that covers the convention space has become a landmark of Vancouver's skyline. Below is a cruise-ship facility, and at the north end are an Imax theater, a restaurant, and an outdoor performance space. A promenade runs along the pier's west side, affording views of the Burrard Inlet harbor and Stanley Park. ⊠ *999 Canada Pl.,* ☎ *604/775–8687.*

❼ **Canadian Craft Museum.** Opened in 1992, the museum is one of the first national cultural facilities dedicated to crafts—historical and contemporary, functional and decorative. Craft embodies the human need for artistic expression in everyday life, and examples here range from elegantly carved utensils with decorative handles to colorful hand-spun and handwoven garments. The two-level museum has exhibits, lectures, and the Museum Shop, which specializes in Canadian crafts. The structure was once a medical building, still evident outside in the restored terra-cotta arch and frieze panels showing scenes of individuals administering care. The restful courtyard is a quiet place to take a break. ⊠ *639 Hornby St.,* ☎ *604/687–8266.* ⊡ *$5.* ☉ *Apr.–Oct., Mon.–Sat. 10–5, Sun. noon–5; Nov.–Mar., Mon. and Wed.–Sat. 10–5, Sun. noon–5.*

⓫ **Canadian Imperial Bank of Commerce (CIBC).** Built between 1906 and 1908, the former headquarters of one of Vancouver's oldest and most powerful chartered banks has columns, arches, and details that reflect a typically Roman influence. It now houses a jewelry store. ⊠ *698 W. Hastings St.*

❻ **Christ Church Cathedral.** This tiny church, built in 1895, is the oldest in Vancouver. Constructed in Gothic style with buttresses and pointed-arch windows, it looks like the parish church of an English village from the outside. By contrast, the cathedral's rough-hewn interior is that of a frontier town, with Douglas-fir beams and ornate woodwork that offer excellent acoustics for the vespers, carols, and Gregorian chants frequently sung here. ⊠ *690 Burrard St.,* ☎ *604/682–3848.* ☉ *Weekdays 10–4.*

❹ **Hotel Vancouver.** Completed in 1939, the Hotel Vancouver (☞ Lodging, *below*) is one of the last railway-built hotels (the final one was the Chateau Whistler, in 1989). With details reminiscent of a medieval French castle, this château style has been incorporated into hotels in almost every major Canadian city. The Depression slowed construction, which began in 1937, and the hotel was finished only in time for the visit of King George VI in 1939. It has been renovated three times, most recently in 1996 at a cost of $12.7 million. During the 1960s the hotel was unfortunately modernized, but the recent refurbishment is more in keeping with the spirit of what is the most recognizable roof on Vancouver's skyline. The exterior of the building has carvings of malevolent-looking gargoyles at the corners, an ornate chimney, native chiefs on the Hornby Street side, and an assortment of grotesque mythological figures. ✉ *900 W. Georgia St.,* ☎ *604/684–3131.*

❽ **Marine Building.** Constructed in 1931, this Art Deco building is ornamented with terra-cotta bas-reliefs depicting the history of transportation: airships, steamships, locomotives, and submarines. These motifs were once considered radical and modernistic adornments, because most buildings were still using classical or Gothic ornamentation. From the east, the Marine Building is reflected in bronze by 999 West Hastings, and from the southeast it is mirrored in silver by the Canadian Imperial Bank of Commerce. Stand on the corner of Hastings and Hornby streets for the best view of the building. ✉ *355 Burrard St.*

❷ **Robson Square.** Built in 1975 and designed by architect Arthur Erickson to be *the* gathering place of downtown Vancouver, Robson Square functions from the outside as a park. Here you'll find the **Vancouver Art Gallery** (☞ *below*), government offices, and law courts woven together by landscaped walkways, as well as a block-long glass canopy over one of the walkways and a waterfall. An ice-skating rink and restaurants occupy the below-street level. ✉ *800 Robson St.*

❶ **Robson Street.** If you're up for a day of shopping, amble down this street (☞ Shopping, *below*), where you'll find any item from souvenirs to high fashions, and nourishment from espresso to sushi.

⓬ **Royal Bank.** Gothic in style, this building was intended to be half of a symmetrical building that was never completed, due to the Depression. Striking, though, is the magnificent hall, reminiscent of a European cathedral. The building is still a bank. ✉ *685 W. Hastings St.*

❿ **Sinclair Centre.** Outstanding Vancouver architect Richard Henriquez has knitted four government office buildings (built between 1905 and 1939) into Sinclair Centre, an office-retail complex. The two Hastings Street buildings—the 1905 **Post Office** with the elegant clock tower and the 1913 **Winch Building**—are linked with the **Post Office Extension** and **Customs Examining Warehouse** to the north. Painstaking and very costly restoration involved finding master masons—the original terrazzo suppliers in Europe—and uncovering and refurbishing the pressed-metal ceilings. ✉ *757 W. Hastings St.,* ☎ *604/666–4438.*

❺ **Sri Lankan Gem Museum.** Housed in a jewelry store with a floor of 9,000 polished Brazilian agates set in pyrite, this museum opened in the impressive Cathedral Place office building in 1993. It has some $5 million worth of gemstones, including moonstones, rubies, lapis lazuli, garnets, jade, and emeralds. **Note:** At press time (summer 1997) the museum closed and was planning to reopen elsewhere. Call information or the Vancouver Tourist Info Center (☞ *below*) for the new address and telephone number.

③ Vancouver Art Gallery. The city's best art museum has sculpture and modern art, as well as some native works, but the most popular permanent collection contains works by artist Emily Carr of British Columbia. This museum was a classical-style 1912 courthouse until architect Arthur Erickson converted it to a spacious gallery in 1980. Notice the detail: lions that guard the majestic front steps and the use of columns and domes—features borrowed from ancient Roman architecture. Behind the old courthouse, a more modest staircase now serves as a speakers' corner. ⊠ *750 Hornby St.,* ☎ *604/662–4719.* 🖼 *$9.50.* ⊙ *Mon.–Wed. and Fri. 10–6, Thurs. 10–9, Sat. 10–5, Sun. noon–5.*

⑨ Vancouver Club. Built between 1912 and 1914, this was a gathering place for the city's elite. Its architecture evokes that of private clubs in England inspired by Italian Renaissance palaces. The Vancouver Club is still the private haunt of city businesspeople. ⊠ *915 W. Hastings St.,* ☎ *604/685–9321.*

Vancouver Tourist Info Centre. Here you'll find brochures and personnel to answer questions, as well as an attractive Northwest Coast native art collection. ⊠ *200 Burrard St.,* ☎ *604/683–2000.*

⑬ Waterfront Station. The third and most imposing of three Canadian Pacific Railway passenger terminals in Vancouver was constructed from 1912 to 1914. It replaced the other two as the western terminus for Canada's transcontinental railway. After Canada's railways merged, the station became obsolete until a 1978 renovation turned it into an office-retail complex and SeaBus terminal. Murals in the waiting rooms (now used by Skytrain, SeaBus, West Coast Express, and BC Transit passengers) show the scenery travelers once saw on journeys across Canada. ⊠ *601 W. Cordova St.,* ☎ *604/521–0400 for BC Transit.*

Chinatown and Gastown

Gastown is where Vancouver originated after smooth talker "Gassy" Jack Deighton arrived at Burrard Inlet in 1867 with his native wife, some whiskey, and few amenities, and managed to con local loggers and trappers into building him a saloon for a barrel of whiskey. When the transcontinental train arrived in 1887, Gastown became the transfer point for trade with the Far East and was soon crowded with hotels and warehouses. The Klondike gold rush encouraged further development until 1912, when the "Golden Years" ended. From the 1930s to the 1950s hotels were converted into rooming houses, and the warehouse district shifted elsewhere. The neglected area gradually became run down. However, both Gastown and Chinatown were declared historic districts in the late 1970s and have been revitalized. Gastown is now chock-a-block with boutiques, cafés, loft apartments, and souvenir shops.

The Chinese were among the first inhabitants of Vancouver, and some of the oldest buildings in the city are in Chinatown, the second-largest such area in North America. There was already a sizable Chinese community in British Columbia because of the 1858 Cariboo gold rush in central British Columbia, but the greatest influx from China came in the 1880s, during construction of the Canadian Pacific Railway, when 15,000 laborers were imported. Even while doing the hazardous work of blasting the rail bed through the Rocky Mountains, however, the Chinese were discriminated against. The Anti-Asiatic Riots of 1907 stopped growth in Chinatown for 50 years, and immigration from China was discouraged by more and more restrictive policies, climaxing in a $500 head tax during the 1920s. In the 1960s the city council planned bulldozer urban renewal for Strathcona, the residential part of Chinatown, as well as freeway connections through the most historic blocks of the district. Fortunately, the project was halted, and today Chinatown is an expanding, vital neighborhood fueled by investment from Vancouver's most notable newcomers—immigrants from Hong Kong. It is best to view the buildings in Chinatown from the south side of Pender Street, where the Chinese Cultural Center stands. From here you'll see important details that adorn the upper stories. The style of architecture in Vancouver's Chinatown is patterned on that of Canton and won't be seen in any other Canadian cities.

A Good Walk

Pick up Water Street at Richards Street and head east into Gastown, named for saloon keeper "Gassy" Jack Deighton. At the corner of Water and Cambie streets, you can see and hear the world's first **steam-powered clock** ⑮ (it chimes on the quarter hour). Along the way you'll pass **Blood Alley and Gaoler's Mews** ⑯, which are tucked behind 12 Water Street. Two buildings of historical and architectural note are the **Byrnes Block** ⑰ on the corner of Water and Carrall streets and the **Hotel Europe** ⑱ (1908–09) at Powell and Alexander streets. A statue of Gassy Jack stands on the west side of Maple Tree Square, at the intersection of Water, Powell, Alexander, and Carrall streets, where he built his first saloon.

From Maple Tree Square it's only three blocks south on Carrall Street to Pender Street, where Chinatown begins. However, this route passes through a rough part of town, so it's far safer to backtrack two blocks on Water Street through Gastown to Cambie Street, then head south to Pender and east to Carrall. The corner of Carrall and Pender streets, now the western boundary of Chinatown, is one of the neighborhood's most historic and photogenic spots. It's here that you'll find the **Chinese Freemasons Building** ⑲ (circa 1901) and the **Sam Kee Building** ⑳ (circa 1913), and, directly across Carrall Street, the **Chinese Times Building** ㉑ (circa 1902). Across Pender are the first living classical Chinese gardens built outside China, the **Dr. Sun Yat-Sen Gardens** ㉒, tucked behind the Chinese Cultural Center, which houses exhibition space, classrooms, and the occasional mah-jongg tournament. Finish up by poking around in the open-front markets and import shops that line several blocks of Pender running east.

TIMING

The walk itself will take from two to three hours depending on your pace; allow extra time for the guided tour of the garden in Chinatown. Daylight hours are best, although shops and restaurants are open into the night in both areas. There are few traffic signals for safe crossings in Gastown, so avoid commuter rush hours.

Sights to See

★ ⑯ **Blood Alley and Gaoler's Mews.** Once the site of the city's first civic buildings—the constable's cabin and customs house, and a two-cell log jail—today the cobblestone street with antique lighting is home to architectural offices. ⊠ *Behind 12 Water St.*

⑰ **Byrnes Block.** This building was constructed on the site of Gassy Jack's second saloon after the 1886 Great Fire. The date is just visible at the top of the building above the door where it says "Herman Block," which was its name for a short time. ⊠ *Water and Carrall Sts.*

⑲ **Chinese Freemasons Building.** Two completely different facades distinguish a fascinating structure on the northwest corner of Pender and

Carrall streets: The side facing Pender presents a fine example of Cantonese-imported recessed balconies; the Carrall Street side displays the standard Victorian style common throughout the British Empire. It was in this building that Dr. Sun Yat-Sen hid for months from the agents of the Manchu dynasty while he raised funds for its overthrow, which he accomplished in 1911. ⊠ *W. Pender St.*

㉑ **Chinese Times Building.** Police officers could hear the clicking sounds of clandestine mah-jongg games played after sunset on the building's hidden mezzanine floor. Attempts by vice squads to enforce restrictive policies against the Chinese gamblers proved fruitless, because police were unable to find the players. The building, on the north side of Pender Street just east of Carrall, dates to 1902. Meandering down Pender Street, you can still hear mah-jongg games going on behind the colorful facades of other buildings in Chinatown. ⊠ *1 E. Pender St.*

★ ㉒ **Dr. Sun Yat-Sen Gardens.** The gardens were built in the 1980s by 52 artisans from Suzhou, the Garden City of the People's Republic. The gardens incorporate design elements and traditional materials from several of that city's centuries-old private gardens. As you walk through the gardens, remember that no power tools, screws, or nails were used in the construction. Free guided tours are offered throughout the day; telephone for times. ⊠ *578 Carrall St.,* ☎ *604/689–7133.* ☞ *$5.50.* ⊙ *Daily 10–7:30.*

⑱ **Hotel Europe.** Once billed as the best hotel in the city, this circa 1908–1909 flatiron building was Vancouver's first reinforced concrete structure. Designed as a functional commercial building, the hotel lacks ornamentation and fine detail, a style unusually utilitarian for the time. ⊠ *Alexander and Powell Sts.*

⑳ **Sam Kee Building.** Constructed in 1913, this six-foot-wide building is recognized by *Ripley's Believe It or Not!* as the narrowest building in the world. Its bay windows overhang the street and the basement burrows under the sidewalk. ⊠ *8 W. Pender St.*

★ ⑮ **Steam-powered clock.** The world's first steam clock is powered by an underground steam system. Every quarter hour the whistle blows, and on the hour a huge cloud of steam spews from the clock. It was built by Ray Saunders of Landmark Clocks (⊠ 123 Cambie St., ☎ 604/669–3525). ⊠ *Water and Cambie Sts.*

Stanley Park

A 1,000-acre wilderness park just blocks from the downtown section of a major city is both a rarity and a treasure. In the 1860s, because of a threat of American invasion, the area that is now Stanley Park was designated a military reserve (though it was never needed). When the city of Vancouver was incorporated in 1886, the council's first act was to request that the land be set aside for a park. In 1888 permission was granted and the grounds were named Stanley Park after Lord Stanley, then governor general of Canada.

A morning or afternoon in Stanley Park gives you a capsule tour of Vancouver that includes beaches, the ocean, the harbor, Douglas fir and cedar forests, and a good look at the North Shore mountains. The park sits on a peninsula, and along the shore is a pathway 9 km (5½ mi) long called the seawall. You can drive or bicycle the mostly flat route all the way around. Bicycles are for rent at the foot of Georgia

Street near the park entrance. Cyclists must ride in a counterclockwise direction and stay on their side of the path.

A Good Biking or Driving Tour

A good place to start is at the foot of Alberni Street beside Lost Lagoon. Go through the underpass and veer right to the seawall past **Malkin Bowl** ㉓, an open amphitheater. Just past the amphitheater is a cutoff to the left that leads to the renowned **Vancouver Aquarium** ㉔, while the main road continues on to the rest of the park's sights. The old wood structure that you pass next is the Vancouver Rowing Club, a private athletic club established in 1903; a bit farther along is the Royal Vancouver Yacht Club. About ½ km (⅓ mi) away is the causeway to **Deadman's Island** ㉕.

If you continue straight past the causeway, just ahead at the water's edge is the **Nine O'Clock Gun** ㉖. To the north is Brockton Point and its small but functional lighthouse and foghorn. The **totem poles** ㉗, which are a bit farther down the road and slightly inland on your left, make a popular photo stop. Continue on and you'll pass the miniature steam train, just five minutes northwest of the aquarium; it's a big hit with children. The children's water park across the road is also popular throughout the summer.

At km 3 (mi 2) is **Lumberman's Arch** ㉘, a huge log archway. About 2 km (1 mi) farther is the Lions Gate Bridge—the halfway point of the seawall. Just past the bridge is **Prospect Point** ㉙, where cormorants build nests. Continuing around the seawall, you'll come to the English Bay side and the beginning of sandy beaches. The imposing rock just offshore is **Siwash Rock** ㉚, the focus of a native legend.

The next attraction along the seawall is the large saltwater pool at **Second Beach** ㉛. You can take a shortcut from here back to Lost Lagoon by walking along the perpendicular road behind the pool, which cuts into the park. The wood footbridge that's ahead will lead you to a path along the south side of the lagoon to your starting point at the foot of Alberni or Georgia street. If you continue along the seawall, you will emerge from the park into a high-rise residential neighborhood, the West End. You can walk back to Alberni Street along Denman Street, where there are places to stop for coffee, ice cream, or a drink.

TIMING

You'll find parking lots near most of the sights in the park; if you're driving, take the time to stop and get a better look or take pictures. With that advice in mind, expect a driving tour to take about an hour. Your biking time will depend on your speed, but with stops to see the sights, expect it to take several hours. Add at least two hours to thoroughly see the aquarium, and you've filled a half- to full-day tour. Stanley Park gets quite crowded on weekends; on weekday afternoons the local jogging and biking traffic is at its lowest.

Sights to See

㉕ **Deadman's Island.** A former burial ground for the local Salish people and the early settlers is now a small naval training base called H.M.C.S. *Discovery* and is not open to the public.

㉘ **Lumberman's Arch.** Made of logs, this large archway is dedicated to the workers in Vancouver's first industry. Beside the arch is an asphalt path that leads back to Lost Lagoon and the Vancouver Aquarium.

㉓ **Malkin Bowl.** An open amphitheater becomes a theater under the stars during the summer. ✉ *1st right off Pipeline Rd. past park entrance,* ☎ *604/687–0174.*

Stanley Park

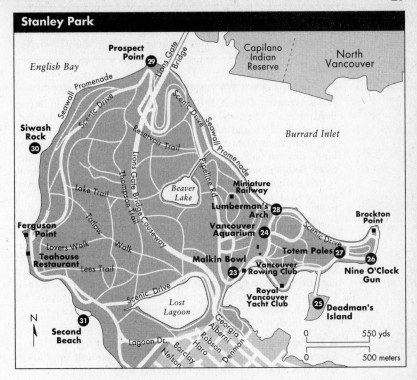

Prospect Point · Lions Gate Bridge · Capilano Indian Reserve · North Vancouver · English Bay · Seawall Promenade · Scenic Drive · Reservoir Trail · Scenic Drive · Seawall Promenade · Burrard Inlet · Siwash Rock 30 · Lions Gate Bridge Causeway · Thompson Trail · Lake Trail · Beaver Lake · Pipeline Rd. · Miniature Railway · Lumberman's Arch · 28 · Brockton Point · Vancouver Aquarium 24 · Scenic Drive · Ferguson Point · Tatlow Walk · Lovers Walk · Walk · Teahouse Restaurant · Lees Trail · Malkin Bowl · 23 · Vancouver Rowing Club · Totem Poles 27 · 26 · Nine O'Clock Gun · Royal Vancouver Yacht Club · 25 · Deadman's Island · Lost Lagoon · 31 · Second Beach · Lagoon Dr. · Georgia · Alberni · Robson · Barclay · Haro · Denman · Nelson · N · 0   550 yds · 0   500 meters

26 Nine O'Clock Gun. This cannonlike apparatus by the water was originally used to alert fishermen to a curfew ending weekend fishing; now it signals 9 o'clock every night.

29 Prospect Point. Here cormorants build their seaweed nests along the cliff's ledges. The large black diving birds are distinguished by their long necks and beaks; when not nesting, they often perch atop floating logs or boulders. Another remarkable bird found along the park's shore is the beautiful great blue heron, which reaches up to 4 feet tall and has a wing span of 6 feet. Herons prey on passing fish in the waters here; the oldest heron rookery in British Columbia is in the trees near the aquarium.

31 Second Beach. In summer a draw is the big saltwater children's pool with lifeguards, but in winter, when the pool is drained, skateboarders perform stunts here.

30 Siwash Rock. Legend tells of a young Native American who, about to become a father, bathed persistently to wash his sins away so that his son could be born pure. For his devotion he was blessed by the gods and immortalized in the shape of Siwash Rock, just offshore. Two small rocks, said to be his wife and child, are on the cliff above the site.

27 Totem poles. Totem poles were not made in the Vancouver area; these, carved of cedar by the Kwakiutl and Haida peoples late in the last century, were brought to the park from the north coast of British Columbia. The carved animals, fish, birds, and mythological creatures were like family coats-of-arms or crests.

★ ✋ **24 Vancouver Aquarium.** The humid Amazon rain-forest gallery has piranhas, giant cockroaches, alligators, tropical birds, and jungle vegetation. Other displays show the underwater life of coastal British Columbia, the Canadian arctic, and other areas of the world. Huge tanks (populated with orca and beluga whales and playful sea otters) have large windows for underwater viewing. ☎ *604/682–1118.* ✉ *$12.* ⏱ *July–Labor Day, daily 9:30–8; Labor Day–June, daily 10–5:30.*

Granville Island

Granville Island was just a sandbar until World War I, when the federal government dredged False Creek for access to the sawmills that lined the shore. The sludge from the creek was heaped up onto the sandbar to create the island and to house much-needed industrial- and logging-equipment plants. By the late 1960s, however, many of the businesses that had once flourished on Granville Island had deteriorated. Buildings were rotted, rat-infested, and dangerous. In 1971 the federal government bought up leases from businesses that wanted to leave and offered an imaginative plan to refurbish the island with a public market, marine activities, and artisans' studios. The opposite shore of False Creek was the site of the 1986 World's Fair and is now part of the largest urban redevelopment plan in North America.

The small island has no residents except for a houseboat community. Most of the former industrial buildings and tin sheds have been retained but are painted in upbeat reds, yellows, and blues. Through a committee of community representatives, the government regulates the types of businesses on Granville Island; most of the businesses permitted involve food, crafts, marine activities, and the arts.

A Good Walk

To reach Granville Island on foot, make the 15-minute walk from downtown Vancouver to the south end of Hornby Street. Aquabuses (☎ 604/689–5858) depart here and deliver passengers across False Creek to Granville Island Public Market. Another option is the Granville Island Ferries (☎ 604/684–7781), which leave every five minutes from a dock behind the Vancouver Aquatic Centre. Still another way to reach the island is to take a 20-minute ride on a B.C. Transit (☎ 604/521–0400) bus; to do this take a University of British Columbia (U.B.C.), Granville, Arbutus, Cambie, or Oak bus from downtown to Granville and Broadway, and transfer to Granville Island Bus 51 or False Creek Bus 50 from Gastown or stops on Granville Street for direct service to Granville Island. Parking is free for one to three hours; paid parking is available in garages on the island.

The ferry will drop you off at the **Granville Island Public Market** ㉜, with its fast food-outlets and fruit and vegetable, meat, coffee, liquor, and flower stalls. At the **Granville Island Information Centre** ㉝, cater-corner to the market, stop to pick up a map of the island.

Walk south on Johnston Street to begin a clockwise loop tour of the island. Ocean Cement is one of the last of the island's former industries; its lease does not expire until the year 2004. Next door is the **Emily Carr Institute of Art and Design** ㉞. Past the art school, on the left, is Sea Village, one of the only houseboat communities in Vancouver. Take the boardwalk that starts at the houseboats and continues partway around the island.

As you circle around to Cartwright Street, stop in Kakali at Number 1249, where you can watch the fabrication of fine handmade paper from such materials as blue jeans, herbs, and sequins. Another unusual artisan on the island is the glassblower at the New-Small Sterling Glass Studio (✉ 1404 Old Bridge St.), around the corner. The next two attractions will make any child's visit to Granville Island a thrill. First, on Cartwright Street, is the **Granville Island Water Park** ㉟. A bit farther down the street, beside Isadora's restaurant, is the **Kids Only Mar-**

Granville Island

ket ㊱, selling anything and everything a child could desire. Cross Anderson Street and walk down Duranleau Street. On your left are the seafaring stores of the **Maritime Market** ㊲. The last place to explore on Granville Island is the **Net Loft** ㊳, a collection of small, high-quality stores. Once you have come full circle, you can either take the ferry back to downtown Vancouver or stay for dinner and catch a play at the Arts Club (☎ 604/687–1644) or the Waterfront Theater (☎ 604/685–6217).

TIMING

If your schedule is tight, you can tour Granville Island in three to four hours; if you're a shopping fanatic, plan for a full day here.

Sights to See

㉞ **Emily Carr Institute of Art and Design.** Just inside the front door of the institute, to your right, is the **Charles H. Scott Gallery**, which hosts contemporary multimedia exhibits. ⊠ 1399 Johnston St., ☎ 604/687–3800. ⊡ Free. ☉ Daily noon–5.

㉝ **Granville Island Information Centre.** Maps are available here, and a slide show depicts the evolution of Granville Island. Ask about special-events days; perhaps there's a boat show, an outdoor concert, a dance performance, or some other happening. ⊠ 1592 Johnston St., ☎ 604/666–5784. ☉ Daily 8–6.

★ ㉜ **Granville Island Public Market.** As the government allows no chain stores, each outlet in the 50,000-square-foot building is unique, and most are of good quality. You probably won't be able to leave the market without a snack, espresso, or fixings for lunch on the wharf. Year-round you'll see mounds of raspberries, strawberries, blueberries, and more exotic fruits like persimmons. There's plenty of outdoor seating on the water side of the market. ⊠ 1669 Johnston St., under Granville Street *bridge, 2nd floor,* ☎ *604/666–6477.* ⊙ *Memorial Day–Labor Day, daily 9–6; Labor Day–Memorial Day, Tues.–Sun. 9–6.*

🐤 ㉟ **Granville Island Water Park.** This kid's paradise has a wading pool, sprinklers, and a fire hydrant made for children to shower one another. ⊠ *1318 Cartwright St.,* ☎ *604/257–8195.* 🎫 *Free.* ⊙ *Late May–early Sept., daily 10–6.*

🐤 ㊱ **Kids Only Market.** Yet another slice of kid's heaven on Granville Island, the Kids Only Market has two floors of small shops selling toys, arts-and-crafts materials, dolls, records and tapes, chemistry sets, and other good kid stuff. ⊠ *1496 Cartwright St.,* ☎ *604/689–8447.* ⊙ *Daily 10–6.*

㊲ **Maritime Market.** These businesses are all geared to the sea. The first walkway to the left, Maritime Mews, leads to marinas and dry docks. ⊠ *1650 Duranleau St.,* ☎ *604/687–1556.*

㊳ **Net Loft.** In this blue building is a collection of small, high-quality stores, including a bookstore, a crafts store-gallery, a kitchenware shop, a post-card shop, a custom-made hat shop, a handmade paper store, a British Columbian native art gallery, and a do-it-yourself jewelry store. ⊠ *1666 Johnston St., across from Public Market,* ☎ *604/876–6637.*

Greater Vancouver

The metropolis of Vancouver includes North Vancouver across Burrard Inlet and the larger, more residential peninsula south of downtown bordered by English Bay to the north, the Strait of Georgia to the west, and the Fraser River to the south. There are wonderful museums, gardens, and natural sights sprinkled throughout Greater Vancouver, but you'll need a car to maximize your time and cover as much ground as your itinerary allows.

A Good Drive
This tour includes numerous museums, so start out early and head south across the Burrard Bridge to Vanier Park. Here you'll find the **Vancouver Museum** ㊴, showcasing the city's history in cheerful, life-size displays; the **Pacific Space Centre** ㊵, a high-tech museum focusing on outer space; and the **Vancouver Maritime Museum** ㊶, which traces the maritime history of the West Coast. There are hands-on exhibits to attract the kids at each of these. Next, follow Cypress Street south out of the park to Fourth Avenue, then go west to the University of British Columbia to visit the **Museum of Anthropology** ㊷, housing an amazing collection of totem poles and other native artifacts, and **Nitobe Memorial Garden** ㊸, a Japanese-style strolling garden.

For more gardens, follow Southwest Marine Drive through the U.B.C. grounds and turn left onto 41st Avenue. Turn left again onto Oak Street to reach the entrance of the **VanDusen Botanical Garden** ㊹ (it'll be on your left); the complex is planted with English-style mazes, water gardens, herb gardens, and more. Return to 41st Avenue, continue farther east, and then turn left on Cambie Street to reach **Queen Elizabeth Park** ㊺, which overlooks the city.

You can head back downtown across the Cambie Bridge (stay in the right lane), which flows onto Smithe Street. Turn right onto Homer and look for parking within the next few blocks so that you can stop to see **Library Square** ㊻, the city's new multimillion-dollar central library project that resembles Rome's coliseum. From there it's only three more blocks to B.C. Place, where you'll find the **B.C. Sports Hall of Fame and Museum** ㊼, devoted to British Columbia's favorite sons and daughters who made a name for themselves in sports. Turn south on Cambie and follow it to Pacific Boulevard (don't cross the Cambie Bridge), which winds east around False Creek and turns into Quebec Street at the head of the creek. Turn right here, and right again into the parking lot of **Science World** ㊽, a hands-on museum.

After a science lesson, head straight across Quebec to Main Street, turn left, and make a second left at the Georgia Viaduct, which leads onto Dunsmuir. Follow it for eight or so city blocks, turn left onto Howe Street, then right onto Georgia, which will take you through town and Stanley Park and across the Lions Gate Bridge to North Vancouver. Follow the signs into the mountains of the North Shore to see the **Capilano Suspension Bridge and Park** ㊾, where a cedar plank footbridge swings high above the Capilano River. Nearby in the Capilano Regional Park, the **Capilano Salmon Hatchery** ㊿ is another good spot to visit. Up the hill a bit farther, at the end of Nancy Greene Way, is **Grouse Mountain** ㉛, where a funicular gives you great city views.

TIMING

To cover all the sights of Greater Vancouver, taking sufficient time at each of the museums and gardens, could easily take two days. Either pick and choose those you really want to see, or limit yourself to the sights south of the city one day and save the remaining sights downtown and on the North Shore for another day.

Sights to See

㊼ **B.C. Sports Hall of Fame and Museum.** Part of the B.C. Place Stadium complex, this museum celebrating the province's sports achievers shows video documentaries and has photographs, costumes, and an array of sporting equipment on display. Bring tennis shoes to wear in the high-tech, hands-on participation gallery. ✉ *B.C. Place, 777 Pacific Blvd. S, Gate A,* ☎ *604/687–5525.* ☞ *$6.* ☉ *Daily 10–5.*

㊿ **Capilano Salmon Hatchery.** In the Capilano Regional Park, the hatchery has viewing areas and exhibits about the life cycle of the salmon. ✉ *4500 Capilano Park Rd., North Vancouver,* ☎ *604/666–1790.* ☞ *Free.* ☉ *Call for seasonal hours.*

㊾ **Capilano Suspension Bridge and Park.** At this, Vancouver's oldest tourist attraction (the original bridge was built in 1889), you can get a taste of the mountains and test your mettle on the swaying, 450-foot cedar plank suspension bridge that hangs 230 feet above the rushing Capilano River. The amusement park also has viewing decks, nature trails amid tall firs and cedars, a gift shop, a totem-carving shed, and displays for the kids. ✉ *3735 Capilano Rd., North Vancouver,* ☎ *604/987–7474.* ☞ *Call for admission fees.* ☉ *Summer, daily 8–dusk; winter, daily 9–5; call for exact hours.*

㉛ **Grouse Mountain.** The Skyride to the top is a great way to take in stunning city, sea, and mountain vistas. In the theater at the peak you can catch a film on Vancouver's transformation from a string of scattered native, trapper, and logger settlements to a bustling modern metropolis. ✉ *6400 Nancy Greene Way, North Vancouver,* ☎ *604/984–0661.* ☞ *Ride and theater $15.* ☉ *Call for seasonal hours.*

㊻ **Library Square.** Built to evoke images of the Colosseum in Rome, the spiraling library building, open plazas, frescoed waterfall, and shaded atriums of the new Library Square were completed in 1995. This architectural stunner is a favorite backdrop for movie productions, so you may see it at the movies or on television before you actually visit it. The book collection is moved about on motorized shelving systems in the ultra-high-tech library that fills the core of the structure; the outer edge of the spiral houses trendy boutiques, coffee shops, and a fine book and gift shop. ⊠ *350 W. Georgia St.,* ☎ *604/331–3600.* ☉ *Mon.–Wed. 10–9, Thurs.–Sat. 10–6; also Oct.–Apr., Sun. 1–5.*

★ ㊷ **Museum of Anthropology.** The MOA is Vancouver's most spectacular museum, focusing on the arts of the Pacific Northwest natives and aboriginals from around the world, including the works of Bill Reid, Canada's most respected Haida carver. His *The Raven and the First Men,* which took five carvers more than three years to complete, is its centerpiece. Reid's Pacific Northwest Coast artworks are world renowned. On the campus of the University of British Columbia, the museum is housed in an award-winning glass-and-concrete structure designed by Arthur Erickson. In the Great Hall are large and dramatic totem poles, ceremonial archways, and dugout canoes—all adorned with carvings of frogs, eagles, ravens, bears, and salmon. Also showcased are exquisite carvings of gold, silver, and argillite (a black stone found in the Queen Charlotte Islands), as well as masks, tools, and costumes from many other cultures. The museum contains a ceramics wing, which houses about 600 pieces from 15th- to 19th-century Europe. ⊠ *6393 N.W. Marine Dr.,* ☎ *604/822–5087.* 🎫 *$5, free Tues.* ☉ *Tues. 11–9, Wed.–Sun. 11–5.*

㊸ **Nitobe Memorial Garden.** This 2½-acre garden is considered the most authentic Japanese garden outside Japan. The circular path around the park symbolizes the cycle of life and provides a tranquil view from every direction. In April and May cherry blossoms are the highlight, and in June the irises are magnificent. ⊠ *1903 West Mall, University of British Columbia,* ☎ *604/822–6038.* 🎫 *$3.* ☉ *Summer, daily 10–6; winter, weekdays 10–3.*

☝ ㊵ **Pacific Space Centre.** After major expansion in 1997, this new facility has a host of interactive exhibits and high-tech learning systems—a virtual reality Cyberwalk, a kinetic space ride simulator, and a theater showcasing Canada's achievements in space—advanced enough to qualify it for NASA Teacher Resource Center status. During the day, catch the astronomy show at the **H.R. MacMillan Planetarium** on site. If the sky is clear, the half-meter telescope at the **Gordon MacMillan Southam Observatory** is focused on whatever stars or planets are worth watching that night. ⊠ *1100 Chestnut St., Vanier Park,* ☎ *604/738–7827, 604/738–2855 special-events schedule.* 🎫 *Observatory free, planetarium fee varies.* ☉ *Observatory daily 7 PM–11 PM; planetarium July–early Sept., daily 11–4.*

㊺ **Queen Elizabeth Park.** Besides views of downtown, the park has lavish gardens brimming with roses and other flowers, an abundance of grassy picnicking spots, and illuminated fountains. In the **Bloedel Conservatory,** you can see tropical and desert plants and 35 species of free-flying tropical birds. Other park facilities include 20 tennis courts, lawn bowling, pitch and putt, and a restaurant. ⊠ *Cambie St. and 33rd Ave.,* ☎ *604/872–5513.* 🎫 *Conservatory $3.* ☉ *Apr.–Sept., weekdays 9–8, weekends 10–9; Oct.–Mar., daily 10–5.*

☝ ㊽ **Science World.** In a gigantic shiny dome built over an Omnimax Theater for Expo '86, this hands-on museum encourages visitors to touch and participate in the theme exhibits. The special Search Gallery is aimed at younger children, as are the fun-filled demonstrations given in Center Stage. ⊠ *1455 Québec St.,* ☎ *604/268–6363.* 🎫 *Science World $9, Omnimax $9, combination ticket $12.* ☉ *Weekdays 10–5, weekends 10–6.*

☝ ㊶ **Vancouver Maritime Museum.** This museum on English Bay traces the history of marine activities on the West Coast. Permanent exhibits depict the port of Vancouver, the fishing industry, and early explorers;

the model ships on display are a delight. Traveling exhibits vary but always have a maritime theme. Guided tours are led through the double-masted schooner *St. Roch*, the first ship to sail in both directions through the treacherous Northwest Passage. A changing variety of restored heritage boats from different cultures is moored behind the museum, and a huge Kwakiutl totem pole stands out front. ⊠ *1905 Ogden Ave., north end of Cypress St., also accessible via Granville Island Ferry,* ☎ *604/257–8300.* ⊡ *$5.* ☉ *May–Aug., daily 10–5; Sept.–Apr., Tues.–Sun. 10–5.*

39 Vancouver Museum. The museum's permanent exhibits focus on the city's early history and native art and culture. Life-size replicas of an 1897 Canadian Pacific Railway passenger car, a trading post, and a Victorian parlor, as well as a real dugout canoe, are highlights. ⊠ *1100 Chestnut St., Vanier Park,* ☎ *604/736–4431.* ⊡ *$5, extra charge for special exhibitions.* ☉ *Summer, daily 10–5; winter, Tues.–Sun. 10–5.*

44 VanDusen Botanical Garden. On what was once a 55-acre golf course grows one of the largest collections of ornamental plants in Canada. Native and exotic plant displays include a shrubbery maze; rhododendrons bloom in May and June. For a bite to eat, stop in Sprinklers Restaurant (☎ *604/261–0011*), on the grounds. ⊠ *5251 Oak St., at 37th Ave.,* ☎ *604/878–9274.* ⊡ *$5, ½ price Oct.–May.* ☉ *July and Aug., daily 10–9; Oct.–Apr., daily 10–4; May, June, and Sept., daily 10–6.*

DINING

Vancouver dining is usually fairly informal; casual but neat dress is appropriate everywhere except the few expensive restaurants that require jacket and tie (indicated in the text).

CATEGORY	COST*
$$$$	over $40
$$$	$30–$40
$$	$20–$30
$	under $20

*per person, including appetizer, entrée, and dessert and excluding drinks, service, and sales tax

American

$$ ✕ Griffin's. Sunday brunch here is cheerful, energetic, and kid-oriented: A special buffet is chock-a-block with favorite foods for the younger set. The rest of the week the emphasis is on the adult crowd. This brasserie uniquely blends the charm of old Italy with sophisticated design. Squash-yellow walls, bold black-and-white tiles, and splashy food art keep it lively. The open kitchen prepares inspired cuisine from fresh, regional ingredients, including such buffet selections as convict bread (a round loaf stuffed with goat cheese, olives, tomatoes, and peppers in olive oil), smoked salmon, chicken pasta al pesto, and baked Pacific cod. ⊠ *900 W. Georgia St.,* ☎ *604/662–1900. Reservations essential. AE, D, DC, MC, V.*

$ ✕ Isadora's. Not only does Isadora's offer good coffee and a "West Coast–fresh" menu that ranges from lox and bagels to vegetarian pastas and seafood platters, but it also has children's specials (the pizzas come with faces here) and an inside play area packed with toys. In summer the restaurant opens onto Granville Island's water park. Service can be slow, but the staff is friendly. The restaurant is no-smoking. Vegan dishes (prepared without animal products) are available on request. ⊠ *1540 Old Bridge St., Granville Island,* ☎ *604/681–8816. DC, MC, V. No dinner Mon. Sept.–May.*

Downtown Vancouver Dining

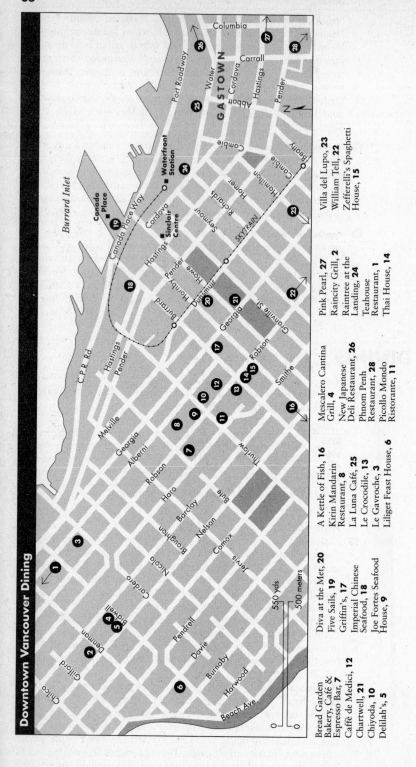

Bread Garden Bakery, Café & Espresso Bar, **7**
Caffè de Medici, **12**
Chartwell, **21**
Chiyoda, **10**
Delilah's, **5**

Diva at the Met, **20**
Five Sails, **19**
Griffin's, **17**
Imperial Chinese Seafood, **18**
Joe Fortes Seafood House, **9**

A Kettle of Fish, **16**
Kirin Mandarin Restaurant, **8**
La Luna Café, **25**
Le Crocodile, **13**
Le Gavroche, **3**
Liliget Feast House, **6**

Mescalero Cantina Grill, **4**
New Japanese Deli Restaurant, **26**
Phnom Penh Restaurant, **28**
Picollo Mondo Ristorante, **11**

Pink Pearl, **27**
Raincity Grill, **2**
Raintree at the Landing, **24**
Teahouse Restaurant, **1**
Thai House, **14**

Villa del Lupo, **23**
William Tell, **22**
Zefferelli's Spaghetti House, **15**

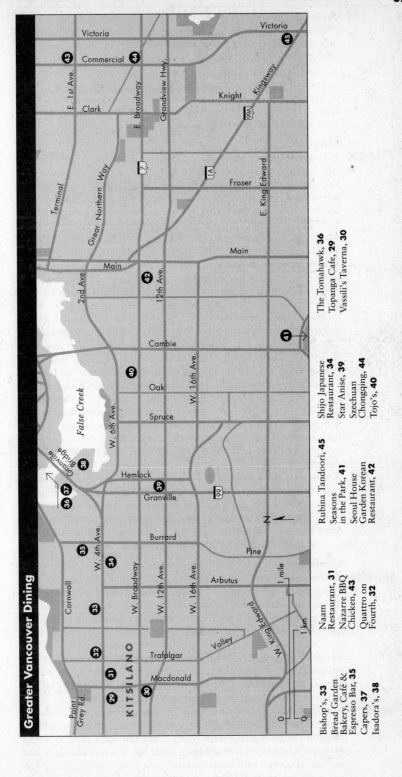

Greater Vancouver Dining

Bishop's, **33**
Bread Garden
Bakery, Café &
Espresso Bar, **35**
Capers, **37**
Isadora's, **38**

Naam
Restaurant, **31**
Nazarre BBQ
Chicken, **43**
Quattro on
Fourth, **32**

Rubina Tandoori, **45**
Seasons
in the Park, **41**
Seoul House
Garden Korean
Restaurant, **42**

Shijo Japanese
Restaurant, **34**
Star Anise, **39**
Szechuan
Chongqing, **44**
Tojo's, **40**

The Tomahawk, **36**
Topanga Cafe, **29**
Vassili's Taverna, **30**

$ ✕ **Nazarre BBQ Chicken.** The best barbecued chicken in town comes from this funky storefront on Commercial Avenue in the Little Italy neighborhood. Owner Gerry Moutal massages his chickens for tenderness before he puts them on the rotisserie and bastes them with a mixture of rum and spices. Chicken comes with roasted potatoes and a choice of mild, hot, or extra spicy garlic sauce. You can eat in, at one of four rickety tables, but the service can be surly at times; we recommend takeout. ⊠ *1859 Commercial Dr.,* ☎ *604/251–1844. Reservations not accepted. No credit cards.*

Chinese

$$–$$$ ✕ **Imperial Chinese Seafood.** This elegant Cantonese restaurant in the
★   Art Deco Marine Building has two-story floor-to-ceiling windows with stupendous views of Stanley Park and the North Shore mountains across Coal Harbour. Any dish featuring lobster, crab, or shrimp from the live tanks is recommended, as is the dim sum served every day from 11 to 2:30. Portions tend to be small and pricey (especially the abalone, shark's fin, and bird's nest delicacies) but never fail to please. ⊠ *355 Burrard St.,* ☎ *604/688–8191. Reservations essential. AE, MC, V.*

$$ ✕ **Kirin Mandarin Restaurant.** Fish swim in tanks set into the slate-green walls, part of the lavish decorations of this restaurant serving a smattering of northern Chinese cuisines. Dishes include Shanghai-style smoked eel, Peking duck, and Szechuan hot-and-spicy scallops. Kirin is just two blocks from most of the major downtown hotels. A second location at Cambie focuses on milder Cantonese seafood creations. ⊠ *102–1166 Alberni St.,* ☎ *604/682–8833;* ⊠ *555 W. 12th Ave., 2nd floor,* ☎ *604/879–8038. Reservations essential. AE, DC, MC, V.*

$$ ✕ **Pink Pearl.** This noisy, 680-seat Cantonese restaurant has tanks of live seafood—crab, shrimp, geoduck, oysters, abalone, rock cod, lobsters, and scallops. Menu highlights include clams in black-bean sauce, crab sautéed with five spices (a spicy dish sometimes translated as crab with peppery salt), and Pink Pearl's version of crisp-skinned chicken. Arrive early for dim sum on the weekend if you don't want to be caught in the lineup. ⊠ *1132 E. Hastings St.,* ☎ *604/253–4316. Reservations essential. AE, DC, MC, V.*

$ ✕ **Szechuan Chongqing.** At this unpretentious, white-tablecloth restaurant, try the Szechuan-style crunchy green beans tossed with garlic and ground pork or the Chongqing chicken—a boneless chicken served on a bed of spinach cooked in dry heat until crisp, giving it the texture of dried seaweed and a salty, rich, and nutty taste. ⊠ *1668 W. Broadway,* ☎ *604/734–1668. Reservations essential. AE, MC, V.*

Continental

$$$–$$$$ ✕ **Chartwell.** Named after Sir Winston Churchill's country home (a
★   painting of which hangs over the green marble fireplace), the flagship dining room at the Four Seasons hotel (☞ Lodging, *below*) looks like an upper-class British club. Floor-to-ceiling dark wood paneling, deep leather chairs, and a quiet setting make this the city's top spot for a power lunch. The chefs cook robust, inventive Continental food as well as lighter offerings and a variety of low-calorie, low-fat entrées. Favorites include tomato basil soup with gin, rack of lamb, and a number of salmon offerings. ⊠ *791 W. Georgia St.,* ☎ *604/844–6715. Reservations essential. Jacket and tie. AE, DC, MC, V.*

$$$–$$$$ ✕ **William Tell.** Silver service plates, embossed linen napkins, and a silver vase on each table set the tone of Swiss luxury in this establishment in the Georgian Court Hotel. Chef Christian Lindner offers excellent sautéed veal sweetbreads with red onion marmalade and marsala sauce and such Swiss specialties as cheese fondue, pickled herring with apples, and *Zürcher Geschnetzeltes* (thinly sliced veal with mushrooms in a light white wine sauce). A bar and bistro area caters

to a more casual crowd. Reserve in advance for the all-you-can-eat Swiss Farmer's Buffet on Sunday nights. ⊠ *765 Beatty St.,* ☎ *604/688–3504. Reservations essential. Jacket and tie. AE, DC, MC, V.*

$$$ ✗ **Seasons in the Park.** Seasons, in Queen Elizabeth Park, has a commanding view over the park gardens to the city lights and the mountains beyond. A comfortable room with lots of light wood and white tablecloths is matched with a conservative Continental menu including such standards as grilled salmon with fresh mint and roast duck with sun-dried cranberry sauce. This is a very popular choice with the weekend brunch crowd. ⊠ *Queen Elizabeth Park, 33rd and Cambie St.,* ☎ *604/874–8008. Reservations essential. AE, MC, V.*

$$$ ✗ **Teahouse Restaurant.** The best of the Stanley Park restaurants is perfectly poised for watching sunsets over the water, especially from a glassed-in wing that resembles a conservatory. The country French and seafood menu includes such specialties as cream of carrot soup, lamb with herb crust, and the perfectly grilled fish. ⊠ *7501 Stanley Park Dr., Ferguson Point, Stanley Park,* ☎ *604/669–3281. Reservations essential. AE, MC, V.*

Deli/Bakery

$ ✗ **Bread Garden Bakery, Café & Espresso Bar.** Once a croissant bakery, this is now the ultimate Kitsilano 24-hour hangout. Salads, quiches, elaborate cakes and pies, giant muffins, and cappuccino draw a steady stream of the young and fashionable. The wait in line may be long here or at any of its other locations. Reports indicate that quality has suffered with the rapid expansion, but the Garden's following is still strong. ⊠ *1880 W. 1st Ave., Kitsilano,* ☎ *604/738–6684;* ⊠ *2996 Granville St.,* ☎ *604/736–6465;* ⊠ *812 Bute St.,* ☎ *604/688–3213. AE, MC, V.*

$ ✗ **La Luna Café.** This unpretentious bi-level deli in the heart of Gastown serves fragrant coffees and teas and fresh soup and salad lunches, but it's the luscious sourdough cinnamon rolls that steal the show. Have one heated and slathered with butter if you plan to eat in at one of the small tables, or get the staff to bag a roll to go. These rolls are not to be missed! ⊠ *117 Water St.,* ☎ *604/687–5862. AE, MC, V.*

East Indian

$$ ✗ **Rubina Tandoori.** For the best East Indian food in the city, try Ru-
★ bina Tandoori, 20 minutes from downtown. The large menu spans most of the subcontinent's cuisines, and the especially popular *chevda* (an East Indian salty snack) is shipped to fans all over North America. Nonsmokers sit in the smaller, funkier back room with paintings of coupling gods and goddesses; smokers have the slightly more subdued front room. ⊠ *1962 Kingsway,* ☎ *604/874–3621. Reservations essential. DC, MC, V. Closed Sun.*

French

$$$ ✗ **Le Gavroche.** At this charming, somewhat formal turn-of-the-century house, a woman dining with a man will be offered a menu without prices. The classic French cooking, lightened—but by no means reduced—to nouvelle cuisine, includes such simple dishes as smoked salmon with blini and sour cream and more complex offerings such as grilled veal tenderloin with chanterelles and lobster sauce. The excellent wine list stresses Bordeaux. Tables by the front window promise mountains-and-water views. ⊠ *1616 Alberni St.,* ☎ *604/685–3924. Reservations essential. AE, DC, MC, V. No lunch weekends.*

$$ ✗ **Le Crocodile.** In a roomy location off Burrard Street, Chef Michael Jacob serves extremely well-cooked, simple food at reasonable prices. His Alsatian background shines with the caramel-sweet onion tart. Anything that involves innards is superb, and even such old standards as duck à l'orange are worth ordering here. Sadly, the quality is not what it was years ago in the smaller incarnation of this well-known restaurant. ⊠ *100–909 Burrard St.,* ☎ *604/669–4298. Reservations essential. AE, DC, MC, V. Closed Sun. No lunch Sat.*

Greek

$$ ✕ **Vassili's Taverna.** The menu in this family-run restaurant in the heart of the city's small Greek community is almost as conventional as the decor: checked tablecloths and mandatory paintings of fishing villages and the blue Aegean Sea. At Vassili's, though, even standards become memorable because of the flawless preparation. The house specialty is a deceptively simple *kotopoulo* (a half chicken, pounded flat, herbed, and charbroiled). ⊠ *2884 W. Broadway,* ☎ *604/733–3231. Reservations essential. AE, DC, MC, V. Closed Mon. No lunch weekends.*

Health Food

$ ✕ **Capers.** Hidden in the back of the most lavish health food store in
★ the Lower Mainland, Capers drips with earth-mother chic: wood tables, potted plants, and heady aromas from the store's bakery. Breakfast starts at 8: free-range eggs and bacon with no additives, or feather-light blueberry pancakes. Top choices from the lunch and dinner menu include roasted squash soup and local mushrooms with capellini. The newer 4th Avenue location, with its dining room above the store, is by far the nicer of the two; the West Vancouver store is somewhat old and dingy. ⊠ *2496 Marine Dr., West Vancouver,* ☎ *604/ 925–3374;* ⊠ *2285 W. 4th Ave.,* ☎ *604/739–6685. MC, V. No dinner Sun. at Marine Dr.*

$ ✕ **Naam Restaurant.** Vancouver's oldest organic eatery is open 24 hours, so if you need to satisfy a late-night tofu-burger craving, rest easy. The Naam also serves wine, beer, cappuccino, fresh juices, and wicked chocolate desserts, along with the vegetarian stir-fries. Wood tables and kitchen chairs help create a homey atmosphere. On warm summer evenings, try the outdoor courtyard at the back of the restaurant. ⊠ *2724 W. 4th Ave.,* ☎ *604/738–7151. MC, V.*

Italian

$$$ ✕ **Caffè de Medici.** This elegant, somewhat formal restaurant has ornate molded ceilings, rich green velvet curtains and chair coverings, portraits of the Medici family, and a courtly, peaceful atmosphere. Although an enticing antipasto table sits in the center of the room, consider the *bresaola* (air-dried beef marinated in olive oil, lemon, and pepper) as a worthwhile appetizer. Try the rack of lamb in a mint, mustard, and vermouth sauce. Any of the pastas is a safe bet. ⊠ *1025 Robson St.,* ☎ *604/669–9322. Reservations essential. AE, D, DC, MC, V. No lunch weekends.*

$$$ ✕ **Villa del Lupo.** Ask the top chefs in town where they go for Italian,
★ and Villa del Lupo is the answer more often than not. Country-house elegant decor sets a romantic tone, but come prepared to roll up your sleeves and mop up the sauce with a chunk of crusty bread. Agnolotti pasta stuffed with roasted duck, veggies, and ricotta cheese; rabbit loin with mushrooms, black olives, and thyme; and braised lamb osso buco in a sauce of tomatoes, red wine, cinnamon, and lemon are favorites here. ⊠ *869 Hamilton St.,* ☎ *604/688–7436. Reservations essential. AE, MC, V. No lunch weekends.*

$$ ✕ **Picollo Mondo Ristorante.** Soft candlelight, elegantly set tables, bountiful flower arrangements, and fine European antiques create a fairly formal, romantic tone at this intimate Northern Italian restaurant on a quiet street a block off Robson. Start with the seafood puff pastry with chive-vermouth cream sauce and follow up with the classic osso buco or the linguine tossed with smoked Alaskan cod, capers, and red onions. The award-winning wine cellar stocks over 3,000 bottles (450 varieties). ⊠ *850 Thurlow St.,* ☎ *604/688–1633. Reservations essential. AE, DC, MC, V. Closed Sun. No lunch weekends.*

$$ ✕ **Quattro on Fourth.** This Northern Italian restaurant in Kitsilano shot to stardom quickly. A mosaic floor, mustard-colored walls with stark-green-and-mauve-stenciled borders, cherry-stained tables, and a wraparound covered porch for al fresco dining enhance the Mediterranean atmosphere. Mushroom lovers usually jump at the truffle fettuccine, but if you can't make up your mind, there's the antipasto platter and combinazione (a plate for two with the five most popular pastas and sauces). The gelato trio is a perfect topper. ⊠ *2611 W. 4th Ave.,* ☎ *604/734–4444. Reservations essential. AE, DC, MC, V. No lunch.*

$$ ✕ **Zefferelli's Spaghetti House.** As you might guess from the name, spaghetti, penne, fusilli, tortellini, and fettuccine dressed in creative but subtle sauces—from roasted garlic, broccoli, feta cheese, and tomato sauce to traditional meat sauce—play first string at Zefferelli's, but grilled prawns and chicken saltimbocca (with prosciutto and sage in marsala wine) are strong competition. Done up in forest green, mustard, and persimmon, the trendy, somewhat rushed dining room has an open kitchen at one end and a wall of windows overlooking busy Robson Street at the other. ⊠ *1136 Robson St.,* ☎ *604/687–0655. Reservations essential. AE, DC, MC, V. No lunch weekends.*

Japanese

$$$ ✕ **Tojo's.** Hidekazu Tojo is a sushi-making legend here, with more than
★ 2,000 special preparations stored in his creative mind. His handsome blond-wood tatami rooms, on the second floor of a modern green-glass tower on West Broadway, provide the proper ambience for intimate dining, but Tojo's 10-seat sushi bar stands as the centerpiece. With Tojo presiding, it offers a convivial ringside seat for watching the creation of edible art. Although tempura and teriyaki dinners will satisfy, the seasonal menu is more exciting. In fall, ask for *dobin mushi,* a soup made from pine mushrooms. In spring, try salad made from scallops and pink cherry blossoms. ⊠ *202–777 W. Broadway,* ☎ *604/872–8050. Reservations essential. AE, DC, MC, V. Closed Sun. No lunch.*

$$ ✕ **Chiyoda.** The *robata* (grill) bar curves through Chiyoda's main room: On one side are the customers and an array of flat baskets full of the day's offerings; on the other side are the chefs and grills. There are 35 choices of things to grill, from squid, snapper, and oysters to eggplant, mushrooms, onions, and potatoes. The finished dishes, dressed with sake, soy sauce, or *ponzu* (vinegar and soy sauce), are dramatically passed over on the end of a long wooden paddle. ⊠ *200–1050 Alberni St.,* ☎ *604/688–5050. Reservations essential. AE, DC, MC, V. Closed Sun. No lunch Sat.*

$$ ✕ **Shijo Japanese Restaurant.** Shijo has an excellent and very large sushi bar, a smaller robata bar, tatami rooms, and a row of tables overlooking bustling Fourth Avenue. The epitome of modern urban Japanese chic is conveyed through the jazz music, handsome lamps with a bronze finish, and lots of black wood. Count on creatively prepared sushi in generous proportions, eggplant *dengaku* (topped with light and dark miso paste and broiled), and shiitake foil *yaki* (fresh shiitake mushrooms cooked in foil with lemony ponzu sauce). ⊠ *1926 W. 4th Ave.,* ☎ *604/732–4676. Reservations essential. AE, DC, MC, V. No lunch weekends.*

$ ✕ **New Japanese Deli Restaurant.** The least expensive sushi in town is served in the high-ceilinged main-floor room of a turn-of-the-century building on Powell Street, once the heart of Vancouver's Japantown. The food is especially fresh and good if you can make it an early lunch: sushi rectangles and rolls are made at 11 AM for the 11:30

opening, and there are all-you-can-eat sushi and tempura lunch specials on weekdays. ✉ *381 Powell St.,* ☎ *604/662–8755. No credit cards. Closed Sun.*

Korean

$ ✕ **Seoul House Garden Korean Restaurant.** This bright, popular restaurant, decorated in Japanese style, serves a full menu of Japanese and Korean food, including sushi. The best bet is the Korean barbecue, which you cook at your table; the dinner of marinated beef, pork, chicken, or fish comes complete with a half dozen side dishes—kimchi, salads, stir-fried rice, and pickled vegetables—as well as soup and rice. Service can be chaotic. ✉ *36 E. Broadway,* ☎ *604/874–4131. Reservations essential. MC, V. No lunch Sun.*

Mexican/Spanish

$$–$$$ ✕ **Mescalero Cantina Grill.** Here you find the look and feel of a Santa
★   Fe cocina, from stucco walls and leather chairs inside to a charming greenery-draped patio for open-air dining. Tapas are the main draw—Cajun beef and black bean tostada; panfried blue cornmeal-crusted oysters; roast chicken and chorizo chimichangas; and grilled salmon, asparagus, and goat cheese burritos—but dinner selections such as blackened red snapper with avocado, corn, black bean, vodka salsa with crème fraîche are equally good. The Bandito Brunch on weekends draws a crowd. ✉ *1215 Bidwell St.,* ☎ *604/669–2399. Reservations essential. AE, MC, V.*

$ ✕ **Topanga Cafe.** Arrive before 6:30 or after 8 PM to avoid waiting in line for this 40-seat Kitsilano classic. The Tex-Mex food hasn't changed much since 1978, when the Topanga started dishing up fresh salsa and homemade tortilla chips. Quantities are still huge and prices low. Kids can color blank menu covers while waiting for food; a hundred of their best efforts are framed on the walls. ✉ *2904 W. 4th Ave.,* ☎ *604/733–3713. Reservations not accepted. MC, V. Closed Sun.*

Nouvelle

$$$$ ✕ **Five Sails.** On the fourth floor of the Pan Pacific Hotel (☞ Lodging, *below*), this special-occasion restaurant has a stunning panoramic view of Canada Place, Lions Gate Bridge, and the lights of the north shore across the bay. Austrian chef Ernst Dorfler has a special flair for presentation, from the swan-shape butter served with breads early in the meal to the chocolate ice-cream bonbon served at the end. The broad-reaching, seasonally changing Pacific Rim menu often includes caramelized swordfish, ahi in red Thai curry vinaigrette, terrine of duck, and such old favorites as medallions of British Columbia salmon or lamb from Salt Spring Island. ✉ *Pan Pacific Hotel, 300–999 Canada Pl.,* ☎ *604/662–8211. Reservations essential. AE, DC, MC, V. No lunch.*

$$$–$$$$ ✕ **Bishop's.** John Bishop established this restaurant as a favorite in 1985 by serving West Coast Continental cuisine with an emphasis on British Columbia seafood. The seasonal menu may include medallions of venison, smoked Alaskan black cod, seared lamb loin, roast rabbit leg, or linguine tossed with fresh acorn squash. The small white rooms—their only ornament some splashy expressionist paintings—are favored by Pierre Trudeau and by Robert De Niro when he's on location in Vancouver. ✉ *2183 W. 4th Ave.,* ☎ *604/738–2025. Reservations essential. AE, DC, MC, V. Closed 1st week in Jan. No lunch.*

$$$ ✕ **Star Anise.** When Sammy Lalji left the highly regarded Bishop's (☞
★   *above*) to open his own restaurant, he built a faithful following in record time. His superior skills in attentive service, imaginative presentation, and excellent preparation of Pacific Rim cuisine with French flair shine in this intimate, no-smoking location just off Granville. Don't miss the crab and shrimp sausage on wilted spinach salad or the grilled enoki

mushrooms with tomato risotto; the juniper-marinated venison with raspberry vinegar and crème fraîche is another fine choice. ⊠ *1485 W. 12th Ave.,* ☎ *604/737–1485. Reservations essential. AE, D, DC, MC, V. No lunch weekends.*

$$ ✕ **Delilah's.** Cherubs dance on the ceiling, candles flicker on the ta-
★ bles, and martini glasses clink in toasts at this incredibly popular restaurant. Under the direction of chef Peg Montgomery, the nouvelle California cuisine is delicious, innovative, and beautifully presented. The menu, which changes seasonally, lets you choose two- or five-course prix-fixe dinners. Try the pancetta, pine nut, Asiago, and mozzarella fritters with sun-dried tomato aioli and the grilled swordfish with blueberry-lemon compote if they're available. Patrons have been known to line up before Delilah's opens for dinner. ⊠ *1739 Comox St.,* ☎ *604/687–3424. Reservations not accepted. DC, MC, V. No lunch.*

$$ ✕ **Diva at the Met.** This new, multitiered restaurant at the Metropolitan Hotel (☞ Lodging, *below*) is quickly becoming a local favorite. Presentation of the innovative nouvelle cuisine is as appealing as the impressionist art adorning the walls. Top creations from the glass-walled kitchen include charred ahi tuna on a warm bean salad with grilled asparagus and red pepper aioli, and veal London broil with foie gras and mushroom risotto and balsamic reduction. The after-theater crowd heads here for the late-evening dessert menu: Fresh sorbets, chocolate anise crème brûlée, and Stilton cream cheesecake draw rave reviews. ⊠ *645 Howe St.,* ☎ *604/687–7788. AE, DC, MC, V.*

Pacific Northwest

$$ ✕ **Liliget Feast House.** Only a few blocks from English Bay, this downstairs "longhouse" serves the original Northwest Coast cuisine: Bannock bread, baked sweet potato with hazelnuts, alder-grilled salmon, toasted seaweed with rice, steamed fern shoots, barbecued venison, and soapberries for dessert. Try the authentic but odd dish—"oolichan grease"—that's prepared from candlefish. Native music is piped in, and Northwest Coast native masks (for sale) peer from the walls. ⊠ *1724 Davie St.,* ☎ *604/681–7044. Reservations essential. AE, MC, V. No lunch.*

$$ ✕ **Raincity Grill.** This West End hot spot across the street from English Bay is a neighborhood favorite. The setting, with candlelit tables, balloon-back chairs, cushioned banquettes, and enormous flower arrangements is very sophisticated. All the same, it plays second fiddle to a creative, fresh weekly menu that highlights the best regional seafood, meats, and produce. Grilled romaine spears are used in the Caesar salad, giving it a delightful smokey flavor. Varying preparations of salmon and duck are usually available, as is at least one vegetarian selection. ⊠ *1193 Denman St.,* ☎ *604/685–7337. Reservations essential. AE, DC, MC, V.*

$$ ✕ **Raintree at the Landing.** In a beautifully renovated heritage building in busy Gastown, this spacious restaurant has waterfront views, a local menu, and a wine list with Pacific Northwest vintages. The kitchen, focusing on healthy cuisine, teeters between willfully eccentric and exceedingly simple; it bakes its own bread and makes luxurious soups. Main courses, which change daily, may include salmon and crab gnocchi, smoked Fraser Valley duck breast, and grilled marlin with basil risotto cakes. ⊠ *375 Water St.,* ☎ *604/688–5570. Reservations essential. AE, DC, MC, V. No lunch weekends.*

$ ✕ **The Tomahawk.** North Vancouver was mostly trees in 1926, when the Tomahawk first opened. Over the years, the original hamburger stand grew and mutated into part Northwest Coast native kitsch museum, part gift shop, and part restaurant. Renowned for its Yukon breakfast—five slices of back bacon, two eggs, hash browns, and toast—the

Tomahawk also serves gigantic muffins, excellent French toast, and pancakes. The menu switches to oysters, trout, and burgers named for native chiefs, at lunch and dinner. ⊠ *1550 Philip Ave.,* ☎ *604/988–2612. AE, MC, V.*

Seafood

$$ ✕ **Joe Fortes Seafood House.** Reserve a table on the second-floor bal-
★ cony at this Vancouver seafood hot spot to take in the view of the broad wall murals, the mounted blue marlins, and, most especially, the ever-entertaining boy-meets-girl scene at the noisy bar downstairs. The signature panfried Cajun oysters, clam and corn fritters, salmon with smoked apple and cider chutney, and seared sea scallops in sesame and oyster glaze are tasty and filling, but often overlooked in favor of the reasonably priced blue-plate special. ⊠ *777 Thurlow St.,* ☎ *604/669–1940. Reservations essential. AE, D, DC, MC, V.*

$$ ✕ **A Kettle of Fish.** Since opening in 1979, this family-run restaurant at the northeast end of Burrard Bridge has attracted a strong local following; count on getting top-quality seafood here. The menu varies daily according to market availability, but there are generally 15 kinds of fresh seafood that are either grilled, sautéed, poached, barbecued, or blackened Cajun-style. The British Columbia salmon and the seafood combo plate are always good choices. ⊠ *900 Pacific Blvd.,* ☎ *604/682–6661. AE, DC, MC, V. No lunch weekends.*

Southeast Asian

$ ✕ **Phnom Penh Restaurant.** Part of a small cluster of Southeast Asian
★ shops on the fringes of Chinatown, this eatery has potted plants and framed views of Angkor Wat. The hospitable staff serves unusually robust Vietnamese and Cambodian fare, including crisp, peppery garlic prawns fried in the shell and slices of beef crusted with ground salt and pepper mixed in the warm beef salad. The decor in the Broadway location is fancier, but the food is every bit as good as at East Georgia Street. ⊠ *244 E. Georgia St.,* ☎ *604/253–8899;* ⊠ *955 W. Broadway,* ☎ *604/734–8988. AE, MC, V. Closed Tues.*

$ ✕ **Thai House.** This sun-filled second-floor diner overlooking Robson Street offers a great lunch deal from 11 to 3: For under $8, patrons feast on a spring roll, soup, salad, rice, and a choice of 18 typical Thai dishes for the main course. The mild, smoky flavor of *kai pad khing* (boneless chicken with ginger, mushroom, and onions) is satisfying, but the tangy Thai garlic chicken is even better. ⊠ *1116 Robson St.,* ☎ *604/683–3383. AE, MC, V.*

LODGING

The hotel industry has become a major business for Vancouver, which hosts large numbers of conventioneers, Asian businesspeople, and others who are used to an above-average level of service. Although by some standards pricey, properties here are highly competitive, and you can expect the service to reflect this. Of the more than 16,000 rooms in greater Vancouver, just over 10,000 are in the downtown core. The chart below shows high-season prices, but from mid-October through May, rates throughout the city can drop as much as 50%.

Vancouver hotels, especially the more expensive properties downtown, are fairly comparable in facilities. Unless otherwise noted, expect to find the following amenities: minibars, in-room movies, no-smoking rooms/floors, room service, massage, exercise room, baby-sitting, laundry service and dry cleaning, concierge, business services, meeting rooms, and parking (there is usually an additional fee). Lodgings in the moderate to inexpensive category do not generally offer much in the way of amenities (no in-room minibar, restaurant, room service, pool, exercise room, and so on).

CATEGORY	COST*
$$$$	over $300
$$$	$200–$300
$$	$125–$200
$	under $125

All prices are for a standard double room for two, excluding 10% provincial accommodation tax, 15% service charge, and 7% GST.

$$$$ 🖽 **Four Seasons.** This bustling 28-story hotel adjacent to the Vancouver Stock Exchange is attached to the Pacific Centre shopping mall. Standard rooms are average in size and comforts; roomier corner rooms are recommended. Service at this luxury property is top notch, and the attention to detail is outstanding. The formal dining room, Chartwell (☞ Dining, *above*), is one of the best in the city. Even pets receive red-carpet treatment here—they're served Evian and pet treats in silver bowls. ⊠ *791 W. Georgia St., V6C 2T4,* ☎ *604/689–9333, 800/268–6282 in Canada, 800/332–3442 in the U.S.,* ℻ *604/844–6744. 274 rooms, 111 suites. 2 dining rooms, bar, lobby lounge, indoor-outdoor pool, hot tub, sauna, aerobics, shops, piano. AE, DC, MC, V.*

$$$$ 🖽 **Hyatt Regency.** The standard rooms of this 34-story hotel are spacious and decorated in deep, dramatic colors and dark wood; all are equipped with irons and ironing boards, coffeemakers, bathrobes, and voice mail. Ask for a corner room with a balcony on the north or west side for the best view. Automated check-in service (via a kiosk) is available in the bustling lobby. For a small fee, the Regency Club gives you the exclusivity of a floor accessed by keyed elevators, your own concierge, a private lounge, and complimentary breakfast. ⊠ *655 Burrard St., V6C 2R7,* ☎ *604/683–1234 or 800/233–1234,* ℻ *604/689–3707. 612 rooms, 34 suites. Restaurant, 2 bars, café, in-room modem lines, in-room safes, pool, sauna, shops, children's programs (ages 6–12), travel services, car rental. AE, D, DC, MC, V.*

$$$$ 🖽 **Pan Pacific Hotel.** Sprawling Canada Place, on a pier right by the financial district, houses the luxurious Pan Pacific, the Vancouver Trade and Convention Centre, and a cruise-ship terminal. The three-story atrium lobby has a dramatic totem pole and waterfall, and the lounge, restaurant, and café all have huge expanses of glass with views of the harbor and mountains. Earth tones and varied textures give the rooms an understated elegance. Corner rooms overlooking the harbor are favorites. ⊠ *300–999 Canada Pl., V6C 3B5,* ☎ *604/662–8111, 800/663–1515 in Canada, 800/937–1515 in the U.S.,* ℻ *604/685–8690. 467 rooms, 39 suites. 3 restaurants, coffee shop, lobby lounge, in-room modem lines, in-room safes, in-room VCRs, pool, barber/beauty salon, hot tubs, saunas, steam rooms, aerobics, health club, indoor track, paddle tennis, racquetball, squash, shops, convention center, travel services. AE, DC, MC, V.*

$$$$ 🖽 **Sutton Place.** The feel here is more exclusive guest house than large
★ hotel: The lobby has sumptuously thick carpets, enormous displays of flowers, and elegant European furniture. The rooms are furnished with rich, dark woods reminiscent of 19th-century France. Despite its size, this hotel maintains a significant level of intimacy and exclusivity. The Fleuri Restaurant serves a great Sunday brunch; Le Club, a fine Continental restaurant, is for special occasions. Le Grande Residence, a luxury apartment hotel suitable for extended stays, adjoins the hotel. ⊠ *845 Burrard St., V6Z 2K6,* ☎ *604/682–5511 or 800/961–7555,* ℻ *604/682–5513. 350 rooms, 47 suites. Restaurant, bar, café, lobby lounge, kitchenettes, indoor pool, beauty salon, sauna, spa, steam room, health club, bicycles, piano. AE, D, DC, MC, V.*

Vancouver Lodging

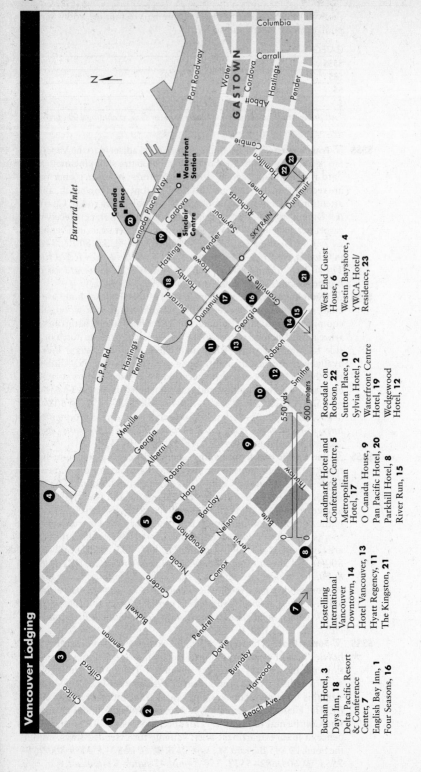

Buchan Hotel, **3**
Days Inn, **18**
Delta Pacific Resort & Conference Center, **7**
English Bay Inn, **1**
Four Seasons, **16**

Hostelling International Vancouver Downtown, **14**
Hotel Vancouver, **13**
Hyatt Regency, **11**
The Kingston, **21**

Landmark Hotel and Conference Centre, **5**
Metropolitan Hotel, **17**
O Canada House, **9**
Pan Pacific Hotel, **20**
Parkhill Hotel, **8**
River Run, **15**

Rosedale on Robson, **22**
Sutton Place, **10**
Sylvia Hotel, **2**
Waterfront Centre Hotel, **19**
Wedgewood Hotel, **12**

West End Guest House, **6**
Westin Bayshore, **4**
YWCA Hotel/ Residence, **23**

$$$$ ★ **⊞ Waterfront Centre Hotel.** Dramatically elegant, the 23-story glass hotel opened in 1991 across from Canada Place, which can be reached from the hotel by an underground walkway. Views from the caramel-color lobby and 70% of the guest rooms are of Burrard Inlet. The rooms are attractively furnished with contemporary artwork; armoires conceal the TV. Large corner rooms have the best views. A string quartet entertains in the lobby restaurant, Herons, during Sunday brunch. ⊠ *900 Canada Place Way, V6C 3L5,* ☎ *604/691–1991 or 800/441–1414,* ℻ *604/691–1999. 460 rooms, 29 suites. Restaurant, pool, steam room, shops, travel services, car rental. AE, D, DC, MC, V.*

$$$–$$$$ ★ **⊞ Wedgewood Hotel.** This small, elegant property is run by an owner who cares fervently about her guests. The intimate lobby is decorated with polished brass, beveled glass, a fireplace, tasteful artwork, and fine antiques. All the extra touches are here, too: nightly turndown service, afternoon ice delivery, dark-out drapes, flowers on the balcony, robes, and a morning newspaper. No tour groups or conventions stop here; the Wedgewood's clients are almost exclusively corporate, except on weekends, when the place turns into a couples' retreat. ⊠ *845 Hornby St., V6Z 1V1,* ☎ *604/689–7777 or 800/663–0666,* ℻ *604/608–5348. 59 rooms, 34 suites. Restaurant, bar, some in-room modems, in-room safes, sauna, piano, travel services. AE, D, DC, MC, V.*

$$$ **⊞ Delta Pacific Resort & Conference Center.** It's the facilities that make this 14-acre site a resort: swimming pools (one indoor, with a three-story tubular water slide), tennis courts with a pro, an outdoor fitness circuit, aqua-exercise classes, outdoor volleyball nets, a play center and summer camps for children, and a playground. In spite of the hotel's size, the atmosphere is casual and friendly. Guest rooms are modern, with contemporary decor and a pleasant blue and green color scheme. ⊠ *10251 St. Edwards Dr., Richmond V6X 2M9,* ☎ *604/278–9611, 800/268–1133 in Canada, 800/877–1133 in the U.S.,* ℻ *604/276–1121. 453 rooms, 5 suites. 2 restaurants, lobby lounge, in-room modem lines, indoor pool, 2 outdoor pools, barbershop, beauty salon, hot tub, saunas, putting green, squash, bicycles, children's programs (ages 5–12), convention center, travel services, car rental, free parking. AE, DC, MC, V.*

$$$ ★ **⊞ Hotel Vancouver.** The copper roof of this grand château-style hotel dominates Vancouver's skyline. Opened in 1939 by the Canadian National Railway, the hotel commands a regal position in the center of town. Even the standard guest rooms have an air of prestige, with mahogany furniture, attractive linens, and the original, deep bathtubs. Suites, with French doors and graceful wing chairs, take up two floors and come with extra services and amenities. Afternoon tea in the lobby lounge is a real treat. ⊠ *900 W. Georgia St., V6C 2W6,* ☎ *604/684–3131 or 800/441–1414,* ℻ *604/662–1937. 504 rooms, 46 suites. 3 restaurants, lobby lounge, in-room modem lines, indoor lap pool, hot tub, spa, steam rooms, shops, piano, travel services, car rental. AE, D, DC, MC, V.*

$$$ **⊞ Metropolitan Hotel.** This 18-story hotel built in 1984 by the Hong Kong Mandarin chain is now a member of the Preferred Hotels group. Although the rates went down, the surroundings were improved during 1996 renovations: The lobby, still restrained and tasteful, now has a view of the hotel's new restaurant, Diva at the Met (☞ Dining, *above*), through an etched-glass wall. A slight Asian theme touches the rich dark-mahogany furnishings. Standard rooms are surprisingly spacious and have narrow balconies, but the studio suites—even bigger and only slightly more expensive than a standard room—are a favorite. ⊠ *645 Howe St., V6C 2Y9,* ☎ *604/687–1122 or 800/667–2300,* ℻ *604/689–7044. 179 rooms, 18 suites. Restaurant, juice bar, piano bar; in-room*

fax, printer, and modem lines in business rooms; indoor lap pool, men's steam room, racquetball, squash. AE, DC, MC, V.

$$$ 🏨 **Westin Bayshore.** The Bayshore, perched right on the best part of the harbor adjacent to Stanley Park, has truly fabulous views. It's the perfect place to stay in summer, especially for a family, because of its huge outdoor pool, sundeck, grassy areas, and extensive recreational facilities. The tower rooms have the best views of the water; rooms in the main wing are decorated in contemporary style. Development along this section of the waterfront was in high gear at press time, robbing the Bayshore of its tranquillity. ✉ *1601 W. Georgia St., V6G 2V4,* ☎ *604/682–3377 or 800/228–3000,* FAX *604/687–3102. 484 rooms, 33 suites. Restaurant, café, 2 bars, in-room modem lines and safes in tower rooms, indoor pool, outdoor pool, barbershop/beauty salon, steam rooms, boating, fishing, bicycles, billiards, piano, travel services, shuttle, car rental. AE, D, DC, MC, V.*

$$–$$$ 🏨 **Parkhill Hotel.** Cool pastel shades echo the colors of impressionist prints decorating the surprisingly spacious rooms in this West End hotel just a block from the seawall and sandy Sunset Beach. Large, comfortable sitting areas, half-moon balconies with city or bay views, mini-refrigerators, hair dryers, and complimentary downtown shuttle services are part of the package. ✉ *1160 Davie St., V6E 1N1,* ☎ *604/685–1311 or 800/663–1525,* FAX *604/681–0208. 191 rooms. 2 restaurants, lounge, in-room safes, pool, sauna, travel services, car rental. AE, D, DC, MC, V.*

$$–$$$ 🏨 **Rosedale on Robson.** If you plan to be in town a while and want
★   to keep expenses down by doing some of your own cooking, look into a room at the all-suite Rosedale on Robson, opened in 1995. Rooms in shades of peach and light green are generous in size and have European kitchens, bleached hemlock furniture, and garden patios or balconies overlooking the city. Rooms on upper floors on the north side have views of Coal Harbour. You'll find charming gardens with strolling paths on the second and third floors of the complex. ✉ *838 Hamilton St., V6B 5W4,* ☎ *604/689–8033 or 800/661–8870,* FAX *604/689–4426. 275 suites. Restaurant, bar, in-room video games, kitchenettes, refrigerators, limited room service, indoor lap pool, hot tub, sauna, steam room, coin laundry. AE, DC, MC, V.*

$$ 🏨 **English Bay Inn.** This renovated 1930s Tudor house is one block from
★   the ocean and Stanley Park. The guest rooms—each with a private bath—have wonderful sleigh beds (in all but one room) with matching armoires and Ralph Lauren linens. The common areas of this no-smoking inn are elegantly furnished with museum-quality antiques: The sophisticated but cozy parlor has wing chairs, a fireplace, a gilt Louis XIV clock and candelabra, and French doors overlooking the front garden. Breakfast is served in a rather formal room with a Gothic dining room suite, a fireplace, and a 17th-century grandfather clock. ✉ *1968 Comox St., V6G 1R4,* ☎ *604/683–8002. 4 rooms, 1 suite. Free parking. AE, MC, V.*

$$ 🏨 **Landmark Hotel and Conference Center.** The towering Landmark is still the tallest hotel (42 stories) in downtown Vancouver and contains some of the prettiest guest rooms in town. The bold jewel tones (emerald, sapphire, and ruby) of paintings by British Columbia's beloved Emily Carr (whose works hang in every room) are repeated on walls and furnishings. All rooms enjoy a fine view, but the Cloud Nine revolving restaurant on the top floor is a great place for an unobstructed view of Vancouver over an early breakfast buffet (in summer only); go elsewhere for dinner. ✉ *1400 Robson St., V6G 1B9,* ☎ *604/687–0511 or 800/325–3535,* FAX *604/687–2801. 351 rooms, 7 suites. Restaurant, café, sports bar, saunas, travel services. AE, DC, MC, V.*

$$ ⌂ **O Canada House.** New to the growing list of bed-and-breakfasts in Vancouver, O Canada House is a beautifully restored 1897 Victorian oozing with period charm inside and out. Each bedroom is fairly spacious and appointed in late-Victorian antiques; modern touches, including TV, VCR, fridge, and phone, are discreetly tucked out of sight. Guests often gather in the evening near the fireplace in the front parlor, and assemble again in the morning in the formal dining room for a gourmet breakfast (though breakfast served on the wraparound porch is also an option). ⌂ *1114 Barclay St., V6E 1H1,* ☎ *604/688–0555,* FAX *604/ 488–0556. 5 rooms. Free parking. AE, MC, V.*

$$ ⌂ **West End Guest House.** This lovely Victorian house, built in 1906,
★ is a true "painted lady," from its gracious front parlor, cozy fireplace, and early 1900s furniture to its green-trimmed pink exterior. Most of the small but handsome rooms have high brass beds, antiques, and gorgeous linens. The basement suite has a gas fireplace in the sitting area and a side garden view. The inn's genial host, Evan Penner, adds small touches such as a pre-dinner glass of sherry, duvets and feather mattress pads, terry bathrobes, and turndown service. The inn is in a residential neighborhood two minutes from Robson Street. Room rates at this no-smoking establishment include a full breakfast. ⌂ *1362 Haro St., V6E 1G2,* ☎ *604/681–2889,* FAX *604/688–8812. 7 rooms. Bicycles, free parking. AE, D, MC, V.*

$–$$ ⌂ **Days Inn.** Business travelers looking for a bargain will find this location convenient. The six-story hotel, which opened as the Abbotsford in 1920, is the only moderately priced hotel in the business core. Recent renovations of the guest rooms and the lobby have made it even more agreeable. Rooms are bright, clean, and utilitarian; standard units are large, but there is no room service and few amenities. Suites 310, 410, 510, and 610 have a harbor view. ⌂ *921 W. Pender St., V6C 1M2,* ☎ *604/681–4335,* FAX *604/681–7808. 74 rooms, 11 suites. Restaurant, 2 bars, in-room safes, billiards, coin laundry, free off-site parking. AE, D, DC, MC, V.*

$–$$ ⌂ **River Run.** This unique bed-and-breakfast rests in the serene Fraser River delta in the village of Ladner, 30 minutes drive south of downtown Vancouver and 10 minutes north of the ferries to Vancouver Island. You can choose among a little gem of a floating house; a room in the owner's larger floating home; a net loft (complete with Japanese soaking tub on the deck and a cozy captain's bed tucked away in the rafters); and a river's-edge cottage with a two-person whirlpool tub, full kitchen, fireplace, and deck. There's a canoe and a kayak for guest use. Afternoon refreshments and breakfast are included in the tariff at this no-smoking inn. ⌂ *4551 River Rd. W, Ladner V4K 1R9,* ☎ *604/ 946–7778,* FAX *604/940–1970. 1 room, 3 suites. Kitchenettes, TV and VCR on request, bicycles, free parking. MC, V.*

$ ⌂ **Buchan Hotel.** The three-story 1930s building is conveniently set in a tree-lined residential street a block from Stanley Park. For the budget price, you rent tiny, institutional rooms with very basic furnishings, ceiling fans, and color TV, but no telephone or air-conditioning. There's also a TV lounge, public telephone, and storage for bikes and skis. The pension-style rooms with shared bath down the hall are perhaps the most affordable accommodations in downtown. This is a no-smoking hotel. ⌂ *1906 Haro St., V6G 1H7,* ☎ *604/685–5354 or 800/668– 6654,* FAX *604/685–5367. 60 rooms, 30 with bath. Coin laundry. AE, DC, MC, V.*

$ ⌂ **Hostelling International Vancouver Downtown.** Vancouver's newest
★ hostel, conveniently located in the West End downtown, is just blocks from Sunset Beach on English Bay and within walking distance of Stanley Park and a quick ferry ride to Granville Island. The hostel itself is very tidy and secure; access to the wings of private rooms and the men's

and women's dorms requires a card key. Amenities include a shared kitchen and dining room, a TV room, a garden patio and rooftop garden, a games room, bicycles, and storage for luggage and bikes. The staff here are extremely friendly and informative, and the prime location and inexpensive price can't be beat. ⊠ *1114 Burnaby St., V6E 1P1,* ☎ *604/684–4565,* FAX *604/684-4540. 220 beds in 7 private and 61 semiprivate rooms. No-smoking floors, library, coin laundry.*

$ 🏨 **The Kingston.** The Kingston is a small budget hotel convenient for shopping. It's an old-style, four-story building, with no elevator—the type of establishment you'd find in Europe. The Spartan rooms, renovated in 1995, are small and immaculate and share a bathroom down the hall. All rooms have phones and a few have TVs and private baths; there's a TV lounge. Rooms on the south side are sunnier. Continental breakfast is included in the price. ⊠ *757 Richards St., V6B 3A6,* ☎ *604/684–9024,* FAX *604/684–9917. 56 rooms, 8 with bath. Sauna, coin laundry, free overnight parking (fee during day). AE, MC, V.*

$ 🏨 **Sylvia Hotel.** To stay at the Sylvia Hotel from June through August you'll need to book six months to a year ahead. This older, ivy-covered hotel is so popular because of its low rates and near-perfect location: about 25 feet from the beach on scenic English Bay, 200 feet from Stanley Park, and a 20-minute walk from Robson Street. The unadorned rooms have worn, plain furnishings. Suites are huge, and all have kitchens. ⊠ *1154 Gilford St., V6G 2P6,* ☎ *604/681–9321. 97 rooms, 18 suites. Restaurant, bistro, lounge, laundry service, dry cleaning. AE, DC, MC, V.*

$ 🏨 **YWCA Hotel/Residence.** Opened in the heart of the entertainment ★   district in late 1995, the secured 12-story building has bright, airy, and very comfortable rooms. All have cheery floral bedspreads, framed floral prints on the wall, white laminated nightstands and desk, a mini-refrigerator, and a phone. Some have sinks in the room and share a bath down the hall, others share a bath between two rooms, and still others have private baths. The hotel is open to both men and women and offers discounts for seniors, students, and YWCA members. ⊠ *733 Beatty St., V6B 2M4,* ☎ *604/895–5830, 800/663–1424 in British Columbia and Alberta,* FAX *604/681–2550. 155 rooms. 3 shared kitchens, 2 shared kitchenettes, no-smoking floors, refrigerators, 3 shared TV lounges, 2 coin laundries, meeting rooms. MC, V.*

NIGHTLIFE AND THE ARTS

For **information on events,** pick up a free copy of the *Georgia Straight* (available at cafés and bookstores around town), or look in the entertainment section of the *Vancouver Sun* (Thursday's paper has listings in the "What's On" column). Call the **Arts Hotline** (☎ 604/ 684–2787) for the latest lineups in entertainment. For tickets, book through **Ticketmaster** (☎ 604/280–3311).

The Arts

Dance
Watch for **Ballet British Columbia**'s (☎ 604/732–5003) Dance Alive! series September through April, presenting visiting or local ballet companies (from the Kirov to Ballet British Columbia). Local modern dance companies worth seeing are **Karen Jamison, Judith Marcuse,** and **JumpStart.** Most performances by these companies can be seen at the Queen Elizabeth Theatre (☞ Music, *below*). Two other top dance venues are the Fireside Arts Centre (⊠ 280 E. Cordova, ☎ 604/689–0926) and the Vancouver East Cultural Centre (☞ Theater, *below*).

Film

For **foreign films and original works,** try the Park Theater (✉ 3440 Cambie St., ☎ 604/876–2747), the Ridge Theatre (✉ 3131 Arbutus St., ☎ 604/738–6311), and the Varsity Theater (✉ 4375 W. 10th Ave., ☎ 604/222–2235). **Pacific Cinématèque** (✉ 1131 Howe St., ☎ 604/688–8202) shows esoteric foreign and art films. Tickets are half price on Tuesdays at all **Cineplex Odeon** theaters. The **Vancouver International Film Festival** (☎ 604/685–0260) is held during September or October in several theaters around town.

Music

The **Vancouver Symphony Orchestra** (☎ 604/684–9100) plays at the restored Orpheum Theatre (✉ 601 Smithe St.). The **CBC Orchestra** (☎ 604/662–6000) is one of the groups that uses the Orpheum Theatre (☞ *above*). **Choral groups** like the Bach Choir (☎ 604/921–8012), the Vancouver Cantata Singers (☎ 604/921–8588), and the Vancouver Chamber Choir (☎ 604/738–6822) play a major role in Vancouver's classical music scene. The **Early Music Society** (☎ 604/732–1610) performs medieval, Renaissance, and Baroque music throughout the year and hosts the Vancouver Early Music Summer Festival, one of the most important early music festivals in North America. Concerts by the **Friends of Chamber Music** (no phone) are worth watching for. Programs of the **Vancouver Recital Society** (☎ 604/736–6034) are always of excellent quality.

Vancouver Opera (☎ 604/682–2871) stages five high-caliber productions a year, usually in October, November, February, March, and June, at the Queen Elizabeth Theatre. The **Queen Elizabeth Theatre** (✉ 600 Hamilton St., ☎ 604/665–3050) is a major venue in Vancouver for traveling Broadway musicals as well as opera and other events.

Theater

The **Vancouver Playhouse** (✉ 160 W. 1st. St., ☎ 604/872–6622) is the best-established venue in Vancouver for mainstream theatrical shows. The newly completed **Ford Centre for the Performing Arts** (✉ 777 Homer St., ☎ 604/876–2808) was built to showcase major productions and attract top touring companies. The **Arts Club Theatre** (✉ 1585 Johnston St., ☎ 604/687–1644) has two stages on Granville Island and theatrical performances all year. **Carousel Theatre** (☎ 604/669–3410) performs off-of-Broadway shows at the Waterfront Theatre (✉ 1405 Anderson St. on Granville Island. **Touchstone** (☎ 604/687–8737), at the Firehall Theatre (✉ 280 E. Cordova St.), is a small but lively company. The **Back Alley Theatre** (✉ 751 Thurlow St., ☎ 604/738–7013) hosts *Theatresports,* a hilarious improv event. The **Vancouver East Cultural Centre** (✉ 1895 Venables St., ☎ 604/254–9578) is a multipurpose performance space that always hosts high-caliber shows.

Bard on the Beach (☎ 604/739–0559) is a summer series of Shakespeare's plays performed under a huge tent on the beach at Vanier Park. **The Fringe** (☎ 604/873–3646), Vancouver's annual live theatrical arts festival, is staged in September at churches, dance studios, and theater halls around town.

Nightlife

Bars and Lounges

The **Gérard Lounge** (✉ 845 Burrard St., ☎ 604/682–5511) at the Sutton Place Hotel is probably the nicest in the city because of its fireplaces, wing chairs, dark wood, and leather; it's also the major film industry hangout in town. The sophisticated lobby bar at the **Hotel Vancouver** (⊠ 900 W. Georgia St., ☎ 604/684–3131) is the place to see and be seen; there's live music in the evenings from 4 PM, and 55 wines are available by the glass. The **Bacchus Lounge** (⊠ 845 Hornby St., ☎ 604/689–7777) in the Wedgewood Hotel is stylish and chic, with a pianist providing soothing background music. The **Garden Lounge** (⊠ 791 W. Georgia St., ☎ 604/689–9333) in the Four Seasons is bright and airy with African flora and a waterfall, plus big soft chairs you won't want to get out of; a pianist plays here on the weekends.

For a more lively atmosphere, try **Joe Fortes** (⊠ 777 Thurlow St., ☎ 604/669–1940), known in town as the local "meet market." Billiards is now tremendously popular in Vancouver, and the **Soho Café and Billiards** (⊠ 1144 Homer, ☎ 604/688–1180) is the place to go. One of the city's "hot" pool halls is the **Automotive Billiards Club** (⊠ 1095 Homer, ☎ 604/682–0040).

Microbreweries have finally hit Vancouver, a few of them taking off in a big way. At **Steam Works** (⊠ 375 Water St., ☎ 604/689–2739) on the edge of bustling Gastown, they use an age-old steam brewing process and large copper kettles (visible through glass walls in the dining room downstairs) to whip up six to nine brews; the espresso ale is interesting. The **Yaletown Brewing Company** (⊠ 1111 Mainland St., ☎ 604/681–2739) is based in a huge renovated warehouse with a glassed-in brewery turning out eight tasty microbrews; it also has a darts and billiards pub and a restaurant with an open-grill kitchen.

On Granville Island, the after-work crowd heads to **Bridges** (☎ 604/687–4400) near the Public Market overlooking False Creek. **Pelican Bay** (☎ 604/683–7373) is a somewhat upscale lounge in the Granville Island Hotel. The **Backstage Lounge** (⊠ 1585 Johnston St., ☎ 604/687–1354), behind the main stage at the Arts Club Theatre on Granville Island, stocks one of the largest selections of scotches in town and is the hangout for local and touring musicians and actors.

Casinos

Vancouver has a few casinos; proceeds go to local charities and arts groups. No alcohol is served. A good bet is the **Royal Diamond Casino** (⊠ 106B-750 Pacific Blvd. S, ☎ 604/685–2340), in the Plaza of Nations Expo site downtown. The **Great Canadian Casino** (⊠ 2477 Heather St., ☎ 604/872–5543), in the Holiday Inn, is an option for gamblers in downtown Vancouver.

Comedy

Yuk Yuks (⊠ 750 Pacific Blvd., ☎ 604/687–5233) is good for a few laughs. The cheerful **Punchlines Comedy Theatre** (⊠ 15 Water St., ☎ 604/684–3015) is in Gastown.

Music

DANCE CLUBS

Although dance clubs come and go, lines still form every weekend at **Richard's on Richards** (⊠ 1036 Richards St., ☎ 604/687–6794) for live and taped dance tunes. **Graceland** (⊠ 1250 Richards St., ☎ 604/688–2648), featuring progressive European, North American and tribal dance music, attracts a slightly younger dance crowd. The nitrogen fog screen, automated lighting, and go-go dancers at **Mars** (⊠ 1320 Richards St., ☎ 604/662–7707) are supposed to be there to get dancers into the swing of things.

JAZZ

A jazz and blues hot line (☎ 604/682–0706) gives you current information on concerts and clubs. The **Alma Street Café** (⊠ 2505 Alma

St., ☎ 604/222–2244), a restaurant, is a traditional venue with good mainstream jazz; live performances have the spotlight Wednesday through Saturday. The venerable **Glass Slipper** (✉ 185 E. 11th Ave., ☎ 604/877–0066) has mainstream to contemporary jazz with a more underground atmosphere and a hushed crowd there to listen to the music. A Big Band dance sound carries into the night at **Hot Jazz** (✉ 2120 Main St., ☎ 604/873–4131). Beatnik poetry readings would seem to fit right in at the **Chameleon Urban Lounge** (✉ 801 W. Georgia St., ☎ 604/669-0806) in the basement of the Hotel Georgia, but it's the sophisticated mix of jazz, R&B, and Latin tunes that draws the crowds.

ROCK

The **Town Pump** (✉ 66 Water St., ☎ 604/683–6695) is the main venue for local and touring rock bands. **The Rage** nightclub (✉ 750 Pacific Blvd. S, ☎ 604/685–5585) has alternative music and draws a young crowd. You'll find taped classic rock and roll, plenty of music memorabilia, and specialty salads and sandwiches dished up at Vancouver's version of the **Hard Rock Cafe** (✉ 686 W. Hastings St., ☎ 604/687–7625). The **Commodore Ballroom** (✉ 870 Granville St., ☎ 604/681–7838), a Vancouver institution, has been restored to its original Art Deco style and offers live music ranging from B.B. King to zydeco bands.

OUTDOOR ACTIVITIES AND SPORTS

Beaches

An almost continuous string of beaches runs from Stanley Park to the University of British Columbia. The water is cool, but the beaches are sandy, edged by grass. Liquor is prohibited in parks and on beaches. For information, call the **Vancouver Board of Parks and Recreation** (☎ 604/257–8400).

Kitsilano Beach, over the Burrard Bridge from downtown, has a lifeguard and is the city's busiest—transistor radios, volleyball games, and sleek young people are ever present. The part of the beach nearest the Maritime Museum is the quietest. Facilities include a playground, tennis courts, a heated saltwater pool, concession stands, and nearby restaurants and cafés.

The **Point Grey beaches** give you a number of different options. Jericho, Locarno, and Spanish Banks, which begin at the end of Point Grey Road, offer a huge expanse of sand, especially in summer and at low tide. The shallow water here, warmed slightly by sun and sand, is best for swimming. Farther out, toward Spanish Banks, you'll find the beach less crowded, but the last concession stand and washrooms are at Locarno. If you keep walking along the beach just past Point Grey, you'll hit Wreck Beach, Vancouver's nude beach.

Among the **West End beaches,** Second Beach and Third Beach, along Beach Drive in Stanley Park, draw families. Second Beach has a guarded saltwater pool. Both have concession stands and washrooms. The liveliest of the West End beaches is English Bay Beach, at the foot of Denman Street. A water slide, live music, a windsurfing outlet, and other concessions here stay jumping all summer long. Farther along Beach Drive, Sunset Beach, surprisingly quiet considering the location, has a lifeguard but no facilities.

Participant Sports

Biking

Stanley Park (☞ Stanley Park *in* Exploring Vancouver, *above*) is the most popular spot for family cycling. Rentals are available here from **Bayshore Bicycles** (⊠ 745 Denman St., ☎ 604/688–2453) or **Spokes Bicycle Rentals & Espresso Bar** (⊠ 1798 W. Georgia St., ☎ 604/688–5141).

A good summer biking route is along the north or south shores of **False Creek.** For bikes, try **Granville Island Bike Rentals** (⊠ 1496 Cartwright, ☎ 604/669–2453) or **Granville Island Water Sports** (⊠ Charter Boat Dock, ☎ 604/662–7245).

Cycling British Columbia (⊠ 1367 W. Broadway, Suite 332, ☎ 604/737–3034) is the best source for bike route maps and biking guidebooks.

Boating

Several charter companies offer a cruise-and-learn vacation, usually to the Gulf Islands. **Sea Wing Sailing Group, Ltd.** (⊠ Granville Island, ☎ 604/669–0840) offers a five-day trip teaching the ins and outs of sailing. If you'd rather rent a speedboat to zip around the bay for a day, contact **Granville Island Boat Rentals** (☎ 604/682–6287).

Fishing

You can fish for salmon all year in coastal British Columbia. **Sewell's Marina Horseshoe Bay** (⊠ 6695 Nelson St., Horseshoe Bay, ☎ 604/921–3474) organizes a daily four-hour trip on Howe Sound or has hourly rates on U-drives. **Bayshore Yacht Charters** (⊠ 1601 W. Georgia St., ☎ 604/691–6936) has fishing charters.

Golf

Lower Mainland golf courses are open all year. Spacious **Fraserview Golf Course** (⊠ 7800 Vivian St., ☎ 604/280–8633), with fairways well defined by hills and mature conifers and deciduous trees, is the busiest in the region. **Seymour Golf and Country Club** (⊠ 3723 Mt. Seymour Parkway, ☎ 604/929–5491), on the south side of Mt. Seymour on the North Shore, is a semiprivate club open to the public on Monday and Friday. North of Vancouver is **Furry Creek** (⊠ Lion's Bay, ☎ 604/896–2224), a challenging but forgiving 6,200-yard all-terrain public course overlooking scenic Howe Sound.

Westwood Golf and Country Club in nearby Coquitlam (⊠ 3251 Plateau Blvd., ☎ 604/552–0777) was recently runner-up in the "Best New Course in Canada" category in *Golf Digest.* One of the finest public courses in the area is **Peace Portal** (⊠ 6900 4th Ave., ☎ 604/538–4818), near White Rock, a 45-minute drive from downtown. **Northview Golf and Country Club** (⊠ 6857 168th St., ☎ 604/574–0324), easily accessible from Vancouver in Surrey, just 15 minutes above the U.S. border, has two Arnold Palmer–designed courses and is the home of the Greater Vancouver Open.

Health and Fitness Clubs

The **YMCA** (⊠ 955 Burrard St., ☎ 604/681–0221) downtown has daily rates; facilities include pools and weight rooms, as well as racquetball, squash, and handball courts. The **YWCA** (⊠ 580 Burrard St., ☎ 604/662–8188) has drop-in rates that let you participate in all activities for the day; the facility has pools, weight rooms, and fitness classes. The **Bentall Centre Athletic Club** (⊠ 1055 Dunsmuir St., lower level, ☎ 604/689–4424), has racquetball and squash courts, weight rooms, and aerobics.

Hiking

Pacific Spirit Park (⊠ 4915 W. 16th Ave., ☎ 604/224–5739), more rugged than Stanley Park, has 61 km (38 mi) of trails, a few washrooms, and a couple of signboard maps. Go for a wonderful walk in the West-Coast arbutus and evergreen woods only 15 minutes from downtown Vancouver. The **Capilano Regional Park** (☞ Greater Vancouver *in* Exploring Vancouver, *above*), on the North Shore, provides a scenic hike.

Jogging

The seawall around **Stanley Park** (☞ Stanley Park *in* Exploring Vancouver, *above*) is 9 km (5½ mi) long and gives an excellent minitour of the city. You can take a shorter run of 4 km (2½ mi) in the park around Lost Lagoon. The **Running Room** (⊠ 1519 Robson St., ☎ 604/684–9771) is a good source for information on fun runs in the area.

Skiing

CROSS-COUNTRY

The best cross-country skiing is at **Cypress Bowl Ski Area** (⊠ Cypress Bowl Ski Area Rd., Exit 8 off Hwy. 1 westbound, ☎ 604/922–0825).

DOWNHILL

Vancouver is two hours from **Whistler/Blackcomb** (☞ Side Trip from Vancouver, *below*), a top-ranked ski destination.

There are three ski areas on the **North Shore mountains,** close to Vancouver, with night skiing. The snow is not as good as at Whistler, and the runs are generally used by novice, junior, and family skiers or those who want a quick ski after work. **Cypress Bowl** (⊠ End of Cypress Bowl Ski Area Rd., Exit 8 off Hwy. 1 westbound, ☎ 604/922–0825; snow report, 604/926–6007) has a large number of runs, and most are long. **Grouse Mountain** (⊠ 6400 Nancy Greene Way, ☎ 604/984–0661; snow report, 604/986–6262) has extensive night skiing, restaurants, and bars. **Mt. Seymour** (⊠ 1700 Mt. Seymour Rd., ☎ 604/986–2261; snow report, 604/879–3999) is high and gets a good snow cover.

Tennis

There are 180 free public courts around town; contact the **Vancouver Board of Parks and Recreation** (☎ 604/257–8400) for locations. **Stanley Park** has 15 well-surfaced outdoor courts near English Bay Beach; many of the other city parks have public courts as well.

Water Sports

KAYAKING

Rent a kayak from **Ecomarine Ocean Kayak Center** (⊠ 1668 Duranleau St., ☎ 604/689–7575) on Granville Island to explore the waters of False Creek and the shoreline of English Bay.

WINDSURFING

Sailboards and lessons are available at **Windsure Windsurfing School** (⊠ Jericho Beach, ☎ 604/224–0615) and **Windmaster** (⊠ English Bay Beach, ☎ 604/685–7245). The winds aren't very heavy on English Bay, making it a perfect locale for learning the sport. You'll have to travel north to Squamish for more challenging high-wind conditions.

Spectator Sports

The **Vancouver Canucks** (☎ 604/899–4600) of the National Hockey League play at General Motors Place (⊠ 800 Griffith Way) October–April. The Pacific Coast League **Canadians** (☎ 604/872–5232) play baseball in an old-time outdoor stadium; their season runs April–September. The **B.C. Lions** (☎ 604/583–7747) football team scrimmages at the B.C. Place Stadium downtown June–November. The **Vancouver**

Eighty-Sixers (☎ 604/299–0086) play soccer in Swangard Stadium in Burnaby from July through mid-September. The **Vancouver Grizzlies** (☎ 604/899–4666), members of the National Basketball Association, hoop it up at the new G.M. Place arena near B.C. Place. New to Vancouver is an in-line roller hockey team, the **Vancouver Voodoo** (☎ 604-899–7400); they scrimmage from June through August at G.M. Place. Tickets for these sports events are available from **Ticketmaster** (☎ 604/280–4400).

SHOPPING

Unlike many cities where suburban malls have taken over, Vancouver is full of individual boutiques and specialty shops. A multitude of antiques stores, ethnic markets, art galleries, high-fashion outlets, and fine department stores dot the city. Stores are usually open daily, Thursday and Friday nights, and Sunday noon to 5.

Auctions

On Wednesday at noon and 7 PM, art and antiques auctions are held at **Love's** (✉ 1635 W. Broadway, ☎ 604/733–1157). **Maynard's** (✉ 415 W. 2nd Ave., ☎ 604/876–6787) has home furnishings auctions on Wednesday at 7 PM.

Department Stores

Among Vancouver's top department stores is Canadian-owned **Eaton's** (✉ 701 Granville St., ☎ 604/685–7112), which carries everything: clothing, appliances, furniture, jewelry, accessories, and souvenirs. Many malls have branches, too. **Holt Renfrew** (✉ 633 Granville St., ☎ 604/681–3121) is smaller, focusing on high fashion for men and women. You'll find this Canadian store in most malls as well.

Flea Market

The huge **Vancouver Flea Market** (✉ 703 Terminal Ave., ☎ 604/685–0666), with more than 360 stalls, is held weekends and holidays from 9 to 5. It is easily accessible from downtown on the SkyTrain, if you exit at the Main Street station.

Shopping Districts

The immense **Pacific Centre Mall** (✉ 550–750 W. Georgia St., ☎ 604/688–7236), on two levels and mostly underground, in the heart of downtown, connects Eaton's and the Bay department stores, which stand at opposite corners of Georgia and Granville streets. A commercial center has developed around **Sinclair Centre** (✉ 757 W. Hastings St., ☎ 604/666–4483), which caters to sophisticated and upscale tastes (☞ Robson to the Waterfront *in* Exploring Vancouver, *above*). **Robson Street,** stretching from Burrard to Bute streets, is chockablock with small boutiques and cafés. Vancouver's liveliest street is not only for the fashion-conscious; it also provides many excellent corners for people-watching and attracts an array of street performers. **Fourth Avenue,** from Burrard to Balsam streets, has an eclectic mix of stores (from sophisticated women's clothing to surfboards). **Oakridge Shopping Centre** (✉ 650 W. 41st Ave., at Cambie St., ☎ 604/261–2511) has chic, expensive stores that are fun to browse.

Ethnic Districts

Chinatown—centered on Pender and Main streets—is an exciting, bustling place for restaurants, exotic foods, and distinctive architecture (☞ Gastown and Chinatown *in* Exploring Vancouver, *above*). Commercial Drive (around East 1st Avenue) is the heart of the Italian community, here called **Little Italy.** You can sip cappuccino in coffee bars where you may be the only one speaking English, or buy sun-dried tomatoes, real Parmesan, or an espresso machine. **Little India** is on Main Street around 50th Avenue. Curry houses, sweet shops, grocery stores, discount jewelry, and silk shops abound. A small **Japantown** on Powell Street at Dunlevy Street is made up of grocery stores, fish stores, and a few restaurants.

Specialty Stores

Antiques
A stretch of antiques stores runs along Main Street from 19th to 35th avenues. **Folkart Interiors** (✉ 3715 W. 10th Ave., ☎ 604/228–1011) specializes in whimsical British Columbia folk art and Western Canadian antiques. **The Vancouver Antique Center** (✉ 422 Richards St., ☎ 604/681–3248) has two floors of antiques and collectibles dealers under one roof. For Oriental rugs, go to **Granville Street** between 7th and 14th avenues.

Art Galleries
There are many private galleries throughout Vancouver. **Buschlen/Mowatt** (✉ 1445 W. Georgia St., 111, ☎ 604/682–1234), among the best in the city, is a showcase for Canadian and international artists. **Diane Farris** (✉ 1565 W. 7th Ave., ☎ 604/737–2629; call first) often spotlights hot new artists. **The Inuit Gallery of Vancouver** (345 Water St., ☎ 604/688–7323) features an array of coastal native art.

Books
Bollum's Books (✉ 710 Granville St., ☎ 604/689–1802) carries 250,000 books and CD-ROM titles, all nicely displayed and well lit, with several comfortable sitting areas, including a little café, for browsers. **Duthie's** (✉ 919 Robson St., ☎ 604/684–4496; ✉ Library Square, 205–345 Robson St., ☎ 604/602–0610), downtown and near the university, is a book-lovers' favorite in Vancouver. **World Wide Books and Maps** (✉ 736A Granville St., downstairs, ☎ 604/687–3320), one of several specialty bookstores in town, sells travel books and maps that cover the world.

Clothing
Fashion is big business in Vancouver, and there are clothing boutiques on almost every corner downtown. If your tastes are traditional, don't miss **George Straith** (✉ 900 W. Georgia St., ☎ 604/685–3301) in the Hotel Vancouver, offering tailored designer fashions for both sexes. Handmade Italian suits, cashmere, and leather for men are sold at stylish **E.A. Lee** (✉ 466 Howe St., ☎ 604/683–2457); there are also a few women's items to browse through. Buttoned-down businesswomen usually shop at **Wear Else?** (✉ 789 W. Pender St., ☎ 604/662–7890), focusing on career women's fashions. For truly unique women's clothing, try **Dorothy Grant** (✉ 757 W. Hastings St., ☎ 604/681–0201), where traditional Haida native designs meld with modern fashion in a boutique that looks more like an art gallery.

At the architecturally stunning **Versus** (✉ 1008 W. Georgia St., ☎ 604/688–8938) boutique, ladies and gents sip cappuccino as they browse through the fashionable Italian designs of Gianni Versace. **Leone** (✉ 757 W. Hastings St., ☎ 604/683–1133) is yet another ultrachic boutique, dividing designer collections in themed areas. Trendy men's and women's casual wear by Ralph Lauren is available at **The Polo Store** (✉ 375 Water St., ☎ 604/682–7656).

Gifts

Want something special to take home from British Columbia? One of the best places in Vancouver for good-quality souvenirs (West Coast native art, books, music, jewelry, and so on) is the **Clamshell Gift Shop** (⌧ Vancouver Aquarium, ☎ 604/685–5911) in Stanley Park. The **Salmon Shop** (☎ 604/666–6477) in the Granville Island Public Market will wrap smoked salmon for travel. Haida, Inuit, and Salish native art is available at Gastown's **Hill's Indian Crafts** (⌧ 165 Water St., ☎ 604/685–4249). Near Granville Island, **Leona Lattimer's** shop (⌧ 1590 W. 2nd Ave., ☎ 604/732–4556), built like a longhouse, is full of native arts and crafts ranging from cheap to priceless.

SIDE TRIP FROM VANCOUVER

If you think of skiing when you hear mention of Whistler, British Columbia, you're thinking on track. Whistler and Blackcomb mountains, part of Whistler Resort (☎ 800/944–7853), are the two largest ski mountains in North America and are consistently ranked the first- or second-best ski destinations on the continent. There's winter and summer glacier skiing, the longest vertical drop in North America, and one of the most advanced lift systems in the world. Whistler has also grown in popularity as a summer destination, with a range of outdoor activities and events filling the warm, sunny months. All this action is just a couple of hours from Vancouver. Take Highway 1 west to the narrow, winding Highway 99, the Sea to Sky Highway, which takes you past Shannon Falls and the Tantalus Range glaciers to Whistler.

Adjacent to the area is the 78,000-acre Garibaldi Provincial Park (☎ 604/898–3678), with dense mountainous forests splashed with hospitable lakes and streams. Even if you don't want to roam much farther than the village, there are five lakes for canoeing, fishing, swimming, and windsurfing, and many nearby hiking and mountain-bike trails.

If you're planning a trip to Whistler, you can also consider the Coast Mountain Circle, which links Vancouver to Cariboo Country. This 702-km (435-mi) route takes in spectacular Howe Sound, the deep-water port of Squamish, Whistler Resort, and Pemberton Valley before heading back to Vancouver through scenic Fraser Canyon and Harrison Hot Springs (☞ Chapter 3). The loop makes a comfortable two- to three-day journey.

Whistler

120 km (74 mi) from Vancouver.

At the base of the mountains are Whistler Village, Village North, and Upper Village—a rapidly expanding, interconnected community of lodgings, restaurants, pubs, gift shops, and boutiques. With dozens of hotels and condos within a five-minute walk of the mountains, the site is frenzied with activity. Culinary options in the resort range from burgers to French, Japanese to deli cuisine; nightly entertainment runs the gamut from sophisticated piano bars to casual pubs.

Whistler Village is a pedestrian-only community. Anywhere you want to go within the resort is at most five minutes away, and parking lots are just outside the village. The bases of Whistler and Blackcomb mountains are also just at the edge; in fact, you can ski right into the lower level of the Chateau Whistler Hotel. With all of the recent expansion in Whistler, there is now space to rest 17,910 sleepy heads within 400 yards of the lifts (which means that more than half of all accommodations are considered ski-in/ski-out).

In winter, the village buzzes with skiers taking to the slopes, but as the scenery changes from winter's snow-white to summer's lush-green landscapes, the mood of Whistler changes, too. Things seem to slow down a bit, and the resort sheds some of its competitive edge and relaxes to a slower pace. Even the local golf tournaments and the triathlon are interspersed with Mozart and bluegrass festivals.

Dining

Dining at Whistler is informal; casual dress is appropriate everywhere. At press time, there were record numbers of promising new restaurants coming on the scene in Whistler, so you're bound to find something worthwhile to suit virtually any craving. Japanese and Mediterranean offerings are especially strong in the village. For price categories, *see* the dining price chart *in* Dining, *above.* You'll need dinner reservations in all but the fast-food joints.

$$$ ✕ **Il Caminetto di Umberto, Trattoria di Umberto.** Umberto offers home-style Italian cooking in a relaxed atmosphere; he specializes in such pasta dishes as crab-stuffed cannelloni or a four-cheese lasagna. Il Caminetto is known for its veal, osso buco, and zabaglione. The Trattoria has a Tuscan-style rotisserie, highlighting a pasta dish served with a tray of chopped tomatoes, hot pepper, basil, olive oil, anchovies, and Parmesan so that you can mix it as spicy and flavorful as you like. ⊠ *Il Caminetto, 4242 Village Stroll,* ☎ *604/932–4442;* ⊠ *Trattoria, Mountainside Lodge, 4417 Sundial Pl.,* ☎ *604/932–5858. Reservations essential. AE, DC, MC, V.*

$$$ ✕ **Les Deux Gros.** The name means "the two fat guys," which may ex-
★ plain the restaurant's motto, "Never trust a skinny chef." Portions of the country French cuisine are generous indeed. Alsatian onion pie, steak tartare, juicy rack of lamb, and salmon Wellington are all superbly crafted and presented, and service is friendly but unobtrusive. Just southwest of the village, this is the spot for a special romantic dinner; request one of the prime tables by the massive stone fireplace. ⊠ *1200 Alta Lake Rd.,* ☎ *604/932–4611. Reservations essential. AE, MC, V. No lunch.*

$$$ ✕ **Wildflower Cafe.** The main dining room of the Chateau Whistler (☞ Lodging, *below*) is an informal, comfortable restaurant with huge windows overlooking the ski slopes. The rustic effect of the Chateau lobby continues in the Wildflower—more than 100 antique wood birdhouses decorate the room, and chairs and tables have a farmhouse look. An à la carte menu focuses on creative concoctions starring fresh B.C. fare; the signature dish is pan-seared, cinnamon-smoked pheasant breast served with roasted corn, spiced squash, sheep's milk brie, and risotto. ⊠ *Chateau Whistler Resort, 4599 Chateau Blvd.,* ☎ *604/938–2033. Reservations essential. AE, D, DC, MC, V.*

$$ ✕ **La Rúa.** One of the brightest lights on the Whistler dining scene is
★ on the ground floor of Le Chamois (☞ Lodging, *below*). Reddish flagstone floors and sponge-painted walls, a wine cellar behind a wrought-iron door, modern oil paintings, and sconce lighting give the restaurant an intimate, Mediterranean ambience. Favorites from the Continental menu include charred rare tuna, loin of deer, rack of lamb, and baked sea bass fillet in red wine and herb sauce. ⊠ *4557 Blackcomb Way,* ☎ *604/932–5011. Reservations essential. AE, DC, MC, V. No lunch.*

$ ✕ **Hard Rock Cafe.** You know you're in a big-time tourist destination when you see a Hard Rock Cafe. Guitars and gold records adorn the walls, but the incredible mural of rock icons on the ceiling of the main dining room is the primary attraction. Steaks, sandwiches, and salads are tasty and filling if rather uninventive at this cheerful, tremendously popular diner. ⊠ *4295 Blackcomb Way,* ☎ *604/938–9922. AE, DC, MC, V.*

$ ✕ **Zeuski's.** This friendly taverna, now in new digs at the Whistler Town
★   Plaza, introduced tasty, inexpensive Greek fare to Whistler. Wall murals of the Greek islands surround candlelit tables, helping create a
Mediterranean atmosphere. There's also a patio for al fresco dining.
It's hard to pass on the spanikopita, souvlaki, and other standards, but
the house special, *katapoulo* (chicken breast rolled in pistachios and
roasted), is not to be missed, nor are the tender, delicately herb-bat-
tered calamari. ⊠ *4314 Main St.,* ☎ *604/932–6009. Reservations essential. AE, MC, V.*

Lodging

At press time, Whistler was undergoing a tremendous building boom,
much of it centered around new lodging complexes. Latest to join the
ranks at the foot of the two mountains is **One Whistler Village,** managed by Pan Pacific Hotels (☎ 800/937–1515); it is scheduled for completion in spring 1998. All lodgings, including hundreds of time-share
condos, can be booked through the **Whistler Resort Association** (☎ 604/
932–3928 or 800/944–7853); summer rates are greatly discounted.

For price categories and facilities information, *see* the price chart *in*
Lodging, *above.* You can add mountain bikes, a hot tub, skiing, and
bike and ski storage to the list of facilities often found in the higher-
priced accommodations.

$$$$ 🏨 **Chateau Whistler.** This large and friendly-looking fortress in the Upper
Village at the foot of Blackcomb Mountain was built and is run by Canadian Pacific. The marvelous lobby is filled with rustic Canadiana,
handmade Mennonite rugs, enormous fireplaces, and enticing overstuffed
sofas. The standard rooms are average, but the suites are fit for royalty, with specially commissioned quilts and artwork, complemented
by antique furnishings. Expansion to be completed sometime in 1998
will add 220 more rooms and new meeting space. ⊠ *4599 Chateau
Blvd., Box 100, V0N 1B0,* ☎ *604/938–8000, 800/441–1414 in the
U.S. and Canada,* 🖷 *604/938–2055. 307 rooms, 36 suites. Restaurant, lobby lounge, tapas bar, indoor-outdoor pool, saunas, steam
rooms, 18-hole golf course, 3 tennis courts, mountain bicycles, ski shop,
shops, piano, travel services. AE, D, DC, MC, V.*

$$$$ 🏨 **Delta Whistler Resort.** The resort, at the base of Whistler Mountain,
catercorner to the Whistler Village Gondola and adjacent to the Whistler
Golf Club, is a large complex, complete with shopping, dining, and
fitness amenities. Rooms are very generous in size (almost every room
will easily sleep four). There are a few standard rooms, but most have
fireplaces, whirlpool bathtubs, balconies, and/or kitchens. ⊠ *4050
Whistler Way, Box 550, V0N 1B0,* ☎ *604/932–1982, 800/877–1133
in the U.S., 800/268–1133 in Canada,* 🖷 *604/932–7318. 276 rooms,
24 suites. Restaurant, sports bar, seasonal pool bar, kitchenettes, pool,
indoor and outdoor hot tubs, steam room, 2 indoor/outdoor tennis
courts, shops, video games, coin laundries. AE, DC, MC, V.*

$$$–$$$$ 🏨 **Le Chamois.** Enjoying the prime ski-in, ski-out location at the base
★   of the Blackcomb runs is this elegant luxury hotel. Of the spacious guest
rooms with convenience kitchens, the most popular are the studios with
Jacuzzi tubs set in front of the living room's bay windows overlook-
ing the slopes and lifts. Guests can also keep an eye on the action from
the glass elevators and the heated outdoor pool. ⊠ *4557 Blackcomb
Way, V0N 1B0,* ☎ *604/932–8700, 800/777–0185 in the U.S. and
Canada,* 🖷 *604/905–2576. 47 suites, 6 studios. 2 restaurants, kitch-
enettes, refrigerators, limited room service, pool, coin laundry. AE, DC,
MC, V.*

$$$ 🏨 **Edgewater.** Next to pretty little Green Lake nestles this intimate cedar
lodge. In traditional Canadian shades of olive, crimson, pale yellow,

and cloudy blue, the interior is simple and relaxing, a true country retreat. You can do everything here from sleigh riding and singing around a campfire to canoeing, bird-watching, and cross-country skiing. An extended Continental breakfast (juice, granola, fruit, and breakfast breads) is included in the tariff at this no-smoking establishment. ⊠ *Off Hwy. 99, 2½ km (1½ mi) north of village, Box 369, V0N 1B0,* ☎ *604/932–0688,* FAX *604/932–0686. 6 rooms, 6 suites. Dining room, fireside lounge with bar, outdoor hot tub, bird-watching gear, hiking, boating, cross-country skiing, ski storage. MC, V.*

$$ ▦ **Durlacher Hof.** Custom fir woodwork and doors, exposed ceiling beams, a *kachelofen* (tiled oven), and antler chandeliers hung over fir benches and tables carry out the rustic European theme of this fancy Tyrolean inn. The green and maroon bedrooms, all named for European mountains, contain more fine examples of custom-crafted wooden furniture. Two upgraded rooms on the third floor have such added amenities as double whirlpool tubs. The inn also has a guest refrigerator, a guest lounge, and a pay phone. A hearty European breakfast is included in the tariff. German is spoken here. ⊠ *7055 Nesters Rd., V0N 1B0,* ☎ *604/932–1924,* FAX *604/938–1980. 7 double rooms, 1 suite. No-smoking rooms, hot tub, sauna, ski storage, airport shuttle. MC, V. Closed Nov.*

$$ ▦ **Pension Edelweiss.** The Edelweiss, one of several charming and very European bed-and-breakfasts around Whistler, is within walking distance of Whistler Village. Rooms have a crisp, spic-and-span feel, in keeping with the Bavarian chalet style of the house; all have private baths and some have balconies and telephones. Each morning a different breakfast (included in the room rate) is served: Scandinavian, American, French, German. A bus stop just outside provides easy access to Whistler Village. Smoking is not permitted here. ⊠ *7162 Nancy Greene Way, Box 850, V0N 1B0,* ☎ *604/932–3641 or 800/665–2003,* FAX *604/938–1746. 8 rooms, 1 suite. Hot tub, sauna, bicycles, ski storage, bus and train stations shuttle. AE, MC, V.*

$ ▦ **Hostelling International Whistler Youth Hostel.** While it's nothing to write home about, it is the cheapest sleep in town. Bunks in men's or women's dorms, a shared kitchen, and a game room make up the basic accommodations of this hostel overlooking Alta Lake. The train passes by twice a day. ⊠ *Alta Lake Rd., V0N 1B0,* ☎ *604/932–5492,* FAX *604/932–4687. 30 beds in 5 dorms, 1 private room (no bath). Kitchen, ski storage. No credit cards.*

Outdoor Activities and Sports

CANOEING, KAYAKING, RAFTING, AND WINDSURFING

You'll see canoes, kayaks, and sailboards at the many lakes and rivers near Whistler. If you want to get in on the fun, rentals are available at **Alta Lake** at both **Lakeside Park** and **Wayside Park.** A spot that's perfect for canoeing is the **River of Golden Dreams,** either from Meadow Park to Green Lake or upstream to Twin Bridges. Kayakers looking for a thrill may want to try **Green River** from Green Lake to Pemberton. There are several rivers with mild rapids around Whistler, and **Whistler River Adventures** (☎ 604/932–3532) offers a variety of half- and full-day rafting trips priced from $50–$150.

You'll find the breezes reliable for windsurfing on **Alpha, Alta,** and **Green** lakes. Call **Whistler Outdoor Experience** (☎ 604/932–3389), **Whistler Sailing and Water Sports** (☎ 604/932–7245), **Whistler Windsurfing** (☎ 604/932–3589), or **Sea to Sky Kayaking** (☎ 604/898–5498) for equipment or guided trips.

Whistler Backcountry Adventures (⊠ No. 36, 4314 Main St., ☎ 604/938–1410) or **Whistler Fishing Guides** (⊠ Carlton Lodge, 4218 Mountain Sq. [base of both gondolas], ☎ 604/932–4267) will take care of anything you need—equipment, guides, and transportation. All five of the lakes around Whistler are stocked with trout, but the area around **Dream River Park** is one of the most popular. Slightly farther afield, try **Cheakamus Lake, Daisy Lake,** and **Callaghan Lake.**

GOLF

Arnold Palmer designed the par-72 championship **Whistler Golf Course** (⊠ 4010 Whistler Way, ☎ 604/932–4544). **Chateau Whistler Golf Club** (⊠ 4612 Blackcomb Way, ☎ 604/938–2092), designed by Robert Trent Jones II, was ranked the best new course in Canada by *Golf Digest* in 1993. The summer of 1995 saw the introduction of **Nicklaus North Golf Course** (Hwy. 99, ☎ 604/938–9898), a challenging 18-hole course designed by Jack Nicklaus.

SKIING

Cross-Country. The meandering trail around the **Whistler Golf Course** in the village is an ideal beginners' route. For more advanced skiing, try the 28 km (17 mi) of track-set trails that wind around scenic **Lost Lake, Chateau Whistler Golf Course,** and the **Nicklaus North Golf Course** and **Green Lake.** Cross-country trail maps and equipment rental information are available at the **Whistler Activity and Information Center** (☎ 604/932–2394) in the village.

Downhill. The vertical drops and elevations at **Blackcomb** (☎ 604/938–7743, FAX 604/938–7527) and **Whistler** (☎ 604/932–3434, FAX 604/938–9174) mountains are, perhaps, the most impressive features to skiers here. The resort covers 6,998 acres of skiable terrain in 12 alpine bowls, on three glaciers, and over 200 marked trails, served by the most advanced high-speed lift system on the continent. Blackcomb has a 5,280-foot vertical drop, North America's longest, while Whistler comes in second, with a 5,020-foot drop. The top elevation is 7,494 feet on Blackcomb and 7,160 on Whistler. Blackcomb and Whistler have more than 100 marked trails each and receive an average of 360 inches of snow per year; Blackcomb is open June–August for summer glacier skiing. **Whistler Ski School** and **Blackcomb Ski School** provide lessons to skiers of all levels.

Heli-Skiing. In Whistler, **Mountain Heli-Sports** (☎ 604/932–2070), **Tyax Heli-Skiing** (☎ 604/932–7007 or 800/663–8126), and **Whistler Heli-Skiing** (☎ 604/932–4105) have guided day trips with up to four glacier runs, or 12,000 vertical feet of skiing, for experienced skiers; the cost is about $350.

SPORTS CENTER

Meadow Park Sports Centre (☎ 604/938–3133) has a six-lane pool, a children's wading pool, a hockey/ice skating rink, a hot tub, a sauna, a steam room, and two squash courts.

Whistler A to Z

Arriving and Departing

BY BUS

Maverick Coach Lines (☎ 604/255–1171, FAX 604/255–5770) has buses leaving every couple of hours for Whistler Village from the depot in downtown Vancouver. The fare is approximately $34 round-trip. During ski season, the last bus leaves Whistler at 9:45 PM. **Perimeter Bus Transportation** (☎ 604/266–5386, FAX 604/266–1628) has daily service, November–April and June–September from Vancouver International Airport to Whistler. Prepaid reservations are necessary 24 hours in advance; the ticket booth is on Level One of the airport. The fare is around $40 one way. **Westcoast City and Nature Sightseeing** (☎ 604/451–1600 in Vancouver) offers a sightseeing tour to Whistler that allows passengers to stay over and return on their date of choice to Vancouver; call for seasonal rates.

BY CAR

Driving time from Seattle to Vancouver is about three hours. Whistler is 120 km (74 mi), or 2½ hours, north of Vancouver on winding Highway 99, the Sea-to-Sky Highway.

BY TRAIN

B.C. Rail (☎ 604/984–5246, FAX 604/984–5505) travels north from Vancouver to Whistler along a beautiful route. The Vancouver Bus Terminal and the North Vancouver Station are connected by bus shuttle. Rates are under $60 round-trip for the train only.

Getting Around

Streets in Whistler Village, Village North, and Upper Village are clearly marked and easy to negotiate by car, and pay parking is readily available. However, there's really no reason to use a car because the resort association operates a free public transit system that loops throughout the resort; call ☎ 604/932–4020 for information and schedules.

Contacts and Resources

B&B RESERVATION AGENCIES

Whistler Bed and Breakfast Inns (☎ 604/932–3282 or 800/665–1892) represents the leading inns of Whistler.

CAR RENTALS

Budget Rent-A-Car (☎ 604/932–1236, FAX 604/932–3026) and **Thrifty Car Rental** (☎ 604/938–0302 or 800/367–2277, FAX 604/938–1228) have rental outlets in the village.

EMERGENCIES

Dial 0 for **police, ambulance,** or **poison control.**

GUIDED TOURS

If you are interested in a tour of the area, **Alpine Adventure Tours** (☎ 604/683–0209) has a Whistler history tour of the valley and a Squamish day trip. If four-wheel-drive and ATV tours of the backcountry appeal to you, contact **Whistler Backcountry Adventures** (☎ 604/932–3474). **Whistler Nature Guides** (☎ 604/932–4595) provides guided alpine hiking tours. Budget-priced, guided camping trips out of Vancouver are available through **Bigfoots Backpacker Adventure Express** (☎ 604/739–1025).

VISITOR INFORMATION

Contact the **Whistler Resort Association** (✉ 4010 Whistler Way, Whistler V0N 1B4, ☎ 604/932–4222, 604/664–5625 in Vancouver, or 800/944–7853 in the U.S. and Canada, FAX 604/938–5758). There is an **information booth** (☎ 604/932–2394) in Whistler Village at the front door of the Conference Center; hours fluctuate, so call before visiting. If you're traveling in the area around Whistler, contact the **Coast & Mountains Tourism Association** (✉ 204–1755 W. Broadway, Vancouver V6J 4S5, ☎ 604/739–9011 or 800/667–3306, FAX 604/739–0153).

A provincial government **Travel Infocentre** (☎ 604/932–5528) is on the main highway, about 1½ km (1 mi) south of Whistler.

VANCOUVER A TO Z

Arriving and Departing

By Bus

Greyhound Lines (☎ 604/662–3222; in Canada, 800/661–8747; in the U.S., 800/231–2222) is the largest bus line serving Vancouver. The Pacific Central Station (✉ 1150 Station St.) is the depot. **Quick Shuttle** (☎ 604/244–3744; in the U.S., 800/665–2122) bus service runs between Vancouver and Seattle five times a day in winter and up to eight times a day in summer. The depot is at 180 West Georgia Street.

By Car

From the south, I–5 from Seattle becomes **Highway 99** at the U.S.–Canada border. Vancouver is a three-hour drive (226 km, or 140 mi) from Seattle. It's best to avoid border crossings during peak times such as holidays and weekends.

Highway 1, the **Trans-Canada Highway,** enters Vancouver from the east. To avoid traffic, arrive after rush hour (8:30 AM).

By Ferry

B.C. Ferries (24-hour recorded schedule information, ☎ 604/277–0277; reservations, ☎ 604/669–1211 or ☎ 800/663–7600 in British Columbia) operates two major ferry terminals outside Vancouver. From Tsawwassen to the south (an hour's drive from downtown), ferries sail to Victoria and Nanaimo on Vancouver Island and to the Gulf Islands (the small islands between the mainland and Vancouver Island). From Horseshoe Bay (30 minutes north of downtown), ferries sail a short distance across the strait and up the coast to Nanaimo on Vancouver Island.

By Plane

Vancouver International Airport (☎ 604/276–6101) is on an island about 14 km (9 mi) south of downtown. An airport improvement fee is assessed on all flight departures: $5 for flights within British Columbia, $10 for flights within Canada, and $15 for international flights. **American Airlines** (☎ 800/433–7300), **Continental Airlines** (☎ 800/231–0856), **Delta** (☎ 604/221–1212), **Horizon Air** (☎ 800/547–9308), and **United** (☎ 800/241–6522) fly into the airport. The two major domestic airlines are **Air Canada** (☎ 604/688–5515 or 800/776–3000) and **Canadian Airlines** (☎ 604/279–6611 or 800/426–7000).

Air B.C. (☎ 604/688–5515 or 800/776–3000) offers 30-minute harbor-to-harbor service (downtown Vancouver to downtown Victoria) several times a day. Planes leave from near the Westin Bayshore Hotel (✉ 1601 W. Georgia St.). **Helijet Airways** (☎ 604/682–1468) has helicopter service from downtown Vancouver to downtown Victoria. The heliport is near Vancouver's Pan Pacific Hotel (✉ 300–999 Canada Pl.).

BETWEEN THE AIRPORT AND DOWNTOWN

The drive from the airport to downtown takes 20 to 45 minutes, depending on the time of day. Airport hotels offer free shuttle service to and from the airport.

The **Vancouver Airporter Service** (☎ 604/244–9888) bus leaves the international and domestic arrivals levels of the terminal building approximately every half hour, stopping at major downtown hotels. It operates from 6 AM until midnight. The fare is $9 one way and $15 round-trip.

Taxi stands are in front of the terminal building on domestic and international arrivals levels. Taxi fare to downtown is about $22. Area cab companies are **Yellow** (☎ 604/681–1111) and **Black Top** (☎ 604/681–2181).

Limousine service from **Airlimo** (☎ 604/273–1331) costs a bit more than the taxi fare to downtown: The current rate is about $30.

By Train
The **Pacific Central Station** (✉ 1150 Station St.) is the hub for rail, bus, and SkyTrain service. The **VIA Rail** (☎ 800/561–8630) station is at Main Street and Terminal Avenue. VIA provides transcontinental service through Jasper to Toronto three times a week. Passenger trains leave the **B.C. Rail** (☎ 604/631–3500) station in North Vancouver for Whistler and the interior of British Columbia. **Amtrak** (☎ 800/835–8725 in the U.S. or 800/872–7245 in B.C.) has one round-trip per day between Seattle and Vancouver.

Getting Around

By Bus
Exact change is needed to ride **B.C. Transit** (☎ 604/521–0400) buses: $1.50. Books of 25 tickets are sold at convenience stores and newsstands; look for a red, white, and blue "Fare Dealer" sign. Day passes, good for unlimited travel after 9:30 AM, cost $4.50 for adults. They are available from fare dealers and any SeaBus or SkyTrain station. Transfers are valid for 90 minutes and allow travel in both directions. Because of traffic and overcrowding, this mode can be time-consuming and uncomfortable; however, you can get just about anywhere you need to go in the city by bus.

By Car
Because no freeways cross Vancouver, rush-hour traffic still tends to be horrendous. The worst bottlenecks outside the city center are the North Shore bridges, the George Massey Tunnel on Highway 99 south of Vancouver, and Highway 1 through Coquitlam and Surrey. Parking downtown is both expensive and tricky to find.

By Ferry
The **SeaBus** is a 400-passenger commuter ferry that crosses Burrard Inlet from the foot of Lonsdale (North Vancouver) to downtown. The ride takes 13 minutes and costs the same as the transit bus (and it's much faster). With a transfer, connection can be made with any B.C. Transit bus or SkyTrain. **Aquabus Ferries** (☎ 604/689–5858) connect several stations on False Creek including Science Center, Granville Island, Stamp's Landing, and the Hornby Street dock.

By Rapid Transit
Vancouver has a one-line, 25-km (16-mi) rapid transit system called **SkyTrain,** which travels underground downtown and is elevated for the rest of its route to New Westminster and Surrey. Trains leave about every five minutes. Tickets, sold at each station from machines (correct change is not necessary), must be carried with you as proof of payment. You may use transfers from SkyTrain to SeaBus (☞ *above*) and B.C. Transit buses and vice versa. The SkyTrain is convenient for transit between Gastown and Science World, but that's about it for points of interest.

By Taxi
It is difficult to hail a cab in Vancouver; unless you're near a hotel, you'd have better luck calling a taxi service. Try **Yellow** (☎ 604/681–3311) or **Black Top** (☎ 604/683–4567).

Opening and Closing Times

Banks traditionally are open Monday through Thursday 10 to 3 and Friday 10 to 6, but many banks have extended hours and are open on Saturday, particularly outside of downtown. **Museums** are generally open 10–5, including weekends. Most are open one evening a week as well. **Department store** hours are Monday through Wednesday and Saturday 9:30 to 6, Thursday and Friday 9:30 to 9, and Sunday noon to 5. Many smaller stores are also open Sunday.

Contacts and Resources

B&B Reservation Agencies

A Home Away From Home (⊠ 1441 Howard Ave., V5B 3S2, ☎ 604/294–1760, FAX 604/294–0799), **Best Canadian Bed and Breakfast Network** (⊠ 1090 W. King Edward Ave., V6H 1Z4, ☎ 604/ 738–7207), and **Town & Country Bed and Breakfast** (⊠ 2803 W. 4th Ave., V6K 1K2, ☎ 604/731–5942) are useful services.

Car Rentals

Avis (☎ 604/606–2847 or 800/331–1212), **Budget** (☎ 604/668–7000; in the U.S., 800/527–0700), and **Thrifty Car Rental** (☎ 604/606–1666 or 800/367–2277) are some firms with offices in the city.

Consulates

United States (⊠ 1075 W. Pender St., ☎ 604/685–4311), **United Kingdom** (⊠ 800–1111 Melville St., ☎ 604/683–4421).

Doctors and Dentists

Doctors are on call through the emergency ward at **St. Paul's Hospital** (⊠ 1081 Burrard St., ☎ 604/682–2344), a downtown facility open around the clock. **Medicentre** (⊠ 1055 Dunsmuir St., lower level, ☎ 604/683–8138), a drop-in clinic in the Bentall Centre, is open weekdays. The counterpart to Medicentre is **Dentacentre** (⊠ 1055 Dunsmuir St., lower level, ☎ 604/669–6700), which is next door and is also open weekdays.

Emergencies

Call 911 for **police, fire** department, and **ambulance**.

Guided Tours

Tour prices tend to fluctuate, so inquire about current rates when booking tours. Kids are generally charged half the adult fare.

AIR TOURS

Tour the mountains and fjords of the North Shore by helicopter for around $200 per person (minimum of three people) for 50 minutes: **Vancouver Helicopters** (☎ 604/270–1484) flies from the Harbour Heliport downtown. You can see Vancouver from the air for $70 for 30 minutes: **Harbour Air**'s (☎ 604/688–1277) seaplanes leave from beside the Westin Bayshore Hotel.

BOAT TOURS

Aquabus Ferries (⊠ 1656 Duranleau St., ☎ 604/689–5858) runs a 25-minute City Skyline cruise departing from Hornby dock or Granville Island for $6. Their English Bay Cruise runs 50 minutes from Granville Island out into the bay, passing Siwash Rock and Stanley Park, and returning along the Kitsilano shoreline; fare is $15.

Fraser River Connection (⊠ 810 Quayside Dr., in Information Centre at Westminster Quay, ☎ 604/525–4465) will take you on a seven-hour tour of a fascinating working river—past log booms, tugs, and houseboats. Between May and October, ride from New Westminster to Fort

Langley aboard a convincing replica of an 1800s-era paddle wheeler for under $50.

Harbour Ferries (⌧ 1 N. Denman St., ☎ 604/688–7246) has several worthwhile excursions. On one, the Royal Hudson, Canada's only functioning steam train, heads along the mountainous coast up Howe Sound to the logging town of Squamish. After a break here, you sail back to Vancouver on the M.V. *Britannia*. The trip costs about $75 and takes 6½ hours; reservations are advised.

Harbour Ferries also operates a 1½-hour narrated tour of Burrard Inlet aboard the paddle wheeler M.V. *Constitution*; the tour operates Wednesday–Sunday and costs less than $20. Sunset cruises are also available.

ECO TOURS

Vancouver is blessed with nature all around, and a growing number of tour operators can help you get a closer look at the wild side of the city. Guided hikes through the rain forests and canyons surrounding the city are available through **Rockwood Adventures** (☎ 604/926–7705). They have many tours to choose from; prices start around $35. A good operator with a number of interpretive day hikes around Vancouver is **Path of Logic Wilderness Adventures** (☎ 604/802–2082). **English Bay Sea Kayaking Company** (☎ 604/898–4979) has guided half-day ($75) and sunset ($45) sea kayaking tours for a closer look at the inlets and bays of Vancouver's waterfront. **Lotus Land Tours** (☎ 604/684–4922) runs a six-hour sea canoe (similar to, but wider than a kayak) trip that visits Twin Island (an uninhabited provincial marine park) to explore the marine life that populates the area's intertidal zone; cost is $120 and includes a salmon barbecue lunch. A unique way to see the heights of the city with an environmental focus is the Grouse Mountain downhill mountain biking trip offered by **Velo-City Cycle Tours** (☎ 604/924–0288).

There are also a few companies with **multiday adventure trips** out of Vancouver. **Wild West Adventures** (☎ 604/688–2008) has a weekend camping tour to Mayne Island that incorporates interpretive hikes, sea kayaking around the island, and wildlife watching (seals, otters, eagles, and more); cost is $200. The company also schedules whale-watching trips to Tofino, using Zodiac boats to explore Clayquote Sound and seek out migrating gray whales each spring; cost is $210. **Nunatak Expeditions** (☎ 604/987–6727) offers three- to six-day guided sea kayaking trips to the islands and sounds in Canada's Inside Passage, including a fantastic six-day trip in Johnstone Straight in search of orca (killer whale) encounters. Costs range from $350 to $850. **Bluewater Adventures** (☎ 604/980–3800) has a multiday natural history cruise to the Gulf Islands and Queen Charlotte Islands, including an Orca and Totems trip that visits long-abandoned Haida native villages to see the fallen totem poles slowly being reclaimed by the landscape. Call for pricing.

ORIENTATION

Gray Line (☎ 604/879–3363), the largest tour operator, offers the 3½-hour Grand City bus tour year-round. Departing from the Sandman Inn in winter and the Plaza of Nations in summer, the tour includes Stanley Park, Chinatown, Gastown, English Bay, and Queen Elizabeth Park and costs about $31. During spring, summer, and fall, **Westcoast City and Nature Sightseeing** (☎ 604/451–1600) accommodates up to 31 people in vans that run a 3½-hour City Highlights tour for about $30 (pickup available from all major hotels downtown). Using minibuses departing from downtown hotels and transit stations, **Vance Tours** (☎ 604/941–5660) has a highlights tour (3½ hours, $33) that includes a visit to the University of British Columbia and a shorter city tour (2½ hours, $30, hotel pickup included).

The **Vancouver Trolley Company** (☎ 604/451–5581) runs turn-of-the-century–style trolleys through Vancouver from April through October on a two-hour narrated tour of Stanley Park, Gastown, English Bay, Granville Island, and Chinatown, among other sights. A day pass allows you to complete one full circuit, getting off and on as often as you like. Start the trip at any of the sights and buy a ticket on board. Adult fare is under $20. During the rest of the year, the trolley runs the same circuit on a 2½-hour trip, but no on-off option is available. Between June and September, **Gray Line** (☎ 604/879–3363) has a narrated city tour aboard double-decker buses; passengers can get on and off as they choose and are allowed to ride free the following day if they haven't had their fill. Adult fare is about $20.

North Shore tours usually include any or several of the following: a gondola ride up Grouse Mountain, a walk across the Capilano Suspension Bridge, a stop at a salmon hatchery, the Lonsdale Quay Market, and a ride back to town on the SeaBus. Half-day tours cost anywhere from $45–$55 and are offered by Landsea Tours (☎ 604/255–7272), Harbour Ferries (☎ 604/688–7246), Gray Line (☎ 604/879–3363), and Pacific Coach Lines (☎ 604/662–7575).

PERSONAL GUIDES

Early Motion Tours (☎ 604/687–5088) will pick you up at your hotel for a tour of Vancouver in a Model-A Ford convertible. For about $70–$80, up to four people can take an hour-long trip around downtown, Chinatown, and Stanley Park; longer tours can also be arranged. **AAA Horse & Carriage** (☎ 604/681–5115) has a one-hour tour of Stanley Park, along the waterfront, and through a cedar forest and a rose garden for about $10 per person ($30 for a family of four); the tour departs from the information booth near the zoo. Individualized tours are available from **VIP Tourguide Services,** run by Marcel Jonker (☎ 604/214–4677).

WALKING TOURS

The **Gastown Business Improvement Society** (✉ 12 Water St., ☎ 604/683–5650) sponsors free 90-minute historical and architectural walking tours daily June–August. Meet the guide at 2 PM at the statue of Gassy Jack in Maple Tree Square.

Late-Night Pharmacy

Shopper's Drug Mart (✉ 1125 Davie St., ☎ 604/669–2424) has 24-hour service daily.

Road Emergencies

BCAA (☎ 604/293–2222) has 24-hour emergency road service for members of AAA or CAA.

Travel Agencies

American Express Travel Service (✉ 666 Burrard St., ☎ 604/669–2813), **Mirage Holidays** (✉ 14–200 Burrard St., ☎ 604/685–4008), and **P. Lawson Travel** (✉ 409 Granville St., Suite 150, ☎ 604/682–4272) are some of the many agencies in the city.

Visitor Information

Vancouver Tourist Info Centre (✉ 200 Burrard St., V6C 3L6, ☎ 604/683–2000, FAX 604/682–6839) provides maps and information about the city and is open daily from 8 to 6 in July and August; for the remainder of the year, hours are weekdays 8:30 to 5, Saturday 9 to 5. Eaton's department store downtown also has a visitor information counter that is open all year. **Super, Natural B.C.** (☎ 800/663–6000) is available year-round to assist with visitor information and reservations.

3 British Columbia

Lush inland valleys and Pacific beaches, rugged mountains and forested islands: In this western province you'll find an abundance of outdoor beauty and action. There are plenty of opportunities for whale- and nature-watching, as well as year-round skiing and superb fishing and kayaking. And whether your visit takes you to the Anglophile city of Victoria, small coastal and island towns, or the re-created native village of 'Ksan, you'll encounter the diversity of the area's residents.

Updated by
Melissa Rivers

BRITISH COLUMBIA, CANADA'S WESTERNMOST
province, harbors Pacific beaches, forested islands,
year-round skiing, world-class fishing—a wealth
of outdoor action and beauty. The people of the province are a simi-
larly heterogeneous mix: descendants of the original Native American
peoples and 19th-century British and European settlers and more recent immigrants from Asia and Eastern Europe. From Anglophile Victoria to the re-created Native American village of 'Ksan, British
Columbia's towns reflect the vigor of its inhabitants.

Canada's third-largest province (only Québec and Ontario are bigger),
British Columbia occupies almost 10% of Canada's total surface area,
stretching from the Pacific Ocean eastward to the province of Alberta,
and from the U.S. border north to the Yukon and Northwest Territories. It spans more than 360,000 square miles, making it larger than
every American state except Alaska.

British Columbia's appeal as a vacation destination stems from its status as the most spectacular part of the nation, with salmon-rich waters, abundant coastal scenery, and stretches of snow-capped peaks.
Outdoor enthusiasts have gravitated here for sports including fishing,
golfing, kayaking, rafting, and skiing. Whale-watching adventures,
whether by charter boat or in a kayak, are increasingly popular along
the Inside Passage and off the west coast of Vancouver Island.

The region's natural splendor has ironically become the source of conflict. For more than a century, logging companies have depended on
the abundant supply of British Columbia timber, and whole towns are
still centered on the industry. Environmentalists and many residents
now see the logging industry as a threat to the natural surroundings.
Compromises have been achieved in recent years, but the issue is far
from resolved.

The province used to be very British and predictable, reflecting its colonial heritage; but no longer. Vancouver (☞ Chapter 2) is an international city whose relaxed lifestyle is spiced by a rich and varied cultural
scene embracing large Chinese, Japanese, Italian, and Greek communities. Even Vancouver Island's Victoria, which clings with restrained
passion to British traditions and lifestyles, has undergone an international metamorphosis in recent years.

No matter how modern the province may appear, evidence remains of
the earliest settlers: Pacific Coast natives (Haida, Kwakiutl, Nootka,
Salish, and others) who occupied the land for more than 12,000 years
before the first Europeans arrived en masse in the late 19th century.
Today's native residents often face social barriers that have kept them
from the mainstream of the province's rich economy. Although some
have gained university educations and have fashioned careers, many
are just now beginning to make demands on the nonnative population.
In dispute are thousands of square miles of land claimed as aboriginal
territory, some of which is within such major cities as Vancouver,
Prince George, and Prince Rupert. Although the issue of ownership remains undecided, British Columbia's roots show throughout the
province, from such native arts as wood-carved objects and etched-sil-
ver jewelry in small-town boutiques to authentic culinary delights
from traditional recipes in big-city dining establishments.

Pleasures and Pastimes

Dining

Throughout British Columbia you'll find a range of cuisines, from Vancouver Island's seafood places to interior British Columbia's wild game–oriented menus. Although Vancouver has the most varied and creative restaurants, a number of fine country inns have helped define a local cuisine based on the best local fare from seafood and lamb to fine produce and herbs. The food here overall is fresh and hearty. Victoria has lots of seafood spots and places serving British-style dishes including fish and chips.

Prices vary from location to location, but ratings reflect the categories listed on the dining chart. Restaurants are generally casual in the region; if a restaurant requires jacket or jacket and tie, it is noted in the service information of the review.

CATEGORY	COST*
$$$$	over $35
$$$	$25–$35
$$	$15–$25
$	under $15

per person, excluding drinks, service, and 7% GST

Lodging

Accommodations across the province range from bed-and-breakfasts and rustic cabins to deluxe chain hotels. In the cities you'll find an abundance of lodgings, but once you get off the beaten path, guest rooms are often a rare commodity and usually require advance booking.

CATEGORY	COST*
$$$$	over $180
$$$	$110–$180
$$	$70–$110
$	under $70

All prices are for a standard double room, excluding 10% provincial accommodation tax, service charge, and 7% GST.

Outdoor Activities and Sports

CANOEING AND KAYAKING

These are favorite ways to explore the miles of extended, interconnected waterways and the breathtaking coastline of British Columbia. The Inside Passage, Queen Charlotte Strait, the Strait of Georgia, and the other island-dotted straits and sounds that border the mainland provide fairly protected sea-going from Washington state to the Alaskan border, with numerous marine parks to explore along the way. Another particular favorite among paddlers is the Powell Forest Canoe Route, a 60-km (37-mi) circuit of 12 lakes connected by streams, rivers, and well-maintained portage trails along the Powell River.

FISHING

Miles of coastline and thousands of lakes, rivers, and streams bring more than 750,000 fishermen to British Columbia each year. The waters of the province hold 74 species of fish (25 of them sport fish), including Chinook salmon and rainbow trout.

GOLF

There are more than 230 golf courses in British Columbia, and the number is growing. The province is now an Official Golf Destination of both the Canadian and American PGA tours. The topography here tends to be mountainous, and many courses have fine views as well as treacherous approaches to greens.

HIKING

Virtually all of British Columbia's provincial parks have fine hiking-trail networks. Heli-hiking is also very popular here; helicopters deliver hikers to high alpine meadows and verdant, untouched mountaintops.

RAFTING

With such beautiful rivers as the Adams, Chilcotin, Chilliwack, Fraser, Illecillewaet, Nahatlach, and Thompson lacing British Columbia, you can choose from a wide range of rafting trips.

SKIING

British Columbia has hundreds of kilometers of groomed cross-country (Nordic) ski trails in the provincial parks and more than 40 cross-country resorts. Most downhill destinations have carved out cross-country routes along the valleys, and there are literally thousands more trails in unmanaged areas of British Columbia.

With more than half the province higher than 4,200 feet above sea level, new downhill areas are constantly opening. Currently, more than 40 major resorts in the province have downhill facilities.

Heli-skiing on a large scale was invented in British Columbia over three decades ago and has grown in popularity ever since. Heli-skiing operators often serve well-established resorts, taking clients into otherwise inaccessible deep-powder regions of the mountains. Sno-cats—which are modified slope-grooming machines—can also transport skiers to pristine, powdery runs.

WHALE-WATCHING

Three resident and several transient pods of orca (killer) whales travel in the waters around Vancouver Island and are the primary focus of nature-watching charter boat tours that depart Victoria from May through October. June and July are actually the best time to see the whales, and harbor seal, sea lion, porpoise, and marine bird sightings are a safe bet anytime. Numerous outfitters in Victoria and other Vancouver Island cities offer outings for a closer look.

Exploring British Columbia

When you travel by car, keep in mind that more than three-quarters of British Columbia is mountainous terrain. Trips that appear relatively short may take longer, especially in the northern regions and along the coast, where roads are often narrow and winding. In certain areas—most of the uninhabited west coast of Vancouver Island, for example—roads do not exist.

British Columbia encompasses a vast range of climates, largely a result of the province's size, its mountainous topography, and its border on the Pacific. Vancouver Island, surrounded by Pacific waters, has relatively mild winters and summers (usually above 32°F winter, below 80°F summer), although winter brings frequent rains. Likewise, the northern coast around Prince Rupert and the Queen Charlotte Islands has wet winter months and few extremes in temperature. As you move inland, especially toward the Peace River region in the north, the climate becomes much colder. In the southern interior, the Okanagan Valley is arid, with temperatures dropping below freezing in winter and sometimes reaching 90°F in summer.

Numbers in the text correspond to numbers in the margin and on the Southern British Columbia, Downtown Victoria, and Vancouver Island maps.

Great Itineraries

IF YOU HAVE 1–3 DAYS

For a short trip, ☎ **Victoria** ①–⑬ is a fine place to begin. There's plenty to explore, from flower-fringed Inner Harbour and the museums and attractions nearby to Bastion Square and the red gates of Chinatown. World-famous Butchart Gardens is only half an hour away by car, and you might take a full day to explore the beautiful grounds. On day three, head out to ☎ **Sooke** ⑭ or to one of the Gulf Islands— ☎ **Galiano** ㉜, ☎ **Mayne** ㉝, or ☎ **Saltspring** ㉞—to stay at a romantic country inn for a night.

Another three-day option is to fly to ☎ **Prince Rupert** ㊱ to tour the region north of Vancouver Island, including the abandoned Haida villages of the ☎ **Queen Charlotte Islands** ㊲ for a day or so before spending a day aboard a ferry cruising the breathtaking **Inside Passage** ㉟ on the way to **Port Hardy** ㉚ on Vancouver Island and a plane home from there.

IF YOU HAVE 4–6 DAYS

A brief stay in ☎ **Victoria** ①–⑬ can be followed by a leisurely tour of Vancouver Island and perhaps a portion of the mainland coast if you have more time. Assuming you plan to stay on Vancouver Island, day four allows time to stop to see the Native Heritage Centre in **Duncan** ⑮, the murals of **Chemainus** ⑯, and the petroglyphs in ☎ **Nanaimo** ⑰. On day five, one alternative is to trek across island to the scenic west coast to visit ☎ **Tofino** ㉒ and ☎ **Ucluelet** ㉑ (pick one for your overnight) and spend some time whale-watching or hiking around **Pacific Rim National Park** ㉓. Another choice is to continue up the east coast to do some salmon fishing in ☎ **Campbell River** ㉙ or ☎ **Port Hardy** ㉚. If you want to go on to the **Queen Charlotte Islands** ㊲ by boat, you'll have a full day of cruising the **Inside Passage** ㉟, but little time to actually tour the islands. If you've gone the eastern route, day six will take you by ferry from **Courtenay and Comox** ㉗ across the Strait of Georgia to **Powell River** ㉘ on the Sunshine Coast, a paradise for outdoors lovers. Ferries and short highway jaunts will carry you down the scenic coast to Vancouver. If you've crossed to the west coast, you can spend day six backtracking to **Victoria** or making your way to **Nanaimo** to catch the ferry to Vancouver and the mainland.

IF YOU HAVE 7–10 DAYS

After visiting Vancouver Island and the upper mainland, tour British Columbia's lower mainland. Day seven takes you through the rolling lowlands of southwestern British Columbia to ☎ **Harrison Hot Springs** ㊹ for some deep relaxation in the natural springs. Points of interest in the vicinity include Hell's Gate on the Fraser River, Minter Gardens, and the Kilby Historic Store and Farm. Days eight through ten are best spent making the loop through the Okanagan Valley, the fruit-growing capital of the province. You can make stops in ☎ **Penticton** ㊸ to see the Kettle Valley Steam Railway and Cathedral Provincial Park, ☎ **Kelowna** ㊷ to tour the vineyards, ☎ **Vernon** ㊶ for the O'Keefe Historic Ranch, and ☎ **Kamloops** ㊵ to fish in one of the many lakes or visit the wildlife preserves. Any of these towns is fine for your overnights.

When to Tour British Columbia

Victoria is at its peak each year from late spring to early fall, but high summer is the most appealing time in a city proud of its gardens. Rooms can be hard to come by, so book well in advance if you plan to visit from June through August. Summer and fall are the best seasons to tour the islands of the province (frequent ferry service to the Gulf Islands, the Queen Charlottes, and Prince Rupert drops off in slower winter and spring months). Vancouver Island is very busy during sum-

Southern British Columbia

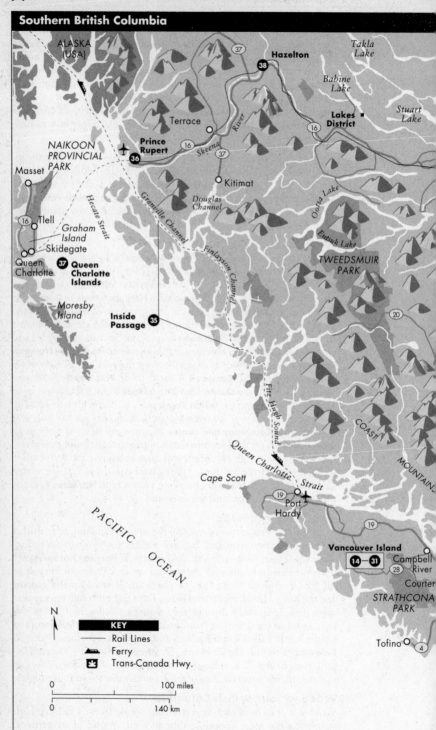

ALASKA (USA)

Takla Lake

37

Hazelton

38

Babine Lake

Terrace

River

Stuart Lake

Lakes District

16

NAIKOON PROVINCIAL PARK

Prince Rupert

36

16

Skeena

37

Masset

Hecate Strait

Grenville Channel

Kitimat

Douglas Channel

Ootsa Lake

16

Tlell

Graham Island

Skidegate

Queen Charlotte

37

Queen Charlotte Islands

Finlayson Channel

Eutsuk Lake

TWEEDSMUIR PARK

Moresby Island

Inside Passage

35

20

Fitz Hugh Sound

COAST

Queen Charlotte Strait

MOUNTAINS

Cape Scott

19

Port Hardy

19

Vancouver Island

14 — 31

28

Campbell River

Courter

STRATHCONA PARK

PACIFIC

OCEAN

N

KEY	
——	Rail Lines
⛴	Ferry
🍁	Trans-Canada Hwy.

Tofino

4

0   100 miles

0   140 km

mer and fall (especially during the fishing derbies and when leaves are changing color); the winter resorts draw more locals than visitors, so the crowds are much smaller than on the mainland. High Country and the Okanagan Valley have year-round appeal: Winter brings snow for downhill and cross-country skiing, spring is filled with blossoms on fruit trees, and summer has warm, dry temperatures conducive to all the outdoor activities. Fall harvest time is a particular favorite; pears, apples, and other produce are readily available, harvest festivals are frequent, and the turning leaves add their color.

VICTORIA

Originally Fort Victoria, Victoria was the first European settlement on Vancouver Island and is the oldest city on Canada's west coast. It was chosen in 1843 by James Douglas to be the Hudson's Bay Company's westernmost outpost, and it became the capital of British Columbia in 1868. Today it's a compact seaside town laced with tea shops and gardens. Though Victoria is quite touristy during the high summer season, it's also at its prettiest, with flowers hanging from turn-of-the-century lampposts and strollers feasting on the beauty of Victoria's natural harbor. A trip to Butchart Gardens (☞ Side Trip from Victoria, *below*), north of the city, adds to the experience. The city is 71 km (44 mi) south of Vancouver; it's about 2½ hours by direct ferry from Seattle.

Downtown Victoria

Great views, lush gardens, and fine museums are the highlights of a visit to Victoria's walkable downtown. There are also many places to shop and stop for a cup of tea along the way. This is as British a city as you'll find outside England, but you'll still see many signs of the distinctive heritage of the Pacific Northwest.

A Good Walk and Tour

For some wonderful views, begin your tour of Victoria on the waterfront at the **Visitors Information Centre** ①. Just across the way is the **Empress Hotel** ②, a majestic railway hotel that originally opened in 1908. A short walk around the harbor leads you to the **Royal London Wax Museum** ③. Next to the wax museum are the **Pacific Undersea Gardens** ④, with more than 5,000 marine specimens. Across Belleville Street is the **Parliament Buildings** ⑤ complex, typical of the style of much of the city's architecture. Follow Belleville Street one block east to reach the **Royal British Columbia Museum** ⑥, where you can explore thousands of years of history. Just behind the museum and bordering Douglas Street is Thunderbird Park, where totem poles and a ceremonial longhouse stand in one corner of the garden of **Helmcken House,** the oldest house in British Columbia. A walk east on Superior Street to Douglas Street will lead you to **Beacon Hill Park** ⑦, a haven for joggers, walkers, and cyclists. From the park, go north on Douglas Street and stop off at the glass-roof **Crystal Gardens** ⑧, where you can see 75 varieties of birds, hundreds of flowers, and monkeys.

From Crystal Gardens, continue north on Douglas Street to View Street, then west to **Bastion Square** ⑨, with its gas lamps, restaurants, cobblestone streets, and small shops. While you're here, you can stop in at the **Maritime Museum of British Columbia** ⑩ and learn about an important part of the province's history. West of Government Street, between Pandora Avenue and Johnson Street, is **Market Square** ⑪, one of the most picturesque shopping districts in the city. Just around the corner from Market Square is Fisgard Street, the heart of **Chinatown** ⑫. A 15-minute walk or a short drive east on Fort Street will take you to

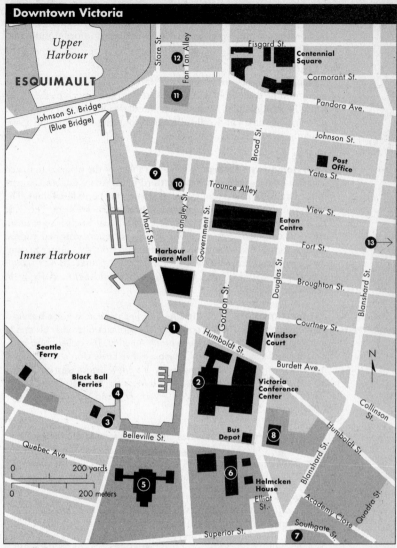

Downtown Victoria

Upper Harbour

ESQUIMAULT

Johnson St. Bridge (Blue Bridge)

Store St.

Fan Tan Alley

Fisgard St.

Centennial Square

Cormorant St.

Pandora Ave.

Broad St.

Johnson St.

Post Office

Yates St.

Trounce Alley

View St.

Langley St.

Government St.

Eaton Centre

Fort St.

Wharf St.

Harbour Square Mall

Douglas St.

Broughton St.

Inner Harbour

Gordon St.

Courtney St.

Blanshard St.

Humboldt St.

Windsor Court

Seattle Ferry

Burdett Ave.

Black Ball Ferries

Victoria Conference Center

Collinson St.

Belleville St.

Bus Depot

Humboldt St.

Quebec Ave.

Helmcken House

Elliot St.

Academy Close

Quadra St.

Superior St.

Southgate St.

0   200 yards
0   200 meters

N

Joan Crescent and lavish **Craigdarroch Castle** ⑬. From downtown Victoria, you can take the Munro bus to **Anne Hathaway's Cottage,** a full-size replica of the original thatched home in Stratford-upon-Avon, England.

TIMING

Many of the sights are within easy walking distance of one another and could be covered in half a day, but there's so much to see at the Royal British Columbia Museum and the other museums that you should plan on a full day. This would allow time for some shopping and a visit to Craigdarroch Castle, too.

Sights to See

Anne Hathaway's Cottage. A full-size replica of the original thatched home of Shakespeare's wife in Stratford-upon-Avon, England, is part of the English Village, a complex with re-created period buildings. The 16th-century antiques inside are typical of Shakespeare's era. The Olde England Inn here is a pleasant spot for tea or an English-style meal, and you can also stay in one of the 50 antiques-furnished rooms. Guided tours leave from the inn in winter and from the cottage in summer. The village is touristy but appeals to many people. ✉ *429 Lampson St.,* ☎ *250/388–4353.* ⌨ *$6.50.* ◷ *June–Sept., daily 9–8; Oct.–May, daily 10–4.*

OFF THE
BEATEN PATH

ART GALLERY OF GREATER VICTORIA – This fine museum is home both to large collections of Chinese and Japanese ceramics and other art and to the only authentic Shinto shrine in North America. The gallery also has a permanent exhibit of British Columbia native Emily Carr's work and numerous temporary exhibitions yearly. It's a few blocks west of Craigdarroch Castle, off Fort Street. ✉ *1040 Moss St.,* ☎ *250/384–4101.* ⌨ *$5, Mon. by donation.* ◷ *Mon.–Wed., Fri., and Sat. 10–5; Thurs. 10–9; Sun. 1–5.*

⑨ Bastion Square. James Douglas chose this spot for the original Fort Victoria in 1843 and the original Hudson's Bay Company trading post. Today fashion boutiques and restaurants occupy the old buildings. The cobblestone streets are lighted by gas lamps.

⑦ Beacon Hill Park. The southern lawns of this spacious haven for joggers, walkers, and cyclists have one of the best views of the Olympic Mountains and the Strait of Juan de Fuca. There are also lakes, walking paths, abundant flowers and gardens, a wading pool, a petting zoo, and an outdoor amphitheater for Sunday afternoon concerts. ✉ *East of Douglas St.*

⑫ Chinatown. The Chinese were responsible for building much of the Canadian Pacific Railway in the 19th century, and their influences still mark the region. If you enter Chinatown (one of the oldest in Canada) from Government Street, you'll walk under the elaborate **Gate of Harmonious Interest,** made from Taiwanese ceramic tiles and decorative panels. Along the street, merchants display paper lanterns, embroidered silks, imported fruits, and vegetables. **Fan Tan Alley,** off Fisgard Street, holds claim not only to being the narrowest street in Canada but also to having been the gambling and opium center of Chinatown, where games of mah-jongg, fan-tan, and dominoes were played.

★ ⑬ Craigdarroch Castle. This lavish mansion was built as the home of British Columbia's first millionaire, Robert Dunsmuir, who oversaw coal mining for the Hudson's Bay Company. He died in 1889, just a few months before the castle's completion. Converted into a museum depicting turn-of-the-century life, the castle has elaborately framed landscape paintings, stained-glass windows, carved woodwork—precut in Chicago for Dunsmuir and sent by rail—and rooms for billiards and smoking. There's a wonderful view of downtown Victoria from the fourth-floor tower. ⌂ *1050 Joan Crescent,* ☎ *250/592–5323.* ⌂ *$6.50.* ☉ *Mid-June–early Sept., daily 9–7:30; mid-Sept.–mid-June, daily 10–4:30.*

❽ Crystal Gardens. Opened in 1925 as the largest saltwater swimming pool in the British Empire, this glass-roof building—owned by the provincial government—is now home to flamingos, macaws, 75 varieties of other tropical birds, monkeys, and hundreds of blooming flowers. At street level there are several boutiques and Rattenbury's Restaurant, one of Victoria's well-frequented establishments. ⌂ *713 Douglas St.,* ☎ *250/381–1213.* ⌂ *$7.* ☉ *Dec.–Apr., daily 10–4:30; May–Aug., daily 8–8; Sept.–Nov., daily 9–6.*

❷ Empress Hotel. Originally opened in 1908, the Empress (☞ Lodging, *below*) is a symbol of both the city and the Canadian Pacific Railway. Designed by Francis Rattenbury, whose works dot Victoria, the property is another of the great châteaus built by Canadian Pacific, still the owners. The ingredients that made the 483-room hotel a tourist attraction in the past—Old World architecture and ornate decor, a commanding view of the Inner Harbour—are still here. Stop in for high tea, served at hour-and-a-half intervals during the afternoon (no jeans, shorts, or T-shirts are permitted in the tea lobby). ⌂ *721 Government St.,* ☎ *250/ 384–8111.*

★ Helmcken House. The oldest house in British Columbia was built in 1852 by pioneer doctor and statesman John Sebastian Helmcken. It is a treasure trove of history, from the early Victorian furnishings to an intriguing collection of 19th-century medical tools. Audio tours last 20 minutes. **Thunderbird Park,** with totem poles and a ceremonial longhouse constructed by Kwakiutl Chief Mungo Martin, occupies one corner of the garden. For further information on these and other Heritage attractions in Victoria (Craigflower Farm and Schoolhouse, Emily Carr House, and Point Ellice House), call 250/387–4697. ⌂ *Helmcken House, 10 Elliot St.,* ☎ *250/361–0021.* ⌂ *$4.* ☉ *May–Sept., daily 10–5; call for winter hours.*

❿ Maritime Museum of British Columbia. In Victoria's original courthouse, dugout canoes, model ships, Royal Navy charts, photographs, uniforms, and ship's bells chronicle Victoria's seafaring history. A seldom-used 100-year-old cage lift, believed to be the oldest in North America, ascends to the third floor. ⌂ *28 Bastion Sq.,* ☎ *250/385–4222.* ⌂ *$5.* ☉ *Daily 9:30–4:30.*

⓫ Market Square. The many specialty shops and boutiques here are enhanced by a historic setting. At the turn of the century this area—once part of Chinatown—provided everything a visitor desired: food, lodging, entertainment. Today the square has been restored to its original, pre-1900s character.

⓸ Pacific Undersea Gardens. Here you can see more than 5,000 marine specimens in their natural habitat. You'll also see a short, rather hokey show of performing scuba divers and a giant Pacific octopus. Unfortunately, there are no washrooms, and the site is not wheelchair accessible. This one is usually a disappointment to all but the youngest visitors. ⌂ *490 Belleville St.,* ☎ *250/382–5717.* ⌂ *$6.75.* ☉ *Oct.–May, daily 10–5; June–Sept., daily 9–9; show every 35 min.*

★ ⓹ Parliament Buildings. The massive stone structures, completed in 1897, dominate the Inner Harbour and are flanked by statues of two men: Sir James Douglas, who chose the site where Victoria was built, and

Sir Matthew Baille Begbie, the man in charge of law and order during the gold-rush era. Atop the central dome is a gilded statue of Captain George Vancouver, the first European to sail around Vancouver Island. A statue of Queen Victoria stands in front of the complex; more than 3,000 lights outline the buildings at night. Another of Francis Rattenbury's creations, the complex is a good example of the rigid symmetry and European elegance that characterize much of the city's architecture. Tours, several times daily, are conducted in at least four languages in summer and three in winter. ⊠ *501 Belleville St.,* ☎ *250/387–3046.* ☞ *Free.* ☉ *Sept.–May, weekdays 8:30–5; June–Aug., daily 9–5.*

★ ☝ ❻ **Royal British Columbia Museum.** At what is easily the best attraction in Victoria, you can spend hours wandering through the centuries, back 12,000 years. In the prehistoric exhibit, you can actually smell the pines and hear the calls of mammoths and other ancient wildlife. Other exhibits allow you to explore a turn-of-the-century town, with trains rumbling past. In the Kwakiutl longhouse, the smell of cedar envelops you, while piped-in potlatch songs tell the origins of the genuine ceremonial house before you. The museum also has fine interpretive displays of native artifacts, including an impressive collection of masks. ⊠ *675 Belleville St.,* ☎ *250/387–3014.* ☞ *$7.* ☉ *Sept.–June, daily 10–5:30; July and Aug., daily 9:30–7.*

☝ ❸ **Royal London Wax Museum.** This museum is in the old CPR Steamship Terminal, designed by Francis Rattenbury and completed in 1924. Today it houses some 300 wax figures, including replicas of Queen Victoria, Elvis, and Marilyn Monroe. ⊠ *470 Belleville St.,* ☎ *250/388–4461.* ☞ *$7.* ☉ *May–Aug., daily 9–9; Sept.–Apr., Mon.–Sat. 9:30–5, Sun. 11–5.*

❶ **Visitors Information Centre.** A convenient waterfront location adds to the center's appeal. The bridge immediately to the south gives you a grand view of the Inner Harbour and, across the water on Songhees Point, the 182½-foot **Welcome Totem** (now the tallest totem pole in the world) erected in 1994 for the Commonwealth Games. ⊠ *812 Wharf St.,* ☎ *250/953–2033.* ☉ *July and Aug., Mon.–Sat. 9–9, Sun. 9–7; May, June, and Sept., daily 9–7; Oct.–Apr., daily 9–5.*

Dining

$$$–$$$$ ✗ **Empress Room.** For a special-occasion dinner, reserve a fireside table in the elegant Empress Room. Innovative and beautifully presented Pacific Northwest cuisine vies for attention with the setting when candlelight dances on the tapestried walls beneath an intricately carved mahogany ceiling. Fresh local ingredients go into imaginative seasonal dishes such as house-cured Pacific salmon with wild blackberry-ginger butter, pan-roasted Arctic char with wild-rice polenta and gooseberry chutney, or peppered Vancouver Island venison with black currant sauce. The dining room is no-smoking. ⊠ *Empress Hotel, 721 Government St.,* ☎ *250/381–8111. Reservations essential. AE, D, DC, MC, V. No lunch.*

$$$ ✗ **Chez Daniel.** One of Victoria's old standbys, Chez Daniel offers rich French dishes, though the nouvelle influence has found its way into some creations. The interior, with a burgundy color scheme, seems to match the traditional caloric cuisine. The award-winning wine list is varied, and the menu has a wide selection of basic dishes including rabbit, salmon, duck, and steak. The romantic atmosphere here encourages you to linger. ⊠ *2524 Estevan Ave.,* ☎ *250/592–7424. Reservations essential. AE, MC, V. Closed Sun. and Mon. No lunch.*

$$–$$$ ✕ **Marina Restaurant.** This lovely, round restaurant overlooking the
★ Oak Bay Marina is so popular with the locals that it's always crowded
and a bit noisy. While seasonings and presentation often change, the
best bets on the imaginative menu are warm salmon salad, grilled
marlin in citrus sesame vinaigrette, rack of lamb in port glaze, and crab
served with drawn butter and Indonesian hot-and-sour sauce. Choose
from more than 500 wines to complement the meal. If you don't have
reservations and the dining room and sushi bar are full, head downstairs to the Café Deli for Mediterranean picnic foods prepared by the
chefs upstairs; go early for the best selection. ⊠ *1327 Beach Dr.,*
☎ *250/598–8555. Reservations essential. AE, DC, MC, V.*

$$–$$$ ✕ **Pescatore's Fish House and Oyster Bar.** Conveniently situated across
from the Inner Harbour, upbeat Pescatore's specializes in fresh seafood
(grilled wild Coho salmon, fresh spinach, and smoked Gruyère on Italian flatbread) and Pacific Northwest specialties such as rosemary-and-
garlic-marinated lamb and oyster mushrooms on angel-hair pasta). Daily
blue plate specials tend to be reasonably priced and creative—for example, pan-seared chicken breast in chanterelle sauce with crushed potatoes and vegetables. A favorite of downtown businesspeople, this
popular spot is frequently too crowded and noisy to be considered romantic. ⊠ *614 Humboldt St.,* ☎ *250/385–4512. Reservations essential. AE, MC, V.*

$$ ✕ **Camilles.** This intimate restaurant is one of the city's few West
Coast–cuisine restaurants. Such house specialties as smoked Gruyère
cheese and carrot cake (an appetizer), roast loin of venison with wild
mushroom polenta, and grainy Dijon-and-mint-crusted lamb with a
blackberry port reduction are all served in generous portions. Camilles
also has an extensive wine cellar; special wine tasting dinners are of-
fered once each week. ⊠ *45 Bastion Sq.,* ☎ *250/381–3433. Reser-
vations essential. AE, MC, V. No lunch.*

$$ ✕ **Don Mee's.** A large neon sign invites you inside this traditional Chinese restaurant. The long, red staircase leads to an expansive, comfortable
dining room; some of the Szechuan and Cantonese entrées are sweet-
and-sour chicken, almond duck, and bean curd with broccoli. Dim sum
is served daily during lunch hours. ⊠ *538 Fisgard St.,* ☎ *250/383–
1032. AE, DC, MC, V.*

$$ ✕ **Il Terrazzo.** A charming redbrick terrace edged by potted greenery,
★ lit by flickering candles, and warmed by fireplaces and overhead heaters
make Il Terrazzo, tucked away off Waddington Alley, and not visible
from the street, the locals' choice for romantic al fresco dining in Vic-
toria. Baked garlic served with warm cambozola cheese and focaccia;
scallops dipped in roasted pistachios and garnished with arugula, Bel-
gian endive, and mango salsa; grilled lamb chops on angel-hair pasta
with tomatoes, garlic, mint, and black pepper; and other hearty North-
ern Italian dishes come piping hot from the restaurant's authentic
wood oven. Anything from the daily fresh sheet is worth a try here.
⊠ *555 Johnson St., off Waddington Alley (call for directions),* ☎ *250/
361–0028. Reservations essential. AE, MC, V.*

$$ ✕ **Pagliacci's.** This fine Italian bistro is a must. Dozens of pasta dishes,
quiches, veal, and chicken in marsala sauce with fettuccine are stan-
dard, and the pastas are freshly made in-house. You'll dine surrounded
by orange walls covered with photos of Hollywood movie stars. Save
room for the divine cheesecake. ⊠ *1011 Broad St.,* ☎ *250/386–1662.
Reservations not accepted. AE, MC, V.*

$$ ✕ **Tomoe.** A long sushi bar, a few tatami rooms, and tables set com-
fortably apart are the elements of this low-key Japanese restaurant.
Choose from satisfying seafood dishes (watch for the occasional ex-
otic offering flown in from Japan) as well as standards such as tem-
pura and teriyaki. The chicken teriyaki salad nesting on a bed of crisp

fried noodles and fresh greens is recommended. ⊠ *726 Johnson St.,* ☎ *250/381–0223. AE, MC, V. Closed Sun.*

$–$$ ✕ **Le Petit Saigon.** An intimate café-style restaurant offers quiet dining with beautifully presented meals and fare that is primarily Vietnamese, with a touch of French. The crab, asparagus, and egg swirl soup is a house specialty, and combination meals are cheap and tasty. ⊠ *1010 Langley St.,* ☎ *250/386–1412. AE, MC, V.*

$ ✕ **Barb's Place.** This funky, blue-painted take-out shack is on Fisherman's Wharf, on the south side of Victoria Harbour west of the Inner Harbour just off Marine Drive, where fishing boats come in. It has become an institution in Victoria, and the locals consider the authentic fish (halibut) and chips to be the best. Pick up an order before taking a quick ride on the little harbor ferry across the bay to Songhees Point for a picnic. ⊠ *310 Lawrence St.,* ☎ *250/384–6515. No credit cards. Closed Nov.–Mar.*

$ ✕ **Cafe Mexico.** Hearty portions of Mexican food, such as *pollo chipotle* (grilled chicken with melted cheddar and spicy sauce on a bed of rice) are served at a spacious, redbrick dining establishment just off the waterfront. Bullfight ads and cactus plants lend a touch of Mexican atmosphere. ⊠ *1425 Store St.,* ☎ *250/386–5454. AE, DC, MC, V.*

$ ✕ **Periklis.** You can order standard Greek cuisine in this warm, taverna-style restaurant, but steaks and ribs are also on the menu. The dolmas and baklava are especially good. At night there's Greek and belly dancing, but brace yourself for the hordes of people who come for this entertainment. ⊠ *531 Yates St.,* ☎ *250/386–3313. Reservations essential. AE, MC, V. No lunch weekends.*

$ ✕ **Siam.** The Thai chefs at Siam work wonders with both hot and mild Thai dishes. The *phad Thai goong* (fried rice noodles with prawns, tofu, peanuts, eggs, bean sprouts, and green onions), *panang* (choice of meat in curry and coconut milk), *bami goreng* (a noodle-based dish with shreds of shrimp, pork, vegetables, and an Indonesian blend of herbs and spices), and *satay* (grilled, marinated cubes of meat served with a spicy peanut sauce) are particularly good options. The restaurant is spacious and conveniently near the Inner Harbour. The well-stocked bar has a variety of beers. ⊠ *512 Fort St.,* ☎ *250/383–9911. Reservations essential. MC, V. No lunch Sun.*

$ ✕ **Six-Mile-House.** Although it's a bit of a drive from downtown, this 1855 carriage house is a Victoria landmark and the oldest pub in British Columbia. The brass, carved oak moldings, and stained glass set a festive mood. The menu constantly changes but always includes seafood selections and burgers. Try the cider or one of the many international beers. ⊠ *494 Island Hwy.,* ☎ *250/478–3121. DC, MC, V.*

Lodging

$$$$ ▣ **The Aerie.** The million-dollar view of Finlayson Arm and the Gulf
★ Islands persuaded Leo and Maria Schuster to build their small, luxury resort here, 30 km (19 mi) north of Victoria. In the Mediterranean-style villa, some plush rooms have a patio; others have fireplaces and whirlpool tubs tucked into window nooks. The dining room is open to the public for stunning dinner views and outstanding cuisine. The maple-smoked salmon, pheasant consommé, and medallions of venison in morel sauce are more than worth the drive from Victoria. A full gourmet breakfast is included in the tariff. ⊠ *600 Ebedora La., Malahat V0R 2L0,* ☎ *250/743–7115,* FAX *250/743–4766. 11 rooms, 11 suites. Dining room, no-smoking rooms, indoor pool, indoor and outdoor hot tubs, sauna, spa, tennis court, exercise room, library, meeting room, helipad. AE, MC, V.*

$$$$ 🏨 **Beaconsfield Inn.** Built in 1905 and restored in 1984, the Beaconsfield has retained its Old World charm. Dark mahogany wood appears throughout the house; down comforters and some canopy beds adorn the rooms, reinforcing its Edwardian style. Some of the rooms in this no-smoking inn have fireplaces and whirlpool bathtubs. Added pluses are the guest library and the conservatory/sun room. Full breakfast, with homemade croissants or scones, and afternoon tea as well as evening sherry are included in the room rates. ⊠ *998 Humboldt St., V8V 2Z8,* ☎ *250/384–4044,* FAX *250/721–2442. 5 rooms, 4 suites. Breakfast room, no-smoking rooms, library. MC, V.*

$$$$ 🏨 **Clarion Hotel Grand Pacific.** One of Victoria's newest and finest hotels has mahogany woodwork and an elegant ambience. Overlooking the harbor, and adjacent to the legislative buildings, the hotel accommodates business travelers and vacationers looking for comfort, convenience, and great scenery; all rooms have terraces, with views of either the harbor or the Olympic Mountains. The elaborate health club is one of the best in the city. ⊠ *450 Québec St., V8V 1W5,* ☎ *250/386–0450 or 800/663–7550,* FAX *250/386–8779. 130 rooms, 15 suites. Dining room, lounge, no-smoking rooms, room service, indoor pool, massage, sauna, aerobics, racquetball, squash, bicycles, laundry service and dry cleaning, business services, convention center, meeting rooms, downtown shuttle, free parking. AE, D, DC, MC, V.*

$$$$ 🏨 **Empress Hotel.** This is Victoria's dowager queen with a face-lift. First opened in 1908, the hotel underwent a major renovation in 1989 that enhanced its Edwardian charm, updated existing guest rooms, and added some 45 new ones (opt for one of the new rooms for more space). Stained glass, carved archways, and hardwood floors are used effectively. Dominating the Inner Harbour area, the Empress is the city's primary meeting place for politicians, locals, and tourists. Afternoon tea has been a tradition since 1908, but it's so popular today that reservations are a must. The Empress Room (☞ Dining, *above*) serves superb regional cuisine. ⊠ *721 Government St., V8W 1W5,* ☎ *250/384–8111 or 800/441–1414,* FAX *250/381–4334. 466 rooms, 17 suites. Restaurant, café, 2 lounges, no-smoking rooms, room service, indoor pool, sauna, health club, laundry service and dry cleaning, concierge, business services, convention center, parking (fee). AE, D, DC, MC, V.*

$$$–$$$$ 🏨 **Chateau Victoria.** Wonderful views from the upper-floor rooms and rooftop restaurant are a plus at this 19-story hotel across from Victoria's new Conference Centre, near the Inner Harbour and the Royal British Columbia Museum. Rooms are fairly standard in size, and some have balconies or sitting areas and kitchenettes. ⊠ *740 Burdett Ave., V8W 1B2,* ☎ *250/382–4221 or 800/663–5891,* FAX *250/380–1950. 71 rooms, 107 suites. Restaurant, lounge, no-smoking rooms, room service, indoor pool, laundry service and dry cleaning, concierge, business services, meeting rooms, ferry shuttle, free parking. AE, D, DC, MC, V.*

$$$–$$$$ 🏨 **Ocean Pointe Resort.** Across the "blue bridge" (Johnson Street
★ Bridge) from downtown Victoria, the Ocean Pointe opened in 1992 on the site of an old shingle mill in an area once claimed by the Songhees natives. From here you have the best possible view of the lights of the Parliament buildings across the Inner Harbour. Public rooms and half of the guest rooms offer romantic evening views of downtown Victoria. Some of the spacious guest rooms come with floor-to-ceiling windows. Amenities include the only full European aesthetics spa in western Canada, with all kinds of beauty treatments. ⊠ *45 Songhees Rd., V9A 6T3,* ☎ *250/360–2999 or 800/667–4677,* FAX *250/360–5856. 213 rooms, 37 suites. 2 restaurants, lounge, kitchenettes, no-smoking rooms, indoor pool, sauna, spa, 2 tennis courts, exercise room, rac-*

quetball, squash, laundry service and dry cleaning, business services, meeting rooms, parking (fee). AE, DC, MC, V.

$$$–$$$$ ☑ **Victoria Regent Hotel.** Originally built as an apartment house, this is now a posh hotel with views of the harbor or city. The outside is plain, with a glass facade, but the interior is sumptuously decorated with warm earth tones and modern furnishings; each suite has a living room, a dining room, a deck, a kitchen, and one or two bedrooms with bath (some with hot tubs). It's a good choice for families. ⊠ *1234 Wharf St., V8W 3H9, ☎ 250/386–2211 or 800/663–7472, FAX 250/386–2622. 10 rooms, 34 suites. Restaurant, kitchenettes, no-smoking rooms, refrigerators, coin laundry, meeting room, free parking. AE, D, DC, MC, V.*

$$$ ☑ **Abigail's Hotel.** A Tudor country inn with gardens and crystal chan-
★ deliers, Abigail's is not only lovely but also convenient—it's within walking distance of the shops and restaurants of downtown. The guest rooms are prettily detailed in soothing pastel colors. Down comforters, together with Jacuzzis and fireplaces in some, add to the pampering atmosphere. The elegant informality in this no-smoking hotel is especially noticeable in the guest library and sitting room, where hors d'oeuvres are served each evening. Breakfast, included in the room rate, is served in the downstairs dining room. ⊠ *906 McClure St., V8V 3E7, ☎ 250/388–5363 or 800/561–6565, FAX 250/361–1905. 16 rooms. Breakfast room, library, concierge, free parking. MC, V.*

$$$ ☑ **Bedford Regency.** This European-style hotel in the heart of downtown is reminiscent of San Francisco's small hotels, with personalized service and careful attention to details. Rooms are in earth colors, and many have goose-down comforters, fireplaces, and whirlpool bathtubs. Four rooms on the west side have views of the harbor and are much quieter than those facing the traffic on Government Street. Meeting rooms and small conference facilities are also available, making this a good business traveler's lodging. ⊠ *1140 Government St., V8W 1Y2, ☎ 250/384–6835 or 800/665–6500, FAX 250/386–8930. 40 rooms. Restaurant, pub, no-smoking rooms, laundry service and dry cleaning, business services, free parking. AE, MC, V.*

$$$ ☑ **Haterleigh Heritage Inn.** The Haterleigh, a 4,400-square-foot 1901 modified Queen Anne just blocks from the Inner Harbour, was opened as a bed-and-breakfast in 1990 after arduous restoration. Leaded- and stained-glass windows, intricate moldings, and ornate plasterwork on 11-foot ceilings transport you to a more gracious time. Mounds of pillows and plump down comforters dress the beds. Extras, like sherry and chocolates delivered to your room on check-in, are nice touches indeed, as are the hearty family-style breakfasts. ⊠ *243 Kingston St., V8V 1V5, ☎ 250/384–9995, FAX 250/384–1935. 5 double rooms, 1 2-bedroom room, 1 suite. Whirlpool tubs in several rooms. MC, V.*

$$$ ☑ **Oak Bay Beach Hotel.** Beside the ocean in Oak Bay, on the southwest side of the Saanich Peninsula, this Tudor-style hotel is just 10 minutes from the bustle of downtown. The hotel overlooks Haro Strait; antiques and flower prints decorating the rooms echo the dreamy landscaped grounds above the pebble beach. Most of the highly individual guest rooms have antiques (lots of slipper chairs and high brass or canopy beds), though a 1992 renovation brought contemporary styling, furniture, and fixtures to some. ⊠ *1175 Beach Dr., V8S 2N2, ☎ 250/598–4556 or 800/668–7758, FAX 250/598–6180. 51 rooms. Restaurant, pub, no-smoking rooms, limited room service, boating, meeting room, downtown shuttle, free parking. AE, DC, MC, V.*

$$–$$$ ☑ **Coast Victoria Harbourside.** Built in 1991 on the more residential
★ section of the harborfront next to Fisherman's Wharf (west of the Inner Harbour), the Coast Victoria has water views but is removed from the traffic on Government Street. Serene relaxation in modern comfort is

a theme here, from the warm mahogany-paneled lobby and the soothing shades of blue-gray and pale pink in average-size guest rooms to an extensive health club. Fishing and whale-watching charters and the harbor ferries stop at the hotel's marina, and the action of the Inner Harbour is a leisurely stroll or quick shuttle ride away. ⊠ *146 Kingston St., V8V 1V4,* ☎ *250/360–1211 or 800/663–1144,* FAX *250/360– 1418. 118 rooms, 14 suites. Restaurant, lounge, no-smoking rooms, room service, indoor-outdoor pool, hot tub, sauna, health club, business services, meeting rooms, downtown shuttle, free parking. AE, DC, MC, V.*

$$–$$$ 🏠 **Holland House Inn.** Two blocks from the Inner Harbour, legislative buildings, and ferry terminals, this no-smoking hotel surrounded by a picket fence possesses a casual elegance. Some of the individually designed rooms have original fine art created by local artists; some have four-poster beds and fireplaces. All but two rooms have their own balconies. A lavish breakfast is included in room rates. ⊠ *595 Michigan St., V8V 1S7,* ☎ *250/384–6644,* FAX *250/384–6117. 10 rooms. No-smoking rooms. AE, MC, V.*

$$ 🏠 **Borthwick Country Manor.** Flower boxes and awnings trim the windows of the Tudor-style Borthwick, built in 1974 on the Saanich Peninsula in the quiet countryside not far from Butchart Gardens or Victoria. Owners Susan and Michael Siems provide afternoon tea and a gourmet four-course breakfast. Rooms are cheerful, with coordinated English floral duvets, shams, and curtains. French doors lead to the backyard, with gardens and a hot tub; on sunny summer mornings, you may breakfast al fresco on the patio. ⊠ *9750 Ardmore Dr., R.R. 2, V8L 5H5,* ☎ FAX *250/656–9498. 5 rooms. Breakfast room, no-smoking rooms, hot tub, fishing, bicycles, library. AE, MC, V.*

$$ 🏠 **Carberry Gardens.** A 1907 gambrel-roof, board-and-shingle home in the historic Rocklands neighborhood, Carberry Gardens is just blocks from Craigdarroch Castle, Antique Row, and the Art Gallery of Greater Victoria. The original fir floors, moldings, and staircase, as well as the fine collection of Welsh, Scottish, and American antiques, are eye-catching. In the spacious second-floor rooms, the sun filters through lace curtains onto fluffy down comforters on antique bedsteads. One bedroom has a detached bathroom across the hall, but that bathroom is fun, with French doors that open to a little balcony. A hot, hearty breakfast is included. ⊠ *1008 Carberry Gardens, V8S 3R7,* ☎ *250/595–8906,* FAX *250/595–8185. 3 rooms. No-smoking rooms, refrigerator. MC, V.*

$$ 🏠 **Mulberry Manor.** The last building designed by Victoria architect Samuel McClure has been restored and decorated to magazine-cover perfection with antiques, sumptuous linens, and tile baths. The Tudor-style mansion sits behind a high stone wall on an acre of carefully manicured, landscaped grounds. Charming hosts Susan and Tony Temple serve sumptuous breakfasts with homemade jams and great coffee. ⊠ *611 Foul Bay Rd., V8S 1H2,* ☎ *250/370–1918,* FAX *250/370–1968. 3 rooms, 1 suite. Breakfast room, no-smoking rooms. MC, V.*

$$ 🏠 **Swans.** When English-born shepherd Michael Williams bought supplies for his kennel at the Buckerfield Company Feed Store during the 1950s, he never dreamed he would one day own the building and turn it into a waterfront hotel. Extensive renovations have given the 1913 brick warehouse a new look: There's a brewery, bistro, and pub on the first floor; and large, apartmentlike guest rooms decorated with Pacific Northwest art fill the upper floors. Swans is a good choice for families. ⊠ *506 Pandora Ave., V8W 1N6,* ☎ *250/361–3310 or 800/668–7926,* FAX *250/361–3491. 29 rooms. Restaurant, pub, no-smoking rooms, coin laundry. AE, DC, MC, V.*

$–$$ ☒ **Admiral Motel.** On Victoria harbor along the tourist strip, this small, modern motel is in the center of things, although it is relatively quiet in the evening. If you're looking for basic, clean lodging, the Admiral is just that. The amiable owners take good care of the rooms, and small pets are permitted. Kids under 12 stay free in their parents' room. ☒ *257 Belleville St., V8V 1X1,* ☎ FAX *250/388–6267. 29 rooms. Kitchenettes, no-smoking rooms, coin laundry, free parking. AE, D, MC, V.*

$ ☒ **Cats Meow.** If you're on a tight budget, you may appreciate this small youth hostel operated by bubbly Daphne Cuthill and resident meow Rufus. The hostel has a dorm room and two private rooms, as well as a guest lounge. Laundry service is available at nominal extra cost; Daphne also arranges discounted day trips. It's only a 15-minute walk east of downtown in the quiet Fernwood neighborhood, not far from Craigdarroch Castle. Dorm space costs under $20 per night, a private room about $45 for two people. ☒ *1316 Grant St., V8R 1M3,* ☎ FAX *250/ 595–8878. 1 dorm with 6 beds shares bath, 2 private rooms share bath. No credit cards.*

Nightlife and the Arts

The Arts

MUSIC

The **Victoria Symphony** has a winter schedule and a summer season, playing in the recently refurbished Royal Theatre (☒ 805 Broughton St., ☎ 250/386–6121) and at the University Centre Auditorium (☒ Finnerty Rd., ☎ 250/721–8480). The **Pacific Opera Victoria** performs three productions a year in the 900-seat McPherson Playhouse (☒ 3 Centennial Sq., ☎ 250/386–6121), adjoining the Victoria City Hall. The **Victoria International Music Festival** (☎ 250/736–2119) showcases internationally acclaimed musicians each summer from the first week in July through late August.

The **Victoria Jazz Society** (☎ 250/388–4423) organizes an annual JazzFest International in late June, which in the past has featured such jazz, blues, and world-beat artists as Dizzy Gillespie, Frank Morgan, and Ellis Marsalis. For listings of clubs and restaurants featuring jazz during the year, call **Jazz Hotline** (☎ 250/658–5255).

THEATER

Live productions can be seen at the **Belfry Theatre** (☒ 1291 Gladstone Ave., ☎ 250/385–6815), the **Phoenix Theatre** (☒ Finnerty Rd., ☎ 250/ 721–8000) at the University of Victoria, **Langham Court Theatre** (☒ 805 Langham Ct., ☎ 250/384–2142), and **McPherson Playhouse** (☒ 3 Centennial Sq., ☎ 250/386–6121).

Nightlife

In addition to live music, darts, and brewery tours, **Spinnakers Brew Pub** (☒ 308 Catherine St., ☎ 250/386–2739) pours plenty of British Columbian microbrewery beer. **Harpo's** (☒ 15 Bastion Sq., ☎ 250/385– 5333) has live rock, blues, and jazz, with visits from internationally recognized bands. For dancing, head to **Sweetwater's** (☒ 27-560 Johnson St., ☎ 250/383–7844), where a younger crowd moves on two dance floors to taped techno and Top 40.

Outdoor Activities and Sports

Golf

Although **Victoria Golf Club** (☒ 1110 Beach Dr., ☎ 250/598–4321) is private, it's open to other private-club members; the windy course is the oldest (built in 1893) in British Columbia and has spectacular views. The **Cordova Bay Golf Course** (⊠ 5333 Cordova Bay Rd., ☎ 250/658–4444), Victoria's newest public course, is an 18-hole, par-72 course set on the shoreline. The **Olympic View Golf Club** (⊠ 643 Latoria Rd., ☎ 250/474–3673), 20 minutes from downtown, offers both challenging and forgiving tees and stunning views.

Hiking

Swan Lake Christmas Hill Nature Sanctuary, just minutes from downtown, has a 23-acre lake set in 110 acres of open fields and wetlands. From the 1½-mile chip trail and floating boardwalk, birders can spot a variety of waterfowl even in winter, as well as nesting birds in the tall grass. ⊠ 3873 Swan Lake Rd. (Bus 70 or 75), ☎ 250/479–0211. ⌑ Free. ☉ Nature House weekdays 8:30–4, weekends and holidays noon–4.

Whale-Watching

To see the pods of orcas (killer whales) that travel in the waters around Vancouver Island, you can take **charter boat tours** from Victoria from May through October. These three-hour Zodiac (motor-powered inflatable boat) excursions cost about $75 per person: **Great Pacific Adventures** (☎ 250/386–2277), **Ocean Explorations** (☎ 250/383–6722), and **Seacoast Expeditions** (☎ 250/383–2254) are the top operators. For a longer trip, contact the **Canadian Outback Adventure Company** (⊠ 1110 Hamilton St., 206, Vancouver, V62 3L6, ☎ 604/688–7206) to learn more about their week-long sea kayaking trips among the orcas in Johnstone Strait off the north coast of Vancouver Island.

Shopping

Shopping Centers

For a wide selection, head to the larger shopping centers downtown, such as **Eaton Centre** (⊠ 1 Victoria Eaton Centre, at Government and Fort Sts., ☎ 250/382–7141), a department store and mall with about 100 boutiques and restaurants. **Market Square** (⊠ 560 Johnson St., ☎ 250/386–2441) has three stories of specialty shops and offbeat stores; there's everything from fudge, music, and comic books to jewelry, local arts, and New Age accoutrements.

Specialty Stores

Shopping in Victoria is easy: Virtually everything can be found in the downtown area on or near Government Street stretching north from the Empress Hotel. **Beautiful B.C.** (⊠ 910 Government St., ☎ 250/384–7773) focuses on products produced in British Columbia, from maple syrup to original art. The **Cowichan Trading Co., Ltd.** (⊠ 1328 Government St., ☎ 250/383–0321) sells native jewelry, moccasins, and Cowichan Indian sweaters. **Hill's Indian Crafts** (⊠ 1008 Government St., ☎ 250/385–3911) has a mixture; you'll have to plow through some schlocky souvenirs to find the good-quality West Coast native art. The **House of Traditions** (⊠ 910 Government St., ☎ 250/361–3020) offers frilly lace blouses and skirts, some Victorian in fashion. As the name would suggest, **Irish Linen Stores** (⊠ 1090 Government St., ☎ 250/383–6812) stocks fine linen and lace items—hankies, napkins, tablecloths, and place mats. The high ceiling, elaborate moldings, and murals at **Munro's Books** (⊠ 1108 Government St., ☎ 250/382–2464) are worth a peek. If the British spirit of Victoria has you searching for fine teas, head to **Murchie's** (⊠ 1110 Government St., ☎ 250/383–3112) for a choice of 40 varieties, plus blended coffees, tarts, and cakes. Men's designer clothes by Ralph Lauren are available at **The Polo Store** (⊠ 1200 Government St., ☎ 250/381–7656). You'll smell the sweets well before you get to **Roger's Chocolates** (⊠ 913 Government St., ☎ 250/384–7021).

A 10-minute drive (or Bus 1 or 2) from downtown out Fort Street to Oak Bay Avenue will take you to **Oak Bay Village,** one of the few residential shopping areas that is not a mall. It's great for browsing, buying, or an afternoon cuppa. Start at the corner of Oak Bay and Foul Bay and work your way east toward the water.

ANTIQUES

At last count, Victoria had 60-plus **antiques shops** specializing in coins, stamps, estate jewelry, rare books, crystal, china, furniture, or paintings and other works of art. A short walk on Fort Street going away from the harbor will take you to Antique Row between Blanshard and Cook streets. You will also find antiques on the west side of Government Street near the Old Town.

ART GALLERIES

The **Fran Willis North Park Gallery** (⊠ 1619 Store St., ☎ 250/381–3422) is in a gorgeously restored warehouse near the waterfront; it shows contemporary paintings and sculpture by local artists. **Eagle's Moon Gallery** (⊠ 1010 Government St., ☎ 250/361–4184) showcases the totems, serigraphs, and original paintings of Tsimishian artist Roy Henry Vickers. Original art and fine Canadian crafts are the focus at the **Northern Passage Gallery** (⊠ 1020 Government St., ☎ 250/381–3380).

Side Trip from Victoria

Butchart Gardens

★ *21 km (13 mi) north of downtown Victoria.*

This impressive 50-acre garden grows more than 700 varieties of flowers and has Italian, Japanese, and English rose gardens. In summer, many of the exhibits are illuminated at night, and fireworks light the sky over the gardens every Saturday night. Also on the premises are a teahouse and restaurants. ⊠ *800 Benvenuto Ave., Brentwood Bay,* ☎ *250/652–5256 or 250/652–4422.* ⊡ *$14.50, discounts in winter.* ☉ *Call for seasonal hours.*

Victoria A to Z

Arriving and Departing

BY BOAT

There is year-round passenger service between Victoria and Seattle on jet catamarans operated by **Clipper Navigation** (☎ 250/480–5555, 800/888–2535 in the U.S.).

Washington State Ferries (☎ 250/381–1551; in the U.S., 206/464–6400) cross daily, year-round, between Sidney, just north of Victoria, and Anacortes, Washington. **Black Ball Transport** (☎ 250/386–2202; in the U.S., 206/457–4491) operates between Victoria and Port Angeles, Washington. Direct passenger and vehicle service between Seattle and Victoria is available mid-May–mid-September on the *Princess Marguerite III,* operated by **Clipper Navigation** (☞ *above*). Reservations are advised if you're traveling with a vehicle.

BY HELICOPTER

Helijet Airways (☎ 604/628–1468 or 250/382–6222) helicopter service is available from downtown Vancouver to downtown Victoria.

BY PLANE

Air B.C. (☎ 604/688–5515 or 250/360–9074; in the U.S., 800/776–3000), the major regional line, and **Horizon Air** (☎ 800/547–9308) both provide service between Seattle and Victoria airports).

Getting Around

BY BUS

The **B.C. Transit System** (☎ 250/382–6161) runs a fairly extensive service in Victoria and the surrounding areas, with an all-day pass that costs $5 for adults, $4 for students and senior citizens.

BY TAXI

Taxis are available from **Empress Taxi** (☎ 250/381–2222) and **Victoria Taxi** (☎ 250/383–7111).

Contacts and Resources

CAR RENTALS

A good local rental agent in Victoria is **ABC Rent a Car** (☎ 250/388–3153, FAX 250/388–0111).

EMERGENCIES

Dial **911.**

GUIDED TOURS

Tally-Ho Horsedrawn Tours (☎ 250/479–1113) offers a get-acquainted session with downtown Victoria that includes Beacon Hill Park. **Victoria Carriage Tours** (☎ 250/383–2207) has horse-drawn tours of the city. From April through September it's possible to tour downtown Victoria by pedicab; contact **Kabuki Kabs** (☎ 250/385–4243). The best way to see the sights of the Inner Harbour is by **Harbour Gondola** (☎ 250/480–8841), complete with an authentically garbed gondolier to narrate the tour. **Gray Line** (☎ 250/388–5248) offers city tours on double-decker buses that visit the city center, Chinatown, Antique Row, Oak Bay, and Beacon Hill Park; a combination tour stops at Butchart Gardens as well. History buffs may want to look into Victoria's background on the intriguing guided cemetery tours put together by the **Old Cemeteries Society** (☎ 250/598–8870).

HOSPITAL

Victoria General Hospital (⊠ 35 Helmcken Rd., ☎ 250/727–4212).

LATE-NIGHT PHARMACY

McGill and Orme Pharmacies (⊠ 649 Fort St., ☎ 250/384–1195).

LODGING RESERVATION SERVICE

Discover B.C. (☎ 800/663–6000), funded by the tourism ministry, is available year-round to assist with visitor information and reservations.

VISITOR INFORMATION

For Victoria, contact **Tourism Victoria** (⊠ 812 Wharf St., V8W 1T3, ☎ 250/953–2033, FAX 250/382–6539).

VANCOUVER ISLAND

The largest island on Canada's west coast, Vancouver Island stretches 450 km (279 mi) from Victoria in the south to Cape Scott in the north. Some 97% of the island's population of 684,000 live between Victoria and Campbell River (halfway up the island); 50% live in Victoria itself. A ridge of mountains crowns the island's center, providing opportunities for skiing, climbing, and hiking. Thick conifer forests blanket it down to soft, sandy beaches on the eastern shoreline and rocky, wave-pounded grottoes and inlets along the western shore.

The western side is wild, often inhospitable, with just a handful of small settlements. Nevertheless, the west coast is invaded every summer by fishermen, kayakers, scuba divers, and hikers. The west-coast towns of Ucluelet and Tofino are the whale-watching capitals of Canada, if not of the whole west coast of North America. The two towns are quite different in character, though both are relaxed in winter and swell to several times their sizes in summer. Virtually all of the island's permanent human habitation is on the eastern coast, where the weather is gentler and the topography is low-lying.

The cultural heritage of the island is from the Kwakiutl, Nootka, and Coastal Salish native groups. Native art and cultural centers flourish throughout the region, especially in the lower end of the island, enabling you to catch a glimpse of contemporary native culture.

Mining, logging, and tourism are the important island industries. Environmental issues, such as the logging practices of British Columbia's lumber companies, are becoming important to islanders—both native and nonnative. Residents are working to establish a balance between the island's wilderness and its economy.

Sooke

⑭ *42 km (26 mi) west of Victoria on Hwy. 14.*

Sooke is a logging, fishing, and farming community. **East Sooke Park,** on the east side of the harbor, has 350 acres of beaches, hiking trails, and wildflower-dotted meadows. You can also visit the **Sooke Regional Museum and Travel Infocentre,** where displays of Salish and Nootka crafts and artifacts from 19th-century Sooke occasionally compete with barbecued salmon and strawberry shortcake on the front lawn in summer. ⊠ *2070 Phillips Rd., Box 774, V0S 1N0,* ☎ *250/642–6351,* FAX *250/642–7089.* 🖼 *Donations accepted.* ☉ *June–Aug., daily 9–6; Sept.–May, Tues.–Sun. 9–5.*

Dining and Lodging

$ ✕ **Seventeen Mile House.** Stop here on the road between Sooke and Victoria for British pub fare, a beer, or fresh local seafood. Built as a hotel, the house is a study in turn-of-the-century island architecture. ⊠ *5121 Sooke Rd.,* ☎ *250/642–5942. MC, V.*

$$$$ ✕🖼 **Sooke Harbour House.** This oceanfront 1931 clapboard farmhouse-
★ turned–country inn has three suites, a 10-room addition, and a dining room—all of which exude elegance. The restaurant is one of the finest in British Columbia: The seafood is just-caught fresh, and the herbs are grown on the property. Four chefs in the kitchen guarantee an abundance of creative dishes. In the romantic guest rooms, natural wood and white finishes add to each unit's unique theme. Rooms range from the Herb Garden Room—decorated in shades of mint, with French doors opening onto a private patio—to the Longhouse Room, complete with Native American furnishings. Breakfast and lunch are included in room rates. At press time an additional 10 rooms were slated to be added by winter 1998. ⊠ *1528 Whiffen Spit Rd., R.R. 4, V0S 1N0,* ☎ *250/642–3421 or 250/642–4944,* FAX *250/642–6988. 13 rooms. Restaurant, no-smoking rooms, beach, meeting room. AE, MC, V.*

$$–$$$ ✕🖼 **Ocean Wilderness.** A large 1940s log cabin sits on 5 forested, beach-front acres, 13 km (8 mi) west of Sooke. Auction-buff owner Marion Rolston built a rough cedar addition in 1990 and has furnished her home with Victorian antiques. Romantic canopies and ruffled linens on high beds dominate the spacious guest rooms, which have sitting areas with views of either the Strait of Juan de Fuca or the pretty gardens in the back, as well as private decks or patios. The dining room fare is innovative West Coast treatments of fresh local fish and meats. ⊠ *109 W. Coast Rd., R.R. 2, V0S 1N0,* ☎ FAX *250/646–2116. 9 rooms. Dining room, no-smoking rooms, hot tub, hiking. MC, V.*

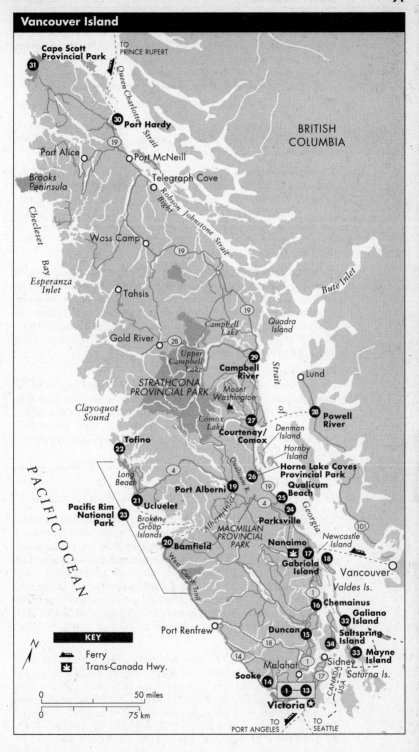

Vancouver Island

TO PRINCE RUPERT

31 Cape Scott Provincial Park

BRITISH COLUMBIA

30 Port Hardy

Port Alice

Port McNeill

Brooks Peninsula

Telegraph Cove

Checleset Bay

Woss Camp

Esperanza Inlet

Tahsis

Bute Inlet

Gold River

Campbell Lake

Quadra Island

Upper Campbell Lake

STRATHCONA PROVINCIAL PARK

29 Campbell River

Lund

Mount Washington

Clayoquot Sound

Comox Lake

28 Powell River

27 Courtenay/Comox

Denman Island

22 Tofino

Hornby Island

Long Beach

Horne Lake Caves Provincial Park

26

Qualicum Beach

21 Ucluelet

Port Alberni 19

19

25

Pacific Rim National Park 23

Broken Group Islands

24 Parksville

MACMILLAN PROVINCIAL PARK

20 Bamfield

Newcastle Island

Nanaimo

17

Gabriola Island

18

Vancouver

Valdes Is.

West Coast Trail

16 Chemainus

Galiano Island 32

Duncan 15

Saltspring Island

34

Mayne Island 33

Port Renfrew

Malahat

Sidney

Saturna Is.

KEY

Ferry

Trans-Canada Hwy.

Sooke 14

1 — 13

0   50 miles

0   75 km

Victoria

TO PORT ANGELES

TO SEATTLE

Shopping

Watercolor artist and author **Sue Coleman** (☎ 250/478–0380) in Metchosin, 35 minutes west of Victoria on the road to Sooke, invites visitors to the island to tour her studio by appointment.

Duncan

⑮ *60 km (37 mi) north of Victoria on the Trans-Canada Hwy. (Hwy. 1).*

Duncan is nicknamed City of Totems for the many totem poles that dot the small community. The two carvings behind the City Hall are worth a short trip off the main road.

The **Native Heritage Centre** covers 13 acres on the banks of the Cowichan River. The center includes a native longhouse, a theater, occasional interpretive dance presentations, an arts-and-crafts gallery that focuses on carvings and weaving traditions, and native fare served in the Bighouse Restaurant. ⊠ *200 Cowichan Way,* ☎ *250/746–8119,* FAX *250/746–4143.* ☎ *$8.* ☉ *Mid-May–mid-Oct., daily 9:30–5:30; mid-Oct.–mid-May, daily 10–4:30.*

The **British Columbia Forest Museum,** more a park than a museum, spans some 100 acres, combining indoor and outdoor exhibits that focus on the history of forestry in the province. You ride an original steam locomotive around the property and over an old wood trestle bridge. The exhibits show logging and milling equipment. ⊠ *Trans-Canada Hwy.,* ☎ *250/746–1251,* FAX *250/715–1113.* ☎ *$7.50.* ☉ *May–Sept., daily 9:30–6; Oct.–Apr. by appointment.*

Shopping

Duncan is the home of Cowichan wool sweaters, hand knitted by the Cowichan people. A large selection of sweaters is available from **Hills Indian Crafts** (☎ 250/746–6731) on the main highway, about 1½ km (1 mi) south of Duncan. **Modeste Wool Carding** (⊠ 2615 Modeste Rd., ☎ 250/748–8983), about a half mile off the highway, also carries a selection of handmade knitwear.

Chemainus

★ **⑯** *85 km (53 mi) north of Victoria, 27 km (17 mi) south of Nanaimo.*

Chemainus is known for the bold epic murals that decorate its townscape. Once dependent on the lumber industry, the small community began to revitalize itself in the early 1980s when its mill closed down. Since then, the town has brought in international artists to paint more than 30 murals depicting local historical events around town. Footprints on the sidewalk lead you on a self-guided tour of the murals. Restaurants, shops, tea rooms, coffee bars, art galleries, antiques dealers, and the new **Chemainus Theater** (☎ 250/246–9820 or 800/565–7738) have added to the town's growth.

Lodging

$$$ 🏠 **Little Inn on Willow.** This fairy-tale-looking little cottage, complete with gingerbread and turret, is a romantic delight. Built for two, it has a lavishly draped bed, a whirlpool tub for two, and a fireplace. The cottage is managed by the Pacific Shores Inn next door, which caters more to families, with simpler accommodations with fully equipped kitchens. ⊠ *Chemainus Rd., Box 958, V0R 1K0,* ☎ *250/246–4987,* FAX *250/246–4785. 1 cottage, 3 rooms (Pacific Shores). MC.*

Nanaimo

⑰ *110 km (68 mi) northwest of Victoria, 115 km (71 mi) southeast of Courtenay, 155 km (96 mi) southeast of Campbell River, 23 km (14 mi) on land plus 38 nautical mi west of Vancouver.*

Throughout the Nanaimo area, there are petroglyphs (rock carvings) representing humans, birds, wolves, lizards, sea monsters, and supernatural creatures. The **Nanaimo District Museum** (⊠ 100 Cameron St., ☎ 250/753–1821) will give you information about local carvings. Eight km (5 mi) south of town at **Petroglyph Provincial Park** (⊠ Hwy. 1, ☎ 250/387–5002), you can follow marked trails that begin at the parking lot to see designs carved thousands of years ago.

Dining and Lodging

$$ ★ **✕ Mahle House.** This casually elegant place serves innovative Northwest cuisine, such as braised rabbit with Dijon mustard and red wine sauce. Among the items on the regular menu are a succulent carrot and ginger soup and a catch of the day. Attention to detail, an intimate setting, and three country-style rooms make this one of the finest dining experiences in the region. ⊠ *Cedar and Heemer Rds.,* ☎ *250/722–3621. MC, V. Closed Mon. and Tues. No lunch.*

$–$$ ★ **✕ The Grotto.** A Nanaimo institution that specializes in a variety of seafood has a casual waterfront setting. Try oysters on the half shell, the spareribs, garlic prawn pasta, or the seafood platter that's big enough for two. The Kitchen Sink, a heaping bowl of clams, shrimp, and salmon steamed in white wine, herbs, and butter, is a favorite. ⊠ *1511 Stewart Ave.,* ☎ *250/753–3303. AE, MC, V. No lunch.*

$$–$$$ **✕⌂ Coast Bastion Inn Nanaimo.** This convenient hotel is downtown near the ferry terminal and train and bus stations. Rooms with balconies and modern furnishings have views of the old Hudson's Bay fort and the ocean. There's an Irish deli/pub. ⊠ *11 Bastion St., V9R 2Z9,* ☎ *250/753–6601, 800/663–1144 in the U.S.,* FAX *250/753–4155. 179 rooms. Restaurant, lounge, no-smoking rooms, room service, hot tub, sauna, exercise room, laundry service and dry cleaning, meeting rooms. AE, DC, MC, V.*

$–$$ ★ **✕⌂ Yellow Point Lodge.** Yellow Point is a very popular resort area on a spit of land 24 km (15 mi) south of Nanaimo, 13 km (8 mi) northeast of Ladysmith. Rebuilt in 1986 after a fire destroyed the original, the lodge lost almost nothing of its homey, summer-camp ambience. Nine large lodge rooms and a range of cottages all have private baths; most are available year-round. Perched on a rocky knoll overlooking the Stuart Channel are beach cabins, field cabins, and beach barracks for the hardy; these are closed mid-October to mid-April, have no running water, and share a central bathhouse. You can stroll the lodge's 178 acres, and there are canoes and kayaks for exploring the shoreline. Three full meals and snacks are included in the rate. ⊠ *3700 Yellow Point Rd., R.R. 3, Ladysmith V0R 2E0,* ☎ *250/245–7422,* FAX *250/245–7411. 50 rooms. Restaurant (for guests only), no-smoking rooms, saltwater pool, hot tub, sauna, 2 tennis courts, badminton, jogging, volleyball, boating, mountain bikes. MC, V.*

$$–$$$ **⌂ Best Western Dorchester Hotel.** Upbeat Mediterranean tones of champagne, ocher, and teal brighten the exterior of the Dorchester. Once the Nanaimo Opera House, this elegant hotel in the city center overlooking the harbor has a distinctive character, with gold knockers on each of the doors, winding hallways, and a rooftop patio. The rooms are small but exceptionally comfortable, and most have views of the harbor. ⊠ *70 Church St., V9R 5H4,* ☎ *250/754–6835 or 800/528–*

1234, FAX *250/754–2638. 65 rooms. Restaurant, lounge, no-smoking rooms, room service, library, laundry service and dry cleaning, meeting rooms. AE, D, DC, MC, V.*

Outdoor Activities and Sports

CANOEING AND KAYAKING

For multiple-day, guided sea-kayak expeditions, contact **Wild Heart Adventures** (✉ Site P, C-5, R.R. 4, Nanaimo, V9R 5X9, ☎ 250/722–3683, FAX 250/722–2175).

GOLF

Fairwinds Golf and Country Club (✉ 3730 Fairwinds Dr., Nanoose Bay, ☎ 250/468–7666 or 800/663–7060).

Gabriola Island

⑱ *3½ nautical mi (20-min ferry ride) east of Nanaimo.*

From rustic, rural Gabriola Island, which has lodging, you can take a further 10-minute ferry ride to **Newcastle Island,** where you can picnic, ride your bicycle, walk on trails leading past old mines and quarries, and catch glimpses of deer, rabbits, and eagles.

Port Alberni

⑲ *80 km (50 mi) west of Nanaimo, 195 km (121 mi) northwest of Victoria.*

Port Alberni is mainly a pulp- and sawmill town and a stopover on the way to Ucluelet and Tofino on the west coast. The salmon-rich waters attract fishermen. From here, you can take a breathtaking trip to towns along the Alberni Inlet and Barkley Sound aboard the *Lady Rose,* a Scottish ship built in 1937. ✉ *Argyle St. dock,* ☎ *250/723–8313, 800/663–7192 reservations Apr.–Sept.* ✉ *Bamfield $36, Broken Group Islands $38, Ucluelet $40.* ☉ *Sailings daily 8* AM.

Bamfield

⑳ *100 km (62 mi) southwest of Port Alberni.*

In Bamfield, a remote village of about 200, the seaside boardwalk affords an uninterrupted view of ships heading up the inlet to Port Alberni. The town is well equipped to handle overnight visitors. Bamfield is also a good base for boating trips to the Broken Group Islands and hikes along the West Coast Trail (☞ Pacific Rim National Park, *below*).

Ucluelet

㉑ *100 km (62 mi) west of Port Alberni, 295 km (183 mi) northwest of Victoria.*

Ucluelet, which in the native language means "people with a safe landing place," is totally focused on the sea. Fishing, water tours, and whale-watching are the primary activities. A variety of charter companies (☞ Contacts and Resources *in* British Columbia A to Z, *below*) take boats to greet the 20,000 gray whales that pass close to Ucluelet on their migration to the Bering Sea every March through May. Sometimes you can even see the migrating whales from the Ucluelet shore.

Dining and Lodging

$$ ✕ **Whale's Tale.** At this no-frills, dark but warmly decorated down-to-earth place, the cooking and the rustic decor go hand in hand. The view isn't much, and the cedar-shingle building, set on pilings, shakes with a good gust of wind. The menu is highlighted by prime rib and a variety of local seafood. ⊠ *1861 Peninsula Rd.,* ☎ *250/726–4621. MC, V. Closed Nov.–Jan. No lunch.*

$$ ✕ **Wickaninnish Restaurant.** Before the Canadian government ac-
★ quired this wonderful wood building for an interpretive center for Pa-
cific Rim National Park, it was a unique inn. It's still a restaurant, and
the beach setting, combined with the building's glass exterior and
stone-and-beam interior, gives the Wickaninnish an ambience that
cannot be matched anywhere else in the area. Seafood is the primary
choice here, especially the West Coast chowder, but if you order the
vegetable or vegetable-seafood stir-fry, you won't be disappointed. ⊠
Long Beach, 16 km (10 mi) north of Ucluelet, ☎ *250/726–7706. AE,
MC, V. Closed mid-Oct.–mid-Feb.*

$$–$$$ 🏨 **Canadian Princess Fishing Resort.** If vintage ships are to your lik-
ing, book a cabin on this converted 230-foot steam-powered survey
ship, which has 36 comfortable, but hardly opulent, staterooms. Each
offers one to four berths, and all share washrooms. Roomier than the
ship cabins, the resort's deluxe shoreside rooms come complete with
more contemporary furnishings; a few have fireplaces. This unique resort provides the bare necessities—mostly to nature enthusiasts and fishermen. ⊠ *Boat Basin, Box 939, V0R 3A0,* ☎ *250/726–7771 or
800/663–7090,* ℻ *250/726–7121. 46 shoreside and 30 shipboard sleeping units. 2 bars, dining room, no-smoking rooms, boating, fishing.
AE, DC, MC, V.*

Whale-Watching
Subtidal Adventures (☎ 250/726–7336) runs trips in the area.

Tofino

㉒ *42 km (26 mi) northwest of Ucluelet, 337 km (209 mi) northwest of
Victoria, 130 km (81 mi) west of Port Alberni.*

The town of Tofino is commercial, with beachfront resorts, motels, and
several unique B&Bs. The surrounding area remains natural; you can
walk along the beach discovering caves, cruise around the ancient
forests of Meares Island, or take an hour-long water taxi ride to the
hot springs north of town.

Dining and Lodging

$$$$ ✕🏨 **The Wickaninnish Inn.** Set on a rocky promontory above Chesterman Beach, this country inn is surrounded by water on three sides, with
old-growth forest as a backdrop. Every spacious room has an ocean
view and its own balcony, fireplace, and soaker tub; the forest green
and beige colors of the decor were taken from the natural surroundings. Local artisans have contributed hand-adzed cedar timbers, driftwood accent furniture, and a bounty of artwork. Chef Rodney Butters
serves up coastal food at the inn's Pointe Restaurant. An exclusively
West Coast wine list complements mussels, clams, and scallops in
Rainforest Ale broth; wild mushroom terrine; steamed Dungeness
crab; or savory crusted wild boar. ⊠ *Osprey La. at Chesterman Beach,
Box 250, V0R 2Z0,* ☎ *250/725–3100 or 800/333–4604,* ℻ *250/725–
3110. 46 rooms, 1 suite. Restaurant, minibars, no-smoking rooms, beach.
AE, DC, MC, V.*

$$$–$$$$ 🏨 **Pacific Sands Beach Resort.** Just a mile north of Pacific Rim National
Park, this beachside resort has motel suites and individual two-bed-
room cottages, each with a beautiful bay view. The motel rooms have
modern furnishings, and fireplaces make them seem cozy. Some of the
specialty suites in the three-story addition have hot tubs outside on the
deck. Dangerous currents and riptides off the beach in front of the re-

sort make it unsuitable for swimming. ⊠ *1421 Pacific Rim Hwy., Box 237, V0R 2Z0,* ☎ *250/725–3322 or 800/565–2322,* FAX *250/725–3155. 54 rooms, 10 cottages. Kitchenettes, no-smoking rooms, beach, coin laundry. AE, MC, V.*

$$–$$$ 🏠 **Chesterman Beach Bed and Breakfast.** This small, romantic bed-
★   and-breakfast on the beach has rolling ocean surf for a front yard. You can walk the beach, search the tidal pools, or—from March through October—watch whales migrate. The self-contained suite in the main house (complete with sauna and full kitchen) and the separate Look-out Suite are romantic and cozy; both have a fireplace, comfortable beds, and a view of the beach. The self-sufficient one-bedroom garden cottage offers no ocean view but accommodates up to four; it's a good option for a family vacation. ⊠ *1345 Chesterman Beach Rd., V0R 2Z0,* ☎ FAX *250/725–3726. 4 rooms, 1 cottage. Beach, no-smoking rooms, kitchenettes, refrigerators. MC, V.*

Outdoor Activities and Sports

CANOEING AND KAYAKING

You can rent canoes and kayaks from **Tofino Sea-Kayaking Company** (⊠ Box 620, V0N 3J0, ☎ 250/928–3117 or 250/725–4222).

GOLF

Long Beach Golf Course (⊠ Pacific Rim Hwy., ☎ 250/725–3332).

WHALE-WATCHING

A number of operators have trips, including **Weigh West Marine Resort** (☎ 250/725–3277), **Sea Trek Tours & Expeditions** (☎ 250/725–4412), **Chinook Charters** (☎ 250/725–3431), and **Remote Passage Whale Watching** (☎ 250/725–3330).

Pacific Rim National Park

★ ㉓   *85 km (53 mi) west of Port Alberni.*

The first national marine park in Canada, Pacific Rim National Park (⊠ Box 280, Ucluelet V0R 3A0, ☎ 250/726–7721, FAX 250/726–4720) comprises three separate areas—Long Beach, the Broken Group Islands, and the West Coast Trail for a combined area of 49,962 hectares (20,243 acres). Each section accommodates a specific interest.

The **Long Beach** unit gets its name from an 11-km (7-mi) strip of hard-packed white sand strewn with twisted driftwood, shells, and the occasional Japanese glass fishing float. It is a favorite spot in summer, and you often have to fight heavy traffic along the twisting Highway 4 from Port Alberni.

The 100 **Broken Group Islands** can be reached only by boat. Many commercial charter tours are available from Ucluelet, at the southern end of Long Beach, and from Bamfield and Port Alberni. The islands and their waters are alive with sea lions, seals, and whales. The sheltered lagoons of Gibraltar, Jacques, and Hand islands offer protection and good boating conditions, but go with a guide.

The third element of the park, the **West Coast Trail,** stretches along the coast from Bamfield to Port Renfrew. After the S.S. *Valencia* ran aground in 1906, killing all but 30 of the crew and passengers, the Canadian government constructed the lifesaving trail to help future victims of shipwrecks reach safe ground. The path remains, with demanding bogs, steep slopes and gullies, cliffs (with ladders), slippery boardwalks, and insects. The rewards of a hike here are the panoramic views of the sea, the dense rain forest, sandstone cliffs with waterfalls, and wildlife that includes gray whales and seals.

The extremely rugged 77-km (48-mi) trail is for experienced hikers. It can be traveled only on foot, takes an average of six days to complete, and is open from May to late September. A permit is necessary to hike this trail; reservations by phone (☎ 800/663–6000) are available from March through September.

En Route Heading back to the east coast from Port Alberni, stop off at **Cathedral Grove** in MacMillan Provincial Park on Highway 4. Walking trails lead you past Douglas fir trees and western red cedars, some as much as 800 years old. Their remarkable height creates a spiritual effect, as though you were gazing at a cathedral ceiling. Another stop along the way is **Butterfly World** (⊠ Hwy. 4, ☎ 250/248–7026) in Coombs, an enclosed tropical garden housing an amazing collection of exotic, free-flying tropical butterflies.

Parksville

㉔ *38 km (24 mi) northwest of Nanaimo, 47 km (29 mi) east of Port Alberni, 72 km (45 mi) southeast of Courtenay, 154 km (95 mi) north of Victoria.*

Parksville is one of the east island's primary resort areas, where lodges and waterfront motels cater to families, campers, and boaters. In **Rathtrevor Provincial Park** (⊠ Off Hwy. 19, ☎ 250/248–9449), 1½ km (about 1 mi) south of Parksville, high tide brings ashore the warmest ocean water in British Columbia, so plan to swim here.

North Island Wildlife Recovery Association's Museum of Nature (1240 Leffler Rd., Errington, ☎ 250/248–8534) showcases the wildlife typical of Vancouver Island. The recovery center houses injured, ill, or orphaned wildlife (primarily birds such as owls, hawks, and eagles) and the largest flight cage in Canada (bald eagles are readied for release here). Errington is a short drive east of Parksville and about a 10-minute drive west of Nanoose Bay.

Lodging

$$–$$$ 🏨 **EcoMed.** Dr. Stefan Kuprowsky ran a successful naturopathic clinic
★ in Vancouver for 10 years before he opened this spa in Nanoose Bay, a few miles southeast of Parksville. EcoMed is in a beautiful spot overlooking Craig Bay (one of the island's warmest swimming bays), adjacent to a bird sanctuary and a nature reserve. You can choose the "bed and healthy breakfast" or select from the extensive spa and natural healing treatments. The suite is an apartment with kitchen, two fireplaces, and a whirlpool bath; the other two rooms are more standard hotel style, in soothing pastel shades. Creative vegetarian meals are a feast for the eyes and the palate. Come to this no-smoking retreat for revitalization. ⊠ *Pacific Shores Nature Resort #515, 1655 Strougler, R.R. 1, Box 50, Nanoose Bay V0R 2R0,* ☎ *250/468–7133,* ℻ *250/468–7135. 3 units. Indoor pool, hot tub, sauna, spa, canoe, kayak, mountain bikes. MC, V.*

$$ 🏨 **Holiday Inn Express.** About a block from the pretty beach in Parksville, this hotel opened in 1994. Kids under 19 stay free with their parents in the motel-modern rooms outfitted with two queen-size beds. King-size rooms have whirlpool tubs. ⊠ *424 W. Island Hwy., V9P 1K8,* ☎ *250/248–2232 or 800/661–3110,* ℻ *250/248–3273. 87 rooms, 3 suites. No-smoking rooms, indoor pool, hot tub, exercise room. AE, DC, MC, V.*

$ 🏨 **Roadhouse Inn.** This small Swiss-style chalet, set on 3 acres, is central to four of the region's golf courses. The rooms, on the second floor, are comfortable, with basic furnishings. ⊠ *1223 Smithers Rd., V9P 2C1,* ☎ *250/248–2912. 6 rooms. Restaurant. MC, V.*

Golf

Morningstar Golf Course (⊠ 525 Lowery Rd., Parksville, ☎ 250/248–8161).

Qualicum Beach

㉕ *10 km (6 mi) north of Parksville.*

Qualicum Beach is known largely for its salmon fishing and opportunities for beachcombing. The nonprofit **Old School House Gallery and Art Centre** (⊠ 122 Fern Rd. W, ☎ 250/752–6133), with seven working studios, shows and sells the work of local artists and artisans.

Horne Lake Caves Provincial Park

㉖ *25 km (16 mi) north of Parksville, then 15 km (9 mi) west off Hwy. 19.*

At Horne Lake you'll find Horne Lake Caves Provincial Park. Three of the six caves are open at all times. If you decide to venture in, bring along a flashlight, warm clothes, and a hard hat, and be prepared to bend and even crawl. Riverbend Cave, 1,260 feet long, requires ladders and ropes in some parts, and can be explored only with a guided tour. Spelunking lessons and tours are offered for all levels, from beginner to advanced. Make reservations for tours. ⊠ *Off Hwy. 19,* ☎ *250/248–7829.* ⬛ *Tour fee varies depending on participants' ability.*

En Route Between the Horne Lake turnoff and the twin cities of Courtenay and Comox is tiny Buckley Bay, where ferries leave for **Denman Island,** with connecting service to **Hornby Island.** Denman offers old-growth forests and long sandy beaches, while Hornby's spectacular beaches have earned it the nickname the Undiscovered Hawaii of British Columbia. Many artists have settled on the islands, establishing studios for pottery, jewelry, wood carving, and sculpture.

Courtenay and Comox

㉗ *220 km (136 mi) northwest of Victoria, 17 nautical mi west of Powell River, 46 km (29 mi) southeast of Campbell River; Comox is 6 km (4 mi) east of Courtenay.*

Courtenay and Comox are commercial towns that also provide a base for Mt. Washington and Forbidden Plateau skiers; Courtenay is the larger of the two. You can also hike along the beach north of here. A ferry from Comox goes to Powell River (☞ *below* and Getting Around *in* British Columbia A to Z).

Dining and Lodging

$$ ✕ **Old House Restaurant.** This bilevel restaurant offers casual dining
★ in a restored 1938 house with large cedar beams and a stone fireplace. People flock here for the West Coast homestyle cuisine—pastas, salads, and sandwiches, along with fancier, more innovative dishes (rack of lamb, panfried flounder, California cioppino)—on the fresh-daily sheet. ⊠ *1760 Riverside La., Courtenay,* ☎ *250/338–5406. AE, DC, MC, V.*

$$ ▦ **Kingfisher Oceanside Inn.** Ten minutes south of Courtenay, this Quality Inn hotel stands among trees and overlooks the Strait of Georgia. Solid furnishings, white stucco walls, a bright lobby with lots of greenery, and rooms with mountain and ocean views make this place special. There's also an RV park. ⊠ *4330 S. Island Hwy., Site 672, R.R. 6, Courtenay V9N 8H9,* ☎ *250/338–1323,* ℻ *250/338–0058. 30 units. Restaurant, lounge, pool, tennis court. AE, D, DC, MC, V.*

$ 🏠 **Greystone Manor.** A no-smoking bed-and-breakfast, set in a 1918 house with period furnishings, looks out on Comox Harbor, where a colony of seals is often visible. The antiques, woodstove, and wood paneling add to the hospitable, cozy feel. Breakfast, which includes fresh fruit, muffins, and fruit pancakes, can keep you filled most of the day. You can walk in the English garden and on trails nearby. ⊠ *4014 Haas Rd., Site 684–C2, R.R. 6, Courtenay V9N 8H9,* ☎ *250/338–1422. 3 rooms. Breakfast room, no-smoking rooms, hiking. MC, V.*

Skiing

Mt. Washington Ski Resort Ltd. (⊠ Box 3069, Courtenay V9N 5N3, ☎ 250/338–1386), with nearly 22 downhill runs and an elevation of 5,200 feet, is the largest ski area on the island, and the third-largest in terms of visitors in the province. The resort also has 29 km (18 mi) of double track–set cross-country trails. It's a modern, well-organized mountain with snowpack averaging 472 inches a year. **Forbidden Plateau** (⊠ Box 3268, Courtenay V9N 5N4, ☎ 250/334–4744), near Mt. Washington, has 15 runs and a vertical drop of 1,150 feet.

Powell River

㉘ *17 nautical mi (75-minute ferry ride) east across Strait of Georgia from Comox, 121 km (75 mi) plus 12.5 nautical mi northwest of Vancouver.*

Powell River was established around the MacMillan pulp-and-paper mill, which opened in 1912. The forestry industry continues to have a strong presence in this area. Renowned as a year-round salmon-fishing destination, the mainland Sunshine Coast town has 30 regional lakes that offer exceptional trout fishing. The town has a few bed-and-breakfasts and restaurants, as well as a park with oceanfront camping. A 60-km (37-mi) canoeing circuit, the **Powell Forest Canoe Route,** can be accessed here. For information, contact the **Powell River Visitor Information Centre** (⊠ 4690 Marine Ave., ☎ 250/485–4701).

Campbell River

㉙ *155 km (96 mi) northwest of Nanaimo, 270 km (167 mi) northwest of Victoria.*

Campbell River draws people who want to fish; some of the biggest salmon ever caught on a line have been landed just off the coast here. You can try for membership in the Tyee Club, which would allow you to fish in a specific area and possibly land a giant chinook. Requirements include registering and landing a tyee (a spring salmon weighing 30 pounds or more). Coho salmon and cutthroat trout are also plentiful in the river.

There are other recreational activities here. The primary access to Strathcona Provincial Park (☞ *below*) is on Highway 28 west from town. You can also arrange to dive in Discovery Passage, where an artificial reef has been sunk; kayak; or take a summer whale-watching tour. For information, contact **Campbell River Visitor Information Centre** (⊠ 1235 Shoppers Row, Box 482, V9W 5B6, ☎ 250/287–4636, FAX 250/286–6490).

Dining and Lodging

$–$$ ✕ **Royal Coachman Inn.** Informal, blackboard-menu restaurants like
★ this one dot the landscape of the island. The menu, which changes daily, is surprisingly daring for what is essentially a high-end pub, and the inn draws crowds nightly, especially on Tuesday and Saturday (prime rib nights). Come early for both lunch and dinner to avoid a wait. ⊠ *84 Dogwood St.,* ☎ *250/286–0231. AE, MC, V.*

$$–$$$ ✕⊡ **April Point Lodge and Fishing Resort.** This popular 1944 cedar lodge
★   is surrounded by refurbished fishermen's cabins and guest houses that
spread across a point of Quadra Island and stretch into Discovery Passage across from Campbell River. Most of the comfortable accommodations are tidy and have kitchen facilities, fireplaces, and sundecks. Kwakiutl and Haida art adorns the lounge and dining room, where fine regional cuisine is served. In summer you can dine on spitted salmon roasted over an open fire and fresh steamed scallops, prawns, and clams. ✉ *1000 April Point Rd., Box 1, V9W 4Z9,* ☎ *250/285–2222,* FAX *250/285–2411. 39 units. 2 bars, breakfast room, coffee shop, dining room, lobby lounge, picnic area, sushi bar, no-smoking rooms, saltwater pool, exercise room, hiking, scuba diving, dock, snorkeling, fishing, bicycles, piano, baby-sitting, coin laundry, laundry service, business services, meeting rooms, airport shuttle, helipad. AE, D, DC, MC, V. Some units closed Nov.–Mar.*

$$–$$$ ⊡ **Tsa-Kwa-Luten Lodge.** Operated by members of the Kwakiutl tribe,
this resort offers authentic Pacific Coast native food and cultural activities. It stands on a high bluff amid 1,100 acres of forest on Quadra Island, a 10-minute ferry ride from Campbell River. Each room in the main lodge has a sea view; many have a fireplace and loft. Four beachfront cabins have fireplaces, whirlpool tubs, kitchen facilities, private verandas, and two to four bedrooms. You can take part in traditional dances in the lounge, which resembles a longhouse, and visit nearby petroglyphs. ✉ *Lighthouse Rd., Box 460, Quathiaski Cove V0P 1N0,* ☎ *250/285–2042 or 800/665–7745,* FAX *250/285–2532. 36 units. Dining room, lounge, no-smoking rooms, room service, hot tub, sauna, exercise room, fishing, mountain bikes, laundry service, business services, meeting rooms. AE, DC, MC, V.*

Outdoor Activities and Sports

CANOEING AND KAYAKING

Island Sauvage (✉ R.R. 1, Sayward V0P 1R0, ☎ 250/282–3644 or 800/667–4354, FAX 250/287–8840) specializes in guided sea kayaking but does have canoes and kayaks for rent.

GOLF

Storey Creek Golf Club (✉ Box 727, Campbell River, ☎ 250/923–3673).

HIKING

Island Sauvage (✉ R.R. 1, Sayward V0P 1R0, ☎ 250/282–3644 or 800/667–4354, FAX 250/287–8840) can arrange heli-hiking.

Strathcona Provincial Park

40 km (25 mi) west of Campbell River.

Strathcona Provincial Park (☎ 250/387–5002), the largest provincial park on Vancouver Island, encompasses **Mt. Golden Hinde,** at 7,220 feet the island's highest mountain; and **Della Falls,** Canada's highest waterfall, reaching 1,440 feet. This wilderness park's multitude of lakes and 161 campsites attract summer canoeists, hikers, fishermen, and campers. The main access is by Highway 28 from Campbell River; Mt. Washington and Forbidden Plateau can be reached by roads out of Courtenay.

The **Strathcona Park Lodge and Outdoor Education Center,** well known for its wilderness-skills programs, has information on the park's facilities. It also has a variety of accommodations. ✉ *Education Center, Hwy. 28, Upper Campbell Lake, about 45 km (28 mi) west of Hwy. 19, Box 2160, Campbell River V9W 5C9,* ☎ *250/286–3122.* ☉ *Call for hours.*

Johnstone Strait

East side of Vancouver Island, roughly between Campbell River and Telegraph Cove.

Pods of resident orcas (killer whales) live year-round in the Inside Passage and around Vancouver Island; in **Robson Bight** they like rubbing against the beaches. Whales are most often seen during the salmon runs of the summer and fall. Because of their presence, Robson Bight has been made into an ecological preserve: Whales there must not be disturbed by human observers. Some of the island's best whale-watching tours, however, are conducted nearby, out of **Telegraph Cove**, a village built on pilings over water.

Outdoor Activities and Sports

CANOEING AND KAYAKING

In Telegraph Cove, you can rent canoes and kayaks from **North Island Boat, Canoe, and Kayak** (☎ 250/949–7707).

WHALE-WATCHING

Most trips run between June and October; call ahead to check.

Half-day whale-watching expeditions are available through **Stubbs Island Whale Watching** (☎ 250/928–3185) on the west coast of Johnstone Strait. **Seasmoke Tours** (☎ 250/974–5225), in Alert Bay on the east coast, has half-day tours.

Contact **Island Sauvage** (✉ R.R. 1, Sayward V0P 1R0, ☎ 250/282–3644 or 800/667–4354, FAX 250/287–8840) or the **Canadian Outback Adventure Company** (✉ 206–1110 Hamilton St., Vancouver, ☎ 250/688–7206) to learn more about their weeklong sea kayaking trips among the orcas in the strait.

Port Hardy

30 *238 km (148 mi) northwest of Campbell River, 499 km (309 mi) northwest of Victoria, 274 nautical mi southeast of Prince Rupert.*

Port Hardy is the departure and arrival point for B.C. Ferries (☞ Getting Around *in* British Columbia A to Z, *below*) going through the scenic Inside Passage to and from Prince Rupert, the coastal port serving the Queen Charlotte Islands. B.C. Ferries has also added a "Discovery Coast Passage" route out of Port Hardy that travels to Bella Coola and other small communities along the scenic mid-coast. In summer the town can be crowded, so book your accommodations early. Ferry reservations for the trip between Port Hardy and Prince Rupert and Port Hardy and Bella Coola should also be made well in advance.

Lodging

$ 🏨 **Glen Lyon Inn.** The rooms have a full ocean view of Hardy Bay and, like most area motels, have clean, modern amenities. Eagles can often be spotted eyeing the water for fish to prey on. The inn is a short ride from the ferry terminal. You can arrange fishing charters here. ✉ 6435 Hardy Bay Rd., Box 103, V0N 2P0, ☎ 250/949–7115, FAX 250/949–7415. 29 rooms. Restaurant, lounge, no-smoking rooms. AE, D, DC, MC, V.

Cape Scott

60 km (37 mi) northwest of Port Hardy on logging roads.

31 The northernmost part of Vancouver Island is Cape Scott. **Cape Scott Provincial Park** (☎ 250/954–4600 or 250/387–5002), a wilderness camping region, is designed for well-equipped and experienced hikers.

At Sand Neck, a strip of land that joins the cape to the mainland of the island, you can see both the eastern and the western shores at once.

THE GULF ISLANDS

Traveling up the northeastern coastline of Vancouver Island in the late 1790s, Captain George Vancouver dubbed the expansive body of water on which he sailed the Gulf of Georgia, thinking that it led to open sea. While the name of the waterway was later changed to the Strait of Georgia when further exploration revealed that the British Columbia mainland lay to the east, the islands dotting the strait continue to be known as the Gulf Islands.

Of the hundreds of islands in this strait, the most popular are Galiano, Mayne, North and South Pender, Saturna, and Saltspring. A temperate Mediterranean climate (warmer, with half the rainfall of Vancouver), scenic beaches, towering promontories, rolling pasturelands, and virgin forests are common to all, but each has its unique flavor. Marine birds are numerous, and unusual vegetation such as arbutus trees (also known as madrones, a leafy evergreen with red peeling bark) and Garry oaks differentiate the islands from other areas around Vancouver. Writers, artists, craftspeople, weekend cottagers, and retirees take full advantage of the undeveloped islands.

For a first visit to the Gulf Islands, make a stopover on Saltspring Island, the most commercialized of the southern islands, or on more subdued, pastoral Mayne Island. Outdoors enthusiasts will find much to their liking on Galiano, which is far less developed than other Gulf Islands. Their proximity to Vancouver makes each of these islands feasible for a one- or two-day trip. Free maps are available on the ferry or in island stores.

Galiano Island

㉜ *20 nautical mi (almost 2 hours by ferry due to interisland stops) from Swartz Bay (32 km, or 20 mi, north of Victoria), 13 nautical mi (a 50-minute ferry ride) from Tsawwassen (39 km, or 24 mi, south of Vancouver).*

The activities on Galiano Island are almost exclusively of the outdoor type. The long, unbroken eastern shoreline is perfect for leisurely beach walks, while the numerous coves and inlets along the western coast make it a prime area for kayaking. Miles of trails through Douglas fir forest beg for exploration by foot or bike. Hikers can climb to the top of **Mt. Galiano** for a view of the Olympic Mountains in Washington or trek the length of **Bodega Ridge**. The best spots to view Active Pass and the surrounding islands are Bluffs Park, Bellhouse Park, and Centennial Park; these are also good areas for picnicking and bird-watching.

Biological studies show that the straits between Vancouver Island and the mainland of British Columbia are home to the largest variety of marine life in North American. The frigid waters offer superb visibility, especially in winter. Acala Point, **Porlier Pass,** and Active Pass are top locations for scuba diving. Fisherman head to the point at **Bellhouse Park** to spin cast for salmon from shore, or head by boat to Porlier Pass and **Trincomali Channel.**

Lodging

$$$ 🏠 **Woodstone Country Inn.** This serene, no-smoking inn sits on the edge of a forest overlooking a meadow that's fantastic for bird-watching. Stenciled walls and tall windows bring the pastoral setting into spacious bedrooms furnished in a mixture of wicker, antiques, and

English country prints. Most of the rooms have fireplaces and patios, and a few have oversize soaker tubs. A hearty gourmet breakfast is included in the cost. Guests and nonguests can have four-course dinners here by advance reservation. ✉ *Georgeson Bay Rd., R.R. 1, V0N 1P0,* ☎ *250/539–2022 or 250/539–5198. 12 rooms. AE, MC, V.*

$ 🔟 **Sutil Lodge.** Family photos from the 1920s and heavy Art Deco furnishings re-create a sense of lodge life in an earlier era at a 1927 British Colonial bungalow set on 20 wooded acres on picturesque Montague Bay. The simple guest rooms have throw rugs on dark hardwood floors and beds tucked into window nooks; the shared bathrooms have antique ball-foot tubs and small corner sinks. Nature-watching and picnic cruises by kayak and sailboat can be arranged. The kayak center on the property attracts folks from around the world who want to paddle the still coves of the Gulf Islands (rentals and guided trips are available). Breakfast is included in the rate. ✉ *637 Southwind Rd., Montague Harbour V0N 1P0,* ☎ *250/539–2930,* FAX *250/539–5390. 7 rooms share 3 baths. Dining room, hiking. MC, V.*

Outdoor Activities and Sports

BIKING

There are miles of trails to explore, and biking is a fun way to do it. Bike rentals are available from **Galiano Bicycle** (☎ 250/539–9906).

DIVING

For **dive charters** on Galiano, contact Martin Karakas (☎ 250/539–5186) or George Parson (☎ 250/539–3109).

FISHING

Mel-n-i Fishing Charters (☎ 250/539–3171) is one of the primary fishing operators on the island. **Bert's Charters** (☎ 250/539–3109) runs fishing charters.

GOLF

The **Galiano Golf Course** (☎ 250/539–5533) is a pleasant nine-hole course in a forest clearing. It's fairly flat and moderate in difficulty.

KAYAKING

The kayaking around Galiano Island is world-class. For equipment rentals and guided kayak tours, contact **Gulf Islands Kayaking** (☎ 250/539–2442). **Canadian Gulf Islands Seakayaking** (☎ 250/539–2930) has rentals and tours.

Mayne Island

③③ *28 nautical mi from Swartz Bay (32 km, or 20 mi, north of Victoria), 22 nautical mi from Tsawwassen (39 km, or 24 mi, south of Vancouver).*

Middens of clam and oyster shells give evidence that tiny Mayne Island—only 21 square km (8 square mi)—was inhabited as early as 5,000 years ago. It later became the stopover point for miners headed from Victoria to the gold fields of Fraser River and Barkersville, and by the mid-1800s had developed into the communal center of the inhabited Gulf Islands, with the first school, post office, police lockup, church, and hotel. Farm tracts and orchards established in the 1930s and 1940s and worked by Japanese farmers until their internment during World War II continue to thrive today, and a farmer's market is open each Saturday during harvest season. There are few stores, restaurants, or historic sites here, but Mayne's manageable size (even if you're on a bicycle) and slower pace make it very popular.

Starting at the ferry dock at **Village Bay**, head toward Miners Bay on Village Bay Road. About a half mile from the ferry landing on the left is the unmarked path to **Helen Point** (pull off on the shoulder near the grouping of power lines that cross the road), previously a native reservation, which currently has no inhabitants. You'll pass middens by the bay and log cabin remains in the woods on the hour-long hike out to Helen Point, where you can look out across Active Pass (named for the turbulent waters).

A quarter mile farther on the right side of Village Bay Road is the entrance to **Mount Parke,** declared a wilderness park in 1989. Drive as far as the gate and the sign that reads NO VEHICLES PAST THIS POINT. From here it's a 15- to 20-minute hike to the highest point on the island and a stunning, almost 360-degree view of Vancouver, Active Pass, and Vancouver Island.

Continue on Village Bay Road toward **Miners Bay,** a little town 2 km (1 mi) away. Here, you'll find Plumbers Pass Lockup (closed September–June), built in 1896 as a jail and now a minuscule museum chronicling the island's history.

From Miners Bay head east on Georgia Point Road to **St. Mary Magdalene Church,** a pretty stone chapel built in 1898 that now doubles as an Anglican and United church. The graveyard beyond is also interesting; generations of islanders—the Bennets, Georgesons, Maudes, and Deacons (whose names are all over the Mayne Island map)—are buried here. Across the road, a stairway leads down to the beach.

At the end of Georgia Point Road is the **Active Pass Lighthouse,** built in 1855, which still signals ships into the busy waterway. The grassy grounds, open to the public every day from 1 to 3, are great for picnicking.

Head Back down Georgia Point Road and turn left on Waugh Road, which turns into Campbell Bay Road. There's a great pebble beach for beachcombing at shallow (and therefore warmer) **Campbell Bay.** Look for a pull-out on the left just past the bottom of the hairpin turn. A fencepost marks the entrance to the path leading to the beach. Campbell Bay Road ends at Fernhill Road; turn right here and you'll end up back in Miners Bay.

Dining and Lodging

$$$–$$$$ ✕⌂ **Oceanwood Country Inn.** This Tudor-style house on 10 quiet,
★ forested acres overlooking Navy Channel has English country decor throughout. Fireplaces, ocean-view balconies, and whirlpool or soaking tubs make several rooms deluxe; all are inviting, with cozy down comforters on comfortable beds, cheerful wall stenciling, and cushioned chairs in brightly lit reading areas. For dinner, the waterfront dining room, which is open to the public, serves outstanding regional cuisine. You may find grilled salmon, tomato and Dungeness crab soup, or wild mushroom and goat cheese ravioli on the prix-fixe, fresh-daily menu. Afternoon tea and breakfast are included in the room rates. ✉ *630 Dinner Bay Rd., V0N 2J0,* ☎ *250/539–5074,* 𝖥𝖠𝖷 *250/539–3002. 12 rooms. Restaurant, no-smoking rooms, hot tub, sauna, hiking, jogging, beach, bicycles, library, meeting room. MC, V.*

$$–$$$ ✕⌂ **Fernhill Lodge.** Constructed of wood from the property, this 1983 West Coast cedar contemporary has fantastical theme rooms—Moroccan, East Indian, Edwardian, Japanese, Colonial, Jacobean, and French. Two of them have outdoor hot tubs. On the 5-acre grounds are a rustic gazebo with a meditation loft, an Elizabethan knot garden, and a medieval "garden of physic." Hosts Mary and Brian Crumblehulme offer historical dinners (Rome, Chaucer, and Cleopatra, to name a few themes) several nights a week; nonguests must reserve in advance. Breakfasts, included in the room rate, are rather less exotic. This is a no-smoking inn, and pets are not allowed. ✉ *Fernhill Rd.,*

R.R. 1 C-4, V0N 2J0, ☎ 250/539–2544. 7 rooms. Dining room, no-smoking rooms, sauna, bicycles, library. MC, V.

Saltspring Island

③④ *28 nautical mi from Swartz Bay (32 km, or 20 mi, north of Victoria), 22 nautical mi from Tsawwassen (39 km, or 24 mi, south of Vancouver).*

Named for the saltwater springs at its north end, Saltspring is the largest and most developed of the Gulf Islands. Among its first nonnative settlers were black Americans who came here to escape slavery in the 1850s. The agrarian tradition they and other immigrants established remains strong, but tourism and art now support the local economy. A government wharf, two marinas, and a waterfront shopping complex at Ganges serve a community of more than 8,500 residents.

In **Ganges,** a pedestrian-oriented seaside village and the island's cultural and commercial center, you'll find dozens of smart boutiques, galleries, and restaurants. Mouat's Trading Company (Fulford–Ganges Road), built in 1912 and still functioning as a community store, is worth a peek. Ganges is also the site of **ArtCraft,** a summer-long art, crafts, theater, music, and dance festival. Dozens of working **artists' studios** are open to the public here; pick up a studio tour map at the Chamber of Commerce on Lower Ganges Road.

From Ganges, you can circle the northern tip of the island by bike or car (on Vesuvius Bay Road, Sunset Road, North End and North Beach Roads, Walker Hook Road, and Robson Road) past fields and peek-a-boo marine views. You can take a shortcut on North End Road past **St. Mary Lake,** your best bet for warm-water swimming.

Near the center of Saltspring, the summit of **Mt. Maxwell Provincial Park** (⊠ Mt. Maxwell Rd., off Fulford–Ganges Rd.) affords spectacular views of south Saltspring, Vancouver Island, and other Gulf Islands. It's also a great picnic spot. The last portion of the drive is steep, winding, and unpaved.

From Mt. Maxwell, follow Fulford–Ganges Road south, then turn east on Beaver Point Road to reach **Ruckle Provincial Park,** site of an 1872 heritage homestead and extensive fields still being farmed by the Ruckle family. The park also has camping and picnic spots and trails leading to rocky headlands.

Dining and Lodging

$$ ✕ **House Piccolo.** Blue and white tablecloths and framed pastel prints on whitewashed walls give this cozy restaurant a casual feel. Broiled sea scallop brochette, roasted British Columbia venison with juniper berries, and the salmon du jour are good choices from the dinner menu, but save room for homemade ice cream or the signature chocolate terrine. ⊠ *108 Hereford Ave., Ganges, ☎ 250/537–1844. Reservations essential. AE, DC, MC, V. Closed Jan. No lunch.*

$–$$ ✕ **Pomodori.** This local favorite is set in a heritage farmhouse warmed
★ by wood-burning fireplaces and overlooking Chemainus across the water. Earthenware pots with dried flowers, antique farm implements, battered wooden tables, bent willow chairs, and international folk music set an eclectic tone for an eatery with a unique menu that changes daily. Roasted tomato, red pepper, and Italian feta in balsamic-vinegar and olive-oil dressing with home-baked focaccia for dipping; chicken, prawn, and mussel jambalaya; and fresh vegetable and herb stew appear often. ⊠ *Booth Bay Resort, 375 Baker Rd., Ganges, ☎ 250/537–2247. Reservations essential. MC, V. No lunch Mon.–Sat.*

\$\$\$\$ ✕⊞ **Hastings House.** Guests are nicely pampered at Hastings House.
★ The centerpiece of this luxurious 30-acre seaside farm estate is a Tudor-style manor built in 1940. Guest quarters are in the manor or the farmhouse, in cliffside or garden cottages, and in lovely suites in the reconstructed barn. All are furnished with fine antiques in an English country theme, with such extras as eiderdowns, fireplaces, and covered porches or decks. Elegant dinners in the manor house are formal and open to the public: The prix-fixe menu may include grilled eggplant with goat cheese, plum tomato and roasted garlic soup, peppered sea bass on wilted spinach with nasturtium butter, and Saltspring lamb loin with rosemary. ⊠ *160 Upper Ganges Rd., Box 1110, Ganges, V0S 1E0,* ☎ *250/537–2362 or 800/661–9255,* FAX *250/537–5333. 3 rooms, 7 suites, 2 2-bedroom suites. Restaurant, minibars, no-smoking rooms, beach, croquet, mountain bikes. AE, MC, V. Closed Jan.–mid-Mar.*

\$\$\$ ⊞ **Beach House on Sunset.** The sunsets over Stuart Channel and Vancouver Island are stunning from this West Coast contemporary house set on a sloping beach. Two upstairs rooms in the bed-and-breakfast have private entrances and balconies; a romantic, cedar-lined cottage with wraparound porch sits over the boathouse at water's edge. There's also a suite with cathedral ceiling, broad windows framing lovely sea views, and a private deck with outdoor shower. Extras include eiderdown comforters, thick terry robes, slippers, fruit platters, decanters of sherry, fresh flowers, and a bountiful breakfast. You can also arrange boat charters and kayak tours. ⊠ *930 Sunset Dr., V8K 1E6,* ☎ *250/537–2879,* FAX *250/537–4747. 4 rooms. Library. MC, V. Closed Dec.–Feb.*

\$\$\$ ⊞ **Old Farmhouse Bed and Breakfast.** Gerti Fuss operates this delightful bed-and-breakfast with the assistance of her husband, Karl. Their gray-and-white saltbox farmhouse sits in a quiet meadow edged by towering trees. The style of the main house, a registered historic property built in 1895, is echoed in the four-room wing added by Karl in 1989, which has country-comfortable guest rooms furnished with pine bedsteads, down comforters, lace curtains, and wicker chairs. Breakfast in the dining room begins with Gerti's fresh-daily baked goods, followed by a hot entrée such as smoked salmon soufflé. ⊠ *1077 Northend Rd., V8K 1L9,* ☎ *250/537–4113,* FAX *250/537–4969. 4 rooms. Breakfast room, no-smoking rooms, boating. MC, V.*

\$\$\$ ⊞ **Salty Springs Resort.** Perched on a 50-foot bluff on the northern shore of Saltspring, this is the only property to take advantage of the island's natural mineral springs. The one-, two-, and three-bedroom Ponderosa pine cabins have Gothic arch ceilings, fireplaces, kitchenettes, and whirlpool massage bathtubs that tap into the mineral springs. Outside are flower boxes, gas grills, picnic tables, and unobstructed ocean or forest views. ⊠ *1460 N. Beach Rd., V8K 1J4,* ☎ *250/537–4111,* FAX *250/537–2939. 12 units. Picnic areas, kitchenettes, refrigerators, boating, bicycles, recreation room, coin laundry. MC, V.*

Shopping

There are bargains galore at Saltspring Island's **Saturday markets,** held each year from April through October. Fresh produce, seafood, crafts, clothing, herbs and aromatherapy mixtures, candles, toys, home-canned items, and more are available at two markets; one is at the top of the hill (next to the Harbour House) overlooking Ganges Harbour, the other in the center of town between Fulford–Ganges Road and Centennial Park.

NORTH OF VANCOUVER ISLAND

Gateway to Alaska and the Yukon, this vast, rugged region is marked by soaring, snowcapped mountain ranges, scenic fjords, primordial islands, and towering rain forests. Once the center of a vast trading network, the "North by Northwest Region" is home to First Nations (native) people who have lived here for 10,000 years and more recent immigrants drawn by the natural resources of fur, fish, and forest. You can explore the ancient native villages of the Queen Charlotte Islands and Hazelton, fish for rainbow trout or giant halibut, and tour cities such as Prince Rupert and Prince George, which grew out of important fur trading posts.

Inside Passage

★ ㉟ *507 km (314 mi), or 274 nautical miles, between Port Hardy on northern Vancouver Island and Prince Rupert.*

The Inside Passage, a sheltered marine highway, follows a series of natural channels behind protective islands along the green-and-blue shaded British Columbia coast. The undisturbed landscape of rising mountains and humpbacked islands has a striking, prehistoric look. You can take a ferry cruise along the Inside Passage or see it on one of the more expensive luxury liners that sail along the British Columbia coast from Vancouver to Alaska.

The comfortable ferry **Queen of the North,** carrying up to 800 passengers and 157 vehicles, takes 15 hours (almost all in daylight during summer sailings) to make the Port Hardy to Prince Rupert trip. Reservations are required for the cruise and advised for hotel accommodations at ports of call. ⊠ *B.C. Ferries, 1112 Fort St., Victoria V8V 4V2,* ☎ *250/386–3431 or 604/669–1211.* 🖃 *Cost varies according to cabin, vehicle, and season.* ☉ *Sailings Oct.–Apr., once weekly; May, twice weekly; June–Sept., daily, departing on alternate days from Port Hardy and Prince Rupert; departure time 7:30 AM, arrival time 10:30 PM; call to verify schedule.*

Prince Rupert

㊱ *1,502 km (931 mi) by highway and 750 km (465 mi) by air northwest of Vancouver; 15 hours by ferry northwest of Port Hardy on Vancouver Island.*

Prince Rupert, the final stop on the B.C. Ferries route through the Inside Passage, has a mild but wet climate, so take rain gear. The town lives off fishing, fish processing, logging, saw- and pulp-mill operations, deep-sea shipping, and tourism.

The **Museum of Northern British Columbia** has one of the province's finest collections of coastal native art, some artifacts dating back 10,000 years. Native artisans work on totem poles in the carving shed and, in summer, the museum runs a 2½-hour boat tour of the harbor and Metlakatla native village. ⊠ *1st Ave. and McBride St.,* ☎ *250/624–3207.* 🖃 *Donations accepted.* ☉ *Sept.–May, Mon.–Sat. 10–5; June–Aug., Mon–Sat. 9–9, Sun. 9–5.*

The **North Pacific Cannery Village Museum** in Port Edward, 20 km (12 mi) south of Prince Rupert, is the oldest salmon cannery on the West Coast. You can step back in time here, touring the cannery buildings, mess hall, company store, and managers' houses, where interpretive displays about the canning process and cannery village life are set up.

✉ *1889 Skeena Dr., Port Edward, V0E 1G0,* ☎ *250/628–3538.* 🖭
$5. ☉ *May–Sept., daily 10–7; Oct.–Apr., Wed.–Sun. 10–4.*

Dining and Lodging

$$$ ✕🏨 **Crest Motor Hotel.** Warm and modern, the Crest is a block from
★ the two shopping centers but stands on a bluff overlooking the har-
bor. Some rooms have minibars and whirlpool tubs. The restaurant,
pleasantly decorated with brass rails and beam ceilings, has a water-
front view and specializes in seafood; particularly outstanding are the
salmon dishes. ✉ *222 1st Ave. W, V8J 3P6,* ☎ *250/624–6771 or
800/663–8150,* 🄵🄰🄷 *250/627–7666. 102 rooms. Restaurant, coffee
shop, lounge, in-room modem lines, no-smoking floor, room service,
outdoor hot tub, steam room, exercise room, fishing, baby-sitting, dry
cleaning, business services, meeting rooms. AE, D, DC, MC, V.*

$$ 🏨 **Best Western Highliner Inn.** This modern high rise near the waterfront is conveniently situated and relatively well priced. It's in the
heart of the downtown shopping district only one block from the airline terminal building. Ask for a room with a private balcony and view
of the harbor. ✉ *815 1st Ave. W, V8J 1B3,* ☎ *250/624–9060 or
800/668–3115,* 🄵🄰🄷 *250/627–7759. 93 rooms. Restaurant, lounge,
beauty salon, coin laundry. AE, DC, MC, V.*

Shopping

Native art and other local crafts are for sale at **Studio 9** (✉ 516 3rd
Ave. W, ☎ 250/624–2366).

Queen Charlotte Islands

★ ㊲ *93 nautical mi southwest of Prince Rupert, 367 nautical mi northwest
of Port Hardy.*

An increasingly popular vacation destination, the beautiful Queen Charlotte Islands, or Misty Islands, were once the remote preserve of the Haida
natives; now they are easily accessible by ferry. Today the Haida make
up only one-sixth of the population, but they continue to infuse the island with a sense of the Haida past and contribute to the logging and
fishing industries, as well as to tourism. Haida elders lead tours—an
essential service if you want to reach the isolated, abandoned villages.

In the Queen Charlottes, 150 km (93 mi) of paved road, most of it on
Graham Island (the northernmost and largest of the group of 150), connect Queen Charlotte city in the south to Masset in the north. Some
of the other islands are laced with gravel roads. The rugged, rocky west
coast of the archipelago faces the ocean; the east coast has many broad
sandy beaches. The incredible scenery makes the islands an artisans'
delight, and kayaking enthusiasts from around the world are drawn
to waterways here. Throughout, the mountains and shores are often
shrouded in fog and rain-laden clouds, adding to the islands' mystery.

Naikoon Provincial Park (☎ 250/557–4390), in the northeast corner
of Graham, preserves a large section of unique wilderness, where low-
lying swamps, pine and cedar forests, lakes, beaches, trails, and wildlife
combine to create an intriguing environment. Take the 5-km (3-mi) walk
from the Tlell Picnic Site to the beach, and on to the bow section of
the old wooden shipwreck of the *Pezuta,* a 1928 log-hauling vessel.

On the southern end of Graham Island, the **Queen Charlotte Islands Museum** has an impressive display of Haida totem poles, masks, and carvings of both silver and argillite (hard black slate). A natural history exhibit
gives interesting background on the wildlife of the islands. ✉ *Box*

1373, Skidegate V0T 1S1, ☎ 250/559–4643. ✉ $2.50. ☉ Apr.–Oct., weekdays 9–5, weekends 1–5; Nov.–Mar., Wed.–Sun. 1–5.

The **Ed Jones Haida Museum,** in Old Masset on the northern coast of Graham Island, exhibits totems and artifacts. Nearby, artists sell their work from their homes. South of Graham, in and around **South Moresby National Park Reserve,** lie most of the better-known abandoned Haida villages, which are accessible by water. Several days' travel time and careful planning for wilderness conditions are required to see some of the villages. Visitors must arrange their trips through Parks Canada (☎ 250/559–8818).

Dining and Lodging

There are many small bed-and-breakfasts and inns in the islands; contact the **Queen Charlotte Islands Travel Infocentre** (✉ 3922 Hwy. 33, Box 819, Queen Charlotte V0T 1S0, ☎ 250/559–4742, FAX 250/559–8188) for a list.

$$ ⊡ **Alaska View Lodge.** On a clear day, you can see the mountains of Alaska from the porch of this bed-and-breakfast. A long stretch of sandy beach borders the lodge on one side and woods on the other. With advance notice and at an additional cost, the owner makes a three-course dinner, using classical recipes based on Queen Charlotte fare, such as home-smoked salmon, scallops, and Dungeness crab. ✉ *Tow Hill Rd., Box 227, Masset V0T 1M0,* ☎ *250/626–3333, 800/661–0019 in Canada,* FAX *250/626–3858. 4 rooms. Dining room, no-smoking rooms. MC, V.*

$$ ⊡ **Spruce Point Lodge.** This cedar-sided building, encircled by a balcony, attracts families and couples because of its low rates and down-home feel. Like most Queen Charlotte accommodations, the Spruce Point tends to the rustic and has locally made pine furnishings. For the rate you get a Continental breakfast and an occasional seafood barbecue, with a menu that depends on the daily catch. Bunk rooms are usually available at a low nightly rate. ✉ *609 6th Ave., Queen Charlotte V0T 1S0,* ☎ FAX *250/559–8234. 7 rooms. Breakfast room, boating, fishing. MC, V.*

Kayaking

Ecosummer Expeditions (✉ 1516 Duranleau St., Vancouver V6H 3S4, ☎ 604/669–7741 or 800/465–8884, FAX 604/669–3244) has multiday guided kayak tours. **Queen Charlotte Adventures** (✉ Box 196, Queen Charlotte V0T 1S0, ☎ 250/559–8990 or 800/668–4288, FAX 250/559–8983) offers multiday guided tours around the islands. For kayak equipment rentals, contact **Moresby Explorers** (✉ Box 109, Sandspit V0T 1T0, ☎ 800/806–7633, FAX 250/637–2215).

Shopping

The Haida of the region carve valuable figurines from a variety of hard, black slate called argillite that is found only on the islands. Other island specialties are silk-screen prints and silver jewelry. Haida works are sold at the **Adams Family House of Silver** (☎ 250/626–3215), in Old Masset, behind the Ed Jones Haida Museum. **Joy's Island Jewellers** (☎ 250/559–4742) in Queen Charlotte carries a good selection of Haida art.

En Route To see interior British Columbia, take Highway 16 east from Prince Rupert. On the way you'll pass through or near such communities as **Terrace,** with a hot-springs complex at the Mt. Layton Resort, skiing at Shames Mountain, and excellent fishing in the Skeena River. At **Kitimat** (Highway 37, south of Terrace), at the head of the Douglas Channel, the fishing is superb.

Hazelton

38 *293 km (182 mi) northeast of Prince Rupert, 439 km (272 mi) northwest of Prince George, 1,217 km (755 mi) northwest of Vancouver.*

★ Hazelton is rich in the culture of the Gitksan and Wet'suwet'en peoples. **'Ksan,** just outside town, is a re-created Gitksan village. The elaborately painted community of seven longhouses is a replica of the one that stood on the same site when the first European explorers arrived in the 19th century. The carving shed, often used by 'Ksan artists, is open to the public, and three other longhouses can be visited: One displays contemporary masks and robes, another has song-and-dance dramas in the summer, and the third exhibits pre-European tools of bone, sinew, stone, and wood. ✉ *Box 326, V0J 1Y0,* ☎ *250/842–5544.* 🎟 *$8.* ⊙ *Apr.–Sept., daily 9–6; Oct.–Mar., Thurs.–Mon. 9–5; tour May–mid-Oct., on the hour.*

The **'Ksan Museum** displays works and artifacts from the Upper Skeena River region as well as modern-day regalia kept at the museum by local natives. ✉ *Box 333, V0J 1Y0,* ☎ *250/842–5723.* 🎟 *Donation.* ⊙ *Mid-Apr.–Sept., daily.*

Prince George

39 *721 km (447 mi) east of Prince Rupert, 786 km (487 mi) north of Vancouver.*

At the crossroads of two railways and two highways, Prince George has grown to become the capital of northern British Columbia and the third-largest city in the province. Nestled on the edge of a vast forested plateau, it has an economy fueled by forest industries, from tree farms to logging to lumber and paper processing. **Canadian Forest Products Ltd.** (☎ 250/561–3947) provides free tours of the area's pulp and sawmills.

In Ft. George Park, you can visit the **Fraser–Ft. George Regional Museum** to see the fine collection of artifacts illustrating local history. ✉ *333 20th Ave.,* ☎ *250/562–1612.* 🎟 *$3.* ⊙ *May–Sept., daily 9–5; Sept.–Apr., Tues.–Sun. noon–5.*

A collection of photos, rail cars, and logging and sawmilling equipment at the **Central BC Railway and Forest Industry Museum** traces the town's origin to the building of the railway and the development of logging. ✉ *150 River Rd.,* ☎ *250/563–7351.* 🎟 *$4.* ⊙ *May–Sept., Thurs.–Mon. 9–5.*

The **Prince George Native Art Gallery** has traditional and contemporary works (carvings, sculpture, jewelry, literature) by the region's native peoples. ✉ *144 George. St., V2L 1P9,* ☎ *250/562–7385.* 🎟 *Free.* ⊙ *June–Sept., daily 9–5; Oct.–May, Tues.–Sat. 9–5.*

Gold Rush Trail

Begins at Prince George and ends at Lilloet, 170 km (105 mi) west of Kamloops, 131 km (81 mi) northeast of Whistler.

From Prince George you can turn south on Highway 97 toward Kamloops and the Okanagan Valley, following the 640-km (397-mi) Gold Rush Trail, along which frontiersmen traveled in search of gold in the 19th and early 20th centuries. It takes you through Quesnel, Williams Lake, Wells, and Barkerville and along the Fraser Canyon and Cache Creek. Most towns and communities through which the trail passes have re-created villages, history museums, or historic sites that help to tell the story of the gold-rush era. For more information contact the **Cariboo Chilcotin Coast Tourist Association** (✉ Box 4900, Williams Lake

V2G 2V8, ☎ 250/392–2226; in the U.S., 800/663–5885; FAX 250/392–2838). Another source of information is **Heritage Attractions of British Columbia** (✉ Ministry of Small Business, Tourism, and Culture, 800 Johnson St., Victoria V8V 1X4, ☎ 250/387–5129).

HIGH COUNTRY AND ENVIRONS
Including Okanagan Valley and Southwestern British Columbia

Diversity of setting differentiates High Country from the other regions of British Columbia. This roughly triangular territory, stretching from Valemount in the north just past Revelstoke in the southeast to Merritt, farther south and west, presents a spectacular array of scenery, from deep canyons carved by the Thompson and Fraser rivers to the towering ranges of the Rockies, Monashees, and Selkirks. Skiing, white-water rafting, heli-skiing, and other challenging outdoor activities can be a focus of any High Country tour. If you were driving here from Prince George, you could continue on Highway 16 to Highway 5 for a spectacular drive through High Country to Kamloops.

The Okanagan Valley region, four hours east of Vancouver by car, or one hour by air, is part of a highland plateau between the Cascade range of mountains on the west and the lower Monashees on the east. Though small in size (only 3% of the province's total land mass), the area contains the interior's largest concentration of people. Dominating the valley is Okanagan Lake, a vacation magnet for visitors from both the west coast and Alberta. In summer, rooms can be scarce here. The largest towns along the lake, bordered by Highway 97—Vernon at the north end, Kelowna in the middle, and Penticton to the south—are actually one large unit. Okanagan Lake is their glue, offering recreation, lodging, and restaurants. Between these towns, and along the lake, are the recreational and resort communities of Summerland, Peachland, Westbank, and Oyama, which are popular destinations and have camping facilities, motels, and cabins. The valley is the fruit-growing capital of Canada, producing apricots, pears, cherries, plums, apples, grapes, and peaches, plus clouds of fragrant blossoms from mid-April through early June.

Kamloops

40 *355 km (220 mi) northeast of Vancouver, 163 km (101 mi) northwest of Kelowna.*

Kamloops is a convenient passageway into the Okanagan Valley from Fraser Canyon and Thompson Valley, and a stop on the Canadian Pacific Railroad. The town is surrounded by 500 lakes, which provide an abundance of trout, Dolly Varden, and kokanee. In late September and October, however, attention turns to the sockeye salmon, when thousands of these fish, intent on breeding, return home to the waters where they were spawned, in the Adams River (65 km, or 40 mi, east of Kamloops off the Trans-Canada Highway).

Once every four years—the next time will be 1998—the sockeye run reaches a massive scale, as more than a million salmon pack the waters and up to 500,000 visitors come to observe. The **Roderick Haig-Brown Conservation Area,** which protects the 11-km (7-mi) stretch of Adams River, is the best vantage point; call the B.C. Parks district office (☎ 604/851–3000) for information.

The **Kamloops Wildlife Park** houses 65 species in fairly natural habitats on 55 acres. Canyon hiking trails, a miniature railway, and adjacent water slides are other attractions. ⊠ *East of Hwy. 1, Box 698, V2C 5L7,* ☎ *250/573–3262.* 🎫 *$6.50.* ☉ *Call for seasonal hours.*

Dining and Lodging

$$ ✕🏨 **Lac le Jeune Resort.** With miles of hiking trails, a lake stocked with trout, and a restaurant that serves robust helpings, this resort lets you enjoy the outdoors. The rustic, self-sufficient cabins have ample space and amenities for families, and pets are permitted. In the large, comfortable rooms in the main lodge, no phones or televisions distract from the beauty of the setting. ⊠ *Off Coquihala Hwy., 29 km (18 mi) southwest of Kamloops, Box 3215, Kamloops V2C 6B8,* ☎ *250/372–2722 or 800/561–5253,* FAX *250/372–8755. 28 rooms, 4-plex chalet, 6 cabins. Restaurant, lounge, no-smoking rooms, sauna, boating, fishing, cross-country skiing, theater, meeting room. AE, D, DC, MC, V. Closed Oct.–Apr.*

$–$$ ✕🏨 **Corbett Lake Country Inn.** The inn's single (with extra beds) and
★ duplex cabins are comfortable and basic, as are rooms in the main lodge. Every night the restaurant presents a different fixed menu; favorites include rack of lamb and chateaubriand. Fly-fishing for rainbow trout on the private lake is a big attraction here, and no fishing license is required. Small pets are allowed. The inn is in Merritt, 20 km (12 miles) south of Kamloops. ⊠ *Off Hwy. 5A, Box 327, Merritt V0K 2B0,* ☎ *250/378–4334. 3 rooms, 10 cabins. Restaurant, boating, fishing. V. Closed mid-Jan.–Apr. and Nov.–Dec. 23.*

Outdoor Activities and Sports

CANOEING AND KAYAKING

Okanagan Canoe Holidays (⊠ R.R. 1, 2910 N. Glenmore Rd., Kelowna V1V 2B6, ☎ FAX 250/762–8156) runs day trips on over a dozen rivers in the region.

GOLF

Rivershore Golf Club (⊠ Off Old Shuswap Rd., ☎ 250/573–4211), a Robert Trent Jones–designed course, is one of British Columbia's longest, at 7,007 yards. At press time, nine of 18 holes at the new **Sun Peaks Resort Golf Course** (☎ 250/578–5431) were open; the other nine were well under way.

RAFTING

One regional operator is **Mount Robson Adventure Holidays** (⊠ Box 687, Valemount V0E 2Z0, ☎ 250/566–4386, FAX 250/566–4351). **Fraser River Raft Expeditions Ltd.** (⊠ Box 10, Yale V0K 2S0, ☎ 250/863–2336; in Canada, 800/363–7238; FAX 250/863–2355) has rafting trips in the area.

SKIING

With 2,844 feet of vertical drop, **Sun Peaks Resort** (⊠ Box 869, Kamloops V2C 5M8, ☎ 250/578–7222 or 800/807–3257, FAX 250/578–7223) has 58 runs.

For High Country heli-skiing, contact **Mike Wiegle Helicopter Skiing** (⊠ Box 159, Blue River V0E 1J0, ☎ 250/762–5846 or 800/661–9170, FAX 250/673–8464), **Cat Powder Skiing** (⊠ Box 1479, Revelstoke V0E 5S0, ☎ 250/837–5151).

Vernon

🄴🄸 *117 km (73 mi) southeast of Kamloops.*

The main businesses in Vernon are forestry and agriculture. The town borders on two other lakes besides Okanagan, the more enticing of which is Kalamalka Lake. Vernon is also the town closest to the ski area and gaslight-era-theme village resort atop Silver Star Mountain.

Kalamalka Lake Provincial Park (☎ 250/387–5002) has warm-water beaches and some of the most scenic viewpoints and hiking trails in the region.

★ North of Vernon, the **O'Keefe Historic Ranch** gives you a window on cattle-ranch life at the turn of the century. The late-19th-century Victorian mansion is opulently furnished with original antiques. On the 50 acres are a Chinese cooks' house, St. Anne's Church, a blacksmith shop, a reconstructed general store, a display of the old Shuswap and Okanagan Railroad, and a modern restaurant and gift shop. Stagecoach rides are available. ⊠ *9830 Hwy. 97, 12 km (7 mi) north of Vernon,* ☎ *250/542–7868.* ▣ *$5.* ⊙ *Mid-May–mid-Oct., daily 9–5.*

Dining and Lodging

$$ ✕ **Craigellachie Dining Room.** The home-cooked meals in the dining room of the Putnam Station Hotel are filling rather than fancy. Soups and sandwiches are on the lunch menu, while old favorites like barbecue ribs, lasagna, pork chops, steaks, and pastas are offered in the evenings. The daily three-course special is generally a good deal. ⊠ *Silver Star Mountain Resort,* ☎ *250/542–2459. Reservations essential. AE, MC, V.*

$$–$$$ ✕▥ **Swiss Hotel Silver Lode Inn.** Owner Isidore Borgeaud serves hearty helpings of real raclette or fondue in her cheerful Silver Lode Restaurant. The inn's no-frills rooms offering the basic comforts are the most reasonably priced in the village; some rooms have kitchenettes. ⊠ *Silver Star Mountain Resort, Box 5, Silver Star Mountain BC V0E 1G0,* ☎ *250/549–5105, ℻ 250/549–2163. 20 rooms. Restaurant, bar, lobby lounge, indoor pool, hot tub, bicycles, ski storage, meeting room. AE, MC, V.*

$$$ ▥ **Vance Creek Hotel.** Looking more like the set of a spaghetti West-
★ ern than a modern hotel, the Vance Creek has a prime location in the heart of the resort. Rooms are simple, with coordinated decor and boxy bathrooms. Those on the first floor are equipped with kitchenettes, bunk beds, and private outside entrances. Willow furniture and fireplaces add a touch more comfort to suites in the 1993 annex. ⊠ *Silver Star Mountain Resort, Box 3002, Silver Star Mountain V0E 1G0,* ☎ *250/ 549–5191, ℻ 250/549–5177. 84 rooms. Bar, dining room, lobby lounge, kitchenettes, no-smoking rooms, refrigerators, bicycles, cross-country and downhill skiing, ski storage, coin laundry, meeting rooms. AE, D, MC, V. Closed mid-Apr.–mid-May.*

Outdoor Activities and Sports

GOLF

Predator Ridge Golf Resort (⊠ 360 Commonage Rd., ☎ 250/542–3436).

SKIING

Silver Star Mountain Resort (⊠ Box 2, Silver Star Mountain V1B 3M1, ☎ 250/542–0224; in the U.S., 800/663–4431; ℻ 250/542–1236), near Vernon, with more than 80 runs, offers the extra bonus of well-lighted night downhill skiing.

Kelowna

🕘 *46 km (29 mi) south of Vernon, 68 km (42 mi) north of Penticton.*

Kelowna is the largest town in the Okanagan Valley and the geographic center of the valley's wine industry. For information about tours, call the individual wineries. **Calona Wines Ltd.** (⊠ 1125 Richter St., ☎ 250/762–9144) is British Columbia's oldest and largest wine maker. One of the area's more intimate wineries is **Gray Monk Estate Winery**

(✉ 1055 Camp Rd., ☎ 250/766–3168), which is 8 km, or 5 mi, west of Winfield, off Highway 97. **CedarCreek Estate Winery** (✉ 5445 Lakeshore Rd., off Hwy. 97, ☎ 250/764–8866) is 12 km, or 7 mi, south of Kelowna; it's a smaller area winery.

Father Pandosy's Mission, the first nonnative settlement in the region, was founded here in 1859. ✉ *3685 Benvoulin Rd.,* ☎ *250/860–8369.* 🖼 *Donations accepted.* ☉ *Daily 8–dusk.*

Dining and Lodging

$$–$$$ ✕ **Agapi's Greek Taverna.** This contemporary-looking restaurant has a Greek menu that lists seafood, lamb, and, of course, standards such as spanakopita, dolma, hummus, and kebabs. The wine list includes a wide selection of imported and local wines. ✉ *375 Leon Ave.,* ☎ *250/763–0997. AE, DC, MC, V.*

$$$$ 🏨 **Grand Okanagan.** On the shore of Okanagan Lake, this new resort is a five-minute stroll from the shops, theaters, and restaurants of downtown Kelowna. The spacious guest rooms in the high-rise tower have peach decor and views of the lake and surrounding mountains. Waterfront condo units have fully equipped kitchens. ✉ *1310 Water St., V1Y 9P3,* ☎ *250/763–4500 or 800/465–4651,* 𝔽𝔸𝕏 *250/763–4565. 205 rooms. Restaurant, lounge, pool, exercise room, laundry service and dry cleaning, convention center, meeting rooms, business services. AE, DC, MC, V.*

$$$ 🏨 **Hotel Eldorado.** Rebuilt in the style of the 1926-vintage Eldorado Arms, which burned down in the early 1990s, the new Eldorado has much of the original's charm intact. Rooms tend to be small and cozy, with light carpets, floral patterns, and Canadian heritage furnishings; many have balconies with views of Okanagan Lake. The dining room serves fresh rack of lamb and seafood dishes. ✉ *500 Cook Rd., V1W 3G9,* ☎ *250/763–7500,* 𝔽𝔸𝕏 *250/861–4779. 20 rooms. Restaurant, lounge, no-smoking rooms, boating. AE, DC, MC, V.*

$$$ 🏨 **Lake Okanagan Resort.** The rooms of this self-contained resort on
★   the west side of Okanagan Lake have either kitchens or kitchenettes and range in size from one-room suites in the main hotel to spacious three-room chalets spread around the 300 acres. Large rooms, functional furnishings, wood-burning fireplaces, perfect views of the lake, and all the resort activities make this a good choice. ✉ *2751 Westside Rd., V1Y 8B2,* ☎ *250/769–3511 or 800/663–3273,* 𝔽𝔸𝕏 *250/769–6665. 150 rooms. Restaurant, café, no-smoking rooms, refrigerators, 3 pools, hot tub, sauna, 9-hole golf course, exercise room, 7 tennis courts, beach, dock, bicycles, video games, children's programs (ages 6–12), playground, coin laundry, laundry service and dry cleaning, meeting rooms, helipad. AE, DC, MC, V.*

Outdoor Activities and Sports

CANOEING AND KAYAKING

Numerous waterways run through the region. For guided trips, try **Okanagan Canoe Holidays** (✉ R.R. 1, 2910 N. Glenmore Rd., V1V 2B6, ☎ 𝔽𝔸𝕏 250/762–8156).

GOLF

Gallaghers Canyon Golf and Country Club (✉ 4320 McCulloch Rd., Kelowna, ☎ 250/861–4240). **Harvest Golf Club** (✉ 2725 KLO Rd., East Kelowna, ☎ 250/862–3103).

HIKING

You can hike the rail bed of the **Kettle Valley Railway** network along Lake Okanagan between Penticton and Kelowna. The Visitors Bureau for Kelowna (☎ 250/861–1515) can provide maps and information.

Kelowna Hike-Bike-Paddle Adventures (✉ R.R. 1, 2910 N. Glenmore Rd., V1V 2B6, ☎ 𝔽𝔸𝕏 250/762–8156) can arrange guided hikes.

SKIING

Cross-Country. Postill Lake Lodge (✉ Box 854, V1Y 7P5, ☎ 250/860–1655) has excellent trails just east of Kelowna.

Downhill. Big White Ski Resort (✉ Box 2039, Station R, V1X 4K5, ☎ 250/765-3101 or 800/663-2772, 𝔽𝔸𝕏 250/765–8200) has almost 70 runs on about 12,000 acres of skiable terrain and is expanding rapidly. Night skiing is available five nights each week.

Shopping

At **Geert Maas Sculpture Gardens, Gallery, and Studio** (✉ Reynolds Rd., ☎ 250/860–7012), in the hills above Kelowna, world-class sculptor Geert Maas exhibits his distinctive bronze, stoneware, and mixed media abstract figures in an indoor gallery and a garden. He also sells medallions, original paintings, and etchings. The **Okanagan Pottery Studio** (☎ 250/767–2010), on Highway 97 in Peachland, south of Kelowna, sells handcrafted ceramics.

Penticton

㊽ *395 km (245 mi) east of Vancouver.*

Although Penticton's winter population is about 25,000, its summer population nears 130,000. Sixteen km (10 mi) north of town, you can take a ride on the historic **Kettle Valley Steam Railway** (✉ 10112 S. Victoria Rd., Summerland, ☎ 250/494–8422), reopened in 1995, which passes through 10 km (6 mi) of orchards, vineyards, and wooded mountain terrain along the 1915 line that opened up the interior of British Columbia by connecting Vancouver with the Kootenays.

The **Okanagan Game Farm** (☎ 250/497–5405), an 11-km (7-mi) drive south from Penticton on Highway 97, has more than 100 species of wild animals from around the world.

West of Penticton is British Columbia's **Kootenay Country,** named for one of the mountain ranges that fill it.

Dining and Lodging

$$–$$$ ✕ **Granny Bogner's.** The theme is determinedly homey: flowing lace
★ curtains, Oriental rugs, wood chairs, cloth-covered tables, and waitresses in long skirts. But the food at this mostly Continental restaurant is excellent. The poached halibut and roasted duck have contributed to the widely held belief that this is the best restaurant in the Okanagan. ✉ *302 Eckhardt Ave. W, ☎ 250/493–2711. Reservations essential. AE, MC, V. Closed Sun., Mon., and Jan. No lunch.*

$$$ 🏨 **Clarion Lakeside Resort and Conference Center.** On the shore of Okanagan Lake, this resort is both a peaceful retreat and right in the center of the action. Vancouver businesspeople love this place for its comfort and conference facilities. The rooms are bright and airy, and half of them have lake views; whirlpool bathtubs were added to some in 1994, and all units were redecorated in 1995. ✉ *21 Lakeshore Dr. W, V2A 7M5, ☎ 250/493–8221 or 800/663–9400, 𝔽𝔸𝕏 250/493–0607. 204 rooms. Coffee shop, dining room, outdoor café, in-room modem lines, no-smoking floor, room service, indoor pool, beauty salon, hot tub, massage, sauna, 2 tennis courts, aerobics, health club, jogging, shuffleboard, volleyball, beach, dock, bicycles, billiards, nightclub, recreation room, video games, baby-sitting, children's programs (ages 5–12), dry cleaning, concierge, business services, convention center, meeting rooms. AE, DC, MC, V.*

$ ⌕ **Riordan House.** John and Donna Ortiz didn't expect to give guided tours of their newly spiffed-up 1921 house. But people seemed to like the place, built by a Prohibition rum-runner and furnished now with family antiques, so the Ortizes bowed to the inevitable and opened it as a bed-and-breakfast. One bedroom has a fireplace and one a sitting area; all look out on the surrounding hills. The Continental breakfast stars home-baked croissants, scones, muffins, and a selection of seasonal fruit; box lunches are packed on request. ⊠ *689 Winnipeg St., V2A 5N1, ☎ FAX 250/493–5997. 3 rooms share 3 baths. Breakfast room, no-smoking rooms, in-room VCRs, bicycles, airport and beach shuttle. MC, V.*

Outdoor Activities and Sports

GOLF

Osoyoos Golf and Country Club (⊠ 12300 46th Ave., off Hwy. 97 S, Osoyoos, ☎ 250/495–7003).

SKIING

Apex Resort (⊠ Box 1060, V2A 7N7, ☎ 250/492–2880 or 800/387–2739, FAX 250/292–8622) has 56 trails, a vertical rise of 2,000 feet, and a peak elevation of 7,187 feet.

In Kootenay Country, **Whitewater** (⊠ Box 60, Nelson V1L 5P7, ☎ 250/354–4944), has 32 runs and plenty of powder skiing. **Red Mountain Resorts** (⊠ Box 670, Rossland V0G 1Y0, ☎ 250/362–7700), which spans two mountains and three mountain faces in Kootenay Country, has 77 marked runs. For heli-skiing in Kootenay Country, try **Kootenay Helicopter Skiing** (⊠ Box 717, Nakusp V0G 1R0, ☎ 250/265–3121 or 800/663–0100), FAX 250/265–4447. With accommodations at the Tenderfoot Lodge, they run three- to seven-day all-inclusive packages in the Selkirks and Monashees.

Cathedral Provincial Park

75 km (47 mi) southwest of Penticton.

Off Highway 3 along the U.S. border, Cathedral Provincial Park (☎ 250/494–6500) preserves 82,000 acres of lakes and rolling meadows, teeming with mule deer, mountain goats, and California bighorn sheep. To reach the main part of the park, either take the steep, eight-hour hike, or arrange (and pay in advance) for the **Cathedral Lakes Lodge** (☎ 250/499–5848, FAX 250/499–5266) to transport you by four-wheel-drive vehicle. There are 16 campsites in the park, which is open mid-June through early October.

Skiing

Manning Park Resort (⊠ Box 1480, Hope V0X 1L0, ☎ 604/840–8822), northwest of Cathedral Provincial Park, has excellent cross-country trails and downhill facilities.

En Route Winding farther west, Highway 3 connects with the Trans-Canada Highway (Highway 1), which parallels the Fraser River. To the north, a glimpse through the mists above roiling **Hell's Gate,** in scenic Fraser Canyon, hints at how the region got its name. An airtram (cable car) carries you across the foaming canyon above the fishway, where millions of sockeye salmon fight their way upriver to spawning grounds four times a year—April, July, August, and October. In addition to displays on the life cycle of the salmon, you'll find a fudge factory, a gift shop, and a restaurant at the lower air-tram terminal. This site is about 2½ hours east of Vancouver. ⊠ *Hell's Gate Airtram, Exit 170 off Hwy. 1, Hope, ☎ 604/867–9277. ☎ $9.50. ☉ Mid-Apr.–mid-Oct., daily 9 AM; closing time between 5 and 7, depending on season.*

Harrison Hot Springs

44 *128 km (79 mi) northeast of Vancouver.*

The small resort community of Harrison Hot Springs lies at the southern tip of picturesque Harrison Lake. Vacationers flock here to relax in this almost pristine natural setting. Mountains surround the 64-km-long (40-mi-long) lake, which, ringed by pretty beaches, provides a broad range of outdoor activities in addition to the hot springs.

The **Harrison Hot Springs Hotel,** across from the beach, has a spring-fed public pool. ⊠ *100 Esplanade,* ☎ *604/796–2244.* ☞ *$7.50.* ☉ *Sun.–Thurs. 8 AM–9 PM, Fri. and Sat. 8 AM–10 PM.*

★ ☾ A tour of **Kilby Historic Store and Farm,** a heritage attraction in nearby Harrison Mills, takes you back in time to the British Columbia of the 1920s. Tour the general store and farm buildings of T. Kilby and other pioneers of the area, chat with the shopkeeper, sniff whatever is simmering on the wood-burning stove, and tramp through the orchards, stockroom, fueling station, barn, and dairy house on the grounds. The kids can enjoy feeding the farm animals. You can sample 1920s-style home cooking in the **Harrison River Tearoom.** This is a fine slice of living history. ⊠ *215 Kilby Rd. (1½ km, or 1 mi, off Hwy. 7 on north shore of Fraser River; follow signs), Harrison Mills,* ☎ *604/796–9576.* ☞ *$4.50.* ☉ *Mid-Apr.–June and Sept.–Nov., Thurs.–Mon. 11–5; July and Aug., daily 11–5.*

Dining and Lodging

$$ ✗ **Black Forest.** Ask the locals where to dine and they'll send you here, to a charming Bavarian dining room on Harrison Village Esplanade, overlooking the lake. It comes as no surprise that the specialties are German standards, from schnitzels to Black Forest cake, with a few Continental dishes (mainly steaks and seafood) for good measure. Hearty German beer and an array of wines round out the selection. ⊠ *180 Esplanade,* ☎ *604/796–9343. AE, MC, V. No lunch.*

$$$ ✗⊡ **Harrison Hot Springs Hotel.** Ever since fur traders and gold miners discovered the soothing hot springs in the late 1800s, Harrison has been a favored stopover spot. Built beside the lake in the 1920s, the hotel has grown over the decades. The most reasonably priced rooms, in the original building and the west tower, have an old English look, with Edwardian furnishings and ceiling moldings; those in the east tower are more modern and plush, with a heftier price tag. Amenities include a PGA-rated nine-hole golf course and, of course, hot spring–fed pools (two new outdoor mineral pools were added in 1996). ⊠ *100 Esplanade, V0M 1K0,* ☎ *604/796–2244 or 800/663–2266,* 𝖥𝖠𝖷 *604/796–3682. 290 rooms, 16 cottages. 2 restaurants, lounge, no-smoking floors, room service, 2 indoor and 1 outdoor pools, beauty salon, 1 indoor and 2 outdoor tennis courts, exercise room, massage, hiking, bicycles, playground, laundry service and dry cleaning, business services, meeting rooms. AE, DC, MC, V.*

Rosedale

45 *8 km (5 mi) southwest of Harrison Hot Springs, 120 km (74 mi) east of Vancouver.*

The attractions in Rosedale are a beautiful garden and a water park. The well-signed **Minter Gardens** is a 27-acre compound containing 11 beautifully presented theme gardens—Chinese, rose, English, fern, fragrance, and more—along with aviaries and ponds. There are playgrounds and a giant evergreen maze. ⊠ *Exit 135 off Hwy. 1, 52892 Bunker*

Rd., ☎ *604/794–7191, 800/661–3919 in Canada.* ⌑ *$10.* ☉ *Apr.–Oct., daily 9–dusk.*

☿ It's hard to miss the **Trans-Canada Waterslides,** a tremendously popular water park that has slides with such names as Kamikaze, Cannonball, Super Heroes, Black Hole, and Flash Flood, along with wave and soaking pools, snack bars, and sunbathing areas. ⌧ *Bridal Falls Rd.,* ☎ *604/794–7455.* ⌑ *$12.50.* ☉ *Mid-May–mid-June, weekends 10–8; mid-June–early Sept., daily 10–9.*

BRITISH COLUMBIA A TO Z

Arriving and Departing

By Boat
For information, *see* Victoria A to Z, *above.*

By Bus
Greyhound (☎ 604/662–3222; in Canada, 800/661–8747; in the U.S., 800/231–2222) connects destinations throughout British Columbia with cities and towns all along the Pacific North Coast.

By Car
Driving time from Seattle to Vancouver is about 3 hours. From other Canadian regions, three main routes lead into British Columbia: through Sparwood, in the south, take Highway 3; from Jasper and Banff, in the central region, travel on Highway 1 or Highway 5; and through Dawson Creek, in the north, follow Highways 2 and 97.

By Plane
British Columbia is served by **Victoria International Airport** and **Vancouver International Airport.** Domestic airports are in most cities. **Air Canada** (☎ 604/688–5515; in the U.S., 800/776–3000) and **Canadian Airlines International** (☎ 604/279–6611; in the U.S., 800/426–7000) are the two dominant carriers. **Kenmore Air** (☎ 206/486–1257 or 800/543–9595) offers direct daily flights from Seattle to Victoria, Nanaimo, Campbell River, and Northeast Vancouver Island.

Getting Around

By Bicycle
GULF ISLANDS

Because **Mayne Island** is so small (only 21 square km, or 8 square mi), with mild hills and wonderful scenery, it is great territory for a vigorous bike ride. On Mayne, you can rent bikes at the Miner's Bay gas station. At 100 km (62 mi) on the circular route, **Saltspring Island** offers more of a challenge. Some bed-and-breakfasts have bicycles; ask that they be set aside for you when you make your reservations. For rentals on Saltspring, try Island Spoke Folk (☎ 250/537–4664) at the Trading Company Building in Ganges.

By Bus
VICTORIA AND VANCOUVER ISLAND

Pacific Coach Lines (☎ 800/661–1725) operates daily connecting service between Victoria and Vancouver on B.C. Ferries. **Island Coach Lines** (☎ 250/385–4411) serves the Vancouver Island area. **Maverick Coach Lines** (☎ 250/662–8051) serves Nanaimo from Vancouver on B.C. Ferries (☞ By Ferry, *below*).

Greyhound Lines of Canada (☎ 604/662–3222; in Canada, 800/231–2222) serves the area north of Vancouver. Among its hundreds of stops in the province are Prince Rupert, Terrace, and Smithers.

By Car

Major roads in British Columbia, and most secondary roads, are paved and well engineered. Mountain driving is slower but more scenic. There are no roads on the mainland coast once you leave the populated areas of the southwest corner near Vancouver.

VICTORIA AND VANCOUVER ISLAND
Highway 17 connects the Swartz Bay ferry terminal on the Saanich Peninsula with downtown Victoria. The **Trans-Canada Highway** (Highway 1) runs south from Nanaimo to Victoria. **Highway 14** connects Sooke to Port Renfrew, on the west coast of Vancouver Island, with Victoria.

GULF ISLANDS
The roads on the islands are narrow and winding. Exercise extreme caution around the many cyclists, especially thick on the roads in summer.

By Ferry

B.C. Ferries (in Vancouver, ☎ 604/669–1211; in Victoria, 250/386–3431; reservations, 604/669–1211 or 250/629–3215; in Nanaimo, 250/753–6626) provides frequent year-round passenger and vehicle service between Vancouver and Vancouver Island, from Tsawwassen (south of Vancouver) to Swartz Bay (30 minutes by car north of Victoria); Tsawwassen to Nanaimo; and Horseshoe Bay (north of Vancouver) to Nanaimo. B.C. Ferries also provides service from outside Vancouver and Victoria to the northern and southern Gulf Islands (reserve ahead), the Sunshine Coast, Nanaimo, through the Inside Passage between Port Hardy and Prince Rupert, and from Prince Rupert to the Queen Charlotte Islands. When you travel with a vehicle in summer, plan to arrive at the terminal well in advance of the scheduled sailing time.

GULF ISLANDS
Mayne and Saltspring Islands are an hour to an hour and a half via ferry from Swartz Bay and Tsawwassen.

QUEEN CHARLOTTE ISLANDS
The *Queen of Prince Rupert* (☎ 250/386–3431), a B.C. Ferries ship, sails six times a week between late May and September (three times a week the rest of the year), and can easily accommodate recreational vehicles. The crossing from Prince Rupert to Skidegate, near Queen Charlotte on Graham Island, takes about six hours. Schedules vary and reservations are required. The **M.V. *Kwuna,*** another B.C. Ferries ship, connects Skidegate Landing to Alliford Bay on Moresby Island. Access to smaller islands is by boat or air; plans should be made in advance through a travel agent.

By Plane

GULF ISLANDS
Harbour Air Ltd. (☎ 250/537–5525 or 800/665–0212, FAX 250/627–8307) and **Hanna Air Saltspring** (☎ 250/537–9359; in British Columbia, 800/665–2359) provide several regularly scheduled 20- to 30-minute daily floatplane flights from Ganges on Saltspring Island to Coal Harbour in downtown Vancouver and to Vancouver Airport. **Air B.C.** (☎ 800/776-3000) provides both airport-to-airport and harbor-to-harbor service from Vancouver to Victoria at least hourly. Both flights take about 35 minutes.

Harbour Air Ltd. (☎ 250/627–1341 or 800/665–0212, ℻ 250/627–8307) runs scheduled floatplanes between Sandspit, Masset, Queen Charlotte City, and Prince Rupert daily except December 25 and 26 and January 1.

By Train
MAINLAND

B.C. Rail (☎ 604/984–5246, 604/631–3500, or 800/663–8238) travels from Vancouver to Prince George, a route of 747 km (463 mi), and offers daily service to Whistler. **Via Rail** (in British Columbia, ☎ 800/561–8630) provides service between Prince Rupert and Prince George.

VANCOUVER ISLAND

Esquimalt & Nanaimo Rail Liner (✉ 450 Pandora Ave., Victoria V8W 1N6, ☎ 250/383–4324; in British Columbia, 800/561–8630), operated by Via Rail, makes the round-trip from Victoria's Pandora Avenue Station to Courtenay; schedules vary seasonally.

Contacts and Resources

B&B Reservation Agencies
Garden City Reservation Service (✉ 660 Jones Terr., Victoria V8Z 2L7, ☎ 250/479–1986, ℻ 250/479–9999) specializes in Victoria but can book bed-and-breakfast accommodations throughout British Columbia.

Car Rentals
Most major agencies, including **Avis, Budget,** and **Hertz,** serve cities throughout the province (☞ Car Rentals *in* the Gold Guide). Car rentals are available on Saltspring Island through **Heritage Rentals** (☎ 250/537–4225, ℻ 250/537–4226).

Emergencies
Except in Vancouver and Victoria (☞ Vancouver A to Z *in* Chapter 2 *and* Victoria A to Z, *above*), dial 0 for **police, ambulance,** or **poison control.** On the Gulf Islands, dial 911 for **police, fire,** or **ambulance service.**

Guided Tours
ECOLOGICAL TOURS

Ecosummer Expeditions (✉ 1516 Duranleau St., Vancouver V6H 3S4, ☎ 604/669–7741 or 800/465–8884, ℻ 604/669–3244), **Queen Charlotte Adventures** (✉ Box 196, Queen Charlotte V0T 1S0, ☎ 250/559–8990 or 800/668–4288, ℻ 250/559–8983), and the **Canadian Outback Adventure Company** (✉ 1110 Hamilton St., Vancouver V6C 3L6, ☎ 604/688–7206) run ecological tours of the Queen Charlotte and Gulf Islands.

ORIENTATION

Classic Holidays Tour & Travel (102–75 W. Broadway, Vancouver V5Y 1P1, ☎ 604/875–6377) and **Sea to Sky** (1928 Nelson Ave., West Vancouver V7V 2P4, ☎ 604/922–7339) offer tours throughout the province.

SPECIAL-INTEREST

The history and culture of the First Nations (native) people of the region are the focus of new summer tours including **Lheit-Lit'en Nation Elders Salmon Camp Tours** (✉ Lheit-Lit'en Native Heritage Society, R.R. 1, Site 27, Compartment 60, Prince George V2N 2H8, ☎ 250/963–8451, ℻ 250/963–8324) on the mainland and **Yuquot History Tours** (✉ Ahaminaquis Tourist Centre, Box 459, Gold River V0P 1G0, ☎ 250/283–7464, ℻ 250/283–2335) on Vancouver Island. The **Canadian Outback Adventure Company** (✉ 1110 Hamilton St., Vancouver V6C 3L6, ☎ 604/688–7206) and **Queen Charlotte Adventures** (✉ Box

196, Queen Charlotte V0T 1S0, ☎ 250/559–8990 or 800/668–4288, FAX 250/559–8983) offer unique summer tours of the abandoned Queen Charlotte Islands villages of the Haida Gwai, including the United Nations–designated World Heritage Site at Ninstints.

WHALE-WATCHING

A few Vancouver Island–based companies that conduct whale-watching tours are: **Jamie's Whaling Station** (⌧ Box 590, Tofino V0R 2Z0, ☎ 250/725–3919; in Canada, 800/667–9913), **Tofino Sea-Kayaking Company** (⌧ Box 620, Tofino V0R 2Z0, ☎ 250/725–4222) on the west coast, **Robson Bight Charters** (⌧ Box 99, Sayward V0P 1R0, ☎ 250/282–3833) near Campbell River, and, near Port Hardy, **Stubbs Island Charters** (⌧ Box 7, Telegraph Cove, V0N 3J0, ☎ 250/928–3185).

Hospitals

British Columbia has hospitals in virtually every town, including: on the Gulf Islands, **Lady Minto Hospital** (☎ 250/537–5545) in Ganges on Saltspring Island; in Prince George, **Prince George Regional Hospital** (⌧ 2000 15th Ave., ☎ 250/565–2000; emergencies, 250/565–2444); in Kamloops, **Royal Inland Hospital** (⌧ 311 Columbia St., ☎ 250/374–5111); in Kelowna, **Kelowna General Hospital** (⌧ 2268 Pandosy St., ☎ 250/862–4000).

Late-Night Pharmacies

In Prince George, **Hart Drugs** (⌧ 3789 W. Austin Rd., ☎ 250/962–9666). In Kamloops, **Kipp-Mallery I.D.A. Pharmacy** (⌧ 273 Victoria St., ☎ 250/372–2531). In Hope, **Pharmasave Drugs** (⌧ 235 Wallace St., ☎ 604/869–2486).

Outdoor Activities and Sports

CANOEING

Mt. Robson Adventure Holidays (⌧ Box 687, Valemount V0E 2Z0, ☎ 250/566–4386, FAX 250/566–4351) arranges canoe trips at the northern end of the High Country near Mt. Robson Provincial Park.

FISHING

A saltwater-fishing license for one day costs $3.75 for both Canadian residents and non-Canadians and is available at virtually every fishing lodge and sporting-goods outlet along the coast. Annual licenses are about $11 for non–British Columbia Canadians and $38 for non-Canadians.

For updated fishing information and regulations, contact the **B.C. Fish Branch** (⌧ Ministry of Environment, Parliament Buildings, Victoria V8V 1X4, ☎ 250/387–9688). For a guide to saltwater fishing, contact the **Department of Fisheries and Oceans** (⌧ Recreational Fisheries Division, ⌧ 555 W. Hastings St., Vancouver V6B 5G3, ☎ 604/666–3545).

GOLF

Greens fees are about $25–$50 in the province. **Tee-Time Central Booking Service** (⌧ 412–4004 Bluebird Rd., Kelowna V1W 1X3, ☎ 250/764–4118 or 800/930–4622), for out-of-town golfers, lists courses throughout Vancouver Island and mainland British Columbia. It's open May 15–October 15, weekdays 9–5.

HIKING

B.C. Parks (⌧ 800 Johnson St., 2nd floor, Victoria V8V 1X4, ☎ 250/387–5002) offers detailed information.

For heli-hiking, **Highland Helicopter** (⌧ 1685 Tranmer, Agassiz V0M 1K0, ☎ 604/796–9610), **Crescent Spur Helicopter Holidays** (⌧ Crescent Spur V0J 3E0, ☎ 250/569–2730), **Peak Experiences** (⌧ 29 Oersted. St., Kitimat V8C 1J6, ☎ 250/632–7512, FAX 250/635–3404) and **Mt. Robson Adventure Holidays** (⊠ Box 687, Valemount V0E 2Z0, ☎ 250/566–4386) on the mainland can provide further information.

RAFTING

Hyak Wilderness Adventures (⊠ 204B–1975, Maple St., Vancouver V6J 3S9, ☎ 604/734–8622 or 800/663–7238, FAX 604/734–5718), **Canadian River Expeditions** (⊠ 301–9571 Emerald Dr., Whistler V0N 1B9, ☎ 604/938–6651; 800/898–7238 in Canada), **Alpine Rafting Company** (⊠ Box 1409, Golden V0A 1H0, ☎ 250/344–5016 or 800/663–7080, FAX 250/344–7102), and **Suskwa Adventure Outfitters** (⊠ Box 3262ag, Smithers V0J 2N0, ☎ FAX 250/847–2885) provide options ranging from lazy half-day floats to exhilarating white-water journeys of up to a week.

SKIING

The **Canada West Ski Areas Association** (⊠ 3313 32nd Ave., Suite 103, Vernon V1T 2M8, ☎ 250/542–9020, FAX 250/542–5070) has information about the top heli- and Sno-cat ski operators in British Columbia.

Visitor Information

For information concerning the province contact **Tourism B.C.** (⊠ 802–865 Hornby St., Vancouver V6Z 2G3, ☎ 604/660–2861 or 800/663–6000). More than 140 communities in the province have **Travel Infocentres.**

For Prince George, contact **Tourism Prince George** (⊠ 1198 Victoria St., V2L 2L2, ☎ 250/562–3700, FAX 250/563–3584).

The principal regional tourist offices are: **Tourism Association of Southwestern B.C.** (⊠ 204–1755 W. Broadway, Vancouver V6J 4S5, ☎ 604/739–9011 or 800/667–3306, FAX 604/739–0153), **Tourism Association of Vancouver Island** (⊠ 302–45 Bastion Sq., Victoria V8W 1J1, ☎ 250/382–3551, FAX 250/382–3523), **Okanagan–Similkameen Tourist Association** (⊠ 1332 Water St., Kelowna V1Y 9P4, ☎ 250/860–5999, FAX 250/861–7493), **High Country Tourist Association** (⊠ 2–1490 Pearson Pl., Kamloops V1S 1J9, ☎ 250/372–7770 or 800/567–2275, FAX 250/828–4656), **North By Northwest Tourism** (⊠ 3840 Alfred Ave., Box 1030, Smithers V0J 2N0, ☎ 250/847–5227, FAX 250/847–7585), **Rocky Mountain Visitors Association** (⊠ 495 Wallinger Ave., Box 10, Kimberley V1A 2Y5, ☎ 250/427–4838, FAX 250/427–3344), **Prince Rupert Convention and Visitors Bureau** (⊠ 100 McBride St., Box 669, Prince Rupert V8J 3S1, ☎ 250/624–5637 or 800/667–1994, FAX 250/627–8009), **Kootenay Country Tourist Association** (⊠ 610 Railway St., Nelson V1L 1H4, ☎ 250/352–6033, FAX 250/352–1656), **Cariboo Chilcotin Coast Tourist Association** (⊠ 190 Yorston St., Box 4900, Williams Lake V2G 2V8, ☎ 250/392–2226 or 800/663–5885, FAX 250/392–2838), **Peace River Alaska Highway Tourist Association** (⊠ 10631 100th St., Box 6850, Fort St. John V1J 4J3, ☎ 250/785–2544, FAX 250/785–4424).

Saltspring Island Visitor Information Centre (⊠ 121 Lower Ganges Rd., Ganges V8K 2T1, ☎ 250/537–5252, FAX 250/537–4276), **Galiano Island Visitor Information Centre** (⊠ Sturdies Bay, Box 73, Galiano V0N 1P0, ☎ 250/539–2233, and **Mayne Island Chamber of Commerce** (⊠ General Delivery, Mayne Island V0N 2J0, no phone) provide information on the Gulf Islands. For information on the Queen Charlotte Islands, contact the **Queen Charlotte Islands Travel Infocentre** (⊠ 3922 Hwy. 33, Box 819, Queen Charlotte V0T 1S0, ☎ 250/559–4742, FAX 250/559–8188).

4 The Canadian Rockies

The ranges that form the rugged Canadian Rockies arch north-northwest for more than 1,000 miles from the U.S. border in the south to the Yukon in the north. Here you'll find sights as varied as wildflower-filled alpine meadows and windswept blue-white glaciers. The majestic beauty of the Rockies has been preserved in provincial and national parks that hold some of the most spectacular drives in the world. In these mountains you can also fish, ski, hike, climb, boat, ride, and stay at some of the best resort facilities anywhere.

Updated by
Don Thacker

COMPARING MOUNTAINS IS A SUBJECTIVE and imprecise business. Yet few would argue that the 640-km (397-mi) stretch of the Canadian Rockies that marks part of the Alberta–British Columbia border easily ranks as one of the most extravagantly beautiful ranges on earth. Approaching the mountains from the east, you are struck by the wall of rock on the western horizon, made more dramatic by the white snowfields that cling to the upper slopes until well into the summer. First visible from about 100 km (about 62 mi) away, the mountains become progressively more imposing with each passing mile. Near the south end of the range (Waterton Lakes National Park), the view is particularly dramatic as gently rolling prairie butts up abruptly against the edge of the mountains. Farther north, in Banff and Jasper national parks, tree-covered foothills roll out of the mountains.

It is obvious how the Rockies got their name. Wildly folded sedimentary and metamorphic rocks have been thrust up to form ragged peaks and high cliffs; you can't help but be awed by the forces of nature that operated here. Add glaciers and snowfields to the high peaks, carpet the valleys with forests, mix in a generous helping of large mammals, wildflowers, rivers, and lakes, and you've got the recipe for the Canadian Rockies.

The peaks of the Rockies are aligned in long, closely spaced ranges that run in approximately a north–south direction. From east to west these can be grouped into the foothills, front ranges, main ranges, and a small area of west ranges. Apart from forming distinct sets of mountains, these groupings differ somewhat in geology and age—which increases from 40 to 50 million years in the foothills to 110 to 120 million years in the west ranges. The main ranges have the highest peaks.

The Columbia Mountains, a series of parallel ranges just west of the Rockies, are often grouped with the Rockies. Many recreational activities that are prohibited in the national parks of the Rockies (notably helicopter-assisted skiing and heli-hiking) are allowed in the Columbias. The Columbias were formed about 180 million years ago and consist of four subranges: the Cariboos to the north and, farther south, the Purcells, Selkirks, and Monashees (from east to west).

Recognizing early the region's exceptional natural beauty, the Canadian government began shielding the area from human development and resource exploitation in the 1880s. In 1885, the government created a park preserve around the Cave and Basin Hot Springs in Banff. Two years later, Canada's first national park, Rocky Mountain Park (later Banff National Park), was officially established. Lands that would later become Yoho National Park and Glacier National Park in the Columbias were set aside in 1886.

Today, about 25,000 square km (roughly 10,000 square mi)—an area larger than the state of New Hampshire—are protected in seven national parks in the Rockies and the Columbias. Because they were protected early on, the parks of the Rockies—Waterton Lakes, Banff, Kootenay, Yoho, and Jasper—have remained relatively untouched by human development. The only significant clusters of human settlement are in the town centers of Banff, Jasper, Waterton Park, and the area around Lake Louise. Several thousand more square kilometers are also protected as wilderness areas and provincial parks, most notably Mt. Robson and Mt. Assiniboine provincial parks and Kananaskis Country.

Most of the facilities and roads of the Rockies are concentrated in the valleys, where the elevations are 3,500 to 4,500 feet, only about 1,000 feet higher than in the major prairie cities to the east. Consequently, temperatures in the mountain towns are rather similar to those in Calgary and Edmonton. The mountains themselves rise to elevations above 10,000 feet, and the alpine areas (above tree line) may be whitened by snowfalls even in midsummer.

The Icefields Parkway runs down the heart of the Rockies for 230 km (143 mi) from Jasper to Lake Louise. While all roads in the Rockies offer stunning scenery, the Icefields Parkway is without doubt the most impressive. More than 100 glaciers show off their blue ice along this drive; at the Columbia Icefields, the Athabasca Glacier reaches almost to the roadway (a short walk takes you right up to the ice). Large animals such as elk, moose, deer, and bighorn sheep are fairly common along this route; occasionally you can see bears and mountain goats. Two high passes, the Bow Pass in the south and the Sunwapta Pass about halfway along the route, rise almost to tree line, offering a chance to see carpets of alpine wildflowers in summer. Hiking trails abound along the route if you want to explore the land more closely. Even if you're on a tight schedule, make a point of driving at least part of the Icefields Parkway.

Pleasures and Pastimes

Dining

Eating out in the Canadian Rockies is, for the most part, a casual affair. Given the mix of travelers to the region—families, active outdoorspeople, and sightseers—the emphasis is on good food served in large quantities, at slightly inflated prices. This is not the place for the traveler who expects haute service and cuisine; the region can claim only a handful of top-caliber restaurants. However, people who like fresh game and fish will not be disappointed. Trout, venison, elk, moose, quail, and other game are items that even modest dining establishments list on their menus. One new trend in the region is the appearance of Japanese restaurants.

CATEGORY	COST*
$$$$	over $35
$$$	$25–$35
$$	$15–$25
$	under $15

per person, excluding drinks, service, and sales tax

Lodging

The hotels, inns, and lodges of the Canadian Rockies comprise an eclectic list, ranging from rustic, backcountry lodges without electricity or running water to numerous standard roadside motels, to hotels of supreme luxury. With just a few exceptions (ski resorts being the main one) they share one common trait—room rates that are considerably higher in the summer than during the rest of the year. The week between Christmas and New Year's, as well as February university break, often commands a higher rate as well. For this reason, flexibility in travel planning can mean considerable savings—a room that goes for $150 a night in summer may well drop to $75 from early or mid-October through May.

Lodgings are categorized according to their peak-season rates. Low-season discounts are noted within each listing, where applicable. High-season rates generally run from mid-June to late September or early October. You would be wise to check in advance for off-season rates—

over the past few years the Rockies have become much busier in summer, and the period considered peak season has been getting longer.

Bed-and-breakfast accommodations are plentiful in and around the parks, but most are simply ordinary rooms in small, ordinary homes. The main attractions are price and the fact that you can often find a B&B with a room available if you arrive in town without a reservation.

Most cabin-style accommodations are not insulated (though they have gas heat) and are open almost exclusively in peak season, along with perhaps a brief shoulder season of a few weeks at each end of peak season.

Backcountry lodges have been an integral part of Canadian Rockies travel since the '20s. They vary considerably in terms of accommodations and accessibility. At the luxurious end are lodges with private rooms, private baths, full electricity, telephones, and restaurant-style dining; at the rugged extreme are lodges with bunk beds, kerosene lamps for evening light, and outhouses. A few are accessible by car in summer; some can be reached only by hiking or skiing, or by helicopter. Note that most backcountry lodges are priced on a per-person basis (the price generally includes meals) rather than the double-room rate used for more standard accommodations. Rating classes for these are based on a single-person rate.

Guest ranches, mainly in the ranching area just east of Kananaskis Country, are another alternative accommodation. These comfortable accommodations have a definite ranching theme; horseback riding and pack trips are standard visitor activities.

Of the more than 40 public campgrounds within the national parks (not including backcountry sites for backpackers and climbers), most operate on a first-come, first-served basis, though some allow reservations a few days in advance. The season generally runs from mid-May through October, although some campgrounds remain open year-round. Hookups are available at most of the 40 national park campgrounds and at four of the 30 Kananaskis campgrounds. Prices for a one-night stay are $18 to $22 at hook-up sites, $13 to $16 at sites without hookups, and $10 at sites with pit toilets only.

Numerous privately run campgrounds, which usually take reservations, can be found outside park boundaries.

CATEGORY	COST*
$$$$	over $200
$$$	$150–$200
$$	$100–$150
$	under $100

All prices are for a standard double room (or an equivalent, where not applicable), excluding 7% goods and services tax, 5% room tax in Alberta, 8% room tax in British Columbia, and, in some areas, a small municipal tax.

Outdoor Activities and Sports

See individual towns or Contacts and Resources *in* Canadian Rockies A to Z, *below,* for addresses and telephone numbers.

BIKING

Biking is a popular pastime in the Rockies, whether for a short spin around town or on a multiday guided tour. Around Banff, the Vermilion Lakes loop and the more strenuous loop over Tunnel Mountain are popular half-day bike tours. For a longer ride, Highway 1A between Banff and Lake Louise is a good choice. For a rugged workout you can test lungs and legs on the steep switchbacks leading up to Mt.

Norquay ski area. Highway 93 is a long and strenuous route for cycling but is becoming increasingly popular because of the wide paved shoulders along most of the way and, of course, the beautiful scenery. The Overlander Bike Trail in Jasper National Park takes you through four different scenic zones: marshland, river, meadow, and mountain.

Mountain biking has become increasingly popular in recent years, leading to controversy in the Canadian Rockies. Park officials have reported problems resulting from breakdowns (flat tires, broken frames, and so on) in remote areas, occasionally requiring rescue. Problems have also been reported with mountain bikers unwittingly breaking scent lines between mother bears and cubs. As a result, although mountain bikes provide good access to the backcountry, they are restricted to relatively few trails, primarily fire roads in the parks. Check with the nearest park warden or bike store before heading off-road. Mountain bikers may find Kananaskis Country, with its more lenient restrictions, preferable.

CLIMBING

Except for Waterton Lakes, where the rock is generally crumbly, the Canadian Rockies is one of the world's great climbing regions. Among the classic ascents are Mt. Assiniboine, the "Matterhorn of the Rockies"; glacier-cloaked Mt. Athabasca; Mt. Sir Donald, in Glacier National Park; the daunting Mt. Robson; and, in the Purcells, the spires of the Bugaboos. Climbing and mountaineering are year-round activities in the Canadian Rockies, although October and November—after the summer and before icefalls are solid enough for winter climbing—are the least desirable months.

FISHING

The principal game fish in the Canadian Rockies is trout—cutthroat and rainbow are the most common varieties. The best fishing tends to be in streams, rivers, and lakes in the valleys, rather than in waters from glacial sources. Fishing is usually better outside the national parks because fish-stocking programs are more common. The Bow River, the lakes of British Columbia, and the streams of Crowsnest Pass are prime fishing spots outside the national parks.

GOLF

The golf season is short, running from about mid-May through mid-October. Golf courses are generally in excellent playing condition, with lush grasses and well-kept greens. If hole lengths seem long, keep in mind that at the elevation of Canadian Rockies courses (about 4,000 feet), a golf ball tends to travel 10% farther than at sea level. The area between Golden and Kimberley in British Columbia is growing as a golfing hotbed: Golfers here can now choose from ten 18-hole courses and two 9-hole courses.

HIKING

The four contiguous parks (Banff, Jasper, Kootenay, and Yoho) have 2,900 km (1,798 mi) of hiking trails. In Waterton Lakes there are 183 km (113 mi) of trails, with further access to more than 1,200 km (744 mi) of trails in adjacent Glacier National Park in the United States. Kananaskis Country has numerous hiking and backpacking opportunities (water can be in short supply, especially in late summer and fall), while Revelstoke and Glacier parks in British Columbia are generally best for shorter day hikes.

The snow-free hiking season usually runs from early April to early November for trails in the valleys, and mid-June to mid- or late September for trails that extend into alpine areas. Though most trails are restricted to foot traffic, horses and mountain bikes are permitted in some areas; check with the park warden.

HORSEBACK RIDING

A unique way to explore the Canadian Rockies is on horseback. Horses are prohibited on many trails within the national parks, but there are still some opportunities; among the most attractive areas for pack trips within the parks is Tonquin Valley in Jasper. More options are available in Kananaskis Country, the provincial parks, and the British Columbia Rockies region.

RAFTING

Rafting opportunities range from gentle floats along the Bow River near Banff to rollicking white-water rides on the Kicking Horse River near Golden. Most trips are half- or full-day. The season runs from May through October; if you want white water at its frothiest, June is usually the best month, when rivers are still swollen with the snowmelt, but not dangerously so.

SKIING

There are 11 lift-service ski areas in the region, five of which are within an hour's drive of Banff; daily lift tickets cost between $25 and $50. Cross-country opportunities are also plentiful, and many backcountry lodges are winterized and offer guide services for backcountry touring. Numerous tour operators have ski packages designed to fit a variety of interests, abilities, and budgets.

Heli-skiing was once considered an activity exclusively for experienced, well-conditioned skiers. But in recent years, heli-ski operators also have introduced programs for intermediate skiers with little or no powder-skiing experience. Daily tours start above $200 per person, and weekly packages (including meals and lodging but not airfare) begin at about $2,000 off-season and climb up to $5,000 in the busy months.

WATER SPORTS

Swimmers generally avoid the icy, glacier-fed waters of the Rockies. However, several lakes near Jasper can become relatively temperate during spells of warm summer weather. Motorized boats are not allowed on most lakes in the parks, but rowboat and canoe rentals are available at Lake Louise and Moraine Lake in Banff National Park, at Emerald Lake and Lake O'Hara in Yoho, and at Lac Beauvert, Pyramid Lake, and Patricia Lake in Jasper National Park.

Spray Lakes Reservoir and Kananaskis Lake are the main sites of boating activity in Kananaskis Country—where motorized boating is allowed. Lake Windermere, in British Columbia, is popular among sailors, board sailors, and water-skiers and is pleasant for swimming in the midsummer months. To the north, the long, dam-controlled Kinbasket and Revelstoke lakes give boaters, canoeists, and fishermen more of a wilderness experience. There are several boat ramps on the lakes but few services.

For sailors and board sailors who like strong winds, Waterton Lakes, with winds often exceeding 50 km (31 mi) per hour, is the place to be. The water is numbingly cold, though, so be sure to wear a wetsuit. The Athabasca, Bow, Kicking Horse, and Maligne rivers provide various levels of river-running challenges for canoeists and kayakers—from relatively still water to roaring white water.

Exploring the Canadian Rockies

The Canadian Rockies can be divided into four broad regions. The Banff and Lake Louise area is the main hub of tourism and makes a convenient reference point for the other regions.

North and west of Banff lie the spectacular Icefields Parkway and Jasper National Park (north), and the smaller Kootenay, Yoho, and Glacier national parks (west). Jasper National Park includes the townsite (meaning the town and surrounding cabins and campgrounds) of Jasper—a smaller and more relaxed version of Banff. Kootenay, Yoho, and Glacier parks have comparatively few visitor facilities but make good destinations to escape the crowds of Banff and Jasper parks.

The region south of Banff includes Kananaskis Country and Waterton Lakes National Park. Kananaskis Country, adjacent to Banff National Park but outside the national park system, allows many activities— for example, snowmobiling and hunting—that are prohibited in the national parks. Waterton, a small park along the United States border contiguous with Glacier National Park in Montana, has smaller mountains but a very unhurried atmosphere in contrast to the main parks of the Canadian Rockies.

The British Columbia Rockies region, west of the main Rocky Mountains, consists of a series of parallel, somewhat more weathered mountain ranges. The parks here are smaller and more scattered, interspersed with mostly functional rather than visitor-oriented towns.

A word about fees: The national parks system in Canada has a complex fee structure. Different annual and day pass fees apply depending on which parks you plan to visit. In general an annual pass covering all 11 national parks in western Canada costs $35 per person and a day pass costs about $5 per person. There are extra daily charges for some of the National Historic Sites in the parks, too.

Numbers in the text correspond to numbers in the margin and on the Canadian Rockies and Banff maps.

Great Itineraries

The Canadian Rockies region is a sizable chunk of real estate, about twice the area of New York State. You could easily spend a month and still just skim the surface. The heart of the Canadian Rockies—the adjoining national parks of Banff, Jasper, Kootenay, and Yoho—puts the major attractions relatively close together. Ten days would allow for a leisurely tour of the main parks, with time left over for hiking or exploring some of the outlying regions of the Rockies. Five days would be sufficient for a visit to the major attractions in both Banff and Jasper parks, but there wouldn't be much time spent sitting about. A weekend would be time enough to get a flavor for Banff and Lake Louise, the hub of the region.

IF YOU HAVE 2 DAYS
The best option is to visit the Banff/Lake Louise region. One day could be spent in and around **Banff** ①–⑩—exploring, shopping, or just relaxing, perhaps with visits to one or two of the attractions on the outskirts of town—the **Upper Hot Springs** ④, the **Sulphur Mountain Gondola** ⑤, the **Cave and Basin National Historic Site** ⑥, or one of the short drives near town. The second day would allow a visit to the **Lake Louise** ⑪ area, including scenic Moraine Lake, where you can hike, rent a boat, or just sightsee.

Alternatively, you could choose to make **Jasper** ⑭ your destination, and spend one day in and around the town (shopping, taking the **Jasper Tramway** ⑮, exploring **Pyramid and Patricia lakes** ⑯). The second day could be filled with a visit to one or two of the scenic attractions within an hour's drive of Jasper—**Mt. Edith Cavell** ⑰, **Athabasca Falls** ⑱, **Maligne Lake** ⑲, **Miette Hot Springs** ⑳, or **Mt. Robson** ㉑.

The Canadian Rockies

Edmonton

Morinville

Wetaskiwin

Red Deer

Olds

ALBERTA

Hwy.

Yellowhead

Drayton Valley

Edson

Rocky Mountain House

Saskatchewan River

Athabasca River

Hinton

Grande Cache

Miette Hot Springs

Pyramid and Patricia Lakes **20**

Jasper **14**

Maligne Lake **19**

Icefield Centre **13**

Bow Pass **12**

Jasper Tramway **15**

Mt. Edith Cavell **17**

Medicine Lake

Athabasca Falls **18**

Sunwapta Falls

Columbia Icefields

Athabasca Glacier

Sunwapta Pass

Icefields Pkwy.

BANFF NATIONAL PARK

YOHO NATIONAL PARK

Takakkaw Falls **11**

Emerald Lake **26**

Takakkaw Falls **24**

Burgess Shale site **25**

Lake O'Hara Lake

Rogers

JASPER NATIONAL PARK

WILLMORE WILDERNESS PARK

Indian R.

Mt. Robson **21**

Valemount

Canoe Reach

THE COLUMBIAS

McBride

Hobson Lake

WELLS GRAY PROVINCIAL PARK

Murtle Lake

IF YOU HAVE 5 DAYS

More days allow either a more vigorous or a more relaxed schedule. If you are feeling energetic, an ideal option would be a two-day visit to the **Banff** ①–⑩ and **Lake Louise** ⑪ area, a day spent exploring the Icefields Parkway between Lake Louise and Jasper, and a two-day visit to the **Jasper** ⑭ area.

IF YOU HAVE 10 DAYS

This is enough time to do some serious exploring. You could spend five days touring the **Banff** ①–⑩ and **Lake Louise** ⑪ area, the **Icefields Parkway,** and **Jasper** ⑭ and environs. You can spend the additional five days just relaxing, or you can focus on a specific activity such as hiking (which could easily fill up the remaining time).

If you aren't one to sit around in the same spot for too long, spend the extra five days visiting and overnighting in the out-of-the-way regions—**Yoho** (perhaps visiting the famous **Burgess Shale** ㉕ fossil beds), **Waterton Lakes** ㉚, **Glacier** ㉝, or **Mt. Revelstoke** ㉞ national parks, or the **British Columbia Rockies.**

When to Tour the Canadian Rockies

The main places of interest in the Rockies attract crowds in the peak summer season, so try to reach them early in the day if you want a sense of seclusion. If hiking is your passion, remember that high-altitude trails may be snow covered until well into June. Animals are more common before the July crowds arrive, although midsummer visitors are still certain to see plenty. Wildflowers, especially in the alpine meadows, reach their peak from early July to mid-August.

Although the weather is best during the mid-June to mid-September period, you can avoid crowds and make substantial savings on lodgings by scheduling your visit outside this period. Check on rates, though, as many hotel operators are waking up to the fact that they can keep rates high to early October and still fill their rooms.

BANFF AND LAKE LOUISE

Most people who come to the Canadian Rockies make the Banff and Lake Louise area their first destination, perhaps their only destination; both towns are within Banff National Park. Banff, just an hour's drive west of Calgary, is the largest townsite in the parks and a logical first stop in the mountains. It has plenty of lodging, dining, recreation, and shopping opportunities, but most people also make a point of visiting smaller, but majestic, Lake Louise, a half hour's drive north of Banff. If you're on a tight schedule, the Banff–Lake Louise area has just about every type of activity and scenic highlight available in the Canadian Rockies.

From Banff, the most popular excursions are the spectacular drive north along the Icefields Parkway (Highway 93) to Jasper, 280 km (174 mi) away, and the short trip immediately south into Kananaskis Country. Excursions into the less frequented Yoho and Kootenay parks offer the same magnificent scenery without the crowds.

Banff National Park

Eastern boundary of park: 113 km (70 mi) west of Calgary.

★ With an area of 6,641 square km (2,564 square mi), majestic **Banff National Park** is the second largest of Canada's mountain parks. Bordered by Jasper National Park to the north, Kootenay and Yoho national parks to the west, the Bighorn Wildland Recreation Area to the east, and

Kananaskis Country and Peter Lougheed Provincial Park to the south, Banff is at the center of a huge block of protected wilderness.

You can soak up the rugged alpine scenery, hike on more than 1,600 km (992 mi) of trails, tour the region by automobile or tour bus, watch wildlife, visit historic sites, or enjoy fine dining, lodging, and shopping in the town of Banff. The Banff–Lake Louise hub (☞ Banff *and* Lake Louise, *below*) is not only the geographic center of the park but also the cultural, dining, lodging, and activity center. Expect crowds here, but pristine wilderness in the rest of the park.

Hiking

The trails of Banff National Park tend to get a lot of traffic during the summer peak season. The most interesting hikes are north of the townsite of Banff. The most popular day-hiking areas, both accessible and scenic, are around **Lake Louise** and **Moraine Lake.** The short (2½-km, or 1½-mi), steep **Parker Ridge Trail** at the northern end of the park along the Icefields Parkway is one of the easiest hikes in the national parks to bring you into the alpine world above tree line. There's an excellent view of the Saskatchewan Glacier, where the river of the same name begins. Snowbanks can persist into early summer, but sunshine lays intricate carpets of wildflowers across the trail in late July and August. Trail information is available from any Parks Canada office (☞ Visitor Information *in* the Canadian Rockies A to Z, *below*).

Banff

128 km (79 mi) west of Calgary.

Unlikely contrasts are the rule in Banff: Amid the bustle of commercialism, elk regularly wander into town to graze the lush grass on the town common; tour-bus sightseers carrying souvenir-stuffed bags mix on Banff Avenue (the main drag) with rugged outdoorspeople, among them some of the world's most accomplished mountaineers. For almost all who come to the Canadian Rockies, Banff is the central depot in their travel.

Banff straddles a thin line between mountain resort town and tourist trap. The town was governed by Parks Canada until January of 1990, when the residents voted to become an autonomous municipality (a move rejected by the residents of Jasper to the north). This allowed Banff to reduce the strict and vigilant zoning laws the park authorities had in place. An expansion of both commercial and residential properties has followed. Thus Banff is certainly no quaint little western outpost; except for the oft-photographed Banff Springs Hotel, its architecture is mostly modern, simple, and undistinguished. But the park authorities placed limits on the acreage of the town and so, instead of expanding, Banff has compressed itself. The result is a hub of hyperactivity, especially during the summer—a hub that seems all the more hectic in contrast to the surrounding wilderness.

❶ An amazing number of shops and restaurants have been crammed together on the short stretch of **Banff Avenue** that composes the core of downtown. Clustered together in about a half-dozen indoor malls are art galleries, clothing stores, photo shops, bookstores, and confectioners whose fudge and cookie output makes Banff Avenue a minefield for anyone with a sweet tooth. Items sold in the galleries range from trinkets to kitsch to genuine art; price does not necessarily indicate real value.

Banff

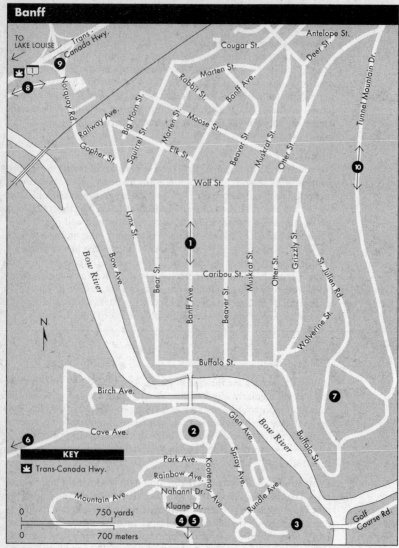

TO LAKE LOUISE

Trans-Canada Hwy.

Antelope St.

Cougar St.

Deer St.

Marten St.

Rabbit St.

Banff Ave.

Tunnel Mountain Dr.

Norquay Rd.

Railway Ave.

Big Horn St.

Marten St.

Moose St.

Muskrat St.

Otter St.

Squirrel St.

Gopher St.

Elk St.

Beaver St.

Wolf St.

N

Lynx St.

Bear St.

Banff Ave.

Caribou St.

Beaver St.

Muskrat St.

Otter St.

Grizzly St.

St. Julien Rd.

Wolverine St.

Bow River

Bow Ave.

Buffalo St.

Birch Ave.

Cave Ave.

KEY

Bow River

Buffalo St.

Trans-Canada Hwy.

Glen Ave.

Park Ave.

Rainbow Ave.

Nahanni Dr.

Kluane Dr.

Kootenay Ave.

Spray Ave.

Rundle Ave.

Mountain Ave.

Golf Course Rd.

0   750 yards

0   700 meters

Banff Avenue, **1**
Banff Centre, **7**
Banff Springs
Hotel, **3**
Cave and Basin
National Historic
Site, **6**

Norquay Road, **9**
Parks Administration
Building, **2**
Sulphur Mountain
Gondola, **5**

Tunnel Mountain
Drive, **10**
Upper Hot Springs, **4**
Vermilion Lakes
Drive, **8**

The Victorian **Banff Park Museum** houses a taxidermy collection of animals indigenous to Banff National Park, as well as wildlife art and a library on natural history. ⊠ *92 Banff Ave.,* ☎ *403/762–1558.* ☞ *$2.25.* ☉ *June–Labor Day, daily 10–6; Sept.–May, daily 1–5.*

The **Whyte Museum** displays art, photography, historical artifacts, and exhibits about life in the Canadian Rockies. The museum hosts special events for families in summer. ⊠ *111 Bear St.,* ☎ *403/762–2291.* ☞ *$3.* ☉ *July and Aug., daily 10–9; mid-May–June and Sept.–mid-Oct., daily 10–6; off-season hours vary.*

❷ For a pleasant after-dinner walk, stroll to the **Parks Administration Building** (⊠ 1 Cave Ave.) with its splendid summertime flower gardens at the rear. It stands at the south end of Banff Avenue, across a stone bridge over the Bow River. For park information, such as maps, park regulations, and so on, the **Information Centre** can provide a wealth of help. ⊠ *224 Banff Ave.,* ☎ *403/762–1550.* ☉ *June–Sept., daily 8–8; Oct.–May, daily 9–5.*

★ ❸ The **Banff Springs Hotel** (☞ Dining and Lodging, *below*) is the architectural highlight of Banff and can at times resemble a year-round three-ring circus. Built in 1888, the hotel is easily recognized by its castlelike exterior; inside, the visitor can expect to get lost in the crazy-quilt network of restaurants, shops, salons, and ballrooms. Even renovators got confused; evidently, the hotel has a hidden room—one that was accidentally sealed off by an overzealous plasterer. It was left that way to add a chapter to the hotel lore. ⊠ *Spray Ave., 2 km (1 mi) south of downtown Banff.*

❹ The **Upper Hot Springs** is a sulphur pool that can be soothing, invigorating, or both. The hot spring water is especially inviting on a dull, cold day. Lockers, period bathing suits, and towels are available to rent. ⊠ *Mountain Ave., 3 km (2 mi) south of downtown Banff; or via 20-min hike up steep trail from Banff Springs Hotel parking area,* ☎ *403/762–1515.* ☞ *$5–$7.* ☉ *Late May–Sept., daily 9 AM–11 PM; Oct.–late May, daily 10–10.*

❺ For great vistas, ride the **Sulphur Mountain Gondola.** Views during the steep eight-minute ride to and from the 7,500-foot summit are spectacular, but they are hardly private. The observation decks and short trails are well visited, especially in summer. From the main deck you can hike the short distance to the summit of Samson Peak and frolic among the lazy Rocky Mountain bighorn sheep that graze there or visit the gift shop or the reasonably priced restaurant. ⊠ *Mountain Ave., 3 km (2 mi) south of downtown Banff, lower terminal next to Upper Hot Springs,* ☎ *403/762–5438 or 403/762–2523.* ☞ *$10–$12.*

❻ The **Cave and Basin National Historic Site** became the birthplace of the Canadian Rockies park system when the region was given national park protection in 1885. Two interpretive trails provide good insight into geology and plant life here, with half-hour and one-hour ranger-guided tours available. Cave and Basin also has hands-on interpretive displays on the wildlife and history of the national park. The **Cave and Basin Centre Pool** is no longer open for swimming, but you can take a guided tour. A boardwalk leads to a marsh where the warm spring water supports a variety of tropical fish. ⊠ *Cave Ave., 2 km (1 mi) west of downtown Banff,* ☎ *403/762–1557.* ☞ *$2.25.* ☉ *June–early Sept., daily 9–6; Sept.–May, daily 9:30–5.*

❼ The **Banff Centre,** a 50-year-old, highly renowned training center for musicians, artists, and writers, is *the* place in town and in the parks for performances ranging from poetry readings to rock concerts. The

Banff Festival of the Arts is held here every summer. Within the center, the **Walter Philips Gallery** focuses on contemporary works by Canadian and international artists. ⊠ *St. Julien Rd., ☎ 403/762–6300, 403/762–6281 gallery.* ⊠ *Free.* ☉ *Tues.–Sun. noon–5.*

⑧ For a pleasant, short ride near town, try the **Vermilion Lakes Drive,** just off the west Banff exit from Highway 1. Wildlife sightings are excellent: elk, bighorn sheep, muskrat, and the occasional moose. Dawn and dusk are the best times.

⑨ The short drive up the steep **Norquay Road** leads to a parking lot with a prize view of Banff townsite and the Bow River valley. Just below, bighorn sheep, deer, goats, elk, and Columbian ground squirrels negotiate their pastoral existence on some extremely treacherous slopes.

⑩ **Tunnel Mountain Drive** (east side of Banff) makes a scenic 5-km (3-mi) loop. The drive is closed in winter, but just off the drive, the **Hoodoos**—fingerlike rock formations caused by erosion—are accessible year-round.

Dining and Lodging

$$$$ ✕ **Le Beaujolais.** Elegantly decorated in neoclassical style, this restau-
★ rant is strikingly out of place in casual Banff. Tapestries on the wall lend a hint of baronial splendor, and the rich food is a suitable match. Traditional French preparations of beef, veal, and lamb are menu highlights. Fish and seafood specialties include arctic char, salmon, sea bass, and lobster. For dessert, spoil yourself with the Raspberry Balloon—a mixture of fresh raspberries, raspberry-flavored ice cream, and raspberry liqueur, all smothered in whipped cream. The wine cellar is lavishly and imaginatively stocked. ⊠ *212 Buffalo St., at Banff Ave., ☎ 403/762–2712. Reservations essential. AE, MC, V. No lunch.*

$$$$ ✕ **Ristorante Classico.** The Rimrock hotel's (☞ *below*) restaurant jux-
★ taposes northern Italian cuisine with a backdrop of the Bow Valley. The dining room—complete with abstract paintings and intricate moldings on the high ceiling—is divided into three cozy sections. Tables are surrounded by grand old armchairs. Chef Hans Sauter creates such daring originals as *roulade di salmone picante* (seared peppered salmon roulade with gazpacho), *cotoletta di vitello ai ferri al rosmarino* (grilled veal chop with rosemary), and rack of lamb baked in an aromatic crust. Fresh fruit desserts and an extensive wine list will complete your epicurean evening. ⊠ *Rimrock Resort Hotel, Mountain Ave., ☎ 403/762–3356. Reservations essential. AE, D, DC, MC, V. No lunch.*

$$–$$$$ ✕ **Banff Springs Hotel.** Restaurants, bars, and lounges of varying formality and cuisine—from coffeehouses to a grand dining room—create a small culinary universe in this hotel in the heart of the Rockies. **Samurai,** a Japanese restaurant, may have the best food—the standard of its sushi and *shabu-shabu* (thin strips of beef, chicken, or fish cooked in a copper bowl full of boiling water) must be high enough to satisfy the hotel's large Japanese clientele. The best overall dining experience may be at the **Waldhaus,** (closed mid-November–mid-December), where a Bavarian-style meal—they specialize in fondues—is often followed by a Bavarian-style sing-along. The **Grapes Wine Bar,** which serves a light-fare menu with adventurous salads, pâtés, and a choice selection of cheeses, is tucked away in a small, quiet room on the mezzanine level. Big windows provide nice views here. The **Alhambra,** open in summer only, specializes in steak and seafood. A summer highlight is the barbecue lunch on the **Red Terrace.** The flavor of the traditional fare—steaks, corn on the cob, roast potatoes—seems greatly enhanced by the view of Rundle Mountain and the Bow River. ⊠ *Spray Ave., ☎ 403/762–2211. Reservations essential. AE, D, DC, MC, V.*

$$$ ✕ **Buffalo Mountain Lodge.** An exposed, rough-hewn post-and-beam interior gives the dining room a comfortable likeness to a converted barn. This is a woodcrafter's showcase, highlighted by the large polished wine cabinet that separates the dining and bar areas. On the menu is Rocky Mountain cuisine—fish, meat, and numerous game dishes with sweet nouvelle sauces, supplemented by hearty soups, fresh-baked breads, and a superbly extensive and frequently updated wine list. ✉ *Tunnel Mountain Rd.,* ☎ *403/762–2400. AE, DC, MC, V.*

$$$ ✕ **Caboose.** In the railway depot, the Caboose recalls of the bygone train era. Old train-engine, rail-car, and train-depot paraphernalia fills the dining room; dim lighting adds to the spirit of nostalgia. The Continental dishes, served with salad, are good but basic: slow-roasted prime rib and steaks, plus crab legs, salmon, lobster, prawns, and trout. ✉ *Elk and Lynx Sts.,* ☎ *403/762–3622. AE, MC, V. No lunch.*

$$$ ✕ **Ticino.** This stucco-and-wood-beam dining room has Swiss-Italian fare. There are numerous standard pasta and meat dishes, as well as more adventurous Alpine cuisine. Fondue is a house specialty; the *mar-e-mont* (Italian for "ocean and mountain") is a beef-and-shrimp fondue you cook yourself in hot broth. Baked salmon, beef medallions, and panfried veal are among the other entrées. ✉ *High Country Inn, 415 Banff Ave.,* ☎ *403/762–3848. AE, MC, V. No lunch.*

$$ ✕ **Balkan Restaurant.** The bright blue-and-white decor, with tile trim, cane-back chairs, and plants, evokes the Mediterranean. You can choose between classic Greek dishes, such as moussaka and souvlaki, or creative ethnic mixes, such as Greek stir-fry (rice and veggies with feta cheese). ✉ *120 Banff Ave.,* ☎ *403/762–3454. MC, V.*

$$ ✕ **Giorgio's Trattoria.** This split-level eatery serves high-quality Italian food that is immensely popular with the local crowd, so you might have to wait a bit during the busy hours. Philippine mahogany tables and bar, Tuscany-style sponged walls, a beamed ceiling, and detailed wrought-iron work on the stairway create an elegant look. The menu consists mainly of pizzas—try the exotic pizza *mare* with tiger shrimp, mussels, cilantro, sun-dried tomatoes, and roast garlic topping—and such pasta dishes as the ricotta ravioli *con gamberetti* (ravioli tossed with baby shrimps in oregano butter and virgin olive oil). ✉ *219 Banff Ave.,* ☎ *403/762–5114. AE, MC, V. No lunch.*

$–$$ ✕ **Barbary Coast.** Paraphernalia from all manner of sport, from base-
★ ball to bobsledding, decorates the plant-filled, skylighted dining room. The food is neo-California: New York steak is a house specialty, pizzas with pesto sauce are always a favorite, and the menu also includes a variety of pastas. Live blues bands play in the bar after 10 PM daily. ✉ *119 Banff Ave.,* ☎ *403/762–4616. AE, MC, V.*

$ ✕ **Joe Btfsplk's Diner.** This place, named for an Al Capp cartoon char-
★ acter, is fun, camp, or overbearing, depending on your taste. It's a re-created '50s-style diner, with red vinyl banquettes, chrome-trimmed tables with individual jukeboxes, and waitresses in '50s attire. The menu is straight from a true-Americana cookbook: burgers, meat loaf, mashed potatoes, and apple pie for lunch or dinner, and eggs and bacon for breakfast. Fresh-baked cookies and muffins, available for take-out, are the culinary highlight. ✉ *221 Banff Ave.,* ☎ *403/762–5529. Reservations not accepted. AE, DC, MC, V.*

$$$$ 🏨 **Banff Rocky Mountain Resort.** Numerous outdoor facilities are a draw at this resort 5 km (3 mi) east of Banff. Inside the chalet-style building, rooms are bright, with white walls, wall-to-wall carpeting, and lots of blond-wood trim. Many rooms have fireplaces and kitchens with microwave ovens. Rates decrease by 40% off-season. ✉ *Banff Ave. and Tunnel Mountain Rd., Box 100, T0L 0C0,* ☎ *403/762–5531 or 800/661–9563, 🖷 403/762–5166. 171 studio, 1-bedroom, and 2-bed-*

room units. Indoor pool, 2 tennis courts, exercise room, squash, shuttle to downtown. AE, DC, MC, V.

$$$$ 🏨 **Banff Springs Hotel.** Built in 1888, this massive, castlelike hotel marked the beginning of Banff's tourism boom. The 87 different styles of guest rooms are linked by their blue, burgundy, and green color schemes and such old-hotel characteristics as high ceilings, tapestries and oil paintings on the walls, antique furniture, and marble sinks. A world-class spa, opened in 1995, is an oasis of pampering and luxury. Guest rooms are not soundproof. Tour groups may receive preferential treatment over individual travelers, and overbooking can be a problem in peak season. Rates decrease about 25% off-season. ✉ *Spray Ave., Box 960, T0L 0C0,* ☎ *403/762–2211 or 800/441–1414,* 🆑 *403/762–5755. 804 rooms, 80 suites. 12 restaurants, 3 bars, indoor pool, spa, 27-hole golf course, 5 tennis courts, bowling, health club, horseback riding, nightclub, convention center. AE, D, DC, MC, V.*

$$$$ 🏨 **Buffalo Mountain Lodge.** Part of the Canadian Rocky Mountain Re-
★ sorts group, along with Emerald Lake Lodge in Yoho and Deer Lodge in Lake Louise, this complex shares their ambience and style. Polished pine, rough-hewn beams, and a stone hearth set the tone in the lobby. There is a hotel-condo cluster built in 1987, as well as 42 renovated rooms that reopened in 1997. Rooms are dressed in pastel shades and have fireplaces, willow chairs, and pine cabinetry. Rates decrease by 35% off-season. ✉ *Tunnel Mountain Rd., Box 1326, T0L 0C0,* ☎ *403/762–2400 or 800/661–1367,* 🆑 *403/762–4495. 82 rooms, 20 studios. 2 restaurants, lobby lounge, hot tub, steam room. AE, DC, MC, V.*

$$$$ 🏨 **Rimrock Resort Hotel.** Perched on the flank of Sulphur Mountain,
★ with a gondola and hot pools nearby, this hotel looks deceptively small and simple from the front. But the mountain-modern–style structure, clad in broken-face Tyndall stone and built into the steeply sloping mountain, is eight stories high. The huge lobby has a 25-foot ceiling, giant windows facing the Rockies, and an oversize marble fireplace. Nearly all rooms have views of the Bow Valley; each is decorated individually, but all have dark color schemes of burgundy, brown, and blue, and plush leather and velvet furnishings. Rates decrease by one-third off-season. ✉ *Mountain Ave., Box 1110, T0L 0C0,* ☎ *403/762–3356 or 800/661–1587,* 🆑 *403/762–4132. 304 rooms, 41 suites. 2 restaurants, lobby lounge, indoor pool, sauna, exercise room, squash, shuttle downtown. AE, DC, MC, V.*

$$$ 🏨 **Banff Park Lodge.** The high, slanted ceiling and dark cedar paneling, in addition to the modern and unembellished style, exude a Scandinavian feeling. On a quiet street in downtown Banff, the lodge is within walking distance of shops and restaurants. Rooms are bright, with lots of beige and ecru. Rates are cut in half off-season. ✉ *222 Lynx St., Box 2200, T0L 0C0,* ☎ *403/762–4433 or 800/661–9266,* 🆑 *403/762–3553. 211 rooms. 2 restaurants, indoor pool, sauna, steam room. AE, DC, MC, V.*

$$$ 🏨 **Castle Mountain Village.** Six different chalet styles can satisfy a variety of budgets. The smallest have kitchens, bathrooms, and sleeping areas with fireplaces. Although cramped and on the dark side, they are clean and quiet. Larger and newer pine-log chalets, which make up the vast majority of the units, have two bedrooms, Jacuzzis, and sleep up to six. For four people, the large chalets are a comfortable, economical choice. Five new one-bedroom cabins (one wheelchair accessible) opened in 1997. Request a room with a view of Castle Mountain. Rates decrease 35% off-season; pets are $10 extra each. ✉ *Hwy. 1A, halfway between Banff and Lake Louise, Box 1655, Banff T0L 0C0,* ☎ *403/762–3868,* 🆑 *403/762–8629. 24 chalets. Steam room, exercise room, groceries, coin laundry. MC, V.*

$$ ⊞ **High Country Inn.** There is nothing fancy here—just clean, simple, comfortable motel rooms. The units are of standard size, cedar-covered walls give some rooms a touch of regional character, and many rooms have a balcony. Ask for a room in the back, away from the heavy traffic on Banff Avenue. Rates decrease by 40% off-season. ⊠ *419 Banff Ave., Box 700, T0L 0C0,* ☎ *403/762–2236, 800/661–1244 in Canada,* ℻ *403/762–5084. 70 rooms. Restaurant, indoor pool. AE, MC, V.*

$$ ⊞ **Red Carpet Inn.** Under the same management as the High Country Inn next door, the no-frills Red Carpet is one of the few moderately priced lodging options in downtown Banff. Small motel-style rooms are decorated in pastel shades, right down to the pastel-painted wooden furnishings. Front rooms, on Banff Avenue, can be noisy. Rates decrease 50% off-season. ⊠ *425 Banff Ave., Box 1800, T0L 0C0,* ☎ *403/762– 4184, 800/563–4609 in Canada,* ℻ *403/762–4894. 52 rooms. Hot tub. AE, MC, V.*

$$ ⊞ **Storm Mountain Lodge.** This is one of the original Canadian Pacific
★ Railway backcountry lodges, built in 1922. Not nearly as back-country today, it is on Highway 93, just east of Vermilion Pass. The sitting area of the main, log cabin–style lodge is dominated by a large fireplace crowned by the head of a bighorn sheep. The dining area embodies simple elegance: straight-back wood chairs and white tablecloths on an enclosed porch with big glass windows overlooking the pass. Cabins, tucked in the woods, are smallish but cozy, made so by fireplaces, old lamps, and down comforters. ⊠ *Hwy. 93, 5 km (3 mi) west of Hwy. 1, Box 670, T0L 0C0,* ☎ ℻ *403/762–4155. 12 cabins. Restaurant, lounge, hiking. AE, MC, V. Closed late Sept.–late May.*

Nightlife and the Arts

THE ARTS

Most of the cultural activity in the Canadian Rockies is in and around Banff, and unquestionably the hub of this activity is the **Banff Centre** (⊠ St. Julien Rd., ☎ 403/762–6300; in Alberta and British Columbia, 800/413–8368). Presenting a performing-arts grab bag throughout the year, with pop and classical music, theater, and dance, the center peaks in summer with the three-month **Banff Festival of the Arts.**

The **Lux Cinema** (⊠ Wolf and Bear Mall, ☎ 403/762–8595) plays major releases.

NIGHTLIFE

For cocktails and socializing, the **Banff Springs Hotel** (☞ Dining and Lodging, *above*) has lounges and dining rooms with entertainment and dancing. **Wild Bill's** (⊠ Banff Ave. and Caribou St., ☎ 403/762–0333) is a cowboy bar with live music where two-steppers can strut their stuff. If you prefer rock and roll with your drink, try **Eddy's Back Alley** (⊠ 137 Banff Ave., ☎ 403/762–8434). **Barbary Coast** (⊠ 119 Banff Ave., ☎ 403/762–4616) has late-night blues and good food (☞ Dining, *above*).

Outdoor Activities and Sports

BIKING

Bikes can be rented from **Park and Pedal Bike Shop** (⊠ 229 Wolf St., ☎ 403/762–3190).

BOATING

Lake Minnewanka Boat Tours (⊠ Box 2189, T0L 0C0, ☎ 403/762– 3473) offers 1½-hour tours in summer on Lake Minnewanka, near town. The cost is $20.

GOLF

The **Banff Springs Hotel** (☎ 403/762–6801) has a 27-hole course (advance bookings required).

HORSEBACK RIDING

Arrangements for hourly or daily rides, as well as lessons, can be made through the concierge at the **Banff Springs Hotel. Sundance Stables** (☎ 403/762–2832) and **Brewster's Kananaskis Guest Ranch** (☎ 403/673–3737), on the Bow River 30 minutes east of Banff, have horses to rent.

RAFTING

Rocky Mountain Raft Tours (⊠ Box 1771, T0L 0C0, ☎ 403/762–3632) has one- to three-hour trips on the Bow River and also offers canoe rentals.

SKIING

Cross-country. Banff Alpine Guides (⊠ Box 1025, T0L 0C0, ☎ 403/678–6091) leads backcountry ski tours.

Downhill. Mt. Norquay (⊠ Mt. Norquay Rd., Box 219, Suite 7000, T0L 0C0, ☎ 403/762–4421) runs are generally short and steep with a growing range of expert terrain. At **Sunshine Village** (⊠ Box 1510, T0L 0C0, ☎ 403/762–6500 or 800/661–1363) the terrain is mostly intermediate and above the tree line. These resorts and **Lake Louise** (☞ *below*) have dining options, ski schools, day-care facilities, and licensed day lodges. A good bargain is the $146 3-day pass from **Ski Banff/Lake Louise** (⊠ Box 1805, T0L 0C0, ☎ 403/762–4561), which allows you to ski at the three areas and includes free shuttle service to the slopes.

Heli-skiing. Mike Wiegele Helicopter Skiing (⊠ Box 249, T0L 0C0, ☎ 403/762–5548 or 800/661–9170) serves the Banff region. *See also* Skiing *in* Canadian Rockies A to Z, *below*.

SPORTING GEAR

Mountain Magic (⊠ 224 Bear St., ☎ 403/762–2591) has three floors of hiking, climbing, skiing, running, and biking equipment, and a 30-foot indoor climbing wall for gear testing. **Monod's** (⊠ 111 Banff Ave., ☎ 403/762–3725; ⊠ 129 Banff Ave., ☎ 403/762–4571) sells a wide array of sports equipment and clothing.

Shopping

When shopping in the Canadian Rockies, you'll find the best selection in Banff, but you may pay a resort premium for souvenirs as well as native crafts, sporting gear, landscape paintings, woolens, and outdoor wear.

Of the numerous galleries and shops along Banff Avenue, perhaps the best for crafts and other art items, principally by Canadian craftspeople, is **The Quest for Handcrafts** (⊠ 105 Banff Ave., ☎ 403/762–2722). For arts and crafts, including handmade jewelry and watercolor paintings, check out **Canada House** (⊠ 201 Bear St., ☎ 403/762–3757). The **Banff Indian Trading Post** (⊠ Birch and Cave Aves., ☎ 403/762–2456) has a good selection of crafts.

If you have a sweet tooth, one place too good to miss is **Welch's Chocolate Shop** (⊠ 126 Banff Ave., near Wolf St., ☎ 403/762–3737). Its selection of homemade candies includes licorice jelly beans and chocolate and sugar sculptures of local wildlife.

Lake Louise

★ ⓫ *56 km (35 mi) north of Banff, 184 km (114 mi) west of Calgary.*

Ask people what pops to mind when they think of the Canadian Rockies and they are as likely to say Lake Louise as Banff. What they are really thinking of is the lake itself, with the impressive Victoria Glacier flowing off the mountain at the lake's end, and the hotel located at the lakeshore—the classy Chateau Lake Louise. The scenery here is among the most spectacular in all of Banff National Park, and the Chateau Lake Louise is comparable in quality to the Banff Springs Hotel in Banff—both are owned and operated by the Canadian Pacific chain of luxury hotels.

The town of Lake Louise, though, is another story; blink and you'll miss it on your way through. That's not to say there aren't hotels, restaurants, shopping, and other services here—there are, and some very good ones at that.

Most people traveling from Banff to Lake Louise take Highway 1 for about 56 km (35 mi) north along the Bow River. But if you aren't in a hurry, the two-lane Highway 1A, running approximately parallel to Highway 1, is the more scenic option.

In summer you can ride the **Lake Louise Summer Sightseeing Lift** to the summit of Mt. Whitehorn for a stunning view that includes over a dozen glaciers. Interpretive guides give free tours of mountain flora and fauna. In good weather, the sun deck of the Whitehorn Tea House, at the top of the lift, is a good place to break for lunch. The ski area here is generally regarded as one of Canada's best and is frequent home to World Cup downhill races. ⊠ *Lake Louise exit, Hwy. 1,* ☎ *403/522– 3555.* ⊠ *$10.* ⊙ *June–Sept., daily.*

The **Chateau Lake Louise** (☞ Dining and Lodging, *below*), built in 1923, overlooks blue-green Lake Louise and the Victoria Glacier at the far end of the lake. The hotel's setting is as scenic as it is popular. Canoe rentals are available at the boat house. The château is also a departure point for several short, moderately strenuous, well-traveled hiking routes. The most popular hike (about 3½ km, or 2¼ mi) is to Lake Agnes. The tiny lake hangs on a mountain-surrounded shelf that opens to the east with a distant view of the Bow River valley. ⊠ *6 km (4 mi) south of Hwys. 93 and 1, 6 km (4 mi) northwest of Hwy. 1 and Bow Valley Pkwy.; follow signs.*

Moraine Lake, 11 km (7 mi) south of Lake Louise, is a photographic highlight in Banff National Park. Set in the "Valley of the Ten Peaks," the lake reflects the snow-clad peaks of sedimentary rock that rise abruptly around it. As beautiful as it is, don't expect Moraine Lake necessarily to offer an escape from the Lake Louise crowd; it is a major stop for tour buses as well as a popular departure point for hikers. However, a hiking path that runs along the lakeshore will quickly take you away from the crowds. ⊠ *Moraine Lake Rd. off Great Divide Hwy.*

If you are seeking solitude, several moderate hiking trails lead from Moraine Lake into some spectacular country. A popular day hike is the trek over Sentinel Pass and through Paradise Valley to Lake Louise. For great views, the short (3-km, or 2-mi) but steep hike from Moraine Lake to Larch Valley is well worth the effort. From June through September, another option is to rent a canoe from the office of Moraine Lake Lodge (☎ 403/522–3733).

Dining and Lodging

$$$$ ✕ **Post Hotel.** Here is one of the true epicurean experiences in the Cana-
★ dian Rockies. A low, exposed-beam ceiling and a stone, wood-burning hearth in the corner lend a warm, in-from-the-cold atmosphere; white tablecloths and fanned napkins provide an elegant touch. Daring European cuisine is combined with a lighter, California influence. The house specialty is Alberta rack of lamb; veal and venison are also good choices. You might try the free-range duck sausage served with gnocchi and mango-lime salsa, or salmon with one of the house spe-

cialty sauces, which change twice a year. Homemade pastries and desserts cap off the meal. ✉ *200 Pipestone Rd.,* ☎ *403/522–3989. Reservations essential. AE, MC, V.*

$$–$$$$ ✕ **Chateau Lake Louise.** The many choices at the Chateau range from light snacking in the **Poppy Room** to night-on-the-town elegance in the **Edelweiss Dining Room** (jacket required for dinner). Wherever you eat, dining inevitably defers to the view through the 10-foot-high windows. The size of the **Victoria Dining Room,** with seating for more than 300, is nicely tempered by plush carpeting, upholstered chairs, and standing plants. The food and ambience are European hotel-style—croissants and jam for breakfast, Continental fare for lunch and dinner—with white cotton tablecloths and polished silver. For something different, try **Walliser Stube,** a Swiss wine bar with warm, cherry-wood decor and a good selection of fondues. From early June to early September, afternoon tea in the **Lakeside Lounge** is a highlight that usually includes fresh scones, pastries, or croissants—along with coffee and tea—served on silver. In summer you can sample Continental cuisine at the **Tom Wilson dining room.** Dinner reservations are necessary in summer for most of the restaurants. ✉ *Lake Louise Dr.,* ☎ *403/522–3511, Ext. 1818. AE, D, DC, MC, V.*

$$$ ✕ **The Station.** Housed in a lovingly restored railway station and two
★   early 20th-century burgundy Canadian Pacific rail cars, this restaurant stands on the site of the original railway station in Lake Louise. The narrow cars are decorated with period furnishings, paintings, and photographs. After your meal you can retire to the original observation room, with its brocade tapestry and deep upholstered couch, for coffee or tea. The centerpiece of the station is a huge three-sided fireplace that faces out onto each of three small dining rooms. The fresh fare on the menu is expertly prepared but quite predictable, with Alberta beef, chicken, and fish dishes dominating. ✉ *200 Sentinel Rd.,* ☎ *403/522–2600. Reservations essential. MC, V.*

$ ✕ **Laggan's Mountain Bakery and Deli.** This six-table coffee shop in the Samson Mall is where the local work crews, mountain guides, and park wardens come for an early-morning muffin and a cup of coffee. Laggan's has excellent baked goods, especially the sweet poppy-seed breads. You can pick up a sandwich here if you're driving north on the Icefields Parkway. ✉ *Samson Mall, off Hwy. 1,* ☎ *403/522–2017. Reservations not accepted. No credit cards.*

$$$$ 🏨 **Chateau Lake Louise.** There's a good chance that no hotel—anywhere—has a more dramatic view out its back door. Terraces and lawns reach to the famous aquamarine lake, backed up by the Victoria Glacier. Inside, off-white walls, polished wood and brass, and burgundy carpeting blend well with the lake view, seen through large, horseshoe-shape windows. Guest rooms have neo-colonial furnishings; some have terraces. The stone-facade hotel was built in 1923, and rooms lack soundproofing. Reader feedback suggests that preferred service may be reserved for tour groups during busy times; some individual travelers have felt neglected. There's a minimal off-season rate decrease. ✉ *Lake Louise Dr., T0L 1E0,* ☎ *403/522–3511 or 800/441–1414,* ℻ *403/522–3834. 511 rooms, 60 suites. 6 restaurants, 2 lounges, indoor pool, steam room, exercise room, horseback riding, boating. AE, D, DC, MC, V.*

$$$$ 🏨 **Post Hotel.** This hotel makes up for a rather ordinary location in
★   several ways. Amber-color wood dominates the decor, lending an atmosphere of muted elegance. Rooms come in 15 different configurations, from standard doubles to units with sleeping lofts, balconies, fireplaces, and whirlpool tubs. Two streamside log cabins evoke a mood of old-fashioned, in-the-mountains romance. Seven deluxe, two-level suites come with a king-size bed and a large living room with a

river-stone fireplace. The restaurant (☞ *above*) is regularly rated as one of the best in the Canadian Rockies. Rates decrease about 40% off-season. ⊠ *Box 69, T0L 1E0,* ☎ *403/522–3989 or 800/661–1586,* 𝖥𝖠𝖷 *403/522–3966. 98 units. Restaurant, lounge, pub, indoor pool, steam room. AE, MC, V. Closed late Oct.–early Dec.*

$$$ 🏨 **Lake Louise Inn.** Five buildings hold a variety of accommodations, from small one-bedrooms to two-bedroom condo units, some with a balcony, a fireplace, and/or a kitchenette. A three-story building has 12 one-room suites and 24 motel-style rooms with private entrances. For economy-minded travelers, the Pinery, a separate 56-room building, has spare but comfortable accommodations. In winter there's a shuttle to the mountain, and multiday ski packages. Rates decrease 50% in the off-season. ⊠ *210 Village Rd., Box 209, T0L 1E0,* ☎ *403/522–3791 or 800/661–9237,* 𝖥𝖠𝖷 *403/522–2018. 222 rooms and condo units. Restaurant, pizzeria, pub, indoor pool, hot tub, sauna, ice skating. AE, DC, MC, V.*

$$ 🏨 **Paradise Lodge & Bungalows.** Only 2 km (1 mi) down the access road from Lake Louise, this lodge has one- and two-bedroom suites with wood furnishings and oak paneling in the two main log buildings. One-bedroom units come with a full kitchen and a fireplace, while the two-bedroom option includes a balcony. The bungalows, or log-sided cabins (some with kitchenettes), are more rustic from the outside than on the inside. Set in a spruce and pine grove, they can be somewhat dark and feel cramped, but they are well maintained. ⊠ *Box 7, T0L 1E0,* ☎ *403/522–3595,* 𝖥𝖠𝖷 *403/522–3987. 24 suites, 21 bungalows. Playground, coin laundry. MC. V. Closed mid-Oct.–mid-May.*

$$ 🏨 **Skoki Lodge.** An 11-km (7-mi) hike or ski from the Lake Louise ski area, Skoki is the kind of backcountry lodge you must work to get to. The high-alpine scenery of Skoki Valley makes the trek well worthwhile, as does the small lodge itself, built in 1930. The log walls and big stone fireplace epitomize backcountry coziness, but don't expect such luxuries as private baths, running water, or electricity. Meals are included in the rates. An afternoon tea, with freshly baked bread and sweets, is also served to lodge guests and day-trippers. Reserve far in advance. ⊠ *Box 5, T0L 1E0,* ☎ *403/522–3555,* 𝖥𝖠𝖷 *403/522–2095. 4 rooms, 3 cabins. Dining room. AE, MC, V. Closed late Sept.–Dec. 21 and Easter–late June.*

Nightlife

If you don't want to spend the evening outdoors, the **Chateau Lake Louise** has lounges and dining rooms with entertainment and dancing.

Outdoor Activities and Sports

HORSEBACK RIDING

The concierge at **Chateau Lake Louise** can arrange for trail rides and lessons.

SKIING

At **Lake Louise Ski Area** (⊠ Box 5, T0L 1E0, ☎ 403/522–3555) the downhill terrain is large and varied, with a fairly even spread of novice, intermediate, and expert runs (☞ Skiing *in* Banff, *above*).

SPORTING GEAR

Monod's (⊠ Chateau Lake Louise, ☎ 403/522–3837) has a wide selection of gear and clothing.

NORTH AND WEST OF BANFF

Just north of Lake Louise, Highways 1 and 93 diverge. Highway 93, the spectacularly scenic Icefields Parkway, continues northward for 230 km (143 mi) to Jasper National Park and Jasper. Highway 1 bears west over Kicking Horse Pass—named, according to local lore, after an unpleasant encounter between a pack animal and a member of an exploratory expedition in the mid-1800s—into Yoho National Park and British Columbia (if you're continuing in this direction, *see* the British Columbia Rockies, *below*).

The Icefields Parkway

230 km (143 mi), running from Lake Louise to Jasper.

★ Powerfully rugged mountain scenery, more than 100 glaciers, waterfalls and icefalls, and close encounters with big-game animals: The **Icefields Parkway** has all these and more as it snakes its way between Lake Louise and Jasper. The original highway was built in the Depression but has since been completely reconstructed and is now a good two-lane road, with wide paved shoulders along most of the route. It needs to be: Some 4 million people drive the parkway each year.

For the best views, try to choose a clear day for your trip. There aren't many facilities along the route, so be sure to check the gas gauge and pack some food if you plan to travel its entire length. Although you could drive this winding road in three to four hours if you were in a hurry, it's more likely to be a full-day trip with stops. The road rises to near tree line at several points, and it can be chilly at these high elevations even in midsummer—bring some warmer clothing along.

The most dramatic scenery is in the north end of Banff National Park and the south end of Jasper National Park, where ice fields and glaciers become common on the high mountains surrounding the route (ice fields are massive reservoirs of ice; glaciers are the slow-moving rivers of ice that flow from the ice fields). Scenic overlooks and hiking trails of varying lengths abound along the route.

⑫ **Bow Pass,** at 6,787 feet the highest drivable pass in the national parks of the Canadian Rockies, may be covered with snow as late as May and as early as September. On the south side of the pass is Bow Lake, source of the Bow River, which flows through Banff. Above Bow Lake hangs the edge of Crowfoot Glacier; to the south, across the lake, is the beginning of the Waputik Icefield. Around the lake are stubby trees and underbrush—this is where the trees end and high-alpine country begins. On the north side of the pass is **Peyto Lake**; its startlingly deep aqua blue color comes from the minerals in glacier runoff. ⊠ *41 km (25 mi) north of Lake Louise, 190 km (118 mi) south of Jasper.*

Sunwapta Pass marks the juncture of Banff and Jasper national parks. Wildlife abounds here and is most visible in spring and autumn after a snowfall, when herds of bighorn sheep come to the road to lick up the salt used to melt snow and ice. Drive cautiously: At 6,675 feet, Sunwapta is the second-highest drivable pass in the national parks of the Canadian Rockies. Regardless of whether you approach it from the north or south, be prepared for a series of hairpin turns as you switchback your way up to the pass summit. ⊠ *122 km (76 mi) north of Lake Louise, 108 km (67 mi) south of Jasper.*

The **Athabasca Glacier** is a 7-km (4½-mi) tongue of ice flowing from the immense Columbia Icefield almost to the highway. Several other glaciers are visible from here; they all originate from the Columbia Icefield—a giant alpine lake of ice covering 325 square km (130 square mi), whose edge is visible from the highway. You can take a trip onto the Athabasca Glacier on buses (called snow-coaches) modified to drive on ice (tickets available at the Icefield Centre). Hikers can also walk onto the tongue of the glacier, but venturing very far without a trained guide is dangerous due to hidden crevasses and slippery, sharp *ice. ⊠ 127 km (79 mi) north of Lake Louise, 103 km (64 mi) south of Jasper. Bus tour, Brewster Tours, ☏ 403/762–6700. ☏ $21.50, ☉ May–mid-Oct. Guided ½-day walking tour, ⊠ Athabasca Glacier Ice Walks, ☏ 403/347–1828 in-season, 403/852–3803 off-season. ☏ 3-hr walk $28, 5- to 6-hr walk $32. Reserve through Jasper Adventure Centre, ☏ 403/852–5595 or 800/565–7547; tickets also available at Icefield Centre (☞ below).*

⑬ The **Icefield Centre,** the interpretive center for the Athabasca Glacier and Columbia Icefield, houses a wealth of interpretive exhibits, a gift shop, and two dining facilities (one cafeteria style, one buffet style). There are even 32 hotel rooms, available from early May to mid-October (book through Brewster's Transport in Banff, ☏ 403/762–6735). Keep in mind that the summer midday rush between 11 and 3 can be so intense that even the Icefield Centre's promotional materials suggest you choose another time of day to come. ⊠ *Opposite Athabasca Glacier on Hwy. 93, 127 km (79 mi) north of Lake Louise, 103 km (64 mi) south of Jasper,* ☏ *403/852–7030 summer, 403/852–6176 winter.* ☉ *Late May–mid-June and Sept., daily 10–5; mid-June–Aug., daily 10–7.*

Jasper

⑭ *287 km (178 mi) north of Banff, 362 km (224 mi) west of Edmonton.*

The town of Jasper, a less-hectic version of Banff and about one-half the size of its larger cousin, is a convenient central location for exploring the sights in Jasper National Park. The shopping and dining scene is even more casual than Banff's, and the center of town has space for adults to hang out and for kids to play. Jasper has grown considerably in recent years and has become a major tourist destination, with prices to match. Still, it remains a relaxed and less commercialized place to stay in the parks—for now.

Jasper is set in one of the preeminent backpacking areas in North America. Multiday loops of more than 160 km (99 mi) are possible on well-maintained trails. Backpacking and horse-packing trips in the northern half of the park offer legitimate wilderness seclusion, if not the dramatic glacial scenery of the park's southern half. However, day trips are much more common, especially around Mt. Edith Cavell, Pyramid Lake, Jasper Park Lodge, and Maligne Lake.

The main drag in Jasper is **Connaught Drive;** railroad tracks border one side of the road, a dense collection of shops, restaurants, and motels line the other. This strip gets crowded; drive it with an eye out for pedestrians.

★ ⑮ The **Jasper Tramway** whisks riders 3,191 vertical feet up the steep flank of Whistlers Mountain to an impressive overlook of the town of Jasper. You can see the summit of Mt. Robson (when that mountain is clear) and the Miette valley to the west and the Athabasca valley to the east. On the seven-minute ride, the lift operator doubles as a guide, revealing the geological and historical secrets of key elements in the surrounding landscape. The upper station is above tree line (be sure to bring warm clothes). From it, a 20-minute scramble will take you to the summit, where you can sign a register to prove you were there. ⊠ *Whistlers Mountain Rd., 3 km (2 mi) south of Jasper off Hwy. 93,* ☏ *403/852–3093.* ☏ *$14.* ☉ *Mid-May–Aug., daily 8:30 AM–10 PM; Sept., daily 9:30–9; Apr.–mid-May and Oct., daily 9–4:30.*

The **Jasper-Yellowhead Museum** has historical exhibits showing what life in the area was like when prospectors, surveyors, settlers, and others arrived more than a century ago. ✉ *400 Pyramid Lake Rd.,* ☎ *403/852–3013.* 🎫 *Donations accepted.* ☉ *Mid-May–early Sept., daily 10–9; early Sept.–mid-May, call for hours.*

🅒 **Jasper Aquatic Center** pleases children with an indoor water slide, the Kidspool, and a huge regular pool. ✉ *Pyramid Lake Rd.,* ☎ *403/852–3663.* 🎫 *$4.* ☉ *Public swim Mon.–Thurs. 6 PM–8:30 PM, Fri. 4–9:30, weekends 2–9:30; call for other hours.*

⑯ **Pyramid** and **Patricia lakes** are on the outskirts of Jasper. Motorboats, sailboats, rowboats, canoes, kayaks, catamarans, and 4-seater pedal boats can be rented from Pyramid Lake Resort. Pyramid Lake is one of only two lakes in Jasper National Park where boat motors are allowed (the other is a section of Maligne Lake). There are picnic tables and a sandy beach at Pyramid Lake, but you're likely to find the water too cold for swimming even in midsummer. At Patricia Lake Bungalows, you can rent from a small selection of canoes and rowboats. ✉ *Pyramid Lake Resort, Pyramid Lake Rd., 6 km (4 mi) north of Jasper,* ☎ *403/852–4900.* 🎫 *Boat rentals start at $10 per hr per boat.* ☉ *May–Oct., approximately 8 AM–10 PM.* ✉ *Patricia Lake Bungalows, Pyramid Lake Rd., 5 km (3 mi) north of Jasper,* ☎ *403/852–3560.* 🎫 *Boat rentals $6 per hr.*

Dining and Lodging

$$$$ ⨯ **Becker's Gourmet Restaurant (L'Auberge).** French cuisine is served
★ in this small mountain-lodge retreat with panoramic views of the Athabasca River from a glass-enclosed dining room. The menu is creatively assembled from French classics such as brie baked in puff pastry or veal with wild mushrooms. Breakfast begins at 8 AM. ✉ *Near Becker's Chalets, 8 km (5 mi) south of Jasper on Hwy. 93,* ☎ *403/852–3535. Reservations essential. MC, V. Closed mid-Oct.–Apr. No lunch.*

$$$$ ⨯ **Jasper Park Lodge.** For fancy dining and a wide-ranging Continental menu, the **Beauvert Room** is the place to go around Jasper. The huge dining room, with its stone pillars and hard angles, conveys a big-hotel–style ambience. Menu favorites include the warm artichoke pâté with water biscuits and garden crudités, and the slow-roasted loin of Alberta pork, honey-glazed and served with apricot chutney. The **Edith Cavell Dining Room** overlooks a mountain of the same name and is slightly smaller and more private than the Beauvert Room, with tall wooden pillars, wall tapestries, and live classical piano music. The menu is very French, with a few local nuances. The chowder of wild mushrooms and mixed grains and the hearts of romaine lettuce with roast garlic in anchovy dressing are each meals in themselves. **Moose's Nook,** more intimate but retaining a modern coolness, offers imaginative Continental dishes, including pastas and Alberta prime rib of beef, as well as a popular salad and dessert bar. Moose's Nook is open for breakfast; the Edith Cavell Dining Room and the Beauvert Room are open for dinner only. ✉ *Off Hwy. 16, 4 km (2½ mi) northeast of Jasper, off Hwy. 16,* ☎ *403/852–3301 or 800/441–1414. Reservations essential. AE, D, DC, MC, V.*

$$$–$$$$ ⨯ **Le Beauvallon.** This is often the restaurant of choice for Jasperites
★ going out for a special meal. Upholstered chairs, blue tablecloths, and wood-trimmed crimson walls give the dining room an air of elegance that is enhanced by the strains of a world-class harpist playing in the nearby lounge. The menu has some seafood items, but meat and game dishes are the highlight, including lamb and venison. The giant Sunday-brunch buffet is an epic feast. Try Le Beauvallon for breakfast, too. ✉ *Chateau Jasper, 96 Giekie St.,* ☎ *403/852–5644. Reservations essential. AE, DC, MC, V.*

$$ ✕ **Palisades.** A surprisingly rich Greek streak runs through Jasper, and this restaurant is a good place to get a feel for it. Bright white walls, a greenhouse ceiling over part of the dining room, and numerous plants evoke a sunny Mediterranean mood. The walls are adorned with local artwork (for sale). Moussaka and souvlaki, along with baklava for dessert, are the characteristic Greek items; there's pizza, too. ✉ *Cedar Ave. near Connaught Dr.,* ☎ *403/852–5222. AE, DC, MC, V.*

$ ✕ **Mountain Foods.** This is a good place to pick up a morning cup of coffee or sandwiches for a picnic lunch. The café has a health-food store in the back and a deli counter up front. Though the emphasis is on health foods, you can still get an old-fashioned three-meat hero to eat in or take out. The tabbouleh salad is especially good. Browse through the store's book rack while waiting for your sandwich to be made. ✉ *606 Connaught Dr.,* ☎ *403/852–4050. MC, V.*

$$$$ 🏨 **Chateau Jasper.** Large wood beams cantilevered over the front door of this two-story inn suggest a Scandinavian interior, but rooms are of the American motel style, with a Colonial motif that's most notable in the Colonial-style headboards. Burgundy carpets and low ceilings add coziness to largish rooms. The hotel's restaurant, Le Beauvallon (☞ *above*), is excellent. Rates drop by more than half October–May. ✉ *96 Giekie St., T0E 1E0,* ☎ *403/852–5644,* 𝔽𝔸𝕏 *403/852–4860. 119 rooms. Restaurant, indoor pool, hot tub. AE, DC, MC, V.*

$$$$ 🏨 **Jasper Park Lodge.** This lakeside village northeast of town hums ★ with on-site recreational amenities and is a notable mountain destination in itself, whether or not you stay here. Rooms vary: Some are modern in style; others have an exposed-log, rustic character, with fireplaces. Most are arranged in long one-story rows of attached "cabins," with one room or one or two bedrooms; eight specialty cabins have up to eight bedrooms each. The cabins have bright down comforters, a porch, patio, or balcony. There's year-round outdoor swimming in a heated pool—a major draw for winter guests. Note that tour groups may receive preferential treatment to individual travelers, and overbooking can be a problem during peak season. Rates drop by almost one-half October–May. ✉ *Off Hwy. 16, 4 km (2½ mi) northeast of Jasper, Box 40, T0E 1E0,* ☎ *403/852–3301 or 800/441–1414,* 𝔽𝔸𝕏 *403/ 852–5107. 442 rooms. 4 restaurants, 3 bars, coffee shop, pool, 18-hole golf course, 4 tennis courts, horseback riding, boating, bicycles, ice skating, rollerblading, sleigh rides. AE, D, DC, MC, V.*

$$ 🏨 **Jasper Inn.** A modern interpretation of chalet-style architecture, this inn has oblique angles and hard edges, with sleek, low-slung furniture to match. The angular coolness is warmed by slanted cedar ceilings and redbrick fireplaces. During breakfast, the skylighted dining area can be as bright as the beach on a sunny day. Accommodations vary, but living areas in condo-style units are particularly spacious. Most units have kitchenettes and fireplaces. Rates drop by more than half October–May. ✉ *Giekie St. and Bonhomme Ave., Box 879, T0E 1E0,* ☎ *403/852–4461,* 𝔽𝔸𝕏 *403/852–5916. 129 rooms, 14 suites. Restaurant, lobby lounge, indoor pool, sauna, steam bath. AE, DC, MC, V.*

$–$$ 🏨 **Alpine Village.** One of Jasper's bargains is just south of town. Logs ★ in many cabins are left exposed on interior walls, adding to the warm, rustic feeling of this family-run operation. Rooms have pine furnishings, fieldstone fireplaces, and beamed ceilings. Most units have sundecks; two-bedroom cabins have full kitchens. Mt. Edith Cavell rises in the distance, and the Athabasca River runs out front, though you must cross a small road to reach it. Rates decrease by one-third off-season. ✉ *Hwy. 93A, 1 km (½ mi) south of Jasper, Box 610, T0E 1E0,* ☎ *403/ 852–3285. 42 units. Outdoor hot tub. MC, V. Closed mid-Oct.–Apr.*

$ 🏠 **Patricia Lake Bungalows.** On the shores of Patricia Lake, this great place for peace and quiet is just a short drive from Jasper. The clean, bright, and roomy cabins have basic furnishings—queen-size beds, dressers and tables, kitchen facilities, and TV. Shower stalls are the rule here, not bathtubs. This is one of the few remaining bargain accommodations in Jasper. The motel-style rooms have recently been remodeled into large family units, but the cabins remain the most popular choice for most visitors. Rates decrease 20% off-season. ⊠ *Pyramid Lake Rd., 5 km (3 mi) from Jasper, Box 657, Jasper, T0E 1E0,* ☎ *403/ 852–3560,* FAX *403/852–4060. 7 rooms, 29 cabins. Boating, bicycles, coin laundry. Closed mid-Oct–Apr.*

Nightlife and the Arts

THE ARTS

The **Jasper Activity Centre** (⊠ 303 Pyramid Ave., ☎ 403/852–3381) hosts local theater, music, and dance troupes throughout the year. The **Jasper Folk Festival,** on the first weekend in August, presents Canadian folk music in the town center and at other venues. The **Chaba Movie Theatre** (⊠ Connaught Dr., ☎ 403/852–4749) plays major releases.

NIGHTLIFE

The **Astoria Hotel** (⊠ 404 Connaught Dr., ☎ 403/852–3351) is a popular spot that can become crowded and raucous. The **Athabasca Hotel**'s nightclub (⊠ 510 Patricia St., ☎ 403/852–3386) has dancing to Top-40 music and live bands. For cocktails and socializing, the **Jasper Park Lodge** (⊠ Off Hwy. 16, ☎ 403/852–3301) has lounges and dining rooms with entertainment and dancing. The **Whistle Stop** (⊠ Whistlers Inn, Connaught Dr., ☎ 403/852–3361) is a local haunt with the ambience of a British pub.

Outdoor Activities and Sports

The **Jasper Adventure Centre** (⊠ Box 1064, T0E 1E0, ☎ FAX 403/852–5595) provides guided tours of popular sights in Jasper National Park as well as more specialized offerings such as birding trips, ice walks, and snowshoeing tours. Rates are about $22–$30 per adult, with most tours lasting about three hours. The center rents skis, snowboards, and snowshoes. It also handles bookings for a number of other adventure companies (canoeing, rafting, and other sports).

BIKING

Bikes can be rented from **Freewheel Cycle** (⊠ 611 Patricia St., ☎ 403/852–3898).

CLIMBING

The **Jasper Climbing School and Mountaineering Service** (⊠ Box 452, T0E 1E0, ☎ 403/852–3964) offers daylong guided trips as well as climbing instruction.

GOLF

Jasper Park Lodge (☎ 403/852–6090) has an 18-hole course.

HIKING

For information on Skyline and Tonquin Valley trail quotas, contact **Jasper National Park Information Centre** (⊠ 500 Connaught Dr., T0E 1E0, ☎ 403/852–6177). **Rocky Mountain Hiking** (⊠ Box 2623, T0E 1E0, ☎ 403/852–5015) has trained backcountry guides to take visitors on customized multiday hikes and also offers interpretive programs, day hikes, and some caving.

HORSEBACK RIDING

For trail rides or lessons contact the concierge at **Jasper Park Lodge** or **Pyramid Riding Stables** (⊠ Box 787, T0E 1E0, ☎ 403/852–3562).

RAFTING

Jasper Raft Tours (⌧ Box 398, T0E 1E0, ☎ 403/852–3613) runs half-day float trips on the Athabasca. **Maligne River Adventures** (⌧ Box 280, 616 Connaught Dr., T0E 1E0, ☎ 403/852–3370) runs half-day white-water trips on the Maligne. Prices begin at $50.

SCUBA DIVING

For scuba divers **Patricia Lake,** near Jasper, is a popular spot to explore the remains of the *Habakkuk.* This was a ship made of ice: a military prototype, secretly designed during World War II to take advantage of the fact that the plastic nature of ice (maintained by a cooling system) could absorb an impact without major structural damage to the vessel. What remains is mostly a skeleton of cooling pipes, but it makes for an interesting historical dive.

SKIING

Cross-Country. Jasper National Park has excellent groomed trails at Pyramid and Patricia lakes and on the Icefields Parkway near town. Maligne Lake has a range of moderate-to-challenging lakeside and forest cross-country ski trails. Reservations for backcountry huts in Tonquin Valley can be made through **Tonquin Valley Pack and Ski Trips** (⌧ Box 550, 712 Connaught Dr., T0E 1E0, ☎ 403/852–3909).

Downhill. Marmot Basin (⌧ Box 1300, Jasper T0E 1E0, ☎ 403/852–3816), near Jasper, has a wide mix of terrain, and slopes are a little less crowded than those around Banff.

SPORTING GEAR

Totem Ski Shop (⌧ 408 Connaught Dr., ☎ 403/852–3078 or 800/363–3078) is the major sporting goods outlet.

SWIMMING

Pyramid Lake has a large beach, although it would be unusual for the water to warm above 20°C (68°F). Lake Annette and Lake Edith, near Jasper Park Lodge, also have beaches and somewhat warmer water that reaches the low 20s°C (low 70s°F) during warm spells. These waters are among the clearest anywhere—crystalline views of the lake bottom fool swimmers into trying to put a foot onto rocks that are hopelessly beyond their reach.

Shopping

In Jasper the main **shopping streets** are Patricia Street and Connaught Drive; expect to pay a resort premium for most goods.

You'll find a large selection of native arts and crafts at **E&A Studio** (⌧ 105 Miette Ave., ☎ 403/852–3606). **Jasper Originals** (⌧ Beauvert Promenade, Jasper Park Lodge, ☎ 403/852–5378) has regional arts and crafts.

Jasper National Park

South border of park: 178 km (110 mi) north of Banff townsite, 152 km (94 mi) south of Jasper townsite. East border of park: 323 km (200 mi) west of Edmonton, 50 km (31 mi) east of Jasper townsite.

Apart from the innumerable scenic vistas and hiking trails, a number of special attractions in Jasper National Park make for easy half-day trips south, east, north, or west from the Jasper townsite. Don't expect much in the way of accommodations, though; apart from a single motel at Miette Hot Springs, and two cabin-type facilities near the east gate, all the lodging in this huge park—almost as large as the entire state of Connecticut—is clustered in the town.

⓱ **Mt. Edith Cavell** is the highest mountain in the vicinity of the town of Jasper. Named after a heroic nurse who was shot by the Germans during the First World War, it towers above the surroundings at 11,033 feet and shows off its permanently snow-clad north face to the town. From Highway 93A, a narrow, winding 14½-km (9-mi) road (often closed until the beginning of June) leads to the base of the mountain. Traffic is one way only, with the direction reversed every 1½ hours. Trailers are not permitted on this road, but they can be dropped off at a parking lot near the junction with 93A. There are several pullouts along the road that offer spectacular views, as well as access to trails leading up the **Tonquin Valley,** one of the premier hiking (as well as horse-packing and backcountry skiing) areas in the park.

The mountain itself is arguably the most spectacular site in Jasper National Park, reachable by automobile. From the parking lot—which can become quite congested—there is a short trail that leads to the base of an imposing mile-high cliff. The Angel Glacier drips out of a valley partway up the cliff, highlighting the scene. If you feel ambitious, a steep 3-km (2-mi) trail climbs up the valley opposite the mountain, opening into an alpine meadow—**Cavell Meadows.** The meadow is carpeted with wildflowers from mid-July to mid- or late August, and there's an excellent view of the Angel Glacier on the opposite slope. ⊠ *27 km (17 mi) south of Jasper.*

⑱ At **Athabasca Falls,** the Athabasca River is compressed through a narrow gorge, producing a violent torrent of water. The falls are especially dramatic in early summer, when the river is swollen by snowmelt. Trails and overlooks provide numerous vantage points to view the falls and the nearby montane forest. ⊠ *31 km (19 mi) south of Jasper at Icefields Pkwy. and Hwy. 93A.*

Maligne Canyon, along the way to Maligne Lake, is where the Maligne River cuts a narrow 165-foot-deep gorge through limestone bedrock. An interpretive trail winds its way from a picnic area across six bridges where you can catch the spray from the thundering Maligne River. It is an impressive sight, but the 4-km (2½-mi) trail along the canyon can be crowded, especially near the start of the trail. Just off the path, you'll find a restaurant and native crafts store at the Maligne Canyon Chalet. ⊠ *Maligne Lake Rd., 11 km (7 mi) south of Jasper.*

Medicine Lake has a complex, underground drainage system that causes the lake to empty almost completely at times. This led the early natives to suspect that spirits were responsible for the dramatic fluctuations in the level of the placid waters. ⊠ *Maligne Lake Rd., 26 km (16 mi) south of Jasper.*

★ ⑲ The remarkably blue, 22-km-long (14-mi-long) **Maligne Lake** is one of the largest glacier-fed lakes in the world. You can explore it on a 1½-hour guided cruise or in a rented boat. Several day hikes (approximately 4 hours round-trip), with some steep sections, lead to alpine meadows that have panoramic views of the lake and the surrounding mountain ranges. You can also take horseback riding and fishing trips, and there's an excellent cafeteria here. ⊠ *Maligne Lake Rd., 44 km (27 mi) southeast of Jasper. Tour reservations, ⊠ Maligne Lake Scenic Cruises, 626 Connaught Dr., ☎ 403/852–3370. ⊡ Boat tour $31. ☉ Mid-May–Oct., daily 10–5, every hr on the hr.*

⑳ **Miette Hot Springs** is a relaxing spot, especially when the weather turns inclement. You can soak in naturally heated mineral waters originating from three springs that reach 54°C (129°F) and have to be cooled to 40°C (104°F) to allow bathing. There are two hot pools and one cool pool (27°C, or 80°F). A short walk leads to the remnants of the original hot spring facility, where several springs still pour heated sulphurous water into the adjacent creek. Day passes and suit, locker, and towel rentals are available. ⊠ *Miette Hot Springs Rd. off Hwy. 16, 58 km (36 mi) northeast of Jasper,* ☎ *403/866–3939.* ☒ *$4–$5.* ☉ *Late May–mid-June and early Sept.–early Oct., daily 10:30–9, late-June–early Sept., daily 8:30 AM–10:30 PM.*

Hiking

Jasper National Park, with nearly 1,000 km (620 mi) of hiking trails, is popular with hikers who want to go deep into the wilderness for several days at a time. In an effort to minimize environmental impact, park officials in Jasper have set quotas for some of the park's most popular backpacking routes. In the height of the summer season, be prepared to encounter filled quotas for such areas as the Skyline Trail and Tonquin Valley. About a third of each trail's quota is prebooked by reservations, which can be made up to three weeks in advance by contacting the Jasper National Park Information Centre (☞ Outdoor Activities and Sports *in* Jasper, *above*). **Tonquin Valley,** near Mt. Edith Cavell, is one of Canada's classic backpacking areas. Its high mountain lakes, bounded by a series of steep, rocky peaks known as the Ramparts, attract many visitors in the height of summer. The **Skyline Trail** wanders for 44 km (27 mi), at or above the tree line, past some of the park's most spectacular scenery. Good **day-hiking areas** in Jasper are around Maligne Lake, Mt. Edith Cavell, and Miette Hot Springs.

Mt. Robson Provincial Park

80 km (50 mi) west of Jasper.

This provinical park, contiguous with Jasper National Park, makes a nice hour-long trip from Jasper townsite on Highway 16. The terrain and scenery are similar to Jasper's, although the vegetation is a bit more lush because of higher rainfall. The park has a number of hiking trails, plus some campgrounds. Another draw is the Fraser River. The **visitor center** (☎ 250/566–4325), open mid-May to early October, has a fine view of Mt. Robson, and a small restaurant.

㉑ At 12,972 feet, towering **Mt. Robson** is the highest mountain in the Canadian Rockies. The peak was not successfully scaled until 1913, despite numerous attempts. Certain routes on Robson are still considered by experienced mountaineers to be among the world's most challenging. Mt. Robson's weather is notoriously bad even when the weather elsewhere is perfectly fine; it is a rare day that the summit is not encircled by clouds. A favorite backpacking trip on the mountain is the strenuous 18-km (11-mi) hike to **Berg Lake,** through the wonderfully named Valley of a Thousand Falls. Berg Lake is no tranquil body of water; the grunt and splash as Robson's glaciers calve chunks of ice into the lake are regular sounds in summer. The 5-km (3-mi) mostly level hike to **Kinney Lake,** along the Berg Lake trail, is a good option for day hikers.

Kootenay National Park

34 km (21 mi) west of Banff townsite, 162 km (100 mi) west of Calgary.

Named for the Kootenai people who settled in the area, Kootenay National Park is just over the border in British Columbia, touching the west side of Banff National Park and the south end of Yoho National Park. When the tourist population of Banff swells during the busy summer months, Kootenay park remains surprisingly quiet, although not for lack of natural beauty; the scenery can certainly match that of Banff and Jasper parks. Facilities are few here, so most people see the park only as they drive through on Highway 93, which traverses the length of the park, while on their way to other points in British Columbia.

㉒ **Vermilion Pass** is at the juncture of Banff and Kootenay national parks. At 5,416 feet, this is not one of the highest passes in the Canadian Rockies, but it marks the boundary between Alberta and British Columbia and the Continental Divide—rivers east of here flow to the Atlantic Ocean; rivers to the west flow to the Pacific Ocean.

Just beyond the Vermilion Pass summit is the head of the **Stanley Glacier trail,** one of the fine choices for a day hike in the park. The trail climbs easily for 4 km (2½ mi) through fire remnants and new growth, across rock debris and glacial moraine, ending in the giant amphitheater of the Stanley Glacier basin. ⊠ *3 km (2 mi) from east gate of Kootenay park.*

㉓ **Floe Lake,** at the base of a 3,300-foot-high cliff called the Rockwall, is one of the most popular hiking destinations in Kootenay National Park. The 10-km (6-mi) trail from the highway passes through characteristic Kootenay backcountry terrain. Plan a full day for this one. ⊠ *Trailhead, 22 km (14 mi) from east gate of Kootenay park.*

Hiking

The trail that best characterizes the hiking in Kootenay is the strenuous **Rockwall Trail,** which runs along the series of steep rock facades that are the predominant feature of the park. Floe Lake, sitting at the base of a sheer 3,300-foot wall, is a trail highlight. Several long day-hike spurs connect the trail with Highway 93.

En Route Along the stretch of Highway 93 that leads through Kootenay National Park from Banff National Park to Radium Hot Springs, 63 km (39 mi) to the south, the only service area is at **Vermilion Crossing,** the approximate halfway point. Here, you'll find fuel and basic groceries (summer only). Between Vermilion Crossing and Radium, the mountains open up gradually, their flanks covered by thick stands of Douglas fir, as the Vermilion River joins with the wider Kootenay River. The highway then heads west, winding through the narrow limestone canyon cut by the Sinclair River.

Yoho National Park

57 km (35 mi) northwest of town of Banff, 185 km (115 mi) west of Calgary.

The name "Yoho" is a native word that translates, approximately, to "awe inspiring." Indeed, Yoho National Park is awe inspiring, containing some of the most outstanding scenery in the Canadian Rockies and a well-known fossil site. Yoho National Park adjoins Banff National Park to the east and Kootenay National Park to the south, but it is quieter than its eastern neighbor. The park is divided by Highway 1 into the northern half, which includes Takakkaw Falls, the Yoho River Valley, and Emerald Lake, and the southern half, of which Lake O'Hara is the physical and spiritual epicenter.

㉔ In the northern half of Yoho park, **Takakkaw Falls,** 833 feet high, is the highest waterfall in Canada. The falls are spectacular in early summer when melting snow and ice provide ample runoff. (The flow of the falls can also increase during summer hot spells, which speed the melt of glacial ice.) But the falls are just a taste of what lies ahead for day hikers and backpackers who choose to explore the region's trail network through the Yoho River Valley with its ice fields and high cliffs. ⊠ *Access from 13-km (8-mi) Yoho Valley Rd., off Hwy. 1, 13 km (8 mi) west of Banff National Park.*

㉕ The **Burgess Shale site,** halfway between the Takakkaw Falls road and the Emerald Lake Lodge road, contains the fossilized remains of 120 marine species dating back 515 million years. Burgess Shale was designated a World Heritage Site in 1981; guided hikes are the only way to see the actual fossil sites, and they're popular, so make reservations. The hikes are conducted July through mid-September, and the going is fairly strenuous; the round-trip distance is 20 km (12 mi). There is a shorter, steeper hike to the Mt. Stevens trilobite fossil beds. Guided hikes are also offered to extensions of the Burgess Shale fossils in Kootenay and Banff national parks. Allow a full day for any of the hikes. ⊠ *Trailhead, 16 km (10 mi) west of Banff National Park. Reservations for guided hikes,* ⊠ *Canadian Wilderness Tours, 1010 Larch Pl., Canmore, AB T1W 1S7,* ☎ *403/678–3795; or* ⊠ *Yoho-Burgess Shale Research Foundation, Box 148, Field, BC V0A 1G0,* ☎ *800/343–3006.* 🖅 *Guided hike $35–$45.*

㉖ **Emerald Lake** is a vivid turquoise shimmer at the base of the President Range, where you can rent a canoe, have a cup of tea at the teahouse by the lodge, or take a stroll around the lake. The lake also is a trailhead for hikers, as well as a frequent haunt of cross-country and backcountry skiers in winter. ⊠ *Access from 8-km (5-mi) road off Hwy. 1, 19 km (12 mi) west of Banff National Park.*

㉗ **Lake O'Hara,** in Yoho's southern half, is widely regarded as one of *the* ultimate destinations for outdoor enthusiasts in the Canadian Rockies. For summer, Lake O'Hara Lodge (☞ Dining and Lodging, *below*) is booked months in advance. Although the forest-lined fire road between Highway 1 and the lake can be hiked, it makes more sense to ride the lodge-run bus even if you aren't staying at the lodge. (Call the lodge for times and space availability.) Save your legs for hiking any of several moderately strenuous trails that radiate from the lodge into a spectacular, high-alpine world of small lakes surrounded by escarpments of rock and permanent snowpack. Keep in mind, however, that the bus makes the Lake O'Hara area accessible to many other people, too. If you're looking for a true wilderness experience, other places (notably Kootenay National Park) are better choices. ⊠ *Access from 11-km (7-mi) Lake O'Hara Fire Rd. off Lake Louise/Great Divide Dr., 3 km (2 mi) west of Banff National Park.*

Dining and Lodging

$$$$ ✕🏨 **Emerald Lake Lodge.** This enchanted place at the edge of a secluded,
★ glacier-fed lake is only a 20-minute drive from Lake Louise and an hour from Banff. You can get light meals in a comfortable sitting area by the large stone hearth in the log-cabin main lodge. Guest rooms have fireplaces and balconies. The main dining room is a glass-enclosed terrace, with views of the lake through tall stands of evergreens. The menu mixes traditional Canadian and American fare—steaks, game, and fish—with such nouvelle sauces as ginger-tangerine glaze. Cilantro-on-the-Lake serves café-style light meals (summer only). Rates are reduced by half in off-season. ⊠ *Yoho National Park, 9½ km (6 mi) north of Field, Box 10, Field, BC V0A 1G0,* ☎ *250/343–6321 or 800/663–6336,* FAX *250/343–6724. 85 units in 2- and 4-room cottages. 2 restaurants, bar, tea shop, sauna, outdoor hot tub, exercise room, horseback riding, boating. AE, DC, MC, V.*

$$$$ 🏨 **Lake O'Hara Lodge.** In summer guests are ferried by a lodge-operated bus along an 11-km (7-mi) fire road between Highway 1 and the grounds. In winter guests must ski the distance. The lodge and lakeside cabins offer fairly luxurious backcountry living; the rooms have baths, and a dining room serves three meals a day (included in the room

rates). Avoid the smaller, cramped, noisy rooms near the gentlemen's bathroom. Reservations for the high summer season (mid-June–September) should be booked several months in advance. Rates are based on double-occupancy rooms; there are no off-season rates. ⊠ *Off Hwy. 1, Yoho National Park, Box 55, Lake Louise, AB T0L 1E0,* ☎ *250/ 343–6418, or 403/678–4110. 23 units in lodge and cabins. Dining room, hiking, cross-country skiing, boating. No credit cards. Closed mid-Apr.–mid-June and Oct.–mid-Feb.*

Outdoor Activities and Sports

HIKING

Yoho is divided into two parts: the popular hiking area around Lake O'Hara, dotted with high-alpine lakes, and the less-traveled Yoho River valley, terminating at the Yoho Glacier. Access to the Lake O'Hara region is somewhat restricted by the long, rather uneventful fire road from Highway 1. Most hikers and climbers take the Lake O'Hara Lodge shuttle bus. Entry into the Yoho River valley is more immediate, either from Takakkaw Falls or from Emerald Lake.

HORSEBACK RIDING

The concierge at **Emerald Lake Lodge** (☎ 250/343–6321) can arrange for horseback riding expeditions and lessons.

SOUTH OF BANFF

The region immediately southeast of Banff—the town of Canmore and, south of it, the group of provincial parks and recreation areas jointly known as Kananaskis Country—attracted mostly locals from Calgary and Banff until the 1988 Olympics brought brand-new facilities—ski jumps, cross-country trails, and other sports installations, as well as hotels and restaurants—to the region. Farther south, Waterton Lakes National Park marks the meeting of the prairie and the mountains. With Glacier Park in Montana, it forms Waterton-Glacier International Peace Park.

Canmore

28 *24 km (15 mi) southeast of Banff townsite, 106 km (66 mi) west of Calgary.*

A modern boomtown, Canmore is attracting high-end tourism developments and residents who crave a mountain lifestyle. The handsome, boutique-lined Main Street and several good restaurants are indications that it is no longer a locals-only town, although much of its character and charm remains. Canmore has become the regional center for outdoor activities—climbing, hiking, and mountain biking in summer, cross-country and alpine skiing in winter. Several outfitters, climbing schools, and guide services are based here, and the town makes a good base for exploring the national parks or Kananaskis Country. This version of Canmore didn't really emerge until the 1988 Winter Olympics, when new facilities around Canmore and Kananaskis Country gave this area widespread appeal.

Dining and Lodging

$$–$$$ ✕ **Pepper Mill.** The small dining room is simply adorned with off-white walls, green tablecloths, and hanging lamps. Known for its pepper steak, the restaurant also serves well-prepared pasta dishes, fish, and seafood. ⊠ *726 9th St.,* ☎ *403/678–2292. AE, MC, V. No lunch.*

$$ ✕ **Faro's.** Colorful drawings of Canmore hung against white walls and blond-wood tabletops contribute to a bright, casual environment. The menu is eclectic, listing barbecued dishes, pizzas, and steaks, but such

Greek entrées as souvlaki are the house specialties. ⊠ *8th St. and 8th Ave.,* ☎ *403/678–2234. AE, MC, V.*

$$$ ⊡ **Mt. Assiniboine Lodge.** Built in 1928, this lodge appears to have changed little in 70 years. The backcountry setting is classically alpine—at the edge of mile-long Lake Magog, with the rocky pyramid of Mt. Assiniboine in full view. Guests can hike in (20–30 km, or 12–19 mi) or fly in by helicopter from Canmore. Hearty meals are served family-style. There are cabins that sleep two to four people, as well as lodge rooms. The lodge has some electricity and running water, but guests should be prepared to use outhouses. Room rates include all meals and hiking (or skiing) guide service. Rates decrease about 15% in off-season. ⊠ *Box 8128, T1W 2T8,* ☎ *403/678–2883,* FAX *403/678–4877. 6 rooms, 6 cabins. Dining room. MC, V. Closed Oct.–mid-Feb. and mid-Apr.–late June.*

$–$$ ⊡ **Rocky Mountain Ski Lodge.** Several motels in Canmore provide lower-price alternatives to Banff accommodations. Of these, Rocky Mountain Ski Lodge is a notch above the rest. It's really three separate motel properties rolled into one. Slanting, exposed wood-and-beam ceilings give a chaletlike feel to otherwise simple motel rooms. Rooms in the older section have kitchenettes, but the decor is more '60s American than Swiss-chalet. Rates drop 40% in off-season. ⊠ *Hwy. 1A, Box 8070, T1W 2T8,* ☎ *403/678–5445, 800/665–6111in Canada,* FAX *403/ 678–6484. 82 units. Sauna, hot tub, playground. AE, MC, V.*

$ ⊡ **Bow Valley Motel.** This two-story, few-frills motel in the center of Canmore is enhanced by its friendly management. If you put a premium on being able to walk to dining and shopping, this is the place to stay. Rooms are clean and simply furnished, with a bed, a dresser, a small fridge, and a 20-inch TV. Five rooms have kitchens. Rates drop 50% in off-season. ⊠ *610 8th St., T1W 2B5, T0L 0M0,* ☎ *403/678–5085,* FAX *403/678–6560. 25 rooms. Outdoor hot tub, coin laundry. AE, D, MC, V.*

Nightlife

Join Canmore's locals and kick back at **Sherwood House** (⊠ 738 8th St., ☎ 403/678–5211), which occasionally has live bands on weekends.

Outdoor Activities and Sports

CROSS-COUNTRY SKIING

Canmore Nordic Centre (⊠ 1988 Olympic Way, Suite 100, T0L 0M0, ☎ 403/678–2400) has 70 km (43 mi) of groomed trails. The **Canadian School of Mountaineering** (⊠ 629 10th St., T1W 2E5, ☎ 403/678–4134) leads backcountry tours.

GOLF

Canmore Golf Course (⊠ Off Hwy 1, ☎ 403/678–4784) has 18 holes.

Shopping

Stonecrop Studios & Gallery (⊠ 8th Ave. and Main St., ☎ 403/678–4151) displays the works in progress of local artists using bronze, ceramics, pottery, and silver, among other media.

Kananaskis Country

㉙ *North entrance: 26 km (16 mi) southeast of Canmore, 80 km (50 mi) west of Calgary.*

Three provincial parks make up the 4,200-square-km (1,600-square-mi) recreational region known as Kananaskis Country. It has great mountain scenery, though not quite as spectacular as that in the adjacent national parks. Kananaskis, however, has a multitude of outdoor activities, some of which are prohibited or discouraged in the national parks. Camping, hiking, bicycling, fishing, hunting, golfing, boating, canoeing, horseback riding, and exploring in all-terrain vehicles predominate in spring, summer, and fall. Downhill skiing, cross-country skiing, snowshoeing, ice skating, snowmobiling, dogsledding, ice fishing, and camping are popular winter activities.

The main highway through Kananaskis Country is Highway 40, also known as the **Kananaskis Trail.** It runs north–south through the impressive scenery of the front ranges of the Rockies. Only the northern 40 km (25 mi) of the road remain open from December 1 to June 15, in part because of the extreme conditions of the **Highwood Pass** (at 7,280 feet, the highest drivable pass in Canada), and in part to protect winter wildlife habitat in **Peter Lougheed Provincial Park** and southward. Highway 40 continues south to join Highway 541, west of Longview. Access to East Kananaskis Country, a popular area for horseback-riding trips, is on Highway 66, which heads west from Priddis.

The **Canmore Nordic Centre,** built for the 1988 Olympic Nordic skiing events, has dozens of miles of groomed cross-country trails. This state-of-the-art facility is in the northwest corner of Kananaskis Country, just south of Canmore. Some trails are lighted for night skiing, and a 1½-km (1-mi) paved trail is open in summer for roller skiing and in-line skating. Lessons and rentals are available. ⊠ *Box 1979, Canmore T0L 0M0,* ☎ *403/678–2400.* ☞ *Trail use free.* ☉ *Lodge daily 9–5:30, some trails until 9.*

Kananaskis Village (☞ Dining and Lodging, *below*), a full-service resort built for the 1988 Olympics, brings first-class lodging, dining, and golf to Kananaskis Country. A lodge, a hotel, and an inn cluster next to an attractively landscaped artificial pond on a small plateau between the Nakiska ski area and two 18-hole golf courses. Many visitors to the region stay at one of the several campgrounds, most of which can accommodate recreational vehicles.

The **William Watson Lodge** is unique in the Canadian Rockies in that it is designed exclusively for senior citizens and people who have disabilities. Access points have been built along Mt. Lorette Ponds north of Kananaskis Village to accommodate anglers using wheelchairs, and many hiking trails near the village have been cut wide and gentle enough for wheelchair travel. Overnight and day-use facilities, including cabins, are available to people with disabilities and Alberta senior citizens. Albertans get preference; people with disabilities from out of the province must book 60 days in advance. ⊠ *30 km (19 mi) south of Kananaskis Village on Hwy. 40, Box 130, Kananaskis T0L 2H0,* ☎ *403/591–7227.* ☉ *Office weekdays 8 AM–9 PM.*

Dining and Lodging

$$$$ ✕ **L'Escapade.** This is the signature dining room of the Hotel at Kananaskis (☞ *below*). The atmosphere is intimate and the service attentive. On the menu are innovative Canadian dishes such as Brome Lake duck, Arctic musk ox, Yukon char, and desserts flambéed at the table. Soft, live music plays nightly for dancing. ⊠ *Hotel at Kananaskis, Hwy. 40, Kananaskis Village,* ☎ *403/591–7711 or 800/441–1414. Reservations essential. AE, D, DC, MC, V.*

$$$$ ✕▥ **Hotel and Lodge at Kananaskis.** The Hotel and the Lodge are part of Canadian Pacific's chain of luxury hotels. Many of the Hotel's large, lavish rooms have fireplaces, Jacuzzi tubs, and large sitting areas. Several restaurants, skewed toward high-end elegance, serve food from Spanish tapas to haute cuisine. For casual dining, try the **Peaks Din-**

ing **Room** in the Lodge, with family favorites, including burgers for lunch or dinner and a buffet-style breakfast, plus nightly family entertainment. Rates drop by 50% off-season. ✉ *Hwy. 40, 28 km (17 mi) south of Hwy. 1, Kananaskis Village T0L 2H0,* ☎ *403/591–7711 or 800/441–1414,* 🖷 *403/591–7770. 243 rooms, 78 suites. 3 restaurants, 2 lounges, indoor pool, sauna, steam room, 2 18-hole golf courses, health club. AE, D, DC, MC, V.*

$$$ 🏨 **Homeplace Ranch.** Just east of the Kananaskis Country foothills, this guest ranch is what its name suggests: homey. The principal activity is horseback riding over the rolling land near the ranch. Multiday pack trips into Kananaskis Country are available, but there's no riding mid-October–spring. The small living-dining area is cluttered with books and magazines that provide good reading, the main evening activity. Meals, included in the guest rate, are served family-style. A "south ranch," 1½ hours away, opened in 1995. It is similar to the main ranch, but accommodation is in 6 bunkhouses (no electricity). Rates decrease by one-third in off-season. There's a minimum three-night stay during summer. ✉ *Main ranch, off Hwy. 2, 10 km (6 mi) west of Priddis; south ranch, 30 km (19 mi) south of Longview; R.R. 1, Box 6, Priddis, AB T0L 1W0,* ☎ 🖷 *403/931–3245. Main ranch, 7 rooms; south ranch, 6 bunkhouses. Dining room. No credit cards.*

$$ 🏨 **Kananaskis Inn.** Part of the complex built for the 1988 Olympics, and overlooking the resort's pond, the Inn has log pillars and an inviting redwood exterior. Some of the motel-style rooms have private balconies, kitchenettes, or fireplaces. Rates drop by one-third off-season. ✉ *Hwy. 40, 28 km (17 mi) south of Hwy. 1, Box 10, Kananaskis Village T0L 2H0,* ☎ *403/591–7500,* 🖷 *403/591–7633. 94 rooms. Restaurant, bar, indoor pool, hot tub, steam room, coin laundry. AE, MC, V.*

$–$$ 🏨 **Kananaskis Guest Ranch.** Cabins and larger "chalets" surround the main lodge of this ranch near the Bow River, at the edge of Kananaskis Country. Cedar walls and, in some units, cedar-beam ceilings give a rustic flavor to otherwise plain, double-bed bedrooms. The Donut Tent—a log-and-wood-roof "tent" with a large hole in the middle, where bonfires are built for family-style barbecues—is the ranch's claim to fame. In addition to the obligatory horseback riding, the ranch also has jet-boat trips on the Bow River. ✉ *Ranch Rd., from Seebe-Exshaw exit on Hwy. 1 east of Canmore, General Delivery, Seebe T0L 1X0,* ☎ *403/673–3737 or 800/691–5085,* 🖷 *403/673–2100. 33 units in cabins and chalets. Dining room, lounge, hot tub, boating, horseback riding. AE, MC, V. Closed mid-Oct–Apr.*

$–$$ 🏨 **Mt. Engadine Lodge.** Hiking and cross-country skiing trails lead out
★ the back door of this backcountry lodge to the mountains and lakes of Kananaskis Country. Rooms (shared as well as private) have a scrubbed simplicity to them, as do the common areas. Meals, served family-style, are included in the rate. Small decrease in off-season rates. The lodge operators are also backcountry guides, and hiking packages are available. ✉ *At Mt. Shark, turn onto Spray Tr., 38 km (24 mi) south of Canmore, Box 8239, Canmore T1W 2T9,* ☎ *403/678–4080,* 🖷 *403/678–2109. 10 rooms and 2 cabins, all with shared baths. Restaurant, outdoor hot tub, sauna, hiking. MC, V. Closed May–mid-June, Oct.–Dec. 25, and weekdays Jan.–Apr.*

Nightlife

For the most part, nightlife in Kananaskis is of the do-it-yourself variety, but the **Hotel and Lodge at Kananaskis** (☞ Dining and Lodging, *above*) has lounges and dining rooms with entertainment and dancing.

Outdoor Activities and Sports

GOLF

Kananaskis Country Course (☎ In season, 403/591–7272; off-season, 403/591–7070) has two 18-hole links.

HORSEBACK RIDING

Boundary Ranch (✉ Box 44, Kananaskis Village T0L 2H0, ☎ 403/591–7171) has horses to rent for trail rides.

SKIING

Nakiska (✉ Box 1988, Kananaskis Village T0L 0M0, ☎ 403/591–7777), about 45 minutes southeast of Banff, was the site of the 1988 Olympic alpine events and has wide-trail intermediate skiing and not always reliable snow.

Waterton Lakes National Park

③⓪ *354 km (219 mi) south of Banff, 267 km (166 mi) south of Calgary.*

The mountains at Waterton Lakes National Park, near the southern end of the Canadian Rockies, seem a bit friendlier—not quite so high, not quite so rugged. This is a small park compared to Jasper or Banff, and you can cover its highlights in a day or two and still have time to relax.

Several hundred kilometers of highway separate Waterton from the other six mountain parks. As a result, the park is a rare side trip from Banff—it's generally a destination in itself or combined with a vacation in the much larger Glacier National Park across the U.S. border in Montana.

Waterton is the meeting of two worlds—the flatlands of the prairie and the abrupt upthrust of the mountains. In this juncture of worlds, the park squeezes into a relatively small area (525 square km, or 200 square mi) an unusual mix of wildlife, flora, and climate zones.

Politically, too, Waterton represents a meeting of worlds. Although the park was officially established in 1895, it was joined in 1932 with Glacier National Park in Montana to form **Waterton/Glacier International Peace Park**—a symbol of friendship and peaceful coexistence between Canada and the United States. In fact, some services in the park, including the Prince of Wales Hotel—perhaps the park's most recognizable landmark—are under Glacier Park management in the United States. In 1995 this park was designated a World Heritage Site by UNESCO.

Whether it is a pervading spirit of international peace or the park's isolation, Waterton is decidedly low-key. The townsite of Waterton Park is a small, quiet community, located in roughly the geographical center of the park. In winter it essentially closes down; in summer several hundred residents call the park home. Hiking, horseback riding, and boating are the main activities. The park contains numerous short hikes for day-trippers and some longer treks for backpackers. Boats (non-motorized) can be rented at Upper Waterton Lake or Cameron Lake. For windsurfing enthusiasts, the winds that rake across Upper Waterton Lake create an exciting ride. Bring a wetsuit, though; the water remains numbingly cold throughout the summer.

Because of Waterton's proximity to the U.S. border and its bond with Glacier National Park, many visitors come to the park from the south. You can fly into Great Falls or Kalispell, Montana, and drive to Waterton. If you drive from Calgary (via Highways 2, 3, and 6), you can take an interesting side trip to Crowsnest Pass (☞ Off the Beaten Path, *below*).

Red Rock Canyon is one of the more popular natural attractions in Waterton park. "Canyon" is stretching the term, as it is little more than a gully carved into the rock by a mountain stream. But "red rock" is appropriate; the exposed rock throughout the canyon displays a remarkably red hue. This is a popular spot for a picnic and a stroll along the paths that line the canyon. ⊠ *10 km (6 mi) north of Waterton Park; watch for signs to access road.*

Cameron Lake, the jewel of Waterton, sits in a land of high basins and glacially carved cirques. In summer the area is filled with hundreds of varieties of alpine wild flowers, including 22 varieties of wild orchids. You also can rent canoes and paddleboats to explore Cameron Lake. ⊠ *Akima Pkwy., 13 km (8 mi) southwest of Waterton Park.*

One of the park's most popular activities is the two-hour cruise on Upper Waterton Lake from the townsite of Waterton Park south to **Goat Haunt,** Montana. From here several short, easy hikes are possible before you return to Waterton; properly equipped overnighters can also camp out at Goat Haunt. (Because Goat Haunt is in the United States, travelers going to and from must clear Customs. Stops are included only from mid-June to mid-September, as customs office is closed at other times.) ⊠ *Waterton International Shoreline Cruise Company, Box 126, Waterton Park, AB T0K 2M0,* ☎ *403/859–2362.* 🎫 *$17.* ◷ *Mid-May–Sept.*

Lodging

$$$ 🏨 **Prince of Wales Hotel.** Perched between two lakes, the hotel has breath-
★ taking views of both a mountain backdrop and a lake-and-prairie setting. Fantastically ornamented with eaves, balconies, and turrets, it's crowned by a high steeple. The baronial, dark-paneled interior evokes the feeling of a royal Scottish hunting lodge. Expect creaks and rattles at night—the old hotel (built in the 1920s) is exposed to rough winds. Rates decrease about 25% off-season. ⊠ *Waterton Park. Reservations, Station 0928, Phoenix, AZ 85077, or General Delivery, Prince of Wales Hotel, Waterton Lakes National Park, Waterton, AB T0K 2M0,* ☎ *403/859–2231 or 403/236–3400. 81 rooms. Restaurant. MC, V. Closed late-Sept.–mid-May.*

$$ 🏨 **Bayshore Inn.** As the name suggests, this two-story inn is on the lakeside, and rooms with balconies take full advantage of the setting. Otherwise, the inn's common areas and motel-style rooms are rather ordinary. The lakeside patio is a great spot for light meals and drinks. Rates decrease 25% off-season. ⊠ *Main St., Box 38, Waterton Park, AB T0K 2M0,* ☎ *403/859–2211, 403/238–4847 off-season,* FAX *403/859–2291. 62 rooms, 8 suites. Restaurant, bar, coffee shop, lobby lounge, pizzeria. AE, D, MC, V. Closed mid-Oct.–Mar.*

$ 🏨 **Kilmorey Lodge.** This 60-year-old inn with a log-cabin facade sits
★ at the edge of Waterton Park. Rooms are steeped in country-cottage atmosphere, with pine walls, eiderdown comforters, sloped floors, and homespun antique furnishings. Some rooms have additional sleeping or sitting areas. ⊠ *Box 100, Waterton Park, AB T0K 2M0,* ☎ *403/859–2334,* FAX *403/859–2342. 23 rooms. Restaurant, lounge. AE, D, DC, MC, V.*

Golf

Waterton Golf Course (2 km, or 1 mi, east of Waterton Park, ☎ 403/859–2114) has 18 holes.

....

OFF THE
BEATEN PATH

CROWSNEST PASS – Between Calgary or Banff and Waterton, you can take a side trip to the site of a turn-of-the-century coal-mining settlement. From the outset, the industry here was ill-fated. In April 1903, some 90 million tons of rock from Turtle Mountain buried a portion of the town of

Frank, killing about 70 people. Then in 1914 a massive mine explosion killed 189 people, and a few years later the coal-mining industry all but collapsed. The story of the slide and the history of coal mining in the region are well recorded at the **Frank Slide Interpretive Center.** ⊠ *Hwy. 3, 35 km (22 mi) west of Hwy. 6,* ☎ *403/562-7388.* ⊠ *$4.* ⊙ *June–Labor Day, daily 9–8; Labor Day–May, daily 10–4.*

THE BRITISH COLUMBIA ROCKIES

In the national and provincial parks of the British Columbia Rockies, the sense of isolation and grandeur easily rivals that found in the parks to the east. Much of the British Columbia Rockies are not protected within park boundaries, however. This means that enthusiasts of activities such as motorboating, heli-skiing or heli-hiking, or hunting, which are severely restricted in the protected parks, will find more opportunities here than elsewhere in the region.

"British Columbia Rockies" is in part a misnomer. The term is often used to refer to the Columbia Mountains of southeastern British Columbia, which flank the western slope of the Rockies but geologically are not a part of the Rockies. If differentiating the Columbias from the Rockies seems confusing, at least their separation is made obvious by the broad, low valley of the Columbia River, known colloquially as the Columbia River trench. Four separate ranges form the Columbias themselves: To the north are the Cariboos, west of Jasper and Mt. Robson parks; reaching south like three long talons from the Cariboos are (west to east) the Monashees, the Selkirks, and the Purcells. Finally, there are the Bugaboos—a few dramatic peaks in the Purcells that are often thought of as encompassing the entire region.

The British Columbia Rockies are a bit older than the true Rockies. Numerous peaks exceed 10,000 feet in height, the upper slopes have extensive areas of alpine meadows above tree line, evergreen forests cover the valleys and lower slopes, and glaciers and snowfields are not uncommon (especially in Glacier National Park, not to be confused with the U.S. Glacier National Park, in Montana).

As the first ranges to capture storms moving from the west across the plains of interior British Columbia, the Columbias get much more rain and snow than do the Rockies. Annual precipitation in many areas exceeds 60 inches, and in the Monashees, the most westerly of the subranges, annual snowfalls can exceed 65 feet.

Such precipitation has helped create the large, deep glaciers that add to the high-alpine beauty of the Columbias. Lower down, the moist climate has contributed to much more lush forests than those found in the Rockies to the east. In winter, the deep snows make the Columbias a magnet for deep-powder and helicopter skiers.

Because only a relatively small portion of the British Columbia Rockies is protected from development, human encroachment from residential and commercial development, farming, mining, and lumbering is rather common in the accessible portions of these ranges. The towns reflect this difference—tourism is a secondary pursuit; their primary function is to serve the local residents and industries. The advantage for visitors is that prices, for the most part, are substantially less than in the Alberta Rockies.

From Banff, there are two main routes to the British Columbia Rockies. The first follows the Trans-Canada Highway (Highway 1), northwest from Banff to Lake Louise, then west through Golden, Glacier

National Park, Mt. Revelstoke National Park, and finally the town of Revelstoke. The second route follows the Trans-Canada from Banff halfway to Lake Louise, then cuts south on Highway 93 through the southern British Columbia Rockies and Kootenay National Park (☞ North and West of Banff, *above*), then through Radium Hot Springs, Invermere, Fairmont Hot Springs, Fort Steele, Cranbrook, Kimberley (a small side trip), and finally through Fernie on a return swing to southern Alberta through the Crowsnest Pass.

Golden

㉛ *80 km (50 mi) west of Lake Louise, 105 km (65 mi) north of Radium Hot Springs.*

For the most part, the towns of the Columbia River trench are not beautiful, nor do they aspire to be. Golden—a town best described as a service center—is the epitome of this unassuming character. Primarily a stopping-off point for anyone journeying elsewhere, Golden is a base for several river runners, outfitters, and guide services.

Lodging

$ ▦ **Swiss Village.** A combination motel and campground, this complex has a little more modern polish than some of its Golden neighbors. There is nothing special here, just basic motel rooms—bed, bathroom, TV—at a fair price. The RV sites have electrical hookups and water. Rates drop 40% off-season. ⊠ *Off Hwy. 1, west end of Golden, Box 765, V0A 1H0,* ☎ *250/344–2276,* ℻ *250/344–5259. 40 rooms, 10 RV sites. Sauna. AE, MC, V.*

Rafting

Alpine Rafting Company (⊠ Box 2446, V0A 1H0, ☎ 250/344–5016 or 888/666–9494) runs a variety of white-water trips on the Kicking Horse River, including multiday trips.

En Route The 105 km (65 mi) south from Golden to Radium Hot Springs, where Highway 93 joins Highway 95, is a pleasant drive, rambling along the rolling **flood plain of the Columbia River.** To the right are the river and the Purcell Mountains; more immediately to the left are the Rockies, although the major peaks are hidden by the ranges in the foreground. Resorts catering to RVs—hard to find in the parks—abound here.

Bugaboo Recreation Area

㉜ *Access on unpaved roads off Hwy. 95 out of Spillimacheen and Brisco, between 65 and 77 km (40 and 48 mi) south of Golden.*

Climbers and hikers in search of solitude can find it in the Bugaboo Recreation Area. The Bugaboos are especially popular among experienced rock climbers. Rock spires that rise from glaciers like giant rocket cones are both dramatic to look at and challenging to climb. This is wild country: Except for the Bugaboo Lodge—reserved mainly for heli-hiking and heli-skiing guests—and remote alpine huts, there are no facilities in this area.

Glacier National Park

㉝ *58 km (36 mi) west of Golden, 45 km (28 mi) east of Revelstoke.*

Relatively small Glacier National Park is marked by rugged mountains and, not surprisingly, an abundance of glaciers (more than 400). The glaciers result not because of the exceptionally high elevation—although some peaks here do exceed 10,000 feet—but because of the high winter snowfalls in the park. Many of the glaciers can be seen from the highway, but to fully appreciate Glacier National Park, you must take to the trail (☞ Hiking, *below*).

At **Rogers Pass,** near the center of Glacier National Park, the heavy winter snowfalls made rail and road construction particularly difficult. Avalanches claimed the lives of hundreds of railway-construction workers in the early 1900s and continued to be a threat during highway construction in the 1950s.

Today, the Rogers Pass war against avalanches is both active and passive. Heavy artillery—105mm howitzers—is used to shoot down snow buildups before they become so severe as to threaten a major avalanche. (If you're traveling in the backcountry, even in summer, be alert to unexploded howitzer shells that pose a potential hazard.) On the passive side, train tunnels and long snow sheds along the highway shield travelers from major slide paths.

Glacier National Park's history is well documented at the **Rogers Pass Centre**—worth a visit whether you're staying in Glacier or just passing through. Open year-round, the center displays geology and wildlife and screens 30-minute movies on subjects from avalanches to bears. ⊠ *Hwy. 1,* ☎ *250/837–6274.* 🎫 *Free with park pass.* ☉ *May–June 15 and Sept. 15–Oct., daily 9–5; June 16–Sept. 14, daily 8–8; Nov.–Apr., daily 7–5.*

Lodging

$$ 🏨 **Glacier Park Lodge.** This modern, two-floor Best Western at the top of Rogers Pass—the only lodging within Glacier National Park boundaries—offers ambience in the chain's familiar format: wood-veneer tables and chairs, and pink wall-to-wall carpeting. The steep-sloping A-frame roof is a design concession to the heavy winter snows. On Highway 1, the lodge accommodates long-distance travelers with its 24-hour service station, 24-hour coffee shop, and gift shop. Rates drop 40% off-season. ⊠ *The Summit, Rogers Pass, BC V0E 2S0,* ☎ *250/837–2126 or 800/528–1234,* FAX *250/837–2126. 51 rooms. Restaurant, coffee shop, pool, outdoor hot tub. AE, D, DC, MC, V.*

Hiking

From the Illecillewaet Campground, a few kilometers west of the park's Rogers Pass Centre, several trails lead to good overlooks and glacier tongues, offering day-hiking opportunities. One of the best, although fairly strenuous, is the Asulkan Valley trail. This 13-km (8-mi) loop passes waterfalls and yields views of the Asulkan Glacier and three massifs—the Ramparts, the Dome, and Mt. Jupiter. A much easier hike is the 1½-km (1-mi) loop Brook trail (6 km, or 4 mi, west of the Rogers Pass Centre), with views of the glaciers of Mt. Bonney.

Mt. Revelstoke National Park

❸❹ *Eastern edge, 20 km (12 mi) west of Glacier National Park; western edge is by town of Revelstoke.*

Conceived primarily as a day-use park, Mt. Revelstoke National Park covers just 260 square km (100 square mi). The park's principal attraction is the 26-km (16-mi) **Summit Road** to the top of the mountain, at 6,395 feet. The gravel road begins from Highway 1, 2 km (1 mi) before the turnoff to the town of Revelstoke, and its last few kilometers may be closed off by melting snows until well into July. You can choose among several easy hikes from the summit parking lot that meander past small lakes and have views of the Selkirk and Monashee ranges as well as mountain meadows full of wildflowers.

Revelstoke

35 *148 km (92 mi) west of Golden, on western edge of Mt. Revelstoke National Park.*

The town of Revelstoke is a skiers' headquarters in winter. The downtown district, an attractive, authentic turn-of-the-century renovation, today houses modern shops, restaurants, and businesses.

Dining and Lodging

$$$$ ✕ **One-Twelve.** In the Regent Inn (☞ *below*), this restaurant has low cedar ★ ceilings and an abundance of historic photos that lend warmth to the atmosphere. Continental dishes, such as salmon, chicken Cordon Bleu, and beef brochette, are the basic fare, but the blue ribbon of the menu is the lamb broiled with rosemary and red wine. ⊠ *Regent Inn, 112 1st St. E,* ☎ *250/837–2107. Reservations essential. AE, D, DC, MC, V.*

$$ ☷ **Regent Inn.** The inn mixes many styles: Colonial, with its brick-arcade facade; true Canadian, in its pine-trimmed lobby area and restaurant; and Scandinavian, in the angular, low-slung wood furnishings of the guest rooms. Rooms are on the large side but have no spectacular views. Continental breakfast is complimentary. There are no off-season rate reductions. ⊠ *112 Victoria Rd., Box 450, V0E 2S0,* ☎ *250/837–2107,* ᴲᴬˣ *250/837–9669. 38 rooms. Restaurant, pub, outdoor hot tub, sauna. AE, D, DC, MC, V.*

Outdoor Activities and Sports

BIKING

In Revelstoke, try **Spoketacular** (⊠ 11 Mackenzie Ave., ☎ 250/837–2220) for rentals.

SKIING

Selkirk Tangiers Helicopter Skiing (⊠ Box 1409, Golden V0A 1H0, ☎ 250/344–5016 or 800/663–7080, ᴲᴬˣ 250/344–7012) runs three-, five-, and seven-day all-inclusive packages in the Selkirk and Monashee mountains from their base in Revelstoke. **Cat Powder Skiing** (⊠ Box 1479, 1601 W. 3rd St., Revelstoke V0E 2S0, ☎ 250/837–5151) organizes two-, three-, and five-day all-inclusive packages that run into the Selkirks and on the upper slopes of Mt. MacKenzie in Revelstoke.

Radium Hot Springs

36 *127 km (79 mi) southwest of Banff, 103 km (64 mi) south of Golden, at junction of Hwys. 93 and 95.*

Radium Hot Springs is little more than a service town for the busy highway traffic passing through it. The town makes a convenient access point for Kootenay National Park and has lower prices than in the national parks.

Radium Hot Springs, the springs that give the town its name, are the town's longest-standing attraction and the summer lifeblood for the numerous motels in the area. There are two outdoor pools tucked beneath the walls of Sinclair Canyon. The hot pool is maintained at 41°C (106°F); in a cooler pool the hot mineral water is diluted to 28°C (82°F). Lockers, towels, and suits are available to rent. ⊠ *Hwy. 93, 2 km (1 mi) northeast of Hwy. 95,* ☎ *250/347–9485 or 800/767–1611.* ᴿ *$5, day passes available.* ◷ *Hot pool summer, daily 9 AM–10:30 PM; mid-Oct.–Apr., daily noon–9; cooler pool schedule varies with weather.*

Lodging

$$–$$$ ☷ **Radium Hot Springs Resort.** Recreational facilities and activities bring this resort to life. Accommodations are in hotel rooms or one-, two-, or three-bedroom condo units. Rooms are modern, with hardwood furnishings and sponge-painted walls, and each has a sundeck, a wet bar, and a view overlooking the golf fairways. Condos have full kitchens. Golf packages are available. There's a small rate reduction off-season. ⊠ *Off Hwy. 93 south of Radium Hot Springs, Box 310, V0A 1M0,* ☎ *250/347–9311 or 800/665–3585,* ℻ *250/347–6299. 90 rooms, 30 condo units. Dining room, indoor pool, hot tub, sauna, 18-hole golf course, 2 tennis courts, exercise room, racquetball, squash, mountain bikes, cross-country skiing. AE, DC, MC, V.*

$–$$ 🏨 **The Chalet.** The hotel sits on a crest above town; all rooms have expansive views of the Columbia River valley. The decor is nothing special—lots of browns, navy blue, and wood veneer—but each room comes with a sitting area and minikitchen (microwave, refrigerator, sink), and all have balconies. Rates drop one-third off-season. ⊠ *Madsen Rd., Box 456, V0A 1M0,* ☎ *250/347–9305,* ℻ *250/347–9306. 17 suites. Sauna, hot tub. AE, DC, MC, V.*

Golf

Arrangements for golfing can be made through **Fairmont Hot Springs Resort** (☎ 250/345–6514 or 800/663–4979), with two 18-hole courses on site (☞ Fairmont Hot Springs, *below*). **Radium Hot Springs Resort** (☎ 250/347–9652 or 800/665–3585) has one 18-hole course on site (☞ Lodging, *above*).

Invermere

18 km (11 mi) south of Radium Hot Springs.

Invermere is another of the many highway-service towns in the British Columbia Rockies. It is the central access point for Windermere Lake, Panorama Resort, and the Purcell Wilderness area.

For summer water sports, **Windermere Lake**—actually an extra-wide stretch of the Columbia River—is popular among swimmers, boaters, and board sailors. Invermere has a good beach on the lake.

If you're visiting the Invermere area between May and September, one of the best museums in the area is the **Windermere Valley Pioneer Museum** (⊠ 622 3rd St., ☎ 250/342–9769), which depicts the life of 19th-century settlers through artifacts and memorabilia.

Panorama Resort (☞ Dining and Lodging *and* Skiing, *below*) is a year-round accommodation known best for skiing in winter. For summer visitors it has tennis courts, an outdoor pool, and hiking and biking trails. The resort is on the edge of the **Purcell Wilderness**—a large section of the southern British Columbia Rockies devoted to backcountry hiking, camping, and fishing, with relatively few facilities.

Dining and Lodging

$$$$ ✕ **Toby Creek Dining Lounge.** The restaurant, part of a 1960s-era ski lodge, has cedar walls, a slanted ceiling, and—in winter—a big roaring fire in the central fireplace. In summer an outside deck offers fresh air, though not much of a view. The varied menu lists salads, steaks, stir-fries, and chicken dishes, as well as breakfast in summer. ⊠ *Panorama Resort, 18 km (11 mi) west of Invermere,* ☎ *250/342–6941. Reservations essential. AE, D, MC, V.*

$$ 🏨 **Panorama Resort.** This resort near the edge of the Purcell Wilderness has a variety of rooms. While the lodge at the base of the ski lift conveys a college-dorm atmosphere, other accommodations are in condo villas that look to be part of a mountainside suburb. Many have fireplaces, patios, or balconies. Skiing, hiking, biking, an outdoor pool, and tennis courts are available, depending on the season. The restaurants are open only during winter. Peak season is Christmas week, February break, and late June–early September; rates decrease 25% in off-season. ⊠ *18 km (11 mi) west of Invermere, BC V0A 1T0,* ☎ *250/342–6941 or 800/663–2929,* FAX *250/342–3395. 105 lodge rooms, 250 condo units. 3 restaurants, 3 bars, cafeteria, pool, sauna, 8 tennis courts, downhill skiing, nightclub. AE, D, MC, V.*

$ 🏨 **Delphine Lodge.** Originally built in 1899, the hotel has been restored
★ and now feels like a cozy bed-and-breakfast. Big, lace-curtained windows shed lots of light on a living-dining area distinguished by its polished, wide-board floors, huge stone hearth, and antique straight-back chairs and wicker rockers. Handcrafted pine furnishings and down comforters fill the smallish, pastel-shade bedrooms. All rooms are no-smoking. Full breakfast is served every morning. ⊠ *Main St., 5 km (3 mi) west of town, Box 2797, V0A 1K0,* ☎ *250/342–6851. 6 rooms, 1 with private bath, 5 sharing 2 baths. V.*

Skiing

DOWNHILL

Panorama Resort (☞ Dining and Lodging, *above*), in the Purcells, has the second-highest lift-served vertical rise (4,300 feet) in North America.

HELI-SKIING

R.K. Heli-Ski (⊠ Box 695, V0A 1K0, ☎ 250/342–3889 or 800/661–6060), based at the Panorama ski area, has daily tours.

Fairmont Hot Springs

❸❼ *20 km (12 mi) south of Invermere, 94 km (58 mi) north of Fort Steele.*

Fairmont Hot Springs is named for the hot springs and the resort that has sprouted around it. The "town" is little more than a service strip along the highway, but turn in to the resort and things become more impressive. The town is also close to Columbia Lake, popular with boaters and board sailors. Golf is a growing attraction at several fine courses in the area.

Lodging

$$ 🏨 **Fairmont Hot Springs Resort.** With a wide selection of activities from golf to heli-hiking, vacationing at this resort is like being at camp. In addition to the recreational facilities, Fairmont also has hot springs, a spa, and an airport. Inside the attractive, low-slung bungalow-style structure, rooms are contemporary, many with wood paneling; some are equipped with kitchens and have balconies or patios. Other options are the RV sites. Golf, ski, and spa packages are available. Rates decrease 40% in off-season. ⊠ *Hwy. 93/95, Box 10, V0B 1L0,* ☎ *250/ 345–6311, 800/663–4979 in Canada,* FAX *250/345–6616. 140 rooms, 294 RV sites. 7 restaurants, lobby lounge, snack bar, 4 pools, hot springs, spa, 2 18-hole golf courses, 2 tennis courts, private airstrip. AE, D, DC, MC, V.*

Fort Steele

❸❽ *94 km (58 mi) south of Fairmont Hot Springs.*

Fort Steele and nearby Kimberley were home to many German and Swiss immigrants who arrived in the late 19th century to work as miners and loggers. Southeastern British Columbia was not unlike the Tyrol region they had left, so it was easy to settle here. Later, a demand for experienced alpinists to guide and teach hikers, climbers, and skiers brought more settlers from the Alpine countries, and Tyrolean influence is evident throughout southeastern British Columbia. Schnitzels and fondues appear on menus as often as burgers and fries.

★ **Fort Steele Heritage Town,** a reconstructed 19th-century mining outpost consisting of more than 60 buildings, is a step back to silver- and lead-mining days. Its theater, milliner's, barbershop, and dry-goods store breathe authenticity, helping to preserve the 1890s flavor. Plan a half-day or more; there is enough here to hold the interest of children and adults alike. ⊠ *3 km (2 mi) south of Fort Steele on Hwy. 93/95,* ☎ *250/426–7352.* 💰 *2 consecutive days $5.50; grounds free Sept.–mid-June, weather permitting.* ☉ *Concessions and museum mid-June–early Sept., daily 9:30–8; grounds daily 9:30–dusk.*

The Arts

The **Wild Horse Theater** (⊠ Fort Steele Heritage Town, ☎ 250/426–6923) has college presentations from late June to mid-September.

Cranbrook

16 km (10 mi) southwest of Fort Steele, 27 km (17 mi) southeast of Kimberley.

Cranbrook is primarily a service center for motorists and the surrounding mining and logging industries. As one of the largest towns in the region, it has correspondingly more choice in the way of moderately priced basic motels and restaurants.

Dining

$$–$$$ ✕ **City Cafe.** If you find yourself stuck for lunch in the fast-food world of Cranbrook, City Cafe will be a breath of fresh air. The low ceilings and pine banquettes give the small dining room a French country-bistro air. Sandwiches served on fresh, crusty French bread are tasty and very reasonably priced. A German side to the menu lists schnitzel, a popular choice. ⊠ *1015 Baker St.,* ☎ *250/489–5413. DC, MC, V.*

Kimberley

③⑨ *40 km (25 mi) west of Fort Steele, 98 km (61 mi) south of Fairmont Hot Springs.*

A cross between quaint and kitschy, Kimberley is rich with Tyrolean character. The Platzl ("small plaza," in German), a walking mall of shops and restaurants styled after a Bavarian village, is crowned by what is reputed to be the world's largest cuckoo clock. Chalet-style buildings are as common here as log cabins are in the national parks. In summer Kimberley plays its alpine theme to the hilt: Merchants dress up in lederhosen and dirndls, and promotional gimmicks abound.

Dining and Lodging

$$–$$$ ✕ **Chef Bernard's Kitchen.** Dining in this small, homey storefront
★ restaurant on the Kimberley pedestrian mall is like dining in someone's pantry. Goat horns, cowbells, and photos fill the walls and set an alpine mood. The menu is international, ranging from German to Thai to Cajun. Homemade desserts are always a favorite. Breakfast is served in summer. ⊠ *170 Spokane St.,* ☎ *250/427–4820. Reservations essential. AE, D, DC, MC, V.*

$ 🏠 **Inn of the Rockies.** In keeping with downtown Kimberley's Bavarian theme, the hotel's exterior is exposed-wood beams and stucco. Large rooms have a small sitting area and are plainly furnished with dark brown wood–veneer furniture, including a bed, bureau, and TV. The restaurant serves good, reasonably priced food. Just a block from the Platzl, this is *the* hotel in Kimberley. There is a minimal rate decrease during the off-season. ✉ *300 Wallinger Ave., V1A 1Z4,* ☎ *250/427–2266 or 800/661–7559,* FAX *250/427–7621. 43 rooms. Restaurant, lounge, hot tubs, exercise room, coin laundry. AE, DC, MC, V.*

The Arts
In summer Bavarian bands in Kimberley strike up with oompah music on the Platzl, especially when festivals are in swing. The **Old Time Accordion Championships,** in early July, is a Kimberley highlight.

Skiing
Kimberley Ski Resort (✉ Box 40, V1A 2Y5, ☎ 250/427–4881) has a vertical drop of more than 2,000 feet and on-mountain facilities.

Fernie

96 km (60 mi) east of Fort Steele, 331 km (205 mi) southwest of Calgary.

Fernie is primarily a winter destination, serving skiers at the Fernie Snow Valley ski area. One of the largest towns between Cranbrook and Calgary, it has a wider selection of motels and restaurants than the other centers along this route.

Skiing
Fernie Snow Valley (✉ Ski Area Rd., V0A 1M1, ☎ 250/423–4655) has a vertical rise of more than 2,000 feet and on-mountain facilities.

CANADIAN ROCKIES A TO Z

Arriving and Departing

By Bus
Greyhound Lines (call local listing) provides regular service to Calgary, Edmonton, and Vancouver, with connecting service to Jasper and Banff. **Brewster Transportation and Tours** (☎ 800/661–1152) offers service between the Calgary International Airport and Banff, Jasper, and Lake Louise. **Laidlaw Transportation** (☎ 403/762–9102) also operates between Calgary Airport and the Banff–Lake Louise area.

By Car
Highway 1, the Trans-Canada Highway, is the principal east–west route into the region. Banff is 128 km (79 mi) west of Calgary on Highway 1 and 858 km (532 mi) east of Vancouver. The other major east–west routes are Highway 16 to the north, the main highway between Edmonton and Jasper, and Highway 3 to the south. The main routes from the south are Route 89 (Highway 2 in Canada), which enters Canada east of Alberta's Waterton Lakes National Park from Montana, and Highway 93, also from Montana, which provides access to the British Columbia Rockies.

By Plane
Calgary is the most common gateway for travelers arriving by plane. If you plan to visit only Jasper and northern park regions, you may prefer to use Edmonton as a gateway city. Both cities have international airports served by several major carriers; the Calgary flight schedule is somewhat more extensive. For airline information, *see* Calgary A to Z *and* Edmonton A to Z *in* Chapter 5.)

Air Canada and **Canadian Airlines** have daily flights to and from many points in southern British Columbia; most of these flights connect with flights through the international airports in Vancouver, Calgary, and Edmonton. **Westjet** is a new regional discount airline with an increasing number of connections between points in Alberta and British Columbia.

By Train

VIA Rail (☎ 800/561–8630) trains stop in Jasper, with connecting overnight runs to and from Toronto, Edmonton, and Vancouver. A specialty train-tour service, **Rocky Mountaineer RailTours** (✉ 1150 Station St., Suite 130, Vancouver, BC, V6A 2X7, ☎ 604/606–7200 or 800/665–7245, FAX 604/606–7201) connects Vancouver, Kamloops, Banff, Jasper, and Calgary. Dome cars allow panoramic mountain views, and friendly staff provide excellent food and service. A luxury bi-level dome coach caters specifically to people accustomed to five-star hotels. It has two spiral staircases, a private dining area, an open-air observation platform, and on-board hosts. The RailTour coaches travel through the Rockies during daylight only.

Getting Around

By Car

Automobile is the way to travel in the Canadian Rockies, though some guided tour operators have good sightseeing trips by bus and train. Unless you plan to go off the beaten path (in Kananaskis Country or in the Columbias only; vehicles aren't permitted off major roadways in the national parks), a four-wheel-drive vehicle is not necessary. Major roadways are well maintained. Keep in mind, however, that snow arrives in early fall and remains until late spring. When traveling between October and April, stay informed of local road conditions, especially if you're traveling over mountain passes or along the Icefields Parkway (Highway 93). A few roads, such as Highway 40 over Highwood Pass in Kananaskis Country, are closed in winter.

CAR RENTALS

Car-rental outlets are at the Calgary and Edmonton airports, as well as in Banff and Jasper, Alberta, and Cranbrook, British Columbia. Daily rentals for sightseeing are available but should be reserved well ahead of time, especially in summer.

Contacts and Resources

B&B Reservation Agencies

In Alberta, **Gem B&B Reservation Agency** (☎ 403/434–6098) represents licensed B&Bs and charges a booking fee. The **Bed-and-Breakfast Agency of Alberta** (☎ 403/277–8486 or 800/425–8160) handles about 50 B&Bs and inspects each property. For the British Columbia Rockies, contact the **British Columbia Bed-and-Breakfast Association** (☎ 604/276–8616).

Emergencies

Ambulance (☎ 911). **Police** (☎ 911).

Guided Tours

BICYCLE TOURS

Several operators offer guided on-road and off-road bicycle tours. **Rocky Mountain Cycle Tours** (✉ 333 Baker St., Nelson, BC V1L 4H6, ☎ 250/354–1241 or 800/661–2453) runs one- to seven-day tours in the Banff area and in British Columbia. Prices begin at $80.

BUS TOURS

Brewster Transportation and Tours (✉ Box 1140, Banff, AB T0L 0C0, ☎ In Banff, 403/762–6700; in Jasper, 403/852–3332; in Calgary, 403/221–8242; or 800/661–1152, FAX 403/762-2090) offers half-, full-, and multiday sightseeing tours of the parks. Prices start at about $33 per person.

Tauck Tours (✉ 276 Post Rd. W, Box 5027, Westport, CT 06880, ☎ 800/468–2825) conducts multiday bus tours through the region.

DRIVING TOURS

Audiocassette tapes for self-guided auto tours of the parks are produced by **Auto Tape Tours** (☎ 201/236–1666) and **Rocky Mountain Tape Tours. Canadian Wilderness Videos** (✉ 1010 Larch Pl., Canmore, AB T1W 1S7, ☎ 403/678–3795) produces a series of videotapes illustrating highlights along specific routes. Tapes can be rented or purchased at news or gift shops in Banff, Lake Louise, and Jasper.

HELI-TOURS

Alpine Helicopters (✉ 91 Bow Valley Trail, Canmore, AB T1W 1N8, ☎ 403/678–4802) is 20 minutes southeast of Banff and provides year-round, guided "flightseeing" tours (25–45 minutes) above the Banff and Kananaskis valleys. They also offer half- or full-day heli-hiking tours. Prices begin at $110.

SEASONAL TOURS

Challenge Enterprises (✉ Box 8127, Canmore, AB T1W 2T8, ☎ 403/678–2628) specializes in half-day to multiday guided snowmobile tours. Prices start at $120 per person.

Kingmik Expeditions (✉ Box 227, Lake Louise, AB T0L 1E0, ☎ 250/344–5298) specializes in dogsledding tours through the mountains. You can even have a go at being the musher; tours range from 35 minutes to five-day outings, with prices starting at $68 per sled (2 adults and 1 small child per sled).

Mountain Fly Fishers (✉ 909 Railway Ave., Canmore, AB T1W 1P3, ☎ In season 403/678–9522, off-season 403/678–2915) offers fly-fishing instruction, guide services, float-fishing tours, and equipment rentals. "Hike and wade" programs start at $110 per person, two people per guide.

Outdoor Activities and Sports

BACKPACKING AND HIKING

Backpackers need to register with the nearest park warden for permits. This is principally for safety reasons—so that you can be tracked down in case of emergency—as well as for trail-usage records. The fee is $6 per person per night (to a maximum of $30 per person per trip or $42 annually) for the use of backcountry campsites. You can make reservations up to three weeks in advance by contacting the park office. The office can also supply trail and topographical maps and information on current trail conditions.

If you're interested in hiking or backpacking, several good books describe various routes and route combinations. One of the best, *The Canadian Rockies Trail Guide,* by Brian Patton and Bart Robinson (Summerthought Ltd., $14.95), is available in most bookstores in Banff, Lake Louise, and Jasper.

CAMPING

Campground information is available from **Parks Canada** (✉ Canadian Heritage—Parks Canada, Information Services, Room 552, 220 4th Ave. SE, Calgary, AB T2G 4X3, ☎ 403/292–4401 or 800/651–7959, ℻ 403/292–6004) and from **Kananaskis Country** (✉ #100, 3115-12th St. NE, Calgary, AB T2E 7J2, ☎ 403/297–3362, ℻ 403/297–2180). Contact **Discover British Columbia** or **Travel Alberta** (☞ Visitor Information, *below*) for special camping publications.

CLIMBING

Climbing permits are required within the parks and can be obtained at park warden offices. Except for very experienced mountaineers, guide and instruction services are essential here. Climbing gear can be rented at outdoor stores in Banff. **Banff Alpine Guides** (⊠ Box 1025, Banff, AB T0L 0C0, ☎ 403/678–6091), the **Canadian School of Mountaineering** (⊠ 629 10th St., Canmore, AB T1W 2E5, ☎ 403/678–4134), and **Yamnuska Mountain Adventures** (⊠ 1316 Railway Ave., Canmore, AB T1W 1P6, ☎ 403/678–4164, FAX 403/678–4450), catering to all ability levels, lead trips throughout the parks.

Climbers or backpackers interested in extended stays of more than three or four days might consider membership in the **Alpine Club of Canada** (⊠ Box 8040, Indian Flats Rd., Canmore, AB T1W 2T8, ☎ 403/678–3200). The club maintains several mountain huts in the parks.

FISHING

You need a fishing license, which you can buy at information centers and sports shops throughout the region. A British Columbia license is good only in British Columbia; an Alberta license is good only in Alberta. If you are fishing in the national parks, you need a national parks fishing license (but not provincial licenses).

In Alberta the fee for an annual license for nonresident Canadians is $18 and for non-Canadians $36. Non-Canadians can also purchase a 5-day license for $24. In British Columbia, the fees for one-day, eight-day, and annual licenses for nonresident Canadians are $10, $20, and $28, respectively; for non-Canadians the fees are $10, $25, and $40. The fee for a 7-day national park license is $6; an annual license is $13.

GOLF

In Alberta parks, peak-season greens fees range from $35 to $60 and cart rental costs from $20 to $30. All courses have full pro-shop services, including cart rentals, which are mandatory at some courses. Most courses enforce a standard dress code, requiring shirts with collars and Bermuda-length shorts or long pants.

HORSEBACK RIDING

Travel Alberta and **Tourism British Columbia** (☞ Visitor Information, *below*) can provide listings of pack-trip outfitters, which proliferate on the fringes of the national parks. They also have information about guest ranches; riding is generally a major part of a stay. In British Columbia, further information is available from the **Guide-Outfitters Association** (⊠ Box 94675, Richmond, BC V64 4A4, ☎ 250/278–2688).

SKIING

Cross-Country. Groomed trails (and rental equipment) can be found near the Banff Springs Hotel, Chateau Lake Louise, Jasper Park Lodge, Fairmont Hot Springs Resort, and Mt. Engadine Lodge. Lake O'Hara Lodge, Mt. Assiniboine Lodge, and Skoki Lodge offer guided backcountry ski touring. For information, see the individual towns in this chapter.

Downhill. For information, see individual towns throughout the chapter.

Heli-Skiing. The original, and by far the largest, heli-skiing operator in the region is **Canadian Mountain Holidays** (⊠ Box 1660, Banff, AB T0L 0C0, ☎ 403/762–7100 or 800/661–0252, FAX 403/762–5879). They have heli-skiing (and in summer, heli-hiking) packages in the Cariboo and Purcell Ranges in the British Columbia Rockies, with accommodation at their relatively luxurious but remote lodges. Reserve several months in advance.

Safety

Visitors to the backcountry must register with the nearest park warden's office. Very few of the natural hazards in the Rockies are marked with warning signs. Be wary of slippery rocks and vegetation near rivers and canyons, snow-covered crevasses on glaciers, avalanche conditions in winter, and potentially aggressive animals. Each year there are several fatalities from natural hazards in the Rockies.

Visitor Information

The region's three major sources of visitor information are **Travel Alberta** (⊠ Box 2500, Edmonton, AB T5J 2Z4, ☎ 800/661–8888), **Tourism British Columbia** (⊠ 802–865 Hornby St., Vancouver V6Z 2G3, ☎ 800/663–6000), and **Parks Canada** (⊠ Canadian Heritage-Parks Canada, 220 4th St. SE, Room 552, Calgary, AB T2G 4X3, ☎ 403/292–4401 or 800/651–7959, FAX 403/292–6004). Parks Canada information is also available at the **Parks Information Centre** (⊠ Box 900, 224 Banff Ave., Banff, AB T0L 0C0, ☎ 403/762–1550).

You can contact individual offices of the four contiguous Rockies parks directly: **Banff** (☎ 403/762–1550), **Jasper** (☎ 403/852–6176), **Kootenay** (in summer, ☎ 250/347–9505; in winter, 250/347–9551), or **Yoho** (☎ 250/343–6783). For local information, contact **Banff–Lake Louise Tourism Bureau** (⊠ 224 Banff Ave., Banff, AB T0L 0C0, ☎ 403/762–8421), **Lake Louise Visitor Centre** (⊠ Village Rd. beside Samson Mall, Box 213, Lake Louise, AB T0L 1E0, ☎ 403/522–3833), **Jasper Tourism and Commerce** (⊠ Box 98, 632 Connaught Dr., Jasper, AB T0E 1E0, ☎ 403/852–3858), **Kananaskis Country** (⊠ 3115-12th St. NE, #100, Calgary, AB T2E 7J2, ☎ 403/297–3362), **Waterton Lakes National Park** (⊠ Superintendent, Waterton Park, AB T0K 2M0, ☎ 403/859–2224), **Waterton Park Chamber of Commerce** (⊠ Box 55, Waterton Park, AB T0K 2M0, ☎ 403/859–2203), **Mt. Revelstoke and Glacier National Parks** (⊠ Visitor Centre, Box 350, Revelstoke, BC V0E 2S0, ☎ 250/837–6274), and **Rocky Mountain Visitors Association** (⊠ Box 10, Kimberley, BC V1A 2Y5, ☎ 250/427–4838).

5 The Prairie Provinces

Alberta, Saskatchewan, Manitoba

Between the eastern slopes of the Rockies and the wilds of western Ontario lie Canada's three prairie provinces: Alberta, Saskatchewan, and Manitoba. Their northern sections are sparsely populated expanses of lakes, rivers, and forests. The fertile southern plains support farms and ranches—interspersed with river valleys, lakes, badlands, dry hills of sand, and oil wells—and five busy cities: Calgary, Edmonton, Saskatoon, Regina, and Winnipeg. Here you'll also find stunning national parks, dinosaur sites, and attractions that preserve the area's native and frontier heritage.

ALBERTA, SASKATCHEWAN, AND MANITOBA contain Canada's heartland, the principal source of such solid commodities as wheat, oil, and beef. These provinces are also home to a rich stew of ethnic communities that make the area unexpectedly colorful and cosmopolitan. You will find exceptional outdoor recreational facilities and a spectrum of historical attractions that focuses on Mounties, Métis, dinosaurs, and railroads; excellent accommodations and cuisine at reasonable (but not low) prices; and quiet, crowdless expanses of extraordinarily wide-open spaces.

Updated by
Jens Nielsen

The term "prairie provinces" is a bit of a misnomer, as most of this region (the northern half of Alberta and Saskatchewan, and the northern two-thirds of Manitoba) consists of sparsely populated expanses of lakes, rivers, and forests. Most of northern Saskatchewan and Manitoba belongs to the Canadian Shield, the bedrock core of North America, with a foundation of Precambrian rock that is some of the oldest in the world. On the fertile plains of the south, wheat is still king, but other crops, as well as livestock, help boost the economy. The landscape is quite diverse, with farms and ranches interspersed with wide river valleys, lakes, rolling hills, badlands, and even dry hills of sand.

Early milestones in the history of this region include the period 75 million years ago when dinosaurs roamed what was then semitropical swampland, and the epoch when the first human settlers crossed the Bering Strait from Asia 12,000 years ago. Later, Plains Indians of the Athabascan, Algonquian, and Siouan language groups developed a culture and hunted buffalo here. In the 17th century European fur traders began to arrive, and in 1670 the British Crown granted the Hudson's Bay Company administrative and trading rights to "Rupert's Land," a vast territory whose waters drained into Hudson Bay. A hundred years later, the North West Company went into direct competition by building outposts throughout the area. From this fur-trading tradition arose the Métis—mostly French-speaking offspring of native women and European traders who followed the Roman Catholic religion but adhered to a traditional native lifestyle.

By 1873 the North West Mounted Police was established in Manitoba, just six years after the formation of the Canadian government. In 1874, the Mounties began their march west: Their first chores included resolving conflicts between the native peoples and American whiskey traders and overseeing the orderly distribution of the free homesteads granted by the Dominion Lands Act of 1872. The Mounties played a role in the Northwest Rebellion—a revolt by Métis, who feared that the encroachment of western settlement would threaten their traditions and freedom. Although the Métis eventually succumbed, and their leader, Louis Riel, was hanged in 1885, Riel is now hailed as a martyr of the Métis and a statue of him stands on the grounds of Manitoba's Legislature Building.

Railroads arrived in the 1880s, and with them came a torrent of immigrants seeking free government land. An influx of farmers from the British Isles, Scandinavia, Holland, Germany, Eastern Europe, Russia, and especially Ukraine, plus persecuted religious groups such as the Mennonites, Hutterites, Mormons, and Jews, made the prairies into a rich wheat-growing breadbasket and cultural mosaic that is still in evidence today. In 1947, a big oil strike transformed Edmonton and Calgary into gleaming metropolises full of western oil barons.

The people of the prairie provinces are relaxed, reserved, and irascibly independent. They maintain equal suspicion toward "Ottawa" (big government) and "Toronto" (big media and big business). To visitors, the people of this region convey western openness and Canadian-style courtesy: no fawning, but no rudeness. It's an appealing combination.

Pleasures and Pastimes

Dining

Although places specializing in generous helpings of Canadian beef still dominate the scene, restaurants throughout the prairie provinces now tastily reflect the region's ethnic makeup and offer a wide variety of cuisine to fit every price range. Dress in the prairie cities tends to formality in expensive restaurants and is casual in moderate and inexpensive restaurants.

CATEGORY	COST*
$$$$	over $25
$$$	$20–$25
$$	$15–$20
$	under $15

per person for a three-course dinner, excluding drinks, service, and taxes

Lodging

Although lodging has never been a problem in the major cities in the prairies, there's been a welcome improvement at many of the lakes and parks in recent years. Prince Albert National Park in Saskatchewan, for instance, once essentially a summer getaway, has in recent years added several excellent properties and become a legitimate four-season resort.

CATEGORY	COST*
$$$$	over $150
$$$	$75–$150
$$	$50–$75
$	under $50

All prices are for a standard double room, excluding taxes.

National and Provincial Parks

Throughout this vast region, some special places have preserved unique landscapes, from Riding Mountain National Park in the rolling hills of Manitoba to the vast wilderness and waterways of Prince Albert National Park in Saskatchewan. You can explore grasslands, badlands, lakes, or forests, and participate in a number of activities, including fishing in the provincial parks.

Regional History

The larger history of these provinces encompasses a number of special elements, from the dinosaurs that roamed here to the native peoples and the fur traders and frontier settlers who came from around the world. Each province has highlights, whether it's the dinosaur sites around Drumheller, Alberta; the Wanuskewin Heritage Park in Saskatoon, which intereprets native culture; the Mennonite Heritage Village in Steinbach, Manitoba; or the Western Development Museum in North Battleford, Saskatchewan, a re-created 1920s farming village.

Exploring the Prairie Provinces

As you leave the Rockies, the landscape becomes dramatically flatter. From the foothills of Alberta to the Great Lakes, you can explore the prairies from west to east, with visits to the region's five major cities, Calgary, Edmonton, Regina, Saskatoon, and Winnipeg.

Numbers in the text correspond to numbers in the margin and on the Alberta, Downtown Calgary, Greater Calgary, Downtown Edmonton, Saskatchewan, Regina, Saskatoon, Manitoba, and Downtown Winnipeg maps.

Great Itineraries

Enormous distances separate many of the region's major attractions. If you're ambitious and want to include all three prairie provinces, you will need considerable time.

IF YOU HAVE 2 DAYS

If you're interested in the rich history of the Plains Indians, take the time to delve into the area around Saskatoon known as the Heart of the Old Northwest. Start in **Saskatoon** ㊸–㊾ and use it as the base for day trips. On the first day, you can go to nearby **Wanuskewin Heritage Park** (50), a wonderfully cerebral onetime buffalo hunting ground. Less than an hour's drive away is **Batoche** (51) and Batoche National Historic Site, where Louis Riel fought his last battle against the North West Mounted Police. **Duck Lake** (52), 30 minutes north of Batoche along Highway 11, a series of colorful murals on town buildings depict the 1885 Northwest Rebellion. Fort Carlton Provincial Park, another 15 minutes west, is a reconstructed stockade from the fur-trade days. On the second day, go to **North Battleford** (54), 138 km (86 mi) northwest of Saskatoon, for the Fort Battleford National Historic Site, also dealing with the North West Mounted Police.

IF YOU HAVE 4 DAYS

If you're particularly interested in dinosaurs and fossil hunting, travel from **Calgary** ①–⑯, Alberta, to **Regina** ㉘–㉞, Saskatchewan, by way of Drumheller, Alberta, and Eastend, Saskatchewan. In **Drumheller** ⑰, just over an hour east of Calgary on the Trans-Canada Highway, you can spend an entire day at the world-class Royal Tyrell Museum of Paleontology. East on the Trans-Canada Highway en route to **Dinosaur Provincial Park,** you pass through the unique badlands areas, where rivers flowed more than 70 million years ago. South along the Trans-Canada, the thriving oil-rich city of **Medicine Hat** ⑱ is a good choice for an overnight stop. Farther east, south of the Trans-Canada, you come to the small community of **Eastend** ㊴, where you can view a recently discovered, fully preserved Tyrannosaurus rex skeleton in a working lab—the Eastend Fossil Research Station.

IF YOU HAVE 12 DAYS

You can choose between two major routes westward from **Winnipeg** (56)–(68)—north on the Yellowhead (Highway 16) to **Edmonton** ㉑–㉕ via **Saskatoon** ㊸–㊾, or south on the Trans-Canada to **Calgary** ①–⑯ via **Regina** ㉘–㉞. Either is approximately 1,370 grueling km (850 mi). On the Yellowhead route, you can stop for one or two nights in **Riding Mountain National Park,** a half hour north of Highway 16 on Highway 10, near **Wasagaming** (77). Here you'll find forested landscape and sparkling clear lakes, as well as comfortable amenities. Langenburg, just inside the Saskatchewan border, has a provincial tourism information center. Less than four hours to the northwest you come to Saskatoon, Saskatchewan's largest city. Plan on staying at least two nights. Ninety minutes farther westward is the historic community of **North Battleford** (54), where the Western Development Museum and Fort Battleford National Historic Site rate as the two must-see attractions. From here it is approximately three hours to Edmonton.

If you take the more southerly Trans-Canada route, you'll stop in such major centers as **Brandon** (73), **Regina** ㉘–㉞, **Swift Current** ㊱, and 🚆 **Medicine Hat** ⑱ en route to Calgary. All offer interesting diversions and adequate facilities for dining and accommodation.

When to Tour the Prairie Provinces

From June through August you're likely to encounter more festivals and the greatest number of open lodgings (some close seasonally). However, the spring and fall months offer a more tranquil experience for travelers; September can be particularly rewarding, with a combination of warm weather and some autumn foliage. Unless you enjoy bone-chilling cold temperatures, you would be well-advised to skip winter.

CALGARY

With the eastern face of the Rockies as its backdrop, the crisp concrete-and-steel skyline of Calgary, Alberta, seems to rise from the plains as if by sheer force of will. In fact, all the elements in the great saga of the Canadian West—Mounties, native peoples, railroads, cowboys, oil—have converged to create a city with a brand-new face and a surprisingly traditional soul.

Calgary, believed to be derived from the Gaelic phrase meaning "bay farm," was founded in 1875 at the junction of the Bow and Elbow rivers as a North West Mounted Police post. The Canadian Pacific Railroad arrived in 1883, and ranchers established major spreads on the plains surrounding the town. Incorporated as a city in 1894, Calgary grew quickly, and by 1911 its population had reached 43,000.

The major growth came with the oil boom in the 1960s and 1970s, when most Canadian oil companies established their head offices in the city. Today, Calgary is a city of more than 750,000 mostly easy-going and downright neighborly people. It is Canada's second-largest center for corporate head offices. Downtown is still evolving, but Calgary's planners have made life during winter more pleasant by connecting most of the buildings with the Plus 15, a network of enclosed walkways 15 feet above street level.

Calgary supports professional football and hockey teams, and in July the rodeo events of the Calgary Stampede attract visitors from around the world. The city is also the perfect starting point for one of the preeminent dinosaur-exploration sites in the world (☞ Drumheller *in* Elsewhere in Southern Alberta, *below*). Glenbow Museum is one of the top four museums in Canada, and the Calgary Centre for the Performing Arts is a showcase for the arts. Calaway Park, on the western edge of Calgary, is a playground for children of all ages.

Downtown Calgary

In the Calgary grid pattern, numbered streets run north–south in both directions from Centre Street, and numbered avenues run east–west in both directions from Centre Avenue.

A Good Walk

Start at **Calgary Tower** ① for a bird's-eye view of the city. Take the Plus 15 walkway over 9th Avenue Southeast to the **Glenbow Museum** ②, a major showcase of art and history. Next use the Plus 15 walkway above 1st Street Southeast to join a walking tour of the **Calgary Centre for the Performing Arts** ③ theater complex. You can step outside on **Olympic Plaza** ④, where Olympic medals were presented in 1988. Nearby, you'll see the **Municipal Building** ⑤, whose mirror-glass walls reflect other city landmarks. Hop on the C-Train, Calgary's light rail system, for a free ride (along 7th Avenue downtown only) to the center of the downtown shopping district. Here, the top attraction is **De-**

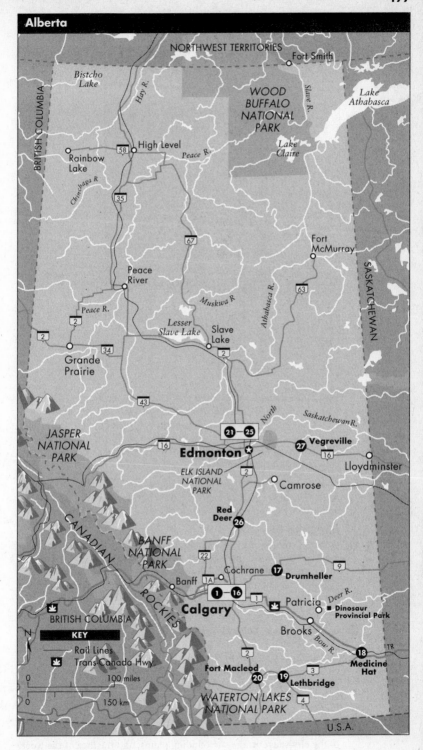

NORTHWEST TERRITORIES

Fort Smith

Bistcho Lake

Hay R.

WOOD BUFFALO NATIONAL PARK

Slave R.

Lake Athabasca

BRITISH COLUMBIA

58 High Level

Peace R.

Lake Claire

Rainbow Lake

Chinchaga R

35

67

Fort McMurray

Peace River

Muskwa R.

Athabasca R.

63

SASKATCHEWAN

Peace R.

2

34

Lesser Slave Lake

Slave Lake

2

Grande Prairie

43

North

Saskatchewan R.

JASPER NATIONAL PARK

21 — 25

27 Vegreville

16 **Edmonton** ★

16

Lloydminster

2

ELK ISLAND NATIONAL PARK

Camrose

CANADIAN

Red Deer 26

BANFF NATIONAL PARK

22

9

Cochrane 17 Drumheller

Banff 1A

1 — 16

1

Patricia

Deer R.

Dinosaur Provincial Park

ROCKIES

Calgary

BRITISH COLUMBIA

Brooks

Bow R.

KEY

— Rail Lines
Trans-Canada Hwy.

N

2

3

18 Medicine Hat

1TR

0   100 miles
0   150 km

Fort Macleod 20

19 Lethbridge

4

WATERTON LAKES NATIONAL PARK

U.S.A.

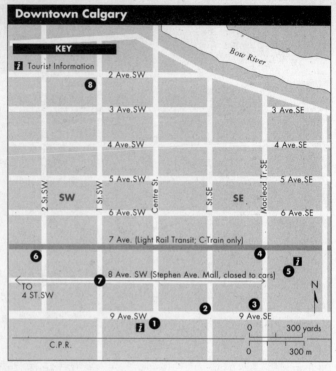

Downtown Calgary

vonian Gardens ⑥, an enclosed roof garden above Toronto Dominion Square. On 8th Avenue, between Macleod Trail and 4th Street Southwest, you'll find **Stephen Avenue Mall** ⑦, for shopping in the ground floors of Calgary's oldest structures. Head north on 1st Street Southwest to the ornate **Calgary Chinese Cultural Centre** ⑧ to take in the architecture and the museum.

TIMING

Allow the better part of a day for this tour, for time in the museums and a bit of shopping.

Sights to See

★ ❸ **Calgary Centre for the Performing Arts.** A complex of three theater spaces, a concert hall, and a shopping area, the center was pieced together with the historic **Calgary Public Building** (1930) and the **Burns Building** (1913). Come at night for a performance, or take a one-hour walking tour at noon most weekdays. ⊠ *Plus 15 walkway above 1st St. SE,* ☎ *403/294–7455.*

❽ **Calgary Chinese Cultural Centre.** This ornate building is in the heart of Chinatown beside the Bow River. Its focal point is the Hall of Prayers of the **Temple of Heaven**; the column details and paintings include 561 dragons and 40 phoenixes. The center also houses a cultural museum, a craft store, an herbal medicine store, and a 330-seat Chinese restaurant. ⊠ *197 1st St. SW,* ☎ *403/262–5071.* 🎫 *Centre free, museum $2.* ☉ *Daily 9:30–9.*

❶ **Calgary Tower.** The 626-foot, scepter-shape edifice affords great views of the city's layout, the surrounding plains, and the face of the Rockies rising 80 km (50 mi) to the west. A flame on top is lit for special occasions; the revolving **Panorama Dining Room** provides refreshment. ⊠ *9th Ave. and Centre St. S,* ☏ *403/266–7171.* ⌑ *$4.95.* ◷ *Weekdays and Sat. 7:30 AM–11:30 PM, Sun. 7:30 AM–10:30 PM.*

❻ Devonian Gardens. Above Toronto Dominion Square, atop Toronto Dominion Centre shopping center, is a 2½-acre enclosed roof garden with 20,000 mostly tropical plants, nearly a mile of lush walkways, a sculpture court, and a playground. Reached by a glass-enclosed elevator just inside the 8th Avenue door, the Devonian Gardens has a reflecting pool that turns into a skating rink in winter and a small stage for musical performances year-round. ⊠ *Between 2nd and 3rd Sts. and 7th and 8th Aves. SW,* ☏ *403/268–3830.* ⌑ *Free.* ◷ *Daily 9–9.*

★ ❷ Glenbow Museum. Calgary's premier showcase of both art and history is ranked among the top four museums in Canada. Along with traveling exhibits, the Glenbow has comprehensive displays devoted to Alberta's native (Indian and Inuit) inhabitants, early European settlers, and latter-day pioneers. A highlight of the museum's recent extensive redevelopment is the new **Alberta Children's Museum.** The mineralogy collection and the cache of arms and armor are superb. ⊠ *130 9th Ave. SE,* ☏ *403/268–4100 or 403/237–8988.* ⌑ *$5.* ◷ *Mid-Oct.–May, Tues.–Sun. 9–5; June–mid-Oct., daily 9–5.*

❺ Municipal Building. This angular, mirror-walled structure reflects a number of city landmarks. One is the stunning **City Hall,** a stately 1911 sandstone building that still houses the mayor's office and some city offices. The City Information Centre, on the main floor, has brochures on historical walking tours. ⊠ *8th Ave. SE and Macleod Tr. SE,* ☏ *403/268–4656.*

❹ Olympic Plaza. The site of the Olympic medals presentation, the plaza is a popular year-round venue for city festivals, arts, and entertainment. You can go skating here in winter. ⊠ *7th Ave. SE and Macleod Tr. SE,* ☏ *403/268–2300.*

❼ Stephen Avenue Mall. In this pedestrian-only shopping area, shops, nightclubs, and restaurants occupy the ground floors of Calgary's oldest structures, mostly sandstone buildings erected after an 1886 fire destroyed almost everything older.

Greater Calgary

With a car you can easily visit a number of top Calgary sights, from Heritage Park to the Stampede Park and Canada Olympic Park. Some kid favorites such as the Calgary Zoo are found here.

A Good Drive

From downtown, drive east on 9th Avenue about a half mile to **Fort Calgary Interpretive Centre** ⑨, at the confluence of the Bow and Elbow rivers, to learn the history of the region. Directly across the 9th Avenue Bridge is the **Deane House** ⑩, dating from 1906. Continue east on 9th Avenue, turn north on 12th Street and cross the bridge to St. George's Island and the **Calgary Zoo, Botanical Gardens, and Prehistoric Park** ⑪. Next head south and west to Olympic Way and **Stampede Park** ⑫ for tours of the grounds and a visit to the Grain Academy museum. Follow Macleod Trail south and go west on Heritage Drive to **Heritage Park** ⑬, where you can see authentic historic structures from all over western Canada. East across Glenmore Reservoir, turn north on Crowchild Trail to reach the **Museum of the Regiments** ⑭ and the **Naval Museum of Alberta.** Continuing north on Crowchild Trail, turn east on 9th Avenue Southwest and then north again on 11th Street Southwest to the **Calgary Science Centre** ⑮ and new multimedia theater for hands-on exhibits and star shows.

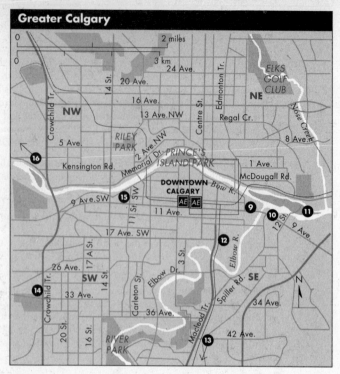

Greater Calgary

Another drive from downtown takes you west on 6th Avenue, following signs to Crowchild Trail, which you take north to 16th Avenue Northwest (Highway 1). Head west on Highway 1 about 8 km (5 mi) to **Canada Olympic Park** ⑯, site of the 1988 Winter Olympics, where you can visit ski jumps and try the bobsled and luge rides. A 20-minute drive beyond the Olympic Park is **Calaway Park,** western Canada's largest amusement park.

TIMING

Because of the distances and the size of the sights, you'd need more than a day to do everything on this tour. Pick sights based on your interests or location. If you have kids, for example, allow a day with the zoo as the main component in the morning, leaving Calaway Park for the afternoon and evening.

Sights to See

Calaway Park. Western Canada's largest outdoor amusement park also has live entertainment, miniature golf, a driving range, a maze, a petting farm, food outlets, and shops. ⊠ *Hwy. 1, 10 km (6 mi) west of Calgary,* ☎ *403/240–3822.* ☉ *May–Sept., hours vary.*

⑮ **Calgary Science Centre.** More than 35 hands-on exhibits of scientific marvels—including holograms, frozen shadows, and laser beams—fascinate visitors; user-friendly demonstrations add to the fun. The Discovery Dome features the latest in computer graphics, with motion picture images that fill an entire dome; the sound system is state-of-the-art. ⊠ *701 11th St. SW,* ☎ *403/221–3700.* ⊡ *$8, but fee varies with program.* ☉ *Tues.–Sun. 10–5.*

★ ⑪ **Calgary Zoo, Botanical Gardens, and Prehistoric Park.** On St. George's Island, in the middle of the Bow River, Canada's second-largest zoo houses more than 1,400 animals in natural settings. The Canadian Wilds section replicates endangered Canadian ecosystems. The Prehistoric Park displays 22 dinosaur replicas in a re-creation of their bygone natural habitat. ⊠ *1300 Zoo Rd. NE,* ☎ *403/232–9372.* ☑ *$7.50.* ☉ *Apr.–June, weekdays 9–4, weekends 9–6; July–Sept., daily 9–6; Oct.– Mar., daily 9–4.*

⑯ Canada Olympic Park. The site of the 1988 Winter Olympics is today a year-round attraction. A one-hour bus tour goes over, under, around, and through the 70- and 90-meter ski jumps and the bobsled and luge tracks (in summer you have the option of walking down the slopes). In winter the slopes are open to the public (lessons available). Visitors can try Olympic-size thrills on the scarifying one-minute bobsled simulator—the Bobsled Bullet ($39)—and the slightly briefer Tourist Luge Ride ($12); safety equipment is provided. On the premises are a day lodge with a cafeteria and the **Olympic Hall of Fame,** a collection of Olympic memorabilia and video displays. ⊠ *88 Olympic Rd. SW,* ☎ *403/286–2632.* ☑ *Bus or self-guided tour $6, tour and Hall of Fame $8.* ☉ *Park mid-June–Sept. 2, daily 7 AM–9 PM; Sept. 3–mid-June, daily 8 AM–9 PM. Hall of Fame, daily 10–5.*

⑩ Deane House. Part of Fort Calgary, this is the restored 1906 post commander's house; it has free tours and a restaurant. ⊠ *809 9th Ave. SE,* ☎ *403/269–7747.*

⑨ Fort Calgary Interpretive Centre. At the confluence of the Bow and Elbow rivers, the fort was established in 1875 by the North West Mounted Police to subdue Montana whiskey traders, who were raising havoc among the native people. The original fort is being rebuilt by a group of volunteers. An ultracontemporary interpretive center traces the history of area aboriginal peoples, Mounties, and European settlers. ⊠ *750 9th Ave. SE,* ☎ *403/290–1875.* ☑ *$2.* ☉ *May–Oct., daily 9–5.*

☝ ⑬ Heritage Park. More than 100 authentic structures have been collected from all over western Canada and relocated here beside Glenmore Reservoir. The "neighborhoods," inhabited by costumed staff, range from an 1850s fur-trading post to a 1910-era town. Steam trains, horse-drawn buses, and paddle-wheel steamers provide transportation, and North America's only antique amusement park re-creates bygone thrills. Theme snacks—sarsaparilla, beef jerky, fresh apple pie—abound. ⊠ *1900 Heritage Dr. SW,* ☎ *403/259–1900.* ☑ *$10; rates vary with season.* ☉ *Late May–June, weekdays 10–4, weekends 10–6; July–Sept. 2, daily 10–6; Sept. 3–early Oct., weekends 10–5.*

⑭ Museum of the Regiments. A collection of military memorabilia depicts the history of Calgary-based regiments dating back to 1900. ⊠ *4520 Crowchild Tr. SW,* ☎ *403/240–7674.* ☑ *Free.* ☉ *July–Labor Day, daily 10–6; Labor Day–June, daily 10–4.*

Naval Museum of Alberta. Canada's second-largest naval museum focuses on the unlikely role of the Prairie Provinces in the Navy. ⊠ *1820 24th St. SW,* ☎ *403/242–0002.* ☑ *Free.* ☉ *July–Labor Day, daily 10– 6; Labor Day–June, daily 10–4.*

⑫ Stampede Park. International attention focuses here each July for the rodeo events of the Calgary Stampede (☞ Outdoor Activities and Sports, *below*). Throughout the year, the Roundup Centre, Big Four Building, and Agriculture Building host trade shows; the **Canadian Airlines Saddledome** (☎ 403/261–0400) has concerts and Calgary Flames hockey games; and the Grandstand holds Thoroughbred and harness racing (☞ Outdoor Activities and Sports, *below*). Visitors can wander the grounds, take free one-hour tours of the Saddledome, and visit the free **Grain Academy** in Roundup Centre, an interesting little museum that proudly proclaims itself "Canada's only grain interpretive centre." ☒ *17th Ave. and 2nd St. SE,* ☎ *403/261–0101, 403/263–4594 Grain Academy in Stampede Park.* ⌨ *Free.* ☉ *Weekdays 10–4, Sat. noon–4.*

Dining

$$$$ ✕ **Owl's Nest Dining Room.** Plush armchairs and dark-wood booths
★   express the subdued confidence of a restaurant long proclaimed the best in town. Standards are maintained, and all dishes are served with impeccable Continental flair. Alberta beef entrées are ample and tender; British Columbia salmon is memorably fresh; the wine list is exhaustive. ☒ *Westin Hotel, 320 4th Ave. SW,* ☎ *403/266–1611. Reservations essential. AE, DC, MC, V.*

$$$ ✕ **Grand Isle Seafood Restaurant.** This large second-floor Chinese restaurant has a riverfront view and modern, very appealing decor. Dim sum is featured, but it's also well known for seafood. ☒ *128 2nd Ave. SE,* ☎ *403/269–7783. AE, D, DC, MC, V.*

$$$ ✕ **Hy's Steak House.** This is where Calgary (and Edmonton, Winnipeg, Toronto, and more) goes for immense portions of charcoal-broiled steaks, fresh seafood, chicken, and a huge selection of wines. Wood paneling and earthy decor help create a sedate Victorian ambience. ☒ *316 4th Ave. SW,* ☎ *403/263–2222. Reservations essential. AE, DC, MC, V. Closed Sun.*

$$ ✕ **Billy MacIntyre's Cattle Company.** This western restaurant chain serves up authentic Alberta-style home cooking, following the recipes used by Alberta ranchers in the early 1900s. Try the baby-back ribs. ☒ *No. 500, 3630 Brentwood Rd. NW,* ☎ *403/282–6614;* ☒ *7104 Macleod Tr. S,* ☎ *403/252–2260. Reservations not accepted. AE, DC, MC, V.*

$$ ✕ **Mescalero.** The casual dining at this popular spot is influenced by the *cucina rustica* of the American Southwest and Latin America. There's an apple-wood grill, and tasty tapas (small dishes) are the star. The daily menu is fresh and creative. In the restaurant's Crazy Horse Bar you can sip margaritas and order from a café menu. ☒ *1315 1st St. SW,* ☎ *403/266–3339. Reservations essential. AE, MC, V.*

$ ✕ **Buzzards Café.** This lively European-style downtown café serves 70
★   wines by the bottle or glass and the exclusive home brew, Buzzard Breath Ale. Wine-theme prints and posters adorn the walls. Food selections include 8-ounce Alberta beef Buzzard Burgers, pub grub, and low-priced entrées, such as teriyaki chicken and fettuccine Alfredo. In summer dine out on the patio. Adjoining the café is Bottlescrew Bill's Old English Pub. ☒ *140 10th Ave. SW,* ☎ *403/264–6959. Reservations not accepted. AE, DC, MC, V.*

$ ✕ **Kaos Café.** Rapidly becoming Calgary's premiere jazz club, this relaxed New York–style café specializes in a jazzy selection of entrées, coffees, and desserts. The outdoor patio is a pleasant choice in summer, and the Saturday and Sunday brunches are popular. ☒ *718 17 Ave. SW,* ☎ *403/228–9997. Reservations essential. AE, DC, MC, V.*

$ ✕ **Osteria de Medici Restaurant.** An authentic, family-run Italian eatery serves up a wide variety of homemade pastas, seafood, and veal, along with such extras as bruschetta and rich desserts. If you're enamored enough, you can purchase the restaurant's cookbook here. ☒ *201 10th St. NW,* ☎ *403/283–5553. AE, DC, MV, V.*

Lodging

$$$$ 🏨 **Delta Bow Valley.** The bright, 24-story high rise occupies a relatively quiet street on the southern edge of downtown. Decent-size contemporary rooms, with rose-and-green furnishings, have good views from upper floors. For the brightest and most colorful units, request a room with a northern exposure. The sunny lobby—decorated in pink tones and with lush foliage—is an uplifting addition to an already lively setting. ⊠ *209 4th Ave. SE, T2G 0C6,* ☎ *403/266–1980 or 800/268–1133,* ⅨX *403/266–0007. 400 rooms. 2 restaurants, bar, no-smoking floors, indoor pool, sauna, exercise room. AE, DC, MC, V.*

$$$$ 🏨 **The Palliser.** The downtown area of every Canadian city has a grand
★ old railroad hotel, and the Palliser is Calgary's. This landmark, built in 1914, was restored in the early 1990s. Guest rooms are tastefully appointed with traditional furnishings and have ornate moldings and high ceilings. ⊠ *133 9th Ave. SW, T2P 2M3,* ☎ *403/262–1234 or 800/268–9411,* ⅨX *403/260–1260. 406 rooms. Restaurant, bar, no-smoking floor, exercise room. AE, DC, MC, V.*

$$$$ 🏨 **Radisson Plaza Hotel.** This business-class hotel in the heart of downtown is connected to the Calgary Convention Centre. Nearby are the Glenbow Museum and the Calgary Centre for Performing Arts. The warm, inviting lobby sets the tone; rooms are done in pastels and maroons. ⊠ *110 9th Ave., T2G 5A6,* ☎ *403/266–7331 or 800/661–7776,* ⅨX *403/262–8442. 387 rooms. 2 restaurants, 2 bars, no-smoking floors, indoor pool, sauna, health club. AE, DC, MC, V.*

$$$$ 🏨 **Sheraton Cavalier.** In northeast Calgary, the hotel has a lobby decorated with pale colors, a multitude of plants, and a large marble water fountain. Barlow's Lounge hosts live entertainment from Thursday through Saturday. For sports fans, Henry's Pub, the hotel's sports bar, has large TV screens. Oasis River Country, on the second floor of the hotel, has two 200-foot water slides and a recreation and exercise area. ⊠ *2620 32nd Ave. NE, T1Y 6B8,* ☎ *403/291–0107 or 800/325–3535,* ⅨX *403/291–2834. 307 rooms. Restaurant, bar, lounge, no-smoking rooms, indoor pool. AE, DC, MC, V.*

$$$$ 🏨 **Westin Hotel.** Calgary's Plus 15 pedway (walkway) system connects
★ this luxury high rise in the midst of downtown to most other important nearby structures. Rooms are large and decorated with tasteful contemporary furniture and pastel and neutral tones. The rooftop pool is one of this lodging's unique attractions. The Owl's Nest restaurant (☞ Dining, *above*) is one of the best dining spots in town. For lighter meals stop in at the Lobby Court, which has Fitness Buffet breakfasts. ⊠ *320 4th Ave. SW, T2P 2S6,* ☎ *403/266–1611 or 800/228–3000,* ⅨX *403/265–7908. 525 rooms. 2 restaurants, 2 bars, no-smoking rooms, indoor pool, sauna, health club. AE, DC, MC, V.*

$$$ 🏨 **Carriage House.** This unique, locally owned property, almost 10 km (6 mi) south of downtown, has a lobby with fish tanks, caged songbirds, and a waterfall. Room decor is comfortably mismatched. Nighttime entertainment options include a disco and rock club, a country and rock saloon, and an English pub. Guests receive discounts at the nearby Family Leisure Centre (☞ Outdoor Activities and Sports, *below*). ⊠ *9030 Macleod Tr. S, T2H 0M4,* ☎ *403/253–1101 (call collect from the U.S.), 800/661–9566 in Canada,* ⅨX *403/259–2414. 175 rooms. 2 restaurants, 3 bars, no-smoking rooms, pool, sauna. AE, DC, MC, V.*

$$ 🏨 **Prince Royal Inn.** Calgary's bargain inn has a great deal going for it within its 28 floors: a convenient downtown location, all-suite (studios, one-, and two-bedroom) accommodations with fully equipped kitchens, free parking, free Continental breakfast, and a health club. It's a great deal for families. ⊠ *618 5th Ave. SW, T2P 0M7,* ☎ *403/263–0520, 800/661–1592 in Canada,* ⅨX *403/262–9991. 300 suites. Restaurant, bar, no-smoking floors, sauna, exercise room. AE, DC, MC, V.*

$$ 🏨 **Ramada Inn Airport.** This convenient and comfortable property is on the northeast side of town a few minutes from Calgary International Airport. Bright rooms are large, with standard furnishings, and are tastefully decorated with a rose-and-mauve scheme. ⊠ *1250 McKinnon Dr. NE, T2E 7T7, ☎ 403/230–1999 or 800/661–5095, FAX 403/277–2623. 168 rooms. Restaurant, bar, no-smoking rooms, indoor pool, sauna. AE, DC, MC, V.*

Nightlife and the Arts

Tickets for events at the Calgary Centre for the Performing Arts, Jubilee Auditorium, and the Saddledome are available at Ticketmaster outlets at the Calgary Centre box office or can be charged over the phone (☎ 403/270–6700 or 403/266–8888).

The Arts

MUSIC AND DANCE

Calgary Philharmonic Orchestra (☎ 403/294–7420) concerts, chamber groups, and a broad spectrum of music and dance shows are presented in the 1,755-seat Jack Singer Concert Hall in the **Calgary Centre for the Performing Arts** (⊠ 205 8th Ave. SE, ☎ 403/294–7455). The **Jubilee Auditorium** (⊠ 1415 14th Ave. NW, ☎ 403/297–8000) hosts the Alberta Ballet company and a variety of classical music, opera, dance, pop, and rock concerts. Concerts are performed at **University of Calgary Theatre** (⊠ 2500 University Dr. NW, ☎ 403/220–4900).

THEATER

Calgary's showcase theater facility is the **Calgary Centre for the Performing Arts** (⊠ 205 8th Ave. SE, ☎ 403/294–7455), with three modern auditoriums in two contiguous historic buildings. Productions by resident Alberta Theatre Projects (ATP) of works by principally Canadian playwrights are highly recommended. More than 20 local companies use the stage of the **Pumphouse Theatre** (⊠ 2140 9th Ave. SW, ☎ 403/263–0079). The **University of Calgary Theatre** (⊠ Reeve Theatre, 2500 University Dr. NW, ☎ 403/220–4900) stages classic and contemporary works. **Loose Moose** (⊠ 2003 McKnight Blvd. NE, ☎ 403/291–5682) features competitive "Theatresports" and all sorts of improvisational fun and games.

Nightlife

BARS AND CLUBS

Gargoyle's (⊠ 1213 1st St. SW, ☎ 403/263–4810) caters to an older, upscale crowd. The club atmosphere at **Republik** (⊠ 219 17th Ave. SW, ☎ 403/244–1884) attracts a young crowd for alternative rock. The Mexican accent at **Señor Frog's** (⊠ 739 2nd Ave. SW, 403/264–5100) is popular with all ages.

CASINOS

You can play blackjack, roulette, and wheel of fortune at **River Park Casino** (⊠ 1919 Macleod Trail S, ☎ 403/269–6771). **Cash Casino Place** (⊠ 4040B Blackfoot Trail SE, ☎ 403/287–1635) has games of chance and a restaurant. At **Tower Casino** in Tower Centre you can place wagers. **Frontier Casino** is in the Big Four Building in Stampede Park.

COMEDY

Yuk Yuk's (⊠ Blackfoot Inn, 5940 Blackfoot Trail, ☎ 403/258–2028), part of the Canadian comedy chain, has name performers from Canada and the United States. **Jester's** (⊠ 239 10th Ave. SE, ☎ 403/269–6669) has comedians and Wednesday night open mikes.

MUSIC

For western sights and sounds, head for **Ranchman's** (⊠ 9615 Macleod Trail S, ☎ 403/253–1100). The **Longhorn Dance Hall** (⊠ 9631 Macleod Trail S, ☎ 403/258–0528) is one of Calgary's western hangouts. The

Rocking Horse Saloon (✉ 24 7400 Macleod Trail S, ☎ 403/255–4646) features country music every night but Sunday.

Outdoor Activities and Sports

Participant Sports

BICYCLING AND JOGGING

Calgary has about 300 km (186 mi) of bicycling and jogging paths, most of which wind along rivers and through city parks. Maps are available at visitor centers and bike shops. You can rent bikes at **Sports Rent** (✉ 4424 16th Ave. NW, Calgary, ☎ 403/292–0077) and from **Budget Rent-A-Car** (✉ 140 6th Ave. SE, ☎ 403/264–5212).

HEALTH AND FITNESS CLUBS

Three **Leisure Centre** water parks in Calgary have wave pools and water slides, plus gymnasiums and training facilities; Southland and Family have racquetball and squash courts. ✉ *Village Square Leisure Centre, 2623 56th St. NE,* ☎ *403/280–9714;* ✉ *Family Leisure Centre, 11150 Bonaventure Dr. SE,* ☎ *403/278–7542;* ✉ *Southland Leisure Centre, 2000 Southland Dr. SW,* ☎ *403/251–3505.*

Just south of downtown, the striking white-dome **Lindsay Park Sports Centre** (✉ 2225 Macleod Trail SW, ☎ 403/233–8393) encompasses a 50-meter natatorium, a 200-meter track, racquetball and squash courts, and a weight room.

Spectator Sports

FOOTBALL

The **Calgary Stampeders** of the Canadian Football League play home games in **McMahon Stadium** (✉ 1817 Crowchild Trail NW, ☎ 403/289–0205) throughout the season, which runs July through November.

HOCKEY

The **Calgary Flames** play National Hockey League matches October–April at the **Canadian Airlines Saddledome** (✉ 17th Ave. and 2nd St. SE, ☎ 403/261–0475) in Stampede Park.

HORSE RACING

There's racing year-round (except March) in **Stampede Park** (✉ 17th Ave. and 2nd St. SE, ☎ 403/261–0101). Thoroughbreds race April–May and September–November; trotters May–September and December–February. **Spruce Meadows** (✉ southwest of Calgary city boundary, ☎ 403/974–4200) is one of the world's finest show-jumping facilities, with major competitions held June–September.

RODEO

For 10 days each July, rodeo events draw the world's top cowboys and plenty of greenhorns to one of Canada's most popular events, the **Calgary Stampede** (☎ 800/661–1260), held in Stampede Park. Besides rodeo events, there are livestock shows, concerts, and high-spirited western-style entertainment. Make room and ticket reservations well in advance if you plan to attend.

Shopping

Calgary's best shopping is in the center of the downtown district, where you can wander through various shopping centers connected by indoor walkways. **Bankers Hall** has exclusive specialty shops, restaurants, and cinemas. **Scotia Centre** has fashion, accessory, and other retail outlets. **Penny Lane Mall** is in renovated, early 20th-century buildings. **Toronto Dominion Centre** is home to the indoor park—Devonian Gardens—as well as more than 100 stores. The **Eaton Centre** has more than 500 stores. For outdoor shopping, the six-block stretch of 8th Avenue Southwest between 3rd Street Southwest and Macleod Trail Southeast has been turned into the traffic-free **Stephen Avenue Mall** (although traffic is allowed during the evenings). **Uptown 17** and **Kensington** are trendy shopping districts northwest of the city center on 10th Street and Kensington Road, respectively; here you'll find craft shops, antiques stores, boutiques, galleries, cafés, and coffee shops.

Side Trip from Calgary

Cochrane
25 km (16 mi) west of Calgary.

Cochrane is a popular center for trail rides and canoe trips on the Bow River. Its western-style buildings hold some thriving craft shops. **The Western Heritage Centre** is a new interactive interpretive center dedicated to the history of ranching, farming, and rodeos; the people who operated the first ranches in Alberta; and the men and women who still perform those same chores today. ⊠ *Near junction of Hwys. 22 and 1A,* ☎ *403/932–3514.* ☞ *$7.50.* ☉ *Late May–Labor Day, daily 9–8; Labor Day–late May, daily 9–5.*

Calgary A to Z

Arriving and Departing
BY CAR

The Trans-Canada Highway (Highway 1) runs west to southeast across Alberta, through Calgary. Highway 2 passes through Calgary on its way from the U.S. border to Edmonton and points north. Calgary is 690 km (428 mi) northwest of Helena, Montana; it's 670 km (415 mi) northeast of Seattle, via the Trans-Canada Highway.

BY PLANE

Calgary International Airport (☎ 403/735–1372) is 20 minutes northeast of the city center. Airlines serving Calgary include Air Canada, Canadian Airlines International, Air BC, American, Delta, United, and KLM. Taxis make the trip between the airport and downtown for about $18.

Getting Around
BY BUS AND LRT

Calgary Transit (⊠ 206 7th Ave. SW, ☎ 403/276–7801) operates a comprehensive bus system and light rail transit system (the C-Train or LRT) throughout the area. Fares on both are $1.50. Books of 10 tickets are $12. A Calgary Transit (CT) Day Pass good for unlimited rides costs $4. The C-Train has lines running northwest (Brentwood), northeast (Whitehorn), and south (Anderson) from downtown. The C-Train is free within the downtown core.

BY CAR

Although many sights are in the downtown area and can be reached on foot, a car is useful for visiting outlying attractions.

BY TAXI

Taxis are fairly expensive, at $2.05 for the drop and about $1 for each additional mile. Major taxi services are **Checker** (☎ 403/299–9999), **Yellow Cab** (☎ 403/974–1111), **Red Top** (☎ 403/974–4444), **Associated Cabs** (☎ 403/299–1111), and **Co-op** (☎ 403/531–8294).

Contacts and Resources
EMERGENCIES

Dial 911 for all emergencies; **police,** ☎ 403/266–1234; **poison center,** ☎ 403/670–1414.

Several companies offer tours of Calgary and environs, although none operate on regular schedules. Call the **Calgary Convention and Visitors Bureau** (☎ 403/263–8510 or 800/661–1678) for up-to-date information.

HOSPITALS
Emergency rooms are at **General Hospital** (✉ 841 Centre Ave. E, ☎ 403/268–9111), **Foothills Hospital** (✉ 1403 29th Ave. NW, ☎ 403/670–1110), **Alberta Children's Hospital** (✉ 1820 Richmond Rd. SW, ☎ 403/229–7211), and **Rocky View Hospital** (✉ 7007 14th St. SW, ☎ 403/541–3000).

LATE-NIGHT PHARMACY
The **Super Drug Mart** (✉ 504 Elbow Dr. SW, ☎ 403/228–3338) is open daily until midnight.

VISITOR INFORMATION
The main **Calgary Convention and Visitors Bureau** (✉ 237 8th Ave. SE, T2G 0K8, ☎ 403/263–8510 or 800/661–1678) is open daily 8–5. There are also walk-in visitor service centers at the base of the Calgary Tower and at the Calgary International Airport.

ELSEWHERE IN SOUTHERN ALBERTA

A number of cities and varied sights in the southern part of the province provide a look at key elements of Alberta's history. You can study the world of the dinosaurs in Drumheller, learn about the role of native peoples, settlers, and the North West Mounted Police in Fort MacLeod, and explore prosperous, modern Medicine Hat.

Drumheller

🔟 *20 km (12 mi) east of Calgary on Trans-Canada Hwy. (Hwy. 1), then 120 km (75 mi) north on Rte. 9.*

The road to Drumheller takes you through the vast Canadian prairie of seemingly endless expanses of flat country in every direction. Once a coal-mining center, the town lies in the rugged valley of the Red Deer River, where millions of years of wind and water erosion exposed the "strike" that produced what amounts to present-day Drumheller's major industry: dinosaurs.

★ The **Royal Tyrrell Museum of Paleontology** explores the geological and paleontological history of Alberta. The barren lunar terrain of stark badlands and eerie rock cylinders (called hoodoos) may seem an ideal setting for the dinosaurs that stalked the countryside 75 million years ago, but in fact, when the dinosaurs were here the area had a semitropical climate and verdant marshlands not unlike the Florida Everglades. Participate in hands-on exhibits and meet the local hero, *Albertosaurus*, a smaller, fiercer version of *Tyrannosaurus rex*, the first dinosaur discovered around here. ✉ *Rte. 838, 6 km (4 mi) west of Drumheller*, ☎ *403/823–7707 or 403/294–1992.* ⊠ *$6.50.* ☉ *Mid-May–early Sept., daily 9–9; mid-Sept.–mid-May, Tues.–Sun. 10–5.*

Capitalizing on its rich paleontological past, Drumheller has a number of dinosaur-related businesses. **Reptile World** (✉ Rte. 9, ☎ 403/823–8623) has a crowd-pleasing collection of poisonous snakes. The **Homestead Antique Museum** (✉ Rte. 838, ☎ 403/823–2600) packs 4,000 native artifacts, medical instruments, pieces of period clothing, and other items of Canadiana into a roadside Quonset hut. **Prehistoric Park** (✉ Off Rte. 575, ☎ 403/823–7625) depicts life-size dinosaurs in a badlands setting and sells a vast selection of fossils, bones, rocks, and petrified wood. No visit to Drumheller is complete without a family portrait beside the comic-book *Tyrannosaurus rex* guarding the Route 9 bridge over the Red Deer River.

Dinosaur Provincial Park

142 km (88 mi) south of Drumheller, 190 km (118 mi) southeast of Calgary.

Dinosaur Provincial Park encompasses 73 square km (28 square mi) of Canada's greatest badlands, as well as prairie and riverside habitats. A United Nations World Heritage Site, the park contains some of the world's richest fossil beds, including many kinds of dinosaurs. Much of the area is a nature preserve with restricted public access. Self-guiding trails explore different habitats, and a public loop road leads to two outdoor fossil displays. The Royal Tyrrell Museum Field Station has ongoing fossil excavations. Interpretive programs run daily from mid-May to early September and on weekends until mid-October, but many require tickets; call for reservations. You should allow at least 1½ days for an in-depth experience. The campground has a food service center. To get here from Drumheller, take Route 56 to the Trans-Canada Highway (Highway 1) east, go north at Brooks on Route 873 and then east on Route 544, and follow signs. ⊠ *Rte. 544, Patricia,* ☎ *403/378–4342 for information, 403/378–4344 for tour reservations (mid-May–Aug.), 403/378–3700 for campground reservations (May–Aug.).* ▧ *Free, bus tour $4.50.* ☉ *Daily 24 hrs; Tyrrell Museum Field Station mid-May–Aug., daily 8:15 AM–9 PM; Sept.–mid-Oct., weekdays 8:15–4:30, weekends 9–5; mid-Oct.–mid-May, weekdays 8:15–4:30.*

Medicine Hat

🔞 *95 km (59 mi) southeast of Patricia, 293 km (182 mi) southeast of Calgary on Trans-Canada Highway.*

Medicine Hat is a prosperous and scenic city built on high banks overlooking the South Saskatchewan River. Much local lore concerns the origin of its name, but one legend tells of a battle between Cree and Blackfoot peoples: The Cree fought bravely until their medicine man deserted, losing his headdress in the South Saskatchewan River. The site's name, *Saamis,* meaning "medicine man's hat," was later translated by white settlers into Medicine Hat. Roadside views on the way to Medicine Hat consist of small well pumps and storage tanks amid endless expanses of "prairie wool," spear and blue grama grass.

Alberta's fifth-largest city's wealth derives from vast deposits of natural gas below, some of which is piped up to fuel quaint gas lamps in the turn-of-the-century downtown area. Prosperity is embodied in the striking, glass-sided **Medicine Hat City Hall,** which won the Canadian Architectural Award in 1986. Guided group and self-guided tours are available. ⊠ *1st St. SE and 6th Ave. SE,* ☎ *403/529–8100.* ☉ *Weekdays 8:30–4:30.*

Medicine Hat's greatest achievement was turning the land alongside the South Saskatchewan River and Seven Persons Creek into **parkland and environmental preserves** interconnected by 15 km (9½ mi) of walking, biking, and cross-country ski trails. Detailed trail maps are available at the **Tourist Information Centre** (⊠ 8 Gehring Rd. SW, ☎ 403/527–6422). There is a half mile of falling water at **Riverside Amusement Park** (⊠ Hwy. 1 and Power House Rd., ☎ 403/529–6218), with water slides, go-carts, and inner tubing. **Echo Dale Regional Park** (⊠ Holsom Rd. off Rte. 3, ☎ 403/529–6225) provides a riverside setting for swimming, boating, fishing, a 1900s farm, and a historic coal mine.

Dining and Lodging

$$ ✕📶 **Medicine Hat Lodge.** On the edge of town adjacent to a shopping mall, this hotel has several rooms with inward views of the indoor pool and the huge, curving water slide. The Atrium Dining Room serves fine Continental meals. J.D.'s is a hotel country-and-western club with live music. ⊠ *1051 Ross Glen Dr. SE, T1B 3T8,* ☎ *403/529–2222 or 800/661–8095. 190 rooms. 2 restaurants, 2 bars, no-smoking rooms, indoor pool, steam room. AE, DC, MC, V.*

Lethbridge

⑲ *164 km (102 mi) west of Medicine Hat on Crowsnest Hwy. (Rte. 3); 217 km (135 mi) south of Calgary via Hwy. 2 and Route 3.*

Alberta's third-largest city, Lethbridge is an 1870s coal boomtown that is now a center of agriculture, oil, and gas. The main attraction, **Fort Whoop-Up,** part of the **Indian Battle Park,** is a reconstruction of a southern Alberta whiskey fort. Along with weapons, relics, and a 15-minute audiovisual historical presentation, Fort Whoop-Up has wagon-train tours of the river valley and other points of local historical interest. ⊠ *Indian Battle Park, Whoop-Up Dr. and Oldman River,* ☎ *403/329–0444.* 🎟 *Fort Whoop-Up $2.50.* 🕙 *Late May–Labor Day, Mon.–Sat. 10–6, Sun. 2–8; off-season, call for hours.*

Henderson Lake Park, 3 km (2 mi) east of downtown Lethbridge, is filled with lush trees, a golf course, a baseball stadium, tennis courts, a swimming pool, and a 60-acre man-made lake. Alongside the lake, **Nikka Yuko Japanese Gardens** is a tranquil setting for manicured trees and shrubs, miniature pools and waterfalls, a teahouse, and pebble designs originally constructed in Japan and reassembled alongside Henderson Lake. ⊠ *Henderson Lake Park, Mayor Magrath Dr. and S. Parkside Dr.,* ☎ *403/320–3020, 403/328–3511 gardens.* 🎟 *$3.* 🕙 *Mid-May–mid-June, daily 9–5; mid-June–Aug., daily 9–8; Sept.–early Oct., daily 9–5.*

Dining and Lodging

$$$ ✕ **Cafe Martinique.** This locally renowned fine dining spot, in the El Rancho Motor Hotel, specializes in aged steaks and chateaubriand made with tender Alberta beef. For something lighter in a more informal setting, try the El Rancho coffee shop on the same property. There's live music and dancing most nights. ⊠ *526 Mayor Magrath Dr.,* ☎ *403/ 327–5701. Reservations essential. AE, DC, MC, V.*

$$ ✕ **Sven Eriksen's Family Restaurant.** Tasty versions of Canadian prairie standards, including chicken and an especially good prime rib, are cooked up at this homey, colonial-style eatery. "Family Restaurant" label notwithstanding, there's a full bar. ⊠ *1715 Mayor Magrath Dr.,* ☎ *403/328–7756. Reservations essential. AE, MC, V.*

$$ 📶 **Lethbridge Lodge Hotel.** Besides great Oldman River views, this modern lodge has a pleasant tropical indoor courtyard filled with exotic plants, a swimming pool, a whirlpool, a waterfall, and chairs. There are two restaurants: At the more formal **Anton's,** the waiters wear tuxedos, and reservations are needed. ⊠ *320 Scenic Dr., T1J 4B4,* ☎ *403/ 328–1123 or 800/661–1232. 190 rooms. 2 restaurants, bar, no-smoking rooms, indoor pool, hot tub. AE, MC, V.*

$ 📶 **Parkside Inn.** This comfortable, nearly 40-year-old hotel is a good bargain, conveniently situated across the street from a golf course and within walking distance of Henderson Lake Park and the Japanese gardens. The lobby is done in muted burgundies and blues, while rooms are styled in grays and rusts. The hotel's tavern has live country-and-western music on weekends and the lounge has video lottery machines. ✉ *1009 Mayor Magrath Dr., T1K 2P7,* ☎ *403/328–2366. 65 rooms. Restaurant, bar, no-smoking rooms. AE, MC, V.*

Fort Macleod

⓴ *50 km (31 mi) west of Lethbridge on Rte. 3, 167 km (104 mi) from Calgary.*

Fort Macleod, southern Alberta's oldest town, was founded by the Mounties in 1874 to maintain order among the farmers, native people, whiskey vendors, and ranchers beginning to settle here. The pre-1900 wood-frame buildings and the more recent sandstone-and-brick buildings have established this as Alberta's first historic area. For information about guided and self-guided tours, visit the information booth (☎ 403/553–2500) beside the Fort Macleod Museum. An authentic reconstruction of the 1874 fort, the **Fort Macleod Museum** grants almost equal exhibitory weight to settlers, native peoples, old North West Mounted Police, and today's Royal Canadian Mounted Police. ✉ *25th St.,* ☎ *403/553–4703.* *$4.* ⏲ *May–mid-June and early Sept.–mid-Oct., daily 9–5; mid-June–early Sept., daily 9–8:30.*

Head-Smashed-In Buffalo Jump, about 18 km (11 mi) northwest of Fort Macleod, is a World Heritage Site. At the large, seven-level interpretive center built into the side of a cliff, you can learn how Plains Indians herded buffalo over the edge to their death in order to harvest meat and fur from the carcasses. Museum displays describe the tradition and offer insight into the life and customs of the Plains Indians, especially the Blackfoot. Guided walks and audiovisual exhibits are presented. ✉ *Rte. 785 off Hwy. 2,* ☎ *403/553–2731.* *$6.50.* ⏲ *May 16–Labor Day, daily 9–8; Labor Day–May 15, daily 9–5.*

EDMONTON

Lucky Edmonton is a recidivist boomtown that never seems to go bust. The first boom arrived in 1795, when the North West Company and Hudson's Bay Company both established fur-trading posts in the area. Boom II came in 1897, when Edmonton became principal outfitter on the overland "All Canadian Route" to the Yukon goldfields; as a result, Edmonton was named capital when the province of Alberta was formed in 1905. The latest boom began on February 13, 1947, when oil was discovered in Leduc, 40 km (25 mi) to the southwest. More than 10,000 wells were eventually drilled within 100 km (62 mi) of the city, and with them came fields of refineries and supply depots. By 1965 Edmonton had solidified its role as the "oil capital of Canada."

More interesting is how wisely Edmonton has spread the wealth to create a beautiful and livable city. Shunning the uncontrolled development of some other oil boomtowns, Edmonton turned its great natural resource, the North Saskatchewan River valley, into a 27-km (17-mi) greenbelt of parks and recreational facilities. With a population of 875,000, Edmonton is the fifth-largest city in Canada and also Canada's second-largest city in land area—270 square miles. As the seat of the provincial government and home to the University of Alberta, the city has an unusually sophisticated atmosphere that has generated many fine restaurants and a thriving arts community. Another of its attractions, the West Edmonton Mall, is a year-round drawing card for shoppers and families, complete with facilities ranging from an amusement park to a shopping center and hotel, and from a cinema complex to a water park. The city also has professional football and hockey teams, as well as Triple A baseball.

Downtown Edmonton

The city's striking physical feature, where most recreational facilities are located, is the broad green valley of the North Saskatchewan River, running diagonally northeast to southwest through the city center. The downtown area lies just north of the river, between 95th and 109th streets.

The Edmonton street system is a grid with numbered streets running north–south (numbers decrease as you go east) and numbered avenues running east–west (numbers decrease as you go south). Edmontonians often use the last digit or two of large numbers as shorthand for the complete number: The Inn on 7th is on 107th Street; the 9th Street Bistro can be found on 109th Street. Edmonton's main drag is Jasper Avenue, which runs east–west through the center of downtown.

A Good Walk and Ride

Start at the **Edmonton Convention Centre** ㉑, an architecturally inventive space built into a hillside with terraced levels accessed by glass-enclosed escalators. Head west along Jasper Avenue and turn north on 99th Street to **Sir Winston Churchill Square** ㉒, where you'll find many of the city's major cultural institutions. Across 99th Street is the **Edmonton Art Gallery** ㉓. Directly west of Churchill Square begins a maze of multilevel shopping malls, department stores, cinemas, and office buildings—all climatically controlled and interconnected by a network of tunnels and second-floor pedways (☞ Shopping, *below*). Enter the LRT station on Jasper Avenue at 103rd or 104th Street for the ride to Grandin Station and the **Alberta Government Centre** ㉔, where you can tour the **Alberta Legislature Building** ㉕.

TIMING

You can do this tour in a few hours any day of the week, although you may choose to linger to explore the cultural institutions or to shop.

Sights to See

㉔ **Alberta Government Centre.** The seat of Alberta's government, this complex encompasses several acres of carefully manicured gardens and fountains. The gardens are open for strolling. ⊠ *109th St. and 97th Ave.*

㉕ **Alberta Legislature Building.** The stately 1912 Edwardian structure overlooks the river on the site of an early trading post. Frequent free tours of the building help explain the intricacies of the Albertan and Canadian systems of government. ⊠ *109th St. and 97th Ave.,* ☎ *403/427–7362.* ⊡ *Tour free.* ☉ *Daily, call for hours.*

㉓ **Edmonton Art Gallery.** More than 30 annual exhibits of classical and contemporary art from Canada and the rest of the world are mounted here. ⊠ *2 Sir Winston Churchill Sq.,* ☎ *403/422–6223.* ⊡ *$3, free Thurs. after 4.* ☉ *Mon.–Wed. 10:30–5, Thurs. and Fri. 10:30–8, weekends 11–5.*

㉑ **Edmonton Convention Centre.** This most unconventional building is filled with surprises. The center has been built onto a slope, and the terraced levels are reached by glass-enclosed escalators with great views of the North Saskatchewan River valley. On the Pedway (walkway) Level check out the **Canadian Country Music Hall of Honor,** actually a wall filled with plaques memorializing such good old boys as Hank Snow, Wilf Carter, and Orval "the Canadian Plowboy" Prophet. ⊠ *9797 Jasper Ave.,* ☎ *403/421–9797.*

Downtown Edmonton

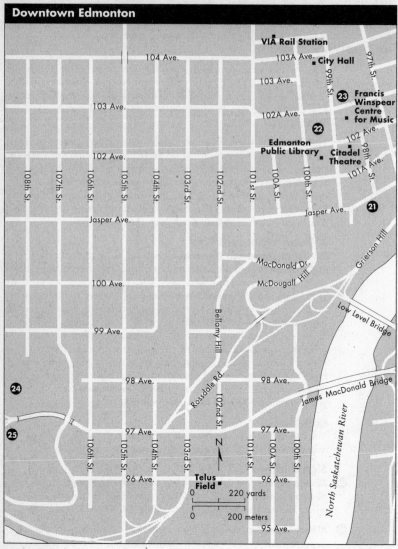

Alberta Government
Centre, **24**

Alberta Legislature
Building, **25**

Edmonton Art
Gallery, **23**

Edmonton Convention
Centre, **21**

Sir Winston Churchill
Square, **22**

㉒ **Sir Winston Churchill Square** is the focus of the Civic Centre, a six-block area that incorporates many of Edmonton's major institutions. The newest addition, scheduled to open by 1998, will be the **Francis Winspear Centre for Music,** with an 1,800-seat concert hall that will be home to the Edmonton Symphony Orchestra. Also housed here is the largest theater complex in Canada, the **Citadel Theatre,** which houses five different venues (plus workshops and classrooms) and an indoor garden with a waterfall. The **Edmonton Public Library** (✉ 7 Sir Winston Churchill Sq., ☎ 403/423–2331) augments books and art exhibits with a lively round of activities in the Children's Department. The **Chinatown Gate** is a symbol of friendship between Edmonton and its sister city, Harbin, China; it spans the portal to Edmonton's meager Chinatown. Nearby, the **City Hall** (✉ 1 Sir Winston Churchill Sq., ☎ 403/496–8200) is more than a place for civic government. This architectural showcase contains a grand stairway, a large art exhibition space, and a 200-foot tower with an enormous 23-bell carillon.

Greater Edmonton

You'll find everything from historical sights and museums to water parks and the world's largest mall outside downtown Edmonton.

A Good Drive

To make a circuit, start northwest of city center at the **Edmonton Space and Science Centre,** where you can play with high-tech equipment in hands-on displays. On the western edge of the city is the **Wild Waters Waterslide Park,** a great place to cool off the kids. Moving toward the center again, you can visit the **West Edmonton Mall,** the world's largest. On the south side of the North Saskatchewan River, just off Whitemud Drive, is **Fort Edmonton Park,** where costumed interpreters take you back in time. Still on the south side of the river, but around a few bends just off Groat Road, is **William Hawrelak Park,** a perfect place for kids to fish. After fishing, you can visit the **Valley Zoo,** just across the river. A few blocks north is the **Provincial Museum of Alberta,** which focuses on natural and human history. Across the river again, via the 109th Street Bridge, you'll come to the **Old Strathcona Historic Area,** the **Old Strathcona Model and Toy Museum,** and the **Telephone Historical Centre,** all within a few blocks of one another. To the northeast, still on the south side of the river, lies **Muttart Conservatory,** an important botanical facility. You can end your tour with thrills at the **Whitemud Drive Amusement Park,** toward the southeastern side of the city.

TIMING

You can spend several days taking in these places of interest outside downtown, depending on how much time you want to devote to shopping or playing in the amusement parks. If you have only a day, choose based on your interests.

Sights to See

Edmonton Space and Science Centre. Explore the heavens using a stunning variety of high-tech techniques. Standing exhibits and a fascinating science shop are always of interest, but the star attractions include laser-light concerts and IMAX films. ✉ 11211 142nd St., ☎ 403/493–9000. ᴁ $12. ⊙ Mid-June–early Sept., daily 10–10; early Sept.–mid-June, Tues.–Sun. 10–10.

Fort Edmonton Park. Canada's largest historical park (158 acres) is home to an authentic re-creation of several periods in Edmonton history. There is a fur press (an apparatus for bundling pelts for shipping) in the 1846 Hudson's Bay Company fort; a blacksmith shop, a saloon, and a jail along 1885 Street; photo studios and a firehouse on 1905 Street; and relatively modern conveniences on 1920 Street. Horse wagon, street-car, stagecoach, and pony rides are available, as well as a short trip on a steam-powered train. ⊠ *Whitemud and Fox Drs.,* ☎ *403/496–8787.* ☎ *$6.75.* ☉ *Mid-May–June, daily 10–4; July–early Sept., daily 10–6; Sept., Mon.–Sat. 11–2, Sun. 10–6.*

Muttart Conservatory. At one of North America's most important botanical facilities, separate greenhouses each contain flora of a different climate: arid, tropical, and temperate. A show pavilion has special seasonal floral displays. ⊠ *9626 96A St.,* ☎ *403/496–8755.* ☎ *$4.25.* ☉ *Sun.–Wed. 11–9, Thurs.–Sat. 11–6.*

Old Strathcona Historic Area. The area surrounding 104th Street and Whyte (82nd) Avenue on the south side of the river is a district of restored houses and shops built mainly when Strathcona Town amalgamated with Edmonton, in 1912. The low buildings and wide streets have a decidedly Old West air, and Old Strathcona is a good place to get out and wander. There's a farmer's market, theaters, museums, and 75 restaurants and coffee houses, which add to the ambience of the area. Call the Old Strathcona Foundation (☎ 403/433–5866) for information.

☾ **Old Strathcona Model and Toy Museum.** Here you'll find intricate models of planes, buildings, wildlife, and much more, all made of paper. ⊠ *8603 104th St.,* ☎ *403/433–4512.*

Provincial Museum of Alberta. At the province's foremost natural and human history museum, four main galleries depict Alberta's heritage. The Aboriginal Peoples Gallery has a collection of native artifacts that is among North America's finest. ⊠ *12845 102nd Ave.,* ☎ *403/453–9100.* ☎ *$5.* ☉ *May–Sept., daily 9–5; Oct.–Apr., Tues.–Sun. 9–5.*

Telephone Historical Centre. The largest telephone museum in Canada is filled with hands-on exhibits. ⊠ *10437 83rd Ave.,* ☎ *403/441–2077.*

☾ **Valley Zoo.** This small but imaginative zoo in riverside Laurier Park places exotic species in well-known storybook settings. ⊠ *134th St. and Buena Vista Rd.,* ☎ *403/496–6911.* ☎ *Summer $4.95, winter $3.35.*

West Edmonton Mall. Listed in the *Guinness Book of World Records* as the world's largest mall, this is Edmonton's preeminent shopping attraction. Its sheer magnitude and variety transform it from a mere shopping center to an indoor city with high-rent districts, blue-collar strips, and hidden byways waiting to be discovered. There are 800 stores and services, including six major department stores, 19 movie theaters, and 90 places to eat; the mall also contains an amusement park, an ice-skating rink, a replica of Columbus's ship the *Santa Maria,* an 18-hole miniature-golf course, the Deep Sea Adventure submarine ride and dolphin show, the 5-acre World Waterpark water amusement park, Fantasyland Hotel (☞ Lodging, *below*), a playhouse, a chapel, a bingo parlor, and a casino. If you don't feel like walking the mall, rent an electric scooter or hitch a ride on a rickshaw. ⊠ *8770 170th St.,* ☎ *403/444–5300.* ☎ *Amusement park day pass $29.95, individual ride tickets $1 (rides cost 1–7 tickets), World Waterpark day pass $29.95, Deep Sea Adventure $13.* ☉ *Weekdays 10–9, Sat. 10–6, Sun. noon–5.*

☾ **Whitemud Drive Amusement Park.** Here you can enjoy go-carts, bumper-boats, miniature golf, and batting cages. ⊠ *7411 51st Ave.,* ☎ *403/465–1190.*

☾ **Wild Waters Waterslide Park.** For plenty of wet fun, try the equipment at this facility. ⊠ *21515 103rd Ave.,* ☎ *403/447–4476.*

☝ **William Hawrelak Park.** Children only—or adults in their company—may fish in this rainbow trout–stocked pond. The park includes paddleboats and an adventure playground. ✉ *Off Groat Rd. south of North Saskatchewan River,* ☎ *403/496–7275.*

Dining

$$$$ ✕ **La Boheme.** On the historic east-side Gibbard Block, this fittingly splendid restaurant presents classic French cuisine, prepared with invention and served with solicitous care. Edwardian pressed-tin ceilings and a French provincial fireplace enhance the setting. Specialties include lamb sausages and varieties of fresh fish. The restaurant is part of a bed-and-breakfast. ✉ *6427 112th Ave.,* ☎ *403/474–5693. Reservations essential. AE, MC, V.*

$$$$ ✕ **Unheardof Dining Lounge.** Hardly "unheard-of" any longer, this is ★ an extremely popular restaurant in an antiques-filled old house. The seven-course prix-fixe dinner changes weekly but is likely to include game in autumn, and poultry or beef the rest of the year. Dinners begin with a light pâté and are punctuated by surprising salads and refreshing sorbets. Desserts, especially the Danish cream-cheese cheesecake, are light and delicious. ✉ *9602 82nd Ave.,* ☎ *403/432–0480. Reservations essential. AE, MC, V. No lunch Tues.–Sat.*

$$$ ✕ **Bistro Praha.** Table lamps and paintings of Prague street scenes make this European-style café feel as homey as Grandma's living room. The background music is classical, the clientele mainly urban young professional. The menu includes such Eastern European favorites as cabbage soup and Wiener schnitzel. A rich selection of desserts and a wide choice of teas make this a perfect stop for snacks. ✉ *10168 100A St., at Jasper Ave.,* ☎ *403/424–4218. AE, DC, MC, V.*

$$$ ✕ **Bourbon Street.** This is actually an assemblage of moderately priced restaurants around a cul-de-sac on the main floor of West Edmonton Mall. "Exterior" decor features New Orleans street lamps and wrought-iron balconies. **Café Orleans** serves such Cajun/Creole dishes as jambalaya and oysters. **Sherlock Holmes** is a popular English pub with imported draft beer and such dishes as Mrs. Hudson's Home Made Pies. **Albert's** has deli fare including the Montréal favorite, smoked meat. Other spots are **Kokomo's California Bar and Grill** and the **Hard Rock Cafe.** One of the newest additions, the visually stunning **Modern Art Cafe,** offers an assortment of designer pizzas. ✉ *West Edmonton Mall, 8770 170th St., Entrance 6. AE, MC, V.*

$$$ ✕ **La Spiga.** Admirable northern Italian cuisine is served in a flower-filled 1913 house that feels more like Montréal than the western plains. Menu highlights include rack of lamb with grappa, breast of chicken with fresh tomato, and various renditions of veal. Portions are large and accompanied by fettuccine; the wine list is long. ✉ *10133 125th St., at 102nd Ave.,* ☎ *403/482–3100. Reservations essential. AE, MC, V. Closed Sun. No lunch.*

$$ ✕ **Frank's Place.** This restaurant satisfies landlocked Edmonton's appetite for fresh seafood with daily fly-ins. Order oysters Rockefeller and whiskey shrimp as appetizers, and anything charbroiled over mesquite turns out fine. Decor runs to deck flooring, corrugated walls, and nets dangling overhead. ✉ *10020 101A Ave.,* ☎ *403/422–0282. Reservations essential. AE, MC, V.*

$ ✕ **Chianti Café.** This extremely popular spot occupies part of the main ★ floor of Strathcona Square, a converted post office in the lively Old Strathcona. A mostly young crowd gathers for square meals with tasty shellfish appetizers, more than 20 varieties of pasta, a couple dozen veal dishes, and a discriminating selection of desserts. Be prepared to wait for seating on weekend evenings. ⊠ *10501 82nd Ave.,* ☎ *403/ 439–9829. AE, DC, MC, V.*

$ ✕ **Vi's.** In summer, this old house has outdoor seating on a deck overlooking the river; in winter, patrons are warmed by a blazing fire. The menu emphasizes the basics: hearty soups, fresh salads, extravagant sandwiches, and desserts such as chocolate pecan pie. Try Vi's for Sunday brunch. ⊠ *9712 111th St.,* ☎ *403/482–6402. AE, MC, V.*

Lodging

$$$$ 🏨 **Hotel Macdonald.** The city's landmark 1915 hotel underwent a
★ massive but sensitive restoration in the late 1980s. Far from its former dowager state, the hotel now boasts first-class modern facilities in both the traditionally furnished guest rooms and the ornate public areas. The royal suite, located in the former attic, is spectacular. There's fine dining in the elegantly restored **Empire Ballroom** or the **Wedgewood Room.** The hotel offers a sweeping view of the riverbank. ⊠ *10061 100th St., T5J ON6,* ☎ *403/424–5181,* 𝐅𝐀𝐗 *403/424–8017. 198 rooms. 4 restaurants, bar, pool, massage, steam room, health club, tennis courts. AE, MC, V.*

$$$$ 🏨 **Sheraton Grande.** This financial-district luxury high rise connects by second-level passageways to five major office buildings and two shopping centers. Rooms—with bay windows and blue-and-gray color schemes—are decorated with sophistication and include marble tabletops, walnut furniture, and brass accents. The **Rose and Crown** is an English-style pub. ⊠ *10235 101st St., T5J 3E9,* ☎ *403/428–7111 or 800/268–9275,* 𝐅𝐀𝐗 *403/441–3098. 313 rooms. 3 restaurants, 2 bars, no-smoking floors, indoor pool, sauna. AE, DC, MC, V.*

$$$ 🏨 **Edmonton House.** The building's cylindrical design creates oddly
★ shaped but large and comfortable one- and two-bedroom and executive suites. All units have balconies with views of the skyline or the river valley, and kitchens are fully equipped (down to a toaster). A small mezzanine-level convenience store supplies basics. Weekend and long-term rates are available. ⊠ *10205 100th Ave., T5J 4B5,* ☎ *403/424–5555 or 800/661–6562,* 𝐅𝐀𝐗 *403/425–5485. 293 suites. Restaurant, bar, no-smoking floors, indoor pool, sauna, exercise room, parking. AE, DC, MC, V.*

$$$ 🏨 **Fantasyland Hotel.** This important component of the massive West Edmonton Mall (☞ Greater Edmonton, *above*) has regular and theme rooms; the latter include Victorian coach rooms, where guests sleep in open carriages; Roman rooms, with classic round beds; truck rooms, where the bed is the back of a pickup; and Polynesian rooms, with catamaran beds and waterfalls. All theme rooms have Jacuzzis, and non-theme quarters are comfortable and tidy. ⊠ *17700 87th Ave., T5T 4V4,* ☎ *403/444–3000 or 800/661–6454,* 𝐅𝐀𝐗 *403/444–3294. 459 rooms. 2 restaurants, bar. AE, DC, MC, V.*

$$$ 🏨 **Inn on 7th.** Edmonton shorthand provides the name for this cheerful property on 107th Street. In the foliage-filled lobby stand Paul Bunyan–size easy chairs. Run by the Courtyard Inn chain, this hotel caters to tourists and government employees. Rooms are comfortably modern, and the location is convenient. ⊠ *10001 107th St., T5J 1J1,* ☎ *403/429–2861 or 800/661–7327,* 𝐅𝐀𝐗 *403/426–7225. 180 rooms. Restaurant, bar, deli, no-smoking floors. AE, DC, MC, V.*

$$$ 🏨 **Westin Hotel.** This brown block structure in the heart of downtown has an atrium lobby with a decorative mobile, trees, and plants that convey comfort and luxury. The large, comfortable beige-and-pastel rooms are tastefully decorated with attractive artwork. The experienced staff speaks a total of 29 languages. Some of the finest food in the downtown area can be found in the **Carvery.** ⊠ *10135 100th St., T5J 0Z1,* ☎ *403/*

426–3636 or 800/228–3000, FAX *403/428–6060. 420 rooms. 2 restaurants, 2 bars, no-smoking floors, indoor pool, sauna. AE, DC, MC, V.*

$$ ⌂ **West Harvest Inn.** The clean, modern three-story West Harvest caters to families; it's on the western edge of town, only five minutes from the West Edmonton Mall. Rooms in the new wing are slightly larger and more expensive than those in the older wing, but all are comfortable. **Grainfield's** family restaurant is on the premises. ⌂ *17803 Stony Plain Rd. (Rte. 16), T5S 1B4,* ☎ *403/484–8000 or 800/661–6993,* FAX *403/486–6060. 162 rooms. Restaurant, bar. AE, MC, V.*

$ ⌂ **Travelodge.** The budget chain operates two clean and functional motels in Edmonton: Travelodge West is on the edge of town, not far from West Edmonton Mall, while Travelodge South is on the road to the airport. ⌂ *18320 Stony Plain Rd., T5S 1A7,* ☎ *403/483–6031 or 800/ 661–9563,* FAX *403/484–2358. 227 rooms.* ⌂ *10320 45th Ave. S, T6H 5K3,* ☎ *403/436–9770. 222 rooms. Restaurant, bar, no-smoking rooms, indoor pool. AE, DC, MC, V.*

$ ⌂ **YMCA of Edmonton.** This Y has an outstanding location: in the heart of downtown adjacent to Edmonton Centre shopping mall. Rooms are small and spare but carpeted and cheerfully furnished. Singles and couples are invited to stay for $30 to $50 a night; families are accommodated as well. All the Y's facilities are available to overnight guests. ⌂ *10030 102A Ave., T5J 0G5,* ☎ *403/421–9622,* FAX *403/428–9469. 113 rooms, 30 with bath. Cafeteria, indoor pool, health club, jogging, racquetball. MC, V.*

Nightlife and the Arts

Tickets for events in Edmonton are available from TicketMaster (☎ 403/451–8000) at various locations, as well as at Champions in West Edmonton Mall and at Sears stores.

One huge event that encompasses plenty of music, shows, and special events is the 10-day **Klondike Days,** held late in July. The festivities celebrate the prosperity that the Yukon gold rush brought the city, which served as a supply route and stopping point for miners.

The Arts

FILM

Edmonton's **Metro Cinema** (⌂ NFB Theatre, Canada Place, 9700 Jasper Ave., ☎ 403/425–9212) presents classics, imports, and new films on weekend nights. The **Edmonton Film Society** screens an ambitious program at a theater in the Provincial Museum of Alberta (⌂ 12845 102nd Ave., ☎ 403/453–9100). The **Princess Theatre** (⌂ 10337 Whyte Ave., ☎ 403/433–5785), an old-time movie house in the Old Strathcona district, presents revivals, experiments, and foreign films.

MUSIC AND DANCE

The **Edmonton Opera** (☎ 403/424–4040) and **Alberta Ballet Company** (☎ 403/428–6839) perform in the **Northern Alberta Jubilee Auditorium** (⌂ 87th Ave. and 114th St., ☎ 403/427–9622) at the University of Alberta. By 1998, the **Edmonton Symphony Orchestra** (☎ 403/428–1414) is slated to move to the new Francis Winspear Centre for Music in Sir Winston Churchill Square.

THEATER

Edmonton has 13 professional theater companies. The paramount facility is the glass-clad downtown **Citadel Theatre** complex (⌂ 99th St. and 101A Ave., ☎ 403/425–1820), where four theaters present a mix of esoteric works and classics. **Northern Light Theatre** (⌂ Kaasa Theatre, Jubilee Auditorium, 87th Ave. and 114th St., ☎ 403/471–1586) stages avant-garde productions that usually succeed.

Nightlife

BARS AND CLUBS

The **Rose & Crown** English-style pub in the Edmonton Hilton (✉ 10235 101st St., ☎ 403/428–7111) is a popular downtown gathering place with dart boards and a huge selection of beers. **Elephant & Castle Pubs** are pleasant watering holes in downtown Edmonton's Eaton Centre (☎ 403/424–4555) and the West Edmonton Mall (☎ 403/444–3555).

CASINOS

Roulette, blackjack, and wheel of fortune action usually takes place in Edmonton between noon and midnight daily except Sunday at the **Casino ABS Downtown** (✉ 10549 102 St., ☎ 403/424–9461). For games of chance you can also go to **Casino ABS South** (✉ 7055 Argyll Rd., ☎ 403/466–0199). The **Palace Casino** at the West Edmonton Mall (☎ 403/444–2112) offers shoppers another way to part with their money. The newest casino in town is the **Baccarat Casino** (✉ 101st St and 104th Ave, ☎ 403/413–3178).

COMEDY

Edmonton has a branch of **Yuk Yuk's,** Canada's comedy chain, at West Edmonton Mall (☎ 403/481–9857).

MUSIC

The **Sidetrack Cafe** (✉ 10333 112th St., ☎ 403/421–1326) has top-name entertainers, big-screen telecasts of sports events, Variety Night on Sunday, and the Monday-Night Comedy Bowl. **Yardbird Suite** (✉ 10203 86th Ave., ☎ 403/432–0428) is Edmonton's premiere jazz showcase. **Club Malibu** (✉ 10310 85th Ave., ☎ 403/432–7300) blasts out Top 40 hits in a converted armory. **Thunderdome** (✉ 9920 63rd Ave., ☎ 403/433–3661) has classic rock. **Cook County Saloon** (✉ 8010 103rd St., ☎ 403/432–2665) has a mellow honky-tonk ambience and country-and-western music.

Outdoor Activities and Sports

Participant Sports

BICYCLING AND JOGGING

The North Saskatchewan River valley is the longest stretch of urban parkland in Canada. For information about jogging and cycling trails call the **River Valley Outdoor Centre** (✉ 10125 97th Ave., ☎ 403/496–7275).

HEALTH AND FITNESS CLUBS

The **Kinsmen Sports Centre** (✉ 9100 Walterdale Rd., ☎ 403/496–7300) and **Mill Woods Recreation Centre** (✉ 7207 28th Ave., ☎ 403/496–2929) have swimming pools and facilities for the entire family.

Spectator Sports

AUTO RACING

Capital Raceway (✉ Rte. 19, 2 km west of Hwy. 2S, on the way to Devon, ☎ 403/462–8901), a multiuse motor-sport complex, has events most weekends from May through October.

BASEBALL

The **Edmonton Trappers** play in the Pacific Coast League (AAA) at Telus Field (✉ 10233 96th Ave., ☎ 403/429-2934).

FOOTBALL

The **Edmonton Eskimos** play in the Canadian Football League June through November at Commonwealth Stadium (✉ 9022 111th Ave., ☎ 403/448–3757 or 403/448–1525).

HOCKEY

The **Edmonton Oilers** play National Hockey League hockey October through April at the Edmonton Coliseum (⊠ 118th Ave. and 74th St., ☎ 403/471–2191 or 403/451–8000).

HORSE RACING

Northlands Park (⊠ 112th Ave. and 74th St., ☎ 403/471–7379) hosts harness racing from early March to mid-May and from mid-September through December. Thoroughbred racing occupies the summer months, mid-May through early September.

Shopping

In the heart of **downtown,** between 100th and 103rd streets, is a complex of shopping centers—Eaton Centre (⊠ 102nd Ave.), ManuLife Place (⊠ 102nd Ave.), and Edmonton Centre (⊠ 100th St.)—and department stores (the Bay, Eaton's) connected by tunnels or second-level pedways. **West Edmonton Mall** (⊠ 87th Ave. and 170th St.) has 800 stores and services, including such department stores as Sears, the Bay, Eaton's, Zeller's, and Canadian Tire (☞ Greater Edmonton, *above*). **Old Strathcona Historic Area** (⊠ Whyte [82nd] Ave. and 104th St.) has restaurants and enticing boutiques. **High Street/124th Street** (⊠ Along 124th and 125th Sts. between 102nd and 109th Aves.) is an outdoor shopping area full of boutiques, bistros, bookstores, and galleries.

Side Trips from Edmonton

Sites relating to Alberta's Ukrainian heritage and some beautiful natural areas make good side trips from the city.

Red Deer

❷❻ *149 km (92 mi) south of Edmonton, 145 km (90 mi) north of Calgary.*

Red Deer, midway between Calgary and Edmonton on Highway 2, is on the Red Deer River. Along the riverbank winds **Waskasoo Park,** with nearly 30 miles of pedestrian and bike paths, equestrian trails, and canoeing and fishing. At the **Red Deer and District Museum,** you can see a pioneer home and other historic items. ⊠ *4525 47A Ave.,* ☎ *403/343–6844.* ☞ *Donation accepted.* ☉ *Weekdays noon–5 and 7–9, weekends 1–5.*

Elk Island National Park

48 km (30 mi) east of Edmonton on Rte. 16.

Probably Canada's least-known national park, Elk Island was established in 1906 as the country's first federal wildlife sanctuary for large mammals. It covers 194 square km (75 square mi) and is dedicated to protecting the environment. A herd of 850 plains and 350 wood bison roam the park, as well as elk, moose, white-tail deer, and more than 240 species of birds, including herons. There are 80 campsites, an interpretive center, a nine-hole golf course, and a lake. ⊠ *Rte. 16,* ☎ *403/922–5790 or 403/992–2950.* ☞ *$4.* ☉ *Daily.*

Ukrainian Cultural Heritage Village

3 km (2 mi) east of Elk Island National Park, 51 km (32 mi) from Edmonton.

The village consists of 34 historic buildings from around the province that have been assembled to typify the lifestyle of a pre-1930s village of Ukrainian settlers. Guides in period dress interpret the displays. It's good background for a visit to Vegreville (☞ *below*). ⊠ *Rte. 16,* ☎ *403/662–3640.* ☞ *$6.50.* ☉ *Mid-May–Labor Day, daily 10–6; Sept.– mid-Oct., daily 10–4.*

Vegreville

 50 km (31 mi) from Ukrainian Cultural Heritage Village, 101 km (63 mi) east of Edmonton.

Vegreville is the center of eastern Alberta's Ukrainian culture and home of the "world's largest Easter egg" (*pysanka*), measuring 30 feet high, at the east end of the town's main street. Colorfully decorated, it consists of more than 3,500 pieces of aluminum. A Ukrainian festival takes place here annually the first weekend in July. ⊠ *Rte. 16.*

Edmonton A to Z

Arriving and Departing

BY CAR

Edmonton is situated on the Yellowhead Highway (Highway 16), which runs from Winnipeg through the central parts of Saskatchewan and Alberta. This highway is four lanes and divided through most of Alberta; it intersects with the four-lane divided Highway 2, which runs south to Calgary.

BY PLANE

All flights use **Edmonton International Airport** (☎ 403/890–4306). Along with the major Canadian airlines (Air Canada, Canadian Airlines International, Air BC, NWT Air, Horizon Air), Edmonton is served by Delta and Northwest.

Taxi rides from Edmonton International cost approximately $29 to the city center. The Sky Shuttle (☎ 403/463–7520) provides frequent service between the airport and major downtown hotels; fare is $11 one way, $18 round-trip.

Getting Around

BY BUS AND LRT

Edmonton Transit (☎ 403/496–1611) operates a comprehensive system of buses throughout the area and a light rail transit (LRT) line from downtown to the northeast side of the city. The fare is $1.65; transfers are free. Buses operate from 5:30 AM to 2 AM. The LRT is free in the downtown area (between Churchill and Grandin stations) weekdays 9–3 and Saturday 9–6. The **Downtown Information Centre** above Central LRT Station (⊠ 100A St. and Jasper Ave.) provides free information, timetables, and maps, weekdays 9–5.

BY TAXI

Taxis tend to be costly: $2 for the first 105 meters, and 10¢ for each additional 105 meters. Cabs may be hailed on the street, but phoning is recommended. Call **Alberta Co-op Taxi** (☎ 403/425–8310), **Checker** (☎ 403/455–2211), or **Yellow** (☎ 403/462–3456).

Contacts and Resources

DENTISTS

For 24-hour dental care, contact **Denta Care** (⊠ 472 Southgate Shopping Centre, 111th St. and 51st Ave., ☎ 403/434–9566).

EMERGENCIES

Dial 911 for **police, fire, ambulance,** and **poison center.**

GUIDED TOURS

From early May to early October three **Royal Tours** (☎ 403/488–9090) itineraries hit the high points of Edmonton. **Klondike Jet Boats** (☎ 403/486–0896) ply the North Saskatchewan River, May–October.

Emergency rooms are at the **Royal Alexandra Hospital** (⊠ 10240 Kingsway Ave., ☎ 403/477–4111) and **University of Alberta Hospitals** (⊠ 8440 112th St., ☎ 403/492–8822).

Shopper's Drug Mart (⊠ 11408 Jasper Ave., ☎ 403/482–1171; ⊠ 8210 109 St., ☎ 403/433–3121) is open 24 hours.

Edmonton Tourism Information Centres are at Gateway Park (⊠ Hwy. 2, ☎ 403/496–8400 or 800/463–4667) and City Hall. Other offices are open around Edmonton; for locations call the above number.

REGINA

Regina, Saskatchewan, was originally dubbed Pile O'Bones, in reference to the remnants left by years of buffalo hunting by native peoples and later European hunters. The city was renamed after the Latin title of Queen Victoria, the reigning monarch in 1883. It was at this time that the railroad arrived and the city became the capital of the Northwest Territories. The Mounties made it their headquarters. When the province of Saskatchewan was formed in 1905, Regina was chosen as its capital. At the beginning of the 20th century, immigrants from the British Isles, Eastern Europe, and East Asia rushed in to claim parcels of river-fed prairie land for $1 per lot. Oil and potash were discovered in the 1950s and 1960s, and Regina became a major agricultural and industrial distribution center as well as the head office of the world's largest grain-handling cooperative.

The centerpiece of this city of 185,000 is Wascana Centre, created by expanding meager Wascana Creek into the broad Wascana Lake and surrounding it with 2,000 acres of parkland. This unique multipurpose site contains the city's major museums, the Saskatchewan provincial legislature, the University of Regina campus, and all the amenities of a big-city park and natural-habitat waterfowl sanctuary.

Exploring Regina

Streets in Regina run north–south; avenues, east–west. The most important north–south artery is Albert Street (Route 6); Victoria Avenue is the main east–west thoroughfare. The Trans-Canada Highway (Highway 1) bypasses the city to the south and east.

A Good Drive

Begin at the northwest corner of Wascana Centre, at the **Royal Saskatchewan Museum** ㉘, and check out the Earth Sciences Gallery and the First Nations Gallery. Continue south on Albert Street past Speakers Corner, where, as in London's Hyde Park, free speech is volubly expressed. Turn left onto Legislature Drive to the **Legislative Building** ㉙, for a tour of its marble interior. Take Saskatchewan Road (west on Legislature) south to the **MacKenzie Art Gallery** ㉚, which displays European and Canadian art. Continuing along Saskatchewan Road, turn north onto Avenue G and then east onto Lakeshore Drive to the **Wascana Waterfowl Park Display Ponds** ㉛ to see the many breeds of migratory birds that stop here. Return to Broad Street (Wascana Parkway), cross the bridge to Wascana Drive, and head toward Winnipeg Street and the **Saskatchewan Science Centre** ㉜ for hands-on exhibits demonstrating various scientific phenomena. Next, take a car or bike to Broad Street and follow it north to Dewdney Avenue, then head west

Saskatchewan

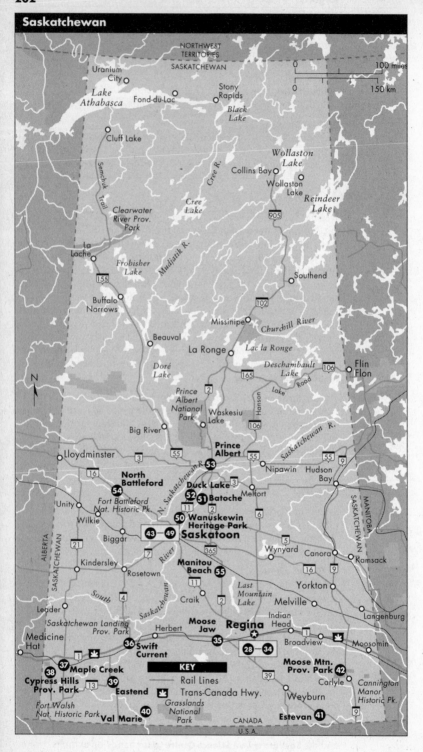

NORTHWEST
TERRITORIES
SASKATCHEWAN

100 miles

150 km

Uranium
City

*Lake
Athabasca*

Fond-du-Lac

Stony
Rapids

*Black
Lake*

Cluff Lake

*Semchuk
Trail*

*Clearwater
River Prov.
Park*

Cree R.

Collins Bay

*Wollaston
Lake*

Wollaston
Lake

*Reindeer
Lake*

905

La
Loche

155

*Frobisher
Lake*

*Cree
Lake*

Mudjatik R.

Southend

Buffalo
Narrows

Beauval

102

Missinipe

Churchill River

La Ronge

Lac la Ronge

*Deschambault
Lake*

106

Flin
Flon

*Doré
Lake*

165

Hanson *Lake* *Road*

2

*Prince
Albert
National
Park*

Waskesiu
Lake

106

Big River

55

Prince
Albert

55

Saskatchewan R.

55

9

Lloydminster

3

16

**North
Battleford**

54

N. Saskatchewan R.

53

Duck Lake

3

Nipawin

Hudson
Bay

Unity

*Fort Battleford
Nat. Historic Pk.*

52 **51** **Batoche**

11

Melfort

6

Wilkie

50

**Wanuskewin
Heritage Park**

Biggar

43 — 49

Saskatoon

5

21

River

Saskatchewan

Kindersley

7

**Manitou
Beach**

365

Wynyard

Canora

Kamsack

55

MANITOBA

SASKATCHEWAN

Rosetown

11

*Last
Mountain
Lake*

16

9

Yorkton

South

4

Craik

2

Melville

Langenburg

Leader

*Saskatchewan Landing
Prov. Park*

Herbert

**Moose
Jaw**

Indian
Head

Regina

35

1

Broadview

Moosomin

Medicine
Hat

1

37

36

**Swift
Current**

28 — 34

**Moose Mtn.
Prov. Park**

42

38

Maple Creek

**Cypress Hills
Prov. Park**

13

39

Eastend

39

Carlyle

*Cannington
Manor
Historic Pk.*

*Fort Walsh
Nat. Historic Park*

Val Marie

40

*Grasslands
National
Park*

Weyburn

9

Estevan **41**

CANADA
U.S.A.

KEY

— Rail Lines

⬧ Trans-Canada Hwy.

ALBERTA

SASKATCHEWAN

N

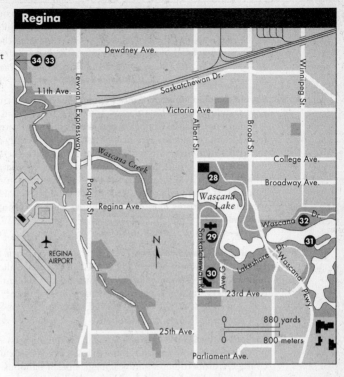

to **Government House** ㉝, once the residence of Saskatchewan's lieutenant governors. Continue west on Dewdney Avenue to the **Royal Canadian Mounted Police Depot Division** ㉞, the Mounties' national training center.

TIMING

The tour will take most of the day, but time your visit to catch the RCMP training academy's daily drill parade at about 1. Call to check the time for this.

Sights to See

㉝ **Government House.** Between 1891 and 1945 this was the lavish home of Saskatchewan's lieutenant governors. It has been restored with period furnishings and mementos of the governors and their families. ⊠ *4607 Dewdney Ave.,* ☎ *306/787–5726.* ☜ *Free.* ☉ *Oct.–Mar. and July–Aug. Tues.–Fri. 1–4, Sun. 1–5; Apr.–June and Sept., Tues.–Sat. 1–4, Sun. 1–5.*

㉙ **Legislative Building.** Dominating the skyline in the provincial capital is the dome of this quasi-Versailles–style structure. "The Ledge" was built in 1908–12, with Tyndall stone from Manitoba on the exterior and 34 types of marble from all over the world in the interior. As you tour the Legislative Assembly Chamber, note the huge picture of Queen Elizabeth—a reminder that Canada retains a technical allegiance to the British monarchy. Free tours leave on the half hour. ⊠ *Legislature Dr.,* ☎ *306/787–5357.* ☜ *Free.* ☉ *Victoria Day–Labor Day, daily 8–9; winter, daily 8–5.*

㉚ **MacKenzie Art Gallery.** Here you will find 19th- and 20th-century European art and Canadian historical and contemporary works, with a special emphasis on western Canadian art. The popular Prairie Artists Series allows emerging Saskatchewan artists to display recent work.

For three nights a week in August, a stage becomes the courtroom setting for the production of *The Trial of Louis Riel*. Riel led rebellions of the Métis against the new Canadian government in the 1870s and 1880s and was tried in Regina (and ultimately hanged) for treason. ☒ *3475 Albert St.,* ☎ *306/522–4242.* ☒ *Free, extra charge for play.* ☉ *Fri.–Tues. 11–6, Wed. and Thurs. 11–10.*

★ ❸ **Royal Canadian Mounted Police Depot Division.** This is the Mounties' only training center. Visitors can tour the grounds and the nondenominational RCMP Chapel, a converted cookhouse originally built in 1883 and considered Regina's oldest building. In July and August, the spectacular Sunset Retreat Ceremony takes place Tuesday evening; try to arrive by 6:30. On the grounds is the **Centennial Museum,** which has exhibits and mementos of the Mounties (originally the North West Mounted Police). The order's proud history is revealed by weaponry, uniforms, photos, and oddities, such as Sitting Bull's rifle case and tobacco pouch. ☒ *11th Ave. W,* ☎ *306/780–5838.* ☒ *Free.* ☉ *June–mid-Sept., daily 8–6:45; mid-Sept.–May, daily 10–4:45.*

☾ ❷❽ **Royal Saskatchewan Museum.** Here a time line traces local history from before the dinosaur era to today. The Earth Sciences Gallery depicts 2 billion years of Saskatchewan geological history, while the First Nations Gallery highlights aspects of native life and history. ☒ *College Ave. and Albert St.,* ☎ *306/787–2815.* ☒ *Free.* ☉ *May–Sept. 2, daily 9–8:30; Sept. 3–Apr., daily 9–4:30.*

☾ ❸❷ **Saskatchewan Science Centre.** Housed in the refurbished City of Regina powerhouse, the museum has more than 80 hands-on exhibits that encourage visitors to build bubbles, juggle hot-air balloons, make voice prints, and take apart models of human bodies. Demonstrations of biological, geological, and astronomical phenomena begin on the hour. The Kramer IMAX Theatre shows breathtaking films several times daily on a five-story screen. ☒ *Winnipeg St. and Wascana Dr.,* ☎ *306/352–5811, 306/522–4629 IMAX.* ☒ *$5.50.* ☉ *May and June, Mon.–Thurs. 9–6, Fri. 9–8, Sat. 10–8, Sun. 10–6; July and Aug., daily 10–8; Sept.–Apr., Tues.–Fri. 9–4, Sat. noon–8, Sun. noon–6.*

❸❶ **Wascana Waterfowl Park Display Ponds.** The serenity and beauty of the park attract nature lovers. A boardwalk constructed over a marsh is accompanied by display panels that help identify the more than 60 breeds of migrating waterfowl found here. ☒ *Lakeshore Dr.,* ☎ *306/522–3661.* ☒ *Free.* ☉ *Daily 9–9; guided tour (if there is a group) June–Sept., daily at 3.*

Dining

$$$$ ✗ **The Diplomat.** One of Regina's most elegant restaurants is an upscale, traditional steak house in an old brick building downtown. The decor suggests the Victorian era, with paintings of Canada's prime ministers on the walls and dusty-rose cloths and candles on the tables. It offers an extensive selection of seafood and steaks and an outstanding rack of lamb, as well as a high-quality wine list. ☒ *2302 Broad St.,* ☎ *306/359–3366. Reservations essential. AE, D, MC, V.*

$$ ✗ **Bartleby's.** This good-time downtown "dining emporium and gathering place" is a veritable museum of western memorabilia, musical instruments, and old-time carnival games. Victorian lamp shades and heavy leather armchairs further convey the whimsical tone. Karaoke music at night adds a bit of fun. The menu runs to big sandwiches and western beef, especially prime rib. ☒ *1920 Broad St.,* ☎ *306/565–0040. Reservations essential. AE, DC, MC, V.*

$$ ✕ **C.C. Lloyd's.** Locals esteem the fine service and casual elegance of the dining room in the downtown Chelton Inn. The decor evokes the atmosphere of Manhattan circa 1930, and the menu features such international classics as rack of lamb, chicken en croûte dijonnaise (in a mustard crust), fillet of beef Madeira, shrimp Provençal, and a variety of tasty steaks. ⊠ *1907 11th Ave.,* ☎ *306/569–4650. Reservations essential. AE, MC, V.*

$ ✕ **Brewsters.** The copper kettle and shiny fermentation tanks are proudly prominent in Saskatchewan's first brew pub. This full-mash brewery has 11 in-house concoctions on tap, as well as a large selection of imports and domestic beers, wine, and spirits. The menu consists of pub snacks and full meals. ⊠ *Victoria East Plaza, 1832 Victoria Ave. E,* ☎ *306/761–1500. Reservations not accepted. AE, MC, V.*

$ ✕ **Simply Delicious.** Everything is homemade in this small country-style café. Offerings include cinnamon buns, fresh pies, chicken noodle and vegetable soups, several salads, and specialty coffees. ⊠ *826 Victoria Ave.,* ☎ *306/352–4929. Reservations not accepted. No credit cards.*

Lodging

$$$ ⊞ **Hotel Saskatchewan Radisson Plaza.** This former railway hotel built in 1927 has old-time charm and up-to-date facilities. High-ceiling rooms are decorated in an early 1930s style, with lots of wood and lace curtains. The Victoria Room serves high tea each afternoon, and there's fine dining in the Cortlandt Hall Dining Room. For a light lunch or evening cocktails visit the cozy and casually elegant Monarch Lounge. ⊠ *2125 Victoria Ave., S4P 0S3,* ☎ *306/522–7691 or 800/333–3333,* ℻ *306/757–5521. 215 rooms. 2 restaurants, bar, no-smoking rooms, health club. AE, DC, MC, V.*

$$$ ⊞ **Ramada Plaza Hotel.** The tallest building in Saskatchewan, Regina's newest and most luxurious hotel rises 25 stories over the city and is attached to the Saskatchewan Trade and Convention Centre. Rooms are furnished in subtle pastels and have modern amenities. The pool has a three-story water slide. ⊠ *1919 Saskatchewan Dr., S4P 4H2,* ☎ *306/525–5255 or 800/268–8998,* ℻ *306/781–7188. 255 rooms. 2 restaurants, bar, no-smoking rooms, indoor pool. AE, DC, MC, V.*

$$$ ⊞ **Regina Inn Hotel.** A plant-filled lobby welcomes you into this modern downtown hotel, where all the guest rooms—decorated with blues, grays, and browns—have balconies overlooking either Broad or Victoria street. On the ground floor is Lauderdale's, a local hot spot. Applause Feast & Folly, Regina's dinner theater, is downstairs in the Catalina Theatre. ⊠ *1975 Broad St., at Victoria Ave., S4P 1Y2,* ☎ *306/525–6767 or 800/667–8162,* ℻ *306/352–1858. 237 rooms. 2 restaurants, bar, 2 outdoor hot tubs, exercise room, nightclub, indoor parking. AE, DC, MC, V.*

$$$ ⊞ **Regina Travelodge Hotel.** The hotel's convenient location, on Regina's main thoroughfare and close to downtown, is the biggest draw for its guests. The other feature is the well-known water-slide complex on the property. In the evenings the pub, the Blarney Stone, is a cheerful place to grab a beer or soda. ⊠ *4177 Albert St., S4S 3R6,* ☎ *306/586–3443 or 800/255–3050,* ℻ *306/586–9311. 200 rooms. Restaurant, pub, indoor pool, hot tub. AE, DC, MC, V.*

$$$ ⊞ **Sands Hotel and Resort.** This modern downtown property has a dra-
★ matic multilevel, sun-filled lobby enhanced by abundant foliage and a charming waterfall. A second-floor oasis is the perfect setting for such water-theme pastimes as a soothing soak in the whirlpool or, for the children, a dip in either the kiddie or the standard pool. The modern rooms are airy and furnished in light colors and dusty-rose tones. ⊠ *1818 Victoria Ave., S4P 0R1,* ☎ *306/569–1666 or 800/268–1133,*

FAX *306/525–3550. 251 rooms. 2 restaurants, bar, pub, 2 indoor pools, sauna. AE, DC, MC, V.*

$$ ▥ **Chelton Suites Hotel.** An older hotel in the heart of downtown is one of Regina's biggest bargains. Its modernized rooms are downright huge. Contemporary, light-wood furnishings match the earth tones that are used in the draperies and upholstery. Service is particularly friendly. The food at C.C. Lloyd's (☞ *Dining, above*) is among the best in town. ⊠ *1907 11th Ave., S4P 0J2,* ☎ *306/569–4600 or 800/667–9922,* FAX *306/569–3531. 56 rooms. Restaurant, bar, coffee shop. AE, DC, MC, V.*

$ ▥ **West Harvest Inn.** Rebuilt and refurbished in 1995, this five-story brick 1960s-vintage hotel is dependable. The average-size rooms have low-key beige-patterned drapes and spreads and modern, dark-cherry furniture. ⊠ *4025 Albert St. (Rte. 6), S4S 3R6,* ☎ *306/586–6755 or 800/667–3529,* FAX *306/584–1345. 105 rooms. Restaurant, bar, 2 hot tubs, sauna, exercise room. AE, DC, MC, V.*

Nightlife and the Arts

The Arts

MUSIC AND DANCE

The **Saskatchewan Centre of the Arts** (⊠ Wascana Centre, 200 Lakeshore Dr., ☎ 306/565–0404) is the venue for the **Regina Symphony Orchestra** (Canada's longest-running symphony orchestra), pop concerts, dance performances, and Broadway musicals and plays.

THEATER

On a theater-in-the-round stage inside the old Regina City Hall, the **Globe Theatre** (⊠ 1801 Scarth St., ☎ 306/525–9553) offers classic and contemporary Saskatchewan works from October through April. **Regina Little Theatre** (⊠ Regina Performing Arts Centre, 1077 Angus St., ☎ 306/352–5535 or 306/543–7292) presents lighthearted original productions.

Nightlife

BAR

Caper's, in the Ramada Plaza Hotel (⊠ 1919 Saskatchewan Dr., ☎ 306/525–5255), is where local movers and shakers mingle with visitors from the convention center next door.

CASINO

The city's newest marquee attraction, the posh **Casino Regina** (⊠ 1880 Saskatchewan Dr., ☎ 800/555–3189) in the extensively refurbished former Union Station railroad passenger terminal, has slot machines and table games such as blackjack, roulette, and baccarat.

MUSIC

The Pump (⊠ 641 Victoria Ave. E, ☎ 306/522–0977) features Canadian and American country-and-western bands. **Delbert's** (⊠ 1433 Hamilton St., ☎ 306/757–7625) is known for high-energy rock and roll. **Longbranch Saloon** (⊠ 1400 McIntyre St., ☎ 306/525–8336) specializes in country-and-western music.

Outdoor Activities and Sports

Participant Sports

BICYCLING AND JOGGING

Wascana Place (⊠ 2900 Wascana Dr., ☎ 306/522–3661) provides maps of the many jogging, biking, and hiking trails in Wascana Centre. The

Devonian Pathway—8 km (about 5 mi) of paved trails that follow Wascana Creek and pass through six city parks—is a favorite of walkers, joggers, and cyclists.

The **Regina Sportplex & Lawson Aquatic Centre** (✉ 1717 Elphinstone St., ☎ 306/777–7156 or 306/777–7323) comprises a pool and diving well, a 200-meter track, tennis and badminton courts, weight rooms, a sauna, and drop-in aerobic and aqua exercise sessions.

Spectator Sports

CURLING
Check out this incredibly popular local sport at the **Caledonian Curling Club** (✉ 2225 Empress Rd., near airport, ☎ 306/525–8171).

FOOTBALL
The **Saskatchewan Roughriders** (☎ 306/525–2181) of the Canadian Football League play their home games at Taylor Field.

HOCKEY
The **Regina Pats** play other Western Hockey League (minor league) teams in the Agridome (✉ Exhibition Park, Lewvan Expressway and 11th Ave., Regina, ☎ 306/522–5604).

HORSE RACING
Queensbury Downs (✉ Exhibition Park, Lewvan Dr. and 11th Ave., Regina, ☎ 306/781–9310) hosts Standardbred racing in summer and televised racing year-round.

Shopping

Art and Antiques
The **Strathdee Shoppes** (✉ Dewdney Ave. and Cornwall St.) have arts, crafts, antiques, and specialty stores—plus a food court. The **Antique Mall** (✉ 1175 Rose St., ☎ 306/525–9688) encompasses 28 antiques, art, and collectibles sellers. **Patchworks** (✉ 3026 13th Ave., ☎ 306/522–0664), features arts and crafts. **Sarah's Corner** (✉ 1853 Hamilton St., ☎ 306/565–2200) has crafts and artwork. **Affinity's Antiques** (✉ 1178 Albert St., ☎ 306/757–4265) sells vintage collectibles.

Malls
Cornwall Centre (✉ 11th Ave. and Saskatchewan Dr.), downtown, is an indoor mall with more than 100 shops, including Eaton's and Sears. Indoor passages connect Cornwall Centre to the **Galleria** (✉ 11th Ave. and Saskatchewan Dr.), an indoor mall with more than 50 stores.

Side Trips from Regina

In and around the modern city of Moose Jaw are attractions that will give you a feeling for the area's past and present.

Moose Jaw
③ *71 km (44 mi) west of Regina.*

Saskatchewan's third-largest city, Moose Jaw is a prosperous railroad and industrial center, renowned as a wide-open Roaring-'20s haven for American gangsters. It is said that Al Capone visited here from Chicago. Today, Moose Jaw's most prominent citizen stands right on the Trans-

Canada Highway: Mac the Moose, an immense sculpture that greets travelers from beside the visitor information center (⊠ Hwy. 1, east of Hwy. 2, ☎ 306/692–6414).

The **Western Development Museum** (⊠ 50 Diefenbaker Dr., ☎ 306/693–6556), which focuses on air, land, water, and rail transportation, houses the Snowbirds Gallery, filled with memorabilia, including vintage airplanes, of Canada's air demonstration team, the Snowbirds, who are stationed at the nearby Armed Forces base. **The Moose Jaw Art Museum** (⊠ Crescent Park, Athabasca St. and Langdon Crescent, ☎ 306/692–4471) displays native art and small farm implements. While you're here, pick up *A Walking Tour of Downtown Moose Jaw* ($1.50), a guide to the city's notable and notorious landmarks. As you drive around, notice the historical murals on the walls of many downtown buildings. A quirky attraction that chronicles aspects of the city's history is the **Tunnels of Little Chicago** (☎ 306/693–5251). You can view these tunnels, rumored to have been built by the Chinese in the late 1800s and later supposedly used by Al Capone to smuggle liquor during the Prohibition era. Tours start at the old Canadian Pacific Railroad station.

Moose Jaw's newest attraction, the **Temple Gardens Mineral Spa** (⊠ 108 Main St. N, ☎ 306/694–5055), is in the heart of downtown. It has naturally heated indoor and outdoor pools (40°C) supplied by an artesian well, 4,500 feet below the earth's surface. The four-story geothermal spa complex adjoins a 69-room hotel. Costs for various treatments and massages range from about $16 to $70.

Pioneer Village and Museum
13 km (8 mi) south of Moose Jaw, 84 km (52 mi) from Regina.

At the offbeat Pioneer Village and Museum, in addition to a series of old buildings and cars, you can see the *Sukanen,* a large, unfinished ship made by a Finnish settler between 1928 and 1941 and patterned after a 17th-century Finnish fishing vessel. ⊠ *Hwy. 2,* ☎ *306/693–7315.* ◱ *$2.50.* ◷ *June–Sept., daily 9–5.*

Regina A to Z

Arriving and Departing
BY CAR

Regina stands at the crossroads of the Trans-Canada Highway (Highway 1) and Highway 11, which goes north to Saskatoon.

BY PLANE

Regina Airport (☎ 306/780–5750), 8 km (5 mi) southwest of downtown, is served by Air Canada, Canadian Airlines International, Northwest Airlines, and several Canadian commuter airlines. Cabs charge about $7 for the 10- to 15-minute ride downtown.

Getting Around
BY BUS

Regina Transit's (☎ 306/777–7433) 19 bus routes serve the metropolitan area daily except Sunday. The fare is $1.10.

BY TAXI

Taxis are easy to find outside major hotels, or they can be summoned by phone. Call **Regina Cabs** (☎ 306/543–3333), **Capital Cab** (☎ 306/781–7777), or **Co-op Taxis** (☎ 306/586–6555).

Contacts and Resources
EMERGENCIES

Dial 911 for emergency **fire, police,** or **ambulance service.**

GUIDED TOURS

Classic Carriage Service (☎ 306/543–9155) offers horse-drawn carriage rides around the city in summer and horse-drawn sleigh and hayrides around Wascana Centre in winter. Both tours accommodate 15 to 20 people and cost $60 to $75 per hour.

HOSPITALS

Emergency rooms are located at **Regina General Hospital** (⊠ 1140 14th Ave., ☎ 306/766-4444), **Plains Health Centre** (⊠ 4500 Wascana Pkwy., ☎ 306/766–6211), and **Pasqua Hospital** (⊠ 4101 Dewdney Ave., ☎ 306/766–2222).

LATE-NIGHT PHARMACY

Shopper's Drug Marts (⊠ Northgate Mall, ☎ 306/777–8010; ⊠ Broad St. and 14th Ave., ☎ 306/757–8100; ⊠ Gordon Rd. and Albert St., ☎ 306/777–8040; and ⊠ Victoria Sq., ☎ 306/777–8060) are open until midnight.

VISITOR INFORMATION

Tourism Regina (⊠ Box 3355, S4P 3H1, ☎ 306/789–5099) has an information center on the Trans-Canada Highway (Highway 1) on the eastern approach to the city and is open Victoria Day (late May) to Labor Day 8–6; Labor Day to Victoria Day, weekdays 8:30–4:30. The **Tourism Saskatchewan information center** (⊠ 500–1900 Albert St., ☎ 306/787–2300) is open weekdays 8–5.

ELSEWHERE IN SOUTHERN SASKATCHEWAN

Spread from west to east across the southern part of the province are varied attractions, including a fossil research station in Eastend, sites that interpret pioneer and native life, and unique natural areas such as Grasslands National Park in Val Marie.

Swift Current

③⑥ *174 km (108 mi) west of Regina on the Trans-Canada Highway.*

West of Regina, the square townships and straight roads of the grain-belt prairie farms gradually give way to the arid rolling hills of the upland plains ranches. The Trans-Canada Highway skirts the edge of the Missouri Coteau—glacial hills that divide the prairie from the dry western plain—on its way west to Swift Current (population 16,000). The town cultivates its western image during Frontier Days Regional Fair and Rodeo (☞ Festivals and Seasonal Events *in* Chapter 1). At the **Swift Current Museum**, pioneer and native artifacts and exhibits of local natural history are displayed. ⊠ *105 Chaplin St.,* ☎ *306/778–2775.* ☜ *Free.* ☉ *May–Aug., weekdays 1:30–4:30 and 7–9, weekends 1:30–4:30; Sept.–Apr., weekdays 1:30–4:30.*

Dining and Lodging

$$ ✕ **Wong's Kitchen.** This longtime Swift Current favorite serves fine Canadian food and an even better Asian menu: Dry garlic ribs are the star attraction. Count on live entertainment nightly. ⊠ *Hwy. 1, S. Service Rd.,* ☎ *306/773–6244. Reservations essential. AE, MC, V.*

$ ☷ **Horseshoe Lodge.** It's conveniently situated along the Trans-Canada Highway service road, yet the rooms still have fine views of the surrounding countryside. The cocktail lounge is a popular meeting spot, and the restaurant offers solid Canadian cooking. ⊠ *Mobile Rte. 35,*

S9H 3X6, ☎ 306/773–4643, FAX 306/773–0309. 49 rooms. 2 restaurants, bar, pool. AE, DC, MC, V.

OFF THE BEATEN PATH

A 50-km (31-mi) drive north from Swift Current on Highway 4 will bring you to **Saskatchewan Landing Provincial Park.** The 54-square-km (21-square-mi) natural preserve lies at the point where Indians and pioneers forded the South Saskatchewan River en route to northern Saskatchewan. It has campsites, picnic facilities, and an interpretive center. ⊠ Hwy. 4, ☎ 306/375–2434. ⊠ $6 per day per car; camping mid-Sept.–mid-May $8; camping mid-May–mid-Sept. $14. ⊙ Daily.

Maple Creek

③⑦ 128 km (79 mi) west of Swift Current, 302 km (187 mi) from Regina.

The Trans-Canada Highway skirts the southern edge of the Great Sand Hills. These desertlike remnants of a huge glacial lake now abound with such native wildlife as pronghorn, mule deer, coyote, jackrabbit, and kangaroo rats. Maple Creek, a self-styled "old cow town" just south of the Trans-Canada Highway on Route 21, has a number of preserved Old West storefronts. Saskatchewan's oldest museum, the **Old Timer's Museum,** displays pictures and artifacts of Mounties, early ranchers, and natives. ⊠ 218 Jasper St., ☎ 306/662–2474. ⊠ $2. ⊙ June–Sept., daily 9–5; Oct., Apr., and May, weekdays 1–4.

Cypress Hills Provincial Park

③⑧ 27 km (17 mi) south of Maple Creek, 330 km (205 mi) from Regina.

Cypress Hills Provincial Park consists of two sections, a Centre Block and a West Block, which are about 25 km (16 mi) apart and separated by nonpark land. The larger West Block abuts the border with Alberta and is connected to Alberta's Cypress Hills Provincial Park. Within the Centre Block, the Cypress Hills plateau, rising more than 4,000 feet above sea level, is covered with spruce, aspen, and lodgepole pines erroneously identified as cypress by early European explorers. From Lookout Point you have an 80-km (50-mi) view of Maple Creek and the hills beyond. Maps are available at the Administrative Building near the park entrance. ⊠ Cypress Hills Provincial Park, Rte. 21, ☎ 306/662–4411. ⊠ $6 per day per car. ⊙ Daily.

In the West Block, you'll find **Fort Walsh National Historic Park.** The original fort was built by the Mounties in 1875 to establish order between the "wolfers" (whiskey traders) and the Assiniboine. Fort Walsh remained the center of local commerce until its abandonment in 1883. Today, free bus service links the Visitor Reception Centre and the reconstructed fort itself, Farwell's Trading Post, and a picnic area. No private vehicles are permitted beyond the parking area. A rough gravel road connects the Cypress Hills Centre Block plateau with the West Block plateau. During wet weather, take Route 21 north to Maple Creek and Route 271 southwest to the West Block. ⊠ Rte. 271, 55 km (34 mi) southwest of Maple Creek, ☎ 306/662–2645. ⊠ Free. ⊙ Mid-May–mid-Oct., daily 9–5.

Lodging

$$ ⛺ **Cypress Four Seasons Resort.** This resort in the Centre Block of Cypress Hills Provincial Park is set in the middle of a lodgepole-pine forest. Comfortable contemporary rooms are done in pastels or earth tones. The woodsy restaurant has picture windows that overlook the forest. Standard Canadian fare is more successful than the Chinese dishes. Note that this resort is not part of the Four Seasons chain. ⊠ Box 1480,

Maple Creek, S0N 1N0, ☎ 306/662–4477, FAX 306/662–3238. 31 rooms, 15 cabins, 10 condos. Restaurant, bar, indoor pool. MC, V.

Eastend

③⑨ *120 km (74 mi) east of Cypress Hills on Rte. 13, 360 km (223 mi) southwest of Regina.*

In the tiny Frenchman River valley town of Eastend, paleontologists in 1994 found one of only 12 *Tyrannosaurus rex* fossils unearthed thus far anywhere in the world. The T-rex, believed to be 65 million years old, is one of a number of fossils that have been discovered in the area. You can visit a fully operational laboratory in Eastend (with a viewing area), the **Eastend Fossil Research Station** (⊠ 118 Maple Ave. S, ☎ 306/295–4009), where paleontologists are working on the T-rex fossil. There are also trips on which you can dig for fossils yourself; contact the **Eastend Tourism Authority** (☎ 306/295–4144].

Val Marie

④⓪ *152 km (94 mi) south of Swift Current, 37 km (23 mi) north of U.S. border, 375 km (232 mi) southwest of Regina.*

The information center for a unique national park is in Val Marie. **Grasslands National Park** is between Val Marie and Killdeer in southwestern Saskatchewan. The Frenchman River valley, part of which is within the Grasslands, was the first portion of mixed-grass prairie in North America to be set aside as a park, and is marked by strange land formations and badlands. Colonies of black-tailed prairie dogs are the most numerous of the many animal species found here. Interpretive and visitor services are limited. Tent camping is permitted, and electrical hookups are provided; all sites cost $10 per night. ⊠ *Off Hwys. 4 and 18, Box 150, S0N 2T0, ☎ 306/298–2257. ⊙ Park office June–Aug., daily 8–6 and Sept.–May, weekdays 8–4:30; information center in Val Marie, late May–early Sept., daily 8–6.*

Estevan

④① *205 km (127 mi) southeast of Regina on Route 39.*

Estevan, within 16 km (10 mi) of the U.S. border, has a rich history dating back to Prohibition days in the United States, when rum-running was popular here. In summer, the town hosts popular stage plays in an outdoor tent setting. For information call **Estevan Tourism** (☎ 306/634–6044).

Moose Mountain Provincial Park

④② *139 km (86 mi) east of Weyburn, which is 115 km (71 mi) southeast of Regina via Rtes. 6 and 39.*

Moose Mountain Provincial Park is 401 square km (155 square mi) of rolling poplar and birch forest that forms a natural refuge for moose and elk and a wide variety of birds. A 24-km (15-mi) gravel road goes in to moose and elk grazing areas (best times: early morning and early evening). Visitors can vary their wildlife experiences with beaches, golf, tennis, and horseback riding. Of the 330 campsites, ⅓ have electric hookups. The Kenosee Inn (⊠ Kenosee Village, Saskatchewan S0C 2S0, ☎ 306/577–2099) is a 30-room accommodation on the park grounds. ⊠ *Rte. 9, ☎ 306/577–2131, 306/577–2144 camping reservations. ⛺ $6 per day per car; camping $14 per night with electricity, $12 without electricity. ⊙ Daily.*

CANNINGTON MANOR HISTORIC PARK – A site southeast of Moose Mountain Provincial Park preserves the 1880s lifestyle of an experimental Victorian settlement that attempted to re-create upper-class life in England and was abandoned after only 15 years when the railway bypassed the town. What remain to be seen are the original manor house, a church, shops, and a museum in the original schoolhouse. ⊠ *Rte. 603, 16 km (10 mi) northeast of Manor on gravel roads,* ☎ *306/787-9573.* ⊠ *Donations accepted.* ☉ *Late May–early Sept., daily 10–6.*

SASKATOON

Saskatchewan's largest city is Saskatoon (population 200,000), nicknamed "City of Bridges" because it has seven spans across the South Saskatchewan River, which cuts the city in half diagonally. It is considered one of the most beautiful of Canada's mid-size cities, in part because a zealous protectionist campaign has allowed the riverbanks to flourish largely in their natural state. Many visitors are impressed by the richness of the city's cultural life, particularly the thriving theater scene.

Saskatoon was founded in 1882 when a group of Ontario Methodists was granted 200,000 acres to form a temperance colony. Teetotaling Methodists controlled only half the land, however, and eventually the influence of those who controlled the other half turned the town wet. The coming of the railroad in 1890 made it the major regional transportation hub, but during the 20th century it became known for its three major resources: potash, oil, and wheat. Saskatoon today is the high-tech hub of Saskatchewan's agricultural industry and is also home to the University of Saskatchewan—a major presence in all aspects of local life.

Exploring Saskatoon

Reasonably compact for a western city, Saskatoon proper is easily accessible to drivers and cyclists. Idylwyld Drive divides the city into east and west; 22nd Street divides the city into north and south. The downtown area and the Spadina Crescent are on the west side of the South Saskatchewan River.

A Good Drive

Begin exploring at **Meewasin Valley Centre** ㊸, which traces Saskatoon history back to temperance-colony days. Follow Spadina Crescent north along the river to the **Ukrainian Museum of Canada** ㊹. Just north of the museum is **Kinsmen Park** ㊺, with riverside amusements. From Spadina Crescent, head east over the river on the University Bridge to the picturesque **University of Saskatchewan** ㊻ campus. You can detour into the northeastern part of the city to the **Saskatoon Zoo Forestry Farm Park** ㊼ for animals and hiking trails. Return to the university campus, head west on College Drive, and then pick up University Drive, lined with grand old houses. University Drive eventually joins Broadway Avenue, the city's oldest business district. Follow Broadway Avenue south to 8th Street; head west to Lorne Avenue and then south to the **Western Development Museum** ㊽, on the **Saskatoon Prairieland Exhibition Grounds** ㊾, to see a re-creation of a 1910 boomtown. To return to downtown Saskatoon, take the scenic route: Head north on Lorne Avenue, then west on Ruth Street to the river. Follow St. Henry Avenue, Taylor Street, Herman Avenue, and Saskatchewan Crescent past the fine old homes that overlook one of the prettier stretches of the South Saskatchewan River. Cross over the 19th Street Bridge.

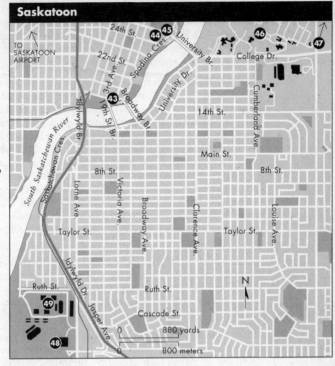

Saskatoon

TIMING

By car this tour can easily be done without stops in a morning or afternoon. If you want to explore museums or take a hike, leave more time and choose any day except Monday, when the Ukrainian Museum is closed.

Sights to See

Kinsmen Park. This riverside amusement park includes a children's play village. ✉ *Spadina Crescent and 25th St.,* ☎ *306/975–3366.*

Meewasin Valley Centre. This small museum traces Saskatoon history back to the time when it was a Methodist temperance colony. Meewasin is Cree for "beautiful valley," and this is a fitting place to embark upon the **Meewasin Valley Trail,** a 19-km (12-mi) biking and hiking trail along both banks of the beautiful South Saskatchewan River. ✉ *402 3rd Ave. S,* ☎ *306/665–6888.* ⌨ *Free.* ☉ *Weekdays 9–5, weekends 10:30–5.*

Saskatoon Prairieland Exhibition Grounds. This vast plot encompasses space for agricultural shows, rodeos, and horse races, and the Western Development Museum (☞ *below*). ✉ *Ruth St. and Lorne Ave.,* ☎ *306/931–7149.*

Saskatoon Zoo Forestry Farm Park. More than 300 animals live here. The zoo spotlights species native to Saskatchewan, such as deer, wolf, bear, coyote, and fox. The park offers barbecue areas, nature displays, cross-country ski trails, and sports fields. It also has a trout pond for fishing and train rides in the zoo area. ✉ *Off Attridge Dr., northeast Saskatoon,* ☎ *306/975–3382.* ⌨ *May–Labor Day $3, Labor Day–Apr. free, vehicle charge $2.* ☉ *May–Labor Day, daily 9–9; Labor Day–Apr., daily 10–4.*

㊹ Ukrainian Museum of Canada. This collection celebrates—through photos, costumes, textiles, and of course the famous *pysanky* (Easter eggs)—the rich history of the Ukrainian people who make up 10% of Saskatchewan's population. ⊠ *910 Spadina Crescent E,* ☎ *306/244–3800.* ⊡ *$2.* ⊘ *Tues.–Sat. 10–5, Sun. 1–5.*

㊻ University of Saskatchewan. The parklike riverside campus occupies a 2,550-acre site on the east bank of the river. The university grounds, among the most picturesque in Canada, contain several museums and galleries, including the **Natural Sciences Museum,** the **Little Stone School House,** the **Museum of Antiquities,** the **Biology Museum,** and the **Gordon Snelgrove Gallery.** A highlight is the **Diefenbaker Canada Centre,** a museum, art gallery, and research center in Canadian studies commemorating Canada's 13th prime minister. The center explores John Diefenbaker's life and times. Two replica rooms represent the Privy Council Chamber and the prime minister's Ottawa office, where he served in the late 1950s and early 1960s. ⊠ *Diefenbaker Canada Centre,* ☎ *306/966–8384.* ⊘ *Weekdays 9:30–4:30, weekends 12:30–5.*

㊽ Western Development Museum. One of four such museums in Saskatchewan, the Saskatoon branch is called "1910 Boomtown" and re-creates early 20th-century life in western Canada. ⊠ *2610 Lorne Ave. S,* ☎ *306/931–1910.* ⊡ *$4.50.* ⊘ *Daily 9–5.*

Dining

$$$ ✕ **R.J. Willoughby's.** Stands of bamboo and other foliage enhance the lush, tropical, pink-and-green color scheme of the Ramada Hotel's main dining room. Menu highlights are Continental entrées plus themed evenings with specialty buffets (prime rib on Wednesday, pasta on Friday, seafood on Sunday). The very popular Sunday brunch has an impressive array of selections, including custom-made omelets and flambéed fruit. ⊠ *Ramada Hotel, 90 22nd St. E,* ☎ *306/665–7576. Reservations essential. AE, DC, MC, V.*

$$ ✕ **St. Tropez Bistro.** This sophisticated spot a short stroll from downtown hotels offers intimate French bistro decor, with blue-and-pink florals, candlelit tables, and imaginative preparations that change daily. Veal, fish, pastas, quiches, and outstanding homemade bread are often on the menu. A tasty specialty is the blackened chicken. For dessert, try the chocolate fondue. ⊠ *243 3rd Ave. S,* ☎ *306/652–1250. Reservations essential. AE, MC, V. Closed Sun.*

$$ ✕ **Saskatoon Station Place.** The station is newly built, but the vintage railroad cars and decorative antiques are fascinatingly authentic. The newspaper-style menu headlines Canadian prime rib and steaks, seafood, and Greek specialties, such as Greek ribs and souvlaki. ⊠ *221 Idylwyld Dr. N,* ☎ *306/244–7777. Reservations essential. AE, MC, V.*

$ ✕ **Lydia's.** This Broadway Avenue–neighborhood pub presents a wide selection of international beers and has a full menu, including beef and chicken kebabs as well as Cajun chicken, Caesar salad, and a variety of pasta dishes. There's music every weekend. ⊠ *650 Broadway Ave.,* ☎ *306/652–8595. DC, MC, V.*

$ ✕ **Taunte Maria's.** At this Mennonite restaurant, you're served hearty soups, huge farmer's sausages, potato salad, homemade bread, and noodles steeped in gravy. The decor, too, reflects the Mennonite tradition: simple, functional, and comfortable. Try to save room for Ho-Ho Cake (chocolate cake with cream filling and chocolate icing) or bread pudding with ice cream. ⊠ *51st St. and Faithfull Ave.,* ☎ *306/931–3212. Reservations not accepted. MC, V. Closed Sun.*

Lodging

$$$ **Delta Bessborough.** Saskatoon's majestic old landmark, opened in 1935,
★ looks like a castle and dominates the skyline from its riverfront setting.
The hotel has recently been restored and upgraded with modern ameni-
ties, but it still retains its grand details. Rooms differ in size but all have
traditional furniture. ⊠ *601 Spadina Crescent E, S7K 3G8,* ☎ *306/244–
5521 or 800/268–1133,* FAX *306/653–2458. 227 rooms. 2 restaurants,
2 bars, no-smoking rooms, indoor pool, sauna. AE, DC, MC, V.*

$$$ **Radisson Hotel Saskatoon.** One of Saskatoon's newest luxury prop-
erties has a prime riverfront location downtown and 19 floors of clas-
sically styled rooms. Units are large, and the peach, gray, and pastel
colors make them bright and airy; for still more atmosphere, request
a river view. The elaborate Waterworks Recreation Complex has an
indoor pool, a whirlpool, a sauna, and two three-story water slides.
⊠ *405 20th St. E, S7K 6X6,* ☎ *306/665–3322 or 800/228–9898,* FAX
*306/665–5531. 291 rooms. Restaurant, bar, no-smoking rooms, in-
door pool, sauna. AE, DC, MC, V.*

$$$ **Sheraton Cavalier.** Downtown, opposite Kiwanis Park, this eight-
story property has unusually large rooms that face either the city or
the river, and an elaborate water-sports complex. Benedict's Dining Room
is the place for elegant dining, while Windows Café is more informal
and offers a view of the river from every table. ⊠ *612 Spadina Cres-
cent E, S7K 3G9,* ☎ *306/652–6770 or 800/325–3535,* FAX *306/244–
1739. 250 rooms. 2 restaurants, pub, no-smoking rooms, 2 indoor pools,
sauna. AE, DC, MC, V.*

$$ **Travelodge.** A sprawling property near the airport has two flora-
filled indoor pool complexes; there's a water slide, too. Rooms come
in a variety of sizes and shapes; many have balconies overlooking the
pool. The Gardens Terrace Restaurant has informal poolside dining.
⊠ *106 Circle Dr. W, S7L 4L6,* ☎ *306/242–8881 or 800/255–3050,*
FAX *306/665–7378. 220 rooms. 2 restaurants, 2 bars, no-smoking
rooms, 2 indoor pools, sauna. AE, DC, MC, V.*

$ **Colonial Square Motel.** This pink-stucco, two-story motel is east of
the river, along a fast-food strip. Rooms are furnished in pastel colors
and have two queen-size beds or a double bed plus a pullout sofa. Across
the parking lot is the Venice Pizza House and Lounge. ⊠ *1301 8th St.
E, S7H 0S7,* ☎ *306/343–1676 or 800/667–3939,* FAX *306/956–1313.
80 rooms. Restaurant, bar, no-smoking rooms. AE, MC, V.*

$ **Patricia Hotel.** Conveniently located in the center of downtown, this
★ older hotel is appealing if you're looking for a bargain. Some rooms
are also available as a youth hostel. There's a dining room, Karz Kafe,
and a lounge. ⊠ *345 2nd Ave. N,* ☎ *306/242–8861,* FAX *306/242–
8861. 45 rooms. Restaurant, bar. MC, V.*

Nightlife and the Arts

The Arts

MUSIC AND DANCE

The **Saskatoon Symphony** (☎ 306/665–6414) performs an October–April season. When the city symphony isn't in concert, the 2,003-
seat **Saskatoon Centennial Auditorium** (⊠ 35 22nd St. E, ☎ 306/
975–7777) hosts ballet, rock and pop concerts, comedians, musical
comedies, and opera. The **Mendel Art Gallery** (⊠ 950 Spadina Crescent E, ☎ 306/975–7610) has a regular concert program. The **Saskatoon Jazz Society** performs in its permanent space, The Bassment (⊠
245 3rd Ave. S, ☎ 306/668–2277). Each summer Saskatoon is home
to the popular **Saskatchewan Jazz Festival** (☎ 306/652–1421) when
jazz musicians from around the world play more than 125 performances
throughout the city.

Saskatoon's oldest professional theater, **25th Street Theatre Centre** (⊠ 420 Duchess St., ☎ 306/664–2239), produces mostly works by Saskatchewan playwrights, as well as the Fringe Festival every summer. **Persephone Theatre** (⊠ 2802 Rusholme Rd., ☎ 306/384–7727) presents six plays and musicals a year. **Gateway Players** (⊠ 709 Cumberland St., ☎ 306/653–1200) presents five productions from October through April. A popular summertime tradition, **Shakespeare on the Saskatchewan** (☎ 306/653–2300) is staged in a riverside tent during July and August. **Saskatoon Soaps** present midnight improvisational comedy at the Broadway Theatre (⊠ 715 Broadway Ave., ☎ 306/652–6556).

Nightlife

BARS AND CLUBS

One Up (⊠ 410 22nd St. E, ☎ 306/244–7770) is a civilized rooftop place with great river views. Saskatoon's businesspeople mingle with traveling executives at **Caper's Lounge** (⊠ 405 20th St. E, ☎ 306/665–3322) in the Radisson Hotel Saskatoon. See top rock groups at **Bud's On Broadway** (⊠ 817 Broadway Ave., ☎ 306/244–4155). **Amigos** (⊠ 632 10th St. E, ☎ 306/652–4912) is a rock hangout. The **Artful Dodger** (⊠ 100–119 4th Ave. S, ☎ 306/653–2577) pub has live entertainment. Go out to **Texas T** (⊠ 3331 8th St. E, ☎ 306/373–8080) for country sights and sounds around the city's largest dance floor.

Outdoor Activities and Sports

Participant Sports

BICYCLING AND JOGGING

The **Meewasin Valley Trail** (☎ 306/665–6888) is a gorgeous 19-km (12-mi) biking and jogging trail along both banks of the South Saskatchewan River in Saskatoon.

HEALTH AND FITNESS CLUBS

The **Riverraquet Athletic Club** (⊠ 322 Saguenay Dr., ☎ 306/242–0010) has racquetball and squash courts, a weight room, aerobics classes, miniature golf, and beach volleyball in summer. The **Saskatoon Field House** (⊠ University of Saskatchewan, 2020 College Dr., ☎ 306/975–3354) has tennis courts, a weight room, a gymnastics area, an indoor track, a fitness dance area, and drop-in fitness classes.

Spectator Sports

HOCKEY

The **Saskatoon Blades** play major junior hockey league action in the Western Hockey League at Saskatchewan Place (⊠ 3515 Thatcher Ave., ☎ 306/938–7800).

HORSE RACING

Marquis Downs Racetrack (⊠ Prairieland Exhibition Centre, enter on Ruth St., ☎ 306/242–6100) has Thoroughbred racing from early May through mid-October.

Shopping

Malls and Shopping Districts

Midtown Plaza (⊠ 22nd St. and 1st Ave., ☎ 306/652–9366) and **Scotia Centre Mall** (⊠ 123 2nd Ave., ☎ 306/665–6120) are enclosed malls downtown. Two interesting suburban choices are the recently linked **Centre at Circle and 8th** and the **Market Mall** (⊠ Louise and Preston), with its indoor miniature golf. If you enjoy funkier, smaller boutiques and restaurants, head to **Broadway Avenue** (⊠ between 8th and 12th

Sts. east of river), the city's oldest business district and location of more than 150 shops and restaurants and a cinema.

Specialty Stores

Trading Post Limited (✉ 226 2nd Ave. S, ☎ 306/653–1769) carries an extensive and reasonably priced selection of Inuit and Indian crafts and Canadian foodstuffs—including Saskatoon berry products. Local crafts are available at **Handmade House** (✉ 710 Broadway Ave., ☎ 306/665–5542). The **Homespun Craft Emporium** (✉ 250A 2nd Ave. S, ☎ 306/652–3585) has crafts.

Side Trips from Saskatoon

Day trips to a number of sites outside the city can deepen your understanding of native and frontier life, including the heritage of the Métis. Prince Albert National Park may be a bit far for a day trip but is well worth an overnight stay.

Wanuskewin Heritage Park

★ 50 *5 km (3 mi) north of Saskatoon just off Hwy. 11.*

Wanuskewin Heritage Park portrays 6,000 years of Northern Plains native culture. The Interpretive Centre has an archaeological laboratory, displays, films, and hands-on activities. Outside, walking trails take you to archaeological sites, including a medicine wheel, tepee rings, bison kills and pounds, habitation sites, and stone cairns. ✉ *R.R. 4, Saskatoon,* ☎ *306/931–6767.* ✐ *$6.* ☼ *June–Sept., daily 9–9; Sept.–May, daily 9–5.*

Batoche

51 *100 km (62 mi) northeast of Saskatoon.*

This small town is most notable for being near a significant historic
★ site. **Batoche National Historic Site** is a center of the Métis' heritage. It was here that the Métis under Louis Riel fought and lost their last battle against the Canadian militia in 1885. The large historical park includes a visitor center, displays, a historic church and rectory, and walking trails that take you by many of the battle sites. ✉ *Off Hwy. 11 (follow signs),* ☎ *306/423–6227.* ✐ *$3.* ☼ *July and Aug., daily 10–6; May, June, Sept., and Oct., daily 9–5.*

Duck Lake

52 *20 km (12 mi) north of Batoche, 120 km (74 mi) north of Saskatoon.*

Duck Lake lies along Highway 11, between the North and South Saskatchewan rivers. Town buildings are decorated with life-size murals depicting the area's history, including the 1885 Northwest Rebellion. The **Regional Interpretive Centre** has more than 2,000 artifacts from the period of the Métis' last rebellion. ✉ *Hwy. 11,* ☎ *306/467–2057.* ✐ *$4.* ☼ *Mid-May–Labor Day, daily 10–5:30.*

OFF THE   **FORT CARLTON PROVINCIAL HISTORIC PARK** – This site, 24 km (15 mi)
BEATEN PATH   west of Duck Lake, has a reconstructed stockade and buildings from the mid-1800s fur-trade days. ✉ *Rte. 212,* ☎ *306/787-2854.* ✐ *$2.50.* ☼ *Mid-May–Labor Day, daily 10-6.*

Prince Albert

53 *141 km (87 mi) north of Saskatoon on Hwy. 11 and Rte. 2.*

Prince Albert is Saskatchewan's fourth-largest city (population 34,000), the center of the lumber industry, and the self-proclaimed "Gateway to the North." The prosperous modern city straddles the North Saskatchewan River; its most interesting attractions are downtown. The

Prince Albert Historical Museum, housed in the old Fire Hall, also has a walk-tour pamphlet. ⊠ *River St. and Central Ave.,* ☎ *306/764–2992.* 🎟 *$1.* ☉ *Mid-May–Aug., Mon.–Sat. 10–6, Sun. 10–9.*

Prince Albert National Park

80 km (50 mi) north of Prince Albert, 221 km (137 mi) north of Saskatoon.

★ **Prince Albert National Park** encompasses nearly a million acres of wilderness and waterways and is divided into three landscapes: wide-open fescue grassland, rolling wooded parkland, and dense boreal forest. In addition to hiking trails, the park has three major campgrounds, with more than 500 sites, plus rustic campgrounds and primitive sites in the backcountry. Pick up maps and information at the **Waskesiu Lake Visitor Centre** in Waskesiu, a townsite with restaurants, motels, and stores, and a golf course within the park. The **Nature Centre,** inside the visitor center, orients you to the plant and animal life of the area. Hiking along the marked trails, you have a good chance of spotting moose, deer, bear, elk, and red fox. Canoes, rowboats, and powerboats can be rented from Waskesiu Lake Marina. Lodging in Waskesiu includes **Chateau Park Chalets** (☎ 306/663–5556), the **Hawood Inn** (☎ 306/663–5911), and **Waskesiu Lake Lodge** (☎ 306/663–6161); all offer year-round accommodation. ⊠ *Prince Albert National Park, off Rte. 2,* ☎ *306/663–5322;* ⊠ *Waskesiu Lake Visitor Centre, Rtes. 263 and 264,* ☎ *306/663–5322.* 🎟 *Free.* ☉ *Park daily; visitor center May–Sept., daily 8 AM–10 PM, and Oct.–Apr., weekdays 8–4:30.*

North Battleford

54 *138 km (86 mi) northwest of Saskatoon on Rte. 16.*

The attractions in this town represent different aspects of the area's history. The **Western Development Museum** presents a re-created 1920s farming village, complete with homes, offices, churches, and a Mountie post. The museum also exhibits vintage farming tools and provides demonstrations of agricultural skills used. ⊠ *Rtes. 16 and 40,* ☎ *306/445–8033.* 🎟 *$4.50.* ☉ *Call for hours.*

While you're in town, visit the **Allen Sapp Gallery,** which features the paintings of Cree artist Allen Sapp. ⊠ *1091 100th St.,* ☎ *306/445–1760.* 🎟 *Free.* ☉ *May–Sept., daily 1–5; Oct.–Apr., Wed.–Sun. 1–5.*

Fort Battleford National Historic Site pays tribute to the role of mounted police in the development of the Canadian west. The fort was established in 1876 as the North West Mounted Police headquarters for the District of Saskatchewan. Costumed guides explain day-to-day life at the post, and an interpretive center has exhibits relating to the history of the Mounted Police and ways of life of natives and settlers. ⊠ *Central Ave.,* ☎ *306/937–2621.* 🎟 *$3.* ☉ *July and Aug., daily 9–6; May, June, Sept., and Oct., daily 9–5.*

Manitou Beach

55 *124 km (77 mi) southeast of Saskatoon, via Rtes. 16 and 365.*

Fifty years ago the town of Manitou Beach was a world-famous spa nicknamed the "Carlsbad of Canada." The mineral water in Little Manitou Lake is said to be three times saltier than the ocean and dense enough to make anyone float. Today **Manitou Springs Mineral Spa** (⊠ Rte. 365, ☎ 306/946–2233) attracts vacationers as well as sufferers from arthritis, rheumatism, and skin disorders to the spa resort (☞ *below*).

DINING AND LODGING

$$ ✕🏨 **Manitou Springs Resort.** On the lake shore, it has rooms and suites with balconies and good views. The rooms are comfortable, with cushy fabrics in muted pastels; the spa is lined with cedar. There's Continental cuisine, including a small selection of seafood, as well as prairie fare—steaks and roasts—in a light and airy dining room overlooking the lake. ⊠ *Box 610, Watrous, SK S0K 4T0,* ☎ *306/946–2233 or 800/667–7672 in Canada. 56 rooms, 4 suites. Dining room, massage, mineral baths, exercise room, bicycles, shops, meeting rooms. MC, V.*

Saskatoon A to Z

Arriving and Departing

BY CAR

The two-lane Yellowhead Highway (Highway 16) passes through Saskatoon on its journey from Winnipeg through to Edmonton and west. There is also access to Saskatoon along Highway 11 from Regina.

BY PLANE

Saskatoon Airport (☎ 306/975–4274), 7 km (4½ mi) northwest of downtown, is served by Canadian Airlines International, Air Canada, Northwest Airlines, Westjet and Canadian commuter carriers. Taxis to the downtown area cost about $10–$12.

Getting Around

BY BUS

Saskatoon Transit (☎ 306/975–3100) buses offer convenient service to points around the city. Tickets cost $1.25.

BY TAXI

Taxis are plentiful, especially outside downtown hotels, but they are fairly expensive. For service, call **United Yellow Cab** (☎ 306/652–2222), **Blueline Taxi** (☎ 306/653–3333), or **Saskatoon Radio Cab** (☎ 306/242–1221).

Contacts and Resources

EMERGENCIES

Dial 911 for **police, fire, ambulance, poison,** and **emergency services.**

GUIDED TOURS

W.W. Northcote River Cruises depart on the hour for 11-km (7-mi) tours of the South Saskatchewan River. Cruises run June–August, daily 10–8. **The Delta Lady** (☎ 306/934–7642) offers one-hour river cruises from May through October, daily 9:30–9. Departures are directly behind the Delta Bessborough Hotel, and tickets can be purchased in the lobby.

HOSPITALS

There are emergency rooms at **City Hospital** (⊠ Queen St. and 6th Ave. N, ☎ 306/655–8230), **Royal University Hospital** (⊠ University Grounds, ☎ 306/655–1362), and **St. Paul's Hospital** (⊠ 1702 20th St. W, ☎ 306/665–5113).

LATE-NIGHT PHARMACY

Shopper's Drug Mart (⊠ 610 Taylor St. E, at Broadway Ave., ☎ 306/343–1608) is open till midnight; another branch (⊠ 2410 22nd St. W, ☎ 306/382–5005) is open 24 hours.

VISITOR INFORMATION

Tourism Saskatoon (⊠ 6-305 Idylwyld Dr. N, S7L 0Z1, ☎ 306/242–1206) is open weekdays 8:30–5 during most of the year and 8:30–7 mid-May–early September. In summer, visitor information centers open at various points along Highway 16.

WINNIPEG

Though geographically isolated, Manitoba's provincial capital has become a center for both commerce and culture, home to a symphony orchestra, ballet and opera companies, a lively theater scene, and a thriving community of local and native artists. The first stop on the great Canadian land rush of the late 19th century, Winnipeg still counts among its citizens descendants of the original French and British settlers, and it has distinct neighborhoods of Ukrainians, Jews, Italians, Mennonites, Hungarians, Portuguese, Poles, and Chinese.

Unlike the boom-and-bust towns farther west, Winnipeg has enjoyed steady growth, with a diversified economy based on manufacturing, banking, transportation, and agriculture. With a population of more than 650,000, it ranks as Canada's seventh-largest city and the largest population center between Toronto and Calgary. Winnipeg looks like the cosmopolitan centers of midwestern America—Minneapolis, Milwaukee, Chicago—with a downtown area filled with cast-iron buildings and established neighborhoods of older homes along curving, tree-lined streets.

Originally, buffalo-hunting Plains Indians were the only inhabitants of the area, which was franchised by the British Crown to the Hudson's Bay Company. That was until 1738, when Pierre Gaultier de Varennes established a North West Company fur-trading post at the junction of the Red and Assiniboine rivers. Lord Selkirk, a Scot, brought a permanent agricultural settlement in 1812; Winnipeg was incorporated as a city in 1873; and soon after, in 1886, the Canadian Pacific Railroad arrived, bringing a rush of European immigrants. Winnipeg boomed as a railroad hub, a center of the livestock and grain industries, and a principal market city of western Canada.

Exploring Winnipeg

It's somewhat difficult to get your bearings in Winnipeg. The downtown area lies just north of the junction of the Red and Assiniboine rivers, and its streets interconnect at skewed angles with the curving rivers, creating diagonal streets in all directions. Much of downtown Winnipeg is linked by a network of enclosed pedestrian overpasses and underground concourses. The intersection of Portage Avenue and Main Street is the focal point of the city, with Portage Avenue (Highway 1) the principal artery heading west and Main Street (Route 52) heading north. South of Winnipeg, the main drag is Pembina Highway (Route 42). Streets in St. Boniface, east of the Red River, are labeled in French—evidence of the community's ethnic heritage.

A Good Walk and Drive

Begin at the southeast corner of downtown Winnipeg at the visitor information center, housed in the **Legislative Building** ⑯. Walk east on Broadway and south on Carlton Street to tour **Dalnavert Museum** ⑰, the 1895 house built for Manitoba's premier. Back at the Legislature, head north on Osborne Street past the stately The Bay store (the legacy of the Hudson's Bay Company) to the **Winnipeg Art Gallery** ⑱ to view Inuit sculpture and art. Turn east at the north end of the Winnipeg Art Gallery to Portage Avenue for a look at the shopping district (☞ Shopping, *below*). Continue east on Portage Avenue to Main Street and what's reputed to be the windiest intersection in the world. Five floors above the breeze, visit the **Winnipeg Commodity Exchange** ⑲, the oldest and largest futures exchange in Canada. Below ground is Winnipeg Square, a concourse with shops and fast-food stores. Emerge to street level on the north side of Portage Avenue and into the **Exchange District** ⑳—a

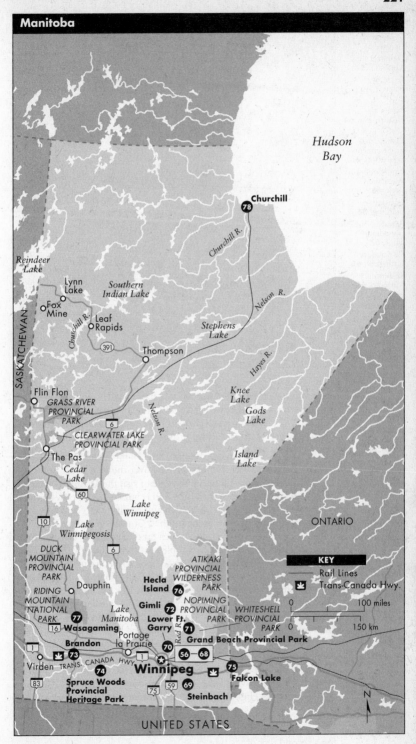

222

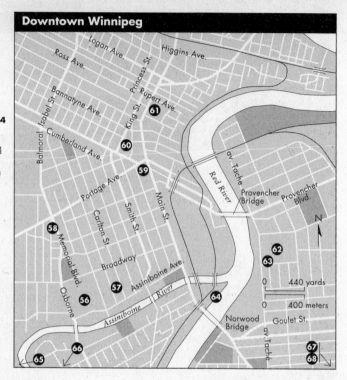

Downtown Winnipeg

concentration of renovated warehouses, banks, and insurance companies now thriving as a nightlife center and Sunday open-air market. Continue north on Main Street to Rupert Avenue and **Centennial Centre** ⑥, site of a concert hall, a natural history museum, and a planetarium.

The suburb of St. Boniface, about 2½ km (1½ mi) away, can be reached by crossing the Provencher Bridge east over the Red River and turning right onto avenue Taché. Here you can visit the **St. Boniface Cathedral** ⑥, in whose churchyard Louis Riel is buried, and the **St. Boniface Museum** ⑥, which focuses on French and Métis history and culture in Manitoba. Follow avenue Taché south to Goulet Street, turn right, and follow it onto Norwood Bridge, which takes you to the **Forks National Historic Site** ⑥ and the Forks complex, at the junction of the Assiniboine and Red rivers. A longer drive—left on River Avenue, left on Donald Street, and right on Corydon Avenue—will bring you to **Assiniboine Park** ⑥, where the zoo and several lovely gardens are. South of the park, you can follow Shaftsbury Boulevard past Assiniboine Forest across Wilkes Avenue to McCreary Road, where the **Fort Whyte Center for Environmental Education** ⑥ re-creates natural habitats of Manitoba in a former cement quarry. To see where Canadian money is made, drive 6½ km (4 mi) southeast of downtown off Highway 1 or take Bus 50 (available on the east side of Fort Street between Portage and Graham avenues on weekdays) to the **Royal Canadian Mint** ⑥. Also southeast of the center off Highway 1 is **Fun Mountain Waterslide Park** ⑥.

TIMING

This makes for a busy day's tour; you might want to save a few sights for a second day of visiting.

Sights to See

⑥ **Assiniboine Park.** West of town along the river of the same name, the park encompasses 376 acres of cycling paths, picnic areas, playgrounds, a miniature railway, formal English and French gardens, a conservatory, and a cricket pitch. **Assiniboine Zoo,** also on the grounds, houses more than 1,200 species in reasonably natural settings. ☎ 204/986–6921 or 204/986–3130. ☒ Zoo $3, free Tues. ☉ Zoo Oct.–Mar., daily 10–4; Apr., May, and Sept., daily 10–7; June and July, daily 10–9; Aug., daily 10–8. Park daily 7–10.

61 **Centennial Centre.** A concert hall, the **Manitoba Museum of Man and Nature,** and the dazzling **Manitoba Planetarium** are the highlights of this complex. Exhibits at the museum focus on prehistoric Manitoba, local wildlife, the native peoples of the region, and the exploration of Hudson Bay. Downstairs, the planetarium presents a variety of cosmic adventures in the multimedia Star Theater; 60 interactive multisensory exhibits in Touch the Universe explain laws of nature. ☒ 190 Rupert Ave., ☎ 204/943–3139 or 204/943–3142. ☒ Museum $4, planetarium $3.50, science gallery $3.50, 3-day all-inclusive Omni pass $9. ☉ Mid-May–early Sept., daily 10–6; Sept.–mid-May, Tues.–Thurs. 10–6, weekends noon–6.

57 **Dalnavert Museum.** This Queen Anne Revival–style house was built in 1895 for Sir Hugh John Macdonald, who became premier of Manitoba. Costumed guides escort visitors around the premises. ☒ 61 Carlton St., ☎ 204/943–2835. ☒ $3.21. ☉ Jan. and Feb., weekends noon–4; Mar.–May, weekends and Tues.–Thurs. noon–4:30; June–Aug., weekends and Tues.–Thurs. 10–5:30; Sept.–Dec., weekends and Tues.–Thurs. noon–4:30.

60 **Exchange District.** A concentration of renovated warehouses, banks, and insurance companies built during Winnipeg's turn-of-the-century boom period now stands as a thriving nightlife spot. On Sunday, from May through October, attention focuses on **Old Market Square Park** (☒ King St. and Bannatyne Ave.), a new marketplace bursting with fresh produce, fish, crafts, and street performers. ☒ Between Portage Ave. and Main St.

★ **64** **Forks National Historic Site.** Winnipeg began here, at the junction of the Red and Assiniboine rivers, with native settlements that date back 6,000 years. On 10 landscaped acres, you can learn about the region's history through interpretive displays as you stroll paths or rest on benches overlooking the river. There's also a playground and an amphitheater. Interpretive programs are presented as well; check at the Forks information center at the back of the Manitoba Children's Museum (☞ below). Next to the Historic Site and sharing the 2-mile riverside promenade with it is **The Forks,** a 56-acre complex of renovated railway buildings and parkland now hosting a public market in former stables; a playground; a small boat dock; Johnston terminal, with shops and restaurants; and the **Manitoba Children's Museum.** The museum is western Canada's first hands-on museum for children. In five galleries, kids can climb aboard a 1952-vintage steam engine and passenger car, try out a fully functioning TV studio, and more. ☒ Forks Market Rd. off Main St., ☎ 204/983–2007 Historic Site, 204/943–7752 the Forks, 204/956–1888 Children's Museum. ☒ Museum: $4. ☉ Victoria Day–Labor Day, daily 9:30–5; Labor Day–Victoria Day, weekdays 8–4:30.

☾ **66** **Fort Whyte Center for Environmental Education.** This center, on 200 acres of land in the city's southwest corner, re-creates the natural habitats of Manitoba's lakes and rivers in and around several former cement quarries. Self-guided nature trails and an interpretive center explain it all. ☒ 1961 McCreary Rd., ☎ 204/989–8355. ☒ $3.50. ☉ Weekdays 9–5, weekends 10–5.

✋ ➏➑ **Fun Mountain Water Slide Park.** Bumper boats, a mammoth hot tub, rides, and a playground are all part of the fun at the water park 13 km (8 mi) east of downtown. ⌧ *Hwy. 1, east at Murdock Rd.,* ☎ *204/255–3910.* ➳ *$11.* ☉ *June–Aug., daily 10–8.*

➎➏ **Legislative Building.** The classic Greek-style structure made of local Tyndall stone contains the offices of Manitoba's premier and members of the cabinet, as well as the chamber where the legislature meets. The 240-foot dome supports Manitoba's symbol, Golden Boy—a gold-sheathed statue with a sheaf of wheat under his left arm and the torch of progress in his right hand. In the grounds fronting the river stand statues that celebrate Manitoba's ethnic diversity, including Scotland's Robert Burns, Iceland's Jon Sigurdson, Ukrainian poet Taras Ahevchenko, and Métis leader and "Father of Manitoba" Louis Riel. ⌧ *450 Broadway, at Osborne St.,* ☎ *204/945–5813.* ☉ *Guided tour July–Labor Day, weekdays 9–6:30; Labor Day–June by appointment.*

➏➐ **Royal Canadian Mint.** You can see Canadian coins rolling off the presses at this facility. ⌧ *520 Lagimodière Blvd., at Trans-Canada Hwy.,* ☎ *204/257–3359.* ➳ *$2.* ☉ *Tour May–Aug., weekdays 9–5, Sat. noon–5.*

➏➋ **St. Boniface Cathedral.** The largest French community in western Canada was founded as Fort Rouge in 1783 and became an important fur-trading outpost for the North West Company. Upon the arrival of Roman Catholic priests, the settlement was renamed St. Boniface. Remnants of a 1908 basilica that survived a 1968 fire can be seen outside the perimeter of the present cathedral, built in 1972. The grave of Louis Riel, the St. Boniface native son who led the Métis rebellion, is in the churchyard. ⌧ *Av. de la Cathedral and av. Taché,* ☎ *204/233–7304.*

➏➌ **St. Boniface Museum.** Housed in the oldest (1846) structure in Winnipeg and the largest oak log building in North America, the museum tells the French and Métis side of Manitoba history. Artifacts include an altar crafted from papier-mâché, the first church bell in western Canada, and a host of innovative household gadgets. ⌧ *494 av. Tache,* ☎ *204/237–4500.* ➳ *$2.14.* ☉ *Mid-May–mid-June and Sept., weekdays 9–5, weekends 10–5; mid-June–Aug., Sun. 10–8, Mon.–Thurs. 9–8, Fri. and Sat. 9–5; Oct.–mid-May, weekdays 9–5.*

★ ➎➑ **Winnipeg Art Gallery.** The gallery, has the world's largest collection of Inuit sculpture and art; it also houses contemporary Canadian art and sculpture. ⌧ *300 Memorial Blvd.,* ☎ *204/786–6641.* ➳ *$3, free Wed.* ☉ *Thurs.–Tues. 11–5, Wed. 11–9; times may vary with season.*

➎➒ **Winnipeg Commodity Exchange.** At the oldest and largest futures exchange in Canada, you can observe the controlled chaos of wild men (and a few women) involved in the buying and selling of grains, cooking oils, gold, and silver. Below the exchange is **Winnipeg Square,** with shops and fast-food stores. ⌧ *360 Main St.,* ☎ *204/949–0495.* ☉ *Weekdays 9:30–1:20.*

Dining

$$$$ ✕ **Le Beaujolais.** This sophisticated, bright spot in the French St. Boniface district presents waiters in black tie; a softly lit ambience with French blue, coral, and burgundy decor; fresh-cut flowers; and a menu that combines classic French with lighter nouvelle cuisine. Fresh salmon with herb vinaigrette is the recommended seafood; tournedos with green peppercorns, veal with Roquefort and leeks, and rack of lamb are other
★

entrée suggestions. Save room for dessert. ⊠ *131 Provencher Blvd.,* ☎ *204/237–6306. Reservations essential. AE, DC, MC, V.*

$$$ ✕ **Restaurant Dubrovnik.** The setting is a romantic Victorian town house, with seating on an enclosed veranda overlooking the Assiniboine River. An extensive menu blends Continental specialties, such as rack of lamb, breast of duck, and pheasant, with southern Yugoslavian dishes. Two good choices are *gibanica* (feta cheese in phyllo pastry) and *muckalica* (pork, lamb, chicken, and sausage casserole). A lengthy wine list is available. ⊠ *390 Assiniboine Ave.,* ☎ *204/944–0594. Reservations essential. Jacket required. AE, MC, V. Closed Sun.*

$$$ ✕ **Victor's.** In the Ramada Marlborough (☞ *below*), with its rich wood paneling and chandeliers, Victor's serves Continental cuisine in a stylish, upscale atmosphere. **Joanna's Café,** in the same hotel, is a more casual dining spot for before- or after-dinner drinks. In both restaurants, poppy-seed cake is a must for dessert. ⊠ *331 Smith St.,* ☎ *204/947–2751. Reservations essential. AE, DC, MC, V. Closed Sun.*

$$ ✕ **Amici.** The sophisticated and posh downtown *ristorante* is the local avatar of *cucina nuova,* the Italian version of nouvelle cuisine. Clever pastas and such dishes as roast quail on radicchio and chicken stuffed with goat cheese are served in a second-floor dining room that's divided by partitions of frosted glass. Downstairs, the Bombolini Wine Bar serves many simpler dishes at lower prices. ⊠ *326 Broadway,* ☎ *204/943–4997. Reservations essential. AE, DC, MC, V. Closed Sun.*

$$ ✕ **Bistro Dansk.** Wood tables, bright red chairs, and strains of classi-
★ cal music convey a cozy European air. Dinner entrée selections mingle Danish specialties like *frikadeller* (meat patties) and salmon topped with crab, with such dishes as roast chicken. A less expensive lunch menu has a vast variety of open-face sandwiches. ⊠ *63 Sherbrook St.,* ☎ *204/775–5662. Reservations essential. DC, V. Closed Sun.*

$$ ✕ **Picasso's.** It may be named for a Spanish painter, but this is a Portuguese restaurant that serves outstanding seafood. On the street level it's a bustling neighborhood café; upstairs there's a subdued atmosphere where white tablecloths, candlelight, and soft music prevail. Try the salmon or Arctic char; Portuguese favorites are paella and octopus stew. ⊠ *615 Sargent Ave.,* ☎ *204/775–2469. Reservations essential. AE, DC, MC, V.*

$ ✕ **d'8 Schtove.** The name is Mennonite for "the eating room," and,
★ true to its name, the menu has heavyweight servings of soup, salads, and Mennonite concoctions, usually involving meat, potatoes, onions, and vegetables. Try the *klopz* (ground-beef-and-pork meatballs) or *wrenikje* (cottage-cheese pierogi). The south-side location is bright and immaculately clean, and the restaurant looks spacious, although you may still have to wait for a table. Service is quick and friendly. ⊠ *1842 Pembina Hwy.,* ☎ *204/275–2294. Reservations not accepted. AE, DC, MC, V.*

$ ✕ **Homer's.** This good-time downtown place, with a definite Mediterranean atmosphere, has been one of the city's favorite Greek restaurants for more than 15 years. Greek specialties include roast leg of lamb and moussaka, but Homer's is also famous for ribs, steak, seafood, pasta, and fresh hot bread. In summer you can eat outdoors. ⊠ *520 Ellice Ave.,* ☎ *204/788–4858. Reservations essential. AE, DC, MC, V.*

$ ✕ **Kelekis.** This north-end shrine has purveyed legendary burgers, hot dogs, and fries for more than 60 years. A photo montage of family history and autographed photos of celebrities set the tone. Breakfast, lunch, and dinner are served daily. ⊠ *1100 Main St.,* ☎ *204/582–1786. Reservations not accepted. No credit cards.*

$ ✕ **Mandarin.** The Sargent Avenue Mandarin is a crowded, 12-table, west-side place with unique and reasonably exotic northern Chinese dishes. Complete Gourmet Delight dinners include soup, dumplings, entrées, and dessert. Wine is the only alcohol served. The River Mandarin, a spin-off, has a slightly different menu, a calmer pace, and a full liquor license. ⊠ *Mandarin, 613 Sargent Ave.,* ☎ *204/775–7819; River Mandarin,* ⊠ *252 River Ave.,* ☎ *204/284–8963. Reservations essential. AE, MC, V.*

Lodging

$$$ 🏨 **Crowne Plaza Winnipeg Downtown.** Winnipeg's largest hotel, this Holiday Inn is 17 stories high and connects to the convention center. Rooms are decorated in pastels and have pleasant modern furnishings—some rooms overlook the skylighted pool. Ticker's lobby bar is a lively spot for a rendezvous. ⊠ *350 St. Mary Ave., R3C 3J2,* ☎ *204/942–0551 or 800/465–4329,* FAX *204/943–8702. 406 rooms. 3 restaurants, no-smoking rooms, indoor pool, outdoor pool, sauna, exercise room, cabaret. AE, DC, MC, V.*

$$$ 🏨 **Holiday Inn Airport/West.** This bright and sumptuous modern prop-
★ erty stands next to the Trans-Canada Highway's western approach to Winnipeg, near the airport, the racetrack, and shopping areas. Rooms are large, with modern earth-tone furnishings. Executive suites, decorated in blue and green, are a bit fancier. The atrium is a lush setting for the pool and poolside lounge. ⊠ *2520 Portage Ave., R3J 3T6,* ☎ *204/885–4478 or 800/465–4329,* FAX *204/831–5734. 210 rooms. 2 restaurants, indoor pool, sauna, exercise room. AE, DC, MC, V.*

$$$ 🏨 **Hotel Fort Garry.** Built in 1913 and known far and wide as the Grand Castle, the old railroad hotel is one of Winnipeg's gathering places. On the south edge of downtown, near Union Station, the hotel and its hushed, spacious lobby are furnished with inviting armchairs and original marble, brass, and crystal accents. Large guest rooms still have classic, dark-wood furnishings and floral wallpapers. ⊠ *222 Broadway, R3C 0R3,* ☎ *204/942–8251 or 800/665–8088,* FAX *204/956–2351. 246 rooms. 2 restaurants, cabaret, casino. AE, DC, MC, V.*

$$$ 🏨 **The Lombard.** The top luxury hotel in town is near Winnipeg's
★ hub—Portage and Main streets—and is connected by skywalk to office buildings and Portage Place Mall. The 21st-floor rooftop indoor pool makes a dramatic setting for a swim. Chimes has a contemporary atmosphere and light meals; other restaurants are the elegant Velvet Glove Dining Room and Café Express for quick meals at affordable prices. Formerly the Westin, the hotel is owned by a local family and managed by Canadian Pacific Hotels. ⊠ *2 Lombard Pl., R3B 0Y3,* ☎ *204/957–1350 or 800/228–3000,* FAX *204/956–1791. 350 rooms. 3 restaurants, no-smoking rooms, indoor pool, sauna, exercise room. AE, DC, MC, V.*

$$$ 🏨 **Place Louis Riel.** This luxury-class bargain is a converted apartment
★ building that has contemporary suites with living rooms, dining areas, and fully equipped kitchens. Though all rooms are up-to-date, the suites on the upper floors facing west are preferred because of their view of the Legislative Building. The excellent downtown location—adjacent to Eaton Place mall—is only one of the hotel's advantages. ⊠ *190 Smith St., R3C 1J8,* ☎ *204/947–6961, 800/665–0569 in Canada,* FAX *204/947–3029. 255 suites. Restaurant, lounge, no-smoking rooms, free parking. AE, DC, MC, V.*

$$$ 🏨 **Travelodge Hotel Downtown Winnipeg.** Canada's oldest budget chain placed this high-rise venture in a strategically desirable location, next to the bus depot and adjacent to The Bay department store and the Winnipeg Art Gallery. Rooms on the south side look out on the Legislative Building, and north-side rooms overlook the city. Guest rooms have subdued modern furnishings in either neutral or pastel colors. ⊠

360 Colony St., R3B 2P3, ☎ *204/786–7011 or 800/661–9563,* FAX *204/772–1443. 157 rooms. Restaurant, no-smoking rooms, indoor pool. AE, DC, MC, V.*

$$ 🖃 **Charter House.** Half the rooms in this five-story low rise on the south
★ side of downtown have balconies. Furnishings are contemporary motel style, and the atmosphere is friendly. The Rib Room is a popular and moderately priced. ✉ *330 York Ave., R3C 0N9,* ☎ *204/942–0101, 800/782–0175 in Manitoba,* FAX *204/956–0665. 90 rooms. 2 restaurants, no-smoking rooms, pool. AE, DC, MC, V.*

$$ 🖃 **Gordon Downtowner Motor Hotel.** There's nothing fancy here, but it's a good deal on the edge of downtown, a block from the Portage Place mall. Most rooms are decorated in dusty rose with gray carpeting. Modern two-room suites are the best bargains. ✉ *330 Kennedy St., R3B 2M6,* ☎ *204/943–5581,* FAX *204/947–3041. 40 rooms. Restaurant, pub, free parking. AE, DC, MC, V.*

$$ 🖃 **Journey's End.** This south-side lodging is a reliable choice. The adequate-size rooms are furnished in contemporary style, with rose or beige carpets, dusty-rose and earth-tone accessories. There is no charge for local phone calls, and morning coffee is free. ✉ *3109 Pembina Hwy., R3T 4R6,* ☎ *204/269–7390 or 800/668–4200,* FAX *204/261–7565. 80 rooms. Restaurant. AE, DC, MC, V.*

$$ 🖃 **Ramada Marlborough.** This ornate, 1914 Gothic structure in the financial district has vaulted ceilings and a stained-glass window and is home to Joanna's Café and Victor's (☞ Dining, *above*). The public areas and guest rooms are freshly decorated. Soft sofas provide comfortable seating in a spacious lobby that has marble floors, high ceilings, and wood paneling. ✉ *331 Smith St., R3B 2G9,* ☎ *204/942–6411, 204/942–2017, or 800/667–7666,* FAX *204/942–2017. 121 rooms. 2 restaurants. AE, DC, MC, V.*

Nightlife and the Arts

The Arts

FILM

In Winnipeg, the best places to find imports, art films, oldies, and midnight cult classics are **Cinémathèque** (✉ 100 Arthur St., ☎ 204/942–6795) and **Cinema 3** (✉ 585 Ellice Ave., ☎ 204/783–1097). The **Winnipeg Art Gallery** (✉ 300 Memorial Blvd., ☎ 204/786–6641) also has a cinema series.

MUSIC AND DANCE

Winnipeg's principal venue for serious music, dance, and pop concerts is the magnificent 2,263-seat Centennial Concert Hall in the **Manitoba Centennial Centre** (✉ 555 Main St., ☎ 204/956–1360). From September to mid-May Centennial Centre is the home of the **Winnipeg Symphony Orchestra** (☎ 204/949–3999). The acclaimed **Royal Winnipeg Ballet** (☎ 204/956–2792 or 800/667–4792) performs in Centennial Concert Hall in October, December, March, and May; it's a must for dance fans. The **Manitoba Opera** (☎ 204/942–7479) presents three operas a year—in November, February, and May—in Centennial Concert Hall.

The **Winnipeg Art Gallery** (✉ 300 Memorial Blvd., ☎ 204/786–6641) hosts jazz, blues, chamber music, and contemporary groups. For contemporary dance and new music, check out **Le Rendez-Vous** (✉ 768 av. Taché, ☎ 204/233–9214 or 204/237–7692) in St. Boniface. Other performance spaces include **Pantages Playhouse Theatre** (✉ 180 Market Ave. E, ☎ 204/986–3003) and the **Winnipeg Convention Centre** (✉ 375 York Ave., ☎ 204/956–1720).

THEATER

One of Canada's most acclaimed regional theaters, the **Manitoba Theatre Centre,** produces serious plays from many sources at the 785-seat Mainstage (⊠ 174 Market Ave., ☎ 204/942–6537) and more experimental work in the MTC Warehouse Theatre (⊠ 140 Rupert Ave., ☎ 204/942–6537). The **Prairie Theatre Exchange** focuses on local playwrights in an attractive facility in the Portage Place mall (⊠ Portage Ave. and Carlton St., ☎ 204/942–5483).

Nightlife

BARS AND CLUBS

Hy's Steak Loft (⊠ 216 Kennedy St., ☎ 204/942–1000) is convenient for cocktails and has a late-evening piano bar. A most convincingly British pub in the Exchange District is **The King's Head** (⊠ 120 King St., ☎ 204/957–1479).

CASINOS

Play blackjack, baccarat, la boule, and roulette at the **Crystal Casino** (⊠ 7th floor, Hotel Fort Garry, 222 Broadway Ave., ☎ 204/957–2600). There's state-of-the-art gaming at **McPhillips Street Station** (⊠ 484 McPhillips St., ☎ 204/957–3900). You can try your luck at **Club Regent** (⊠ 1425 Regent Ave., ☎ 204/957–2700).

MUSIC

The **Palomino Club** (⊠ 1133 Portage Ave., ☎ 204/772–0454) is a country-and-western hangout. Rhythm-and-blues fans can check out **Mustang Sally's** (⊠ 114 Market Ave., ☎ 204/957–2700). A somewhat sedate dance floor comes alive after 9 PM in **Windows Lounge** in the Sheraton Winnipeg (⊠ 161 Donald St., ☎ 204/942–5300).

Outdoor Activities and Sports

Participant Sports

BICYCLING AND JOGGING

Most public parks in Manitoba have marked biking and jogging paths. For information on routes, pick up maps from **Travel Manitoba** (☞ Visitor Information *in* Manitoba A to Z, *below*).

HEALTH AND FITNESS CLUBS

Drop-in rates and a full slate of classes and equipment are available at **Body Options** (⊠ 1604 St. Mary's Rd., ☎ 204/255–6600) and **Bodyworks** (⊠ 2 Donald St., ☎ 204/477–1691).

Spectator Sports

BASEBALL

The **Winnipeg Goldeyes** (☎ 204/982–2273] play AA baseball in the Northern League, with games at Winnipeg Stadium.

BASKETBALL

The **Winnipeg Cyclones** (☎ 204/944–8932) play in the International Basketball League at Winnipeg Convention Centre.

FOOTBALL

The **Winnipeg Blue Bombers** (☎ 204/784–2583) of the Canadian Football League play home games at the Winnipeg Arena.

HOCKEY

The **Manitoba Moose** (☎ 204/987–7825) of the International Hockey League play home games at the Winnipeg Arena.

HORSE RACING

Assiniboia Downs (⊠ 3975 Portage Ave., at Perimeter Hwy. W, ☎ 204/885–3330) hosts Thoroughbred racing May–October.

Shopping

Art and Crafts

The **Crafts Guild of Manitoba** (⌧ 183 Kennedy St., ☎ 204/943–1190) displays works by Manitoba carvers, weavers, and jewelers. **Northern Images** (⌧ 216 Portage Place Mall, 393 Portage Ave., ☎ 204/942–5501; Airport Executive Centre, 1790 Wellington Ave., ☎ 204/788–4806) markets the work of the Inuit and Déné members of the North Territories Co-operative, which owns the stores. Check out the **Great Canadian Print Company** (⌧ 75 Albert St., ☎ 204/942–1002) for native art. **The Upstairs Gallery** (⌧ 266 Edmonton St., ☎ 204/943–2734) has prints, drawings, wall hangings, and sculpture.

Malls and Shopping Districts

Downtown shopping is dominated by **Portage Place** (⌧ Portage Ave. between Balmoral and Carlton Sts.) and **Eaton Place** (⌧ Bounded by Graham Ave., Hargrave St., St. Mary Ave., and Donald St.), two malls with numerous stores, fast-food joints, and movie theaters. Across the Assiniboine River, the **Osborne Village** area (⌧ Osborne St. between River and Corydon Aves.) has 150 trendy boutiques and specialty shops, cafés, restaurants, and crafts shops.

Side Trips from Winnipeg

On day trips outside the city you can experience the area's fur-trading, Mennonite, and Icelandic heritage or head for a lovely beach.

Steinbach

69 *48 km (30 mi) southeast of Winnipeg.*

The town of Steinbach is populated with nearly 10,000 descendants of Mennonites who fled religious persecution in late-19th-century Europe. Note all the automobile dealerships: Manitoban car buyers flock here because of the Mennonite reputation for making square deals.

In the **Mennonite Heritage Village,** a 40-acre museum, guides demonstrate blacksmithing, wheat grinding, and old-time housekeeping chores while conversing in the Mennonite German dialect. During the Pioneer Days festival in early August, everyone wears costumes and demonstrates homespun crafts. An authentic and extremely low-priced restaurant serves Mennonite specialties, such as borscht, pierogi, and *ukrenky* (cheese or potato torte). ⌧ *Rte. 12, 2 km (1 mi) north of Steinbach,* ☎ *204/326–9661.* ⌧ *$4.* ☉ *May and Sept., Mon.–Sat. 10–5, Sun. noon–5; June–Aug., Mon.–Sat. 10–7, Sun. noon–7; Oct. and Apr., weekdays 10–4.*

Selkirk

32 km (20 mi) north of Winnipeg.

This town is notable for a structure that recalls Canada's early days. **70** **Lower Fort Garry,** built in 1830, is the oldest stone fort remaining from the Hudson's Bay Company fur-trading days. Nowadays, costumed employees describe daily tasks and recount thrilling journeys by York boat, the "boat that won the West." Beaver, raccoon, fox, and wolf pelts hang in the fur loft as a reminder of the bygone days. ⌧ *Rte. 9,* ☎ *204/785–6050.* ⌧ *$5.* ☉ *Grounds daily dawn–dusk; buildings mid-May–Sept. 2, daily 10–6.*

Grand Beach Provincial Park

71 *87 km (54 mi) northeast of Winnipeg.*

This park is on the eastern shore of Lake Winnipeg, the seventh-largest lake in North America. On summer weekends, crowds flock here from

Winnipeg for the white-powder sand, the grass-crowned 30-foot dunes, and a lagoon that makes bird-watchers' dreams come true. Grand Marais, at the southern portal of the park, has a few services such as a gas station and restaurant. ⊠ *Rte. 12,* ☎ *204/754–2212.* ☉ *May–Sept., daily.*

Gimli

 76 km (47 mi) north of Winnipeg.

Gimli, the largest Icelandic community outside the homeland, was once the center of the independent state of New Iceland. It still has an impressive harbor and marina on Lake Winnipeg. A giant Viking statue proclaims allegiance to the far-off island. The **Gimli Historical Museum,** on the Gimli harbor waterfront, preserves the ethnic heritage of early Ukrainian and Icelandic settlers and records the history of the Lake Winnipeg commercial fishing industry. ⊠ *Rte. 9,* ☎ *204/642–5317.* ☑ *$2.* ☉ *Mid-May–June, Wed.–Sun. 10–5; July and Aug., daily 10–6.*

Winnipeg A to Z

Arriving and Departing

BY CAR

Two main east–west highways link Winnipeg with the prairie provinces. The Trans-Canada Highway (Highway 1) runs through Winnipeg, Regina, and Calgary. West of Winnipeg the Yellowhead Highway (Highway 16) branches off the Trans-Canada and heads northwest toward Saskatoon and Edmonton.

Travelers from the United States can reach the Manitoba capital from Minneapolis along I–94 and I–29, connecting to Route 75 at the Canadian border. The driving distance between Minneapolis and Winnipeg is 691 km (428 mi).

BY PLANE

Winnipeg International Airport (☎ 204/983–8400), 8 km (5 mi) from the city, is served by Northwest, Air Canada, Canadian Airlines International, and several commuter airlines. Taxi fare downtown runs about $10–$12. Some airport-area hotels provide complimentary airport shuttles.

Getting Around

BY BUS

The **City of Winnipeg Transit System** (☎ 204/986–5700) operates an extensive network of buses throughout the city and metropolitan area. Adult fare is $1.40, and it's 80¢ for senior citizens and children over four; exact change is required and transfers are free.

BY TAXI

Taxis—relatively expensive by U.S. standards—can be found outside downtown hotels or summoned by phone. Car services are **Unicity** (☎ 204/947–6611) and **Duffy's Taxi** (☎ 204/775–0101).

Contacts and Resources

EMERGENCIES

Dial 911 for **fire, police, ambulance,** or **poison control.**

GUIDED TOURS

Several lines ply the Red and Assiniboine rivers between May and mid-October. The ***Paddlewheel River Rouge*** (☎ 204/942–4500) has a variety of cruises (dining, dinner-dance, evening), combining sailings with double-decker bus tours.

The **Prairie Dog Central Steam Train** (☎ 204/832–5259) follows a 58-km (36-mi) route from the Canadian National Railways (CNR) St. James

Station (⊠ 1661 Portage Ave.) to Grosse Isle on Sunday, from mid-May through September, departing at 11 AM and 3 PM.

Walking tours of the turn-of-the-century Exchange District begin at the Manitoba Museum of Man and Nature (⊠ 190 Rupert Ave., ☎ 204/943–3139 or 204/956–2830) during July and August.

HOSPITALS

Emergency rooms are located at the **Health Sciences Centre** (⊠ 700 William Ave., ☎ 204/787–3167 or 204/787–2306), **Riverview Health Centre** (⊠ 1 Morley Ave., ☎ 204/452–3411), and **Misericordia General Hospital** (⊠ 99 Cornish Ave., ☎ 204/788–8188).

LATE-NIGHT PHARMACY

Shopper's Drug Mart (⊠ 471 River Ave., ☎ 204/950–7000) is open 24 hours.

VISITOR INFORMATION

The **Government Tourist Reception Office** (⊠ Broadway and Osborne St., ☎ 204/945–3777 or 800/665–0040), housed in the Manitoba Legislative Building, is open May–Labor Day, daily 8:30 AM–9 PM; Labor Day–April, weekdays 8:30–4:30. The **Explore Manitoba Idea Centre** is open weekdays at The Forks ((⊠ 21 Forks Market Rd., ☎ 204/945–3777 or 800/665–0040). **Tourism Winnipeg** (⊠ 320–25 The Forks Market Rd., ☎ 204/943–1970) is open weekdays 8:30–4:30; and there's an airport location (☎ 800/665–0204) that's open 8 AM–9:45 PM.

ELSEWHERE IN MANITOBA

A clutch of sites from the city of Brandon to superb parks and the Hudson Bay polar-bear mecca of Churchill are some highlights of the province.

Brandon

73 *197 km (122 mi) west of Winnipeg.*

Brandon, Manitoba's second-largest city (population 40,000), is west of Winnipeg, along the Trans-Canada Highway. The **Commonwealth Air Training Plan Museum** contains pre–World War II aircraft from the time when the Royal Canadian Air Force had a major training school here. ⊠ *Airport, Hangar 1, Brandon Airport,* ☎ *204/727–2444.* ☞ *$3.* ☉ *May–Oct., daily 10–4; Nov.–Apr., daily 1–4.*

Spruce Woods Provincial Heritage Park

74 *180 km (112 mi) west of Winnipeg.*

In this park, among rolling hills covered with spruce and basswood, lies the desertlike **Spirit Sands**, a 16-square-km (7-square-mi) tract of cactus-filled sand dunes. Walk the self-guided trail through the dunes, but keep your eyes peeled for lizards and snakes! Your final destination will be **Devil's Punch Bowl**, a dramatic pit dug out by an underground stream. You can also tour the park in a horse-drawn covered wagon. The nearest town is Carberry, north of the park. ⊠ *Rte. 5,* ☎ *204/827–2543.* ☉ *May–Sept., daily.*

Falcon Lake

75 *143 km (89 mi) east of Winnipeg.*

The Falcon Lake development, within a lovely provincial park, has a shopping center, a golf course, tennis courts, a very good beach, a sailing club, and top-grade accommodations in the 34-room **Falcon Lake**

Resort & Club (☎ 204/349–8400). **Whiteshell Provincial Park,** a 2,590-square-km (984-square-mi) tract on the edge of the Canadian Shield, has 200 lakes with some of the best northern-pike, perch, walleye, and lake-trout fishing in western Canada. **Beaver Creek** trail is a short walk to such wilderness denizens as beaver and deer. Farther on, **West Hawk Lake** (or Crater Lake)—formed a few thousand years ago by a falling meteor—is 365 feet deep and full of feisty smallmouth bass. Scuba divers love it. ⊠ *Hwy. 1E,* ☎ *204/369–5232.* ⊙ *Daily 8 AM–11 PM.*

Hecla Island

76 *175 km (109 mi) north of Winnipeg.*

Hecla Provincial Park, about a 2½-hour drive from Winnipeg, is a densely wooded archipelago named for the Icelandic volcano that drove the area's original settlers to Canada. The park is on the central North American flyway, and 50,000 waterfowl summer here. **Moose Tower** is a good spot in the early morning and evening to view moose and other wildlife. The original 1880s **Hecla Icelandic Fishing Village** is restored near Gull Harbour, the tourist center of the park and site of the luxurious **Gull Harbour Resort** (☎ 204/475–2354), complete with a marina, hiking trails, and a devilishly difficult golf course. ⊠ *Rte. 8,* ☎ *204/378–2945.* ⊙ *May–Sept., daily.*

Wasagaming

77 *304 km (188 mi) northwest of Winnipeg via Rtes. 1 and 10.*

★ The town of Wasagming serves Manitoba's only national park. **Riding Mountain National Park** lies among rolling hills south of Dauphin in the western part of the province. It covers 3,026 square km (1,150 square mi) and comprises forests and grasslands that support a herd of bison. The townsite of Wasagaming is on Clear Lake, which is ideal for fishing and boating and offers supervised swimming. There is also a highly acclaimed 18-hole golf course. The **Elkhorn Ranch and Resort** (⊠ Box 40, Rte. 10, Dauphin, R0J 2H0, ☎ 204/848–2802) offers a nine-hole golf course, tennis, and trail rides. There is also plenty of camping, as well as other hotels and cabins nearby. ⊠ *Riding Mountain National Park, Wasagaming R0J 2H0,* ☎ *204/848–2811.*

Churchill

★ **78** *1,600 km (992 mi) north of Winnipeg.*

Churchill is Canada's northernmost seaport, on the shore of Hudson Bay. It has become a mecca for international travelers wanting to see polar bears up close. **Tundra Buggy Tours** (☎ 204/675–2121 or 800/544–5049) has specially designed vehicles that go out on the tundra for better viewing. Half-day tours, offered July–September, cost $74; full-day tours, offered in October and early November, cost $162. You can ride a Tundra Buggy to the **Tundra Buggy Lodge** ($312.50 per person per night, including meals), similar to a train, with viewing balconies, berths, and a dining car, which is stationed in the Churchill wilderness wherever wildlife viewing is best.

THE PRAIRIE PROVINCES A TO Z

Arriving and Departing

By Bus

Greyhound Lines (consult local directory) and local bus companies provide service from the United States, other parts of Canada, and throughout the prairie provinces.

By Plane

Air Canada and **Canadian Airlines International** have direct or connecting service from Boston, New York, Chicago, San Francisco, and Los Angeles to Winnipeg, Regina, Saskatoon, Calgary, and Edmonton. Commuter affiliates serve other U.S. and Canadian destinations. U.S. airlines serving the prairie provinces include **Northwest** to Winnipeg; **American, Delta,** and **United** to Calgary; **American, Delta,** and **Northwest** to Edmonton.

By Train

There is no direct rail service between the United States and the prairie provinces. **VIA Rail** trains (from New York and Connecticut, ☎ 800/361–3677; from the Atlantic seaboard, 800/561–3949; from the Midwest, 800/387–1144; from the western United States, 800/665–0200) connect eastern Canada and the West Coast through Winnipeg–Saskatoon–Edmonton.

Getting Around

By Car

Two main east–west highways link the major cities of the prairie provinces. The Trans-Canada Highway (Highway 1), mostly a four-lane divided freeway, runs through Winnipeg, Regina, and Calgary on its nationwide course. The two-lane Yellowhead Highway (Highway 16) branches off the Trans-Canada Highway west of Winnipeg and heads northwest toward Saskatoon, Saskatchewan, and Edmonton, Alberta. Traveling north–south, four-lane divided freeways connect Saskatoon–Regina (Highway 11) and Edmonton–Calgary (Highway 2).

From the United States, interstate highways cross the Canadian border, and two-lane highways continue on to major cities of the prairie provinces. From Minneapolis, I–94 and then I–29 connect to Route 75 at the Manitoba border south of Winnipeg. A main route to Alberta is I–15 north of Helena, Montana, which connects to Highway 2 and Routes 3 and 4 to Calgary.

By Plane

Canadian Airlines International (☎ 204/632–1250) offers flights to cities and towns throughout the Prairie Provinces.

By Train

VIA Rail (☎ 800/561–8630) operates train service between major cities and towns on two east–west routes through the Prairie Provinces.

Contacts and Resources

Visitor Information

Travel Alberta (✉ Box 2500, Edmonton T5J 2Z4, ☎ 403/427–4321; 800/222–6501 in Alberta; in the U.S. and Canada, 800/661–8888) distributes extremely comprehensive and useful free promotional literature. The office is open weekdays 9 to 4:30. **Travel Manitoba** (✉ 155 Carlton St., 7th floor, Winnipeg R3C 3H8, ☎ 204/945–3777 or 800/665–0040) distributes a free road map and several useful brochures.

The office is open weekdays 8:30 to 4:30. **Manitoba Travel Idea Centre** (✉ 21 Forks Market Rd., Winnipeg R3C 4T7, ☎ 204/945–3777) is intended primarily for walk-in traffic and is open Monday through Thursday, 10 to 6 and Friday, 10 to 8. **Manitoba Travel Information Centres,** just inside the Manitoba border along major routes, are open mid-May through early September, 8 AM to 9 PM. **Tourism Saskatchewan** (✉ 1900 Albert St., Suite 500, Regina S4P 4L9, ☎ 800/667–7191) can provide you with brochures and maps of attractions, accommodations, and parks inside and outside the province. The main office is open weekdays 8 to 7, Saturday 10 to 4. **Information centers,** in cities throughout Saskatchewan, also open in summer along major highways leading into the province.

6 Toronto

Founded by Scots who set up banks and built churches, Toronto now thrives on a mix of cultures. You'll experience these in attractions that range from the staid architecture of its abundant bank buildings to the sensual overload of ethnic markets and eateries. This cosmopolitan city on Lake Ontario has high-tone temples of art and culture, a vibrant theater scene, and plenty of fun spots, whether you want to shop in tony Yorkville or funky Queen Street West, or explore the action along the city's revived waterfront.

MUCH OF TORONTO'S EXCITEMENT is explained
by its ethnic diversity. Nearly two-thirds of the
3.2 million people who now live in the
metropolitan area were born and raised somewhere else. A half million Italians live here, as do the largest Chinese community in Canada and the biggest Portuguese population in North America. What this has meant to Toronto is the rather rapid creation of a mix of cultures—but without the slums, crowding, and tensions found in many other large cities around the world.

Updated by
Wendy Lindsay

Still, to give to its developing ethnic population all, or even most, of the credit for Toronto's becoming a cosmopolitan, world-class city in just a few decades would be a kind of reverse racism, and not totally correct, either. Much of the thanks must be given to the so-called dour Scots who set up the banks, built the churches, and created a solid base for a community that would come to such a healthy fruition in the four decades following World War II. Toronto, Canada's largest city, is clearly this country's center of culture, commerce, and communications—"New York run by the Swiss," according to Peter Ustinov.

Toronto has gained the nickname Hollywood North, because many major films have been made in this city, especially over the past decade, from *Moonstruck* to David Cronenberg's *Naked Lunch* and Tim Allen's *The Santa Clause* to such popular TV series as *Road to Avonlea*. Indeed, it is hard to walk about the city nowadays without tripping over a movie crew and a number of celebrities.

Toronto's roots go back to 1615, when a French explorer named Etienne Brûlé was led by Hurons to the land between the Humber and Don rivers, which was known to the Indians as Toronto ("a place of meetings"). Over the following two centuries it became a busy native village named Teiaiagon, a French trading post, and a British town named York. Finally, on March 6, 1834, the city was officially named Toronto again.

Pleasures and Pastimes

Dining
The formal haute cuisine establishments have all but faded into Toronto's gastronomic history, making way for bistros, cantinas, tavernas, trattorias, tapas bars, noodle bars, wine bars, and smart cafés. Steak houses are proliferating, and the cuisines of the world have appeared on Toronto's doorstep. The restaurants of Little Italy, a half dozen individual Chinatowns, urban and suburban, and Little India, have long served up fine cooking. Now, a tidal wave of restaurants specializing in the cuisines of Southeast Asia has hit. Korean, Vietnamese, Laotian, Thai, and Malaysian dishes are taking taste buds by storm with their assertive flavors: chili, ginger, lemongrass, coconut, lime, and tamarind. Toronto's brilliant young chefs recognize that when most customers start requesting "sauce on the side," the public's taste is changing; those with vision are looking over their shoulders toward California for a more creative marriage of fresh-market ingredients.

Museums
This metropolis by the lake possesses miles of museums. The Royal Ontario Museum, affectionately known as the ROM, is a sprawling giant that presents a brilliant and wildly diverse collection from mummies to Chinese art, totem poles to musical instruments. For art lovers, Toronto is the place to explore Canadian art, which is definitely overlooked by most American and European curators. Another outstanding institu-

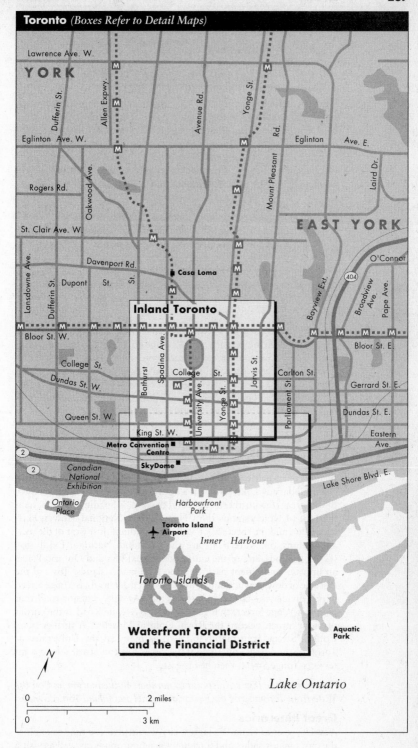

Toronto *(Boxes Refer to Detail Maps)*

Lawrence Ave. W.

YORK

Dufferin St.

Allen Expwy.

Avenue Rd.

Yonge St.

Eglinton Ave. W.

Eglinton Ave. E.

Rogers Rd.

Oakwood Ave.

Mount Pleasant Rd.

EAST YORK

Laird Dr.

St. Clair Ave. W.

Landsowne Ave.

Dufferin St.

Davenport Rd.

Dupont St. St.

■ **Casa Loma**

O'Connor

Bayview Ext.

Broadview Ave.

Pape Ave.

404

Inland Toronto

Bloor St. W.

Spadina Ave.

Bathurst

College

St.

Jarvis St.

Bloor St. E.

College St.

Dundas St. W.

University Ave.

Yonge St.

Carlton St.

Gerrard St. E.

Queen St. W.

Parliament St.

Dundas St. E.

King St. W.

■ **Metro Convention Centre**

Eastern Ave.

■ **SkyDome**

2

2

Canadian National Exhibition

Lake Shore Blvd. E.

Ontario Place

Harbourfront Park

✈ **Toronto Island Airport**

Inner Harbour

Toronto Islands

Waterfront Toronto and the Financial District

Aquatic Park

Lake Ontario

0   2 miles

0   3 km

tion is the Ontario Science Centre. Then, too, the city has offbeat museums devoted to the study of hockey, design, history, and even shoes.

Outdoor Activities and Sports

In Canada's largest city, sports are more of a religion than a pastime. The big professional baseball, basketball, football and hockey teams are considered civic treasures. When the Toronto Blue Jays won the World Series in 1992 and 1993, the province-wide celebration was felt across Canada. In 1996 the Toronto Argonauts football team won the 84th annual national contest for the coveted Grey Cup. When Toronto residents aren't watching sports, many pursue fitness. In the warmer months, the streets and lakefront brim with bikers, runners, in-line skaters, and walkers. When winter comes, outdoor skating is very popular, especially at Harbourfront and at Nathan Phillips Square.

Performing Arts

Toronto is not only Canada's capital of the lively arts; it has also become the third most important theater city in the English-speaking world, after New York and London. Productions range from the finest in classic and contemporary drama to West End and Broadway productions. True, Winnipeg has a very fine ballet, and Montréal's orchestra is superb. But no other city in Canada, and few in North America, can compete with the variety of music, opera, dance, and theater found here.

Shopping

Toronto prides itself on having some of the finest shopping in North America; indeed, most of the world's name boutiques can be found here. There's also a large artistic and crafts community, with many art galleries, custom jewelers, clothing designers, and artisans selling everything from sophisticated glass sculpture to native art, traditional crafts, antiques, quilts, wood carvings, and pine furniture. Local food items include wild rice, available in bulk or in gift packages, and maple syrup in jars or cans.

EXPLORING TORONTO

Imagine the downtown area of Toronto as a large rectangle. The southern boundary is Lake Ontario. The western edge, shooting north to Bloor Street (the northern edge) and beyond, is Spadina Avenue, near the foot of which stands the CN (Canadian National) Tower, Harbourfront, and the spectacular SkyDome Stadium. Just west of the rectangle along the waterfront are the Canadian National Exhibition (CNE) grounds, site of the enormous annual fair, and Ontario Place, an upscale amusement park built on man-made islands. Toward the east side of downtown, running from the lakefront north, is Yonge Street, which divides the city in half. University Avenue, a major road that parallels Yonge Street, changes its name to Avenue Road at the corner of Bloor Street, next to the Royal Ontario Museum. A further note: College Street, legitimately named, as many of the University of Toronto's buildings run along it, becomes Carlton Street where it intersects Yonge Street, then heads east.

Numbers in the text correspond to numbers in the margin and on the Waterfront Toronto and the Financial District and Inland Toronto maps.

Great Itineraries

A week's visit to Canada's largest city would give you time to explore the city's major sights and intriguing neighborhoods, as well as visit a few outstanding attractions outside the center. In three days, however, you can take in the cultural and architectural highlights downtown and near the waterfront, and get a taste of Toronto's cultural life, whether you see a play or attend a concert. With a few more days, you'd have time to visit the Toronto Islands, explore some city markets and shop in a number of neighborhoods, and check out some museums; you'd also be able to savor the city's varied dining scene more fully.

IF YOU HAVE 3 DAYS

Start an exploration of downtown Toronto at the grandiose Union Station; glance upward at the famed Royal York Hotel, which has defined Toronto's cityscape since 1928. Head north on Yonge, surveying the towering edifices of pride and progress above, before arriving at the Eaton Centre with its more than 300 shops, services and restaurants. Exit on Queen Street West and behold the magnificent New City Hall. Cold weather permitting, rent skates and glide across Nathan Phillips Square. On Day 2, ride the subway to Bloor and Yonge. Walk west along Bloor Street—an upscale shopping thoroughfare—to Avenue Road, where the Royal Ontario Museum awaits; plan on spending two to four hours at the museum. Exit the ROM on University Avenue, walking south to Queen's Park, home of Ontario's Romanesque-inspired Provincial Parliament Building. On Day 3, visit the Art Gallery of Ontario, which contains the largest collection in the world of Henry Moore sculptures. Then stroll along the waterfront, stopping at the Queen's Quay Terminal at Harbourfront and passing by the Sky-Dome. On a clear day, ride to the peak of the CN Tower.

IF YOU HAVE 5 DAYS

Extra time offers the opportunity to experience the city as locals live it. Besides the attractions mentioned in the three-day tour, you might try these: On a Saturday, conquer either the Kensington or St. Lawrence Market (☞ Shopping, *below*). Both are vibrant ventures, although the St. Lawrence at Front and Jarvis streets is larger and indoors. In summer, buy fresh ingredients for a picnic lunch before cruising across Lake Ontario on a ferry boat to the Toronto Islands. Plan to either walk or bike on the islands—no automobiles are permitted. In the late afternoon, you can explore Queen Street West—an exotic mix of the avant-garde. On Day 5, return to the Yorkville district, the epicenter of wealthy Toronto. Beyond the designer boutiques and elegant restaurants, check out the Bata Shoe Museum and, farther north, Casa Loma, a 20th-century medieval-style castle.

IF YOU HAVE 7 DAYS

Follow the three- and five-day itineraries above; then, on Day Six, rent a car (or use subways and buses) and choose among some easy, first-rate excursions (☞ Side Trips from Downtown Toronto, *below*). North of downtown, the Black Creek Pioneer Village re-creates a rural community of the 1880s; it's open May–December. Farther north and west, you can visit the stunning McMichael Canadian Art Collection, on over 100 acres of meadows. Its collection champions Canada's landscape artists known as the Group of Seven and is augmented by native and contemporary artworks. Northeast of downtown are the Ontario Science Centre and the Metro Toronto Zoo. These are great for kids; either could occupy a day. Day 7 would be a good time for exploring overlooked neighborhoods and sights, such as the Design Exchange and the Hockey Hall of Fame.

The Toronto Islands

The islands form a pleasant park with numerous attractions, including a stunning view of the Toronto skyline. The four thin, curved, tree-lined islands—Centre, Ward's, Algonquin, and Olympic—have been attracting visitors since 1833, four years before Victoria became queen and just a year before the town of York changed its name to Toronto.

A Good Walk

Just behind the giant Westin Harbour Castle is the debarkation point for ferries to the **Toronto Islands** ①. It takes only eight minutes for the quaint little ferries to chug across the tiny bay to different landings. On these islands, all transportation comes to you compliments of your feet: No cars are allowed anywhere. Your nostrils will wonder at the lack of exhaust fumes, while your feet will wonder why you insist on walking all the way along the boardwalk from Centre to Ward's Island (2½ km, or 1½ mi). You'll be wise to rent a bike (on Centre Island, a five-minute walk from the ferry) for an hour or more and work your way across the interconnected islands, perhaps with a stop at one of the island's **beaches.** If you are traveling with children, Centre Island is certainly the one to check out first. A few hundred yards from the ferry docks lies **Centreville,** an amusement park that's supposed to be a turn-of-the-century children's village. Perhaps most enjoyable for children is **Far Enough Farm,** which is near enough to walk to. Ward's Island has **Gibraltar Lighthouse.**

TIMING

Take the earliest possible ferry and return at your leisure. Plan on at least staying for a picnic lunch. Families may want to stay longer. If you love the outdoors and the weather is right, plan for the entire day.

Sights to See

Beaches. There are free changing rooms near each area but no facilities for checking your clothes. Swimming in the various lagoons and channels is prohibited. Yet there are great swimming areas at Hanlon's Point, Manitou Beach, and Ward Island. The beaches on Ward tend to be the least crowded. They're also the cleanest; there have been problems with the cleanliness of Lake Ontario's water over the past decade. Except for the hottest days in August, the Great Lake tends to be uncomfortably chilly, so bring appropriate clothing.

Centreville. The concept works wondrously well: True, the pizza, fries, and hot dogs are barely edible—pack a lunch!—but on the little Main Street there are charming shops, a town hall, a little railroad station, and more than a dozen rides, including a restored 1890s merry-go-round with more than four dozen hand-carved animals. There's no entrance fee to the modest, 14-acre amusement park, although you'll have to pay a nominal charge for each ride or buy an all-day pass. ⊠ *Centre Island,* ☎ *416/203–1113.* ⊠ *Day pass, $15.95.* ☉ *Mid-May–Labor Day, weekdays 10:30–6, weekends 10:30–8; Labor Day–Oct., weekends 10:30–6 weather permitting.*

Far Enough Farm. It has all kinds of animals to pet and feed, ranging from piglets to geese, cows to birds. This is a great treat for youngsters, especially the wee ones. ⊠ *Centre Island,* ☎ *416/393–8195.* ⊠ *Free.* ☉ *Daily, dawn–dusk.*

Gibraltar Lighthouse. Built in 1808 near the southwestern tip of Ward's Island, it is the oldest monument in the city still standing on its original site, but it cannot be entered. Right next to it is a pond stocked with rainbow trout and a concession for buying bait and renting rods. ⊠ *Gibraltar Point.*

❶ **Toronto Islands.** These are surely among the highlights of any trip to the city—especially from May through October. The more than 550 acres of parkland are irresistible for renting a bike, hiking, snowshoeing, or skiing cross-country with downtown Toronto over your shoulder. Encircling the islands are sandy **beaches** (☞ *above*); the best are on the southeast tip of Ward's Island, the southernmost edge of Centre Island, and the west side of Hanlan's Point. ☎ *416/392–8195*

for island information. Ferries, foot of Bay St., ☎ 416/392–8193 or
416/392–8186. 🖃 $4. ☉ Ferries: winter, daily every ½ hr or so until
10 or 11 AM, every hr or so thereafter; summer, daily 3 times per hr.

Harbourfront

Until the early 1980s, Toronto was notoriously negligent about its waterfront. The Gardiner Expressway, Lake Shore Boulevard, and a network of rusty rail yards stood as hideous barriers to the natural beauty
of Lake Ontario. Some 15 years ago the various levels of government
began a struggle to change this unfortunate situation. First came the
handsome Westin Harbour Castle Hotel and an attractive tower of condominiums at the foot of Yonge Street on Harbourfront. Today these
buildings are just part of a group of hotels, condominiums, shopping
malls, and recreational and cultural attractions that stretch for almost
a mile along the lakefront west of Yonge Street. Taxis and a transit line
can help you get around this area.

A Good Tour

Harbourfront ②, a lakefront cultural and recreational center, is within
walking distance of Union Station (☞ The Financial District, *below*).
If you're driving, head for the foot of Bay Street or Spadina Avenue and
park in one of the many lots. A streetcar also swings around from Union
Station to Harbourfront and on to Spadina Avenue. Begin at the Queen's
Quay Terminal, an eight-story shopping and cultural complex. Just west
of Queen's Quay is the Power Plant, which hosts art shows. Next door
is the Harbourfront Centre, which has ice skating, canoeing, and concerts. You can rent boats at the nearby Nautical Centre. On Maple Leaf
Quay, visit the outdoor antique market, especially on the weekends. Otherwise, you can visit the very popular and indoor Harbourfront Antique
Market. About a half-hour walk west of Harbourfront (you can use the
transit line along Queen's Quay to take you part of the way) is **Ontario
Place,** a 96-acre family-oriented experience that showcases the province
and Canada. Visible from Ontario Place and a 10-minute cab ride away
is the **CN Tower** ③, which has observation decks with great views of the
area; it's on Front Street, near Spadina Avenue, not far from the waterfront. In the shadow of the CN Tower is the **SkyDome** ④ stadium.
SkyDome and the CN Tower are linked to Union Station by a covered
walkway lined with fast-food outlets.

TIMING

While Harbourfront buzzes throughout the year, it is especially pleasant to visit from May through October, when Lake Ontario's breezes
aren't so bitterly cold. As the natives do their best to cope with the below-
zero temperatures, the district remains a year-round destination. A Harbourfront visit can easily stretch across an entire day, particularly if
there are children along. Be sure to check the local papers and magazines for special activities and events. Set aside at least one to two hours
for the CN Tower, a required stop for first-time visitors.

Sights to See

🖑 ❸ **CN Tower.** It's the tallest freestanding structure in the world, fully
1,815 ft, 5 inches high, and it really is worth a visit despite the steep
fee, if the weather is clear. Four elevators zoom up the outside of the
tower. The ride takes but a minute, going at 20 ft a second, a rate of
ascent similar to that of a jet-plane takeoff. But each elevator has only
one floor-to-ceiling glass wall, preventing vertigo. The CN Tower resembles a self-contained amusement park: The **Skypod,** about two-thirds
of the way up the tower, is seven stories high and has two observation
decks, a nightclub, and a fine-dining restaurant that revolves 360°. The
tower was originally constructed to house microwave communication

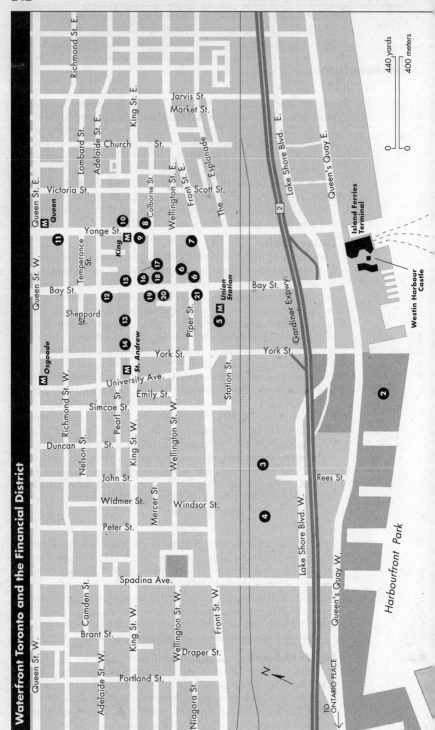

Waterfront Toronto and the Financial District

Richmond St. E.
Jarvis St.
Market St.
King St. E.
Lombard St.
Adelaide St. E.
Church St.
The Esplanade
Wellington St. E.
Front St. E.
Scott St.
Queen St. E.
Victoria St.
Queen
Colborne St.
Yonge St.
King
Temperance St.
Queen St. W.
Bay St.
Bay St.
Union Station
Sheppard St.
Osgoode
St. Andrew
York St.
York St.
Richmond St. W.
University Ave.
Emily St.
Simcoe St.
Pearl St.
Station St.
Duncan St.
Nelson St.
John St.
Widmer St.
Mercer St.
Windsor St.
Peter St.
King St. W.
Wellington St. W.
Lake Shore Blvd. E.
Queen's Quay E.
Island Ferries Terminal
Westin Harbour Castle
Queen's Quay W.
Gardiner Expwy.
Rees St.
Lake Shore Blvd. W.
Spadina Ave.
Camden St.
Brant St.
King St. W.
Wellington St. W.
Front St. W.
Draper St.
Adelaide St. W.
Portland St.
Niagara St.
Harbourfront Park
TO ONTARIO PLACE
Piper St.
N

440 yards
400 meters

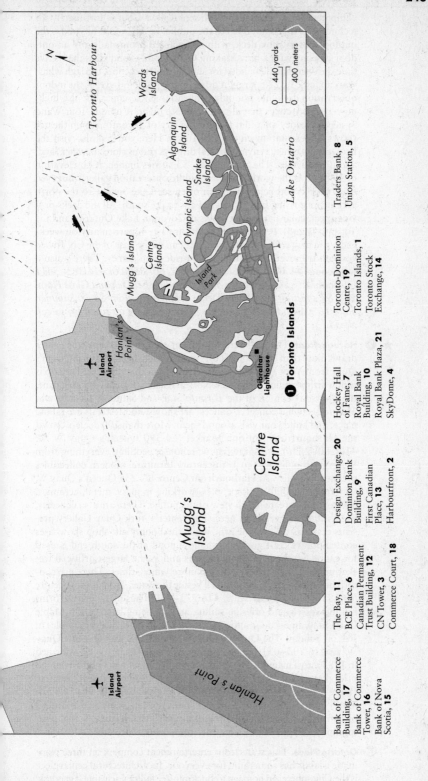

1 Toronto Islands

Bank of Commerce Building, **17**
Bank of Commerce Tower, **16**
Bank of Nova Scotia, **15**

The Bay, **11**
BCE Place, **6**
Canadian Permanent Trust Building, **12**
CN Tower, **3**
Commerce Court, **18**

Design Exchange, **20**
Dominion Bank Building, **9**
First Canadian Place, **13**
Harbourfront, **2**

Hockey Hall of Fame, **7**
Royal Bank Building, **10**
Royal Bank Plaza, **21**
SkyDome, **4**

Toronto-Dominion Centre, **19**
Toronto Islands, **1**
Toronto Stock Exchange, **14**

Traders Bank, **8**
Union Station, **5**

equipment for the Canadian National Railway, but unfortunately for techno buffs this is not open to the public. Level 2 of the Skypod is the **outdoor observation deck,** with an enclosed promenade and an outdoor balcony with a breathtaking **Glass Floor**—solid glass that is five times heavier than demanded for standard construction, through which you can look 1,122 ft straight down to the ground. Level 3, the **indoor observation deck,** has not only conventional telescopes but also high-powered periscopes that almost simulate flight. A unique Tour Wand System provides an audio tour of the city of Toronto. A minitheater shows a presentation on the CN Tower. Here you can also visit the **EcoDek,** multimedia environmental displays that explore air, water, land, and urban issues. The **Space Deck,** 33 stories higher, at an elevation of 1,465 ft, is the world's highest public observation gallery. But even from the Skypod below, you can often see Lake Simcoe to the north and the mist rising from Niagara Falls to the south. All the decks provide spectacular panoramic views of Toronto, Lake Ontario, and the Toronto Islands. Peak visiting hours are 11–4, particularly on weekends; you may wish to work around them. At the base of the CN Tower, you can try several high-tech action rides and games. There's also a food court. ⊠ *301 Front St. W,* ☎ *416/360–8500 or 416/362–5411 (restaurant).* ✆ *Observation deck, including EcoDek and Glass Floor, $12; $3 additional for Space Deck; action attractions $6.* ☉ *Summer, daily 10 AM–midnight; fall–spring times vary by up to an hr, so call ahead.*

★ ❷ **Harbourfront.** This 100-acre waterfront culture and recreation center draws more than 3 million visitors each year. It stretches along Queen's Quay from York Street for nearly a mile to Bathurst Street. The trip is well worth planning for: Check *Now* magazine, *Eye Weekly* magazine, the Thursday edition of the *Toronto Star,* and Saturday's *Globe and Mail* to see what concerts, dances, art shows, and festivals are taking place, and build your visit around them. More than 100 dealers crowd the **Harbourfront Antique Market** (⊠ 390 Queen's Quay W, ☎ 416/260–2626) in a sprawling warehouse, peddling everything from Victorian candlesticks to 18th-century furniture, modern collectibles to vintage jewelry. At **Harbourfront Centre** (⊠ 235 Queen's Quay W, ☎ 416/973–3000) craftspeople—working in glass, metal, ceramics, and textiles—create in full view of the public. There are also concerts, live theater, and readings here. The center's York Quay Gallery presents crafts as well as fine arts, while the Bounty gift shop showcases contemporary craft goods. A shallow pond at the south end is used for canoe lessons in warmer months and as the largest artificial ice-skating rink in North America in more wintry times. There are concerts at Molson Place, a band shell beside the water. The **Nautical Centre** (⊠ 283 Queen's Quay W, ☎ 416/973–4600) has many private firms renting vessels and offering sailing and canoeing lessons. On **Maple Leaf Quay,** an outdoor antiques market of 70 or so dealers doubles in size on Sunday. The **Queen's Quay Terminal** (⊠ 207 Queen's Quay W, ☎ 416/203–0510) is a 57-year-old food warehouse transformed in 1983 into a magnificent eight-story structure with delightful (though pricey) specialty shops, eateries, and the handsome 450-seat Premiere Dance Theatre. The **Power Plant** (⊠ 231 Queen's Quay W, ☎ 416/973–4949), in a 1927 building with a tall red smokestack, hosts exhibitions of contemporary arts—painting, sculpture, architecture, video, photography, design, installation, file, and performance art.

☾ **Ontario Place.** This waterfront entertainment complex on three manmade islands has something for everyone. Its architectural centerpiece is the **Cinesphere,** an homage to Buckminster Fuller's acclaimed geodesic dome at Expo '67. Inside the dome a six-story movie screen shows IMAX and 70mm films. You can explore the *Haida,* a World War II destroyer. Nightly concerts take place at the outdoor **Molson Canadian Amphitheatre. Children's Village** has water games, slides, puppet shows, clowns, magicians, and a children's theater. From mid-May through September, Ontario Place brims with people and concerts. ⊠ *South of Lake Shore Blvd.,* ☎ *416/314–9900.* 🎟 *Free; charge for some individual attractions.* ☯ *Mid-May–mid-Sept., daily 10 AM–midnight.*

🕲 ❹ **SkyDome.** One of Toronto's newest, and already one of its most famous, landmarks is the home of the Blue Jays. It is the world's only stadium with a fully retractable roof. Toronto has lost no opportunity to honor its World Series–winning baseball team—the official address of SkyDome is 1 Blue Jays Way. One way to see the huge 52,000-seat stadium is to buy tickets for a Blue Jays game or one of the many other events that take place here. These may include cricket matches, Wrestlemania, monster truck races, Peter Pan on ice, or even the opera *Aïda.* You can take a one-hour walking tour (including a 15-minute film). The tours are not available, however, when daytime events are scheduled. ⊠ *Tour entrance: Front and John Sts., between Gates 1 and 2, northeast corner of SkyDome,* ☎ *416/341–2770.* 🎟 *Tour $9.50.* ☯ *Tour leaves daily on the hr 10–3 or 4; call ahead.*

The Financial District

This is the epicenter of Canada's commercial life. To prove it, the nation's leading banks have erected towering skyscrapers, handsome and modern monuments to their achievements. You'll notice that many banks have more than one building named for them: This reflects the new ethic of recycling and reusing old buildings even if corporate pride requires the building of a fancier, more up-to-date headquarters. Many of the 20th century's best and brightest architects have contributed to Toronto's skyline, including I.M. Pei, Edward Durrell Stone, Mies van der Rohe, and Santiago Calatrava, among others. Running below all of this design splendor is the Underground City, a dazzling maze of tunnels that links the Financial District and keeps the businesspeople warm during the city's long cold season.

A Good Walk

On the south side of Front Street, between York and Bay streets across from the handsome Royal York Hotel, stands the monumental **Union Station** ⑤. On Bay Street just north of Front Street, a number of historic buildings have been incorporated into the striking **BCE Place** ⑥ with its huge, sophisticated galleria. At the northwest corner of Front Street and Yonge Street, you'll find the **Hockey Hall of Fame** ⑦ in a former branch of the Bank of Montréal now incorporated into BCE Place. Continue north on Yonge Street until you reach the northeast corner of Yonge and Colborne, where you will see the 1905–06 **Traders Bank** ⑧, the first "skyscraper" of the city. The next building to the north, built in 1913, is owned by Canadian Pacific, the famous company whose transcontinental railroad literally helped build a country. At the southwest corner of King and Yonge streets is the **Dominion Bank Building** ⑨, erected in 1913. Diagonally across the intersection is the first **Royal Bank Building** ⑩. Farther north along Yonge Street, at Richmond Street West, is the original Simpsons department store, now **The Bay** ⑪. Outside, continue a few steps west to Bay Street, a name synonymous with finance and power in Canada, as Wall Street is in the United States. Head south (left), back toward the lakefront. Just south of Adelaide Street, on the west side of Bay Street, is the **Canadian Permanent Trust Building** ⑫. Turn right (west) along King Street, and on your right stands the first of the towering bank buildings that have defined Toronto's skyline over the past two decades. Here is **First Canadian Place** ⑬, built in the early 1970s. Farther along you come to the second phase of the project, opened in 1983, which houses the ultramodern **Toronto Stock Exchange** ⑭. Returning to Bay Street, on the northeast corner of King and Bay streets, you see the **Bank of Nova Scotia** ⑮, built between 1949 and 1951, and partially replaced by the modern Scotia Tower just to the east. On the southeast corner of King and Bay streets is the "old" **Bank of Commerce Tower** ⑯, which for a third of a century was the tallest building in the British Commonwealth. Tucked behind this tower is the **Bank of Commerce Building** ⑰, built between 1929 and 1931 and one of Toronto's premiere bank buildings. The company's 57-story glass and stainless steel **Commerce Court** ⑱ is just south of the "old tower." Due west, across Bay Street, also on the south side of King Street, are the five black towers of the **Toronto-Dominion Centre** ⑲, the first International-style skyscrapers built in Toronto, which houses the bank's Gallery of Inuit Art, one of the finest of its kind in Canada. Immediately to the south of the Toronto-Dominion Centre towers is the fabulous **Design Exchange** ⑳, an exposition complex housed in the former Toronto Stock Exchange Building of 1937. Walk south another block to the northwest corner of Bay and Front streets: Here, in all its golden glory, is the **Royal Bank Plaza** ㉑. Running beneath the financial district is Toronto's **Underground City,** a sprawling maze of convenience shops, lobbies, and even trees.

TIMING
Plan on spending an entire day in the Financial District, especially if you stop at the various museums and shops along the way. Since many of these acclaimed buildings are closed on Saturday and Sunday, schedule this walk during a weekday. Be aware that during the cold season these marvelous edifices create chilling wind tunnels; dress appropriately and use the walkways of the Underground City if you need to.

Sights to See

⑰ **Bank of Commerce Building.** Nearly 70 years after its completion in 1931, this ranks as the best office tower in the financial district, combining monumentality and grace in a stunning 34-story structure. The Romanesque exterior is awe-inspiring, as is the equally compelling interior of marble floors, limestone walls, and bronze vestibule doors decorated with masks, owls, and animals. In the alcoves on each side of the entrance, murals trace the history of transportation. The bronze elevator doors are richly decorated; the vaulted banking hall is illuminated by period chandeliers. It's so beautiful that visitors are inclined to snap a photo, but bank officials forbid it. ✉ *25 King St. W.*

⑯ **Bank of Commerce Tower.** For 30 years the tallest building in the British Commonwealth, the tower has a set-back top; huge, carved human heads adorn all four sides. The base has bas-relief carvings, and there is marvelous animal and floral ornamentation around the vaulted entrance. ✉ *King and Bay Sts.*

⑮ **Bank of Nova Scotia.** This 25-story 1949 building by architect John Lyle has successfully been joined to a 68-story 1989 postmodern tower, **Scotia Tower.** The original building is in neoclassical style. Above the large exterior windows are sculptural panels inspired by Greek mythology. In the lobby, reliefs symbolizing four regions of Canada fill the walls below a brightly colored, gilded plaster ceiling. The north wall relief depicts some of the industries and enterprises financed by the bank. The original stainless-steel-and-glass stairway decorated with marine motifs leads up to the marble counters and floors. All this opens graciously into the recent Scotia Plaza building. ✉ *30–44 King St. W.*

⓫ **The Bay.** Built in 1895 as Simpson's department store, it was one of the city's first buildings with a steel-frame construction. Later bought by The Bay, the store no longer possesses the allure of Simpson's, but the top floor's **Thompson Gallery** (☎ 416/861–4571), a private collection of about 395 paintings by mainly Canadian artists, is worth a visit and the $2.75 admission fee. This emporium's melange of buildings blankets an entire block. The most stunning is the six-story 1907 structure at Queen and Yonge streets, with attractive terra-cotta decorations. The Bay is owned by Hudson's Bay Company, North America's oldest company, which received a fur-trading charter from King Charles II in 1670. ✉ *160–184 Yonge St.*

➏ **BCE Place.** Completed in 1990, this granite-and-glass mixed-use structure offers a dramatic contrast of old and new and represents the last hurrah of Toronto's 1980s building boom. What a triumph! Two towers—51 and 44 stories—incorporate 12 historic buildings, including the original Bank of Montréal building, plus a magnificent six-story galleria atrium designed by Santiago Calatrava. ✉ *161 Bay St.*

⓬ **Canadian Permanent Trust Building.** This stout skyscraper in the New York wedding-cake style was built in 1929. Ornate stone carvings decorate both the lower stories and the top, where carved, stylized faces peer down to the street below. The imposing vaulted entrance has polished brass doors, and even the elevator doors in the foyer are embossed brass. The spacious banking hall has a vaulted ceiling, marble walls and pillars, and a marble floor with mosaic borders. ✉ *320 Bay St.*

⓲ **Commerce Court.** The Bank of Commerce's (☞ *above*) sister structure is a 57-story glass and stainless steel tower built in 1968. ✉ *243 Bay St.*

⓴ **Design Exchange.** Since its opening in 1994, the DX has emerged as North America's most innovative design exposition and promotion center, encompassing architecture, decorative arts, graphics, and interiors. All this glory stands in a stunning Art Deco structure of polished pink granite and smooth buff limestone that once housed the Toronto Stock Exchange. The Toronto-based architectural firm of KPMB Associates gracefully blended the past with the present here, preserving Charles Comfort's famed murals above the historic trading floor. ✉ *234 Bay St.,* ☎ *416/363–6121.* 🎟 *$5.* ☼ *Tues.–Fri. 10–6, weekends noon–5.*

➒ **Dominion Bank Building.** Erected in 1913, this classic Chicago-style skyscraper has a marble and bronze stairway leading to the second floor. Upstairs, the opulent banking hall has a marble floor and marble walls. On the ornate plaster ceiling are reproduced the coats of arms of the nine Canadian provinces in existence at the time it was built. ✉ *King and Yonge Sts., southwest corner.*

⓭ **First Canadian Place.** This 72-story office tower is difficult to miss. Designed in the early 1970s by Edward Durrell Stone for the Bank of Montréal, the edifice is covered in Italian white marble. He deliberately faced it with white to contrast with the black of the Toronto-Dominion Centre, to the south, and with the silver of the Commerce Court tower, diagonally opposite. The marble theme continues inside the glamorous lobby. ✉ *50 King St. W.*

🐥 ➐ **Hockey Hall of Fame.** Writer John Robert Columbo observed that the two distinctly Canadian institutions are the United Church of Canada and the National Hockey League. So, it is appropriate that in this world hockey capital sits a first-rate tribute to the fast and furious winter sport. In addition to showcasing the coveted Stanley Cup trophy, the Hall of Fame contains 13 zones, including one where visitors can take shots at a computer-generated target; another is a precise replica (right down to the trainer's whirlpool) of the Montréal Canadiens' dressing room. There's also a store that carries an array of hockey jerseys, skates, and other apparel, as well as souvenirs. Even non-hockey fans can appreciate this multimedia exhibition, which is inventively based in a historic branch of the Bank of Montréal from 1893. An archive and resource library is also available by appointment. ⊠ *BCE Place, Concourse Level,* ☎ *416/360–7765.* 🎟 *$9.50.* ⊙ *Weekdays and Sun. 10:30–5, Sat. 9:30–6.*

❿ **Royal Bank Building.** Built in 1913 for the Royal Bank, it has a distinctive cornice, an overhanging roof, a decorative pattern of sculpted ox skulls above the ground-floor windows, and classically detailed leaves at the top of the Corinthian columns. ⊠ *King and Yonge Sts., northeast corner.*

㉑ **Royal Bank Plaza.** This 1976 building is already a classic of its kind. Go into the 120-ft-high banking hall to see the hanging sculpture by Jesus Raphael Soto. ⊠ *Bay and Front Sts., northwest corner.*

⓳ **Toronto-Dominion Centre.** Mies van der Rohe, a master of modern architecture, designed this austere five-building masterwork, even though he died in 1969 before it was fully realized. As in his acclaimed Seagram Building in New York, Mies stripped these buildings to their skin and bones of bronze-color glass and black metal I-beams. The tallest tower reaches 56 stories. The only decoration consists of geometric repetition, and the only extravagance is the use of rich materials, such as marble counters and leather-covered furniture. Walk inside the low-rise square banking pavilion at King and Bay to experience a virtually intact Mies interior. Here you can visit the **Gallery of Inuit Art,** one of the few galleries in North America devoted to Inuit art. The Toronto-Dominion Bank's incredible collection equals that of the Smithsonian Institution. The gallery focuses attention on Canada's huge and unexplored northern frontier. ⊠ *Centre: 55 King St. W.* ⊠ *Gallery: 79 Wellington St.,* ☎ *416/982–8473.* 🎟 *Free.* ⊙ *Weekdays 8–6, weekends 10–4.*

⓮ **Toronto Stock Exchange.** At North America's second-largest stock exchange, go to the fourth-floor visitor center, where you can learn about the securities industry through colorful displays or even join in daily presentations. The attractions are many: a 140-seat auditorium, an educational audiovisual presentation, a real-time stock-quotation terminal, and avant-garde artworks by General Idea and Robert Longo. ⊠ *Exchange Tower, 2 First Canadian Pl.,* ☎ *416/947–4700.* 🎟 *Free.* ⊙ *Tues.–Thurs. 10, 2; Fri. 2.*

❽ **Traders Bank.** Built in 1905–06, the first "skyscraper" in the city, 15 stories high, came complete with an observation deck, now closed. The building has been dwarfed by 50-story giants. ⊠ *67 Yonge St.*

Underground City. The origins of what is known as the largest pedestrian walkway in the world go back over a generation. One can walk—and shop, eat, and browse—without ever seeing the light of day, from beneath Union Station to the Royal York Hotel, the Toronto-Dominion Centre, First Canadian Place, the Sheraton Centre, the Eaton Centre, and the Atrium-on-Bay. Altogether, it extends through nearly 5 km (3 mi) of tunnels and seven subway stops. If you become disoriented, head for a subway station: Maps of the underground area are posted near the turnstiles. Enter the subterranean community from anywhere between Dundas Street on the north and Union Station on the south, and you'll encounter art exhibitions, buskers, fountains, and trees growing as much as two stories high, as well as crowds of businesspeople on breaks from their offices in the towers above.

⑤ Union Station. Designed in 1907, when trains were still as exciting as space shuttles are today, the station was opened in 1927 by the Prince of Wales. If any building in Toronto can be called monumental, this is it. Over 750 ft long and set well back along its Front Street block, this landmark borrows from classical architecture to create a magnificently powerful yet simple structure. Walk along the lengthy concourse; bask in the light flooding through the high, arched windows at each end of the mammoth hall. Try to imagine the awe of the immigrants who poured into Toronto between the wars by the tens of thousands, staring up at the towering ceiling of Italian tile or leaning against one of the 22 pillars, each 40 ft tall and weighing 75 tons. ✉ *65–75 Front St. W.*

Central Toronto

This walk highlights Toronto's commercial and cultural diversity. It begins at Eaton Centre on Yonge Street and extends westward to Spadina Avenue, the city's bustling discount thoroughfare. In between lie the New City Hall and the Art Gallery of Ontario. A walk through Chinatown provides a sense of the city's ethnic diversity.

A Good Walk

Start at **Eaton Centre** ㉒, a 3-million-square-ft shopping complex extending along the west side of Yonge Street all the way from Queen Street up to Dundas Street (with subway stops at each end) that has become the city's number-one tourist draw. Exit the Eaton Centre at Queen Street and walk just one long block west to Toronto's city halls. The **Old City Hall** ㉓ is the very beautiful building at the northeast corner of Queen and Bay streets, sweetly coexisting with the futuristic **New City Hall** ㉔, just across the street, on the west side. West of University Avenue on Queen Street stands **Campbell House** ㉕, a living museum. Walk up University Avenue; just north of the New City Hall begins Toronto's main **Chinatown.** Huge Chinese characters hang over the **52nd Division Police Station** ㉖, on the west side of Simcoe Street, just south of Dundas Street. Turn left off Dundas Street onto McCaul Street to enter the **Ontario College of Art and Design Gallery** ㉗. Directly across the street is **Village by the Grange** ㉘, an apartment and shopping complex. Return to Dundas Street and head west to the **Art Gallery of Ontario** ㉙. The stretch of **Spadina Avenue** from Queen Street to College Street has never been fashionable, but on it you'll find a treasure trove of offbeat stores. **Kensington Market** ㉚ is a delightful side tour off Spadina Avenue, where you'll find bargains of the more edible kind. Afterward, you can rest in **Bellevue Square.**

TIMING

Set aside at least a half day for this tour. It is an excellent weekend adventure, although the New City Hall is closed on Saturday and Sunday. One of the best times to explore Chinatown is on a Sunday, when business booms; Kensington Market is closed that day, however. You can plan an entire sojourn around Eaton Centre. A visit to the Art Gallery of Ontario can easily extend from two to four hours; note that the gallery is closed Monday and Tuesday.

Sights to See

★ ㉙ **Art Gallery of Ontario.** From extremely modest beginnings in 1900, the AGO (as it's known) is now in the big leagues in terms of exhibits and support. A 1992 renovation has won international acclaim and put it among North America's top 10 art galleries. The **Henry Moore Sculpture Centre** has the largest public collection of Moore's sculpture in the world. The **Canadian Wing** includes major works by such northern lights as Emily Carr, Cornelius Krieghoff, David Milne, and Homer Watson. Visitors of any age can drop by the **Anne Tannenbaum Gallery**

250

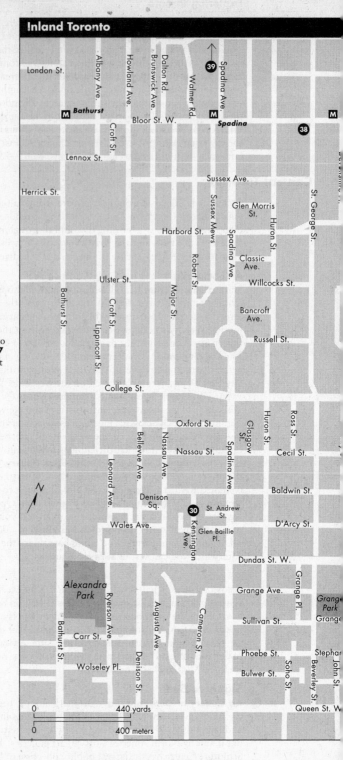

Inland Toronto

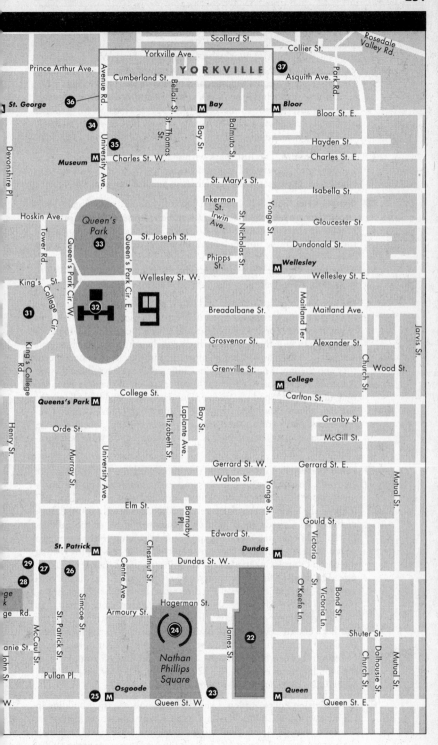

Scollard St.

Rosedale Valley Rd.

Collier St.

Yorkville Ave.

Prince Arthur Ave.

YORKVILLE

Cumberland St.

Asquith Ave.

Park Rd.

St. George

M *Bay*

M *Bloor*

Bloor St. E.

Hayden St.

Museum

Charles St. W.

Charles St. E.

St. Mary's St.

Isabella St.

Inkerman St.

Irwin Ave.

Gloucester St.

Hoskin Ave.

Queen's Park

St. Joseph St.

Phipps St.

Dundonald St.

Yonge St.

Wellesley

King's

Wellesley St. W.

Wellesley St. E.

Breadalbane St.

Maitland Ave.

Maitland Ter.

Grosvenor St.

Alexander St.

Jarvis St.

Grenville St.

Wood St.

Church St.

College

College St.

Carlton St.

Orde St.

Granby St.

McGill St.

Gerrard St. W.

Gerrard St. E.

Walton St.

Yonge St.

Elm St.

Barnaby Pl.

Edward St.

Gould St.

Victoria St.

Mutual St.

St. Patrick

Dundas

Dundas St. W.

Chestnut St.

O'Keefe Ln.

Hagerman St.

Armoury St.

James St.

Shuter St.

Nathan Phillips Square

Bond St.

Victoria St.

Dalhousie St.

Church St.

Mutual St.

Osgoode

Queen

Queen St. W.

Queen St. E.

Pullan Pl.

Henry St.

Murray St.

University Ave.

Laplante Ave.

Elizabeth St.

Bay St.

Simcoe St.

St. Patrick St.

McCaul St.

Centre Ave.

John St.

Devonshire Pl.

Tower Rd.

St. College Cir.

King's College Cir.

King's College Rd.

Queen's Park Cir. W.

Queen's Park Cir. E.

Avenue Rd.

University Ave.

Bellair St.

St. Thomas St.

Bay St.

Balmuto St.

St. Nicholas St.

School on Sunday and explore painting, printmaking, and sculpture in Toronto's most spectacular studio space. The museum arranges numerous other workshops and special activities. The AGO also has a growing collection of works by Rembrandt, Hals, Van Dyck, Hogarth, Reynolds, Chardin, Renoir, de Kooning, Rothko, Oldenburg, Picasso, Rodin, Degas, Matisse, and many others. The **Grange,** a historic house just behind the AGO, is a perfect place to browse, either before or after a visit to the gallery. ⊠ *317 Dundas St. W, 3 blocks west of St. Patrick station on University subway line,* ☎ *416/979–6648.* ⬚ *$7.50, Wed. evening free.* ☉ *Wed. 10–10, Thurs.–Sun., 10–5:30.*

Bellevue Square. This little park with shady trees, benches, and a wading pool and playground is a good place to rest after a visit to Kensington Market (☞ *below*). ⊠ *Denison Sq. and Augusta Pl.*

㉕ **Campbell House.** Built in 1822 and tastefully restored with elegant 18th- and early 19th-century furniture, Campbell House is one of Toronto's most charming living museums. Costumed hostesses will tell you about the social life of the upper class of the period. Guided tours are available. ⊠ *160 Queen St. W,* ☎ *416/597–0227.* ⬚ *$3.50.* ☉ *Oct.–mid-May, weekdays 9:30–4:30; mid-May–Oct., weekdays 9:30–4:30, weekends noon–4:30.*

Chinatown. Diverse, exciting, and lively, this is the largest Chinatown in Canada and one of the largest in North America. You'll pass shops selling reasonably priced silk blouses and antique porcelain, silk kimonos for less than half the price elsewhere, lovely sake sets, and women's silk suits. More than 100,000 Chinese live in the city; just over a century ago there was only one—Sam Ching, who ran a hand laundry on Adelaide Street. Today, Chinatown covers much of the area bounded by Queen Street, Spadina Avenue, Dundas Street, and Bay Street. On Sunday, up and down Spadina Avenue and along Dundas Street, Chinese music blasts from storefronts, cash registers ring, abacuses clack, and bakeries, markets, herbalists, and restaurants do their best business of the week.

㉒ **Eaton Centre.** Even if you rank shopping with the flu, you may be charmed, possibly dazzled, by this impressive environment, Toronto's number-one tourist attraction. From its graceful glass roof, arching 127 ft above the lowest of the mall levels, to Michael Snow's exquisite flock of fiberglass Canada geese floating in the open space of the galleria, to the glass-enclosed elevators, porthole windows, and nearly two dozen graceful escalators, there are plenty of good reasons for visiting the Eaton Centre. Galleria Level 1 contains two food courts; popularly priced fashions; photo, electronics, and record stores; and much "convenience" merchandise. Level 2 is directed to the middle-income shopper; Level 3 has the highest fashion and prices. **Eaton's,** one of Canada's classic department-store chains, has a nine-floor branch here. At the southern end of Level 3 is a skywalk over Queen Street that connects the Eaton Centre with **The Bay,** a seven-floor department store. Dozens of restaurants can be found here. A 17-theater cinema complex is at the Dundas Street entrance. ⊠ *220 Yonge St.,* ☎ *416/598–2322.* ☉ *Weekdays 10–9, Sat. 9:30–6, Sun. noon–5.*

㉖ **52nd Division Police Station.** Even the large police station building in Chinatown has a Chinese flavor. Large Chinese characters identify it, demonstrating the Asian community's strong influence here. Otherwise, the postmodern building of 1977 recalls the Art Deco craze of the 1930s. ⊠ *225 Dundas St. W,* ☎ *416/808–2222.*

㉚ **Kensington Market.** This old, steamy, smelly, raucous, colorful, European-style marketplace titillates all the senses. Go and explore, especially during warmer weather, when the goods pour out into the narrow streets: Russian rye breads, barrels of dill pickles, fresh fish on ice, mountains of cheese, bushels of ripe fruit, and crates of chickens and rabbits that will have your children both giggling and horrified. Jewish and Eastern European stores sit side by side with Portuguese, Caribbean, Latin American, and East Indian shops—with Vietnamese, Japanese, and Chinese establishments sprinkled throughout. ⊠ *Northwest of Dundas St. and Spadina Ave.,* ☎ *416/979–3757.* ☉ *Daily 6– 6; hrs vary; many stores closed Sun.*

㉔ New City Hall. The futuristic-looking complex was the result of a massive international competition in 1958. The winning presentation, by Finnish architect Viljo Revell, was very controversial: two towers of differing height, and curved! But there is a logic to it all: An aerial view of the New City Hall shows a circular council chamber sitting like an eye between the two tower "eyelids." Within months of its opening in 1965, the New City Hall became a symbol of a thriving city. Annual events here include the Spring Flower Show in late March; the Toronto Outdoor Art Exhibition early each July, and the Cavalcade of Lights from late November through Christmas each year, when more than 100,000 sparkling lights are illuminated across both city halls (☞ Old City Hall, *below*). The underground garage holds 2,400 cars. ⊠ *100 Queen St. W,* ☎ *416/392–9111, TDD 416/392–7354.* ⌂ *Tour free.* ☉ *Weekdays 8:30–4:30; cafeteria daily 7:30–4; guided tour weekdays 10, 11, and 2.*

㉓ Old City Hall. Considered one of North America's most impressive municipal halls in its heyday, the building was designed by E. J. Lennox; it opened in 1899. When the New City Hall debuted in 1965, the Friends of Old City Hall organized to ensure its preservation, while also heightening Toronto's awareness of its architectural heritage. Since the opening of its younger sister, Old City Hall has been the site for the provincial courts, county offices, and thousands of low-cost marriages. The fabulous gargoyles above the front steps were apparently the architect's witty way of mocking certain turn-of-the-century politicians. There is a great stained-glass window as you enter. The handsome old structure stands in delightful contrast to its daring and unique sibling. ⊠ *60 Queen St. W,* ☎ *416/327–5675.* ☉ *Weekdays 8:30–4:45.*

㉗ Ontario College of Art and Design Gallery. Across the street from the Art Gallery of Ontario (AGO), the college's third-floor gallery shows works by students, faculty, and alumni. It is one of Canada's major art institutions and an important exhibit space for emerging artists and designers. ⊠ *291 Dundas St. (enter on McCaul St.),* ☎ *416/977–6000, ext. 262.* ⌂ *Free.* ☉ *Wed.–Sat. noon–6.*

Spadina Avenue. Toronto's widest street has been pronounced "Spa*dye*-nah" for a century and a half. For decades it has contained a collection of inexpensive stores, factories that sell wholesale if you have connections, ethnic food and fruit stores, and eateries, including some often first-class, if modest-looking, Chinese restaurants sprinkled throughout the area. Each new wave of immigrants—Jewish, Chinese, Portuguese, East and West Indian, South American—has added its own flavor to the mix, but Spadina-Kensington's basic bill of fare is still bargains galore. Here you'll find gourmet cheeses at gourmet prices, fresh (no, not fresh-frozen) ocean fish, fine European kitchenware at half the prices you'll see in stores in the Yorkville area, yards of remnants piled high in bins, designer clothes minus the labels, and the occasional rock-and-roll night spot and interesting greasy spoon. ⊠ *Spadina, between College and Queen Sts.*

㉘ **Village by the Grange.** This apartment and shopping complex has more than 100 shops selling everything from ethnic fast food to serious art. It's a perfect example of wise, careful blending of the commercial and the residential. ⊠ *89 McCaul St.,* ☎ *416/598–1414.*

North-Central Toronto

The competing interests of academia, culture, and commerce all converge at the corner of University Avenue and Bloor Street. Before reaching this landmark intersection—where the Royal Ontario Museum stands—the major forces of Toronto metropolitan life unfold: government, industry, and the University of Toronto. Even though all these sites lie in the middle of a busy city, the area is surprisingly tranquil, particularly on weekends.

A Good Tour

University Avenue runs from downtown Toronto at Front Street to Bloor, where it becomes Avenue Road and runs to the city's northern fringes. West of the avenue, north of College Street, lies the **University of Toronto** ㉛. Follow King's College Road north from College Street to King's College Circle. At the top of the circle is Hart House, the Gothic-style student center. Continue around the circle to the Romanesque University College. Next is Knox College, whose Scottish origins are evident in the bagpipe music that escapes from the building at odd hours. On the west side of the circle, the Medical Sciences Building is a giant assemblage of Brutalist architecture. Return to College Avenue and walk west to St. George, where you can proceed north to the Forestry Building and Sidney Smith Hall. At the crossroads of Hardord and Hoskin Avenue, turn right onto Hoskin and walk past Massey College.

From Massey, follow Queen's Park Circle south. The **Provincial Parliament Buildings** ㉜ sit in the middle of **Queen's Park** ㉝. East of the park is the Ontario Legislative Building. Just to the north of Queen's Park is the revered **Royal Ontario Museum** ㉞ (ROM), which could occupy you for most of a day. Across University Avenue stands the **George R. Gardiner Museum of Ceramic Art** ㉟, home to a rarefied $25 million collection of European ceramics. Next, you can visit the upscale shopping area of **Yorkville** ㊱, just to the north. A block north of Bloor and Yonge streets, east of Yorkville, stands the magnificent **Metropolitan Toronto Reference Library** ㊲. Several blocks west, across the street from the St. George subway station near Bloor Street, is the **Bata Shoe Museum Collection** ㊳. A subway ride will take you to the final stop, **Casa Loma** ㊴, a spectacular castlelike mansion north of the center just off Spadina Avenue.

TIMING

Schedule your tour between Tuesday and Saturday, when the museums and shops are open. Give yourself a full day: Even a highly abbreviated visit to the ROM takes a minimum of two hours, and shoppers will want to allow time to browse in Yorkville.

Sights to See

㊳ **Bata Shoe Museum Collection.** The collection, the only one of its kind in North America, contains more than 10,000 items of footwear from nearly every country in the world, some dating back more than 4,000 years. Items such as pressurized sky-diving boots, iron-spiked shoes used for crushing chestnuts, and smugglers' clogs are just a few of the pieces you'll see. ⊠ *327 Bloor St. W,* ☎ *416/979–7799.* 🖃 *$6, free 1st Tues. of month.* ☉ *Tues., Wed., Fri., and Sat. 10–5, Thurs. 10–8, Sun. noon–5.*

🐾 ③⑨ **Casa Loma.** Architect E. J. Lennox, who also designed Toronto's Old City Hall and the King Edward Hotel, created a 20th-century castle here, with 98 rooms, two towers, secret panels, long, creepy passageways, and some superb views of Toronto. The medieval-style castle cost over $3 million to build shortly before World War I. You tour it at your own speed, guided by a tape recording. Wear sensible shoes: You'll have walked a good mile by the time you're done. ⊠ *1 Austin Terr., Spadina Ave. south of St. Clair Ave., near Dupont subway stop,* ☎ *416/923–1171.* ⊡ *$8.* ⊙ *Daily 9:30–4.*

③⑤ **George R. Gardiner Museum of Ceramic Art.** The collection focuses on 17th-century English delftware and 18th-century yellow European porcelain but also has pre-Columbian works from Olmec and Maya times. There's also a display of Italian commedia dell'arte figures, especially Harlequin. Don't miss the museum's gift shop, which stocks many unusual items. ⊠ *111 Queen's Park, across University Ave. from ROM,* ☎ *416/586–8080.* ⊡ *Free.* ⊙ *Mon.–Sat. 10–5 (Tues. until 8), Sun. 11–4.*

③⑦ **Metropolitan Toronto Reference Library.** This impressive library was designed by one of Canada's most admired architects, Raymond Moriyama, who also created the Ontario Science Centre. Arranged around an interior atrium, the library gives a delightful sense of open space. Fully one-third of the more than 1.3 million books—spread across 28 mi of shelves—are available to the public. In the headphone-equipped audio carrels, you may listen to any one of more than 10,000 albums. Open on Saturday from 2 to 4 and by appointment, the **Arthur Conan Doyle Room** houses the finest public collection of Holmesiana anywhere, with records, films, photos, books, manuscripts, and letters. ⊠ *789 Yonge St., north of Bloor St.,* ☎ *416/393–7000 or 416/393–7131.* ⊡ *Free.* ⊙ *Mon.–Thurs. 10–8, Fri. and Sat. 10–5, Sun. 1:30–5.*

③② **Provincial Parliament Buildings.** You can get a taste of Ontario's history and government here. Surrounded by Queen's Park, the pink, 1889 buildings have a heavy, almost Romanesque quality. Inside are huge, lovely halls that echo a half millennium of English architecture. The long hallways are hung with hundreds of oils by Canadian artists. If you take one of the frequent (and free) tours, you will see the chamber where the 130 elected representatives from across Ontario, called MPPs (Members of Provincial Parliament), meet on a regular basis. There are two heritage rooms—one each for the parliamentary histories of Great Britain and Ontario—filled with old newspapers, periodicals, and pictures. The lobby holds a fine collection of minerals and rocks of the province. On the lawn in front of the Parliament Buildings, facing College Street, stand many statues, including one of Queen Victoria and one of Canada's first prime minister, Sir John A. Macdonald. ⊠ *1 Queen's Park, University Ave. subway, Queen's Park stop,* ☎ *416/325–7500.* ⊡ *Free.* ⊙ *Guided tour mid-May–Labor Day, daily on the hr 9–4, weekends every ½ hr 9–11:30 and 1:30–4; frequent tours rest of the year; also at 6:45 PM when evening sessions are held.*

③③ **Queen's Park.** Many visitors consider this to be the soul of Toronto. Surrounding the large oval-shaped patch of land are medical facilities to the south, the University of Toronto to the west, and the Royal Ontario Museum to the north. To most natives, Queen's Park is chiefly synonymous with politics, as the Provincial **Parliament Buildings** sit in the middle of this charming urban oasis. ⊠ *Queen's Park Circle, between College St. and Bloor St. W.*

★ 🐾 ③④ **Royal Ontario Museum** (ROM). Ongoing renovations have restored the ROM to its status as—in the words of the Canada Council—

"Canada's single greatest cultural asset." Since its inception in 1912, Canada's largest museum has continued to collect—always with brilliance—reaching more than 6 million items altogether. What makes the ROM unique is the fact that science, art, and archaeology exhibits are all appealingly presented under one roof. **The Dinosaur Collection** absorbs children and adults alike. The **Evolution Gallery** has an ongoing audiovisual program on Darwin's theories of evolution. The **Sigmund Samuel Canadiana Collection,** a worthy assemblage of 18th- and 19th-century Canadian furnishings, glassware, silver, and period rooms, is part of the Canadian Heritage gallery. A particular strength of the ROM is the **T.T. Tsui Galleries of Chinese Art,** with stunning sculptures, paintings, and many other artifacts. The **Roman Gallery** has the most extensive collection of Roman artifacts in Canada. The brilliant **Ancient Egypt Gallery** is connected with the newer **Nubia Gallery**; both exhibit artifacts that illuminate the ancient cultures. And the **European Musical Instruments Gallery** has a revolutionary audio system and more than 1,200 instruments dating back to the late 16th century. The **Discovery Gallery** allows children (over age six) to handle objects from the ROM's collections and to study them, using microscopes, ultraviolet light, and magnifying glasses. There's even a **Bat Cave,** which contains 4,000 freeze-dried and artificial bats in a lifelike presentation; piped-in narration directs visitors on a 15-minute walk through a dimly lit replica of an 8-ft-high limestone tunnel in Jamaica, filled with sounds of dripping water and bat squeaks. ⊠ *110 Queen's Park, University Ave. subway to Museum stop,* ☎ *416/586–5549.* ⊠ *$10, free Tues. after 4:30.* ☉ *Mon. and Wed.–Sat. 10–6, Tues. 10–8, Sun. 11–6; Discovery Gallery hrs vary, so call ahead.*

㉛ University of Toronto. One of Canada's largest and most revered institutions of higher learning began in 1827, when King George IV signed a charter for a "King's College in the Town of York, Capital of Upper Canada." The Church of England had control then, but by 1850 the college was proclaimed nondenominational, renamed the University of Toronto, and put under the control of the province. Then, in a spirit of Christian competition, the Anglicans started Trinity College, the Methodists began Victoria, and the Roman Catholics begat St. Michael's; by the time the Presbyterians founded Knox College, the whole thing was almost out of hand. The 17 schools and faculties are now united, and they welcome anyone who can pass the entrance exams and afford the tuition. Like that of most large universities built over several decades, the quality of the institution's architecture catalog is mixed. There is much to see and do around the main campus. One highlight is **Hart House** (⊠ 7 Hart House Circle), the Gothic-style student center built in the second decade of this century; the dining hall has stained glass windows and cheap and rather good food. The ravishing **Rosebrugh Building** (⊠ 4 Taddle Creek Rd.) of 1921 features an eye-catching display of energetic brickwork, making it one of the university's most delightful structures. Romanesque **University College** (⊠ 15 King's College Circle) was built in 1859. **Knox College** (⊠ 59 St. George St.) has been training ministers since 1844, although the building was erected in 1915. On the site of the **Medical Sciences Building** (⊠ 1 King's College Circle), Drs. Banting, Best, and others discovered the insulin that has saved the lives of tens of millions of diabetics around the world. The handsome redbrick **Forestry Building** (⊠ 45 St. George St.) and the modern and massive **Sidney Smith Hall** (⊠ 100 St. George St.), with its two wings, are also worth a look. **Massey College** (⊠ 4 Devonshire Pl.), of 1963, blends medieval ideas and forms into a modern architectural idiom. ⊠ *Public and Community Rela-*

tions Office, 27 King's College Circle, Room 133S, ☎ 416/978–2021; call about summer walking tours.

36 **Yorkville.** This is one of the most dynamic and expensive areas of the city; some call it Toronto's Rodeo Drive, others call it Toronto's Fifth Avenue. One thing is certain: These blocks are packed with restaurants, galleries, specialty shops and high-price stores specializing in designer clothes, furs, and jewels. ⊠ *Bordered by Avenue Rd., Yonge and Bloor Sts., and Yorkville Ave.*

DINING

By Sara
Waxman

Most restaurants have smoking and no-smoking sections, and some maintain a totally smoke-free environment. If this is important to you, call to check. Unless noted in the reviews, dress in Toronto is casual but neat. In the more elegant and/or expensive restaurants, men are likely to feel more comfortable in a jacket.

CATEGORY	COST*
$$$$	over $40
$$$	$30–$40
$$	$20–$30
$	under $20

per person without 7% GST and 8% provincial sales tax, tip, or drinks

American Fusion

$$$–$$$$ ✕ **North 44.** Textured walls hung with mirrored sconces hold exotic
★ floral arrangements; a steel compass is embedded in a gorgeous marble floor. This is the place to awaken your taste buds with appetizers of roasted pancetta-wrapped Mission figs with Gorgonzola center, tomato parfait and baby arugula, or grilled scallop brûlée with spun Yukon Gold potatoes, Sevruga caviar, and herb beurre blanc. Innovation and creative alchemy is owner/chef Marc McEwen's credo. Try main courses like roasted Australian lamb rack with pecan honey mustard crust, zinfandel sauce and vegetable ragout, or grilled Atlantic swordfish with charred tomato onion and coriander salsa. A delightful private dining room seats 12 to 15 people. ⊠ *2537 Yonge St.,* ☎ *416/487–4897. AE, DC, MC, V. No dinner Sun.*

$$$ ✕ **Mercer Street Grill.** Sensory thrills abound in this casual, sophisticated, witty room. Southeast Asian sentiments are joined with the finest fresh local ingredients. The city's designers and fashion-mongers, as well as socialites, ease menu-monotony with a steamer basket of Chilean sea bass with steamed and grilled vegetables, or grilled five-spice duck breast with sweet-and-sour glaze and hazelnut exotic rice. A light meal is grilled tiger shrimps with crispy noodles. Dine-alones love sitting at the open kitchen's eating counter, watching culinary theater in motion. ⊠ *36 Mercer St.,* ☎ *416/599–3399. AE, DC, MC, V. No lunch Sat.–Wed.*

$$$ ✕ **Pangaea.** A tranquil room has an aura of restrained sophistication. Partners Peter Geary and Chef Martin Kouprie use unprocessed, seasonal ingredients and the bounty of produce the world has to offer. Soups are celestial, cream-free compositions; salads are creative constructions. Terrine of foie gras is velvet; grilled calamari sings and dances with vivacious flavors. Vegetarians will find bliss in this caring kitchen. And, on the other side of the food chain, New York steak gets dolled up with sweet potato, leek, and Oka cheese gratin. ⊠ *1221 Bay St.,* ☎ *416/920–2323. AE, DC, MC, V.*

258

Toronto Dining

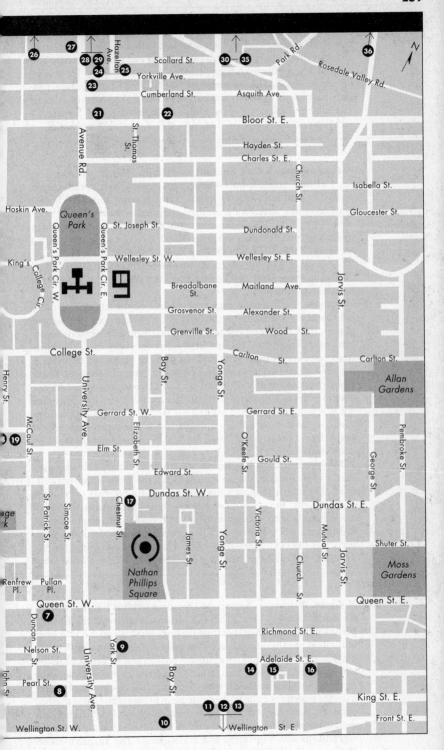

Scollard St.

Yorkville Ave.

Cumberland St.

Hazelton Ave.

St. Thomas St.

Avenue Rd.

Park Rd.

Rosedale Valley Rd.

Asquith Ave.

Bloor St. E.

Hayden St.

Charles St. E.

Isabella St.

Gloucester St.

Hoskin Ave.

Queen's Park

Queen's Park Cir. W.

Queen's Park Cir. E.

St. Joseph St.

Wellesley St. W.

Wellesley St. E.

Dundonald St.

King's

College Cir.

Breadalbane St.

Maitland Ave.

Grosvenor St.

Alexander St.

Grenville St.

Wood St.

College St.

Carlton St.

Carlton St.

Allan Gardens

Henry St.

Bay St.

Yonge St.

University Ave.

Jarvis St.

McCaul St.

Gerrard St. W.

Gerrard St. E.

Elm St.

Elizabeth St.

O'Keefe St.

Gould St.

George St.

Pembroke St.

Edward St.

Dundas St. W.

Dundas St. E.

Chestnut St.

Simcoe St.

St. Patrick St.

James St.

Yonge St.

Victoria St.

Mutual St.

Jarvis St.

Shuter St.

Moss Gardens

Nathan Phillips Square

Renfrew Pl.

Pullan Pl.

Church St.

Queen St. E.

Queen St. W.

Duncan St.

Nelson St.

York St.

Bay St.

University Ave.

Richmond St. E.

Adelaide St. E.

John St.

Pearl St.

King St. E.

Front St. E.

Wellington St. W.

Wellington St. E.

$$ ✕ **Atlas.** This restaurant/bar/jazz club combines California cool, New York glitz, and Italian passion. At the lower-level oyster bar, fish swim in built-in wall tanks. The main floor bar, with its high grazing tables and divine tapas menu, opens in summer to a vast streetside patio. You can watch it all from a balcony table in the dining room. There is an intensity to roasted boneless pheasant served with Arctic cloudberries, and a savory crunch to phyllo pastry–wrapped, baked Atlantic salmon. The Satellite Lounge on the top floor is for smoking and dancing. ⊠ *129 Peter St,* ☎ *416/977–7544. AE, MC, V. No lunch weekends.*

Cafés

$ ✕ **Future Bakery & Café.** Students love this place for its generous portions of beef borscht, buckwheat cabbage rolls, and potato-cheese *varenycky* slathered with thick sour cream. It's also adored by homesick Europeans hungry for goulash and knishes, by the cheesecake-and-coffee crowd, by health-conscious foodies, and by people-watchers looking for people worth watching from 7 AM to 2 AM. ⊠ *1535 Yonge St.,* ☎ *416/944–1253; ⊠ 438 Bloor St. W, ☎ 416/922–5875; ⊠ 2199 Bloor St. W, ☎ 416/769–5020; ⊠ 739 Queen St. W, ☎ 416/504–4235; ⊠ St. Lawrence Market, 95 Front St. E, ☎ 416/366–7259. Reservations not accepted. MC, V.*

$ ✕ **Marché.** A self-service restaurant has created the atmosphere of an old-world market square in the belly of an office tower. Herbs grow in pots; fresh fruits and vegetables are piled high; an enormous snowbank holds bright-eyed fish and fresh seafood; oysters await shucking; fresh pasta spews from pasta makers, ready to be cooked to order. A rotisserie roasts lacquer-crisp game birds and European sausages. Bread and croissants are mixed, placed on racks to rise, and baked before your eyes. Pizza is prepared to order. This high-concept, low-price dining adventure is open 7:30 AM to 2 AM Wednesday through Saturday and 7:30 AM to 1 AM Sunday through Tuesday; there are smaller versions all over town. ⊠ *42 Yonge St.,* ☎ *416/366–8986. Reservations not accepted. AE, DC, MC, V.*

$ ✕ **Masquerade Caffè Bar.** An eclectic array of primary-color furnishings, stoves, and Murano glass mosaics fills this Felliniesque environment. The daily-changing Italian menu includes a variety of risottos, divine ravioli, and a choice of *panini*—Italian sandwiches on homemade breads with scrumptious meat, cheese, and veggie fillings. Zabaglione, whipped to a thick, frothy cream and poured over fresh berries, is a knockout dessert. ⊠ *BCE Place, Front and Yonge Sts.,* ☎ *416/363–8971. Reservations not accepted. AE, MC, V. Closed Sun.*

Canadian

$$$ ✕ **Canoe.** A delicious homage to Canadian foods is filtered through the world's finest cuisines. There's a breathtaking view of the Toronto Islands and the sparkling lake from the huge windows on the 54th floor of the Toronto Dominion Bank Tower. Some inspirational dishes here are goat cheese and sunflower blossom terrine, and an Atlantic salmon trio—smoked, gravlax, and tartar. Canadiana courses through the menu with dishes like fusilli with maple-smoked chicken, and poetry from the prairies, a grilled Alberta striploin of beef with Canoe mashed potatoes, roast vegetables, and five-onion gravy. The adventurous meat eater might enjoy roast of wild Yukon caribou with caramelized vegetable gâteau. Vegetarian and spa dishes are also available. ⊠ *66 Wellington St. W, 54th floor,* ☎ *416/364–0054. Reservations essential. AE, DC, MC, V. Closed weekends.*

Chinese

$$$ ✕ **Lai Wah Heen.** If you are in the mood for Cantonese culinary fire-works, phone and preorder Lustrous Peacock as your first dish. An explosion of white vapor reveals a feathery yet robust salad of melon, barbecued duck, chicken, and honeyed walnuts. The hundred-dish menu includes wok-fried shredded beef and vegetables in a crisp potato nest, and barbecue duck in a thick taro blanket, braised in a casserole with coconut milk. At lunch the dim sum is divine. Translucent pouches burst with juicy fillings of shark's fin sprinkled with bright red lobster roe; shrimp dumplings have green tops that look like baby bok choy. The service is French in an elegant room with a sculptured ceiling, etched-glass turntables, and silver serving dishes. ⊠ *Metropolitan Hotel, 118 Chestnut St., 2nd floor,* ☎ *416/977–9899. AE, DC, MC, V.*

$ ✕ **Tiger Lily's Noodle House.** If you want to know what real egg rolls
★ taste like, you'll find them in this clean and bright hand-painted café. It's worth a visit for one dish alone: shrimp and spinach dumplinglike potstickers in a light lemony sauce. But most people come for the noodles, cooked in many ways and combinations: Hawaiian duck long rice soup, redolent with coconut lemongrass, plump with chicken and seafood, is one option. Soups include noodles, wontons, meat or vegetable broth, and garnishes of barbecued pork, Shanghai chicken, or veggies. If you want your Chinese food steeped in tradition, not grease, you'll find double happiness here. ⊠ *257 Queen St. W,* ☎ *416/977–5499. AE, MC, V.*

$ ✕ **Wah Sing.** Just one of a jumble of Asian restaurants clustered together on a tiny Kensington Market street, this meticulously clean and spacious restaurant has two-for-the-price-of-one lobsters (in season, which is almost always). With black bean sauce or ginger and green onion, they're scrumptious and tender. ⊠ *47 Baldwin St.,* ☎ *416/599–8822. AE, MC, V.*

Fish and Seafood

$$$–$$$$ ✕ **Joso's.** Joso Spralja—artist, musician, and restaurateur—has filled
★ his two-story midtown restaurant with objets d'art: sensual paintings of nudes and the sea, stylized busts of women, signed celebrity photos, and intriguing wall hangings. The kitchen prepares dishes of the Dalmatian side of the Adriatic Sea, utterly fresh fish, and unique risottos. *Risotto carajoi* is Joso's own creation of rice and sea snails simmered in an aggressively seasoned tomato sauce. Try tiger prawns from Vietnam, porgy from Boston, salmon trout from northern Ontario, or baby clams from New Zealand. A dish often carried aloft by speed-walking servers is flame-grilled prawns, their charred tails pointing skyward. ⊠ *202 Davenport Rd.,* ☎ *416/925–1903. Reservations essential. AE, DC, MC, V. Closed Sun. No lunch Sat.*

$$$ ✕ **Chiado.** Service is bilingual (Portuguese and English) and the fish are flown in from the Azores and Madeira. French doors lead to polished wood floors, tables set with starched white napery, and plum velvet armchairs. Most days you'll find bluefin tuna, piexe aspado, swordfish, and boca negra, along with monkfish, sardines, squid, and salmon. Traditional Portuguese dishes like *parrilhada* of fresh fish and seafood, a kind of soufflé, are served from a silver tureen. If you want meat, rabbit is braised in Madeira wine. Beef tenderloin is blessed with a wild mushroom tawny port sauce, and roasted rack of lamb sparkles with Duoro wine sauce. ⊠ *864 College St. W,* ☎ *416/538–1910. Reservations essential. AE, DC, MC, V.*

$$$ ✕ **Rodney's Oyster Bar.** Table-for-one diners and showbiz and agency types frequent this hotbed of bivalve variety. The offerings include salty Lewis Islands from Cape Breton, perfect Malpeques from Rodney

Clark's own oyster beds in Prince Edward Island, New York Pine Islands, and more. State-of-the-art equipment turns out soft-shell steamers, quahogs, oyster slapjack chowder, and an array of oceanic delights. "Sharing and half-orders are okay here," says Rodney. Ask for the daily "white-plate specials." ✉ *209 Adelaide St. E,* ☎ *416/363–8105. AE, DC, MC, V. Closed Sun.*

French

$$$$ ✕ **Truffles.** Through the impressive wrought-iron gates of Truffles,
★ pale wood walls glow in the reflected soft light of handcrafted candelabra. Chef Xavier Deshayes has won the hearts of discerning gastronomes with dishes like velvet foie gras gilded with quinoa lemon preserves and diffused lemon vodka sauce; a splendid duo of rack and tenderloin of wild boar; and a triumphant bouillabaisse of sea scallops, shrimp, lobster, and scampi. This is considered to be one of the finest restaurants in Canada. ✉ *Four Seasons Hotel, 21 Avenue Rd.,* ☎ *416/ 928-7331. Reservations essential. AE, DC, MC, V. Closed Sun. No lunch.*

Indian

$$ ✕ **Cuisine of India.** Chef Shishir Sharma has mastered the art of blending spices, herbs, and roots with other ingredients and achieves a delicate balance of flavors and visual appeal. He lifts a whole salmon trout from its marinade, fits it onto a forged steel skewer, and plunges it deep into the tandoor oven. A whole leg of lamb for two, halved chicken breasts, and giant shrimp can all be ordered oven-baked, too. Vegans can also enjoy elaborate dinners here. It's worth the 20-minute taxi ride from the city center. ✉ *5222 Yonge St.,* ☎ *416/229–0377. Reservations essential. AE, DC, MC, V.*

Italian

$$$ ✕ **Bellini.** From the street you might miss this comfortable, flower-filled, romantic spot. The tuna or beef carpaccio and the layered goat cheese and grilled eggplant are excellent. Try the Provimi veal, either with caramelized shallots and roasted artichokes or grilled with wild mushrooms and splashed with Cabernet Franc. Service pampers, and a friendly host greets you at the door. ✉ *101 Yorkville Ave.,* ☎ *416/929– 9111. AE, DC, MC, V. No lunch.*

$$$ ✕ **Il Posto.** Foodies, socialites, and the powers of the business world recognize the sophistication of Piero Maritano's kitchen, and wife Nella's charm in the dining room. In a rather plain space tucked into the hip of Hazelton Lanes, Il Posto serves excellent traditional Italian dishes. An iced trolley of fresh fish and seafood is wheeled over for your choosing, or you may want the perfectly grilled veal chop or angelhair pasta with a whole lobster. Signature desserts are peeled whole oranges marinated in Grand Marnier and Italian cake topped with fluffy meringue. In summer the flower-filled outdoor patio is a peoplewatcher's delight. ✉ *148 Yorkville Ave.,* ☎ *416/968–0469. AE, DC, MC, V. Closed Sun.*

$$$ ✕ **Prego de la Piazza.** Tucked into a chic shopping passage, this Italian eatery is filled with the who's who of the city's highly visible film and TV industry. The stars of Hollywood North nibble on carpaccio della casa and Caesar salad and indulge in pappardelle capra (rabbit sauce) and spaghetti calamari. Chef Massimo strolls through the plush contemporary room, gaining accolades for his roasted and stuffed Cornish game hen and seared sea scallops with shiitake mushrooms. Next door at Enoteca della Piazza, a design award–winning wine bar, the chic and cheerful sip wine and nibble on pizza and antipasti. A third separate room is called Black and Blue, a tribute to fine steaks and wines. Upstairs, the lounge is a luxe cigar smoke-easy. ⊠ *150 Bloor St. W,* ☎ *416/920–9900. AE, DC, MC, V. Closed Sun.*

$$$ ✕ **Pronto.** On the cutting edge of innovative, modern Italian cuisine, the menu marries the sunny flavors of California with solid Italian tradition. Mahogany-color grilled quails dance atop shiitake mushroom risotto. Braised veal osso buco on mashed potatoes with *gremolata* (a garnish of minced parsley, lemon peel, and garlic) is fine, home-style cuisine. From the selection of pasta, try venison ravioli or fettuccine tossed with lobster morsels in tarragon and shrimp cream. Desserts, too, are outstanding in this neighborhood eatery. ⊠ *692 Mt. Pleasant Rd.,* ☎ *416/486–1111. Reservations essential. AE, D, MC, V.*

$$$ ✕ **Splendido.** Everyone loves the ambience and respects this kitchen where chef/owner Arpi Magyar presents a sparkling Cal-Ital contemporary menu. He roasts tiger shrimp with Cajun spices and sets them on angel-hair pasta. Ricotta and potato are coaxed into plump gnocchi and served splashed with lemon butter, Parmesan, cracked pepper, and sage. Veal is the chef's masterpiece: Oven-baked rack set on garlic mashed potatoes comes with fresh horseradish, pesto sauce, sautéed kale, and sun-dried tomato mayonnaise. Casual, sophisticated good taste meets the eye at every turn. The bar is popular for nightcaps. ⊠ *88 Harbord St.,* ☎ *416/929–7788. AE, DC, MC, V.*

$$ ✕ **Grano.** What started as a bakery and takeout antipasto bar has grown
★ into a joyful collage of the Martella family's Italy. There's a small espresso bar to perch at while you wait for a table or takeout. Choose, if you can, from 40 delectable vegetarian dishes and numerous meat and fish antipasti. Lucia's homemade gnocchi and ravioli are divine, as are the tiramisù or the white chocolate and raspberry pie. ⊠ *2035 Yonge St.,* ☎ *416/440–1986. AE, DC, MC, V. Closed Sun.*

$$ ✕ **KitKat Bar & Grill.** Walls are crammed with autographed memorabilia, and the kitchen is built around a massive tree. This eclectic and eccentric southern Italian eatery is in the middle of the theater district, so pre- and post-theater hours are really busy. Choose from window tables in the front, perch at the long bar, enjoy the privacy of an old-fashioned wooden booth, or sit at a picnic table in the rear. Portions are enormous. An antipasto platter for two is a meal; pastas, seafood, roast chicken, and grilled steak are all delectable. Owner Al Carbone welcomes everyone like long-lost family. ⊠ *297 King St. W,* ☎ *416/977–4461. AE, DC, MC, V. Closed Sun. No lunch Sat.*

$$ ✕ **Verona.** The kitchen sends over homemade savories as soon as you're seated: diced marinated vegetables in olive oil, lush olive spread, and a basket of fresh breads. You might start with opulent pan-seared sea scallops on truffled asparagus spears with champagne cream, or goat cheese wrapped in prosciutto with marinated eggplant. The kitchen blesses angel-hair pasta with tiger shrimp, scallops, and woodland mushrooms. Calves' liver is infused with rosemary, matched with double-smoked grilled bacon, peppered onions, and garlic mashed potatoes. A specialty is hazelnut-crumbed pork tenderloin. Upstairs, a comfortable lounge served by the same kitchen offers cigars, fine wines, and live music on weekends. ⊠ *335 King St. W,* ☎ *416/593–7771. AE, DC, MC, V. Closed Sun. No lunch Sat.*

$ ✕ **Il Fornello.** Pizza aficionados especially love this thin-crust pie,
★ baked in a wood-burning oven. Orchestrate your own medley from over 100 traditional and exotic toppings that include braised onion, *capicolla* (spicy Italian sausage), pancetta, provolone, and calamari. Pastas, veal dishes, and salads are available, too. Wheat-free pizza crust and dairy-free cappuccino are now on the menu—your taste buds won't know the difference. ⊠ *55 Eglinton Ave. E,* ☎ *416/486–2130;* ⊠ *86 Bloor St. W,* ☎ *416/588–5658;* ⊠ *214 King St. W,* ☎ *416/977–*

2855; ⊠ *1560 Yonge St.,* ☎ *416/920–8291;* ⊠ *486 Bloor St. W,* ☎
416/588–9358; ⊠ *1968 Queen St. E,* ☎ *416/691–8377;* ⊠ *1218 St.*
Clair Ave. W, ☎ *416/658–8511;* ⊠ *35 Elm St.,* ☎ *416/598–1766;* ⊠
576 Danforth Ave., ☎ *416/466–2931. AE, MC, V.*

Japanese

\$\$\$ ✕ **Nami.** In this large, attractive restaurant, diners can choose to eat
at the sushi bar, in tatami rooms with nontraditional wells under the
tables, or at the *robatayaki* (a cooking grill surrounded by an eating
counter). The chef douses soft-shell crabs with a special sauce and puts
them on the grill. Scallops, shrimp, Atlantic salmon, mackerel and ocean
perch sizzle on skewers. Special dinner combos at a table or booth include soup, salad, tempura, yakitori (skewers of chicken), or a beef or
salmon teriyaki dish, rice, and dessert. ⊠ *55 Adelaide St. E,* ☎ *416/*
362–7373. AE, DC, MC, V. Closed Sun. No lunch Sat.

Mixed Menu

\$\$\$\$ ✕ **Scaramouche.** Consistent, perfectly beautiful dishes belie the idea
that you can't get a good view (the city's southern skyline) and good
food at the same table. Fresh lobster and scallop sausage with grilled
vegetables in a rich lobster broth with roasted pepper mayonnaise is
a popular appetizer or light supper. The city's best grilled filet mignon
with truffle mashed potatoes is polished with a red wine glaze. The
height of elegance is coconut cream pie with white chocolate shavings
and dark chocolate sauce. The adjacent Pasta Bar, alas, takes no reservations. ⊠ *1 Benvenuto Pl.,* ☎ *416/961–8011. Reservations essen-*
tial. Jacket required. AE, DC, MC, V. Closed Sun. No lunch.

\$\$\$–\$\$\$\$ ✕ **Centro.** This is Toronto's trendsetter restaurant. Massive columns
★ that hold up a bright blue ceiling combine with salmon-color walls lined
with comfortable banquettes to create an intimate space in the 182-
seat eatery. Owners Tony Longo and award-winning chef Marc Thuet
continually set standards of excellence. French/Mediterranean experience filters through fine regional ingredients into a menu with specialties
like an exquisite appetizer of Québec foie gras served with a compote
of dried fruits, Ice Wine jelly, and sesame brioche. Entrées include steamed
Rendezvous of Seafood on a bed of braised leeks and potatoes in a bouillabaisse broth, and Northwest Territories Caribou chops with spätzle,
red cabbage, chestnuts, cloudberry sauce, and orange and lemon preserve. Service is flawless. ⊠ *2472 Yonge St.,* ☎ *416/483–2211. Reser-*
vations essential. AE, DC, MC, V. Closed Sun.

\$\$\$ ✕ **Boba.** Barbara Gordon and Bob Bermann are a sophisticated culi-
nary couple now ensconced in a charming brick house personalized
with robust and gorgeous color. The dishes they've dreamed up are original and delicious: Rice paper–wrapped chicken breast on Thai black
rice and big-eye tuna grilled rare with coconut noodles, mango and avocado salsa, and black bean sauce are favorites, or try the traditional
grilled bone-in rib steak with Yukon Gold frites. Vegetable dinners are
spontaneously created. The couple's flamboyant presentations bring
to mind gourmet chefs at play. ⊠ *90 Avenue Rd.,* ☎ *416/961–2622.*
AE, MC, V. No lunch weekdays.

\$\$\$ ✕ **Jump Café & Bar.** Look up through the atrium and you'll see that
you're surrounded by towering skyscrapers. From May through September, the interior courtyard becomes a vast flower- and fountain-filled
patio with a menu of appetizers such as grilled calamari with an-
chovies, capers, and olives. The chef's pasta of the moment is gnocchi
malfatti of roast garlic, spinach, corn, and ricotta cheese, panfried with
roasted pepper cream sauce. Chef Herbert Barnsteiner roasts honeyed
rack of lamb with a pumpkinseed crust and presents Provimi veal liver

with buttermilk mashed potatoes. From 5 to 7, a smartly dressed, downtown office crowd packs the bar. ⊠ *Commerce Court E, Yonge and Wellington Sts., Court Level,* ☎ *416/363–3400. AE, DC, MC, V. Closed Sun. No lunch Sat.*

$$$ ✕ **Rosewater Supper Club.** A historic landmark building with 22-ft-high ceilings, hardwood and marble floors, and thronelike blue velvet banquettes for two is a place to go when you're in the party mood. The exciting appetizers and beautifully presented entrées include sea bass marinated in sake-flavored dashi, crispy five-spice chicken, and barbecued rack of baby pig. Not ready to commit to dinner? A lounge with a baby grand and a slinky torch singer can hold your attention. Or play a game of billiards, nibble from a tapas menu, and relax in luxe comfort in the downstairs lounge. ⊠ *19 Toronto St.* ☎ *416/214–5888. AE, DC, MC, V. Closed Sun. No lunch Sat.*

South American

$$–$$$ ✕ **Xango.** The beautiful people know that the discreet red capital X on a black tile is where the action is. A three-tiered rack of appetizers can include Honduran Fire and Ice, fresh tuna loin ceviche with coconut chilies and ginger; and fried oysters with sweet plantain, bacon, and spinach. Salvadorean chicken perched on saffron mashed potatoes or sea bass baked on a cedar plank with calamari rice and Cuban mojo has blasts of flavor. Coco Cabana, a coconut custard, and flan Borracho are dazzling desserts. Upstairs is for tango and tapas fans. ⊠ *106 John St.,* ☎ *416/593–4407. AE, MC, V. Closed Sun. No lunch.*

Swiss

$$ ✕ **Mövenpick.** Swiss hospitality and a cosmopolitan atmosphere make these downtown restaurants all things to all people. Among the dinner specialties are *Zürcher G'Schnatzlets,* the famous Swiss dish of thinly sliced veal and mushrooms in a creamy white wine sauce served with *rosti* (panfried) potatoes; *Kasseler,* a thick, smoked, juicy pork chop grilled to perfection and served with braised savoy cabbage; and red wine herring from Iceland marinated in wine and selected spices. The Swiss Farmers Sunday Brunch (York Street location only) is a vast buffet of food stations. The Yorkville location is renowned for superb fresh fish and seafood, as well as a vast selection of ice creams and desserts. ⊠ *165 York St.,* ☎ *416/366–5234;* ⊠ *133 Yorkville Ave.,* ☎ *416/926–9545. AE, DC, MC, V.*

Thai

$$ ✕ **Mata Hari Grill.** Dusky mauves and plums give this jewel-box interior a calm yet exotic aura, and there's a clean, fresh scent in the room. Sticky rice mixed with shrimp and spices is wrapped in a banana leaf and grilled. Crackling spring rolls filled with shrimp and jicama arrive with little dishes of hot sweet-and-sour sauce. Satays sizzle with the heat of freshly ground spices; sea scallops and red pepper, marinated beef, and chicken speak eloquently with mysterious Malay-Thai flavor. ⊠ *39 Baldwin St.,* ☎ *416/596–2832. AE, DC, MC, V. Closed Mon. No lunch weekends.*

$$ ✕ **Thai Magic.** Bamboo trellises, cascading vines, fish and animal carvings, and a shrine to a mermaid goddess make a magical setting for coolly saronged waiters and hot-and-spicy Thai food. Hurricane Kettle is a dramatic presentation of fiery seafood soup. Whole coriander lobster sparkles with flavor; chicken with cashews and whole dried chilies is for the adventurous. ⊠ *1118 Yonge St.,* ☎ *416/968–7366. Reservations essential. AE, MC, V. Closed Sun. No lunch Sat.*

$ ✗ **Vanipha Lanna.** Every night this tidy, colorful restaurant is crowded
★ with people who can't get enough of the clean, bright flavors, grease-
free cooking (everything's made from scratch), and lovingly garnished
Lao-Thai presentations. The bamboo steamer of dumplings with
minced chicken and seafood, sticky rice in a raffia cylinder, and chicken
and green beans stir-fried in lime sauce are exceptional. Rice is served
from a huge silver tureen. ⊠ *471 Eglinton Ave. W,* ☎ *416/484–0895.
MC, V. Closed Sun.*

LODGING

Places to stay in this cosmopolitan city range from luxurious hotels to
budget motels to bed-and-breakfasts. Prices are cut over weekends and
during quiet times of the year (many hotels drop their rates a full 50%
in January and February). Wherever you stay in Toronto, try to bargain for a lower-than-standard rate. You can request corporate prices
or inquire about special deals.

CATEGORY	COST*
$$$$	over $200
$$$	$150–$200
$$	$80–$150
$	under $80

*All prices are for a standard double room, excluding 7% GST, 5% room
tax, and optional service charge.*

$$$$ ⊞ **Four Seasons Toronto.** It's hard to imagine a hotel more exclusive
★ than the elegant Four Seasons. The location is ideal: on the edge of
Yorkville, a few yards from the Royal Ontario Museum. Rooms are
tastefully appointed and come with comfortable bathrobes and oversize towels; maids come twice a day. Even special rates will not drop
the cost much below $200 a night, but the hotel does offer some in-
ventive packages. Its restaurants include Truffles (☞ Dining, *above*)
for delectable formal dining, the Studio Cafe for all-day dining, and
La Serre and the Lobby Bar for cocktails and afternoon tea. ⊠ *21 Avenue Rd., 1 block north of Bloor St., M5R 2G1,* ☎ *416/964–0411,
800/332–3442 in the U.S., or 800/268–6282 in Canada,* 🆛 *416/964–
1489. 380 rooms. 4 restaurants, indoor-outdoor pool, sauna, health
club, meeting rooms. AE, DC, MC, V.*

$$$$ ⊞ **Inter-Continental.** This handsome postmodern high-rise, part of a
respected international chain, is just a half block west of the major intersection of Bloor Street, Avenue Road, and University Avenue, making it a two-minute walk to the Royal Ontario Museum and the
Yorkville shopping area. Edwardian and art deco touches enhance the
public areas and the spacious, well-appointed guest rooms. The lobby
lounge is especially nice for tea after a hard morning of shopping. Service here is top-notch. ⊠ *220 Bloor St. W, M5S 1T8,* ☎ *416/960–5200
or 800/327–0200,* 🆛 *416/960–8269. 20l rooms, 12 suites. Restaurant, lobby lounge, outdoor café, in-room modem lines, indoor lap pool,
massage, sauna, exercise room. AE, DC, MC, V.*

$$$$ ⊞ **King Edward.** The grande dame of downtown Toronto hotels, this
beauty built in 1903 attracts a well-heeled clientele. The "King Eddie,"
a member of the worldwide Forte chain, still has an air of understated
elegance, with its vaulted ceiling, marble pillars, and palm trees. A highlight here is the Chef's Table: for $110 per person, executive chef John
Higgins will prepare an eight-course meal for up to eight people, at a
table right next to the stoves in his kitchen. The hotel's restaurants,
Chiaro's and the Café Victoria, are favorites among Toronto power
brokers. For a genteel afternoon pastime, take tea in the lobby lounge.
⊠ *37 King St. E, M5C 1E9,* ☎ *416/863–9700 or 800/225–5843,* 🆛

416/367–5515. *315 rooms. 2 restaurants, lobby lounge, spa, health club, business services, meeting rooms. AE, DC, MC, V.*

$$$$ 🏨 **Park Plaza Hotel.** The Park Plaza has one of the best locations in
★ the city, near the Royal Ontario Museum, Queen's Park, and the affluent Yorkville shopping district. An extensive renovation in 1997 added a pool and health club, and rooms are now fresh but still cozy. If you request a south-facing room in the older tower, you'll have stunning cityscape views—with glimpses of Lake Ontario. The Roof Restaurant, with an adjoining bar, was once described by novelist Mordecai Richler as "the only civilized place in Toronto." ✉ *4 Avenue Rd., at Bloor St. W, M5R 2E8,* ☎ *416/924–5471 or 800/977–4197,* FAX *416/924–4933. 348 rooms. 3 restaurants, bar, lounge, pool, health club, ballroom, business services. AE, DC, MC, V.*

$$$$ 🏨 **Westin Harbour Castle.** The Westin, just steps from Harbourfront and the Toronto Islands ferry, offers the best views of Lake Ontario of any hotel in the city. A free shuttle bus and the Harbourfront LRT (light rail transit) provide links to Union Station, the subway, and downtown business and shopping. It's a favorite with conventioneers because of its enclosed bridge to the large convention center across the street. Rooms are modern in style, and frequent family and weekend rates help bring the regular price down by as much as a third. The revolving Lighthouse restaurant, atop the 37th floor, has a spectacular view. ✉ *1 Harbour Sq., M5J 1A6,* ☎ *416/869–1600 or 800/228–3000,* FAX *416/869–3682. 980 rooms. 2 restaurants, lobby lounge, pool, health club, tennis court, playground. AE, DC, MC, V.*

$$$ 🏨 **Metropolitan Hotel.** This contemporary 26-story hotel could hardly
★ be more convenient: behind City Hall, a few short blocks from the Eaton Centre, and near the theater district. The guest rooms, which include eight for travelers with disabilities, are decorated with finely crafted modern furniture; some have king-size beds, and executive rooms have a work center with printer and fax. Restaurants include Lai Wah Heen (☞ Dining, *above*), Hemispheres, and Alibi Bar & Grill. The hotel is adjacent to the Museum of Textiles. ✉ *108 Chestnut St., north of Nathan Phillips Sq., M5G 1R3,* ☎ *416/977–5000,* FAX *416/977–9513 or 800/323–7500. 481 rooms. 3 restaurants, 2 bars, indoor pool, sauna, hot tub, health club, business services. AE, DC, MC, V.*

$$$ 🏨 **Royal York Hotel.** One of Canada's famous railway hotels, this
★ grand hostelry was built by the Canadian Pacific Railway for the convenience of passengers using the nearby train station. An award-winning refurbishment of the hotel has returned the lobby to its classic 1929 decor. Business floors and a work center cater to travelers' needs; the health club has picturesque views of the city. You can have full afternoon tea at the Royal Tea Room or sample wine from the Acadian Room's extensive wine list. The hotel's links to Union Station and the Underground City make it very handy in cold weather. ✉ *100 Front St. W, M5J IE3,* ☎ *416/368–2511 or 800/441–1414,* FAX *416/368–9040. 1,408 rooms. 6 restaurants, 4 bars, indoor lap pool, massage, sauna, health club, business services, travel services, airport shuttle. AE, DC, MC, V.*

$$$ 🏨 **Sheraton Centre.** This busy conventioneer's favorite is across from the New City Hall, just a block from Eaton Centre, which is accessible through an underground passage. The belowground level is part of Toronto's labyrinth of shop-lined corridors, the Underground City. The Long Bar, overlooking Nathan Phillips Square, is a great place to meet friends for a drink. ✉ *123 Queen St. W, M5H 2M9,* ☎ *416/361–1000 or 800/325–3535,* FAX *416/947–4854. 1,382 rooms. 4 restaurants, 2 bars, coffee shop, no-smoking floors, indoor-outdoor pool, hot tub, sauna, exercise room, children's program (ages 18 months–12 years). AE, DC, MC, V.*

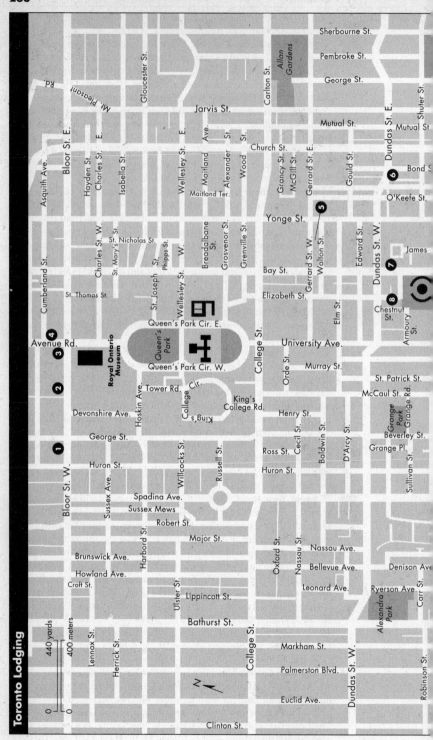

Toronto Lodging

Sherborne St.

Pembroke St.

Allan Gardens

George St.

Gloucester St.

Carlton St.

Jarvis St.

Mt. Pleasant Rd.

Bloor St. E.

Asquith Ave.

Hayden St.

Charles St. E.

Isabella St.

Wellesley St. E.

Maitland St.

Alexander St.

Wood St.

Church St.

Maitland Ter.

Mutual St.

Grancy St.

McGill St.

Gerrard St. E.

Gould St.

Dundas St. E.

Mutual St.

Shuter St.

Bond St.

O'Keefe St.

Yonge St.

Charles St. W.

St. Mary's St.

St. Nicholas St.

Phipps St.

St. Joseph St.

Breadalbane St.

Grosvenor St.

Grenville St.

Gerrard St. W.

Walton St.

Edward St.

Dundas St. W.

James

Cumberland St.

St. Thomas St.

Wellesley St. W.

Bay St.

Elizabeth St.

Elm St.

Chestnut St.

Avenue Rd.

Royal Ontario Museum

Queen's Park

Queen's Park Cir. E.

Queen's Park Cir. W.

College St.

University Ave.

Murray St.

Orde St.

St. Patrick St.

McCaul St.

Grange Rd.

Grange Park

Armoury St.

Devonshire Ave.

Hoskin Ave.

Tower Rd.

College Cir.

King's College Rd.

King's

Henry St.

Cecil St.

Baldwin St.

D'Arcy St.

Beverley St.

Grange Pl.

Sullivan St.

Bloor St. W.

George St.

Huron St.

Sussex Ave.

Willcocks St.

Russell St.

Ross St.

Huron St.

Spadina Ave.

Sussex Mews

Robert St.

Major St.

Oxford St.

Nassau St.

Nassau Ave.

Bellevue Ave.

Denison Ave.

Brunswick Ave.

Harbord St.

Howland Ave.

Croft St.

Ulster St.

Lippincott St.

Leonard Ave.

Ryerson Ave.

Alexandra Park

Carr St.

440 yards

400 meters

Lennox St.

Herrick St.

Bathurst St.

College St.

Markham St.

Palmerston Blvd.

Euclid Ave.

Clinton St.

Dundas St. W.

Robinson St.

N

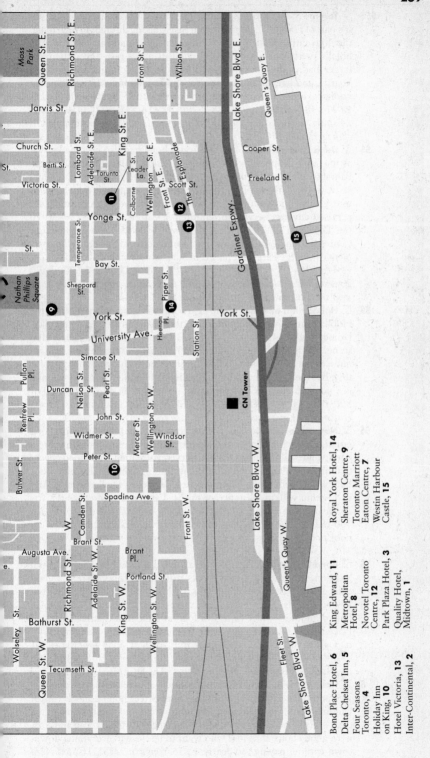

Mass Park

Queen St. E.

Richmond St. E.

Front St. E.

Wilton St.

Lake Shore Blvd. E.

Queen's Quay E.

Jarvis St.

Church St.

Berti St.

Victoria St.

Lombard St.

Adelaide St. E.

King St. E.

St.

Toronto St.

Leader La.

Colborne

Wellington St. E.

Front St. E.

Scott St.

The Esplanade

Cooper St.

Freeland St.

Yonge St.

11

12

13

15

Gardiner Expwy.

St.

Nathan Phillips Square

Bay St.

Sheppard St.

Temperance St.

Piper St.

York St.

University Ave.

Simcoe St.

Nelson St.

Pearl St.

Duncan

John St.

Widmer St.

Mercer St.

Wellington St. W.

Windsor St.

Peter St.

9

14

Heenan Pl.

Station St.

York St.

CN Tower

Renfrew Pl.

Pullan Pl.

Bulwer St.

10

Spadina Ave.

Camden St.

W.

Brant St.

Brant Pl.

Front St. W.

Lake Shore Blvd. W.

Queen's Quay W.

Augusta Ave.

e.

Richmond St.

Adelaide St. W.

Portland St.

Wolseley St.

St.

Bathurst St.

Queen St. W.

Tecumseth St.

King St. W.

Wellington St. W.

Fleet St.

Lake Shore Blvd. W.

Queen's Quay W.

Royal York Hotel, **14**
Sheraton Centre, **9**
Toronto Marriott
Eaton Centre, **7**
Westin Harbour
Castle, **15**

King Edward, **11**
Metropolitan
Hotel, **8**
Novotel Toronto
Centre, **12**
Park Plaza Hotel, **3**
Quality Hotel,
Midtown, **1**

Bond Place Hotel, **6**
Delta Chelsea Inn, **5**
Four Seasons
Toronto, **4**
Holiday Inn
on King, **10**
Hotel Victoria, **13**
Inter-Continental, **2**

$$$ ⚏ **Toronto Marriott Eaton Centre.** The Marriott has a terrific location: It's part of Eaton Centre and within easy walking distance of SkyDome, the convention center, and the theater and financial districts. The hotel's pretty guest rooms, decorated in dusty rose and gray, have larger bedrooms than most you'll find in Toronto; irons, ironing boards, and hair dryers are standard. The indoor rooftop swimming pool provides a fabulous view of the city. ⊠ *525 Bay St., M5G 2L2,* ☎ *416/597–9200 or 800/228–9290,* 🖷 *416/597–9211. 459 rooms, 24 suites. 2 restaurants, lobby lounge, sports bar, indoor pool, health club. AE, DC, MC, V.*

$$ ⚏ **Delta Chelsea Inn.** Toronto's largest hotel has also become known as the city's theater hotel because it is within walking distance of the Pantages, Elgin, and Winter Garden theaters, and guests can book tickets with their rooms. This friendly spot has long been popular with tour groups and with business travelers on a budget. A creative, supervised day-care service for children 3–8 runs from 9:30 AM to 10 PM. The Delta Chelsea is a couple of short blocks north of the Eaton Centre, and the College subway station is across the street in the basement of College Park shopping center. ⊠ *33 Gerrard St. W, M5G 1Z4,* ☎ *416/595–1975 or 800/877–1133,* 🖷 *416/585–4302. 1,600 rooms. 2 restaurants, 3 lounges, 2 pools, hot tub, sauna, exercise room, business services, children's program. AE, DC, MC, V.*

$$ ⚏ **Holiday Inn on King.** In the heart of the entertainment district, the Holiday Inn is just three blocks north of the convention center, SkyDome, and CN Tower; also nearby is Queen Street and its lively club scene. The hotel occupies floors 9–20 of a 20-story tower; you can request views of the lake, skyline, or SkyDome. The swimming pool is tiny, but the exercise room is appealing. All in all, this chain offering is a good value. ⊠ *370 King St. W, M5V 1J9,* ☎ *416/599–4000 or 800/465–4329,* 🖷 *416/599–7394. 426 rooms. 3 restaurants, refrigerators, pool, massage, sauna, exercise room. AE, DC, MC, V.*

$$ ⚏ **Novotel Toronto Centre.** The moderately priced Novotel—part of a popular French chain—offers comfortable modern rooms that are a good value. All rooms have a hair dryer, voice mail, and video checkout, and there are a good number of fitness facilities. This nine-floor hotel is just behind the Hummingbird Centre for the Performing Arts and within walking distance of the St. Lawrence market. ⊠ *45 The Esplanade, M5E 1W2,* ☎ *416/367–8900 or 800/668–6835,* 🖷 *416/ 360–8285. 266 rooms. Restaurant, minibars, no-smoking floors, indoor pool, hot tub, sauna, exercise room, banquet facilities. AE, DC, MC, V.*

$ ⚏ **Bond Place Hotel.** If you're on a limited budget but want a central location, this hotel just two blocks from the Eaton Centre is a good choice. It has clean, spacious rooms with color TVs and phones, but few other frills. The Garden Café serves breakfast, lunch, and dinner, but you'll find a wider variety of food at the Eaton Centre. The Bond Place is also a few minutes' walk from the Elgin, Pantages, and Winter Garden theaters. ⊠ *65 Dundas St. E, M5B 2G8,* ☎ *416/362–6061 or 800/268–9390 in Canada and N.E. USA,* 🖷 *416/360–6406. 286 rooms. Restaurant, no-smoking floors. AE, DC, MC, V.*

$ ⚏ **Hotel Victoria.** Travelers on budgets will appreciate the personal ser-
★   vice and quiet atmosphere of this Yonge Street hotel a block east of Union Station. At press time, the public areas and guest rooms of the eight-story Victorian-era building were being renovated. Clean and cozy, it's a good choice for those who want to be close to everything downtown without paying too dearly. ⊠ *56 Yonge St., M5E 1G5,* ☎ *416/ 363–1666, 800/363–8228 in Canada and NY.* 🖷 *416/365–7327. 48 rooms. Restaurant, bar. AE, DC, MC, V.*

$ ⊞ **Quality Hotel, Midtown.** The Choice Hotel chain has four down-town locations plus four hotels near the airport. This one is close to the University of Toronto, the Royal Ontario Museum, and the Yorkville shopping district. Rooms are comfortable but not luxurious. The St. George subway stop is steps away, and underground parking is available. It's hard to beat the combination of convenience and price here. ⊠ *280 Bloor St. W, M5S 1V8,* ☎ *416/968–0010 or 800/228-5151. 210 rooms. Restaurant, coffee shop. AE, D, MC, V.*

NIGHTLIFE AND THE ARTS

Toronto's performing arts scene has flourished in recent years, aided by the introduction of some dazzling new venues and the refurbishment of some magnificent old ones. The influence of the burgeoning film industry has made nightlife in this once-staid town a lot more glamorous, too.

The Arts

The best places to get information on cultural happenings are in the Thursday editions of the *Toronto Star,* the Saturday *Globe and Mail,* the free weeklies *Now* and *Eye Weekly,* and *Toronto Life* magazine. For half-price tickets on the day of a performance, try the **Five Star Tickets booth,** located in the Royal Ontario Museum lobby in winter and the rest of the year at the corner of Yonge and Dundas streets, outside the Eaton Centre. The museum booth is open daily 10–7; the Yonge and Dundas booth is open (in good weather) Monday–Saturday noon–7:30 and Sunday 11–3. Tickets are sold for cash only, all sales are final, and a service charge is added to the price of each ticket. The booth outside the Eaton Centre also gives out superb brochures and pamphlets on the city. Tickets for almost any event in the city can be obtained through **Ticketmaster** (☎ 416/872–2222). Tickets can be picked up at the door on the night of the event or at any Ticketmaster location; note that a service charge applies to all orders.

Classical Concerts

The Toronto Symphony has achieved world acclaim, with conductors the quality of Seiji Ozawa, Walter Susskind, Sir Thomas Beecham, and Andrew Davis. Maestro Jukka-Pekka Sarasti has reinvigorated the repertory with 20th-century pieces to complement older masterworks. When the orchestra is home, it presents about three concerts weekly from September through May in Roy Thomson Hall (☞ Concert Halls and Theaters, *below).*

The **Toronto Mendelssohn Choir** (☎ 416/598–0422) often performs with the Toronto Symphony. This 180-singer group, going since 1894, has been applauded worldwide, and its *Messiah* is handled well every Christmas. For tickets call 416/598–0422 or Roy Thomson Hall (☞ Concert Halls and Theaters, *below).*

Concert Halls and Theaters

The **Hummingbird Centre for the Performing Arts** is the home of the Canadian Opera Company and the National Ballet of Canada. It also hosts visiting comedians, pre-Broadway musicals, rock stars, and almost anyone else who can fill its 3,167 seats. Avoid the extreme front rows (lettered AA, BB, and so on). ⊠ *1 Front St. E, 1 block east of Union Station,* ☎ *416/872–2262.* ☜ *Tickets $20–$50.*

Massey Hall is cramped and dingy, but its near-perfect acoustics and its handsome, U-shape tiers sloping down to the stage have made it a happy place to hear the Toronto Symphony, or anyone else in the world of music, for almost a century. The best seats are in Rows G–M center and Rows 32–50 in the balcony. ⊠ *178 Victoria St., at Shuster, east of Eaton Centre,* ☎ *416/593–4828.* 🎟 *Tickets $20–$60.*

The **Roy Thomson Hall** has become the most important concert hall in Toronto. It is the home of the Toronto Symphony and the Toronto Mendelssohn Choir. It also hosts orchestras from around the world and popular entertainers. The best seats are in Rows H and J in the orchestra and Row L upstairs. Rush seats are sold two hours before curtain. ⊠ *60 Simcoe St., at King St. W, 1 block west of University Ave.,* ☎ *416/593–4828.* 🎟 *Tickets $20–$60, theater tour $3, organ tour $5.* ☉ *Theater tour Mon., Tues., and Thurs. 12:30; organ tour Wed. 12:30; phone ahead regarding tours.*

The **Royal Alexandra,** which opened in 1907, has plush red seats, gold brocade, and baroque swirls and curlicues that make theater-going a refined experience here. The best seats are in Rows C–L center; avoid Rows A and B; for musicals try the first rows of the first balcony. ⊠ *260 King St. W,* ☎ *416/872–3333 or 416/872–1212.* 🎟 *Tickets $35–$75 (more for major musicals); student tickets $15 and up.*

Since 1970 the **St. Lawrence Centre for the Arts** has been presenting everything from live theater to string quartets and forums on city issues. The main hall, the luxuriously appointed **Bluma Appel Theatre,** hosts the often brilliant productions of the **Canadian Stage Company** and **Theatre Plus.** Classical and contemporary plays are often on a level with the best of Broadway and London's West End. The best seats are Rows E–N, Seats 1–10. ⊠ *Front St. and Scott St.,* ☎ *416/366–7723.* 🎟 *Tickets $20–$45.*

Dance

Since its debut in 1951, the **National Ballet of Canada** has done some extraordinary things, with such principal dancers as Karen Kain, Rex Harrington, Kimberly Glasco, and Jeremy Ramson all wowing audiences. ⊠ *Hummingbird Centre for the Performing Arts, 1 Front St. E,* ☎ *416/345–9686 or 416/872–1111.* 🎟 *Tickets $15–$55.* ☉ *Performances Nov., Dec., Feb., and May.*

Toronto Dance Theatre, which has roots in the Martha Graham tradition, tours Canada and has played major festivals in England, Europe, and the United States. ⊠ *Premiere Dance Theatre, Harbourfront, 235 Queen's Quay W,* ☎ *416/973–4000.* 🎟 *Tickets $19–$31.*

Film

Toronto has a devoted film audience. The result is an embarrassment of riches: commercial first- and second-run showings, festivals, lecture series for every taste. In September Toronto hosts the world-class **Toronto International Film Festival** (☎ 416/967–7371 or 416/968–3456). You can see new work from around the world, retrospectives of the films of major directors, or tributes to particular actors.

Carlton Cinemas shows rare, important films from Canada and around the world in nearly a dozen screening rooms. ⊠ *20 Carlton St., east of College St. subway,* ☎ *416/598–2309.*

Opera

Since its founding in 1950, the **Canadian Opera Company** (☎ 416/363–8231) has grown into the largest producer of opera in Canada. Each year, at the Hummingbird Centre for the Performing Arts (☞ Concert Halls and Theaters, *above*), more than 150,000 people attend the season of seven operas and hear world-class performers. The COC also performs free outdoor concerts during the summer at Harbourfront.

Theater

Toronto, after London and New York, is the largest center for English-speaking theater in the world. There are more than four dozen performing spaces here, presenting everything from the finest in classic and contemporary drama to well-produced Broadway and West End fare. Full-price tickets can range from about $20 to $100.

The **Elgin and Winter Garden theaters** (⊠ 189 Yonge St., north of Queen St. W, ☎ 416/872–5555 for tickets, 416/314–2901 for biweekly tours) are two recently renovated old vaudeville palaces, stacked upon one another. The Elgin, downstairs, has about 1,500 seats; the Winter Garden is some 500 seats smaller; both are stunningly attractive. These landmark theaters from 1913 showcase traveling as well as locally based artistic productions of all kinds.

The **Ford Centre for the Performing Arts** (⊠ 5040 Yonge St., ☎ 416/872–2222 or 416/733–9388), less than a half-hour drive north of the waterfront, close to the North York subway stop, often hosts megamusicals and classical music concerts. The stunning **Pantages Theatre** (⊠ 263 Yonge St., ☎ 416/872–2222), a restored 1920 vaudeville palace, has been home to *The Phantom of the Opera* for over eight years. The **Princess of Wales Theatre** (⊠ 300 King St. W, ☎ 416/872–1212) hosts productions such as the musical *Beauty and the Beast.*

The **Factory Theater** (⊠ 125 Bathurst St., ☎ 416/504–9971) is an alternative theater devoted to original and experimental work.

The **Tarragon Theatre** (⊠ 30 Bridgman Ave., ☎ 416/531–1827), in an old warehouse and railroad district, is the natural habital for excellent indigenous Canadian theater.

Théâtre Passe Muraille (⊠ 16 Ryerson Ave., ☎ 416/504–7529), in the unfashionable area of Bathurst and Queen streets, has long been the home of fine Canadian collaborative theater.

The **Young People's Theatre** (⊠ 165 Front St. E, near Sherbourne, ☎ 416/862–2222), the only theater center in the country devoted solely to children, does not compromise its dramatic integrity.

Nightlife

The area bounded by Front, Adelaide, Peter, and John streets has become the center of Toronto's club and bar scene in recent years.

Bars

The **Loose Moose Tap & Grill** (⊠ 220 Adelaide St. W, ☎ 416/971–5252) is a popular bar. In 1993 hockey superstar Wayne Gretzky opened **Wayne Gretzky's** (⊠ 99 Blue Jay Way, ☎ 416/979–7825), a sports bar and restaurant.

Comedy Clubs

Second City (⊠ Old Firehall Theatre, 110 Lombard St., at Jarvis, ☎ 416/863–1111), just east of the heart of downtown, has long provided some of the best comedy in North America. Among those who have cut their teeth here are Dan Aykroyd, Martin Short, Andrea Martin, Catherine O'Hara, and the late John Candy. Shows can be seen alone or in a dinner-theater package. By 1998 the club plans to move into new quarters on Blue Jays Way in the entertainment district.

Yuk-Yuk's Komedy Kabaret (⊠ 2335 Yonge St., north of Eglinton Ave.; ⊠ 5165 Dixie St., Mississauga; ☎ 416/967–6425 for tickets for both locations) has always been a major place for comedy. This is where Howie Mandel and Jim Carrey got their starts and where such comic luminaries as George Carlin, Rodney Dangerfield, Robin Williams, and Mort Sahl have presented their best routines. It's open Thursday–Sunday.

Dancing

At **Big Bop** (✉ 651 Queen St. W, ☎ 416/504–6699), DJs play '60s music downstairs and '90s music upstairs in a four-story, century-old fun house. At **Fluid** (✉ 217 Richmond St. W, ☎ 416/593–6116), which caters to a Yorkville-ish older (25–35) crowd, the decor is metallic and modular, with custom-made furnishings. **The Guvernment** (✉ 132 Queen's Quay, ☎ 416/869–1462), near Harbourfront, draws lovers of dance, rock, and alternative music, while professional dancers perform above the crowd.

Gay and Lesbian Clubs

Fab and *X-Extra* chronicle the gay and lesbian scene. These free publications can be readily found in the Church and Wellesley district. Near or along Church Street are several nightlife options. **Woody's** (✉ 467 Church St., ☎ 416/972–0887) is fashionable yet neighborly. **Crews** (✉ 508 Church St., ☎ 416/972–1662) is youthful. The Sunday night window drag show at **Bar 501** (✉ 501 Church St., ☎ 416/944–3272) is an institution. For the aspiring Versace-model crowd, **Boots** (✉ 592 Sherbourne, ☎ 416/921–0665) rocks in a fabulous warehouse space.

Jazz Clubs

Chick 'n Deli (✉ 744 Mt. Pleasant Rd., near Eglinton Ave., ☎ 416/489–3363 or 416/489–7931), long one of the great jazz places in Toronto, now has jazz only on Saturday; there's a dance floor, and dark wood everywhere gives it a casual, neighborhood-pub feel. **Top O' The Senator** (✉ 249 Victoria St., ☎ 416/364–7517), this city's first club exclusively for jazz and cabaret, has the atmosphere of a 1930s lounge. It's closed on Monday.

Lounges

The **Consort Bar** (✉ 37 King St. E, ☎ 416/863–9700), in the King Edward Hotel, has jazz on Thursday, Friday, and Saturday evenings, and Sunday afternoons. In the classy Four Seasons Hotel, **La Serre** (✉ Avenue Rd. and Yorkville Ave., ☎ 416/964–0411), which looks like a library in a mansion, has a stand-up piano bar and a pianist worth standing for. Up on the 51st floor of the ManuLife Centre, the **Panorama** (✉ 55 Bloor St. W, at Bay St., ☎ 416/967–5225) features Latin American music. The gorgeous and tasteful **Park Plaza Roof Lounge** (✉ Avenue Rd. and Bloor St., ☎ 416/924–5471) has been used as a setting in the writings of such Canadian literary luminaries as Margaret Atwood and Mordecai Richler.

Rhythm and Blues

The modern—brass, black, polished oak—**Network** (✉ 138 Pears Ave., near Davenport Rd., ☎ 416/323–0164) entertainment lounge is a supper club and show specializing in name acts such as the Stylistics, Junior Walker, and Goodman and Brown.

Rock and Popular Music

Most major international recording companies have offices in Toronto, so the city is a regular stop for top musical performers of today. Tickets ($15–$100) can usually be booked through **Ticketmaster** (☎ 416/872–1111).

Major venues include the SkyDome (✉ 1 Blue Jays Way, Front St. W and Peter St., ☎ 416/341–3663), Maple Leaf Gardens (✉ 60 Carlton St., ☎ 416/977–1641), the Hummingbird Centre for the Performing Arts (✉ 1 Front St. E, ☎ 416/872–2262), and Exhibition Stadium (✉ CNE grounds, Dufferin St. at waterfront, ☎ 416/393–

6000). **Ontario Place** (⊠ Lake Shore Blvd. W between Dufferin and Bathurst Sts., ☎ 416/314–9900) has pop, rock, and jazz concerts all summer at very reasonable prices. You may pay around $10 to see/hear a fabulous singer or group (or orchestra or ballet corps) that would cost you $25–$50 elsewhere. This is one of the loveliest and least expensive places for concerts in the city. **Kingswood Music Theatre** (⊠ Hwy. 400, 10 min north of Hwy. 401, ☎ 905/832–8131) has important rock and pop concerts during the warmer months. **The Phoenix Concert Theatre** (⊠ 410 Sherbourne St., ☎ 416/323–1251) has a wide variety of music, with DJs from local radio stations broadcasting live on Monday (classic rock) and Saturday (alternative music). A major showcase for more daring acts has long been the **Rivoli** (⊠ 332 Queen St. W, west of University Ave., ☎ 416/597–0794), where the backroom functions as a club, with theater happenings, progressive rock and jazz, and comedy troupes with very funny improvisations.

OUTDOOR ACTIVITIES AND SPORTS

Participant Sports

Contact the **Ministry of Tourism and Recreation** (⊠ Queen's Park, M7A 2R2) for pamphlets on various activities. For information on sports in the province, call 800/668–2746 from anywhere in the continental United States and Canada (except the Northwest Territories and the Yukon). In Toronto contact Ontario Travel (☎ 416/314–0944).

A number of fine **conservation areas** circle metropolitan Toronto. Most have large swimming areas, sledding, and cross-country skiing, as well as skating, fishing, and boating. For information call Metro Region Conservation (☎ 416//661–6600).

Biking
More than 29 km (18 mi) of street bike routes cut across the city and dozens more follow safer paths through Toronto's many parks. Maps are available at most local bike shops. Bikes can be rented on the Toronto Islands. The 19-km (12-mi) **Martin Goodman Trail** runs along the waterfront from the Balmy Beach Club in the east end past the western beaches southwest of High Park.

Metro Parks Department (⊠ 55 John St., ☎ 416/392–8186) has maps that show bike (and jogging) routes that run through Toronto parkland. **Ontario Cycling** (⊠ 1185 Eglinton Ave. E, ☎ 416/426–7242) has maps, booklets, and information.

Boating
You can rent canoes, punts, and/or sailboats at Grenadier Pond in High Park, at Centre Island, at Ontario Place, at Harbourfront, and at most of the conservation areas surrounding metro Toronto.

Fitness Facilities
Nearly every major hotel has a decent indoor swimming pool; some even have indoor/outdoor swimming pools. Among the best are those at the Sheraton Centre (⊠ 123 Queen St. W, at Bay St., ☎ 416/361–1000). Many also have health clubs; call ahead to inquire about availability and fees, particularly if you're not a guest.

Golf
The season lasts only from April to late October. For information about courses, contact Metro Parks (☎ 416/392–8186) or Ontario Travel (☎ 416/314–0944). The top course is **Glen Abbey** (⊠ 1333 Dorval Dr., Oakville, ☎ 905/844–1800), where the Canadian Open Cham-

pionship is held in late summer; cart and greens fees will cost up to $75 on weekends, but this 18-hole course is a real beauty.

Horseback Riding

Sunnybrook Stables (✉ Leslie St. and Eglinton Ave., ☎ 416/444–4044), in Sunnybrook Park, has an indoor arena, an outdoor ring, and about 19 km (nearly 12 mi) of bridle trails through the Don valley.

Ice-Skating

Toronto operates some 30 outdoor artificial rinks and 100 natural-ice rinks—and all are free. Among the most popular are those in Nathan Phillips Square, in front of the New City Hall at Queen and Bay streets; down at Harbourfront, which has Canada's largest outdoor artificial ice rink; College Park, at Yonge and College streets; Grenadier Pond, within High Park, at Bloor and Keele streets; and inside Hazelton Lanes, the classy shopping mall on the edge of Yorkville, on Avenue Road, just above Bloor Street. Bring your own skates to most outdoor rinks; one exception is Nathan Phillips Square, where equipment can be rented. For details on any city rink, call 416/392–1111.

Jogging

The Martin Goodman Trail (☞ Bicycling, *above*) is ideal. Also try the boardwalk of The Beaches in the east end, High Park in the west end, the Toronto Islands, or any of Toronto's parks. Some hotels will provide maps of popular jogging routes.

Sailing

This can be a breeze, especially between April and October. Contact the **Ontario Sailing Association** (✉ 1185 Eglinton Ave., North York M3C 3C3, ☎ 416/426–7271). The **Royal Canadian Yacht Club** (✉ 1441 St. George St., ☎ 416/967–7245) has its summer headquarters in a beautiful Victorian mansion on Centre Island.

Skiing

CROSS-COUNTRY

Try Toronto's parks and ravines; High Park; the lakefront along the southern edge of the city; Tommy Thompson Park; Toronto Islands; and Centennial Park, in the western borough of Etobicoke, only a 20-minute drive from downtown.

DOWNHILL

The best alpine hills are a good 45 to 60 minutes north of the city (☞ Barrie, Collingwood, and Huntsville *in* Chapter 7).

Tennis

The city provides dozens of free courts, many of them floodlighted. Parks with courts open from 7 AM to 11 PM, in season, include High Park, off Bloor Street at Keele Street, in the west end; Stanley Park, on King Street West, three blocks west of Bathurst Street; and Eglinton Park, on Eglinton Avenue West, just east of Avenue Road. A number of indoor courts are open throughout winter. Call the Ontario Tennis Association (☎ 416/426–7135).

Spectator Sports

Auto Racing

For the past several years, the **Molson Indy** has been roaring around the Canadian National Exhibition grounds for three days in mid-July. You'll pay more than $85 for a three-day "red" reserved seat, but general admission can be as cheap as $10–$20, depending upon the day. For tickets and information call Ticketmaster (☎ 416/872–4639). Less than a half-hour drive away is the **Cayuga International Speed-**

way (☎ 705/743–6671), where international stock-car races are held from May through September.

Baseball

The **Toronto Blue Jays** (☎ 416/341–1111) play at SkyDome. Tickets range from $4 (for seats near heaven) to $25. Games usually sell out, so plan way ahead of your Toronto visit.

Canoeing and Rowing

One of the world's largest **canoeing and rowing regattas** is held every July 1, as it has been for more than a century, on Toronto Island's Long Pond. For information call Canoe Ontario at 416/426–7170.

Football

The Canadian Football League has teetered near extinction in recent years, but it continues to draw fans. The **Toronto Argonauts** (☎ 416/341–5151), which are partly owned by hockey superstar Wayne Gretzky, have been as erratic as the league itself. The Argos play their home games at the SkyDome.

Golf

The site of the **Canadian Open Golf Championship** is Glen Abbey (☞ Participant Sports, *above*), a course designed by Jack Nicklaus. This tournament is one of golf's Big Five and is played in late summer.

Hockey

The **Toronto Maple Leafs** (✉ Box office: 60 Carlton at Church St., ☎ 416/977–1641, at 9 AM sharp on day of game you wish to see) play 40 home games each season (October–April), usually on Wednesday and Saturday nights, in the big, ugly Maple Leaf Gardens. There are always tickets available at each game—at least from scalpers (scalping is illegal, but they're there) in front of the stadium on Carlton Street, a half block east of the corner of Yonge and College streets.

Horse Racing

HARNESS AND THOROUGHBRED RACING
The **Ontario Jockey Club** (☎ 416/675–7223 or 888/675–7223) operates three major racetracks. **Woodbine Race Track** (✉ Hwy. 427 and Rexdale Blvd., 30 min northwest of downtown Toronto, near the airport, is the showplace of Thoroughbred and harness racing in Canada. Horses run late April through late October. **Mohawk** (✉ Hwy. 401, 30 min west of Toronto, beyond Milton, in the heart of Ontario's Standardbred breeding country, has a glass-enclosed, climate-controlled grandstand. **Fort Erie** (✉ 230 Catherine St., Queen Elizabeth Way/Bertie St. exit) is one of the most picturesque racetracks in the world, with willows, manicured hedges, and flower-bordered infield lakes.

ROYAL HORSE SHOW
This highlight of Canada's equestrian season is part of the Royal Winter Fair each November. It's held at the CNE grounds (✉ Dufferin St., at waterfront, ☎ 416/393–6400).

Soccer

Although Toronto keeps getting and losing and getting a professional soccer team, you can catch this exciting sport, as well as collegiate football, at **Varsity Stadium** (✉ Bloor St. W at Bedford, 1 block west of Royal Ontario Museum and University Ave., ☎ 416/978–7388).

SHOPPING

Toronto, the shopping capital of Canada, has a fine selection of British Isles imports and Canadiana, as well as everything from Gianni Versace suits to Ikea furnishings. Books, antiques, and clothing are plentiful and interesting. The biggest sale day of the year is Boxing Day, the first business day after Christmas, when nearly everything in the city is half price. As winter fades, clothing prices tend to drop even further. Summer sales start in late June and continue through August.

Shoppers can haggle at flea markets, including the Harbourfront Antique Market, and perhaps in the Chinatown and Kensington Market/Spadina Avenue areas. In some small boutiques, where the owner is in attendance, you may be able to negotiate for a better price than what you see on the ticket.

Most shops are open Monday through Wednesday and Saturday 10 to 6, Thursday and Friday until 8, and Sunday noon to 5. Many stores are closed on major holidays, including Good Friday, Easter Monday, and Victoria Day (third Monday in May).

Shopping Districts and Malls

On **Bloor Street** you'll find such wonderful stores as **Zoe,** with haute couture designs; **The Bay,** a department store with clothes for men and women; **Holt Renfrew,** possibly the most stunning store in Toronto, with marble, chrome, glass, and glittering fashions for both sexes; **Harry Rosen** for men; and such shoe shops as **Boutique Quinto** and **David's.** In **The Colonnade,** on the south side of Bloor Street, a few doors east of University Avenue, is another upscale cluster of stores. Even with the invasion of such American chains as The Gap and Banana Republic, the tone is très expensive, and très good.

The **Eaton Centre** (✉ 220 Yonge St., ☎ 416/598–2322) is a large galleria-style shopping center downtown, on Yonge Street between Queen and Dundas streets. With scores of stores and restaurants, all sheltered from the weather, it's a major tourist attractions. Generally, the lower levels are lower priced and the higher levels are more expensive. Hours are Monday–Saturday 10–9, Sunday noon to 5.

Harbourfront includes an antiques market (✉ 390 Queen's Quay W, ☎ 416/260–2626) that is Canada's biggest on Sunday, when it draws about 200 dealers. The market is open Tuesday–Friday 11–5, weekends 10–6. The **Queen's Quay Terminal** (✉ 207 Queen's Quay W, ☎ 416/203–0501) is a renovated warehouse that houses a collection of unique boutiques, craft stalls, patisseries, and so on; it's a great place to buy gifts. There's frequent streetcar service from Union Station, but it's a fairly easy walk. Parking is expensive.

Queen Street West, starting just west of University Avenue and continuing past Spadina Avenue, creeping ever westward past Bathurst Street, is a trendy area near the Ontario College of Art and Design. Here, you'll find young, hip designers; new- and used-book bookstores; vintage clothes; two comic-book stores, including the biggest in North America (**Silver Snail,** No. 367; also check out the **Dragon Lady Comic Shop** at No. 200); and the more progressive private galleries.

Spadina Avenue (☞ Central Toronto *in* Exploring Toronto, *above*), from Wellington Street north to College Street, has plenty of low-price clothing for the family, as well as fur and leather factory outlets. **Winner's** (✉ South of King St.) is a good discount outlet for women and children. This area can be very crowded on weekends.

The **Underground City** is a vast maze of shopping warrens that burrow between and underneath the office towers downtown. The tenants are mostly chain and convenience stores, and the shopping is rather dull. The network runs roughly from the Royal York Hotel near Union Station north to the Eaton Centre.

Yorkville is where you'll find the big fashion names, fine leather goods, important jewelers, some of the top private art galleries, upscale shoe stores, and discount china and glassware. Streets to explore include Yorkville Avenue, Cumberland Street, and Scollard Street, all running parallel to Bloor Street, and Hazelton Avenue, running north from Yorkville Avenue near Avenue Road. **Hazelton Lanes**, between Hazelton Avenue and Avenue Road, and the adjacent **York Square** are among the most chichi shopping areas in Canada, and they are headquarters for café society during the brief annual spell of warm weather.

Department Stores

The major department stores have branches around the city and flagship stores downtown. Service tends to be very slow and uninformed compared with that of boutiques. The exclusive **Holt Renfrew** (⊠ 50 Bloor St. W, ☎ 416/922–2333) sings with élan and quality. One big name is **Eaton's**, in the Eaton Centre (☞ *above*). **The Bay** is on Yonge Street between Queen and Richmond streets (☎ 416/861–9111) and at Yonge and Bloor streets (☎ 416/975–0009).

Specialty Shops

Antiques
Yorkville is the headquarters of establishment antiques dealers. There are several other pockets around town, including a strip along Queen Street East, roughly between Sherbourne and George streets. The antiques market at Harbourfront (☞ Shopping Districts and Malls, *above*) is another choice.

The Allery (⊠ 322½ Queen St. W, ☎ 416/593–0853) specializes in antique prints and maps. **Art Metropole** (⊠ 788 King St. W, ☎ 416/703–4400) specializes in limited-edition, small-press, or self-published artists' books from around the world. **Quasi Modo** (⊠ 789 Queen St. W, ☎ 416/703–8300) has a quirky collection of 20th-century furniture and design; you never know what will be on display: vintage bicycles, Noguchi lamps, or a corrugated cardboard table by Frank Gehry. **20th Century** (⊠ 23 Beverley St., north of Queen St., ☎ 416/598–2172) is for serious collectors of 20th-century design, particularly furniture, lamps, jewelry, and decorative arts.

Art Galleries
Toronto is a cosmopolitan art center with more than 300 commercial galleries offering every kind of art for viewing and sale, from representational to abstract, from Inuit to other native art. You can stroll from gallery to gallery in two major districts—the Yorkville area and Queen Street west of University Avenue. Many galleries are closed Sunday and Monday, but call to check.

For avant-garde works, look in **Cold City** (⊠ 686 Richmond St. W, ☎ 416/504–6681). **Jane Corkin Gallery** (⊠ 179 John St., north of Queen St., ☎ 416/979–1980) specializes in photography. The **Isaacs/Inuit Gallery** (⊠ 9 Prince Arthur Ave., ☎ 416/921–9985), owned by Av Isaacs, showcases fine arts and crafts produced in the Canadian Arctic, including prints, sculptures, and wall hangings. **Mercer Union** (⊠ 439 King St. W, ☎ 416/977–1412) is in the forefront of the arts. **Prime Canadian Gallery** (⊠ 52 McCaul St., ☎ 416/593–5750) has an ever-changing array of crafts from across Canada. **YYZ** (⊠ 1087 Queen St. W, ☎ 416/531–7869) has a good collection of contemporary pieces.

Bookstores
Toronto is rich in specialty bookstores selling new books, used books, best-sellers, and remainders. If you just need a current magazine or a

paperback for the plane, there are good chain stores including Chapters and W.H. Smith.

Albert Britnell Book Shop (⊠ 765 Yonge St., north of Bloor St., ☎ 416/924–3321) has been a Toronto legend since 1893, with a marvelous British ambience and great browsing. **Ballenford Architectural Books** (⊠ 600 Markham St., ☎ 416/588–0800) has Canada's largest selection of architectural titles and a gallery with usually interesting exhibits of architectural drawings and related work. **Edward's Books and Art** (⊠ 356 Queen St. W, near Spadina Ave., ☎ 416/593–0126; ⊠ 2179 Queen St. E, the Beaches, ☎ 416/698–1442; ⊠ Park Plaza Hotel, 170 Bloor St. W, ☎ 416/961–2428; ⊠ 2200 Yonge St., south of Eglinton Ave., ☎ 416/487–5431; ⊠ 8147 Yonge St., ☎ 905/731–3050), one of the city's nicest local chains, discounts best-sellers and remainders and carries an impressive catalog of current and rare artists' monographs. **Glad Day Books** (⊠ 598 Yonge St., ☎ 416/961-4161), one block north of the Church and Wellesley gay mecca, is the city's leading gay and lesbian bookstore. **Bob Miller Book Room** (⊠ 180 Bloor St. W, northwest of ROM, ☎ 416/922–3557) has the best literature and philosophy section in the city and a fine staff. **Pages Books and Magazines** (⊠ 256 Queen St. W, ☎ 416/598–1447) has a wide selection of international and small-press literature; fashion and design books and magazines; and books on film, art, and literary criticism. **Theatrebooks** (⊠ 11 St. Thomas St., ☎ 416/922–7175) has an astounding collection of performing arts books: theater, film, opera, jazz, television, and media studies. **This Ain't the Rosedale Library** (⊠ 483 Church St., south of Wellesley Ave., ☎ 416/929–9912) stocks the largest selection of baseball books in Canada, as well as a good range of fiction, poetry, photography, design, rock, and jazz books. **The World's Biggest Book Store** (⊠ 20 Edward St., 1 block north of Eaton Centre, ☎ 416/977–7009) is Canada's largest book shop. It's particularly strong in business, computers, and travel; the store also showcases an array of Canadian books. **Writers & Co.** (⊠ 2005 Yonge St., near Davisville, a few blocks south of Eglinton, ☎ 416/481–8432) is arguably Canada's finest literary bookstore, with hard-to-find poets, essayists, and world novelists.

Clothing
Queen Street West is well known for its stores catering to the young, hip, and zany. Among those in the neighborhood are **Boomer** (⊠ No. 309, ☎ 416/598–0013), **Due West** (⊠ No. 431, ☎ 416/593–6267), **No. 6 Clothing Company** (⊠ No. 290A, ☎ 416/593–2745), and **Rag Tag** (⊠ No. 359, ☎ 416/979–3939). **Yonge Street** is also a popular area for clothes shopping; try **Soul Underground** (⊠ No. 673, ☎ 416/924–4119).

Brown's (⊠ 1975 Avenue Rd., south of Hwy. 401, ☎ 416/489–1975) provides classic clothing for short men and women. There's a **Brown's** store for men only (⊠ 545 Queen St. W, ☎ 416/504–5937). **Fetoun** (⊠ Four Seasons Hotel, 162 Cumberland St., ☎ 416/923–3434) sells high-fashion gowns and evening clothes. **Linda Lundstrom** (⊠ 2507 Yonge St., ☎ 416/480–1602; ⊠ 136 Cumberland St., ☎ 416/927–9009) is an award-winning designer of high-fashion winter clothing. This is the place to buy an eye-catching parka. **Muskat & Brown** (⊠ 2528 Yonge St., ☎ 416/489–4005) is for petite women. **Venni** (⊠ 274 Queen St. W, ☎ 416/597–9360; ⊠ 2638 Yonge St., ☎ 416/489–9561; ⊠ Bayview Village Shopping Centre, ☎ 416/223–4304) highlights trendy Canadian-designed clothing at three locations.

Food Markets

Kensington Market (⊠ Northwest of Dundas St. and Spadina Ave., ☎ 416/979–3757) is an outdoor market open every day (although many stores are closed Sunday), with a vibrant ethnic mix. Saturday is the best day to go, preferably by public transit, because parking is difficult. **St. Lawrence Market** (⊠ Front and Jarvis Sts., ☎ 416/392–7219) is best early on Saturday, when, in addition to the permanent indoor market on the south side of Front Street, there's a farmer's market in the building on the north side. The historic south market was once Toronto's city hall, and it fronted the lake before extensive landfill projects were undertaken.

Gifts

The Guild Shop (⊠ 118 Cumberland St., ☎ 416/921–1721) is an outlet for a wide variety of Canadian artists. Soapstone carvings from Inuit communities in the Arctic, aboriginal paintings from British Columbia and Ontario, and even woolen ties from Nova Scotia are among the items for sale. It's worth a visit for an appreciation of indigenous Canadian arts and crafts. **Arts-on-King** (⊠ 169 King St. E, ☎ 416/777–9617) is a bright and spacious store with a varied selection of glass, ceramic, wood, and other creations. **Filigree** (⊠ 1156 Yonge St., ☎ 416/961–5223) has a good assortment of linens, as well as drawer liners, silver frames, and other Victorian pleasures.

Robin Kay Home and Style (⊠ 276 Queen St. W, ☎ 416/585–7731; ⊠ 922 Eglinton Ave. W, ☎ 416/785–0968; ⊠ 394 Spadina Rd., ☎ 416/932–2833; ⊠ 2599 Yonge St., ☎ 416/485–5097), this country's answer to Martha Stewart, carries lovely Canadian products to enliven any interior, from bibelots to linens.

Jewelry

Secrett Jewel Salon (⊠ 150 Bloor St. W, ☎ 416/967–7500) is a reputable source of unusual gemstones and fine new and estate jewelry; local gemologists consider it the best in town.

SIDE TRIPS FROM DOWNTOWN TORONTO

If you're staying in the city for more than a couple of days, you may have time for one or more worthwhile excursions. These easy day trips, less than an hour from downtown, appeal to a variety of interests; each could easily occupy half a day or more. North Yorkville is home to the Black Creek Pioneer Village living history site. The excellent McMichael Canadian Art Collection is farther north and west, in the village of Kleinburg. East of downtown, you can try a host of technical marvels at the Ontario Science Centre. The sprawling Metro Toronto Zoo is farther north and east of downtown Toronto in Scarborough.

Black Creek Pioneer Village

☪ *20 km (12 mi) north of downtown.*

This living history site is as good a reproduction as you'll find of a rural Victorian community in the 1860s. Roblin's Mill, powered by a big wooden waterwheel, grinds wheat as it was done 130 years ago. At the weaver's shop, a costumed interpreter explains the magic of the loom. At other artisans' shops around the village, you can watch blacksmiths, clock makers, tinsmiths, coopers, and broom makers at their trades. Seasonal festivals are celebrated in grand style. You can drive or take a subway and bus here. ⊠ *1000 Murray Ross Pkwy., cor-*

ner of Jane St. and Steeles Ave., North York, ☎ *416/736–1733.* ▦ *$8; parking is $4.* ☉ *May–Dec., 10–4.*

McMichael Canadian Art Collection

25 km (15½ mi) north of downtown.

★ A 45-minute drive north of downtown, in the village of Kleinburg, the celebrated **McMichael Canadian Art Collection** is superb. The landscape paintings of Canada's Group of Seven artists, including Tom Thomson, and extensive holdings of Inuit and native art are only part of the McMichael's charm. The gallery is set in 100 acres of woodland, with strategically placed windows so that visitors can appreciate the scenery as they admire art that took its inspiration from the vast outdoors. ⊠ *10365 Islington Ave., west of Hwy. 400 and north of Major Mackenzie Dr., Kleinburg,* ☎ *905/893–1121.* ▦ *$7.* ☉ *Mid-Oct.–mid-May, Tues.–Sat. 10–4, Sun. 10–5; mid-May–mid-Oct., daily 10–5.*

Ontario Science Centre

11 km (7 mi) northeast of downtown.

★ ♻ The **Ontario Science Centre,** a stunningly successful blend of education and entertainment, has thrilling space, communications, laser, nutrition, and electricity exhibits. Live demonstrations—lasers, glassblowing, papermaking, and more—take place throughout the day; check the schedule when you arrive. There's an Omnimax Theatre (extra charge for movies) and a fine permanent exhibit called "the Sport Show." You need at least two hours to scratch the surface; you can spend an entire day here. ⊠ *770 Don Mills Rd.; Yonge St. subway from downtown to Eglinton station and Eglinton East bus to Don Mills Rd. stop), North York,* ☎ *416/696–3127 or 416/429–4100.* ▦ *$8, parking $5.* ☉ *Daily 10–5, Wed. until 8, Fri. until 9.*

Metro Toronto Zoo

35 km (22 mi) northeast of downtown.

♻ The 710 acres of the **Metro Toronto Zoo** were developed for animals, not people. In the varied terrain of the Rouge Valley, from river valley to dense forest, mammals, birds, reptiles, and fish have been grouped according to where they live in the wild. In most regions, you'll find botanical exhibits in enclosed, climate-controlled pavilions. Don't miss the 3-ton banyan tree in the **Indo-Malayan Pavilion,** the fan-shape traveler's palm from Madagascar in the **African Pavilion,** or the perfumed flowers of the jasmine vines in the **Eurasian Pavilion.** The "round-the-world tour" takes about three hours and is suitable for any kind of weather, because most of the time is spent inside pavilions. It's been estimated that it would take four full days to see everything, so study the map you'll get at the zoo entrance and decide what you wish to see most. For younger children, the delightful **Littlefootland** allows contact with tame animals, such as rabbits and sheep. In winter cross-country skiers follow groomed trails that skirt the animal exhibits; lessons and rentals are available. An electrically powered train moves silently among the animals without frightening them. It can accommodate wheelchairs (available free inside the main gate), and all pavilions have ramp access. If you're on a very tight budget, the zoo is free if you show up the last hour of the day, enough time for a taste of this world-class institution. ⊠ *Meadowvale Rd. north of Hwy. 401, 30-min drive from downtown, or take Bus 86A from Kennedy subway station, Scarborough,* ☎ *416/392–5900.* ▦ *$9.95; parking in winter free, parking Mar.–Oct. $4.* ☉ *Daily 9:30–4:30.*

TORONTO A TO Z

Arriving and Departing

By Bus

The bus terminal (✉ 610 Bay St., north of Dundas St., ☎ 416/393–7911) serves a number of lines. **Greyhound** (☎ 416/367–8747 or 800/231–2222) has regular bus service into Toronto from all over the United States and Canada. From Detroit the trip takes five hours, from Buffalo two to three hours, and from Chicago and New York City 11 hours. Several other bus companies, such as **Trentway-Wagar,** Ontario Northland, Penetang-Midland Coach Lines (PMCL), and **Can-AR** offer a variety of bus services.

By Car

Detroit–Windsor and Buffalo–Fort Erie crossings can be slow, especially on weekends and holidays. The wide Highway 401—reaching up to 16 lanes as it slashes across metro Toronto from the airport on the west almost as far as the zoo on the east—is the major link between Windsor, Ontario (and Detroit), and Montréal. It's also known as the Macdonald-Cartier Freeway but is generally called simply "the 401." There are no tolls, but be warned: In weekday rush hours the 401 can become dreadfully crowded, even stop-and-go.

From Buffalo or Niagara Falls, take the Queen Elizabeth Way (known as the QEW), which curves up along the western shore of Lake Ontario, eventually turns into the Gardiner Expressway, and flows right into the downtown core.

Yonge Street, which begins at the lakefront, is called Highway 11 once you get north of Toronto and continues all the way to the Ontario–Minnesota border, at Rainy River. At 1,896 km (1,175 mi), it is the longest street in the world.

By Plane

Flights into Toronto land at the **Lester B. Pearson International Airport** (☎ 416/247–7678), commonly called "the Toronto airport" or "Malton" (after the once-small town where it was built, just northwest of the city).

Toronto is served by **American** (☎ 800/433–7300), **Delta** (☎ 800/221–1212), **Northwest** (☎ 800/225–2525), **United** (☎ 800/241–6522), **USAir** (☎ 800/428–4322), **Air Canada** (☎ 16/925–2311 or 800/268–7240), **Canadian Airlines International** (☎ 416/798–2211 or 800/665–1177), as well as more than a dozen European and Asian carriers with easy connections to many U.S. cities. **Air Ontario,** affiliated with Air Canada (☎ 416/925–2311), flies from the small, downtown Island Airport to and from Ottawa, Montréal, and London (Ontario). It is a convenient alternative to Pearson International if you're staying downtown and making trips to these cities.

BETWEEN THE AIRPORT AND CENTER CITY

Although Pearson is not far from downtown (about 32 km, or 18 mi), the drive can take well over an hour during weekday rush hours. Taxis and limos to a hotel or attraction near the lake typically cost $35 or more. Airport cabs have fixed rates to different parts of the city. You must pay the full fare from the airport, but it is often possible to negotiate a lower fare from downtown, where airport cabs compete with regular city cabs. It is illegal for city cabs to pick up passengers at the airport, unless they are called—a time-consuming process, but sometimes worth the wait. Note that some airport and downtown hotels offer free shuttle bus service from the airport.

If you rent a car at the airport, ask for a street map of the city. Highway 427 runs south some 6 km (4 mi) to the lakeshore. Here you pick up the Queen Elizabeth Way east to the Gardiner Expressway, which runs east into the heart of downtown. If you take the QEW west, you'll find yourself swinging around Lake Ontario, toward Hamilton, Niagara-on-the-Lake, and Niagara Falls.

Pacific Western (☎ 905/564–6333) offers express coach service linking the airport to three subway stops in the southwest and north-central areas of the city. Buses depart several times each hour from 8 AM to 11:30 PM. Fares average $6–$7. The service to and from several downtown hotels operates every 20 minutes from 6:25 AM to at least 10:45 PM daily and costs approximately $12.50.

By Train
Amtrak (☎ 800/872–7245) runs a daily train to Toronto from Chicago (a 12-hour trip), and another from New York City (12 hours). From Union Station (✉ Front St. between Bay and York Sts.) you can walk underground to many hotels—a real boon in inclement weather. There is a cab stand outside the main entrance of the station.

Getting Around

Most of Toronto is laid out on a grid. Yonge Street (pronounced "young") is the main north–south artery. Most major cross streets are numbered east and west of Yonge Street. If you are looking for 180 St. Clair Avenue West, you want a building a few blocks *west* of Yonge Street; 75 Queen Street East is a block or so *east* of Yonge Street.

At press time the fare for buses, streetcars, and trolleys was $2 in exact change, but 10 adult tickets/tokens cost $15. Two-fare tickets are available for $3.50 for adults. If you plan to stay in Toronto for more than a month, consider the **Metropass,** a photo-identity card that currently costs $83 for adults plus $3 extra for the photo.

Families can take advantage of the **Day Pass.** It costs $6.50 and is good for unlimited travel for one person, weekdays after 9:30 AM, and all day Saturday. On Sunday and holidays, it's good for up to six persons (maximum two adults) for unlimited travel. Call the TTC (☎ 416/393–4636) from 7 AM to 11:30 PM for information on how to take public transit to any street or attraction in the city. The TTC publishes a very useful **Ride Guide** each year. It shows nearly every major place of interest and how to reach it by public transit. These guides are available in most subways and many other places around the city. The subways stop running at 2 AM, but the TTC has bus service from 1 to 5:30 AM on many major streets, including Queen, College, Bloor, Yonge, part of Dufferin, and as far north as Finch and Eglinton.

By Bus
All buses and streetcars accept exact change, tickets, or tokens. Paper transfers are free; pick one up from the driver when you pay your fare.

By Car
Pedestrian crosswalks are sprinkled throughout the city; they are marked clearly by yellow overhead signs and very large painted Xs. All a pedestrian has to do is stick out a hand, and cars (you hope!) screech to a halt in both directions. Right turns on red lights are nearly always permitted, except where otherwise posted. You must come to a complete stop before making the turn.

By Subway
The Toronto Transit Commission (TTC) runs one of the safest, cleanest, most trustworthy systems of its kind anywhere. There are two major

subway lines, with 60 stations along the way: the **Bloor/Danforth Line,** which crosses Toronto about 5 km (3 mi) north of the lakefront, from east to west, and the **Yonge/University/Spadina Line,** which loops north and south, like a giant "U," with the bottom of the "U" at Union Station. Tokens and tickets are sold in subway stations and at hundreds of convenience stores along the many routes of the TTC. Get your transfers just after you pay your fare and enter the subway; you'll find them in machines on your way down to the trains.

By Taxi

The meter begins at $2.50 and includes the first .2 km (roughly .1 mi). Each additional .235 km (.145 mi) is 25¢—as is each passenger in excess of four. The waiting time "while under engagement" is 25¢ for every 33 seconds—and in a traffic jam, this could add up. Still, it's possible to take a cab across downtown Toronto for $8 to $9. The largest companies are **Beck** (☎ 416/461–1131), **Co-op** (☎ 416/504–2667), **Diamond** (☎ 416/366–6868), **Metro** (☎ 416/504–8294), and **Royal** (☎ 416/785–3322). For more information call the Metro Licensing Commission (☎ 416/392–3000).

Contacts and Resources

B&B Reservation Services

More than two dozen private homes are affiliated with **Toronto Bed & Breakfast** (✉ 21 Kingswood Rd., M4E 3N4, ☎ 416/690–1407, FAX 416/690–5089), most of them scattered around metro Toronto. Rooms cost as little as $50 a night and include breakfast. **Metropolitan Bed & Breakfast** (✉ 615 Mt. Pleasant Rd., Suite 269, M4S 3C5, ☎ 416/964–2566, FAX 416/960–9529) registry service has about 30 city and suburban homes on its books. Some 15–20 homes in various parts of the city have signed up with **Bed and Breakfast Homes of Toronto** (✉ Box 46093, College Park Postal Station, M5B 2L8, ☎ 416/363–6362); write for a brochure detailing individual homes.

Consulates

Consulate General of the United States (✉ 360 University Ave., north of Queen St., M56 1S4, ☎ 416/595–0228). **British Consulate General** (✉ 777 Bay St., at College St., M56 2G2, ☎ 416/593–1267).

Doctors and Dentists

Ask at your hotel desk or call **Dial-a-Doctor** (☎ 416/756–6259) or the **Dental Emergency Service** (☎ 416/967–5649).

Emergencies

Ambulance or **Police** (☎ 911).

Guided Tours

ORIENTATION

Greyhound Sightseeing Bus Tours (☎ 416/367–8747) has tours from April through November. The 2-hour tours start at the bus terminal (✉ Bay and Dundas Sts.) and include the Eaton Centre, the old and new city halls, Queen's Park, the University of Toronto, Yorkville, Ontario Place, and Casa Loma—the latter, for a full hour. The fare is $18.

In winter, city bus tours are provided by **Niagara Tours** (☎ 416/868–0400). These full-day tours make a circuit of the city's high points. Pickups are made at all major downtown hotels between 9:30 and 10 AM, returning around 6. The fare is $98.

You can take tours of the Toronto harbor and islands on comfortably equipped **Toronto Tours** (☎ 416/869–1372) boats for about $15. The hourly tour passes the Toronto Islands, with lovely city views. Boats leave from the Pier Six Building next to Queen's Quay Terminal from early May through mid-October, daily 10–6. Tours leave as late as 7:15 PM in summer. Other boats depart from the Westin Harbour Castle hotel at the foot of Yonge Street.

SPECIAL-INTEREST

The **Bruce Trail Association** (☎ 416/690–4453 or 800/665–4453) arranges day and overnight hikes around Toronto and its environs.

Ghost Walk (☎ 416/922–6289) takes you on a walking tour of the haunted places in Toronto. This first-rate adventure is available from mid-May through October (and throughout the winter for groups that make reservations). The cost of the tour is $10 per person.

Mosaic Environ Excursion Toronto (☎ 416/778–9686) offers a five-hour tour that visits some of the ethnic neighborhoods and green spaces that give Toronto its special character. This tour, which starts at Union Station, goes beyond the downtown area to include Cabbagetown, Little Italy, and the picturesque area around the Humber River. The cost is $34.95 and includes a picnic lunch.

Underground City Tours (☎ 905/886–9111), Marius Frederick's fascinating 2½-hour tour full of tidbits about the city's life and history, meets at the south door of the Eaton Centre across from the Bay on Queen Street Tuesday and Wednesday at 10 and 1:30. The cost is $15.

WALKING TOURS

Downtown Toronto Walking Tour (☎ 416/922–7606) is just that—the closest look possible at central Toronto, with the emphasis on architecture. The 2- to 2½-hour tours take place daily Tuesday–Sunday between May and October, starting in front of Old City Hall on the northeast corner of Bay and Queen streets. Starting times vary, so call in advance. The cost is $10.

Hotel Reservation Service

Accommodation Toronto (☎ 905/629–3800), a service of the Hotel Association of Toronto, is an excellent source for finding the room and price you want. Ask about family deals and special packages.

Late-Night Pharmacies

Pharma Plus Drugmart (✉ Church St. and Wellesley Ave., ☎ 416/924–7760). **Shoppers Drug Mart** (✉ 700 Bay St., ☎ 416/979–2424; ✉ 2500 Hurontario St., Mississauga, ☎ 905/896–2500).

Road Emergencies

The **Canadian Automobile Association** (☎ 416/222–5222) has 24-hour road service; membership benefits are extended to U.S. AAA members.

Visitor Information

The **Metropolitan Toronto Convention & Visitors Association** (✉ 207 Queen's Quay W, Suite 509, M5J 1A7, ☎ 416/203–2500 or 800/363–1990) has its office at Queen's Quay Terminal. Booths providing brochures and pamphlets about the city and its attractions, as well as accommodations, are set up in the summer outside the Eaton Centre, on Yonge Street just below Dundas Street, and outside the Royal Ontario Museum.

The **Traveller's Aid Society** (✉ Union Station, arrivals level and basement level, Room B23, ☎ 416/366–7788; ✉ Pearson Airport, Terminal I, arrivals level, past Customs, near Area B, ☎ 905/676–2868; Pearson Airport, Terminal 2, between international and domestic arrivals, ☎ 905/676–2869; ✉ Pearson Airport, Terminal 3, arrivals level, near international side, ☎ 905/612–5890) recommends restaurants and hotels and distributes subway maps and Ontario sales tax rebate forms.

7 Province of Ontario

Ottawa, Algonquin Park, Windsor, Niagara, London

With shorelines on four of the five Great Lakes, Ontario is Canada's second-largest and most urbanized province, but only 10 million people live in this vast area, and 90% of them are within a narrow strip just north of the U.S. border. A bit north of the strip, Ottawa, Canada's capital, gathers government workers and parliamentarians.

ONTARIO IS AN IROQUOIAN WORD variously interpreted as: beautiful lake, beautiful water, or rocks standing high beside the water (the last an apparent reference to Niagara Falls). The province contains 156,670 square km (68,490 square mi) of fresh water—one quarter of all there is in the world.

Updated by
Wendy Lindsay

Ontario is Canada's most urban province; half of its population lives in four cities whose boundaries have spread to such an extent that they almost adjoin. Metropolitan Toronto has more than 2 million people. To the east, Oshawa has 175,000 people and heavily populated suburbs. South and west of Toronto are Hamilton with 550,000 people and St. Catharines with 290,000. Half of Ontario's population is of British stock, but successive waves of immigrants over the past century have turned the province into a mini-United Nations. Thunder Bay contains the largest settlement of Finns outside Finland. Toronto has a half-million Italians, the largest Chinese community in Canada, and the most Portuguese in North America. More recent arrivals include thousands of West Indians, Vietnamese, Somalis, South Africans, and east Europeans, giving Ontario—Toronto in particular—a cosmopolitan flavor rivaling New York's or Chicago's.

The towns and cities of northern Ontario are strung along the railway lines that brought them into being. The discovery of immense deposits of gold, silver, uranium, and other minerals by railway construction gangs sparked mining booms that established such communities as Sudbury, Cobalt, and Timmins, which continue to owe their existence to mining.

Ontario has the most varied landscape of any Canadian province. The most conspicuous topographical feature is the Niagara Escarpment, which runs from Niagara to Tobermory at the tip of the Bruce Peninsula in Lake Huron. The northern 90% of Ontario is covered by the Canadian Shield, worn-down mountain ranges of the world's oldest rock, reaching only 2,183 ft above sea level at their highest point.

East of Hamilton toward Niagara Falls is a narrow strip along the south shore of Lake Ontario in a partial rain shadow of the Niagara Escarpment. The climate, moderated in winter by Lakes Ontario and Erie, allows the growing of tender fruits and grapes, making it Canada's largest wine-producing area.

Pleasures and Pastimes

The Arts
By combining public and private resources, Ontario has fostered one of North America's most supportive environments for the arts. Each year thousands flock to see great Shakespeare at the Stratford Festival and top-notch music at the Shaw Festival. Better still, each city claims an arts prize. In Hamilton it's the Hamilton Opera, while in Ottawa it's the National Arts Centre Orchestra. Beyond these stalwarts, there are plenty of upstart dance, music, and theater companies.

Dining
The cuisine of this vast province runs the gamut from fresh-caught fish in cottage country to French-influenced dishes in Ottawa and great home-style Canadian fare such as maple-syrup pie in southern Ontario. Given the enormous British influence here, there's plenty of roast beef, shepherd's pie, and rice pudding, especially in the English-dominated enclaves of London, Stratford, and Hamilton. Ontarians crave Tim Horton's doughnuts, found at franchise shops in virtually every city.

CATEGORY	COST*
$$$$	over $50
$$$	$35–$50
$$	$15–$35
$	under $15

per person, excluding drinks, service, 7% GST, 8% food tax, and 10% bar tax

Lodging

Reservations are strongly recommended anywhere in Ontario during summer months. Generally you get what you pay for at Ontario hotels and motels, though rates are often double those charged in the United States for comparable accommodation. Bed-and-breakfast associations exist in most cities, but, again, many of those rates exceed what you'd pay for a good hotel or motel room south of the border. In Niagara Falls the closer the hotel is to the falls, or the better the view is of them, the higher the rate.

CATEGORY	COST*
$$$$	over $100
$$$	$75–$100
$$	$35–$75
$	under $35

All prices are for a standard double room, excluding taxes.

Museums

The diverse museums of Canada's most populous province document Ontario's evolution from a rough-hewn outpost to a lively cosmopolitan society. Living history museums, such as Upper Canada Village, reveal the early years. Numerous institutions, particularly in southern Ontario, chronicle the War of 1812. The National Gallery of Canada in Ottawa, among others, is the place to examine the region's fascinating artistic tradition.

Outdoor Activities and Sports

CAMPING

Most of the provincial parks offer a variety of services for campers, from electrical outlets and sturdy, covered picnic shelters to laundry facilities and camp stores for provisions. Some also have cottages for rent. Additionally, many sponsor educational programs that teach children wilderness survival techniques and aim to offer a better understanding of nature.

In southern Ontario most provincial parks operate from mid-May until Labor Day weekend; in northern Ontario provincial parks open from early June until Labor Day weekend. Even when "closed," however, the parks never completely shut down, and visitors are welcome in the off-season, though few facilities are maintained. Some parks may be gated to prevent vehicular entry, but all are accessible to pedestrians from sunrise to sunset. Expect vault privies to be open, fireplace grates should be available, and fees usually will be collected through self-serve registration. Winter camping, which is becoming a popular pastime, is allowed in some provincial parks, though most are unsupervised and facilities are limited. During the fall and winter months reservations are not required at most parks.

FISHING

Ontario has about 250,000 lakes and 150,000 rivers that contain myriad species of fish. The favorite trophies of most anglers are salmon and trout, but others lust after pike or muskie and still others swear that battling a frenzied black bass on light tackle is life's ultimate piscatorial challenge.

SKIING

This province is rich with cross-country and downhill ski trails. Nordic ski trails exist just about anywhere in the province where you find snow and accommodations for skiers. Ontario has hundreds of alpine slopes, although most are under 660 ft in vertical drop. All major Ontario ski centers have high-tech snow-making equipment, which has guaranteed good skiing from late November through early April.

Shopping

Visitors from the States often relish Ontario's handsome inventory of things British, scooping up everything from china teacups and cashmere clothing to crumpet tins. Others marvel at the province's rich handicraft tradition. Ottawa, Sault Ste. Marie, Midland, and Thunder Bay have museum shops and galleries that specialize in native and Inuit crafts. Antiques stores abound. Some of the best antiques can be found at small shops in Cobourg, Peterborough, and St. Jacobs.

Exploring Ontario

You could spend a lifetime exploring this enormous province and still not see it all. But by using three cities—Ottawa, Sault Ste. Marie, and Toronto—as bases for one- and two-day excursions, you can visit all the major sights and some special little corners that even many Ontarians don't know about.

Numbers in the text correspond to numbers in the margin and on the Lower Ontario Province, Downtown Ottawa, Greater Ottawa and Hull, Niagara Falls, and Upper Ontario maps.

Great Itineraries

IF YOU HAVE 3 DAYS

Spend two days in **Ottawa** ①–⑲, beginning at the Parliament Buildings, where a variety of indoor sights and outdoor events could keep you occupied for an afternoon. Ottawa's colorful downtown and excursions to neighboring Hull are full of activities based on history and culture. On day three, drive to **Upper Canada Village** ⑳, which captures the spirit of the United Empire Loyalists' struggle to sustain Canadian independence during the War of 1812. Afterward, explore the Heritage Highways, stopping at historic **Kingston** ㉒, the country's capital from 1841 to 1844. Besides the massive Fort Henry, Kingston is home to the International Hockey Hall of Fame. Consider taking a jaunt to **Prince Edward County** ㉓, a Loyalist enclave with strong ties to Sir John A. MacDonald, Canada's first prime minister. If you're ambitious, you can try to make it to ⛺ **Peterborough** ㉖ by nightfall.

IF YOU HAVE 5 DAYS

After spending three days in **Ottawa** ①–⑲, **Kingston** ㉒, and **Prince Edward County** ㉓, you can use **Peterborough** ㉖ as a springboard from which to explore Ontario's "cottage country." Native rock carvings can be found at the **Petroglyphs Provincial Park** ㉗, northeast of Peterborough on Highway 26. To the west via Highways 12 and 93, dash to the towns of **Penetanguishene** and **Midland** ㉙, on the shores of Georgian Bay. To experience the bay's beauty, take a cruise from either town. Drive south to **St. Jacobs** ⑳, in the heart of Mennonite and Hutterite country. On day five, travel to **Kitchener/Waterloo** ㉙. If you're there on a Saturday, don't miss the Kitchener Market, where you can ogle a variety of goods. Head south to **Stratford** ㉑, home to the acclaimed Stratford Festival, a centerpiece of Canada's rich artistic landscape.

IF YOU HAVE 7 DAYS

After five days of visits to **Ottawa** ①–⑲, **Kingston** ㉒, the towns around Georgian Bay ㉙–㉜, **Kitchener/Waterloo** ㉙, and **Stratford** ⑳, head for

London ⑫, city of trees, via Highways 7 and 4. Its Storybook Gardens is one of the least expensive theme parks around. Next, drive along Highway 3 through United Empire Loyalist territory—the villages of **Port Stanley** ㊸, **St. Thomas** ㊷, **Port Dover** ㊶, and **Port Colborne** ㊴. By nightfall on Day 6, you will have reached 🔅 **Niagara Falls** ㊿–㊅, using it as a base from which to explore the diverse Niagara Peninsula. Drive through the wine region, making sure to stop for a few tastings, to 🔅 **Niagara-on-the-Lake** ㊅, home to several beautifully kept homes that date back 100 years. Devote the last day to taking in the Falls and its environs, where high- and low-brow attractions flourish.

When to Tour the Province of Ontario

In winter Ontario's weather veers toward the very severe, making road travel difficult, and many museums and attractions are either closed or have limited hours. Plan to visit between April and October, when most sites are open longer hours. Try to avoid touring over the crazy July 1 Canada Day weekend. The warm months also offer travelers the chance to catch some of the province's many cultural highlights, especially the Stratford and Shaw festivals, as well as to enjoy outdoor action such as boating and hiking, or even just resting on a beach.

OTTAWA

Only a few scattered settlers lived in what is now Ottawa when, in 1826, Colonel John By and his Royal Engineers arrived to build the Rideau Canal, which links the Ottawa River to Lake Ontario. This new waterway was intended to protect a supply route from Montréal to the Great Lakes in the event of a repeat of the War of 1812 against the Americans. Once By's headquarters had been established, the settlement, then called Bytown, grew rapidly and fast became a rowdy, rough-and-tumble backwoods town as hordes arrived seeking employment on the largest construction project on the continent. The canal, completed in 1832, was hacked through 200 km (124 mi) of swamp, rock, and lakes whose different levels were overcome by locks.

By 1837, when its population had reached 2,400, Bytown was declared a town by the attorney general of Upper Canada. Government moved slowly even then, and it was not legally incorporated until 1850. Five years later, when the population had reached 10,000, Bytown became a city and was farsightedly given the name Ottawa, a word of Native American origin meaning "a place for buying and selling."

Canadians are taught in school that it was Queen Victoria's fault their capital is inconveniently situated off the main east–west corridor along the U.S. border. From 1841 to 1857, politicians dithered, trying to decide among five possible sites, including Québec City, Montréal, Cobourg, Kingston, and Ottawa. In 1857 they passed the buck to Buckingham Palace, and Queen Victoria got them off the hook. She chose Ottawa for five reasons, all valid at the time: The site was politically acceptable to both Canada east and Canada west. It was also centrally located, reassuringly remote from the hostile United States, and industrially prosperous. And it had a naturally beautiful setting at the confluence of the Ottawa and Rideau rivers.

In 1859 construction began on the Parliament Buildings. The buildings are magnificent, but their location in the mid-1850s earned Ottawa the nickname "Westminster in the Wilderness." Today, neo-Gothic towers and spires are undergoing their first major restoration and renovation, with parts of the building promised to be shrouded in scaffolding until the year 2000.

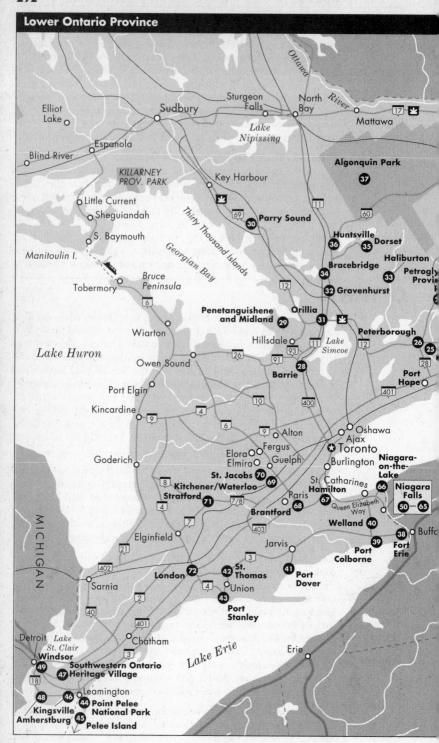

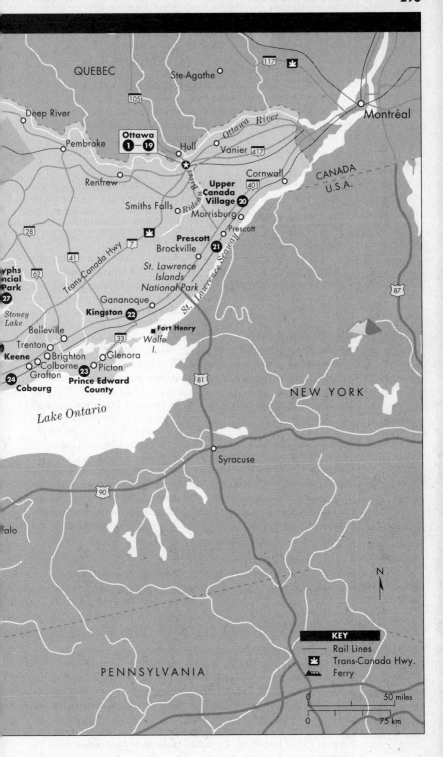

As early as 1899, federal politicians were concerned with more than just the grounds around the Parliament Buildings, known as "the Hill." A variety of commissions and committees and plans have become today's National Capital Commission (NCC). The NCC works with all municipalities within the 2,903-sq-km (1,800-sq-mi) National Capital Region, which includes neighboring Hull and a big chunk of Québec, to coordinate development in the best interests of the region. The result is a profusion of festivals, beautiful parks, bicycle paths, jogging trails, and the world's longest skating rink, on an 8-km (5-mi) stretch of the Rideau Canal in use from January to March.

Exploring Ottawa

Given Ottawa's architectural beauty and the fact that parking is at a premium here, one of the best ways to see many of the gems in this metropolis of 720,000 is on foot. A car, taxi, or bus is needed to visit some other major attractions and museums.

A Good Walk and Drive

Begin your walk at the **Parliament Buildings** ①. The Centre Block and the Peace Tower are surrounded by 29 acres of lawn interspersed by statues of celebrated Canadians. Turn right onto Wellington Street and walk past Bank Street to the Bank of Canada. At Sparks Street you can access the entrance to **Bank of Canada Currency Museum** ②, where seven galleries chronicle the evolution of notes and coins within the context of Canadian history. On Kent Street is the **Supreme Court** ③, housed in a stunning Art Deco edifice. At the end of Wellington Street is the **Garden of the Provinces** ④. Across from the park are the **National Archives of Canada** and **National Library of Canada** ⑤, two centers of Canadian history. Head back toward Parliament Hill via the friendly **Sparks Street Pedestrian Mall** ⑥. Emerging from the mall, you'll face **Confederation Square** ⑦, where homage is paid to those Canadians who didn't survive World War I. Adjacent to the square stands the **National Arts Centre** ⑧, a huge complex home to a fine orchestra plus English and French theater and dance performances. Walk northward along the Rideau Canal to Ottawa's older buildings: The **Bytown Museum** ⑨ houses a collection of 3,500 artifacts that once belonged to Colonel By. Next door are the **Rideau Locks** ⑩. Farther down the canal, toward Wellington Street, is the **Canadian Museum of Contemporary Photography** ⑪. Several blocks away, between George and York streets, is the site of **Byward Market** ⑫, with food shops that date back a century. About a five-minute walk up Sussex Drive, the **National Gallery of Canada** ⑬ reflects the Parliament Buildings in its modern mirror-and-granite facade. The **Canadian Museum of Nature** ⑭, a brisk 20-minute walk or short car ride from the Parliament Buildings, has a fabulous dinosaur display.

The remaining Ottawa highlights are more easily seen by car, taxi, or tour bus. Continue down Sussex Drive to view Ottawa's embassy row. Take a glimpse at the entrance to 24 Sussex Drive—the **Residence of the Prime Minister** ⑮—before finding the **Rideau Hall** ⑯, the governor-general's home, at 1 Sussex Drive. Continue on Sussex Drive to the Rockcliffe Driveway, and watch for the signs that proclaim 4 km (2½ mi) to the **National Aviation Museum** ⑰. It's worth the drive to the **National Museum of Science and Technology** ⑱, where children, in particular, will enjoy the institution's hands-on exhibits. Across the Ottawa River in Hull, Quebec, the **Canadian Museum of Civilization** ⑲ has an Imax/Omnimax theater and stunning collections documenting the country's history in a fresh interactive way.

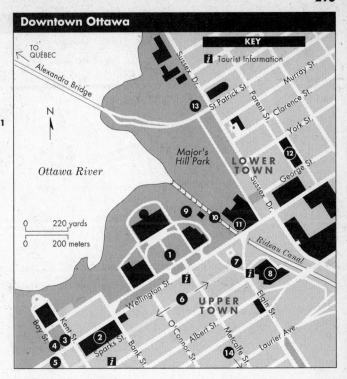

TIMING

You'll need at least a day to visit the sights on the walking portion of
the tour and a day to drive to the more distant attractions; allow more
time if you wish to tour the museums. Most museums are closed Monday, but the staff at the Capital Infocentre (☞ Visitor Information *in*
Ottawa A to Z, *below*) will help you locate those open if that happens
to be your only day in town.

Sights to See

② Bank of Canada Currency Museum. The ancestors of the credit card
are all here: bracelets made from elephant hair, cowrie shells, whale's
teeth, and what is believed to be the world's largest coin. Here, too,
of course, is the country's most complete collection of Canadian notes
and coins. ⊠ *245 Sparks St.,* ☎ *613/782–8914.* ⌾ *$2, free Tues.* ☉
Tues.–Sat. 10:30–5, Sun. 1–5 in summer.

⑨ Bytown Museum. In the former commissariat used by the Royal Engineers and Colonel John By during the building of the Rideau Canal—
the oldest stone masonry building in the city—you'll find exhibits that
record the life and times of Bytown and Ottawa. ⊠ *Wellington St. at
bottom of Ottawa Locks, behind Chateau Laurier Hotel,* ☎ *613/234–
4570.* ⌾ *$2.50.* ☉ *May–mid-Oct., Mon.–Sat. 10–5, Sun. 1–5; mid-
Oct.–late Nov., weekdays 10–4; Nov. 30–Apr. 1 by appointment only.*

⑫ Byward Market. The excellent fresh produce and maple products have
been attracting shoppers to this farmers' market since 1840. Surrounding the market stalls are permanent specialty food shops, some
well over 100 years old, as well as cafés and boutiques. ⊠ *Between
George and York Sts.* ☉ *Sun.–Wed., 8–6, Thurs.–Sat., 8–9.*

⑲ Canadian Museum of Civilization. Across the Ottawa River in Hull,
Québec, is one of the area's most architecturally stunning museums. Here,

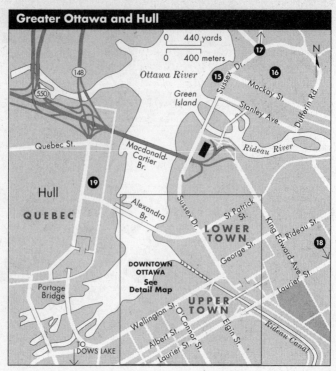

Greater Ottawa and Hull

visitors can trace Canada's history from prehistoric times to the present. In the Grand Hall are six Canadian West Coast Native longhouses, towering totem poles, and life-size reconstructions of an archaeological dig. Kids can enjoy hands-on activities in the newly expanded Children's Museum. In the Cineplus you'll find the larger-than-life IMAX and Omnimax. ⊠ *100 Laurier St., Hull,* ☎ *819/776–7000 or 800/555-5621, 819/776–7010 Cineplus.* 🎫 *Museum $5 (free Sun. 9–noon), Cineplus $7 (varies with show).* ☉ *Tues.–Sun. 9–5, Thurs. 9–9.*

⑪ Canadian Museum of Contemporary Photography. Opened in 1992, this museum holds more than 158,000 images, spotlighted in changing exhibitions. There are also a 50-seat theater and a boutique. ⊠ *1 Rideau Canal,* ☎ *613/990–8257.* 🎫 *Free.* ☉ *Wed., Fri., and weekends 11–5, Thurs. 11–8; closed Wed. and Thurs. in winter.*

⑭ Canadian Museum of Nature. In a castlelike building, the museum and its exhibits explore the evolution of the Earth, plus the birds, mammals, and plants of Canada. The dinosaur collection is outstanding. The Viola MacMillan Mineral Gallery displays a world-class collection. ⊠ *McLeod St. at Metcalfe St.,* ☎ *613/566-4700.* 🎫 *$4; ½ price Thurs. until 5, free 5–8.* ☉ *Fri.–Wed. 10–5, Thurs. 10–8.*

⑦ Confederation Square. In the center of this triangular junction in the heart of the city stands the **National War Memorial,** honoring the 66,651 Canadian dead of World War I. ⊠ *Wellington, Sparks, and Elgin Sts.*

④ Garden of the Provinces. Two fountains and the arms and floral emblems of Canada's 10 provinces and two territories commemorate confederation in this park. ⊠ *Southwest corner of Bay and Wellington Sts.*

⑤ National Archives of Canada and **National Library of Canada.** The archives, Canada's oldest cultural institution, contain more than 60 million manuscripts and government records, 1 million maps, and about 11 million photographs. The National Library collects, preserves, and promotes the published heritage of Canada and exhibits books, paintings, maps, and photographs. Both institutions mount exhibitions regularly. ⊠ *395 Wellington St. at Bay St.,* ☎ *613/995–5138 archives, 613/995–9481 library.* 🖼 *Free.* ⊙ *Daily 9–9.*

❽ **National Arts Centre.** Completed in 1969, the complex includes an opera hall, a theater, a studio theater, and a salon for readings and concerts. The grounds are populated with sculptures by Canadian artists. The canal-side café, **Le Café,** spills outside in warm weather and is popular for a meal or drink; in winter it's a cozy vantage spot from which to watch skaters on the canal. ⊠ *53 Elgin St.,* ☎ *613/996–5051.*

🦢 ⓱ **National Aviation Museum.** Among over 100 aircraft are a replica of the model that made the first powered flight in Canada. Engines, propellers, and aeronautical antiques complete the collection. ⊠ *Rockcliffe and Aviation pkwys.,* ☎ *613/993–2010 or 800/463–2038.* 🖼 *$5, free Thurs. 5–9.* ⊙ *Sept. 3–May 1, Tues.–Sun. 10–5, Thurs. 10–10; May 2–Sept. 2, daily 9–5, Thurs. 9–9.*

⓭ **National Gallery of Canada.** In a magnificent, glass-towered structure engineered by Canadian architect Moshe Safdie is one of the premier collections of Canadian art in the world. Inside is the reconstructed **Rideau Convent Chapel,** a classic example of French Canadian 19th-century architecture with the only neo-Gothic fan-vaulted ceiling on the continent. The building has three restaurants and a large bookstore with publications on the arts. ⊠ *380 Sussex Dr.,* ☎ *613/990–1985.* 🖼 *Free, except special exhibits.* ⊙ *Daily 10–6 (Thurs. until 8); closed Mon. and Tues. in winter.*

🦢 ⓲ **National Museum of Science and Technology.** Canada's largest museum has permanent displays of printing presses, antique cars, steam locomotives, and agricultural machinery, as well as ever-changing exhibits, many of which are hands-on, or "minds-on." The evening "Discover the Universe" program uses the largest refracting telescope in Canada to stargaze into the world of astronomy. ⊠ *1867 St. Laurent Blvd.,* ☎ *613/991–3044.* 🖼 *$6.* ⊙ *Labor Day–Apr., daily 9–5; May–Labor Day, Sat.–Thurs. 9–6, Fri. 9–9.*

🦢 ❶ **Parliament Buildings.** Three beloved Gothic-style buildings with copper roofs dominate the nation's capital from Parliament Hill on a promontory overlooking the Ottawa River. Originally built in 1867, they were destroyed by fire and rebuilt in 1916. Currently, they are undergoing extensive restoration, slated for completion in 2000. The **Centre Block** is where the Senate and House of Commons, the two houses of Parliament, work to shape the laws of the land. The wonderfully detailed stone frieze in the foyer, which depicts Canadian history, and the masterfully carved stone pillars and provincial emblems in stained glass in the House of Commons, are all works of the nationally renowned artist Eleanor Milne.

The central **Peace Tower** houses a Memorial Chamber with an Altar of Sacrifice, which bears the names of 66,651 Canadians killed during service in World War I, and the 44,895 Canadians who died in World War II. Also in the Tower is the 53-bell carillon; concerts are performed daily in summer by the Dominion Carillonneur. Outside on the lawn, there's plenty of room to observe the colorful **Changing of the Guard ceremony** that takes place daily, late June to late August, weather permitting. The Ceremonial Guard brings together two of Canada's most historic regiments, the Canadian Grenadier Guards and the Governor General's Foot Guards.

North of the Centre Block and reached via its corridors is the **Library of Parliament.** A statue of a young Queen Victoria is the centerpiece of the octagonal-shaped chamber. The walls are ornately carved pine galleries lined with books, many of them priceless.

In front of, and to either side of, the Centre Block are the **East Block** and the **West Block.** The East Block has four historic rooms open to the public: the original Governor General's office restored to the period of Lord Dufferin, 1872–1878; the offices of Sir John A. Macdonald and Sir George Étienne Cartier, Fathers of the Confederation in 1867; and the Privy Council Chamber. The West Block, originally designed to house the civil service, has been converted to offices for parliamentarians and is not open to the public.

Against the backdrop of the imposing Parliament Buildings, a free half-hour laser **Sound and Light Show** highlights Canada's history. ⊠ *Parliament Hill,* ☎ *613/992–4793 or 613/996–0896.* ☞ *Free.* ☉ *Mid-May–Labor Day, daily 9–8:30; Labor Day–mid-May, daily 9–4:30; 20-min tours in English or French every ½ hr; same-day reservations for tours available at white Infotent east of Centre Block; sound-and-light shows late May–Labor Day, twice nightly (1 in English, 1 in French).*

⑮ Residence of the Prime Minister. It has been home to men named Laurier, Massey, and Trudeau, among others. Unlike the White House, it is not open for public inspection. Lacking an invitation, you can hope only for a drive-by glimpse of a couple of roof gables. Don't even try parking near the mansion; security is tight. ⊠ *24 Sussex Dr.*

⑯ Rideau Hall. The official residence of the governor-general of Canada since 1865 houses visiting heads of state, royalty, and the monarch when any of them are here on official business. The 1830 mansion has a ballroom, a skating rink, and a cricket pitch. Sentries of the Canadian Grenadier Guards and the Governor General's Foot Guards are posted outside the main gate of Rideau Hall in summer. Free guided tours of the public rooms and grounds are conducted, but days and times change frequently. ⊠ *1 Sussex Dr.,* ☎ *613/998–7113.*

⑩ Rideau Locks. On the Rideau Canal, which runs southward through the city from the Ottawa River, the locks are a downtown landmark. ⊠ *Junction of Rideau Canal and Wellington St., where Wellington becomes Rideau St.*

⑥ Sparks Street Pedestrian Mall. Here, the automobile has been banished and browsers can wander carefree in warm weather among fountains, rock gardens, sculptures, and outdoor cafés. ⊠ *1 block south of Wellington St., between Confederation Square and Kent St.*

⑨ Supreme Court. Established in 1875, this body became the ultimate court of appeal in the land in 1949. The nine judges sit in their stately Art Deco building for three sessions each year. ⊠ *Kent and Wellington Sts.,* ☎ *613/995–4330.* ☞ *Free.* ☉ *Tours May–Aug., daily 9–5; Sept.–Apr., by appointment.*

Dining

$$ ✕ Chequers. In this three-story, Gothic-style 1868 country inn 25 km (16 mi) southwest of Ottawa, the specialties are French and Spanish haute cuisine. The service is European and so is the decor. ⊠ *5816 Hazeldean Rd., Stittsville,* ☎ *613/836–1665. Reservations essential. AE, MC, V.*

$$ ✕ Courtyard Restaurant. Fine French cuisine is served in this lovely, historic limestone building on a quiet cul-de-sac near Byward Market, a five-minute stroll from the Parliament Buildings. The forerunner of today's elegant dining establishment was a log tavern built in 1827, probably to take advantage of the construction of the nearby Rideau Canal. The humble tavern was replaced by the limestone Ottawa Hotel a decade later. Extensive renovations created the Courtyard Restaurant, and its cuisine and ambience attracted a dedicated following. ⊠ *21 George St., ☎ 613/241–1516. Reservations essential. AE, MC, V.*

$$ ✕ **Fresco.** This cozy Italian restaurant's dominant feature is the mural of mountains in Tuscany on the back wall, although the dizzying number of food options is impressive, too. You can choose from 10 sauces to accompany such house specialties as scallops, salmon, and veal. ⊠ *354 Elgin St., ☎ 613/235–7541. AE, DC, MC, V.*

Lodging

$$$$ 🏨 **Westin Hotel.** Attached to the Rideau Centre shopping mall and convention hall, this 24-story hotel in the heart of Ottawa has modern rooms done in pastel hues. Floor to ceiling windows provide one of the best views in Ottawa ($20 extra for rooms facing the Rideau Canal and the Parliament Buildings). ⊠ *11 Colonel By Dr., K1N 9H4, ☎ 613/560–7000 or 800/228–3000, FAX 613/234–5396. 484 rooms. Restaurant, lounge, night club, indoor pool, 2 saunas, whirlpool, exercise room, 2 squash courts. AE, MC, V.*

$$$–$$$$ 🏨 **Albert at Bay.** One- and two-bedroom suites make up this 12- story hotel close to the Sparks Street Mall, with fully equipped kitchens and laundry facilities. ⊠ *435 Albert St. (corner Bay and Albert), ☎ 613/238–8858 or 800/267–6644, FAX 613/238–1433. Restaurant, hot tub, sauna, exercise room, 24-hr convenience store, indoor parking. AE, MC, V, DC.*

$$$–$$$$ 🏨 **Château Laurier Hotel.** Ottawa has all kinds of posh new hotels with
★ great service and food, but this grand hotel is an institution. It's one of Canada's greatest railroad hotels, built in 1912 and named for Sir Wilfrid Laurier, who served as prime minister from 1896 to 1911. Rooms that were formerly on the small side have been combined into suites. Zoe's, the glassed-in conservatory lounge, serves afternoon tea and coffee and a sumptuous Sunday brunch. The Château, as it's known, is truly part of the Ottawa experience. ⊠ *1 Rideau St., K1N 8S7, ☎ 613/241–1414 or 800/441–1414, FAX 613/562–7030. 425 rooms. Restaurant, lounge, bar, indoor pool, health club, children's programs. AE, MC, V.*

Nightlife and the Arts

The Arts

More than 900 performances are showcased at the **National Arts Centre** (⊠ 53 Elgin St., ☎ 613/996–5051) annually, and it is the home of the National Arts Centre Orchestra. In summer the Centre is one of the hosts of the **Ottawa International Jazz Festival, Cultures Canada,** and the biennial **Canada Dance Festival.**

Nightlife

Barrymore's (⊠ 53 Elgin St., ☎ 613/996–5051) has transformed the Imperial Theatre of 1914, strategically located on the Bank Street promenade, into one of the city's most energetic nightclubs. It draws a twenty-to-thirty-something crowd. Live musicians take center stage from Wednesday through Saturday until midnight, after which dance music thumps through the three-tiered hall until 2 AM.

Outdoor Activities and Sports

Biking

Ottawa has 150 km (93 mi) of bicycle paths. On Sunday **Queen Elizabeth Drive** and **Colonel By Drive** are closed to traffic until noon for cyclists. Rent A Bike, in the Château Laurier Hotel (☞ Lodging, *above*), rents a variety of bicycles for all ages, including tandems.

Hiking

The **Rideau Trail** runs 406 km (252 mi) along the Rideau Canal from Kingston to Ottawa. Access points from the highway are marked with orange triangles. Contact Rideau Trail Association (⊠ Box 15, Kingston K7L 4V6).

Skating

In winter the Rideau Canal transforms into the longest skating rink in the world, stretching from the National Arts Centre to Dows Lake. Across from The National Arts Centre, skates can be rented and sharpened, and wooden sleds for towing children can also be rented. Along the route are a few warmup/changing shelters and food concessions. Call the NCC (☎ 613/239–5234) for daily skating conditions.

Shopping

Antiques

John Coles at the Astrolabe Gallery (⊠ 112 Sparks St., ☎ 613/234–2348) is a good source for 19th-century prints of Ottawa scenes or antique maps of North America.

Shopping Center

Rideau Centre (⊠ Rideau St. and Colonel By Dr.) has more than 200 stores, including The Bay and Eaton department stores.

Ottawa A to Z

Arriving and Departing

BY BUS

Voyageur Colonial Bus Lines (⊠ 265 Catherine St., ☎ 613/238–5900) offers frequent service from Montréal and Toronto to Ottawa, including some express buses.

BY CAR

Highway 417 links Ottawa to Quebec from the east; Highway 16 connects Ottawa with the Trans-Canada Highway to the south.

BY PLANE

Ottawa International Airport (☎ 613/998–3151), 18 km (11 mi) from downtown, is served by Air Canada (☎ 613/247–5000 or 800/268–7240), First Air (☎ 613/839–1247 or 800/267–1247), Canadian Airlines International (☎ 613/237–1380 or 800/665–1177), Delta Airlines (☎ 800/363–2857 or 800/843–9378), and US Airways (☎ 800/428–4322).

BY TRAIN

Trans-Canada **ViaRail** serves the Ottawa rail station (⊠ 200 Tremblay Rd., ☎ 613/244–8289) at the southeastern end of town. It's a $12 taxi ride to downtown.

Getting Around

BY BUS

OC Transpo (☎ 613/741–4390) serves the metropolitan region of Ottawa–Carleton on the Ontario side of the Ottawa River. It operates buses on city streets and on the Transitway, a system of bus-only roads. All bus routes in downtown Ottawa meet at the Rideau Centre (⊠ Rideau St. between Nicholas and Sussex and the Mackenzie King Bridge).

BY TAXI

Major cab companies such as **Blue Line** (☎ 613/238–1111) and **Capital** (☎ 613/746–2233) operate in and around Ottawa.

Contacts and Resources

EMERGENCIES

If you are in need of emergency assistance, dial 911. The main hospitals in Ottawa are **Ottawa General Hospital** (☎ 613/737–7777) and **Ottawa Civic Hospital** (☎ 613/761–4000). **Shoppers Drug Mart** (✉ 1460 Merivale Rd., ☎ 613/224–7270) is a 24-hour pharmacy.

GUIDED TOURS

Paul's Boat Lines Limited (☎ 613/225–6781) offers seven 75-minute cruises daily on the Rideau Canal and four 90-minute cruises daily on the Ottawa River from mid-May to mid-October. Canal boats dock across from the National Arts Centre; river cruise boats dock at the Bytown Museum at the foot of the Ottawa Locks on the Rideau Canal. **Ottawa Riverboat Company** (☎ 613/562–4888) operates two-hour sightseeing boat tours on the Ottawa River from May through October.

Gray Line (☎ 613/748–4426) operates frequent, two-hour, 50-km (31-mi) orientation bus tours ($16) from mid-May through October. **Picadilly Bus Tours** (☎ 613/820–6745) has a regular schedule of 1¼-hour tours in double-decker London buses to Ottawa's major sites, May through October.

VISITOR INFORMATION

Just across from the Parliament Buildings is the **Capital Infocentre** (✉ 90 Wellington St., ☎ 613/239–5000 or 800/465–1867).

THE HERITAGE HIGHWAYS

Most of Ontario's first French, English, and Loyalist settlers entered the province from the southeast. You can retrace some of their routes on southern Ontario's Heritage Highways. Highway 2, parallel to Highway 401, is smaller than the cross Ontario freeway and more picturesque. It's the original 19th-century route that linked Québec and Kingston to "Muddy York" (Toronto) in the west. And with appropriate detours it can afford you a good glimpse into many of this area's diverse attractions.

Upper Canada Village

★ ⑳ *86 km (53 mi) southeast of Ottawa on Hwys. 2 and 401.*

Eight villages disappeared under rising waters when the St. Lawrence Seaway opened in 1959, but their best historic buildings were moved to a new site, called Upper Canada Village, a faithful re-creation of an Ontario community from the 1800s. The village occupies 66 acres of the 2,000-acre Crysler's Farm Battlefield Memorial Park, which figured prominently in the War of 1812. Such anachronisms as radios and tape players are banned in this throwback to the days of the United Empire Loyalists. The village has three mills, two farms, two churches, two hotels, and 25 other buildings. A leisurely tour takes three to four hours. More than 150 staff people are on site, all in early 1800s costume, to answer questions. The Village Store sells Canadian crafts and village-made bread, cheese, and flour. Willard's Hotel serves lunches, full-course meals, and teas. ✉ *Hwy. 2E, Morrisburg,* ☎ *613/543–3704.* ⌑ *$12.50.* ☉ *Mid-May–mid-Oct., daily 9:30–5; group tours may be arranged year-round.*

Prescott

★ ㉑ *40 km (25 mi) west of Morrisburg on Hwy. 2.*

Both Prescott's Fort Wellington and the Old Lighthouse saw action in the War of 1812. Both have been restored and are open to the public.

Fort Wellington was built by the British in 1813 to protect goods and troops moving between Montréal and Upper Canada after the outbreak of the War of 1812. No harm ever came to the fort, which was completed when the war ended. The Ottawa–Kingston Rideau Canal eliminated its need and the fort was abandoned. In 1837 rebellion broke out in Upper and Lower Canada, and the British built a new and stronger Fort Wellington on the same site. The buildings are furnished in 1846 period style. ✉ *370 Vankoughnet St.,* ☎ *613/925–2896.* ✉ *$2.25.* ⏰ *Mid-May–Aug., daily 10–6; Sept.–mid-Oct., daily 10–5; mid-Oct.–mid-May, by reservation only.*

Ontario's oldest barracks building is one block west of Fort Wellington and open in summer as a museum. Lunches and dinners at **Stockade Barracks and Hospital Museum** feature historic menus. By prior arrangement, groups of 15–40 can have five- or six-course meals of 1812-style dishes served by mess waiters in military uniforms. ✉ *356 East St.,* ☎ *613/925–4894.* ✉ *$2.* ⏰ *June–Sept., weekends 10–5.*

Kingston

🄬 *100 km (62 mi) southwest of Prescott on Hwy. 401.*

Kingston's imposing architecture has been impressing visitors since 1673, when La Salle chose the location as the site for a meeting between Governor Frontenac and the Iroquois. Before the meeting, Frontenac built a stockaded fort to impress the Native Americans and thus tap into the fur trade. The city occupied a strategic site at the junction of the St. Lawrence River and the Rideau Canal system, making it a major military site in upper Canada. Four Martello towers still guard the harbor. Thanks to misguided American strategy, Kingston survived the War of 1812 almost totally unscathed; Many of its beautiful limestone buildings remain in mint condition today.

From 1841 to 1844, Kingston was the national capital; today the gorgeous, cut-limestone **City Hall** (✉ 216 Ontario St., ☎ 613/546–4291) dominates the downtown core, facing a riverfront park. Tours are given weekdays in summer, but you can wander through the lobby any time of year.

Point Frederick, a small peninsula at the junction of the Cataraqui River and St. Lawrence River, is connected to downtown Kingston by a bridge. The site of the Royal Navy Dockyard until 1850, Point Frederick became home to the **Royal Military College of Canada** in 1876. Explore the relics of the dockyard on the college grounds. Of particular note is the **Royal Military College Museum,** housed in the largest of the four Martello towers that guarded the Kingston harborfront. The museum contains the internationally renowned Douglas Arms Collection, which includes the small arms owned by General Porfirio Díaz, president of Mexico from 1886 to 1912. ✉ *Off Hwy. 2, east of Kingston,* ☎ *613/541–6000, Ext. 6652.* ✉ *Free.* ⏰ *Last weekend in June–Labor Day, daily 10–5.*

★ The massive **Fort Henry** was built during the War of 1812 to repel a possible American invasion, which never came. Staff in period military costume guide visitors, hold parades, and re-create an era past. ✉ *Hwys. 2 and 15,* ☎ *613/542–7388.* ✉ *$8.75.* ⏰ *Mid-May–late Sept., daily 10–5; Oct. by reservation only.*

Locals have nicknamed it Tea Caddy Castle, Molasses Hall, and Pekoe Pagoda, but Canada's first prime minister, Sir John A. Macdonald, who lived in the house for a year, called it **Bellevue** because of its view of the St. Lawrence River. Today the 1840 house is a National Historic

Park site, restored and furnished in the style of 1848, when Macdonald lived here. ⊠ *35 Centre St.,* ☎ *613/545–8666.* ⊠ *$2.50.* ☉ *June–Labor Day, daily 9–6; Apr., May, Sept., and Oct., daily 10–5.*

The **Pump House Steam Museum** (⊠ 23 Ontario St., ☎ 613/546–4696), a restored Victorian-style 1849 municipal water-pumping station, is maintained by the Marine Museum of the Great Lakes at Kingston (☞ *below*). All exhibits run on steam; models range from miniatures to an 1897-model Toronto-built engine with a 9-ton flywheel. ⊠ *23 Ontario St.,* ☎ *613/546–4696.* ⊠ *$3.75.* ☉ *June–Labor Day.*

The rambling display area at the **Marine Museum of the Great Lakes at Kingston,** at the historic former Kingston dry dock, traces Great Lakes shipping since 1678. The museum's *Alexander Henry,* a 3,000-ton, 210-ft retired icebreaker, is open for tours in summer; visitors can rent a stateroom and sleep aboard. ⊠ *55 Ontario St.,* ☎ *613/542–2261.* ⊠ *$5.75.* ☉ *Apr.–Dec., daily 10–5; Jan.–Mar., weekdays 10–4.*

Kingston is the birthplace of organized ice hockey—the first league game was played in the city in 1885. So it seems fitting that the city is also home to an **International Ice Hockey Federation Museum,** a shrine to puck-chasing. (Canada's other Hockey Hall of Fame opened at a larger venue in Toronto in 1993.) ⊠ *York and Alfred Sts., 1 block north of Princess St. (Hwy. 2),* ☎ *613/544–2355.* ⊠ *$2.* ☉ *Mid-June–mid-Sept., Mon.–Sat., 10–5; Sun. noon–5; late Sept.–early June, weekends by appointment.*

Lodging

$$$ ⊞ **Hochelaga Inn.** This Victorian inn, built more than a century ago, is in a quiet residential and historic neighborhood, yet only a five-minute walk from downtown. All the rooms have private baths, and all but one have a queen-size bed. The inn has neither bar nor restaurant, but a Continental breakfast is included in the room rate. ⊠ *24 Sydenham St. S, K7L 3G9,* ☎ ⊞ *613/549–5534 or 800/267–0525. 23 rooms. AE, MC, V.*

Prince Edward County

㉓ *80 km (50 mi) southwest of Kingston.*

Though the island county of Prince Edward can be reached by car via Highway 33, a free, 10-minute car ferry ride, which departs from Adolphustown every 15 minutes in summer, is another option. New Englanders wandering this island county may find themselves wondering if they've ever left home—so similar are the scenery and the pages of history that brought both regions into being. The island was one of the earliest parts of Ontario to be settled after the American Revolution, and a Loyalist influence remained dominant for generations. The Loyalist church erected in 1822 is still used as a parish meeting hall.

Picton, the island's capital of sorts, is a serene town of 4,300 with fine old buildings and strong associations with Sir John A. Macdonald, Canada's first prime minister, who practiced law at the 1834 county courthouse, which is still in use. Within the town is the **Macaulay Heritage Park,** which sits on about 15 acres of land and includes picnic facilities, the **Macaulay House,** and the **County Museum.** Tours of the park and the town's attractions are available by prior arrangement and may include a visit to the jail, where a double gallows is kept handy (although it hasn't been used since 1884). ⊠ *1 block south of Hwy. 33 at Union and Church Sts.,* ☎ *613/476–3833.* ⊠ *Macaulay House $2.* ☉ *June–Labor Day, weekdays 10–4:30, weekends 1–4:30.*

Dining and Lodging

$$$–$$$$ ✕⊞ **Isaiah Tubbs Resort.** A dozen km (7 mi) west of Picton, this posh 60-room property has rooms and suites with fireplaces as well as 12 sea-

sonal cottages. There's fine dining in the Restaurant on the Knoll Overlooking the Sandbanks at West Lake. (That's the correct name of the restaurant and that's what it overlooks!) ⊠ *R.R. 1, K0K 2T0,* ☎ *613/393–2090 or 800/267–0525,* FAX *613/393–2812. 60 rooms. Restaurant, indoor pool, outdoor pool, hot tub, sauna, exercise room. AE, MC, V.*

$$$ 🖫 **Merrill Inn.** This beautiful 1870 house is a short stroll from the heart of downtown Picton. It has been converted to a cozy 15-room inn by the same folks who created Idlewylde Inn at London (☞ Hamilton and Festival Country, *below*). The refrigerator is stocked with soft drinks and the sideboard with croissants, muffins, tea, and coffee 24 hours a day, but no meals are served. ⊠ *343 Main St. E, K0K 2T0,* ☎ *613/476– 7451 or 800/567–5969. 14 rooms. AE, D, MC, V.*

Cobourg

㉔ *75 km (47 mi) west of Picton on Hwy. 401 or Hwy. 2.*

Cobourg once expected to be chosen as the provincial capital. It was passed over, but not before the town nearly went bankrupt building the magnificent **Victoria Hall,** officially opened in 1860 by the young Prince of Wales, later King Edward VII. A courtroom modeled after London's Old Bailey was on the ground floor, and town council meetings, formal balls, and concerts were held on the second floor. Today you can tour some of the building's 41 rooms. ⊠ *55 King St. W,* ☎ *905/372–5831,* FAX *905/372–2411.* 🖾 *Free.* ☉ *Guided tours in summer or by prior arrangement.*

Keene

㉕ *27 km (17 mi) north of Port Hope via Hwys. 28 and 2.*

Keene's most noteworthy attraction is an unusual gravesite. About 2,000 years ago, a nomadic native tribe buried its dead in nine earth mounds, the largest of which is shaped like a 200-ft-long serpent. The burial ground is preserved in **Serpent Mounds Park.** An interpretation center explains the site and displays artifacts. ⊠ *R.R. 3, Hwy. 34,* ☎ *705/295–4421,* FAX *705/295–4424.* 🖾 *$5 per vehicle.* ☉ *Mid-May–Labor Day, daily.*

About 3 km (2 mi) north of the village of Keene is the well-signed **Lang Pioneer Village,** with its museum and 26 pioneer buildings. You can see displays and demonstrations of pioneer arts and crafts in summer. ⊠ *Off Hwy. 34, Lang,* ☎ *705/295–6694.* 🖾 *$5.* ☉ *June–Labor Day, weekdays 11–5, Sat. 1–5, Sun. noon–5; visitor center only Labor Day–May, weekdays 9–4.*

Peterborough

㉖ *13 km (8 mi) northeast of Keene via Hwys. 34 and 7.*

The small city of Peterborough is home to Trent University. The lift locks on the **Trent-Severn Waterway** are among the world's highest and are in operation from mid-May through October. Built in 1904, they have floated boats straight up 65 ft in less than 10 minutes. If you want to learn more about the way the locks work, you can see slides and films at the **Peterborough Lift and Lock Visitor Centre** (⊠ Hunter St. E, ☎ 705/750–4950, FAX 705/750–4958), also open from mid-May through October.

Dining and Lodging

$$$ ✕🖫 **Ramada Inn.** This hotel is connected to the city's largest downtown indoor shopping complex. Guest rooms are comfortably furnished. Sir William's restaurant offers Continental fare and lighter meals (be

30%* more charming.

(*depending on the exchange rate)

AIR CANADA

Air Canada can't take credit for the very generous exchange rate on American currency. But, in all modesty, we do pride ourselves on getting a lot of other things right. *Like more nonstops* between the USA and Canada than any other airline. Not to mention convenient connections to our vast global network. We even offer you your choice of Mileage Plus[®1], OnePass[®2] or our own Aeroplan[®3] miles.

So to say that we are eager to please would be a remarkable understatement. However, this may help to explain why Americans polled by Business Traveler International Magazine declared Air Canada *The Best Airline to Canada.* For the fifth year in a row (wow, thanks guys). And why more people fly Air Canada from the USA to Canada than any other airline. Air Canada. We're like a regular airline, only nicer.

For more details, please call your travel agent or Air Canada at **1-800-776-3000.** For great holiday packages, call **Air Canada's Canada at 1-800-774-8993 (ext. 8045).** And feel free to visit us on our Internet site at this address: http://www.aircanada.ca

[1]Mileage Plus is a registered trademark of United Airlines. [2]OnePass is a registered trademark of Continental Airlines. [3]Aeroplan is a registered trademark of Air Canada.

The nicer way to fly.[TM]

Pick up the phone.
Pick up the miles.

1-800-FLY-FREE

Is this a great time, or what? :-)

Now when you sign up with MCI you can receive up to 8,000 bonus frequent flyer miles on one of seven major airlines.

Then earn another 5 miles for every dollar you spend on a variety of MCI services, including MCI Card® calls from virtually anywhere in the world.[*]

You're going to use these services anyway. Why not rack up the miles while you're doing it?

sure to reserve), and snacks are served at the Garden Cafe in the pool area. ⊠ *100 Charlotte St., K9J 7L4,* ☎ *705/743–7272,* FAX *705/749–0845. 170 rooms. 2 restaurants, indoor pool, hot tub, sauna, free parking. AE, D, MC, V.*

Petroglyphs Provincial Park

㉗ *50 km (31 mi) northeast of Peterborough on Hwy. 28.*

Canada's largest concentration of native rock carvings was found at the east end of Stony Lake, outside the hamlet of Stonyridge, in 1954. The site is now within Petroglyphs Provincial Park. The well-preserved symbols and figures are carved on a flat expanse of white marble almost 70 ft wide, which are sheltered in a protective building. The more than 900 carvings are believed to be of Algonquin spirit figures. ⊠ *East of Hwy. 28 on Northey's Bay Rd., Stonyridge,* ☎ *705/877–2552.* ⊡ *$6 per vehicle.* ☉ *Mid-May–mid-Oct., daily.*

NORTH OF TORONTO TO THE LAKES

There are several ways to explore this picturesque area, known to Torontonians as "Cottage Country." You can take a day trip from Toronto, driving through the area and perhaps stopping for a picnic lunch at one of the lakes or at one of numerous roadside restaurants. Alternatively, spend up to a week exploring the district from one of many lakeside resorts near towns such as Orillia, Gravenhurst, Bracebridge, and Huntsville. A cheaper—but equally satisfying choice—is to rent a cottage for a week or two. "Cottages" range from log cabins to palatial homes that would not look out of place in a wealthy urban neighborhood. Rentals are available through local real estate agents.

Barrie

㉘ *75 km (47 mi) north of Toronto on Hwy. 400.*

Barrie is on the shores of Lake Simcoe. A winter carnival brings ice fishing, dogsledding, and ice motorcycling. From late June through Labor Day, there's informal drama in **Gryphon Theatre** at Georgian College and harness racing at **Barrie Raceway.**

More than a dozen artists have studios in the Barrie area; most of the work spaces are attached to their homes. For studio tour maps, call tour organizer Chris Symes (☎ 705/329–0842). Among those studios worth a visit is the home of **Henni Stoffregen,** who sells lamp shades, place mats, cards, and numerous other items made from pressed wildflowers, leaves, and grasses. ⊠ *Mill St. and Mt. St. Louis Rd. near Hillsdale,* ☎ *705/835–3296.*

Dining and Lodging

$$$$ ✕⌂ **Inn at Horseshoe.** On a ski hill at the Horseshoe Resort, this top-drawer lodge has modern guest rooms with down comforters. Many suites have sunken living rooms, wood-burning fireplaces, and whirlpools. Dining options range from the distinctive Continental menu of the formal Silks restaurant to the informal fare at the Santa Fe–style Go West Grill. When the snow melts, you can tee off on the 18-hole or the nine-hole golf courses. ⊠ *Horse Valley Rd., L4M 4Y8,* ☎ *705/835–2790,* FAX *705/835–5232. 57 rooms, 53 suites, 172-condominium complex. 2 restaurants, lounge, 1 indoor and 2 outdoor pools, hot tub, 27-hole golf course, 2 tennis courts, exercise room, squash, mountain bikes, downhill skiing. AE, MC, V.*

$$$–$$$$ ✕⌂ **Blue Mountain Resort.** In addition to being the largest ski resort in Ontario, this acclaimed lodge at the base of the slopes has an out-

standing 18-hole golf course. The guest rooms are fairly standard, and suites as well as condominium units have kitchens and fireplaces. At the Pottery dining room, you'll find Continental interpretations of Canadian standards, or you can opt for the Mexican-influenced Montero Pavilion restaurant. ⊠ *R.R. 3, Collingwood L9Y 3Z2,* ☎ *705/445–0231,* FAX *705/444–1751. 98 rooms, 2 suites, 100 condominiums. 2 restaurants, lounge, indoor and outdoor pools, outdoor hot tub, massage, sauna, 18-hole golf course, 9 tennis courts, exercise room, squash, beach. AE, MC, V.*

Skiing

Blue Mountain (☎ 705/445–0231 or 416/869–3799), near Collingwood, west of Barrie on Highway 26, is Ontario's most extensively developed and heavily used ski area, with a vertical drop of 720 ft. It has 32 pistes served by a high-speed quad lift, three triple chairs, eight double chairs, two pomas, and a rope tow. **Horseshoe Valley Resort** (☎ 705/835–2790), near Barrie, is among the few resorts that offer both Nordic and downhill skiing facilities. It has 22 runs served by a quad and two triple and three double lifts. The vertical drop is only 309 ft, but seven of the runs are rated for advanced skiers.

Penetanguishene and Midland

㉙ *80 km (50 mi) north of Barrie on Hwys. 400 and 93.*

The quiet towns of Penetanguishene (known locally as Penetang) and Midland occupy a small corner of northern Simcoe County known as Huronia. Both towns sit on a snug, safe harbor at the foot of a bay that leads out to Georgian Bay.

Just 5 km (3 mi) east of Midland on Highway 12, visitors can explore a complete reconstruction of **Ste-Marie among the Hurons.** Jesuit missionaries built the Ste-Marie mission at this spot in 1639. The Jesuits preached Christianity, and the Hurons—also called Wendat—taught the French settlers how to survive in the harsh climate. By 1648 the mission was home to one-fifth of the European population of New France. The villagers built Ontario's first hospital, farm, school, and social service center here and constructed a canal from the Wye River. A combination of disease and Iroquois attacks led to the mission's demise. Twenty-two structures, faithfully reproduced from a scientific excavation, including a native longhouse and a wigwam, can now be toured. The canal is working again; staff in period costume saw timber, repair shoes, sew clothes, and grow vegetables. ⊠ *Hwy. 12,* ☎ *705/526–7838.* 🎫 *$7.25.* ☉ *May–mid-Oct., daily 10–5, last admittance at 4:15; mid-Oct.–Apr., by appointment.*

On a hill overlooking Ste-Marie among the Hurons is **Martyrs' Shrine,** a twin-spired stone cathedral built in 1926 to honor the eight missionaries who died in Huronia; in 1930 five of the priests were canonized by the Roman Catholic church. The grounds include a theater, a souvenir shop, a cafeteria, and a picnic area. ⊠ *Off Hwy. 12,* ☎ *705/526–3788.* ☉ *Mid-May–mid-Oct., daily 9–9.*

The best artifacts from several hundred archaeological digs in the area are displayed at **Huronia Museum and Gallery of Historic Huronia** in Little Lake Park, Midland. Behind the museum and gallery building is **Huron Indian Village,** a full-scale replica of a 16th-century Huron settlement. ⊠ *Little Lake Park,* ☎ *705/526–2844.* 🎫 *Museum and village $5.* ☉ *Daily 9–5; call for exceptions.*

Cruises leave from the town docks of both Midland and Penetang to explore the 30,000 Islands region of Georgian Bay from May to

Thanksgiving (the second Monday in October). The 300-passenger MS *Miss Midland* (☎ 705/526–0161, 800/461–1767 in Ontario), which leaves from the Midland town dock, offers one to four 2½-hour sight-seeing cruises daily. From the Penetang town dock, the 200-passenger MS *Georgian Queen* (☎ 705/549–7795) takes passengers on three-hour tours of the islands, from late May through mid-October. The cruises leave once daily at 2 PM. Call ahead.

Parry Sound

30 *110 km (68 mi) north of Penetang or Midland on Hwys. 12 and 69.*

Parry Sound is home to Canada's largest sightseeing cruise ship. The **Island Queen,** which offers an extensive three-hour cruise of Georgian Bay once or twice daily, depending on season. There's free parking at the town dock. ⊠ *9 Bay St.,* ☎ *705/746–2311.* 🎫 *$16.* ☉ *June–Thanksgiving (mid-Oct.).*

From mid-July to mid-August, the **Festival of the Sound** (☎ 705/746–2410) fills the auditorium of Parry Sound High School and the decks of the *Island Queen* with jazz, popular music, classical piano, and show tunes.

Lodging

$$ 🏨 **Highland Inn.** An enormous atrium anchors this completely self-contained hotel/motel/resort. Honeymoon suites have heart-shape tubs or sunken Jacuzzis. Sunday brunches by the pool in the Garden Cafe are popular; there are three other dining areas (reserve ahead) as well. ⊠ *924 King St. and Hwy. 12, L4R 4L3,* ☎ *705/526–9307 or 800/461–4265,* 📠 *705/526–0099. 119 rooms, 13 suites. 2 restaurants, indoor pool, sauna, exercise room. AE, MC, V.*

Orillia

31 *35 km (22 mi) northeast of Barrie on Hwy. 11.*

Orillia will be recognized by readers of Canada's great humorist, Stephen Leacock, as Mariposa, the "little town" he described in *Sunshine Sketches of a Little Town.* Leacock's former summer home is now a museum, the **Stephen Leacock Memorial Home.** In the Mariposa Room, characters from the book are matched with the Orillia residents who inspired them. ⊠ *Off Hwy. 12B in the east end of Orillia,* ☎ *705/329–1908.* 🎫 *$7.50.* ☉ *Daily 9–5.*

Gravenhurst

32 *39 km (24 mi) northeast of Barrie on Hwy. 11.*

North along Highway 11, rolling farmland suddenly changes to lakes and pine trees amid granite outcrops of the Canadian Shield. This region, called Muskoka, is the playground of people who live in the highly urbanized areas around Toronto. Gravenhurst is a town of approximately 6,000 and the birthplace of a Canadian hero. In China, Norman Bethune's name is almost as well known as Wayne Gretzky's is in Canada. Bethune is remembered for his heroic work in China as a field surgeon and medical educator. The **Bethune Memorial House,** an 1880-vintage frame structure, has become a shrine of sorts to Chinese diplomats visiting North America. ⊠ *235 John St. N,* ☎ *705/687–4261.* 🎫 *$2.25.* ☉ *Late May–mid-Oct., daily 10–5; mid-Oct.–late May, weekdays 10–noon and 1–5.*

The **RMS Segwun** (the initials stand for Royal Mail Ship) is the sole survivor of a fleet of steamships that once provided transportation through the Muskoka Lakes. The 128-ft boat carries 99 passengers on cruises from mid-June to mid-October. Cruises range from 90 minutes to two days in length (passengers dine aboard but sleep in one of Muskoka's grand resorts). ⊠ *Muskoka Lakes Navigation and Hotel Company Limited, 820 Bay St., Sagamo Park, Gravenhurst P1P 1G7,* ☎ *705/687–6667.*

Haliburton

㉝ *60 km (37 mi) northeast of Gravenhurst via Hwy. 11 and Hwy. 118, 250 km (155 mi) northeast of Toronto.*

Close to huge Algonquin Provincial Park, Haliburton is a Nordic skiing and winter sports base. In summer the self-guided trails of **Leslie Frost Natural Resources Center** (⊠ Hwy. 35 at St. Nora's Lake, ☎ 705/766–2451) offer a great primer in Ontario's wildlife.

Outdoor Activities and Sports

SKIING LODGE-TO-LODGE

Three- and four-night guided lodge-to-lodge cross-country ski packages are available along the Haliburton Nordic Trail system. There are groups for skiers of all levels, and the trips cover 8 to 25 km (5 to 16 mi) per day, depending on the group's abilities. Eight lodges participate in the program, and skiers stay and dine at a different lodge each night. Packages include all meals, trail passes, and a guide. Contact Brian Dean, General Manager, or John Teljeur of the **Haliburton Nordic Trail Association** (⊠ Box 670, K0M 1S0, ☎ 800/461–7677).

SNOWMOBILING

C Mac Snow Tours (⊠ R.R. 3, Walton N0K 1Z0, ☎ 519/887–6686 or 800/225–4258) has three- and five-night all-inclusive excursions in Haliburton Highlands/Algonquin Park.

Bracebridge

㉞ *11 km (8 mi) north of Gravenhurst via Hwy. 11.*

Holiday cheer brightens Bracebridge in summer with Christmas-oriented amusements. The Bracebridge Falls on the Muskoka River are a good option for those who prefer a more peaceful excursion. After letting Santa know what they'd like to find under the Christmas tree, youngsters can ride the Kris Kringle Riverboat, the Candy Cane Express Train, minibikes, bumper boats, paddleboats, ponies, and more ⟳ at **Santa's Village.** ⊠ *Santa's Village Rd. (west of Bracebridge),* ☎ *705/645–2512.* ⊠ *$14.95.* ⊙ *Mid-June–Labor Day, daily 10–6.*

⟳ **Funland,** for children 12 and older, offers go-carts, batting cages, in-line skating, 18-hole mini-putt, laser tag, and an indoor activity center with video games. A separate ticket is required for each amusement. ⊠ *Santa's Village Rd. (west of Bracebridge),* ☎ *705/645–2512.* ⊠ *$2 per ticket.* ⊙ *Mid-May–mid-June, weekends 10–10; mid-June–Labor Day, daily 10–10.*

Dining and Lodging

$$$ ✕⊡ **Inn at the Falls.** This Victorian inn and its annex of motel-style
★ rooms command a magnificent view of the pretty Bracebridge Falls. Accommodations include rooms, cottages, and suites; six of the units have fireplaces. The outdoor pool is heated. The main dining room (reserve ahead) and pub-lounge offer food and live entertainment; there's an outdoor patio for dining and sipping as well. Try the steak-and-kidney pie. ⊠ *17 Dominion St., Box 1139, P1L 1V3,* ☎ *705/645–2245,* ℻ *705/645–5093. 27 rooms, 1 cottage, 7 suites. Dining room, pub, pool. AE, MC, V.*

Dorset

35 *48 km (30 mi) northeast of Bracebridge via Hwys. 11 and 117.*

Dorset is a pretty village on a narrows between two bays of the Lake of Bays. The village is home to **Robinson's General Store** (☎ 705/766–2415), which, with the exception of the World War II years, has been continuously owned and operated by a Robinson since its 1921 opening. You'll find everything here from moose-fur hats to stoves and pine furniture. You can circle back to Toronto on scenic Highway 35 or make Dorset a stop on a circle tour from Huntsville (☞ *below*) around the Lake of Bays.

Huntsville

36 *34 km (21 mi) north of Bracebridge on Hwy. 11; 215 km (133 mi) north of Toronto via Hwys. 400 and 11.*

The Huntsville region is filled with lakes and streams, stands of virgin birch and pine, and deer and smaller forest dwellers that browse along the trails. Because the area is part of Toronto's summer playground, there is no shortage of year-round resorts.

Dining and Lodging

$$$$ ✕🏨 **Deerhurst Resort.** This spectacular, ultradeluxe Canadian Pacific resort is a self-contained community on 800 acres. The flavor is largely modern, although the main lodge, complete with dining room and Cypress Lounge, dates from 1886 and is appointed with a rustic flair. The menu offers such delicacies as Ontario game—buffalo and caribou—as well as Mediterranean dishes. ⊠ *1235 Deerhurst Dr., P18 2E8,* ☎ *705/789–6411. 400 rooms. Indoor pool, 2 golf courses, tennis court, exercise room, racquetball, squash, cross-country skiing, snowmobiling. AE, MC, V.*

$$$ ✕🏨 **Walker Lake Resort.** In winter the rustic cottages here overlook deer-feeding stations on either side of the frozen lake. The Norseman Restaurant serves formal Continental meals. ⊠ *R.R. 4, P1H 2J6,* ☎ *705/635–2473. 7 cottages. Restaurant. MC, V.*

Cross-Country Skiing

In southern Ontario the Huntsville area is usually the cross-country skier's best bet for an abundance of natural snow. Both Deerhurst and Walker Lake resorts (☞ *above*) have trails.

Algonquin Park

37 *50 km (31 mi) northeast of Huntsville on Hwy. 60.*

Algonquin Provincial Park stretches across 7,600 square km (3,040 square mi) of lakes, forests, rivers, and cliffs. It is a hiker's, canoeist's, and camper's paradise. But don't be put off if you're not the athletic or rough-outdoors sort. About a third of all visitors to Algonquin come for the day to visit a museum, walk one of the 14 interpretive trails, or enjoy a swim or a picnic. Swimming is especially good at the Lake of Two Rivers, about halfway between the west and east gates along Highway 60. A morning drive through the park in May or June is often rewarded by a sighting of moose, which are attracted to the highway by the slightly salty water in roadside ditches. Wolf-howling expeditions, led by a park naturalist, take place in August. Two newly added attractions near the east side of the park are the **visitor center**, which includes a bookstore, a restaurant, and a viewing deck, and the **Algonquin Logging Museum**, which depicts life at an early Canadian logging camp. ⊠ *Box 219, Whitney K0J 2M0,* ☎ *705/633–5572.* 🎫 *$8 per vehicle.* ☺ *Park daily 8 AM–10 PM. Museum mid-June–Labor Day, daily 10–6; Labor Day–Oct., weekends 10–5.*

Skiing

Radcliffe Hills ski area (☎ 613/756–2931 or 800/668–8249, ᶠᴬˣ 613/756–2931), near Barry's Bay, south of the park on Highway 60, has a vertical drop of 400 ft and a tubing run with a tube lift.

FORT ERIE AND WEST TO WINDSOR

Fort Erie

㊳ *155 km (96 mi) south of Toronto via the Queen Elizabeth Way.*

Fort Erie, at the extreme southeast tip of the Niagara Peninsula, is a drab, boom-or-bust town of fast-food chains, taverns, and gas stations whose profits rise or fall with the exchange rate between Canadian and U.S. dollars.

Old Fort Erie, at the south end of Fort Erie, has been reconstructed to look as it did before it was destroyed at the end of the War of 1812. The Old Fort's colorful and bloody history reveals that thousands of soldiers lost their lives within sight of the earthworks, drawbridges, and palisades. The fort itself was destroyed in 1779 and again in 1803 by spectacular storms that drove masses of ice ashore at the foot of Lake Erie. Visitors are conducted through the display rooms by guards in period British army uniforms. In summer the guards stand sentry duty, fire the cannon, and demonstrate drill and musket practice. ⊠ *350 Lakeshore Rd.,* ☎ *905/871–0540.* ⊠ *$3.50.* ☉ *May, weekdays 10–4, weekends 9:30–6; June–early Oct., daily 9:30–6.*

Though it dates back to 1897, **Fort Erie Race Track** is one of the most modern—and picturesque—tracks in North America. Glass-enclosed dining lounges overlook a 1-mi dirt track and a seven-furlong turf course. Also in view are gardens, ponds, and waterways. ⊠ *Bertie St. and Queen Elizabeth Way,* ☎ *905/871–3200.* ☉ *May–Sept., Fri.–Mon. at 1; Oct., Fri.–Sun. at 1.*

Port Colborne

㊴ *30 km (19 mi) west of Fort Erie on Hwy. 3.*

Port Colborne, a shipping center on Lake Erie, is at the southern end of the 44-km-long (27-mi-long) Welland Canal, which connects Lake Ontario to Lake Erie, bypassing Niagara Falls. You can view **Lock 8** from a platform. The town (population 18,800) remains an enclave for descendants of United Empire Loyalist stock. Chronicling the town's rich history and development is the **Port Colborne Historical and Marine Museum,** a six-building complex. ⊠ *280 King St.,* ☎ *905/834–7604.* ⊠ *Free.* ☉ *May–Dec., daily noon–5.*

Welland

㊵ *10 km (6 mi) north of Port Colborne on Hwy. 58 or 140.*

In 1988 Welland staged a Festival of Arts Murals to attract the 14–16 million tourists who were bypassing the town on their way to Niagara Falls. Thirty giant murals decorate downtown buildings; the longest is 130 ft, and the tallest is three stories high. You can pick up a free mural tour map from **Welland Tourism** (⊠ 32 E. Main St., ☎ 905/735–8696) or from brochure racks at City Hall and in local restaurants and hotels. Welland is also the home of the annual **Niagara Food Festival.** Held in the downtown Market Square around the end of September or early October, this festival brings together an array of local farmers, wineries, and restaurants to provide the food.

OFF THE
BEATEN PATH
WELLAND CANAL – At St. Catharines, about 25 km (15 mi) north of Welland, you may see a ship pass through Lock 3 of the Welland Canal, which joins Lake Erie and Lake Ontario. Also on the site, the **St. Catharines Museum** (☎ 905/984–8880) has displays about the construction of the canal, part of the St. Lawrence Seaway; there are historical exhibits, too. To get here from Welland, take Highway 406 north to the Queen Elizabeth Way and head west to St. Catharines; Lock 3 is on Government Road, near the QEW.

Port Dover

❹❶ *107 km (66 mi) west of Welland via Hwys. 58, 23, 3, and 6.*

Port Dover is the home of the world's largest fleet of freshwater fishing boats. It's a pretty beach resort town where freshwater fish is served up steamy and golden at a number of restaurants.

St. Thomas

❹❷ *75 km (47 mi) west of Port Dover on Hwy. 3 and 28 km (17 mi) east of London on Hwy. 3.*

St. Thomas's first buildings went up in 1810, over a decade and a half ahead of the first building in London, Ontario (☞ Hamilton and Festival Country, *below*). However, while St. Thomas's population has leveled at 29,000, London's has hit 310,000. Note the **statue of Jumbo** (⊠ 555 Talbot St.), the Barnum and Bailey circus elephant, killed here in a freak railway accident in 1885. The monument is a 10%-larger-than-life-size statue of the largest elephant ever in captivity. Adjacent to the Jumbo monument are a railway caboose, the St. Thomas Chamber of Commerce, and the **St. Thomas–Elgin Tourist Association** (⊠ 555 Talbot St., ☎ 519/631–1981), open May through Labor Day until 9 PM.

Port Stanley

❹❸ *15 km (9 mi) south of St. Thomas on Hwy. 4.*

The fishing village of Port Stanley has the largest natural harbor on the North shore of Lake Erie. Its fine brown sand beach, boutiques, snack bars, and kitsch stands make for a lively summer destination.

� The **Port Stanley Terminal Railroad,** originally built in 1856, was intended to be a main trade link between Canada and the United States. The trade didn't materialize, but the railroad survived on excursion traffic until 1957. Railroad buffs later restored some passenger cars and repaired the line as far as Union, in 1992 extending it to St. Thomas. You can take a 45-minute excursion to Union on Sunday afternoons year-round, on Saturdays from May through November, and daily in July and August. ⊠ *Port Stanley Railway Station,* ☎ *519/782–3730.* 🎫 *Round-trip fare to Union $8, to St. Thomas $11.* ☉ *Call ahead.*

Dining and Lodging

$$–$$$$ ⨯🏨 **Kettle Creek Inn.** All the rooms and suites in this small, elegant
★ country inn and its modern annex have views of a landscaped courtyard and gazebo. Some rooms have whirlpool baths and gas fireplaces. There are other nice touches, such as old-fashioned pedestal sinks and interesting local artwork. Continental breakfast is included in the room rate. The three dining rooms (reserve ahead) in the original inn offer daily specials, including fresh Lake Erie fish just brought ashore by the local fishing fleet and fresh Ontario lamb and pork tenderloin. ⊠ *216 Joseph St., N5L 1C4,* ☎ *519/782–3388,* 🇫🇦🇽 *519/782–4747. 10 rooms, 5 suites. 3 dining rooms. AE, D, DC, MC, V.*

Point Pelee National Park

★ **㊹** *150 km (93 mi) west of Port Stanley/St. Thomas on Hwy. 401 or Hwy. 3, near Leamington on Hwy. 33.*

The southernmost tip of mainland Canada, Point Pelee National Park has the smallest dry land area of any Canadian national park, yet it draws more than a half-million visitors every year. At the park's visitor center you'll find exhibits, slide shows, and a keen, knowledgeable staff to answer questions. Some 700 kinds of plants and 347 species of birds have been recorded here, including a number of endangered species. A tram operates seasonally to "the tip." September is the best time to see monarch butterflies resting in Pelee before they head south to Mexico's Sierra Madres. The park is also world renowned for bird-watching, especially during spring and fall migrations. This is a day-use park only. ⊠ *R.R.1, Leamington N8H 3V4,* ☎ *519/322–2365.* ▨ *$3.25 Apr.–Labor Day; $2.25 Labor Day–Mar.* ☉ *Daily 6 AM -10 PM.*

Pelee Island

㊺ *25 km (16 mi) and 90 min by ferry from Point Pelee via Hwy. 33 and Leamington ferry.*

Pelee is a small, flat island, roughly 13 by 6 km (8 by 4 mi), at the west end of Lake Erie, served spring through fall by a ferry boat (for which reservations are necessary) that links it with Essex County on the Canadian mainland and Sandusky in Ohio. In winter there are scheduled flights from Windsor. The island's permanent population is under 300, but in summer that quadruples as vacationers cram into private cottages. Still, Pelee maintains its "island pace." Enjoy the beaches, cycle around the island, tour the Wine Pavilion, or visit the ruins of Vin Villa winery, dating back to the mid-1800s. Pelee Island is Canada's southernmost inhabited point, on the same latitude as northern California and northern Spain.

Kingsville

㊻ *10 km (7 mi) west of Leamington on Hwy. 18.*

Kingsville, one of the southernmost towns in Ontario, is best known for its bird sanctuary. **Jack Miner's Bird Sanctuary** is well signposted. Jack Miner was an avid hunter who realized no species could survive both its natural enemies *and* man. In 1904 he dug ponds, planted trees, and introduced four Canada geese with clipped wings to the ponds. That number grew to the 50,000 that now winter here. From 1910 to 1940 Miner lectured kings and presidents on the importance of conservation, earning him the Order of the British Empire in 1943. His former home is now a trust, open year-round. No admission is charged and nothing is sold on the grounds. A two-story museum (closed Sunday) in the former stables has a wealth of Miner memorabilia, and at a pond beside the house you can feed for free far-from-shy geese and ducks. At 4 PM daily, the birds are flushed for "air shows," and circle wildly overhead. The best times to view migrations are late March, October, and November. ⊠ *Essex County Rd. 29, 5 km (3 mi) north of Kingsville,* ☎ *519/ 733–4034.* ▨ *Free.* ☉ *Mid-Mar.–Dec., Mon.–Sat. 9–5.*

The **John R. Park Homestead and Conservation Area,** 8 km (5 mi) west of Kingsville, is a pioneer village anchored by one of Ontario's few examples of American Greek Revival architecture, an 1842 home. The village's 10 buildings include the house of John R. Park, a shed built without nails, a smokehouse, an icehouse, an outhouse, a blacksmith shop, a sawmill, and a livestock stable. ⊠ *County Rd. 50 at Iler Rd.,*

☎ 519/738–2029. ⊠ $3. ⏱ July–Labor Day, daily 11–5; Labor Day–June, Sun.–Fri 11-4.

Southwestern Ontario Heritage Village

47 About 10 km (6 mi) north of Kingsville on Hwy. 23.

This turn-of-the-century Southwestern Ontario Heritage Village has 20 historic buildings spread across 54 wooded acres. Volunteers in period dress show visitors how pioneers baked, operated looms, and dipped candles. The **Transportation Museum** of the Historic Vehicle Society of Ontario, Windsor Branch, also on the grounds, displays a fine collection of travel artifacts, from snowshoes to buggies to vintage automobiles. The gem of the collection is the world's only 1893 Shamrock. This two-seater was the second effort at a workable prototype built by the Mira Brothers. When it failed to run properly, the brothers abandoned their brief careers as auto manufacturers. ⊠ County Rd. 23, ☎ 519/776–6909. ⊠ $3. ⏱ Village and museum Apr.–Nov., Wed.–Sun. 11–5; July–Aug., daily 11–5.

Amherstburg

48 25 km (16 mi) west of Kingsville on Hwy. 18.

The riverside parks in the quiet town of Amherstburg are great places to watch the procession of Great Lakes shipping. **Navy Yard Park,** with flower beds ringed by old anchor chains, has benches overlooking Bois Blanc Island and the narrow main shipping channel.

Fort Malden was the British base in the War of 1812 from which Detroit was captured, though the site dates back to 1727, when a Jesuit mission began occupying lands in the area. Now the fort is an 11-acre National Historic Park, with original earthworks, restored barracks, a military pensioner's cottage, two exhibit buildings, and picnic facilities. ⊠ 100 Laird Ave., ☎ 519/736–5416. ⊠ $2. ⏱ Jan.–Apr., weekdays 1–5, weekends 10–5; May–Dec., daily 10–5.

The **North American Black Historical Museum** commemorates the U.S. slaves and the Underground Railroad system many used to flee to Canada. It is one of several heritage sites related to this history in the area. Between 1800 and 1860, 30,000 to 50,000 U.S. slaves made the pilgrimage to Canada, and many of those crossed the Detroit River at Amherstburg because it was the narrowest point. An 1848-vintage church and log cabin contain exhibits, artifacts, and biographies. ⊠ 277 King St., ☎ 519/736–5433. ⊠ $4.50. ⏱ Wed.–Fri. 10–5, weekends 1–5.

Windsor

49 30 km (19 mi) north of Amherstburg on Hwy. 18 and 150 km (93 mi) west of London on Hwy. 401.

Long an unattractive industrial city that hosted Ford, General Motors, and Chrysler manufacturing plants, Windsor has become a pleasant place to visit. The riverfront has pretty parks, some with fountains and statues, all overlooking the spectacular Detroit skyline. The cities are linked by the Ambassador Bridge and the Windsor–Detroit Tunnel. If you're traveling by car, start your Windsor visit at the **Convention & Visitors Bureau** (⊠ 333 Riverside Dr. W, Suite 103, ☎ 800/265–3633).

The **Art Gallery of Windsor** mounts changing displays of contemporary and historic Canadian and foreign art. ⊠ Devonshire Mall, 3100 Howard Ave., ☎ 519/969–4494. ⊠ Free. ⏱ Tues–Fri. 10–7, Sat. 10–5, Sun. noon–5.

The **Windsor's Community Museum** houses a collection of area artifacts in the 1812 house where the Battle of Windsor, the final incident
in the Upper Canada Rebellion, was fought in 1838. ⊠ *254 Pitt St.
W,* ☎ *519/253–1812.* ☞ *Free.* ☉ *Tues.–Sat. 10–5, Sun. 2–5.*

Willistead Manor is the former home of Edward Chandler Walker, second son of Hiram, who founded Walker's Distillery in 1858. The 15-
acre estate is now a city park. Call to confirm tour schedule. ⊠
Niagara St. and Kildare Rd., ☎ *519/253–2365.* ☞ *$3.50.* ☉ *Tours:
Sept.–June, 1st and 3rd Sun. of each month 1–4; July and Aug., Sun.
and Wed. 1–4.*

Since 1959, Windsor and Detroit have combined their national birthday parties (Canada Day, July 1; and Independence Day, July 4) into
a massive bash called **International Freedom Festival.** The two-week
party includes nonstop entertainment with more than 100 special
events on both sides of the river and a spectacular fireworks display,
billed as the largest in North America. For information, call the I.F.F.
Offices (☎ 519/252–7264).

With over 100 exhibits displaying more than 400 animals, **Windsor
Reptile World** (⊠ 853 Division Rd., ☎ 519/966–1762) is home to
Canada's largest live display of reptiles and amphibians.

Dining and Lodging

$$ ✕ **Brigantino's.** This popular establishment serves traditional home-
style Italian cooking with original twists, such as veal with cognac and
portobello mushrooms, and pasta stuffed with ricotta cheese and
spinach and smothered in your choice of pesto, hot red, or cream
sauce. Nightly entertainment adds festivity to the atmosphere, espe-
cially when accordion players are scheduled. ⊠ *851 Erie St. E,* ☎
519/254–7041. Reservations essential. AE, D, DC, MC, V.

$$ ✕ **Old Fish Market.** A wonderful ambience is created here with hanging plants, brass railings, and lovely woodwork. The menu, predictably,
is heavy on seafood. It has a deserved reputation of excellence. ⊠ *156
Chatham St. W,* ☎ *519/253–7417. Reservations essential. AE, DC,
MC, V.*

$$$$ ⊡ **Hilton International Windsor.** Each of the guest rooms in this downtown riverbank hotel has a view of Detroit's impressive skyline and
the shipping activity on the world's busiest inland waterway. The Park
Terrace Restaurant and Lounge offers a wide menu and a spectacular
river view. In the River Runner Bar and Grill, there's music and dancing. ⊠ *277 Riverside Dr. W, N9A 5K4,* ☎ *519/973–5555 or 800/463–
6655,* FAX *519/973–1600. 303 rooms. 2 restaurants, bar, room service,
indoor pool, hot tub, sauna, meeting rooms. AE, MC, V.*

THE NIAGARA PENINSULA

The two most visited towns on the Niagara peninsula have very different flavors. Home to a wildly popular natural attraction, Niagara
Falls can have a certain tacky quality, while Niagara-on-the-Lake,
which draws theatergoers to its annual Shaw festival, epitomizes ye olde
British tastefulness. Still, Niagara Falls has something for everyone, from
water slides and wax museums to honeymoon certificates. Because they
are in such close proximity to each other, however, there's no need to
choose; base your decision on the day's mood. This is also one of the
three best regions for wine production in Canada—Point Pelee (☞ Fort
Erie and West to Windsor, *above*) and British Columbia are the others.
More than 20 small, quality vineyards produce fine wines; most of them
offer tastings and tours.

Niagara Falls

130 km (81 mi) south of Toronto via the Queen Elizabeth Way.

★ Cynics have had a field day with **Niagara Falls,** calling it everything from "water on the rocks" to "the second major disappointment of American married life" (Oscar Wilde). Others have been far more glowing. Missionary and explorer Louis Hennepin, whose books were widely read across Europe, first described the falls in 1678 as "an incredible Cataract or Waterfall which has no equal." Nearly two centuries later, Charles Dickens wrote, "I seemed to be lifted from the earth and to be looking into Heaven. Niagara was at once stamped upon my heart, an image of beauty, to remain there changeless and indelible." Henry James recorded in 1883 how one stands there "gazing your fill at the most beautiful object in the world."

Understandably, all these rave reviews began to bring out professional daredevils, as well as self-destructive amateurs. In 1859 the French tightrope walker Blondin walked across the Niagara Gorge, from the American to the Canadian side, on a 3-inch-thick rope, while some 100,000 spectators watched from both shores. "Thank God it is over!" exclaimed the future King Edward VII of England, after completion of the walk. "Please never attempt it again." But sadly, others did. From the early 18th century, dozens went over in boats and barrels. Not a single one survived, until 1901, when schoolteacher Annie Taylor made the attempt. Emerging from her barrel, she asked, "Did I go over the falls yet?" The endless stunts were finally outlawed in 1912, but not before the province of Ontario created the first provincial park in all of Canada—Queen Victoria Park—in 1887.

It all started more than 10,000 years ago, when a group of glaciers receded, diverting the waters of Lake Erie northward into Lake Ontario. The force and volume of the water as it flowed over the Niagara Escarpment caused the phenomenon we know as the falls. The area's human history is fairly interesting, too. The War of 1812 had settlers on both sides of the river killing one another, with the greatest battle taking place in Niagara Falls itself, at Lundy's Lane. Soon after, at the Treaty of Ghent, two modest cities of the same name arose on each side of the river—one in the United States, the other in Canada.

The Niagara Parks Commission (NPC) was formed in 1885 to preserve the area around the falls. Beginning with a small block of land, the NPC has gradually acquired most of the land fronting on the Canadian side of the Niagara River, from Niagara-on-the-Lake to Fort Erie. This 56-km (35-mi) riverside drive is a 3,000-acre ribbon of parkland lined with parking overlooks, picnic tables, and barbecue pits; the public is welcome to use the facilities at no charge.

And don't allow winter to put you off from coming. The **Winter Festival of Lights** is a real stunner. Seventy trees are illuminated with 34,000 lights in the parklands near the Rainbow Bridge, plus "The Enchantment of Disney," lighted displays based on cartoon characters and movies. The Falls are illuminated nightly from 5 to 10 PM, late November through mid-January.

🔟 The **Niagara Parks Botanical Gardens and School of Horticulture** has been graduating professional gardeners since 1936. The art of horticulture is celebrated by its students with 80 acres of immaculately maintained gardens. Within the Botanical Gardens is the **Niagara Parks Butterfly Conservatory** (☎ 905/356–8119), home to one of North America's largest collections of free-flying butterflies—at least 2,000 are protected in a lush rain forest setting by a glass-enclosed conservatory. The cli-

Niagara Falls

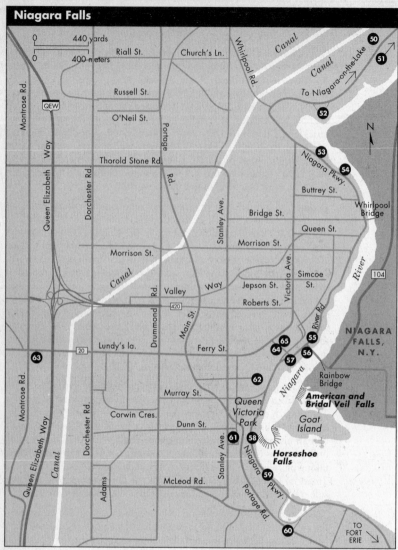

440 yards
400 meters

Riall St.
Church's Ln.
Whirlpool Rd.
Canal
Canal
To Niagara-on-the-Lake
Montrose Rd.
QEW
Russell St.
O'Neil St.
Portage Rd.
Thorold Stone Rd.
Stanley Ave.
Niagara Pkwy.
Buttrey St.
Whirlpool Bridge
Queen Elizabeth Way
Morrison St.
Canal
Bridge St.
Morrison St.
Queen St.
Valley Way
Drummond Rd.
420
Main St.
Jepson St.
Roberts St.
Victoria Ave.
Simcoe St.
River
104
Lundy's la.
20
Ferry St.
NIAGARA FALLS, N.Y.
River Rd.
Montrose Rd.
Dorchester Rd.
Murray St.
Corwin Cres.
Dunn St.
Niagara
Rainbow Bridge
American and Bridal Veil Falls
Queen Victoria Park
Goat Island
Horseshoe Falls
Stanley Ave.
Queen Elizabeth Way
Canal
Adams
McLeod Rd.
Portage Rd.
TO FORT ERIE

Casino Niagara, 65
Clifton Hill, 64
Floral Clock, 51
Great Gorge Adventure, 54
Greenhouse and Plant Conservatory, 59

Journey Behind the Falls, 58
Maid of the Mist boats, **57**
Marineland, 60
Minolta Tower, 61
Niagara Falls Museum, 55

Niagara Glen, 52
Niagara Parks Botanical Gardens and School of Horticulture, 50
Niagara Spanish Aero Car, 53

Ride Niagara, 56
Skylon Tower, 62
White Water Park, 63

mate-controlled conservatory operates year-round and contains 50 species from around the world, each with its own unique and colorful markings. In 1997, a new outdoor butterfly garden was added with 120 domestic species. ⊠ *2565 North Niagara Pkwy.,* ☎ *905/356–8554.* *Botanical Gardens free, Butterfly Conservatory $4.50.* ☉ *Botanical Gardens dawn–dusk; Butterfly Conservatory, daily 9–9.*

A short distance (downriver) from the Botanical Gardens and School of Horticulture (☞ *above*) on the Niagara Parkway is one of the **⑤①** world's largest **floral clocks**; its 40-ft "living" face is designed by the NPC and planted in a different design twice every season.

⑤② You'll find trails maintained by the NPC in the **Niagara Glen.** A bicycle trail that parallels the Niagara Parkway from Fort Erie to Niagara-on-the-Lake winds between beautiful homes on one side and the river, with its abundant bird life, on the other.

⑤③ The **Niagara Spanish Aero Car,** in operation since 1916, is a cable car that crosses the Whirlpool Basin in the Niagara Gorge. This trip is not for the fainthearted; when you're swinging high above the roiling whirlpool, those cables seem awfully thin. ⊠ *4.5 km (3 mi) north of the falls,* ☎ *905/354–5711.* *$5.* ☉ *Mid-May–Labor Day, daily 9– 9; Labor Day–mid-Oct., shorter hrs, weather permitting.*

⑤④ The **Great Gorge Adventure** involves taking an elevator to the bottom of the Niagara Gorge, where you can walk a boardwalk beside the roaring torrent of the Niagara River. There the gorge is rimmed by sheer cliffs as it enters the giant whirlpool. ⊠ *3 km (2 mi) north of falls,* ☎ *905/354–5711.* *$4.75.* ☉ *Mid-May–Labor Day, daily 9–9; Labor Day–mid-Oct., shorter hrs, weather permitting.*

⑤⑤ The **Niagara Falls Museum,** founded in 1827, claims to be North America's oldest museum. It contains everything from stuffed birds and Egyptian mummies to the **Daredevil Hall of Fame,** where the barrels and other contraptions in which people have gone over the falls pay tribute to two centuries of Niagara Falls rebels. There are 26 galleries on four floors and 700,000 exhibits, so gauge your time accordingly— this museum is well worth two hours of browsing. ⊠ *5651 River Rd.,* ☎ *905/356–2151.* *$6.75.* ☉ *June–early Oct., daily 8:30 AM–11 PM; mid-Oct.–May, daily 10–5.*

⑤⑥ **Ride Niagara** is divided into three portions: a theater presentation, an elevator ride down to the tunnel, and the shuttle that simulates plunging over the falls and down the rapids in a barrel. The entire event takes about 20–25 minutes. Children under 3 are not admitted. ⊠ *5755 River Rd.,* ☎ *905/374–7433.* *$7.95.* ☉ *Daily 11:30–5.*

⑤⑦ *Maid of the Mist* boats have been operating since 1846, when they were wooden-hulled, coal-fired steamboats. Today, boats tow fun-loving passengers on 30-minute journeys to the foot of the falls where the spray is so heavy that raincoats must be distributed. ⊠ *Boats leave from foot of Clifton Hill,* ☎ *905/358–5781.* *$10.10.* ☉ *Mid-May–late June and Labor Day–mid-May, daily 9:45–4:45 (weekends until 5:45), every 15 min; late June-Labor Day, daily 9:45–7:45, every 15 min.*

⑤⑧ At **Journey Behind the Falls** your admission ticket includes use of rubber boots and a hooded rain slicker. An elevator will take you to an observation deck, which allows a fish-eye view of the Canadian Horseshoe Falls and the Niagara River. From there a walk through three tunnels cut into the rock takes you behind the wall of crashing water. ⊠ *Tours begin at Table Rock House, Queen Victoria Park,* ☎ *905/354– 1551.* *$5.75.* ☉ *Mid-Nov.–mid-Apr., daily 9–5:30; mid-Apr.–mid-Nov., daily 9–sunset.*

59 The NPC's enormous **Greenhouse and Plant Conservatory** (☎ 905/356–4699), just south of the Horseshoe Falls, is open daily. Here you can see myriad plants and flowers year-round.

60 **Marineland,** a theme park with a marine show, wildlife displays, and rides, is 1½ km (1 mi) south of the falls. The daily marine show includes performing killer whales, dolphins, harbor seals, and sea lions. Children can pet and feed members of a herd of 500 deer and get nose-to-nose with North American freshwater fish. Among the many rides is Dragon Mountain, the world's largest steel roller coaster. Marineland is signposted from Niagara Parkway or reached from the Queen Elizabeth Way by exiting at McLeod Road (Exit 27). ⊠ *7657 Portage Rd.,* ☎ *905/356–8250 or 905/356–9565.* ☜ *$21.95.* ☼ *Apr.–June and Sept., daily 10–5; July–Aug., daily 9–6.*

Niagara Falls Imax Theatre/The Daredevil Adventure Gallery. See the wonder of the falls up close and travel back in time for a glimpse of its 12,000-year-old history with *Niagara: Miracles, Myths and Magic.* The movie screen, Canada's largest, is over 6 stories high. The Daredevil Adventure Gallery chronicles the brave expeditions of those who tackled the falls. ⊠ *6170 Buchanan Ave,* ☎ *905/358–3611.* ☜ *$7.50.* ☼ *Sept.–Oct. and late Apr.–June, daily 11–8; Oct.–Apr., weekdays and Sun. 11–4, Sat. 11–7; movies run every hr on the hr.*

61 **Minolta Tower,** 525 ft above the base of the falls, affords panoramic views of the Horseshoe Falls and the surrounding area. Also in the tower are a variety of high-tech games: Cybermind Virtual Reality, offering precisely what its name suggests; Galaxian Adventure, a laser action game played from seated consoles; and Thrill Ride Simulator, a simulated roller coaster ride through a volcano mine. ⊠ *6732 Oakes Dr.,* ☎ *905/356–1501 or 800/461–2492.* ☜ *Tower $5.95, Cybermind Virtual Reality $5.95, Galaxian Space Adventure $2.95, Thrill Ride Simulator $5.95.* ☼ *9 AM until lights go off at the falls (as late as midnight in summer).*

62 Rising 775 ft above the falls, **Skylon Tower** offers the best view of both the great Niagara and the entire city. An indoor/outdoor observation deck facilitates the view. Amusements for children plus a revolving dining room (☞ Dining and Lodging, *below*) are other reasons to visit. ⊠ *5200 Robinson St.,* ☎ *905/356–2651.* ☜ *$6.95.* ☼ *Mid-June–Labor Day, daily 8 AM–1 AM; Labor Day–early June, daily 10–9.*

63 **White Water Park** offers just about every means of getting wet there is, including Canada's biggest water slide, two hot tubs, and a wave pool. If you arrive within the first hour of the park's opening, you'll receive $1 off the admission price. ⊠ *7430 Lundy's La.,* ☎ *905/357–3380.* ☜ *$13.95.* ☼ *June–Labor Day, daily 10–8.*

64 **Clifton Hill,** almost directly opposite the American falls, is probably the most crassly commercial district of Niagara Falls. Sometimes referred to as "Museum Alley," this area encompasses the Guinness World of Records Museum, Ripley's Believe It Or Not Museum, Louis Tussaud's Waxworks Museum, the Haunted House, the Funhouse, the House of Frankenstein, Castle Dracula, and Super Star Recording (where you can record the musical number of your choice), Movieland Wax Museum, Criminals Hall of Fame Wax Museum, the Elvis Presley Museum, and the That's Incredible Museum. Admission for most attractions usually runs about $6 or $7.

65 **Casino Niagara,** set in an architectural design reminiscent of the 1920s, has a total of 3,000 slot machines and 123 gambling tables such as Blackjack, Roulette, Baccarat, Caribbean Stud Poker, Let it Ride, Pai Gow Poker, and Big Six. Within the casino are several restaurants and lounges. ✉ *5705 Falls Ave.,* ☎ *888/946–3255 or 905/374–5964.* ⊙ *Year-round, daily 24 hrs.*

Dining and Lodging

$$$ ✕ **Casa Mia.** This off-the-tourist-track restaurant, in a pink stucco villa
★ about 10 minutes from the center of town, is airy and modern with a comfortable piano lounge (there's live music Friday and Saturday). All the pasta is kitchen-made. Fresh-grated beets impart a shocking pink color to the gnocchi, divine with fresh Gorgonzola sauce. If you've ever wondered what real cannelloni was like, these light pasta pancakes, filled with coarse-ground veal and spinach, will tell you. The veal chop, grilled with lemon and caper juice, is a thing of beauty. Heart-smart menu selections are indicated, and even the desserts, particularly cassata—a light cake with homemade ice-cream terrine—are not overly heavy. ✉ *3518 Portage Rd., about 10 km (6 mi) from Niagara-on-the-Lake,* ☎ *905/356–5410. AE, MC, V.*

$$$ ✕ **Skylon Tower.** Don't come here for surprises—this tower is owned by the same people who own the local Holiday Inn—but for the view from the Revolving Dining Room, which rotates at one revolution per hour. Traditionally prepared rack-of-lamb, baked salmon, steak, and chicken make up the list of entrées. It's an eclectic crowd, with cocktail wear and casual clothes seated side-by-side. Even with a reservation there may be a short wait in summer. ✉ *5200 Robin St.,* ☎ *905/356–2651, ext. 259. AE, MC, V.*

$$ ✕ **Capri.** This award-winning restaurant is not only family-owned, but—
★ a rarity in this business—it's had the same chef for 43 years. Chef Carmen continues to prepare huge, Italian-style platters such as linguine with chicken cacciatore. The three separate dining rooms, decorated in the traditional dark wood paneling, draw traditional Italian families daily. ✉ *5348 Ferry St. (Hwy. 20), about ½ mi from falls,* ☎ *905/354–7519. AE, DC, MC, V.*

$$$$ ✕🏨 **Sheraton Fallsview Hotel and Conference Centre.** Overlooking the spectacular Canadian and American Falls, this modern high-rise hotel has oversized guest rooms and suites, most with breathtaking views of the falls and upper rapids. Business facilities are excellent; the hotel has fiber optic and satellite uplinks to provide high-quality teleconferencing. The fine dining room has snagged the best view in town. In the evening, candlelight adds romance, and the kitchen does its part with a French/Continental menu that might include tournedos with a three-peppercorn sauce. ✉ *6755 Oakes Dr.,* ☎ *905/374–1077 or 800/267–8439,* ℻ *905/374–6224. 295 rooms. 2 restaurants, lobby lounge, pool, hot tub, sauna, spa, children's programs, convention center, meeting rooms. AE, DC, MC, V.*

$$ 🏨 **Renaissance Fallsview Hotel.** Many rooms overlook the falls at this luxuriously appointed hotel, about ½ km (⅓ mi) from the mighty cataracts. There are lots of recreational facilities on the premises and golf and fishing nearby. Free morning coffee is available for guests year-round, and in summer a light breakfast is also included in the room tab. ✉ *6455 Buchanan Ave.,* ☎ *905/357–5200,* ℻ *905/357–3422. 262 rooms. 2 restaurants, indoor pool, hot tub, sauna, exercise room, racquetball, squash, business services, meeting rooms. AE, D, DC, MC, V.*

Nightlife and the Arts

There are free band concerts on summer Sundays at **Queenston Heights Park, Queen Victoria Park,** and **Old Fort Erie** (☞ Fort Erie and West to Windsor, *above*), as well as **Rainbow Bridge Carillon** recitals.

Biking

The NPC (☎ 905/356–2241) maintains 55 km (34 mi) of **bicycle trails** along the Niagara River between Fort Erie and Niagara-on-the-Lake.

Guided Tours

BY BUS

Double Deck Tours (☎ 905/295–3051), operates 4½- to 5-hour tours in double-decker English buses. The tours operate daily from mid-May through October and include most of the major sights of Niagara Falls. The fare ($34.55) includes admissions to Journey Behind the Falls, *Maid of the Mist,* and a trip in the Niagara Spanish Aero Car. A shorter tour ($14.75) does not stop at attractions to which admission is charged.

From late April to mid-October, the NPC operates a **People Mover System** in which air-conditioned buses travel on a loop route between its public parking lot above the falls at Rapids View Terminal (well marked) and the Niagara Spanish Aero Car parking lot about 8 km (5 mi) downriver. With a day's pass (available at any booth on the system: $3) you can get on and off as many times as you wish at the well-marked stops along the route.

BY HELICOPTER

Niagara Helicopters Ltd. takes you on a nine-minute flight over the Giant Whirlpool, up the Niagara Gorge, and past the Canadian Falls and then banks around the curve of the Horseshoe Falls for a never-to-be-forgotten thrill. ⊠ *3731 Victoria Ave.,* ☎ *905/357–5672.* ⊠ *$70 per person.* ☉ *Daily 9 AM–½ hr after sunset.*

Wine Region

Some of the Niagara Peninsula's 23 wineries are on the Niagara Parkway between Niagara Falls and Niagara-on-the-Lake, or on Highway 55 from the Queen Elizabeth Way. As the quality of Ontario wines has improved in recent years, wine makers have stepped up their marketing and promotional activities. Look for the **Wine Regions Welcome Centre** (⊠ Casablanca Blvd., Grimsby), just off Queen Elizabeth Way East. The center is open in July, Friday 3 to 8, Saturday 9 to 5, and Sunday 10 to 3.

For a map of the wine region, including locations of individual wineries and details of summer events, write to **Wine Council of Ontario** (⊠ 110 Hanover Dr., Suite B205, St. Catharines L2W 1A4, ☎ 905/684–8070). Several wineries offer wine tasting and tours; for exact times, call ahead. The best-known wineries include **Château des Charmes Wines Ltd.** (☎ 905/262–4219), **Hillebrand Estates Winery** (☎ 905/468–7123), **Iniskillin Wines** (☎ 905/468–3554), **Konzelmann Winery** (☎ 905/935–2866), **Reif Winery** (☎ 905/468–7738), and **Willowbank Estate Wines** (☎ 905/468–4219).

Niagara-on-the-Lake

66 *15 km (9 mi) north of (downriver from) Niagara Falls.*

Since 1962, Niagara-on-the-Lake has been considered the southern outpost of fine summer theater in Ontario because of its acclaimed Shaw Festival. But it offers more than Stratford (☞ Hamilton and Festival Country, *below*), its older theatrical sister to the north: Stately homes sit back from tree-shaded streets; Most are at least a century old, and their owners maintain their original charm by keeping rose trellises freshly painted and brass door knockers gleaming. Any proposed new business is screened by the village council to ensure that neither chrome, glass, nor neon-girdled atrocity will mar the Victorian character.

Though the town of 14,000 is worth a visit anytime of the year, it's most attractive from April through October, when both the Shaw Festival and the flowers are in full bloom. **Antours** (☎ 416/424–4403) provides several tours of Niagara-on-the-Lake, which include lunch and major performances at the Shaw Festival.

The **Niagara Apothecary Museum** was built in 1866 and restored in 1971. Note the exquisite walnut and butternut fixtures, crystal pieces, and a rare collection of apothecary glasses. ⊠ *5 Queen St.,* ☎ *905/468–3845.* 🎫 *Free.* ⊙ *Mid-May–Labor Day, daily noon–6.*

The **Niagara Historical Society Museum,** built in 1906, houses a collection of artifacts from prehistory through the arrival of the Loyalists and the War of 1812. ⊠ *43 Castlereagh St.,* ☎ *905/468–3912.* 🎫 *$2.50.* ⊙ *May–Oct., daily 10–5; Jan.–Feb., weekends 1–5; Mar., Apr., Nov., and Dec., daily 1–5.*

Originally, **Fort George** was built by the British in the late 1700s to protect the trafficking of supplies on the Niagara River. In the War of 1812, the fort was lost to the Americans, and by the time the British regained it, it had fallen into ruins. Fort George was reconstructed in the 1940s. Today, soldiers in period dress perform drills and musical programs on the parade square. ⊠ *Queens Parade, Niagara Pkwy.,* ☎ *905/468–4257.* 🎫 *$4.* ⊙ *Apr.–June, daily 9:30–4:30; July–Labor Day, daily 10–5; Labor Day–Nov., daily 9:30–4:30.*

Dining and Lodging

$$$$ ✕🎭 **Prince of Wales.** A visit from the Prince of Wales at the turn of the
★ century prompted the name of this hotel, built in 1864. It's in the heart of town and has been tastefully restored. The Prince of Wales Court, adjacent to the main hotel, has many larger, newer rooms at higher prices; some housekeeping units are available. The suede-walled dining room has a tree-filled patio that looks out to the street. Entrées might include veal tenderloin with shiitake mushrooms, Osaka mustard, and a balsamic glaze, and the dessert menu is exquisite. The more casual Queens's Royal Lounge offers soups and sandwiches daily, plus lunch and dinner buffets, all for under $10. ⊠ *6 Picton St.,* ☎ *905/468–3246 or 800/263–2452,* 🆑 *905/468–1310. 90 rooms, 11 suites. 3 dining rooms, lounge, indoor pool, hot tub, sauna, health club. AE, MC, V.*

$$$ ✕🎭 **Oban Inn.** This elegant, historic country inn has a view of Lake Ontario. Each room is distinct, embellished with antiques in an old-world English tone; some have fireplaces. While away the day on broad verandas and beautifully manicured gardens. The popular dining room spotlights Canadian beef favorites with a fresh twist of vegetables and fruits (reserve ahead). ⊠ *160 Front St., L0S 1J0,* ☎ *905/468–2165,* 🆑 *905/468–4165. 22 rooms. Dining room, lounge. AE, DC, MC, V.*

$$$ ✕🎭 **Queen's Landing.** The views are a knockout, since Queen's Land-
★ ing is just across from the historic Fort Niagara, at the mouth of the Niagara River. Rooms are nicely decorated with antiques, including canopy beds; many have working fireplaces and modern whirlpool baths. Unlike the other century-old country inns of this town, Queen's Landing has a full range of fitness facilities. It's a most appealing new/old inn. ⊠ *Melville and Bryon Sts., Box 1180, L0S 1J0,* ☎ *905/468–2195 or 800/361–6645,* 🆑 *905/468–2227. 137 rooms. Dining room, lounge, indoor pool, lap pool, hot tub, sauna, exercise room, babysitting. AE, DC, MC, V.*

The Arts

The **Shaw Festival** began modestly back in the early 1960s with a single play and a premise: To perform the plays of George Bernard Shaw and his contemporaries, who include Noel Coward, Bertholt Brecht, J.M.

Barrie, and J.M. Synge. The season now runs from the beginning of April through mid-October, staging close to a dozen plays. The Festival operates in three buildings, within a few blocks of each other. The handsome **Festival Theatre,** the largest of the three, stands on Queen's Parade near Wellington Street and houses the box office. The **Court House,** on Queen Street between King and Regent streets, served as the town's municipal offices until 1969. At the corner of Queen and Victoria streets is the slightly smaller **Royal George Theater,** the most intimate of the Festival's theaters. ⊠ *Shaw Festival Box Office, Box 774, Niagara-on-the-Lake L0S 1J0,* ☎ *905/468–2153 or 800/511–7429.*

En Route   The Niagara Peninsula is Ontario's fruit basket. From mid-summer to late fall, fruit and vegetable stands proliferate along the highways and byways, and there are several farmers' markets along the Queen Elizabeth Way between Niagara Falls and Hamilton. Some of the best displays of fruits and vegetables are on Highway 55, between Niagara-on-the-Lake and the Queen Elizabeth Way. **Harvest Barn Market** (⊠ R.R. 3, Hwy. 55, Niagara-on-the-Lake, ☎ 905/468–3224), marked by a red-and-white-striped awning, not only features regional fruits and vegetables but also tempts with a bakery offering sausage rolls, tiny loaves of bread, and fruit pies. You can test the market's wares at the picnic tables, where knowledgeable locals have lunch.

HAMILTON AND FESTIVAL COUNTRY

A combination of rural pleasures and sophisticated theater draw visitors to this region. Stratford, a small industrial city, made a name for itself with its Shakespeare festival, while Kitchener and Waterloo attract thousands with an annual Oktoberfest. Once you're in these areas, you'll also enjoy the less famous lures—parks, gardens, and country trails. Hamilton, known for its exceptionally productive iron and steel mills, maintains acre upon acre of lush gardens, and London is spread across with riverside parks.

Hamilton

67 *75 km (47 mi) west of Niagara Falls on the Queen Elizabeth Way.*

Hamilton is Canada's steel capital—the Dofasco and Stelco mills produce 60% of the country's iron and steel. This isn't the sort of city where you'd expect to find 2,700 acres of gardens and exotic plants, a symphony orchestra, a modern and active theater, 45 parks, and a developed waterfront. But they're all here in Hamilton, Ontario's second-largest city and Canada's third-busiest port. The city's downtown is on a plain between the harbor and the base of "the mountain," a 250-ft-high section of the Niagara Escarpment. Downtown Hamilton is a potpourri of glass-walled high rises, century-old mansions, a convention center, a coliseum, and a shopping complex.

With 176 stalls spread over more than 20,000 square ft, **Hamilton Farmers' Market** is Canada's largest farmers' market. It's been around since 1837. ⊠ *Adjoining Jackson Square and new Eaton Centre,* ☎ *905/546–2096.* ☉ *Tues. and Thurs. 7–6, Fri. 9–6, Sat. 6–6.*

The Art Gallery of Hamilton houses 8,000 works of art, both Canadian and international, in an acclaimed three-level modern structure in the central business district. ⊠ *123 King St. W,* ☎ *905/527–6610.* ⊠ *$4.* ☉ *Wed., Fri., and Sat. 10–5; Thurs. 10–9; Sun. 1–5.*

The **Royal Botanical Gardens,** opened in 1932, encompass five major gardens and 48 km (30 mi) of trails that wind across marshes and ravines, past the world's largest collection of lilacs, 2 acres of roses, and all manner of shrubs, trees, plants, hedges, and flowers. Two tea houses are open May 1 to Thanksgiving (mid-October). ⊠ *Plains Rd. (Hwy. 2), Burlington, accessible from Queen Elizabeth Way and Hwys. 6 and 403,* ☎ *905/527–1158 or 800/668–9449 in Ontario and Québec.* ☞ *Mid-May–Labor Day, $5.25; Labor Day–mid-May, grounds free, greenhouse $2.* ☉ *Main building daily 9–5, outdoor garden daily 9:30–6.*

Plant lovers will marvel at **Gage Park**'s 70-acre botanical greens, a beautiful oasis in the center of the city. Its rose garden, with more than 30 varieties, is especially stunning. ⊠ *Main St. E and Gage Ave., east of downtown.*

★ Sir Allan Napier MacNab, a War of 1812 hero and Upper Canada's pre-confederation prime minister, built a 35-room mansion called **Dundurn Castle** in 1832 through 1835. Now a museum, it has been furnished to reflect the opulence in which MacNab lived at the height of his political career. ⊠ *Dundurn Park and York Blvd.,* ☎ *905/546–2872.* ☞ *$5.40.* ☉ *June–Labor Day, daily 11–4; Labor Day–May, Tues.–Sun. 1–4; closed nonholiday Mon.*

Flamboro Downs harness-racing track, just west of Hamilton, has matinee and evening races year-round, though not on a daily basis. The clubhouse has two dining areas that overlook the track. ⊠ *Hwy. 5.,* ☎ *905/627–3561.*

☾ At **African Lion Safari,** lions, tigers, cheetahs, elephants, and zebras abound. You can drive your own car or take an air-conditioned tram over a 9-km (6-mi) safari trail through the wildlife park. ⊠ *Rockton, near Hamilton, off Hwy. 8, south of Cambridge,* ☎ *519/623–2620 or 800/461–WILD.* ☞ *$14.50.* ☉ *Grounds early Apr.–Oct., daily 9–6:30; tour weekdays 9–4, weekends 9–5.*

Dining and Lodging

$$
★
✕ Ancaster Old Mill. This historic mill is just outside Hamilton and worth the trip if only to sample the bread, baked daily with flour ground on millstones installed in 1863. The dining rooms are light and bright with hanging plants. Try to get a table overlooking the mill stream and a waterfall. ⊠ *548 Old Dundas Rd., Ancaster,* ☎ *905/648–1827. Reservations essential. AE, DC, MC, V.*

$$$ **✕▤ Howard Johnson Royal Connaught Plaza Hotel.** This venerable 1914 hotel in the heart of downtown Hamilton is a grand old place complete with a ballroom. The indoor swimming pool has one of Canada's longest water slides. Fran's is the hotel's very popular dining room (reserve ahead). Meat is broiled over an open mesquite fire. There's a marble floor and, after you've eaten—or while you're waiting for your entrée to be flamed—you can dance in the gazebo. ⊠ *112 King St. E, L8N 1A8,* ☎ *905/546–8111,* ℻ *905/546–8144. 206 rooms, 21 suites. Restaurant, lounge, indoor pool, hot tub, sauna, cabaret, comedy club. AE, MC, V.*

Nightlife and the Arts

Hamilton Place's Great Hall can accommodate 1,193 on the orchestra level, 560 in the first balcony, and 428 in the second balcony. Opera Hamilton holds performances here from September through April. Its repertoire embraces works from *Aida* to *Nixon in China.* ⊠ *10 MacNab St.,* ☎ *905/546–3050.*

Hiking

The 680-km (422-mi) **Bruce Trail** stretches northwest along the Niagara Escarpment from the orchards of the Niagara Peninsula to the cliffs and bluffs at Tobermory, at the end of the Bruce Peninsula. You can access the Bruce Trail at just about any point along the route, so your hike can be as long or as short as you wish. Contact the Bruce Trail Association (✉ Box 857, Hamilton L8N 3N9, ☎ 905/592–6821).

Brantford

68 *40 km (25 mi) west of Hamilton on Hwy. 403.*

Brantford is named for Joseph Brant, the Loyalist Mohawk chief who brought members of the Six Nations Confederacy into Canada after the American Revolution. King George III showed gratitude to Chief Brant by building the **Mohawk Church.** In 1904, by royal assent, it was given the name His Majesty's Chapel of the Mohawks (now changed to Her Majesty's). This simple, white-painted frame building with eight stained-glass windows depicting the colorful history of the Six Nations people is the oldest Protestant Church in Ontario and the only Indian Royal Chapel in existence. A guide is available. ✉ *292 Mohawk St.,* ☎ *519/758–5444.* ⊠ *$1.* ☉ *Daily 1–5.*

Woodland Indian Cultural Educational Centre is a museum of sorts that aims to preserve and promote the culture and heritage of the native people of the First Nation. The modern building contains displays and exhibits showing early Woodland Indian culture. ✉ *184 Mohawk St., near Mohawk Chapel,* ☎ *519/759–2650.* ⊠ *$3.* ☉ *Weekdays 8:30– 4, weekends 10–5.*

Though Brantford is the hometown of hockey star Wayne Gretzky, it is better known as "the Telephone City" because Alexander Graham Bell invented the device here and made the first long-distance call from his parents' home to nearby Paris, Ontario, in 1874. The **Bell Homestead** is now a National Historic Site. Next door is the house of the Reverend Thomas Henderson, a Baptist minister who left the church when he recognized the profit potential in telephones. His home served as the first telephone office and now is a museum of telephone artifacts and displays. Guided tours can be arranged. ✉ *94 Tutela Heights Rd.,* ☎ *519/756– 6220.* ⊠ *$2.50.* ☉ *Mid-Mar.–Thanksgiving, Tues.–Sun. 9:30–4:30.*

Outdoor Activities and Sports

BIKING

Brantford is protected by a flood-control dam on top of which is a bicycle trail that passes many attractions.

HIKING

The **Grand Valley Trail** runs 128 km (79 mi) between Elora and Brantford. Contact the Grand Valley Trail Association (✉ Box 1233, Kitchener N2G 4G8) for more information.

Kitchener and Waterloo

69 *Approximately 27 km (17 mi) north of Brantford on Hwy. 24.*

Kitchener and Waterloo, which merge into one another, are usually referred to as K–W. Settled around 1800 by Swiss-German Mennonites from Pennsylvania, the region's German origins remain obvious: There's a huge glockenspiel downtown by Speakers' Corner, and each October since 1967 the city has hosted Oktoberfest. The event now draws more than 600,000 people, who swarm to more than a dozen festival halls where they dance, gorge on German-style food, listen to oompah bands, and drink with a fervor that seems driven by an irrational fear that all Canadian breweries are about to go on strike.

The **Kitchener Market** isn't the oldest or the largest farmers' market in Ontario, but it's been around since 1869 and since 1986 has been housed in spacious quarters at Market Square. The block-long complex is wrapped in green-tinted glass and contains 70 shops and snack bars, and an Eaton's department store. ⊠ *Frederick and Duke Sts.,* ☎ *519/741–2287.* ⊙ *Sat. 6–2.*

William Lyon Mackenzie King, who was prime minister of Canada for almost 22 of the years between 1921 and 1948, spent his teenage years in a rented 10-room house called Woodside, now **Woodside National Historic Sites.** There's no particular imprint here of the bachelor prime minister whose diaries reveal his belief in mysticism, portents, and communications with the dead, but the house has been furnished to reflect the Victorian period of the King family's occupancy. ⊠ *528 Wellington St., Kitchener,* ☎ *519/571–5684.* ⊡ *$2.50.* ⊙ *May–Dec., daily 10–5; Jan.–Apr., by appointment only.*

The **Seagram Museum** is a shrine to booze, and every exhibit in the enormous former barrel warehouses and new exhibition building relates to the product. ⊠ *57 Erb St. W, Waterloo,* ☎ *519/885–1857.* ⊡ *Free.* ⊙ *May–Dec., daily 10–6; Jan.–Apr., Tues.–Sun. 10–6.*

Doon Heritage Crossroads is a complete living history site including a restored 1914 village with two farms located on Homer Watson Boulevard, just north of Highway 401 in Kitchener. The village recalls the tranquility of rural lifestyles in the early 1900s. You can cross a covered bridge and wander tree-shaded roads to visit with costumed staff who perform authentic period trades and activities. ⊠ *From Hwy. 401 exit Homer Watson Blvd. North (interchange #275),* ☎ *519/748–1914.* ⊡ *$5.* ⊙ *May–Labor Day, daily 10–4:30; Labor Day–Dec., weekdays 10–4:30.*

Dining and Lodging

$$$$ ✕🖭 **Langdon Hall Country House Hotel.** This magnificent colonial-re-
★ vival-style mansion on 50 landscaped acres has grand public rooms and huge fireplaces. It was built in 1898 as a summer home for a great-granddaughter of John Jacob Astor and has been sensitively converted to a grand country hotel with 13 guest rooms in the original building and 30 in a modern annex. The house has a billiard room, a conservatory, a card room, and a drawing room. The dining room (reserve ahead) specializes in Regional cuisine such as Waterloo County pork tenderloin and Woolwich goat cheese in phyllo pastry. Call for directions. ⊠ *R.R. 33, Cambridge N3H 4R8,* ☎ *519/740–2100 or 800/268–1898,* ℻ *519/740–8161. 43 rooms. Dining Room, room service, pool, hot tub, sauna, tennis court, croquet, exercise room, boating, billiards, meeting rooms. AE, DC, MC, V.*

$$$ ✕🖭 **Four Points Sheraton.** This modern hotel has a major sports complex in its basement and is connected by a glassed-in skywalk to the Market Square shopping mall and Farmers' Market. Shatz's, the main, more formal restaurant (reserve ahead), is candlelit and decorated in earth tones. Continental fare dominates the menu. A smaller café is fine for casual meals. ⊠ *105 King St. E, N2G 2K8,* ☎ *519/744–4141,* ℻ *519/578–6889. 203 rooms. Café, dining room, lounge, indoor pool, hot tub, sauna, miniature golf, bowling. AE, MC, V.*

St. Jacobs

★ ⑳ *10 km (6 mi) north of Kitchener and Waterloo on Hwy. 8.*

The villages of St. Jacobs and Elmira (10 km, or 6 mi, north of St. Jacobs via Route 86 and County Road 21) are in the heart of Mennonite and Hutterite country. "The Meetingplace" interpretation center in St. Jacobs offers visitors a chance to learn more about the Old Order Mennonite community in the area (seasonal hours). St. Jacobs is also a unique shopping destination with over 100 shops that run the gamut from antiques to fashion wear. The St. Jacobs Farmers Market and Flea Market has over 350 vendors selling fresh produce and crafts on Thursday and Saturday from 7 AM to 3:30 PM year-round and on Tuesday from 8 AM to 3 PM June through August.

Dining and Lodging

$$$$ ✕🏨 **Millcroft Inn.** This 19th-century stone knitting mill has been con-
★ verted to an exquisite full-service country inn beside the millpond. About 40 km (25 mi) northeast of Elmira (80 km, or 50 mi, northwest of Toronto) in Alton, it is one of Canada's finest hostelries. Some large suites have fireplaces. Rooms are available in both the older inn and a more modern annex, where they tend to be more spacious. In addition to sports facilities, there's a year-round outdoor whirlpool. The dining room menu offers a relatively limited choice of traditional Continental dishes, but quality more than makes up for the lack of variety (reserve ahead). ⊠ 55 John St., Alton, L0N 1A0, ☎ 519/941–8111, FAX 519/941–0192. 52 rooms. Dining room, pool, hot tub, 2 saunas, 2 tennis courts, exercise room, recreation room. AE, DC, MC, V.

$$$ ✕🏨 **Benjamins.** This is a lovely re-creation of the original 1852 Farmer's Inn. Nine guest rooms on the second floor are furnished in antiques, and every bed is covered with a locally made Mennonite quilt. The licensed, 120-seat restaurant (reserve ahead) has pine ceiling beams, an open-hearth fireplace, lots of greenery, and imaginative French cuisine. ⊠ 17 King St., N0B 2N0, ☎ 519/664–3731, FAX 519/664–2218. 9 rooms. Restaurant. AE, MC, V.

$$$ ✕🏨 **Elora Mill.** This is one of Canada's few remaining five-story grist-
★ mills. It has been converted to luxury accommodations and offers superb dining. There are 16 guest rooms in the 1859 mill building and 16 more in four other historic stone buildings in the immediate vicinity of the mill. The inn is in the heart of Elora, a village about 15 km (9 mi) north of Elmira full of stone buildings that could have been lifted from England's Cotswolds or southern France. The cuisine is a mix of imaginative Canadian and European dishes (reserve ahead). ⊠ 77 Mill St. W, Elora N0B 1S0, ☎ 519/846–5356, FAX 519/846–9180. 32 rooms. Dining room. AE, MC, V.

Outdoor Activities and Sports

BIKING

Two popular bike routes can be reached from **Fergus,** 18 km (11 mi) northwest of Elmira: One is a 32-km (20-mi) tour around Lake Belwood, the other a 40-km (25-mi) loop around Eramosa Township. There is little traffic on these scenic routes, and restaurants are few and far between, so take a picnic lunch.

HIKING

The 5-km (3-mi) pathway along the **Elora Gorge** between Fergus and Elora, 15 km (9 mi) north of Elmira is a great minihike. You'll pass a whirlpool at Templin Gardens, a restored English garden, and cross a bridge at Mirror Basin.

Stratford

71 *46 km (29 mi) west of Kitchener on Hwys. 7 and 8.*

The city of Stratford was named by homesick English settlers; all that the town had in common with England's Stratford was a river called Avon meandering through rolling countryside—and not even particularly similar countryside. Nowadays the village is famous for hosting the annual Stratford Festival, which welcomes more than 400,000 people to its acclaimed performances of music, opera, and drama.

Dining and Lodging

$$$$ ✗ **Church Restaurant and Belfry.** One block from the Avon Theatre, this church—complete with organ pipes and stained-glass windows—has been converted into a restaurant. There's even an old pew outside the rest room. Specialties include Ostrich, Noisette of lamb and Atlantic salmon. The Belfry upstairs is more casual and less expensive. ⊠ *Brunswick and Waterloo Sts.,* ☎ *519/273–3424. Reservations essential. AE, DC, MC, V.*

$$ ✗ ⬚ **La Brassine.** Near the edge of Lake Huron northwest of Stratford,
★ this large farm home–cum–country inn has a kitchen that produces some of the finest French cuisine west of the Québec border. Book ahead at least 24 hours for Wednesday–Saturday dinners or daily if you're a resident of one of the guest rooms in the inn. Everything served is created in-house; the linen-covered tables are set with crystal and silver. There is no liquor license. The management accepts the credit cards noted below, but prefers cash or check payment. Call for directions. ⊠ *R.R. 2, Goderich N78 3X8,* ☎ *519/524–6300. 4 rooms. MC, V.*

$$ ✗ ⬚ **Queen's Inn at Stratford.** This country-style inn dating from 1850 is in the heart of Stratford. The restaurant, Soltar, serves flavorful Santa Fe cuisine at reasonable prices. The Boar's head is a popular pub-lounge with light snacks and a great variety of brews. ⊠ *161 Ontario St., N5A 3H3,* ☎ *519/271–1400,* ℻ *519/271–7373. 30 rooms. Restaurant, lounge. AE, MC, V.*

$$$–$$$$ ⬚ **Woods Villa Bed and Breakfast.** This elegant 1875 home once belonged to a wealthy magistrate; it has since been restored to its 19th-century grandeur. The public rooms hold an astonishing collection of restored vintage jukeboxes, music boxes, and player pianos. Start the day on the right foot with a grand breakfast accompanied by full table service. Five of the six rooms have fireplaces. Woods Villa does not accept children or pets; the latter might ruffle the feathers of the owner's five tropical birds. Note that while the credit cards listed below are accepted, cash is preferred. ⊠ *62 John St. N, N5A 6K7,* ☎ *519/271–4576. 6 rooms. Outdoor pool. MC, V.*

The Arts

★ The **Stratford Festival** hosts music, opera, and drama annually. It all started in 1953, in a massive tent, with Sir Alec Guinness playing Richard III. The next year musical programs were added to supplement Shakespeare's plays. The venture was a huge success, and the 1957 season opened in a permanent home with 2,262 seats, none of which is more than 65 ft from the stage. The 1901-vintage, 1,107-seat Avon Theatre became a partner in the festival in 1967, and the Tom Patterson Theatre, seating 496, opened in 1971. The Stratford Festival now starts around the beginning of May and runs until late October. ⊠ *55 Queens St.,* ☎ *519/273–1600 or 800/567–1600.*

London

72 *75 km (47 mi) southwest of Stratford on Hwys. 7 and 4.*

Nicknamed Forest City, London has more than 50,000 trees on city property and 1,500 acres of parks, including 1,000 acres along the Thames River. It's a quiet, provincial city where old money rules the arts and development projects, and it's become famous for its hospitals, which specialize in organ-transplant operations. London has been called a microcosm of Canadian life; it is so "typically Canadian," it's often used as a test market for new products—if something will sell in London, it will probably sell anywhere in Canada.

From mid-May through October you can get another view of London by cruising on the Thames River in a 60-passenger boat. Afternoon cruises (✉ Spring Bank Park, ☎ 519/473–0363) depart every hour from Storybook Gardens. The easiest way to get an overview of the town is to take a tour on a big, red, double-decker—what else?—London bus. They operate from City Hall, July 1 to Labor Day (at 10 and 2).

Because **Storybook Gardens** is owned and operated by the city's Public Utility Commission, this is one of the least expensive children's theme parks in the country. It's on the Thames River in the 281-acre Springbank Park. You'll see a castle, storybook characters, and a zoo with foreign and indigenous animals, including some from Old MacDonald's Farm. Children can slide down Jack and Jill's hill and the throat of Willie the Whale. ✉ *929 Springbank Dr.,* ☎ *519/661–5770.* ✆ *$5.* ☉ *May–Labor Day, daily 10–8; Labor Day–Thanksgiving (mid-Oct.), weekdays 10–5, weekends 10–6.*

London Regional Art and Historical Museum is as interesting from the outside as its exhibits are on the inside. The gallery is contained in six joined, glass-covered structures whose ends are the shape of croquet hoops. An impressive collection of fine art and artifacts plus regularly changing exhibitions are complemented by films, lectures, music, and live performances. ✉ *Forks of the Thames,* ☎ *519/672–4580.* ✆ *Donation requested.* ☉ *Tues.–Sun. noon–5.*

The **London Museum of Archaeology** maintains more than 40,000 native artifacts plus a gallery of artists' conceptions of the lives of the Attawandaron natives who lived on the Lawson site, a nearby archaeological dig, some 500 years ago. Within proximity is a reconstructed multifamily longhouse on its original site. ✉ *1600 Attawandaron Rd., south of Hwy. 22,* ☎ *519/473–1360.* ✆ *$3.50.* ☉ *May–Labor Day, daily 10–5; Labor Day–Oct., Tues.–Sun. 10–5; Jan.–Apr., Wed.–Sun. 1–4.*

London's oldest building is also one of its most impressive. The wrecker's ball came awfully close to the **Old Courthouse Building,** and it got one wall of the former Middlesex County Gaol. But a citizens' group prevailed, and the Old Courthouse, modeled after Malahide Castle in England, reopened as the home of the Middlesex County council. ✉ *399 Ridout St. N,* ☎ *519/434–7321.* ✆ *Free.* ☉ *June–Aug., weekdays 8:30–noon and 1–4:30.*

Dining and Lodging

$$ ✕ **Marienbad and Chaucer's Pub.** Among the reasonably priced Czech fare is great goulash, schnitzels, and sauerbraten are among the choices. ✉ *122 Carling St.,* ☎ *519/679–9940. AE, MC, V.*

$$ ✕ **Michael's on the Thames.** This popular lunch and dinner spot overlooks the Thames River. The Canadian and Continental cuisine includes flambéed dishes, fresh seafood, chateaubriand, and flaming desserts and coffees. ✉ *1 York St., at Thames River,* ☎ *519/672–0111,* FAX *519/672–2892. Reservations essential. AE, DC, MC, V.*

$$$$ 🏨 **Delta London Armouries.** This 20-story, silver-mirrored tower rises from the center of the 1905 London Armoury. The lobby is a greenhouse of vines, trees, plants, and fountains, wrapped in marble and accented by rich woods and old yellow brick. The architects left as much of the original armory intact as possible. A set of steps through manicured jungle takes you to the indoor swimming pool, sauna, and whirlpool. Guest rooms are spacious and decorated in pastel shades. Suites vary in size and grandeur—the Middlesex Suite has a grand piano. ✉ *325 Dundas St., N6B 1T9,* ☎ *519/679-6111 or 800/668–9999,*

FAX *519/679–3957. 242 rooms, 8 suites. Restaurant, lounge, indoor pool, sauna, miniature golf, racquetball, squash. AE, MC, V.*

$$$$ ☉ **Idlewylde Inn.** Though an elevator was installed in this converted 1878 mansion, the architects succeeded in preserving its original detail. Complimentary breakfast, snacks, and parking are included in your room rate. ⊠ *36 Grand Ave., N6C 1K8,* ☎ FAX *519/433–2891. 27 rooms. AE, DC, MC, V.*

Biking

Scenic **Springbank Park** has miles of pretty bicycle trails.

SAULT STE. MARIE AND WEST TO THUNDER BAY

Sault Ste. Marie

73 *700 km (434 mi) northwest of Toronto.*

Sault Ste. Marie has always been a natural meeting place and cultural melting pot. Long before Etienne Brulé "discovered" the rapids in 1622, Ojibwa tribes gathered here. Whitefish, their staple food, could easily be caught year-round, and the rapids in the St. Mary's River linking lakes Huron and Superior were often the only sources of open water for miles during the winter. When Father Jacques Marquette opened a mission in 1668, he named it Sainte Marie de Sault. Sault is French for rapids, which generate hydroelectric power for the city. Today locals call the city simply "the Sault," pronounced "the Soo."

The elegant **Ermatinger Stone House** was built by Montréal fur trader Charles Oakes Ermatinger in 1814 and is the oldest building in Canada west of Toronto. Ermatinger married a daughter of the influential Indian chief Katawebeda, a move that didn't hurt his business. Today, costumed interpreters guide visitors through the house. ⊠ *831 Queen St. E,* ☎ *705/759–5443.* ▣ *Donation requested.* ◷ *Apr.–May, weekdays 10–5; June–Sept., daily 10–5; Oct.–Nov., weekdays 1–5.*

Lock Tours Canada runs two-hour excursions through the 21-ft-high **Soo Locks,** the 16th and final lift for ships bound for Lake Superior from the St. Lawrence River. Tours aboard the 200-passenger MV *Chief Shingwauk* leave from the Roberta Bondar Dock next door to the Holiday Inn, May 15 through October 15, and up to eight times daily July 1 through Labor Day. ⊠ *Roberta Bondar Dock off Foster Dr.,* ☎ *705/253–9850.* ▣ *$17.*

★ The Algoma Central Railway not only operates a main line track between the Sault and iron mines at Hearst and Michipicoten Harbor, but it also runs the **Agawa Canyon Train Tours,** a lucrative sideline of tour trains that provide day trips to and from scenic Agawa Canyon, a deep valley 19 km (12 mi) long with 800-ft-high cliff walls through which the Agawa River flows. In summer the Agawa Canyon Train makes a two-hour stopover in the canyon during which passengers can lunch in a park, hike to their choice of three waterfalls, or climb to a lookout 250 ft above the train. In colder months, the Snow Train makes the same trip, minus the Agawa Canyon layover. ⊠ *129 Bay St.,* ☎ *705/946–7300 or 800/242–9287.* ▣ *Agawa Canyon Train: $49–$59, Snow Train $55.* ◷ *Agawa Canyon Train: June–mid-Oct., daily; Snow Train: Jan.–mid-Mar., weekends; trains depart 8 AM and return at 5 in warmer seasons and 4 in cooler weather.*

Dining and Lodging

$$$ ✕☉ **Quality Inn Bayfront.** If you're planning to take an Agawa Canyon Train Tour (☞ *above*), book a room at this popular hotel. The rooms

Upper Ontario

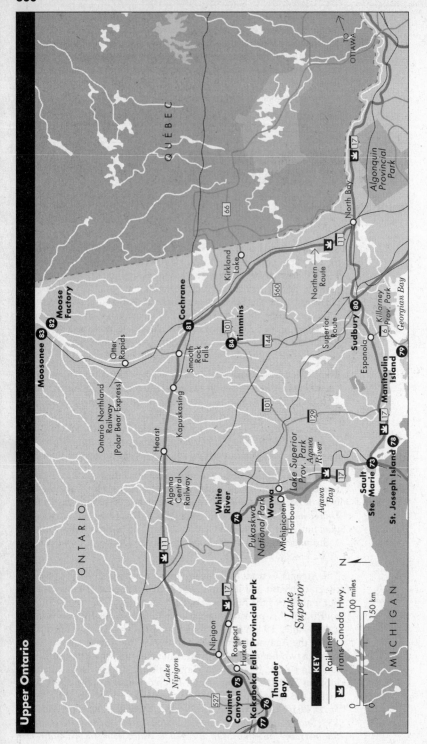

QUÉBEC

ONTARIO

TO OTTAWA

Algonquin Provincial Park

North Bay

17

111

Sudbury 80

Killarney Prov. Park

Georgian Bay

79

Espanola

Manitoulin Island

17

78

St. Joseph Island

Sault Ste. Marie

75

Aqawa Bay

Lake Superior Prov. Park
Aqawa River

17

129

101

Michipicoten Harbour

Wawa

74

Pukaskwa National Park

White River

Hearst

Algoma Central Railway

Kapuskasing

Smooth Rock Falls

Cochrane 81

Kirkland Lake

66

560

84

Timmins

101

144

Northern Route

Superior Route

Moosonee 83

82 Moose Factory

Otter Rapids

Ontario Northland Railway (Polar Bear Express)

111

17

Nipigon

Rossport
Hurkett

Kakabeka Falls Provincial Park

Ouimet Canyon 75

76 Thunder Bay

77

527

Lake Nipigon

Lake Superior

MICHIGAN

N

KEY

Rail Lines

Trans-Canada Hwy.

0   100 miles

0   150 km

and suites are clean and modern with many comforts, including a sauna and in-house movies. Most important—because the train leaves at 8 AM and you should be at the station by 7:30 AM at the latest—the hotel is directly across the street from the Algoma Central Railroad station. When you return at night, the hotel's swimming pool and dining room await you. The hotel's Gran Sesta Ristorante (reserve ahead), bright and airy with lots of brass and greenery, serves southern Italian dishes garnished with edible flowers. ⊠ *180 Bay St., P6A 6S2,* ☎ *705/945–9264 or 800/228–5151,* ⅨⅩ *705/945–9766. 109 rooms, 13 suites. Dining room, indoor pool, hot tub, sauna, exercise room, meeting rooms. AE, MC, V.*

Guided Tours

Hiawathaland Tours (☎ 705/759–6200) operates three city tours by double-decker bus and a wilderness tour by minivan to Aubrey Falls from June 15 to October 15. There's also a 75-minute evening tour.

En Route　　**Wawa,** 225 km (140 mi) north of Sault Ste. Marie on Trans-Canada Highway 17, is the first town north of the Lake Superior Provincial Park. It's name is derived from an Ojibwa word meaning "wild goose," and the 3,700 residents of Wawa have erected a massive goose monument at the entrance to town from Highway 17. Next door is the town's new log-cabin tourist information office.

White River

❼❹ *90 km (56 mi) north of Wawa on Trans-Canada Hwy. 17.*

This town is marked by a huge thermometer indicating 72 degrees below zero and a sign that advises: "White River—coldest place in Canada." White River is hard to miss. The town has another claim to fame: It was the home of Winnie-the-Pooh, the bear cub immortalized in the children's stories by British author A. A. Milne. A 25-ft-high statue honoring Winnie was put up in 1992, and each August the town holds a three-day Winnie's Homecoming Festival, with parades, street dances, and a community barbecue.

Dining and Lodging

$$　✕▣ **Rossport Inn.** The hamlet of Rossport, about 200 km (124 mi) west of White River, on a harbor off Lake Superior, is about as close as you can get to an unspoiled outpost on the Great Lakes. The inn was built in 1884 as a railroad hotel. Now it has six small guest rooms sharing two bathrooms. This is one of the nicest country inns in the province. It's cozy and down-home—the nightlife consists of swapping lies with the innkeepers and other guests about the fish that got away. Breakfast is included in the room rate. The dining room's home-style cooking of locally caught fish, as well as of steak, chicken, pork chops, and lobster, is irresistible. ⊠ *Rossport Loop, ½ mi from Trans-Canada Hwy., Bowman St., P0T 2R0,* ☎ *807/824–3213. 6 rooms. Dining room. MC, V. Closed Nov.–May.*

Ouimet Canyon Provincial Park

★ **❼❺** *300 km (186 mi) west of White River on Trans-Canada Hwy. 17.*

Just past the town of Hurkett, west of Nipigon, watch for signs to Ouimet Canyon. This geological anomaly is spectacular; Botanists have discovered arctic plants native to the Tundra growing in areas where the sun never shines. A walking path stops short at the edge of the canyon, where viewing platforms allow you to look straight down 350 ft. The far wall is only 492 ft away, and the chasm is 2½ km (1½ mi) long. Geologists believe the canyon could be a gigantic fault in the earth's surface or the result of glacial action. (Note: access to the canyon floor is restricted due its fragile nature.) ⊠ *11 km (7 mi) off Hwy. 17, 10 km (6 mi) west of Hurkett,* ☎ *807/977–2526.* ⚐ *Free.* ☉ *Mid-May–Thanksgiving (mid-Oct.), daily 9–5.*

En Route   Ontario's gemstone is an imperfect quartz tinted violet or purple. There are five amethyst mines between Sleeping Giant Provincial Park and Ouimet Canyon, a distance of 50 km (31 mi) along Highways 11 and 17 east of Thunder Bay. All are signposted from the highway, and each offers the opportunity to hand-pick some samples (paid for by the pound). **Amethyst Mine Panorama** is closest to Thunder Bay (☞ *below*). Tours of the mine run four times daily at 11, 12:30, 3, and 5. To get there follow Loon Lake Road from Highways 11 and 17, east of Thunder Bay. ⊠ *E. Loon Rd.,* ☎ *807/622-6908.* ⚐ *$3.* ☉ *Mid-May–mid-Oct., daily 10–5; July–Aug., daily 10–7.*

Thunder Bay

76 *67 km (42 mi) southwest of Ouimet Canyon on Trans-Canada Hwy. 17.*

Although they amalgamated into one city in 1970, there are still Port Arthur and Fort Williams sections of Thunder Bay. The city is one of the world's largest grain-handling centers. It has an extraordinary ethnic mix, with 42 nationalities and the largest Finnish population outside Finland. The area has Ontario's best alpine and cross-country skiing with the longest ski season, superb fishing and hunting, great camping and hiking, unlimited canoe and boating routes, and even ice climbing. Several amethyst mines have shops in the city. There are also an art gallery, dozens of good restaurants, and nine shopping malls.

Be sure to visit **Old Fort William,** where costumed interpreters bring to life a reconstructed fur-trading fort with 42 historic buildings on a 125-acre site. ⊠ *Broadway Ave.,* ☎ *807/577–8461.* ⚐ *$10.* ☉ *mid-May–mid-Oct., daily 10–5.*

Dining and Lodging

$$$ ✕🏨 **Valhalla Inn.** The warm lobby is based on old Scandinavian design, with plenty of wood and brass. The guest rooms are large with queen-size beds and local art. The Nordic dining room offers signature Scandinavian dishes, including smoked salmon and Swedish fish chowder. ⊠ *1 Valhalla Inn Rd., P7E 6J1,* ☎ *807/577–1121 or 800/268–2500,* 🖷 *807/475–4723. 220 rooms. Dining room, indoor pool, hot tub, sauna, exercise room. AE, D, MC, V.*

Outdoor Activities and Sports

ICE CLIMBING

North of Superior Climbing Company (⊠ Box 2204, P7B 5E8, ☎ 807/344–9636) offers ice climbing lessons, professionally led climbs, and two-day packages. Accommodations in rustic cabins or motels are provided, but meals are not included.

SKIING

The highest ski slopes in Ontario are **Candy Mountain Resort** and **Loch Lomond** (☎ 807/475–5250), both just outside Thunder Bay and both with 750 ft of vertical drop. Lift tickets are interchangeable between the two areas.

Kakabeka Falls Provincial Park

77 *40 km (25 mi) northwest of Thunder Bay off Hwys. 11 and 17.*

Kakabeka Falls Provincial Park, on the Kaministikwia River, drops 154 ft over a limestone ledge into a deep gorge. The falls can be seen from either side, and there are large, free parking lots.

EAST ALONG GEORGIAN BAY AND SOUTH TO MANITOULIN ISLAND

On a half-day journey by car you can see the stunning beauty of Georgian Bay and the stark landscape of industrial Sudbury. Highlights include the wild flowers of St. Joseph Island, the rugged simplicity of Manitoulin Island, and the Big Nickel Mine Tour in Sudbury.

St. Joseph Island

㊆ *40 km (25 mi) southeast of Sault Ste. Marie via Hwy. 17.*

St. Joseph Island is a sparsely settled bit of land about 24 by 30 km (16 by 20 mi) in the mouth of the St. Mary's River, connected by causeway and bridge to the mainland. In spring the island is a scented riot of wild lilac, and you're likely to see moose and deer along the quiet side roads.

In fur-trading days, **Fort St. Joseph,** established by the British at the southeast tip of the island, guarded the trade route from Montréal to the upper Great Lakes. Today, visitors can wander the national historic park on the rounded peninsula on which the fort and commercial buildings once stood and see the outlines and few above-ground stone ruins of the 42 building sites that have been identified. Free walking tours and a free booklet are available at the visitor center, which is about 30 minutes by car southeast of the Gilbertson Bridge. Call ahead for directions. ☎ *705/246–2664.* ☉ *Late May–Thanksgiving (mid-Oct.), daily 10–5.*

Manitoulin Island

㊖ *149 km (92 mi) east of St. Joseph Island and south of Espanola via Hwys. 17 and 6.*

Manitoulin Island, the world's largest freshwater island, which sits at the top of Lake Huron plugging the mouth of Georgian Bay, is 160 km (99 mi) long and varies in width from 3 to 64 km (2 to 40 mi). The island is pretty and rugged, with granite outcrops, forests, meadows, rivers, and rolling countryside. Only 20% of the land is arable, and much of the rest is used for grazing sheep and cattle. Yachters rate the waters around the islands among the best in the world, and hunters and fishermen have taken advantage of the island's riches for generations. Hikes and exploration could easily turn this "side trip" into a week-long stay. For the most part it has not been ravaged by time and human incursions. Archaeological digs on Manitoulin Island have unearthed traces of human habitation that are more than 30,000 years old, making them the oldest on the North American continent. There is no interim record of people living on the island until explorer Samuel de Champlain met some island residents in 1650. The towns on the island, such as Little Current (closest to the mainland), Sheguiandah, and Wikwemikong, are simple and picturesque.

As an alternative to driving that is especially convenient if you are heading up the Bruce Peninsula from southern Ontario, you can take a ferry. The **MS *Chi-Cheemaun,*** connects the picturesque town of Tobermory, at the northern tip of the peninsula, with South Baymouth on the island. The trip takes 1 hour and 45 minutes each way. There are four sailings in each direction daily between mid-June and Labor Day, and three during spring and fall. Reservations are advised. ✉ *Ontario Northland Marine Services, 343 8th St. E, Owen Sound N4K 1L3,* ☎ *519/596–2510 or 800/265–3163.* 💳 *One-way $11, plus $24 per car.*

Little Current–Howland Centennial Museum, in the village of Sheguiandah about 11 km (7 mi) south of Little Current, displays local native and pioneer artifacts. ⊠ *Hwy. 6,* ☎ *705/368–2367.* ⊑ *$3.* ☉ *Mid-May–mid-Oct., daily 10–4:30.*

Wikwemikong Unceded Indian Reserve encompasses the entire southeastern peninsula of Manitoulin Island. One of Manitoulin's most colorful events is the Wikwemikong Pow Wow, held on Civic Holiday (the first weekend in August). Dancers accompanied by drummers and singers compete while performing the steps of their ancestors.

Sudbury

⑧⓪ *60 km (37 mi) east of Espanola on Trans-Canada Hwy. 17.*

The mining town of Sudbury used to bear the brunt of frequent unkind jokes. After all, didn't the U.S. astronauts go there to train in the type of terrain they were likely to encounter on the moon? Today, the Greening of Sudbury, an ongoing community-wide land-reclamation project has revived much of the landscape that suffered from years of logging, smelter emissions, and soil erosion. What you see today is typical of Canadian Shield country with beautiful lakes, rocky outcroppings, and trees. In addition, there are outdoor concerts, art centers, museums, and cruises on Ramsey Lake, the largest freshwater lake inside city limits in North America.

Science North is Northern Ontario's largest tourist attraction, encompassing a world-renowned Science Centre, a giant-screen IMAX Theatre, an underground mine tour, and a new Virtual Voyages Motion Theatre. Explore science in your everyday world at Northern Ontario's Science Centre. Touch live animals, gaze at the stars, test your senses, play with technology, watch a 3-D film, listen to 3-D sound, and more. Friendly scientists are always available to share their knowledge. ⊠ *100 Ramsey Lake Rd.,* ☎ *705/522–3700.* ⊑ *Museum and IMAX theatre $8.95.* ☉ *Daily 9–5.*

The **Big Nickel,** a 30-ft replica of the 1951 Canadian commemorative coin, has been synonymous with Sudbury for almost three decades. It stands on a barren hillside on the west side of the city, overlooking Inco's smokestacks. Near the Big Nickel is the entrance to the **Big Nickel Mine.** At 73 ft, it is one of the shallowest mines in the area. Science North (☞ *above*) offers tours of the mine in summer. Visitors are given hard hats, coats, and boots and lowered into the mine shaft in a "cage" elevator. In the 437-yard-long drifts, or tunnels, miners demonstrate mining techniques. ⊠ *Hwy. 17 and Big Nickel Mine Rd.,* ☎ *705/673–5659 or 705/522–3701.* ⊑ *$8.50.* ☉ *Tour: May–Nov., daily 9–5.*

FROM COCHRANE TO MOOSE FACTORY ISLAND AND MOOSONEE

For many people these northern outposts are simply fly-over land, but you can find undiscovered Canada here. The terrain is densely packed with pines; moose and bear are common. Nearby lies the expansive, awe-inspiring James Bay.

Cochrane

⑧① *400 km (248 mi) north of Sudbury via Hwys. 17 east and 11 north.*

Cochrane is Ontario's gateway to the Arctic, Moose Factory, and Moosonee, at the southern end of James Bay. There's train service to Cochrane from Toronto and North Bay. Although you can fly to Moosonee via Air Creebec (⊠ Timmons Airport, R.R. 4, Timmons P4N 7C3, ☎ 705/264–9521 or 800/567–6567), which provides service from

★ Timmins, Ontario Northland's (✉ 65 Front St. W, Toronto M5J 1E6, ☎ 416/314–3750) *Polar Bear Express* train is the more popular option. Everyday except Friday from late June to Labor Day, the *Polar Bear* leaves Cochrane at 8:30 AM and arrives at Moosonee just before 1 PM and departs Moosonee at 5:15 PM and returns to Cochrane by 9:20 PM. Meals, light lunches, and snacks are available in the snack car. It's a 20-minute boat ride from Moosonee aboard the *Polar Princess* to Moose Factory Island.

Dining and Lodging

If you plan to take the *Polar Bear Express* train, you'll probably need to overnight in Cochrane. There are seven motels in and around the town. Not all have restaurant facilities, but they are geared to early wake-up calls for guests taking the train and late check-ins for those returning from the excursion. The three largest are 🏨 **Westway Motor Motel** (✉ 21 1st St., Cochrane P0L 1CO, ☎ 705/272–4285, FAX 705/272–4429), 🏨 **Cochrane Station Inn** (✉ 200 Railway St., Cochrane P0L 1CO, ☎ 705/272–3500, FAX 705/272–5713), and 🏨 **Chimo Motel** (✉ Box 2326, Cochrane P0L 1CO, ☎ 705/272–6555, FAX 705/272–5666).

Moose Factory Island

82 *300 km (186 mi) north of Cochrane via Hwys. 11 and 634.*

One of a number of islands in the delta of the Moose River, Moose Factory Island is 8 km (5 mi) long and just over a km wide. The island was the site of the second Hudson's Bay Company trading post, established in 1672 on what was then called Hayes Island, 24 km (15 mi) up the Moose River from James Bay. It was captured by the French in 1686 and renamed Fort St. Louis. Contrary to popular myth, the holes in the floor of **St. Thomas Anglican Church** (✉ Front Rd., ☎ 705/658–4800) are to let floodwater *out* and to ventilate the foundation. When the church was being built in 1864, the foundation floated a short distance in a spring flood, but the church itself has never floated anywhere. The altar cloths and lectern hangings are of moose hide decorated with beads.

The Hudson's Bay post—now known as the North West Company after the group of fur traders who competed against the Bay in the 19th century—is a modern building. Beside it is the 1850 **Hudson's Bay Staff House** in which animal pelts, carvings, snowshoes, gloves, slippers, and beadwork are sold.

The **Blacksmith's Shop** in Centennial Park isn't the oldest wooden building in Ontario, but the stone forge inside it may be the oldest "structure" in the province. The original shop was built in the late 1600s but moved back from the riverbank in 1820. The forge stones had to be transported a long distance and were dissembled and rebuilt at the present location. In summer an apprentice smith runs the forge and explains its operation.

Moosonee

83 *2 km (1 mi) from Moose Factory; 24 km (15 mi) from James Bay.*

Summer tides average 5 ft in Moosonee, Ontario's only tidal port. The community came into existence only in 1903, when the Revillon Frères Trading Company of France established a post to compete with the Hudson's Bay Company. It wasn't until the Ontario Northland Railway arrived in 1932 that the region's population began to catch up to that of Moose Factory. The **Moosonee visitor center** (✉ Ferguson Rd. at 1st St., ☎ 705/336–2364) is in a small, one-story office building. Down Revillon Road is the modern **Ministry of Natural Resources Interpretive Cen-**

tre (☎ 705/336–2489), with exhibits of regional wildlife and of the area's geological and geographical history. During tourist season, locals open stalls on Revillon Road to sell handcrafts ranging from moccasins and buckskin vests to jewelry, beadwork, and wood and stone carvings.

Dining and Lodging

$$$ ✕🏨 **Polar Bear Lodge, Moosonee Lodge.** Both face the Moose River. Their rates are high for the caliber of accommodation offered, but these are the only choices. Both hotels serve meals, but alcohol is available only during the dinner hour, and only to those dining at the hotel. *Mailing address for both:* ⊠ *Polar Bear Lodge, 65 Enterprise Rd., Rexdale M9W 1C4;* ⊠ *Moosonee Lodge, Revillon St., Moosonee POL 1Y0,* ☎ *705/336–2351,* 📠 *705/336–2773; Polar Bear Lodge,* ☎ *705/336–2345,* 📠 *705/336–2185. Polar Bear Lodge, 28 rooms; Moosonee Lodge, 21 rooms. Restaurant. MC, V.*

Timmins

🔢 *96 km (60 mi) southwest of Cochrane on Hwys. 11 and 101.*

The mining center of Timmins prides itself on being the largest city in Canada (geographically, that is). Despite its vastness, there's not much to see in Timmins, except for one of Canada's few underground mine tours.

At **Timmins Underground Gold Mine Tour,** visitors dress in full mining attire for the 2½-hour tour of the old Hollinger gold workings. Surface attractions include a headframe, a prospector's trail with a view of mineral outcrops and ore samples, and a refurbished miner's house. The road to the tour site, near downtown Timmins, is well marked. ⊠ *Park Rd. off Hwy. 101,* ☎ *705/267–6222 or 800/387–8466.* 🎫 *$16 (in winter as low as $8).* ☯ *Mid-May–late June and Sept.–late Oct., Wed.–Sun. at 10:30 and 1:30; July and Aug., daily at 9:30, 10:30, noon, 1:30, and 3.*

ONTARIO A TO Z

Arriving and Departing

By Car

The **Macdonald–Cartier Freeway,** known as Highway 401, is Ontario's major highway link. It runs from Windsor in the southwest through Toronto, along the north shore of Lake Ontario, and along the north shore of the St. Lawrence River to the Québec border west of Montréal. The **Trans-Canada Highway** follows the west bank of the Ottawa River from Montréal to Ottawa and on to North Bay. From North Bay to Nipigon at the northern tip of Lake Superior, there are two Trans-Canada highways, and from just west of Thunder Bay to Kenora, near the Manitoba border, another two. For 24-hour road-condition information anywhere in Ontario, call 416/235–1110.

By Plane

Toronto (☞ Chapter 6), the area's chief city, is served by most major international airlines.

By Train

Ontario is served by cross-Canada **VIA Rail** (☎ 416/366–8411, 800/361–1235 outside Toronto, Kingston, London, Windsor, Hamilton; within those cities check local listings) and connects with **Amtrak** (☎ 800/872–7245) service at Windsor (Detroit) and Fort Erie (Buffalo).

Getting Around

For information on Toronto travel options, *see* Chapter 6.

In case you want to be welcomed there.

We're here to see that you're always welcomed at establishments everywhere. That's why millions of people carry the American Express® Card — for peace of mind, confidence, and security, around the world or just around the corner.

do more ®

Cards

In case you're running low.

We're here to help with more than 118,000 Express Cash locations around the world. In order to enroll, just call American Express before you start your vacation.

do more

Express Cash

And just in case.

We're here with American Express® Travelers Cheques and Cheques *for Two.*® They're the safest way to carry money on your vacation and the surest way to get a refund, practically anywhere, anytime.

Another way we help you...

do more®

Travelers Cheques

By Car

Ontario is a no-fault province, and minimum liability insurance is $200,000. If you're driving across the Ontario border, either bring the policy or the vehicle registration forms and a free Canadian Non-Resident Insurance Card from your insurance agent. If you're driving a borrowed car, also bring a letter of permission signed by the owner. Driving motorized vehicles (including boats, all-terrain vehicles, and motorbikes) while impaired by alcohol is taken seriously in Ontario and results in heavy fines, imprisonment, or both. You can be convicted for refusing to take a Breathalyzer test. Radar warning devices are not permitted in Ontario even if they are turned off. Police can seize them on the spot, and heavy fines may be imposed.

Studded tires and window coatings that do not allow a clear view of the vehicle interior are forbidden in Ontario. Right turns on red lights are permitted unless otherwise noted. Pedestrians crossing at designated crosswalks have the right of way.

By Taxi

Cabs are plentiful in Ontario's major cities.

Contacts and Resources

B&B Listing

A comprehensive bed-and-breakfast guide listing about 200 establishments is published by the **Federation of Ontario Bed and Breakfast Accommodation** (⊠ Box 437, 253 College St., Toronto M5T 1R5, ☎ 416/964–2566).

Emergencies

Dial 911 for **police, fire,** or **ambulance** anywhere in Ontario.

Outdoor Activities and Sports

CAMPING

Peak season in Ontario's parks is June through August, and it is advised that you reserve a campsite, if reservations are accepted; sites can be guaranteed by phone, by mail, or in person by using a Visa or MasterCard. All provincial parks have some sites available on a first-come, first-served basis. In an effort to avoid overcrowding on canoe routes and hiking or backpacking trails, daily quotas have been established governing the number of people permitted in the parks. Permits can be reserved ahead of time. For more detailed information on parks and campgrounds in Ontario, write to the **Ministry of Economic Development, Trade and Tourism** (☞ Visitor Information, *below*) for a free camping guide.

DOGSLEDDING

Burton Penner (⊠ Box 151, Vermilion Bay POV 2VO, ☎ 807/227–5593) of Vermilion Bay, 91 km (56 mi) east of Kenora (490 km, or 304 mi, west of Thunder Bay), offers guided dogsled tours of varying length into the wilderness, overnighting in an outpost cabin or heated wall tent. Rates run from $300 per person for a one-night trip, everything included, but are reduced to $250 per person for a group of three.

FISHING

Licenses are required for fishing in Ontario and may be purchased from the Ministry of Natural Resources district offices and from most sporting goods stores, outfitters, and resorts. Seasons and catch limits change annually, and some districts infringe closed seasons. Restrictions are published in *Summary of the Fishing Regulations*, free from the Ministry of Natural Resources (⊠ Public Information Centre, Macdonald Block, Room M1-73, 900 Bay St., Toronto M7A 1W3, ☎ 416/314–2000).

There are about 500 fishing resorts and lodges listed in the current catalogue of fishing packages available free from the **Ministry of Economic Development, Trade and Tourism** (☞ Visitor Information, *below*). The establishments listed are not hotels that happen to be located near bodies of water that contain fish, but businesses designed to make sport fishing available to their guests. To that end, each property offers all the accoutrements of the modern fisherman, including boats, motors, guides, float planes, and freezers. Rates at these lodges are hefty.

HIKING

Call 800/665−4453 or **Hike Ontario** (☎ 416/462−7362) for information about hiking in the province.

RAFTING

A growing number of companies in Eastern Ontario offer packages ranging from half-day to week-long trips between May and September. **River-Run** (⊠ Box 179, Beachburg K0J 1C0, ☎ 800/267−8504), a 90-minute drive west of Ottawa, has a one-day tour on the Ottawa River. **Owl Rafting** (⊠ Box 29, Forester's Falls K0J 1V0, ☎ 613/646−2263 or 613/238−7238) offers half-day excursions on the nearby Ottawa and Madawaska rivers. **Esprit Rafting Adventures** (⊠ Box 463, Pembroke K8A 6X7, ☎ 819/683−3241) offers trips such as rafting on the Ottawa River, canoeing in Algonquin Park, or mountain biking in the Upper Ottawa Valley.

SKIING

For a recorded snow report, call 416/314−0998.

SNOWMOBILING

Overnight guided excursions are available in Haliburton Highlands/Algonquin Park (☞ Haliburton, *above*) and out of Kenora. At Kenora, **Halley's Camps** (⊠ Box 608, Kenora P9N 3X6, ☎ 807/224−6531, 800/465−3325 in Ontario and Manitoba) has guided all-inclusive excursions on wilderness trails to outpost camps for three to six nights.

Visitor Information

Ontario has a wealth of excellent and free tourist information. The best source is the **Travelinx Ontario** (⊠ Hearst Block, 900 Bay St., Toronto M7A 231, ☎ 800/668−2746 in Canada and the U.S., except the Yukon, Northwest Territories, and AK).

Ontario's principal regional and municipal tourist offices are: **Greater Hamilton, Visitor and Convention Services** (⊠ 1 James St., 3rd Floor, Hamilton L8P 4R5, ☎ 905/546−4222 or 800/263−8590, ℻ 905/546−4107), **Kingston Tourist Information Office** (⊠ 209 Ontario St., Kingston K7L 2Z1, ☎ 613/548−4415, ℻ 613/548−4549), **Kitchener and Waterloo Visitor and Convention Bureau** (⊠ 2848 King St. E, Kitchener N2A 1A5, ☎ 519/748−0800 or 800/265−6959, ℻ 519/748−6411), **Midland Chamber of Commerce** (⊠ 208 King St., Box 158, Midland L4R 4K8, ☎ 705/526−7884, ℻ 705/526−1744), **Niagara Falls, Canada Visitor and Convention Bureau** (⊠ 5433 Victoria Ave., Niagara Falls L2G 3L1, ☎ 905/356−6061 or 800/563−2557, ℻ 905/356−5567), **Ontario Northland** (⊠ 65 Front St. W, Toronto M5J 1E6, ☎ 416/314−3750), **Peterborough–Kawartha Tourism & Convention Bureau** (⊠ 175 George St. N, Peterborough K9J 3G6, ☎ 705/748−2201 or 800/461−6424, ℻ 705/742−2494), **Sault Ste. Marie Chamber of Commerce** (⊠ 360 Great Northern Rd., Sault Ste. Marie P6A 2A3, ☎ 705/949−7152, ℻ 705/759−8166), **Tourism Thunder Bay** (⊠ 500 E. Donald St., Thunder Bay P7E 5V3, ☎ 807/625−2149 or 800/667−8386), **Convention and Visitors Bureau of Windsor, Essex County, and Pelee Island** (⊠ 333 Riverside Dr. W, Suite 103, Windsor N9A 5K4, ☎ 519/255−6530 or 800/265−3633, ℻ 519/255−6192).

8 Montréal

Traces of this island city's long history are found everywhere, from the 17th-century buildings in Vieux-Montréal to grand cathedrals and verdant parks such as Mont-Royal. But Montréal, with its atmosphere of romantic elegance, is also full of very modern pleasures: fine dining, whether you want French cuisine or any kind of ethnic fare; good shopping for everything from antiques to high fashion; and nightlife, arts events, and festivals that provide diversions year-round.

By Paul and
Julie Waters

MONTRÉAL IS CANADA'S most romantic metropolis, an island city that seems to favor grace and elegance over order and even prosperity; a city full of music, art, and joie de vivre. It is rather like the European capital Vienna—past its peak of power and glory, perhaps, but still a vibrant and beautiful place full of memories, dreams, and festivals.

That's not to say Montréal is ready to fade away. It may not be so young anymore—it celebrated its 350th birthday in 1992—but it remains Québec's largest city and an important port and financial center. Its office towers are full of young Québécois entrepreneurs, members of a new breed who are ready and eager to take on the world.

Montréal is the only French-speaking metropolis in North America and the second-largest French-speaking city in the world, but it's a tolerant place that over the years has made room for millions of immigrants who speak dozens of languages. Today about 15% of the 3.1 million people who live in the metropolitan area claim English as their mother tongue and another 15% claim a language that's neither English nor French. The city's gentle tolerance has won recognition: Several times it has been voted one of the world's most livable cities.

The city's grace, however, has been sorely tested. Since 1976, Montréal has twice weathered the election of a separatist provincial government, a law banning all languages but French on virtually all public signs and billboards, and four referendums on the future of Québec and Canada. The latest chapter in this long constitutional drama was the cliffhanger referendum on Québec independence on October 30, 1995. In that showdown Québécois voters chose to remain part of Canada but by the thinnest of possible margins. More than 98% of eligible voters participated, and the final province-wide result was 49.42% in favor of independence and 50.58% against. In fact 60% of the province's Francophones voted in favor of establishing an independent Québec. But Montréal, where most of the province's Anglophones and immigrants live, bucked the separatist trend and voted nearly 70% against independence. The drama has since cooled. The separatist Parti-Québécois still controls the provincial government, but it has switched its focus to the flagging economy, and its leader, Lucien Bouchard, has tried to steer clear of divisive arguments about language.

In spite of uncertainty about the future, most Montrealers still delight in their city, which has weathered all these storms with aplomb. It is, after all, a city that's used to turmoil. It was founded by the French, conquered by the British, and occupied by the Americans. It has a long history of reconciling contradictions and even today is a city of contrasts. The glass office tower of La Maison des Coopérants, for example, soars above a Gothic-style Anglican cathedral that squats gracefully in its shadow. The neo-Gothic facade of the Basilique Notre-Dame-de-Montréal glares across Place d'Armes at the pagan temple that is the head office of the Bank of Montréal. And while pilgrims still climb the steps to the Oratoire St-Joseph on their knees on one side of the mountain, thousands of their fellow Catholics line up to get into the very chic Casino de Montréal on the other side—certainly not what the earnest French settlers who founded Montréal envisioned when they landed on the island in May 1642.

Those 54 pious men and women under the leadership of Paul de Chomedey, Sieur de Maisonneuve, hoped to do nothing less than create a new Christian society. They named their settlement Ville-Marie in honor of the mother of Christ and set out to convert the natives. Those early years were marked by the heroism of two women—Jeanne Mance, a French noblewoman who arrived with de Maisonneuve, and Marguerite Bourgeoys, who came 11 years later. Jeanne Mance, working alone, established the Hôpital Hôtel-Dieu de St-Joseph, still one of the city's major hospitals. In 1659 she invited members of a French order of nuns to help her in her efforts. That order, the Religieuses Hospitalières de St-Joseph, now has its motherhouse in Montréal and is the oldest nursing group in the Americas. Marguerite Bourgeoys, with Jeanne Mance's help, established the colony's first school and taught both French and native children how to read and write. Bourgeoys founded the Congrégation de Notre Dame, a teaching order that still has schools in Montréal, across Canada, and around the world. She was canonized a saint by the Roman Catholic church in 1982.

Piety wasn't the settlement's only raison d'être, however. Ville-Marie was ideally located to be a commercial success as well. It was at the confluence of two major transportation routes—the St. Lawrence and Ottawa rivers—and fur trappers used the town as a staging point for their expeditions. But the city's religious roots were never forgotten. Until 1854, long after the French lost possession of the city, the island of Montréal remained the property of the Sulpicians, an aristocratic order of French priests. The Sulpicians were responsible for administering the colony and for recruiting colonists. They still run the Basilique Notre-Dame-de-Montréal, and are still responsible for training priests for the Roman Catholic archdiocese.

The French regime in Canada ended with the Seven Years' War—what Americans call the French and Indian Wars. British troops took Québec City in 1759 and Montréal fell less than a year later. The Treaty of Paris ceded all New France to Britain in 1763, and soon English and Scottish settlers poured into Montréal to take advantage of the city's geography and economic potential. By 1832 Montréal was a leading colonial capital of business, finance, and transportation and had grown far beyond the walls of the old settlement. Much of that business and financial leadership has since moved to Toronto, the upstream rival Montrealers love to hate.

Pleasures and Pastimes

Dining
Montrealers are passionate about food. They love to dine on classic dishes in restaurants like Les Halles and the Beaver Club, or swoon over culinary innovations in places like Toqué, but they can get equally passionate about humbler fare. They'll argue with some heat about where to get the juiciest smoked meat, the crispiest barbecued chicken, and the soggiest *stimés* (steamed hot dogs). You'll find great French food here but also cuisines from around the world; the city's restaurants represent more than 75 ethnic groups.

Faith and History
Traces of the city's long history are found everywhere, including in its churches. Some buildings in Vieux-Montréal date to the 17th century. Other parts of the city are full of wonderful examples of Victorian architecture. Museums like the Musée McCord de l'Histoire Canadienne, the Musée d'Archéologie de la Pointe-à-Callière, and the Stewart Museum in the Old Fort on Ile Ste-Hélène attest to the city's fascination with its past.

Montréal's two most popular attractions are monuments dedicated to a Jewish couple who lived 2,000 years ago—the oratory dedicated to

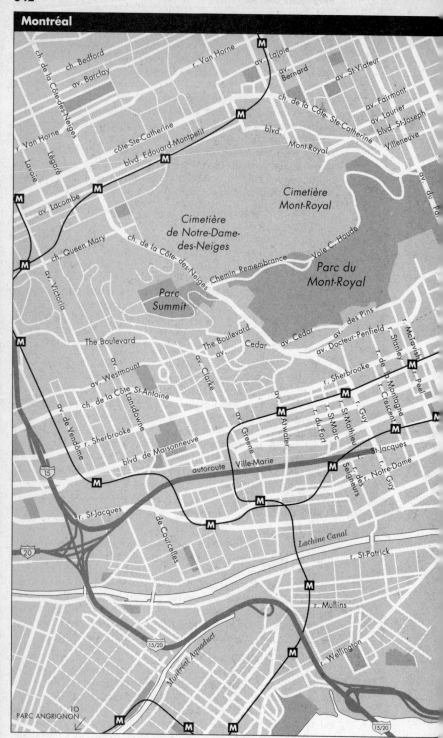

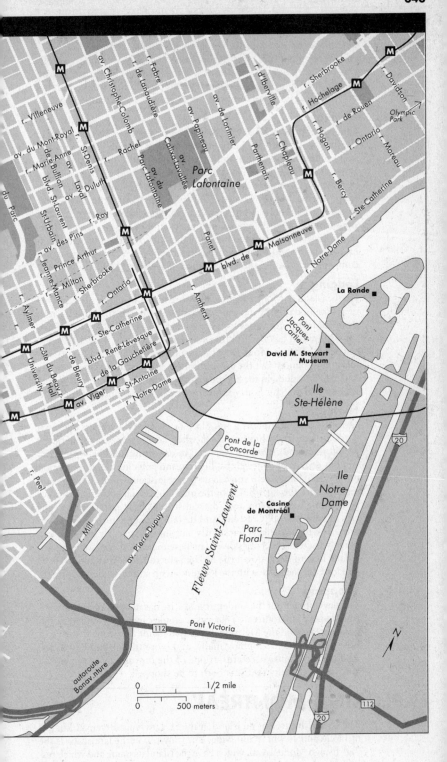

r. Villeneuve

av. du Mont-Royal

r. Marie-Anne

r. de Bullion
av. Laval
av. Duluth
blvd. St-Laurent
St-Urbain
av. des Pins
Roy
Jeanne-Mance
Prince Arthur
Milton
Sherbrooke
Ontario
r. Ste-Catherine
côte du Beaver Hall
University
r. de Bleury
blvd. René-Lévesque
de la Gauchetière
av. Viger
r. St-Antoine
r. Notre-Dame
St-Denis

av. Christophe-Colomb
r. Fabre
r. de Lanaudière
Rachel
av. du Parc Lafontaine
av. Calixa-Lavallée
av. Papineau
av. de Lorimier
Parthenais
r. Chapleau
Panet
r. Amherst

du Parc
r. Peel
r. Mill
av. Pierre-Dupuy
autoroute Bonaventure

Parc Lafontaine

blvd. de Maisonneuve

r. d'Iberville
r. Sherbrooke
r. Hochelage
de Rouen
r. Hogan
r. Bercy
Ontario
r. Davidson
Moreau
r. Ste-Catherine
r. Notre-Dame

Olympic Park

La Ronde

Pont Jacques-Cartier

David M. Stewart Museum

Ile Ste-Hélène

Pont de la Concorde

Ile Notre-Dame

Casino de Montréal

Parc Floral

20

Fleuve Saint-Laurent

Pont Victoria

112

112

20

N

0   1/2 mile

0   500 meters

St. Joseph on the north side of Mont-Royal and the Basilique Notre-Dame-de-Montréal dedicated to his wife in the old city. These are just two of dozens of beautiful churches built in the days when the Québécois were among the most devout adherents to the Roman Catholic church. Other gems of ecclesiastical architecture are St. Patrick's Basilica and the Chapelle Notré-Dame-de-Lourdes. Even humble churches in working-class neighborhoods are as grand as some cathedrals.

Festivals
Summer and fall are just one long succession of festivals that begin in late June with a 10-day Festival International de Jazz, when as many as a million fans descend on the city to hear more than 1,000 musicians, including giants like guitarist John Scofield and tenor saxophonist Joe Lovano. In August there's the World Film Festival and the lively Just for Laughs Comedy Festival in the Vieux-Port area. Other festivals celebrate beer, alternative films, French-language music and song from around the world, and international cuisine. Every Saturday in June and every Sunday in July the skies over the city waterfront erupt in color and flame as fireworks teams from around the world compete for prizes in the International Fireworks Competition.

Lodging
On the island of Montréal alone there are rooms available in every type of accommodation, from world-class luxury hotels to youth hostels, from student dormitories to budget executive motels. The Ritz-Carlton Kempinski has been setting standards of luxury since 1912, and the nearby Westin Mont-Royal is one of the best modern luxury hotels in the country. But the city also offers more intimate charm, at the Château Versailles on rue Sherbrooke, for example, or the tiny Auberge les Passants du Sans Soucy in the heart of Vieux-Montréal.

Nightlife
Montréal's reputation as a fun place to visit for a night on the town dates at least to Prohibition days, when hordes of thirsty Americans would flood the city every weekend to eat, drink, and be merry. The city has dozens of dance clubs, bistros, and jazz clubs, not to mention hundreds of bars where you can go to argue about sports, politics, and religion until the early hours of the morning. Much of the action takes place along rue St-Denis and adjacent streets in the eastern part of the city or rues Bishop, Crescent, and de la Montagne in the downtown area. The night scene is constantly shifting—last year's hot spot can quickly become this year's dive. The best and easiest way to figure out what's in is to stroll down rue St-Denis or rue Bishop at about 10:30 and look for the place with the longest lineup and the rudest doorman.

Shopping
The development of the Underground City has made shopping a year-round sport in Montréal. That vast complex linked by underground passageways and the Métro includes two major department stores, at least a dozen huge shopping malls, and more than 1,000 boutiques. Add to this Montréal's status as one of the fur capitals of the world, and you have a city that was born to be shopped.

EXPLORING MONTRÉAL

The Ile de Montréal is an island in the St. Lawrence River, 51 km (32 mi) long and 14 km (9 mi) wide. The only rise in the landscape is the 764-ft-high Mont-Royal, which gave the island its name and which residents call simply "the mountain." The city of Montréal is the oldest and by far the largest of the 24 municipalities on the island, which together make up the Communauté Urbaine de Montréal (the Montréal

Urban Community), the regional government that runs, among other things, the police department and the transit system. There is a belt of off-island suburbs on the South Shore of the St. Lawrence, and just to the north across the narrow Rivière-des Prairies, on an island of its own, is Laval, a suburb that has grown to be the second-largest city in the province. But the countryside is never far away. The pastoral Eastern Townships, first settled by Loyalists fleeing the American Revolution, are less than an hour's drive away, and the Laurentians, an all-season playground full of lakes and ski hills, are even closer.

For a good overview of the city, head for the lookout at the Chalet du Mont-Royal. You can drive most of the way, park, and walk ½ km (¼ mi) or hike all the way up from chemin de la Côte-des-Neiges or avenue des Pins. If you look directly out—southeast—from the belvedere, at the foot of the hill will be the McGill University campus and, surrounding it, the skyscrapers of downtown Montréal. Just beyond, along the banks of the river, are the stone houses of Vieux-Montréal. Hugging the South Shore on the other side of the river are the Iles Ste-Hélène and Notre-Dame, sites of La Ronde amusement park, the Biosphere, the Casino de Montréal, acres of parkland, and the Lac de l'Ile Notre-Dame public beach—all popular excursions. To the east is rue St-Denis and the Quartier Latin with its rows of French and ethnic restaurants, bistros, chess hangouts, designer boutiques, antiques shops, and art galleries. Even farther east you can see the flying-saucer-shaped Olympic Stadium with its leaning tower.

Montréal is easy to explore. Streets, subways, and bus lines are clearly marked. The city is divided by a grid of streets roughly aligned east–west and north–south. (This grid is tilted about 40° off—to the left of—true north, so west is actually southwest and so on.) North–south street numbers begin at the St. Lawrence River and increase as you head north. East–west street numbers begin at boulevard St-Laurent, which divides Montréal into east and west halves. The city is not so large that seasoned walkers can't see all the districts around the base of Mont-Royal on foot. Nearly everything else is easily accessible by the city's quiet, clean, and very safe bus and Métro (subway) system. If you're planning to visit a number of museums, look into the city's museum pass (☞ Contacts and Resources *in* Montréal A to Z, *below*).

Numbers in the text correspond to numbers in the margin and on the Vieux-Montréal, Downtown Montréal (Centre-Ville), Quartier Latin and Parc du Mont-Royal, and Olympic Park and Botanical Garden maps.

Great Itineraries

Getting any real feel for this bilingual, multicultural city takes some time. An ideal stay would be seven days, but you should spend at least three days walking and soaking up the atmosphere. That's enough time to visit Mont-Royal, explore Vieux-Montréal, do some shopping, and perhaps visit the Parc Olympique. It also includes enough nights for an evening of bar-hopping on rue St-Denis or rue Crescent and another for a long, luxurious dinner at one of the city's excellent restaurants.

IF YOU HAVE 3 DAYS

Any visit to Montréal should start with Mont-Royal, Montréal's most enduring symbol. Afterward wander down to avenue des Pins and then through McGill University to downtown. Make an effort to stop at the Musée des Beaux-Arts and St. Patrick's Basilica. Day 2 should be spent exploring Vieux-Montréal, with special emphasis on the Basilique Notre-Dame-de-Montréal and the Musée d'Archéologie Pointe-à-Callière. On Day 3 you can either visit the Parc Olympique (recommended for children) or stroll through the Quartier Latin.

Once again start with a visit to Parc du Mont-Royal, but instead of going downtown after you've viewed the city from the Chalet du Mont-Royal, visit the Oratoire St-Joseph. You should still have enough time to visit the Musée des Beaux-Arts before dinner. That will leave time on Day 2 to get in more shopping as you explore downtown, with perhaps a visit to the Centre Canadien d'Architecture. Spend all of Day 3 in Vieux-Montréal, and on Day 4 stroll through the Quartier Latin. On Day 5, visit the Parc Olympique and then do one of three things: visit the islands, take a ride on the Lachine Rapids, or revisit some of the sights you missed in Vieux-Montréal or downtown.

A week will give you enough time to do the five-day itinerary, expanding your Vieux-Montréal explorations to two days and adding a shopping spree on rue Chabanel and a visit to the Casino de Montréal.

Vieux-Montréal

When Montréal's first European settlers arrived by river in 1642 they stopped to build their houses just below the treacherous Lachine Rapids that blocked the way upstream. They picked a site near an old Iroquois settlement on the bank of the river nearest Mont-Royal. In the mid-17th century Montréal consisted of a handful of wood houses clustered around a pair of stone buildings, all flimsily fortified by a wood stockade. For almost three centuries this district—bounded by rues Berri and McGill on the east and west, rue St-Jacques on the north, and the river to the south—was the financial and political heart of the city. Government buildings, the largest church, the stock exchange, the main market, and the port were here. The narrow but relatively straight streets were cobblestone and lined with solid, occasionally elegant houses, office buildings, and warehouses—also made of stone. A thick stone wall with four gates protected the city against native people and marauding European powers. Montréal quickly grew past the bounds of its fortifications, however, and by World War I the center of the city had moved toward Mont-Royal. The new heart of Montréal became Dominion Square (now Square Dorchester). For the next two decades Vieux-Montréal (Old Montréal), as it became known, was gradually abandoned, the warehouses and offices emptied. In 1962 the city began studying ways to revitalize Vieux-Montréal, and a decade of renovations and restorations began.

Today Vieux-Montréal is a center of cultural life and municipal government. Most of the summer activities revolve around Place Jacques-Cartier, which becomes a pedestrian mall with street performers and outdoor cafés, and the Vieux-Port, one of the city's most popular recreation grounds. The Orchestre Symphonique de Montréal performs all year at Basilique Notre-Dame-de-Montréal, which has one of the finest organs in North America, and English-language plays are staged in the Centaur Theatre in the old stock-exchange building. This district has six museums devoted to history, religion, and arts.

A Good Walk

Take the Métro to the Square-Victoria Station and follow the signs to the **Centre de Commerce Mondial de Montréal** ①, one of the city's more appealing enclosed spaces, with a fountain and frequent art exhibits. Exit on the east side of the complex and turn right on rue St-Pierre, walk south to **rue St-Jacques,** and turn left. Walking east you'll see the Victorian office buildings of the country's former financial center. This area can seem tomblike on weekends when the business and legal offices close down, but things get livelier closer to the waterfront.

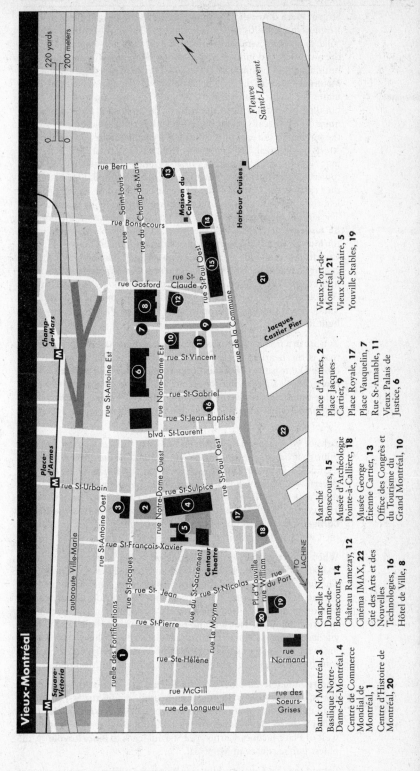

Stop at **Place d'Armes** ②, a square that was the site of battles with the Iroquois in the 1600s and later became the center of Montréal's Haute-Ville, or Upper Town. There are calèches at the south end of the square; the north side is dominated by the **Bank of Montréal** ③, an impressive building with Corinthian columns. The **Basilique Notre-Dame-de-Montréal** ④, one of the most beautiful churches in North America, dominates the south end of Place d'Armes. The low, more retiring stone building behind a wall to the west of the basilica is the **Vieux Séminaire** ⑤, Montréal's oldest building. Unlike the basilica, it is closed to the public. To the east of the basilica is **rue St-Sulpice,** one of the first streets in Montréal, and catercorner from it is the Art Deco Aldred Building. Next to that is Montreal's first skyscraper, a nine-story red-stone tower built by the now defunct Québec Bank in 1888. One block farther east on rue Notre-Dame, just past boulevard St-Laurent, on the left, rises the black-glass-sheathed **Palais de Justice** (1971), a courthouse. The large domed building at 155 rue Notre-Dame Est is the **Vieux Palais de Justice** ⑥ (1857). Across the street, at 160 rue Notre-Dame Est, is the **Maison de la Sauvegarde,** one of the city's oldest houses. The Old Courthouse abuts the small **Place Vauquelin** ⑦, named after an 18th-century naval hero. North of this square is **Champs-de-Mars,** a former military parade ground and now a public park crisscrossed by archaeologists' trenches. The ornate building on the east side of Place Vauquelin is the Second Empire–style **Hôtel de Ville** ⑧, or City Hall, built in 1878.

You are in a perfect spot to explore **Place Jacques-Cartier** ⑨, the square that is the heart of Vieux-Montréal. At the western corner of rue Notre-Dame is the **Office des Congrès et du Tourisme du Grand Montréal** ⑩. Both sides of the square are lined with two- and three-story stone buildings that were originally homes or hotels. In summer the one-block **rue St-Amable** ⑪ near the bottom of the square becomes a marketplace.

Retrace your steps to the north end of Place Jacques-Cartier and continue east on rue Notre-Dame. On the right, at the corner of rue St-Claude, is **Château Ramezay** ⑫, built as the residence of the 11th governor of Montréal, Claude de Ramezay, and now a museum. Continue east to rue Berri. On the corner are two houses from the mid-19th century that have been transformed into the **Musée George-Étienne Cartier** ⑬, a museum honoring one of the leading figures in founding the Canadian federation in 1867.

When you come out of the museum, walk south on rue Berri to rue St-Paul and then start walking west again toward the center of the city. The first street on your right is rue Bonsecours, one of the oldest in the city. On the corner is the charming Maison du Calvet, now a restaurant and small bed-and-breakfast. Opposite it is the small but beautiful **Chapelle Notre-Dame-de-Bonsecours** ⑭, built by St. Marguerite Bourgeoys, Montréal's first schoolteacher. The long, domed building to the west of the chapel is the **Marché Bonsecours** ⑮, a public market transformed into a cultural center with exhibits on Montréal.

The fashionable 20 blocks of **rue St-Paul** are lined with restaurants, shops, and nightclubs. In an old stone building on rue St-Paul Ouest is an exhibit that focuses on the very new: **Cité des Arts et des Nouvelles Technologies** ⑯ is devoted to exploring cyberspace. Eight blocks west of Place Jacques-Cartier, rue St-Paul leads to **Place Royale** ⑰, the oldest public square in Montréal.

Behind the Old Customs House is **Pointe-à-Callière,** a small park that commemorates the settlers' first landing, and the **Musée d'Archéolo-**

gie **Pointe-à-Callière** ⑱, Montréal's dazzling museum of history and archaeology. A 1½-block walk down rue William takes you to the **Youville Stables** ⑲ on the left. These low stone buildings enclosing a garden now house offices, shops, and a restaurant.

Across rue William from the stables is the old fire station that houses the **Centre d'Histoire de Montréal** ⑳, a museum that chronicles the day-to-day life of Montrealers throughout the years. Now walk back east on rue William and turn right down rue du Port to rue de la Commune. Across the street is the **Vieux-Port-de-Montréal** ㉑, a pleasant and popular waterfront park that makes a fitting close to any walk in Vieux-Montréal. If you have time, you can arrange for a harbor excursion or a daring ride on the Lachine Rapids. The Vieux-Port is also home to the **Cinéma IMAX** ㉒, which shows films on a seven-story screen. The impact can be more terrifying than the rapids.

TIMING

If you walk briskly and don't stop, you could get through this route in under an hour. A more realistic and leisurely pace would take about 90 minutes—still without stopping—longer in winter when the streets are icy. The Basilique Notre-Dame is one of Montréal's most famous landmarks and deserves at least a 45-minute visit; Château Ramezay deserves the same. Pointe-à-Callière could keep an enthusiastic history buff occupied for a whole day, but give it at least two hours. If you're visiting any museums, check ahead for seasonal hours.

Sights to See

❸ Bank of Montréal. The head office of Canada's oldest chartered bank is an impressive building with Corinthian columns, built in 1847 and remodeled by the renowned architectural firm McKim, Mead & White in 1905. It has a one-room museum that recounts the early history of banking in Canada. ⊠ *119 rue St-Jacques Ouest.* ☉ *Weekdays 10–4.* ☐ *Museum free.*

★ **❹ Basilique Notre-Dame-de-Montréal** (Notre-Dame Basilica). The first church called Notre-Dame was a bark-covered structure built in 1642. Three times it was torn down and rebuilt, each time larger and more ornate. The present church is an enormous (3,800-seat), neo-Gothic structure that opened in 1829. Its architect was an American Protestant named James O'Donnell, who converted to Catholicism during construction and is buried in the church crypt. The twin towers are 228 ft high, and the western one holds one of North America's largest bells. The interior is neo-Gothic, with stained-glass windows, pine and walnut carvings, and a vaulted blue ceiling studded with thousands of 24-carat gold stars. With more than 7,000 pipes, the pipe organ is one of the largest on the continent. If you just want to hear the organ roar, drop in for the 11 AM solemn Mass on Sunday and pay special attention to the recessional. Behind the main altar is the **Sacré-Coeur Chapel,** which was destroyed by fire in 1978 and rebuilt in five different styles. The chapel is often called the Wedding Chapel because of the hundreds of Montrealers who get married in it every year. When pop star Céline Dion married her manager in 1994, however, the lavish and elaborate ceremony was in the main church. Also in the back of the church is a small museum of religious paintings and historical objects. Please note: Notre-Dame is an active house of worship and visitors should dress accordingly. Also, it is advisable to plan your visit around the daily 12:15 PM Mass in the chapel and the 5 PM Mass in the main church. ⊠ *116 rue Notre-Dame Ouest,* ☎ *514/849–1070 basilica, 514/842–2925 museum.* ☐ *Basilica donation requested, tour free; museum $1.* ☉ *Basilica Labor Day–June 24, daily 7–6, and June 25–Labor Day, daily 7 AM–8 PM. Guided tour (except Sun. morning)*

May–June 24, daily 9–4; June 25–Labor Day, daily 8:30–4:30; Labor Day–mid-Oct., daily 9–4. Museum weekends 9:30–4:30.

❶ Centre de Commerce Mondial de Montréal (Montréal World Trade Center). This is one of the nicest enclosed spaces in Montréal, with a fountain, frequent art exhibits, and Montréal's own chunk of the Berlin Wall, complete with colorful graffiti. The center covers a block of the run-down ruelle des Fortifications, a narrow lane that marks the place where the city walls stood. Developers glassed it in and sandblasted and restored 11 of the 19th-century buildings that lined it. It's home to the Hôtel Inter-Continental Montréal (☞ Lodging, *below*), some boutiques and restaurants, and an imaginative food court. ⊠ 747 sq. Victoria. Métro: Square-Victoria Station and follow signs.

❷⓿ Centre d'Histoire de Montréal. Video games, soundtracks, and more than 300 artifacts re-create the day-to-day life of the ordinary men and women who have lived in Montréal, from precolonial to modern times. Some of the most touching exhibits depict family life in Montréal's working-class tenements in the 20th century. ⊠ 335 Pl. d'Youville, ☎ 514/872–3207. ☞ $4.50. ⊙ Tues.–Sun. 10–5.

Champs-de-Mars. This park on rue St-Antoine Ouest between boulevard St-Laurent and rue Gosford used to be a parade ground in colonial days. Archaeologists have excavated the foundations of the old city walls on the site.

❶❹ Chapelle Notre-Dame-de-Bonsecours. St. Marguerite Bourgeoys dedicated this chapel to the Virgin Mary in 1657. It became known as a sailor's church, and small wood models of sailing ships hang from the ceiling. In the basement there's a gift shop and a small museum that tells the story of the saint's life with a series of little tableaux. From the museum you can climb to the rather precarious bell tower (beware of the slippery metal steps in winter) for a fine view of the Vieux-Port. At press time the chapel was due to reopen in September 1997 after a year-long renovation. ⊠ 400 rue St-Paul Est, ☎ 514/845–9991. ☞ Museum $2. ⊙ Museum May–Nov., Tues.–Sat. 9–4:30, Sun. 11:30–4:30, and Dec.–Apr., Tues.–Fri. 10:30–2:30, Sat. 10–4:30, Sun. 11:30–4:30; chapel May–Nov., daily 9–5, and Dec.–Apr., daily 10–3.

❶❷ Château Ramezay. This elegant colonial building was the residence of the 11th governor of Montréal, Claude de Ramezay. In 1775–76 it was the headquarters for American troops seeking to conquer Canada; Benjamin Franklin stayed here during that winter occupation. The château became a museum of city and provincial history in 1895, and it has been restored to the style of Governor de Ramezay's day. It underwent a major renovation early in 1997. ⊠ 280 rue Notre-Dame Est, ☎ 514/861–3708. ☞ $5. ⊙ June–Sept., daily 10–6; Oct.– May, Tues.–Sun. 10–4:30.

NEED A BREAK? In summer there are few places lovelier and livelier than **Place Jacques-Cartier.** You could stop at a *terasse* (sidewalk café) for a beer or a coffee or just sit on a bench amid the flower vendors and listen to the street musicians or watch a juggler perform. If you're peckish, there are several snack bars and ice cream stands. If you're really daring, you could try *poutine,* Québec's very own contribution to junk-food culture. It consists of french fries covered with cheese curds and smothered in gravy—an acquired taste.

❷❷ Cinéma IMAX. Nausea and vertigo are some of the more negative things people experience the first time they see an IMAX film roar at them from a seven-story screen. Wonder and excitement are among the more positive. The content of the films—most under an hour long—is decidedly educational. It's best to reserve ahead. ✉ *Vieux-Port, Shed No. 7,* ☎ *514/790–1245.* 🎫 *$11.75.* ⊙ *Tues.–Sun. from 9:45 AM.*

⑯ Cité des Arts et des Nouvelles Technologies. The center, dedicated to art and modern technology, has revolving exhibits that explore virtual reality, interactive art, computer animation, and other wonders of the cyber universe. In the electronic café you can have coffee and a sandwich and plug into the Internet on one of 40 computers. ✉ *85 rue St-Paul Ouest,* ☎ *514/849–1612.* 🎫 *$11.75.* ⊙ *Sun.–Thurs. 10–6, Fri.–Sat. 10–9; call for show times.*

➑ Hôtel de Ville. Montréal's ornate City Hall was built in 1878 in the Second Empire style. On July 24, 1967, President Charles de Gaulle of France stood on the central balcony here and made his famous *"Vive le Québec libre"* speech. There are no tours, but there are occasional exhibitions in the main hall. ✉ *275 rue Notre-Dame Est.*

Maison de la Sauvegarde. One of the oldest houses in the city (1811) is now home to the European sausage restaurant, **Chez Better** (☞ Dining, *below*). ✉ *160 rue Notre-Dame Est.*

⑮ Marché Bonsecours. Built in 1845, this was for years Montréal's main produce, meat, and fish market. It now houses municipal offices and a cultural center with exhibits on Montréal. ✉ *350 rue St-Paul Est.*

★ **⑱ Musée d'Archéologie Pointe-à-Callière.** Here you can get to the very foundations of New France. This museum in the ☞ Pointe-à-Callière park was built around the excavated remains of structures dating to Montréal's beginnings, including the city's first Catholic cemetery. It's a labyrinth of stone walls and corridors, illuminated by spotlights and holograms of figures from the past. An audiovisual show gives a historical overview of the area. It also has an excellent gift shop, full of interesting books on Montréal's history, as well as pictures and reproductions of old maps, engravings, and other artifacts. ✉ *350 pl. Royale,* ☎ *514/872–9150.* 🎫 *$7.* ⊙ *June 24–Labor Day, Tues.–Sun. 10–8; Sept. 6–June 23, Tues. and Thurs.–Sun. 10–5, Wed. 10–8.*

⑬ Musée George-Étienne Cartier. This museum, which honors one of the architects of the 1867 Canadian federation, comprises two houses. The west house was the Cartiers' home in 1862 and has been meticulously restored to the style of that period, with plush Victorian furniture. The house on the east focuses on the political career of one of the most important French-Canadian statesmen of his day. Costumed guides act out the roles of the Cartiers' friends and servants. From mid-November to mid-December the Cartiers' home is festooned with Victorian decorations. ✉ *458 rue Notre-Dame Est,* ☎ *514/283–2282.* 🎫 *$3.* ⊙ *Late May–Labor Day, daily 10–6; Labor Day–mid-May, Wed.–Sun. 10–noon and 1–5.*

⑩ Office des Congrès et du Tourisme du Grand Montréal. This small building (1811) was the site of the old Silver Dollar Saloon, so named because there were 350 silver dollars nailed to the floor. Today it's now one of two visitor information offices operated by Info-Touriste; the other is at 1001 square Dorchester. ✉ *174 rue Notre-Dame Est.*

Palais de Justice. Built in 1971, this black glass building is the main courthouse for the judicial district of Montréal. Criminal law in Canada falls under federal jurisdiction and is based on British common law, but civil law is a provincial matter and Québec's is based on France's Napoleonic Code, which governs all the minutiae of private life—from setting up a company and negotiating a mortgage to drawing up a marriage contract and registering the names of children. Lawyers and judges in Québec courts wear the same elaborate gowns as their British counterparts, but not the wigs. This building is not open for tours. ⊠ *1 rue Notre-Dame Est.*

② **Place d'Armes.** Montréal's founder, Paul de Chomedy, slew an Iroquois chief in a battle here in 1644 and was wounded in return. His statue stands in a fountain in the middle of the square. Tunnels beneath the square protected the colonists from the winter weather and provided an escape route; unfortunately they are too small and dangerous to visit. ⊠ *Bordered by rues Notre-Dame Ouest and St-Jacques.*

★ **⑨** **Place Jacques-Cartier.** This two-block-long square, at the heart of Vieux-Montréal, opened in 1804 as a municipal market, and every summer it is transformed into a flower market. The 1809 monument at the top of the square celebrates Lord Nelson's victory over Napoléon Bonaparte's French navy at Trafalgar. It was built not by patriotic British residents of Montréal but by the Sulpician priests, who didn't have much love for the Corsican emperor either. ⊠ *Bordered by rues Notre-Dame Est and de la Commune.*

⑰ **Place Royale.** The oldest public square in Montréal served as a public market during the French regime and later became a Victorian garden. The severely beautiful neoclassical Vielle Douane (Old Customs House) on its south side serves as the gift shop for the ☞ **Musée d'Archéologie Pointe-à-Callière.**

⑦ **Place Vauquelin.** The statue in this little square is of Admiral Jacques Vauquelin, a naval hero of the French regime.

Pointe-à-Callière. This small park commemorates the settlers' first landing. A small stream used to flow into the St. Lawrence here, and it was on the point of land between the two waters that the colonists landed their four boats on May 17, 1642. The settlement was almost washed away the next Christmas by a flood. When it was spared, Paul de Chomedey, Sieur de Maisonneuve, placed a cross on top of Mont-Royal as thanks to God. ⊠ *Bordered by rues de la Commune and William.*

⑪ **Rue St-Amable.** A one-block lane near Place Jacques-Cartier is a summer marketplace for local jewelers, artists, and craftspeople.

Rue St-Jacques. This was once the financial heart, not just of Montréal, but of Canada. As you walk here, note the fine decorative stone flourishes—grapevines, nymphs, angels, and goddesses—on the Victorian office buildings.

Rue St-Paul. The most fashionable street in Vieux-Montréal, rue St-Paul is lined with restaurants, shops filled with Québécois handicrafts, and nightclubs for almost 20 blocks.

Rue St-Sulpice. This is one of the oldest streets in Montréal. A plaque on the eastern side marks the spot where Jeanne Mance built Hôpital Hôtel-Dieu, the city's first hospital, in 1644.

⑥ **Vieux Palais de Justice.** The old courthouse, a domed building in the Classical Revival style, was built in 1857. It once housed the civil courts but is now a warren of city offices. ⊠ *155 rue Notre-Dame Est.*

㉑ **Vieux-Port-de-Montréal.** The port is no longer the heart and soul of the city's commercial life. Its docks are too small and its channels too shallow for modern megaships, and only a few freighters use it now. However, the area is a popular waterfront park with a promenade and a giant indoor flea market (☞ Shopping, *below*) in summer. Several companies offer boat excursions on the river (☞ Guided Tours *in*

Montréal A to Z, *below*). Cruise ships dock here and so do visiting naval vessels. The port also marks the start of one of the city's most popular bicycle paths. Every weekend hundreds of Montrealers follow the route of the old Lachine Canal (built in 1825 to bypass the Lachine Rapids and rendered obsolete by the St. Lawrence Seaway) to Parc René-Lévesque in Lachine, a narrow spit of land jutting into Lac St-Louis.

⑤ Vieux Séminaire. Montréal's oldest building is considered the finest, most elegant example of 17th-century Québec architecture. It was built in 1685 as a headquarters for the Sulpician priests who owned the island of Montréal until 1854, and it is still a residence for the Sulpicians who administer the basilica. The clock on the roof over the main doorway is the oldest (pre-1701) public timepiece in North America. Behind the seminary building is a garden, which is unfortunately closed to the public as is the seminary itself. ⊠ *116 rue Notre-Dame Ouest, behind wall west of Basilique Notre-Dame-de-Montréal.*

⑲ Youville Stables. These low stone buildings enclosing a garden were originally built as warehouses in 1825 (they never were stables). They now house offices, shops, and Gibby's restaurant (☞ Dining, *below*). ⊠ *298 Pl. d'Youville.*

Downtown

On the surface Montréal's downtown, or *centre-ville,* is much like the downtown core of many other major cities—full of life and noisy traffic, its streets lined with department stores, boutiques, bars, restaurants, strip clubs, amusement arcades, and bookstores. But, in fact, much of the area's activity goes on beneath the surface, in Montréal's Cité Souterrain (Underground City). Development of this unique endeavor began in 1966 when the Métro opened. Now it includes (at last count) seven hotels, 1,500 offices, 30 movie theaters, more than 1,600 boutiques, 200 restaurants, three universities, two colleges, two train stations, a skating rink, 40 banks, a bus terminal, an art museum, a complex of concert halls, the home ice of the Montréal Canadiens, and a church. All this is linked by Métro lines and more than 30 km (19 mi) of well-lit, boutique-lined passages that protect shoppers and workers from the hardships of winter and the heat of summer. A traveler arriving by train could book into a fine hotel and spend a week shopping, dining, and going to a long list of movies, plays, concerts, sports events, and discos, without once stepping outside.

Aboveground, the downtown core is a sprawling 30-by-8-block area bounded by avenue Atwater and boulevard St-Laurent on the west and east, respectively, avenue des Pins on the north, and rue St-Antoine on the south. In the early days of European settlement, this area was a patchwork of farms, pastures, and woodlots. In 1701 the French administration signed a peace treaty with the Iroquois, and the colonists began to feel safe about building outside Vieux-Montréal's fortifications. The city inched northward, toward Mont-Royal, particularly after the British conquest in 1760. By the end of the 19th century, rue Ste-Catherine was the main commercial thoroughfare, and the city's elite built mansions on the slope of the mountain.

A Good Walk

This downtown walk begins underground at the McGill Métro station, one of the central points in the Underground City. It's linked to a half-dozen office towers and two of the "Big Three" department stores, **Eaton** ㉓ and La Baie (the other is Ogilvy). Passages also link the station to such major shopping malls as Le Centre Eaton, Les Promenades de la Cathédrale, and Les Cours Mont-Royal.

354

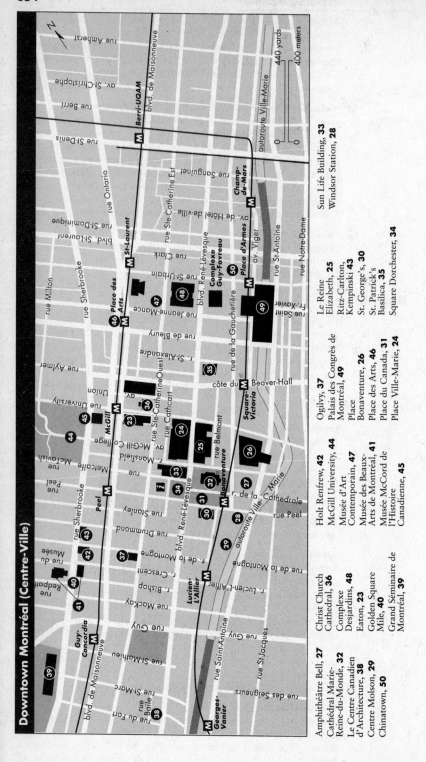

Downtown Montréal (Centre-Ville)

Amphithéâtre Bell, **27**
Cathédral Marie-Reine-du-Monde, **32**
Le Centre Canadien d'Architecture, **38**
Centre Molson, **29**
Chinatown, **50**

Christ Church Cathedral, **36**
Complexe Desjardins, **48**
Eaton, **23**
Golden Square Mile, **40**
Grand Séminaire de Montréal, **39**

Holt Renfrew, **42**
McGill University, **44**
Musée d'Art Contemporain, **47**
Musée des Beaux-Arts de Montréal, **41**
Musée McCord de l'Histoire Canadienne, **45**

Ogilvy, **37**
Palais des Congrès de Montréal, **49**
Place Bonaventure, **26**
Place des Arts, **46**
Place du Canada, **31**
Place Ville-Marie, **24**

Le Reine Elizabeth, **25**
Ritz-Carlton, Kempinski **43**
St. George's, **30**
St. Patrick's Basilica, **35**
Square Dorchester, **34**

Sun Life Building, **33**
Windsor Station, **28**

A tunnel links the Centre Eaton to **Place Ville-Marie** ㉔. The mall complex underneath this skyscraper was the first link in the Underground City. From here head south via the passageways toward **Le Reine Elizabeth** ㉕, or Queen Elizabeth, hotel, which straddles the entrance to the Gare Centrale (Central Station). Follow the signs marked "Métro/Place Bonaventure" to **Place Bonaventure** ㉖, which has shops, restaurants, and offices on its lower floors.

When you've finished exploring Place Bonaventure, go to the northwest corner of the building and descend the escalator into the Underground City. This time follow the signs for Le 1000 rue de la Gauchetière, a skyscraper that's home to the **Amphithéâtre Bell** ㉗, a $5 million indoor ice rink. Return to the tunnels and follow signs to the Bonaventure Métro station and then to the Canadian Pacific Railway Company's **Windsor Station** ㉘, with its massive stone exterior and steel-and-glass roof. The rail station and the Place Bonaventure Métro station below it are all linked to **Centre Molson** ㉙, the home of the Montréal Canadiens.

Exit the Underground City at the north end of Windsor Station and cross rue de la Gauchetière to **St. George's** ㉚, the prettiest Anglican church in the city. Just to the east across rue Peel is **Place du Canada** ㉛, a park with a statue of Sir John A. Macdonald, Canada's first prime minister. Cross the park and rue de la Cathédrale to **Cathédrale Marie-Reine-du-Monde** ㉜, which is modeled after St. Peter's Basilica in Rome. People sometimes call the gray granite building across boulevard René-Lévesque from the cathedral the "Wedding Cake," because it rises in tiers of decreasing size and has lots of columns, but its real name is the **Sun Life Building** ㉝. The park that faces the Sun Life Building just north of boulevard René-Lévesque is **Square Dorchester** ㉞, for many years the heart of Montréal. Walk east along boulevard René-Lévesque to beautiful old **St. Patrick's Basilica** ㉟ (1847).

After visiting the church, backtrack a half block, cross boulevard René-Lévesque, and walk north on rue Phillips (which becomes rue Aylmer) to rue Ste-Catherine, the main retail shopping street of Montréal. At the northwest corner of rues Ste-Catherine and Aylmer is La Baie department store. The church just west of La Baie is **Christ Church Cathedral** ㊱ (1859), the main church of the Anglican diocese of Montréal.

As you continue your walk west, pause briefly to admire the view at the corner of rue Ste-Catherine and avenue McGill College. Look north up this broad boulevard and you can see the Victorian-era buildings of the McGill University campus with Mont-Royal looming in the background. The grim-looking gray castle you can see high on the slopes to the right is the Royal Victoria Hospital.

Another six blocks farther west is **Ogilvy** ㊲, the last of the Big Three department stores. The houses in **rue de la Montagne and rues Crescent and Bishop,** the two streets just west of it, are filled with trendy restaurants, shops, and bars. **Le Centre Canadien d'Architecture** ㊳ is just four blocks west at rue St-Marc on rue Baile. From the center, walk north on rue Fort three blocks to rue Sherbrooke. On the north side of the street you will see a complex of fine neoclassical buildings in a shady garden. This is the **Grand Séminaire de Montréal** ㊴, which trains priests for Montréal's Roman Catholic parishes.

Three blocks east at rue Bishop you'll enter the exclusive neighborhood known as the **Golden Square Mile** ㊵. In the heart of this district at the corner of rues Sherbrooke and du Musée is the **Musée des Beaux-Arts de Montréal** ㊶, the Museum of Fine Arts, with a large collection from around the world. Walking east on rue Sherbrooke brings you to the small and exclusive **Holt Renfrew** ㊷ department store, perhaps the city's fanciest, at the corner of rue de la Montagne. One block farther east at rue Drummond stands the **Ritz-Carlton Kempinski** ㊸, the grande dame of Montréal hotels.

The campus of **McGill University** ㊹ is on the north side of rue Sherbrooke just three blocks east of the Ritz-Carlton. Just across rue Sherbrooke is the **Musée McCord de l'Histoire Canadienne** ㊺, one of the best history museums in Canada. Turn right on rue University and walk a block to the McGill Métro station. Take the train one stop in the direction of Honoré-Beaugrand to the **Place des Arts** ㊻ station and follow the signs to the theater complex of the same name. The **Musée d'Art Contemporain** ㊼, the city's modern art museum, is in Place des Arts. While still in Place des Arts, follow the signs to the **Complexe Desjardins** ㊽, an office building, hotel, and mall along the lines of Place Ville-Marie (☞ *above*). The next development south is the Complexe Guy-Favreau, a huge federal office building named after the Canadian minister of justice in the early '60s. If you continue in a straight line, you will hit the **Palais des Congrès de Montréal** ㊾ above the Place d'Armes Métro stop. But if you take a left out of Guy-Favreau onto rue de la Gauchetière, you will be in **Chinatown** ㊿, a relief after all that enclosed retail space.

TIMING

Just to walk this route briskly will take a minimum of two hours, even on a fine day. Several of the museums along the route—the McCord, the Centre Canadien d'Architecture, the Musée d'Art Contemporain, and the Musée des Beaux-Arts—are worthy of visits of at least two hours each. So if you want to see everything, it would be wise to spread the tour of downtown over two days, ending the first day after the Musée des Beaux-Arts. Another possibility is to walk the route in one day, stopping briefly at places like St. Patrick's Basilica and perhaps going for a skate at the Amphithéâtre Bell, and then doing the museums on another day (note that they're not open on Monday).

Sights to See

🖐 ㉗ **Amphithéâtre Bell.** Skating is a passion in Montréal and you can do it year-round in this $5-million indoor ice rink on the ground floor of a skyscraper. The rink is bathed in natural light and surrounded by cafés, a food court, and a winter garden. It's open to skaters of all levels of experience; skate rentals and lockers are available. There are also skating lessons, Saturday- and Sunday-night disco skating, and scheduled ice shows. To find the rink once you're inside the building, remember the French word for skating rink is *patinoire*. ⊠ *1000 rue de la Gauchetière,* ☎ *514/395–0555, ext. 237.* ⊠ *$5, skate rental $4.* ☉ *Weekdays 11:30–10, Sat. 11:30–7, Sun. 11:30–6; dancing on ice for those 16 or over, weekends 7 PM–midnight.*

㉜ **Cathédrale Marie-Reine-du-Monde** (Mary Queen of the World Cathedral). Seat of the Roman Catholic archbishop of Montréal, this church (1894) is modeled after St. Peter's Basilica in Rome. Victor Bourgeau, the same architect who did the interior of Notre-Dame in Vieux-Montréal, thought the idea of the cathedral's design terrible but completed it after the original architect proved incompetent. Inside there is even a canopy over the altar that is a miniature copy of Bernini's baldachin in St. Peter's. ⊠ *1085 rue de la Cathédral; through main doors on blvd. René-Lévesque.*

㊳ **Le Centre Canadien d'Architecture** (Canadian Center for Architecture). Architect Phyllis Lambert transformed one of the city's mansions into the centerpiece of what is probably the world's premier architectural collection. The center traces the history and development of all architecture (not just Canadian), with exhibits that include blueprints, photographs, scale models, and hands-on demonstrations. The main exhibit is in the Shaughnessy Mansion, a 19th-century home that gave its name to Shaughnessy Village, the surrounding neighborhood of homes and apartments. ⊠ *1920 rue Baile,* ☎ *514/939–7000.* ⊡ *$5.* ☉ *Wed. and Fri. 11–6, Thurs. 11–8, weekends 11–5.*

㉙ Centre Molson. Opened in spring 1996, this arena is the new home of the Montréal Canadiens, the hockey team devoted hometown fans call simply *les Glorieux.* The brown-brick building replaces the old Forum that had been the Canadiens' home since 1917. The name refers to the Molson family, who established Montréal's first brewery in the 18th century and whose company, Molson-O'Keefe, owns the hockey team. ⊠ *1260 rue de la Gauchetière Ouest,* ☎ *517/932–2582 or 514/989–2841 (for tours).* ⊡ *Tour $7.* ☉ *Tour in English at 10:30 and 3:30, in French at 11 and 2.*

㊿ Chinatown. The Chinese first came to Montréal in large numbers after 1880, following the construction of the transcontinental railroad. They settled in an 18-block area between boulevard René-Lévesque and avenue Viger to the north and south, and near rues Hôtel de Ville and Bleury on the west and east, an area now full of restaurants, food stores, and gift shops. If you have enough energy, stroll south on rue St-Urbain for a block to rue St-Antoine. A half block east is **Steve's Music Store** (⊠ 51 rue St-Antoine Ouest, ☎ 514/878–2216), a shabby warren of five storefronts jammed with just about everything you need to be a rock star except talent. Sooner or later every musician and wannabe musician in the city wanders through it.

Pho Bang New York (⊠ 970 blvd. St-Laurent, ☎ 514/954–2032) is a small Vietnamese restaurant on the edge of Chinatown that specializes in traditional noodle soups served in bowls big enough to bathe a small dog. And it's cheap, too—for less than $5, you get soup, a plate of crispy vegetables, and a small pot of tea. The restaurant does not accept credit cards.

㊱ Christ Church Cathedral. This is the main church (1859) of the Anglican diocese of Montréal. In early 1988 the diocese leased the land and air rights to a consortium of developers. The consortium then built **La Maison des Coopérants,** a 34-story office tower behind the cathedral, and a huge retail complex, **Les Promenades de la Cathédrale,** under it. The church has a quiet graceful interior and frequent organ recitals and concerts. ⊠ *535 rue Ste-Catherine Ouest.* ☉ *Daily 8–6.*

㊽ Complexe Desjardins. The large galleria space in this boutique-rich mall is the scene of all types of performances, from lectures on Japanese massage techniques to pop music. ⊠ *Bounded by rues Ste-Catherine, Jeanne-Mance, and St-Urbain and blvd. René-Lévesque.*

㉓ Eaton. The largest of Montréal's department stores is a central point in the Underground City (☞ *Shopping, below*). ⊠ *677 rue Ste-Catherine Ouest,* ☎ *514/284–8411.*

㊵ Golden Square Mile. This was once the richest neighborhood in Canada. At the turn of the century, the people who lived here—mostly of Scottish descent—controlled 70% of the country's wealth. Their baronial homes filled an area that stretched from avenue Atwater in the west to rue de Bleury in the east and from rue de la Gauchetière in the south to avenue des Pins halfway up the mountain. Most of those palatial homes have been leveled to make way for high rises and office towers, and the few left are either consulates or conference centers associated with McGill University.

39 Grand Séminaire de Montréal. The Montréal archdiocese trains its priests here in buildings that date to 1860. Two squat towers in the gardens date to the 17th century, and it was in one of these that St. Marguerite Bourgeoys set up her first school for native girls. The towers, among the oldest buildings on the island, are visible from the street; there is a little area just by the gates with three plaques that explain the towers and their history in French. The seminary is private, but you can go to Mass at 10:30 on Sunday morning from September through June in the lovely neoclassical chapel. ⊠ *2065 rue Sherbrooke Ouest.*

42 Holt Renfrew. This is perhaps the city's fanciest department store (☞ Shopping, *below*). ⊠ *1300 rue Sherbrooke Ouest,* ☎ *514/842–5111.*

44 McGill University. James McGill, a wealthy Scottish fur trader, bequeathed the money and the land for this institution, which opened in 1828 and is perhaps the finest English-language university in the nation. The student body numbers 15,000, and the university is best known for its medical and engineering schools. Most of the campus buildings are fine examples of Victorian architecture. ⊠ *845 rue Sherbrooke Ouest.*

NEED A
BREAK?
> The **McGill University campus** is an island of green in a sea of traffic and skyscrapers. On a fine day you can sit on the grass in the shade of a 100-year-old tree and just let the world drift by.

🌤 47 Musée d'Art Contemporain. The museum's large permanent collection of modern art represents works by Québécois, Canadian, and international artists in every medium. The museum often has weekend programs, with many child-oriented activities, and almost all are free. There are guided tours; hours vary. ⊠ *185 rue Ste-Catherine Ouest,* ☎ *514/847–6226.* 🎟 *$5, Wed. evening free.* ☉ *Tues. and Thurs.–Sun. 11–6, Wed. 11–9.*

41 Musée des Beaux-Arts de Montréal (Museum of Fine Arts). The oldest museum in the country was founded by a group of English-speaking Montrealers in 1860. The art collection is housed in two buildings—the older Benaiah-Gibb Pavilion on the north side of rue Sherbrooke and the glittering glass-fronted Pavilion Jean-Noël-Desmarais right across the street. The two buildings are connected by underground tunnels and hold a large collection of European and North American fine and decorative art; ancient treasures from Europe, the Near East, Asia, Africa, and America; art from Québec and Canada; and Native American and Eskimo artifacts. The museum has a gift shop, an art-book store, a restaurant, a cafeteria, and a gallery from which you can buy or rent paintings by local artists. ⊠ *1380 rue Sherbrooke Ouest,* ☎ *514/285–1600.* 🎟 *Permanent collection free, special exhibitions $10.* ☉ *Tues. and Thurs.–Sun. 11–6, Wed. 11–9.*

🌤 45 Musée McCord de l'Histoire Canadienne. A grand, eclectic attic of a museum, the McCord documents the life of ordinary Canadians, using costumes and textiles, decorative arts, paintings, prints and drawings, and the 450,000-print-and-negative Notman Photographic Archives, which highlights 19th-century life in Montréal. The McCord is the only museum in Canada with a permanent costume gallery. There are guided tours (call for times), a reading room and documentation center, a gift shop and bookstore, and a tearoom. ⊠ *690 rue Sherbrooke Ouest,* ☎ *514/398–7100.* 🎟 *$7.* ☉ *Tues., Wed., and Fri. 10–6; Thurs. 10–9; weekends 10–5; closed Mon. except statutory holidays.*

37 Ogilvy. A kilted piper still closes this department store every afternoon (☞ Shopping, *below*). ⊠ *1307 rue Ste-Catherine Ouest,* ☎ *514/942–7711.*

49 Palais des Congrès de Montréal. Montréal's convention center is built on concrete pillars over an expressway and can accommodate 10,000 conventioneers. ⊠ *201 rue Viger Ouest.*

26 Place Bonaventure. The lower floors of this building have shops, restaurants, and exhibition halls and offices. On top is the Bonaventure Hilton International (☞ Lodging, *below*).

46 Place des Arts. The Place des Arts theater is a government-subsidized complex of three very modern theaters. Guided tours of the halls and backstage are available for groups of at least 15. The ☞ **Musée d'Art Contemporain**, the city's modern art museum, moved here in 1991. ⊠ *183 rue Ste-Catherine Ouest,* ☎ *514/842–2112, 514/285–4275 guided tour.*

31 Place du Canada. This park has a statue of Sir John A. Macdonald, Canada's first prime minister. In October 1995 the park was the site of a huge rally for Canadian unity that drew more than 300,000 participants from across the country. That patriotic demonstration was at least partly responsible for preserving a slim victory for the pro-unity forces in the subsequent referendum on independence for Québec. At the south end of Place du Canada is **Le Marriott Château Champlain** (☞ Lodging, *below*), known as the Cheese Grater because of its rows and rows of half-moon-shape windows. ⊠ *Bordered by blvd. René-Lévesque and rue de la Gauchetière.*

24 Place Ville-Marie. This cross-shaped 1962 office tower was Montréal's first modern skyscraper; the mall complex underneath it was the first link in the Underground City. ⊠ *Bounded by blvd. René-Lévesque and rues Mansfield, Cathcart, and University.*

NEED A BREAK? The once grim passageways at the back of Central Station just below the escalators leading to Place Ville-Marie now house a trendy food court, **Les Halles de la Gare.** The food includes some of the city's best bread and pastries, salads, and sandwiches made with fresh terrines and pâtés. If it's nice out, you can take your snack up the escalator to the mall under Place Ville-Marie and then up the stairs in the middle of its food court to the terrace, a wide area with a fine view.

25 Le Reine Elizabeth. One of the city's major hotels (☞ Lodging, *below*) straddles the **Gare Centrale** (Central Station), where most trains from the United States and the rest of Canada arrive. ⊠ *900 blvd. René-Lévesque,* ☎ *514/861–3511.*

43 Ritz-Carlton Kempinski. The grande dame of Montréal hotels (☞ Lodging, *below*) has been in business since 1912. ⊠ *1228 rue Sherbrooke Ouest,* ☎ *514/842–4212.*

Rues de la Montagne, Crescent and Bishop. Today dozens of trendy bars, restaurants, and bistros are ensconced in the old row houses that line these streets between boulevard René-Lévesque and rue Sherbrooke. This area once formed the playing fields of the Montréal Lacrosse and Cricket Grounds. Later it became an exclusive suburb lined with millionaires' row houses.

30 St. George's. Built in 1872, this is the prettiest Anglican church in the city, a jewel of neo-Gothic architecture. ⊠ *1101 rue Stanley.*

★ **35 St. Patrick's Basilica.** This church (1847) is one of the purest examples of the Gothic Revival style in Canada. It is to Montréal's English-speaking Catholics what the Basilique Notre-Dame is to the city's French-speaking Catholics. The church's colors are soft and the vaulted ceiling over the sanctuary glows with green and gold mosaics. The old pulpit has panels depicting the Apostles, and a huge lamp decorated with six 6-ft-high angels hangs over the main altar. If you're named after some obscure saint, you might find his or her portrait in one of the 150 painted panels that decorate the oak wainscoting along the nave. ✉ *460 blvd. René-Lévesque Ouest,* ☎ *514/866–0491.* ⏲ *Daily 8:30–6.*

㉞ **Square Dorchester.** Until 1870 a Catholic burial ground occupied this downtown park, and there are still bodies buried beneath the grass. The statuary includes a monument to the Boer War and a statue of the Scottish poet Robert Burns. ✉ *Bordered by rues Peel, Metcalfe, and McTavish.*

㉝ **Sun Life Building.** At one time this was the largest building in the British Commonwealth. During World War II much of England's financial reserves and national treasures were stored in Sun Life's vaults. ✉ *1155 rue Metcalfe.*

㉘ **Windsor Station.** This magnificent building with its massive stone exterior and steel-and-glass roof was once the eastern passenger terminus for the Canadian Pacific Railway, Canada's first transcontinental link. Alas, today it is a trainless shell. ✉ *1100 rue de la Gauchetière.*

Quartier Latin

Early in this century, rue St-Denis cut through a bourgeois neighborhood of large, comfortable residences. The Université de Montréal was established here in 1893, and the students and academics who moved into the area dubbed it the Quartier Latin, or Latin Quarter. The university eventually moved to a larger campus on the north side of Mont-Royal, and the area went into decline. It revived in the early 1970s, largely as a result of the 1969 opening of the Université du Québec à Montréal and the launch of the International Jazz Festival in the summer of 1980. Plateau Mont-Royal, the neighborhood just north of the Quartier Latin, shared in this revival. Residents are now a mix of immigrants, working-class Francophones, and young professionals eager to find a home they can renovate close to the city center. The Quartier Latin and Plateau Mont-Royal are home to rows of French and ethnic restaurants, charming bistros, coffee shops, designer boutiques, antiques shops, and art galleries. When night falls, these streets are always full of omnilingual hordes—young and not so young, rich and poor, established and still studying.

Many of the older residences in this area have graceful wrought-iron balconies and twisting staircases that are typical of Montréal. They were built that way for practical reasons. The buildings are what Montrealers call duplexes or triplexes, that is, two or three residences stacked on top of each other. To save interior space, the stairs to reach the upper floors were put outside. The stairs and balconies are treacherous in winter, but in summer they are often full of families and couples, gossiping, picnicking, and partying. If Montrealers tell you they spend the summer in Balconville, they mean they don't have the money or the time to leave town and won't get any farther than their balcony.

A Good Walk

Begin at the Berri-UQAM Métro stop. The "UQAM" in the subway name is pronounced "oo-kam" by local Francophones and "you-kwam" by local Anglophones. It refers to the **Université du Québec à Montréal** (51), whose drab brick campus fills up much of three city blocks between rues Sanguinet and Berri. A few splendid fragments of the old Eglise St-Jacques poke up amid this modern dreck. A more substantial religious monument that has survived intact right in UQAM's resolutely secularist heart is the ornate **Chapelle Notre-Dame-de-Lourdes** (52), on rue Ste-Catherine.

Quartier Latin and Parc du Mont-Royal

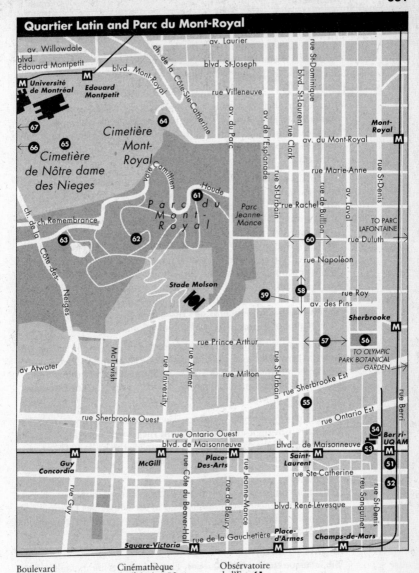

Just west of rue St-Denis you find the **Cinémathèque Québécoise** ⑬, which houses one of the largest cinematic reference libraries in the world. Around the corner and a half block north on rue St-Denis stands the 2,500-seat **Théâtre St-Denis** ⑭, the city's second-largest auditorium. On the next block north is the **Bibliothèque Nationale du Québec,** which houses Québec's official archives.

Turn left on Sherbrooke and left again on boulevard St-Laurent for the **Musée Juste pour Rire** ⑮, the world's first museum of humor. Backtrack east on rue Sherbrooke, turn left on rue St-Denis, and walk north to **Square St-Louis** ⑯, one of the most attractive green spaces in Montréal.

The stretch of **rue Prince Arthur** ⑰, beginning at the western end of Square St-Louis and continuing several blocks west, is a center of youth culture. When you reach **boulevard St-Laurent** ⑱, take a right and stroll north through Montréal's ethnic diversity. This area was still partly rural in the mid-19th century, with lots of fresh air, which made it healthier than overcrowded Vieux-Montréal. So in 1861 the Hôpital Hôtel-Dieu, the hospital Jeanne Mance founded in the 17th century, moved into a new building at what is now the corner of avenue des Pins and rue St-Urbain, just a block west of boulevard St-Laurent. Hôtel-Dieu, one of the city's major hospitals, is still there, and right next to it is the **Musée des Hospitalières de l'Hôtel-Dieu** ⑲, which gives a remarkable picture of the early days of colonization.

Merchants are attempting to re-create rue Prince Arthur on **rue Duluth** ⑳. Turn right and walk four blocks east to rue St-Denis, where you will find Greek and Vietnamese restaurants and boutiques and art galleries. Walk east another nine blocks and you come to **Parc Lafontaine,** the smallest of Montréal's three major parks.

After exploring the park's 100 acres, walk south to rue Sherbrooke Est and then turn right and walk west on rues Sherbrooke and Cherrier to the Sherbrooke Métro station to complete the walk. Or head west to explore Parc du Mont-Royal (☞ *below*).

TIMING

This is a comfortable afternoon walk, lasting perhaps two hours, longer if you linger for an hour or so in the Musée des Hospitalières and spend some time shopping. There's a bit of a climb from boulevard de Maisonneuve to rue Sherbrooke.

Sights to See

Bibliothèque Nationale du Québec. This Beaux-Arts library built in 1915 houses Québec's official archives. ☒ *1700 rue St-Denis,* ☎ *514/873–1100.* ☉ *Tues.–Sat. 9–5.*

⑱ **Boulevard St-Laurent.** Depending on how you look at it, this street divides the city into east and west or it's where East and West meet. After the first electric tramway was installed on boulevard St-Laurent, working-class families began to move in. In the 1880s the first of many waves of Jewish immigrants escaping pogroms in eastern Europe arrived. They called the street the Main, as in "Main Street." The Jews were followed by Greeks, Eastern Europeans, Portuguese, and, most recently, Latin Americans. The 10 blocks north of rue Sherbrooke are filled with delis, junk stores, restaurants, luncheonettes, and clothing stores, as well as fashionable boutiques, bistros, cafés, bars, nightclubs, bookstores, and galleries. The block between rues Roy and Napoléon is particularly rich in delights.

⑫ **Chapelle Notre-Dame-de-Lourdes.** This tiny Roman Catholic chapel is one of the most ornate pieces of religious architecture in the city. It was built in 1876 and decorated with brightly colored murals by artist Napoléon Bourassa, who lived nearby. It's a mixture of Roman and Byzantine styles, and its beautifully restored interior is a must-see, despite the panhandlers that cluster at its doors and the somewhat eccentric devotees it attracts. ⊠ *430 rue Ste-Catherine Est.* ⊙ *Daily 8–5.*

⑬ Cinémathèque Québécoise. This museum and repertory movie house is one of Montréal's great bargains. For $3 you can visit the permanent exhibition on the history of filmmaking equipment and see two movies. Expansion in 1997 added two exhibition rooms and a TV documentary center. ⊠ *335 blvd. de Maisonneuve Ouest,* ☎ *514/842– 9763.* ⊡ *$3.* ⊙ *Tues.–Sun. 11–9.*

⑭ Musée des Hospitalières de l'Hôtel-Dieu. More than just a fascinating and sometimes chilling exhibit on the history of medicine and nursing, this museum captures the spirit of an age. France in the 17th century was consumed with religious fervor, and aristocratic men and women often built hospitals, schools, and churches in distant lands. The nuns of the Religieuses Hospitalières de St-Joseph who came to Montréal in the mid-17th century to help Jeanne Mance run the Hôpital Hôtel-Dieu were good examples of this fervor, and much of their spirit is evident in the letters, books, and religious artifacts displayed here. Pay special attention to the beautiful wooden stairway in the museum's entrance hall. ⊠ *201 av. des Pins Ouest,* ☎ *514/849–2919.* ⊡ *$5.* ⊙ *Mid-June–mid-Oct., Tues.–Fri. 10–5, weekends 1–5; mid-Oct.–mid-June, Wed.–Sun. 1–5.*

NEED A BREAK? | **Café Santropol** (⊠ 3990 rue St-Urbain, ☎ 514/842–3110) serves hearty soups, cake, salads, and unusual high-rise sandwiches garnished with fruit (the Jeanne Mance mixes pineapples and chives in cream cheese). The atmosphere is homey, with a molded tin ceiling and a little *terasse* out back. One percent of the profits go to charity, and the staff runs a meals-on-wheels program. Credit cards are not accepted.

⑮ Musée Juste pour Rire (International Humor Museum). This is the first museum in the world to be dedicated to laughter. Its multimedia exhibits explore and celebrate humor by drawing visitors into their plots. Some of the visiting exhibits have a serious side, too. There is a large collection of humor videos, a cabaret where budding comics can test their material, and a restaurant where you can watch old tapes while you eat. ⊠ *2111 blvd. St-Laurent,* ☎ *514/845–2322.* ⊡ *$9.95.* ⊙ *Tues.–Sun. 1–8.*

Parc Lafontaine. Montréal's two main cultures are reflected in the layout of this very popular park: the eastern half is pure French, with paths, gardens, and lawns laid out in geometric shapes; the western half is very English, with meandering paths and irregularly shaped ponds that follow the natural contours of the land. In summer there are two artificial lakes where you can rent paddleboats, bowling greens, tennis courts, and an open-air theater with free arts events. In winter the two artificial lakes form a large skating rink. ⊠ *3933 av. Parc Lafontaine,* ☎ *514/872–6211.* ⊙ *Daily 9 AM–10 PM.*

⑯ Rue Duluth. Modest little ethnic restaurants with outdoor terraces have sprouted along the street, along with crafts boutiques and a few shops selling collectibles such as cookie jars and bottles.

⑰ Rue Prince Arthur. In the 1960s the young people who moved to the neighborhood transformed this street into a small hippie bazaar of clothing, leather, and smoke shops. It remains a center of youth culture, although it's now much tamer and more commercial. The city turned the blocks between avenue Laval and boulevard St-Laurent into a pedestrian mall. Hippie shops have metamorphosed into inexpensive Greek, Vietnamese, Italian, Polish, and Chinese restaurants and little neighborhood bars. ⊠ *Beginning at western end of sq. St-Louis and stretching a few blocks west.*

56 **Square St-Louis.** This graceful square has a fountain, benches, and trees and is surrounded by 19th-century homes built in the large, comfortable style of the Second Empire. Originally a reservoir, these blocks became a park in 1879 and attracted upper-middle-class families and artists to the area. French-Canadian poets were among the most famous creative people to occupy the houses back then, and the neighborhood is now home to painters, filmmakers, musicians, and writers. On the wall of 336 Square St-Louis you can see—and read, if your French is good— a long poem by Michel Bujold. ⊠ *Bordered by av. Laval and rue St-Denis.*

54 **Théâtre St-Denis.** This is the second-largest auditorium in Montréal (after Salle Wilfrid Pelletier in Place des Arts). Sarah Bernhardt and many other famous actors have graced its stage. ⊠ *1594 rue St-Denis,* ☎ *514/849–4211.*

51 **Université du Québec à Montréal.** Part of a network of provincial campuses set up by the provincial government in 1969, UQAM is housed in a series of massive, modern brick buildings that clog much of the three city blocks bordered by rues Sanguinet and Berri and boulevards de Maisonneuve and René-Lévesque. The splendid fragments of Gothic grandeur sprouting up among the modern brick hulks like flowers in a swamp are all that's left of Église St-Jacques.

Parc du Mont-Royal

Parc du Mont-Royal is 494 acres of forest and paths in the heart of the city. The park was designed by Frederick Law Olmsted, the architect of New York's Central Park. He believed that communion with nature could cure body and soul, and the park follows the natural topography and accentuates its features, in the English style. You can jog, cycle, stroll the miles of paths, or just scan the horizon from one of two lookouts. Horse-drawn transport is popular year-round: sleigh rides in winter and calèche rides in summer. On the eastern side of the hill stands the 100-ft steel cross that is the symbol of the city. Not far away from the park and perched on a neighboring crest of the same mountain is the Oratoire St-Joseph, a shrine that draws millions of visitors and pilgrims every year.

A Good Walk

Begin by taking the Métro's Orange Line to the Mont-Royal station and transfer to Bus 11 (be sure to get a transfer—*correspondance* in French—from a machine before you get on the Métro). The No. 11 drives right through the park on the Voie Camillien Houde. Get off at the **Obsérvatoire de l'Est** 61, a lookout. Climb the stone staircase at the end of the parking lot and follow the trails to the **Chalet du Mont-Royal** 62, a baronial building with a terrace that overlooks downtown Montréal. The next stop is **Lac aux Castors** 63, and there are at least three ways to get to this lake. You can take the long way and walk down the steep flight of stairs at the east end of the terrace and then turn right to follow the gravel road that circles the mountain. The shortest way is to leave the terrace at the west end and follow the crowds along the road. The middle way is to leave at the east end, but then to turn off the main road and follow one of the shaded paths that leads through the woods and along the southern ridge of the mountain.

Across Chemin Remembrance from Lac aux Castors is what looks like one vast cemetery. It is in fact two cemeteries—one Protestant and the other Catholic. The **Cimetière Mont-Royal** ⑥④ is toward the east in a little valley that cuts off the noise of the city; it is the final resting place of Anna Leonowens, the real-life heroine of *The King and I*. The yellow-brick buildings and tower on the north side of the mountain beyond the cemetery belong to the Université de Montréal, the second-largest French-language university in the world with nearly 60,000 students. If you're now humming "Getting to Know You," you'll probably change your tune to Canada's national anthem when you enter the **Cimetière Notre-Dame-des-Neiges** ⑥⑤, as the song's composer, Calixa Lavallée, is buried here.

Wander northwest through the two cemeteries, and you will eventually emerge on Chemin Queen Mary on the edge of a decidedly lively area of street vendors, ethnic restaurants, and boutiques. Walk west on Queen Mary across Chemin Côte-des-Neiges, and you come to Montréal's most grandiose religious monument, the **Oratoire St-Joseph** ⑥⑥. Across the street is the ivy-covered **Collège Notre Dame** ⑥⑦, where the oratory's founder, Brother André, worked as a porter.

After visiting the church, retrace your steps to Chemin Côte-des-Neiges and walk to the Côte-des-Neiges station to catch the Métro.

TIMING
Allot at least the better part of a day for this tour, longer if you plan on catching some rays or ice skating in the park.

Sights to See

★ ⑥② **Chalet du Mont-Royal.** The view here overlooks downtown Montréal. In the distance you can see Mont-Royal's sister mountains—Mont St-Bruno, Mont St-Hilaire, and Mont St-Grégoire. These isolated peaks—called the Montérégies, or Mountains of the King—rise quite dramatically from flat surrounding countryside. Be sure to take a look inside the chalet, especially at the murals that depict scenes from Canadian history. There's a snack bar in the back. ◔ *Daily 9–5.*

⑥④ **Cimetière Mont-Royal.** This cemetery was established in 1852 by the Anglican, Presbyterian, Unitarian, and Baptist churches, and was laid out like a landscaped garden with monuments that are genuine works of art. The cemetery's most famous permanent guest is Anna Leonowens, who was governess to the children of the King of Siam and the real-life model for the heroine of the musical *The King and I*. There are no tours of the cemetery. ⊠ *1297 Chemin de la Forêt.*

⑥⑤ **Cimetière Notre-Dame-des-Neiges.** This Catholic graveyard is the largest in the city, and the final resting place of hundreds of prominent artists, poets, intellectuals, politicians, and clerics. Among them is Calixa Lavallée, who wrote "O Canada." Many of the monuments and mausoleums—scattered along 55 km (34 mi) of paths and roadways—are the work of leading artists. There are no tours of the cemetery. ⊠ *4601 Côte-des-Neiges.*

⑥⑦ **Collège Notre Dame.** Brother André, founder of the Oratoire St-Joseph, worked as a porter here. It's still an important private school, and one of the few in the city that still accepts boarders. Its students these days, however, include girls, a situation that would have shocked Brother André. ⊠ *3791 chemin Queen Mary.*

⑥③ **Lac aux Castors.** Beaver Lake was reclaimed from boggy ground and so violates Olmsted's purist vision of a natural environment. But children like to float boats on it in summer, and it makes a fine skating rink in winter. ⊠ *Off Chemin Remembrance.*

61 **Obsérvatoire de l'Est.** This lookout gives a spectacular view of the east end of the city and the St. Lawrence River.

66 **Oratoire St-Joseph.** St. Joseph's Oratory, a huge domed church perched high on a ridge of Mont-Royal, is the largest shrine in the world dedicated to the earthly father of Jesus. It is the result of the persistence of a remarkable little man named Brother André, who was a porter in the school that his religious order ran. He dreamed of building a shrine dedicated to St. Joseph—Canada's patron saint—and began in 1904 by building a little chapel. Miraculous cures were reported and attributed to St. Joseph's intercession, and Brother André's project caught the imagination of Montréal. The result is one of the most important shrines in North America. The oratory dome is one of the biggest in the world, and the church has a magnificent setting. It's also home to Les Petits Chanteurs de Mont-Royal, the city's finest boys' choir. But alas, the interior is oppressive and drab. There's a more modest and quite undistinguished crypt church at the bottom of the structure, and right behind it is a room that glitters with hundreds of votive candles lit in honor of St. Joseph. The walls are festooned with crutches discarded by the cured. Right behind that is the simple tomb of Brother André, who was beatified in 1982. Brother André's heart is displayed in a glass case upstairs in a small museum depicting events in his life. From early December through February the oratory features a display of crèches (nativity scenes) from all over the world. High on the mountain beside the main church is a beautiful garden, commemorating the passion of Christ with life-size representations of the 14 traditional Stations of the Cross. Carillon, choral, and organ concerts are held weekly at the oratory during the summer. To visit the church you can either climb the more than 300 steps to the front door (many pilgrims do so on their knees, pausing to pray at each step) or you can take the shuttle bus that runs from the front gate. ⊠ *3800 Chemin Queen Mary, near Côte-des-Neiges Métro station,* ☎ *514/733–8211.* ☼ *Sept.–May, daily 6 AM–9:30 PM; June–Aug., daily 6 AM—10 PM.*

Olympic Park and Botanical Garden

The Parc Olympique (Olympic Park) and the Jardin Botanique (Botanical Garden) are in the east end of the city. You can reach them via the Pie-IX or Viau Métro stations (the latter is nearer the stadium entrance). The giant, mollusk-shaped Stade Olympique and the leaning tower that supports the stadium's roof dominate the skyline of the eastern end of the city. But the area has more to recommend it than just the stadium complex; there's the city's world-class botanical garden, the world's largest museum dedicated to bugs, and Parc Maisonneuve.

Daily guided tours of the Olympic complex leave from the Tourist Hall (☎ 514/252–8687) in the base of the tower. Tours at 12:40 and 3:40 are in English and the ones at 11 and 2 are in French; cost is $5.25.

A Good Walk

Start with a ride on the Métro's Green Line and get off at the Viau station, which is only a few steps from the main entrance to the 70,000-seat **Stade Olympique** 68, a stadium built for the 1976 summer games. A trip to the top of the **Tour Olympique** 69, the world's tallest tilting structure, can give you a view up to 80 km (50 mi) on a clear day. The six pools of the **Centre Aquatique** 70 are under the tower.

Right next to the tower is the **Biodôme** 71, where you can explore both a rain forest and an arctic landscape. Continuing your back-to-nature experience, cross rue Sherbrooke to the north of the park (or take the free shuttle bus) to reach the **Jardin Botanique** 72, a botanical garden

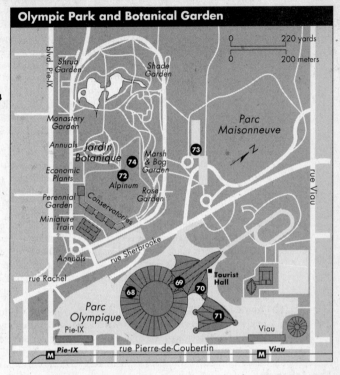

Olympic Park and Botanical Garden

that is the second-largest attraction of its kind in the world. It includes the **Insectarium** ⑦ and the 5-acre **Montréal-Shanghai Lac de Rêve** ⑦, an elegant Ming-style garden.

After you've looked at the flowers, return to boulevard Pie-IX, which runs along the western border of the gardens. The name of this traffic artery (and the adjoining Métro station) puzzles thousands of visitors every year. The street is named for the 19th-century pope, Pius IX, or Pie IX in French. It's pronounced Pee-neuf, however, which isn't at all how it looks from an English-speaker's standpoint.

TIMING

To see all the sights at a leisurely pace, you'll need a full day.

Sights to See

⌚ ⑦ **Biodôme.** Not everyone thought it was a great idea to change an Olympic bicycle-racing stadium into a natural-history exhibit, but the result is one of the city's most popular attractions. It combines four ecosystems—the boreal forest, tropical forest, polar world, and St. Lawrence River—under one climate-controlled dome. You follow protected pathways through each environment, observing flora and fauna of each ecosystem. A word of warning: The tropical forest really is tropical. If you want to stay comfortable, dress in layers. ⊠ *4777 av. Pierre-de-Coubertin,* ☎ *514/868–3000.* ⊡ *$9.50.* ⊙ *June 18–Sept. 9, daily 9–8; Sept. 10–June 17, daily 9–6.*

⌚ ⑦ **Centre Aquatique.** Olympic swimmers competed here in 1976, but anyone can use the six swimming pools now. ⊠ *4141 av. Pierre-de-Coubertin,* ☎ *514/252–4622.* ⊙ *Weekdays 9–9, weekends 1–4.* ⊡ *$3.30.*

⌚ ⑦ **Insectarium.** A bug-shape building in the ☞ **Jardin Botanique** houses more than 250,000 insect specimens. Visit in February and you can taste such delicacies as deep-fried bumblebees.

★ ☞ ⑦ **Jardin Botanique.** This botanical garden, with 181 acres of gardens in summer and 10 exhibition greenhouses open all year, is the second-largest attraction of its kind in the world (after England's Kew Gardens). The garden was founded in 1931 and has more than 26,000 species of plants. The poisonous plant garden is a perennial favorite. You can see a traditional tea ceremony in the Japanese Garden, which also has one of the best bonsai collections in the West. Other highlights are the ☞ Insectarium and the ☞ Montréal-Shanghai Lac de Rêve. ⊠ 4101 rue Sherbrooke Est, ☎ 514/872–1400. ☜ May–Oct. $8.75; Nov.–Apr. $6.50; combined ticket for Biodôme and Jardin Botanique $14.75. ☉ Daily 9–6. Metro: Pie-IX.

⑭ **Montréal-Shanghai Lac de Rêve.** These five acres in the ☞ Jardin Botanique are the largest Ming-style Chinese garden outside Asia, with seven elegant pavilions and a 30-ft rockery built around a reflecting pool.

⑱ **Stade Olympique.** The stadium, built for the 1976 summer games, is beautiful to look at but not very practical. It's hard to heat and the retractable fabric roof, supported by the tower, has never worked properly. Nevertheless, it's home to the National League's Expos and is used for events like Montréal's annual car show. ⊠ 4141 av. Pierre-de-Coubertin, ☎ 514/252–8687.

⑲ **Tour Olympique.** A trip to the top of this tower, the world's tallest tilting structure, is very popular; a two-level cable car can whisk 90 people up the exterior of the 890-ft tower. On a clear day you can see up to 80 km (50 mi) from the tower-top observatory.

The Islands

Expo '67—the world fair staged to celebrate the centennial of the Canadian federation—was the biggest party in Montréal's history, and it marked a defining moment in the city's evolution as a modern metropolis. That party was held on two islands in the middle of the St. Lawrence River—Ile Ste-Hélène, which was formed by nature, and Ile Notre-Dame, which was created by humans out of the stone rubble excavated for Montréal's Métro. The two islands are still a playground—the Parc des Iles has a major amusement park, acres of flower gardens, a beach with clean filtered water, and the Casino de Montréal. There's history, too, at the Old Fort where soldiers in colonial uniforms display the military skills of ancient wars. In winter you can skate on the old Olympic rowing basin or slide down iced trails on an inner tube. You can get information on most of the activities and attractions at Parc des Iles by phoning (☎ 514/872–6222).

A Good Walk

Start at the Ile Ste-Hélène station on the Métro's Yellow Line. The first thing you'll see when you emerge will be the huge geodesic dome that houses **Biosphere,** an environmental exhibition center. From the Biosphere walk to the northern shore and then east through the Parc des Iles to the **Old Fort,** now a museum of colonial life and a parade ground. Just east of the Old Fort past the Pont Jacques-Cartier (Jacques Cartier Bridge) is **La Ronde,** an amusement park.

Now cross over to the island's southern shore and walk back along the waterfront to the Cosmos Footbridge that leads to Ile Notre-Dame. On the way you'll pass the Restaurant Hélène de Champlain (☞ Dining, *below*), which probably has the prettiest setting of any restaurant in Montréal, and the military cemetery of the British garrison stationed on Ile Ste-Hélène from 1828 to 1870.

Ile Notre-Dame is laced by a network of canals and ponds, and the grounds are brilliant with flower gardens left from the 1980 Floralies Internationales flower show. Most of the Expo '67 buildings are gone, the victims of time and weather. One that has remained, however, is the fanciful French Pavilion. It and the neighboring Québec Pavilion have been turned into the **Casino de Montréal.** A five-minute walk west of the Casino is the Lac de l'Ile Notre-Dame, site of **Plage de l'Ile Notre Dame,** Montréal's only beach. In mid-June Ile Notre-Dame is the site of the Player's Grand Prix du Canada, a top Formula 1 international auto race at the **Circuit Gilles Villeneuve.**

After your walk you can either return to the Métro or walk back to the city via the Pont de la Concorde and the Parc de la Cité du Havre to Vieux-Montréal. If you walk, you'll see **Habitat '67,** an irregular pile of prefabricated concrete blocks that was built as an experiment in housing for Expo.

TIMING

This is a comfortable two-hour stroll, but the Biosphere and the Old Fort (try to time your visit to coincide with a drill display by the colonial troops of the Fraser Highlanders and the Compagnie Franche de la Marine, ☞ *below*) deserve at least an hour each, and you should leave another half hour to admire the flowers. Children will want to spend a whole day at La Ronde, but the best time to go is in the evening when it's cooler. Try to visit the casino during a weekday when the crowds are at their thinnest.

Sights to See

Biosphere. An environmental center in the huge geodesic dome designed by Buckminster Fuller as the American Pavilion at Expo '67 successfully brings fun to an earnest project—heightening awareness of the St. Lawrence River system and its problems. ⊠ *Ile St-Hélène,* ☎ *514/496–8300.* ☞ *$6.50.* ☉ *June–Sept., daily 10–5; Oct.–May, Tues.–Sun., 10–5.*

★ **Casino de Montréal.** This spectacular building was built as the French Pavilion for Expo '67, Montréal's world fair. It's now one of the biggest gambling palaces in the world (☞ Nightlife and the Arts, *below*). ⊠ *Ile Notre-Dame.*

Circuit Gilles Villeneuve. All the big names in motor sports gather at this track every summer for the Player's Grand Prix, one of the racing season's most important Formula 1 events. One of the hottest stars these days is Québécois driver Jacques Villeneuve. The track is named for his father, Gilles, who was killed in a racing crash in Belgium in 1982. ⊠ *Ile Notre-Dame.*

Habitat '67. This private apartment complex, a pile of concrete blocks that resembles an updated version of a Hopi cliff dwelling, was designed by Moshe Safdie and built as an experiment in housing for Expo. ⊠ *Av. Pierre-Dupuy.*

☾ **Old Fort.** In summer the grassy parade square of this fine stone fort comes alive with the crackle of colonial musket fire. The French are represented by the Compagnie Franche de la Marine and the British by the kilted 78th Fraser Highlanders, one of the regiments that participated in the conquest of Québec in 1759. The fort itself, built to protect Montréal from American invasion, is now Stewart Museum at the Fort, which tells the story of colonial life in Montréal through displays of old firearms, maps, and uniforms. The two companies of colonial soldiers raise the flag every day at 11, practice their maneuvers at 1, put on a combined display of precision drilling and musket fire at 2:30, and lower the flag at 5. Children can participate. ⊠ *Ile Ste-Hélène,* ☎ *514/861–6701.* ☞ *$5.* ⊘ *Summer, Wed.–Mon. 10–6; winter, Wed.–Mon. 10–5.*

Plage de l'Ile Notre-Dame. This strip of sand is often filled to capacity in summer. The swimming beach is an oasis, with clear, filtered lake water, and an inviting stretch of lawn and trees. Lifeguards are on duty; there is a shop that rents swimming and boating paraphernalia, and there are picnic areas and a restaurant. ☞ *$3.* ⊘ *Daily.*

🐥 **La Ronde.** A world-class amusement park has Ferris wheels, boat rides, simulator-style rides, and the second-highest roller coaster in the world. It is also the site of the popular Benson & Hedges International Fireworks Competition, which takes place every weekend in June and July. ⊠ *Ile Ste-Hélène,* ☎ *514/872–6222.* ☞ *$24.75, grounds only (no rides) $13.* ⊘ *May, weekends 10–9; June 1–20, daily 10–9; June 21–Sept. 2, daily 11–11; fireworks June–July, weekends, 10 AM–midnight.*

DINING

Montréal has more than 4,500 restaurants of every price range, representing dozens of ethnic groups. When you dine out, you can, of course, order à la carte, choosing each course yourself. But look for the table d'hôte, a kind of two- to four-course package deal. It's usually cheaper, often offers interesting special dishes, and may also take less time to prepare. If you want to splurge with your time and money, indulge yourself with the *menu de dégustation,* a five- to seven-course dinner executed by the chef. It generally includes soup, salad, fish, sherbet (to refresh the taste buds), a meat dish, dessert, and coffee or tea. At the city's finest restaurants, such a meal for two, along with a good bottle of wine, can cost more than $200 and last four hours; it's worth every cent and every second.

A word about language: Menus in many restaurants are bilingual, but some are in French only. If you don't understand what a dish is, don't be shy about asking; a good server will be delighted to explain. If you feel brave enough to order in French, remember that in French an entrée is an appetizer and what English-speakers call an entrée is a *plat principal,* or main dish.

CATEGORY	COST*
$$$$	over $30
$$$	$20–$30
$$	$10–$20
$	under $10

per person without tax (combined GST of 7% and provincial tax of 6.5% on all meals), service, or drinks.

Chinese

$$–$$$ ✕ **Chez Chine.** The restaurant sits beside a miniature lake full of fat goldfish and crossed by little stone bridges that zig and zag to fool evil spirits. The menu has more than a page of shark-fin specialties, along with such delicacies as a clay pot full of sautéed beef slices that have been stir-fried with fresh ginger, green onions, and oyster sauce. ⊠ *Holiday Inn Select, 99 rue Viger Ouest,* ☎ *514/878–9888.* AE, D, DC, MC, V.

$$–$$$ ✕ **Zen.** This very fine modern restaurant specializes in "Zen fusion." Asian dishes combining styles from China, Thailand, Indonesia, and Malaysia are all presented with artistic flair. For $26 try the "Zen Ex-

perience," picking as many items as you want from a menu of 40 magnificently prepared Szechuan items. ⊠ *Le Westin Mont-Royal, 1050 rue Sherbrooke Ouest,* ☎ *514/499–0801. Reservations essential. AE, DC, MC, V.*

$$ ✕ **Maison Kam Fung.** This bright, airy restaurant serves the most reliable dim sum lunch in Chinatown. Every day from 10 to 3, waiters push a parade of trolleys through the restaurant, carting treats like firm dumplings stuffed with pork and chicken, stir-fried squid, and delicate pastry envelopes filled with shrimp. ⊠ *1008 rue Clark,* ☎ *514/878–2888. Reservations not accepted for dim sum. AE, MC, V.*

Continental

$$$$ ✕ **Nuances.** The main restaurant at the Casino de Montréal on Ile Notre-
★ Dame is simply stunning. Diners sit amid rosewood paneling and have a magnificent view of the city. Start with sautéed duck foie gras with exotic fruits and progress to lightly grilled red tuna with vegetables marinated in balsamic vinegar and olive oil. Even dishes that have been approved by the Québec Heart and Stroke Foundation sound exciting, like the saddle of rabbit pot-au-feu served with mushrooms. ⊠ *1 av. de Casino,* ☎ *514/392–2708. Reservations essential. AE, DC, MC, V. No lunch.*

Delicatessens

$ ✕ **Bens.** This big brassy deli features cheesecake smothered in chocolate sauce, drinks the color of electric cherry juice, and a "Big Ben Sandwich"—two slices of rye bread enclosing a pink pile of juicy smoked meat (Montréal's version of corned beef). The decor is strictly '50s, with yellow and green walls and institutional furniture. The waiters are often wisecracking characters but incredibly efficient. Beer, wine, and cocktails are served. ⊠ *990 blvd. de Maisonneuve Ouest,* ☎ *514/844–1000. Reservations not accepted. MC, V.*

$ ✕ **Schwartz's Delicatessen.** Its proper name is the Montreal Hebrew Delicatessen, but everyone calls it Schwartz's. The sandwiches are huge; the steaks are tender and come with grilled liver appetizers. To drink you'll find nothing stronger than a Coke. The furniture looks like it was rescued from a Salvation Army depot and the waiters are briskly efficient. Don't ask for a menu (there isn't one) and avoid the lunch hour unless you don't mind long lines. ⊠ *3895 blvd. St-Laurent,* ☎ *514/842–4813. Reservations not accepted. No credit cards.*

$ ✕ **Wilensky's Light Lunch.** Since 1932 the Wilensky family has served up its special: salami and bologna on a "Jewish" (kaiser) roll, generously slathered with mustard. You can also get a chopped-egg sandwich, which comes with a pickle and a cherry or pineapple cola from the fountain (there's no liquor license). This neighborhood haunt was a setting for the film *The Apprenticeship of Duddy Kravitz,* from the novel by Mordecai Richler. ⊠ *34 rue Fairmount Ouest,* ☎ *514/271–0247. Reservations not accepted. No credit cards. Closed weekends.*

French

$$$$ ✕ **Beaver Club.** This fine French restaurant was a social club for the city's elite in the 19th century, and it still has the atmosphere of an exclusive men's club, even if it's open to anyone with a reservation. The Beaver Club specializes in such classics as roast prime rib of beef au jus and duck à l'orange, but in keeping with the times, lunch offerings tend to be lighter and include three fish dishes. There's dancing here on Saturday. Service is excellent, and the bar serves the best martini in the city. ⊠ *Le Reine Elizabeth hotel, 900 blvd. René-Lévesque Ouest,*

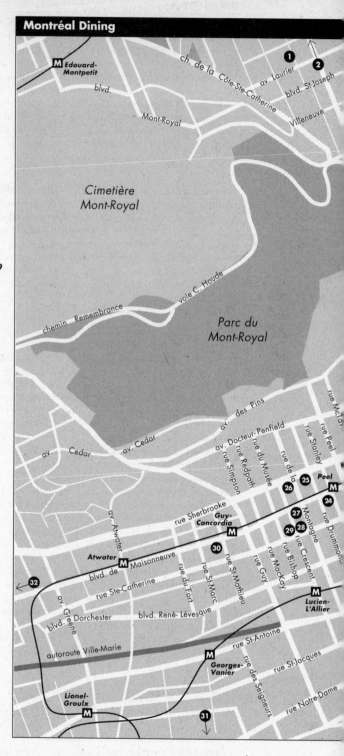

Montréal Dining

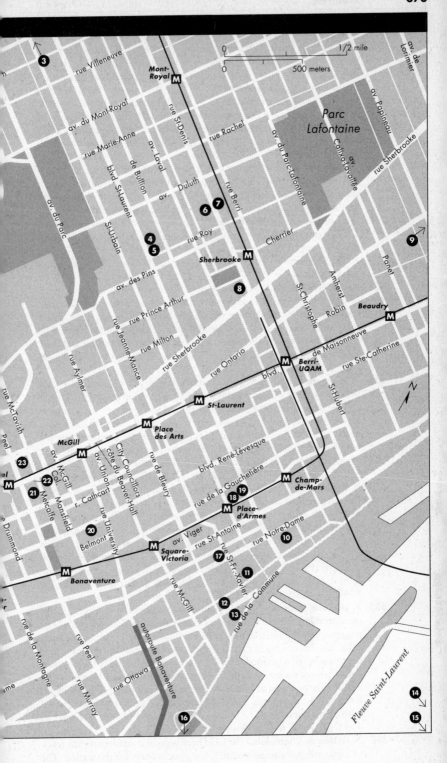

☎ 514/861–3511. *Jacket and tie. AE, D, DC, MC, V. Closed Sun. and July. No dinner Mon.*

$$$$ ╳ **Le Café de Paris.** Patrons sit at large, well-spaced tables in a room ablaze with flowers and with light streaming through the French windows. The Ritz garden, with its picturesque duck pond, is open for summer dining alfresco. You can choose from such classics as *escalope de veau Viennoise* or steak tartare. At meal's end the waiter will trundle over the dessert cart; the *royale chocolat* and the *îles flottant* (puffs of soft meringue in custard) are favorites. ⊠ *Ritz-Carlton Kempinski, 1228 rue Sherbrooke Ouest,* ☎ *514/842–4212. Reservations essential. Jacket required. AE, D, DC, MC, V.*

$$$$ ╳ **Les Halles.** The restaurant brightened its Paris-market decor of mirrors and murals with lighter colors in 1996, but the cuisine hasn't changed. Main dishes like Grapefruit Marie-Louise with scallops and lobster or roasted duck with pears sit comfortably beside the chef's ventures into nouvelle cuisine, such as his lobster with herbs and butter. The desserts are classic—the Paris-Brest, a puff pastry with praline cream inside, is one of the best in town. ⊠ *1450 rue Crescent,* ☎ *514/844–2328. Reservations essential. AE, DC, MC, V. Closed Sun. No lunch Mon. or Sat.*

$$$$ ╳ **Les Trois Tilleuls.** About an hour southeast of town, you can lunch or dine on delectable food right on the Rivière Richelieu. This small, romantic inn, one of the prestigious Relais et Châteaux chain, has a terrace and a large, airy dining room with beautiful sunset views. The chef specializes in cream of onion soup, sweetbreads, and game dishes. ⊠ *290 rue Richelieu, St-Marc sur Richelieu,* ☎ *514/584–2231. Reservations essential. AE, DC, MC, V.*

$$$ ╳ **Allumette.** This exciting little restaurant with rich red walls and plain
★   white tables has won rave reviews since it opened in mid-1996. Dishes include such delicacies as cream of prawn and split-pea soup, rabbit-stuffed ravioli, pasta with snails, oven-cooked salmon with baby navy beans and tomato confits, and honey-and-lemon-braised suckling pig with fried ginger. For dessert, try the soup of fresh apricot slices in fresh orange juice with an apple and lime sherbet in the middle. ⊠ *3434 rue St-Denis,* ☎ *514/284–4239. AE, D, DC, MC, V. No lunch weekends.*

$$$ ╳ **Bonaparte.** In this wonderful little restaurant in the heart of Vieux-
★   Montréal, piped-in Mozart serenades diners surrounded by exposed brick walls. The traditional French dishes here have a light touch. You could start with a wild-mushroom ravioli seasoned with fresh sage and move on to a lobster stew flavored with vanilla and served with a spinach fondue, or a roast rack of lamb in a Port wine sauce. Lunch is a good value. In 1997 the restaurant added a room with a fireplace and is planning a little auberge upstairs. ⊠ *443 rue St-François-Xavier,* ☎ *514/844–4368. AE, D, DC, MC, V. No lunch weekends.*

$$$ ╳ **Guy and Dodo Morali.** Pale yellow walls and lots of art decorate this comfortable restaurant in the very exclusive Cours Mont-Royal shopping plaza. In summer, dining spills out onto a little terrace on rue Metcalfe. Guy's cooking is classic French with a splash of modern flair; his menu is 70% seafood. His daily table d'hôte menu is the best bet, with openers such as excellent lobster bisque followed by *agneau en croute* (lamb in a pastry) with thyme sauce (a house specialty), or fillet of halibut with leeks. For dessert try the *tatan,* apples and caramel with crème anglaise. ⊠ *Les Cours Mont-Royal, 1444 rue Metcalfe,* ☎ *514/842–3636. Reservations essential. AE, D, DC, MC, V.*

$$$ ╳ **Hélène de Champlain.** The food here is good if unadventurous (rack of lamb, fillet of sole amandine), but people come for the setting. The restaurant is in the middle of the park on Ile Ste-Hélène, with views over the river and the city. The large dining room with its fireplace and antique furnishings is delightful. ⊠ *Ile Ste-Hélène near Métro station,* ☎ *514/395–2424. Reservations essential. AE, DC, MC, V.*

$$$ ✕ **Le Passe-Partout.** New York–born James MacGuire might make the
★ best bread in Montréal—moist but airy with a tight, crispy crust. He and his wife, Suzanne Baron-Lafrenière, sell this delicacy, along with homemade pâtés and terrines, in a bakery next door to their restaurant. The handwritten menu is short and changes according to mood and availability. You might start with smoked salmon, a potage of curried sweet potatoes, or perhaps a venison terrine. Entrées include swordfish steak served with a purée of red cabbage or loin of veal with poached cucumbers and noodles. ⊠ *3857 blvd. Décarie (5-min walk south from Ville-Marie Métro),* ☎ *514/487–7750. Reservations essential. AE, DC, MC, V. No lunch Sat.–Mon., no dinner Sun.–Wed.*

$$$ ✕ **Toqué.** The name means "a bit crazy." Its young and innovative chef-
★ owner, Normand Laprise, and partner Christin LaMarche are among the best and most eccentric chefs in the city. They whip market-fresh ingredients into dazzling combinations and colors. The menu often features salmon tournedos, smoked salmon, and warm foie gras, all flavored with fresh ingredients like red peppers, thinly shredded leeks, celery roots, and Québec goat cheese. The portions don't look big but are surprisingly filling. ⊠ *3842 rue St-Denis,* ☎ *514/499–2084. Reservations essential. MC, V.*

$$–$$$ ✕ **L'Express.** This Paris-style bistro has mirrored walls, a smoky atmosphere and noise levels that are close to painful on weekends. But the food's good, the service fast, and the prices reasonable. The steak tartare with French fries, the salmon with sorrel, and the calves' liver with tarragon are marvelous. Jars of gherkins, fresh baguettes, and cheeses aged to perfection make the pleasure last longer. L'Express has one of the best and most original wine cellars in town. ⊠ *3927 rue St-Denis,* ☎ *514/845–5333. Reservations essential. AE, DC, MC, V.*

Greek

$$$$ ✕ **Milos.** Nets, ropes, and floats hang from Milos's walls and ceilings. The real display, however, is in the refrigerated cases and on the beds of ice in the back by the kitchen—octopus, squid, shrimp, crabs, oysters, and sea urchins. The main dish at Milos is usually fish grilled over charcoal and seasoned with parsley, capers, and lemon juice. It's done to a turn and is achingly delicious. The fish are priced by the pound, and you can order one large fish to serve two or more. You'll also find lamb and veal chops, cheeses, and olives. Milos is a healthy walk from Métro Laurier. ⊠ *5357 av. du Parc,* ☎ *514/272–3522. Reservations essential. AE, D, DC, MC, V. No lunch Sat.*

Indian

$$–$$$ ✕ **Le Taj.** The cuisine of the north of India is produced here, less spicy and more refined than that of the south. The tandoori ovens seal in the flavors of the grilled meat and fish. Vegetarian dishes include the *taj-thali,* made of lentils; basmati rice; and *saag panir*—spicy white cheese with spinach. A nine-course lunch buffet is under $10, and at night there's an "Indian feast" for $20. The desserts—pistachio ice cream or mangoes—are often decorated with pure silver leaves. ⊠ *2077 rue Stanley,* ☎ *514/845–9015. AE, MC, V.*

Italian

$$$ ✕ **Bocca d'Oro.** This restaurant next to Métro Guy has a huge menu. One pasta specialty is *tritico di pasta*: one helping each of spinach ravioli with salmon and caviar, shellfish marinara, and spaghetti prima-

vera. Also recommended is the *pasta mistariosa*—no cream, no butter, no tomatoes, but delicious nonetheless. With dessert and coffee, the waiters bring out a bowl of walnuts for you to crack at your table. The two-floor dining area is inexplicably decorated with a huge display of golf pictures, and Italian pop songs play in the background. The staff is extremely friendly and professional; if you're in a hurry, they'll serve your meal in record time. ⊠ *1448 rue St-Mathieu,* ☎ *514/933–8414. Reservations essential. AE, DC, MC, V. Closed Sun.*

$$ ✕ **Pizzaiole.** Pizzaiole brought the first wood-fired pizza ovens to Montréal, and it's still the best in the field. Whether you choose a simple tomato-cheese or a ratatouille on a whole-wheat crust—there are about 30 possible combinations—all the pizzas are made to order and brought to your table piping hot. The calzone is worth the trip. ⊠ *1446-A rue Crescent,* ☎ *514/845–4158;* ⊠ *5100 rue Hutchison,* ☎ *514/274–9349. AE, DC, MC, V.*

Japanese

$$$–$$$$ ✕ **Katsura.** The sushi chefs in this elegant Japanese restaurant create an assortment of raw seafood delicacies, as well as their own delicious invention, the cone-shaped Canada roll (smoked salmon and salmon caviar). Service is excellent, but if you sample all the sushi, the tab can be exorbitant. ⊠ *2170 rue de la Montagne,* ☎ *514/849–1172. Reservations essential. AE, DC, MC, V. No lunch weekends.*

Polish

$$–$$$ ✕ **Café Stash.** On chilly nights many Montrealers turn to Café Stash in Vieux-Montréal for sustenance—for pork chops or duck, hot borscht, pierogies, or cabbages and sausage—in short, for all the hearty specialties of a Polish kitchen. Diners sit on pews from an old chapel at refectory tables from an old convent. ⊠ *200 rue St-Paul Ouest,* ☎ *514/845–6611. AE, MC, V.*

Québécois

$–$$ ✕ **Chez Clo.** Deep in east-end Montréal, where seldom is heard an English word, lies that rarest of the city's culinary finds—authentic Québécois food. A meal could start with a bowl of the best pea soup in the city, followed by a slab of *tourtière* (meat pie), mounds of mashed potatoes, carrots and turnips, and a bowl of gravy on the side. Desserts include bread pudding and several flavors of *renversées* (upside-down cakes). But the restaurant specialty is *pudding au chomeur* (literally, pudding for the unemployed), a kind of shortcake smothered in a thick brown sugar sauce. The service is noisy and friendly and the clientele mostly local. ⊠ *3199 rue Ontario Est,* ☎ *514/522–5348. No credit cards.*

Sausages

$ ✕ **Chez Better.** Rustic fieldstone walls and casement windows create a classy ambience for this North American branch of a popular European sausage house. Although the decor is upscale, the limited menu keeps prices down, to only $3.95 in the case of the "Better Special," a satisfying sandwich of a sausage on freshly baked bread. It's a convenient refueling stop if you're touring Vieux-Montréal. This Notre-Dame restaurant is the most elegant of three "Betters." ⊠ *160 rue Notre-Dame Est,* ☎ *514/861–2617;* ⊠ *5400 chemin Côte-des-Neiges;* ⊠ *2133 boulevard le Carrefour. AE, MC, V.*

Seafood

$$$ ✕ **Bleu Marin.** Fish here comes with an Italian touch. You can start, for example, with antipasto Bleu Marin, which includes little plates of baby clams, mussels, and oysters with a light gratinée of crumbs and cheese. All fish are baked or steamed; a main course could be fillets of sea bass, baked in their own juices along with traces of olive oil, lemon juice, white wine, and capers.✉ *1437-A rue Crescent,* ☎ *514/847–1123. AE, D, DC, MC, V.*

$$$ ✕ **Chez Delmo.** The long shiny wooden bar at Chez Delmo is crammed at lunchtime with lawyers and businessmen gobbling oysters and fish. In the back is a more relaxed and cheerful dining room. The poached salmon with hollandaise is a nice slab of perfectly cooked fish served with potatoes and broccoli. Also excellent are the Arctic char and the Dover sole. The service is efficient and low-key. ✉ *211–215 rue Notre-Dame Ouest,* ☎ *514/849–4061. Reservations essential. AE, DC, MC, V. Closed Sun., 3 wks in midsummer and 3 wks at Christmas.*

Steak

$$$ ✕ **Gibby's.** While the extensive menu is rich in items like broiled lob-
★ ster, Dover sole meunière, and Cajun-blackened grouper, it was Gibby's first-class steaks—some say the best in the city—that made this restaurant famous. Gibby's also boasts its own on-site bakery and makes its own ice cream. The thick gray stone walls here date to 1825, and the attention to service and detail also seems to belong to another age. ✉ *298 Pl. d'Youville,* ☎ *514/282–1837. AE, D, DC, MC, V.*

$$$ ✕ **Moishe's.** The steaks here are big and marbled, and the Lighter brothers still age them in their own cold rooms for 21 days before charcoal grilling them, just the way their father did when he opened Moishe's more than 50 years ago. There are other things on the menu, such as lamb and grilled Arctic char—but people come for the beef. There's an exquisite selection of single-malt Scotches. ✉ *3961 blvd. St-Laurent,* ☎ *514/845–3509. AE, DC, MC, V. No lunch.*

$–$$ ✕ **Magnan.** The atmosphere in this tavern in working-class Pointe St-Charles is decidedly and defiantly masculine. The decor is upscale warehouse and the half-dozen television sets are noisily stuck on professional sports. You can't beat the roast beef, though, and the industrial-strength steaks that range from 6 to 22 ounces. And everyone eats here—from dock workers to corporate executives. It also has excellent beer from several local microbreweries on tap. ✉ *2602 rue St-Patrick,* ☎ *514/935–9647. Reservations essential. AE, DC, MC, V.*

LODGING

Keep in mind that during peak season (May–August) it may be difficult to find a bed without reserving, and most, but not all, hotels raise their prices. Rates often drop from mid-November to early April. Throughout the year a number of the better hotels have two-night, three-day, double-occupancy packages that offer substantial discounts.

CATEGORY	COST*
$$$$	over $160
$$$	$120–$160
$$	$85–$120
$	under $85

All prices are for a standard double room, excluding 13.5% tax and gratuities.

$$$$ ⊞ **Bonaventure Hilton International.** The large Hilton occupies the top
★ three floors of the Place Bonaventure exhibition center. From the outside the massive building is uninviting, but you step off the elevator
into an attractive reception area flanked by an outdoor swimming pool
(heated year-round) and 2½ acres of gardens. All rooms have sleek modern furniture, pastel walls, and TVs in the bathrooms. The Bonaventure has excellent access to the Métro and the Underground City.
✉ *1 Pl. Bonaventure, H5A 1E4,* ☎ *514/878–2332 or 800/267–2575,*
FAX *514/028–1442. 393 rooms. 3 restaurants, minibars, room service,
pool, shops, business services. AE, D, DC, MC, V.*

$$$$ ⊞ **Le Centre Sheraton.** This huge 37-story complex is well placed between the downtown business district and the restaurant-lined streets
of Crescent and Bishop. It offers services to both the business and tourist
crowds. Rooms have coffee makers, irons, and ironing boards. The 10-
story Club section is geared toward business travelers, and there are
lots of meeting rooms for conventions. The hotel began renovating its
guest rooms in 1996. The bar in the busy lobby is in a pleasant forest
of potted trees, some of them 30 ft tall. ✉ *1201 blvd. René-Lévesque
Ouest, H3B 2L7,* ☎ *514/878–2000 or 800/325–3535,* FAX *514/878–
3958. 784 rooms, 25 suites. Restaurant, 2 bars, indoor pool, beauty
salon, health club with whirlpool and sauna, baby-sitting, business services. AE, D, DC, MC, V.*

$$$$ ⊞ **Hôtel Complexe Desjardins.** A 12-story hotel rises from the center
of the Complexe Desjardins, a boutique-rich mall in the middle of the
Underground City. The ultramodern property has blond wood and
leather chairs, a huge lobby overlooking a glassed-in swimming pool,
and a stainless-steel-and-glass elevator that looks like a space module.
Guest rooms have sleek modern furniture with rounded edges and a
shiny finish. Chinatown is a five-minute walk away. ✉ *4 Complexe
Desjardins, C.P. 130, H5B 1E5,* ☎ *514/285–1450 or 800/543–4300,*
FAX *514/285–1243. 572 rooms, 28 suites. 3 restaurants, piano bar, indoor pool, hot tub, sauna, exercise room, baby-sitting, business services. AE, D, DC, MC, V.*

$$$$ ⊞ **Hotel Inter-Continental Montréal.** On the edge of Vieux-Montréal,
this luxury hotel is part of the Montréal World Trade Center, a block-
long retail and office development. Rooms are in a modern 24-story
brick tower with fanciful turrets and pointed roofs. They're large,
with lush carpets, pastel walls, heavy drapes, and big windows overlooking either downtown or Vieux-Montréal and the waterfront. The
main lobby is home to Le Continent Restaurant, which serves fine
international cuisine. ✉ *360 rue St-Antoine Ouest, H2Y 3X4,*
☎ *514/987–9900 or 800/327–0200, 800/361–3600 in the U.S. and
Canada,* FAX *514/847–8550. 335 rooms, 22 suites. 2 restaurants, bar,
room service, indoor pool, sauna, health club, concierge, meeting
rooms. AE, D, DC, MC, V.*

$$$$ ⊞ **Loews Hôtel Vogue.** Tall windows and a facade of polished rose gran-
★ ite grace this chic hotel in the heart of downtown, right across the street
from Ogilvy department store. The lobby's focal point, L'Opéra Bar,
has an expansive bay window overlooking the trendy rue de la Montagne. Room furnishings are upholstered with striped silk, and the
beds are draped with lacy duvets. The bathrooms have whirlpool
baths, televisions, and phones. ✉ *1425 rue de la Montagne, H3G 1Z3,*
☎ *514/285–5555 or 800/465–6654,* FAX *514/849–8903. 126 rooms,
16 suites. Restaurant, bar, exercise room. AE, D, DC, MC, V.*

$$$$ ⊞ **Le Reine Elizabeth.** In the center of the city, this Canadian Pacific
hotel sits on top of the Gare Centrale train station. The lobby is a bit
too much like a railroad station—hordes march this way and that—
but upstairs the rooms are modern, spacious, and spotless, with lush
pale carpets, striped Regency wallpapers, and chintz bedspreads. The

Penthouse floors—20 and 21—have business services, and the Gold Floor is a hotel within a hotel with its own elevator, check-in, and concierge. The hotel is home to the Beaver Club (☞ Dining, *above*). Conventions are a specialty here. ⊠ *900 blvd. René-Lévesque Ouest, H3B 4A5,* ☎ *514/861–3511 or 800/441–1414,* ℻ *514/954–2256. 1,020 rooms. 2 restaurants, 3 bars, indoor pool, beauty salon, health club, baby-sitting. AE, D, DC, MC, V.*

$$$$ 🏨 **Ritz-Carlton Kempinski.** This is the closest Montréal comes to a grand
★ hotel. Power meals are the rule at the elegant Café de Paris (☞ Dining, *above*). Guest rooms are a successful blend of Edwardian style— some suites have working fireplaces—with such modern accessories as electronic safes. Careful and personal attention are hallmarks of the Ritz-Carlton's service: your shoes get shined, there's fresh fruit in your room, and everyone calls you by name. It was good enough for Elizabeth Taylor and Richard Burton, who celebrated one of their weddings here. ⊠ *1228 rue Sherbrooke Ouest, H3G 1H6,* ☎ *514/842–4212 or 800/223–6800,* ℻ *514/842–3383. 201 rooms, 39 suites. Restaurant, bar, piano bar, room service, barbershop. AE, DC, MC, V.*

$$$$ 🏨 **Le Westin Mont-Royal.** Service and hospitality make the Westin
★ stand out among Montréal's best hotels. Its concierge desk can organize anything. The clientele here is primarily corporate, and the large rooms are decorated to serve that market: floral chintzes, plush carpeting, and traditional English furnishings. One of the city's best Chinese restaurants is the Zen (☞ Dining, *above*), downstairs. In 1997 the Westin revamped its ground floor, opening Opus II, a contemporary French restaurant, with a glassed-in atrium. ⊠ *1050 rue Sherbrooke Ouest, H3A 2R6,* ☎ *514/284–1110 or 800/228–3000,* ℻ *514/845– 3025. 300 rooms, 28 suites. 2 restaurants, lobby lounge, minibars, room service, pool, hot tub, 2 saunas, health club. AE, D, DC, MC, V.*

$$$ 🏨 **Delta Montréal.** The Delta has the most complete exercise and pool facility in Montréal and an extensive business center. The hotel's public areas spread over two stories and are decorated to look a bit like a French château, with a huge baronial chandelier and gold patterned carpets. Rooms are big, with plush broadloom, pastel walls, mahogany-veneer furniture, and windows that overlook the mountain or downtown. The jazz bar serves lunch on weekdays. ⊠ *475 av. President-Kennedy, H3A 1J7,* ☎ *514/286–1986 or 800/268–1133,* ℻ *514/284–4306. 453 rooms, 10 suites. 2 restaurants, bar, indoor and outdoor pools, hot tub, sauna, aerobics, health club, squash, recreation room, video games, baby-sitting, business services. AE, D, DC, MC, V.*

$$$ 🏨 **Holiday Inn Select.** This Chinatown hotel is full of surprises, from
★ the two pagodas on the roof to the Chinese garden in the lobby. The hotel restaurant, Chez Chine (☞ Dining, *above*), is one of the best Chinese restaurants in Montréal. There's an executive floor with all the usual business facilities. The hotel has a pool and a small exercise room, but guests also have access to a plush private health and leisure club downstairs with a whirlpool, saunas, a billiard room, and a bar. The hotel is catercorner to the Palais des Congrès and a five-minute walk from the World Trade Center. ⊠ *99 av. Viger Ouest, H2Z 1E9,* ☎ *514/878–9888 or 888/878–9888,* ℻ *514/878–6341. 235 rooms. Restaurant, bar, pool, exercise room, business services. AE, D, DC, MC, V.*

$$$ 🏨 **Hôtel de la Montagne.** Upon entering the reception area you'll be
★ greeted by a naked, butterfly-winged nymph who rises out of a fountain; an enormous crystal chandelier hangs from the ceiling. The decor resembles Versailles rebuilt with a dash of Art Nouveau, although management prefers to describe it as a mix of Early American and Rococo. The rooms are tamer, large and comfortable. There's a piano bar

Auberge de la
Fontaine, **27**
Auberge du
Vieux-Port, **24**
Auberge Les Passants
du Sans Soucy, **22**
Bonaventure Hilton
International, **18**
Le Centre Sheraton, **7**
Château Versailles, **3**
Delta Montréal, **15**
Holiday Inn Select, **23**
Hostelling Montréal, **5**
Hôtel Complexe
Desjardins, **20**
Hôtel de la
Montagne, **8**
Hôtel du Fort, **2**
Hôtel du Parc, **14**
Hôtel Inter-Continental
Montréal, **21**
Hôtel Lord Berri, **25**
Hôtel Radisson des
Gouverneurs de
Montréal, **19**
Hôtel Thrift Lodge, **26**
Loews Hôtel Vogue, **9**
Le Marriott Château
Champlain, **16**
McGill Student
Apartments, **13**
Le Nouvel Hôtel, **4**
Le Reine Elizabeth, **17**
Ritz-Carlton
Kempinski, **11**
Université de Montréal
Residence, **1**
Le Westin
Mont-Royal, **12**
YMCA, **10**
YWCA, **6**

Montréal Lodging

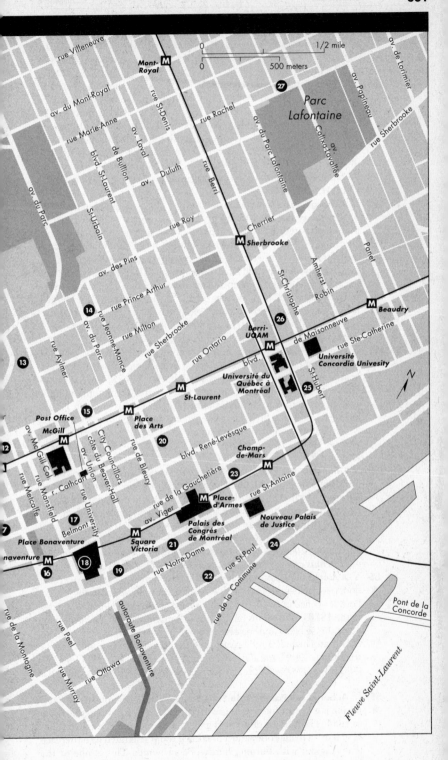

rue Villeneuve

Mont-
Royal M

av. du Mont-Royal

rue Marie-Anne

blvd. St-Laurent

av. du Parc

St-Urbain

rue St-Denis

de Bullion

av. Laval

Duluth

rue Roy

av. des Pins

rue Prince Arthur

rue Milton

rue Sherbrooke

rue Jeanne-Mance

av. du Parc

rue Aylmer

14

13

rue Rachel

rue Berri

27

Parc
Lafontaine

av. du Parc Lafontaine

av. Calix-Lavallée

av. Papineau

av. de Lorimier

rue Sherbrooke

Cherrier

Sherbrooke M

St-Christophe

Amherst

Robin

Panet

Beaudry M

de Maisonneuve

rue Ste-Catherine

Université
Concordia Univesity

Berri-
UQAM

26

rue Ontario

M

blvd.

Université du
Québec à
Montréal

St-Hubert

25

½ mile

500 meters

N

St-Laurent M

Place
des Arts

Post Office

McGill M

av. McGill Col.

15

M

20

City Councillor's

côte du Beaver-Hall

av. Union

blvd. René-Levésque

Champ-
de-Mars M

12

rue Mansfield

r. Cathcart

rue University

rue de Bleury

rue de la Gauchetière

23

rue St-Antoine

Place-
d'Armes M

av. Viger

Palais des
Congrés
de Montréal

Nouveau Palais
de Justice

rue St-Paul

24

7

Belmont

17

Place Bonaventure

Square
Victoria M

21

rue Notre-Dame

22

rue de la Commune

Pont de la
Concorde

naventure M

16

18

19

rue de la Montagne

rue Peel

autoroute Bonaventure

rue Ottawa

rue Murray

Fleuve Saint-Laurent

and a rooftop terrace, and a tunnel connects the hotel to Thursdays/ Les Beaux Jeudis—a popular singles bar, restaurant, and dance club. ⊠ *1430 rue de la Montagne, H3G 1Z5,* ☎ *514/288–5656 or 800/361– 6262,* FAX *514/288–9658. 135 rooms. 2 restaurants, bar, pool, concierge. AE, D, DC, MC, V.*

$$$ ⊡ **Le Marriott Château Champlain.** At the southern end of Place du Canada is this 36-floor skyscraper with distinctive half moon–shape windows that give the rooms a Moorish feel. The furniture is elegantly French and the bedspreads are brightly patterned. Underground passageways connect the Champlain with the Bonaventure Métro station and Place Ville-Marie. ⊠ *1050 rue de la Gauchetière, H3B 4C9,* ☎ *514/878–9000 or 800/200–5909,* FAX *514/878–6761. 616 rooms, 33 suites. Restaurant, bar, no-smoking rooms, indoor pool, sauna, health club. AE, DC, MC, V.*

$$–$$$ ⊡ **Auberge de la Fontaine.** The decor of this small hotel in the heart ★   of the trendy Plateau Mont-Royal district sounds wild—contrasting purple and bare-brick walls, a red molding separating yellow walls from a green ceiling—but the hotel is delightful. Its 21 rooms are scattered over three floors in two turn-of-the-century residences. Some of them have whirlpool baths and a few have private balconies. Guests can use the little ground-floor kitchen and take whatever they like from its fridge full of snacks. The hotel is right on one of the city's bicycle paths and just across the street from Parc Lafontaine. ⊠ *1301 rue Rachel Est, H2J 2K1,* ☎ *514/597–0166 or 800/597–0597,* FAX *514/597–0496. 21 rooms with bath. Meeting room. AE, DC, MC, V.*

$$–$$$ ⊡ **Hôtel du Fort.** All rooms here have good views of the city, the river, or the mountain. The hotel is in the west end of downtown in a residential neighborhood known as Shaughnessy Village, close to shopping at the Faubourg Ste-Catherine and Square Westmount, and just around the corner from the Canadian Center for Architecture. Rates include Continental breakfast served in the charming Louis XV Lounge, which doubles as a bar in the evening. ⊠ *1390 rue du Fort, H3H 2R7,* ☎ *514/938–8333 or 800/565–6333,* FAX *514/938–2078. 127 rooms. Exercise room. AE, DC, MC, V.*

$$–$$$ ⊡ **Hôtel du Parc.** This L-shaped brick tower northwest overlooks Parc du Mont-Royal; the McGill University campus is a 5-minute walk to the west. The hotel is a briskly efficient operation, the rooms are large, and the decor is modern with lots of blond wood and pastel shades. A large, comfortable bar dominates the lobby. ⊠ *3625 av. du Parc, H2X 3P8,* ☎ *514/288–6666 or 800/363–0735,* FAX *514/288–2469. 429 rooms, 20 suites. Restaurant, bar, café, no-smoking floors, indoor pool, tennis court, health club, squash. AE, D, DC, MC, V.*

$$ ⊡ **Auberge du Vieux-Port.** A splendid little hotel—27 rooms over five ★   floors—backs onto fashionable rue St-Paul and overlooks the Vieux-Port. It opened in August 1996 in a Vieux-Montréal building that dates to the 1880s. The rooms have stone or brick walls, tall casement windows, brass beds, and massive exposed beams; many have whirlpool tubs. Rates include a full breakfast in Les Remparts, the hotel's French restaurant. ⊠ *97 rue de la Commune Est, H2Y 1J1,* ☎ *514/876– 0081,* FAX *514/876–8923. 27 rooms. Restaurant, coffee shop. AE, DC, MC, V.*

$$ ⊡ **Auberge Les Passants du Sans Soucy.** A little gem on rue St-Paul, ★   the inn is a former fur warehouse dating to 1836—the foundations date to 1684. The lobby is also an art gallery that opens onto the street. Behind it are a living room and a breakfast room separated by a fireplace that crackles with burning hardwood in winter. This is one of the most romantic city hostelries you'll find anywhere, with brass beds, bare stone walls, exposed beams, soft lighting, whirlpool baths, and lots of fresh-cut flowers. A full breakfast is included in the rates.

✉ *171 rue St-Paul Ouest, H2Y 1Z5,* ☎ *514/842–2634,* 𝖥𝖠𝖷 *514/842–2912. 8 rooms, 1 suite. Breakfast room. AE, DC, MC, V.*

$$ ★ 🛏 **Château Versailles.** This charming hotel occupies a row of four converted mansions on rue Sherbrooke Ouest near Métro Guy-Concordia. The owners have decorated it with antique paintings and tapestries; some rooms have ornate moldings and plaster decorations. Across the street, at 1808 rue Sherbrooke Ouest, is the 107-room Tour Versailles, a converted apartment hotel that the Villeneuve family added as an annex to the original town houses. There is a fine French restaurant, the Champs-Elysées, in La Tour, and a breakfast room in the Château. The staff is extremely helpful and friendly. ✉ *1659 rue Sherbrooke Ouest, H3H 1E3,* ☎ *514/933–3611 or 800/361–3664, 800/361–7199 in Canada,* 𝖥𝖠𝖷 *514/933–7102. 70 rooms in Château; 105 rooms, 2 suites in La Tour. Restaurant, breakfast room. AE, DC, MC, V.*

$$ 🛏 **Hôtel Lord Berri.** Rooms in this moderately priced hotel near the restaurants and nightlife of rue St-Denis have brightly colored bedspreads, modern furniture, and in-room movies. The restaurant, Il Cavaliere, serves Italian food and is popular with locals. ✉ *1199 rue Berri, H2L 4C6,* ☎ *514/845–9236 or 888/363–0363,* 𝖥𝖠𝖷 *514/849–9855. 154 rooms. Restaurant, no-smoking floors, meeting rooms. AE, DC, MC, V.*

$$ 🛏 **Hôtel Radisson des Gouverneurs de Montréal.** Abutting the stock exchange, the Radisson rises above a three-story atrium-reception area and is attractive to convention crowds. It's near Place Bonaventure, the western fringe of Vieux-Montréal, and the Square Victoria Métro (accessible via an underground passage). There's an exclusive floor for higher-paying guests and a shopping arcade on the underground level. The Tour de Ville on the top floor is the city's only revolving restaurant, and its bar has live music nightly. ✉ *777 rue University, H3C 3Z7,* ☎ *514/879–1370 or 800/333–3333,* 𝖥𝖠𝖷 *514/879–1831. 550 rooms, 25 suites. 2 restaurants, bar, indoor pool, steam room, health club. AE, DC, MC, V.*

$$ 🛏 **Le Nouvel Hôtel.** This hotel has brightly colored and functional studios and 2½-room apartments. It is near the restaurants and bars on rues Crescent, de la Montagne, and Bishop, and is two blocks from the Guy-Concordia Métro station. It is also home to the Comedy Nest Cabaret (☞ Nightlife, *below*). ✉ *1740 blvd. René-Lévesque Ouest, H3H 1R3,* ☎ *514/931–8841 or 800/363–6063,* 𝖥𝖠𝖷 *514/931–3233. 126 rooms. Restaurant, bar, pool, comedy club. AE, DC, MC, V.*

$ 🛏 **Hostelling Montréal.** This hostel in the heart of downtown has same-sex dorms that sleep 4, 6, or 10 people. Members pay $17.50 for a bed and nonmembers $22. Some rooms are available for couples and families. There are kitchen facilities and lockers for valuables. Reserve early during summer. ✉ *1030 rue Mackay, H3G 2H1,* ☎ *514/843–3317,* 𝖥𝖠𝖷 *514/934–3251. 263 beds. Coin laundry. DC, MC, V.*

$ 🛏 **Hôtel Thrift Lodge.** The Thrift Lodge is adjacent to the Terminus Voyageur bus station (buses park directly beneath one wing of the hotel), and some of the bus-station aura has rubbed off on the place: It's a little dingy. But if you're stumbling after a long bus ride and want somewhere to stay *now,* the rooms are large and clean, the service is friendly, and the price is right. It's also handy to the Berri-UQAM Métro station. ✉ *1600 rue St-Hubert, H2L 3Z3,* ☎ *514/849–3214,* 𝖥𝖠𝖷 *514/849–9812. 147 rooms. Restaurant. AE, MC, V.*

$ 🛏 **McGill Student Apartments.** From mid-May to mid-August, when McGill is on summer recess, you can stay in its dorms on the grassy, quiet campus in the heart of the city. Nightly rates are $28 students, $36.75 nonstudents (single rooms only). As a visitor, you may use the campus swimming pool and gym facilities for a fee. The university cafeteria is also open during the week, serving breakfast and lunch. ✉ *3935*

rue University, H3A 2B4, ☎ 514/398–6367, FAX 514/398–6770. 1,000
rooms. MC, V.

$ 🏨 **Université de Montréal Residence.** The university's student housing
accepts visitors from early May to late August. It's on the other side
of Mont-Royal from downtown and Vieux-Montréal, but is right next
to the Edouard-Monpetit Métro station. The rooms have phones for
local calls; common lounges have microwaves and TVs. For a fee you
may use the campus sports facilities. Rates are $23 per night or $141
per week. ⊠ 2350 blvd. Edouard-Montpetit, H3C 3J7, ☎ 514/343–
6531, FAX 514/343–2353. 750–800 rooms. AE, MC, V.

$ 🏨 **YMCA.** This clean Y is downtown, next to Peel Métro station. Men
should book at least two days in advance; women should book seven
days ahead because there are fewer rooms with showers for them. Anyone staying summer weekends must book at least a week ahead. There
is a full gym facility and a typical Y cafeteria. ⊠ 1450 rue Stanley, H3A
2W6, ☎ 514/849–8393, FAX 514/849–8017. 331 rooms, 429 beds. Cafeteria, health club. AE, MC, V.

$ 🏨 **YWCA.** Very close to dozens of restaurants, the Y is right downtown,
one block from rue Ste-Catherine. Although men can eat at the café,
the overnight facilities and health club are for women only. If you want
a room with any amenities, you must book in advance; not all the rooms
come with a sink and bath. ⊠ 1355 blvd. René-Lévesque, H3G 1P3,
☎ 514/866–9941, FAX 514/861–1603. 107 rooms. Café, pool, sauna,
aerobics, exercise room, shops. MC, V.

NIGHTLIFE AND THE ARTS

The Friday Preview section of the *Gazette,* the English-language daily
paper, has an especially good list of all events at the city's concert halls,
theaters, clubs, dance spaces, and movie houses. Other publications
listing what's on include the *Mirror, Hour, Scope,* and *Voir* (in French),
distributed free at restaurants and other public places. You can also
phone **Info-Arts (Bell)** (☎ 514/790–2787) for events information.

For **tickets** to major pop and rock concerts, shows, festivals, and
hockey and baseball games, go to the individual box offices or call **Admission** (☎ 514/790–1245 or 800/361–4595); call **Ticketmaster** (☎
514/790–1111) for tickets to Théâtre St-Denis. Place des Arts tickets
may be purchased at its box office underneath the Salle Wilfrid-Pelletier, next to the Métro station.

The Arts

Dance

Traditional and contemporary dance companies thrive in Montréal,
though many take to the road or are on hiatus in the summer. **Ballets
Classiques de Montréal** (☎ 514/866–1771) performs mostly classical
programs. **Les Grands Ballets Canadiens** is the leading Québec company (☎ 514/849–8681 or 514/849–0269). **Ouest Vertigo Danse** (☎
514/251–9177) stages innovative, postmodern performances. **Montréal Danse** (☎ 514/845–2031) is a postmodern dance repertory company. **LaLaLa Human Steps** (☎ 514/277–9090) is an avant-garde,
exciting powerhouse of a company. **Les Ballets Jazz de Montréal** (☎
514/982–6771) experiments with new musical forms. **Margie Gillis
Fondation de Danse** (☎ 514/845–3115) gives young dancers and
choreographers opportunities to develop their art. **Tangente** (☎
514/525–1860) is a nucleus for many of the more avant-garde dance
troupes. When not on tour, many dancers can be seen at Place des Arts
or at any of the **Maisons de la Culture** (☎ 514/872–6211) performance
spaces around town. Montréal's dancers have a downtown performance

and rehearsal space, the **Agora Dance Theatre** (✉ 840 rue Chérrier Est, ☎ 514/525–1500), affiliated with the Université de Montréal dance faculty. Every other September (that is, in the odd-numbered years, such as 1997), the **Festival International de Nouvelle Danse** brings "new" dance to various venues around town. Tickets for this event always sell quickly.

Music

The **Orchestre Symphonique de Montréal** (☎ 514/842–9951) has gained world renown under the baton of Charles Dutoit. When not on tour, its regular venue is the Salle Wilfrid-Pelletier at the Place des Arts. The orchestra also gives Christmas and summer concerts in Notre-Dame Basilica and pop concerts at the Arena Maurice Richard in Olympic Park. Also check the *Gazette* listings for its free summertime concerts in Montréal's city parks. The **Orchestre Métropolitain de Montréal** (☎ 514/598–0870) stars at Place des Arts most weeks during the October–April season. McGill University's **Pollack Concert Hall** (☎ 514/398–4547) is the site of concerts, notably by the **McGill Chamber Orchestra.** The city is home to one of the best chamber orchestras in Canada, **I Musici de Montréal** (☎ 514/982–6037). **L'Opéra de Montréal** (☎ 514/985–2258) stages four productions a year at Place des Arts.

Stade Olympique (✉ Olympic Park, ☎ 514/252–8687) hosts rock and pop concerts. The 2,500-seat **Théâtre St-Denis** (✉ 1594 rue St-Denis, ☎ 514/849–4211) is the second-largest auditorium in Montréal (after Salle Wilfrid-Pelletier in Place des Arts). The **Spectrum** (✉ 318 rue Ste-Catherine Ouest, ☎ 514/861–5851) is an intimate concert hall.

Theater

French-speaking theater lovers will find a wealth of dramatic productions. There are at least 10 major companies in town, some that have an international reputation. Anglophones have less to choose from. **Théâtre de Quat'Sous** (✉ 100 av. des Pins Est, ☎ 514/845-7277) performs modern, experimental, and cerebral plays. **Théâtre du Nouveau Monde** (✉ 84 rue Ste-Catherine Ouest, ☎ 514/866–8667) is the North American temple of French classics. **Théâtre du Rideau Vert** (✉ 4664 rue St-Denis, ☎ 514/844–1793) specializes in modern French repertoire. **Centaur Theatre** (✉ 453 rue St-François-Xavier, ☎ 514/288–3161), the best-known English theatrical company, stages Beaux-Arts-style productions in the former stock exchange building in Vieux-Montréal. English-language plays can also be seen at the **Saidye Bronfman Centre** (✉ 5170 chemin de la Côte Ste-Catherine, ☎ 514/739–2301 or 514/739–7944), a multidisciplinary institution that is a focus of cultural activity for Montréal as a whole and for the Jewish community in particular. Many of its activities, such as gallery exhibits, lectures on public and Jewish affairs, performances, and concerts, are free. The center is home to the **Yiddish Theatre Group**, one of the few Yiddish companies performing today in North America. Touring companies of Broadway productions can often be seen at the **Théâtre St-Denis** (✉ 1594 rue St-Denis, ☎ 514/849–4211), as well as at Place des Arts (☎ 514/842–2112)—especially during summer.

Festivals

Montréal loves a party and every summer there are festivals celebrating everything from beer to Yiddish theatre; this section lists just some of the largest.

Festival International de Jazz de Montréal, the world's biggest jazz festival, brings together more than 2,000 musicians for more than 400 concerts over a period of 11 days, from the end of June to the beginning of July. Some big-name players have included B.B. King, Buddy Guy, Etta James, Sonny Rollins, and Chick Corea. About 75% of concerts are presented free on outdoor stages. You can also hear blues, Latin rhythms, gospel, Cajun, and world music. **Bell Info-Jazz** (☎ 514/871–1881 or 888/515–0515) answers all queries about the festival and about travel packages. You can charge tickets over the phone (☎ 514/790–1245 or 800/678–5440, 800/361–4595 in Canada).

At the **Concours d'Art International Pyrotechnique** (International Fireworks Competition, ☎ 514/935–5161 in Montréal, 800/678–5440, 800/361–4595 in Canada), held every Saturday and Sunday in June and July, teams from around the world compete to see who can best light up the sky. Their launch site is La Ronde on Ile Ste-Hélène, and you can buy a ticket, which includes an amusement park pass, to watch from a reserved seat. But thousands of Montrealers take their lawn chairs and blankets down to the Vieux-Port or across the river to the park along the South Shore and watch the show for nothing.

The **Festival Juste Pour Rire** (Just for Laughs Comedy Festival, ☎ 514/790–4242) begins in early July; the comics show up for a 12-day festival that attracts about 650 performers and 350,000 spectators. Highlight acts have included Bobby Slayton and illusionists Penn and Teller.

At the **Festival International des Films du Monde** (World Film Festival, ☎ 514/848–3883) at the end of August and the beginning of September, international stars and directors show off their best.

Nightlife

Comedy

The **Comedy Nest** (⊠ 1740 blvd. René-Lévesque Ouest, ☎ 514/932–6378) has shows by name performers and up-and-comers.

Dance Clubs

Club 737 (⊠ 1 Place Ville-Marie, ☎ 514/397–0737), on top of Place Ville-Marie, does the disco number every Thursday, Friday, and Saturday night. This has become very popular with the upscale, mid-20s to mid-30s crowd. The view is magnificent and there's an open-air rooftop bar. **Kokino** (⊠ 3556 blvd. St-Laurent, ☎ 514/848–6398) is *the* place for the beautiful people, with jazz, Brazilian, and house music. **Hard Rock Café** (⊠ 1458 rue Crescent, ☎ 514/987–1420) is Montréal's version of this establishment. **Thursdays/Les Beaux Jeudis** (⊠ 1449 rue Crescent, ☎ 514/288–5656) is a popular dance club.

Folk Music

Hurley's Irish Pub (⊠ 1225 rue Crescent, ☎ 514/861–4111) attracts some of the city's best Celtic musicians and dancers. An enthusiastic crowd sings along with Québécois performers at the **Deux Pierrots Boîte aux Chansons** (⊠ 104 rue St-Paul Est, ☎ 514/861–1270).

Gambling

The **Casino de Montréal** (⊠ 1 av. du Casino, ☎ 514/392–2746 or 800/665–2274), on Ile Notre-Dame in the St. Lawrence River, is one of the world's 10 biggest, with 1,835 slot machines and 88 tables for baccarat, blackjack, and roulette. The government has tried to capture the elegance of Monte Carlo: The building glitters with glass and murals and offers stunning city views. There's a strict dress code, and croupiers are trained in politeness as well as math. The casino has five restaurants, including Nuances (☞ Dining, *above*) and a delightfully bilingual cabaret theater. Some oddities for those used to Vegas—no drinking on the floor, no crap games (dice games are illegal in Canada), and no tipping the croupiers. The casino is a $10 cab ride from downtown, or you can take the Métro to the Ile Ste-Helene station and transfer to Bus 167. Driving here is a hassle. It's open daily 9 AM–5 AM.

Jazz

The best-known jazz club is Vieux-Montréal's **L'Air du Temps** (✉ 191 rue St-Paul Ouest, ☎ 514/842–2003). This small, smoky club presents 90% local talent and 10% international acts from 5 PM on into the night. Downtown, duck into **Biddle's** (✉ 2060 rue Aylmer, ☎ 514/842–8656), where bassist Charles Biddle holds forth most evenings. Biddle's serves pretty good ribs and chicken. You might try the **Quai des Brumes Dancing** (✉ 4481 rue St-Denis, ☎ 514/499–0467).

Rock

Rock clubs seem to spring up, flourish, then fizzle out overnight. **Club Soda** (✉ 5240 av. du Parc, ☎ 514/270–7848), the granddaddy of them all, sports a neon martini glass complete with neon effervescence outside. Inside it's a small hall with a stage, three bars, and room for about 400 people. International rock acts play here, as does local talent. It's also a venue for the comedy and jazz festivals. The club is open only for shows. Phone the box office to find out what's on. **Déjà Vu** (✉ 1224 rue Bishop, ☎ 514/866–0512), a rock club with a nostalgia theme, is popular with young English-speakers. **L'Ours Qui Fume** (✉ 2019 rue St-Denis, ☎ 514/845–6998), or the Smoking Bear, is loud, raucous, and very Francophone.

OUTDOOR ACTIVITIES AND SPORTS

Most Montrealers would probably claim they hate winter, but the city is rich in cold-weather activities—skating rinks, cross-country ski trails, toboggan runs, and even a downhill ski run. In summer there are tennis courts, miles of bicycle trails, golf courses, and two lakes for boating and swimming.

Participant Sports

Biking

The island of Montréal—except for Mont-Royal itself—is quite flat, and there are more than 20 cycling paths in the metropolitan area. Bikes are welcome on the first and last cars of Métro trains during non-rush hours. Ferries at the Vieux-Port will take you to Ile Ste-Hélène and the south shore of the St. Lawrence River. You can rent 10-speed bicycles at **Cyclo-Touriste at the Centre Info-Touriste** (✉ 1001 sq. Dorchester, ☎ 514/393–1528). One interesting path follows the **Lachine Canal** (1825) from Vieux-Montréal to the shores of Lac St-Louis in suburban Lachine. Along the way you can stop at the bustling **Atwater Farmer's Market** (✉ 110 av. Atwater) to buy the makings of a picnic or take a break at **Magnan** (☞ Dining, *above*) in summer for a steak or a cheap lobster. In Lachine you can visit the **Fur Trade at Lachine Historic Site** (✉ 1255 blvd. St-Joseph, Lachine, ☎ 514/637–7433). **Parks Canada** (☎ 514/283–6054 or 514/637–7433) conducts guided cycling tours along the Lachine Canal every summer weekend.

Golf

For a complete listing of the many golf courses in the Montréal area, call **Tourisme-Québec** (☎ 514/873–2015 or 800/363–7777).

Ice Skating

The city has at least 195 outdoor and 21 indoor rinks. There are huge ones on Ile Ste-Hélène and at the Vieux-Port. Call the **Parks and Recreation Department** (☎ 514/872–6211) for further information. You can skate year-round in the **Amphithéatre Bell** (☎ 514/395–0555, ext. 237) in Le 1000 rue de la Gauchetière.

Jogging

There are paths in most city parks, but for running with a panoramic view, head to the dirt track in **Parc du Mont-Royal** (take rue Peel, then the steps up to the track).

Rafting

In Montréal you can get in a boat at a downtown wharf and be crashing through Class V white water minutes later. Jack Kowalski of **Lachine Rapids Tours Ltd.** (✉ 105 rue de la Commune [Quai de l'Horloge or Clock Tower Pier], ☎ 514/284–9607) takes thrill seekers on a 45-minute voyage through the rapids in big, sturdy aluminum jet boats. He supplies heavy-water gear, but it's impossible to stay dry—or have a bad time. You can also choose a half-hour trip around the islands in 10-passenger boats that can go 60 miles an hour. Reservations are required; trips are narrated in French and English. There are five trips daily through the rapids from May through September; cost is $48.

Skiing

CROSS-COUNTRY

Trails crisscross most of the city's parks, including Parc des Iles, Maisonneuve, and Mont-Royal, but the best are probably in the 900-acre **Cap St-Jacques Regional Park** (✉ Off blvd. Gouin, ☎ 514/280–6871) in suburban Pierrefonds on the west end of Montréal Island.

DOWNHILL

For the big slopes you'll have to go northwest to the Laurentians (☞ Chapter 10) or south to the Eastern Townships (☞ Chapter 10), an hour or two away by car. There is a small slope in Parc du Mont-Royal. Pick up the "Ski-Québec" brochure at **Tourisme-Québec** offices (☎ 514/873–2015 or 800/363–7777).

Squash

Reserve court time three days ahead at **Nautilus Centre St-Laurent Côte-de-Liesse Racquet Club** (✉ 8305 chemin Côte-de-Liesse, ☎ 514/739–3654).

Swimming

There is a large indoor pool at the Olympic Park's **Centre Aquatique** (✉ Métro Viau, ☎ 514/252–4622). **Centre Sportif et des Loisirs Claude-Robillard** (✉ 1000 av. Emile Journault, ☎ 514/872–6900) has a big indoor pool. The outdoor pool on **Ile Ste-Hélène** is an extremely popular (and crowded) summer gathering place, open June–Labor Day. The city-run **beach** at Ile Notre-Dame is the only natural swimming hole in Montréal (☎ 514/872–6211).

Tennis

There are public courts in the Jeanne-Mance, Kent, Lafontaine, and Somerled parks. For details call the **Parks and Recreation department** (☎ 514/872–6211).

Windsurfing and Sailing

Sailboards and small sailboats can be rented at **L'Ecole de Voile de Lachine** (✉ 2105 blvd. St-Joseph, Lachine, ☎ 514/634–4326) and the Société du Parc des Iles (☎ 514/872–6093).

Spectator Sports

Baseball

The National League's **Montréal Expos** (☎ 514/253–3434 or 800/463–9767) play at the Olympic Stadium from April through September.

Grand Prix

The annual **Player's Grand Prix du Canada** (☎ 514/392–0000 or 514/392–4731), which draws top Formula 1 racers from around the world, takes place every June at the **Gilles Villeneuve Race Track** on Ile Notre-Dame.

Hockey

The **Montréal Canadiens,** winners of 23 Stanley Cups, meet National Hockey League rivals at the Centre Molson (✉ 1250 rue de la Gauchetière Ouest, ☎ 514/932–2582). Buy tickets well in advance if you want to attend a game.

SHOPPING

Montrealers *magasinent* (go shopping) with a vengeance, so it's no surprise that the city has 160 multifaceted retail areas encompassing some 7,000 stores. The law allows shops to stay open weekdays 9–9 and weekends 9–5. However, many merchants close Monday–Wednesday evenings and on Sunday. You'll find many specialty service shops closed on Monday.

Just about all stores, with the exception of some bargain outlets and a few selective art and antiques galleries, accept major credit cards. Buying with plastic usually gets you the best daily exchange rate on the Canadian dollar. If you're shopping with cash, buy your Canadian money at a bank or exchange bureau beforehand. Most purchases are subject to a federal goods and services tax (GST) of 7% as well as a provincial tax of 8%.

If you think you might be buying fur, it is wise to check with your country's customs officials before leaving to find out which animals are considered endangered and cannot be imported. Do the same if you think you might be buying Inuit carvings, many of which are made of whalebone and ivory and cannot be brought into the United States.

Montréal Specialties

Many visitors usually reserve at least one day to hunt for either exclusive fashions along rue Sherbrooke or bargains at the Vieux-Montréal flea market. But there are specific items that you should seek out in Montréal.

Antiques and Secondhand Books

The fashionable place for antiquing is a once run-down five-block strip of rue Notre-Dame Ouest between rue Guy and avenue Atwater (a five-minute walk south from the Lionel-Groulx Métro station). A Sunday tour might begin with brunch at **Salon de Thé Ambiance** (✉ 1874 rue Notre-Dame Ouest, ☎ 514/939–2609), a charming restaurant that also sells antiques. Try **Antiquités Landry** (✉ 1726 rue Notre-Dame Ouest, ☎ 514/937–7040) for solid pine furniture. **Viva Gallery** (✉ 1970 rue Notre-Dame Ouest, ☎ 514/952–3200) specializes in Asian antiques. **Héritage Antique Métropolitain** (✉ 1645 rue Notre-Dame Ouest, ☎ 514/931–5517) has elegant English and French furniture. **Deuxième Moment** (✉ 1880 rue Notre-Dame Ouest, ☎ 514/933–8560) sells a fascinating jumble of objects from every age.

Antique stores are beginning to pop up along **rue Amherst** between rues Ste-Catherine and Ontario (a five-minute walk west of the Beadry Métro station). The area is shabbier than rue Notre-Dame but a lot cheaper. **Intérieurs** (✉ 1863 rue Amherst, ☎ 514/525–2235) blends antique furniture and modern art works along with imported lamps from Europe. **Antiquités Curiosités** (✉ 1769 rue Amherst, ☎ 514/525–

8772) has a wide selection of well-priced wooden toys and Victorian-era tables and tallboys. **L'Antiquaire Joyal** (⊠ 1475 rue Amherst, ☎ 514/524–0057) includes rosaries, crucifixes, and religious art among its two floors of Victorian and earlier furniture. **Cité Déco** (⊠ 1761 rue Amherst, ☎ 514/528–0659) specializes in the chrome and plastic furnishings of the '50s.

Lovers of old books can browse the shelves at **S.W. Wlech** (⊠ 3878 boulevard St-Laurent, ☎ 514/848–9358). **Biblomania** (⊠ 1841-A rue Ste-Catherine Ouest, ☎ 514/933–8156) has some gems among its extensive shelves of secondhand books. One of the most fascinating bookstores in Montréal is **Russell Books** (⊠ 275 rue St-Antoine Ouest, ☎ 514/866–0564), a huge dusty place full of remainders, secondhand paperbacks, children's books, and shelves of old volumes on every subject from algebra to zoology. The back rooms are full of treasures that have never been catalogued.

Fur
Montréal is one of the fur capitals of the world. Close to 85% of Canada's fur manufacturers are based in the city, as are many of their retail outlets. Many of them are clustered along rue Mayor and boulevard de Maisonneuve between rue de Bleury and rue Aylmer. **McComber** (⊠ 402 blvd. de Maisonneuve Ouest, ☎ 514/845–1167) has been in business for 100 years; its present owner has a flair for mink designs. **Grosvenor** (⊠ 400 blvd. de Maisonneuve Ouest, ☎ 514/288–1255) caters more to the wholesale trade, but has several showrooms where customers can view its decidedly European styles. **Alexandor** (⊠ 2055 rue Peel, ☎ 514/288–1119), is nine blocks west of the main fur trade area, and its storefront showroom caters to the downtown trade. **Birger Christensen at Holt Renfrew** (⊠ 1300 rue Sherbrooke Ouest, ☎ 514/842–5111) is perhaps the most exclusive showroom of the lot, with prices to match.

Downtown

Downtown is Montréal's largest retail district. It takes in rue Sherbrooke, boulevard de Maisonneuve, rue Ste-Catherine, and the side streets between them. Because of the proximity and variety of shops, it's the best shopping bet if you're in town overnight or over a weekend. The area bounded by rues Sherbrooke and Ste-Catherine, and rues de la Montagne and Crescent has antiques and art galleries in addition to designer salons. Rue Sherbrooke is lined with fashion boutiques and art and antiques galleries. Rue Crescent is a tempting blend of antiques, fashions, and jewelry displayed beneath colorful awnings.

Complexe Desjardins
Complexe Desjardins (⊠ blvd. René-Lévesque and rue Jeanne Mance) is filled with splashing fountains and exotic plants. To get there take the Métro to the Place des Arts and follow the tunnels to Desjardins' multitiered atrium mall. The roughly 80 stores include budget outlets like Le Château for clothing as well as the exclusive Jonathan Roche Monsieur for men's fashions.

Les Cours Mont-Royal
Les Cours Mont-Royal (⊠ 1550 rue Metcalfe) is *très élégant*. This mall is linked to both the Peel and McGill Métro stations and caters to expensive tastes, but even bargain hunters find it an intriguing spot for window shopping. Beware: The interior layout can be disorienting.

Department Stores
La Baie—The Bay in English—(⊠ 585 rue Ste-Catherine Ouest, ☎ 514/281–4422) has been a department store since 1891. It's known for its

duffel coats and its Hudson Bay red-, green-, and white-striped blankets. It also sells the typical department store fare.

Eaton (✉ 677 rue Ste-Catherine Ouest, ☎ 514/284–8411) is the city's leading department store and part of Canada's largest chain. Founded in Toronto by Timothy Eaton, the first Montréal outlet appeared in 1925. It now sells everything—from fashions and furniture to meals in the Art Deco top-floor restaurant and zucchini loaves in the basement bakery. Everything, that is, except tobacco. Timothy was a good Methodist and his descendants honor his principles.

Exclusive **Holt Renfrew** (✉ 1300 rue Sherbrooke Ouest, ☎ 514/842–5111) is known for furs and fashions. It has supplied coats to four generations of British royalty, and when Queen Elizabeth II got married in 1947, Holt's gave her a priceless Labrador mink. Holt's carries the pricey line of furs by Denmark's Birger Christensen, as well as the haute couture and prêt-à-porter collections of Yves St-Laurent.

A kilted piper regales shoppers at **Ogilvy** (✉ 1307 rue Ste-Catherine Ouest, ☎ 514/942–7711) every day at noon. Founded in 1865, the once-homey department store has undergone a face-lift. Fortunately, it preserved its delicate pink glass chandeliers and still stocks traditional apparel by retailers like Aquascutum and Jaeger. The store has been divided into individual designer boutiques selling pricier lines than La Baie or Eaton. It used to be Ogilvy's (just as Eaton used to be Eaton's) before Québec's French-only sign laws made apostrophes illegal.

Faubourg Ste-Catherine

The Faubourg Ste-Catherine (✉ 1616 rue Ste-Catherine Ouest, at rue Guy) is a vast bazaar abutting the Grey Nuns' convent grounds. There are three levels of clothing and crafts boutiques, as well as food counters and kiosks. You can pick up Québec maple syrup at a street-level boutique or a fine French wine for about $30 at the government-run Société d'Alcools du Québec. Prices at most stores here are generally reasonable, especially if you're sampling the varied ethnic cuisines of the snack counters.

Place Bonaventure

Place Bonaventure (✉ Rues de la Gauchetière and University) is one of Canada's largest commercial exhibition centers. It's directly above the Bonaventure Métro station and has a mall with some 120 stores, including the trendy Au Coton and Bikini Village and the practical Bata Shoes. There are also a number of fun shops: Ici-Bas for outrageous hose, Le Rouet for handicrafts, and Miniatures Plus for exquisite dolls' furniture and tiny gifts.

Place Montréal Trust

Place Montréal Trust (✉ 1600 rue McGill College, at rue Ste-Catherine Ouest) is the lively entrance to an imposing glass office tower. Shoppers, fooled by the aqua and pastel decor, may think they have stumbled into a California mall. Prices at the 110 outlets range from hundreds (for designs by Alfred Sung, haute couture at Gigi, or men's fashions at Rodier) to only a few dollars (for sensible cotton T-shirts or steak-and-kidney pies at the outpost of famed British department store Marks & Spencer). This shopping center is linked to the McGill Métro station.

Place Ville-Marie

Weatherproof shopping began in 1962 beneath the 42-story cruciform towers of Place Ville-Marie (✉ blvd. René-Lévesque and rue University). Stylish men and women head to Place Ville-Marie's 100-plus retail outlets for the clothes—Tristan & Iseut, Cactus, and Aquascutum at the upper end and Dalmys and Reitmans for more affordable fashions. For shoes try Mayfair, Brown's, François Villon, and French.

Les Promenades de la Cathédrale

The Promenades de la Cathédrale (✉ 625 rue Ste-Catherine Ouest) are directly beneath Christ Church Cathedral, the seat of Montréal's Anglican (Episcopalian) bishop. Les Promenades, which is connected to the McGill Métro station, has Canada's largest Linen Chest outlet, with hundreds of bedspreads and duvets draped over revolving racks plus aisles of china, crystal, linen, and silver. It's also home to the Anglican Church's Diocesan Book Room, which sells an unusually good and ecumenical selection of books as well as religious objects.

Rue Chabanel

In the north end of the city, rue Chabanel is the soul of Montréal's extensive garment industry. Every Saturday, from about 8:30 to 1, many of the manufacturers and importers in the area open their doors to the general public. At least they do if they feel like it. What results is part bazaar, part circus, and often all chaos—but friendly chaos. When Montrealers say "Chabanel," they mean the eight-block stretch just west of boulevard St-Laurent. The factories and shops there are tiny—dozens of them are crammed into each building. The goods seem to get more stylish and more expensive the farther west you go. For really cheap leather goods, sportswear, children's clothes, and linens, try the shops at 99 rue Chabanel. For more deluxe options drop into 555 rue Chabanel. The manufacturers and importers here have their work areas on the upper floors and have transformed the mezzanine into a glitzy mall with bargains in men's suits, winter coats, knitted goods, and stylish leather jackets. A few places on Chabanel accept credit cards, but bring cash anyway. It's easier to bargain if you can flash bills, and if you pay cash, the price will often "include the tax."

Square Westmount and Avenue Greene

Square Westmount (✉ rue Ste-Catherine Ouest and av. Greene) has some of the city's finest shops (and the most luxurious public washrooms on the island), which is hardly surprising—it serves the mountainside suburb of Westmount, home to executives and former prime ministers. Humbler types can get there easily by taking the Métro to the Atwater station and following the tunnel to Square Westmount. **Collange** (☎ 514/933–4634) sells lacy lingerie. **Ma Maison** (☎ 514/933–0045) stocks quality housewares. **Hugo Nicholson** (☎ 514/937–1937) sells exclusive fashions for men and women. The very elegant **Marché de Westmount** has an array of gourmet boutiques that sell pastries, cheeses, pâtés, fruits, cakes, and chocolates. You can assemble your own picnic and eat it at one of the little tables scattered among the stalls. If shopping tires you out, you can stop in at the **Spade Westmount** (☎ 514/933–9966) for a massage. Square Westmount opens onto **avenue Greene,** two flower-lined blocks of restored redbrick row houses full of boutiques, restaurants, and shops. **Double Hook** (✉ 1235A av. Greene, ☎ 514/932–5093) sells only Canadian books. Try the **Coach House** (✉ 1325 av. Greene, ☎ 514/937–6191) for antique silverware.

Upper Boulevard St-Laurent and Avenue Laurier Ouest

Upper boulevard St-Laurent—which runs roughly from avenue du Mont-Royal north to rue St-Viateur and climbs the mountain to rue Bernard—has blossomed into one of Montréal's most chic *quartiers*. It's not entirely surprising, given that much of this area lies within or adjacent to Outremont, an enclave of wealthy Francophone Montrealers, with restaurants, boutiques, nightclubs, and bistros catering to the upscale visitor. **Scandale** (✉ 3639 blvd. St-Laurent, ☎ 514/842–4707) has designs for the very hip as well as great lingerie and a secondhand clothes store. **J. Schrecter** (✉ 4350 blvd. St-Laurent, ☎ 514/845–4231) had been supplying work duds for blue-collar workers for decades when the grunge look suddenly made the store trendy.

Shoppers flock to the two blocks of **avenue Mont-Royal** just east of boulevard St-Laurent for a series of shops that sell secondhand clothes and recycled clothes (things like housecoats chopped into sassy miniskirts). **Scarlett O'Hara** (✉ 254 av. Mont-Royal Est, ☎ 514/844–9435) started the whole secondhand trend. **Eva B** (✉ 2013 blvd. St-Laurent, ☎ 514/849–8246) sells new clothes as well as used. **Hatfield & McCoy** (✉ 156 av. Mont-Royal Est, ☎ 514/982–0088) recycles elegant lounge clothes from the 1930s to the 1970s.

Avenue Laurier Ouest, from boulevard St-Laurent to chemin de la Côte-Ste-Catherine, is roughly an eight-block stretch; you'll crisscross it many times as you explore its fashionable and trendy shops, which carry everything from crafts and clothing to books and paintings. **Tilley Endurables** (✉ 1050 av. Laurier Ouest, ☎ 514/272–7791) sells the famous Canadian-designed Tilley hat and other easy-care travel wear. **Boutique Gabriel Filion** (✉ 1127 av. Laurier Ouest, ☎ 514/274–0697) sells interesting imported toys and marvelous dolls, doll clothes, stuffed animals, and music boxes. For Asian and African crafts, try **Artefact** (✉ 102 av. Laurier Ouest, ☎ 514/278–6575).

Vieux-Montréal

Despite Vieux-Montréal's abundance of garish souvenir shops, a shopping spree there can be worthwhile. Both rues Notre-Dame and St-Jacques, from rue McGill to Place Jacques-Cartier, are lined with low to moderately priced fashion boutiques and shoe stores. **Desmarais et Robitaille** (✉ 60 rue Notre-Dame Ouest, ☎ 514/845–3194), a store that supplies churches with vestments and liturgical aids, has Québécois carvings and handicrafts as well as tasteful religious articles. **Rue St-Paul** has some interesting shops and art galleries. **Drags** (✉ 367 rue St-Paul Est, ☎ 514/866–0631) is crammed with fragments of military uniforms and loads of clothes, shoes, hats, and accessories from the '30s and '40s. **L'Empreinte Coopérative** (✉ 272 rue St-Paul Est, ☎ 514/861–4427) has a fine collection of Québec handicrafts. **Rita R. Giroux** (✉ 206 rue St-Paul Ouest, ☎ 514/844–4714) makes flamboyant creations with fresh, dried, and silk flowers. At the **Cerf Volanterie** (✉ 224 rue St-Paul Ouest, ☎ 514/845–7613), Claude Thibaudeau makes sturdy, gloriously colored kites that he signs and guarantees for three years. The **Galerie Art & Culture** (✉ 227 rue St-Paul Ouest, ☎ 514/843–5980) specializes in Canadian landscapes. **Galerie des Arts Relais des Epoques** (✉ 234 rue St-Paul Ouest, ☎ 514/844–2133) sells some fascinating work by contemporary Montréal painters.

The Vieux-Port hosts a sprawling flea market, the **Marché aux Puces.** Dealers and pickers prowl through the huge hangar searching for secondhand steals and antique treasures. ✉ *King Edward Pier.* ☺ *May 5–28, Fri. and Sun. 11–9, Sat. 11–10; May 31–Aug. 27, Wed., Thurs., and Sun. 11–9, Sat. 11–10; July–Aug., Tues. 11–9.*

MONTRÉAL A TO Z

Arriving and Departing

By Bus

For information about bus companies, contact the city's downtown bus terminal, **Terminus Voyageur** (✉ 505 blvd. de Maisonneuve Est, ☎ 514/842–2281), which connects with the Berri-UQAM Métro station. **Greyhound** has coast-to-coast service and serves Montréal with buses arriving from and departing for various cities in North America. **Vermont Transit** serves Montréal via Boston, New York, and other points in New England. **Voyageur** and **Voyageur-Colonial** service destinations primarily within Québec and Ontario.

By Car

Montréal is accessible from the rest of Canada via the Trans-Canada Highway, which enters the city from the east and west via Routes 20 and 40. The New York State Thruway (I–87) becomes Route 15 at the Canadian border, and then it's 47 km (29 mi) to the outskirts of Montréal. U.S. I–89 becomes two-lane Route 133, which eventually joins Route 10, at the border. From I–91 from Massachusetts, you must take Routes 55 and 10 to reach Montréal. At the border you must clear Canadian Customs, so be prepared with proof of citizenship and your vehicle's ownership papers. On holidays and during the peak summer season, expect waits of a half hour or more at the major crossings.

Once you're in Québec, the road signs will be in French, but they're designed so you shouldn't have much trouble understanding them. The speed limit is posted in kilometers; on highways the limit is 100 kph (about 62 mph). There are heavy penalties for driving while intoxicated, and drivers and front-seat passengers must wear over-the-shoulder seat belts. Gasoline is sold in liters (3¾ liters equal 1 U.S. gallon), and lead-free is called *sans plomb*. New York, Maine, and Ontario residents should drive with extra care in Québec: Traffic violations in the province are entered on their driving records back home (and vice versa).

By Plane

Montréal is served by two airports. Flying time from New York is 1½ hours; from Chicago, two hours; from Los Angeles, 6½ hours (with a connection). **Dorval International** (☎ 514/633–3105), 22½ km (14 mi) west of the city, handles domestic and most U.S. flights. **Mirabel International** (☎ 514/476–3010), 54½ km (34 mi) northwest of the city, is a hub for the rest of the international trade.

Air Canada (☎ 514/393–3333 or 800/361–8620) offers nonstop service from New York, Miami, and Tampa and from Boston via its connector airline, Air Alliance. Direct service is available from Los Angeles and San Francisco. **American Airlines** (☎ 800/433–7300) has nonstop service from Chicago with connections from the rest of the United States. **Canadian Airlines International** (☎ 514/847–2211 or 800/426–7000, 800/363–7530 in Canada) has a nonstop charter from Fort Lauderdale and direct or connecting service from Hawaii and Los Angeles. **Delta Air Lines** (☎ 514/337–5520 or 800/221–1212, 800/361–1970 in Québec Province) has nonstops from Boston; Hartford, Connecticut; New York; Cincinnati; and Atlanta and connecting service from most major U.S. cities. **USAir** (☎ 800/428–4322) has service from Philadelphia and Pittsburgh.

A **taxi** from Dorval to downtown will cost $25, from Mirabel about $56. All taxi companies in Montréal must charge the same rates by law. It is best to have Canadian money with you, because the exchange rate for U.S. dollars is at the driver's discretion. **Autobus Connaisseur** (☎ 514/934–1222) is a much cheaper alternative to taxis into town from Mirabel and Dorval. Shuttle service from Mirabel to the terminal next to the Gare Centrale (✉ 777 rue de la Gauchetière) is frequent and costs only $14.50. The shuttle from Dorval runs about every half hour and stops at Le Centre Sheraton, Le Château Champlain, Le Reine Elizabeth, and the Voyageur terminal. It costs $9. If you plan to use the bus to go back to either airport, you can save $6 by buying a round-trip ticket. Connaisseur also runs a shuttle between Dorval and Mirabel.

By Train

The Gare Centrale, on rue de la Gauchetière between rues University and Mansfield (behind Le Reine Elizabeth), is the rail terminus for all trains from the United States and from other Canadian provinces. It is connected by underground passageway to the Bonaventure Métro station.

Amtrak (☎ 800/872–7245) refurbished the cars on its *Adirondack* in 1996. The train leaves New York's Penn Station every morning for the 10½-hour trip through the spectacular scenery of upstate New York to Montréal. Amtrak also has bus connections with the *Vermonter* in St. Albans, Vermont.

VIA Rail (☎ 514/871–1331 or 800/561–3949, 800/361–5390 in Québec Province) connects Montréal with all the major cities of Canada, including Québec City, Halifax, Ottawa, Toronto, Winnipeg, Edmonton, and Vancouver.

Getting Around

By Bus and Métro

Public transportation is easily the best and cheapest way to get around. The Métro (subway) is clean, quiet (it runs on rubber wheels), and safe, and it's heated in winter and cooled in summer. Métro hours on the Orange, Green, and Yellow lines are weekdays 5:30 AM–12:58 AM, Saturday 5:30 AM–1:28 AM, and Sunday 5:30 AM–1:58 AM. The Blue Line runs daily from 5:30 AM to 11 PM. Trains run as often as every three minutes on the most crowded lines—Orange and Green at rush hours. The Métro is also connected to the 29 km (18 mi) of the Underground City, so you may not need to go outside during bad weather. Each of the 65 Métro stops has been individually designed and decorated; Berri-UQAM has stained glass, and at Place d'Armes a small collection of archaeological artifacts is exhibited. The stations between Snowdon and Jean-Talon on the Blue Line are worth a visit, particularly Outremont, with its glass-block design. Each station connects with one or more bus routes, which cover the rest of the island. The STCUM (Société de Transport de la Communauté Urbaine de Montréal) administers both the Métro and the buses, so the same tickets and transfers (free) are valid on either service. You should be able to get within a few blocks of anywhere in the city on one fare. At press time rates were: single ticket $1.85, six tickets $7.75, monthly pass $44.50. Visitors can buy a day pass for $5 or a three-day pass for $12. They're available at most major hotels and at Info-Touriste (☞ Visitor Information *in* Contacts and Resources, *below*).

Free maps may be obtained at Métro ticket booths. Try to get the *Carte Réseau* (system map); it's the most complete. Transfers from Métro to buses are available from the dispenser just beyond the ticket booth inside the station. Bus-to-bus and bus-to-Métro transfers may be obtained from the bus driver. For more information on reaching your destina-

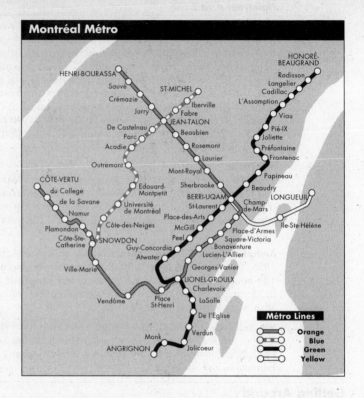

Montréal Métro

Métro Lines
- Orange
- Blue
- Green
- Yellow

tion call the **Société de Transport de la Communauté de Montréal**
(☎ 514/288–6287).

By Car

Finding your way around Montréal by car is not difficult. The streets
are laid out in a fairly straightforward grid and one-way streets are
clearly marked. But parking is difficult and the narrow cobbled streets
of Vieux-Montréal can be a trial. It's much easier to park near a Métro
station and walk and use public transit.

Montréal police have a diligent tow-away and fine system for cars dou-
ble-parked or stopped in no-stopping zones in downtown Montréal
during rush hours and business hours. A parking ticket will cost between $35 and $40. All Montréal parking signs are in French, so
brush up on your *gauche* (left), *droit* (right), *ouest* (west), and *est*
(east). If your car is towed away while illegally parked, it will cost an
additional $35 to retrieve it. Be especially alert during winter: Mont-
réal's snow-clearing crews are the best in the world and a joy to watch
in action after a major blizzard—but they're ruthless in dealing with
any parked cars in their way. If they don't tow them, they'll bury
them.

In winter, remember that your car may not start on extra-cold mornings unless it has been kept in a heated garage. And if you drive in the
city, remember two things: Québec law forbids you to turn right on a
red light and Montrealers are notorious jaywalkers.

By Taxi

Taxis in Montréal all run on the same rate: $2.25 minimum and $1 a
km. They're usually reliable, although they may be hard to find on rainy
nights after the Métro has closed. Each carries on its roof a white or
orange plastic sign that is lit when available and off when occupied.

Contacts and Resources

Car Rentals

Avis (☎ 514/866–7906 or 800/321–3652). **Budget** (☎ 514/938–1000). **Discount** (☎ 514/286–1554). **Dollar** (☎ 514/990–0074 or 800/800–4000). **Hertz** (☎ 514/842–8537 or 800/263–0678). **National/Tilden** (☎ 514/878–2771 or 800/387–4747). **Via Route** (☎ 514/521–5221).

Consulates

United States (✉ 1155 rue St-Alexandre, ☎ 514/398–9695) is open weekdays 8:30–4:30. **United Kingdom** (✉ 1000 rue de la Gauchetière Ouest, ☎ 514/866–5863) is open weekdays 9–5.

Doctors and Dentists

The U.S. Consulate cannot recommend specific doctors and dentists but does provide a list of various specialists in the Montréal area. Call in advance (☎ 514/398–9695) to make sure the consulate is open.

Dental clinic (☎ 514/342–4444) is open 24 hours; Sunday appointments are for emergencies only. **Montréal General Hospital** (☎ 514/937–6011). **Québec Poison Control Centre** (☎ 800/463–5060). **Touring Club de Montréal–AAA, CAA, RAC** (☎ 514/861–7111).

Emergencies

Police, fire, ambulance: Dial 911.

English-Language Bookstores

Chapters (✉ 1171 rue Ste-Catherine Ouest, ☎ 514/849–8825), a branch of the Canadian chain, has a wide selection of books and magazines, as well as a coffee shop. **Double Hook** (✉ 1235A av. Greene, ☎ 514/932–5093) sells only Canadian books. **Paragraphe** (✉ 2065 rue Mansfield, ☎ 514/845–5811) has a café.

Guided Tours

BOAT TOURS

From May through October, **Amphi Tour** (☎ 514/849–5181 or ☎ 514/386–1298 for cell phone in season only) offers a unique one-hour tour of Vieux-Montréal and the Vieux-Port on both land and water in an amphibious bus. **Bateau-Mouche** (☎ 514/849–9952) runs four harbor excursions and an evening supper cruise every day from May through October. The boats are reminiscent of the ones that cruise the canals of the Netherlands—wide-beamed and low-slung, with a glassed-in passenger deck. Boats leave from the Jacques Cartier Pier at the foot of Place Jacques-Cartier in the Vieux-Port (Métro Champs-de-Mars).

CALÈCHE RIDES

Open horse-drawn carriages—fleece-lined in winter—leave from Place Jacques-Cartier, Square Dorchester, Place d'Armes, and rue de la Commune. An hour-long ride costs about $50 (☎ 514/653–0751).

ORIENTATION

Gray Line (☎ 514/934–1222) has nine different tours of Montréal in the summer and one tour during the winter. It offers pickup service at the major hotels, or you may board the buses at Info-Touriste (✉ 1001 sq. Dorchester). **Murray Hill Trolley Buses** (☎ 514/871–4733) follow a 14-stop circuit of the city. Passengers can get off and on as often as they like and stay at each stop as long as they like. There's pickup service at major hotels.

Late-Night Pharmacies

Many pharmacies are open until midnight. **Jean Coutu** (✉ 501 Mont-Royal Est, ☎ 514/521–3481; ✉ 5510 Côte-des-Neiges, ☎ 514/344–8338) is open until midnight. **Pharmaprix** (✉ 1500 rue Ste-Catherine Ouest, ☎ 514/933–4744; ✉ 5157 rue Sherbrooke Ouest, ☎ 514/484–

3531) stays open until midnight. **Pharmaprix** (⊠ Promenades du Musée; ⊠ 5122 Côte-des-Neiges, ☎ 514/738–8464; ⊠ 901 rue Ste-Catherine Est, ☎ 514/842–4915) is open 24 hours.

Lodging Reservations

Bed and Breakfast à Montréal represents more than 50 homes in downtown and in the elegant neighborhoods of Westmount and Outremont. Singles run $40–$55; doubles $55–$85. ⊠ *Marian Kahn, Box 575, Snowdon Station, H3X 3T8,* ☎ *514/738–9410,* FAX *514/735–7493.*

Downtown B&B Network represents 75 homes and apartments, mostly around the downtown core and along rue Sherbrooke, that have one or more rooms available for visitors. Singles are $25–$40, doubles $35–$55. Even during the height of the tourist season, this organization has rooms open. ⊠ *Bob Finkelstein, 3458 av. Laval (at rue Sherbrooke), H2X 3C8,* ☎ *514/289–9749 or 800/267–5180.*

There is a room reservation service at **Info-Touriste** (☎ 800/665–1528), which can find you a room in one of 80 hotels, motels, and bed-and-breakfasts.

Museum Pass

The Montréal museum pass allows you access to 19 major museums, including most of the ones mentioned in this chapter. A day pass costs $15, a three-day pass $28; family passes are $30 for one day and $60 for three days. They are available at museums or Centre Info-Touriste (⊠ 1001 sq. Dorchester).

Travel Agencies

American Express (⊠ 1141 blvd. de Maisonneuve Ouest, ☎ 514/284–3300). **Canadian Automobile Club** (⊠ 1180 rue Drummond, ☎ 514/861–5111). **Vacances Tourbec** (⊠ 595 blvd. de Maisonneuve Ouest, ☎ 514/842–1400). **Voyages Campus** (⊠ McGill University, 3480 rue McTavish, ☎ 514/398–0647).

Visitor Information

Centre Info-Touriste (⊠ 1001 sq. Dorchester, ☎ 514/873–2015 or 800/363–7777) on Square Dorchester is open June 10–Labor Day, daily 8:30–7:30, and Labor Day–June 9, daily 9–6. A second branch (⊠ 174 rue Notre-Dame Est, at pl. Jacques-Cartier, ☎ 514/873–2015) is open Labor Day–mid-May, daily 9–1 and 2–5, and mid-May–Labor Day, daily 9–7.

9 Québec City

Whether you're strolling along the Plains of Abraham or exploring the Vieux-Port, Québec City will give you a feeling for centuries of history and French civilization. The city, which has one of the most spectacular settings in North America, is perched on a cliff above a narrow point in the St. Lawrence River. It is the capital of, as well as the oldest municipality in, Québec province.

Updated by
Dorothy
Guinan

NO EXCURSION TO FRENCH-SPEAKING Canada is complete without a visit to exuberant, romantic Québec City, which can claim one of the most beautiful natural settings in North America. The well-preserved Vieux-Québec (Old Québec) is small and dense, steeped in four centuries of history and French tradition. Here you can explore 17th- and 18th-century buildings, the ramparts that once protected the city, and numerous parks and monuments. The Québec government has completely restored many of the centuries-old buildings of Place Royale, one of the oldest districts on the continent. Because of its immaculate preservation as the only fortified city remaining in North America, UNESCO has designated Vieux-Québec a World Heritage Site.

Perched on a cliff above a narrow point in the St. Lawrence River, Québec City is the oldest municipality in Québec province. In the 17th century the first French explorers, fur trappers, and missionaries came here to establish the colony of New France. Today it still resembles a French provincial town in many ways; its family-oriented residents have strong ties to their past. More than 95% of its metropolitan population of 500,000 are French-speaking.

In 1535 French explorer Jacques Cartier first came upon what the Algonquin Indians called "Kebec," meaning "where the river narrows." New France, however, was not actually founded in the vicinity of what is now Québec City until 1608, when another French explorer, Samuel de Champlain, recognized the military advantages of the location and set up a fort. On the banks of the St. Lawrence, on the spot now called Place Royale, this fort developed into an economic center for fur trade and shipbuilding. Twelve years later, Champlain realized the French colony's vulnerability to attacks from above and expanded its boundaries to the top of the cliff, where he built the fort Château St-Louis on the site of the present-day Château Frontenac.

During the early days of New France, the French and British fought for control of the region. In 1690, when an expedition led by Admiral Sir William Phipps arrived from England, Comte de Frontenac, New France's most illustrious governor, defied him with the statement, "Tell your lord that I will reply with the mouth of my cannons."

The French, preoccupied with scandals at the courts of Louis XV and Louis XVI, gave only grudging help to their possessions in the New World. The French colonists built walls and other military structures and had the strong defensive position on top of the cliff, but they still had to contend with Britain's naval supremacy. On September 13, 1759, the British army, led by General James Wolfe, scaled the colony's cliff and took the French troops led by General Louis-Joseph Montcalm by surprise. The British defeated the French in a 20-minute battle on the Plains of Abraham, and New France came under British rule.

The British brought their mastery of trade to the region. During the 18th century, Québec City's economy prospered because of the success of the fishing, fur-trading, shipbuilding, and timber industries. Wary of new invasions, the British continued to expand upon the fortifications left by the French. They built a wall encircling the city and a star-shape citadel, both of which mark the city's urban landscape today. The constitution of 1791 established Québec City as the capital of Lower Canada until the 1840 Act of Union united Upper and Lower Canada and made Montréal the capital. The city remained under British rule until 1867, when the Act of Confederation united several Canadian provinces (Québec, Ontario, New Brunswick, and Nova Scotia) and established Québec City as capital of the province of Québec.

In the mid-19th century, the economic center of eastern Canada shifted west from Québec City to Montréal and Toronto. Today, government is Québec City's main business: About 27,000 civil-service employees work and live in the area. Office complexes continue to spring up outside the older part of town; modern malls, convention centers, and imposing hotels now cater to an established business clientele.

Pleasures and Pastimes

Dining

Gone are the days when Québec City dining consisted mostly of classic French and hearty Québécois cuisine, served in restaurants in the downtown core. Nowadays the city's finest eateries are found inside and outside the city's walls, offering lighter contemporary fare, often with Asian, Italian, French, and Québécois influences. You will still find fine French restaurants, though, and be able to sample French-Canadian cuisine, composed of robust, uncomplicated dishes that make use of the region's bounty of foods, including fowl and wild game (quail, caribou, venison), maple syrup, and various berries and nuts. Other specialties include *cretons* (pâtés), *tourtière* (meat pie), and *tarte au sucre* (maple-syrup pie).

Lodging

With more than 35 hotels within its walls and an abundance of family-run bed-and-breakfasts, Québec City has a range of lodging options. Landmark hotels stand as prominent as the city's most historic sites; modern high rises outside the ramparts have spectacular views of the old city. Another choice is to immerse yourself in the city's historic charm by staying in one of the many old-fashioned inns where no two rooms are alike.

Walking

Québec City is a wonderful place to wander on foot. From Parc Montmorency, you can see the Laurentian Mountains jutting majestically above the St. Lawrence River. Even more impressive vistas are revealed if you walk along the city walls or climb to the city's highest point, Cap Diamant. You can spend days investigating the narrow cobblestone streets of Vieux-Québec, visiting historic sites or browsing for local arts and crafts in the boutiques of quartier Petit-Champlain. Strolling the Promenade des Gouverneurs and the Plains of Abraham, you have a view of the river as well as the Laurentian foothills and the Appalachian mountains.

EXPLORING QUÉBEC CITY

Québec City's split-level landscape divides Upper Town on the cape from Lower Town, along the shores of the St. Lawrence. If you look out from the Terrasse Dufferin boardwalk in Upper Town, you will see the rooftops of Lower Town buildings directly below. Separating these two sections of the city is steep and precipitous rock, against which were built the city's more than 25 *escaliers* (staircases). At press time the *funiculaire* (funicular)—a cable car that climbs and descends the cliff between Terrasse Dufferin and the Maison Jolliet in Lower Town—was closed and under investigation. There's plenty to see in the oldest sections of town, as well as in the modern city beyond the walls. Outside the city are a number of worthwhile side trips, too.

Metropolitan Québec City

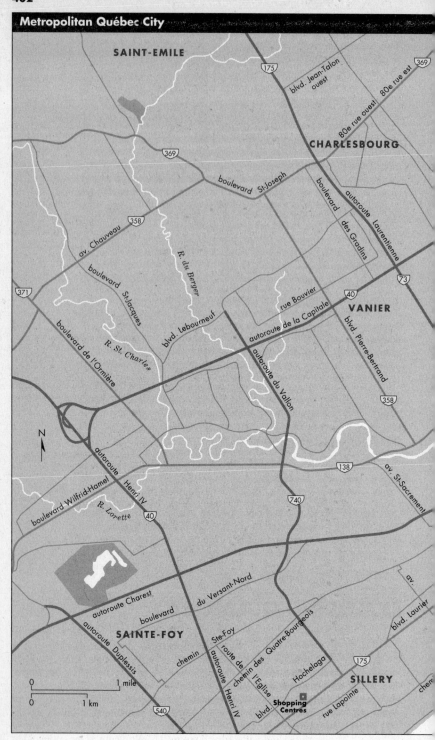

SAINT-EMILE

175

blvd. Jean-Talon ouest

80e rue ouest

80e rue est

369

369

CHARLESBOURG

boulevard St-Joseph

boulevard des Gradins

autoroute Laurentienne

av. Chauveau

358

R. du Berger

boulevard St-Jacques

371

blvd. Lebourneuf

rue Bouvier

40

73

VANIER

autoroute de la Capitale

boulevard de l'Ormière

R. St. Charles

autoroute du Vallon

blvd. Pierre-Bertrand

358

N

autoroute Henri IV

boulevard Wilfrid-Hamel

R. Lorette

40

138

av. St-Sacrement

740

autoroute Charest

du Versant-Nord

av.

boulevard Ste-Foy

blvd. Laurier

SAINTE-FOY

autoroute Duplessis

chemin

route de l'Église

chemin des Quatre-Bourgeois

Hochelaga

175

SILLERY

0   1 mile

0   1 km

540

autoroute Henri IV

blvd

Shopping Centres

rue Lapointe

chem

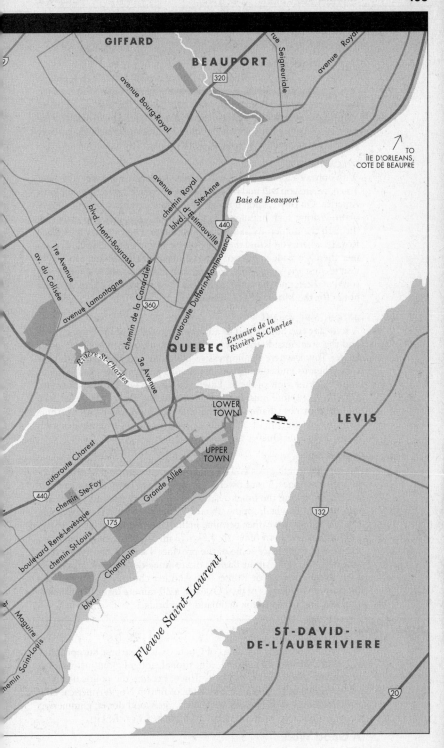

GIFFARD

BEAUPORT

320

rue Seigneuriale

avenue Royal

↗
TO
ÎLE D'ORLEANS,
COTE DE BEAUPRE

avenue Bourg-Royal

avenue

chemin Royal

blvd. Ste-Anne

blvd. de Jestimauville

Baie de Beauport

440

blvd. Henri-Bourassa

1re Avenue

av. du Colisée

avenue Lamontagne

chemin de la Canardière

360

autoroute Dufferin-Montmorency

Estuaire de la
Rivière St-Charles

QUEBEC

Rivière St-Charles

3e Avenue

LOWER
TOWN

LEVIS

UPPER
TOWN

autoroute Charest

chemin Ste-Foy

440

boulevard René-Levèsque

chemin St-Louis

175

Grande Allée

Champlain

blvd.

Maguire

chemin Saint-Louis

Fleuve Saint-Laurent

132

ST-DAVID-
DE-L'AUBERIVIERE

20

Numbers in the text correspond to numbers in the margin and on the Upper and Lower Towns (Haute-Ville, Basse-Ville), Outside the City Walls, and Ile d'Orléans maps.

Great Itineraries

Whether you take a weekend or a almost a week, there's enough history, scenery, and entertainment to delight the most seasoned traveler. On a weekend or four-day trip, you can take in the historic sights of Vieux-Québec, walking along ancient streets and the boardwalk by the river before dining at some of the city's fine restaurants. A longer stay allows you to wander beyond the city proper.

IF YOU HAVE 2 DAYS

With only a couple of days, it makes sense to devote your time to Lower Town, where you will find the earliest site of French civilization in North America. On Day 1, stroll through the narrow streets of the Petit-Champlain, visiting such highlights as the Maison Chevalier and browsing through the numerous handicraft boutiques. Then move on to Place Royale, where you'll find the Eglise Notre-Dame-des-Victoires; in summer there's a wide variety of entertainment in the square. On Day 2 visit the historic Vieux-Port, with exhibits about the old port and a seasonal market, and the antiques district. You should also reserve a few hours for the Musée de la Civilisation.

IF YOU HAVE 4 DAYS

A four-day trip allows you to add the main sights of the Upper Town and the area outside the city walls to your itinerary. On Day 3, visit Upper Town, where the impressive buildings of 17th- and 18th-century religious and educational institutions predominate. Take time to appreciate the view of the St. Lawrence River from Terrasse Dufferin. On Day 4, explore outside the walls, including the fortified Citadelle and the Parc des Champs-de-Bataille, which holds the Plains of Abraham, where the fate of New France was decided. Cultural sites such as the Musée de Québec are also here.

IF YOU HAVE 6 DAYS

A visit this length gives you the opportunity to discover Québec City at a leisurely pace. Visit Lower Town and Upper Town during the first four days, taking the time to savor some fine French and Québécois cuisine, and maybe hopping aboard a calèche. Spend Day 5 outside the walls, and if weather permits, include a tour of the fortifications of Québec, a rampart of nearly 4½ km (3 mi) that encircles the old city. On Day 6, experience some of the province's scenic countryside on a side trip. You can visit the Basilica of Ste-Anne-de-Beaupré, taking historic avenue Royale or Route 360. Another choice is to explore the farms and woodlands of Ile d'Orléans, a 20-minute drive from Vieux-Québec, connected to the mainland by a bridge.

Upper Town

The most prominent buildings of Québec City's earliest European inhabitants, who set up political, educational, and religious institutions, stand here. Haute-Ville, or Upper Town, became the political capital of the colony of New France and, later, of British North America. Historic buildings with thick stone walls, large wood doors, glimmering copper roofs, and majestic steeples fill the heart of the city.

A Good Walk

Begin your walk where rue St-Louis meets rue du Fort at **Place d'Armes** ①, a large plaza bordered by government buildings. To your right is the colony's former treasury building, **Maison Maillou,** interesting for its 18th-century architecture. A little farther along, at 25 rue

St-Louis, is Maison Kent, where the terms of the surrender of Québec to the British were signed in 1759. South of the Place d'Armes towers is Québec City's most celebrated landmark, **Château Frontenac** ②, an impressive green-turreted hotel on the site of what was once the administrative and military headquarters of New France. As you head to the boardwalk behind the Frontenac, notice the glorious bronze statue of Samuel de Champlain, standing where he built his residence.

Walk south along the boardwalk called the **Terrasse Dufferin** ③ for a panoramic view of the city and its surroundings. As you pass to the southern side of the Frontenac, you will come to a small park called **Jardin des Gouverneurs** ④. From the north side of the park follow rue Mont-Carmel until you come to another small park, **Cavalier du Moulin** ⑤. After 1693, it was used as protective fortifications.

Retrace your steps down rue Mont-Carmel, turn left on rue Haldimand and left again on rue St-Louis; then make a right and follow rue du Parloir until it intersects with a tiny street called rue Donnacona where you'll find the **Couvent des Ursulines** ⑥, a private school that houses a museum and has a lovely chapel next door.

On the nearby rue des Jardins, you'll see the **Holy Trinity Anglican Cathedral** ⑦, a dignified church with precious objects on display. Next come two buildings interesting for their Art Deco details: the **Hôtel Clarendon** ⑧, just east of the cathedral, on the corner of rue des Jardins and rue Ste-Anne and, next door, the **Edifice Price** ⑨. Head back on rue Ste-Anne past the cathedral and continue straight until the street becomes a narrow, cobblestone thoroughfare lined with shops and restaurants.

Turn left onto the outdoor art gallery of **rue du Trésor** ⑩ and at its end, turn left on rue Buade. When you reach the corner of côte de la Fabrique, you'll see the historic **Basilique Notre-Dame-de-Québec** ⑪, which has an ornate interior. The basilica marks the beginning of Québec City's **Latin Quarter.**

Head down côte de la Fabrique and turn right when it meets rue Collins. The cluster of stone buildings at the end of the street is the **Monastère des Augustines de l'Hôtel-Dieu de Québec** ⑫, which can be toured. Retrace your steps on rue Collins and côte de la Fabrique. When you reach rue Ste-Famille on the left, you will find the iron entrance gates of the **Séminaire du Québec** ⑬. Head north across the courtyard to the **Musée de l'Amérique Française.** Next, you can visit the seminary's Chapelle Extérieure, at the seminary's west entrance.

Exit the seminary from the east at rue de l'Université and head south to côte de la Montagne, where **Parc Montmorency** ⑭ straddles the hill between Upper Town and Lower Town. Walk through the park and cross côte de la Montagne to the escalier Frontenac, a stairway that leads to the north end of the Terrasse Dufferin. Turn right at the top for the 30-minute recap of the six sieges of Québec City at the **Musée du Fort** ⑮. As you leave the museum, head east to return to the top of the escalier Frontenac along Terrasse Dufferin.

TIMING

Plan on spending at least a day visiting the sites and museums in Upper Town. Lunchtime should find you at the Basilique Notre-Dame-de-Québec. Those who prefer a leisurely pace could take two days, stopping to watch street performers and enjoy long lunches. May through October are the best months for walking, July and August being the busiest.

406

Upper and Lower Towns (Haute-Ville, Basse-Ville)

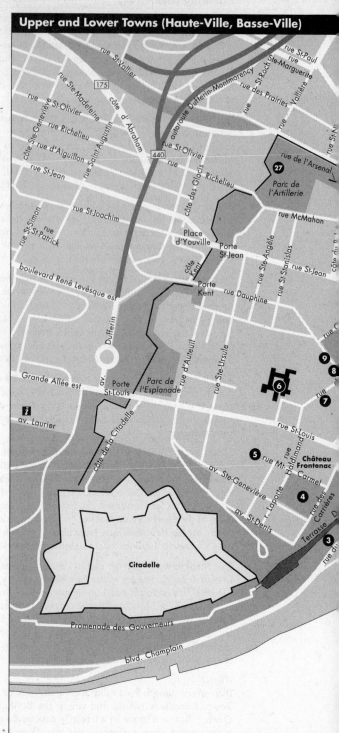

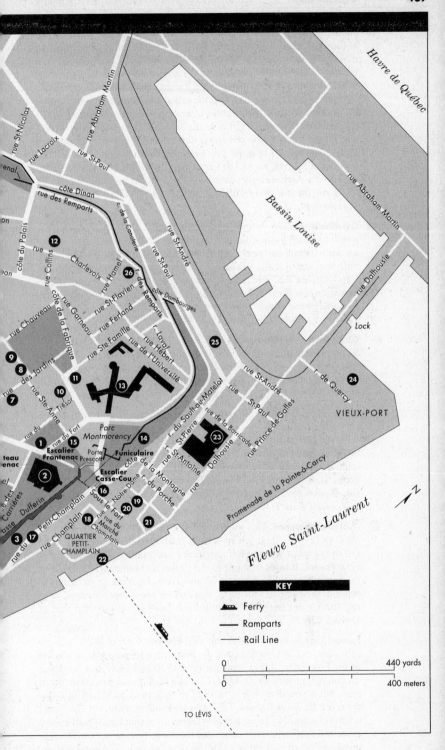

Havre de Québec

rue Abraham Martin

rue St-Nicolas

rue Lacroix

rue St-Paul

côte Dinan

rue des Remparts

côte du Palais

rue Collins

Charlevoix

rue Chauveau

rue Garneau

rue de la Fabrique

rue St-Flavien

rue Ferland

rue Ste-Famille

rue Hamel

r. de la Canoterie

r. des Remparts

rue St-André

rue St-Paul

côte Dambourges

Bassin Louise

rue Abraham Martin

rue Dalhousie

Lock

rue Laval

rue Hébert

rue de l'Université

rue St-André

rue St-Paul

r. de Quercy

VIEUX-PORT

9
8
rue des Jardins

7

rue Ste-Anne

10 rue St-Trésor

11

13

1

15

Parc Montmorency

Escalier Frontenac

Porte Prescott

Funiculaire

14

r. du Sault-au-Matelot

rue St-Pierre

r. de la Barricade

rue St-Antoine

23

2

Escalier Casse-Cou

côte de la Montagne

rue St-Paul

St-Pierre

rue Prince-de-Galles

Dalhousie

16

19

r. Notre-Dame

r. du Porche

20

rue Sous le Fort

17

3

18

rue Petit-Champlain

rue du Marché Champlain

21

QUARTIER PETIT-CHAMPLAIN

Promenade de la Pointe-à-Carcy

22

rue du Petit-Champlain

e des Carrières

Dufferin

teau enac

N

Fleuve Saint-Laurent

KEY
🚢 Ferry
— Ramparts
— Rail Line

0 _____ 440 yards

0 _____ 400 meters

TO LÉVIS

12

26

25

24

Sights to See

⑪ **Basilique Notre-Dame-de-Québec.** This basilica has the oldest parish in North America, dating from 1647. It's been rebuilt three times: in the early 1700s, when François de Montmorency Laval was the first bishop; in 1759, after cannons at Lévis fired upon it during the siege of Québec; and in 1922, after a fire. The basilica's somberly ornate interior includes a canopy dais over the episcopal throne, a ceiling of clouds decorated with gold leaf, richly colored stained-glass windows, and a chancel lamp that was a gift of Louis XIV. The large and famous crypt was Québec City's first cemetery; more than 900 people are interred here, including 20 bishops and four governors of New France. The founder of the city, Samuel de Champlain, is believed to be buried near the basilica: Archaeologists have been searching for his tomb since 1950. ⊠ *16 rue Buade,* ☎ *418/692–2533.* ▦ *Free.* ⊙ *Oct.–May, daily 8– 4; June–Sept., daily 8–6.*

❺ **Cavalier du Moulin.** A small park landscaped with flower beds that are interlaced with footpaths, the Cavalier du Moulin is the former site of a stone windmill that became part of the French fortifications. The windmill was strategically placed so that its cannons could destroy the Cap-Diamant Redoubt (near Promenade des Gouverneurs) and the St-Louis Bastion (near St-Louis Gate) in the event that New France was captured by the British. ⊠ *Between rue St. Louis and av. Ste.-Geneviève.* ▦ *Free.* ⊙ *May–Nov., daily 7 AM–9 PM.*

Centre Marie-de-l'Incarnation. Next to the **Musée des Ursulines** (☞ *below*) is this bookstore with an exhibit on the life of the Ursulines' first superior, who came from France and co-founded the convent. ⊠ *10 rue Donnacona,* ☎ *418/692–1569.* ▦ *Free.* ⊙ *Feb.–Nov., Tues.–Sat. 10–11:30 and 1:30–4:30, Sun. 1:30–4:30.*

Chapelle des Ursulines (Ursuline Chapel). On the grounds of the **Couvent des Ursulines** stands a little chapel where French General Montcalm was buried after he died in the 1759 battle. The exterior was rebuilt in 1902, but the interior contains the original chapel, which took sculptor Pierre-Noël Levasseur from 1726 to 1736 to complete. The votive lamp was lit in 1717 and has never been extinguished. ⊠ *12 rue Donnacona.* ▦ *Free.* ⊙ *May–Oct., Tues.–Sat. 10–11:30 and 1:30–4:30, Sun. 1:30–4:30.*

★ ❷ **Château Frontenac.** This imposing green-turreted castle with its slanting copper roof, Québec City's most celebrated landmark, stands on the site of what was the administrative and military headquarters of New France. It owes its name to the Comte de Frontenac, governor of the French colony between 1672 and 1698. Looking at the magnificence of the château's location, you can see why Frontenac said, "For me, there is no site more beautiful nor more grandiose than that of Québec City."

Samuel de Champlain, who founded Québec City in 1608, was responsible for Château St-Louis, the first structure to appear on the site of the Frontenac; it was built between 1620 and 1624 as a residence for colonial governors. In 1784, Château Haldimand was constructed here, but it was demolished in 1892 to make way for Château Frontenac (☞ Lodging, *below*). The latter was built as a hotel in 1893, and it was considered to be remarkably luxurious at that time: Guest rooms contained fireplaces, bathrooms, and marble fixtures, and a special commissioner purchased antiques for the establishment. The hotel was designed by New York architect Bruce Price, who also worked on Québec City's Gare du Palais (rail station) and other Canadian landmarks, such as Montréal's Windsor Station. The Frontenac was completed in 1925 with the addition of a 20-story central tower. Owned by Canadian Pacific Hotels, it has accumulated a star-studded guest roster, including Queen Elizabeth as well as Franklin Roosevelt and Winston Churchill, who convened here in 1943 and 1944 for two wartime conferences. ⊠ *1 rue des Carrières,* ☎ *418/692–3861.*

★ ❻ **Couvent des Ursulines** (Ursuline Convent). The site of North America's oldest teaching institution for girls, still a private school, was founded in 1639 by two French nuns. The convent has many of its original walls still intact. On its property are the **Musée des Ursulines** (☞ *below*) and the **Chapelle des Ursulines** (☞ *above*), which you may visit. Next door is an interesting bookstore, the **Centre Marie-de-l'Incarnation** (☞ *above*). ⊠ *18 rue Donnacona.*

★ ❾ **Edifice Price** (Price Building). The city's first skyscraper, the 15-story Art Deco building was built in 1929 and served as headquarters of the Price Brothers Company, the lumber firm founded in Canada by Sir William Price. Today it is owned by the provincial government and houses the offices of Québec City's mayor. Don't miss the interior: Exquisite copper plaques depict scenes of the company's early pulp and paper activities, while the two artfully carved maple-wood elevators are '30s classics. ⊠ *65 rue Ste-Anne.*

❼ **Holy Trinity Anglican Cathedral.** This stone church dates from 1804 and was one of the first Anglican cathedrals built outside the British Isles. Its simple, dignified facade is reminiscent of London's St. Martin-in-the-Fields. The cathedral's land was originally given to the Recollet fathers (Franciscan monks from France) in 1681 by the king of France for a church and monastery. When Québec came under British rule, the Recollets made the church available to the Anglicans for services. Later, King George III of England ordered construction of the present cathedral, with an area set aside for members of the royal family. A portion of the north balcony still remains exclusively for the use of the reigning sovereign or her representative. The church houses precious objects donated by George III; wood for the oak benches was imported from the Royal Forest at Windsor. The cathedral's impressive rear organ has more than 2,500 pipes. ⊠ *31 rue des Jardins,* ☎ *418/692–2193.* ▣ *Free.* ☉ *May–June, daily 9–5; July–Aug., daily 9–9; Sept.–Oct., weekdays 10–4; Nov.–Apr., offices only; Sun. services in English 8:30 and 11 AM, and in French 9:30 AM.*

❽ **Hôtel Clarendon.** One of Québec City's finest Art Deco structures is the Clarendon, Québec's oldest hotel (☞ Lodging, *below*). Although the Clarendon dates from 1866, it was reconstructed in its current Art Deco style—with geometric patterns of stone and wrought iron decorating its interior—in 1930. ⊠ *57 rue Ste-Anne, at rue des Jardins,* ☎ *418/692–2480.*

❹ **Jardin des Gouverneurs** (Governors' Park). This small park on the southern side of the Frontenac is home to the **Wolfe-Montcalm Monument,** a 50-ft obelisk that is unique because it pays tribute to both a winning (English) and a losing (French) general. The monument recalls the 1759 battle on the Plains of Abraham, which ended French rule of New France. British General James Wolfe lived only long enough to hear of his victory; French General Louis-Joseph Montcalm died shortly after Wolfe with the knowledge that the city was lost. During the French regime, the public area served as a garden for the governors who resided in Château St-Louis. On the south side of the park is **avenue Ste-Geneviève,** lined with well-preserved Victorian houses dating from 1850 to 1900 that have been converted to quaint old-fashioned inns.

Latin Quarter. Beginning at the Basilique Notre-Dame-de-Québec (☞ *above*), this area extends to the streets northwest of the Seminaire de Québec (☞ *below*)—rue Buade, rue des Remparts, côte de la Fabrique, and côte du Palais—as far as rue St-Jean. The district was dubbed the Latin Quarter because Latin was once a required language course at the seminary and was spoken among the students. Although Latin is no longer compulsory and Québec Seminary–Laval University has moved, students still cling to this neighborhood.

Maison Maillou. The colony's former treasury building typifies the architecture of New France with its sharply slanted roof, dormer windows, concrete chimneys, shutters with iron hinges, and limestone walls. Built between 1736 and 1753, it stands at the end of **rue du Trésor** (☞ *below*). Maison Maillou now houses the Québec City Chamber of Commerce and is not open for tours. ⊠ *17 rue St-Louis.*

⓬ **Monastère des Augustines de l'Hôtel-Dieu de Québec** (Augustine Monastery). Augustine nuns arrived from Dieppe, France, in 1639 with a mission to care for the sick in the new colony; they established the first hospital north of Mexico, the **Hôtel-Dieu hospital**, the large building west of the monastery. The **Musée des Augustines** (Augustine Museum) is in hospital-like quarters with large sterile corridors leading into a ward that has a small exhibit of antique medical instruments, such as a pill-making device from the 17th century. Upon request the Augustines also offer guided tours of the **chapel** (1800) and the cellars used by the nuns as a shelter, beginning in 1659, during bombardments by the British. ⊠ *32 rue Charlevoix,* ☎ *418/692–2492.* 🎟 *Free.* ☉ *Tues.–Sat. 9:30–noon and 1:30–5, Sun. 1:30–5.*

Musée de l'Amérique Française. Housed in a former student residence of the Québec Seminary–Laval University (☞ Séminaire du Québec, *below*), this museum focuses on the history of the French presence in North America. There are more than 400 landscape and still-life paintings dating to the 15th century, rare Canadian money from colonial times, and scientific instruments acquired through the centuries for the purposes of research and teaching. The museum uses historical documents and movies to tell the story as well. A former chapel has been renovated and is used for exhibits, conferences, and cultural activities. ⊠ *9 rue de l' Université,* ☎ *418/692–2843.* 🎟 *$3, free Tues. Sept.–June 23.* ☉ *Sept.–June 23, Tues.–Sun. 10–5; June 24–Aug., daily 10–5:30.*

Musée des Ursulines (Ursuline Museum). Within the walls of the ☞ **Couvent des Ursulines** is this former residence of one of the convent's founders, Madame de la Peltrie. It offers an informative perspective on 120 years of the Ursulines' life under the French regime, from 1639 to 1759. You'll see why it took an Ursuline nun nine years of training to attain the level of a professional embroiderer; the museum contains magnificent pieces of ornate embroidery, such as altar frontals with gold and silver threads intertwined with precious jewels. ⊠ *12 rue Donnacona,* ☎ *418/694–0694.* 🎟 *$3.* ☉ *May–Oct., Tues.–Sat. 10–noon and 1–5, Sun. 12:30–5.*

....

NEED A   At the neon-lit **Bistro Taste-Vin** (⊠ 32 rue St-Louis, ☎ 418/692-4191),
BREAK?   on the corner of rue des Jardins and rue St-Louis, sample delicious sal-
                ads, pastries, and desserts.

....

⓯ **Musée du Fort** (Fort Museum). This museum's sole exhibit is a sound-and-light show that reenacts the region's most important battles, including the Battle of the Plains of Abraham and the 1775 attack by American generals Arnold and Montgomery. ⊠ *10 rue Ste-Anne,* ☎ *418/692–2175.* 🎟 *$5.50.* ☉ *June–Aug., daily 10–6; Apr.–May,*

Sept.–Oct., daily 10–5; Nov. and Jan.–Mar., weekdays 11–noon and 1:45–3:30, weekends 11–5.

⓮ Parc Montmorency. This park marks the spot where Canada's first wheat was grown in 1618 and where the colony's first legislation was passed in 1694 (in a building no longer standing) ⊠ *Off côte de la Montagne.*

❶ Place d'Armes. For centuries, this square atop a cliff has been a gathering place for parades and military events. Upper Town's most central location, the plaza is bordered by government buildings; at its west side is the majestic **Ancien Palais de Justice** (Old Courthouse), a Renaissance-style building from 1887. The plaza is on land that was occupied by a church and convent of the Recollet missionaries (Franciscan monks), who in 1615 were the first order of priests to arrive in New France. The Gothic-style fountain at the center of Place d'Armes pays tribute to their arrival. ⊠ *rue St-Louis and rue du Fort.*

❿ Rue du Trésor. The road colonists took on their way to pay rent to the king's officials is now a narrow alley where hundreds of colorful prints, paintings, and other artworks are on display. You won't necessarily find masterpieces here, but this walkway is a good stop for a souvenir sketch or two. In summer, activity on this street and nearby rue Ste-Anne, lined with eateries and boutiques, starts early in the morning and continues until late at night. Stores stay open, artists paint, and street musicians perform as long as there is an audience, even if it's one o'clock in the morning. At 8 rue du Trésor is the **Québec Experience** (☎ 418/694–4000), a multimedia sound-and-light show that takes you into the heart of Québec's history, from the first explorers until modern days; cost is $6.75.

⓭ Séminaire du Québec. Behind these gates lies a tranquil courtyard surrounded by austere stone buildings with rising steeples; these structures have housed classrooms and student residences since 1663. Québec Seminary was founded by François de Montmorency Laval, the first bishop of New France, to train priests of the new colony. In 1852 the seminary became Université Laval, the first Catholic university in North America. In 1946 the university moved to a larger, modern campus in the suburb of Ste-Foy. Today priests live on the premises, and Laval's architecture school occupies part of the building. The **Musée du Séminaire** offers guided tours of the seminary during the summer. The small Roman-style chapel, **Chapelle Extérieure** (Outer Chapel), at the west entrance of Québec Seminary, was built in 1888 after fire destroyed the first chapel, which dated from 1750. ⊠ *1 côte de la Fabrique,* ☎ *418/692–3981.*

❸ Terrasse Dufferin. This wide boardwalk with an intricate wrought-iron guardrail allows a panoramic view of the St. Lawrence River, the town of Lévis on the opposite shore, Ile d'Orléans, and the Laurentian Mountains. It was named for Lord Dufferin, governor of Canada between 1872 and 1878, who had this walkway constructed in 1878. At its western end begins the **Promenade des Gouverneurs,** which skirts the cliff and leads up to Québec's highest point, Cap Diamant, and also to the Citadelle (☞ *Outside the Walls, below*).

Lower Town

New France first began to flourish in the streets of the Basse-Ville, or Lower Town, along the banks of the St. Lawrence River. These streets became the colony's economic crossroads, where furs were traded, ships came in, and merchants established their residences.

Despite the status of Lower Town as the oldest neighborhood in North America, its narrow and time-worn thoroughfares have a new and polished look. In the 1960s, after a century of decay as the commercial boom moved west and left the area abandoned, the Québec government committed millions of dollars to restore the district to the way it had been during the days of New France. Today modern boutiques, restaurants, galleries, and shops catering to visitors occupy the former warehouses and residences.

A Good Walk

Begin this walk on the northern tip of rue du Petit-Champlain at **Maison Louis-Jolliet** ⑯ at the foot of the **Escalier Casse-Cou.** Heading south on **rue du Petit-Champlain** ⑰, the city's oldest street, you'll notice the cliff on the right that borders this narrow thoroughfare, with Upper Town on the heights above. At the point where rue du Petit-Champlain intersects with boulevard Champlain, make a U-turn to head back north on rue Champlain. One block farther, at the corner of rue du Marché-Champlain, you'll find **Maison Chevalier** ⑱, a stone house in the style of urban New France. Walk east to rue Notre-Dame, which leads directly to **Place Royale** ⑲, formerly the heart of New France. The small stone church at the south side of Place Royale is the **Église Notre-Dame-des-Victoires** ⑳, the oldest church in Québec.

On the east side of Place Royale, take rue de la Place, which leads to an open square, **Place de Paris** ㉑. At this point of the tour you may conveniently catch the 15-minute **Lévis–Québec ferry** ㉒ to the opposite shore of the St. Lawrence River for the view. Back on the Québec side of the river, you may want to stop at **Explore,** a sound-and-light show on rue Dalhousie. Continue north on rue Dalhousie until you come to the **Musée de la Civilisation** ㉓, devoted to Québécois culture and civilization. Head east toward the river to the **Vieux-Port de Québec** ㉔, at one time the busiest on the continent. The breezes here from the St. Lawrence provide a cool reprieve on a hot summer's day, and you can browse through a farmer's market here. You are now in the ideal spot to explore Québec City's **antiques district** ㉕.

Walk west along rue St-Paul and turn left onto a steep brick incline called côte Dambourges; when you reach côte de la Canoterie, take the stairs back on the cliff to rue des Remparts. Continue approximately a block west along rue des Remparts until you come to the last building in a row of purple houses, **Maison Montcalm** ㉖, the former home of General Montcalm. Continue west on rue des Remparts and turn left on côte du Palais and then immediately right on rue de l'Arsenal, which brings you to the **Parc de l'Artillerie** ㉗, a complex of 20 military, industrial, and civilian buildings.

TIMING

This is a good day of sightseeing. A morning stroll will take you to two of the city's most famous squares, Place Royale and Place de Paris. Take the time for a brisk 15-minute ferry ride to Lévis and back and you'll be ready for a mid-morning snack. You may want to take in the Explore light show or tour the Musée de la Civilisation before a late lunch in the antiques district. After browsing along rue St-Paul, explore Parc de l'Artillerie and its adjoining buildings.

Sights to See

㉕ **Antiques district.** Antiques shops cluster along rue St-Pierre and rue St-Paul. Rue St-Paul was once part of a business district where warehouses, stores, and businesses abounded. After World War I, shipping and commercial activities plummeted; low rents attracted antiques dealers.

Today numerous cafés, restaurants, and art galleries have turned this area into one of the town's more fashionable sections.

20 **Eglise Notre-Dame-des-Victoires** (Our Lady of Victory Church). The oldest church in Québec was built on the site of Samuel de Champlain's first residence, which also served as a fort and trading post. The church was built in 1688 and was restored twice. Its name comes from two French victories against the British: one in 1690 against Admiral William Phipps and another in 1711 against Sir Hovendon Walker. The interior contains copies of paintings by such European masters as Van Dyck, Rubens, and Boyermans; its altar resembles the shape of a fort. A scale model suspended from the ceiling represents *Le Brezé*, the boat that transported French soldiers to New France in 1664. The side chapel is dedicated to Ste-Geneviève, the patron saint of Paris. ⊠ *Pl. Royale*, ☎ 418/692–1650. ▨ *Free.* ☉ *Mid-May–mid-Oct., Sun.–Fri. 9–4:30, Sat. 9–4, except during Mass (Sun. at 9:30, 11, and noon; Sat. at 7 PM), marriages, and funerals; mid-Oct.–mid-May, Mon.–Sat. 9–4:30, except during marriages and funerals.*

Escalier Casse-Cou. The steepness of the city's first iron stairway, an ambitious 1893 design by city architect and engineer Charles Baillairgé, is ample evidence of how it got its name: Breakneck Steps. The steps were built on the site of the original 17th-century stairway that linked the Upper Town and Lower Town during the French regime. Today shops, quaint boutiques, and restaurants are at various levels.

Explore. This 30-minute sound-and-light show uses high-tech visual art to re-create the story of the founding of the city. You can sail up the St. Lawrence River with Jacques Cartier and Samuel de Champlain to Québec and witness their first encounter with the area's native people. ⊠ *63 rue Dalhousie*, ☎ 418/692–2063. ▨ *$5.50.* ☉ *May–Aug., daily 10–6; Sept.–Apr., by reservation only.*

22 **Lévis–Québec ferry.** En route to the opposite shore of the St. Lawrence River, you get a striking view of Québec City's skyline, with the Château Frontenac and the Québec Seminary high atop the cliff. The view is even more impressive at night. ⊠ *Rue Dalhousie, 1 block south of Place de Paris*, ☎ 418/644–3704. ▨ *$1.25.* ☉ *Daily, 1st ferry leaves at 6:30 AM; crossings every ½ hr 7:30 AM–6:30 PM, every hr 7:30 PM–2:30 AM; final crossing 3:45 AM. May–Nov., extra ferry service runs every 20 min during rush hours: 7:20AM–9AM and 4PM–6PM.*

NEED A BREAK?　**Café du Monde** (⊠ 57 rue Dalhousie, ☎ 418/692–4455), with an impressive view of the St. Lawrence River, specializes in brunch on Saturday and Sunday. Croissants, sausages, waffles with maple syrup, and *moules et frites* (mussels with French fries) are popular.

18 **Maison Chevalier.** This old stone house was built in 1752 for shipowner Jean-Baptiste Chevalier; the house's style, of classic French inspiration, clearly reflects the urban architecture of New France. Fire walls, chimneys, vaulted cellars, and original wood beams and stone fireplaces are some of its noteworthy features. ⊠ *50 rue du Marché-Champlain*, ☎ 418/643–2158. ▨ *Free.* ☉ *May 6–June 22 and Sept. 8–Oct., Tues.–Sun. 10–6; June 23–Sept. 7, daily 10–6; Nov.–May 5, weekends 10–5.*

16 **Maison Louis-Jolliet.** Built in 1683, this house is the lower station of the funicular (closed at press time) and was used by the first settlers of New France as a base for further westward explorations. A monument commemorating Louis Jolliet's discovery of the Mississippi River in 1672 stands in the park next to the house. At the north side of the house is Escalier Casse-Cou (☞ *above*). ⊠ *16 rue du Petit-Champlain*.

❷❻ **Maison Montcalm.** This was the home of French General Louis-Joseph Montcalm from 1758 until the capitulation of New France. A plaque dedicated to the general is on the right side of the house. ⊠ *rue des Remparts between rues Hamel and St-Flavien.*

⟲ ❷❸ **Musée de la Civilisation** (Museum of Civilization). Wedged into the foot of the cliff, this spacious museum with a striking limestone-and-glass facade has been artfully designed by architect Moshe Safdie to blend into the landscape. Its campanile echoes the shape of church steeples throughout the city. The museum has innovative exhibits devoted to aspects of Québec's culture. It tells the story of how the first settlers lived, and how they survived such harsh winters. It illustrates to what extent the Roman Catholic Church dominated the people and explains the evolution of Québec nationalism. Several of the shows, with their imaginative use of artwork, video screens, computers, and sound, will appeal to both adults and children. Its thematic, interactive approach also extends to exhibits of an international nature. ⊠ *85 rue Dalhousie,* ☎ *418/643–2158.* ▣ *$6; free Tues. in winter.* ⊙ *June 24– Aug., daily 10–7; Sept.–June 23, Tues.–Sun. 10–5.*

★ ❷❼ **Parc de l'Artillerie** (Artillery Park). This national historic park is a complex of 20 military, industrial, and civilian buildings that were situated to guard the St. Charles River and the Old Port. Its earliest buildings served as headquarters for the French garrison and were taken over in 1759 by the British Royal Artillery soldiers. The defense complex was used as a fortress, barracks, and cartridge factory during the American siege of Québec in 1775 and 1776. The area served as an industrial complex providing ammunition for the Canadian army from 1879 until 1964. One of the three buildings you can visit is a former **powder magazine,** which in 1903 became a shell foundry. The building houses a detailed model of Québec City in 1808, rendered by two surveyors in the office of the Royal Engineers Corps. Sent to Britain in 1813, it was intended to show officials the strategic importance of Québec so that more money would be provided to expand the city's fortifications. The model details the city's buildings, streets, and military structures. From April through October, the powder magazine is open daily 10–5; admission is $2.75. The **Dauphin Redoubt,** named in honor of the son of Louis XIV (the heir apparent), was constructed from 1712 to 1748. It served as a barracks for the French garrison until 1760, when it became an officers' mess for the Royal Artillery Regiment. It's open late June–early September, daily 10–5. The **Officers' Quarters,** a dwelling for Royal Artillery officers until 1871 when the British army departed, houses an exhibit on military life during the British regime. The Officers' Quarters are open late June–early September, daily 10–5. ⊠ *2 rue d'Auteuil,* ☎ *418/648–4205.*

❷❶ **Place de Paris.** This square, a newcomer to these historic quarters, is dominated by a black-and-white geometric sculpture, *Dialogue avec l'Histoire* (Dialogue with History), a gift from France positioned on the site where the first French settlers landed. ⊠ *rue Dalhousie.*

❶❾ **Place Royale.** The cobblestone square is encircled by the former homes of wealthy merchants, which have steep Normandy-style roofs, dormer windows, and several chimneys. Until 1686 the area was called Place du Marché, but its name was changed when a bust of Louis XIV was erected at its center. During the late 1600s and early 1700s, when Place Royale was continually under threat of attacks from the British, the colonists progressively moved to higher and safer quarters atop the cliff in Upper Town. Yet after the French colony fell to British rule in 1759, Place Royale flourished again with shipbuilding, logging, fishing, and fur trading. An **information center** (⊠ 215 Marché Finlay, ☎ 418/646–3167) about the square is open June 3–September 29.

⑰ **Rue du Petit-Champlain.** The oldest street in the city, this was the main street of a former harbor village, with trading posts and the homes of rich merchants. Today it has pleasant boutiques and cafés. Natural-fiber weaving, Inuit carvings, hand-painted silks, and enameled copper crafts are some of the local specialties that are good buys here.

㉔ **Vieux-Port de Québec** (Old Port of Québec). The old harbor dates from the 17th century, when ships first arrived from Europe bringing supplies and settlers to the new colony. At one time this port was among the busiest on the continent: Between 1797 and 1897, Québec shipyards turned out more than 2,500 ships, many of which passed the 1,000-ton mark. The port saw a rapid decline after steel replaced wood and the channel to Montréal was deepened to allow larger boats to reach a good port upstream. Today the 72-acre area encompasses several parks. You can stroll along the riverside promenade, where merchant and cruise ships are docked. At the port's northern end, where the St. Charles meets the St. Lawrence, a lock protects the marina in the Louise Basin from the generous Atlantic tides that reach even this far up the St. Lawrence. In the northwest section of the port, an exhibition center, **Port de Québec in the 19th Century** (⊠ 100 rue St-André, ☎ 418/648–3300), presents the history of the port in relation to the lumber trade and shipbuilding. Admission to the center is $2.75; it is open May–November, daily 10–5; December–April, by reservation only. At the port's northwestern tip is the **Marché du Vieux-Port** (Old Port Market), where farmers sell their fresh produce. The market is open May–October, daily 8–8.

Outside the Walls

In the 20th century, Québec City grew into a modern metropolis outside the confines of the city walls. Yet beyond the walls lies a great deal of the city's military history, in the form of its fortifications and battlements, as well as a number of cultural and other attractions.

A Good Walk

Start close to St-Louis Gate at **Parc de l'Esplanade** ㉘, the site of a former military parade ground. From the powder magazine in the park, head south on côte de la Citadelle, which leads directly to the **Citadelle** ㉙, a historic fortified base. Retrace your steps down côte de la Citadelle to Grande Allée. Continue west until you come to the Renaissance-style **Parliament Buildings** ㉚, which mark Parliament Hill, headquarters of the provincial government. Across from the Parliament on the south side of Grande Allée is the Manège Militaire, a turreted armory built in 1888 that is still a drill hall for the 22nd Regiment.

Continue along **Grande Allée** ㉛, Québec City's version of the Champs-Elysées, with its cafés, clubs, and restaurants. If you turn left on Place Montcalm, you'll be facing the **Montcalm Monument** ㉜. Continue south on Place Montcalm to the historic and scenic **Parc des Champs-de-Bataille** ㉝. Within the park are the **Plains of Abraham** ㉞, the site of the famous 1759 battle that decided the fate of New France.

Take avenue Laurier, which runs parallel to the park, a block west until you come to a neatly tended garden called **Parc Jeanne d'Arc** ㉟. If you continue west on avenue Laurier, you'll see a stone oval defense tower, **Tour Martello no. 2** ㊱; on the left, toward the south end of the park, stands **Tour Martello no. 1** ㊲. Continue a block west on rue de Bernières and then follow avenue George-VI along the outskirts of the Parc des Champs-de-Bataille until it intersects with avenue Wolfe-Montcalm. You'll come to the tall **Wolfe Monument** ㊳, which marks the place where

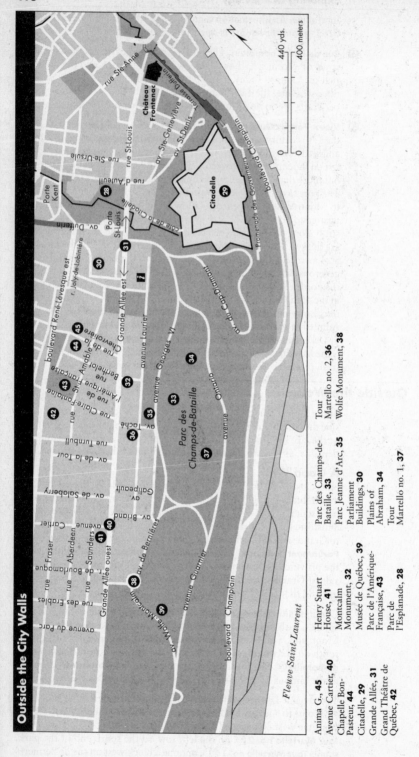

Outside the City Walls

416

Fleuve Saint-Laurent

Anima G., **45**
Avenue Cartier, **40**
Chapelle Bon-
Pasteur, **44**
Citadelle, **29**
Grande Allée, **31**
Grand Théâtre de
Québec, **42**

Henry Stuart
House, **41**
Montcalm
Monument, **32**
Musée de Québec, **39**
Parc de l'Amérique-
Française, **43**
Parc de
l'Esplanade, **28**

Parc des Champs-de-
Bataille, **33**
Parc Jeanne d'Arc, **35**
Parliament
Buildings, **30**
Plains of
Abraham, **34**
Tour
Martello no. 1, **37**

Tour
Martello no. 2, **36**
Wolfe Monument, **38**

the British general died. Turn left on avenue Wolfe-Montcalm for a stroll through the **Musée de Québec** ㊴. From the museum head north on avenue Wolfe-Montcalm, turning right on Grande Allée and walking a block to **avenue Cartier** ㊵. At the corner of avenue Cartier is the **Henry Stuart House** ㊶, home to the same family from 1918 to 1987.

If you continue north along avenue Cartier, the first major intersection is boulevard René-Lévesque Est. Turn right and walk two blocks to the concrete modern building of the **Grand Théâtre de Québec** ㊷, a center for the city's performing arts. High-waving flags east of the Grand Théâtre are displayed in the **Parc de l'Amérique-Française** ㊸, dedicated to places in North America with a French-speaking population. Take rue Claire-Fontaine a block south, turn left on rue St-Amable, and then left again on rue de la Chevrotière. On the west side of the street you'll see the **Chapelle Bon-Pasteur** ㊹, a church surrounded by modern office complexes. Across rue de la Chevrotière is the entrance of Edifice Marie-Guyart, whose observation tower, **Anima G.** ㊺, provides a great view. Two sights not in walking distance are the **Aquarium du Québec** and the **Jardin Zoologique du Québec.**

TIMING

This is a full day of sightseeing. You should be able to visit the Musée de Québec before lunch. In the afternoon, you can visit the Henry Stuart House, but check the limited times. Spend a little more time on avenue Cartier, then visit the Grand Théâtre du Québec or, if you prefer, continue exploring the Plains of Abraham. Other afternoon choices are to head to the aquarium or the zoo.

Sights to See

㊺ **Anima G.** This observation gallery is on top of Edifice Marie-Guyart, Québec City's tallest office building. The gray, modern concrete tower, 31 stories high, has by far the best view of the city and the environs. There's an express elevator. ⊠ *1037 rue de la Chevrotière,* ☎ *418/644–9841.* ☞ *Free.* ☉ *Late Jan.–early Dec., weekdays 10–4, weekends and holidays 1–5.*

㊳ **Aquarium du Québec.** This aquarium, about 10 km (6 mi) from the city center, contains more than 300 species of marine life, including reptiles, exotic fish, and seals from the lower St. Lawrence River. A wooded picnic ground makes this spot ideal for a family outing. The Québec City transit system, Société de Transport de la Communauté Urbaine de Québec, or STCUQ (☎ 418/627–2511), runs Buses 13 and 25 here. ⊠ *1675 av. des Hôtels, Ste-Foy,* ☎ *418/659–5264 or 418/659–5266 (reservations are needed for groups of 15 or more).* ☞ *$8.* ☉ *Daily 9–5; seals are fed and put on a show at 10:15 and 3:15.*

㊵ **Avenue Cartier.** Here you can indulge in the pleasures offered by the many good restaurants, clubs, and cafés lining the block.

㊹ **Chapelle Bon-Pasteur.** This slender church with a steep sloping roof was designed by Charles Baillargé in 1868. Its ornate baroque-style interior has carved-wood designs painted elaborately in gold leaf. The chapel houses 32 religious paintings done by the nuns of the community from 1868 to 1910. Classical concerts are performed here year-round. ⊠ *1080 rue de la Chevrotière,* ☎ *418/641–1069 or 418/648–9710.* ☞ *Free.* ☉ *July–Aug., Tues.–Sun. 1:30–4; Sept.–June by reservation; musical artists' Mass Sun. 10:45.*

㉙ **Citadelle** (Citadel). Built at the city's highest point, on Cap Diamant, the Citadelle is the largest fortified base in North America still occupied by troops. The 25-building fortress was intended to protect the port, prevent the enemy from taking up a position on the Plains of Abraham, and provide a refuge in case of an attack. Having inherited incomplete fortifications, the British sought to complete the Citadelle to protect themselves against retaliations from the French. By the time the Citadelle was completed in 1832, the attacks against Québec City had ended. Since 1920 the Citadelle has served as a base for the Royal 22nd Regiment. Firearms, uniforms, and decorations from the 17th century are displayed in the **Royal 22nd Regiment Museum,** in the former powder house, built in 1750. If weather permits, you can watch the Changing of the Guard, a ceremony in which the troops parade before the Citadelle in red coats and black fur hats. Admission is by guided tour only. ⊠ *1 côte de la Citadelle,* ☎ *418/694–2815.* ☞ *$5.* ◷ *Apr.–mid-May, daily 10–4; mid-May–June 23, daily 9–5; June 24–Aug., daily 9–6; Sept., daily 9–4; Oct., daily 10–3, Nov.–Mar., groups only (reservations required). Changing of the guard, mid-June–Labor Day, daily at 10 AM. Retreat ceremony, July and Aug., daily at 6 PM.*

③① **Grande Allée.** One of the city's oldest streets, Grande Allée was the route people took from outlying areas to sell their furs in town. Now trendy cafés, clubs, and restaurants line the road. The street actually has four names: inside the city walls, it is rue St-Louis; outside the walls, Grande Allée; farther west, chemin St-Louis; and farther still, boulevard Laurier.

④② **Grande Théâtre de Québec.** Opened in 1971, the theater incorporates two main halls, both named for 19th-century Canadian poets. The Grande Salle of Louis-Frechette, named for the first Québec poet and writer to be honored by the French Academy, holds 1,800 seats and is used for concerts, opera, and theater. The Petite Salle of Octave-Crémazie, used for experimental theater and variety shows, derives its name from the poet who stirred the rise of Québec nationalism in the mid-19th century. As the complex was being constructed, Montréal architect Victor Prus commissioned Jordi Bonet, a Québec sculptor, to work simultaneously on a three-wall mural. The themes depicted in the three sections are death, life, and liberty. Bonet wrote "La Liberté" on one wall to symbolize the Québécois' struggle for freedom and cultural distinction. The theater has a full repertory in winter, but no shows in summer. ⊠ *269 blvd. René-Lévesque Est,* ☎ *418/646–0609.* ◷ *Guided tours (reservations required) daily 9–4.*

④① **Henry Stuart House.** Built in 1849, this English-style cottage was home to the Stuart family from 1918 to 1987, when it was designated a historic monument by the Ministry of Culture. Its decor has remained unchanged since 1930. Most of the furniture was imported from England in the second half of the 19th century. ⊠ *82 Grande Allée Ouest,* ☎ *418/647–4347.* ☞ *$5.* ◷ *June–Aug., Wed.–Mon. 11–5; Sept.–May, Thurs. and Sun. 11–5 or by reservation.*

NEED A BREAK?
Halles Petit-Cartier (⊠ 1191 av. Cartier, ☎ 418/688–1630), a food mall near the Henry Stuart House, has restaurants and shops that sell French delicacies—cheeses, pastries, breads, vegetables, and candies. It's good for lunch.

☙ **Jardin Zoologique du Québec.** This zoo is especially scenic because of the DuBerger River, which traverses the grounds. About 250 animal species live here, including bears, wildcats, primates, and birds of prey. There are farm animals and horse-drawn carriage rides, and you can cross-country ski here in winter. The zoo is 11 km (7 mi) west of Québec City on Route 73. The city transit system (☎ 418/627–2511) operates Bus 801 here. ⊠ *9300 rue de la Faune, Charlesbourg,* ☎ *418/*

622–0313. ✉ *Apr.–Sept., $7.50; Oct.–Mar., weekdays free, weekends $5.* ⊙ *Daily 9–5.*

㉜ Montcalm Monument. France and Canada joined together to erect this monument honoring Louis-Joseph Montcalm, who claimed his fame by winning four major battles in North America. His most famous battle, however, was the one he lost, when the British conquered New France on September 13, 1759. Montcalm was north of Québec City at Beauport when he learned that the British attack was imminent. He quickly assembled his troops to meet the enemy and was wounded in battle in the leg and stomach. Montcalm was carried into the walled city, where he died the next morning. 🚇 *Pl. Montcalm.*

★ **㊳ Musée de Québec** (Québec Museum). This neoclassical beaux-arts showcase has more than 18,000 traditional and contemporary pieces of Québec art. The portraits by artists well known in the area, such as Ozias Leduc (1864–1955) and Horatio Walker (1858–1938), are particularly notable. This museum's very formal and dignified building in Parc des Champs-de-Bataille was designed by Wilfrid Lacroix and erected in 1933 to commemorate the tricentennial of the founding of Québec. The museum has renovated the original building, incorporating the space of an abandoned prison dating from 1867. A hallway of cells, with the iron bars and courtyard still intact, has been preserved as part of a permanent exhibition of the prison's history. ✉ *1 av. Wolfe-Montcalm,* ☎ *418/643–2150.* ✉ *$5.75; Sept.–mid-May, free Wed.* ⊙ *Sept.–mid-May, Tues., Thurs.–Sun., 11–5:45, Wed. 11–8:45; mid-May–Aug., Thurs.–Tues. 10–5:45, Wed. 10–9:45.*

㊸ Parc de l'Amérique-Française. Inaugurated in 1985 by the late René Lévesque, former Québec premier, the park is dedicated to places in North America with a French-speaking population. Flags are flown from Acadia, British Columbia, Louisiana, Manitoba, Saskatchewan, and Ontario, but Québec's own Fleur de Lys leads the way. Blue and white, the colors of Sun King Louis XIV, constitute a reminder of Québec's French origins, culture, and language. ✉ *rues St. Amable and Claire-Fontaine.*

㉘ Parc de l'Esplanade (Esplanade Park). In the 19th century, this was a clear space surrounded by a picket fence and poplar trees. Today you'll find the **Poudrière de l'Esplanade** (✉ Powder Magazine, 100 rue St-Louis, ☎ 418/648–7016), which the British constructed in 1820; it houses a model depicting the evolution of the wall surrounding Vieux-Québec. There's a $2.50 charge to enter the magazine; it's open April–October, daily 10–5. The French began building ramparts along the city's natural cliff as early as 1690 to protect themselves from British invaders. The colonists had trouble convincing the French government back home, though, to take the threat of invasion seriously, and by 1759, when the British invaded for control of New France, the walls were still incomplete. The British, despite attacks by the Americans during the War of Independence and the War of 1812, took a century to finish them. The park is also the starting point for walking the city's 4½ km (3 mi) of walls; in summer, guided tours begin here.

㉝ Parc des Champs-de-Bataille (Battlefields Park). One of North America's largest and most scenic parks, this 250-acre area of gently rolling slopes has unparalleled views of the St. Lawrence River. Within the park and just west of the Citadelle are the ☞ **Plains of Abraham**, the site of the famous 1759 battle that decided the fate of New France.

㉟ Parc Jeanne d'Arc. This park, bright with colorful flowers, has an equestrian statue of Joan of Arc as its focal point. A symbol of courage, the statue stands in tribute to the heroes of 1759 near the place where New

France was lost to the British. The park also commemorates the Canadian national anthem, "O Canada"; it was played here for the first time on June 24, 1880. ⊠ *Avs. Laurier and Taché.*

㉚ Parliament Buildings. These buildings, erected between 1877 and 1884, are the seat of L'Assemblée Nationale (the National Assembly) of 125 provincial representatives. Québec architect Eugène-Étienne Taché designed the stately buildings in the late 17th-century Renaissance style of Louis XIV, with four wings set in a square around an interior court. In front of the Parliament, statues pay tribute to important figures of Québec history: Cartier, Champlain, Frontenac, Wolfe, and Montcalm. There's a 30-minute tour (in English or French) of the President's Gallery, the Legislative Council Chamber, and the National Assembly Chamber, which is green, white, and gold—colors that correspond to the House of Commons in both London and Ottawa. ⊠ *Av. Dufferin and Grande Allée Est, door 3,* ☎ *418/643–7239.* ⊡ *Free.* ⊙ *Guided tours (reservations required) Jan.–May and Sept.–Nov., weekdays 9– 4:30; late June–Aug., daily 9–4:30.*

★ ㉞ Plains of Abraham. This park, named after the river pilot Abraham Martin, is the site of the famous 1759 battle that decided the fate of New France. People cross-country ski here in winter. The interpretation center is open year-round; a bus serves as shuttle and guided tour, with commentary in French and English, around the Plains of Abraham, making 11 stops. Call Pavillon Baillargé, Québec Museum (☎ 418/648–4071), for departure times. ⊡ *Tour $1.* ⊙ *Tours mid-June–1st Mon. in Sept., daily 10–6.*

㊲ Tour Martello no. 1. Of the 16 Martello towers in Canada, four were built in Québec City because the British government feared an invasion after the American Revolution. Tour Martello no. 1, which exhibits the history of the four structures, was built between 1802 and 1810. For Tour Martello no. 2, *see below.* Tour no. 3 guarded westward entry to the city, but it was demolished in 1904. Tour no. 4 is on rue Lavigueur overlooking the St. Charles River but is not open to the public. ⊠ *South end of Parc Jeanne d'Arc.*

㊱ Tour Martello no. 2. This Martello tower, which has an astronomy display, was built in the early 19th century to slow an enemy approach (☞ Tour Martello no. 1, *above*). ⊠ *Avs. Taché and Laurier.*

㊳ Wolfe Monument. This tall monument marks the place where the British general James Wolfe died. Wolfe landed his troops about 3 km (less than 2 mi) from the city's walls; the 4,500 English soldiers scaled the cliff and opened fire on the Plains of Abraham. Wolfe was mortally wounded in battle and was carried behind the lines to this spot. ⊠ *Rue de Bernières and av. Wolfe-Montcalm.*

DINING

Most dining establishments usually have a selection of dishes à la carte, but you'll often discover more creative specialties by opting for the table d'hôte, a two- to four-course meal chosen daily by the chef. At dinner many restaurants will offer a *menu de dégustation,* a five- to seven-course dinner of the chef's finest creations. If you're budget-conscious, try the more expensive establishments at lunchtime. Lunch usually costs about 30% less than dinner, and many of the same dishes are available. Lunch is usually served 11:30 to 2:30; dinner, 6:30 until about 11. You should tip about 15% of the bill.

CATEGORY	COST*
$$$$	over $35
$$$	$25–$35
$$	$15–$25
$	under $15

per person, excluding drinks, service, 7% GST, and 6.5% provincial sales tax.

Upper Town

$$$$ ✕ **A la Table de Serge Bruyère.** This restaurant put Québec on the map
  ★ of great gastronomic cities and serves classic French cuisine presented
with plenty of crystal, silver, and fresh flowers. Opened in 1980 by the
late Serge Bruyère, native of Lyon, France, the restaurant is now run
by Henriette Barré. The *menu gourmand* is a seven-course meal for about
$50. Specialties include scampi in puff pastry with fresh tomatoes, scal-
lop stew with watercress, and duckling supreme with blueberry sauce.
Only one sitting is offered each night. Downstairs, **A la Petite Table** is
less formal and less expensive, with such dishes as seafood terrine and
pork with tarragon sauce. ✉ *1200 rue St-Jean,* ☎ *418/694–0618. Reservations essential. Jacket required. AE, DC, MC, V.*

$$$ ✕ **Aux Anciens Canadiens.** This establishment is named for a book by
Philippe-Aubert de Gaspé, who once resided here. The house, dating
from 1675, has five dining rooms with different themes. The *vaisse-
lier* (dish room) is bright and cheerful, with colorful antique dishes and
a fireplace. Come for the authentic French-Canadian cooking; hearty
specialties include duck in maple glaze and caribou with blueberry wine
sauce. The restaurant also serves the best caribou drink (a local bev-
erage made with sweet red wine and whiskey, known for its kick) in
town. ✉ *34 rue St-Louis,* ☎ *418/692–1627. AE, DC, MC, V.*

$$$ ✕ **Le Continental.** If there were a Québec City dining hall of fame, Le
Continental would be there among the best. Since 1956, the Sgobba
family has been serving award-winning Continental cuisine to Québe-
cers. Deep blue walls, mahogany paneling, and crisp white tablecloths
create a stately ambience, and house specialties like orange duckling
and filet mignon Continental are flambéed at your table. Other favorites
are rack of lamb Victoria, partridge Périgourdine, and fish and seafood
dishes. ✉ *26 rue St-Louis,* ☎ *418/694–9995. AE, DC, MC, V.*

$$$ ✕ **Le Saint-Amour.** Here are all the makings of a true haute-cuisine es-
  ★ tablishment without the pretentious atmosphere. A light and airy
atrium, with a retractable roof for outdoor dining in summer, creates
a relaxed dining ambience. Chef Jean-Luc Boulay returns regularly to
France for inspiration; his studies pay off in such specialties as stuffed
quail in port sauce and salmon with chive mousse. Sauces here are light,
with no flour or butter. The *menu de decouvert* has nine courses, and
the *menu de dégustation* has seven. If you plan to order one of these
menus, mention it when you make your reservation. The chef's true
expertise shines in his desserts—try the crème brûlée sweetened with
maple syrup or the royal chocolate cake made with caramelized hazel-
nuts. ✉ *48 rue Ste-Ursule,* ☎ *418/694–0667. Reservations essential
on weekends. AE, DC, MC, V.*

$$ ✕ **L'Apsara.** The Cambodian family that owns this restaurant near the
St-Louis Gate excels at using both subtle and tangy spices to create unique
flavors. It's ideal if you're seeking a reprieve from French fare. Decor
combines Western and Eastern motifs, with flowered wallpaper, Asian
art, and small fountains. Innovative dishes from Vietnam, Thailand,
and Cambodia include such starters as *fleur de pailin* (a rice-paste roll
filled with fresh vegetables, meat, and shrimp) and *mou sati* (pork ke-
babs with peanut sauce and coconut milk). The assorted miniature Cam-

422

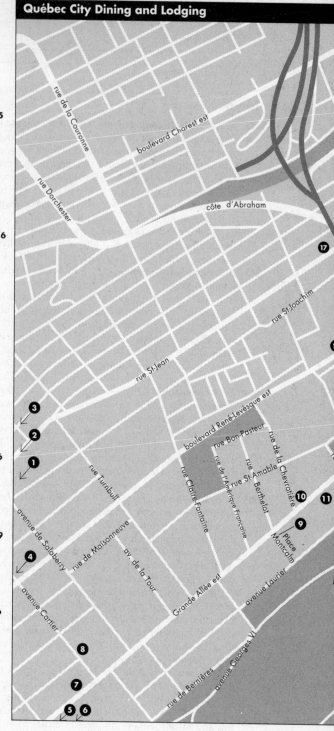

Québec City Dining and Lodging

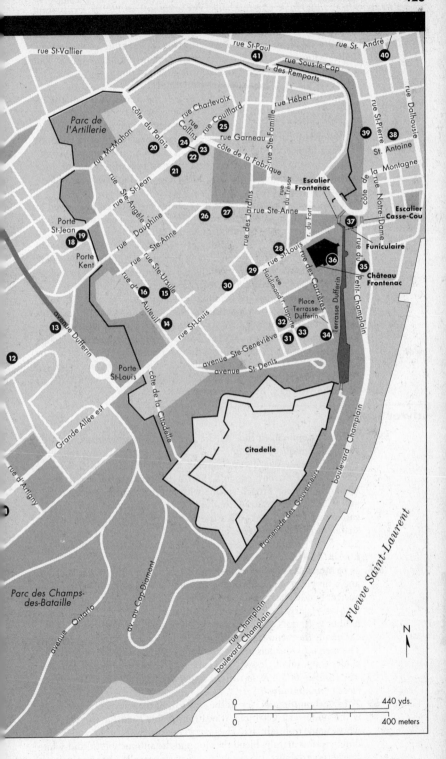

rue St-Vallier

rue St-Paul

rue St-André

41

40

rue Sous-le-Cap

r. des Remparts

Parc de
l'Artillerie

rue Charlevoix

rue Hébert

côte du Palais

rue Couillard

25

rue Collins

rue Garneau

39

rue St-Pierre

rue Dalhousie

38

St. Antoine

rue McMahon

24

23

22

20

côte de la Fabrique

rue Ste-Famille

côte de la Montagne

rue Notre-Dame

rue St-Jean

21

rue du Trésor

Escalier
Frontenac

Escalier
Casse-Cou

26

27

rue Ste-Anne

37

Funiculaire

rue Dauphine

rue des Jardins

28

r. du Fort

36

35

Château
Frontenac

Porte
St-Jean

18

19

rue Ste-Angèle

rue Ste-Anne

rue Ste-Ursule

29

rue St-Louis

rue Haldimand

rue du Petit-Champlain

Porte
Kent

16

15

30

F. Lapointe

Place
Terrasse
Dufferin

rue d'Auteuil

14

rue St-Louis

32

33

34

13

avenue Dufferin

avenue Ste-Geneviève

31

rue des Carrières

Terrasse Dufferin

12

Grande Allée est

avenue St-Denis

Porte
St-Louis

côte de la Citadelle

Promenade des Gouverneurs

boulevard Champlain

rue d'Artigny

Fleuve Saint-Laurent

Citadelle

Parc des Champs-
des-Bataille

avenue Ontario

av. au Cap-Diamont

rue Champlain

boulevard Champlain

N

0   440 yds.

0   400 meters

bodian pastries are delicious with tea served from a little elephant container. ✉ *71 rue d'Auteuil,* ☏ *418/694–0232. AE, DC, MC, V.*

$$ ✕ **Portofino Bistro Italiano.** By joining two 18th-century houses, owner James Monti has created a cozy restaurant with a bistro flavor. The room is distinctive: burnt sienna walls, a wood pizza oven set behind a semicircular bar, deep-blue tablecloths and chairs. Service in this lively restaurant is excellent. Not to be missed: the thin-crust pizza and its accompaniment of oils flavored with pepper and oregano, and *pennini al'arrabiata*—tubular pasta with a spicy tomato sauce. Don't miss the homemade tiramisu—ladyfingers dipped in espresso with a whipped cream and mascarpone-cheese filling. There's a prix-fixe meal of the day, and from 3 to 7 the restaurant serves a beer and pizza meal for about $10. ✉ *54 rue Couillard,* ☏ *418/692–8888. Reservations essential. AE, DC, MC, V.*

$ ✕ **Casse-Crêpe Breton.** Crepes in generous proportions are served in this diner-style restaurant on rue St-Jean. From a menu of more than 20 fillings, pick your own chocolate or fruit combinations, or design a larger meal with cheese, ham, and vegetables. The tables surround three round hot plates at which you watch your creations being made. Crepes made with two to five fillings cost under $6. ✉ *1136 rue St-Jean,* ☏ *418/692–0438. No credit cards.*

$ ✕ **Chez Temporel.** Tucked behind rue St-Jean and côte de la Fabrique,
★ this homey café is an experience *très français.* The aroma of fresh coffee fills the air. The rustic decor incorporates wooden tables, chairs, and benches, and a tiny staircase winds to an upper level. Croissants are made in-house; the staff will fill them with Gruyère and ham or anything else you want. Try the equally delicious *croque monsieur* (grilled ham and cheese sandwich) and quiche Lorraine. ✉ *25 rue Couillard,* ☏ *418/694–1813. No credit cards.*

Lower Town

$$$$ ✕ **Laurie Raphaël.** At this new hot spot in town, the setting is classic
★ yet unpretentious, with high ceilings, white linen tablecloths, and sheer white drapery. Award-winning chef Daniel Vezina was nominated Québec Chef of the Year in 1996 for his bold, innovative recipes, which mix classic French cuisine with international flavors. His creations include goat cheese fondue, wrapped in nuts and served with caramelized pears, and an Australian rack of lamb that comes with a shallot sauce, blue potatoes, and goat cheese. The wine list ranges from $24–$400 per bottle; some wines are sold by the glass. ✉ *117 rue Dalhousie,* ☏ *418/692–4555. Reservations essential. AE, D, MC, V.*

$$$ ✕ **Le Marie Clarisse.** Wood-beam ceilings, stone walls, sea-blue decor, and a fireplace make this dining spot one of the coziest in town. In an ancient building at the bottom of Escalier Casse-Cou near Place Royale, Le Marie Clarisse is well known for its unique seafood dishes, such as halibut with nuts and honey or scallops with port and paprika. Occasionally the menu lists a good game dish, such as caribou with curry. The *menu du jour* has about seven entrées to choose from; dinner includes soup, salad, dessert, and coffee. ✉ *12 rue du Petit-Champlain,* ☏ *418/692–0857. Reservations essential. AE, DC, MC, V. In winter, closed Sun.; no lunch Sat.*

$$ ✕ **Le Cochon Dingue.** Across the street from the ferry in Lower Town is the boulevard Champlain location of this chain, a cheerful café whose name translates to "The Crazy Pig." Sidewalk tables and indoor dining rooms artfully blend the chic and the antique; black-and-white checkerboard floors contrast with ancient stone walls. Café fare includes dependably tasty homemade quiches, thick soups, and such desserts as fresh raspberry tart and maple-sugar pie. ✉ *46 blvd. Champlain,*

☎ 418/692–2013; ✉ 46 blvd. René- Lévesque, ☎ 418/523–2013; ✉ 1326 av. Maguire, Sillery, ☎ 418/684–2013. AE, DC, MC, V.

\$\$ ✕ **L'Echaudé.** This chic black-and-white bistro attracts a mix of busi-
★ ness and tourist clientele because of its location between the financial
and antiques districts in Lower Town. The modern decor consists of
a stark dining area with a mirrored wall and a stainless-steel bar where
you dine atop high stools. Lunch offerings include *cuisse de canard confit* (duck confit) with French fries and fresh seafood salad. Highlights
of the three-course brunch for Sunday antiques shoppers are giant croissants and a tantalizing array of desserts. ✉ *73 Sault-au-Matelot,*
☎ *418/692–1299. Reservations essential. AE, DC, MC, V. No dinner Sun. or Mon. Sept.–May.*

\$–\$\$ ✕ **Mistral Gagnant.** Don't be surprised if the pottery bowl on your table
or the antique armoire you are sitting beside is sold midway through
your meal: Much of what you see in this sunny tea room comes from
Provence and is for sale. Though limited, the menu á la carte is delicious and includes a gourmet salad that changes with the season, daily
quiches, and a few desserts. An ever-changing table d'hôte offers more
hearty meat, seafood, and pasta dishes; the restaurant is famous for
its lemon meringue pie. ✉ *160 rue St-Paul,* ☎ *418/692–4260. V.
Closed some evenings in winter; call ahead.*

Outside the Walls

\$\$\$–\$\$\$\$ ✕ **La Fenouillère.** Don't let the outside of this restaurant discourage
you. Though it is connected to a standard chain hotel, inside you will
find an elegant, spacious dining room, with a view of the Pierre Laporte bridge. Chef Yvon Godbout has served a constantly rotating table
d'hôte since 1986, going out of his way to offer seasonal products. The
house specialty is salmon, but you may want to ask for the lamb, as it
is done to a turn and very popular among the restaurant's regular customers. ✉ *Hotel Best Western Aristocrate, 3100 chemin St-Louis,
Ste-Foy,* ☎ *418/653–3886. AE, DC, MC, V.*

\$\$ ✕ **Le Graffiti.** A good alternative to Vieux-Québec dining, this restaurant housed in a modern gourmet food mall serves the cuisine of
Provence. The romantic setting has dark mahogany-paneled walls and
large bay windows that look out onto the passersby along avenue Cartier.
On the distinctive seasonal menu are such dishes as scampi spiced with
basil and red pepper, and chicken liver mousse with pistachios. There's
a reasonably priced table d'hôte. ✉ *1191 av. Cartier,* ☎ *418/529–4949.
AE, DC, MC, V.*

\$\$ ✕ **Le Lapin Sauté.** Elegant quality dining at a reasonable price is the
hallmark of this eatery near avenue Cartier. Its country-style cuisine
matches the decor; armoires, pots, and aprons appear throughout the
yellow and blue dining room. As the name (which means sautéed rabbit) suggests, rabbit appears on the menu, with a choice of three sauces:
mustard, Normándy, and honey with herbs. You'll also find other
meats, salads, and pasta—and delicious homemade desserts. ✉ *120
blvd. René Lévesque Ouest.,* ☎ *418/523–8777. AE, D, MC, V.*

\$\$ ✕ **Montego Resto Club.** A 15-minute drive west of the old city, the sun
shines year-round at this trendy bistro—where you will find Californian, Italian, French, and Szechuan cuisine all under one roof. The red
and yellow Sante Fe decor pays close attention to detail; each rainbow-
colored light is a work of art and every table setting has a unique twist.
The menu has a variety of inventively prepared dishes, such as rib steak
served with avocado, peppers, and fresh and sun-dried tomatoes, and
linguine al Montego, with prosciutto, sun-dried tomatoes, cantaloupe,
and peppers. ✉ *1460 av. Maguire, Sillery,* ☎ *418/688–7991. AE, D,
MC, V.*

$$ ✗ **Paparazzi.** An Italian restaurant a 15-minute drive west of Vieux-Québec, Paparazzi has a sleek bistro ambience—bare wood tables, halogen lighting, and wrought-iron accents. Its food competes with that of many of the finer dining establishments in town, but without the high prices. A specialty is pizza paparazzi, with wild mushrooms, fresh tomatoes, and a mix of cheeses. The dessert list is interesting. ⊠ *1365 av. Maguire, Sillery,* ☎ *418/683–8111. AE, DC, MC, V.*

$$ ✗ **Le Paris Brest.** This busy restaurant on Grande Allée serves a gregarious crowd attracted to its tastefully prepared French dishes. Its angular halogen lighting and soft yellow walls add a fresh, modern touch to the historic building. Traditional fare, such as *escargots au Pernod* (snails with Pernod) and steak tartare, is presented artistically. Some popular dishes are lamb with *herbes de Provence* and beef Wellington. À la carte and main-course dishes are accompanied by a generous side platter of vegetables. Wine prices range from $22 to $400. ⊠ *590 Grande Allée Est,* ☎ *418/529–2243. AE, DC, MC, V.*

$$ ✗ **La Pointe des Amériques.** Adventurous pizza lovers should explore the fare at this bistro where the Old World meets the New. The original brick walls of the century-old building just outside the St-Jean Gate contrast boldly with modern mirrors and arty wrought-iron lighting. You're likely to find some strange pizza combos like marinated alligator, smoked Gouda, Cajun sauce, and hot peppers. But don't worry—there are more than 25 different pizzas to choose from, as well as meat and pasta dishes, soups, and salads. Connected to the restaurant is the Biloxi Bar, where you can listen to live jazz and enjoy the same menu. ⊠ *964 rue St-Jean,* ☎ *418/694–1199. AE, DC, MC, V.*

$ ✗ **Chez Victor.** It's no ordinary burger joint: Located on rue St-Jean where trendy turns dreary, this cozy café with brick walls and bold red tables attracts an artsy crowd. Hearty gourmet burgers are topped with lettuce, tomatoes, onions, mushrooms, pickles, hot mustard, mayonnaise, and a choice of five cheeses (mozzarella, Swiss, blue, goat or cream). French fries are served with a dollop of mayo and poppy seeds. You will find salads, sandwiches, and a daily dessert as well. ⊠ *145 rue St-Jean,* ☎ *418/529–7702. MC, V.*

$ ✗ **Le Commensal.** This eatery is like an upscale cafeteria. Diners serve themselves from an outstanding informal vegetarian buffet, then grab a table in the vast dining room, where brick walls and green plants add a touch of class. Plates are weighed to determine the price). Hot and cold dishes run the gamut of health-conscious cooking and include stir-fry tofu and ratatouille (vegetables in mild sauce with couscous). ⊠ *860 rue St-Jean,* ☎ *418/647–3733. AE, DC, MC, V.*

LODGING

Be sure to make a reservation if you visit during peak season (May through September) or during the Winter Carnival, in February. During busy times, hotel rates usually rise 30%. From November through April, many lodgings offer discount weekend packages and other promotions.

CATEGORY	COST*
$$$$	over $160
$$$	$120–$160
$$	$85–$120
$	under $85

All prices are for a standard double room, excluding 7% GST, 6.5% provincial sales tax, and an optional service charge.

Upper Town

$$$$ ⊞ **Château Frontenac.** Towering above the St. Lawrence River, the
★ Château Frontenac is Québec City's most renowned landmark. Its public rooms—from the intimate piano bar to the 700-seat ballroom reminiscent of Hall of Mirrors at Versailles—have the opulence of years gone
by, and almost all the guest rooms have excellent views. Reserve well
in advance, especially from the end of June to mid-October. The Frontenac has one of the finer restaurants in town, Le Champlain, where
classic French cuisine is served by waiters dressed in traditional French
costumes. ⊠ *1 rue des Carrières, G1R 4P5,* ☎ *418/692–3861 or
800/441–1414,* ⦿ *418/692–1751. 613 rooms. 2 restaurants, piano bar,
snack bar, indoor pool, beauty salon, health club. AE, DC, MC, V.*

$$$ ⊞ **L'Hôtel du Théâtre.** In 1992 this abandoned, turn-of-the-century the-
ater just outside the St-Jean Gate was transformed into an exclusive
lodging, an Italian bistro, and an elaborate 1920s cabaret-style dinner
theater, Théâtre Capitole (☞ Nightlife and the Arts, *below*). A glitzy
showbiz theme prevails throughout the hotel, with stars on carpets,
doors, and keys. Rooms are small and simple, highlighted with a few
rich details. Painted ceilings have a blue-and-white sky motif; white
down-filled comforters dress the beds. ⊠ *972 rue St-Jean, G1R 1R5,*
☎ *418/694–4040 or 800/363–4040,* ⦿ *418/694–1916. 40 rooms.
Restaurant, bar, theater. AE, DC, MC, V.*

$$$ ⊞ **Hôtel Manoir Victoria.** This European-style hotel with a good fit-
ness center is well situated near the train station. Its discreet, old-fash-
ioned entrance gives way to a large, wood-paneled foyer. A substantial
buffet breakfast is included in some packages. ⊠ *44 Côte du Palais,
G1R 4H8,* ☎ *418/692–1030,* ⦿ *418/692–3822. 144 rooms, 4 suites.
2 restaurants, indoor pool, beauty salon, sauna, health club, meeting
rooms. AE, D, DC, MC, V.*

$–$$$ ⊞ **Manoir d'Auteuil.** Originally a private home, this lodging is one of
★ the more lavish manors in town. In 1995 a major renovation reinstated
many of its Art Deco and Art Nouveau details. An ornate sculpted iron
banister wraps around four floors; guest rooms blend modern design
with the Art Deco structure. Each room is different; one was formerly
a chapel, and another has a tiny staircase leading to its bathroom. The
room with a blue bathroom has a shower with seven showerheads. Some
rooms look out onto the wall between the St-Louis and St-Jean gates.
Note that rooms on the fourth floor are cheaper. ⊠ *49 rue d'Auteuil,
G1R 4C2,* ☎ *418/694–1173,* ⦿ *418/694–0081. 16 rooms. Break-
fast room. AE, D, DC, MC, V.*

$$ ⊞ **Le Château de Pierre.** Built in 1853, this tidy Victorian manor on
a picturesque street has kept its English origins alive. The high-ceilinged
halls have ornate chandeliers, and Victorian rooms are imaginatively
decorated with floral themes; some have either a balcony, fireplace, or
vanity room. Several rooms in the front have bay windows with a view
of Governors' Park. ⊠ *17 av. Ste-Geneviève, G1R 4A8,* ☎ *418/694–
0429,* ⦿ *418/694–0153. 15 rooms. AE, MC, V.*

$$ ⊞ **Hôtel Château Bellevue.** Just behind the Château Frontenac, this hotel
offers comfortable accommodations at reasonable prices in a good lo-
cation. Guest rooms are modern, with standard hotel furnishings;
many have a view of the St. Lawrence River. The rooms vary consid-
erably in size, and package deals are available. ⊠ *16 rue Laporte, G1R
4M9,* ☎ *418/692–2573 or 800/463–2617,* ⦿ *418/692–4876. 57
rooms. Meeting rooms. AE, DC, MC, V.*

$$ ⊞ **L'Hôtel du Vieux Québec.** In the heart of the Latin Quarter on rue
St-Jean, this brick hotel is surrounded by striking historic structures.
Once an apartment building, it still has the long-term visitor in mind.
The interior design is simple, with sparsely furnished but comfortable

rooms decorated in pastel colors. Many rooms have kitchens (dishes and cooking utensils can be rented for $10); some have air-conditioning. ⊠ *1190 rue St-Jean, G1R 1S6,* ☎ *418/692–1850,* FAX *418/692–5637. 38 rooms. AE, MC, V.*

$$ 🏨 **Hôtel Marie Rollet.** An intimate little inn in the heart of Vieux-Québec, built in 1876 by the Ursulines Order, is an oasis of warm woodwork and antique charm. Two rooms have working fireplaces. A rooftop terrace has a garden view. ⊠ *81 rue Ste-Anne, G1R 3X4,* ☎ *418/694–9271. 10 rooms. MC, V.*

$$ 🏨 **Manoir Ste-Geneviève.** Quaint and elaborately decorated, this hotel dating from 1880 stands near the Château Frontenac, on the southwest corner of Governors' Park. A plush Victorian ambience is created with fanciful wallpaper and precious stately English manor furnishings, such as marble lamps, large wooden bedposts, and velvet upholstery; you'll feel as if you are staying in a secluded country inn. Service here is personal and genteel. Some rooms have air-conditioning. ⊠ *13 av. Ste-Geneviève, G1R 4A7,* ☎ FAX *418/694–1666. 9 rooms. No credit cards.*

$–$$ 🏨 **Château de la Terrasse.** This four-story inn has something that many others lack: a view of the St. Lawrence River from rooms in the front. The interior, with its high ceilings and stained glass in the large bay windows, hints at having once possessed a refined and elegant decor. These days rooms are furnished in a mix of styles, yet tastefully put together. ⊠ *6 Pl. Terrasse Dufferin, G1R 4N5,* ☎ *418/694–9472,* FAX *418/694–0055. 18 rooms. AE, MC, V.*

$ 🏨 **L'Auberge St-Louis.** If you're looking for convenience, this inn's central location on the main street of the city can't be beat. A lobby resembling one in a European pension and tall staircases lead to small guest rooms with comfortable but bare-bones furniture. Six budget rooms are on the fourth floor. The service here is friendly. ⊠ *48 rue St-Louis, G1R 3Z3,* ☎ *418/692–2424,* FAX *418/692–3797. 27 rooms, 14 with bath. MC, V.*

Lower Town

$$$$ 🏨 **Auberge Saint-Antoine.** This charming little find is within comfortable walking distance of all the old town's attractions. The hotel seems much older than it is because of its location in an old maritime warehouse and the generally rustic atmosphere. Each room is styled differently, but all have a combination of antiques and contemporary pieces. Some rooms have river views; others have terraces. ⊠ *10 rue St-Antoine, G1K 4C9,* ☎ *418/692–2211 or 800/267–0525,* FAX *418/692–1177. 31 rooms. AE, DC, MC, V.*

Outside the Walls

$$$$ 🏨 **Hôtel Loews Le Concorde.** When Le Concorde was built in 1974,
★   the shockingly tall concrete structure aroused controversy because it supplanted 19th-century Victorian homes. Still, visitors love its location on Grande Allée, where cafés, restaurants, and bars dot the street. Rooms have good views of Battlefields Park and the St. Lawrence River, and nearly all have been redone in modern decor combined with traditional furnishings. Amenities for business travelers have expanded; one of the VIP floors is reserved for female executives. ⊠ *1225 Pl. Montcalm, G1R 4W6,* ☎ *418/647–2222 or 800/463–5256,* FAX *418/647–4710. 424 rooms. 2 restaurants, bar, pool, sauna, health club. AE, D, DC, MC, V.*

$$$$ 🏨 **Hôtel Radisson Gouverneurs Québec.** This large, full-service establishment opposite the Parliament Buildings is part of a Québec chain. Its light and spacious rooms have luminous pastel decor, wood furni-

ture, and marble bathrooms. VIP floors were designed to lure the business traveler. The hotel occupies the first 12 floors of a tall office complex; views of Vieux-Québec are limited to the higher floors. ⊠ *690 blvd. René-Lévesque Est, G1R 5A8,* ☎ *418/647–1717 or 800/333– 3333,* FAX *418/647–2146. 377 rooms. Restaurant, pool, sauna, health club. AE, D, DC, MC, V.*

$$$–$$$$ ⌕ **Hilton International Québec.** Just outside St-Jean Gate, the Hilton rises from the shadow of Parliament Hill. It has spacious facilities and efficient services and hosts groups as well as individual travelers. The lobby, which can be chaotic at times, has a bar and an open-air restaurant. The hotel is next to the Parliament Buildings and connected to a mall, Place Québec, that has 37 shops. Standard yet ultramodern rooms have tall windows; those on upper floors have fine views of Vieux-Québec. Guests on executive floors are offered a free breakfast and an open bar from 5 to 10 PM. ⊠ *1100 blvd. René Lévesque Est, G1K 7M9,* ☎ *418/647–2411 or 800/447–2411,* FAX *418/647–6488. 565 rooms, 36 suites. Restaurant, piano bar, pool, sauna, health club. AE, D, DC, MC, V.*

$$$ ⌕ **Germain des Près.** One of the newly popular hotels for the business crowd is in Ste-Foy, close to Place Laurier and with easy access to Québec City and the airports. Its ultramodern rooms—in black and white or black and tan—have white comforters on the beds. ⊠ *1200 av. Germain-des-Près, Ste-Foy, G1V 3M7,* ☎ *418/658–1224,* FAX *418/658–8846. 126 rooms with shower or bath. Restaurant, business services, meeting room. AE, DC, MC, V.*

$$$ ⌕ **Hôtel Clarendon.** Built in 1870 and considered the oldest hotel in Québec, the Clarendon has been entirely refurbished in its original Art Deco and Art Nouveau styles. Most rooms have excellent views of old Québec. ⊠ *57 rue Ste-Anne, G1R 3X4,* ☎ *418/692–2480 or 800/463– 5250,* FAX *418/692–4652. 96 rooms. Restaurant, café, meeting rooms. AE, D, DC, MC, V.*

$$ ⌕ **Manoir Lafayette.** In 1882 this gray stone building was a lavish, private home; today it is a simple hotel. Considering the location on Grande Allée—a street crowded with restaurants and trendy bars— the clean, comfortable accommodations are reasonably priced. The lobby is open and welcoming, with floral sofas surrounding a fireplace and television. Rooms in the newer wing—although fresher—resemble those in the old part: All are quite small, with high ceilings, wooden furniture, and floral bedspreads and drapes. Rooms facing Grande Allée may be noisy. ⊠ *661 Grande Allée Est, G1R 2K4,* ☎ *418/522–2652 or 800/363–8203,* FAX *418/522–4400. 67 rooms. Restaurant, babysitting. AE, DC, MC, V.*

$ ⌕ **L'Auberge du Quartier.** A small, amiable inn in a house dating from
★ 1852 benefits from a personal touch. The cheerful rooms are modestly furnished but well maintained. A suite of rooms on the third floor can accommodate a family at a reasonable cost. A 20-minute walk west from the old city, L'Auberge du Quartier is convenient to avenue Cartier and Grande Allée nightlife; joggers can use Battlefields Park across the street. ⊠ *170 Grande Allée Ouest, G1R 2G9,* ☎ *418/525– 9726. 11 rooms. Breakfast room. AE, DC, MC, V.*

NIGHTLIFE AND THE ARTS

Considering its size, Québec City has a wide variety of cultural institutions, from the renowned Québec Symphony Orchestra to several small theater companies. The arts scene changes significantly depending on the season. From September through May, a steady repertory of concerts, plays, and performances is presented in theaters and halls around town. In summer, indoor theaters close to make room for out-

door stages. For arts and entertainment listings in English, consult the
Québec Chronicle-Telegraph, published on Wednesday. The French-
language daily newspaper, *Le Soleil,* has listings on a page called "Où
Aller à Québec" ("Where to Go in Québec"). Also, *Voir,* a weekly devoted to arts listings and reviews, appears on the street every Thursday.

Tickets for most shows can be purchased through **Billetech,** with outlets at the Grand Théâtre de Québec (⊠ 269 blvd. René-Lévesque Est,
☎ 418/643–8131), Bibliothèque Gabrielle-Roy (☎ 418/691–7400),
Colisée (☎ 418/691–7211), Théâtre Périscope (☎ 418/529–2183),
Palais Montcalm (☎ 418/670–9011), Salle Albert-Rousseau (☎
418/659–6710), La Baie department store, (⊠ Pl. Laurier, 2nd level,
☎ 418/627–5959), and Provigo supermarkets. Hours vary and in
some cases tickets must be bought at the outlet.

The Arts

Dance

Grand Théâtre de Québec (⊠ 269 blvd. René-Lévesque Est, ☎ 418/643–
8131) presents a dance series with both Canadian and international
companies. Dancers appear at Bibliothèque Gabrielle-Roy (☞ Music,
below), Salle Albert-Rousseau, and the Palais Montcalm (☞ Theater,
below).

Film

Most theaters present French films and American films dubbed into
French. Three popular theaters are **Cinéma Cinéplex Odéon** (⊠ 5900
blvd. des Gradins, ☎ 418/622–1077), **Cinéma de Paris** (⊠ 966 rue
St-Jean, ☎ 418/694–0891) and **Cinéma Place Charest** (⊠ 500 rue du
Pont, ☎ 418/529–9745). **Cinémas Ste-Foy** (⊠ Pl. Ste-Foy, Ste-Foy, ☎
418/656–0592) almost always shows films in English. **Le Clap** (⊠
2360 chemin Ste.-Foy, Ste-Foy, ☎ 418/650–2527) has a repertoire of
foreign, offbeat, and art films. **Imax Theatre,** (⊠ Galeries de la Capitale, 5401 blvd. des Galeries, ☎ 418/627–4629, 418/627–4688, or
800/643–4629) has extra-large-screen movies.

Music

L'Orchestre Symphonique de Québec (Québec Symphony Orchestra)
is Canada's oldest. It performs at Louis-Frechette Hall in the Grand
Théâtre de Québec (⊠ 269 blvd. René-Lévesque Est, ☎ 418/643–8131).

Tickets for children's concerts at the **Joseph Lavergne auditorium** must
be purchased in advance at the Bibliothèque Gabrielle-Roy (⊠ 350 rue
St-Joseph Est, ☎ 418/691–7400). For classical concerts at the **Salle
de l'Institut Canadien** (⊠ 42 rue St-Stanislaus), buy tickets in advance
at the Bibliothèque Gabrielle-Roy (☞ *above*).

Popular music concerts are often booked at the **Colisée de Québec** (⊠
Parc de l'Exposition, 2205 av. du Colisée, Parc de l'Exposition, ☎ 418/
691–7211).

An annual highlight is the July **Festival d'Eté International de Québec**
(☎ 418/692–4540), an 11-day music festival with more than 400 shows
and concerts (many of them free) from classical music to Francophone
song. Events are held in over 10 locations, including outdoor stages
and public squares.

Theater

All theater productions are in French. The following theaters schedule shows from September through April. **Grand Théâtre de Québec**
(⊠ 269 blvd. René-Lévesque Est, ☎ 418/643–8131) is a theater where
classic and contemporary plays are staged by the leading local theater

company, le Théâtre du Trident (☎ 418/643–5873). **Palais Montcalm** (✉ 995 Pl. d'Youville, ☎ 418/670–9011), a municipal theater outside St-Jean Gate, presents a broad range of productions. A diverse repertoire, from classical to comedy, is staged at **Salle Albert-Rousseau** (✉ 2410 chemin Ste-Foy, Ste-Foy, ☎ 418/659–6710). **Théâtre Capitole** (✉ 972 rue St-Jean, ☎ 418/694–4444), a restored turn-of-the-century cabaret-style theater, offers a broad repertory of classical and pop music, plays, and comedy shows. **Théâtre Périscope** (✉ 2 rue Crémazie Est, ☎ 418/529–2183), a multipurpose theater, stages about 200 shows a year, including performances for children.

SUMMER THEATER

During the summer, open-air concerts are presented at **Place d'Youville,** just outside St-Jean Gate.

Nightlife

Québec City nightlife is centered on the clubs and cafés of rue St-Jean, avenue Cartier, and Grande Allée. In winter, evening activity is livelier toward the end of the week, beginning on Wednesday. But as warmer temperatures set in, the café-terrace crowd emerges, and bars are active seven days a week. Most bars and clubs stay open until 3 AM.

Bars and Lounges

Le Pub Saint-Alexandre (✉ 1087 rue St-Jean, ☎ 418/694–0015), a popular English-style pub, was formerly a men-only tavern. It's a good place to look for your favorite brand of beer—there are approximately 200 kinds, 20 on tap. You'll find mainly yuppies at **Vogue** (✉ Upstairs at 1170 d'Artigny, ☎ 418/529–9973), which has dancing. **Sherlock Holmes** (✉ Downstairs at 1170 d'Artigny, ☎ 418/529–8271) is a pub-restaurant.

Dance Clubs

There's a little bit of everything—live rock bands to loud disco—at **Chez Dagobert** (✉ 600 Grande Allée Est, ☎ 418/522–0393), a large and popular club. **Merlin** (✉ 1179 av. Cartier, ☎ 418/529–9567), a second-story dance club with an English pub below, is packed nightly.

Folk, Jazz, and Blues

Maison de la Chanson (✉ Théâtre Petit Champlain, 68 rue du Petit-Champlain, ☎ 418/692–4744) is an excellent spot for contemporary Québec music. French-Canadian folk songs fill **Chez Son Père** (✉ 24 St-Stanislas, ☎ 418/692–5308), a smokey pub on the second floor of an old building in the Latin Quarter. Singers perform nightly. At **Le d'Auteuil** (✉ 35 rue d'Auteuil, ☎ 418/692–2263), a converted church across from Kent Gate, rhythm and blues, jazz, and blues emanate. The first jazz bar in Québec City, **L'Emprise at Hôtel Clarendon** (✉ 57 rue Ste-Anne, ☎ 418/692–2480), is the preferred spot for enthusiasts. The Art Deco decor sets the mood for Jazz Age rhythms.

OUTDOOR ACTIVITIES AND SPORTS

Two parks are central to Québec City: the 250-acre Battlefields Park, with its panoramic views of the St. Lawrence River, and Cartier-Brébeuf Park, which runs along the St. Charles River. Both are favorites for jogging, biking, and cross-country skiing. Scenic rivers and mountains close by (no more than 30 minutes by car) make this city ideal for the sporting life. For information about sports and fitness, contact **Québec City Tourist Information Office** (✉ 835 av. Laurier, G1R 2L3, ☎ 418/692–2471) or **Québec City Bureau of Parks and Recreation** (✉ 65 rue Ste-Anne, 5th floor, G1R 3S9, ☎ 418/691–6278).

Participant Sports and Outdoor Activities

Biking

Bike paths along rolling hills traverse Battlefields Park, at the south side of the city. For a longer ride over flat terrain take the path north of the city skirting the St. Charles River; this route can be reached from rue St-Roch, rue Prince-Edouard, and Pont Dorchester (Dorchester Bridge). Paths along the côte de Beaupré, beginning at the confluence of the St. Charles and St. Lawrence rivers, are especially scenic. They begin northeast of the city at rue de la Verandrye and boulevard Montmorency or rue Abraham-Martin and Pont Samson (Samson Bridge) and continue 10 km (6 mi) along the coast to Montmorency Falls.

You can rent bicycles by the day at **Auberge de la Paix** (⊠ 31 rue Couillard, ☎ 418/694–0735).

Boating

Lakes in the Québec City area have facilities for boating. Take Route 73 north of the city to St-Dunstan de Lac Beauport, then take Exit 157, boulevard du Lac, to **Lac Beauport** (☎ 418/849–2821), one of the best nearby resorts. Boats can be rented at **Campex** (⊠ 8 chemin de l'Orée, Lac Beauport, ☎ 418/849–2236) for canoeing and kayaking.

Dogsledding

Learn how to mush in the forest with **Adventure Nord-Bec** (⊠ 665 rue St. Aimé, St. Lambert de Lévis, G0S 2W0, ☎ 418/889–8001), 20 minutes from the city. Overnight camping trips are available.

Fishing

Permits are needed for fishing in Québec. Most sporting goods stores and all Canadian Tire stores sell them; try **Canadian Tire** (⊠ 1170 rte. de l'Eglise, Ste-Foy, ☎ 418/659–4882). The **Ministry of Wildlife and the Environment** (⊠ Pl. de la Capitale, 150 blvd. René-Lévesque Est, ☎ 418/643–3127) publishes a pamphlet on fishing regulations that is available at tourist information offices.

Réserve Faunique des Laurentides (☎ 418/686–1717) is a wildlife reserve with good lakes for fishing, approximately 48 km (30 mi) north of Québec City via Route 73.

Golf

The Québec City region has 18 golf courses, and several are open to the public. Reservations during summer months are essential. **Club de Golf de Cap Rouge** (⊠ 4600 rue St-Felix, ☎ 418/653–9381) in Cap Rouge, with 18 holes, is one of the courses closest to Québec City. **Club de Golf de Beauport** (⊠ 3533 rue Clemenceau, ☎ 418/663–1578), a nine-hole course, is 20 minutes by car via Route 73 North. **Parc du Mont Ste-Anne** (⊠ Rte. 360, Beaupré, ☎ 418/827–3778), a half-hour drive north of Québec, has one of the best 18-hole courses in the region.

Health and Fitness Clubs

One of the city's most popular health clubs is **Club Entrain** (⊠ Pl. de la Cité, 2600 blvd. Laurier, ☎ 418/658–7771). Facilities include a weight room with Nautilus, a sauna, a whirlpool, aerobics classes, and squash courts. Nonguests at **Hôtel Radisson des Gouverneurs** (⊠ 690 blvd. René-Lévesque Est, ☎ 418/647–1717) can use the health club facilities, which include weights, a sauna, a whirlpool, and an outdoor heated pool, for a $5 fee. **Hilton International Québec** (⊠ 1100 blvd. René Lévesque Est, ☎ 418/647–2411) has a health club with weights, a sauna, and an outdoor pool available to nonguests for a $10 fee. Nonmembers can use the pool at the **YMCA du Vieux-Québec** (⊠ 650 av.

Wilfred Laurier, ☎ 418/522–0800) for a $2.25 fee. Pool facilities cost $2.35 at the **YWCA** (✉ 855 av. Holland, ☎ 418/683–2155).

Hiking and Jogging

The Parc Cartier-Brébeuf, north of Vieux-Québec along the banks of the St. Charles River, has about 13 km (8 mi) of hiking trails. For more mountainous terrain, head 19 km (12 mi) north on Route 73 to Lac Beauport. For jogging, Battlefields Park, Parc Cartier-Brébeuf, and Bois-de-Coulonge park in Sillery are the most popular places.

Horseback Riding

Jacques Cartier Excursions (✉ 978 av. Jacques-Cartier Nord, Tewkesbury, ☎ 418/848–7238), also known for rafting, offers summer and winter horseback riding. An excursion includes an hour of instruction and three hours of riding; the cost is $40–$55. Reservations are required.

Horticulture

Visitors who enjoy gardening will delight in the botanical **Jardin Roger-Van den Hende.** Included is a water garden, more than 2,000 plant species from North and South America, Europe, and Asia, and a collection of trees, small shrubs, and remarkable rhododendrons. The Metrobus and Buses 11 and 801 run to the gardens. ✉ *Pavillon de l'Environtron, 2480 blvd. Hochelaga, Ste-Foy, G1K 7P4,* ☎ *418/656–3410.* ⎙ *Free.* ☉ *May–Oct., daily 9–8.*

Villa Bagatelle is an interpretation center on the villas and garden estates of Sillery. Its English garden, where you can have tea, has more than 350 varieties of indigenous and exotic plants. ✉ *1563 chemin St-Louis, Sillery G1S 1G1,* ☎ *418/688–8074.* ⎙ *$2.* ☉ *Jan.–Oct., Wed.–Sun. 1–5; Nov.–Dec., Wed., Thurs., and Sun. 1–5, Fri.–Sat. 1–9.*

Ice Canoeing

If people windsurf on the ice, why not canoe? This exhilarating sport entails propelling the vessel (a cross between a canoe and a rowboat) over the uneven ice of the St. Lawrence, dipping and sliding and rocking and dragging until you get to open water, at which time you jump in the boat and row. When you return, just hop on the nearest iceberg. To propel the boat on the ice, you straddle it, one knee in a padded rest inside, the other leg pushing like a skateboard. This sport is not for the unfit. The professional guides at **Le Mythe des Glaces** (✉ 737 blvd. du Lac, Charlesbourg, G1H 7B1, ☎ 418/849–6131) will suit you up from head to toe. A half day costs $59, a full day with dinner costs $109, and a two-day excursion costs $259.

Ice Skating

The ice-skating season runs December through March. There is a 4-km (2½-mi) stretch for skating along the **St. Charles River,** between the Dorchester and Lavigueur bridges; season is January through March, depending on the ice. Rentals and changing rooms are nearby. For information contact Marina St-Roch (☎ 418/691–7188).

Place d'Youville, just outside St-Jean Gate, has an outdoor rink open from November through April. From December through March, try the **Patinoire de la Terrasse** adjacent to the Château Frontenac (☎ 418/692–2955), open from 11 to 11; skates can be rented for $4 daily. Nighttime skating is an option at **Village des Sports** (✉ 1860 blvd. Valcartier, St-Gabriel-de-Valcartier, ☎ 418/844–3725).

Rafting

Jacques Cartier River, about 48 km (30 mi) northwest of Québec City, provides good rafting.

Jacques Cartier Excursions (⊠ 978 av. Jacques-Cartier Nord, Tewkesbury, G0A 4P0, ☎ 418/848–7238) offers rafting trips on the Jacques Cartier River. Tours originate from Tewkesbury, a half-hour drive from Québec City, from May through September. A half-day tour costs about $45 and a full day about $65. Wet suits are $16 extra. In winter, snow-rafting excursions are available and include a two-hour sleigh ride and all-day mountain sliding in river rafts. The total cost is $49. Reservations are required.

Nouveau Monde Québec (⊠ 960 av. Jacques-Cartier Nord, Tewkesbury, ☎ 418/848–4144 or 800/267–4144) has excursions on the Jacques Cartier River from mid-May through September. A three-hour excursion costs $44, a two-day package $99. Nouveau Monde Québec also offers boogie boarding—running the Jacques Cartier rapids on surfboards. The activity is available between June and early September. A 3½-hour excursion costs $65. For both activities, wet suits cost $14 extra. Reservations should be made two weeks in advance for weekends, one day in advance for weekdays.

Skiing

Brochures about ski centers in Québec are available at the Québec Tourism and Convention Bureaus or by calling 800/363–7777.

The **Winter Shuttle** is a taxi service between major hotels in Vieux-Québec, Ste Foy, ski centers, and the Village des Sports (☞ Snow Slides, *below*). It leaves hotels at 8:30 and returns at 4:30. The cost is $18–$22; reserve in advance at hotels. The service is also available for people staying in ski areas who want to visit the city; the bus leaves at 9:30 and returns at 3:30.

CROSS-COUNTRY

You can ski cross-country on many trails; **Battlefields Park,** which you can reach from Place Montcalm, has scenic marked trails. Thirty-two ski centers in the Québec area offer 2,000 km (1,240 mi) of groomed trails and heated shelters; for information, call **Regroupement des stations de ski de fond** (☎ 418/653–5875). Lac Beauport, 19 km (12 mi) north of the city, has more than 20 marked trails (150 km, or 93 mi); contact **Les Sentiers du Moulin** (⊠ 99 chemin du Moulin, ☎ 418/849–9652). **Parc du Mont Ste-Anne** (⊠ Rte. 360, Beaupré, ☎ 418/827–4561), 40 km (25 mi) northeast of Québec City, has 215 km (133 mi) of cross-country trails. **Le Centre de Randonnée à Skis de Duchesnay** (⊠ 143 rue de Duchesnay, St-Catherine-de-Jacques-Cartier, ☎ 418/875–2147), just north of Québec City, has 11 marked trails totaling 125 km (77 mi).

DOWNHILL

Four alpine ski resorts, all with night skiing, are within a 30-minute drive of Québec City. **Station Mont Ste-Anne** (⊠ Rte. 360, C.P. 400 Beaupré, G0A 1E0, ☎ 418/827–4561, 800/463–1568 lodging) is the largest resort in eastern Canada, with 51 downhill trails, 11 lifts, and a gondola. **Station Touristique Stoneham** (⊠ 1420 av. du Hibou, Stoneham, G0A 4P0, ☎ 418/848–2411) is known for its long, easy slopes with 25 downhill runs and 10 lifts. A smaller alpine center is at Lac Beauport: 16 trails at **Mont St-Castin** (⊠ 82 chemin du Tour du Lac, Box 1129, Lac Beauport G0A 2C0, ☎ 418/849–6776 or 418/849–1893). There are 25 trails at the smaller **Le Relais** (⊠ 1084 blvd. du Lac, Lac Beauport, G0A 2C0, ☎ 418/849–1851).

Snow Slides

At **Glissades de la Terrasse** (☎ 418/692–2955), adjacent to the Château Frontenac, a wooden toboggan takes you down a 700-ft snow slide. Cost is $1 per ride.

Visitors to **Village des Sports** can use inner tubes or carpets on the two 300-ft snow slides, or join 6–12 others for a snow raft ride down one of seven groomed trails. ⊠ *1860 blvd. Valcartier, St-Gabriel-de-Valcartier,* ☎ *418/844–3725.* ✍ *Rafting and sliding $17.50 per day; with skating $20.* ☼ *Sun.–Thurs. 10–10, Fri.–Sat. 10AM–10:30PM.*

Tennis and Racquet Sports

At **Montcalm Tennis Club** (⊠ 901 blvd. Champlain, Sillery, ☎ 418/687–1250), south of Québec City in Sillery, four indoor and seven outdoor courts are open daily from 8 AM to 10 PM. At **Tennisport** (⊠ 6280 blvd. Hamel, Ancienne Lorette, ☎ 418/872–0111) there are 11 indoor tennis courts, two squash courts, seven racquetball courts, and eight badminton courts.

Winter Carnival

One of the highlights of the winter season in Québec is the **Québec Winter Carnival** (⊠ 290 rue Joly, GIL 1N8, ☎ 418/626–3716), famous for its joie de vivre. The whirl of activities over three weekends in January and/or February includes night parades, a snow-sculpture competition, and a canoe race across the St. Lawrence River. You can participate in or watch every activity imaginable in the snow from dogsledding to ice climbing. Dates for 1998 are January 30 to February 15.

Spectator Sports

Tickets for sporting events can be purchased at **Colisée de Québec** (⊠ Québec Coliseum, 2205 av. du Colisée, ☎ 418/691–7211). You can order tickets through **Billetech** (☞ Nightlife and the Arts, *above*).

Harness Racing

There's horse racing at **Hippodrome de Québec** (⊠ Parc de l'Exposition, ☎ 418/524–5283).

Hockey

An International Hockey League team, the **Québec Rafales,** plays at the Colisée de Québec (⊠ 2205 av. du Colisée, Parc de l'Exposition, ☎ 418/522–5225 or 418/691–7211).

SHOPPING

Shopping is European-style on the fashionable streets of Québec City. The boutiques and specialty shops clustered along narrow streets such as rue du Petit-Champlain, and rue Buade and rue St-Jean in the Latin Quarter, have one of the most striking historic settings on the continent. Prices in Québec City tend to be on a par with those in Montréal and other North American cities, so you won't have much luck hunting for bargains. When sales occur, they are usually listed in the French daily newspaper, *Le Soleil.*

Stores are generally open Monday through Wednesday 9:30–5:30, Thursday and Friday until 9, Saturday until 5, and Sunday noon–5. In summer, shops may be open seven days a week, and most have later evening hours.

Department Stores

Large department stores can be found in the malls of the suburb of Ste-Foy, but some have outlets inside Québec City's walls.

Holt Renfrew & Co., Ltd. (⊠ Pl. Ste-Foy, Ste-Foy, ☎ 418/656–6783), one of the country's more exclusive stores, carries furs, perfume, and tailored designer collections for men and women. **La Baie** (⊠ Pl. Laurier, Ste-Foy, ☏ 418/627–5959) is Québec's version of the Canadian Hudson's Bay Company conglomerate, founded in 1670 by Montréal trappers Pierre Radisson and Medard de Groseiller. Today La Baie carries clothing for the entire family and household wares. **Simons** (⊠ 20 côte de la Fabrique, ☏ 418/692–3630), one of Québec City's oldest family stores, used to be its only source for fine British woolens and tweeds; now the store also has a large selection of designer clothing, linens, and other household items.

Food and Flea Markets

At **Marché du Vieux-Port,** farmers from the Québec countryside sell fresh produce in the Old Port near rue St-André, from May through October, 8–8.

Rue du Trésor hosts a flea market near the Place d'Armes that shows sketches, paintings, and etchings by local artists. Fine portraits of the Québec City landscape and region are plentiful. Good, inexpensive souvenirs also may be purchased here.

Shopping Centers

Place Québec (⊠ 880 autoroute Dufferin-Montmorency, ☏ 418/529–0551), the mall closest to the old city, is a multilevel shopping complex and convention center with 37 stores; it is connected to the Hilton International Hotel. **Halles Petit-Cartier** (⊠ 1191 av. Cartier, ☏ 418/688–1630), off Grande Allée and a 15-minute walk from St-Louis Gate, is a food mall for gourmets, with everything from utensils to petits fours.

The following shopping centers are approximately a 15-minute drive west along Grande Allée. **Place Ste-Foy** (⊠ 2450 blvd. Laurier, Ste-Foy, ☏ 418/653–4184) had 115 stores at press time, but was undergoing a major expansion. **Place de la Cité** (⊠ 2600 blvd. Laurier, Ste-Foy, ☏ 418/657–6920) has 125 boutiques. The massive **Place Laurier** (⊠ 2700 blvd. Laurier, Ste-Foy, ☏ 418/653–9318) has more than 350 stores.

Quartier Petit-Champlain (☏ 418/692–2613) in Lower Town is a pedestrian mall with some 40 boutiques, local businesses, and restaurants. This popular district is the best area to find native Québec arts and crafts, such as wood sculptures, weaving, ceramics, and jewelry. Try **Pot-en-Ciel** (⊠ 27 rue du Petit-Champlain, ☏ 418/692–1743) for ceramics. **Pauline Pelletier** (⊠ 38 rue du Petit-Champlain, ☏ 418/692–4871) has porcelain.

Specialty Stores

Antiques

Québec City's antiques district is on rue St-Paul and rue St-Pierre, across from the Old Port. French Canadian, Victorian, and Art Deco furniture, along with clocks, silverware, and porcelain, are some of the rare collectibles that can be found here. Authentic Québec pine furniture, characterized by simple forms and lines, is becoming increasingly rare and costly.

Centre d'Antiquités Héritage (⊠ 110 rue St-Paul, ☏ 418/692–1681) specializes in precious Québécois furniture from the 18th century. **Antiquités Zaor** (⊠ 112 rue St-Paul, ☏ 418/692–0581), the oldest store on rue St-Paul, is still the best place in the neighborhood to find excellent English, French, and Canadian antiques.

Art

Aux Multiples Collections (⊠ 43 rue Buade, ☎ 418/692–4298) has Inuit art and antique wood collectibles. **Galerie Brousseau et Brousseau** (⊠ Château Frontenac, 1 rue des Carrières, ☎ 418/694–1828) has Inuit art. **Galerie Madeleine Lacerte** (⊠ 1 côte Dinan, ☎ 418/692–1566), in Lower Town, sells contemporary art and sculpture.

Books

English-language books are difficult to find in Québec. One of the city's first bookstores, **Librairie Garneau** (⊠ 24 côte de la Fabrique, ☎ 418/692–4262), near City Hall, carries mostly volumes in French. **La Maison Anglaise** (⊠ 2600 blvd. Laurier, Pl. de la Cité, Ste-Foy, ☎ 418/654–9523), has English-language titles only, specializing in fiction. **Librairie du Nouveau-Monde** (⊠ 103 rue St-Pierre, ☎ 418/694–9475) stocks titles in French and English. **Librairie Smith** (⊠ 2700 blvd. Laurier, Pl. Laurier, ☎ 418/653–8683) is popular.

Clothing

François Côté Collections (⊠ 35 rue Buade, ☎ 418/692–6016) is a chic boutique with fashions for men and women. **La Maison Darlington** (⊠ 7 rue Buade, ☎ 418/692–2268) carries well-made woolens, dresses, and suits for men, women, and children by fine names in couture. **Louis Laflamme** (⊠ 1192 rue St-Jean, ☎ 418/692–3774) has a large selection of stylish men's clothes.

Crafts

Les Trois Colombes Inc. (⊠ 46 rue St-Louis, ☎ 418/694–1114) sells handmade items including clothing made from handwoven fabric, native and Inuit carvings, jewelry, pottery, and paintings.

Fur

The fur trade has been an important industry here for centuries. Québec City is a good place to purchase high-quality furs at fairly reasonable prices. Since 1894, one of the best furriers in town has been **Robitaille Fourrures** (⊠ 1500 des Taneurs, ☎ 418/681–7297). The department store **J. B. Laliberté** (⊠ 595 rue St-Joseph Est, ☎ 418/525–4841) carries furs.

Gifts

Collection Lazuli (⊠ 774 rue St-Jean, ☎ 418/525–6528; ⊠ 2600 blvd. Laurier, Pl. de la Cité, Ste. Foy, ☎ 418/652–3732) offers a good choice of unusual art objects and international jewelry.

Jewelry

Joaillier Louis Perrier (⊠ 48 rue du Petit-Champlain, ☎ 418/692–4633) has Québec-made gold and silver jewelry. Exclusive jewelry can be found at **Zimmermann** (⊠ 46 côte de la Fabrique, ☎ 418/692–2672).

SIDE TRIPS FROM QUÉBEC CITY

A number of easy excursions from the city will show you another side of the province and provide more insight into its past. The spectacular Montmorency Falls and the Basilique Ste-Anne-de-Baupré can be seen in a day trip. To experience rural Québec, drive around the Ile d'Orléans just east of the city. The farms, markets, and churches here evoke the island's long history. You can tour the island in an energetic day, though if you have time, you may be tempted to stay overnight in a rural inn.

Côte de Beaupré and Montmorency Falls

As legend tells it, when explorer Jacques Cartier first caught sight of the north shore of the St. Lawrence River in 1535, he exclaimed, *"Quel beau pré!"* ("What a lovely meadow!"), because the area was the first inviting piece of land he had spotted since leaving France. Today this fertile meadow, first settled by French farmers, is known as Côte de Beaupré (Beaupré Coast), stretching 40 km (25 mi) east from Québec City to the famous pilgrimage site of Ste-Anne-de-Beaupré. Historic Route 360, or avenue Royal, winds its way from Beauport to St-Joachim, east of St-Anne-de-Beaupré. The impressive Montmorency Falls are midway between Québec City and Ste-Anne-de-Beaupré.

Montmorency Falls

㊻ *10 km (6 mi) east of Québec City.*

As it cascades over a cliff into the St. Lawrence River, the Montmorency River (named for Charles de Montmorency, who was a governor of New France) is one of the most beautiful sights in the province. The falls, at 274 ft, are 50% higher than Niagara Falls. A cable car runs to the top of the falls in **Parc de la Chute-Montmorency** (Montmorency Falls Park) from late in April through early November. During very cold weather, the falls' heavy spray freezes and forms a giant loaf-shape ice cone (hill) known to Québécois as the Pain du Sucre (Sugarloaf); this phenomenon attracts sledders and sliders from Québec City. Ice climbers come to scale the falls; a school trains novices for only a few days to make the ascent. In the warmer months, you can visit an observation tower in the river's gorge that is continuously sprayed by a fine drizzle from water pounding onto the cliff rocks. The top of the falls can be observed from avenue Royale.

The park is also a historic sight. The British general Wolfe, on his way to conquer New France, set up camp here in 1759. In 1780, Sir Frederick Haldimand, then the governor of Canada, built a summer home—now a good restaurant called Manoir Montmorency—on top of the cliff. Prince Edward, Queen Victoria's father, rented this villa from 1791 to 1794. Unfortunately, the structure burned several years ago; what now stands is a re-creation. ✉ *2490 av. Royale, Beauport,* ☎ *418/663–2877.* ☞ *Cable car $6 round-trip; parking $6.* ☉ *Cable car: Apr. 26–June 20, 9–7; June 21–Aug. 3, 9 AM–11 PM; Aug. 4–Sept. 1, 9–9; Sept. 2–Oct. 26, 9–7; Oct. 27–Nov. 9, 9–4. It also functions on winter weekends for the sugarloaf slide.*

Ste-Anne-de-Beaupré

40 km (25 mi) from Québec City.

★ **㊼** The small town of Ste-Anne-de-Beaupré is famous for an impressive shrine with the same name. The monumental and inspiring **Basilique Ste-Anne-de-Beaupré** is surrounded by aged, modest homes and tacky souvenir shops that emphasize its grandeur. The basilica has become a popular attraction as well as an important Catholic shrine: More than a half-million people visit the site each year.

The French brought their devotion to St. Anne (the patron saint of those in shipwrecks) with them when they sailed across the Atlantic to New France. In 1650, Breton sailors caught in a storm vowed to erect a chapel in honor of this patron saint at the exact spot where they landed. The present-day neo-Roman basilica constructed in 1923 was the fifth to be built on the site where the sailors first touched ground.

According to local legend, St. Anne was responsible over the years for saving voyagers from shipwrecks in the harsh waters of the St. Lawrence. Tributes to her miraculous powers can be seen in the shrine's various

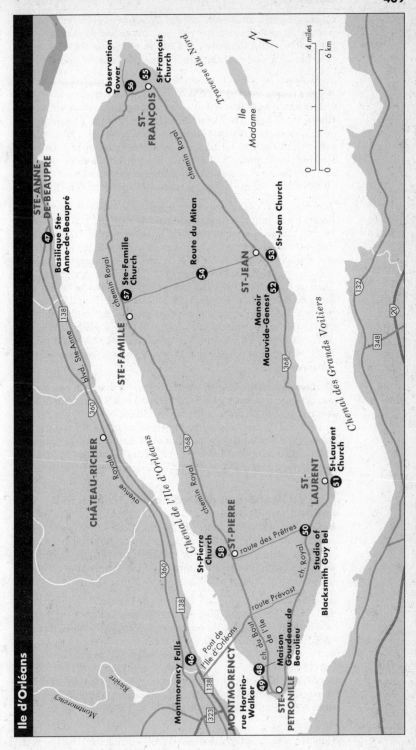

Traverse du Nord

Ile Madame

4 miles

6 km

Observation Tower

ST-FRANÇOIS

St-François Church

55

56

STE-ANNE-DE-BEAUPRÉ

Basilique Ste-Anne-de-Beaupré

47

chemin Royal

Route du Mitan

St-Jean Church

53

54

Ste-Famille Church

57

STE-FAMILLE

blvd. Ste-Anne

138

ST-JEAN

Manoir Mauvide-Genest

52

368

Chenal des Grands Voiliers

132

20

348

360

CHÂTEAU-RICHER

avenue Royale

Chenal de l'Ile d'Orléans

368

chemin Royal

St-Pierre Church

58

ST-PIERRE

route des Prêtres

ST-LAURENT

St-Laurent Church

51

50

Studio of Blacksmith Guy Bel

ch. royal

route Prévost

360

138

Montmorency Falls

46

Pont de l'Ile d'Orléans

MONTMORENCY

rue Horatio-Walker

ch. du Bout de l'Ile

48

49

Maison Gourdeau de Beaulieu

STE-PÉTRONILLE

323

Rivière Montmorency

mosaics, murals, altars, and ceilings. A bas-relief at the entrance depicts St. Anne welcoming her pilgrims, and ceiling mosaics represent her life. Numerous crutches and braces posted on the back pillars have been left by those who have felt the saint's healing powers.

The basilica, which is in the shape of a Latin cross, has two granite steeples jutting from its gigantic structure. Its interior has 22 chapels and 18 altars, as well as round arches and numerous ornaments in the Romanesque style. The 214 stained-glass windows by Frenchmen Auguste Labouret and Pierre Chaudière, finished in 1949, tell a story of salvation through personages who were believed to be instruments of God over the centuries. Other features of the shrine include intricately carved wood pews decorated with various animals and several smaller altars (behind the main altar) that are dedicated to different saints.

The original, 17th-century wood chapel in the village of Ste-Anne-de-Beaupré was built too close to the St. Lawrence and was swept away by river flooding. In 1676 the chapel was replaced by a stone church that was visited by pilgrims for more than a century, but this structure was also demolished in 1872. The first basilica, which replaced the stone church, was destroyed by a fire in 1922. The following year architects Maxime Rosin from Paris and Louis N. Audet from Québec province designed the basilica that now stands. Tours are given daily in summer at 1 and begin at the information booth at the southwest corner of the courtyard outside the basilica. ✉ *10018 av. Royale,* ☎ *418/827–3781.* 🎫 *Free.* ☉ *Reception booth mid-May–mid-Oct., daily 8:30–7:30; guided tours Sept.–mid-May can be arranged by calling in advance.*

The **Commemorative Chapel,** across from the basilica on avenue Royale, was designed by Claude Bailiff and built in 1878. The memorial chapel was constructed on the location of the transept of a stone church built in 1676 and contains the old building's foundations. Among the remnants housed here are the old church's bell dating from 1696, an early 18th-century altar designed by Vezina, a crucifix sculpted by François-Noël Levasseur in 1775, and a pulpit designed by François Baillargé in 1807.

Côte de Beaupré and Montmorency Falls A to Z

ARRIVING AND DEPARTING

By Car. To reach Montmorency Falls, take Route 440 (Autoroute Dufferin-Montmorency) east from Québec City approximately 9½ km (6 mi) to the exit for Montmorency Falls. To drive directly to Ste-Anne-de Beaupré, continue east on Route 440 for approximately 29 km (18 mi) and exit at Ste-Anne-de-Beaupré.

An alternative way to reach Ste-Anne-de-Beaupré is to take Route 360, or avenue Royale. Take Route 440 from Québec City, turn left at d'Estimauville, and right on boulevard Ste-Anne until it intersects with Route 360. Also called *le chemin du Roi* (the King's Road), this panoramic route is one of the oldest in North America, winding 30 km (19 mi) along the steep ridge of the Côte de Beaupré. The road borders 17th- and 18th-century farmhouses, historic churches, and Normandy-style homes with half-buried root cellars. Route 360 goes past the Ste-Anne-de-Beaupré Basilica.

GUIDED TOURS

Companies such as **Gray Line** (☎ 418/653–9722, 🖷 418/653–9834) and **Maple Leaf Sightseeing Tours** (☎ 418/649–9226) lead day excursions along the Côte de Beaupré, with stops at Montmorency Falls and the Ste-Anne-de-Beaupré Basilica. Cost is about $30 per tour.

Beau Temps, Mauvais Temps (✉ 22 rue du Quai, Suite 101, Ste-Pétron-ille, Ile d'Orléans, ☎ 418/828–2275) has guided bus tours of the Côte de Beaupré.

VISITOR INFORMATION

Beaupré Coast Interpretation Center, in the old mill Petit-Pré, built in 1695, has displays on the history and development of the region. ✉ *7007 av. Royale, Château-Richer,* ☎ *418/824–3677.* 🖃 *$2.* ⏱ *Mid-May–mid-Oct., daily 10–5.*

Quebec City Tourist Information has a bureau in Beauport (✉ 4300 blvd. Ste-Anne, Rte. 138) in Montmorency Falls Park. It's open mid-June–October 12, daily 9–5:45.

Ile d'Orléans

Ile d'Orléans, an island slightly downstream in a northeasterly direction from Québec City, exemplifies the historic charm of rural Québec province with its quiet, traditional lifestyle. A drive around the island will take you past stone churches that are among the oldest in the region and centuries-old houses amid acres of lush orchards and cultivated farmland. Horse-drawn carriages are still a means of transport. Ile d'Orléans is also an important marketplace that provides fresh produce daily for Québec City; roadside stands on the island sell a variety of local products, such as crocheted blankets, woven articles, maple syrup, homemade breads and jams, and fruits and vegetables. The island is known for its superb fruits, and you won't find better strawberries anywhere else in the province. There are about two dozen spots where you can pick your own.

The island was discovered at about the same time as Québec City, in 1535. Explorer Jacques Cartier noticed an abundance of vines on the island and called it the "Island of Bacchus," after the Greek god of wine. In 1536 Cartier renamed the island in honor of the duke of Orléans, son of the king of France, François I. Long considered part of the domain of Côte de Beaupré, the island was not given its seignorial autonomy until 1636.

Ile d'Orléans, about 9 km (5½ mi) wide and 34 km (21 mi) long, is now composed of six small villages. These villages have sought over the years to remain relatively private residential and agricultural communities; the island's bridge to the mainland was built only in 1935.

Ste-Pétronille
17 km (10½ mi) from Québec City.

The lovely village of Ste-Pétronille, the first to be settled on Ile d'Orléans, lies to the west of the bridge to the island. Founded in 1648, the community was chosen in 1759 by British general James Wolfe for his headquarters. With 40,000 soldiers and a hundred ships, the English bombarded French-occupied Québec City and Côte de Beaupré.

During the late 19th century, the English population of Québec developed Ste-Pétronille into a resort village. This region is considered by many to be the island's most beautiful, not only because of the spectacular views it offers of Montmorency Falls and Québec City but also for the stylish English villas and exquisitely tended gardens that can be seen from the roadside.

At the **Plante family farm** (✉ 20 chemin Royal) you can stop to pick apples (in season) or buy fresh fruits and vegetables.

❹⓼ The island's first home, the **Maison Gourdeau de Beaulieu** (✉ 137 chemin Royal) was built in 1648 for Jacques Gourdeau de Beaulieu, who was the first seigneur (a landholder who distributed lots to tenant farmers) of Ste-Pétronille. Today this white house with blue shutters is still privately owned by his descendants. Remodeled over the years, it now incorporates both French and Québécois styles. Its thick walls and dormer windows are characteristic of Breton architecture, but its sloping bell-shape roof, designed to protect buildings from large amounts of snow, is typically Québécois. The house is not open to the public.

49 The tiny street called **rue Horatio-Walker** was named after the turn-of-the-century painter known for his landscapes of the island. Walker lived on this street from 1904 until his death in 1938. At 11 and 13 rue Horatio-Walker are his home and workshop, but they are not open to the public. The street is by the river, off chemin Royal.

At the border of Ste-Pétronille and St-Laurent, look for a large boulder in the middle of nowhere: The **roche à Maranda** (just before the intersection of chemin Royal and route Prévost), named for the owner of the property where the rock was discovered in the 19th century, is one of the oldest such rock formations in the world. When the glaciers melted in 9,000 BC, such rocks as this one rolled down with glacial water from the Laurentians onto lower land.

DINING AND LODGING

$$–$$$ ✕🗆 **La Goéliche.** This English-style country manor was rebuilt in 1996 and 1997 following a fire. The new building stands just steps away from the St. Lawrence River, and Québécois antiques decorate light, spacious rooms. All rooms have a view of the river; some have a kitchenette. The classic French kitchen here uses only the freshest ingredients from the island's farms. Lunch is a moderately priced à la carte selection of salads, quiches, and omelets. The evening's menu is more expensive and includes quail with red vermouth and chicken with pistachio mousseline. Desserts, such as maple syrup mousse with strawberry syrup, have a regional flavor. The romantic dining room overlooks the St. Lawrence. ✉ *22 chemin du Quai,* ☎ *418/828–2248,* ℻ *418/828–2745. 18 rooms. Restaurant. AE, MC, V.*

St-Laurent

9 km (5½ mi) from Ste-Pétronille.

Founded in 1679, St-Laurent is one of the island's maritime villages. Until as late as 1935, residents here used boats as their main means of transportation. As you approach the village on chemin Royal, you'll **50** see the **studio of blacksmith Guy Bel** (✉ 2200 chemin Royal, ☎ 418/ 828–9300), which belongs to the talented and well-known local artisan who has done ironwork restoration for Québec City. He was born in Lyon, France, and studied there at the Ecole des Beaux Arts. In summer you can watch him hard at work daily; his stylish candlesticks, mantels, and other ironworks are for sale. In winter his workshop is closed on weekends.

The **Parc Maritime de St-Laurent,** at a former boatyard, is where craftspeople specializing in boat building practiced their trade. Now you can picnic here, rent a rowboat, and visit the Chalouperie Godbout (Godbout Longboat), which houses a complete collection of tools used during the golden era of boat building. You can try your hand at some boat-building skills and practice tying sailors' knots. ✉ *120 chemin de la Chalouperie,* ☎ *418/828–2322.* ✉ *$2.* ☉ *Mid-June–Aug., daily 10–5; Sept.–early Oct., weekends 10–5.*

51 The tall, inspiring **St-Laurent Church,** which stands next to the village marina on chemin Royale, was built in 1860 on the site of an 18th-century church that had to be torn down. One of the church's procession chapels is a miniature stone replica of the original. ⊠ *1532 chemin Royal.* ☎ *Free.* ☼ *Summer, daily.*

DINING

✗ **Moulin de Saint-Laurent.** This is an early 18th-century stone mill in which you can dine in the herb-and-flower garden out back. Scrumptious snacks, such as quiches, bagels, and salads, are available at the café-terrace. ⊠ *754 chemin Royal,* ☎ *418/829–3888. DC, MC, V. Closed Nov.–Apr.*

St-Jean
12 km (7 mi) from St-Laurent.

The southernmost point of the island, St-Jean is a village whose inhabitants were once river pilots and navigators. Most of its small, homogeneous row homes were built between 1840 and 1860. Being at sea most of the time, the sailors did not need large homes and plots of land as did the farmers. The island's sudden drop in elevation is most noticeable in St-Jean.

52 St-Jean's beautiful Normandy-style manor, **Manoir Mauvide-Genest,** was built in 1734 for Jean Mauvide—surgeon to Louis XV—and his wife, Marie-Anne Genest. Most notable about this house, which still has its original thick walls, ceiling beams, and fireplaces, is the degree to which it has held up over the years, in spite of being targeted by English guns during the 1759 siege of Québec City. The home is a pleasure to roam; all rooms are furnished with antiques from the 18th and 19th centuries. There's also an exhibit on French architecture and a downstairs restaurant that serves French cuisine. ⊠ *1451 chemin Royal,* ☎ *418/829–2630.* ☎ *$4.* ☼ *June–Aug., daily 10–5; Sept.–mid-Oct., weekends by reservation.*

53 At the eastern end of the village, you'll see **St-Jean Church,** a massive granite structure with large red doors and a towering steeple built in 1749. The church resembles a ship; it is big and round and appears to be sitting right on the St. Lawrence River. Paintings of the patron saints of seamen line the interior walls. The church's cemetery is also intriguing, especially if you can read French. Back in the 18th century, piloting the St. Lawrence was a dangerous profession; the boats could not easily handle the rough currents. The cemetery tombstones recall the tragedies of lives lost in these harsh waters. ⊠ *2001 chemin Royal,* ☎ *418/829–3182.* ☎ *Free.* ☼ *Summer, daily 9–5.*

54 Outside St-Jean, chemin Royal crosses **route du Mitan.** In old French, *mitan* means "halfway." This road, dividing the island in half, is the most direct route from north to south. It is also the most beautiful on the island, with acres of tended farmland, apple orchards, and maple groves. If you need to end your circuit of the island here, take route du Mitan, which brings you to Ste-Famille; head west on chemin Royal to return to the bridge to the mainland.

St-François
12 km (7 mi) from St-Jean.

When you come to 17th-century farmhouses separated by sprawling open fields, you know you've reached the island's least-toured and most rustic village, St-François. At the eastern tip of the island, this community was originally settled mainly by farmers. St-François is also the perfect place to visit one of the island's *cabanes à sucre* (maple-sugaring shacks), found along chemin Royal. Stop at a hut for a tasting tour; sap is gathered from the maple groves and boiled until it turns to syrup. When it is poured on ice, it tastes like a delicious toffee. The maple syrup season is late March through April.

55 **St-François Church** (✉ Chemin Royal), built in 1734, is one of eight provincial churches dating from the French regime. At the time the English seized Québec in 1759, General Wolfe knew St-François to be among the better strategic points along the St. Lawrence. Consequently, he stationed British troops here and used the church as a military hospital. In May 1988, a fatal car crash set the church on fire and most of the interior treasures were lost.

56 A picnic area with a wood **observation tower** is situated for perfect viewing of the majestic St. Lawrence at its widest point, 10 times as wide as it is near Québec City. During the spring and autumn months, you can observe wild Canada geese here. This area is about a mile north on chemin Royal from the St-François Church.

DINING AND LODGING

$$–$$$ ✕⊠ **Auberge le Chaumonot.** This medium-size hotel near the St. Lawrence River's widest point has large bay windows that capitalize on the view of the river. The decor is uninspired, however, with simple wood furniture of the island. The service here is efficient and friendly. The restaurant serves Continental cuisine, with table d'hôte and à la carte menus. ✉ 425 chemin Royal, G0A 3S0, ☎ 418/829–2735. 8 rooms. Restaurant, pool. AE, MC, V. Closed Nov.–Apr.

Ste-Famille
14 km (9 mi) from St-François.

The village of Ste-Famille, founded in 1661, has exquisite scenery; there are abundant apple orchards and strawberry fields with views of Côte de Beaupré and Mont Ste-Anne in the distance. But the village also has plenty of historic charm; it has the area's highest concentration of stone houses dating from the French regime.

57 Take a quick look at **Ste-Famille Church,** which was constructed in 1749, later than some of the others on the island. This impressive structure is the only church in the province to have three bell towers at the front. Its ceiling was redone in the mid-19th century with elaborate designs in wood and gold. The church also holds a famous painting, *L'Enfant Jésus Voyant la Croix* ("Baby Jesus Looking at the Cross"), done in 1670 by Frère Luc (Father Luc), who was sent from France to decorate churches in the area. ✉ 3915 chemin Royal. ☐ Free. ⊙ Summer, daily.

DINING

$$$ ✕ **L'Atre.** After you park your car, you'll be driven in a 1954 Chevy to the 17th-century Normandy-style house furnished with Québécois pine antiques. True to the establishment's name, which means "hearth," all the traditional dishes are cooked and served from a fireplace. The menu emphasizes hearty fare, such as beef bourguignonne and tourtière, with maple-sugar pie for dessert. Halfway through the meal, you visit the attic for a nip of maple-syrup liqueur. ✉ 4403 chemin Royal, ☎ 418/829–2474. Reservations essential. AE, MC, V. Closed Nov.–Apr.

St-Pierre
14 km (9 mi) from St-Famille.

St-Pierre, on the northwest side of the island, was established in 1679. Situated on a plateau with the island's most fertile land, the town has long been the center of traditional farming industries. The best products grown here are potatoes, asparagus, and corn, and the many dairy farms have given the village a renowned reputation for butter and other dairy products. If you continue west on chemin Royal, just up ahead is the bridge back to the mainland and Route 440.

58 **St-Pierre Church,** the oldest on the island, dates to 1717. It is no longer open for worship, but it was restored during the 1960s and is open to visitors. Many of its original components are still intact, such as benches with compartments below, where hot bricks and stones were placed to keep people warm during winter services. ⊠ *1243 chemin Royal.* ☎ *Free.* ☉ *Summer, daily.*

Ile d'Orléans A to Z

ARRIVING AND DEPARTING

From Québec City, take Route 440 (Dufferin-Montmorency Autoroute) northeast. After a drive of about 10 km (6 mi) take the bridge, Pont de l'Ile d'Orléans, to the island.

Ile d'Orléans has no public transportation; cars are the only way to get around, unless you take a guided tour (☞ Guided Tours, *below*). Parking on the island is never a problem; you can always stop and explore the villages on foot. The main road, chemin Royal (Route 368), extends 67 km (42 mi) through the island's six villages; street numbers along chemin Royal begin at No. 1 for each municipality.

B&B RESERVATION SERVICE

You can get to know the island by staying at one of its 40 B&Bs. Reservations are necessary. The price for a room, double occupancy, runs about $50–$75 per night. **The Chamber of Commerce** (☎ 418/828–9411) is a referral service for these accommodations.

EMERGENCIES

Centre Médical (⊠ 1015 Rte. Prévost, St-Pierre, ☎ 418/828–2213) is the only medical clinic on the island.

GUIDED TOURS

Beau Temps, Mauvais Temps (⊠ 22 rue du Quai, Suite 101, Ste-Pétron-ille, ☎ 418/828–2275) leads guided walking tours of the island. Québec City touring companies, including **Maple Leaf Sightseeing Tours** (☎ 418/649–9226) and **Gray Line** (☎ 418/653–9722, FAX 418/653–9834) offer bus tours of the western tip of the island, combined with sightseeing along the Côte de Beaupré.

Any of the offices of the **Québec City Region Tourism and Convention Bureau** (☞ Visitor Information *in* Québec City A to Z, *below*) can provide information on tours and accommodations on the island.

VISITOR INFORMATION

Beau Temps, Mauvais Temps has a tourist office in Ste-Pétronille. ⊠ *22 rue du Quai, Suite 101, Ste-Pétronille,* ☎ *418/828–2275.* ☉ *May–Oct., weekdays 8:30–4; Nov.–Apr., leave message on answering machine.*

The island's **Chamber of Commerce** operates a tourist information kiosk situated at the west corner of côte du Pont and chemin Royal in St-Pierre. ⊠ *490 côte du Pont, St-Pierre,* ☎ *418/828–9411.* ☉ *June–Sept., daily 8:30–7; Oct.–May, weekdays 8:30–noon, 1–4.*

QUÉBEC CITY A TO Z

Arriving and Departing

By Bus

Voyageur Inc. provides regular service from Montréal to Québec City daily, departing hourly 6 AM–9 PM, with an additional bus at 11 PM. The cost of the three-hour ride is $35.90 one way, and a round-trip is double that; but a round-trip costs $53.27 if you return within 10 days and do not travel on Friday. You can purchase tickets only at one of the terminals (☞ *below*).

TERMINALS

Montréal: Terminus Voyageur (☒ 505 blvd. de Maisonneuve Est, ☎ 514/842–2281). **Québec City:** Downtown Terminal (☒ 320 rue Abraham-Martin, ☎ 418/525–3000); Ste-Foy Terminal (☒ 925 ave. de Rochebelle, ☎ 418/525–3000).

By Car

Montréal and Québec City are linked by Autoroute 20 on the south shore of the St. Lawrence River and by Autoroute 40 on the north shore. On both highways, the ride between the two cities is about 240 km (149 mi) and takes some three hours. U.S. I–87 in New York, U.S. I–89 in Vermont, and U.S. I–91 in New Hampshire connect with Autoroute 20. Highway 401 from Toronto also links up with Autoroute 20.

Driving northeast from Montréal on Autoroute 20, follow signs for Pont Pierre-Laporte (Pierre Laporte Bridge) as you approach Québec City. After you've crossed the bridge, turn right onto boulevard Laurier (Route 175), which becomes the Grande Allée leading into Québec City. Also *see* Getting Around by Car, *below.*

By Plane

Jean Lesage International Airport (☒ 500 rue Principale, Ste-Foy, ☎ 418/640–2600) is about 19 km (12 mi) from downtown. Few U.S. **airlines** fly directly to Québec City. You usually have to stop in Montréal, Toronto, or Ottawa and take one of the regional and commuter airlines, such as Air Canada's Air Alliance (☎ 418/692–0770 or 800/361–8620) or Canadian Airlines International (☎ 418/692–1031). Air Alliance has a daily direct flight between Newark, New Jersey, and Québec City.

BETWEEN THE AIRPORT AND QUÉBEC CITY

The ride from the airport into town should be no longer than 30 minutes. Most hotels do not have an airport shuttle, but they will make a reservation for you with a bus company. If you're not in a rush, a shuttle bus offered by Maple Leaf Sightseeing Tours (☞ *below*) is convenient and half the price of a taxi.

By Bus. Maple Leaf Sightseeing Tours (☒ 240 3ᵉ rue, ☎ 418/649–9226) has a shuttle bus from the airport to hotels; cost is under $10 one way. Reservations are necessary for the trip to the airport.

By Car. If you're driving from the airport, take Route 540 (Autoroute Duplessis) to Route 175 (blvd. Laurier), which becomes Grande Allée and leads right to Vieux-Québec. The ride is about 30 minutes and may be only slightly longer (45 minutes or so) during rush hours (7:30–8:30 AM into town and 4–5:30 PM leaving town).

By Limousine. Private limo service is expensive, starting at $45 for the ride from the airport into Québec City. Try **Groupe Limousine A-1** (☒ 361 rue des Commissaires Est, ☎ 418/523–5059). **Maple Leaf Sightseeing Tours** (☞ *above*) acts as a referral service for local companies offering car service.

By Taxi. Taxis are available immediately outside the airport exit near the baggage claim area. Two local taxi firms are **Taxi Québec** (☒ 975 8ᵉ av., ☎ 418/522–2001) and **Taxi Coop de Québec** (☒ 496 2ᵉ av., ☎ 418/525–5191), the largest company in the city. A ride into the city costs about $25.

By Train

VIA Rail (☎ 418/692–3940; 800/361–5390 in Québec province), Canada's passenger rail service, runs trains from Montréal to Québec City four times daily Tuesday through Friday, and three times daily on Saturday, Sunday, and Monday. The trip takes less than three hours, with a stop in Ste-Foy. Tickets must be purchased in advance at any VIA Rail office or travel agent. The basic one-way rate is about $50, but a limited quantity of seats are reduced to $30 if bought at least five days in advance (not including Friday, Sunday, or holidays). First-class service costs about $90 each way and includes early boarding and a three-course meal with wine.

The train arrives in Québec City at the 19th-century **Gare du Palais** (⊠ 450 rue de la Gare du Palais, ☎ 418/524–6452), in the heart of the old city.

Getting Around

By Bus

The city's transit system, **Société de Transport de la Communauté Urbaine de Québec (STCUQ)** (☎ 418/627–2511) runs buses approximately every 15 or 20 minutes that stop at major points around town. The cost is $1.85; you'll need exact change. Bus tickets are available for $1.50 ($4 for day pass) at major convenience stores. All buses stop in Lower Town at Place Jacques-Cartier or outside St-Jean Gate at Place d'Youville in Upper Town. Transportation maps are available at visitor information offices.

By Car

It is necessary to have a car only if you are planning to visit outlying areas. The narrow streets of the old city leave few two-hour metered parking spaces available. However, there are several parking garages at central locations, with rates running approximately $10 a day. Main garages are at City Hall, Place d'Youville, Edifice Marie-Guyart, Complex G, Place Québec, Château Frontenac, Québec Seminary, rue St-Paul, and the Old Port.

By Ferry

The **Québec–Lévis ferry** (☎ 418/644–3704) makes a 15-minute crossing of the St. Lawrence River to the town of Lévis; cost is $1.25. From December through April, the first ferry leaves daily at 6:30 AM from the pier at rue Dalhousie, across from Place Royale. Crossings run every half hour from 7:30 AM until 6:30 PM, then hourly until 2:30 AM, with a final crossing at 3:45 AM. From May through November, the ferry adds extra service every 20 minutes during rush hours—7:20 AM–9 AM and 4 PM–6 PM.

By Foot

Walking is the best way to explore the city. Vieux-Québec measures 11 square km (about 6 square mi), and most historic sites, hotels, and restaurants are within the walls or a short distance outside. City maps are available at visitor information offices.

By Horse-Drawn Carriage

Hire a calèche on rue d'Auteuil between the St-Louis and Kent gates from **André Beaurivage** (☎ 418/687–9797), **Balades en Calèche** (☎ 418/624–3062), or **Les Calèches de Vieux Québec** (☎ 418/683–9222). The cost is about $50 without tax or tip for a 45-minute tour of Vieux-Québec. Some drivers talk about Québec's history and others don't; if you want a storyteller, ask in advance.

By Limousine

Groupe Limousine A-1 (✉ 361 rue des Commissaires Est, ☎ 418/523–5059) has 24-hour service.

By Taxi

Taxis are stationed in front of major hotels and the Hôtel de Ville (City Hall), along rue des Jardins, and at Place d'Youville outside St-Jean Gate. For radio-dispatched cars, try **Taxi Coop de Québec** (☎ 418/525–5191) and **Taxi Québec** (☎ 418/522–2001). Passengers are charged an initial $2.25, plus $1 for each km.

Contacts and Resources

B&B Reservation Agencies

Québec City has a large number of B&B and hostel accommodations. To guarantee a room during peak season, be sure to reserve in advance. **Québec City Tourist Information** (✉ 835 av. Laurier, G1R 2L3, ☎ 418/692–2471) has B&B listings.

Car Rentals

Hertz Canada (Airport: ☎ 418/871–1571; Vieux-Québec, ✉ 44 Côte du Palais, ☎ 418/694–1224 or 800/263–0600 in English and 800/263–0678 in French). **Tilden** (Airport: ☎ 418/871–1224, ✉ 295 St. Paul St., ☎ 418/694–1727). **Via Route** (✉ 2605 Hamel Blvd., ☎ 418/682–2660).

Consulate

The **U.S. Consulate** (✉ 2 Pl. Terrasse Dufferin, ☎ 418/692–2095) faces the Governors' Park near the Château Frontenac.

Dentists and Doctors

Clinique Dentaire Darveau, Dablois and Tardis (✉ 1175 rue Lavigerie, Edifice Iberville 2, Room 100, Ste-Foy, ☎ 418/653–5412) is open Monday and Tuesday 8–8, Wednesday and Thursday 8–5, Friday 8–4.

Hôtel-Dieu Hospital (✉ 11 côte du Palais, ☎ 418/691–5151, 418/691–5042 emergency) is the main hospital inside Vieux-Québec. **Centre Hospitalier de l"Université Laval (CHUL)** (✉ 2705 blvd. Laurier, ☎ 418/656–4141) is in Ste-Foy.

Emergencies

Distress Center (☎ 418/686–2433). **24-hour Poison Center** (☎ 418/656–8090). **Police and fire**(☎ 911 or 418/691–6911). **Provincial police** (☎ 418/623–6262).

English-Language Bookstore

La Maison Anglaise (✉ 2600 blvd. Laurier, Pl. de la Cité, Ste-Foy, ☎ 418/654–9523).

Guided Tours

BOAT TRIPS

Croisières AML Inc. (✉ Pier Chouinard, 10 rue Dalhousie, beside the Québec-Lévis ferry terminal, ☎ 418/692–1159) runs cruises on the St. Lawrence River aboard the MV *Louis-Jolliet*. One- to three-hour cruises from May through mid-October start at $20.

ORIENTATION

Tours cover such sights as Québec City, Montmorency Falls, and Ste-Anne-de-Beaupré; combination city and harbor cruise tours are also available. Québec City tours operate year-round; excursions to outlying areas may operate only in summer.

Tickets for **Gray Line** bus tours (☎ 418/653–9722) can be purchased at most major hotels or at the kiosk at Terrasse Dufferin at Place d'Armes. Tours run year-round and cost $20–$80; departure is from Château Frontenac terrace. **Maple Leaf Sightseeing Tours** (⊠ 240 3ᵉ rue, ☎ 418/649–9226) offers guided tours in a minibus. Call for a reservation, and the company will pick you up at your hotel. Prices are $20–$89. **La Tournée du Québec Inc.** (☎ 418/836–8687) is a smaller company that has tours.

WALKING TOURS

Adlard Tours (⊠ 13 rue Ste-Famille, ☎ 418/692–2358) leads walking tours of the old city amid the narrow streets where buses cannot enter. The $14 cost includes a refreshment break; unilingual tours are available in many languages.

Late-Night Pharmacy

Pharmacie Brunet (⊠ Les Galeries Charlesbourg, 4250 1ʳᵉ av., north of Québec City in Charlesbourg, ☎ 418/623–1571) is open daily, 24 hours a day.

Opening and Closing Times

Most **banks** are open Monday through Wednesday 10–3 and close later on Thursday and Friday. **Bank of Montréal** (⊠ Pl. Laurier, 2700 blvd. Laurier, Ste-Foy, ☎ 418/525–3786) is open on Saturday 9:30–2. For currency exchange, **Echange de Devises Montréal** (⊠ 12 rue Ste-Anne, ☎ 418/694–1014) is open September–mid-June, daily 9–5, and mid-June–Labor Day, daily 8:30–7:30.

Museum hours are typically 10–5, with longer evening hours during summer months. Most are closed on Monday.

For **store** hours, *see* Shopping, *above*.

In winter many attractions and shops change their hours; visitors are advised to call ahead.

Road Conditions

Seasonal information is available from November through April (☎ 418/643–6830).

Travel Agency

Inter-Voyage (⊠ 1095 rue de l'Amérique Francâise, ☎ 418/524–1414). **American Express** (⊠ 46 rue Garneau, ☎ 418/692–0997).

Visitor Information

Québec City Region Tourism and Convention Bureau has two visitor information centers that are open year-round and a mobile information service that operates between mid-June and September 7 (look for the mopeds with a big question mark).

The **Québec City** (⊠ 835 av. Laurier, G1R 2L3, ☎ 418/692–2471) center is open June–September 7, daily 8:30–7:45; September 8–October 12, daily 8:30–5:15; October 13–March, daily 9–4:45; April–May, daily 8:30–5:15.

The **Ste-Foy** (⊠ 3300 av. des Hôtels, G1W 5A8: look for the big question mark) center, a drop-in office (no telephone) is open June–September 7, daily 8:30–7:45; September 8–October 12, daily 8:30–5:45; October 13–March, daily 9–4:45; April–May, daily 8:30–5:45.

Québec Government Tourism Department (⊠ 12 rue Ste-Anne, on Pl. d'Armes, ☎ 418/643–2280 or 800/363–7777) has a center that is open fall–winter, daily 9–5, and summer, daily 8:30–7:30.

10 Province of Québec

The Laurentians, the Eastern Townships, Charlevoix, the Gaspé Peninsula

Québec has a distinct personality forged by its French heritage and culture. The land, too, is memorable: Within its boundaries lie thousands of lakes, streams, and rivers—the highways for intrepid explorers, fur traders, and pioneers. Echoes of the past remain in the charming rural communities of Charlevoix and the Eastern Townships. The Laurentians with their many ski resorts and the forested coastline of the Gulf of St. Lawrence also lend a unique flavor to La Belle Province.

By Dorothy
Guinan

Updated by
Helga
Loverseed

AMONG THE PROVINCES OF CANADA, Québec is set apart by its strong French heritage, a matter not only of language but of customs, religion, and political structure. Québec covers a vast area—almost one-sixth of Canada's total—although the upper three-quarters is only sparsely inhabited. Most of the population lives in the southern cities, especially Montréal (☞ Chapter 8) and Québec City (☞ Chapter 9). Outside the cities, however, you'll find serenity and natural beauty in the province's innumerable lakes, streams, and rivers; in its farmlands and villages; in its great mountains and deep forests; and in its rugged coastline along the Gulf of St. Lawrence. Though the winters are long, there are plenty of winter sports to while away the cold months, especially in the Laurentians, with their many ski resorts.

The first European to arrive in Québec was French explorer Jacques Cartier, in 1534; another Frenchman, Samuel de Champlain, arrived in 1603 to build French settlements in the region, and Jesuit missionaries followed in due course. Louis XIV of France proclaimed Canada a crown colony in 1663, and the land was allotted to French aristocrats in large grants called seigneuries. As tenants, known as habitants, settled upon farms in Québec, the Roman Catholic church took on an importance that went beyond religion. Priests and nuns also acted as doctors, educators, and overseers of business arrangements between the habitants and between French-speaking fur traders and English-speaking merchants. An important doctrine of the church in Québec, one that took on more emphasis after the British conquest of 1759, was "survivance," the survival of the French people and their culture. Couples were encouraged to have large families, and they did—until the 1950s families with 10 or 12 children were common.

Québec's recent threats to secede from the Canadian union are part of a long-standing tradition of independence. Although the British won control of Canada in the French and Indian War, which ended in 1763, Parliament passed the Québec Act in 1774, which ensured the continuation of French civil law in Québec and left provincial authority in the hands of the Roman Catholic church. In general the law preserved the traditional French-Canadian way of life. Tensions between French- and English-speaking Canada have continued throughout the 20th century, however, and in 1974 the province proclaimed French its sole official language, much the same way the provinces of Manitoba and Alberta had taken steps earlier in the century to make English their sole official language. In 1990 the Canadian government failed to add Québec's signature to changes it had brought about in the Canadian Constitution, and in 1992 failed to have its proposed constitutional changes accepted by the Canadian population in a referendum. Today Québec is part of the Canadian union and a signatory to its constitution, but it has not accepted the changes made in that document during the 1980s.

Being able to speak French can make your visit to the province more pleasant—many locals, at least outside Montréal, do not speak English. If you don't speak French, arm yourself with a phrase book or at least a knowledge of some basic phrases. It's also worth your while to sample the hearty traditional Québécois cuisine, for this is a province where food is taken seriously.

Lower Québec

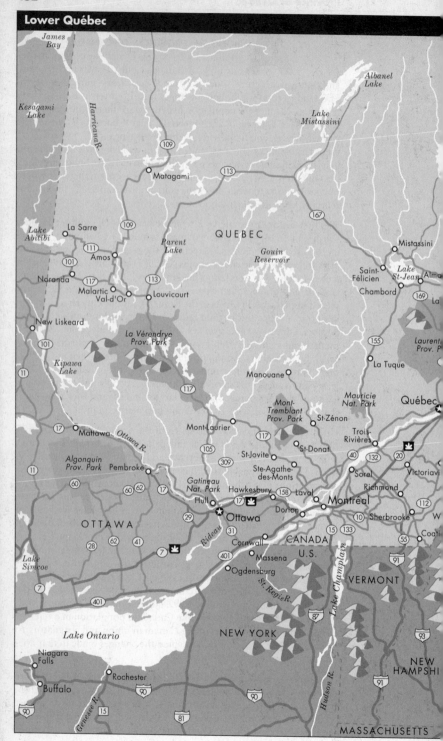

James Bay

Kesagami Lake

Harricana R.

Albanel Lake

Lake Mistassini

109

Matagami

113

167

QUEBEC

Parent Lake

Gouin Reservoir

Mistassini

Saint-Félicien

Lake St-Jean

Alma

La Sarre

109

111

Amos

101

Noranda

117

Malartic

Val-d'Or

Louvicourt

113

Chambord

169

La

New Liskeard

101

Kipawa Lake

11

La Vérendrye Prov. Park

117

155

Laurent Prov. P

Manouane

La Tuque

Mauricie Nat. Park

Québec

17

Mattawa

Ottawa R.

Mont-Tremblant Prov. Park

St-Zénon

Trois-Rivières

Algonquin Prov. Park

Pembroke

Mont-Laurier

117

St-Donat

40

132

20

60

60

62

17

105

309

St-Jovite

Ste-Agathe-des-Monts

Sorel

Victoriavi

11

60

Gatineau Nat. Park

Hawkesbury

158

Laval

Richmond

62

41

29

Hull

17

Dorion

Montréal

112

28

Ottawa

10

Sherbrooke

W

7

Rideau

31

Cornwall

CANADA

15

133

Coati

55

Lake Simcoe

28

62

41

7

401

Massena

U.S.

91

7

Ogdensburg

St. Regis R.

VERMONT

401

NEW YORK

87

Lake Champlain

93

Niagara Falls

Buffalo

Rochester

90

90

Genesee R.

15

81

Lake Ontario

90

Hudson R.

91

NEW HAMPSHI

MASSACHUSETTS

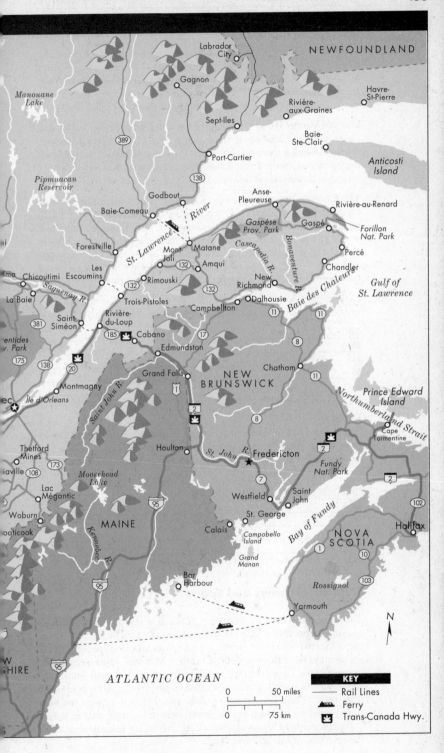

NEWFOUNDLAND

Manouane
Lake

Labrador
City

Gagnon

Havre-
St-Pierre

Rivière-
aux-Graines

Sept-Iles

Baie-
Ste-Clair

(389)

Port-Cartier

Anticosti
Island

*Pipmuacan
Reservoir*

Godbout

Anse-
Pleureuse

Rivière-au-Renard

(138)

Baie-Comeau

St. Lawrence River

Gaspése
Prov. Park

Gaspé

Forillon
Nat. Park

Forestville

Mont-
Joli

Matane

Cascapedia R.

Percé

ma

Chicoutimi Les
Escoumins

(132)

Rimouski

(132)

Amqui

New
Richmond

Chandler

Gulf of
St. Lawrence

Saguenay R.

(132)

(132)

Bonaventure R.

La Baie

Trois-Pistoles

Campbellton

Dalhousie

Baie des Chaleurs

Saint-
Siméon

Rivière-
du-Loup

(11)

(11)

(381)

(185)

Cabano

*rentides
v. Park*

(175)

Edmundston

(17)

(8)

(138)

(20)

NEW
BRUNSWICK

Chatham

(11)

Prince Edward
Island

Grand Falls

Montmagny

Northumberland Strait

Île d'Orleans

(2)

(8)

Cape
Tormentine

ec

Thetford
Mines

Houlton

St. John R. Fredericton

(2)

iaville (108)

(173)

Fundy
Nat. Park

(2)

Lac
Mégantic

*Moosehead
Lake*

(7)

Westfield

Saint
John

(102)

Woburn

MAINE

St. George

Halifax

aticook

(95)

Calais

*Campobello
Island*

Bay of Fundy

NOVA
SCOTIA

Kennebec R.

*Grand
Manan*

(1)

(10)

Rossignol

(103)

Bar
Harbour

(95)

Yarmouth

N

W
HIRE

(95)

ATLANTIC OCEAN

KEY
—— Rail Lines
Ferry
Trans-Canada Hwy.

0   50 miles

0   75 km

Pleasures and Pastimes

Dining

Whether you enjoy a croissant and espresso at a sidewalk café or order *poutine* (a heaped plate of *frites*—French fries—smothered with gravy and melted cheese curds) from a fast-food emporium, you won't soon forget your meals here. There is no such thing as simply "eating out" in the province; restaurants are an integral slice of Québec life.

Outside Montréal and Québec City, you can find both good value and classic cuisine. Cooking in the province tends to be hearty, with such fare as cassoulet, *tourtières* (meat pies), onion soup, and apple pie heading up menus. In the Laurentians, chefs at some of the finer inns have attracted international followings.

The Eastern Townships are one of Québec's foremost regions for fine cuisine and for traditional Québécois dishes. Specialties include such mixed-game meat pies as *cipaille* and sweet, salty dishes like ham and maple syrup. Actually, maple syrup—much of it produced locally—is a mainstay of Québécois dishes. In addition, cloves, nutmeg, cinnamon, and pepper—spices used by the first settlers—have never gone out of style here, and local restaurants make good use of them.

Early reservations are essential. Monday or Tuesday is not too soon to book weekend tables at the best provincial restaurants.

CATEGORY	COST*
$$$$	over $35
$$$	$25–$35
$$	$15–$25
$	under $15

per person, excluding drinks, service, 7% GST, and 6.5% provincial tax.

Lodging

You'll find a full spectrum of accommodation options in Québec: from large resort hotels in the Laurentians and elegant Relais & Châteaux properties in the Eastern Townships to simple accommodations near the heart of the Gaspé.

CATEGORY	COST*
$$$$	over $125
$$$	$90–$125
$$	$50–$90
$	under $50

Prices are for a standard double room, excluding 10% service charge, 7% GST, and 6.5% provincial tax.

Outdoor Activities and Sports

FISHING

There are more than 60 outfitters (some of whom are also innkeepers) in the northern Laurentians area, where provincial parks and game sanctuaries abound. Pike, walleye, and lake and speckled trout are plentiful just a three-hour drive north of Montréal. Open year-round in most cases, their lodging facilities range from the most luxurious first-class resorts to log cabins. As well as supplying trained guides, all offer services and equipment to allow neophytes or experts the best possible fishing in addition to boating, swimming, river rafting, windsurfing, ice fishing, cross-country skiing, hiking, or just relaxing amid the splendor of this still spectacularly unspoiled region.

RIVER RAFTING

Rivière Rouge in the Laurentians rates among the best in North America, so it's not surprising that this river has spawned a miniboom in the sport. Just an hour's drive north of Montréal, the Rouge cuts across the rugged Laurentians through canyons and alongside beaches. From April through October, you can experience what traversing the region must have meant in the days of the voyageurs, though today's trip is much safer and more comfortable. (For outfitter information, *see* Contacts and Resources *in* Québec A to Z, *below*).

SKIING

The Laurentians are well-known internationally as a downhill destination, from St-Sauveur to majestic Mont-Tremblant. Cross-country skiing is popular throughout the area from December to the end of March, especially at Val David, Val Morin, and Ville l'Estérel. Each has a cross-country ski center and at least a dozen groomed trails.

The Eastern Townships have more than 900 km (558 mi) of cross-country trails. Three inns here offer a weeklong package of cross-country treks from one inn to another. The area is also popular as a downhill ski center, with ski hills on four mountains that dwarf anything the Laurentians have to offer, with the exception of Mont-Tremblant.

Charlevoix has three main ski areas with excellent facilities for both the downhill and cross-country skier.

Sugar Shacks

Every March the combination of sunny days and cold nights causes the sap to run in the maple trees. *Cabanes à sucre* (sugar shacks) go into operation, boiling the sap collected from the trees in buckets (now, at some places, complicated tubing and vats do the job). The many commercial enterprises scattered over the area host "sugaring offs" and tours of the process, including the tapping of maple trees, the boiling of the sap in vats, and *tire sur la neige,* when hot syrup is poured over cold snow to give it a taffy consistency just right for "pulling" and eating. A number of cabanes offer hearty meals of ham, baked beans, and pancakes, all drowned in maple syrup.

Exploring Québec

There are two major recreational areas beyond the city limits of Montréal where stressed-out urbanites go to relax: the Laurentians and the Eastern Townships. The Laurentians are a resort area with thousands of miles of wilderness and world-famous ski resorts. The mountains begin only 60 km (37 mi) north of Montréal. Rolling hills and farmland make the Eastern Townships, in the southeast corner of the province, popular year-round, with outdoor activities on ski slopes and lakes and in provincial parks. Cultural attractions are other pleasures here; the Townships start just 80 km (50 mi) east of Montréal.

Charlevoix is often called the Switzerland of Québec because of its landscape, which includes mountains, valleys, streams, and waterfalls. Charming villages draw visitors to an area that stretches along the north shore of the St. Lawrence River for about 200 km (124 mi), from Ste-Anne-de-Beaupré east of Québec City to the Saguenay River. The knobby Gaspé Peninsula is where the St. Lawrence River meets the Gulf of St. Lawrence. This isolated peninsula, about 200 km (124 mi) east of Québec City, has a wild beauty all its own; mountains and cliffs tower above its beaches. The drive around the Gaspé is 848 km (526 mi).

Numbers in the text correspond to numbers in the margin and on the Laurentians (les Laurentides), Eastern Townships (les Cantons de l'Est) and Montérégie, Charlevoix, and Gaspé Peninsula (Gaspésie) maps.

Great Itineraries

IF YOU HAVE 2 DAYS

If you have only a few days for a visit, you'll need to concentrate on one area, and the Laurentians, outside Montréal, are a good choice. This resort area has recreational options (depending on the season) that include golf, hiking, and great skiing. Pick a resort town to stay in, whether it's ⊞ **St-Sauveur-des-Monts** ④, ⊞ **Ste-Adèle** ⑥, or ⊞ **Mont-Tremblant,** near the vast **Parc Mont-Tremblant** ⑪, and use that as a base to visit some of the surrounding towns. There's good eating and shopping here—and even a reconstructed historic village in Ste-Adèle.

If your starting point is Québec City, you could take two days to explore the towns of Charlevoix (☞ If You Have 10–12 Days, *below*) east of the city, with an overnight in the elegant resort town of ⊞ **La Malbaie** ㉖.

IF YOU HAVE 5 DAYS

You can combine a taste of the Eastern Townships with a two-day visit to the Laurentians. Get a feeling for the Laurentians by staying overnight in ⊞ **St-Sauveur-des-Monts** ④ or ⊞ **Ste-Adèle** ⑥ and exploring such surrounding towns as **St-Jérôme** ③ and **Morin Heights** ⑤. Then head back south of Montréal to the Townships, which extend to the east along the border with New England. Overnight in ⊞ **Granby** ⑫ or ⊞ **Bromont** ⑬; Granby has a zoo and Bromont is known for its factory outlets. The next day, you can shop in pretty **Knowlton** ⑯ and explore regional history in such towns as **Valcourt** ⑰, where a museum is dedicated to the inventor of the snowmobile. Spend a night or two in the appealing resort town of ⊞ **Magog** ⑱, along Lac Memphrémagog, or the quieter ⊞ **North Hatley** ⑳, on Lac Massawippi. You'll have good dining in either. Save a day for some outdoor activity, whether it's golfing, skiing, biking on former railroad lines, or hiking.

IF YOU HAVE 10–12 DAYS

A longer visit can show you a number of regions in Québec, but you must do some driving between them. You can spend a few days in either the Laurentians or the Eastern Townships before heading east to Québec City and historic Charlevoix, the heart of what was New France, along the St. Lawrence River. The drive from Montréal or Sherbrooke to Québec City is over 240 km (149 mi); Charlevoix begins 33 km (20 mi) to the east, at **Ste-Anne-de-Beaupré** ㉓, with its famous basilica. Colonial-era homes and farmhouses dot several villages; some are still homes, and others are theaters, museums, or restaurants. Spend time in ⊞ **Baie St-Paul** ㉔ and ⊞ **La Malbaie** ㉖, or just driving lovely roads such as Route 362. There's whale-watching in **Tadoussac** ㉗. To go on to the Gaspé Peninsula, you have to cross the St. Lawrence River. An hour-long ferry ride from St-Siméon, between La Malbaie and Tadoussac, takes you to Rivière-du-Loup. From there it's a day to get to ⊞ **Carleton** ㉘ on the Gaspé's southern shore. With mountains on one side and the ocean on the other, the peninsula offers one of the most scenic drives in North America; you can stop in ⊞ **Percé** ㉙ and spend a day visiting **Bonaventure Island** ㉚ with its fascinating bird colony. The drive around the entire peninsula is over 800 km (500 mi).

When to Tour Québec

The Laurentians are mainly a winter ski destination, but you can drive up from Montréal to enjoy the fall foliage, to hike, bike, or play golf, or to engage in spring skiing—and still get home before dark. The only slow periods are early November, when there is not much to do, and June, when there is plenty to do but the area is plagued by blackflies, admittedly less of a problem now than formerly, thanks to effective biological control programs.

The Eastern Townships are best in fall, when the colors are at their peak. The region borders Vermont and has the same dramatic foliage. You can also visit wineries at this time, although you should call ahead to see if visitors are welcome during the harvest, which can be busy. Charlevoix is lovely in fall, but winter is particularly magical. Although the roads aren't great in winter, the whole region, with its cozy villages and New France architecture, is charming. In summer you get a special silvery light, born of the mountains and the proximity of the sea: This is why the area attracts so many painters. Summer is really the only time to tour the Gaspé. Some attractions have already closed by Labor Day, and few hotels are open during winter. The weather can be harsh, too, and driving the coast road can be difficult.

THE LAURENTIANS

The Laurentians (les Laurentides) are divided into two major regions—the Lower Laurentians (les Basses Laurentides) and the Upper Laurentians (les Hautes Laurentides). But don't be fooled by the designations; they don't signify great driving distances.

Avid skiers might call Montréal a bedroom community for the Laurentians; just 56 km (35 mi) to the north, they are home to some of North America's best-known ski resorts. The Laurentian range is ancient, dating to the Precambrian era (more than 600 million years ago). These rocky hills are relatively low, worn down by glacial activity, but they include eminently skiable hills, with a few peaks above 2,500 ft. World-famous Mont-Tremblant, at 3,150 ft, is the tallest.

The P'tit Train du Nord—the former railroad line that is now a 200-km (124-mi) linear park used by cyclists, hikers, skiers, and snowmobilers—made it possible to easily transport settlers and cargo to the Upper Laurentians. It also opened them up to skiing by the turn of the century. Before long, trainloads of skiers replaced settlers and cargo as the railway's major trade. The Upper Laurentians became known worldwide as the number-one ski center in North America—a position they still hold today. Initially a winter weekend getaway for Montrealers who stayed at boardinghouses and fledgling resorts while skiing its hills, the Upper Laurentians soon began attracting an international clientele.

Ski lodges, originally private family retreats for wealthy city dwellers, were accessible only by train until the 1930s, when Route 117 was built. Once the road opened up, cottages became year-round family retreats. Today there is an uneasy alliance between the longtime cottagers and resort-driven entrepreneurs. Both recognize the other's historic role in developing the Upper Laurentians, but neither espouses the other's cause. At the moment, commercial development seems to be winning out. A number of large hotels have added indoor pools and spa facilities, and efficient highways have brought the country closer to the city—45 minutes to St-Sauveur, 1½–2 hours to Mont-Tremblant.

The Lower Laurentians start almost immediately outside Montréal and are rich in historic and architectural landmarks. Beginning in the mid-17th century, the governors of New France, as Québec was then called, gave large concessions of land to its administrators, priests, and top-ranking military, who became known as seigneurs. In the Lower Laurentians, towns like St-Eustache and Oka are home to the manors, mills, churches, and public buildings these seigneurs had built for themselves and their habitants—the inhabitants of these quasi-feudal villages.

The resort vacation area truly begins at St-Sauveur-des-Monts (Exit 60 on Autoroute 15) and extends as far north as Mont-Tremblant, where it turns into a wilderness of lakes and forests best visited with an outfitter. Laurentian guides planning fishing trips are concentrated around Parc Mont-Tremblant. To the first-time visitor, the hills and resorts around St-Sauveur, Ste-Adèle, Morin Heights, Val Morin, and Val David, up to Ste-Agathe, form a pleasant hodgepodge of villages, hotels, and inns that seem to blend one into another.

Oka

❶ *40 km (25 mi) west of Montréal.*

The town of Oka is known for a monastery that produces cheeses, a calvary, and its provincial park. To promote piety among the native people, the Sulpicians erected the **Oka Calvary** (⊠ Rte. 344, across from Oka Provincial Park), representing the Stations of the Cross, between 1740 and 1742. Three of the seven chapels are still maintained, and every September 14 since 1870, Québécois pilgrims have congregated here from across the province to participate in the half-hour ceremony that proceeds on foot to the calvary's summit. A sense of the divine is inspired as much by the magnificent view of Lac-des-Deux-Montagnes as by religious fervor.

The **Abbaye Cistercienne d'Oka** is one of the oldest in North America. In 1887 the Sulpicians gave about 865 acres of their property near the Oka Calvary to the Trappist monks, who had arrived in New France in 1880 from Bellefontaine Abbey in France. Within 10 years they had built their monastery and transformed this land into one of the most beautiful domains in Québec. Famous for creating Oka cheese, the Trappists established the Oka School of Agriculture, which operated until 1960. Today, the monastery is a noted prayer retreat. The gardens and chapel are open to visitors. ⊠ *1600 chemin d'Oka,* ☎ *514/479–8361.* 🎟 *Free.* ☉ *Chapel daily 8–12:15 and 1–8; gardens and boutique weekdays 9:30–11:30 and 1–4:30, Sat. 9–4.*

Kanesatake, a Mohawk reserve near Oka, made headlines in 1990 when a 78-day armed standoff between Mohawk Warriors (the reserve's self-proclaimed paramilitary force) and Canadian and provincial authorities took place. The Mohawks of Kanesatake said they opposed the expansion of the Oka golf course, claiming the land was stolen from them 273 years before. When the standoff ended peacefully, the golf course was not expanded.

Lodging

$$$ 🏨 **Hotel du Lac Carling.** This modern hotel near Lachute (about 40 km, or 25 mi, from Oka) caters to an upmarket clientele. Besides a large sports center and cross-country ski trails, there's an 18-hole golf course—one of Canada's best. The hotel is owned by a real estate magnate with 23 castles and manor houses in his native Germany, and the rooms have oil paintings and priceless antiques shipped over from his various properties. ⊠ *Rte. 327, Pinehill, J0V 1A0,* ☎ *514/533–9211 or 800/661–9211,* ⨳ *514/533–9197. 100 rooms. Restaurant, bar, pool, sauna, 18-hole golf course, exercise room, racquetball, squash, crosscountry skiing. EP, MAP. AE, DC, MC, V.*

St-Eustache

❷ *25 km (16 mi) northeast of Oka.*

St-Eustache is a must for history buffs. One of the most important and tragic battles in Canadian history took place here during the 1837 Re-

The Laurentians (les Laurentides)

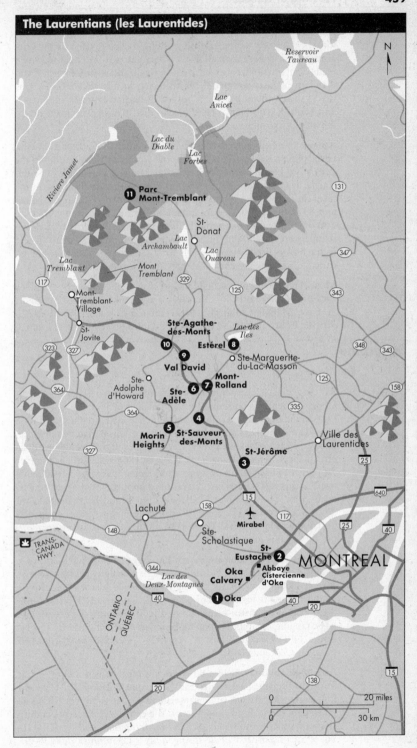

N

Reservoir Taureau

Lac Anicet

131

Lac du Diable

Lac Forbes

11 **Parc Mont-Tremblant**

St-Donat

Lac Archambault

347

Lac Ouareau

Rivière Janet

Lac Tremblant

Mont Tremblant

117

329

125

343

Mont-Tremblant-Village

St-Jovite

Ste-Agathe-des-Monts

Lac des Îles

348

343

323

327

10

9

Estérel **8**

Ste-Marguerite-du-Lac-Masson

158

364

Ste-Adolphe d'Howard

Val David

6 **7** **Mont-Rolland**

125

364

Ste-Adèle

335

5

4

St-Sauveur-des-Monts

327

Morin Heights

St-Jérôme

Ville des Laurentides

25

3

15

640

Lachute

158

117

25

40

148

✈ Mirabel

Ste-Scholastique

TRANS-CANADA HWY.

344

Lac des Deux-Montagnes

St-Eustache **2**

MONTREAL

Oka Calvary

■ Abbaye Cistercienne d'Oka

1 **Oka**

40

40

20

ONTARIO

QUÉBEC

20

138

15

0   20 miles

0   30 km

bellion. Since the British conquest of 1759, French Canadians had been confined to preexisting territories while the new townships were allotted exclusively to the English. Adding to this insult was the government's decision to tax all imported products from England, which made them prohibitively expensive. The result? In 1834 the French Canadian Patriot party defeated the British party locally. Lower Canada, as it was then known, became a hotbed of tension between the French and English, with French resistance to the British government reaching an all-time high.

Rumors of rebellion were rife, and in December 1837, some 2,000 English soldiers led by General Colborne were sent in to put down the "army" of North Shore patriots by surrounding the village of St-Eustache. Jean-Olivier Chénier and his 200 patriots took refuge in the local church, which Colborne's cannons bombed and set afire. Chénier and 80 of his comrades were killed during the battle, and more than 100 of the town's houses and buildings erected during the seignorial regime were looted and burned down by Colborne's soldiers. Traces of the bullets fired by the English army cannons are visible on the facade of St-Eustache's church at 123 rue St-Louis.

Most of the town's period buildings are open to the public. For a guided tour or for a free brochure that serves as a good walking-tour guide, visit the **Manoir Globinsky** (✉ 235 rue St-Eustache, ☎ 514/977–5055/6. Tours are offered from June 23 until September 1 at 1 and 3.

St-Jérôme

❸ *25 km (16 mi) north of St-Eustache.*

Rivaling St-Eustache in Québec's historic folklore is St-Jérôme, in the Upper Laurentians on Route 117. Founded in 1834, it is today a thriving economic center and cultural hub. It first gained prominence in 1868 when Curé Antoine Labelle became pastor of this parish on the shores of Rivière du Nord. Curé Labelle devoted himself to opening up northern Québec to French Canadians. Between 1868 and 1890, he founded 20 parish towns—an impressive achievement given the harsh conditions of this vast wilderness. But his most important legacy was the famous P'tit Train du Nord railroad line, which he persuaded the government to build in order to open St-Jérôme to travel and trade. Today the railroad is a 200-km (124-mi) **linear park** for recreational use that begins in St-Jérôme.

Follow St-Jérôme's **promenade,** a 4-km-long (2½-mi-long) boardwalk, alongside the Rivière du Nord from rue de Martigny bridge to rue St-Joseph bridge for a walk through the town's history. Descriptive plaques en route highlight episodes of the Battle of 1837. The **Centre d'Exposition du Vieux-Palais,** housed in St-Jérôme's old courthouse, has changing exhibits of contemporary art, featuring mostly Québec artists. ✉ *185 rue du Palais,* ☎ *514/432–7171.* ▣ *Free.* ☉ *Tues.–Fri. noon–5, weekends 1–5.*

Parc Régional de la Rivière-du-Nord was created as a nature retreat. Trails through the park lead to the spectacular **Wilson Falls.** The **Pavillon Marie-Victorin** has summer weekend displays and workshops devoted to nature, culture, and history. You can hike, bike, cross-country ski, snowshoe, or snow slide. ✉ *1051 blvd. International,* ☎ *514/431–1676.* ▣ *$3 per car.* ☉ *Fall–spring, daily 9–5; summer, daily 9–7.*

St-Sauveur-des-Monts

❹ *25 km (16 mi) north of St-Jérôme.*

A focal point for area resorts, St-Sauveur-des-Monts has gone from a 1970s sleepy Laurentian village of 4,000 residents that didn't even have a traffic light to a thriving year-round town attracting some 30,000 cottagers and visitors on weekends. Its main street, rue Principale, once dotted with quaint French restaurants, now has dozens of eateries at all price levels; they serve everything from lamb brochettes to spicy Thai cuisine (a current craze among Québeckers). The narrow strip is so choked in summertime with cars and tourists that it has earned the sobriquet "Crescent Street of the North," borrowing its name from the action-filled street in Montréal. Despite all this development, St-Sauveur has maintained some of its charming, rural character.

For those who like their vacations—winter or summer—lively and activity-filled, St-Sauveur is the place where the action rolls nonstop. In winter, skiing is the main thing. (Mont-St-Sauveur, Mont-Avila, Mont-Gabriel, and Mont-Olympia all offer special season passes and programs, and some ski-center passes can be used at more than one center in the region.) From Mont-St-Sauveur to Mont-Tremblant, the area's ski centers (most situated in or near St-Sauveur, Ste-Adèle, Ste-Agathe, and St-Jovite) have night skiing. All have ski instructors—many are members of the Canadian Ski Patrol Association.

☙ Just outside St-Sauveur, the Mont-St-Sauveur **Water Park** and tourist center will keep children occupied with slides, a giant wave pool, a shallow wading pool, snack bars, and more. The rafting river attracts the older, braver crowd; the nine-minute ride follows the natural contours of steep hills and requires about 12,000 gallons of water to be pumped per minute. The latest attraction is tandem slides where plumes of water flow through figure-eight tubes. ⊠ *350 rue St-Denis,* ☎ *514/871–0101 or 800/363–2426.* ☞ *Full day $22, half-day $17, evening (after 5) $9; cost includes access to all activities.* ◷ *June 3–June 21, daily 10–4; June 22–Aug. 25, daily 10–7; Aug. 26–Sept. 2, daily 11–6.*

Skiing
Station Touristique Mont-St-Saveur (☎ 800/363–2426), with a total of 26 downhill runs, is the collective name for the peaks around the village of St-Saveur-des-Monts. The runs are linked to Mont-Avila. **Station de Ski Mont-Christie** (☎ 514/226–2412) has 12 runs. **Station de Ski Mont-Habitant** (☎ 514/393–1821) has 9 runs.

Shopping
Rue Principale has shops, fashion boutiques, and outdoor café terraces decorated with bright awnings and flowers. Housed in a former bank, **Solo Mode** (⊠ 239B rue Principale, ☎ 514/227–1234) carries such international labels as Byblos. **Les Factoreries St-Sauveur** (⊠ 100 rue Guindon, Exit 60 from Autoroute 15, ☎ 514/227–1074) is a factory outlet mall with 12 boutiques. Canadian, American, and European manufacturers sell a variety of goods at reduced prices, from designer clothing to household items.

Morin Heights

❺ *10 km (6 mi) west of St-Sauveur-des-Monts.*

The town's architecture and population reflect its English settlers' origins, and most residents are English-speaking. Morin Heights has escaped the overdevelopment of St-Sauveur but still provides a good range of restaurants, bookstores, boutiques, and crafts shops to explore.

During the summer months, windsurfing, swimming, and canoeing on the area's two lakes are popular pastimes.

In the summer, vacationers also head for the region's golf courses (including the 18-hole links at Mont-Gabriel), campgrounds at Val David, Lacs Claude and Lafontaine, and beaches; in the fall and winter, they come for the foliage as well as alpine and Nordic skiing.

There's a new spin on an old sport at **Ski Morin Heights** (✉ Autoroute 15 N, Exit 60, ☎ 514/227–2020 or 800/661–3535), where snowboarding is the latest craze. Although it doesn't have overnight accommodations, Ski Morin Heights has a 44,000-square-ft chalet with hospitality services and sports-related facilities, eateries, après-ski activities, a pub, and a day-care center. There are special ski-lesson programs for children ages 2 and up.

Dining and Lodging

$$$ ✕⊞ **Auberge le Clos Joli.** This farmhouse turned country inn, only two minutes from the ski slopes, is considered one of the top five hostelries in the Laurentians. Intimate and cozy, the inn is decorated with original artwork by Québécois painters; the dining room has a fireplace. The menu highlights French cuisine but with some local touches, such as roast venison cooked with bilberries and ravioli stuffed with wild mushrooms. A specialty is *ris de veau*—veal sweetbreads—flavored with lemon and thyme. ✉ *19 chemin du Clos Joli, J0R 1H0,* ☎ *514/226–5401. 9 rooms. Restaurant, cross-country skiing, downhill skiing. AE, MC, V.*

Ste-Adèle

❻ *12 km (7 mi) north of Morin Heights.*

The busy town of Ste-Adèle is full of gift and Québec-crafts shops, boutiques, and restaurants. It also has an active nightlife, including a few dance clubs.

The reconstructed **Village de Seraphin**'s 20 small homes, grand country house, general store, and church recall the settlers who came to Ste-Adèle in the 1840s. This award-winning historic town also has a train tour through the woods. ✉ *Rte. 117,* ☎ *514/229–4777.* 🎟 *$9.* ☺ *Late May–late June and early Sept.–mid-Oct., weekends 10–6; late June–early Sept., daily 10–6.*

Dining and Lodging

$$$$ ✕ **La Clef des Champs.** A family-owned hillside restaurant, with its gourmet French cuisine and cozy, romantic atmosphere, is tucked away among trees and faces a mountain. Elegant dishes include *noisette d'agneau en feuilleté* (lamb in pastry) and poached salmon in red wine sauce. Top off your meal with the *gâteau aux deux chocolats* (two-chocolate cake). ✉ *875 chemin Ste-Marguerite,* ☎ *514/229–2857. AE, DC, MC, V. Closed Mon. Oct.–May.*

$$$$ ✕⊞ **L'Eau à la Bouche.** Superb service, stunning rooms awash with color,
★ and a terrace with a flower garden are highlights of this elegant inn. The auberge faces Le Chantecler's ski slopes, so skiing is literally at the door. Tennis, sailing, horseback riding, and a golf course are nearby. The highly recommended restaurant superbly marries nouvelle cuisine and traditional Québec dishes. The care and inventiveness of chef-proprietor Anne Desjardins is extraordinary. Her menus change with the seasons, but some representative dishes are marinated Atlantic salmon and smoked scallops on a bed of julienned cucumber with a blend of mustards, and roast veal in a cognac and Roquefort sauce. ✉ *3003*

blvd. Ste-Adèle, J0R 1L0, ☎ *514/229–2991,* FAX *514/229–7573. 25 rooms. Restaurant, pool. EP, MAP. AE, DC, MC, V.*

$$$$ 🏨 **Le Chantecler.** This Montrealer favorite on Lac Ste-Adèle is nestled at the base of a mountain with 22 downhill ski runs. Skiing is the obvious draw—trails begin almost at the hotel entrance. The condominium units, hotel rooms, and chalets all have a rustic appeal, furnished with Canadian pine. ✉ *1474 chemin Chantecler, C.P. 1048, J0R 1L0,* ☎ *514/229–3555, 800/363–2420 in Québec,* FAX *514/229–5593. 300 rooms, 20 suites. Restaurant, indoor pool, spa, 18-hole golf course, tennis court, beach, boating. EP, MAP. AE, D, DC, MC, V.*

$$ 🏨 **Auberge aux Croissants.** At the foot of the Laurentian Mountains, the inn is only a five-minute drive from Mont-St-Sauveur. Although most rooms have no TV or telephone, such conveniences are found in one of the two lounges, and an impressive buffet-breakfast is included with the price of the room. One room has a whirlpool bath. ✉ *750 chemin Ste-Marguerite, J0R 1L0,* ☎ *514/229–3838. 13 rooms, 1 suite. Pool. MC, V.*

Outdoor Activities and Sports

GOLF

Club de Golf Chantecler (✉ Off Autoroute 15, Exit 67, 2520 chemin du Golf, ☎ 514/229–3742) has 18 holes.

SKIING

Ski Chantecler (☎ 514/229–3555) has 22 runs (☞ Dining and Lodging, *above*). **Station de Ski Côtes** (☎ 514/229–2921) has 5 runs.

Mont-Rolland

❼ *3 km (2 mi) east of Ste-Adèle.*

Mont-Rolland is the jumping-off point for the Mont-Gabriel ski area, about 16 km (10 mi) to the northeast.

Dining and Lodging

$$$ ✕🏨 **Auberge Mont-Gabriel.** At this deluxe resort spread out on a 1,200-acre estate, you can relax in a cozy, modern room with a view of the valley or be close to nature in a log cabin with a fireplace. The dining is superb here. Tennis, golf, and ski-week and -weekend packages are available. ✉ *Autoroute 15 (Exit 64), J0R 1G0,* ☎ *514/229–3547 or 800/668-5253,* FAX *514/229–7034. 127 rooms, 10 suites. Restaurant, indoor and outdoor pools, 18-hole golf course, 6 tennis courts. EP, MAP. AE, DC, MC, V.*

Nightlife

If live music is what you want, head to **Bourbon Street** (✉ 2045 Rte. 117, ☎ 514/229–2905).

Outdoor Activities and Sports

DELTAPLANING

If white-water rafting isn't adventure enough, there is always deltaplaning, a form of hang gliding. The **Vélidelta Free-Flying School** (✉ C.P. 631, Mont-Rolland G0R 1J0 ☎ 514/565–4246) offers lessons on free-flying and the more advanced tricks of the trade you'll need to earn the required deltaplane pilot's license, including flight maneuvers, speed, and turns. Equipment is provided. You can choose a one-day initiation flying lesson, or a four-day course.

SKIING

Ski Mont-Gabriel (☎ 514/227–1100) has 12 superb downhill trails primarily for intermediate and advanced skiers. The most popular runs are the Tamarack and the O'Connell trails for advanced skiers and Obergurgl for intermediates.

Estérel

8 *12 km (7 mi) north of Mont-Rolland.*

The permanent population of the town of Estérel is a mere 95 souls, but visitors to **Hôtel l'Estérel,** a resort off Route 370, at Exit 69, near Ste-Marguerite Station, swell that number into the thousands. Founded in 1959 on the shores of Lac Dupuis, this 5,000-acre domain was bought by Fridolin Simard from Baron Louis Empain. Named Estérel by the baron because it evoked memories of his native village in Provence, Hotel l'Estérel soon became a household word for holiday vacationers in search of a first-class resort area.

Dining and Lodging

$$$$ ✕ **Bistro à Champlain.** An astonishing selection of wines—26,000 bottles at last count—have made the bistro famous. Diners can tour the cellars, where some 2,000 brands are represented, with prices from $28 to $25,000. The restaurant is in a former general store built in 1864; next to the 150-seat dining room is a comfy lounge for cigar smokers. The paintings of Jean-Paul Riopelle adorn the walls. The *menu dégustation* gives you a different wine with several courses for $55; typical dishes are marinated Atlantic smoked salmon, scallops with buttered asparagus, and roast duckling with rosemary. ⊠ *75 chemin Masson, Ste-Marguerite du Lac Masson,* ☎ *514/228–4988 or 514/225–4949. AE, DC, MC, V.*

$$$$ 🏨 **Hôtel l'Estérel.** If this all-inclusive resort were in the Caribbean, it would probably be run by Club Med, given the nonstop activities. Dogsledding and an ice-skating disco are two of the more unusual options. Comfortable rooms offer a view of either the lake or the beautiful flower gardens. ⊠ *39 blvd. Fridolin Simard, J0T 1E0,* ☎ *514/228–2571 or 800/363–3623,* 𝖥𝖠𝖷 *514/228–4977. 135 rooms. Restaurant, indoor pool, 18-hole golf course, tennis courts, exercise room, beach, dock, cross-country skiing, downhill skiing, snowmobiling. EP, MAP. AE, DC, MC, V.*

Val David

9 *18 km (11 mi) west of Estérel.*

Val David is a rendezvous for mountain climbers, hikers, and summer or winter campers, besides a center for arts and crafts. Children know Val David for its **Santa Claus Village.** This is Santa Claus's summer residence, where children can sit on Santa's knee and speak to him in French or English. On the grounds is a petting zoo, with goats, sheep, horses, and colorful birds. Bumper boats and games are run here as well. ⊠ *987 rue Morin,* ☎ *819/322–2146.* ⊡ *$8.* ☼ *Late May–early June, weekends 10–6; early June–late Aug., daily 10–6.*

Dining and Lodging

$$$$ ✕🏨 **Hôtel La Sapinière.** Comfortable, freshly redecorated accommodations are offered in this homey, dark-brown frame hotel. The rooms, with country-style furnishings and pastel floral accents, come with such luxurious extras as thick terry-cloth bathrobes and hair dryers. Relax in front of a blazing fire in one of several lounges. The property is best known for its fine dining room and wine cellar. ⊠ *1244 chemin de la Sapinière, J0T 2N0,* ☎ *819/322–2020 or 800/567–6635,* 𝖥𝖠𝖷 *819/322–6510. 70 rooms. Dining room. MAP. AE, DC, MC, V.*

Skiing
Mont-Alta (☎ 819/322–3206) has 22 runs. **Station de Ski Vallée-Blue** (☎ 819/322–3427) has 16 runs.

Shopping
Val David is a haven for artists, many of whose studios are open to the public. The **Atelier Bernard Chaudron, Inc.** (✉ 2449 chemin de l'Ile, ☎ 819/322–3944), sells hand-shaped and hammered lead-free pewter objets d'art.

Ste-Agathe-des-Monts

⑩ *5 km (3 mi) north of Val David, 96 km (60 mi) northwest of Mont-réal.*

Overlooking Lac des Sables is Ste-Agathe-des-Monts, the largest commercial center for ski communities farther north. You'll find many shops and a variety of restaurants and bars.

Dining and Lodging

$$-$$$ ✕ **Chatel Vienna.** Run by Eberhards Rado and his wife, who is also the chef, this Austrian restaurant serves traditional, hearty Viennese and other Continental dishes in a lakeside setting. You may want to try the home-smoked trout, served with an herb-and-spice butter and garden-fresh vegetables. Other options are a variety of schnitzels, a sauerkraut plate, or venison. Try the hot spiced wine, Czech pilsner beer, or dry Austrian and other international white wines. A Sunday buffet brunch has approximately 35 dishes. ✉ *6 rue Ste-Lucie,* ☎ *819/326–1485. Reservations essential. MC, V.*

$$$ ☷ **Auberge du Lac des Sables.** A favorite with couples, this inn offers a quiet, relaxed atmosphere in a country setting with a magnificent view of Lac des Sables. All rooms have contemporary decor and a balcony. ✉ *230 St-Venant, J8C 2Z7,* ☎ *819/326–3994,* FAX *819/326–9159. 19 rooms. Dining room. CP, MC, V.*

$ ⚠ **Au Parc des Campeurs.** This lively resort area attracts campers with this spacious campground. ✉ *Tour du Lac and Rte. 329, J8C 1M9,* ☎ *819/324–0482. 556 sites. Miniature golf, tennis court, volleyball, coin laundry.*

Boating
The *Alouette* touring launch (✉ Municipal dock, rue Principal, ☎ 819/326–3656) has guided tours of Lac des Sables. Sailing is the favorite summer sport, especially during the *"24 Heures de la Voile,"* a weekend sailing competition (☎ 819/326–0457) that takes place each year in June.

Mont-Tremblant

25 km (16 mi) north of Ste-Agathe-des-Monts.

Mont-Tremblant, more than 3,000 ft high, is the highest peak in the Laurentians and a major center for skiing. The resort village at the foot of the mountain has accommodations and many restaurants, bars, and shops. An exciting ongoing development here has been the redevelopment of the Tremblant resort (☞ *below*).

The mountain and the hundreds of square miles of wilderness beyond ⑪ it constitute **Parc Mont-Tremblant** (☎ 819/688–2281). Created in 1894, the park was once the home of the Algonquin people, who called this area Manitonga Soutana, meaning "mountain of the spirits." Today it is a vast wildlife sanctuary of more than 400 lakes and rivers protecting about 230 species of birds and animals, including moose, deer, bear, and beaver. In winter its trails are used by cross-country skiers, snowshoers, and snowmobile enthusiasts. Moose hunting is allowed in season, and camping and canoeing are the main summer activities.

Dining and Lodging

$$$–$$$$ ✕▥ **Club Tremblant.** Built as a private retreat in the 1930s by a wealthy American, this hotel is across the lake from Station Mont-Tremblant. The original large, log-cabin lodge is furnished in colonial style, with wooden staircases and huge stone fireplaces. The rustic but comfortable main lodge has excellent facilities and an outstanding dining room serving Continental cuisine. Both the main lodge and the 122-unit deluxe condominium complex (with fireplaces, private balconies, kitchenettes, and split-level design), built just up the hill from the lodge, offer magnificent views of Mont-Tremblant and its ski hills. There is a golf course nearby. ✉ *Av. Cuttle, J0T 1Z0,* ☎ *819/425–2731,* FAX *819/425–9903. 121 rooms. Restaurant, indoor pool, tennis court, exercise room, boating, fishing. EP, MAP. AE, MC, V.*

$$–$$$$ ✕▥ **Auberge du Coq de Montagne.** Owners Nino and Kay Faragalli have earned a favorable reputation for their auberge on Lac Moore. The cozy, family-run inn is touted for its friendly service, great hospitality, and modern accommodations. Kudos have also been garnered for the great Italian cuisine served up nightly, which also draws a local crowd; reservations are essential. Year-round facilities and activities, on-site or nearby, include canoeing, kayaking, sailboarding, fishing, badminton, tennis, horseback riding, skating, and skiing. ✉ *2151 chemin Principale, C.P. 208, J0T 1Z0,* ☎ *819/425–3380 or 800/895–3380,* FAX *819/425–7846. 16 rooms. Restaurant, sauna, exercise room, beach. MAP in winter; EP, MAP in summer. AE, MC, V.*

$$–$$$$ ▥ **Château Mont-Tremblant.** A new property built by Canadian Pacific
★ Hotels is the attractive centerpiece of Tremblant's (☞ *below*) pedestrian village. Similar in style to the company's historic railway "castles" scattered throughout Canada—Banff Springs Hotel and Château Frontenac are two examples—the hotel has been decorated with wood paneling, copper, stained glass, stone fireplaces, and wrought-iron lamps with parchment shades. The ambience is elegant but sporty. Skiers can zoom off the mountain, right into the ground-level deli or opt for a more formal meal in the dining room. On the menu are Brie wrapped in filo pastry, Laurentian rainbow trout, and pork chops grilled with local maple syrup. ✉ *3045 chemin Principal, Box 100, J0T 1Z0,* ☎ *819/681–7000. 360 rooms. Indoor pool, sauna, exercise room. AE, DC, MC, V.*

$$–$$$$ ▥ **Tremblant.** This world-class resort, spread around the 14-km-long (9-mi-long) Lac Tremblant, has undergone a radical transformation. Intrawest Corporation has injected a much-needed $350 million (with more investment planned) into the mountain since the early '90s. It has quickly become the most fashionable vacation venue in Québec among sporty types and lovers of the great outdoors. The resort's hub is a pedestrian-only village that looks a bit like a displaced Québec City. The buildings—constructed in the style of New France with dormer windows and steep roofs—hold pubs, restaurants, boutiques, sports shops, a cinema, and accommodations ranging from rooms in hotels to self-catering condominiums. ✉ *3005 chemin Principal, J0T 1Z0,* ☎ *819/425–8711, 800/461–8711, or 800/567–6760 (hotel reservations). 1,050 rooms. 18-hole golf course, tennis courts, hiking, horseback riding, beach, windsurfing, boating, mountain bikes. AE, MC, V.*

Skiing

With the longest vertical drop (2,131 ft) in eastern Canada, **Mont-Tremblant** (☎ 819/425–8711 or 819/681–2000) offers 74 downhill trails,

10 lifts, and 90 km (56 mi) of cross-country trails. Downhill beginners favor the 6-km (4-mi) Nansen trail; intermediate skiers head for the Beauchemin run. Experts choose the challenging Flying Mile on the south side and Duncan and Expo runs on the mountain's north side. The speedy Duncan Express is a quadruple chairlift.

THE EASTERN TOWNSHIPS

The Eastern Townships (also known as les Cantons de l'Est, and formerly as l'Estrie) refers to the area in the southeast corner of the province of Québec, bordering Vermont, New Hampshire, and Maine. Its northern Appalachian hills, rolling down to placid lakeshores, were first home to the Abenaki natives, long before "summer people" built their cottages and horse paddocks here. The Abenaki are gone, but the names they gave to the region's recreational lakes remain—Memphrémagog, Massawippi, Mégantic.

The Eastern Townships (or the Townships, as locals call them) were populated by United Empire Loyalists fleeing the Revolutionary War and, later, the newly created United States of America, to continue living under the English king in British North America. It's not surprising that the Townships, with their covered bridges, village greens, white church steeples, and country inns, are reminiscent of New England. The Loyalists were followed, around 1820, by the first wave of Irish immigrants—ironically, Catholics fleeing their country's union with Protestant England. Some 20 years later the potato famine sent more Irish pioneers to the Townships.

The area became more Gallic after 1850, as French Canadians moved in to work on the railroad and in the lumber industry. Around the turn of the century, English families from Montréal and Americans from the border states discovered the region and began summering at cottages along the lakes. During the Prohibition era, the area attracted even more cottagers from the United States. Lac Massawippi became a favorite summer resort of wealthy families whose homes have since been converted into gracious inns and upscale bed-and-breakfasts.

Today the summer communities fill up with equal parts French and English visitors, though the year-round residents are primarily French. Nevertheless, the locals are proud of both their Loyalist heritage and their Québec roots. They boast of "Loyalist tours" and Victorian gingerbread homes and in the next breath direct visitors to the snowmobile museum in Valcourt, where, in 1937, native son Joseph-Armand Bombardier built the first *moto-neige* (snowmobile) in his garage. (Bombardier's other inventions were the basis of one of Canada's biggest industries, supplying New York City and Mexico City with subway cars and other rolling stock.)

Over the past two decades, the Townships have developed from a series of quiet farm communities and wood-frame summer homes to a thriving all-season resort area. In winter, skiers flock to eight downhill centers and some 900 km (558 mi) of cross-country trails. Three inns—Manoir Hovey, Auberge Hatley, and the Ripplecove Inn—offer the Skiwippi, a weeklong package of cross-country treks from one inn to another. The network covers some 32 km (20 mi). Still less crowded and commercialized than the Laurentians, the area has ski hills on four mountains that dwarf anything the Laurentians have to offer, with the exception of Mont-Tremblant. And, compared to those in Vermont, ski-pass rates are still a bargain. Owl's Head, Mont-Orford, Mont-Sutton, and Bromont have interchangeable lift tickets. The Townships' southerly location also makes this the balmiest corner of Québec, notable for its spring skiing.

By early spring, the sugar shacks are busy with the new maple syrup. In summer, boating, swimming, sailing, golfing, rollerblading, hiking, and bicycling take over. And every fall the inns are booked solid with leaf peepers eager to take in the brilliant foliage.

Granby

⑫ *80 km (50 mi) east of Montréal.*

Granby is the gateway to the Eastern Townships and home to a notable zoo. It also hosts a number of annual festivals—the **Festival of Mascots and Cartoon Characters** (July), a great favorite with youngsters and families; and the **Granby International,** an antique car competition held at the Granby Autodrome (also in July). The **Festival International de la Chanson,** a songfest of budding composers and performers that has launched several of Québec's current megastars, is a nine-day event in mid-September.

★ ⓒ This town is best known for its zoo, the **Jardin Zoologique de Granby.** It houses some 800 animals from 225 species. There are two rare snow leopards here on loan from Chicago's Lincoln Park Zoo and New York's Bronx Zoo. The complex includes amusement park rides and souvenir shops as well as a playground and picnic area. ⊠ *347 rue Bourget,* ☎ *514/372–9113.* ☜ *$16.* ☉ *Late May–early Sept., daily 9:30–5; Sept., weekends 9–5.*

Biking

Cyclists will find outdoor bliss on the paved l'Estriade path, which links Granby to Waterloo, and the Montérégiade between Granby and Farnham, both 21 km (13 mi) long.

Bromont

⑬ *8 km (5 mi) south of Granby.*

The town of Bromont is as lively at night as during the day. It has the only night skiing in the Eastern Townships and a slope-side disco, Le Bromontais, where the après-ski action continues into the night. Bromont and Orford (☞ *below*) are *stations touristiques* (tourist centers), meaning they offer a wide range of activities in all seasons—boating, camping, golf, horseback riding, swimming, tennis, water parks, trail biking, canoeing, fishing, hiking, cross-country and downhill skiing, and snowshoeing. A former Olympic equestrian site, Bromont is horse country, and every year in late June it holds a **riding festival** (☎ 514/534–3255). **Bromont Aquatic Park** (⊠ Autoroute 10, Exit 78, ☎ 514/534–2200) is a water-slide park.

Lodging

$$$–$$$$ 🏨 **Le Château Bromont Hotel Spa.** Massages, electropuncture, algae wraps, facials, and aromatherapy are just a few of the pampering services at this European-style resort spa. Rooms are large and comfortable, with contemporary furniture, but those facing the Atrium are a little somber. L'Equestre Bar, named for Bromont's equestrian interests, has a cocktail hour and live entertainment. ⊠ *90 rue Stanstead, J0E 1L0,* ☎ *514/534–3433 or 800/304–3433,* FAX *514/534–0514. 147 rooms. Restaurant, bar, indoor pool, hot tubs, sauna, spa, badminton, racquetball, squash. EP, MAP. AE, D, DC, MC, V.*

OFF THE BEATEN PATH **SAFARI TOUR LOOWAK –** The brainchild of butterfly collector Serge Poirier, this oddball attraction 10 km (6 mi) from Bromont is a kind of In-

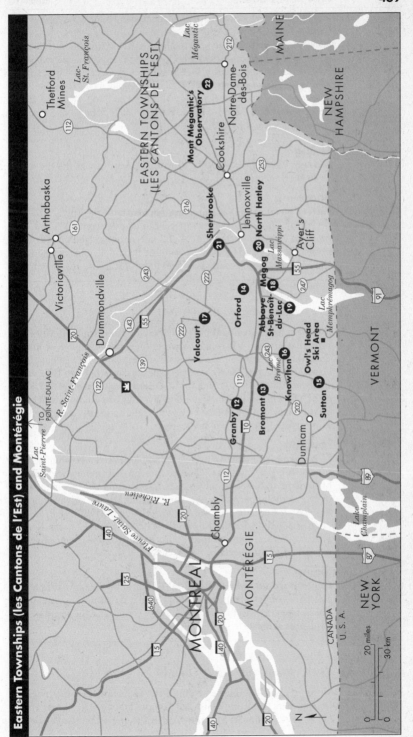

Eastern Townships (les Cantons de l'Est) and Montérégie

diana Jones theme park where participants head off into the bush on treasure hunts and to look for downed planes. To make the game as authentic as possible, Poirier acquired a couple of wrecked aircraft that he has artfully hidden around his land, prompting more than one phone call from alarmed passersby. Needless to say, the place is a great hit with small fry, but parents quickly get caught up in the fantasy, too. Reservations are recommended. ⊠ *475 Horizon Blvd., Waterloo, Exit 88 from Autoroute 10,* ☎ *514/539-0501.* ⊠ *Trips begin at $10 per person (minimum 4 people).*

Skiing

Bromont (☎ 514/534–2200), which has 23 trails, was the site of the 1986 World Cup Slalom.

Shopping

Factory outlet shopping is gaining popularity in the Townships—especially in Bromont, where shoppers can save between 30% and 70% on items carrying such national and international labels as Liz Claiborne, Vuarnet, and Oneida. Versants de Bromont and Promenades de Ma Maison are two centers off Exit 78 of Autoroute 10.

Orford

❿ *25 km (16 mi) northeast of Bromont.*

Orford is near a regional park, the Parc de Récréation du Mont-Orford, that's in use year-round, whether for skiing, camping, or hiking. Orford also has an annual arts festival, Festival Orford, highlighting classical music, pops, and chamber orchestra concerts. Since 1951, thousands of students have come to the **Orford Arts Centre** (☎ 819/843–3981, 800/567–6155 in Canada May–Aug.) to study and perform classical music in the summer. Canada's internationally celebrated Orford String Quartet originated here.

Lodging

$$$ ⊞ **Auberge Estrimont.** An exclusive complex in cedar combining hotel rooms, condos, and larger chalets, Auberge Estrimont is close to ski hills, riding stables, and golf courses. Every room, whether in the hotel or in an adjoining condo unit, has a fireplace and a private balcony. ⊠ *44 av. de l'Auberge, C.P. 98, Orford-Magog J1X 3W7,* ☎ *819/843–1616 or 800/567–7320,* ⅢX *819/843–4909. 76 rooms, 7 suites. Restaurant, bar, indoor and outdoor pools, hot tub, sauna, tennis, exercise room, racquetball, squash. AE, DC, MC, V.*

Skiing

Mont-Orford Ski Area (☎ 819/843–6548), at the center of the provincial park, offers plenty of challenges for alpine and cross-country skiers, from novices to veterans. It has 41 trails and the steepest drop of all area ski resorts.

Sutton

⓯ *65 km (40 mi) southwest of Orford.*

Sutton is a well-established community with crafts shops, cozy eateries, and bars (La Paimpolaise is a favorite among skiers). **Arts Sutton** (⊠ 7 rue Academy, ☎ 514/538–2563) is a long-established mecca for the visual arts.

Lodging

$$–$$$ ⊞ **Auberge la Paimpolaise.** This auberge is on Mont-Sutton, 50 ft from the ski trails. Nothing fancy is offered, but the location is hard to beat. Rooms are simple, comfortable, and clean, with a woodsy appeal. All-inclusive weekend ski packages are available. A complimentary breakfast is served. ⊠ *615 rue Maple, J0E 2K0,* ☎ *514/538–3213 or 800/263–3213,* ℻ *514/538–3970. 28 rooms. EP, MAP. AE, MC, V.*

Outdoor Activities and Sports

GOLF

Reservations must be made in advance at **Les Rochers Bleus** (⊠ 550 Rte. 139, ☎ 514/538–2324), an 18-hole course.

SKIING

Mont-Sutton (⊠ Rte. 139 South, Exit 106 from Autoroute 10, ☎ 514/538–2339), where you pay to ski by the hour, has 53 downhill trails. This ski area attracts a diehard crowd of mostly Anglophone skiers from Québec. It's also one of the area's largest resorts, with trails that plunge and wander through pine, maple, and birch trees slope-side.

Knowlton

16 *15 km (9 mi) northeast of Sutton.*

Along the shore of Lac Brome is the picturesque village of Knowlton, a great place to shop for antiques, clothes, and gifts. The village, which has a pond flanked by a brick church where ducks line up to be fed, is a treasure trove of Victoriana. Renovated clapboard buildings painted every shade of the rainbow have been turned into trendy stores, art galleries, and interesting little eateries. The distinctive Lake Brome ducks—white and plump—are found on local menus and celebrated, with exhibits, activities, and food, during the **Brome Lake Duck Festival** in mid-October.

The Arts

Théâtre Lac Brome (⊠ 267 rue Knowlton, ☎ 514/242–2270 or 514/242–1395) stages plays, musicals, and productions of classic Broadway and West End hits. The company specializes in English productions but also has tried some bilingual productions and some new Canadian works. The 175-seat, air-conditioned theater is behind Knowlton's popular pub of the same name.

Skiing

Many Montrealers come here for the downhill skiing at **Glen Mountain** (⊠ Off Rte. 243, ☎ 514/243–6142).

Valcourt

17 *32 km (20 mi) north of Knowlton.*

Valcourt is the birthplace of the inventor of the snowmobile, so it follows that this is a world center for the sport, with more than 1,500 km (900-plus mi) of paths cutting through the woods and meadows. The **Musée Joseph-Armand Bombardier** displays the innovator's many inventions, including the snowmobile. ⊠ *1001 av. Joseph-Armand Bombardier,* ☎ *514/532–5300.* 🖾 *$5.* ⊙ *Late June–Aug., daily 10–5:30; Sept.–late June, Tues.–Sun. 10–5.*

Magog

18 *32 km (20 mi) south of Valcourt.*

At the northern tip of Lac Memphrémagog, a large body of water reaching into northern Vermont, lies the bustling resort town of Magog, a four-season destination with bed-and-breakfasts, hotels, and restaurants. Sandy beaches, boating, ferry rides, bird-watching, sailboarding, horseback riding, dogsledding, rollerblading, and snowmobiling are just some of the draws here.

You can stroll or picnic (or skate and cross-country ski in winter) along the scenic linear park that skirts the lake, then turns into an off-road recreational trail leading to **Mont-Orford Provincial Park**, 13½ km (8 mi) from the center of town. The trail, which is for cyclists, walkers, and cross-country skiers, hugs the lake, then parallels Route 112 before winding through a forested area into the park.

The streets downtown are lined with century-old homes that have been converted into boutiques, stores, and dozens of eating places— from fast-food outlets to bistros serving Italian and French fare.

Dining and Lodging

$$ ✕ **Auberge de l'Étoile Sur-le-Lac.** This popular restaurant (which also has rooms) serves three meals a day in attractive surroundings. Large windows overlooking mountain-ringed Lac Memphrémagog make the dining room bright and airy. During the summer you can sit outside and take in the smells and sounds, as well as the beautiful view. House specialties include wild game and Swiss fondue. ⊠ *1150 rue Principale Ouest,* ☎ *819/843–6521. AE, DC, MC, V.*

$$$ ✕⊡ **Ripplecove Inn.** The Ripplecove vies with the Hatley and Hovey inns for best in the region. Its accommodations, service, and dining room are consistently excellent. The English pub–style room combines classical and French cuisine in such dishes as *petit timbale de sole et saumon fumé a l'algue nori* (timbale of sole and smoked salmon with seaweed), and the *gateau de foie de volaille a la creme de porto* (gateau of chicken livers in a port-flavored sauce). ⊠ *700 chemin Ripplecove, C.P. 246, Ayer's Cliff (11 km, or 7 mi, south of Magog) J0B 1C0,* ☎ *819/838–4296 or 800/668–4296,* ℻ *819/838–5541. 25 rooms. Restaurant, pool, 2 beaches, windsurfing, boating, cross-country skiing, meeting rooms. MAP. AE, MC, V.*

$$$–$$$$ ⊡ **Centre de Santé Eastman.** The oldest spa in Québec has evolved from a simple health center into a bucolic haven for anyone seeking rest and therapeutic treatments. Owner Jocelyna Dubuc has resisted the temptation to turn the 350-acre property into a glitzy resort. Instead, she has created a relaxing world where people can, at reasonable prices, rejuvenate their bodies and minds through walking programs, massages, algae wraps, oxygen baths, and other energy-boosting programs. The brightly lit restaurant, with its wall of windows, serves flavorful vegetarian cuisine as well as innovative seafood and chicken dishes. Some spa goers, intent on shedding unwanted pounds, walk to nearby Eastman, an attractive hamlet with antiques and gift shops. ⊠ *895 chemin Diligence, Eastman (15 km, or 9 mi, west of Magog) J0E 1P0,* ☎ *514/297–3009 or 800/665–5272. 19 rooms. Restaurant, spa, cross-country skiing. MAP. AE, MC, V.*

Nightlife and the Arts

THE ARTS

One of Magog's many churches has been turned into a theater—**Le Vieux Clocher** (⊠ 64 rue Merry Nord, ☎ 819/847–0470)—that headlines well-known comedians and singers. Most performances are in French but big names, like Jim Corcoran, Edith Butler, and Michel Rivard, perform here regularly.

NIGHTLIFE

Magog is lively after dark, with a variety of bars, cafés, bistros, and restaurants to suit every taste and pocketbook. **La Grosse Pomme** (⊠ 270 rue Principale Ouest, ☎ 819/843–9365) is a multilevel complex with huge video screens, dance floors, and restaurant service. **Resto-bar Au Chat Noir** (⊠ 266 rue Principale Ouest, ☎ 819/843–4337) is a gathering place for local jazz aficionados and musicians, who drop by for impromptu jam sessions that augment the regular performances. **Auberge Orford** (✉ 20 rue Merry Sud, ☎ 819/843–9361) often has live entertainment.

Skiing

Owl's Head Ski Area (✉ Rte. 243 South, Exit 106 from Autoroute 10, ☎ 514/292–3342), 25 km (16 mi) south of Magog, is a mecca for skiers looking for fewer crowds. It has 27 trails and a 4-km (2½-mi) intermediate run, the longest in the Eastern Townships. From the trails you can see nearby Vermont and Lac Memphrémagog. (You might even see the lake's legendary sea dragon, said to have been sighted around 90 times since 1816.)

Abbaye St-Benoît-du-Lac

★ ⑲ *21 km (13 mi) southwest of Magog.*

This abbey's slender bell tower juts up above the trees like a fairy-tale castle. Built by the Benedictines in 1912 on a wooded peninsula on Lac Memphrémagog, the abbey is home to some 60 monks, who sell apples and sparkling apple wine from their orchards as well as distinctive cheeses: Ermite, St-Benoît, and ricotta. Gregorian masses are sung daily and some are open to the public. The abbey was once known as a favorite retreat for some of Québec's best-known politicians. To get to the abbey from Magog, take Route 112 and then follow the signs for the side road (R.R. 2, or rue des Pères) to the abbey. ✉ *R.R. 2, ☎ 819/843–4080 for information about times of masses. ☉ Store open between services; best time is 2–4.*

North Hatley

⑳ *15 km (9 mi) east of Magog.*

North Hatley, the small resort town on the tip of lovely Lac Massawippi, has a theater and a number of excellent inns and restaurants. The town, set among hills and farms, was discovered by well-to-do vacationers early in the century and has been drawing people ever since. A number of special events during the year are additional attractions.

Dining and Lodging

$$–$$$ ✕ **The Pilsen.** Québec's earliest microbrewery no longer brews beer onsite, but you can still get Massawippi pale ale on tap at this lively spot. Good pub food—pasta, homemade soups, burgers, and the like—is served in the upstairs restaurant or the tavern, both of which overlook the water. ✉ *55 Main St.,* ☎ *819/842–2971. AE, MC, V.*

$$$$ ✕⌂ **Manoir Hovey.** Overlooking Lac Massawippi, this retreat has the ★   ambience of a private estate, while offering the activities of a resort. Built in 1900, it resembles George Washington's home at Mount Vernon. Each wallpapered room has a mix of antiques and newer wood furniture, richly printed fabrics, and lace trimmings; many have fireplaces and private balconies. The dining room serves exquisite Continental and French cuisine; if in season, try warm roulades of Swiss chard with spring lamb, preserved apricots, and roasted hazelnuts or grilled tenderloin of beef marinated with juniper berries and a sauce of tarragon and horseradish. Dinner, breakfast, and most sports facilities are included in room rates. ✉ *575 chemin Hovey, C.P. 60, J0B 2C0,* ☎ *819/842–2421 or 800/661–2421,* FAX *819/842–2248. 40 rooms, 1 suite, 1 4-bedroom cottage. Dining room, 2 bars, pool, tennis court, 2 beaches, ice fishing, mountain bikes, cross-country skiing, library, meeting rooms. MAP. AE, DC, MC, V.*

$$$ ✕🖭 **Auberge Hatley.** Chef Alain Labrie specializes in regional dishes at this restaurant/inn, which has three times been voted the best in Québec. The menu changes seasonally, but the rich foie gras and *canard de Barbarie* are recommended if available. The antique yellow room has a panoramic view of Lake Massawippi; linger over your coffee or sip your selection from the wine cellar, which has more than 5,000 bottles. Guest rooms in this 1903 country manor are charmingly decorated; some have a whirlpool and a fireplace. ⊠ *325 chemin Virgin, C.P. 330, J0B 2C0,* ☎ *819/842–2451,* F̃AX *819/842–2907. 25 rooms. Restaurant. MAP. AE, DC, MC, V. Closed last 2 wks in Nov.*

The Arts

The Piggery (⊠ Rte. 108, ☎ 819/842–2432 or 819/842–2431), a theater that was once a pig barn, reigns supreme in the Townships' cultural life. The venue is renowned for its risk taking, often presenting new plays by Canadian playwrights and even experimenting with bilingual productions. The season runs June–August.

Naive Arts Contest (⊠ Galerie Jeannine-Blais, 100 rue Main, ☎ 819/842–2784) shows the work of more than 100 painters of naive art from some 15 countries. This show takes place every two years; the next year is 1998.

L'Association du Festival du Lac Massawippi (☎ 819/563–4141) presents an annual antiques and folk-arts show in July. The association also sponsors a series of classical music concerts performed at the Eglise Ste-Catherine in North Hatley, on Sundays starting in late April and continuing through June.

Sherbrooke

㉑ *16 km (10 mi) north of North Hatley.*

The region's unofficial capital and largest city is Sherbrooke, named in 1818 for Canadian Governor General Sir John Coape Sherbrooke. It was founded by Loyalists in the 1790s along the St-François River. Sherbrooke has a number of art galleries and museums, including the **Musée des Beaux-Arts de Sherbrooke.** This fine-arts museum has mostly oil paintings; there are occasional exhibits by regional artists and other changing shows. ⊠ *241 rue Dufferin, J1H 4M3,* ☎ *819/821–2115.* 🖾 *$2; free Wed. eve.* ☾ *Tues. and Thurs.–Sun. 1–5, Wed. 1–9.*

The **Sherbrooke Tourist Information Center** (⊠ 48 rue Dépôt, ☎ 819/564–8331) conducts city tours from late June through early September. Call for reservations.

Two **sugar shacks** near Sherbrooke give tours of their maple-syrup producing operations in the spring: It's best to call before visiting. **Erablière Patoine** (⊠ 1105 chemin Beauvoir, ☎ 819/563–7455) is in Fleurimont. **Bolduc** (⊠ 525 chemin Lower, ☎ 819/875–3022) is in Cookshire.

Dining and Lodging

$$ ✕ **La Falaise St-Michel.** Chef and part-owner Patrick Laigniel offers up superb French cuisine in a warm redbrick and wood room that takes off any chill even before you sit down. A large selection of wines complements the table d'hôte. ⊠ *Rues Webster and Wellington North, behind Banque National,* ☎ *819/346–6339. AE, DC, MC, V.*

$$ ✕ **Restaurant au P'tit Sabot.** Specialties include dishes with wild boar, quail, and bison. The cozy room is a pleasant refuge from the bustle of Sherbrooke's main drag. A piano in the corner, pink decor, and room for only 35 patrons help set a romantic atmosphere. ⊠ *1410 rue King Ouest,* ☎ *819/563–0262. AE, DC, MC, V.*

$ ⬜ **Bishop's University.** If you are on a budget, the students' residences here are a great place to stay in summer. The prices can't be beat, and the location near Sherbrooke is good for touring. The university's grounds are lovely, with much of the architecture reminiscent of stately New England campuses. Visit the university's 136-year-old chapel, and also look for the butternut tree, an endangered species in the Eastern Townships. Reservations for summer guests are accepted as early as September, so book in advance. ✉ *Rue College, Lennoxville (5 km, or 3 mi, south of Sherbrooke), J1M 1Z7,* ☎ *819/822–9651,* FAX *819/822–9615. 564 beds in single or double rooms. Indoor pool, 18-hole golf course, tennis court, exercise room. MC, V. Closed Sept.–mid-May.*

The Arts

The **Centennial Theatre** (☎ 819/822–9692) at Bishop's University in Lennoxville, 5 km (3 mi) south of Sherbrooke, presents a roster of international, Canadian, and Québécois jazz, classical, and rock concerts, as well as dance, mime, and children's theater.

Mont-Mégantic's Observatory

22 *74 km (46 mi) east of Sherbrooke.*

Both amateur stargazers and serious astronomers are drawn to this site, in a beautifully wild and mountainous part of the Eastern Townships. The observatory is at the summit of the Townships' second-highest mountain (3,601 ft), whose northern face records annual snowfalls rivaling any in North America. The observatory is a joint venture by the University of Montréal and Laval University. Its powerful telescope allows resident scientists to observe celestial bodies 10 million times smaller than the human eye can detect. There's a welcome center, called the Astrolab, on the mountain's base, where you can view an exhibition and a multimedia show and learn about the night sky. ✉ *189 Route du Parc, Notre-Dame-des-Bois,* ☎ *819/888–2822.* 🎫 *Astrolab $8, night tour to summit $8.* ☉ *Astrolab, late June–Labor Day, daily 10–6; night tour to summit late June–Labor Day, daily 8 PM.*

Dining and Lodging

$$$ ✕⬜ **Aux Berges de l'Aurore.** Although this tiny bed-and-breakfast has attractive furnishings and spectacular views (it sits at the foot of Mont-Mégantic), the draw here is the inn's cuisine. The restaurant serves a five-course meal with ingredients supplied from the inn's huge fruit, vegetable, and herb garden, as well as wild game from the surrounding area: boar, fish, hare, and quail. ✉ *51 chemin de l'Observatoire, Notre-Dame-des-Bois,* ☎ *819/888–2715. 4 rooms. MC, V. Closed Jan.–May.*

CHARLEVOIX

Stretching along the St. Lawrence River's north shore, east of Québec City from Ste-Anne-de-Beaupré to the Saguenay River, Charlevoix embraces mountains rising from the sea and a succession of valleys, plateaus, and cliffs cut by waterfalls, brooks, and streams. The roads wind into villages of picturesque houses and huge tin-roof churches. The area has long been popular both as a summer retreat and as a haven for artists and craftspeople. In winter there are opportunities for both downhill and cross-country skiing.

New France's first historian, the Jesuit priest François-Xavier de Charlevoix, gave his name to the region. Charlevoix (pronounced sharle-vwah) was first explored by Jacques Cartier, who landed in

1535, although the first colonists didn't arrive until well into the 17th century. They developed a thriving shipbuilding industry, specializing in the sturdy schooner they called a *goelette,* which they used to haul everything from logs to lobsters up and down the coast in the days before rail and paved roads. Shipbuilding has been a vital part of the provincial economy until recent times; today wrecked and forgotten goelettes lie along beaches in the region.

Ste-Anne-de-Beaupré

㉓ *33 km (20 mi) east of Québec City.*

Charlevoix begins in the tiny town of Ste-Anne-de-Beaupré (named for Québec's patron saint). Each year more than a million pilgrims visit
★ the region's most famous religious site, the **Basilique Ste-Anne-de-Beaupré** (☞ Side Trips from Québec City *in* Chapter 9), which is dedicated to the mother of the Virgin Mary.

At the **Cap Tourmente Wildlife Reserve,** about 8 km (5 mi) northeast of Ste-Anne-de-Beaupré, more than 100,000 greater snow geese gather every October and May. This enclave on the north shore of the St. Lawrence River has 14 hiking trails; the park harbors hundreds of kinds of birds and mammals and more than 700 plant species. Naturalists give guided tours. ⊠ *St-Joachim,* ☎ *418/827–4591 (Apr.–Oct.) and 418/827–3776 (Nov.–Mar.).*

Skiing

Station Mont-Ste-Anne (☞ Outdoor Activities and Sports *in* Chapter 9), outside Québec City, is on the World Cup downhill ski circuit. **Le Massif** (⊠ 1350 rue Principale, Petite Rivière St-François, ☎ 418/632–5876) is a three-peak ski resort that has the province's highest vertical drop—2,500 ft. There are 18 trails, divided into runs for different levels (including one for extremely advanced skiers). Equipment can be rented on site.

Baie-St-Paul

㉔ *60 km (37 mi) northeast of Ste-Anne-de-Beaupré.*

Baie-St-Paul, Charlevoix's earliest settlement after Beaupré, is popular with craftspeople and artists. Here the high hills circle a wide plain, holding the village beside the sea. Many of Québec's greatest landscapists portray the area, and their work is on display year-round at the **Centre d'Art Baie-St-Paul** (⊠ 4 rue Ambroise-Fafard, ☎ 418/435–3681) and the **Centre d'Exposition de Baie-St-Paul** (⊠ 23 rue Ambroise-Fafard, ☎ 418/435–3681).

Dining and Lodging

$$$ ✕ **Auberge la Maison Otis.** Here you can try creative Québec-oriented French cuisine like *ballotine de faisan* (pheasant) stuffed with quail and served in a venison sauce, followed by a delicious assortment of cheeses. The restaurant is in a 150-year-old Norman-style house, elegantly decorated in pastel pink, with a huge stone fireplace. ⊠ *23 rue St-Jean-Baptiste,* ☎ *418/435–2255. MC, V.*

$$ ✕ **Mouton Noir.** French cuisine is served amid flowers on the terrace in the summer or in a cozy rustic setting in the winter. You'll always find a varied menu, with pasta, fish, and meat, for very reasonable prices. ⊠ *43 rue Ste-Anne,* ☎ *418/435–3075. AE, MC, V.*

$$$$ ⌂ **Auberge la Maison Otis.** This inn offers calm and romantic ac-
★ commodations in three buildings, including an old stone house, in the center of the village. Some of the country-style rooms have whirlpools,

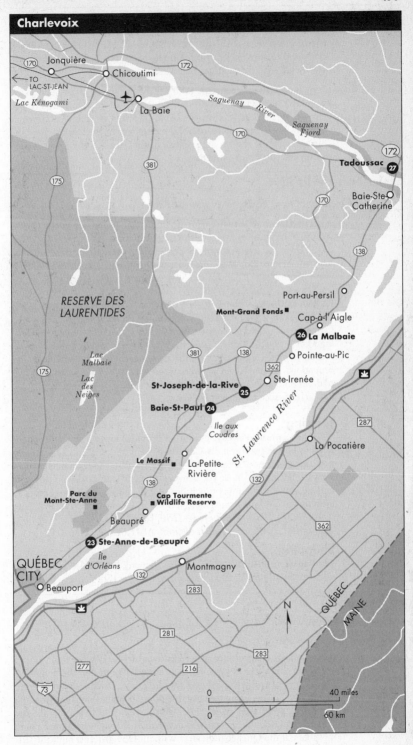

170 Jonquière

Chicoutimi

172

TO
LAC-ST-JEAN

Lac Kénogami

La Baie

Saguenay River

170

Saguenay Fjord

172

381

170

Tadoussac 27

175

Baie-Ste-
Catherine

138

*RESERVE DES
LAURENTIDES*

Port-au-Persil

Mont-Grand Fonds ■

Cap-à-l'Aigle

26 **La Malbaie**

175

*Lac
Malbaie*

381

138

Pointe-au-Pic

362

*Lac
des
Neiges*

St-Joseph-de-la-Rive

Ste-Irenée

25

Baie-St-Paul 24

*Ile aux
Coudres*

St. Lawrence River

287

La Pocatière

Le Massif ■

La-Petite-
Rivière

132

**Parc du
Mont-Ste-Anne**

138

Cap Tourmente
■ Wildlife Reserve

362

Beaupré

23 **Ste-Anne-de-Beaupré**

*Île
d'Orléans*

Montmagny

**QUÉBEC
CITY**

132

Beauport

283

QUÉBEC

MAINE

281

N

277

216

283

73

0 _____ 40 miles

0 _____ 60 km

fireplaces, and antique furnishings. Summer lunches are served on an outdoor terrace. Skiing and ice-skating are available nearby. ⊠ *23 rue St-Jean-Baptiste, G0A 1B0,* ☎ *418/435–2255,* FAX *418/435–2464. 30 rooms, 4 suites. Restaurant, lounge, piano bar, indoor pool, sauna, health club. MAP available. AE, MC, V.*

En Route   From Baie-St-Paul, you can take the open, scenic coastal drive on **Route 362** or the faster Route 138 to Pointe-au-Pic, La Malbaie, and Cap-à-l'Aigle. This section of Route 362 has memorable views of rolling hills—green, white, or ablaze with fiery hues, depending on the season—meeting the broad expanse of the "sea" as the locals like to call the St. Lawrence estuary.

St-Joseph-de-la-Rive

㉕ *15 km (9 mi) northeast of Baie-St-Paul.*

A secondary road leads sharply down into St-Joseph-de-la-Rive, with its line of old houses hugging the mountain base on the narrow shore road. The town has a number of peaceful inns and inviting restaurants. The small **Exposition Maritime** (Maritime Museum, ☎ 418/635–1131) commemorates the days of the St. Lawrence goelettes.

OFF THE   **ILE AUX COUDRES** – From St-Joseph-de-la-Rive you can catch a ferry
BEATEN PATH   (☎ 418/438-2743) to Ile aux Coudres, an island where Jacques Cartier's men gathered *coudres* (hazelnuts) in 1535. Since then, the island has produced many a goelette, and former captains now run several small inns. Larger inns have folk-dance evenings. You can bike around the 16-km (10-mi) island and see windmills, inns, water mills, and old schooners, or stop at boutiques selling paintings and local handicrafts, such as household linens.

Lodging

$$ 🏨 **Hôtel Cap-aux-Pierres.** This hotel provides top-notch accommoda-
★   tions in both a traditionally Canadian main building and a motel section open in the summer only. About a third of the rooms have river views. The restaurant serves a mix of Québec standards and nouvelle cuisine, and entertainment includes folk dancing on summer Saturday evenings. ⊠ *246 rue Principale, La Baleine, Ile aux Coudres, G0A 2A0,* ☎ *418/438–2711 or 800/463–5250,* FAX *418/438–2127. 98 rooms. Restaurant, bar, indoor-outdoor pool. MAP. AE, DC, MC, V.*

Shopping

The **Papeterie St-Gilles** (⊠ 304 rue F.A. Savard, ☎ 418/635–2430) produces unusual handcrafted stationery, using a 17th-century process.

La Malbaie

㉖ *35 km (22 mi) northeast of St-Joseph.*

La Malbaie is one of the most elegant and historically interesting resort towns in the province. It was known as Murray Bay in an earlier era when wealthy Anglophones summered here and in the neighboring villages of Pointe-au-Pic and Cap-à-l'Aigle. Once called the "summer White House," this area became popular with both American and Canadian politicians in the late 1800s when Ottawa Liberals and Washington Republicans partied decorously through the summer with members of the Québec judiciary. William Howard Taft built the first of three summer residences in Pointe-au-Pic in 1894, when he was the American civil governor of the Philippines. He became the 27th president of the United States in 1908.

Now many Taft-era homes serve as handsome inns, guaranteeing an old-fashioned coddling, with such extras as breakfast in bed, gourmet meals, whirlpools, and free shuttles to the ski areas in winter. Many serve lunch and dinner to nonresidents, so you can tour the area going from one gourmet's delight to the next. The cuisine, as elsewhere in Québec, is genuine French or regional fare, rather than a hybrid invented for North Americans.

Musée de Charlevoix traces the region's history as a vacation spot in a series of exhibits and is developing an excellent collection of local paintings and folk art. ⊠ *1 chemin du Havre, Pointe-au-Pic (3 km, or 2 mi, south of La Malbaie),* ☎ *418/665–4411.*

The **Casino de Charlevoix,** styled after European casinos, welcomes visitors year-round. The minimum age is 18. ⊠ *Hôtel Manoir Richelieu, 183 av. Richelieu, Pointe-au-Pic,* ☎ *418/665–5353 or 800/965–5355.* ☉ *Sun.–Thurs. 10 AM–2 AM, Fri. and Sat. 10 AM–3 AM.*

Dining and Lodging

$$$$ ✕ **Auberge des 3 Canards.** This inn has made a name for itself in the region, not only for its accommodations but also for its award-winning restaurant. The menu may include *gratin d'escargots aux bluets* (snails with a blueberry and grapefruit sauce baked au gratin) as an appetizer, and stuffed pheasant—the breasts smothered in mustard sauce and the legs seasoned with spicy maple sauce—as a main course. Homemade desserts include *pomme de l'Ile aux Coudres*—cheese-topped apples with a touch of honey. Meals are elegantly presented in a rustic setting with natural wood and pale and deep blue touches throughout. ⊠ *49 côte Bellevue, Pointe-au-Pic (3 km, or 2 mi, south of La Malbaie),* ☎ *418/665–3761. AE, MC, V.*

$$$–$$$$ ✕ **Auberge sur la Côte.** Simple white tablecloths, natural wood, and stone walls create a casual setting for fine French cuisine. A house specialty is *agneau de Charlevoix,* lamb seasoned with lemon and thyme, served with fresh vegetables. Lunch is served in summer only, but the dining room is open in the evening year-round. ⊠ *205 chemin des Falaises,* ☎ *418/665–3972. AE, MC, V.*

$$$$ ▦ **Auberge la Pinsonnière.** An atmosphere of country luxury prevails
★ at this inn, a Relais & Châteaux property. Each room is decorated differently; some have fireplaces, whirlpools, and king-size four-poster beds. The rooms have a commanding view of Murray Bay on the St. Lawrence River. The food here is excellent, and the auberge has one of the largest wine cellars in North America. ⊠ *124 rue St-Raphael, Cap-à-l'Aigle (3 km, or 2 mi, south of La Malbaie), G0T 1B0,* ☎ *418/665–4431,* FAX *418/665–7156. 26 rooms, 1 suite. 2 restaurants, 3 lounges, indoor pool, sauna, tennis court, beach. MAP. AE, MC, V.*

$$$$ ▦ **Hôtel Manoir Richelieu.** The Manoir Richelieu, an imposing castle nestled amid trees on a cliff overlooking the St. Lawrence River, has been offering first-class accommodations for a hundred years. This hotel was constructed in 1929 on the site of an earlier property, but the Manoir Richelieu retains the air of a turn-of-the-century hostelry. Still, it has kept up with the times: A recent addition is Relaxarium Manoir Richelieu, a health spa with treatments from lymphatic drainage to hydrotherapy. The links-style golf course, similar to those in Scotland, overlooks the St. Lawrence. ⊠ *181 rue Richelieu, Pointe-au-Pic (3 km, or 2 mi, south of La Malbaie), G0T 1M0,* ☎ *418/665–3703 or 800/463–2613,* FAX *418/665–3093. 372 rooms. Restaurant, indoor and outdoor pools, sauna, spa, 18-hole golf course, tennis courts, cross-country skiing, snowmobiling, casino. AE, DC, MC, V.*

The Arts

Domaine Forget, a music and dance academy, presents concerts on summer evenings by fine musicians from around the world, many of whom are teaching or learning at the school. The Domaine also functions as a stopover for traveling musicians, who take advantage of its rental studios. A 600-seat concert hall has recently been added. ⊠ *St-Irenée (15 km, or 9 mi, south of La Malbaie),* ☎ *418/452–8111 or 418/452–2535,* FAX *418/452–3503.* ☉ *Concerts May–Aug.*

Outdoor Activities and Sports

GOLF

Club de Golf de Manoir Richelieu (⊠ 181 rue Richelieu, Pointe-au-Pic, ☎ 418/665–2526 or 800/463–2613) has 18 holes.

SKIING

Mont-Grand Fonds (⊠ 1000 chemin des Loisirs, ☎ 418/665–0095), 10 km (6 mi) north of La Malbaie, has 13 slopes and 141 km (87 mi) of cross-country trails. Two trails meet the standards of the International Ski Federation, and the resort hosts major ski competitions from time to time. Other winter sports include dogsledding, sleigh rides, skating, and tobogganing.

Tadoussac

㉗ *71 km (44 mi) north of La Malbaie.*

The small town of Tadoussac shares the view up the magnificent Saguenay Fjord with Baie-Ste-Catherine. The drive here from La Malbaie, along Route 138, takes you past a lovely series of villages and views along the St. Lawrence. Jacques Cartier made a stop at this point in 1535, and it became an important meeting site for fur traders in the French Territory until the mid-19th century. Whale-watching excursions and cruises of the fjord now depart from Tadoussac, as well as from Chicoutimi, farther up the deep fjord.

As the Saguenay River flows from Lac St-Jean south toward the St. Lawrence, it has a dual character: Between Alma and Chicoutimi, the once rapidly flowing river has been turned into hydroelectric power; in its lower section, it becomes wider and deeper and flows by steep mountains and cliffs, en route to the St. Lawrence. The white beluga whale breeds in the lower portion of the Saguenay in summer, and in the confluence of the fjord and the seaway are many marine species, which attract other whales, such as pilot, finback, humpback, and blues.

Sadly, the beluga is an endangered species; the whales, along with 27 species of mammals and birds and 17 species of fish, are being threatened by pollution in the St. Lawrence River. This has inspired a $100 million project funded by both the federal and provincial governments. An 800-square-km (496-square-mi) **marine park** (☎ 418/235–4703) at the confluence of the Saguenay and St. Lawrence rivers has been created to protect its fragile ecosystem in the hope of reversing some of the damage already done.

Whale-Watching

Croisières Navimex Canada, Inc. (⊠ 124 rue Saint-Pierre, Bureau 300, Québec City G1K 4A7 ☎ 418/692–4643), has three-hour whale-watching cruises ($30) and 4½-hour dinner cruises on the Saguenay Fjord ($40). Cruises depart from Baie-Ste-Catherine, Tadoussac, and Rivière du Loup (the departure from Rivière du Loup costs an additional $5).

THE GASPÉ PENINSULA

Jutting into the stormy Gulf of St. Lawrence like the battered prow of a ship, the Gaspé Peninsula (Gaspésie in French) remains an isolated region of unsurpassed wild beauty. Sheer cliffs tower above broad beaches, and tiny coastal fishing communities cling to the shoreline. Inland rise the Chic-Choc Mountains, eastern Canada's highest, the realm of woodland caribou, black bear, and moose. Townspeople in some Gaspé areas speak mainly English.

The Gaspé was on Jacques Cartier's itinerary—he first stepped ashore in North America in the town of Gaspé in 1534—but Vikings, Basques, and Portuguese fisherfolk had come long before. The area's history is told in countless towns en route. Acadians, displaced by the British from New Brunswick in 1755, settled Bonaventure; Paspébiac still has a gunpowder shed built in the 1770s to help defend the peninsula from American ships; and United Empire Loyalists settled New Carlisle in 1784.

Today the area still seems unspoiled and timeless, a blessing for anyone dipping and soaring along the spectacular coastal highways or venturing on river-valley roads to the interior. Geographically, the peninsula is among the oldest lands on earth. A vast, mainly uninhabited forest covers the hilly hinterland. Local tourist officials can be helpful in locating outfitters and guides to fish and hunt large and small game. The Gaspé's four major parks—Port Daniel, Forillon, Causapscal, and Gaspé—cover a total of 2,292 square km (885 square mi).

Carleton

28 *201 km (125 mi) southeast of Mont-Joli.*

The Notre Dame Oratory on Mont-St-Joseph dominates this French-speaking city. There are lookout points and hiking trails around the site. The views, almost 2,000 ft above Baie des Chaleurs, are spectacular.

Dining and Lodging

$$-$$$ ✕🏨 **Motel Hostelerie Baie-Bleue.** This motel is snuggled up against a mountain beside the Baie des Chaleurs and offers great views. Daily guided bus tours leave from the hotel June–September. The large restaurant, La Seignerie, has been recognized for excellence. Chef Simon Bernard prepares regional dishes, especially seafood. The table d'hôte won't break your budget, and the wine list is extensive and well chosen. ⊠ *482 blvd. Perron, Rte. 132, G0C 1J0,* ☎ *418/364–3355 or 800/463–9099,* FAX *418/364–6165. 95 rooms. Restaurant, pool, tennis courts, beach. AE, MC, V.*

Water Sports

Windsurfers and sailors enjoy the breezes around the Gaspé; there are windsurfing marathons in Baie des Chaleurs each summer.

Percé

29 *193 km (120 mi) east of Carleton.*

A pretty fishing village, Percé has a number of attractions and can get busy in summer. The most famous sight in the region is the huge fossil-embedded rock offshore that the sea "pierced" thousands of years ago. There are many pleasant places to walk and hike near town, and it's also possible to do some fishing or take a whale-watching cruise.

The largest colony of gannets in the world summers off Percé on ★ **30 Bonaventure Island.** From the wharf at Percé, you can take a scenic

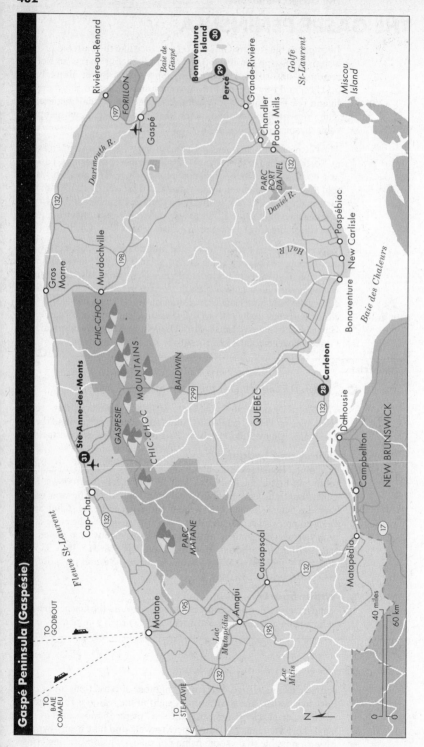

Gaspé Peninsula (Gaspésie)

Rivière-au-Renard

FORILLON

Baie de Gaspé

197

Dartmouth R.

Gaspé

Bonaventure Island ㉚

㉙

Percé

Grande-Rivière

Golfe St-Laurent

Miscou Island

132

Chandler

Pabos Mills

132

Gros Morne

Murdochville

PARC PORT DANIEL

Daniel R.

198

Haf R.

Paspébiac

New Carlisle

CHIC-CHOC

Ste-Anne-des-Monts

BALDWIN

QUÉBEC

Bonaventure

Baie des Chaleurs

GASPÉSIE

CHIC-CHOC MOUNTAINS

299

㉛

Cap-Chat

132

Carleton ㉘

132

Dalhousie

Campbellton

NEW BRUNSWICK

Fleuve St-Laurent

PARC MATANE

Causapscal

17

TO GODBOUT

TO BAIE COMAEU

Matane

195

Amqui

Lac Matapédia

195

Matapédia

132

132

Lac Mitis

40 miles

60 km

TO STE-FLAVIE

N

0

0

boat ride to the island and walk the trails here. Take binoculars and a camera; there are many kinds of birds here.

Dining and Lodging

$ ✕ **La Sieur de Pabos.** Boasting the best seafood in the province, this rustic restaurant overlooks Pabos Bay, south of Chandler, about 40 km (25 mi) south of Percé. The chef suggests *crêpe de la seigneurie*, a seafood crepe with a delicately seasoned white sauce. ✉ *325 Rte. 132, Pabos Mills,* ☎ *418/689–2281. AE, MC, V.*

$$–$$$ ⌂ **La Bonaventure-sur-Mer Hotel.** The waterfront location with views of Percé Rock and Bonaventure Island makes up for the motel-standard decor. Some motel units have kitchenettes. ✉ *Rte. 132, C.P. 339, G0C 2L0,* ☎ *418/782–2166. 90 rooms. Dining room, beach. AE, DC, MC, V. Closed Nov.–May.*

$$–$$$ ⌂ **La Normandie Hotel/Motel.** All but four rooms of this split-level motel face the ocean, with views of Percé Rock and Bonaventure Island. The location in the center of town puts shops and restaurants within walking distance; a beach and a municipal pool are also nearby. Third-floor rooms are more spacious. ✉ *221 Rte. 132 Ouest, C.P. 129, G0C 2L0,* ☎ *418/782–2112 or 800/463–0820. 45 rooms. Restaurant, lounge, sauna, exercise room. EP, MAP. AE, DC, MC, V. Closed Nov.–Apr.*

$$ ⌂ **La Côte Surprise Motor Hotel.** Most of the rooms of this motel have views of Percé Rock and the village. Decor is standard in both motel and second-floor hotel units, but the private balconies and terraces are a plus. ✉ *Rte. 132, C.P. 339, G0C 2L0,* ☎ *418/782–2166,* ℻ *418/782–5323. 36 rooms. Dining room, lounge, snack bar. AE, D, DC, MC, V. Closed Oct.–May.*

Ste-Anne-des-Monts

㉛ *282 km (175 mi) northwest of Percé.*

The area south of this coastal town boasts Québec's highest peaks, the Chic-Choc Mountains. **Parc de Conservation de la Gaspésie** (☎ 418/ 763–3301), off Rte. 299, is undeveloped and full of wildlife. **Parc Ami Chic-Chocs** (☎ 418/763–3301) has climbing, telemark skiing, mountain hiking, and nature interpretation programs such as moose watching. There's also telemark skiing at **Club du Grand Yétis, where overnight accommodation is in cabins heated by wood-burning stoves.** Hardier types can opt for camping out (✉ 85 blvd. Ste-Anne Ouest, ☎ 418/763–7782 or 800/665–6527).

Dining and Lodging

$$ ✕ **Cabillaud.** In this bright restaurant, chef Yvan Belzile serves the local specialty—seafood—as well as his own—duck. This is a good place to unwind with a wine from their fine selection and a view of the everpresent ocean. ✉ *268 rue Notre-Dame Est, Cap-Chat,* ☎ *418/786–2480. MC, V.*

$$ ⌂ **Gîte du Mont-Albert.** In Gaspé Provincial Park, this property is 40 km (25 mi) south of Ste-Anne, nestled in the middle of the Chic-Choc Mountains. It's a perfect retreat for hiking, bicycling, horseback riding, or salmon fishing on the Ste-Anne River. ✉ *Rte. 299, C.P. 1150, G0E 2G0,* ☎ *418/763-2288 or 888/270-4483. 48 rooms. Bar, dining room. AE, MC, V.*

QUÉBEC A TO Z

Arriving and Departing

By Bus
Most major bus lines in the province connect with **Voyageur** (☎ 514/842–2281).

By Car
Major entry points are Ottawa/Hull, U.S. 87 from New York State south of Montréal, U.S. 91 from Vermont into the Eastern Townships area, and the Trans-Canada Highway just west of Montréal.

By Plane
Most airlines fly into either of Montréal's airports (Mirabel or Dorval) or Québec City's airport (☞ Montréal A to Z *in* Chapter 8 *and* Québec City A to Z *in* Chapter 9).

By Train
Regular **VIA Rail** (☎ 800/561–3949 in the U.S., ☎ 800/665–0200 in Canada) passenger service connects all the province with Montréal and Québec City and offers limited service to the Gaspé Peninsula.

Getting Around

Québec
BY BUS

Most bus traffic to the outer reaches of the province begins at the bus terminal in Québec City (✉ 320 rue Abraham-Martin, ☎ 418/525–3000).

BY CAR

Québec has fine roads, along which drivers insist on speeding. Road maps are available at any of the seasonal or permanent Québec tourist offices (call 800/363–7777 for the nearest location).

The major highways are Autoroute des Laurentides 15, a six-lane highway from Montréal to the Laurentians; Autoroute 10 East from Montréal to the Eastern Townships; U.S. 91 from New England, which becomes Autoroute 55 as it crosses the border to the Eastern Townships; and Route 138, which runs from Montréal along the north shore of the St. Lawrence River.

The Laurentians
BY BUS

Frequent bus service is available from the **Terminus Voyageur** (✉ 505 blvd. de Maisonneuve Est, ☎ 514/842–2281) in downtown Montréal. **Limocar Laurentides'** service (☎ 514/435–8899) departs regularly for L'Annonciation, Mont-Laurier, Ste-Adèle, Ste-Agathe-des-Monts, and St-Jovite, among other stops en route. Limocar also has a service to the Lower Laurentians region, departing from the Laval bus terminal at the Métro Henri-Bourassa stop in north Montréal, stopping in many towns and ending in St-Jérôme.

BY CAR

Autoroute des Laurentides 15, a six-lane highway, and the slower but more scenic secondary road, Route 117, lead to this resort country. Try to avoid traveling to and from the region on Friday evening or Sunday afternoon, as you're likely to sit for hours in traffic.

The Eastern Townships

Buses depart daily from the **Terminus Voyageur** in Montréal (⊠ 505 blvd. de Maisonneuve Est, ☎ 514/842–2281) to Granby, Lac-Mégantic, Magog, and Sherbrooke.

Take Autoroute 10 East from Montréal; from New England take U.S. 91, which becomes Autoroute 55 as it crosses the border.

Gaspé Peninsula

Take the Trans-Canada Highway northeast along the southern shore of the St. Lawrence River to just south of Rivière-du-Loup, where you pick up the 270-km (167-mi) Route 132, which hugs the dramatic coastline. At Ste-Flavie, follow the southern leg of Route 132. Note that the entire distance around the peninsula is 848 km (526 mi).

Contacts and Resources

Camping

For information on camping in the province's private trailer parks and campgrounds, write for the free publication "Québec Camping," available from **Tourisme Québec** (⊠ Box 979, Montréal, H3C 2W3 ☎ 514/873–2015 or 800/363–7777). Inquiries about camping in Québec's national parks should be directed to **Parks Canada Information Services** (⊠ 3 rue Buade, Box 6060, Haute Ville, Québec City, G1R 4V7, ☎ 418/648–4177).

Emergencies

Police, fire, ambulance: 911.

Fishing

More than 20 outfitters are members of the Laurentian tourist association; several recommendations follow. **Pourvoirie Baroux** (⊠ St-Jovite, ☎ 819/425–7882). **Pourvoiries Mekoos** (⊠ Mont-Laurier, ☎ 819/623–2336). **Pourvoirie Boismenu** (⊠ Lac-du-Cerf, ☎ 819/597–2619).

Before setting off into the wilds, consult the **Fédération des Pourvoyeurs du Québec** (⊠ Québec Outfitters Federation, 5237 blvd. Hamel, bureau 270, Québec City G2P 2H2, ☎ 418/877–5191) or ask for its list of outfitters available through tourist offices.

Don't forget: Fishing requires a permit, available from the regional offices of the **Ministère de l'Environnement et de la Faune,** (⊠ 150 blvd. René-Lévesque Est, Québec City G1R 4Y1, ☎ 418/643–3127 or 800/561–1616), or inquire at any regional sporting-goods store displaying an "authorized agent" sticker.

Guest Farms

Agricotours (⊠ 4545 av. Pierre de Coubertin, C.P. 1000, Succursale M, Montréal H1V 3R2, ☎ 514/252–3138), the Québec farm-vacation association, can provide lists of guest farms in the province.

Mountain Climbing

Perhaps the best way to view the scenery of the Upper Laurentians is to mountain climb. The **Fédération Québécoise de la Montagne** (⊠ 4545 rue Pierre-de-Coubertin, C.P. 1000, Succursale M, Montréal H1V 3R2, ☎ 514/252–3004) can give you information about this sport, as can the region's tourist offices.

Nature Tours

The **Montréal Zoological Society** (⊠ 2055 rue Peel, Montréal H3A 1V4, ☎ 514/845–8317) is a nature-oriented group that offers lectures, field trips, and weekend excursions. Tours include whale-watching in the St. Lawrence estuary, and hiking and bird-watching in national parks throughout Québec, Canada, and the northern United States.

River Rafting

Four companies specializing in white-water rafting at Rivière Rouge are on-site at the trip's departure point near Calumet. (Take Route 148 past Calumet; turn onto chemin de la Rivière Rouge until you see the signs for the access road to each rafter's headquarters.) **Aventures en Eau Vive** (☎ 819/242–6084 or 800/567–6881), **Nouveau Monde** (☎ 819/242–7238), **Propulsion** (☎ 514/229–6620 or 800/461–3300), and **W-3 Rafting** (☎ 514/334–0889) all offer four- to five-hour rafting trips and provide transportation to and from the river site, as well as guides, helmets, life jackets, and, at the end of the trip, a much-anticipated meal. Most have facilities on-site or nearby for dining, drinking, camping, bathing, swimming, hiking, and horseback riding.

Skiing

For information about ski conditions, call **Tourisme Québec** (☎ 800/363–7777) and ask for the ski report.

Snowmobiling

Jonview Canada (✉ 1227 av. St-Hubert, Suite 200, Montréal H2L 3Y8, ☎ 514/843–8161) offers snowmobile tours in the Laurentians, in Charlevoix, and as far north as the James Bay region. The group also has such adventure packages as "The Magic of the Nunavik Arctic," a weeklong adventure in Québec's Grand Nord, where participants spend one night in an igloo, travel on dogsleds, and go ice fishing.

Visitor Information

QUÉBEC

Tourisme Québec (✉ C.P. 979, Montréal H3C 2W3, ☎ 800/363–7777) can provide information on provincial tourist bureaus throughout the province.

THE LAURENTIANS

The major tourist office is the **Maison du Tourisme des Laurentides** (✉ 14142 rue de Lachapelle, R.R. 1, St-Jérôme J7Z 5T4, ☎ 514/436–8532 or 800/561–6673), just off the Autoroute des Laurentides 15 at Exit 39. The office is open mid-June–August, daily 8:30–8; September–mid-June, Saturday–Thursday 9–5, Friday 9–7.

Year-round regional tourist offices are in the towns of Labelle, Mont-Laurier, Mont-Tremblant, Piedmont, St-Jovite, Ste-Adèle, Ste-Agathe-des-Monts, St-Sauveur-des-Monts, and Val David. **Seasonal tourist offices** (mid-June–Labor Day) are in Grenville, Lachute, L'Annonciation, Ste-Marguerite-du-Lac-Masson, St-Eustache, Oka, Notre-Dame-du-Laus, and St-Adolphe-d'Howard.

THE EASTERN TOWNSHIPS

Year-round regional provincial tourist offices are in the towns of Bromont, Danville, Eastman, Granby, Lac Mégantic, Magog, Sherbrooke, Sutton, Mansonville, and Waterloo. **Seasonal tourist offices** (June–Labor Day) are in Coaticook, Pike River, East Angus, Frelighsburg, Granby, and Lac Brome (Knowlton). Seasonal bureaus' schedules are irregular, so contact the **Association Touristique de les Cantons de l'Est** (✉ 20 rue Don Bosco Sud, Sherbrooke J1L 1W4, ☎ 819/820–2020 or 800/455–5527) before visiting. This association also provides lodging information.

CHARLEVOIX

The regional tourist office is **Association Touristique Régionale de Charlevoix** (✉ 630 blvd. de Comporté, C.P. 275, La Malbaie, G5A 1T8, ☎ 418/665–4454).

GASPÉ PENINSULA

The regional tourist office is **Association Touristique de la Gaspésie** (✉ 357 Rte. de la Mer, Ste-Flavie G0J 2L0, ☎ 418/775–2223 or 800/463–0323).

11 New Brunswick

With the highest tides in the world carving a rugged coast and feeding more whales than you can imagine, New Brunswick can be a phenomenal adventure. White sandy beaches, lobsters in the pot, and cozy inns steeped in history make it easy to have a relaxing interlude, too. And with fine art galleries, museums, and a dual Acadian and Loyalist heritage, the province is an intriguing cultural destination.

Updated by
Ana Watts

NEW BRUNSWICK IS WHERE the great Canadian forest, sliced by sweeping river valleys and modern highways, meets the sea. It's an old place in New World terms, and the remains of a turbulent past are still evident in some of its quiet nooks. Near Moncton, for instance, wild strawberries perfume the air of the grassy slopes of Fort Beausejour, where, in 1755, one of the last battles for possession of Acadia took place—the English finally overcoming the French. The dual heritage of New Brunswick (35% of its population is Acadian French) provides added spice. Other areas of the province were settled by the British and by Loyalists, American colonists who chose to live under British rule after the American Revolution. If you stay in both Acadian and Loyalist regions, a trip to New Brunswick can seem like two vacations in one.

More than half the province is surrounded by coastline—the rest nestles into Québec and Maine, creating slightly schizophrenic attitudes in border towns. The dramatic Bay of Fundy, which has the highest tides in the world, sweeps up the coast of Maine, around the enchanting Fundy Isles at the southern tip of New Brunswick and on up the province's rough and intriguing south coast. To the north and east, the gentle, warm Gulf Stream washes quiet beaches.

New Brunswick is still largely unsettled—85% of the province is forested. Inhabitants have chosen the easily accessible area around rivers, ocean, and lakes, leaving most of the interior to the pulp companies. For years this Cinderella province has been somewhat ignored by tourists who whiz through to better-known Atlantic destinations. New Brunswick's residents can't seem to decide whether this makes them unhappy or not. The government, however, sees tourism as a culturally and economically friendly way of helping the province toward economic self-sufficiency. Money is important in the economically depressed maritime area, where younger generations have traditionally left home for higher-paying jobs in Ontario and "the West." But no one wishes to lose the special characteristics of this still unspoiled province.

This attitude is a blessing in disguise to motorists who do leave the major highways to explore 2,240 km (1,389 mi) of spectacular seacoast, pure inland streams, pretty towns, and historical cities. The custom of hospitality is so much a part of New Brunswick nature that tourists are perceived more as welcome visitors than paying guests. Even cities often retain a bit of naïveté. It makes for a charming vacation, but don't be deceived by ingenuous attitudes. Most residents are products of excellent school and university systems, generally travel widely, live in modern cities, and are well versed in world affairs.

Pleasures and Pastimes

Beaches

There are two kinds of saltwater beaches in New Brunswick: warm-m-m-m-m and c-c-c-c-cold. The warm beaches are along the Northumberland Strait and Gulf of St. Lawrence on the east coast. Here, it's sand castles, sunscreen, and a little beach volleyball on the side. If sand and solitude are more your style, try Kouchibouguac National Park and its 26 km (16 mi) of beaches and dunes.

The cold beaches are on the Bay of Fundy, on the province's southern coast. The highest tides in the world (a *vertical* difference of as much as 48 ft) have carved some spectacular caves, crevices, and cliffs. There are some sandy beaches, and hardy souls do swim in the "invigorating" salt water. But the Fundy beaches are more for adventurers who want to investigate aquatic wildlife on the flats at low tide, hound rocks, or hunt fossils.

Dining

Cast your line just about anywhere in New Brunswick and you catch fish 'n chips, clams 'n chips, and scallops 'n chips. If you want the seafood but not the batter, you'll need a longer line. New Brunswick has never been famous for sophisticated dining, but Saint John, Moncton, and some communities along the Acadian Peninsula offer some interesting options, and resort communities like St. Andrews and Caraquet have consistently good catches.

Silver salmon, once a spring staple when set nets were allowed, is still available but quite costly. Most salmon served in restaurants is farm-reared. Lobster is available in most restaurants but is not always cheap. Residents buy it fresh from the fishermen or shore outlets and devour it in huge quantities. New Brunswick shellfish is especially tasty: Look for oysters, scallops, clams, crab, and mussels. And be sure to try the purple seaweed called dulse, which the natives eat like potato chips. To be truly authentic, accompany any New Brunswick–style feast with hearty Moosehead beer, brewed in Saint John.

In the spring, fiddlehead ferns—a provincial delicacy—are picked from the banks of rivers and streams. Eaten as a vegetable (boiled, drenched with lemon, butter, salt, and pepper), fiddleheads have something of an artichoke taste.

CATEGORY	COST*
$$$$	over $30
$$$	$20–$30
$$	$10–$20
$	under $10

per person, excluding drinks, service, and 15% harmonized sales tax (HST).

Lodging

Among its more interesting options, New Brunswick has a number of officially designated Heritage Inns. These historically significant establishments run the gamut from elegant to homey; many have antique china and furnishings. Hotels and motels in and around Saint John and Fredericton are adequate and friendly. Accommodations in Saint John are at a premium in summer, so reserve ahead.

CATEGORY	COST*
$$$$	over $140
$$$	$85–$140
$$	$50–$85
$	under $50

All prices are for a standard double room, excluding 15% harmonized sales tax (HST).

Outdoor Activities and Sports

BIKING

Byroads, lanes, and rolling secondary highways run through small towns, along the ocean, and into the forest. Set out on your own, or try a guided adventure.

FISHING

Dotted with freshwater lakes, crisscrossed with fish-laden rivers, and bordered by 1,129 km (700 mi) of seacoast, this province is one of Canada's natural treasures. Sports people are drawn by the bass fishing and such world-famous salmon rivers as the Miramichi. Commercial fishermen often take visitors line fishing for groundfish.

GOLF

There are 45 excellent golf courses in New Brunswick. Many provide sparkling views of the sea.

WHALE-WATCHING

Whether you yearn to see a humpback, finback, or minke whale, outfitters along the Bay of Fundy can take you where the action is. Most trips run May through September.

WINTER SPORTS

New Brunswick can get as much as 16 ft of snow each year, so winter fun often lasts well into spring. Dogsledding is taking off, ice-fishing communities pop up on many rivers, and you can always find someone to go tobogganing, skating, or snowshoeing with you. Snowmobiling has boomed: There are more than 9,000 km (5,580 mi) of groomed, marked, and serviced snowmobile trails and dozens of snowmobile clubs hosting special events.

For cross-country skiers, New Brunswick has groomed trails at such parks as Mactaquac Provincial Park near Fredericton, Fundy National Park in Alma, and Kouchibouguac National Park between Moncton and Bathurst. Many communities and small hotels offer groomed trails, but it's also possible to set off on your own. New Brunswick downhill ski areas usually operate from mid-December through April. There are four ski hills—Farlagne, Crabbe, Poley, and Sugarloaf.

Shopping

Fine art galleries proudly display and sell local artists' paintings and sculptures. Craft galleries, shops, and fairs brim with beautiful jewelry, glass, pottery, clothing, furniture, and leather goods. Some of the province's better bookstores even have sections devoted to New Brunswick authors, both literary and popular. You'll find a number of intriguing shopping areas in Saint John, as well as the Old City Market. Fredericton has the Saturday morning Boyce Farmers' Market and shops with crafts, treasures, and a bit of haute couture. The resort town of St. Andrews has some appealing craft stores and shops.

Exploring New Brunswick

In recent years high-tech companies in New Brunswick have helped lead much of the world onto the Information Highway, but all that has done little to change its settlement patterns. The population still clings to the original highways—rivers and oceans. In fact, the Saint John River in the west and the Fundy and Acadian Coasts in the south and east essentially encompass the province.

The Saint John River valley scenery is panoramic—gently rolling hills and sweeping forests, with just enough rocky gorges to keep it interesting. The French, English, Scots, and Danes who settled along the river have ensured its culture is equally intriguing. Here you'll find Fredericton, capital of the province.

The Fundy Coast is phenomenal. Yachts, fishing boats, and tankers bob on the waves at high tide, then sit high and dry on the ocean floor when it goes out. The same tides force the mighty Saint John River to reverse its flow in the old city of Saint John. The southwestern shores have spawned more than their share of world-class artists, authors, actors, and musicians. Maybe it's the Celtic influence; maybe it's the fog.

Along the Acadian Coast the water is warm, the sand is fine, and the accent is French—except in the middle. Where the Miramichi River meets the sea, there is an island of English, Irish, and Scottish tradition that is unto itself, rich in folklore and legend. Many people here find their livelihood in the forests, in the mines, and on the sea.

Numbers in the text correspond to numbers in the margin and on the New Brunswick, Fredericton, Downtown Saint John, and Greater Saint John maps.

Great Itineraries

IF YOU HAVE 3 DAYS

Plan to concentrate on one region if you only have a few days. Otherwise, because distances are so great, you'll spend all your time driving, and you'll have no time to enjoy the scenery, history, and culture. The Saint John River valley is best seen by following the well-marked River Valley Scenic Drive from **Edmundston** ⑦ to **Saint John** ⑪–㉓— a trip of about 380 km (236 mi).

This journey begins in the botanical gardens in **St-Jacques,** just outside Edmundston. The drive from Edmundston to ☒ **Fredericton** ①– ⑤ is about 275 km (171 mi) of panoramic pastoral and river scenery. With its Gothic cathedral, Victorian architecture, museums, theater company, and riverfront pathways, Fredericton is both beautiful and culturally rich. Don't miss nearby **Kings Landing Historical Settlement** ⑥, a faithful depiction of life on the river in the last century.

The drive from Fredericton to ☒ **Saint John** ⑪–㉓ is just over 100 km (62 mi) and passes through the village of **Gagetown** ⑩, a must-see for those who love art and history. Saint John is Canada's oldest incorporated city and celebrates its impressive heritage with enthusiasm.

IF YOU HAVE 6 DAYS

You can easily explore two regions of the province in six days. To the Saint John River valley region (with one night in ☒ **Fredericton** ①–⑤ and the next in ☒ **Saint John** ⑪–㉓) you can add the Fundy Coastal area: Here again it is easily seen by following the well-marked Fundy Coastal Drive. Visit ☒ **St. Andrews by-the-Sea** ㉕, where art, history, nature, and seafood abound. A whale-watching tour, which might entail a ferry ride to either **Grand Manan** ㉖ or **Deer Island** ㉘, is well worth the time and distance.

The Fundy Coastal Drive winds about 100 km (62 mi) along the coast past Saint John to the fishing village of **St. Martins** on Route 111. Follow the Fundy Coastal Route signs inland, over hill and dale to Hampton (back on Route 1) and up the Kennebecasis River Valley to Sussex. The Fundy Coastal Route soon heads back for the bay through Fundy National Park, but travelers would do better to stay on the Trans-Canada Highway for another 75 km (47 mi) and stop in ☒ **Moncton** ㉛ for two nights. This city is a microcosm of New Brunswick in that English and French flow with equal ease. It is also a center of Acadian French culture and education and has several attractions for children.

Moncton is a good starting point for touring the rest of the Bay of Fundy. Drive 80 km (50 mi) down the coast to Alma, the entrance to magnificent **Fundy National Park** ㉚. On the way back to Moncton are **Cape Enrage** and **Hopewell Cape,** where the Fundy Tides have sculpted gigantic flowerpots that turn into islands at high tide.

IF YOU HAVE 10 DAYS

With up to 10 days to explore New Brunswick you can see it all—much of the Acadian Coast as well as the Saint John River valley and the Bay of Fundy coast. For this tour you'll follow the Acadian Coastal Drive, another officially designated provincial tourist route that is well marked from Aulac to Campbellton, a distance of about 400 km (248 mi). But ☒ **Shediac,** about 30 km (19 mi) north of Moncton, is one place to start. Shediac is famous for lobsters and Parlee Beach. Another 65 km (40 mi) north is unspoiled **Kouchibouguac National Park,** which protects beaches, forests, and peat bogs. The coastal drive from the national park to 🖼 **Miramichi City** ㉜, about 75 km (47 mi), follows a fascinating network of fishing villages. Most of the communities are Acadian, but as you approach Miramichi City, English dominates again. Here a variety of cultural influences have created a rich history and tradition. A stopover in one of the city's motels will position you perfectly to begin your exploration of the Acadian Peninsula.

It is only about 120 km (74 mi) from Miramichi City to 🖼 **Caraquet** ㉝, but it might as well be a million. The entire peninsula is so different from the rest of the province it is like a trip to a foreign country: This is a romantic land with a dramatic history and an artistic flair. The **Acadian Historical Village** ㉞ is a faithful re-creation of the traditional Acadian way of life.

When to Tour New Brunswick
Late spring through fall are lovely times to visit, although lovers of winter sports have plenty of options, too. Whales are more plentiful in the Bay of Fundy after the first of August. Festivals celebrating everything from jazz to salmon are held from late spring until early fall.

FREDERICTON

The small inland city of Fredericton spreads itself on a broad point of land jutting into the Saint John River. Its predecessor, the early French settlement of St. Anne's Point, was established in 1642, during the reign of the French governor Villebon, who made his headquarters at the junction of the Nashwaak and the Saint John rivers. Settled by Loyalists and named for Frederick, second son of George III, the city serves as the seat of government for New Brunswick's 723,900 residents. Wealthy and scholarly Loyalists set out to create a gracious and beautiful place, and thus even before the establishment of the University of New Brunswick, in 1785, the town served as a center for liberal arts and sciences. It remains a gracious and beautiful place as well as a center of education, arts, and culture. The river, once the only highway to Fredericton, is now a focus of recreation, and the streets are shaded by leafy plumes of ancient elms.

Exploring Fredericton

Downtown Queen Street runs parallel with the river, and its blocks enclose historic sites and attractions. Most major sites are within walking distance of each other. An excursion to Kings Landing Historical Settlement (☞ Side Trip from Fredericton, *below*), a reconstructed village, can bring alive the province's history.

Dressed in 18th-century costume, actors from the Calithumpians theater company (☎ 506/457–1975) offer free historical walks from City Hall in July and August. Other tours can be arranged.

A Good Walk
Start at City Hall on Phoenix Square, at the corner of York and Queen streets. Once a farmers' market and opera house, its modern council chambers are decorated with tapestries that illustrate Fredericton's history. Walk down (as the river flows) Queen Street to Carleton Street to the **Military Compound** ①, which also contains the New Brunswick Sports Hall of Fame. If you arrive in Officers' Square at lunchtime in summer, you'll be treated to outdoor theater (☞ Nightlife and the Arts, *below*). On a rainy day the show goes on in the nearby College of Craft

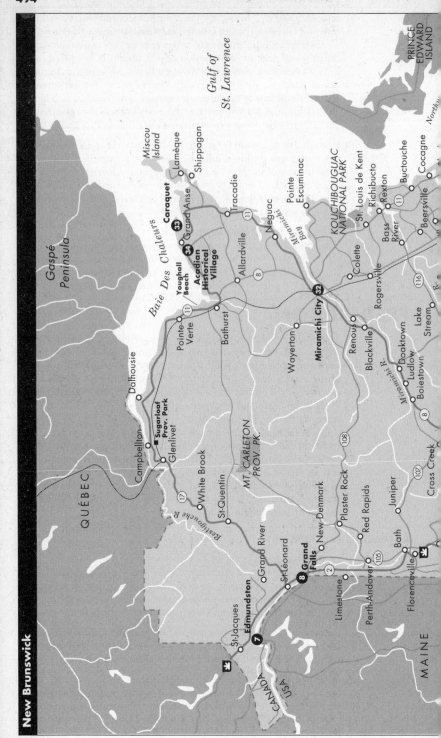

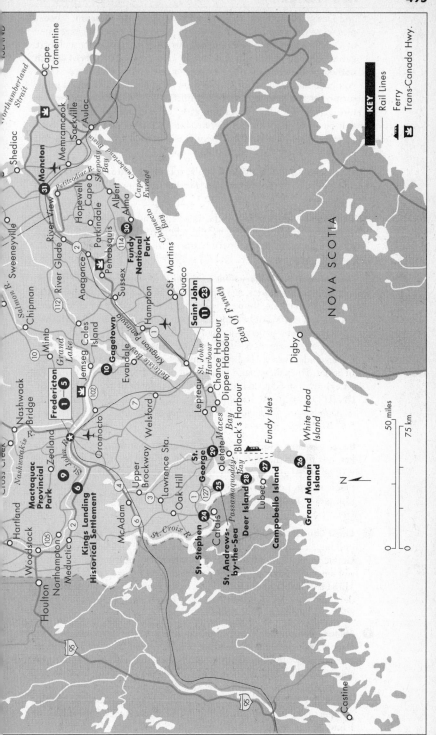

and Design. In Officers' Square, the **York-Sunbury Museum** ② occupies what were the Officers' Quarters. Next stop down the river side of Queen Street is the **Beaverbrook Art Gallery** ③, with its sculpture garden outside. Turn right on Church Street and walk to **Christ Church Cathedral** ④, with gleaming new copper on its renovated steeple. Once you have had your fill of its exquisite architecture and stained glass, turn right and start walking back up Queen. The **Provincial Legislature** ⑤ is on your left. Restaurants and cafés along Queen Street provide plenty of opportunities for refreshment. If you make your way back to **York Street** (across from where you started at City Hall), turn left to visit a chic block of interesting shops.

One variation to this walk: If you're touring on Saturday, start in the morning with the **Boyce Farmers' Market** to get a real taste of the city.

TIMING

The distances are not long, so the time you spend depends on how much you like sports, history, art, and churches. You could do it all in an afternoon, but start at the Boyce Farmers' Market on Saturday.

Sights to See

③ **Beaverbrook Art Gallery.** One of the gifts the late Lord Beaverbrook, former New Brunswick resident and multimillionaire British peer and newspaper magnate, showered upon his native province is this museum, with its collections of historic and contemporary art and the McCain "gallery-within-a-gallery" devoted to Atlantic Canadian artists. Salvador Dalí's gigantic canvas *Santiago el Grande* is here as well as canvasses by Reynolds, Turner, Hogarth, Gainsborough, and the Canadian Group of Seven. The gallery has a major collection of the works of Cornelius Krieghoff, famed Canadian landscape painter of the early 1800s. ⊠ *703 Queen St.,* ☎ *506/458–8545.* ☞ *$3.* ☉ *Mid-June–early-Sept., weekdays 9–6, weekends 10–5; mid-Sept.–mid-June, Tues.–Fri. 9–5, Sat. 10–5, Sun. noon–5.*

Boyce Farmers' Market. You can't miss this Saturday morning market; just follow the crowds. There's lots of local meat and produce, as well as baked goods, craft items, and seasonal items from wreaths to maple syrup. Look for good ready-to-eat food, whether it's German sausages or tasty sandwiches. ⊠ *Bounded by Regent, Brunswick, and George Sts.*

④ **Christ Church Cathedral.** One of Fredericton's prides, this gray stone building, completed in 1853, is an excellent example of decorated Gothic architecture and the first new cathedral foundation built on British soil since the Norman Conquest. Inside you'll see a clock known as "Big Ben's little brother," the test run for London's famous timepiece, designed by Lord Grimthorpe. ⊠ *Church St.,* ☎ *506/450–8500.* ☉ *Free tours June–Aug., daily 9–9.*

① **Military Compound.** The restored buildings of the former British and Canadian post include soldiers' barracks, a guardhouse, and a cell block. It extends two blocks along Queen Street. Redcoats stand guard; in summer a changing-of-the-guard ceremony takes place in Officers' Square at 11 and 7. Within the Military Compound stands the John Thurston Clark Building—an outstanding example of Second Empire architecture that now houses the ☞ **New Brunswick Sports Hall of Fame.** ⊠ *Queen St. at Carleton St.,* ☎ *506/453–2324.* ☞ *Free.*

New Brunswick Sports Hall of Fame. This attraction in the John Thurston Clark Building of the ☞ **Military Compound** celebrates the personalities and events that have shaped New Brunswick's rich sports heritage. Displayed in the main and second-floor galleries are an ex-

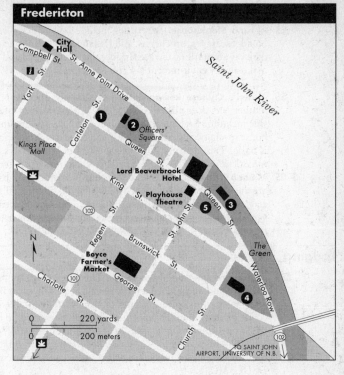

tensive collection of sports memorabilia and the original charcoal portraits of its more than 130 honored members. Special exhibits coincide with national and international sporting events. ✉ *503 Queen St.,* ☎ *506/453–3747.* 🎫 *Free.* 🕐 *Call for hrs of operation.*

⑤ Provincial Legislature. The interior chamber of the legislature, where the premier and elected members govern the province, reflects the taste of the late Victorians. The chandeliers are brass and the prisms are Waterford. Replicas of portraits by Sir Joshua Reynolds of King George III and Queen Charlotte hang here. There is a free-standing staircase, and a volume of Audubon's *Birds of America* is on display. ✉ *Queen St.,* ☎ *506/453–2527.* 🎫 *Free.* 🕐 *Legislature tours June–Aug., daily 9–6; Sept.–May, weekdays 9–4; library weekdays 8:15–5.*

York Street. This is the city's high-fashion block—trendy shops, a hairdresser cum art dealer, and an incense-burning boutique, to name a few. About the middle of the upriver side of the block is Mazucca's Alley, with more shops and the gateway to several pubs and restaurants.

② York-Sunbury Museum. Officers' Quarters houses a museum that offers a living picture of the community from the time when only First Nations peoples inhabited the area, through the Acadian and Loyalist days, to the immediate past. Its penny-farthing bicycle looks impossible to ride, and its World War I trench puts you in the thick of battle. It also contains the shellacked remains of a Fredericton legend, the puzzling Coleman Frog. ✉ *Officers' Sq., Queen St.,* ☎ *506/455–6041.* 🎫 *$2.* 🕐 *May–Labor Day, Mon.–Sat. 10–6 (also July–Aug., Mon. and Fri. 10–9, Sun. noon–6); Labor Day–mid-Oct., weekdays 9–5, Sat. noon–4; mid-Oct.–Apr., Mon., Wed., and Fri. 11–3, or by appointment.*

Dining

$$ ✕ **Luna Steakhouse.** Specialties include huge Caesar salads, garlic bread, escargots, brochettes, and Italian food. In fine weather you can dine on an outdoor terrace. Inside, the stucco walls and dark arches make a cozy environment. ⊠ *168 Dundonald St.,* ☎ *506/455–4020. AE, DC, MC, V.*

$$ ✕ **Mei's Chinese Restaurant.** In this family operation downtown, mother Mei does all the cooking. She serves a variety of Chinese cuisine including Szechuan, Cantonese, and Taiwanese; dumplings are a house specialty. Sushi is available if you call a day in advance. The decor is basic. This is a very popular spot for lunch weekdays. ⊠ *73 Carlton St.,* ☎ *506/454–2177. AE, MC, V. No lunch weekends.*

$–$$ ✕ **Bar B Q Barn.** Special children's menus and barbecued ribs and chicken are the standards; the blackboard lists plenty of other daily dinner specials, such as salmon, scallops, and chili. This local favorite has a convenient downtown location and is great for winding down; the bar serves fine martinis. ⊠ *540 Queen St.,* ☎ *506/455–2742. AE, DC, MC, V.*

Lodging

$$$ ⌸ **Howard Johnson Motor Lodge.** This HoJo is on the north side of the river and at the north end of the Princess Margaret Bridge. It has a terrace bar in a pleasant interior courtyard overlooked by the balconies of many of the rooms. Guest-room decor is standard for the chain. ⊠ *Trans-Canada Hwy., Box 1414, E3B 5E3,* ☎ *506/472–0480 or 800/596–4656,* FAX *506/472–0170. 116 rooms. Restaurant, bar, indoor pool, driving range, miniature golf, 4 tennis courts, exercise room. AE, D, DC, MC, V.*

$$$ ⌸ **Lord Beaverbrook Hotel.** A central location is this modern, seven-story hotel's main attraction. Some rooms have whirlpools or minibars. A veranda off the main dining room overlooks the river, and the bar is lively. ⊠ *659 Queen St., E3B 5A6,* ☎ *506/455–3371,* FAX *506/455–1441. 168 rooms. 2 restaurants, bar, no-smoking rooms, indoor pool. AE, DC, MC, V.*

$$$ ⌸ **Sheraton Fredericton.** Within months of being named Sheraton Inn of the Year for North America in 1996, this property was upgraded to a hotel. The only real difference is some small added amenities. It is still a stately riverside property within walking distance of downtown. The elegant country decor is almost as delightful as the sunset views over the river from the restaurant and many of the modern rooms. The gift shop carries topnotch crafts. ⊠ *225 Woodstock Rd., E3B 2H8,* ☎ *506/457–7000 or 800/325–3535,* FAX *506/457–4000. 223 rooms. Restaurant, bar, minibars, indoor pool, outdoor pool, hot tub, sauna, exercise room. AE, D, DC, MC, V.*

$$–$$$ ⌸ **Carriage House Inn.** This Heritage mansion has lovely bedrooms furnished with Victorian antiques. Homemade breakfast, complete with homemade maple syrup for the fluffy pancakes, is served in the solarium. Breakfast is included in the rates. ⊠ *230 University Ave., E3B 4H7,* ☎ *506/452–9924 or 800/267–6068,* FAX *506/458–0799. 10 rooms, 6 with bath. AE, MC, V.*

Nightlife and the Arts

The Arts

Theatre New Brunswick (⊠ 686 Queen St., ☎ 506/458–8344) performs in the Playhouse and tours the province. The **Playhouse** (⊠ 686 Queen St.) is the venue for theater and most other cultural performances, including Symphony New Brunswick and traveling ballet and dance companies. **The Calithumpians** offer summer outdoor theater daily—

12:15 weekdays, 2 PM weekends—in Officers' Square. Some top musicians and other performers appear at the larger **Aitken Center** (⊠ Rte. 102, ☎ 506/453–5054) on the University of New Brunswick campus near Fredericton.

Nightlife

Fredericton has lively nightlife, with lots of live music in downtown pubs, especially on the weekends. Just wander down **King Street** until you hear your kind of music. **Dolan's Pub** (⊠ 349 King St., ☎ 506/454–7474) has Celtic and folk-style entertainment. At **The Dock** (⊠ 375 King, ☎ 506/458–1254)), you'll hear rock, blues, folk— anything but country. **The Lunar Rogue** (⊠ 625 King St., ☎ 506/450–2065) has an old-world pub atmosphere and showcases acoustic folk, rock, and Celtic music.

Outdoor Activities and Sports

Rowing

Shells, canoes, and kayaks can be rented by the hour, day, or week at the **Aquatic Center** (☎ 506/462–6021), which also arranges guided tours and instruction.

Skiing

Crabbe Mountain Winter Park (⊠ Box 20187, Kings Place Postal Outlet, Fredericton, E3B 7A2, ☎ 506/463–8311) is in Lower Hainesville (about 55 km, or 34 mi, west of Fredericton). There are 14 trails, a vertical elevation of 853 ft, snowboard and ski rentals, instruction, babysitting, and a lounge and restaurant.

Walking

Fredericton has a fine network of walking trails, one of which follows the river from the Green, past the Victorian mansions on Waterloo Row, behind the Beaverbrook Art Gallery, and along the river bank to the Sheraton. Its total length is over 3 km (2 mi), but you can do shorter pieces. If you have a summer evening, walk it upstream, toward the Sheraton, and bask in the glow of a sunset. The visitor information center has a trail map.

Shopping

New Brunswick is known for its crafts, and mammoth **crafts markets** are held occasionally in Fredericton and every Labor Day weekend in Mactaquac Provincial Park (☞ Saint John River Valley to Saint John, *below*). For sale are pottery, blown glass, pressed flowers, metal flowers, turned wood, leather, quilts, and other fine items, many made by members of the New Brunswick Craft Council.

Aitkens Pewter (⊠ 65 Regent St., ☎ 506/453–9474) specializes in pewter goblets, belt buckles, and jewelry. **Gallery 78** (⊠ 96 Queen St., ☎ 506/454–5192), in a Victorian mansion, has works by local artists. **Mulhouse Country Classics** (⊠ Trans-Canada Hwy., ☎ 506/459–8859) is a gem for crafts, Tilley Endurable clothing, and handmade furniture. Excellent men's shoes can be bought at **Hartt's Shoe Factory** (⊠ 401 York St., ☎ 506/458–8358). **The Linen Closet** (⊠ 397 King St., ☎ 506/450–8393) sells Battenburg lace, exquisite bedding, and bathroom accessories.

Side Trip from Fredericton

West of Fredericton, the Kings Landing Historical Settlement was built by moving period buildings to a new shore. The Trans-Canada Highway takes you past some spectacular river and hill scenery. You'll pass the Mactaquac Dam (turn off here if you want to visit Mactaquac Provincial Park). The drive to Kings Landing takes less than a half hour, but to appreciate New Brunswick's background and history, plan to spend most of a day.

Kings Landing Historical Settlement

★ ☺ ❻ *30 km (19 mi) west of Fredericton.*

This excellent outdoor living history museum on the Saint John River evokes the sights, sounds, and society of rural New Brunswick between 1790 and 1900. The winding country lanes and meticulously restored homes will pull you back a century or more so you can learn firsthand how to forge a nail at the blacksmith's shop or bake bread on an open hearth. There are daily dramas in the theater, barn dances, and strolling minstrels. You'll see how the wealthy owner of the sawmill lived and just how different things were for the lowly immigrant farmer or the storekeeper. You can get a hearty meal from the Kings Head Inn. ✉ *Exit 259, Trans-Canada Hwy. (near Prince William)*, ☎ *506/363–5090.* 🎟 *$8.75.* ⊙ *June–mid-Oct., daily 10–5.*

SAINT JOHN RIVER VALLEY TO SAINT JOHN

The Saint John River forms 120 km (74 mi) of the border with Maine and rolls down to Saint John, New Brunswick's largest, and Canada's oldest, city. Gentle hills of rich farmland and the blue sweep of the water make this a pretty drive. The Trans-Canada Highway (Route 2) follows the banks of the river for most of its winding, 403-km (250-mi) course. At the northern end of the valley, near the border with Québec, is the mythical Republic of Madawaska. In the early 1800s the narrow wedge of land was coveted by Québec and New Brunswick; the United States claimed it as well. To settle the issue, New Brunswick governor Sir Thomas Carleton rolled dice all night with the governor of British North America at Québec. Sir Thomas won at dawn—by one point. Settling the border with the Americans was more difficult; even the lumbermen engaged in combat. Finally, in 1842, the British flag was hoisted over Madawaska county. One old-timer, tired of being asked to which country he belonged, replied, "I am a citizen of the Republic of Madawaska." So began the republic, which exists today with its own flag (an eagle on a field of white) and a coat of arms.

St-Jacques

280 km (174 mi) north of Fredericton.

This town near the Québec border contains Les Jardins de la République Provincial Park, with recreational facilities, the Antique Auto Museum, and a botanical garden. In the **New Brunswick Botanical Garden,** roses, rhododendrons, alpine flowers, and dozens of annuals and perennials bloom in the eight gardens while Mozart, Handel, Bach, or Vivaldi plays in the background. Two arboretums have coniferous and deciduous trees and shrubs. ✉ *Main St.,* ☎ *506/739–6335.* 🎟 *$4.75.* ⊙ *Mid-May–mid-Oct., daily 9–dusk.*

Skiing

Mont Farlagne (✉ Box 61, Edmundston E3V 3K7, ☎ 506/735–8401) in St-Jacques, near Edmundston, offers 17 trails on a vertical drop of 182 meters (600 ft). Its 4 lifts can handle 4,000 skiers per hour, and there is night skiing on 6 trails. Snowboarding and a tube slide add to the fun. There are equipment rentals, instruction, and a lounge with live music.

Edmundston

7 *5 km (3 mi) from St. Jacques, 275 km (171 mi) northwest of Fredericton.*

Edmundston, the unofficial capital of Madawaska, has always depended on the wealth of the deep forest around it. Even today, Edmundston looks to the Fraser Company pulp mills as the major source of employment. It was in these woods that the legend of Paul Bunyan was born; tales spread to Maine and even to the West Coast. The **Foire Brayonne** festival (☎ 506/739–6608), held annually during the last week of July, is proud to claim the title of the biggest Francophone festival outside of Québec's Winter Carnival. It is one of the most lively and vibrant cultural events in New Brunswick, offering concerts by acclaimed artists as well as local musicians and entertainers.

Grand Falls

8 *50 km (31 mi) south of St. Jacques.*

At Grand Falls, the Saint John throws itself over a high cliff, squeezes through a narrow rocky gorge, and emerges as a wider river. The result is a magnificent cascade, whose force has worn strange round wells in the rocky bed—some as much as 16 ft in circumference and 30 ft deep. A **pontoon boat** operates June–October at the lower end of the gorge ($8 adults, $4 children) and offers an entirely new perspective of the cliffs and wells. Tickets are available at the Malabeam Tourist Info Centre (✉ 24 Madawaska Rd., ☎ 506/475–7788).

The **Gorge Walk,** which starts at the tourist information center (✉ 24 Madawaska Rd.) and covers the full length of the gorge, is dotted with interpretation panels and interesting monuments. There is no charge for the walk, unless you descend to the wells ($2). According to Indian legend, a young maiden named Malabeam led her Iroquois captors to their deaths over the foaming cataract rather than guide them to her village.

The **Grand Falls Historical Museum** depicts local history. ✉ *209 Sheriff St.,* ☎ *506/473–5265.* ☑ *Free.* ☉ *July–Aug., Mon.–Sat. 9–5, Sun. 2–5; Sept.–June, by appointment.*

Shopping

The studio and store of the **Madawaska Weavers** (✉ Main St., St-Léonard, north of Grand Falls, ☎ 506/423–6341) has handwoven items known the world over. Handsome skirts, stoles, and ties are some of the items for sale.

En Route About 75 km (47 mi) south of Grand Falls, stop in **Florenceville** for a look at the small but reputable Andrew and Laura McCain Gallery (✉ McCain St., ☎ 506/392–5249), which has launched the career of many New Brunswick artists. The Trans-Canada Highway is intriguingly scenic, but if you're looking for less crowded highways and typical small communities, cross the river to Route 105 at Hartland (about 20 km, or 12 mi, south of Florenceville), via the **longest covered bridge** in the world—1,282 ft in length.

Mactaquac Provincial Park

9 *197 km (122 mi) south of Grand Falls.*

Within Mactaquac Provincial Park is Mactaquac Pond, whose existence is attributed to the building of the hydroelectric dam that has caused the upper Saint John River to flood as far up as Woodstock. Park facilities include an 18-hole golf course, two beaches with lifeguards, two marinas, supervised craft activities, and a dining room. There are 300 campsites; reservations are advised for high season. A privately operated power boat marina within the park rents canoes, paddleboats, windsurfers, and kayaks. ⊠ *Rte. 105 at Mactaquac Dam,* ☎ *506/363–4747.* ☒ *$3.50 per vehicle in summer, free off-season.* ☉ *Overnight camping mid-May–Thanksgiving.*

En Route   From Fredericton to Saint John you have a choice of two routes. Route 7 cuts away from the river to run straight south for its fast 109 km (68 mi). Route 102 leads along the Saint John River through engaging communities. You don't have to decide until you hit Oromocto, the site of the Canadian Armed Forces Base, **Camp Gagetown** (not to be confused with the pretty town of Gagetown farther downriver), the largest military base in Canada. Prince Charles completed his helicopter training here. The base has an interesting military museum. ⊠ *Building A5,* ☎ *506/422–1304.* ☒ *Free.* ☉ *July–Aug., weekdays 9–5, weekends and holidays noon–5; Sept.–June, weekdays noon–4. After-hrs tours can be arranged.*

Gagetown

❿ *50 km (31 mi) southeast of Fredericton.*

Gagetown, a pleasant historic community, bustles with artisans' studios and the summer sailors who tie up at the marina. The gingerbread-trimmed **Tilley House** takes you back to Canada's beginnings. Once the home of Sir Leonard Tilley, one of the Fathers of the Confederation, it now houses the **Queens County Museum.** ⊠ *Front St.,* ☎ *506/488–2966.* ☒ *$1.* ☉ *Mid-June–mid-Sept., daily 10–5.*

Shopping
Flo Grieg's (⊠ 36 Front St., ☎ 506/488–2074) carries superior pottery made on the premises. **Claremont House B&B** (⊠ Tilley Rd., ☎ 506/488–2825) displays unusual batik items and copper engravings. **Loomcrofters** (⊠ Loomcroft La. off Main St., ☎ 506/488–2400) is a good choice for handwoven items.

OFF THE   From Gagetown you can ferry across the river to Jemseg and continue
BEATEN PATH   to **Grand Lake Provincial Park** (☎ 506/385–2919), which offers freshwater swimming off the sandy beaches of Grand Lake. At Evandale (30 km, or 19 mi) south of Gagetown, you can ferry to Belleisle Bay and the beautiful **Kingston Peninsula,** with its mossy Loyalist graveyards and pretty churches.

Saint John

70 km (43 mi) south of Gagetown.

Saint John, the first incorporated city (1785) in Canada, has that weather-beaten quality common to so many antique seaport communities. Although the city is sometimes termed a blue-collar town because so many of its residents work for Irving Oil, its genteel Loyalist heritage lingers; you sense it in the grand old buildings, the ladies' teas at the old Union Club, and the lovingly restored redbrick buildings of the downtown harbor district.

In 1604 two Frenchmen, Samuel de Champlain and Sieur de Monts, landed here on Saint John the Baptist Day to trade with the natives. Nearly two centuries later, in May 1785, 3,000 Loyalists escaping from the Revolutionary War poured off a fleet of ships to found a city

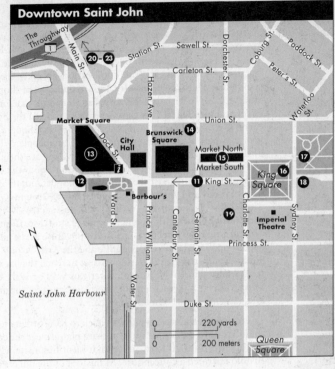

Downtown Saint John

amid the rocks and forests. From those beginnings, Saint John has emerged as a shipbuilding center and a thriving industrial port.

Up until the early 1980s, the buildings around Saint John's waterfront huddled together in forlorn dilapidation, their facades crumbling and blurred by a century of grime. A surge of civic pride sparked a major renovation project that reclaimed these old warehouses as part of a successful waterfront development.

The city has spawned many of the province's major artists—Jack Humphrey, Millar Brittain, and Fred Ross—along with such Hollywood notables as Louis B. Mayer, Donald Sutherland, and Walter Pidgeon. There's also a large Irish population that emerges in a jubilant Irish Festival every March. In July costumed residents reenact the landing of the Loyalists during the Loyalist City Festival.

Brochures for three good self-guided city tours are available at information centers, including one in Market Square. In July and August, free guided walking tours begin at 10 and 2 in Market Square at Barbour's General Store. For information call the Saint John Tourist and Convention Center (☎ 506/658–2990).

A Good Walk

Saint John is a city on hills, and **King Street** ⑪, its main street, slopes steeply to the harbor. A system of escalators/elevators and skywalks inside buildings means you can climb to the top and take in some of the more memorable spots without effort; you can also walk outside if you wish. Start at the foot of King, **Market Slip** ⑫. This is where the Loyalists landed in 1783 and is the site of **Barbour's General Store** and the Little Red Schoolhouse. Here you'll also find **Market Square**, with its visitor information center, restaurants, shops, and the fine **New Brunswick Museum** ⑬.

From the second level of Market Square, a skywalk crosses Dock Street and an escalator takes you up into the City Hall shopping concourse. Here, if you wish, you can branch off to the Canada Games Aquatic Centre and its pools and fitness facilities; and Harbour Station with a busy schedule of concerts, sporting events, and trade shows. Once you are through City Hall, another skywalk takes you across Chipman Hill and into the **Brunswick Square Complex** of shops, hotel, and office space. To visit historic **Loyalist House** ⑭, exit onto Germain Street and turn left: it's on the corner at the top of the hill. In the flavorful **Old City Market** ⑮, across from Brunswick Square, you'll make your way past fishmongers, farmers, and craftspeople. When you leave by the door at the top of the market, you will be at "the head of King" and right across Charlotte Street from **King Square** ⑯. Take a walk through the square, past the statues and bandstand, to Sydney Street. Cross Sydney and you're in the **Loyalist Burial Grounds** ⑰. Make your way back to Sydney Street at King Street East; across King Street is the **Old Courthouse** ⑱ with its amazing spiral staircase. Continue up Sydney; turn right on King Square South and you're at the gilded and gorgeous Imperial Theatre (☞ Nightlife and the Arts, *below*). Follow King Square South and cross Charlotte Street to reach the back door of historic **Trinity Church** ⑲. You can enter this way or walk back to King Street, turn left, and turn left onto Germain Street for the imposing gates and stairs of Trinity's main entrance.

To end your walk, make your way back to King Street and walk down the hill toward the water. You'll notice a plaque near the corner of Canterbury Street (at 20 King Street) that identifies a site where Benedict Arnold operated a coffeehouse. At the foot of the hill is **Prince William Street,** just steps from where you began at Market Slip. Turn left for wonderful shops and historic architecture.

TIMING

Allow the better part of a day for this walk, if you include a few hours for the New Brunswick Museum and some time for shopping. You can walk the route in a couple of hours, though. Note that on Sunday some of the indoor walkways will be closed, and so will the City Market.

Sights to See

Barbour's General Store. This 19th-century shop is filled with the mingled aromas of tobacco, pickles, smoked fish, peppermint sticks, and dulse, an edible seaweed. ⊠ *Market Slip,* ☎ *506/658–2939.*

Brunswick Square Complex. Buildings here include the Delta Brunswick Hotel and Brunswick Square, a multilevel mall and office tower. The major office tower tenant is NB Tel, a highly innovative communications company.

⑯ **King Square.** Laid out in a Union Jack pattern, this green refuge has a two-story bandstand and a number of monuments. In its northeast corner you'll find a strange mass of metal on the ground. It is actually a great lump of melted stock from a neighboring hardware store that was demolished in Saint John's Great Fire of 1877, in which hundreds of buildings were destroyed. ⊠ *Between Charlotte and Sydney Sts.*

⑪ **King Street.** The steep main street of the city is lined with solid Victorian redbrick buildings filled with a variety of shops.

⑰ **Loyalist Burial Grounds.** This cemetery, now a landscaped park, is like a history book published in stone. Brick walkways and a beaver-dam fountain make it a delightful spot. ⊠ *Off Sydney St., between King and E. Union Sts.*

⓮ Loyalist House. Daniel David Merritt, a wealthy Loyalist merchant, built this imposing Georgian structure in 1810. It is distinguished by its authentic period furniture and eight fireplaces. ⊠ *120 Union St.,* ☎ *506/652–3590.* ✍ *$2.* ☉ *June–Sept., daily 10–5; Oct.–May, by appointment.*

⓬ Market Slip. This waterfront area at the foot of King Street is where the Loyalists landed in 1783. Today it's the site of the Saint John Hilton, an information center, and restaurants, but you still get a feeling for the city's maritime heritage.

Market Square. Restored buildings on the waterfront have been attractively developed and hold historic exhibits, shops, restaurants, and cafés. Also here are the Saint John Regional Library and the fine New Brunswick Museum.

★ ☙ **⓭ New Brunswick Museum.** With three floors of natural history, New Brunswick history, and art galleries, this inviting museum has something for everyone. The full-size suspended right whale model and skeleton are impossible to miss. Hike through time on a geologic trail; encounter the industries that shaped the province, from logging to shipping, in displays that re-create the past; and see fine and decorative art from New Brunswick and around the world. There's also a Family Discovery Gallery and a gift shop. ⊠ *Market Sq.,* ☎ *506/643–2300.* ✍ *$6, free Wed. 6–9.* ☉ *Weekdays 9–9, Sat. 10–6, Sun. noon–5.*

⓯ Old City Market. Built in 1876 with a ceiling like an inverted ship's keel, the handsome market occupies a city block between Germain and Charlotte streets. Its temptations include fresh-cooked lobster, great cheeses, dulse, and tasty, inexpensive snacks, along with plenty of souvenir and craft items. ⊠ *47 Charlotte St.,* ☎ *506/658–2820.* ☉ *Mon.–Thurs. 7:30–6, Fri. 7:30–7, Sat. 7:30–5.*

⓲ Old Courthouse. This 1829 neoclassical building has a spiral staircase, built of tons of unsupported stones, that ascends seemingly by miracle for three stories. You can see the staircase year-round during business hours, except when court is in session. ⊠ *King St. E and Sydney St.* ✍ *Free.*

Prince William Street. South of King Street near Market Slip, this street is full of historic bank and business buildings. Today they hold interesting shops and galleries. At the foot of the street is the lamp known as the Three Sisters, which was erected to guide ships into the harbor in 1848.

⓳ Trinity Church. The church dates from 1880, when it was rebuilt after the Great Fire. Inside, over the west door, note the coat of arms—a symbol of the monarchy—rescued from the council chamber in Boston by a British colonel during the American Revolution. It was deemed a worthy refugee and given a place of honor in the church. ⊠ *115 Charlotte St.,* ☎ *506/693–8558 for information about hrs.*

A Good Drive

A car can take you to a number of area sights around downtown. The **Reversing Falls** ⑳ are a fascinating phenomenon. Any bus headed west from downtown will also take you there, or take Dock Street over the viaduct and on to Main Street. For the industrial waterfront route to the falls, turn left off Main at Keddy's Hotel. For a more scenic route, keep going up Main and turn left onto Douglas Avenue, with its grand old homes. A right turn off Douglas Avenue onto Fallsview Drive takes you to a great Reversing Falls lookout. If you continue down Douglas Avenue, keep right, and cross the Reversing Falls Bridge; the Reversing Falls Tourist Bureau and interpretation center are on your left.

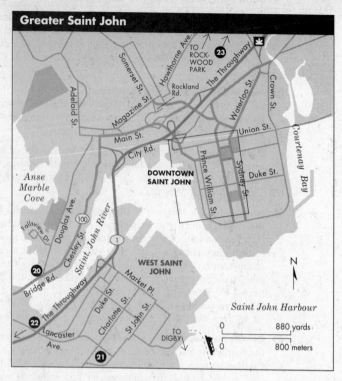

Also west of the city is the historic **Carleton Martello Tower** ㉑. Turn left from the Reversing Falls Tourist Bureau, past the Simms Brush Factory, and bear left when the road splits. The rest of the way is well marked. Off Route 1 at Catherwood Drive, the **Irving Nature Park** ㉒, 600 acres of volcanic rock and forest along the Bay of Fundy shore, has walking trails that make you feel far from the city. If you have children, you may want to visit **Cherry Brook Zoo** ㉓, to the north of downtown Saint John.

TIMING

To fully appreciate the Reversing Falls takes time; you need to visit at high, slack, and low tides. Check with any visitor information office for these times to help you plan a visit.

Sights to See

㉑ **Carleton Martello Tower.** This is a great place to survey the harbor. The tower was built during the war of 1812 as a precaution against American attack. The guides will tell you about the spartan life of a soldier living in the stone fort, and an audiovisual presentation outlines its role in the defense of Saint John during World War II. ⊠ *Whipple St. at Fundy Dr.* ☎ *506/636–4011.* ⊡ *$2.25.* ⊘ *June–mid-Oct., daily 9–5.*

㉓ **Cherry Brook Zoo.** An entertaining monkey house, wildebeests, and other exotic species are highlights of this small zoo. It's at the northern end of **Rockwood Park** (☎ *506/658–2829*), which has plenty of activities. ⊠ *R.R. 1, Sandy Point Rd.,* ☎ *506/634–1440.* ⊡ *$4.75.* ⊘ *Daily 10– dusk.*

㉒ **Irving Nature Park.** At this lovely 600-acre reserve on a peninsula close to downtown you can experience the ecosystems of the southern New Brunswick coast. Roads and seven walking trails up to several miles long make bird- and nature-watching easy. From downtown take

Route 1 west to Exit 107 (Catherwood Rd.) south; follow Sand Cove Road 4½ km (3 mi) to the park. ✉ *Sand Cove Rd*, ☎ *506/634–7135 for seasonal access.* ☜ *Free.*

➋ Reversing Falls. Twice daily at the Reversing Falls rapids, the strong Fundy tides rise faster than the river can empty, and the tide water attempts to push the river water back upstream. When the tide ebbs, the river once again pours over the rock ledges and the rapids appear to reverse themselves. To learn more about the phenomenon, watch the film shown at the **Reversing Falls Tourist Bureau.** There's a restaurant here, too. You can also ride a jet boat (☞ Outdoor Activities and Sports, *below*) for a closer (and wetter) look. A pulp mill on the bank is less scenic, and the stench it occasionally sends out is one of the less-than-charming parts of a visit. ✉ *Rte. 100, Reversing Falls Bridge*, ☎ *506/658–2937.*

Dining and Lodging

$$$ ✕ Top of the Town. This dining room at Keddy's Fort Howe Hotel has a spectacular view of the harbor and city as well as a sophisticated menu. Local seafood is creatively prepared; Fundy scallops are a specialty, and the Maritime Mix—mussels, herring, and lobster—is a favorite. ✉ *Main and Portland Sts.*, ☎ *506/657–7320, 506/657–7325 direct line after 5 PM. Reservations essential. AE, DC, MC, V.*

$$ ✕ Mexicali Rosa's. For a franchise this restaurant has a lot of character. The decor is essentially Santa Fe style, with adobe arches and so forth. The specialty is California-Mexican food, which is heavy on sauces, as opposed to Tex-Mex, which concentrates more on meats. Guests waiting to be seated can order a fine margarita in the large lounge. The chimichangas are with good reason the most popular dish. ✉ *88 Prince William St.*, ☎ *506/652–5252. AE, MC, V.*

$–$$ ✕ Grannan's. Seafood brochette with scallops, shrimp, and lobster tail, sautéed at your table in a white-wine and mushroom sauce, is a favorite in this nautically decorated restaurant, but there are abundant choices. The desserts, including bananas Foster flambéed at your table, are memorable. Dining spills over onto the sidewalk in summer. ✉ *1 Market Sq.*, ☎ *506/634–1555. AE, DC, MC, V.*

$–$$ ✕ Incredible Edibles. Here you can enjoy down-to-earth food—biscuits, garlic-laden hummus, salads, pastas, and desserts—in cozy rooms or, in summer, on the outdoor terrace. The menu also includes beef and chicken dishes. ✉ *42 Princess St.*, ☎ *506/633–7554. AE, DC, MC, V. Closed Sun.*

$$–$$$ ✕▥ Saint John Hilton. Part of the Market Square complex, this Hilton is furnished in Loyalist decor; guest rooms overlook the harbor or the town. Mellow antiques furnish corners of the Turn of the Tide dining room and the medieval-style Great Hall, which hosts banquets. A pedestrian walkway system connects the 12-story property to uptown shops, restaurants, a library, museum, an aquatic center, and a civic center. The large Turn of the Tide restaurant has terrific views of the harbor. Although the dining is pleasant at all times, with seafood and meat choices, the best meal is the Sunday brunch, with a long table full of dishes from the exotic to the tried-and-true. ✉ *1 Market Sq., E2L 4Z6*, ☎ *506/693–8484 or 800/561–8282 (Canada only)*, ℻ *506/657–6610. 197 rooms. Restaurant, bar, pool, exercise room. AE, D, DC, MC, V.*

$$–$$$ ✕▥ Shadow Lawn Country Inn. This charming inn is in an affluent
★ suburb, with tree-lined streets and palatial houses, 10 minutes from Saint John. Tennis, golf, horseback riding, and a yacht club are nearby. The inn has antique-furnished bedrooms, some with fireplaces; one suite has a whirlpool bath. The dining room is open to the public for three

meals a day; seafood is a specialty. Continental breakfast is included in the room rate. ⊠ *3180 Rothesay Rd., Rothesay E2E 5V7,* ☎ *506/ 847–7539 or 800/561–4166,* FAX *506/849–9238. 9 rooms, 2 suites. Restaurant. AE, D, DC, MC, V.*

Nightlife and the Arts

THE ARTS

The **Imperial Theatre** (⊠ King Sq., ☎ 506/633–9494 for box office), a beautifully restored 1913 vaudeville theatre, is home to Saint John's theater, opera, ballet, and symphony productions as well as road shows. **Aitken Bicentennial Exhibition Centre (ABEC)** (⊠ 20 Hazen Ave., ☎ 506/633–4870), in a former Carnegie library, has several galleries displaying the work of local artists and artisans, a hands-on science gallery for children, and a spring/fall Listen and Lunch series. Admission is free.

NIGHTLIFE

Taverns and lounges, usually with music of some kind, provide lively nightlife. Top musical groups, noted professional singers, and other performers regularly appear at **Harbour Station** (⊠ 99 Station St., ☎ 506/ 657–1234). **O'Leary's Pub** (⊠ 46 Princess St., ☎ 506/634–7135) is in the middle of the Trinity Royal Preservation Area and specializes in old-time Irish fun complete with Celtic performers; on Wednesday, Brent Mason, a well-known neo-folk artist, starts the evening with a set and then turns the mike over to the audience.

Outdoor Activities and Sports

BOAT TOURS

The **Reversing Falls Jet Boat** ride (⊠ 55 Fallsview Dr., 1 Market Sq., (☎ 506/634–8987 or 506/634–8824) could be the 20-minute thrill of a lifetime as you view the Reversing Falls close up. At complete low tide passengers must be 16 years or older; at other times children are welcome. Cost is $20 per person. **Harbor tours** are offered by Partridge Island Tours (☎ 506/693–2598) and DMK Marine Tours (☎ 506/ 635–4150).

KAYAKING

Kayaking along the Fundy coast has become very popular. **Eastern Outdoors** (⊠ Brunswick Sq., ☎ 506/634–1530 or 800/565–2925) has single and double kayaks, lessons, tours, and white-water rafting on the world-famous Reversing Falls Rapids and other river systems.

Shopping

Prince William Street provides interesting browsing in antiques shops and crafts boutiques. **House of Tara** (⊠ 72 Prince William St., ☎ 506/ 634–8272) is wonderful for fine Irish linens and woolens. **Brunswick Square** (⊠ King and Germain Sts., ☎ 506/658–1000), a vertical mall, has many top-quality boutiques. **Old City Market,** between Charlotte and Germain streets, bustles Monday–Saturday and stocks delicious local specialties, such as maple syrup and lobster.

THE FUNDY COAST

Bordering the chilly and powerful tidal Bay of Fundy is some of New Brunswick's loveliest coastline. A tour of the region will take you from the border town of St. Stephen and the lovely resort village of St. Andrews, past tiny fishing villages and rocky coves, to Fundy National Park, where the world's most extreme tides rise and fall twice daily. The Fundy Isles—Grand Manan Island, Deer Island, and Campobello—are havens of peace that have lured harried mainlanders for generations.

St. Stephen

24 *107 km (66 mi) west of Saint John.*

St. Stephen is over the St. Croix River from Calais, Maine. There's a provincial visitor information center (☎ 506/466–7390) on King Street. The town is a mecca for chocoholics, who converge on the small town during the Chocolate Festival held early in August. "Choctails," chocolate puddings and cakes, and even complete chocolate meals should come as no surprise when you realize that it was here that the chocolate bar was invented. Sample Ganong's famed, hand-dipped chocolates at the factory store, the **Ganong Chocolatier.** ⊠ *73 Milltown Blvd.,* ☎ *506/465–5611.* ☉ *July–Aug., weekdays 9–8, weekends 9–5; Sept.–Dec., daily 9–5; Jan.–June, Mon.–Sat. 9–5.*

Crocker Hill Studios and Gardens, on the banks of the St. Croix River, is a lovely oasis 3 km (2 mi) east of downtown. Walk down the path to the artists' studio of Steve Smith and his wife, Gail, with its watercolor bird paintings and carved decoys. It is surrounded by a fragrant, tranquil garden with hundreds of herbs and flowers. Relax on one of the comfortable garden benches and watch the osprey and eagles soar over the river. There is a gift shop. ⊠ *R.R. 3, Ledge Rd.,* ☎ *506/466–4251.* ☜ *$3.* ☉ *June–Sept., daily 10–5; Oct.–May, by appointment or chance.*

St. Andrews by-the-Sea

★ **25** *29 km (18 mi) southeast of St. Stephen.*

On Passamaquoddy Bay, St. Andrews by-the-Sea is one of North America's prettiest and least-spoiled resort towns. Long the summer place of the affluent (mansions ring the town), St. Andrews retains its year-round population of fishermen, and little has changed in the past two centuries. Of the town's 550 buildings, 280 were erected before 1880; 14 have survived from the 1700s. Some Loyalists even brought their homes with them piece by piece from Castile, Maine, across the bay, when the American Revolution didn't go their way.

Pick up a walking-tour map at the tourist information center at 46 Reed Avenue (next to the arena) and follow it through the pleasant streets. A particular gem is the **Court House** (⊠ 123 Frederick St., ☎ 506/529–4248), which is still active. Within these old stone walls is the **Old Gaol,** home of the county's archives. Tours are given weekdays 9–5. **Greenock Church,** at the corner of Montague and Edward streets, owes its existence to a remark someone made at an 1822 dinner party about the "poor" Presbyterians not having a church of their own. Captain Christopher Scott, who took exception to the slur, spared no expense on the building, which is decorated with a carving of a green oak tree in honor of Scott's birthplace, Greenock, Scotland. Take time to stroll along **Water Street** down by the harbor, with its assortment of eateries, gift and craft shops, and artists' studios.

The **Ross Memorial Museum** is a monument to an American family, summer residents of St. Andrews, who really appreciated beautiful things. ⊠ *188 Montague St.,* ☎ *506/529–1824.* ☜ *Free.* ☉ *Late May–June and early October, Mon.–Sat. 10–4:30; July–Sept., Mon.–Sat. 10–4:30, Sun. 1:30–4:30; shoulder seasons, Tues.–Sat. 10–4:30.*

Kingsbrae Gardens, a horticultural garden complete with mazes, is scheduled to open in spring 1998 on 27 acres of a historic estate. At press time no specific information was available on admission prices and hours. ⊠ *220 King St.,* ☎ *506/529–3335.*

The **Huntsman Aquarium and Museum** houses marine life and displays, including some very entertaining seals fed at 11 and 4 daily. ✉ *Brandy Cove Rd.,* ☎ *506/529–1202.* ✆ *$4.50.* ☉ *May–June, daily 10–4:30; July–Aug., daily 10–6; Sept.–Oct., Mon.–Tues. noon–4:30, Wed.–Sun. 10–4:30.*

OFF THE
BEATEN PATH   **MINISTERS ISLAND** – Besides being a huge estate, complete with an ocean-fed swimming pool, the house (not fully restored) and buildings on this island retreat are historically significant. Covenhoven was the summer home of Sir William Van Horne, chairman of the Canadian Pacific Railway, who presided over the railroad's push through the Rocky Mountains. Getting here is an adventure: Line up on the Bar Road at low tide (check local schedules), and you drive across the sand bar to the island for a tour. ✉ *Bar Rd., 5 km (3 mi) north of St. Andrews,* ☎ *506/ 529–5081 for tour information.* ✆ *$5.* ☉ *Open June–Oct., daylight hrs at low tide.*

Dining and Lodging

$$–$$$ ✕ **The Gables.** Salads, lobster rolls, fish and seafood fried or grilled, and fresh-made desserts are served in this casual harborside eatery. You can eat outside on the deck in summer. ✉ *143 Water St.,* ☎ *506/529– 3440. MC, V.*

$$$ ✕▥ **The Algonquin.** The wraparound veranda of this grand old resort
★   hotel overlooks wide lawns and lush gardens, and the bellmen wear kilts, setting a mood of relaxed elegance. Rooms, especially those in a new wing, are comfortable and attractively decorated. The excellent dining room is noted for its buffets and seafood. In good weather, meals are served on the veranda. There are fewer services in winter, so call if you plan to visit then. ✉ *Rte. 127, E0G 2X0,* ☎ *506/529–8823 or 800/563–4299,* FAX *506/529–4194. 250 rooms. 2 restaurants, 2 bars, pool, 9-hole and 18-hole golf course, tennis courts, health club, bicycles, children's program. AE, DC, MC, V.*

$$$–$$$$ ▥ **Kingsbrae Arms.** This restored 1897 estate (the first of its kind to receive five stars from the Canada Select rating agency) is an experience as much as it is a property. The many antique furnishings are both eclectic and entertaining. The decor is classy but full of pampering touches, the garden magnificent, and the owners gregarious. Breakfast is included. ✉ *219 King St., E0G 2X0,* ☎ *506/529–1897,* FAX *506/529– 1197. 6 rooms, 3 suites. Pool. MC, V.*

$$$ ▥ **Pansy Patch.** A visit to this B&B, a Normandy-style farmhouse built in 1912, is a bit like a close encounter with landed gentry who are patrons of the arts and who like their gardens as rich and formal as their meals. There's an art gallery. Breakfast is included in the price. Nonguests are welcome for lunch and dinner. ✉ *59 Carleton St., E0G 2X0* ☎ *506/529–3834. 5 rooms. Restaurant. D, MC, V.*

Outdoor Activities and Sports

GOLF

Algonquin Golf Club (☎ 506/529–3062) has a lovely setting.

WATER SPORTS

At the **Adventure Destination Center** on Market Wharf downtown, you can arrange to explore Passamaquoddy Bay on various kinds of boats. **Fundy Tide Runners** (✉ Market Wharf, ☎ 506/529–4481) uses a 24-ft Zodiac to search for whales, seals, and marine birds. **Seascape Kayak Tours** (✉ Market Wharf, ☎ 506/529–4866) provides instruction as well as trips around the area from a half day to a week.

Shopping

The Sea Captain's Loft (⊠ Water St., ☎ 506/529–3190) specializes in English and New Brunswick woolens, English bone china, and marvelous wool yarn. **Cottage Craft** (⊠ Town Sq., ☎ 506/529–3190) employs knitters year-round to make mittens and sweaters from their specially dyed wool. **Tom Smith's Studio** (⊠ Water St., ☎ 506/529–4234) is highly regarded for Asian *raku* pottery.

Grand Manan Island

26 *2 hrs by car ferry from Black's Harbour.*

Grand Manan, the largest of the three Fundy Islands, is also the farthest away from the mainland; you might see spouting whales, sunning seals, or a rare puffin on the way over. Circular herring weirs dot the island's coastal waters, and fish sheds and smokehouses lie beside long wharfs that reach out to bobbing fishing boats. Place names are romantic—Swallowtail, Southern Head, Seven Days Work, and Dark Harbour. It's easy to get around—only about 32 km (20 mi) of road lead from the lighthouse at Southern Head to the one at Northern Head. Grand Manan attracted John James Audubon, that human encyclopedia of birds, in 1831. The puffin is the island's symbol. Whale-watching expeditions can be booked at the Marathon Inn and the Compass Rose (☞ Dining and Lodging *and* Whale-Watching, *below*), and scuba diving to old wrecks is popular. You can make a day trip here or plan a longer stay and really relax. Ferry service is provided by **Coastal Transport** (☎ 506/662–3724).

Lodging

$$–$$$ 🏨 **Marathon Inn.** Perched on a hill overlooking the harbor, this gracious mansion built by a sea captain has guest rooms furnished with antiques. Whale- and bird-watching cruises can be arranged. The dining room specializes in seafood; it does not serve lunch. ⊠ *Box 129, North Head E0G 2M0,* ☎ *506/662–8488. 28 rooms, half with bath. Restaurant, 2 lounges, pool, tennis court. MC, V.*

$$ 🏨 **Compass Rose.** A couple from Montréal fell in love with the lovely guest rooms and comfortable turn-of-the-century furnishings in the two old houses that have been combined into this small, English-style country inn. They bought the inn and upgraded the dining room that overlooks the harbor, where they serve morning and afternoon teas as well as lunch and dinner. A full English breakfast is included in the rate. ⊠ *North Head E0G 2M0,* ☎ *506/662–8570. 8 rooms. Restaurant. MC, V.*

Outdoor Activities and Sports

TOURS

More than 240 species of seabirds nest on Grand Manan Island, which draws painters, nature photographers, hikers, and whale-watchers. Any of these activities can be arranged by calling **Tourism New Brunswick** (⊠ Box 12345, Fredericton E3B 5C3, ☎ 506/453–2170 or 800/561–0123).

WHALE-WATCHING

One New Brunswick experience that is difficult to forget is the sighting of a huge humpback, right whale, finback, or minke. Grand Manan boasts several whale-watching operators: **Ocean Search** (⊠ Marathon Inn, North Head, ☎ 506/662–8488); **Sea Land Adventure** (⊠ Box 86, Castalia E0G 1K0, ☎ 506/662–8997); **Island Coast Boat Tours** (⊠ Box 59, Castalia E0G 1L0, ☎ 506/662–8181); **Sea Watch Tours** (⊠ Box 48, Seal Cove E0G 3B0, ☎ 506/662–8552); **Surfside Boat Tours** (⊠ Box 147, Castalia E0G 1L0, ☎ 506/662–8156).

Campobello Island

★ ㉗   *45 min ferry ride from Deer Island. By road, drive to St. Stephen, cross the border to Maine, drive about 80 km (50 mi) down Rte. 1, then Rte. 190 to Lubec, Maine, and a bridge.*

Neatly manicured, preening itself in the bay, Campobello Island has always had a special appeal to the wealthy and the famous. It was here that the Roosevelt family spent their summers. The 34-room rustic summer cottage of the family of President Franklin Delano Roosevelt is now part of a nature preserve, **Roosevelt International Park,** a joint project of the Canadian and American governments. You can walk miles of trails here. President Roosevelt's boyhood home was also the setting for the movie *Sunrise at Campobello.* ⊠ *Roosevelt Park Rd.,* ☎ *506/752–2922.* 🎟 *Free.* ☉ *House late May–mid-Oct., daily 10–6; grounds daily.*

The island's **Herring Cove Provincial Park** (⊠ Welshpool, ☎ 506/752–7010) has camping facilities and a nine-hole golf course.

Dining and Lodging

$$ ✕🏨 **Lupine Lodge.** Originally a vacation home built by the Adams family (friends of the Roosevelts) around the turn of the century, these three attractive log buildings set on a bluff overlooking the Bay of Fundy are now a modern guest lodge. Nature trails connect it to Herring Cove Provincial Park. Two of the cabins comprise the guest rooms; the third houses the dining room, which specializes in simple but well-prepared local seafood. ⊠ *Box 2, Welshpool E0G 3H0,* ☎ *506/752–2555. 10 rooms, 1 suite. Restaurant, lounge. MC, V.*

$$ 🏨 **Owen House.** Mellow with history, this 200-year-old home, now a bit worn, was built by Admiral Owen, who fancied himself ruler of the island. Its gracious old rooms have hosted such luminaries as actress Greer Garson. Breakfasts are wonderful—pancakes come topped with local berries. ⊠ *Welshpool E0G 3H0,* ☎ *506/752–2977. 3 rooms. MC, V.*

Deer Island

㉘   *40 min by free car ferry from Letete, 13 km (8 mi) south of St. George.*

On Deer Island you'll enjoy exploring the fishing wharves, such as those at Chocolate Cove. Exploring the island takes only a few hours; it's 12 km (7 mi) long, varying in width from almost 5 km (3 mi) to a few hundred feet at some points. At **Deer Point** you can walk through a small nature park while waiting for the ferry to Campobello Island. If you listen carefully, you may be able to hear the sighing and snorting of **"the Old Sow,"** the second largest whirlpool in the world. If you can't hear it, you'll be able to see it, just a few feet offshore.

Lodging

$–$$ 🏨 **West Isles World B&B.** This white frame house overlooks the cove and offers three snug rooms with an informal country feel; the big upstairs bedroom has a water view. A full breakfast is included. The owners will arrange whale-watching cruises for you. ⊠ *Lord's Cove E0G 2J0,* ☎ *506/747–2946. 3 rooms. No credit cards.*

$ 🏨 **45th Parallel Motel and Restaurant.** Deer Island has only one motel—fortunately, it's clean and comfortable. A full breakfast is complimentary, and everything from lobster to hot sandwiches is available at the informal restaurant. Three of the rooms have kitchenettes. Pets are welcome. ⊠ *Fairhaven E0G 1R0,* ☎ *506/747–2231. 10 rooms. Restaurant. AE, MC, V.*

Whale-Watching

Cline Marine Tours (☎ 506/529–2287) offers scenic and whale-watching tours.

St. George

㉙ *40 km (25 mi) east of St. Stephen, 60 km (37 mi) west of Saint John.*

St. George is a pretty town with some excellent bed-and-breakfasts, one of the oldest Protestant graveyards in Canada, and a fish ladder running up the side of a dam. Water runs through this concrete staircase, allowing fish to jump, step by step, to the top and then jump back in the river.

Lodging

$$ 🏨 **Granite Town Hotel.** This hotel, built in 1990, has an old-country-inn feeling to it. The decor is subtle, with pine and washed-birch woodwork. Light blues and pinks dominate in the rooms. One side of the building overlooks an apple orchard; the other sits atop the bank of the Maguadavic River. A Continental breakfast is available but is not included in the rate; there is a barbecue available in summer. Two rooms have whirlpool baths. ⊠ *79 Main St., E0G 2Y0,* ☎ *506/755–6415,* FAX *506/755–6009. 32 rooms. Restaurant, bar, boating, bicycles. AE, D, DC, MC, V.*

Sailing

Fundy Yacht Sales and Charter (⊠ Rte. 2, Dipper Harbour, Lepreau E0G 2H0, ☎ 506/634–1530 or 800/565–2925) charters sailboats.

OFF THE BEATEN PATH

ST. MARTINS – About 45 km (28 mi) east of Saint John on Route 111, the fishing village of St. Martins has a rich shipbuilding heritage, whispering caves, miles of lovely beaches, spectacular tides, and a cluster of covered bridges. If you're tempted to linger, try the **St. Martins Country Inn** (☎ 506/833–4534).

Alma

135 km (84 mi) northeast of Saint John.

Alma is the small seaside town that services Fundy National Park. Here you'll find some motels, great lobster, and the local specialty, sticky buns.

★ **㉚** **Fundy National Park** is an awesome 206-square-km (80-square-mi) microcosm of New Brunswick's inland and coastal climates. Stand on a sandstone ledge above a dark-sand beach and watch the bay's phenomenal tide rise or fall. The park has 110 km (68 mi) of varied hiking and biking trails, as well as some gravel-surface auto trails. There's also golf, tennis, and a restaurant. ⊠ *Hwy. 114, Box 40, E0A 1B0,* ☎ *506/887–6000.* 🎫 *$3.50 in summer.*

Outdoor Activities and Sports

GOLF

The **Fundy National Park Golf Club** (☎ 506/887–2970) is nestled near cliffs overlooking the restless Bay of Fundy; deer grazing on the course are one of its hazards.

SKIING AND SNOWMOBILING

Poley Mountain Ski Area (⊠ Box 1097, Sussex E0E 1P0, ☎ 506/433–3230) is 10 km (6 mi) from Sussex. Its 13 trails and snowboard park mean there's fun for everyone on this 660-ft vertical drop. Poley is also on the groomed Fundy Snowmobile Trail between Saint John and Moncton.

Cape Enrage

15 km (9 mi) from Alma.

Route 915 takes you to the wild driftwood-cluttered beach at Cape Enrage, which juts out into the bay. There's a lighthouse and some spectacular views. You can arrange for rappelling and other adventures here.

Outdoor Activities and Sports

Cape Enrage Adventures (⌧ Site 5-5, R.R. 1, Moncton, ☎ 506/856–6081 off-season, 506/887–2273 mid-May–mid-Sept.) arranges rappelling; fee is $40 per person for 3 hours. Canoeing, kayaking, and hiking are other options.

Hopewell Cape

40 km (25 mi) from Alma.

The coast road (Route 114) from Alma to Moncton winds through covered bridges and along rocky coasts. **The Rocks Provincial Park** (⌧ Rte. 114, ☎ 506/734–2026 or 506/734–3429 in season) is home of the famous Giant Flowerpots—rock formations carved by the Bay of Fundy tides. They're topped with vegetation and are uncovered only at low tide, when you can climb down for a closer study.

MONCTON AND THE ACADIAN PENINSULA

The white sands and gentle tides of the Northumberland Strait and Baie des Chaleurs are as different from the rocky cliffs and powerful tides of the Bay of Fundy as the Acadians are from the Loyalists. This tour takes you from the burgeoning city of Moncton with its high-tech industries, past sandy dunes, and through Acadian fishing villages.

Moncton

31 *80 km (50 mi) north of Alma.*

A friendly town, often called the Gateway to Acadia because of its mix of English and French and its proximity to the Acadian shore, Moncton has a renovated downtown, where wisely placed malls do a booming business. You can pick up a walking tour brochure and see the city's historic highlights, too.

This city has long touted two natural attractions: the Tidal Bore and the Magnetic Hill. You may be disappointed if you've read too much tourist hype, though. In days gone by, before the harbor mouth filled with silt, the **Tidal Bore** was an incredible sight, a high wall of water that surged in through the narrow opening of the river to fill red mud banks to the brim. It still moves up the river, and the moving wave is worth waiting for, but it's nowhere near as lofty as it used to be, except sometimes in the spring. Bore Park on Main Street is the best vantage point; viewing times are posted there.

☾ **Magnetic Hill** creates a bizarre optical illusion. If you park your car in neutral at the designated spot, you'll seem to be coasting uphill without power. Shops, an amusement park, a zoo, a golf course, and a small railroad are part of the larger complex here; there are extra charges for the attractions. ⌧ *North of Moncton off Trans-Canada Hwy. (watch for signs).* ☉ *May–Labor Day, daily 8–8.* ⌑ *2$.*

☾ An excellent family water-theme park, **Magic Mountain,** is adjacent to Magnetic Hill. ⌧ *North of Moncton off Trans-Canada Hwy.,*

☎ *506/857–9283.* ▨ *$17.25.* ☉ *Mid-June–July 1 and mid-Aug.–Labor Day, daily 10–6; July 2–mid-Aug., daily 10–8.*

Among Moncton's notable attractions is the **Acadian Museum,** at the University of Moncton, whose remarkable collection of artifacts reflects 300 years of Acadian life in the Maritimes. ⊠ *Clement Cormier Bldg., Archibald St.,* ☎ *506/858–4088.* ▨ *Free.* ☉ *June–Sept., weekdays 10–5, weekends 1–5; Oct.–May, Tues.–Fri. 1–4:30, weekends 1–4.*

Dining and Lodging

$$ ✕ **Cy's Seafood Restaurant.** This restaurant, decorated in dark wood
★ and brass, has been serving generous portions for decades. Though renowned for its seafood casserole, the restaurant also offers reliable scallop, shrimp, and lobster dishes. You can see the Tidal Bore from the windows. ⊠ *170 Main St.,* ☎ *506/857–0032. AE, DC, MC, V.*

$$ ✕ **Fisherman's Paradise.** In spite of the enormous dining area, which seats more than 350 people, this restaurant serves memorable à la carte seafood dishes in an atmosphere of candlelight and wood furnishings. ⊠ *375 Dieppe Blvd.,* ☎ *506/859–4388. AE, DC, MC, V.*

$$–$$$ ✕⬚ **Chez Françoise.** This lovely old mansion with a wraparound ve-
★ randa has been decorated in Victorian style. There are 9 guest rooms (six with private bath) in this house; another building across the street houses 10 (four with bath). Front rooms in the main house have water views. The dining room, open to the public for dinner, serves excellent traditional French cuisine with an emphasis on seafood. ⊠ *93 Main St., Shediac (30 km/19 mi northeast of Moncton),* ☎ *506/532–4233. 19 rooms, 10 with bath. Restaurant, bar. AE, D, DC, MC, V. Closed Jan.–May 1.*

$$$ ⬚ **Best Western Crystal Palace.** Moncton's newest hotel has theme rooms (want to be Ali Baba or Elvis for a night?) and, for families, an indoor pool and a miniature wonderland of rides, midway stalls, and coin games. Champlain Mall is just across the parking lot. ⊠ *499 Paul St.,* ☎ *506/ 858–8584,* ℻ *506/858–5486. 115 rooms. Restaurant, indoor pool. AE, D, DC, MC, V.*

$$$ ⬚ **Hotel Beausejour.** Moncton's finest hotel, conveniently located
★ downtown, has friendly service. The decor of the guest rooms echoes the city's Loyalist and Acadian roots. L'Auberge, the main hotel restaurant, has a distinct Acadian flavor. The Windjammer dining room is more formal, modeled after the opulent luxury liners of the turn of the century, and reservations are required. ⊠ *750 Main St.,* ☎ *506/854– 4344, 800/441–1414 in Canada and the U.S., 800/561–2328 in the Maritimes and Québec,* ℻ *506/858–0957. 314 rooms. 2 restaurants, bar, café, indoor pool, exercise room. AE, DC, MC, V.*

$$$ ⬚ **Victoria B & B.** This heritage home in the heart of downtown has antique-furnished rooms, with terry robes and aromatic bath gels. The full breakfast, served in the dining room and included in the rate, often features chocolate pecan and orange brandy French toast. ⊠ *71 Park St., E1C 2B2,* ☎ *506/389–8296,* ℻ *506/389–8296. 3 rooms. Dining room, in-room VCRs. MC, V.*

$$ ⬚ **Marshlands Inn.** In this white clapboard inn, a welcoming double
★ living room with fireplace sets the informal country atmosphere. Bedrooms are furnished with sleigh beds or four-posters, and all have telephones. ⊠ *Box 1440, Sackville (53 km/33 mi east of Moncton) E0A 3C0,* ☎ *506/536–0170, 800/561–1256 in Canada,* ℻ *506/536– 0721. 19 rooms. Restaurant. AE, DC, MC, V.*

Nightlife and the Arts

THE ARTS

Top musicians and other performers appear at the **Colosseum** (☎ 506/857–4100).

NIGHTLIFE

Moncton's downtown really rocks at night. **Au Deuxième** (✉ 837 Main St., ☎ 506/383–6192) has live music on the weekends, mostly Francophone artists. **Ziggy's** (✉ 730 Main St., ☎ 506/858–8844) offers dance music and fun promotions. **Club Cosmopolitan** (✉ 700 Main St., ☎ 506/857–9117) is open Wednesday through Saturday for dancing, rock, jazz, or the blues. It's billed as one cool club with four different atmospheres. **Chevy's** (✉ 939 Mountain Rd., ☎ 506/858–5861) has comedy, rock and roll, and traditional music.

Shopping

Five spacious malls and numerous pockets of shops make Moncton and Dieppe the best places to shop in New Brunswick.

En Route   Along the coast from Moncton on Route 11 you'll find **Shediac,** a resort town with the warm waters of Parlee Beach and lots of good lobster feeds.

Kouchibouguac National Park

100 km (62 mi) north of Moncton.

★   The white, dune-edged beaches of **Kouchibouguac National Park** are some of the finest on the continent. Kellys Beach and Callander's Beach are supervised and have facilities. The park also protects forests and peat bogs. You can bicycle, canoe, boat, and picnic. There are 311 campsites; reservations are accepted. ✉ *Off Rtes. 11 and 134, Kent County,* ☎ *506/876–2443.* ☜ *$3.50.*

Miramichi City

❸❷   *150 km (93 mi) north of Moncton.*

The fabled Miramichi region is one of lumberjacks and fishermen. Celebrated for salmon rivers that reach into some of the province's richest forests, and the ebullient nature of its residents (Scottish, English, Irish, and a smattering of native and French), this is a land of stories, folklore, and lumber kings.

Sturdy wood homes dot the banks of Miramichi Bay at newly formed Miramichi City, which in 1995 incorporated the former towns of Chatham and Newcastle and several small villages. This is also where the politician and British media mogul Lord Beaverbrook grew up and is buried.

The **Miramichi Salmon Museum** provides a look at the endangered Atlantic salmon and at life in noted fishing camps along the rivers. ✉ *297 Main St., Doaktown, 80 km (50 mi) southwest of Miramichi City,* ☎ *506/365–7787.* ☯ *June–Sept. daily 9–5.* ☜ *$4.*

The **Woodmen's Museum,** with artifacts that date from the 1700s to the present, is in what looks like two giant logs set on more than 60 acres of land. The museum portrays a lumberman's life through displays, but its tranquil grounds are excuse enough to visit. There are picnic facilities and camping sites. ✉ *Rte. 8, Boiestown, 110 km (68 mi) southwest of Miramichi City,* ☎ *506/369–7214.* ☜ *$5.* ☯ *May–Sept., daily 9–5.*

Lodging

$$ ⊞ **Pond's Chalet Resort.** You'll get a traditional fishing-camp experience in this lodge and the chalets set among trees overlooking a salmon river. The accommodations in Ludlow, 15 km (9 mi) northwest of Boiestown, are comfortable but not luxurious. You can canoe and bicycle here, too. The dining room turns out reliable but undistinguished food. ⊠ *Ludlow E0C 1N0 (watch for signs on Rte. 8),* ☎ *506/369–2612,* FAX *506/369–2293. 10 guest rooms, a 5-bedroom lodge, and 14 cabins. Bar, dining room, tennis court, volleyball, snowmobiling. AE, DC, MC, V.*

$$ ⊞ **Wharf Inn.** Here, in Miramichi country, the staff is friendly and the restaurant serves excellent salmon dinners. This low-rise modern building has two wings; guest rooms in the executive wing have extra amenities. ⊠ *Jane St.,* ☎ *506/622–0302,* FAX *506/622–0354. 70 rooms. Restaurant, bar, patio lounge, no-smoking rooms, indoor pool. AE, DC, MC, V.*

Outdoor Activities and Sports

In winter **Miramichi Four Seasons Outfitters** (⊠ Box 705, R.R. 2, ☎ 506/622–0089) offers custom dogsledding packages for all levels. In summer the outfitter leads hiking tours of the rocky coastline and inland highland tours for both experienced and casual trekkers.

Caraquet

㉝ *118 km (73 mi) north of Miramichi City.*

Caraquet, on the Acadian Peninsula, is perched along the Baie des Chaleurs, with Québec's Gaspé Peninsula beckoning across the inlet. The town is rich in French flavor and hosts an **Acadian Festival** (☎ 506/727–6515) each August. Beaches are another draw here.

★ ☙ **㉞** A highlight of the Acadian Peninsula is the **Acadian Historical Village,** 10 km (6 mi) west of Caraquet. The more than 40 original buildings re-create an early Acadian community between 1780 and 1890. Summer days are wonderfully peaceful: the chapel bell tolls, ducks waddle and quack under a footbridge, wagons creak, and the smell of hearty cooking wafts from cottage doors. Costumed staff act as guides and demonstrate trades; a restaurant serves old-Acadian dishes. ⊠ *Rte. 11,* ☎ *506/726–2600.* ☜ *$8.75.* ☉ *June–Labor Day, daily 10–6; some buildings open in Sept., daily 10–5.*

Dining and Lodging

$–$$ ✕⊞ **Hotel Paulin.** The word *quaint* really fits this property. Each pretty room has its own unique look, with old pine dressers and brass beds, and the colors are as bright and cheerful as the seaside town. An excellent small dining room specializes in fresh fish cooked to perfection, Acadian style. ⊠ *143 blvd. St-Pierre W, E1W 1B6,* ☎ *506/727–9981. 9 rooms, 4 with bath, 1 suite. Dining room. MC, V.*

Skiing

Sugarloaf Provincial Park (⊠ Box 629, Atholville E0K 1A0, ☎ 506/789–2366) is in Atholville, 180 km (112 mi) north of Caraquet. The eight trails on this 507-ft vertical drop accommodate all levels. There are also 25 km (16 mi) of cross-country ski trails. Instruction and equipment rentals are available; the park has a lounge and cafeteria.

NEW BRUNSWICK A TO Z

Arriving and Departing

By Plane

Air Canada and its regional carrier **Air Nova** (☎ 800/776–3000 in the U.S., 800/661–3936 in Canada) serve New Brunswick in Saint John, Moncton, Fredericton, Bathurst, and St-Léonard, and fly to the Atlantic provinces from Montréal, Toronto, and Boston.

Canadian Airlines International operates through **Air Atlantic** (☎ 800/426–7000 in the U.S., 800/665–1177 in Canada) in Saint John, Fredericton, Moncton, Charlo, and Miramichi, and serves the Atlantic provinces, Montréal, Ottawa, and Boston.

By Train

VIA Rail (☎ 800/562–3952) offers passenger service six times a week from Moncton to Montréal and Halifax.

Getting Around

By Bus

SMT Eastern Ltd. (☎ 506/859–5100 or 800/567–5151) runs buses within the province and connects with most major bus lines.

By Car

New Brunswick has an excellent highway system with numerous facilities. The Trans-Canadian Highway, marked by a maple leaf, is the same as Route 2. The only map you'll need is the one available at the tourist information centers listed below. Major entry points are at St. Stephen, Houlton, Edmundston, and Cape Tormentine from Prince Edward Island, and Aulac from Nova Scotia.

Contacts and Resources

Emergencies

Dial 911 for **medical, fire, and police** emergencies anywhere in New Brunswick.

Hospitals

Chaleur Regional Hospital (⊠ 1750 Sunset Dr., Bathurst, ☎ 506/548–8961). **Campbellton Regional Hospital** (⊠ 189 Lilly Lake Rd., Campbellton, ☎ 506/789–5000). **Edmundston Regional Hospital** (⊠ 275 Hébert Blvd., ☎ 506/739–2211). **Dr. Everett Chalmers Hospital** (⊠ Priestman St., Fredericton, ☎ 506/452–5400). **Moncton City Hospital** (⊠ 135 MacBeath Ave., Moncton, ☎ 506/857–5111). **Dr. Georges Dumont Hospital** (⊠ 330 Archibald St., Moncton, ☎ 506/862–4000). **Saint John Regional Hospital** (⊠ Tucker Park Rd., Saint John, ☎ 506/648–6000). **Miramichi Regional Hospital** (⊠ 500 Water St., Miramichi, ☎ 506/623–3000).

Outdoor Activities and Sports

Whale-watching, sea kayaking, trail riding, bird-watching, garden tours, river cruising, and fishing are part of the province's day-adventure program, "Adventures Left and Right." The more than 60 packages cover a variety of skill levels and include equipment. All adventures last at least a half day; some are multiday. Get full details at a New Brunswick Adventure Destination Centre (in some information offices, hotels, and attractions), or contact **Tourism New Brunswick** (⊠ Box 12345, Fredericton E3B 5C3, ☎ 506/453–2170 or 800/561–0123).

BIKING

B&Bs frequently have bicycles for rent and Tourism New Brunswick has listings and free cycling maps. **Covered Bridge Bicycle Tours** (⊠ Dept. F, Box 693, Main Post Office, Saint John E2L 4B3, ☎ 506/849–9028) leads bike trips in the province.

FISHING

New Brunswick Fish and Wildlife (☎ 506/453–2440) can give you information on sporting licenses and tell you where the fish are.

GOLF

Greens fees run about $20–$25, $15 for some nine-hole courses; visitors are generally welcome. For a list of golf courses, contact Tourism New Brunswick (☞ Visitor Information, *below*) or the New Brunswick Golf Association (565 Priestman St, Fredericton, E3B 5X8).

HIKING

For general trail information, contact Eric Hadley at the **New Brunswick Trails Council** (⊠ Dept. of Natural Resources and Energy, Box 6000, Fredericton E3B 5H1, ☎ 506/453–2730).

SNOWMOBILING

For information on snowmobiling in New Brunswick contact the **New Brunswick Federation of Snowmobile Clubs** (⊠ Box 29, Woodstock E0J 2B0, ☎ 506/325–2625).

Visitor Information

Tourism New Brunswick (⊠ Box 12345, Fredericton E3B 5C3, ☎ 506/453–2170 or 800/561–0123) can provide information on day adventures, scenic driving routes, accommodations, and the seven provincial tourist bureaus. Also helpful are information services of the cities of **Bathurst** (☎ 506/548–0410), **Campbellton** (☎ 506/789–2700), **Fredericton** (☎ 506/452–9508), **Moncton** (☎ 506/853–3590), and **Saint John** (☎ 506/658–2990).

12 Prince Edward Island

In the Gulf of St. Lawrence north of Nova Scotia and New Brunswick, Prince Edward Island seems too good to be true, with its crisply painted farmhouses, manicured green fields rolling down to sandy beaches, the warmest ocean water north of Florida, lobster boats in trim little harbors, and a vest-pocket capital city, Charlottetown, packed with architectural heritage.

Updated by
Julie V. Watson

WHEN YOU EXPERIENCE Prince Edward Island, known locally as the Island, you'll understand instantly why Lucy Maud Montgomery's novel of youth and innocence, *Anne of Green Gables,* was framed against this land. What may have been unexpected, however, was how the story burst on the world in 1908 and is still selling untold thousands of copies every year. After potatoes and lobsters, Anne is the Island's most important product.

In 1864, Charlottetown, the Island's capital city, hosted one of the most important meetings in Canadian history, which eventually led to the Dominion of Canada in 1867. Initially, Prince Edward Island was reluctant to join, having spent years fighting for the right to an autonomous government. Originally settled by the French in 1603, the Island was handed over to the British under the Treaty of Paris in 1763. Tension ensued as British absentee governors and proprietors failed to take an active interest in the development of the land, and the resulting parliamentary government that was granted islanders proved ineffective for similar reasons. The development of fisheries and agriculture at the turn of the century strengthened the economy. Soon settlement increased and those who were willing to take a chance on the island prospered.

Around the middle of the century, a modern cabinet government was created and relations between tenants and proprietors worsened. At the same time talk of creating a union with other North American colonies began. After much deliberation, and despite the fact that political upheaval had begun to subside, delegates decided that it was in the Island's best economic interest to join the Confederation.

The recent construction of the Confederation Bridge, which connects Borden-Carleton with Cape Tormentine in New Brunswick, physically seals Prince Edward Island's connection with the mainland, and some islanders are fearful that the province's easygoing character will be sacrificed for the widespread development of unseemly tourist attractions. As you explore the landscape—a vast spectrum of colors giving way to crossroads villages and fishing ports—it's not hard to understand why Islanders love their isolation. Outside the tourist mecca of Cavendish, otherwise known as Anne's land, the Island seems like an oasis of peace in a world of turmoil.

Pleasures and Pastimes

The Arts
The arts, particularly theater, are an integral part of the Island. Summer productions and theater festivals are an Island highlight. The grandest is the Charlottetown Festival, which takes place from June through mid-September at the Confederation Centre of the Arts. Theater in Summerside, Georgetown, and Victoria is also good. Live traditional Celtic music, with fiddling and step dancing, can be heard almost any day of the week.

Beaches
Prince Edward Island is ringed by beaches, and few of them are heavily used. Ask a dozen islanders to recommend their favorites. Basin Head Beach, near Souris, says one—miles of singing sands, utterly deserted. West Point, says a second—lifeguards, restaurants nearby, showers at the provincial park. Greenwich, near St. Peter's Bay, another suggests—a half-hour walk through magnificent wandering dunes brings you to an endless empty beach.

Dining

On Prince Edward Island, wholesome, home-cooked fare is a matter of course. Talented chefs ensure fine cuisine in each region. The service is friendly—though a little laid back at times—and the setting is generally informal. Seafood is usually good anywhere on the island, with top honors being given to lobster.

Look for lobster suppers, offered both commercially and by church and civic groups. These meals feature lobster, rolls, salad, and mountains of sweet, home-baked goods. Regular suppers are held daily in New London from mid-May through September. Check the local papers, bulletin boards at local grocery stores, or Visitor Information Centres for other community suppers.

CATEGORY	COST*
$$$$	over $35
$$$	$25–$35
$$	$15–$25
$	under $15

*per person, excluding drinks, service, 10% sales tax, and 7% GST.

Lodging

Prince Edward Island offers a variety of accommodations at a variety of prices, from full-service resorts and luxury hotels to moderately priced motels, cottages, and lodges, to farms that take guests. Lodgings in summer should be booked early, especially if you are planning a long stay.

CATEGORY	COST*
$$$$	over $75
$$$	$55–$75
$$	$40–$55
$	under $40

*All prices are for a standard double room, excluding 10% provincial sales tax and 7% GST.

Outdoor Activities and Sports

BIKING

Prince Edward Island is popular with bike-touring companies for its moderately hilly roads and stunning scenery. Level areas can be found over most of the island, especially east of Charlottetown to Montague and along the north shore. However, shoulderless, narrow, secondary roads in some areas and summer's car traffic can be challenging for cyclists. A 9-km (5½-mi) path near Cavendish campground loops around marsh, woodland, and farmland. Cycling trips are organized throughout the province, and Prince Edward Island's visitor services can recommend tour operators.

GOLF

Prince Edward Island has several beautiful courses with scenic vistas. Golfing is virtually hassle-free: Tee times are easily booked any day of the week, rates are inexpensive, and courses uncrowded, particularly in the fall.

HIKING

Hiking within the lush scenic areas of Prince Edward Island National Park and provincial parks is encouraged with marked trails. Many of the trails are being upgraded to provide quality surfaces great for walking, hiking, or cycling. One of them is Confederation Trail, a provincial trail system, which will eventually allow outdoors explorers to travel 350 km (217 mi) within the province.

Exploring Prince Edward Island

Prince Edward Island is very irregular in shape, with deep inlets and tidal streams that nearly divide the province into three equal parts, known locally by their county names of Kings, Queens, and Prince (east to west). It is indeed a rich agricultural region surrounded by beautiful sand beaches, delicate dunes, and stunning red sandstone cliffs. The land in the east and central sections consists of gentle hills, creating a rolling landscape that can tax bicyclists. Nevertheless, the land never rises to a height of more than 500 ft above sea level, and you are never more than 15 minutes from a beach or waterway. To the west, from Summerside to North Cape, the land is flatter.

Numbers in the text correspond to numbers in the margin and on the Prince Edward Island and Charlottetown maps.

Great Itineraries

Visitors often tour only the central portion of the Island, taking Confederation Bridge from New Brunswick to Borden-Carleton, and exploring Anne country and the PEI National Park. To more deeply experience the Island's character, stray to the wooded hills of the east—to compact, bustling Montague, straddling its river. Or go west to superb, almost-private beaches, the Acadian parish of Tignish, and the silver-fox country around Summerside. Even if you're in a rush, it won't take long to get off and back on the beaten path: In most places you can cross the Island, north to south, in half an hour or so. The four tours detailed in this chapter are designed to include as many Island essentials as possible; Charlottetown is primarily a walking tour, while the others follow the major scenic highways—Blue Heron Drive, Kings Byway, and Lady Slipper Drive. There are plenty of chances to get out of the car, go fishing, hit the beach, photograph wildflowers, or just watch the sea roll in.

IF YOU HAVE 1 DAY

Leaving ⌾ **Charlottetown** ①–⑨ on Route 2 west, take Route 15 north to **Brackley Beach** ⑪. This puts you onto a 137-km-long (85-mi-long) scenic drive marked with signs depicting a blue heron. Route 6 west will take you to **Cavendish** ⑫, an entryway to **PEI National Park** ⑩. Cavendish is home to the fictional character Anne of Lucy Maud Montgomery's *Anne of Green Gables*. This area has enough attractions for a full day, but if you prefer to keep exploring, continue west on Route 6, where charming museums vie with fishing wharfs and scenic vistas for your attention. Blue Heron Drive joins Route 20, where you'll find the **Anne of Green Gables Museum** at Silver Bush; it offers a glimpse into the life of author Lucy Maud Montgomery in the early 1900s, with a farm, wagon rides, and a family atmosphere. Continue west, then south on Route 20 and rejoin Route 2 south until turning onto Route 1 east and back to Charlottetown.

IF YOU HAVE 2 DAYS

Leaving ⌾ **Charlottetown** ①–⑨ early in the day, follow Highway 1 east to Kings Byway Scenic Drive, marked with signs featuring a king's crown, and on to **Orwell** ⑭, where a period farm re-creates life in the 1800s. Continue on to **Montague** for a seal-watching tour. Overnight in ⌾ **Bay Fortune** ⑮. The next day, a picnic lunch will be the perfect wrap-up to a morning spent at **Basin Head Fisheries Museum** in **Basin Head.** Continue east on Kings Byway to East Point, for a stop at the lighthouse, which marks the most easterly point on the Island. Proceed west along the north shore to the eastern entrance of the **Prince Edward Island National Park** ⑩ and end your tour with a swim or a short hike.

Prince Edward Island

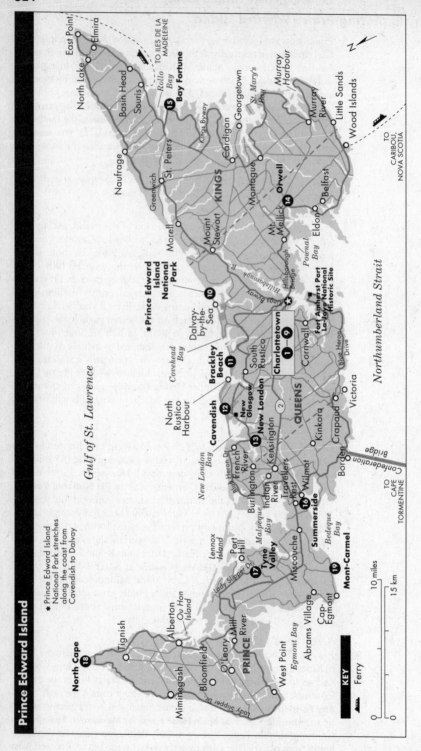

* Prince Edward Island National Park stretches along the coast from Cavendish to Dalvay

Gulf of St. Lawrence

Northumberland Strait

TO ILES DE LA MADELEINE

TO CARIBOU, NOVA SCOTIA

TO CAPE TORMENTINE

East Point
Elmira
North Lake
Basin Head
Souris
Naufrage
Rollo Bay
Bay Fortune 15
Kings Byway
St. Peters
Greenwich
KINGS
Georgetown
Cardigan
St. Mary's Bay
Murray Harbour
Murray River
Little Sands
Wood Islands
Morell
Mount Stewart
Montague
Belfast
Eldon
Orwell 14
Mt. Mellick
Pownal Bay
Prince Edward Island National Park
Prince Edward Island National Park 10
Dalvay-by-the-Sea
Coverhead Bay
Brackley Beach 11
South Rustico
North Rustico Harbour
Hillsborough Bridge
Kings River
Hillsborough R.
Fort Amherst Port La-Joye National Historic Site
Charlottetown 1–9
Cornwall
Blue Heron Drive
Victoria
Cavendish 12
New Glasgow
New London 13
New London Bay
QUEENS
Kensington
Kinkora
Crapaud
Borden
French River
Blue Heron Dr.
Burlington
Indian River
Travellers Rest
Wilmot
Summerside
16
Confederation Bridge
Bedeque Bay
Mont-Carmel 12
Miscouche
Tyne Valley 17
Port Hill
Lennox Island
Malpeque Bay
Ou Hon Island
Lady Slipper Dr.
Alberton
O'Leary
Mill River
PRINCE
Bloomfield
Mimnegash
Lady Slipper Dr.
Egmont Bay
Abrams Village
Cap-Egmont
West Point
Tignish
North Cape 18

N

KEY
Ferry

0   10 miles
0   15 km

IF YOU HAVE 3 DAYS

From **Charlottetown** ①–⑨, explore the peaceful suburban sprawl of ⊞ **Summerside** ⑯ before heading for its bustling waterfront. The relatively undiscovered area west of Summerside is perfect for those who like to pace things slowly. Follow Lady Slipper Drive through Acadian country to the **Acadian Museum of Prince Edward Island** in **Miscouche.** Leave mid-afternoon and take Rte. 12 to ⊞ **Tyne Valley** ⑰, a base from which to visit Lennox Island Reserve, where some of the finest crafts on the Island are sold. That evening, dine at **Seasons In Thyme Restaurant,** then take an evening stroll through Green Park in nearby **Port Hill.** On day three, make your way up to **North Cape** ⑱ and explore its reef. Plan to arrive early in the afternoon at ⊞ **West Point,** where you can enjoy the beach and walking trails. Finish your time in Prince County with a south shore tour to **Mont-Carmel** ⑲, home to one of the province's best French dinner theaters.

When to Tour Prince Edward Island

While Prince Edward Island is considered a summer destination due to its many seasonal attractions, the "shoulder seasons" should not be overlooked. May, June, September, and October usually have spectacular weather and few visitors. The main lobster season is May through June, while Autumn is an excellent time for hiking and golfing. Migratory birds arrive in vast numbers toward the end of summer, many staying until the snow falls. Winters are unpredictable but offer some of the Island's most overlooked activities: cross-country skiing, snowmobiling, and ice-skating on ponds. Nightlife is limited in cold weather.

CHARLOTTETOWN

On an arm of the Northumberland Strait, Prince Edward Island's oldest city is named for the stylish consort of King George III. This small city, peppered with gingerbread-clad Victorian houses and tree-shaded squares, is the largest community on the Island (population 30,000). It is often called "the Cradle of Confederation," a reference to the 1864 conference that led to the union of Nova Scotia, New Brunswick, Ontario, and Québec in 1867, and eventually, Canada itself.

Charlottetown's main activities center on government, tourism, and private commerce. While new suburbs were springing up around it, the core of Charlottetown remained unchanged, and the waterfront has been restored to recapture the flavor of earlier eras. Today the waterfront includes the Prince Edward Hotel; an area known as Peake's Wharf and Confederation Landing Park, with informal restaurants and handicraft and retail shops; and a marked walking path. Irene Rogers's *Charlottetown: The Life in Its Buildings* gives much detail about the architecture and history of downtown Charlottetown.

Exploring Charlottetown

Historic homes, churches, parks, and the waterfront are among the pleasures of a tour of downtown Charlottetown, and you can see many of the sights on foot.

A Good Tour

Before setting out to explore Charlottetown, brush up on local history at the **Confederation Centre of the Arts** ① on Richmond Street in the heart of downtown. Next door is **Province House National Historic Site** ②, where the first meeting to discuss federal union was held. If you have an interest in churches, turn onto Prince Street where **St. Paul's Anglican Church** ③ stands, then backtrack to Great George Street where you'll be summoned to **St. Dunstan's Basilica** ④ by its towering twin

Gothic spires. Great George Street ends at the waterfront, where the boardwalks of **Confederation Landing Park** ⑤ fronts small eateries and shops.

On the city's west end, the work of Robert Harris, Canada's foremost portrait artist, dons the walls of **St. Peter's Cathedral** ⑥ in Rochford Square, flanked by Rochford and Pownal streets. It's a bit of a walk to get there, but **Victoria Park** ⑦ rewards a grassy respite from heavy footwork. Next, climb to the Belvedere on the top floor of the **Beaconsfield Historic House** ⑧ for panoramic views of Charlottetown Harbour. Leave time to observe a favorite Prince Edward Island pastime—harness racing at **Charlottetown Driving Park** ⑨.

TIMING

You can easily explore the downtown area on foot in a couple of hours, but the wealth of historic sites and harbour views warrants full a day.

Sights to See

⑧ **Beaconsfield Historic House.** Designed by architect W. C. Harris and built in 1877, this gracious Victorian mansion near the entrance to Victoria Park is one of the island's finest residential buildings. On site are a gift shop and bookstore. Special events such as theatrical and musical performances, socials, and lectures are held regularly. Also on the grounds is a carriage house where activities for children are held in summer. ⊠ *2 Kent St.,* ☎ *902/368–6600.* ⊠ *$2.50.* ⊘ *June–Labor Day, daily 10–5; Labor Day–June, Tues.–Sun. 1–5.*

⑨ **Charlottetown Driving Park.** Since 1890, this track at the eastern end of the city has been the home of a sport that is dear to the hearts of Islanders—harness racing. Standard-bred horses are raised on farms throughout the island, and harness racing on the ice and on country tracks has been popular for generations. In fact, there are more horses per capita on the Island than in any other Canadian province. August brings **Old Home Week,** when Eastern Canada's best converge for 15 races within an 8-day period. ⊠ *Kensington Rd.,* ☎ *902/892–6823.* ⊠ *$2.* ⊘ *Races: June, July, and most of Aug., 3 nights per week; Old Home Week (mid-Aug.), Mon.–Sat. twice daily.*

❶ **Confederation Centre of the Arts.** Set in Charlottetown's historic red-brick core, this modern, concrete structure opened in 1964 as a tribute to the Fathers of Confederation. The Centre houses a 1,100-seat main-stage theater, two 190-seat second-stage theaters with an outdoor amphitheater, a memorial hall, a gift shop with Canadian crafts, a theater shop, an art gallery and museum, a public library with a special Prince Edward Island collection, including first editions of Lucy Maud Montgomery's famous novel, and a restaurant. The **Charlottetown Festival,** which runs from June through September, includes the professional, musical adaption of *Anne of Green Gables.* ⊠ *145 Richmond St.,* ☎ *902/368–1864, 902/566–1267 box office, or 800/565–0278,* FAX *902/566–4648.* ⊘ *Year-round, 9–5 daily; hrs extended June–Sept.*

❺ **Confederation Landing Park.** This waterfront recreation area at the bottom of Great George Street marks the site of the historic landing of the Fathers of Confederation in 1864. Walkways and park benches offer plenty of opportunity to enjoy the activity of the harbour. The adjacent **Peake's Wharf** has small restaurants, crafts shops, and a marina.

NEED A BREAK?
The **Merchantman Pub** (⊠ 23 Queen St., ☎ 902/892–9150), in a historic building just steps from the waterfront walking path near Confederation Landing Park, is a cozy spot for burgers, crepes, and fish and chips.

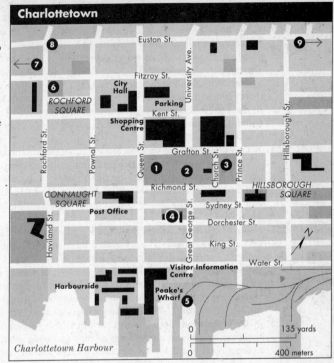

Charlottetown

Charlottetown Harbour

★ ❷ **Province House National Historic Site.** This three-story sandstone building, completed in 1847 to house the colonial government, has been restored to its mid-19th-century appearance. Visit the many restored rooms including the historic Confederation Chamber, where representatives of the 19th-century colonies met to discuss both the creation of a union and the current legislative chamber. ✉ *Richmond St.,* ☎ *902/566–7626.* ⚐ *Donation accepted.* ☉ *Mid-Oct.–mid-June, weekdays 9–5; mid-June, Sept.–mid-Oct., daily 9–5; July and Aug., daily 9–6.*

❹ **St. Dunstan's Basilica.** One of Canada's largest churches, St. Dunstan's is the seat of the Roman Catholic diocese on the island. It's known for its fine Italian carvings. ✉ *Great George St.*

❸ **St. Paul's Anglican Church.** This is actually the third church building, erected in 1896, to stand on this site. The first was built in 1747, making this the oldest parish on the island. ✉ *101 Prince St.*

❻ **St. Peter's Cathedral.** The murals of Robert Harris are found in **All Saints Chapel,** designed in 1888 by his brother W. C. "Willy" Harris, the most celebrated of the island's architects and the designer of many historic homes and buildings. ✉ *Rochford Sq.*

❼ **Victoria Park.** At the southern tip of the city and overlooking Charlottetown Harbour are 40 beautiful acres that provide the perfect place to stroll, picnic, or watch a baseball game. Next to the park, on a hill between groves of white birches, is the white colonial **Government House,** built in 1835 as the official residence for the province's lieutenant governors. The house is not open to the public. ✉ *Park, Lower Kent St.* ☉ *Daily sunrise–sunset.*

Dining

$$$$ ✕ **The Selkirk.** With its wing chairs and live piano entertainment, The Selkirk is the Island's most sophisticated dining room. The extensive, imaginative menu concentrates on regional Canadian fare—locally grown potatoes, smoked Atlantic salmon, lobster, mussels, Malpeque oysters, and Canadian beef to name a few. A four-course extravaganza that begins with Cedar Planked Salmon and closes with a Maple Streusel Apple Tart, will satisfy even the largest of appetites. ⌧ *Prince Edward Hotel, 18 Queen St.,* ☎ *902/566–2222 or 800/441–1414. Reservations essential. AE, DC, MC, V.*

$$$ ✕ **Culinary Institute of Canada.** Students at this internationally acclaimed school cook and present lunch and dinner during the school year as part of their training. Here's an opportunity to enjoy excellent food and top service at reasonable prices. Call for schedule and reservations. ⌧ *Kent St.,* ☎ *902/566–9550. Reservations essential. MC, V. Closed May–Sept.*

$$–$$$ ✕ **Claddagh Room Restaurant.** You'll find some of the best seafood in
★   Charlottetown here. The "Galway Bay Delight," one of the Irish owner's specialties, is a savory combination of fresh scallops and shrimp sautéed with onions and mushrooms, flambéed in Irish Mist, and doused with fresh cream. A pub upstairs has live Irish entertainment every night in summer and on weekends in winter. ⌧ *131 Sydney St.,* ☎ *902/892–9661. Reservations essential. AE, DC, MC, V.*

$$ ✕ **Off Broadway.** Popular with Charlottetown's young professional set, this cozy spot began modestly as a crepe-and-soup joint. You can still make a meal of the lobster or chicken crepe and the spinach or Caesar salad that's served with it, but now the restaurant also has a fairly inventive menu of Continental entrées. The old-fashioned private booths won't reveal your indiscretions—including your indulgence in dessert. ⌧ *125 Sydney St.,* ☎ *902/566–4620. Reservations essential. AE, MC, V.*

$ ✕ **Little Christo's.** Hand-tossed gourmet pizzas like cordon bleu with roasted pine nuts and primavera make this the favorite spot in town for a slice. Soup, salad, pasta, and sandwiches round out the menu. ⌧ *411 University Ave.,* ☎ *905/566–4000. MC, V.*

Lodging

$$$$ ⊡ **The Charlottetown.** This five-story, redbrick hotel with white pillars
★   and a circular driveway is just two blocks from the center of Charlottetown. The rooms have the latest amenities but retain the hotel's old-fashioned flavor with antique-reproduction furnishings. The grandeur and charm of the Confederation Dining Room will take you back to the elegance of a previous era. ⌧ *Kent and Pownal Sts., Box 159, C1A 7K4,* ☎ *902/894–7371,* ℻ *902/368–2178. 107 rooms, 2 suites. Bar, dining room, indoor pool, sauna. AE, DC, MC, V.*

$$$$ ⊡ **Prince Edward Hotel.** A member of the Canadian Pacific chain of
★   hotels and resorts, the Prince Edward has all the comforts and luxuries of its first-rate counterparts—from whirlpool baths in some suites to a grand ballroom and conference center. Guest rooms are modern, and two-thirds of the units in this 10-story hotel overlook the developed Charlottetown waterfront. ⌧ *18 Queen St., Box 2170, C1A 8B9,* ☎ *902/566–2222 or 800/441–1414,* ℻ *902/566–2282. 178 rooms, 33 suites. 2 restaurants, bar, indoor pool, sauna, exercise room. AE, DC, MC, V.*

$$$–$$$$ ⊡ **Dundee Arms.** Depending on your mood, you can choose to stay in
★   either a 1960s motel or a 1904 inn. The motel is simple, modern, and neat; the inn is homey and furnished with brass and antiques. The Griffin Room, the inn's dining room, is filled with antiques, copper, and

brass. The French Continental cuisine includes fresh seafood. Specialties include rack of lamb, chateaubriand, and poached or grilled fillet of salmon in a light lime-dill sauce. ⊠ *200 Pownal St., C1A 3W8,* ☎ *902/892–2496,* FAX *902/368–8532. 16 rooms, 2 suites. Restaurant, pub. CP. MC, V.*

$–$$$ ⊡ **Blue Heron Hideaways.** Just 15 minutes from downtown Charlottetown in Blooming Point, the Blue Heron is a small complex of cottages and beach houses. The private beach has sand dunes and wildlife, and it's great for windsurfing. Outboard motorboat and gas barbecues are available for guest use. ⊠ *Meadowbank, R.R. 2, Cornwall C0A 1H0,* ☎ *902/566–2427,* FAX *902/368–3798. 1 2-bedroom cottage, 2 3-bedroom cottages, 1 waterfront cottage with bunkhouse, 1 6-bedroom oceanfront house with guest house. Pool, windsurfing, boating. Weekly rentals only early June–mid-Oct. No credit cards.*

$$ ⊡ **Sherwood Motel.** This family-oriented motel is about 5 km (3 mi) north of downtown Charlottetown on Route 15. The friendly owners offer help in reserving tickets for events and planning day trips. Don't be daunted by the Sherwood's proximity to the airport—the motel sees very little traffic. Most rooms have kitchenettes. ⊠ *R.R. 9, Winsloe C1E 1Z3,* ☎ *902/892–1622 or 800/567–1622. 30 rooms. MC, V.*

The Arts

Ceilidhs, or live traditional entertainment combining dancing, fiddling, and comedy, can be found throughout Charlottetown and its environs. **The Benevolent Irish Society Hall** (☎ 902/892–2367) stages concerts on Fridays from mid-May through October.

BLUE HERON DRIVE

From Charlottetown, Blue Heron Drive follows Route 15 north to the north shore, then winds along Route 6 through north-shore fishing villages, the spectacular white-sand beaches of Prince Edward Island National Park, through Anne of Green Gables country, and finally along the south shore, with its red sandstone seascapes and historic sites. The drive takes its name from the great blue heron, a stately water bird that migrates to Prince Edward Island every spring to nest in the shallow bays and marshes. The whole circuit roughly outlines Queens County and covers 190 km (118 mi). It circles some of the Island's most beautiful landscapes and best beaches, but its northern section around picturesque Cavendish and the Green Gables farmhouse is also cluttered with tourist traps. If you're looking for unspoiled beauty, you'll have to look beyond the fast-food outlets, tacky gift shops, and expensive carnival-type attractions and try to keep in your mind's eye the Island's simpler days.

Prince Edward Island National Park

🔟 *24 km (15 mi) north of Charlottetown.*

Prince Edward Island National Park stretches for about 40 km (25 mi) along the north shore of the island, from Cavendish to Dalvay, on the Gulf of St. Lawrence. The Park is blessed with nature's broadest brush strokes—sky and sea meet red sandstone cliffs, rolling dunes, and long stretches of sand. Beaches invite you to swim, picnic, or take a quiet walk. Trails lead through woodlands and along streams and ponds. Among more than 200 species of birds are the northern phalarope, Swainson's thrush, and the endangered piping plover. Over 500 campgrounds span the park with varying fees and seasons. In autumn and winter, it's difficult to reach park staff—call the Prince Edward Island

Department of Economic Development and Tourism (☞ Visitor Information *in* Prince Edward Island A to Z, *below*) for exact rates and schedules if you're planning a camping trip ahead of time. Keep in mind that campsites are rented on a first-come, first-served basis; reservations aren't part of the protocol. ☎ 902/672–6350. ✉ *$3 daily pass, $15 seasonal pass, $2.50 off-season.* ⊙ *Year-round.*

Lodging

$$$$ 🏠 **Dalvay-by-the-Sea.** Just within the eastern border of the Prince Edward Island National Park is this Victorian house, built in 1896 as a private summer home. Rooms are furnished with antiques and reproductions. Guests can sip cocktails or tea on the porch while admiring the inn's gardens, Dalvay Lake, or the nearby beach. ⊠ *Rte. 6, Grand Tracadie, near Dalvay Beach; Box 8, York C0A 1P0,* ☎ *902/672–2048. 26 rooms, 4 cottages. Restaurant, bar, driving range, 2 tennis courts, croquet green, boating, gift shop. MAP. AE, MC, V. Closed late Sept.–early June.*

Golf

The 18-hole course at **Stanhope Golf and Country Club** (☎ 902/672–2842) is one of the most challenging and most scenic on the Island. It's a few kilometers west of Dalvay, off Route 6, along beautiful Covehead Bay.

Brackley Beach

⓫ *12 km (7½ mi) west of Dalvay.*

Just outside the National Park, Brackley Beach offers a variety of country-style accommodations and eating establishments. Its bays and waterways attract migratory birds and are excellent for canoeing or kayaking and windsurfing.

Dining and Lodging

$$-$$$ ✕ **Dunes Cafe.** This stunning café shares property with a pottery stu-
★   dio, art gallery, artisans outlet (☞ Shopping, *below*), and outdoor gardens. Soaring wood ceilings lend an airy atmosphere inside, while an outside deck overlooks the dunes and marshlands of Covehead Bay. The chef specializes in local seafood and lamb, incorporating locally grown, fresh produce, much of which comes from the café's own gardens. ⊠ *Rte. 15,* ☎ *902/672–2586. Reservations essential. AE, MC, V. Closed Nov.–May. No dinner weekdays June, Sept., or Oct.*

$$$-$$$$ ✕🏠 **Shaw's Hotel and Cottages.** Each room is unique in this 1860s
★   hotel with antique furnishings, floral-print wallpapers, and hardwood floors. Half the cottages have fireplaces. This country elegance doesn't come cheap; Shaw's is one of the more expensive hotels on the Island, but guests have the opportunity to sail (on small vessels) and windsurf. If you'd like, include in your room rate a home-cooked breakfast and dinner in the Shaw's dining room. ⊠ *Rte. 15, Brackley Beach C1E 1Z3,* ☎ *902/672–3000,* FAX *902/672–6000. 20 rooms, 18 cottages, 2 suites. Restaurant, bar, beach, boating, playground. AE, MC, V. Closed late Sept.–May except for 6 cottages.*

Shopping

The Dunes Studio and Gallery (⊠ Rte. 15, ☎ 902/672–2586) features the work of leading local artists, as well as craftspeople from around the world. The production pottery studio is open for viewing, and a rooftop water garden offers fine views of saltwater bays, sand dunes, rolling hills, and the Gulf of St. Lawrence.

Cavendish

⓬ *21 km (13 mi) west of Brackley.*

Cavendish is the most visited Island community outside of Charlotte-town, due to the heavy influx of visitors to Green Gables, the PEI National Park, and the amusement-park style attractions in the area. Families with children enjoy the entertainment, which ranges from bumper-car rides to water slides to pristine sandy beaches.

Adults will appreciate the **Site of Lucy Maud Montgomery's Cavendish Home,** where the writer lived with her maternal grandparents following the untimely death of her mother. Though the foundation of the home where Montgomery wrote *Anne of Green Gables* and the white picket fence that surrounded it are all that remain, the homestead fields and old apple-tree gardens provide lovely walking grounds. A bookstore and museum are also on the property, which is operated by descendants of the family. ⊠ *Rte. 6,* ☎ *902/963–2231.* ⊡ *$2.* ⊙ *June–mid-Oct.*

★ **Green Gables House,** ½ km (¼ mi) west of Lucy Maud Montgomery's Cavendish home, is the green-and-white farmhouse that served as the setting for *Anne of Green Gables.* The house, frequently visited by Montgomery, belonged to her cousins. Posted walking trails, the Haunted Wood and Balsam Hollow, re-create the landscape reminiscent of Montgomery's day. The site has been part of Prince Edward Island National Park since 1937. ⊠ *Rte. 6, west of Rte. 13,* ☎ *902/672–6350.* ⊡ *$2.75.* ⊙ *Mid-May–late June, daily 9–5; late June–Aug., daily 9–8; Sept.–Nov., daily 9–5.*

Dining and Lodging

$$$ ✕🅷 **Bay Vista Motor Inn.** This clean, friendly motel caters to families. Parents can sit on the outdoor deck and admire the New London Bay panorama while keeping an eye on their children in the large playground. Fiddles 'n Vittles is a great place to eat with the family. ⊠ *R.R. 1, Breadalbane, Cavendish C0A 1E0; in winter,* ⊠ *R.R. 1, North Wiltshire C0A 1Y0; book reservations at R.R. 2, Hunter River, PEI C0A 1N0,* ☎ *902/963–2225. 28 rooms, 2 efficiencies. Restaurant, pool, boating, fishing, playground. AE, MC, V. Closed late Sept.–mid-June.*

$$$$ 🅷 **Kindred Spirits Country Inn and Cottages.** This lovely country estate, a short walk from Green Gables House and golf course, is surrounded by green hills. Relax by its parlour fireplace, and then retreat into a large room or suite, decorated in country-Victorian style with local antiques. ⊠ *Rte. 6, Cavendish C0A 1N0,* ☎ *902/963–2434,* 𝖥𝖠𝖷 *902/963–2434. 14 rooms in the Inn, 13 cottages. Restaurant, pool, whirlpool. MC, V. Closed mid-Oct.–mid-May.*

Golf

Green Gables Course (⊠ Rte. 6, ☎ 902/963–2488), part of the Prince Edward Island National Park, is a scenic 18-hole course.

Sea Kayaking

Sea kayaking with **Outside Expeditions** (☎ 800/207–3899), 8 km (5 mi) east of Cavendish in North Rustico, can be geared to suit either the new or experienced paddler. Tours are catered, from light snacks to full-fledged lobster boils, depending on the expedition you choose.

New London

⓭ *11 km (7 mi) southwest of Cavendish.*

This tiny village is best known as the birthplace of Lucy Maud Montgomery. It's also home to several seasonal gift and craft shops, and a tea shop. The wharf area is a great place to stop, rest, and watch as the fishing boats come and go.

The **Lucy Maud Montgomery Birthplace** is the modest white house where the famous author was born in 1874. Among memorabilia on display are her wedding dress and personal scrapbooks. ⊠ *Rte. 6*, ☎ *902/886–2596.* ⊠ *$2.* ⊙ *June and Sept.–mid-Oct., daily 9–5; July–Aug., daily 9–7.*

Northwest Corner

12 km (7 mi) from New London.

Some of the most beautiful scenery on the Island is on Blue Heron Drive along the north shore. As the drive follows the coastline south to the other side of the Island, it passes rolling farmland and the shores of Malpeque Bay. Three towns of interest round out this scenic corner of the Island: Burlington, Park Corner, and Indian River.

Woodleigh Replicas and Gardens (⊠ Rte. 234, ☎ 902/836–3401), in Burlington, southwest of New London, is a 45-acre park with 30 scale replicas of Britain's best-known architecture, including the Tower of London and Dunvegan Castle. A medieval maze and 10 acres of English Country gardens are also on the grounds. The models that are large enough to enter are furnished with period antiques.

Park Corner's **Anne of Green Gables Museum at Silver Bush** (⊠ Rte. 20, ☎ 902/886–2884) was once the home of Lucy Maud Montgomery's aunt and uncle. Montgomery herself lived here for a time and was married in the parlor in 1911. Fans will appreciate mementos such as photographs and a quilt the writer worked on.

The Arts

The fine acoustics at **St. Mary's Church** (⊠ Hwy. 104, 5 km (3 mi) south of Park Corner, ☎ 902/836–3733) in Indian River draw visiting artists in July and August.

Borden-Carleton

35 km (22 mi) south of Kensington.

Once home port to the Marine-Atlantic car ferries, Borden-Carleton is now linked to the mainland via the Confederation Bridge. The 13-km (8-mi) behemoth, completed in June of 1997, spans the Northumberland Straight and ends in Cape Tormentine, New Brunswick. **Gateway Village,** at the foot of the bridge near the Borden-Carleton toll booths, has a visitor's center and information on the bridge's construction.

En Route   Prior to the late 1800s (when ferry service began), passengers and mail were taken across the straight in ice boats that were rowed and alternately pushed and pulled across floating ice by a fleet of men attached to leather harnesses. A monument on Route 10 in **Cape Traverse** commemorates their journeys.

Victoria

22 km (14 mi) east of Borden-Carleton.

This picturesque fishing village is filled with antiques, art galleries, and handicraft shops. In summer, thespians flock to historic **Victoria Playhouse** (☎ 902/658–2025) for its celebrated theater program.

Fort Amherst Port-La-Joye National Historic Site

36 km (22 mi) east of Victoria.

The drive from Victoria to Rocky Point passes through the Argyle Shore to Fort Amherst Port-La-Joye National Historic Site, at the mouth of Charlottetown Harbour. In 1720 the French founded the first European settlement on the island, Port-La-Joye; 38 years later it was usurped by the British and renamed Fort Amherst. Take time to stroll around the original earthworks of the fort and enjoy a magnificent panoramic view. The Visitor Centre on the grounds has informative exhibits and an audiovisual presentation. ⊠ *Rte. 19,* ☎ *902/672–6350.* 🎫 *$2.25.* ☉ *Visitor's Centre: mid-June–Labor Day, daily 10–6; grounds, year-round.*

THE KINGS BYWAY

For 375 km (233 mi), the Kings Byway follows the coastline of green and tranquil Kings County on the eastern end of the island. The route passes wood lots, patchwork-quilt farms, fishing villages, historic sites, and long, uncrowded beaches. In early summer you can see fields of blue, white, pink, and purple wild lupines sloping down to red cliffs and blue sea. To get there from Charlottetown, take Route 1 east and follow Kings Byway counterclockwise.

Orwell

★ ⓮   *27 km (17 mi) west of Charlottetown.*

For those who like the outdoors, Orwell, lined with farms that welcome guests and offer activities, is ideal.

The **Orwell Corner Historic Village** is a living farm museum that re-creates a 19th-century rural settlement by employing methods used by Scottish settlers in the 1800s. The village contains a beautifully restored 1864 farmhouse, school, church, community hall, blacksmith shop, and barns with handsome draft horses. On Wednesdays in summer the village hosts musical evenings (*ceilidhs*) featuring traditional Scottish fiddle music by local musicians. ⊠ *Rte. 1, Orwell Corner,* ☎ *902/ 651–2013.* 🎫 *$3.* ☉ *Late June–Labor Day, Tues.–Sun. 9–5; mid-May–late June and Labor Day–late Oct., Tues.–Fri. 10–3.*

The **Sir Andrew Macphail Homestead,** a National Historic Site, is a 140-acre farm property that contains an ecological forestry project, gardens, and three walking trails. The restored 1829 house and 19th-century outbuildings commemorate the life of Sir Andrew Macphail (1864–1938), a writer, professor, physician, and soldier. A licensed tea room/restaurant serves traditional Scottish and contemporary fare. ⊠ *Off Rte. 1,* ☎ *902/651–2789.* 🎫 *$3.* ☉ *June and Sept., Tues.–Sun. 10–5; July–Aug., extended hrs.*

OFF THE BEATEN PATH   **BEN'S LAKE TROUT FARM –** This is an enjoyable attraction for the whole family but is especially loved by aspiring young anglers. Not only are you almost guaranteed a fish but the staff will clean it and supply the barbecue and picnic table for a great meal. ⊠ *Rte. 24 (follow gravel road from Sir Andrew Macphail Homestead to Rte. 24; turn right), Bellevue,* ☎ *902/838-2706.* 🎫 *Catch $3.90 per lb.* ☉ *Apr.–Oct.*

En Route   One of the island's most historic churches, St. John's Presbyterian, is in **Belfast,** just off Route 1 on Route 207. This pretty white church, on a hill against a backdrop of trees, was built by settlers from the Isle of Skye who were brought to the Island in 1803 by Lord Selkirk.

Montague

20 km (12 mi) northeast of Orwell.

The business hub of eastern Prince Edward Island, Montague, a lovely fishing village, is a departure point for seal-watching boat tours. **Cruise Manada** (☎ 902/838–3444 or 800/986–3444) sails past a harbor seal colony and mussel farms. Boats leave from Montague Marina on Route 4 and Brudenell Resort Marina on Route 3 from mid-May through October.

Bay Fortune

⑮ *38 km (24 mi) north of Georgetown.*

Bay Fortune, a little-known scenic village, has been a secret refuge of American vacationers for two generations and is home to the wonderful Inn at Bay Fortune, with its old-time style and panache.

Dining and Lodging

$$$$ ×🏠 **Inn at Bay Fortune.** This enticing, unforgettable getaway, the for-
★ mer summer home of Broadway playwright Elmer Harris, and more recently of actress Colleen Dewhurst, is now a charming inn overlooking Fortune Harbour and Northumberland Straight. You'll find superb dining and a taste of genteel living. Local fresh-caught and -harvested ingredients are served in an ambience reminiscent of a bygone era. A full breakfast is included in room rates. ⊠ *Rte. 310, R.R. 4, C0A 2B0,* ☎ *902/687–3745, 203/633–4930 off-season. 11 rooms. Closed late Oct.–mid-May.*

Souris

14 km (9 mi) north of Bay Fortune.

The Souris area is noted for its fine traditional musicians. An outdoor Scottish concert at **Rollo Bay** in July, with fiddling and step dancing, attracts thousands every year. At Souris a car ferry links Prince Edward Island with the Québec-owned Magdalen Islands.

Basin Head

13 km (8 mi) north of Rollo Bay.

This town is noted for an exquisite silvery beach that stretches north-east for miles, backed by high grassy dunes. Scuff your feet in the sand: It will squeak, squawk, and purr at you. Known locally as the "**singing sands,**" they are a phenomenon found in only a few locations world-wide.

At the **Basin Head Fisheries Museum,** spectacularly located on a bluff overlooking Northumberland Straight, boats, gear, and photographs depict the life of an inshore fisherman. There's an aquarium, a smoke-house, a cannery, and coastal-ecology exhibits. ⊠ *Off Rte. 16,* ☎ *902/ 357–2966, 902/368–6600 off-season.* 🎟 *$3.* ☼ *June and Sept., week-days 10–3; July–Aug., daily 10–7.*

En Route Ships from many nations have wrecked on the reef running northeast from the **East Point Lighthouse** (⊠ Off Rte. 16, East Point, ☎ 902/357–2106). Guided tours are offered and numerous detailed books depicting the mysteries and tales of life at sea are available at the gift shop inside the adjacent fog alarm building.

Greenwich

54 km (33 mi) southwest of East Point.

Follow Route 16, the shore road, to Route 2 to St. Peter's Bay and Route 313 to Greenwich. The road ends among sand hills, but from here you can take a half-hour walk through beige dunes to reach the superior beach. These dunes are moving, gradually burying the nearby woods; here and there the bleached skeletons of trees thrust up through the sand like wooden ghosts.

LADY SLIPPER DRIVE

This drive—named for the delicate lady's slipper orchid, the province's official flower—winds along the coast of the narrow, indented western end of the island, known as Prince County, through very old and very small villages, which still adhere to a traditional way of life. Many of these hamlets are inhabited by Acadians, descendants of the original French settlers. The area is known for its oysters and Irish moss, but most famously for its potato farms: The province is a major exporter of seed potatoes worldwide, and half the crop is grown here.

Summerside

16 *71 km (44 mi) west of Charlottetown.*

Summerside, the second-largest city on the Island, has a beautiful waterfront area. A self-guided walking tour arranged by the Eptek National Exhibition Centre (☞ *below*) is a pleasant excursion through the leafy streets lined with large houses. During the third week of July, all of Summerside celebrates the eight-day **Summerside Lobster Carnival,** with livestock exhibitions, harness racing, fiddling contests, and of course, lobster suppers.

Some of the homes in Summerside are known as "fox houses"; silver foxes were first bred in captivity in western Prince Edward Island, and for several decades Summerside was the headquarters of a virtual gold rush based on fox ranching. For more on this unique local history, stop in at the **International Fox Museum and Hall of Fame.** ⊠ *286 Fitzroy St.,* ☎ *902/436–2400 or 902/436–1589.* ☞ *Free.* ☉ *May–Sept., Mon.–Sat. 9–6.*

Eptek National Exhibition Centre and PEI Sports Hall of Fame, on the waterfront, has a spacious main gallery with changing history and fine arts exhibits from all parts of Canada. An adjacent gallery contains the Sports Hall of Fame, a permanent display honoring well-known Island athletes. ⊠ *130 Harbour Dr., Waterfront Properties,* ☎ *902/888–8373,* FAX *902/888–8375.* ☞ *$2.* ☉ *July–Aug., weekdays 10–4, weekends 1–4:30; closed Mon. Sept.–June.*

Spinnaker's Landing, a boardwalk along the peaceful water's edge, is lined with shops and informal eateries. At a boat shed displaying traditional building methods common to the 1800s, you can have your own small ship custom crafted out of wood. ⊠ *130 Waterfront St., Waterfront Properties,* ☎ *902/436–6692.* ☉ *Mid-June–mid-Sept., daily 9:30–9:30.*

Lodging

$$$$ ⊞ **Quality Inn Garden of the Gulf.** Close to downtown Summerside, this clean motel is a convenient place to stay. There's a par-3 golf course on the property slopes to Bedeque Bay. ⊠ *618 Water St. E, C1N 2V5,* ☎ *902/436–2295 or 800/265–5551,* FAX *902/436–6277. 84 rooms.*

Coffee shop, indoor and outdoor pools, 9-hole golf course, gift shop. AE, DC, MC, V.

$$$ 🖭 **Loyalist Country Inn.** A Victorian-street-scene-inspired theme is present throughout this waterfront inn. Ten rooms have whirlpool baths. ⊠ *195 Harbour Dr., C1N 5B2,* ☎ *902/436–3333 or 800/361–2668,* ℻ *902/436–4304. 51 rooms. Dining room, tavern, indoor pool, sauna, tennis court, exercise room. AE, DC, MC, V.*

Nightlife and the Arts

The College of Piping and Celtic Performing Arts of Canada (⊠ 619 Water St. E, ☎ 902/436–5377, ℻ 902/436–4930) puts on a summer-long Celtic Festival incorporating bagpiping, Highland dancing, step dancing, and fiddling. **The Harbourfront Jubilee Theater** (⊠ 130 Water St., Waterfront Properties, ☎ 902/888–2500 or 800/707–6505) is the Maritimes' newest professional theater. Year-round, the main stage celebrates the tradition and culture of the Maritimes with dramatic and musical productions.

Miscouche

10 km (6 mi) northwest of Summerside.

The **Acadian Museum of Prince Edward Island** (☎ 902/436–6237), on Route 2, has a permanent exhibition on Acadian life as well as an audiovisual presentation depicting the history and culture of Island Acadians. Visitors have access to 30,000 genealogical cards listing Acadian descent. The museum is open year-round.

Port Hill

35 km (22 mi) north of Miscouche.

Follow the Lady Slipper signs from Miscouche to Port Hill on Route 12, where you may visit the **Green Park Shipbuilding Museum and Historic House** (☎ 902/831–2206). The house was originally the home of shipbuilder James Yeo, Jr. This 19th-century mansion is topped by the cupola from which Yeo observed his nearby shipyard through a spyglass. The modern museum building, in what has become a provincial park, details the history of the shipbuilder's craft, brought to life at a re-created shipyard with carpenter and blacksmith shops. The park also provides an opportunity for some welcome R&R, with picnic tables and camping facilities, as well as swimming in the river (there may not be a lifeguard on duty). The house and museum are open mid-June through Labor Day, Tuesday through Sunday 9 to 5.

Tyne Valley

⓱ *8 km (5 mi) south of Port Hill.*

The charming community of Tyne Valley has some of the finest food on Prince Edward Island, as well as an annual Oyster Festival, which takes place the first week in August. The area is home to the famous Malpeque oysters; watch for fishermen standing in flat boats wielding rakes to harvest this famous shellfish.

Dining and Lodging

$$–$$$$ ✕ **Seasons In Thyme.** This casual but charming country restaurant is
★   known for its fresh local ingredients such as quail, pheasant, and duck, and organic vegetables. The owner-chef Stefan Czapalay has 27 potato dishes at his fingertips, allowing him to cater to industry officials visiting to check the quality of the island's famous seed potatoes. In recognition of his varied clientele he utilizes the freshest local ingredients from farm and sea in dishes ranging from the most sophisticated

to the most casual. ⊠ *Rte. 178, C0B 2C0,* ☎ *902/831–2124. Reservations essential. AE, MC, V.*

$$ ✕⛫ **Doctor's Inn Bed & Breakfast.** This beautifully landscaped village home is a joy in summer, with its garden of herbs and flowers. In winter cross-country skiers gather 'round the woodstove or fireplace and share good conversation over a warm drink. At the dining room table, the local catch of the day is complemented by produce from the inn's own organic gardens. Dinner is by reservation only. For the horticulturally inclined, there are free tours of the inn's gardens. ⊠ *Rte. 167, C0B 2C0,* ☎ *902/831–3057. 3 rooms share bath. CP. MC, V.*

Shopping

At **Shoreline Sweaters** (⊠ Rte. 12, ☎ 902/831–2950), sometimes known as Tyne Valley Studio, Lesley Dubey produces sweaters with a unique Fair Isle–style lobster pattern and sells local crafts May through October. An art gallery on premises displays original works by Island artists.

Lennox Island Reserve, one of the largest Mi'Kmaq reserves in the province, has a few shops that sell native crafts. To get there, take Route 12 west to Route 163, and follow the road over the causeway. **Indian Art & Craft of North America** (☎ 902/831–2653) sells sweetgrass baskets, pottery, and beadwork. Earthenware figurines depicting native legends can be found at **Micmac Productions** (☎ 902/831–2277).

O'Leary

37 km (23 mi) northeast of Tyne Valley.

The center of Prince County is composed of a loose network of small towns, many of which are merely a stretch of road. Though quality lodging establishments are hard to find in these parts, O'Leary is host to a resort where opportunities for outdoor activities abound. O'Leary is also a good base from which to visit one of the island's best golf courses and a rare woolen crafts shop.

Lodging

$$$$ ⛫ **Rodd Mill River Resort and Aquaplex.** With activities ranging from night skiing and tobogganing to golfing, this is truly an all-season resort. An international dogsled-racing weekend is a popular winter event. Ask about year-round family weekend packages. ⊠ *Box 399, O'Leary C0B 1V0,* ☎ *902/859–3555 or 800/565–7633,* FAX *902/859–2486. 87 rooms, 3 suites. 2 bars, dining room, 2 indoor pools, sauna, 18-hole golf course, tennis court, exercise room, squash, windsurfing, boating, bicycles, ice-skating, cross-country skiing, tobogganing, pro shop. AE, MC, V. Closed Nov.–early Dec., Apr.*

Golf

Mill River Provincial Golf Course (☎ 902/859–2238) in Mill River Provincial Park is among the most scenic and challenging courses in eastern Canada.

Shopping

The **Old Mill Craft Company** (⊠ Rte. 2, Bloomfield, ☎ 902/859–3508) sells hand-quilted and woolen crafts July through August.

En Route   Everything in **Tignish,** a friendly Acadian community on Route 2, 29 km (18 mi) north of Woodstock, seems to be cooperative, including the supermarket, insurance company, seafood plant, service station, and credit union. The imposing parish church of **St. Simon and St. Jude Parish House** (⊠ 315 School St., ☎ 902/882–2049), across from Dalton Square, has a superb Tracker pipe organ, one of the finest such instruments in eastern Canada, and is often used for recitals by world-renowned musicians.

North Cape

★ ⑱ *14 km (9 mi) north of Tignish on Route 12.*

As you proceed north on Route 2, the Island narrows to a north-pointing arrow of land at the tip of which is North Cape with its imposing lighthouse. At low tide, one of the longest reefs in the world gives way to tidal pools teeming with marine life. The curious structures near the reef are wind turbines at the **Atlantic Wind Test Site,** set up on this breezy promontory to evaluate the feasibility of electrical generation by wind power. If you feel you are being watched, you probably are: Look offshore to where the seals gather for some prime people-watching. In summer visit the Interpretive Centre and Aquarium for information on North Cape's natural wonders.

The **Interpretive Centre and Aquarium** has information about marine life, local history, and turbines and windmills. ⊠ *End of Rte. 12,* ☎ *902/882–2991.* ✆ *$2.* ☉ *July–Aug., daily 9–9; mid-May–June and Sept.–Oct., daily 10–6.*

Dining

$$ ✕ **Wind & Reef.** This restaurant serves good seafood, such as Island clams, mussels, and lobster, as well as steaks, prime rib, and chicken. There's a breathtaking view of the Gulf of St. Lawrence and Northumberland Strait. ⊠ *End of Rte. 12,* ☎ *902/882–3535. MC, V. Closed Oct.–May.*

En Route Near North Cape, just off Lady Slipper Drive on the western side of the island, is the very popular natural rock formation called **"Elephant Rock."** You may also see draft horses in the fields or working in the surf. They are "moss horses," used in harvesting a versatile and valuable sea plant known as Irish moss.

Miminegash

20 km (12 mi) south of North Cape.

Find out everything you wanted to know about Irish Moss, the fan-shaped red alga found in abundance on this coast and used as a thickening agent in foods. Visit the **Irish Moss Interpretive Centre** (☎ 902/882–4313) and find out how much Irish moss there was in your last ice cream cone. Then take time for some Seaweed Pie (made from Irish moss) at the adjacent Seaweed Pie Cafe. The Interpretive Centre is open late June through September, weekdays 9 to 5.

West Point

35 km (22 mi) south of Miminegash.

At the southern tip of the western shore is West Point, with a tiny fishing harbor, campsites, and a supervised beach. **West Point Lighthouse** is more than 120 years old and is the tallest on the island. When the lighthouse was automated, the community took over the building and converted it into an inn (☞ *below*) and museum, with moderately priced restaurant attached. The lighthouse is open daily, late May through late October.

Lodging

$$$–$$$$ ⌂ **West Point Lighthouse.** Few can say they've actually spent the night in a lighthouse. Clam-digging is a central activity at this unusual seaside inn. Rooms, most with ocean views, are furnished with local an-

tiques and handmade quilts. This inn books up so make your reservations early. Ask the innkeeper about the region's folklore—buried treasure is reputed to be nearby. ⊠ *Rte. 14,* ☏ *902/859–3605 or 800/764–6854. 9 rooms. Restaurant, beach, fishing, bicycles. AE, MC, V. Closed Oct.–May.*

En Route Lady Slipper Drive meanders from West Point back to Summerside through **Région Évangéline,** the main Acadian district of the island. At **Cape-Egmont,** stop for a look at the **Bottle Houses,** two tiny houses and a chapel built by a retired carpenter entirely out of glass bottles mortared together like bricks.

Mont-Carmel

⓳ *84 km (52 mi) southeast of West Point.*

This community has a magnificent brick church overlooking Northumberland Strait. **Acadian Pioneer Village,** a reproduction of an 1820s French settlement, has a church, school, blacksmith shop, store, restaurant (where you can sample authentic Acadian dishes), and modern accommodations. ⊠ *Rte. 11,* ☏ *902/854–2227.* ☜ *$2.* ☉ *Mid-June–mid-Sept., daily 9–7.*

The Arts

La Cuisine à Mémé (⊠ Rte. 11, ☏ 902/854–2227), a French dinner theater, serves a buffet and has typical Acadian entertainment, such as step dancing and fiddle music.

PRINCE EDWARD ISLAND A TO Z

Arriving and Departing

By Car

The 13-km (8-mi) Confederation Bridge now connects Borden-Carleton, Prince Edward Island, with Cape Tormentine in New Brunswick. The bridge replaces the services of the Marine Atlantic ferries, shortening travel time to a mere 10 minutes. The round-trip cost is $35 per car, $40 for a recreational vehicle.

By Ferry

Northumberland Ferries (☏ 902/566–3838, 800/565–0201 in the Maritimes) sails between Caribou, Nova Scotia, and Wood Islands, from May to mid-December. The crossing takes about 75 minutes, and the round-trip costs approximately $28.25 per automobile and $8.75 per adult. This ferry service will continue after the bridge opens. Reservations are not accepted, and no fares are collected inbound; you pay only on leaving the island.

By Plane

Charlottetown Airport is 5 km (3 mi) north of town. **Air Canada/Air Nova** (☏ 902/892–1007 or 800/776–3000) and **Canadian Airlines International/Air Atlantic** (☏ 902/892–4581 or 800/665–1177) offer daily service to major cities in eastern Canada and the United States via Halifax. **Prince Edward Air** (☏ 902/566-4488) is available for private charters.

Getting Around

By Car

With no public transportation on the Island, your own vehicle is almost a necessity. **Ed's Taxi** (☏ 902/892–6561) can be booked for tours by the hour or day. There are more than 3,700 km (2,300 mi) of paved road in the province, including the three scenic coastal drives called Lady Slipper Drive, Blue Heron Drive, and Kings Byway. The adventurous will enjoy exploring the designated "Heritage Roads," which consist of red clay, the native soil base. These unpaved roads meander through undeveloped areas of rural Prince Edward Island, where you're likely to see lots of wildflowers and birds. A four-wheel-drive vehicle is not necessary, but in spring and inclement weather the mud can get quite deep and the narrow roads become impassable. Keep an eye open for bicycles, motorcycles, and pedestrians.

Contacts and Resources

Emergencies
Police and **fire,** dial 0.

Golf
For a publication listing courses, contact **Golf Prince Edward Island** (✉ Box 2653, Charlottetown C1A 8C3, ☎ 800/463–4734).

Guided Tours
The Island has about 20 sightseeing tours, including double-decker bus tours, taxi tours, cycling tours, harbor cruises, and walking tours. Most tour companies are based in Charlottetown and offer excursions around the city and to the beaches. For a listing of current tour companies, contact **Tourism PEI** (✉ Box 940, Charlottetown C1A 7M5, ☎ 800/463–4734, ℻ 902/368–4438).

Hiking
Island Nature Trust and Island Trails (✉ Ravenwood, Box 265, Charlottetown C1A 7K4, ☎ 902/894–7535, ℻ 902/628–6331) publishes a nature trail map of the island, available for $4.50.

Hospital
Queen Elizabeth Hospital (✉ Riverside Dr., Charlottetown, ☎ 902/566–6200).

Shopping
Information on crafts outlets is provided by the **Prince Edward Island Crafts Council** (✉ 156 Richmond St., Charlottetown C1A 1H9, ☎ 902/892–5152).

Visitor Information
The **Prince Edward Island Department of Economic Development & Tourism** (✉ Quality Service Division, Box 940, Charlottetown C1A 7M5, ☎ 902/368–4444 or 800/463–4734, ℻ 902/629–2428) publishes an excellent annual "Visitor's Guide" and maintains eight **Visitor Information Centres** (VICs) on the island. The main VIC is in Charlottetown (✉ 178 Water St., Box 940, Charlottetown C1A 7M5, ☎ 902/368–4444 or 902/463–4623, ℻ 902/929–2428) and is open mid-May–October, daily; November–mid-May, weekdays.

13 Nova Scotia

Compact and distinctive, this little province on the Atlantic Coast is a mélange of cultures: Gaelic street signs in Pugwash and Mabou, French masses in Chéticamp and Point de l'Eglise, black gospel choirs in Halifax, Mi'Kmaq handicrafts in Eskasoni, onion-dome churches in Sydney, sauerkraut in Lunenburg, and Yankee Puritanism in Clark's Harbour. Though quiet coastal villages may set the tone, urban centers like Halifax and Sydney exist with a pleasant mix of big-city life and small-town charm.

Updated by
Julie V. Watson

INFINITE RICHES IN A LITTLE ROOM,"** wrote Elizabethan playwright Christopher Marlowe. He might have been referring to Nova Scotia, Canada's second-smallest province, which packs an impossible variety of cultures and landscapes into an area half the size of Ohio.

Nova Scotia's landscapes echo every region of Canada. Mountain clefts in Cape Breton Island could pass for crannies in British Columbia. Stretches of the Tantramar Marshes are as board-flat as the prairies. The glaciated interior, spruce-swathed and peppered with lakes, closely resembles the Canadian Shield in northern Manitoba. The apple blossoms in the Annapolis Valley are as glorious as those in Niagara, and parts of Halifax could masquerade as downtown Toronto. A massive Catholic church in a tiny French village recalls Québec. The warm saltwater and long sandy beaches of Prince Edward Island are also found on the mainland side of Northumberland Strait, and the brick-red mud flats of the Bay of Fundy echo their counterparts in New Brunswick. Neil's Harbour looks just like a Newfoundland outport—and sounds like one, too.

The people are as varied as the landscape. The Mi'Kmaq Indians have been here for 10,000 years. The French came to the Annapolis Basin in 1605. In the 1750s, cockneys and Irish settled in Halifax and "Foreign Protestants"—chiefly Germans—in Lunenburg. By then Yankees from New England were putting down roots in Liverpool, Cape Sable Island, and the Annapolis Valley. In the 1780s they were joined by thousands of "Loyalists," many of them black, displaced by the American Revolution. Soon after, the Scots poured into northern Nova Scotia and Cape Breton, evicted from the Highlands by their landlords' preference for sheep. The last wave of immigrants, in the 1890s, became steelworkers and coal miners in Cape Breton; they came from Wales, the West Indies, Poland, Ukraine, and the Middle East. They're all Nova Scotians, and they're all still here, eating their own foods and worshipping in their own churches.

This is a little buried nation, with a capital city the same size as Marlowe's London. Before Canada was formed in 1867, Nova Scotians were prosperous shipwrights and merchants, trading with the world. Who created Cunard Lines? A Haligonian, Samuel Cunard. Those days brought democracy to the British colonies, left Victorian mansions in the salty little ports that dot the coastline, and created a uniquely Nova Scotian outlook: worldly, approachable, and sturdily independent.

Pleasures and Pastimes

Dining

Skilled chefs find their abilities enhanced by the availability of ingredients such as succulent blueberries, crisp apples, wild mushrooms, home-raised poultry, quality beef, fresh-from-the-sea lobster, cultivated mussels, Digby scallops, and the famous Atlantic salmon. The quality of ingredients comes from the closeness of the harvest. Agriculture, fisheries (both wild harvest and aquaculture) are never far from the doorstep of the food and hospitality industry.

Helping travelers discover for themselves the best tastes of this beautiful province, the Nova Scotian culinary industry has formed an organization called the Taste of Nova Scotia. It pulls together the producers and the preparers, setting quality standards to ensure that patrons at member restaurants receive authentic Nova Scotian food. Look for their symbol: a golden oval porthole framing food and a ship.

CATEGORY	COST*
$$$$	over $50
$$$	$35–$50
$$	$15–$35
$	under $15

*per person, excluding drinks, service, 7% GST, and 11% sales tax on meals costing more than $3.

Lodging

Nova Scotia's strength lies within a sprinkling of first-class resorts that have retained the traditional feel, top country inns where a dedication to fine dining with an emphasis on local products and high-level accommodation rule, and a smattering of exceptional corporate hotels. Bed-and-breakfasts, particularly those in smaller towns, are often exceptional. Most of the resorts and many B&Bs are seasonal.

In addition to the reliable chains, Halifax and Dartmouth have a number of excellent hotels; reservations are necessary year-round and can be made by calling Check In (☞ Contacts and Resources *in* Nova Scotia A to Z, *below*). Expect to pay considerably more in the capital district than elsewhere.

CATEGORY	COST*
$$$$	over $80
$$$	$65–$80
$$	$45–$65
$	under $45

*All prices are for a standard double room, excluding 10% service charge.

Music

Talented musicians abound in Nova Scotia, ranging from traditional fiddlers to folk singers and rock bands. Names to watch for include the Rankin Family, the Barra MacNeills, the Minglewood Band, Sam Moon, Rita MacNeil, David MacIsaac, Scott Macmillan, and such traditional fiddlers as Buddy MacMaster, Ashley MacIsaac, Sandy MacIntyre, Lee Cremo, and Jerry Holland.

Outdoor Activities and Sports

BEACHES

The province is one big seashore. The warmest beaches are found on the Northumberland Strait shore. The west coast of Cape Breton and the Bras d'Or Lake also offer fine beaches and warm saltwater.

BIRD-WATCHING

One of the highest concentrations of bald eagles in North America is found in Cape Breton, along the Bras d'Or Lake and in Cape Breton Highlands National Park. July and August are the best eagle-watching months. The Bird Islands, off the coast of Cape Breton, are home to a variety of seabirds, including the rare Atlantic puffin and the endangered Piping Plover.

FISHING

Nova Scotia has more than 9,000 lakes and 100 brooks; practically all lakes and streams are open to anglers. The catch includes Atlantic salmon (June–September), brook and sea trout, bass, rainbow trout, and shad. You can get a nonresident fishing license from any Department of Natural Resources office in the province and at most sporting-goods stores. Before casting a line in national park waters, it is necessary to obtain a transferrable National Parks Fishing License, available at park offices. Licenses are not required for saltwater fishing. South of Shelburne, from Barrington to Digby, is the most prosperous fishing region in the province.

FOSSIL HUNTING AND ROCK HOUNDING

The shoreline along the Bay of Fundy contains some of the oldest rocks and fossils in the world. Fossilized trees, insects, plants, and ferns can be seen at the famous fossil cliffs of Joggins on Chignecto Bay. The Minas Basin near Parrsboro has dinosaur fossils as well as semiprecious stones such as agate and amethyst. Rock hounds are welcome to gather what they find along the beaches, but a permit from the Nova Scotia Museum is required to dig along the cliffs. Organized rock hounding tours are available in Joggins and Parrsboro.

Wineries

Nova Scotian wineries are becoming exceedingly popular. While local wines are featured in many restaurants, they can be sampled for free and bought by the bottle for as little as $6 (U.S.) at the vineyards they come from. Wineries to visit include Jost Vineyards in Malagash and Sainte Famille Winery in Falmouth.

Exploring Nova Scotia

On the eastern edge of North America, Nova Scotia is astonishing in its variety. Along the coast, the North Atlantic breaks on rocky shores and beaches of fine, white sand. To the west the world's largest tides ebb and flow along the Bay of Fundy. Inland, dense forests and country roads weave among hundreds of lakes and rivers. The rugged terrain continues in central Nova Scotia and Cape Breton, where there are spectacular cliffs.

When arriving in Nova Scotia from New Brunswick via the Trans-Canada Highway (Hwy. 104), you are presented with three ways to proceed into the province. Amherst is the first community you will enter upon crossing the border. From Amherst, Highway 104 will take you toward Halifax, only a two-hour drive away. Touring alternatives lie to the north and south. Route 6, to the north, leaves Amherst to follow the shore of the Northumberland Strait; farther east is Cape Breton. Route 2, to the south, is a less travelled road and a favorite with children because of nearby fossil studded shores. Connect to branch roads to reach the Annapolis Valley and other points south. Please be aware that driving on rural roads warrants careful attention; while well surfaced, these roads are often without shoulders and unposted blind crests and sharp curves pop up unexpectedly in keeping with the rugged landscape.

Great Itineraries

The province naturally divides itself into regions that can be explored in three to seven days. Some visitors do a whirlwind drive around, taking in only a few sights. But Nova Scotia's varied cultural landscape deserves careful exploration. If you have the time, try linking up to two or more tours.

Numbers in the text correspond to numbers in the margin and on the Nova Scotia and Halifax maps.

IF YOU HAVE 3 DAYS

Start in **Halifax** ①–⑫, where remnants of a maritime past provide the setting for a surprisingly urban present. Explore the South Shore and Annapolis Valley, taking in the Lighthouse Route and Evangeline Trail. The two trails form a loop that begins and ends in Halifax (via Route 3, 103, or 333, the scenic road around the shore), covering a distance of approximately 850 km (527 mi) with no side trips. Leaving Halifax, head for **Peggy's Cove,** a picturesque fishing village surrounded by bare granite and coastal barrens. Explore **Mahone Bay** and travel on to **Lunenburg** ⑮, where the culture of Atlantic Coast fisheries is explored in the Fisheries Museum. Overnight in Lunenburg before continuing on Route 3 or 103 to **Shelburne** ⑰. Begin day two with a visit to **Yarmouth** ⑱ and travel on to **Digby** for a lunch of scallops. **Annapolis Royal** ㉑, with its gardens, historic sites, and harbor-front boardwalk, is a lovely spot to spend an afternoon. Travel on to ☒ **Wolfville** ㉒ for an overnight stay. The next day check tide times and plan a drive to the shore of Minas Basin, where the tides are the highest in the world. A leisurely drive will put you back in Halifax by late noon.

IF YOU HAVE 5 DAYS

The Eastern Shore, the Atlantic Coast east of Halifax, is perhaps the most scenic and unspoiled stretch of coastline in mainland Nova Scotia. Route 7 winds along a deeply indented, glaciated coastline of rocky waters interspersed with pocket beaches, long, narrow fjords, and fishing villages. **Musquodoboit Harbour** ㉔ is a haven for fishing enthusiasts. Nearby is **Martinique Beach,** one of Nova Scotia's best beaches. Continue north to **Sherbrooke Village** ㉕, full of refurbished late 19th century structures. Route 7 turns inland and follows the St. Mary's River towards **Antigonish** ㉖ on the Sunrise Trail. Historians will appreciate a visit to **Hector Heritage Quay** in ☒ **Pictou** ㉗, where the Scots landed in 1773. From Pictou, Route 6 runs beside an apparently endless string of beaches with many summer homes plunked in the adjoining fields. Turn right to Malagash, where **Jost Vineyards** invites wine tasting and tours. Be sure to visit **Seagull Pewter** in Pugwash ㉘. A half-hour drive will take you to ☒ **Amherst.** Continue on to **Joggins** ㉚ and search for souvenirs in its sandstone cliffs.

IF YOU HAVE 7 DAYS

Cape Breton Island, with its lush natural areas, wonderful small towns, and spectacular National Park, is perfect for a leisurely seven-day tour. Follow the coastal route (described in the following pages), which takes you on a west-to-east loop from the Canso Strait Causeway. Overnight in ☒ **Margaree Harbour** ㉝ so that you can enjoy the Cabot Trail and **Cape Breton Highlands National Park** for at least a full day. Spend a night or more in Margaree Harbour, a good base from which to seek out orchids, photograph spectacular scenery, walk the trails to hidden waterfalls, or go whale-watching (whale-watching opportunities abound on the northeastern side of the peninsula). Allow time for a visit to the **Alexander Graham Bell National Historic Site** in **Baddeck** ㊱, and spend the night in ☒ **Iona** ㊲. ☒ **Sydney** ㊳, with its casino for evening entertainment, will position you for a daylong visit to **Fortress of Louisbourg National Historic Park,** the largest historic restoration in Canada, and the town of **Louisbourg** ㊴, which has an interesting shipwreck museum. Take Route 4 back to Canso Causeway through **Big Pond,** home of singer Rita McNeil.

When to Tour Nova Scotia

The best time of year to visit Nova Scotia is mid-June to mid-September; in fact, many resorts, hotels, and attractions are only open during July and August. Nova Scotia, particularly the Cape Breton area, is a very popular destination in the fall due to the spectacular changing of the leaves. Lobster lovers will find the region's most popular seafood plentiful in May and June. Whale-watching, wildlife cruises, and sea kayaking outfitters generally operate from July to mid-September. Most golf courses stay open from June until late September, and some into October. Skiing (both downhill and cross-country) is popular at a variety of locations including Kejimkujik and Cape Breton Highlands from mid-December to early April.

PRINCE EDW

Borden

Cape Tormentine

Northumberland

NEW BRUNSWICK

Amherst

Oxford

28 Pugwash

6

Malaga

Tatam

Joggins **30**

Trans-Canada

Springhill

29

Balmora
Mills

Chignecto Game
Sanctuary

209

Masstown

Great
Village

Debert

104

Bib

Advocate
Harbour

Parrsboro

Five Islands

2

31

Cape
Split

Cap d'Or
Scots Bay

Cape
Blomidon

Cobequid Bay

Tru

St. John

Bay of Fundy

358

Minas
Basin

Maitland

Stewic

2

Minas Channel

Wolfville

Kentville

22

Hantsport

Shubeno

Windsor

23

Mount
Uniacke

Annapolis
Royal

Evangeline Trail

Berwick

Kingston

101

Middleton

Three
Mile Plains

101

102

Port Royal

21

Bridgetown

Upper Sackville

Lower
Sackville

Clements Port

12

Middle Sackville

Bedford

Digby

Bear
River

8

New Ross

Mahone
Bay

Hubbards

103

St.
Margarets
Bay

13 Dartmout

Eastern F

Long
Island

Digby Neck

Tiverton

St. Bernard

Bridgewater

3

Chester

Peggy's
Cove

333

Herring
Cove

Halifax

1

Westport

19

Evangeline
Trail

Point de
l'Eglise

KEJIMKUJIK
NATIONAL PARK

15

Lunenburg

14

Big and Little
Tancook Islands

Brier
Island

TOBEATIC
WILDLIFE
MANAGEMENT AREA

Lake
Rossignol

La Have

210

Greenfield

103

ATLANT

101

Milton

Brooklyn

16

Liverpool

TO
BAR HARBOR
(MAINE)

1

3

Yarmouth

18

Shelburne

17

103

TO
PORTLAND
(MAINE)

Pubnico

Lockeport

Woods
Harbour

Barrington

330

Cape
Sable
Island

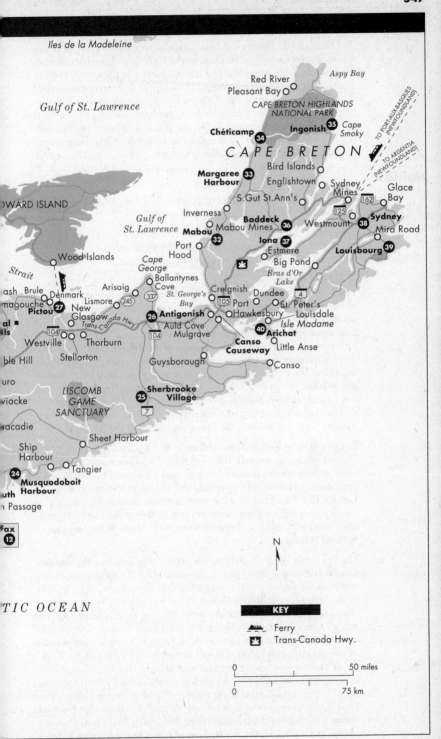

HALIFAX AND DARTMOUTH

The Halifax and Dartmouth metro area, now known, along with the whole former County of Halifax, as the Halifax Regional Municipality, surrounds the second-largest natural harbor in the world, Halifax Harbour. It bustles with activity day and night and flavors the rest of the city with its presence. Pubs, shops, museums, parks, and public gardens buzz with activity. Jazz, buskers, outdoor festivals, and cultural and sporting events abound. Galleries, concerts, theater, and fine dining combine to make the twin cities a destination for any season, with a mix of big-city life and small-town charm.

Halifax

1,137 km (705 mi) northeast of Boston; 275 km (171 mi) southeast of Moncton, New Brunswick.

Salty and urbane, learned and plain-spoken, Halifax is large enough to have the trappings of a capital city, yet small enough to retain the warmth and convenience of a small town.

A Good Walk

Begin on Upper Water Street at **Purdy's Wharf** ①, for unobstructed views of Halifax Harbour and the architectural wonder it inspired. Continue south to the restored warehouses of **Historic Properties** ②, a cluster of boutiques and restaurants linked by cobblestoned footpaths. Stroll along the piers to the **Maritime Museum of the Atlantic** ③: The wharves outside frequently welcome visiting transatlantic yachts and sail-training ships. Walk to the end of the block and cross the street to **Brewery Market** ④, restored waterfront property abundant with eateries. Take the elevator at the office-end of the Brewery Market and emerge on Hollis Street. Turn left, past several elegant Victorian town houses—notably Keith Hall—once the executive offices of the brewery.

Turn right onto Bishop Street and right again onto Barrington Street, Halifax's main downtown thoroughfare. The stone mansion on your right is **Government House** ⑤, the official residence of Nova Scotia's lieutenant governor. Take a detour from Barrington Street onto Spring Garden Road, and head for the **Halifax Public Gardens** ⑥, where you can rest your legs on shaded benches amidst flower beds and rare trees. Only one block away on Summer Street is the **Nova Scotia Museum of Natural History** ⑦.

On your way back to Barrington Street, you'll notice the **Halifax Citadel National Historic Site** ⑧, dominated by the fortress that once commanded the city. On a lot defined by Barrington, Argyle, and Prince streets lies **St. Paul's Church** ⑨; one wall within its historic confines contains a fragment of the great Halifax Explosion of 1917. A block farther and facing City Hall is the Grand Parade, where musicians perform at noon on summer days. From here, the waterfront side of Citadel Hill, look uphill: The tall, stylish brick building is the World Trade and Convention Centre and is attached to the 10,000-seat Halifax Metro Centre—the site of hockey games, rock concerts, and political conventions. Farther to the right are the office towers above Scotia Square, the leading downtown shopping mall. Look also for **Province House** ⑩, Canada's oldest legislative building, and, across from Province House at Cheapside, the **Art Gallery of Nova Scotia** ⑪, which showcases a large collection of folk art. If time permits, end your tour at **Anna Leonowens Gallery** ⑫ on Granville Street and peruse the work of local artists.

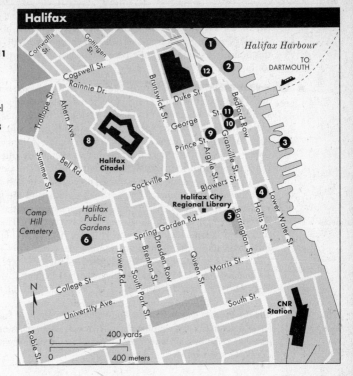

Halifax

TIMING

The city of Halifax is fairly compact: Depending on your tendency to stop and study or sit back and savor the moment, the above tour can take from a half to a full day. You can drive from sight to sight, but parking is a problem, and you will miss out on much of the flavor of the city.

Sights to See

12 **Anna Leonowens Gallery.** Though the gallery is named for the Victorian woman whose memoirs served as fodder for Rodgers' and Hammerstein's *The King and I,* it has nothing to do with the Broadway production—founding the Nova Scotia College of Art and Design is just another of her life's chapters. Three exhibition spaces serve as a public showcase for the college, faculty and students alike, as well as visiting artists. The displays, which change frequently, focus on contemporary studio and media art. ⊠ *1891 Granville St.,* ☏ *902/494–8223.* ▨ *Free.* ◷ *Tues.–Fri. 11–5, Sat. noon–4.*

11 **Art Gallery of Nova Scotia.** Sheltered within this historic building is an extensive permanent collection of over 4,000 works, including an internationally recognized collection of maritime and folk art. ⊠ *1741 Hollis St., at Cheapside,* ☏ *902/424–7542,* ℻ *902/424–0750.* ▨ *$2.50.* ◷ *June–Aug., Tues., Wed., and Fri. 10–5, Thurs. 10–9, weekends noon–5; Sept.–May, Tues.–Fri. 10–5, weekends noon–5.*

4 **Brewery Market.** This sprawling ironstone complex was once Keith's Brewery (named for Alexander Keith, a 19th-century brewer); now it houses offices, restaurants, and shops. It's a favored haunt of Haligonians on Saturday mornings year-round and on Fridays in summer when a farmer's market invites the opportunity to sample local produce, meats, and cheeses. ⊠ *Between Hollis and Lower Water Sts.*

⑤ Government House. Built between 1799 and 1805 for Sir John Wentworth, the Loyalist governor of New Hampshire, and his racy wife, Fannie (Thomas Raddall's novel *The Governor's Lady* tells their story), this house has since been gubernatorial quarters. The house is not open to the public.

★ **⑧ Halifax Citadel National Historic Site.** The Citadel, erected between 1826 and 1856, was the heart of the city's fortifications, and was linked to smaller forts and gun emplacements on the harbor islands and on the bluffs above the harbor entrance. Kilted soldiers drill in front of the **Army Museum,** once the barracks, and a cannon is fired every day at noon. Audiovisual programs and special events are offered several times throughout the year. Before leaving, take in the view from the Citadel: the spiky downtown crowded between the hilltop and the harbor; the wooded islands at the harbor's mouth; and the naval dockyard under the Angus L. MacDonald Bridge, the nearer of the two bridges connecting Halifax with its sister city of Dartmouth. The handsome four-sided **Town Clock** on Citadel Hill was given to Halifax by Prince Edward, Duke of Kent, military commander from 1794 to 1800. ⊠ *Citadel Hill,* ☎ *902/426–5080.* ⊑ *June 15–Aug. $5.75; May 15–June 14 and Sept.–Oct. 15 $3.50; rest of year free.* ☉ *June 15–Aug., daily 9–6; May 15–June 14, Sept.–Oct. 15, and rest of year, daily 9–5.*

NEED A BREAK? **Bud the Spud,** a chip-wagon parked at the curb in front of the Halifax City Regional Library, supplies summer crowds with snacks perfect for listening to the buskers who make stages of the library's lawn. ⊠ *5381 Spring Garden Rd.*

⑥ Halifax Public Gardens. One of the oldest formal Victorian gardens in North America, this city oasis had its start in 1753 as a private garden. Its layout was completed in 1875 by Richard Power, former gardener to the Duke of Devonshire in Ireland. Gravel paths wind among ponds, trees, and flower beds, revealing an astonishing variety of plants from all over the world. The centerpiece is a filigreed gazebo erected in 1887 for Queen Victoria's Golden Jubilee; today it stages Sunday afternoon concerts in summer. ⊠ *Bounded by Sackville, Summer, and S. Park Sts. and Spring Garden Rd.*

② Historic Properties. Dating from the early 19th century when trade and war made Halifax prosperous, these waterfront warehouses are Canada's oldest. They were built by such raffish characters as Enos Collins, a privateer, smuggler, and shipper whose vessels defied Napoléon's blockade to bring American supplies to the Duke of Wellington. Collins was also a prime mover in the Halifax Banking Company, which evolved into the Royal Bank of Canada, the country's largest bank. The buildings have since been taken over by quality shops and restaurants, boisterous pubs, and chic offices.

③ The Maritime Museum of the Atlantic. The exhibits in this restored chandlery and warehouse on the waterfront include small boats once used around the coast, as well as displays describing Nova Scotia's proud sailing heritage, from the days when the province, on its own, was one of the world's foremost shipbuilding and trading nations. Other exhibits explore the Halifax Explosion of 1917, shipwrecks, and lifesaving. Permanently moored outside, after a long life of charting the coasts of Labrador and the Arctic, is the hydrographic steamer *Acadia.* At the next wharf, in summer, is Canada's naval memorial, **HMCS** *Sackville,* the sole survivor of a fleet that escorted convoys of ships from Halifax to England during World War II. ⊠ *1675 Lower Water St.,* ☎ *902/424–7490 or 902/424–7491,* FAX *902/424–0612.* ☉ *June–mid-*

Oct., Mon. and Wed.–Sat. 9:30–5:30, Tues. 9:30–8, Sun. 1–5:30; mid-Oct.–May, Wed.–Sat. 9:30–5, Tues. 9:30–8, Sun. 1–5.

❼ Nova Scotia Museum of Natural History. Nova Scotia's natural wonders are preserved in several galleries that focus on both land and sea. Stand next to a Sei whale skeleton and admire Mi'Kmaq quillwork. The museum is most easily recognized by the huge fiberglass model of the tiny northern spring peeper (a frog), which "clings" to the side of the building May through October. ✉ *1747 Summer St.,* ☎ *902/424–7353,* FAX *902/424–0560.* 🖃 *$3.* ☉ *Mid-May–Oct., Mon., Tues., and Thurs.–Sun. 9:30–5:30, Wed. 9:30–8; Nov.–mid-May, Tues. and Thurs.–Sun. 9:30–5, Wed. 9:30–8.*

Point Pleasant Park. Most of the city's secondary fortifications have been turned into public parks. This one encompasses 186 wooded acres, veined with walking trails and seafront paths. The park was leased from the British Crown by the city for 999 years, at a shilling a year. Its major military installation is a massive round martello tower dating from the late 18th century. Point Pleasant is about 12 blocks down South Park Street from Spring Garden Road.

❿ Province House. Charles Dickens proclaimed this structure "a gem of Georgian architecture." It's now a national historic site. Erected in 1819 to house Britain's first overseas self-government, the sandstone building still serves as the meeting place for the provincial legislature. ✉ *1726 Hollis St.,* ☎ *902/424–4661.* 🖃 *Free.* ☉ *July and Aug., weekdays 9–5, weekends 10–4; Sept.–June, weekdays 8:30–4:30.*

❶ Purdy's Wharf. Named after a famous shipping family from the 19th century, this wharf is composed of a pier and twin office towers that stand right in the harbor. An architectural first, the buildings use ocean water to generate air-conditioning. ✉ *Upper Water St.*

❾ St. Paul's Church. St. Paul's, opened in 1750, is Canada's oldest Protestant church, Britain's first overseas cathedral, and the burial site of many colonial notables. Inside, on the north end, a piece of metal is embedded in the wall. It is a fragment of the *Mont Blanc,* one of the two ships whose collision caused the Halifax Explosion of December 6, 1917, the greatest human-caused explosion prior to Hiroshima. ✉ *1749 Argyle St.,* ☎ *902/429–2240.* ☉ *Sept.–May, weekdays 9–4:30; June–Aug., Mon.–Sat. 9–4:30; services Sun. at 8:30, 10:30, and 7:30.*

Dining and Lodging

$$$ ✕ **MacAskill's Restaurant.** Experience a continuing tradition of Nova Scotian hospitality in this romantic dining room overlooking beautiful Halifax Harbour. Award-winning chefs will delight you with a unique selection of seafood dishes prepared with only the finest, freshest fish available. Specialties include pepper steak, flambéed tableside. ✉ *88 Alderney Dr., Dartmouth Ferry Terminal Bldg.,* ☎ *902/466–3100. AE, DC, MC, V.*

$$–$$$ ✕ **Salty's on the Waterfront.** This restaurant, overlooking Privateer's
★ Wharf and the entire harbor, gets the prize for the best location in the city. Request a table with a window view, and save room for their famous dessert, called "Cadix" (chocolate mousse over praline crust). The **Salty Dog Bar & Grill** on the ground level is less expensive and serves lunches outside on the wharf in summer. ✉ *1869 Upper Water St.,* ☎ *902/423–6818. Reservations essential. AE, DC, MC, V.*

$–$$ ✕ **Privateer's Warehouse.** History surrounds you in this 200-year-old building, where three restaurants share early 18th-century stone walls and hewn beams. **Upper Deck Waterfront Fishery & Grill** (☎ 902/422–1289), done in a nautical theme, affords great views of the harbor, and assures lobsters straight from their holding tank. **Middle Deck Pasta**

Works & Beverage Co. (☎ 902/426–1500) has a bistro-style atmosphere and serves innovative pastas as well as traditional cuisine; there's also a children's menu. **Lower Deck Good Time Pub** (☎ 902/426–1501) is a boisterous bar with long trestle tables and a patio; fish-and-chips and other pub food is served. ⊠ *Historic Properties, Lower Water St. AE, DC, MC, V.*

$ ✕ **Satisfaction Feast.** This small, vegetarian restaurant is informal, friendly, and usually packed at lunchtime. The food is simple and wholesome; try the fresh whole-wheat bread and one of the daily curries. ⊠ *1581 Grafton St.,* ☎ *902/422–3540. AE, MC, V.*

$$$$ ✕🖬 **Hotel Halifax.** This first-class Canadian Pacific hotel has spacious, attractive rooms, the majority with a panoramic view of the harbor. An aboveground pedway network provides easy access to the Scotia Square shopping mall and Historic Properties. The **Crown Bistro** has a unique blend of elegant dishes and lighter fare. **Sam Slicks**, a cozy piano bar, has nightly entertainment and serves great food. ⊠ *1990 Barrington St., B3J 1P2,* ☎ *902/425–6700 or 800/441–1414,* FAX *902/425–6214. 279 rooms, 21 suites. Restaurant, piano bar, indoor pool, hot tub, sauna, exercise room. AE, DC, MC, V.*

$$$$ ✕🖬 **Prince George Hotel.** Contemporary mahogany furnishings in
★   this luxurious and understated business-oriented hotel include writing desks. **Georgio's Restaurant** serves Californian cuisine in a casual setting. The hotel is conveniently connected by underground tunnel to the World Trade and Convention Centre; pedway access to shops, offices, and entertainment is also provided. ⊠ *1725 Market St., B3J 3N9,* ☎ *902/425–1986, 800/565–1567 in Canada. 207 rooms, 9 suites. Restaurant, bar, pool, hot tub, exercise room, concierge. AE, DC, MC, V.*

$$$$ 🖬 **Cambridge Suites.** This hotel, in a convenient location, takes pride in its motto, "A suite for the price of a room." Choose from among three suite sizes; all have sitting rooms and kitchenettes. ⊠ *1583 Brunswick St., B3J 3P5,* ☎ *902/420–0555 or 800/565–1263,* FAX *902/ 420–9379. 200 suites. Restaurant, bar, kitchenettes, hot tub, sauna, exercise room. CP. AE, D, MC, V.*

$$$$ 🖬 **Haliburton House Inn.** Halifax's only four-star registered Heritage property, this hotel is an elegant renovation of three 19th-century town houses. Comfortable rooms are furnished with period antiques, lending a homey ambience. Wild game and Atlantic seafood are served in an elegant dining room. ⊠ *5184 Morris St., B3J 1B3,* ☎ *902/420– 0658,* FAX *902/423–2324. 25 rooms, 2 suites. Dining room, library. CP. AE, DC, MC, V.*

$$$$ 🖬 **Sheraton Halifax.** This waterfront hotel, built low to match neighboring historic ironstone buildings, strays in appearance from others of its chain. Its convenient location in Historic Properties contributes to its elegance. Other assets include an indoor pool with a summer sundeck. Halifax's only casino is in the lobby. ⊠ *1919 Upper Water St., B3J 3J5,* ☎ *902/421–1700 or 800/325–3535,* FAX *902/422–5805. 335 rooms, 19 suites. Restaurant, bar, room service, health club, dock, casino, concierge, meeting rooms. AE, DC, MC, V.*

$$$ 🖬 **Inn on the Lake.** A great value in a quiet, relaxing location, this small country club–style hotel is on 5 acres of parkland on the edge of Fall River Lake, 10 minutes from Halifax and the airport. ⊠ *Box 29, Waverly, B0N 2S0,* ☎ *902/861–3480,* FAX *902/861–4883. 34 rooms, 12 suites. Restaurant, lounge, beach, airport shuttle, free parking. AE, MC, V.*

Nightlife and the Arts

THE ARTS

Halifax has a dynamic film industry, the product of which is presented at the **Atlantic Film Festival** (☎ 902/422–3456), held in Halifax the third week in September. The festival also showcases feature films, TV movies, and documentaries made elsewhere in the Atlantic Provinces.

Wormwood's Dog and Monkey Cinema (⊠ 2112 Gottingen St., ☎ 902/422–3700) shows Canadian, foreign-language, and experimental films.

Scotia Festival of Music (☎ 902/429–9469) presents internationally recognized classical musicians via concert and master classes each May and June. The **du Maurier Atlantic Jazz Festival** (☎ 902/492–2225) takes place in mid-July.

The **Neptune Theatre** (⊠ 1593 Argyle St., B3J 2B2 ☎ 902/429–7300, 902/429–7070 box office), Canada's oldest professional repertory playhouse, stages year-round performances ranging from classics to contemporary Canadian drama. During the first week of September, the **Atlantic Fringe Festival** presents 40 shows in eight venues. The **Historic Feast Company** (☎ 902/420–1840) presents shows set in the 19th-century at Historic Properties on Thursday, Friday, and Saturday evenings. **Grafton Street Dinner Theatre** (⊠ 1741 Grafton St., ☎ 902/425–1961) holds performances Wednesday through Saturday.

NIGHTLIFE

The multilevel entertainment center in Historic Properties, **Privateer's Warehouse** (⊠ Lower Water St., ☎ 902/422–1289), is a popular nighttime hangout. At the ground-level **Lower Deck** tavern you can quaff a beer to Celtic music. **Cheers** (⊠ 1743 Grafton St., ☎ 902/421–1655), with bands and entertainment nightly, is a popular spot. **O'Carroll's** (⊠ 1860 Upper Water St., ☎ 902/423–4405) has a restaurant, oyster bar, and lounge where you can hear live Irish music nightly.

Shopping

The **Spring Garden Road** area has two stylish shopping malls, with shops selling everything from designer clothing to fresh pasta. **Jennifer of Nova Scotia** (⊠ 5635 Spring Garden Rd., ☎ 902/425–3119) sells locally made jewelry, pottery, wool sweaters, and soaps. You can find fine crafts in **Historic Properties** (☞ *above*) and the **Barrington Inn Complex** (⊠ 1875 Barrington St.). **Pewter House** (⊠ 1875 Granville St., ☎ 902/423–8843), across the street from the Barrington Inn Complex, sells locally made and imported pewter goods from knickknacks and tableware to clocks and jewelry. The **Plaid Place** (⊠ 1903 Barrington Pl., ☎ 902/429–6872 or 800/563–1749) has an array of tartans and Highland accessories. The **Wool Sweater Outlet** (⊠ 1870 Hollis St., ☎ 902/422–9209) sells wool and cotton sweaters at reasonable prices.

Dartmouth

⑬ *North of Halifax via the A. Murray Mackay and Angus L. Macdonald bridges.*

You can either drive or take the ferry from Halifax to Dartmouth. If you walk along the water behind the modern Law Courts in Halifax, near Historic Properties, you'll soon reach the Dartmouth ferry terminal, jammed with commuters during the rush hour. The terminal is home to the oldest operational saltwater ferry service in North America, which began operation in 1732. Suburban in demeanor, Dartmouth was first settled by Quaker whalers from Nantucket. The 23 lakes within Dartmouth's boundaries provided the Mi'Kmaqs with a canoe route to the province's interior and to the Bay of Fundy. A 19th-century canal system connected the lakes for a brief time, but today there are only ruins, which have been partially restored as heritage sites.

The **Black Cultural Centre for Nova Scotia,** in Westphal (a neighborhood of Dartmouth), is in the heart of the oldest black community in the area. The museum, library, and educational complex are dedicated to the preservation of the history and culture of blacks in Nova Scotia, who first arrived here in the 1600s. ✉ *Rte. 7 and Cherrybrooke Rd.,* ☎ *902/434–6223.* ✑ *$2.* ☉ *Weekdays 9–5; June–Sept. also Sat. 10–4.*

Lodging

$$$$ 🏨 **Ramada Renaissance.** In Dartmouth's Burnside Industrial Park, this luxury hotel is aimed at the business traveler as well as families. There is a 108-foot indoor water slide. ✉ *240 Brownlow Ave., B3B 1X6,* ☎ *902/468–8888, 800/561–3733 in Canada,* ℻ *902/468–8765. 178 rooms, 30 suites. Restaurant, bar, room service, pool, hot tub, sauna, exercise room, meeting rooms. AE, DC, MC, V.*

THE SOUTH SHORE AND ANNAPOLIS VALLEY

Mainland Nova Scotia is a long, narrow peninsula; no point in the province is more than 56 km (35 mi) from saltwater. The South Shore is on the Atlantic side, the Annapolis Valley on the Fundy side, and though they are less than an hour apart by car, the two destinations seem like different worlds. The South Shore is rocky coast, island-dotted bays, fishing villages, and shipyards; the Annapolis Valley is lumber yards, farms, vineyards, and orchards. The South Shore is German, French, and Yankee; the Valley is stoutly British. The sea is everywhere on the South Shore; in the Valley the sea is blocked from view by a ridge of mountains.

Route 103, Route 3, and various secondary roads form the province's designated Lighthouse Route, which leads from Halifax down the South Shore. It touches the heads of several big bays and small harbors, revealing an ever-changing panorama of shoreline, inlet, and island. Charming little towns and fishing villages are spaced out every 50 km (31 mi). The Lighthouse Route ends in Yarmouth and the Evangeline Trail begins, winding along the shore of St. Mary's Bay, through a succession of Acadian villages collectively known as the French Shore. Here, you'll notice the Acadian flag, tricolored with a gold star representing *stella maris,* the star of the sea. The star guides the Acadians during troubled times, which have been frequent. In 1755, after residing for a century and a half in Nova Scotia, chiefly in the Annapolis Valley, the Acadians were expelled by the British—an event that inspired Longfellow's famous *Evangeline.* Some eluded capture and others slowly crept back, but many settled in New Brunswick and along this shore of Nova Scotia. The villages blend seamlessly into one another for about 32 km (nearly 20 mi), each one, it seems, with its own wharf, fish plant, and enormous Catholic church. This tour mostly focuses on the towns along Route 1, but you should follow the side roads whenever the inclination strikes; the South Shore rewards slow, relaxed exploration.

The Annapolis Valley runs northeast like a huge trench, flat on the bottom, sheltered on both sides by the long ridges of the North and South mountains. Occasional roads over the South Mountain lead to the South Shore; short roads over the North Mountain lead to the Fundy shore. Like the South Shore, the Valley is punctuated with pleasant small towns, each with a generous supply of extravagant Victorian homes and churches. For most visitors, the Valley towns, each with its own distinction, go by like charming milestones. The rich soil of the valley bottom supports dairy herds, hay, grain, root vegetables, tobacco, and fruit. Apple blossom season (late May and early June) and the fall harvest are the loveliest times to visit.

Peggy's Cove

48 km (30 mi) southwest of Halifax.

Peggy's Cove, on Route 333, stands at the mouth of St. Margaret's Bay. The cove, with its houses huddled around the narrow slit in the boulders, is probably the most photographed village in Canada. It also has the only Canadian post office located in a lighthouse (open April–November). Be careful exploring the bald, rocky shore. Incautious visitors have been swept to their deaths by the towering surf that sometimes breaks here.

Dining and Lodging

$$$ ✕⌂ **Dauphinee Inn.** On the shore of Hubbards Cove, about 12 miles before Chester, this charming country inn has first-class accommodations and an excellent restaurant. Try the Hot Rocks, a social dining concept where guests are invited to cook fresh vegetables, seafood, beef, or chicken on a hot slab of South Shore granite. Opportunities abound for bicycling, bird-watching, and deep-sea fishing nearby, and walking trails lead to the shore. ✉ *167 Shore Club Rd., Hubbard B0J 1T0 (Exit 6 off Rte. 103),* ☎ *902/857–1790 or 800/567–1790,* ℻ *902/857– 9555. 6 rooms, 2 suites. Restaurant, lounge, boating, fishing. AE, D, DC, MC. Closed Nov.–Apr.*

Chester

79 km (49 mi) west of Peggy's Cove.

Chester, on Lunenburg County's Mahone Bay, has a population of just over 1,100 people. In summer, however, this seaside retreat swells with a well-established population of U.S. visitors and Haligonians, and with the sailing and yachting community. Mid-August brings **Chester Race Week,** the largest regatta in Atlantic Canada.

The **Ross Farm Museum** is a restored 19th-century living museum that illustrates the evolution of agriculture from 1600 to 1925 and has the types of animals found on a farm of the 1800s—draft horses, oxen, and older breeds or types of animals—not the genetically developed, purebred animals of today. At the Pedlar's Shop, on the premises, you can purchase items made in the community. ✉ *Rte. 12, New Ross (20-min drive inland from Chester),* ☎ *902/689–2210.* ✇ *$3.* ☉ *June–mid-Oct., daily 9:30–5:30; winter programs Jan.–mid-Mar. (call to confirm).*

⓮ A passengers-only ferry runs from the dock in Chester to the scenic **Big and Little Tancook Islands,** 8 km (5 mi) out in Mahone Bay. Reflecting its part-German heritage, Big Tancook claims to make the best sauerkraut in Nova Scotia. Exploration of the island is made easy by walking trails. The boat runs four times daily Monday through Thursday; six times daily Friday; and twice daily on weekends. The 45-minute trip costs $1.

Dining

$ ✕ **The Galley.** Decked out in nautical bric-a-brac and providing a spectacular view of the ocean, this restaurant has a pleasant, relaxed atmosphere. Try the seafood chowder, live lobster from their in-house pond, and homemade desserts. ✉ *Rte. 3, 115 Marina Rd., Marriots Cove (Exit 8 off Rte. 103, 3 km, or 2 mi, west of Chester),* ☎ *902/275–4700. Reservations essential. AE, D, MC, V. Closed mid-Dec.–mid-Mar.*

En Route The town of **Mahone Bay** presents a dramatic face to visitors: Three tall wooden churches—of different denominations—stand side by side, their images reflected in the harbor. Once a shipbuilding community, Mahone Bay is now a crafts center.

Lunenburg

★ **⑮** *9½ km (6 mi) south of the town of Mahone Bay.*

A feast of Victorian-era architecture, wooden boats, steel draggers (a fishing boat that operates a trawl), historic inns, and good restaurants, Lunenburg is, among other things, visually delightful. The center of town, known as **old town,** is a UNESCO world heritage site, and the fantastic old school on the hilltop is the region's finest remaining example of Second Empire architecture, an ornate style that began in France.

Lunenburg is home port to *Bluenose II*, a replica of the great racing schooner depicted on the back of the Canadian dime. Built in 1921, the original *Bluenose,* which sank years ago, was the undefeated champion of the North Atlantic fishing fleet and winner of four international schooner races. Its twin, built in 1963, is open to visitors through the Fisheries Museum (☞ *below*) when in port.

The **Fisheries Museum of the Atlantic** sets off on a nautical journey that explores a day in the life of Canada's Atlantic coast fishermen. Among the attractions are the last of the Grand Bank schooners, the *Theresa E. Connor,* a steel stern trawler, *Cape Sable,* and an aquarium. ⊠ *68 Bluenose Dr.,* ☎ *902/634–4794.* ⊑ *$6. June–mid-Oct., daily 9:30– 5:30; off-season, weekdays by appointment only.*

The **Houston North Gallery** represents both trained and self-taught Nova Scotian artists as well as Inuit (Eskimo) soapstone carvers and printmakers. ⊠ *110 Montague St.,* ☎ *902/634–8869.* ⊙ *Feb.–Dec., Mon.–Sat. 10–6, Sun. 1–6.*

Lodging

$$–$$$ 🏨 **Boscawen Inn and MacLachlan House.** Period antiques adorn and fireplaces warm this elegant 1888 mansion and its 1905 annex, located in the middle of Lunenburg's historic old town. Guests can take afternoon tea in one of the drawing rooms or on the balcony. All rooms and suites have either water or park views. ⊠ *Box 1343, 150 Cumberland St., B0J 2C0,* ☎ *902/634–3325,* FAX *902/634–9293. 20 rooms. Restaurant. AE, D, DC, MC, V. Closed Jan.–Easter.*

$$–$$$ 🏨 **Pelham House Bed & Breakfast.** Close to downtown, this sea captain's home, circa 1906 and decorated to period throughout, has a large collection of books and periodicals about the sea, sailing, and wooden boats. Sit back and relax on the veranda overlooking the harbor. Full breakfast and afternoon tea are included in the room rate. ⊠ *Box 358, 224 Pelham St., B0J 2C0,* ☎ *902/634–7113,* FAX *902/634–7114. 3 rooms. Business services. MC, V.*

Bridgewater

18 km (11 mi) west of Lunenburg.

This is the main market town of the South Shore. The town's main attraction, the **DesBrisay Museum,** explores the nature and people of Lunenburg County and presents exhibits on art, science, technology, and history from museums around the world. The gift shop carries books by local authors and art and crafts by local artisans. ⊠ *130 Jubilee Rd.,* ☎ *902/543–4033.* ⊑ *$2.50.* ⊙ *Mid-May–Sept., Mon.–Sat. 9– 5, Sun. 1–5; Oct.–mid-May, Tues.–Sun. 1–5, Wed. 1–9.*

Liverpool

 46 km (29 mi) south of Bridgewater.

Nestled on the estuary of the Mersey River, Liverpool was settled around 1760 by New Englanders and is now a fishing and paper-milling town. During the American Revolution and the War of 1812, Liverpool was a privateering center; later, it became an important shipping and trading port.

In the center of town is the **Simeon Perkins House,** built in 1766, which was the home of a prominent early settler who kept an extensive and revealing diary. The Perkins diary was used extensively by Thomas Raddall, whose internationally successful novels and stories are sometimes set in and around Liverpool. ⊠ *109 Main St.,* ☎ *902/354–4058.* ▨ *Free.* ☉ *June–mid-Oct., Mon.–Sat. 9:30–5:30, Sun. 1–5:30.*

Fishing

The **Mersey** is the oldest documented canoe route on the continent. It drains Lake Rossignol, Nova Scotia's largest freshwater lake, and provides good trout and salmon fishing. For canoe and fishing outfitters, go to the town of Greenfield, on Route 210, off Route 8.

Kejimkujik National Park

67 km (42 mi) west of Liverpool.

This is a 381-square-km (147-square-mi) inland wilderness about 45 minutes from Liverpool in the interior of the western part of the province. Kejimkujik has many lakes with well-marked canoe routes that have primitive campsites. Nature trails are marked for hikers, boat rentals are available, and there's freshwater swimming. Look for whitetail deer, porcupine, loons, owls and beaver. Kejimkujik also operates the Seaside Adjunct near Port Joli on the Atlantic shore that protects one of the last undeveloped tracts of coastline on the Eastern Seaboard. There are two mile-long beaches, both reached by hiking trails (no visitor services; day use only). Sections of beaches are closed from late April to late July so that nesting birds, such as the endangered piping plover, remain undisturbed. ⊠ *Rte. 8 from Liverpool or Annapolis Royal, Maitland Bridge,* ☎ *902/682–2772.* ▨ *$3 per day, 4-day pass $9, annual pass $15, camping $9–$13.50 per day.*

Shelburne

 69 km (43 mi) south of Liverpool.

The high noon of Shelburne occurred right after the Revolution, when 16,000 Loyalists briefly made it one of the largest communities in North America. Today it is a fishing and shipbuilding town situated at the mouth of the Roseway River.

Many of Shelburne's homes date back to the late 1700s, including the **Ross-Thomson House,** which is now a provincial museum. Inside, the only surviving 18th-century store in Nova Scotia contains all the necessities of the period in which it originated. ⊠ *9 Charlotte La.,* ☎ *902/875–3141.* ▨ *Free.* ☉ *June–mid-Oct., daily 9:30–5:30; call for winter hours.*

Barrington

40 km (25 mi) south of Shelburne.

Barrington harbors a cluster of museums that explore various aspects of life in the 18th and 19th centuries. The **Barrington Woolen Mill Museum** (☎ 902/637–2185), built in 1882, displays machinery and has exhibits that explain how wool is woven into bolts of twills and flannels, blankets, and suitings. Early New England settlers converged at the **Old Meeting House Museum** (☎ 902/637–2185) for town meetings, elections, and religious services. A five-story climb to the top of the **Seal Island Light Museum** affords beautiful views of Barrington Bay. The **Western Counties Military Museum** (☎ 902/768–2161) houses an array of old military artifacts.

Cape Sable Island

8 km (5 mi) south of Barrington over the Causeway.

Connected to the mainland via a bridge, Cape Sable Island has a 13-mile loop that includes Nova Scotia's southernmost extremity. Like Barrington, Cape Sable Island is a Yankee community, as common family names attest; everyone seems to be named "Smith" or "Nickerson." Interestingly, there is a bewildering variety of small evangelical churches, which presumably reflects the Puritan enthusiasm for irreconcilable disagreements over fine points of doctrine. The largest community on Cape Sable is **Clark's Harbour,** where the first Cape Islander fishing boat was developed—with its pilothouse forward and its high, flaring bow and low stern, the Cape Islander is Nova Scotia's standard inshore fishing boat.

Pubnico

48 km (30 mi) west of Barrington.

Upon reaching Pubnico you enter the Acadian milieu; from here to Digby the communities are mostly French-speaking. Favorite local fare includes *fricot,* a stew made mostly of vegetables, sometimes mixed with rabbit meat, and rappie pie, made of meat or poultry with potatoes from which much of the starch has been removed.

You'll no doubt notice that there are no fewer than seven towns bearing the name Pubnico: Lower West Pubnico, Middle West Pubnico, and West Pubnico, all on the west shore of Pubnico Harbour; three East Pubnicos on the eastern shore; and just plain Pubnico, at the top of none other than Pubnico Harbour. These towns were founded by Phillipe Muis D'Entremont, and they once constituted the only barony in French Acadia. D'Entremont was a prodigious progenitor: To this day, many of the people in the Pubnicos are D'Entremonts, and most of the rest are D'Eons or Amiraults.

Yarmouth

 82 km (51 mi) north of Barrington.

The largest town (with some 8,500 inhabitants) in southern Nova Scotia and the biggest port west of Halifax, Yarmouth is the point of entry for travelers arriving by ferry from Maine. The ferries are a major reason for Yarmouth's prosperity as they pull in much revenue by providing quick, inexpensive access for merchants and consumers going to the Boston market for fish, pulpwood, boxes and barrels, knitwear, Irish moss, Christmas trees, and berries.

In the 19th century Yarmouth was an even bigger shipbuilding center than it is now, and its location put the port on all the early steamship routes. The **Yarmouth County Museum,** in a late-19th-century church, unravels the region's history with displays of period furniture, costumes, tools, and toys, as well as a significant collection of ship models and paintings. Also in the building is a research library and archives, where local history and genealogy are documented. ⊠ *22 Collins St.,* ☎ *902/742–*

5539, ℻ 902/749–1120. ☒ $2.50, archive $5 per half day. ⊘ June–mid-Oct., Mon.–Sat. 9–5, Sun. 2–5; mid-Oct.–May, Tues.–Sun. 2–5.

The **Firefighters Museum of Nova Scotia,** one block from the waterfront, presents the evolution of fire fighting through its displays of equipment from the leather bucket to the chemical spray. ☒ 451 Main St., ☎ 902/742–5525. ☒ $2. ⊘ June, Mon.–Sat. 9–5; July and Aug., Mon.–Sat. 9–9, Sun. 10–5; Sept., Mon.–Sat. 9–5; Oct.–May, weekdays 10–noon and 2–4.

NEED A
BREAK?
Harris's Quick 'n' Tasty is the place for good, old-fashioned food such as rappie pie and lobster cooked up in more ways than you can imagine. ☒ Rte. 1, Dayton, ☎ 902/742-3467.

Dining and Lodging

$$ ✗▥ **Manor Inn.** This country inn in a colonial mansion beside Doctors Lake on Rte. 1 offers a choice of four grades of rooms, settings, and price ranges to choose from: coach-house units, lakeside or rose-garden lodges, or the main estate. Prime rib and lobster are the specialties in the dining room; reservations are required. ☒ Box 56, Rte. 1, Hebron, B0W 1X0 (Rte. 1., 5 mi northeast of Yarmouth), ☎ 902/742–2487, 888/626–6746, ℻ 902/742–8094. 53 rooms. 2 dining rooms, 2 bars, outdoor café, pool, tennis court. AE, DC, MC, V.

Point de l'Eglise (Church Point)

⑲ 70 km (43 mi) north of Yarmouth.

Point de l'Eglise is the site of **Université Ste-Anne,** the only French-language institution among Nova Scotia's 17 degree-granting colleges and universities. Founded in 1891, this small university off Route 1 is a focus of Acadian studies and culture in the province.

St. Mary's Church, on the side of the main road that runs through Point de l'Eglise, was finished in 1905. It's the tallest and largest wooden church in North America, at 190 feet long and 185 feet high. The steeple requires 40 tons of rock ballast to keep it steady in the ocean winds and can be seen for miles on the approach. Inside the church is a small museum. Tours are given by appointment. ☒ Main road, ☎ 902/769–2832. ☒ $1. ⊘ July–mid-Oct., daily 9:30–5:30.

En Route **St. Bernard,** a few miles north of Point de l'Eglise, marks the end of the French Shore. It's known for an impressive granite Gothic church that seats 1,000 people.

Digby

35 km (22 mi) north of Point de l'Eglise.

Digby is the terminus of the ferry service from St. John, New Brunswick, and an important fishing port with several good restaurants and a major resort, The Pines (☞ below). The town is on the otherwise-landlocked Annapolis Basin, into which the Annapolis River flows after its long course through the valley. The town is particularly famous for its scallops and for smoked herring known as "Digby Chicks." For a real treat go down to the wharf and visit seafood retailers: They'll cook up the delicious scallops and lobster that you buy.

OFF THE
BEATEN PATH
BEAR RIVER - This jewel of a village, 15 km (9 mi) inland from Digby, is called the "Switzerland of Nova Scotia." It has a large arts-and-crafts community and an Ethnographic Museum (☒ 18 Chute Rd., ☎ 902/467-3762) devoted to folk costumes and artifacts from exotic lands.

Dining and Lodging

$$$$ ✕▥ **Pines Resort Hotel.** Complete with fireplaces, sitting rooms, and a view of the Annapolis Basin, this casually elegant property, composed of a Norman Chateaux–style hotel, 30 cottages, and lavish gardens, offers myriad amenities. Local seafood with a French touch is served daily in the restaurant, and the lounge is perfect for quiet relaxation. ⊠ *Box 70, Shore Rd., B0V 1A0,* ☎ *902/245–2511 or 800/667–4637,* 𝖥𝖠𝖷 *902/245–6133. 144 rooms. Restaurant, bar, pool, sauna, 18-hole golf course, 2 tennis courts, health club, walking trails. AE, D, DC, MC. Closed mid-Oct.–May.*

Long Island and Brier Island

㉑ *10-minute ferry ride between East Ferry and Tiverton.*

Digby Neck is extended seaward by two narrow islands, Long Island and Brier Island. Because the surrounding waters are rich in plankton they attract a variety of whales, including fins, humpbacks, minkes, and right whales, as well as harbor porpoises. This is also an excellent spot for bird-watching.

Ferries going between the islands have to crab sideways against the ferocious Fundy tidal streams that course back and forth through the narrow gaps. They operate hourly, 24 hours a day, with a fare of $1 each way. One of the boats is called *Joshua Slocum* and the other is *Spray;* the former is named after Westport's most famous native, and the latter for the 36-foot oyster sloop that he rebuilt and in which from 1894 to 1896 he became the first man to circumnavigate the world singlehandedly. At the southern tip of Brier Island is a **cairn,** commemorating the voyage.

Whale-Watching

Pirate's Cove Whale Cruises (⊠ Rte. 217, Tiverton, Long Island, ☎ 902/839–2242) operates whale-watching cruises from June through October. The fare is $33.

Annapolis Royal

★ **㉑** *29 km (18 mi) north of Digby.*

This town is well supplied with imposing mansions, particularly along the upper end of St. George Street, the oldest town street in Canada. Local businesses (or the tourist information center in the Annapolis Royal Tidal Power Building) can provide *Footprints with Footnotes,* a self-guided walking tour of the town; guided tours leave from the lighthouse on St. George Street, daily at 10 and 2:30.

Fort Anne National Historic Site was fortified in 1643; the present structures are the remnants of the fourth fort erected here and garrisoned by the British as late as 1854. The officers' quarters are now a museum with exhibits on the site's history. ⊠ *St. George St., Box 9, B0S 1A0,* ☎ *902/532–2397 or 902/532–2321,* 𝖥𝖠𝖷 *902/532–2232.* ▨ *Grounds free, museum $3.* ☽ *Mid-May–mid-Oct., daily 9–6; mid-Oct.–mid-May, by appointment.*

The **Annapolis Royal Historic Gardens** are 10 acres of magnificent theme gardens connected to a wildlife sanctuary. ⊠ *441 St. George St.,* ☎ *902/532–7018.* ▨ *$3.50.* ☽ *Mid-May–mid-Oct., daily 8–dusk.*

The **Annapolis Royal Tidal Power Project,** ¼ mile from Annapolis Royal, was designed to test the feasibility of generating electricity from tidal energy. This pilot project is the only tidal generating station in North America and one of only three operational sites in the world. The interpretive center explains the process with guided tours. ⊠ *Annapolis River Causeway,* ☎ *902/532–5454.* ⊠ *Free.* ⊙ *Mid-May–mid-June, daily 9–5:30; mid-June–Aug., daily 9–8; Sept.–mid-Oct., daily 9–5:30.*

Lodging

$$$ 🏠 **Auberge Wandlyn Royal Anne Motel.** This modern, no-frills motel has a pleasant, quiet setting on 20 acres of land. ⊠ *Box 628, Rte. 1, B0S 1A0,* ☎ *902/532–2323,* FAX *902/532–7277. 30 rooms. Restaurant, hot tubs, sauna, meeting rooms. AE, DC, MC, V.*

$$ 🏠 **Moorings Bed & Breakfast.** Built in 1881, this tall, beautiful home overlooking Annapolis Basin has a fireplace, tin ceilings, antiques, and contemporary art. ⊠ *Box 118, Granville Ferry B0S 1K0,* ☎ FAX *902/532–2146. 1 room with ½ bath, 2 rooms share bath. V.*

Port Royal

8 km (5 mi) downriver from Annapolis Royal on the opposite bank.

One of the oldest settlements in Canada, Port Royal was Nova Scotia's first capital (for both the French and English) until 1749, and the province's first military base. A national historic site commemorates the period.

The **Port Royal National Historic Site,** a reconstructed French fur-trading post, dates back to 1605 when Sieur deMonts and Samuel de Champlain built it. Here, amid the hardships of the New World, North America's first social club—the Order of Good Cheer—was founded, and Canada's first theatrical presentation was written and produced by Marc Lescarbot. ⊠ *Rte. 1 to Granville Ferry, left 12 km (7 mi),* ☎ *902/532–2898, 902/532–5589.* ⊠ *$3.* ⊙ *Mid-May–mid-Oct., daily 9–6.*

OFF THE BEATEN PATH
CAPE BLOMIDON – At Greenwich, take Route 358 to Cape Blomidon via Port Williams and Canning for a spectacular view of the Valley and the Bay of Fundy from the Lookoff.

HALL'S HARBOUR – This is one of the best natural harbors on the upper Bay of Fundy and can be reached via Route 359. Go for a walk on a gravel beach bordered by cliffs; try sea kayaking or wilderness camping, or seek out the intaglio printmaking studio.

Wolfville

㉒ *20 km (12 mi) east of Kentville.*

Settled in the 1760's by New England Planters, Wolfville is a charming college town with stately trees and ornate Victorian homes. Chimney swifts, aerobatic birds that fly in spectacular formation at the brink of dusk, are so abundant there's an interpretive display devoted to them at the **Robie Tufts Nature Centre** on Front Street. At the end of Front, by the harbor, are dikes built by the Acadians in the 1600s.

OFF THE BEATEN PATH
GRAND PRÉ NATIONAL HISTORIC SITE – Follow Route 101 through Wolfville about 5 km (3 mi) to the site that was once an Acadian village. A small stone church commemorates Longfellow's hero in *Evangeline* and houses an exhibit on the 1755 deportation of the Acadians from the Valley. ☎ *902/542–3631.* ⊙ *Mid-May–mid-Oct., daily 9–6.*

Dining and Lodging

$$$–$$$$ ✕🏠 **Blomidon Inn.** This 19th-century sea captain's mansion with 4 acres of lawns and gardens was restored in 1981. Guest rooms are

uniquely furnished, most with four-poster beds, and all with hand-made quilts. Relax over lunch or dinner in one of the dining rooms or on the terrace, enjoying fresh fare from the valley and sea. Lobster bisque and fresh Atlantic salmon are among the menu favorites, and their home-made bread baked with oats and molasses will leave you begging for the recipe. Afternoon tea is served daily, and there's a weekend brunch (reservations advised). ⊠ *127 Main St., Box 839, B0P 1X0,* ☎ *902/542–2291 or 800/565–2291,* ☏ *902/542–7461. 26 rooms. 2 dining rooms, tennis court, horseshoes, shuffleboard, meeting room. MC, V.*

Hiking

A popular hiking trail, 25 km (16 mi) north of Wolfville, leads from the end of Route 358 to the dramatic cliffs of Cape Split, a 13-km (8-mi) round-trip.

Windsor

㉓ *25 km (16 mi) southeast of Wolfville.*

Windsor, the last of the Valley towns, sits midway between the equator and the North Pole and was settled in 1703 as an Acadian community. Here, tide's average rise and fall is over 40 feet; you can see the tidal bore (the leading edge of the incoming tide) rushing up the Meander River and sometimes reaching a height of 3 feet.

Sainte Famille Winery in Falmouth, 5 km (3 mi) west of Windsor, is a family-owned vineyard where tours are offered that combine the region's ecological history with the intricacies of growing grapes and aging wine. Wine tasting is done in the gift shop, where bottles are sold at a steal. ⊠ *Dyke Rd. and Dudley Park La.,* ☎ *902/798–8311 or 800/565–0993,* ☏ *902/798–9418.* ☉ *June–Sept., Mon.–Sat. 9–6, Sun. noon–5; call for off-season hours and tour schedule.*

Fort Edward, one of the assembly points for the expulsion of the Acadians, still stands as the only remaining colonial blockhouse in Nova Scotia. ⊠ *Exit 6 off Rte. 1, 1st left at King St., left up street facing fire station,* ☎ *902/542–3631.* ☉ *Mid-June–Labor Day, daily 10–6.*

The **Haliburton House Museum,** a provincial museum on a manicured 25-acre estate, was the home of Judge Thomas Chandler Haliburton—lawyer, politician, historian, and humorist. His best-known work, *The Clockmaker,* pillories Nova Scotian follies from the viewpoint of a Yankee clock peddler, Sam Slick, whose witty sayings are still commonly used. ⊠ *414 Clifton Ave.,* ☎ *902/798–2915.* ☉ *June–Oct. 15, Mon.–Sat. 9:30–5:30, Sun. 1–5:30.*

OFF THE
BEATEN PATH

UNIACKE ESTATE MUSEUM PARK – Off of Route 1, 25 km (16 mi) east of Windsor, lies a summerhouse built about 1815 for Richard John Uniacke, attorney general and the advocate general to the Admiralty court during the War of 1812. The house, a superb example of colonial architecture on spacious grounds near a lake, is now a provincial museum. It's preserved in its original condition with many authentic furnishings. Several walking trails surround the estate. ⊠ *758 Main Rd., 30 km (19 mi) east of Windsor,* ☎ *902/866-2560.* ☒ *Free.* ☉ *June–Oct. 15, Mon.–Sat. 9:30–5:30, Sun. 1–5:30.*

NORTHERN NOVA SCOTIA

The area that lies between Halifax and Cape Breton Island includes the rugged coastline on the Atlantic, the gentler Bay of Fundy and Northumberland Strait. Fishing villages, sandy beaches, and remote cranberry barrens range along the eastern shore. The salt marshes, Scottish clans, and feasts of lobster along Northumberland Strait give way to mills, rolling hills, hiking trails, and farms as you move inland. A land of high tides, million-year-old fossils, and semiprecious stones borders the Bay of Fundy. Walk on the bottom of the sea when the mighty Fundy tide recedes, or ride the tidal bore as it comes rushing back.

This region takes in parts of three of the official Scenic Trails, including Marine Drive (315 km, or 195 mi), the Sunrise Trail (316 km, or 196 mi), and the Glooscap Trail (365 km, or 226 mi). Any one leg of the routes could be done comfortably as an overnight trip from Halifax; for the whole tour, allow at least three or four days.

Musquodoboit Harbour

24 *45 km (28 mi) east of Dartmouth.*

Musquodoboit Harbour, with about 930 residents, is a substantial village at the mouth of the Musquodoboit River. The river itself offers good trout and salmon fishing, and the village touches on two slender and lovely harbors.

Lodging

$$–$$$ **Salmon River House.** About 35 minutes east of Dartmouth, where Route 7 crosses the Salmon River, is this unpretentious white-frame inn on 30 acres that provides glorious views. The home has a sun room and one room with a waterbed and whirlpool bath. ✉ *9931 #7 Hwy., Salmon River Bridge, B0J 1P0,* ☎ *902/889–3353 or 800/565–3353,* FAX *902/889–3653. 6 rooms with bath or shower. Dining room, boating, fishing. MC, V.*

Beach

One of the Eastern Shore's best beaches, **Martinique Beach,** is about 12 km (7 mi) south of Musquodoboit Harbour. Other fine beaches are at Clam Bay and Clam Harbour, several kilometers east of Martinique.

OFF THE   **MOOSE RIVER GOLD MINES** – This small local museum, about 30 km (19
BEATEN PATH   mi) north of Tangier on Route 224, commemorates the small gold rush
              that occurred during the first part of this century, complete with a 1936
              mine disaster. During the turmoil, the first live, on-the-spot radio news-
              casts were made throughout Canada and the world. It's open July
              through August.

En Route   As you travel through **Ship Harbour** take note of the strings of white buoys, marking one of North America's largest cultivated mussel farms.

Sherbrooke Village

★ **25** *83 km (51 mi) north of Sheet Harbour.*

This living history village, though it has fewer than 400 residents, is this shore's leading tourist center. The St. Mary's River, which flows through the hamlet, is one of Nova Scotia's best salmon rivers. Twenty-five buildings have been restored on their original sites by the Nova Scotia Museum to their late 19th-century character, including a blacksmith shop, water-powered sawmill, horse-drawn wagons, tearooms, and stores. ✉ *Rte. 7,* ☎ *902/522–2400.* 🎟 *$4.* ☉ *June–mid-Oct., daily 9:30–5:30.*

Antigonish

㉖   *62 km (38 mi) north of Sherbrooke Village on Hwy. 104.*

Antigonish is the home of **St. Francis Xavier University,** a center for Gaelic studies and the first coeducational Catholic institution to graduate women.

Dining

$$ ✕ **Lobster Treat Restaurant.** This cozily decorated brick, pine, and stained-glass restaurant was once a two-room schoolhouse. The varied menu includes fresh seafood, chicken, pastas, and bread and pies baked on the premises. Because of its relaxed atmosphere and children's menu, families enjoy coming here. ✉ *241 Post Rd. (Trans-Canada Hwy.),* ☏ *902/863–5465. AE, DC, MC, V. Closed Nov.–mid-Apr.*

En Route   Follow Route 337, the Sunrise Trail, for a glorious drive along St. George's Bay with its many good swimming beaches, before the road abruptly climbs 1,000 feet up and over to Cape George. There's a little take-out shop on the wharf at **Ballantyne's Cove,** a tiny artificial harbor near the tip of Cape George, that has some of the best fish-and-chips in Nova Scotia. Grab an order and enjoy the views. After following the Cape, high above the sea, the road runs along Northumberland Strait through lonely farmlands and tiny villages, such as **Arisaig,** where on the Arisaig shore, you can search for fossils. **Lismore,** just a few kilometers west of Arisaig, affirms the Scottish origin of its people with a stone cairn commemorating Bonnie Prince Charlie's Highland rebels, slaughtered by the English at Culloden in 1746. Lobster is landed and processed in shoreside factories here—a great place to buy some of the freshest lobster possible.

Pictou

★ ㉗   *74 km (46 mi) west of Antigonish.*

First occupied by the Mi'kmaqs, this well-developed town on Pictou Harbour became a Scottish settlement in 1773, when a land grant to the Philadelphia Company gave access to nearly 200 Highland Scots. Now one of the largest communities on the Northumberland Strait, it's considered the "birthplace of New Scotland."

Free factory tours at **Grohmann Knives** introduce the art of knife making. ✉ *116 Water St.,* ☏ *902/485–4224.* ☉ *Weekdays 9–3.*

At the **Hector Heritage Quay,** a replica of the *Hector* is under construction. In 1773 the *Hector*—the nearest thing to a Canadian *Mayflower*—came to Pictou Harbour, inaugurating the torrent of Scottish immigration that permanently altered the character of the province and the nation. An interpretive center with audio and visual displays that tell the story of Pictou's Scottish settlement are on the grounds, as well as working blacksmith and carpentry shops. ✉ *73 Harbour Dr.,* ☏ *902/485–6057.* ▣ *$4.* ☉ *May–Oct., daily 9–8.*

Under the inspired leadership of such men as the pioneering educator Thomas McCulloch, Pictou quickly became a center of commerce, education, theological disputation, and radical politics. **McCulloch House,** a restored 1806 building with displays of McCulloch's scientific collection and such personal items as furniture, is preserved as part of the Nova Scotia Museum. ✉ *Old Haliburton Rd.,* ☏ *902/485–4563.* ▣ *Free.* ☉ *June–mid-Oct., Mon.–Sat. 9:30–5:30, Sun. 11:30–5:30.*

Dining and Lodging

$$–$$$ ✕🖼 **Braeside Inn.** Built in 1938, this inn, on a 5-acre hillside in the center of historic Pictou, has well-appointed accommodations and fine food. Beaches are nearby, and a shuttle services Pictou's two marinas. The dining room specializes in fresh seafood dishes. ✉ *Box 1810, 126 Front St., B0K 1H0,* ☎ *902/485–5046 or 800/613–7701,* 🅵🅰🆇 *902/485– 1701. 20 rooms. 2 dining rooms, meeting room. AE, MC, V.*

$$ 🖼 **Walker Inn.** A hospitable and energetic couple run this downtown inn in their brick Georgian-style town house, built in 1865. Every room is different. ✉ *Box 629, 34 Coleraine St., B0K 1H0,* ☎ *902/485–1433 or 800/370–5553. 10 no-smoking rooms. Dining room (guests only), library, meeting room. AE, MC, V.*

Beach

About 23 km (14 mi) east of Pictou, follow the shore road from Highway 104 to **Melmerby Beach,** one of the warmest beaches on the province.

OFF THE
BEATEN PATH

BALMORAL GRIST MILL MUSEUM – A water-powered gristmill serves as the centerpiece for this museum, 25 km (16 mi) southeast of Pictou. Built in 1860, it's the oldest operating mill in Nova Scotia. Observe the milling demonstrations, then have a picnic in the park on the grounds. ✉ *660 Matheson Brook Rd., Balmoral Mills,* ☎ *902/657-3016.* 🖼 *Free.* ☉ *June–mid-Oct., Mon.–Sat. 9:30–5:30, Sun. 1–5:30; demonstrations daily 10–noon and 2–4.*

Malagash

65 km (40 mi) west of Pictou.

Malagash is best known for a winery that flourishes in the warm climate influenced by the Northumberland Strait. **Jost Vineyards** produces a surprisingly wide range of international award-winning wines, including an ice wine that's making a name for the vineyard. Tours run at 3 PM daily, from mid-June through September. Allow time to enjoy the deli-bar, patio deck, children's playground, and picnic area. ✉ *Off Hwy. 104, on Rte. 6,* ☎ *902/257–2636, 800/565–4567 in Atlantic Canada.*

Pugwash

❷❽ *26 km (16 mi) west of Malagash.*

Pugwash was the home of Cleveland industrialist Cyrus Eaton, at whose estate numerous Thinkers' Conferences brought together leading intellectual figures from the West and the Soviet Union during the 1950s and 1960s. Pugwash is still Scottish terrain, as the Gaelic street signs attest.

Seagull Pewter (✉ Durham St., ☎ 902/243–2516), a husband-and-wife crafts operation that has grown into a $25 million business of exporting pewter vessels, picture frames, and other artifacts worldwide, has a showroom that fronts on the main highway.

Amherst

44 km (27 mi) west of Pugwash.

Amherst stands on one of the glacial ridges that borders the Tantramar Marsh, said to be the largest marsh in the world. It was once a thriving manufacturing center for many products, including pianos and furnaces. In 1917, en route from New York to Russia, the Communist leader Leon Trotsky was confined here for a month in a prisoner-of-war camp.

Lodging

$$$
★

☒ **Amherst Shore Country Inn.** This seaside country inn, with a beautiful view of Northumberland Strait, has comfortable rooms, suites, and cottages fronting 600 feet of private beach. Incredibly well-prepared four-course dinners incorporating home-grown produce are served at one daily seating (7:30, by reservation only). ☒ *Lorneville (32 km, or 20 mi, from Amherst on Rte. 366), R.R. 2, Amherst, B4H 3X9,* ☎ *902/661–4800. 4 rooms, 4 suites, 1 cottage. Dining room. AE, DC, MC, V. Closed late Oct.–Apr.*

Springhill

㉙   *42 km (26 mi) southeast of Amherst.*

Route 2 leads through the coal-mining town of Springhill, the site of the famous mine disaster immortalized in the folk song "The Ballad of Springhill" by Peggy Seeger and Ewen McColl.

Tour a real coal mine at the **Spring Hill Miners Museum.** ☒ *Black River Rd., off Rte. 2,* ☎ *902/597–3449.* ☒ *$5.* ☼ *Mid-May–mid-Oct.*

Springhill is the hometown of internationally acclaimed singer Anne Murray, whose career is celebrated in the **Anne Murray Centre.** ☒ *Main St.,* ☎ *902/597–8614.* ☒ *$5.* ☼ *May–Oct., daily 9–5.*

Joggins

㉚   *40 km (25 mi) west of Springhill.*

Joggins's main draw is the coal-age fossils embedded in its 150-foot sandstone cliffs. Visit the **Joggins Fossil Centre,** where you can learn about the region's geological and archaeological history. Guided tours of the fossil cliffs are available, but departure times depend on the tides. Maps are issued for independent fossil hunters. ☒ *30 Main St.,* ☎ *902/251–2727.* ☒ *Centre $3.50, tour $10.* ☼ *June–Sept., daily 9–6:30.*

En Route   **Advocate Harbour,** 66 km (41 mi) south of Joggins, was named by Champlain for his friend Marc Lescarbot, who was a lawyer, or "avocat." Built on flat shore land with a tall ridge backdrop and a broad harbor before it, Advocate is eerily beautiful.

Cap d'Or

5 km (3 mi) east of Advocate Harbour.

Cape d'Or, land jutting out and dividing the waters of the main Bay of Fundy from the narrow enclosure of the Minas Basin, has a spectacular vista and lighthouse. As the tides change, fierce riptides create stunning waves. The view from the ridge down to the lighthouse is superb—keep your eyes peeled for peregrine falcons. The view from the lighthouse itself is almost equally magnificent, but the road down is rather primitive and should be attempted only in four-wheel-drive vehicles. Those who can handle the steep return climb can park at the top of the hill and walk down.

En Route   **Spencer's Island** (not really an island) is a 19th-century shipbuilding community on Route 209. A cairn commemorates the construction of the famous *Mary Celeste,* which was found in 1872 sailing in the mid-Atlantic without a crew; she had been abandoned at sea with the table still set for dinner.

Parrsboro

③ *45 km (28 mi) east of Spencer's Island.*

Parrsboro, a center for rock hounds and fossil hunters, is the main town on this shore, and hosts the **Rockhound Roundup** every August. Among the exhibits and festivities are geological displays, concerts, and other special events.

Parrsboro is an appropriate setting for the **Fundy Geological Museum** since it's not far from the Minas Basin area, the site where some of the oldest dinosaur fossils in Canada were found. Two-hundred-million-year-old dinosaur fossils are displayed here alongside exhibits of amethysts, agates, zeolites, and other mineral, plant, and animal relics that have washed out of nearby cliffs. ⊠ *6 Two Island Rd.,* ☎ *902/254–3814.* ☞ *$3.* ☉ *June–Oct. 15, daily 9:30–5:30.*

The "world's smallest dinosaur footprints" are on display at the **Parrsboro Rock and Mineral Shop and Museum** (⊠ 39 Whitehall Rd., ☎ 902/254–2981), run by Eldon George.

Although fossils have become Parrsboro's claim to fame, this harbor town was also a major shipping and shipbuilding port, and its history is described at the **Ottawa House Museum-by-the-Sea,** 3 km (2 mi) east of Parrsboro. Ottawa House, which overlooks the Bay of Fundy, was the summer home of Sir Charles Tupper, a former premier of Nova Scotia who was briefly prime minister of Canada. ⊠ *Whitehall Rd.,* ☎ *902/254–2376.* ☞ *$1.* ☉ *July–early Sept., daily 10–8.*

The Arts

Parrsboro's professional **Ship's Company Theatre** (☎ 902/254–3425) has a summer season of plays based on historical events of the region, performed aboard the MV *Kipawo,* a former Minas Basin ferry.

Hiking

Ward's Falls is a beautiful 6 km (4 mi) interpreted hiking trail about 5 km (3 mi) east of Parrsboro.

En Route   The 125-foot-high **Hidden Falls,** near Route 2, are about 5 km (3 mi) east of Parrsboro. Although the falls are located on private property, the path leading from the gift shop is open to the public and parking is available.

Five Islands

24 km (15 mi) east of Parrsboro.

Among the most beautiful scenic areas along Route 2 is Five Islands, which, according to Mi'Kmaq legend, was created when the god Glooscap threw handfuls of sod at beaver. **Five Islands Provincial Park** (⊠ Rte. 2, ☎ 902/254–2980), on the shore of Minas Basin, has a campground, a beach, hiking trails, and some interpretation of the region's unusual geology.

Lodging

$$–$$$ 🏠 **Shady Maple B&B.** Here's a unique property: a working farm where you can breakfast on fresh eggs and the farm's own maple syrup, jams, and jellies. Enjoy the smoke-free rooms and sun-dried bed linen, and take a dip in the pool. One of the three rooms is a deluxe suite with a waterbed. Full breakfast included. ⊠ *R.R. 1, Masstown B0M 1G0,* ☎ *902/662–3565,* ℻ *902/662–3565. 3 rooms. Pool. MC, V.*

CAPE BRETON ISLAND

The highways and byways of the Island of Cape Breton make up one of the most spectacular drives in North America. Wind through the rugged coastal headlands of Cape Breton Highlands National Park where you can climb mountains and plunge back down to the sea in a matter of minutes. The Margaree River is a cultural dividing line: South of the river the settlements are Scottish, up the river they are largely Irish, and north of the river they are Acadian French. Visit villages where ancient dialects can still be heard, and explore a fortress where period players bring history to life. This is a place where heritage is alive, where the atmosphere is maritime, and where inventors Marconi and Bell share the spotlight with coal miners and singers like Rita MacNeil.

Bras d'Or Lake, a vast, warm, almost-landlocked inlet of the sea, occupies the entire center of Cape Breton. The coastline of the lake is more than 967 km (600 mi) long, and people sail yachts from all over the world to cruise its serene, unspoiled coves and islands. Bald eagles have become so plentiful around the lake that they are now exported to the United States to restock natural habitats. Four of the largest communities along the shore are Mi'Kmaq Indian reserves.

If Halifax is the heart of Nova Scotia, Cape Breton is its soul, complete with soul music: flying fiddles, boisterous rock, velvet ballads. Cape Breton musicians—weaned on Scottish jigs and reels—are among Canada's finest, and you can hear them all over the island all summer long at dozens of local festivals and concerts.

Allow three or four days for this meandering tour of approximately 710 km (about 440 mi) that begins by entering the island via the Canso Causeway on Highway 104. Turn left at the rotary and take Route 19, the Ceilidh Trail (129 km, or 80 mi), which winds along the mountainside through green wooden glens and hidden farms, with fine views across St. George's Bay to Cape George. This western shoreline of Cape Breton faces the Gulf of St. Lawrence and is famous for its sandy beaches and warm saltwater.

Mabou

③② *13 km (8 mi) northeast of Port Hood on Rte. 19.*

Mabou has been called "the prettiest village in Canada," and it is also perhaps the most Scottish, with its Gaelic signs and a deep tradition of Scottish music and dancing. This is the hometown of national recording and performing artists such as John Allan Cameron and the Rankin Family; stop at a local gift shop and pick up some tapes to play as you drive down the long fjord of Mabou Harbour.

Lodging

$$$ **⊞ Glenora Inn & Distillery.** This friendly inn is home to North America's only single malt whisky distillery. Sample a "wee dram" of their own whiskey—billed as Canada's first legal moonshine. Stop in for a distillery tour, fine cuisine, and traditional Cape Breton music even if you don't plan to stay overnight. From November through April, rooms are available by reservation only. ⊠ *Glenville (Rte. 19 between Mabou and Inverness), B0E 1X0,* ☎ *902/258–2662. 9 inn rooms, 6 chalets. Restaurant, pub, gift shop, convention facilities. AE, MC, V.*

Mabou Mines

10 km (6 mi) northwest of Mabou.

This town, known as "the mines," is a place so hauntingly exquisite that you expect to meet the *sidhe*, the Scottish fairies, capering on the hillsides. Within the hills of Mabou Mines is some of the finest hiking in the province, and above the land fly bald eagles, plentiful in this region. Inquire locally or at the tourist office on Margaree Forks for information about trails.

En Route Take Route 19 to Route 219 and follow the coast to **Chimney Corner.** A nearby beach has "sonorous sands": When you step on the sand or drag a foot through it, it squeaks and moans.

Margaree Harbour

③ *28 km (17 mi) north of Inverness.*

The Ceilidh Trail joins the Cabot Trail at Margaree Harbour at the mouth of the Margaree River, a famous salmon-fishing stream and a favorite canoe route.

Dining and Lodging

$$$ ✕🏨 **Normaway Inn.** This secluded 1920s inn, nestled on 250 acres in the hills of the Margaree Valley at the beginning of the Cabot Trail, has distinctive rooms and cabins, most with wood stoves and screened porches; some have hot tubs. Take advantage of the traditional entertainment or films featured nightly, and the weekly square dances in the "Barn." The inn is known for its country cuisine, particularly the vegetable chowders and fresh seafood ragoût. ✉ *Box 326, Egypt Rd., 2 mi off Cabot Trail, B0E 2C0,* ☎ *902/248–2987 or 800/565–9463,* 🖷 *902/ 248–2600. 9 rooms, 19 cabins. Restaurant, tennis court, hiking and walking trails, bicycles, travel services. MC, V. Closed mid-Oct.–mid-June.*

$–$$ 🏨 **Heart of Hart's Inn.** This 100-year-old rural farmhouse is within walking distance of the village of North East Margaree. The theme is "very country," with wood stove, antiques, colonial colored glass, and an array of flowers in the gardens. A full breakfast is included in the room rate, and four-course country dinners of local and regional foods are served nightly by reservation, at $30 per person. ✉ *Cabot Trail, Box 21, B0E 2H0,* ☎ *902/248–2765,* 🖷 *902/248–2606. 5 rooms. Travel services. MC, V.*

Chéticamp

④ *26 km (16 mi) north of Margaree Harbour.*

Chéticamp, an Acadian community, has the best harbor and the largest settlement on this shore. With its tall silver steeple towering over the village, it stands exposed on a wide lip of flat land below a range of bald green hills, behind which lies the high plateau of the Cape Breton Highlands. Chéticamp is famous for its hooked rugs, available at many local gift shops.

The **Dr. Elizabeth LeFort Gallery and Museum** displays artifacts and fine hooked embroidery work, rugs, and tapestries. ✉ *Les Trois Pignons.* 🖷 *$3. May–Oct., weekdays 9–5; July and Aug., daily 9–6.*

Whale-Watching

Chéticamp is known for its whale-watching cruises, which depart in June, twice daily, and in July and August, three times daily, from the government wharf. **Whale Cruisers Ltd.** (☎ *902/224–3376 or 800/813–3376*) is a reliable charter company. Cruises cost $25 for adults.

Cape Breton Highlands National Park

★ *At the outskirts of Chéticamp.*

This 950-square-km (361-square-mi) wilderness of wooded valleys, plateau barrens, and steep cliffs stretches across the northern peninsula of Cape Breton from the Gulf Shore to the Atlantic. The highway through the park is magnificent as it rises to the tops of the coastal mountains and descends through tight switchbacks to the sea. In fact the road has been compared to a 106-km (66-mi) roller coaster ride, stretching from Chéticamp to Ingonish. Good brakes and an attentive driver are advised. Pull-offs provide photo opportunities. For wildlife watchers there's much to see, including moose, eagle, deer, bear, fox, and bobcat. Your chances of seeing wildlife are better if you venture off the main road at dusk or dawn. High altitude marshlands are home to delightful wild orchids and other unique flora and fauna. If you plan to hike, fish or camp in the park, or want to maximize your appreciation for the nature and history associated within the park, stop at the Chéticamp Information Centre for advice and necessary permits. A guide to the park's 27 hiking trails, *Walking in the Highlands*, can be purchased. Trails range from easy 20-minute strolls to tough overnight treks. ☎ *902/285–2535, 902/285–2270 in winter.* ✉ *May–Oct. $3.50 per person per day, 4-day pass $10.50, seasonal pass $17.50; Nov.–Apr. free (including use of Cabot Trail lookouts within park, roadside exhibits, walking trails, picnic areas); camping $13–$19.*

OFF THE BEATEN PATH **GAMPO ABBEY –** The most northerly tip of the island is not part of the National Park; a spur road creeps along the cliffs to Red River, beyond which, on a broad flat bench of land high above the sea, is this Tibetan Buddhist monastery. It's the only one in America.

Ingonish

③⑤ *113 km (70 mi) northeast of Chéticamp.*

Ingonish, one of the leading holiday destinations on the island, is actually several villages on two bays, divided by a long narrow peninsula called Middle Head. Each bay has a sandy beach.

Dining and Lodging

$$$$ ✕▥ **Keltic Lodge.** Spread across cliffs overlooking the ocean, the provincially owned Keltic Lodge sits on the Cabot Trail in Cape Breton Highlands National Park (☞ *above*). Guests can choose among the Main Lodge, White Birch Inn, and two- or four-bedroom cottages. A wide variety of activities is offered, including golfing on the world-class Highlands Links. Seafood stars on the menu in the Purple Thistle Dining Room. ✉ *Middlehead Peninsula, Ingonish Beach, B0C 1L0,* ☎ *902/285–2880 or 800/565–0444. 98 rooms. 2 Restaurants, pool, golf, hiking, beaches. Closed Apr., May, Nov., and Dec.*

OFF THE BEATEN PATH **BIRD ISLANDS –** From Big Bras d'Or, 100 km (62 mi) south of Ingonish, notice the small islands on the far side of the mouth of St. Ann's Bay: These are the Bird Islands, breeding grounds for Atlantic puffins, black guillemots, razor-billed auks, and cormorants. Boat tours are available from **Bird Islands Boat Tour** (☎ 902/674–2384). Landing on the islands is forbidden, however.

Englishtown

65 km (40 mi) south of Ingonish on Rte. 312.

Take the short (about 2 minutes) ferry ride from Jersey Cove across St. Ann's Bay to Englishtown, home of the celebrated Cape Breton Giant, Angus MacAskill. Ferries run 24 hours a day, and the fare is 50¢. The **Giant MacAskill Museum** holds artifacts and the remains of the 7′9″ man who traveled with P.T. Barnum's troupe in the 1800s. ⊠ *Rte. 312,* ☎ *902/929–2875.* ⊡ *$1.* ⊙ *May–Oct., daily 9–6.*

South Gut St. Ann's

12 km (7 mi) south of Jersey Cove.

Settled by the Highland Scots, South Gut St. Ann's is home to North America's only **Gaelic College** (☎ 902/295–3441). Its Great Hall of the Clans depicts Scottish history and has an account of the Great Migration. The college offers courses in Gaelic language and literature, Scottish music and dancing, weaving, and other Scottish arts. There's also a Scottish gift shop.

Baddeck

36 *20 km (12 mi) south of South Gut St. Ann's.*

Baddeck, the most highly developed tourist center in Cape Breton, has more than 1,000 motel beds, a golf course, many fine gift shops, and numerous restaurants. It was also the summer home of Alexander Graham Bell until he died here at the age of 75. In summer the town celebrates **Centre Bras d'Or Festival of the Arts,** which offers live music and drama every evening during summer. The annual **regatta** of the Bras d'Or Yacht Club is held in the first week of August. Sailing tours and charters are available locally, as are bus tours along the Cabot Trail.

Discover how Alexander Graham Bell bridged the world between sound and silence at the **Alexander Graham Bell National Historic Site.** Participate in experiments, kite making, and other hands-on activities designed especially for children, and take in a presentation in Mr. Bell Theatre, where you can view films, artifacts, and photographs to learn how ideas led Bell to create man-carrying kites, airplanes, and a marine record-setting hydrofoil boat. ⊠ *Chebucto St.,* ☎ *902/295–2069,* FAX *902/295–3496.* ⊡ *$3.75.* ⊙ *July and Aug., daily 9–8; June and Sept., daily 9–7; Oct.–May (reduced service), daily 9–5.*

Dining and Lodging

$$$$ ✕🖼 **Inverary Inn Resort.** On the shores of the magnificent Bras d'Or Lake, this resort has stunning views and a lot of activities for the money. Choose from cozy pine-paneled cottages, modern hotel units, or the elegant 100-year-old main lodge. There's boating and swimming in close proximity to the village, but the resort remains tranquil. Families will appreciate the on-site children's playground and the choice of dining in the Lakeside Cafe or the elegant main dining room. ⊠ *Box 190, Rte. 205 and Shore Rd., B0E 1B0,* ☎ *902/295–3500 or 800/565–5600,* FAX *902/295–3527. 137 rooms. Restaurant, café, indoor pool, sauna, 3 tennis courts, boat rental. AE, D, MC, V.*

Beach

A free ferry (passengers only) shuttles between the government wharf and the sandy beach by the lighthouse at Kidston Island.

Iona

③⑦ *56 km (35 mi) south of Baddeck.*

From Baddeck, take Trans-Canada Highway 105 to Exit 6, which leads to Little Narrows where you can take a short ferry ride to the Washabuck Peninsula. From here, take Route 223 to Iona, the site of the **Nova Scotia Highland Village,** set high on a mountainside, with a spectacular view of Bras d'Or Lake and the narrow Barra Strait. The village's 10 historic buildings were assembled from all over Cape Breton to depict Highland Scots' way of life from their origins in the Hebrides to the present day. Among the participants at this living-history museum are a smith in the blacksmith shop and a clerk in the store. Ferries run 24 hours a day, and the fare is 25¢. ⊠ *Rte. 233,* ☎ *902/725–2227.* ⊑ *$4.* ☉ *Reception desk and museum June–Sept., Mon.–Sat. 9–5, Sun. 10–6; Welcome Center Oct.–May, weekdays 9–5.*

Dining and Lodging

$$ ✕⊡ **Highland Heights Inn.** The rural surroundings, the Scottish home-style cooking served near the dining room's huge stone fireplace, and the view of the lake substitute nicely for the Scottish Highlands. The inn is on a hillside beside the Nova Scotia Highland Village, overlooking the village of Iona, where some residents still speak the Gaelic language of their ancestors. Enjoy the salmon (or any fish in season), fresh-baked oat cakes, and homemade desserts. ⊠ *Box 19, Rte. 223,* ☎ *902/725–2360,* FAX *902/725–2800. 26 rooms. Dining room. D, MC, V. Closed mid-Oct.–mid-May.*

En Route   The Barra Strait Bridge joins Iona to Grand Narrows. A few kilometers from the bridge, bear right toward East Bay. (If you miss this turn, don't worry; you'll have just as scenic a drive along St. Andrews Channel.) The East Bay route runs through the Mi'Kmaq village of **Eskasoni,** the largest native community in the province. This is one of the friendliest villages, with a fascinating cultural heritage.

Sydney

③⑧ *60 km (37 mi) northeast of Iona.*

The heart of Nova Scotia's second-largest urban cluster, Sydney is known as "Industrial Cape Breton." It encompasses villages, unorganized districts, and a half-dozen towns—most of which sprang up around the coal mines, which fed the steel plant at Sydney. These are warmhearted, interesting communities with a diverse ethnic population, including Ukrainians, Welsh, Poles, Lebanese, West Indians, Italians; most residents descended from the miners and steelworkers who arrived a century ago when the area was booming. Sydney is also the only significantly industrialized district in Atlantic Canada, and it has suffered serious environmental damage.

Sydney has the island's only real airport, its only university, and a lively entertainment scene that specializes in Cape Breton music. The town is also a departure point: Fast ferries leave from North Sydney for Newfoundland, and scheduled air service to Newfoundland and the French islands of St. Pierre and Miquelon departs from Sydney Airport.

Dining and Lodging

$$$ ✕⊡ **Delta Sydney.** This hotel is on the harbor, beside the yacht club, and close to the center of town. The attractively decorated guest rooms each have a view of the harbor. The intimate dining room specializes in seafood and Continental cuisine. ⊠ *300 Esplanade, B1P 6J4,* ☎ *902/562–7500 or 800/887–1133, 800/268–1133 in Canada,* FAX

902/562–3023. *152 rooms. Restaurant, lounge, indoor pool, sauna, exercise room. AE, DC, MC, V.*

Nightlife and the Arts

The **Cape Breton Summertime Revue,** based in Sydney, performs an annual original revue of music and comedy that tours Nova Scotia during June and August. Many leading fiddlers appear at the **Big Pond Concert** in mid-July. At the **Sheraton Casino** (⊠ 625 George St., ☏ 902/563–7777), try the slot machines, roulette, or gaming tables, or enjoy live entertainment in the lounge. Glace Bay's opulent old opera house, the **Savoy Theatre** (⊠ Union St., ☏ 902/842–1577) is the home of the summer-long Festival on the Bay. The **University College of Cape Breton** (⊠ 1250 Grand Lake Rd., ☏ 902/539–5300) has many facilities for the public, such as the **Boardmore Playhouse** and the island's only public **art gallery.**

Louisbourg

㊴ *33 km (20 mi) southeast of Sydney.*

★ Though best known as the home of the largest National Historic Site in Canada, Louisbourg is also an important fishing community with a lovely harborfront. **Fortress of Louisbourg National Historic Park,** the most remarkable site in Cape Breton, is about 30 minutes from Sydney. After the French were forced out of mainland Nova Scotia in 1713, they established their headquarters here in a walled and fortified town on a low point of land at the mouth of Louisbourg Harbour. The fortress was twice captured, once by New Englanders and once by the British; after the second siege, in 1758, it was razed. Its capture essentially ended the French Empire in America. A quarter of the original town has been rebuilt on its foundation, just as it was in 1744, before the first siege. Costumed actors re-create the lives and activities of the original inhabitants; you can watch a military drill, see nails and lace being made, and eat food prepared from 18th-century recipes in the town's two inns. Plan on spending at least a half day. Louisbourg tends to be chilly, so pack a warm sweater or windbreaker. ⊠ *Rte. 22,* ☏ *902/733–2280 or 800/565–9464.* 🎫 *$7.50.* ⏲ *June and Sept., daily 9:30–5; July and Aug., daily 9–6.*

At the **Sydney and Louisburg Historical Society,** a restored 1895 railway station exhibits the history of the S&L Railway, railway technology, and marine shipping. The rolling stock includes a baggage car, coach, and caboose. ⊠ *7336 Main St.,* ☏ *902/733–2720.* 🎫 *Free.* ⏲ *June and Sept., weekdays 9–5; July and Aug., daily 9–7.*

Atlantic Statiquarium is a marine museum devoted largely to underwater treasure. ⊠ *7523 Main St.,* ☏ *902/733–2721.* 🎫 *$2.50.* ⏲ *June–Sept., daily 10–8.*

Big Pond

40 km (25 mi) west of Sydney.

Take Route 22 to Route 125. From here, turn onto Route 4 and follow it to this little town comprised of just a few houses. One of them is the home of singer/songwriter Rita MacNeil, who operates a tearoom in a tranquil setting with seating indoors and out. Stop in for Rita's special blend of tea and home-baked goodies such as oatcakes. A display room contains Rita's awards and memorabilia.

En Route Route 4 rolls along the lake, sometimes close to the shore and sometimes high in the hills. At **St. Peter's** the Atlantic Ocean is connected with the Bras d'Or Lake by the century-old St. Peter's Canal, still heavily used by pleasure craft and fishing vessels. From St. Peter's to Port Hawkesbury the population is largely Acadian French.

Arichat

40 *43 km (27 mi) south of Dundee.*

Take Route 247 to Route 320 and head for Isle Madame, a 27-square-km (10-square-mi) island named for Madame de Maintenon, second wife of Louis XIV. Route 320 leads through the villages of Poulamon and D'Escousse, and overlooks the protected waterway of Lennox Passage, with its spangle of islands. Route 206 meanders through the low hills to a maze of land and water at West Arichat. Together, the two routes encircle the island, meeting at Arichat, the principal town of Isle Madame.

Arichat was once the seat of the local Catholic diocese. Notre Dame de l'Assumption church, built in 1837, still retains the grandeur of its former cathedral status. Its bishop's palace, the only one in Cape Breton, is now a law office. The two cannons overlooking the harbor were installed after the town was sacked by John Paul Jones, founder of the U.S. Navy, during the American Revolution.

The town was an important shipbuilding and trading center during the 19th century, and some fine old houses from that period still remain, along with the 18th-century **LeNoir Forge,** a restored French 18th-century stone blacksmith shop. ⊠ *Rte. 320 off Rte. 4,* ☎ *902/226–9364.* ☉ *May–Sept., weekdays 9–5, Sat. 10–3.*

OFF THE BEATEN PATH   **LITTLE ANSE –** With its rocky red bluffs, cobble shores, tiny harbor, and brightly painted houses, Little Anse is particularly attractive to artists and photographers.

NOVA SCOTIA A TO Z

Arriving and Departing

By Bus

Greyhound Lines (☎ 800/231–2222) from New York, and **Voyageur Inc.** (☎ 613/238–5900) from Montréal, connect with **Scotia Motor Tours** or **SMT** (☎ 506/458–6000) through New Brunswick, which links (rather inconveniently) with **Acadian Lines Limited** (☎ 902/454–8279), which provides inter-urban services within Nova Scotia.

By Car

Throughout Nova Scotia, the highways numbered from 100 to 199 are all-weather, limited-access roads, with 100-km-per-hour (62-mi-per-hour) speed limits. The last two digits usually match the number of an older trunk highway along the same route, numbered from 1 to 99. Thus, Route 102, between Halifax and Truro, matches the older Route 2, between the same towns. Roads numbered from 200 to 399 are secondary roads that usually link villages. Unless otherwise posted, the speed limit on these and any roads other than the 100-series highways is 80 km per hour (50 mi per hour).

Most highways in the province lead to Halifax and Dartmouth. Routes 3/103, 7, 2/102, and 1/101 terminate in the twin cities.

By Ferry

Three car ferries connect Nova Scotia with Maine and New Brunswick. **Marine Atlantic** (☎ 902/794–5700 or 800/341–7981) sails from Bar Harbor, Maine, and **Prince of Fundy Cruises** (☎ 800/341–7540) from

Portland; both arrive in Yarmouth. From Saint John, New Brunswick, to Digby, Nova Scotia, ferry service is provided by **Marine Atlantic** (☎ 800/341–7981; in Canada, 800/565–9470).

Marine Atlantic also operates ferries between New Brunswick and Prince Edward Island, and between Cape Breton and Newfoundland (☎ 902/794–5700, 709/772–7701, or 800/341–7981). Between May and December, **Northumberland Ferries** (☎ 902/566–3838; in Nova Scotia and Prince Edward Island, 800/565–0201) operate between Caribou, Nova Scotia, and Wood Islands, Prince Edward Island.

By Plane
The **Halifax International Airport** is 40 km (25 mi) northeast of downtown Halifax. **Sydney Airport** is 13 km (8 mi) east of Sydney.

Air Canada (☎ 902/429–7111 or 800/776–3000) provides regular, daily service to Halifax and Sydney, Nova Scotia, from New York, Boston, Toronto, Montréal, and St. John's, Newfoundland, as well as Frankfurt, Germany, twice weekly. **Canadian Airlines International** (☎ 800/527–8499) has service to Halifax via Toronto and Montréal. **Air Nova** (☎ 902/429–7111 or 800/776–3000) and **Air Atlantic** (☎ 800/426–7000; in Canada, 800/665–1177) provide regional service to both airports with flights to Toronto, Montréal, and Boston. **Canada 3000** (☎ 902/873–3555) offers service with Toronto, Calgary, Edmonton, Vancouver, London, Amsterdam, and Hamburg. **Northwest Air** (☎ 800/225–2525) provides summer service between Halifax and Detroit. **Icelandair** (☎ 902 873–2029) offers flights from Halifax to Reykjavik.

Visiting pilots will find aviation-related information for the flying tourist from the **Aviation Council of Nova Scotia** (✉ Box 100, Debert, Nova Scotia B0M 1G0, ☎ 902/895–1143). A publication, *Air Tourist Information: Canada,* is available on request from the **Aeronautical Information and Publications Office** (✉ Ministry of Transport, Place de Ville, Tower C, Ottawa, Ontario K1A 0N5).

BETWEEN THE AIRPORT AND CITY CENTER
Limousine and taxi service, as well as car rentals, are available at Halifax, Sydney, and Yarmouth airports. Airport bus service to most Halifax and Dartmouth hotels costs $20 round-trip, $12 one-way. Regular taxi fare is $35 each way, but if you book in advance with **Aero Cab** (☎ 902/445–3393) the fare is $26 if you pay cash, slightly more with a credit card (MC, V). The trip takes 30–40 minutes.

By Train
VIA Rail (☎ 800/561–3949) provides service from Montréal to Halifax via Moncton, in New Brunswick, and Amherst and Truro, in Nova Scotia. **Amtrak** (☎ 800/872–7245) from New York City makes connections in Montréal.

Getting Around

Halifax
BY BUS
Metro Transit (☎ 902/421–6600) provides bus service throughout the cities of Halifax and Dartmouth, the town of Bedford, and (to a limited extent) the county of Halifax. The base fare is $1.35; exact change only.

BY FERRY
Metro Transit (☞ *above*) runs three passenger ferries from the Halifax Ferry Terminal on the hour and half hour from 6:30 AM to 11:57 PM. During the weekday commuter rush, ferries cross continuously to the

Woodside Terminal from 6:52 AM to 10:04 AM and 3:37 PM to 6:19 PM only. Ferries also operate on Sunday during the summer (June–September). Free transfers are available from the ferry to the bus system (and vice versa). The fare for a single crossing is $1.10 and is well worth it considering you get an up-close view of both waterfronts.

BY TAXI

Rates begin at about $2.50 and increase based on mileage and time. A crosstown trip should cost $5–$6, depending on traffic. Hailing a taxi can be difficult, but there are taxi stands at major hotels and shopping malls. Most Haligonians simply phone for a taxi service; try **Aero Cab** (☞ By Plane, *above*).

Elsewhere in Nova Scotia

BY BUS

There are a number of small, regional bus services; however, connections are not always convenient. Outside of Halifax there are no inner-city bus services. For information, call **Nova Scotia Visitors Services** (☎ 800/565–0000).

BY CAR

The recommended mode of travel within the province is by car. As you explore Nova Scotia, be on the lookout for the 10 designated "Scenic Travelways" that appear throughout the province and are easily identified by roadside signs with icons that correspond with trail names. These routes, as well as tourist literature (maps and the provincial *Travel Guide*) published in accordance with this scheme, have been developed by the Nova Scotia Economic Renewal Agency. **Nova Scotia Tourism** (☞ Visitor Information, *below*) provides information and reservation services.

Many of the roads in rural Nova Scotia require attentive driving as they are not well signed, are narrow, and do not always have a paved shoulder. They are generally well surfaced.

BY PLANE

Internal air travel is very limited. **Air Nova** (☎ 902/429–7111 or 800/776–3000) and **Air Atlantic** (☎ 800/426–7000; in Canada, 800/665–1177) provide regional service to other provinces and to Sydney.

Contacts and Resources

Car Rentals

Halifax is the most convenient place from which to begin your driving tour of the province. It is recommended that you book a car through your own travel agent. The following list details city and airport venues of rental-car agencies. **Avis** (✉ 5600 Sackville St., ☎ 902/423–6303; airport, ☎ 902/873–3523). **Budget** (✉ 1558 Hollis St., ☎ 902/421–1242; airport, ☎ 902/873–3509). **Hertz** (✉ Halifax Sheraton, ☎ 902/421–1763; airport, ☎ 902/873–3700). **Thrifty** (✉ 6930 Lady Hammond, ☎ 902/422–4455; airport, ☎ 902/873–3527). **Tilden** (✉ 1130 Hollis St., ☎ 902/422–4433; airport, ☎ 902/873–3505).

Emergencies

Dial **"0"** for operator in emergencies; check the front of the local phone book for specific medical services.

Guided Tours

There are more than 20 tour operators specializing in specific areas, modes of transportation, tour topics, and types of groups. For information, and to connect with the tour company most suited to your needs, contact **Nova Scotia Tourism** (☎ 800/565–0000).

BOAT TOURS

Boat tours have become very popular in all regions of the province. For details contact **Nova Scotia Tourism** (☞ *above*).

Murphy's on the Water (☎ 902/420–1015) sails various vessels: *Harbour Queen I,* a paddle wheeler; *Haligonian III,* an enclosed motor launch; *Stormy Weather I,* a 40-foot Cape Islander (fishing boat); and *Mar II,* a 75-foot sailing ketch. All operate from mid-May to late October from berths at 1751 Lower Water Street on Cable Wharf next to the Historic Properties in Halifax. Costs vary, but a basic tour of the Halifax Harbour ranges from $10 to $15.

BUS TOURS

Both **Gray Line Sightseeing** (☎ 902/454–8279) and **Cabana Tours** (☎ 902/423–6066) run coach tours through Halifax, Dartmouth, and Peggy's Cove. **Halifax Double Decker Tours** (☎ 902/420–1155) offers two-hour tours on double-decker buses that leave daily from Historic Properties in Halifax.

Outdoor Activities and Sports

BIKING

Bicycle Tours in Nova Scotia ($7) is published by **Bicycle Nova Scotia** (✉ Box 3010, 5516 Spring Garden Rd., Halifax B3J 3G6, ☎ 902/425–5450). **Backroads** (✉ 1516 5th St., Suite Q333, Berkeley, CA 94710, ☎ 510/527–1555 or 800/245–3874) offers five- and six-day bike trips in the province.

BIRD-WATCHING

Nova Scotia is located on the "Atlantic Flyway" and is an important staging point for migrating species. An excellent, beautifully illustrated book, *Birds of Nova Scotia,* by Robie Tufts, is a must on every ornithologist's reading list.

CANOEING

Nova Scotia is seamed with small rivers and lakes, by which the Mi'K-maq Indians roamed both Cape Breton and the peninsula. Especially good canoe routes are within Kejimkujik National Park. The publication *Canoe Routes of Nova Scotia* and a variety of route maps are available from the **Nova Scotia Government Bookstore** (✉ Box 637, 1700 Granville St., Halifax B3J 2T3, ☎ 902/424–7580). Canoeing information is also available from **Canoe NS** (✉ Box 3010S, Halifax B3J 3G6, ☎ 902/425–5450, ext. 316; FAX 902/425–5606).

HIKING

The province has a wide variety of trails along the rugged coastline and inland through forest glades, which enable you to experience otherwise inaccessible scenery, wildlife, and vegetation. *Hiking Trails of Nova Scotia* ($12.95) is available through **Gooselane Editions** (✉ 469 King St., Fredericton, New Brunswick, E3R 1E5, ☎ 506/450–4251).

SNOWMOBILING

Visiting snowmobilers can get information on trails, activities, clubs, and dealers through the **Snowmobile Association of Nova Scotia** (✉ Box 3010 South, Halifax B3J 3G6, ☎ 902/425–5450).

Reservation Service

Nova Scotia has a computerized system called **Check In** (☎ 902/425–5781 or 800/565–0000), which provides information and makes reservations with more than 700 hotels, motels, inns, campgrounds, and car-rental agencies. Check In also represents most properties in Prince Edward Island and some in New Brunswick.

Shopping

Changes to the collection of sales tax will combine the current provincial tax and the federal GST to a 15% blended tax, which will be charged on most goods and services. A decision regarding a refund of sales tax for foreign visitors is pending. Contact the **Nova Scotia Government** (☎ 902/421–8736) or the **Provincial Tax Commission** (✉ Tax Refund Unit, Box 755, Halifax B3J 2V4, ☎ 902/424–5946; in Nova Scotia, 902/424–6708) for current information on refunds.

Visitor Information

Nova Scotia Tourism (✉ Box 130, Halifax B3J 2M7, ☎ 902/424–5000 or 800/341–6096; in Canada, 800/565–0000; FAX 902/420–1286) publishes a wide range of literature, including an exhaustive annual travel guide. **Nova Scotia Tourism Information Centre** (✉ Old Red Store at Historic Properties, Halifax, ☎ 902/424–4248) and **Tourism Halifax & Nova Scotia Tourism** (✉ International Visitors Centre, 1595 Barrington St., ☎ 902/421–8736 or 902/421–2842) are open mid-June–Labor Day, daily 9–6; Labor Day–mid-June, weekdays 9–4:30.

14 Newfoundland and Labrador

Canada's easternmost province consists of the island of Newfoundland and Labrador on the mainland. In summer, Newfoundland's stark cliffs, bogs, and meadows become a riot of wildflowers and greenery, and the sea is dotted with boats and buoys. Mountains, lakes, and rivers provide further opportunities for first-class adventures from wildlife viewing to kayaking and fishing. St. John's, the capital, is a classic harbor city offering a lively arts scene and warm hospitality.

Updated by
Ed Kirby

NEWFOUNDLAND WAS THE FIRST PLACE explorers John Cabot (1497) and Gaspar Corte-Real (1500) touched down in the New World. Exactly where they went no one knows, for neither survived a second voyage. But while he was here, Cabot reported that he saw fish in the water so thick you could dip your basket in anywhere and catch as much as you wanted. Within a decade of the explorers' discovery, St. John's had become a crowded harbor. Fishing boats from France, England, Spain, and Portugal vied for a chance to catch Newfoundland's lucrative cod, which was to subsequently shape the province's history and geography.

At one time there were 700 hard-working settlements or "outports" dotting Newfoundland's coast, most devoted to catching, salting, and drying the world's most plentiful fish. Today, only about 400 of these settlements survive. Newfoundland's most famous resource has become so scarce that a partial fishing moratorium was declared in 1992 and extended in 1993. While the province waits for the cod to return, some 25,000 fishers and processors are going to school or looking for other work instead of fishing. The discovery of perhaps the largest nickel deposit in the world at Voisey's Bay in northern Labrador, near Nain, may bring some relief. A mine and mill are expected to begin production in 1999. In addition, a number of offshore oil fields are expected to go into operation between late 1997 and the turn of the century.

Newfoundland and Labrador became part of Canada in 1949. For almost 400 years before this, however, the people had survived the vagaries of a fishing economy on their own, until the Great Depression forced the economy to go belly-up. After almost 50 years of Confederation with Canada, the economy of the province has improved considerably, but the people are still of independent mind: Newfoundlanders regard themselves as North America's first separatists and maintain a unique language and lifestyle as well as their own customs. E. Annie Proulx's Pulitzer Prize–winning novel, *The Shipping News,* brought the attention of many readers to this part of the world.

Visitors to Newfoundland find themselves straddling the centuries. Old accents and customs are common in small towns and outports, yet the major cities of St. John's on the east coast and Corner Brook on the west coast of the island of Newfoundland are very much part of the 20th century. Regardless of where you visit—an isolated outport or lively Duckworth Street—you're sure to interact with some of the warmest, wittiest people in North America. Strangers have always been welcome in Newfoundland, since the days when locals brought visitors in from out of the cold, warmed them by the fire, and charmingly interrogated them for news of events outside the province.

Before you can shoot the breeze, though, you'll have to acclimate yourself to the strong provincial dialects. Newfoundland is one of two provinces with their own dictionaries. Prince Edward Island is the other, but its book has only 873 entries. The *Dictionary of Newfoundland English* has more than 5,000 words, mostly having to do with fishery, weather, and scenery. To get started, you can practice the name of the province—it's *New'fund'land,* with the accent on "land." However, only "livyers" ever get the pronunciation exactly right.

Pleasures and Pastimes

Dining

John Cabot and Sir Humphrey Gilbert raved about "waters teeming with fish." Today, despite the fishing moratorium, seafood is still an excellent value in Newfoundland and Labrador. Many restaurants offer seasonal specialties with a wide variety of traditional wild and cultured species. Although cod may still be available, it may not be locally harvested. It will still, however, be traditionally prepared—pan-fried, baked, or poached. Aquaculture species like steelhead trout, salmon, mussels, and sea scallops are available in better restaurants. Cold-water shrimp, snow crab, lobster, redfish, grenadier, halibut, and turbot are also good seafood choices.

Two other foods you shouldn't leave without trying are partridgeberries and bakeapples. Partridgeberries are a small, lush-tasting berry, called the mountain cranberry in the United States, and locally they are used for just about everything—pies, jams, cakes, pancakes, and even as a sauce for turkey and game. Bakeapples in the wild are a low-growing berry that looks like a yellow raspberry—you'll see them ripening in bogs in August throughout the province. Enterprising pickers sell them by the side of the road in jars. If the ones you buy are hard, wait a few days and they'll ripen into rich-tasting fruit. The berries are popular on ice cream or spread on fresh homemade bread. In Scandinavia they're known as cloudberries and are made into a liqueur.

You may also hear Newfoundlanders talk about the herb they call summer savory. Newfoundlanders are so partial to this peppery herb that they slip it into most stuffings and stews. Growers in the province ship the product all over the world, and Newfoundlanders visiting relatives living outside the province are usually asked to "bring the savory."

Only the large urban centers, especially St. John's and Corner Brook, have gourmet restaurants. Fish is a safe dish to order just about everywhere—even in the lowliest take-out. You'll be surprised by the quality of the meals along the Trans-Canada Highway: Restaurants in the Irving Gas Station chain, for example, have thick homemade soups with dumplings and Sunday dinners that draw in local customers for miles around. Don't be shy about trying some of the excellent meals offered in the province's expanding network of "hospitality homes," where home cooking goes hand in hand with a warm welcome.

CATEGORY	COST*
$$$$	over $50
$$$	$35–$50
$$	$20–$35
$	under $20

per person, excluding drinks, service, and 15% Harmonized Sales Tax (HST).

Festivals and Performing Arts Events

From the Folk Festival main stage in St. John's to the front parlor, Newfoundland and Labrador are filled with music of all kinds. Festivals around the province draw performers and fans from near and far. Newfoundlanders love a party, and from the cities to the smallest towns they celebrate their history and unique culture with events throughout the summer, whether it's music and recitations at a World War II artillery bunker near Cape Spear or a Shakespeare-by-the-Sea event.

Fishing

Newfoundland has over 200 salmon rivers—60% of all salmon rivers in North America—and thousands of trout streams. Angling in these unpolluted waters is a fisherman's dream. The feisty Atlantic salmon is king of the game fish. Top salmon rivers in Newfoundland include the Gander, Humber, and Exploits, while Labrador's top-producing waters are the Sandhill, Michaels, Flowers, and Eagle rivers. Lake trout, brook trout, and landlocked salmon are other favorite species. In Labrador, northern pike and Arctic char can be added to that list.

Hiking

Many provincial and both national parks in Newfoundland and Labrador have hiking and nature trails. Coastal and woods trails radiate from most small communities. However, you can never be sure how far the trail will go unless you ask a local. Be careful: Landmarks are few, the weather is changeable, and it is surprisingly easy to get lost. Many small communities now also have formal walking trails.

Lodging

Newfoundland and Labrador offer lodgings that range from modestly priced "hospitality homes," which you can find through local tourist offices, to luxury accommodations. In between, you can choose from affordable, basic lodging and mid-priced hotels. In remote areas, be prepared to find very basic lodgings. However, the lack of amenities is usually made up for by the home-cooked meals and great hospitality.

CATEGORY	COST*
$$$$	over $110
$$$	$85–$110
$$	$60–$85
$	under $60

All prices are for a standard double room, excluding service charge.

Exploring Newfoundland and Labrador

This chapter divides the province into the island of Newfoundland, beginning with St. John's and the Avalon Peninsula and moving west. Labrador is considered as a whole, with suggested driving and train excursions for a number of areas.

Numbers in the text correspond to numbers in the margin and on the Newfoundland and Labrador map.

Great Itineraries

IF YOU HAVE 3 DAYS

Pick either the west or east coast of Newfoundland. On the west coast, after arriving by ferry at **Port aux Basques** ㉜, drive through the Codroy Valley, heading north to the **Gros Morne National Park** ㉓ and its fjords, and overnight in 🏨 **Rocky Harbour** ㉖ or 🏨 **Woody Point** ㉔. The next day, visit **L'Anse aux Meadows National Historic Site** ㉘, where the Vikings built a village a thousand years ago; here there are reconstructions of the dwellings, plus a Viking boat tour. Then overnight in 🏨 **St. Anthony** ㉙ or nearby.

On the east coast, the ferry docks at Argentia. Explore the Avalon Peninsula beginning in 🏨 **St. John's** ②, where you should spend your first night. The next day, visit **Cape Spear** ①, the most easterly point in North America, and the **Witless Bay Ecological Reserve** ③ for seabirds, whales, and icebergs. Overnight in 🏨 **Placentia** ⑨ and spend your third day at **Cape St. Mary's Ecological Reserve** ⑪, known for its gannets.

IF YOU HAVE 6 DAYS

On Newfoundland's west coast, add southern Labrador to your list. A ferry takes you from St. Barbe to Blanc Sablon on the Québec-Labrador border. Drive 60 mi to **Red Bay** ㉟ to explore the remains of a 17th-century Basque whaling station; then head to **L'Anse Amour** ㉞ to see Canada's second-tallest lighthouse. Overnight at 🏨 **L'Anse au Clair** ㉝. Return through Gros Morne National Park and explore 🏨 **Corner Brook** ㉚, where you should stay overnight. The next day, travel west of **Stephenville** ㉛ to explore the Port au Port Peninsula, home of Newfoundland's French-speaking population.

On the east coast add ⊞ **Trinity** ⑭ to your must-see list, and overnight there or in ⊞ **Clarenville** ⑫. The north shore of Conception Bay is where you will find many picturesque villages, including ⊞ **Cupids** ⑦ or ⊞ **Harbour Grace** ⑧. Several half-day, full-day, and two-day excursions are possible from St. John's, and in each direction a different personality of the region unfolds.

IF YOU HAVE 9 DAYS

In addition to the places already mentioned on the west coast, take a drive into central Newfoundland and visit the lovely villages of Notre Dame Bay. Overnight in ⊞ **Twillingate** ㉑. Catch a ferry to offshore islands like ⊞ **Fogo** or the ⊞ **Change Islands.** Accommodations are available in both towns, but book ahead.

On the east coast add the Burin Peninsula and a trip to France to your itinerary. Yes, France. You can reach the French territory of ⊞ **St-Pierre and Miquelon** ⑰ by passenger ferry from Fortune. Explore romantic **Grand Bank** ⑯, named for the famous fishing area just offshore, and climb Cook's Lookout in ⊞ **Burin** ⑱, where Captain James Cook kept a lookout for smugglers from St-Pierre.

When to Tour Newfoundland and Labrador

Depending on the time of year you visit, your experiences will be dramatically different. In spring icebergs float down from the north, and fin, pilot, minke, and humpback whales hunt for food along the coast. Their preferred cuisine is capelin, a small, smeltlike fish that moves in schools and spawns on Newfoundland's many pebble beaches. During the summer, temperate days turn Newfoundland's stark cliffs, bogs, and meadows into a riot of wildflowers and greenery; and the sea is dotted with boats and buoys marking traps and nets. Fall is a favored season: The weather is usually fine; cliffs and meadows are loaded with berries; and the woods are alive with moose, caribou, partridges, and rabbits, to name just a few residents. In the winter, the forest trails hum with the sound of snowmobiles and ATVs hauling wood home or taking the fishers to their favorite lodges and lakes.

The tourist season runs from June through September, when the province is awash with festivals, fairs, concerts, plays, and crafts shows. The temperature hovers between 75° and 85°, and gently cools off in the evening, providing a good night's sleep.

NEWFOUNDLAND

The rocky coasts and peninsulas of the island of Newfoundland present much dramatic beauty and many opportunities for exploring. Seaport and fishing towns such as St. John's and Grand Bank tell a fascinating history, and parks from Terra Nova National Park on the eastern side of the island and Gros Morne National Park on the west have impressive landscapes. The Avalon Peninsula includes the provincial capital of St. John's as well as the Cape Shore on its west. The Bonavista Peninsula and the Burin Peninsula and Notre Dame Bay have some intriguing sights, from Cape Bonavista, associated with John Cabot's landing, to pretty towns around Notre Dame Bay such as Twillingate. The Great Northern Peninsula on the western side of Newfoundland holds a historic site with the remains of Viking sod houses; the west coast has Corner Brook, a good base for exploring the mountains, as well as farming and fishing communities.

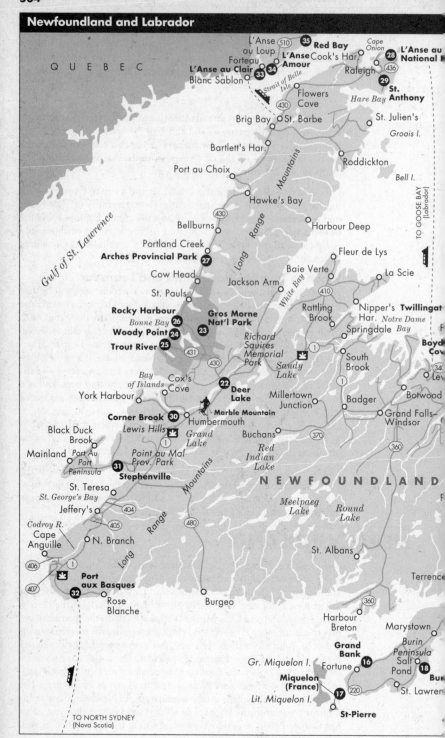

QUEBEC

L'Anse
au Loup (510) **35** **Red Bay**
Forteau **L'Anse** Cook's Har.
L'Anse au Clair **33** **34** **Amour**
Blanc Sablon *Strait of Belle Isle*

Cape
Onion **28** **L'Anse au**
National
Raleigh (436)
29 **St.**
Anthony
Hare Bay

Flowers
Cove
St. Julien's
Groais I.

Brig Bay St. Barbe (430)

Bartlett's Har.

Roddickton

Bell I.

Port au Choix

Hawke's Bay

Harbour Deep

Bellburns (430)

Fleur de Lys

Portland Creek
Arches Provincial Park **27**

Baie Verte
La Scie

Cow Head
Jackson Arm

White Bay

St. Pauls

Rocky Harbour
Bonne Bay **26**
Woody Point **24**
Trout River **25**

(431)

Gros Morne
Nat'l Park **23**

*Richard
Squires
Memorial
Park*

(430)

Rattling
Brook
(410)

Nipper's **Twillingat**
Har. *Notre Dame*
Springdale *Bay*

*Sandy
Lake*
(1)

South
Brook

**Bayd
Cove**

(34

Lev

*Bay
of Islands*
Cox's
Cove
York Harbour

22
**Deer
Lake**
Millertown
Junction

(1)
Badger

Botwood

Corner Brook **30**
Lewis Hills
Marble Mountain
Humbermouth

Buchans
(370)
Grand Falls-
Windsor

Black Duck
Brook
*Grand
Lake*

*Red
Indian
Lake*

(360)

Mainland *Port Au
Port
Peninsula*
(1)
Point au Mal
Prov. Park
31
Stephenville

N E W F O U N D L A N D

St. Teresa
St. George's Bay
Jeffery's
(404)

*Meelpaeg
Lake*

*Round
Lake*

Codroy R.
Cape
Anguille
(405)
N. Branch
(480)

St. Albans

(406)
(1)

Terrence

(407)
**Port
aux Basques**
32
Rose
Blanche

Burgeo

(360)

Harbour
Breton

Marystown

*Burin
Peninsula* Salt
Pond **18**

Gr. Miquelon I.

**Grand
Bank**
Fortune **16**

Bur

TO NORTH SYDNEY
(Nova Scotia)

**Miquelon
(France)**
Lit. Miquelon I.
17
(220)
St. Lawren

St-Pierre

TO GOOSE BAY (Labrador)

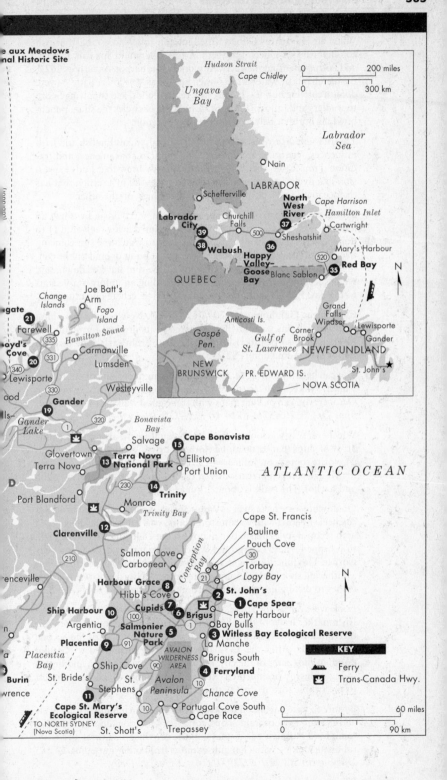

St. John's

When Sir Humphrey Gilbert sailed into St. John's to establish British colonial rule for Queen Elizabeth in 1583, he found Spanish, French, and Portuguese fishermen actively working the harbor. As early as 1627, the merchants of Water Street—then known as "the lower path"—were doing a thriving business buying fish, selling goods, and supplying booze to soldiers and sailors. Today St. John's still encircles the snug, punch-bowl harbor that helped establish its reputation.

This old seaport town, the province's capital, mixes English and Irish influences, Victorian architecture and modern convenience, and traditional music and rock and roll into a heady brew that finds expression in a lively arts scene and a relaxed pace—all in a setting that has the ocean on one side and unexpected greenery on the other.

True early birds can begin a tour of the area at daybreak by filling up a thermos of coffee, getting some muffins, and driving on Route 11 to ★ ❶ **Cape Spear,** so you can be among the first to watch the sun come up over North America. This is the easternmost point of land on the continent. Songbirds begin their chirping in the dim light of dawn, and whales feed directly below the cliffs, providing an unforgettable start to the day. In May and June you may well see icebergs floating by.

Cape Spear Lighthouse (☎ 709/772–5367), Newfoundland's oldest such beacon, has been lovingly restored to its original form and furnishings and is open to visitors, daily 10–6 from early June through Labor Day. Admission is $2.25.

❷ You can begin exploring **St. John's** on the waterfront, site of the Tourist Chalet. This is a converted railway caboose, staffed from May through October; you can pick up maps with some good walking tours. ✉ *Harbour Dr.,* ☎ *709/576–8514.* ☉ *May–Oct., daily 9–7.*

Whichever way you look on the harbor, you'll see the always-fascinating array of ships that tie up along **Harbour Drive.** Walk the harbor front, a favorite route in St. John's, east to the **Battery,** a tiny, still-active fishing village perched precariously at the base of steep cliffs between hill and harbor. The walk is about 1 km (½ mi)

On downtown streets such as **Water Street,** where longtime businesses sit cheek-by-jowl with vacant storefronts, you'll notice the diversity of architectural styles due to two major fires in 1846 and 1892. The 1892 fire stopped where George and Water streets intersect, at **Yellowbelly Corner.** This junction was so-named because in the 19th century it was a gathering spot for Irish immigrants from Wexford who wore yellow sashes to distinguish themselves from their Waterford rivals.

Look west on Water Street, where the block still resembles a typical Irish market town of the 1840s. To the east, Victorian-style architecture predominates, with curved mansard roofs typical of the Second Empire style. After the 1892 fire the city's elite moved to **Circular Road,** in the center of the city, out of reach of future fires, and built a string of highly ornamented Victorian mansions, which bear witness to the sizable fortunes made from the humble cod.

Be sure to take a walk on **Duckworth Street,** which hums with a lively and changing mix of crafts shops, coffee bars, and restaurants. The **Newfoundland Museum** has displays on the province's cultural and natural history, along with changing exhibits from other museums. ✉ *285 Duckworth St.,* ☎ *709/729–0916.* ☜ *Free.* ☉ *Daily.*

While you're downtown, take a look at the **churches of St. John's,** rich in architectural history; many usually schedule summer tours. The

Basilica Cathedral of St. John the Baptist (⊠ Military Rd., ☎ 709/754–2170), with a commanding position above Military Road, overlooks the older section of the city and the harbor. The land was granted to the church by young Queen Victoria, and the edifice was built with stones from both Ireland and Newfoundland. The **Anglican Cathedral of St. John the Baptist** (⊠ 22 Church Hill, ☎ 709/726–5677) is one of the finest examples of Gothic Revival architecture in North America. The imposing **Gower Street United Church** (⊠ Gower St., ☎ 709/753–7286) has redbrick facade and green turrets. The **St. Thomas (Old Garrison) Church** (⊠ Bottom of Military Rd., adjacent to Hotel Newfoundland, ☎ 709/576–6632) is where the English soldiers used to worship during the early and mid-1800s.

The **Commissariat House,** just around the corner from St. Thomas church, has been restored to the way it appeared when it was the residence and office of the British garrison's supply officer in the 1830s. Interpreters dress in period costume. ⊠ *King's Bridge Rd.,* ☎ *709/729–6730.* ◪ *Free.* ☉ *June–mid-Oct., daily 10–5:30.*

★ You can either walk or drive from the Battery to **Signal Hill National Historic Site,** with excellent views of the city to the west. To walk, take the well-maintained 1¾-km (1-mi) walking path that leads along the cliff edge, through the Narrows, and zigzags through the park. To drive, take steep Signal Hill Road. In spite of its height, Signal Hill was difficult to defend: Throughout the 1600s and 1700s it changed hands with every attacking French, English, and Dutch force. A wooden palisade encircles the summit of the hill, indicating the boundaries of the old fortifications. En route to the hill is the **Park Interpretation Centre,** with exhibits describing St. John's history. **Gibbet Hill,** the rocky knob immediately to the west of the Interpretation Centre, got its name—a gibbet is a post with a projecting arm for hanging—because a miscreant was once hanged there and left dangling as a deterrent to other would-be lawbreakers. From the top of the hill it's a 500-ft drop to the narrow harbor entrance below. **Cabot Tower,** at the summit of Signal Hill, was constructed in 1897 to commemorate the 400th anniversary of Cabot's landing in Newfoundland. ⊠ *Cabot Tower,* ☎ *709/772–5367.* ◪ *Free.* ☉ *Labor Day–early June, daily 9–5; mid-June–Labor Day, daily 8:30–8, guides available on summer weekends.*

Quidi Vidi Village is an authentic fishing community whose history goes back to the beginning of St. John's. If you're driving here from Signal Hill, go down from Signal Hill, make a right turn at Quidi Vidi Road, and continue to the right, down Forest Road. If you are walking, paths lead from the summit and the Interpretation Centre to the village. **Quidi Vidi Battery** is a small redoubt that has been restored to the way it appeared in 1812 and is staffed by costumed interpreters who will tell you about the hard, unromantic life of a soldier of the empire. ⊠ *Near entrance to Quidi Vidi harbor,* ☎ *709/729–2460 or 709/729–2977.* ◪ *Free.* ☉ *July–early Sept., daily 10–5:30.*

Quidi Vidi Lake, to the west of Quidi Vidi Village, is encircled by a leisurely path, popular with walkers and joggers. It's the site of the **Royal St. John's Regatta,** the oldest continuing sporting event in North America, which has taken place since at least 1826. Weather permitting, the regatta takes place on the first Wednesday in August.

The **Newfoundland Freshwater Resource Center** has the only public fluvarium in North America; underwater windows let you view a brook. Here you can observe spawning brown and brook trout in their natural habitat. Feeding time for the fish, frogs, and eels is 4 PM daily. If you want to walk here from Quidi Vidi Lake, follow the Rennies

River Trail (4½ km, or 3 mi) that cuts through the city along a wooded stream. ⊠ *Pippy Park,* ☏ 709/754–3474. ⊡ *$2.75.* ☉ *July–Aug., daily 9–5; guided tours at 11, 1, and 3; Sept.–June, Mon.–Tues. and Thurs.–Sat. 9–4:30; Sun. noon–4:30.*

The **Memorial University Botanical Garden** is a 110-acre garden and natural area at Oxen Pond with four pleasant walking trails and many gardens, including rock gardens and scree, a Newfoundland heritage-plants bed, ericaceous borders, peat and woodland beds, a wildlife garden, an alpine house, wildfire cottage and vegetable gardens, an herb wall, and native plant collections. The environmental education programs include seasonal indoor exhibits, and wildflower and bird-watching walks. ⊠ *306 Mt. Scio Rd., Pippy Park,* ☏ 709/737–8590. ⊡ *$1.* ☉ *May–June and Sept.–Nov., Wed.–Sun. 10–5; July–Aug., Fri.–Mon. and Wed. 10–5, Tues. and Thurs. 10–8.*

Bowring Park, an expansive Victorian park west of downtown, was donated to the city by the wealthy Bowring family in 1911. It resembles the famous inner city parks of London, after which it was modeled. Dotting the grounds are ponds and rustic bridges; there's also a statue of Peter Pan. ⊠ *Waterford Bridge Rd.* ⊡ *Free.*

Dining and Lodging

$$$ ✕ **The Cellar.** This restaurant, in a historic building on the waterfront,
★ gets rave reviews for its innovative Continental cuisine featuring the best local ingredients. Menu selections include blackened fish dishes and tiramisu for dessert. ⊠ *Baird's Cove, between Harbour and Water Sts.,* ☏ 709/579–8900. *Reservations essential. AE, MC, V.*

$$$ ✕ **Stone House.** In one of St. John's most historic buildings, a restored
★ 19th-century stone cottage, this dining room serves imported game and Newfoundland specialties. ⊠ *8 Kenna's Hill,* ☏ 709/753–2380. *AE, DC, MC, V.*

$$–$$$ ✕ **Hungry Fishermen.** Salmon, scallops, halibut, mussels, cod, and shrimp top the menu here. Nonfish eaters can choose veal, chicken, or the five-onion soup. This restaurant in a 19th-century historic building overlooking a courtyard has great sauces; desserts change daily and are homemade. ⊠ *Murray Premises, 5 Beck's Cove, off Water St.,* ☏ 709/726–5790. *AE, D, DC, MC, V.*

$$$$ ✕⊡ **Delta St. John's.** In this convention hotel in downtown St. John's,
★ rooms overlook the harbor and the city. The restaurant, Brazil Square, is known for its breakfast and noon buffets. ⊠ *120 New Gower St., A1C 6K4,* ☏ 709/739–6404, FAX 709/570–1622. *276 rooms, 9 suites. Restaurant. AE, DC, MC, V.*

$$$$ ✕⊡ **Hotel Newfoundland.** St. John's residents gather at this comfort-
★ able modern hotel for special occasions. It's noted for its Sunday and evening buffets, charming rooms that overlook St. John's harbor, atrium, and the fine cuisine of the Cabot Club. ⊠ *Box 5637, Cavendish Sq., A1C 5W8,* ☏ 709/726–4980, FAX 709/726–2025. *267 rooms, 20 suites. Restaurant. AE, DC, MC, V.*

$$$ ⊡ **Quality Hotel by Journey's End Motel.** This hotel overlooks St. John's harbor. Like other properties in the chain, it offers clean, comfortable rooms at a reasonable price. The hotel's restaurant, Rumplestiltskins, has a splendid view and an unpretentious menu. ⊠ *Hill O'Chips, A1C 6B1,* ☏ 709/754–7788, FAX 709/754–5209. *162 rooms. Restaurant. AE, DC, MC, V.*

$$ ⊡ **Compton House Bed & Breakfast.** In a charming, restored historic
★ St. John's residence in the west end of the city, this inn is professionally run and beautifully decorated. Twelve-foot ceilings and wide halls

give the place a majestic feeling, and rooms done in pastels and chintzes add an air of coziness. The location, within walking distance of downtown St. John's, is ideal. ⊠ *26 Waterford Bridge Rd., A1E 1C6,* ☎ *709/739–5789. 4 rooms, 2 suites. AE, MC, V.*

$$ 🏠 **Gower Street House Bed & Breakfast.** This gracious former home of the late photographer Elsie Holloway has been designated by the Newfoundland Historic Trust as a point of interest. It's also an ideal setting for paintings by prominent local artists. The location is within walking distance of all the city's main attractions. A full breakfast is included in the room rate. ⊠ *180 Gower St., A1C 1P9,* ☎ *709/754–0047 or 800/563–3959,* FAX *709/754–0047. 4 rooms. MC, V.*

$$ 🏠 **Prescott Inn.** Local art decorates the walls of this house, the city's
★ most popular bed-and-breakfast. The inn has been modernized, tastefully blending the new and the old. It's central to shopping and downtown attractions. ⊠ *17–21 Military Rd., A1C 2C3,* ☎ *709/753–7733,* FAX *709/753–6036. 15 rooms, 7 suites. MC, V.*

Nightlife and the Arts

THE ARTS
St. John's has a lively and, for its size, large arts community. Drop into the **Ship Inn** (☎ 709/753–3870), a pub in Solomon's Lane between Duckworth and Water streets that serves as the local arts watering hole. Actors, musicians, painters, writers, poets, artisans, and their fans and friends hang out here. It's unpretentious and a good place to find out what's happening.

The **Resource Centre for the Arts** (⊠ LSPU Hall, 3 Victoria St., ☎ 709/753–4531, FAX 709/753–4537) is one of the country's oldest and most innovative experimental theaters. In addition to a busy fall and winter season, the center has a busy summer, with cabarets, outdoor concerts, plays, and alternative concerts.

The **Newfoundland and Labrador Folk Festival** (☎ 709/576–8508), held in St. John's in early August, is the province's best-known traditional music festival. **The Newfoundland International Irish Festival** (☎ 709/754–0700), held in Mount Pearl (south of St. John's) each July, features international performers and a Leprechaun Festival for the kids. **Shakespeare by the Sea** (☎ 709/576–0980) summer performances use the ocean as a backdrop.

NIGHTLIFE
It has been a long-standing claim (since at least the 1700s) that St. John's has more bars per mile than any city in North America. Each establishment has its own personality. **Erin's Pub** (⊠ 186 Water St., ☎ 709/722–1916) is famous for its Irish music. The **Blarney Stone** (⊠ 342 Water St., 2nd floor, ☎ 709/754–1798) also has Irish music. **George Street,** downtown, a beautifully restored street of pubs and restaurants, often has open-air concerts.

Shopping

ANTIQUES
Murray's Antiques (⊠ 414 Blackmarsh Rd., ☎ 709/579–7344) is renowned for silver, china, and fine mahogany and walnut furniture. **Livyers** (⊠ 202 Duckworth St., ☎ 709/726–5650) carries locally crafted furniture and is a great spot for digging through books, prints, and maps.

ART GALLERIES
St. John's has a dozen commercial and public art galleries, nearly all of which carry works by local artists. Newfoundland's unique landscape, portrayed realistically or more experimentally, is a favorite subject. **The Art Gallery of Newfoundland and Labrador** (⊠ Allandale Rd.

and Prince Philip Dr., ☎ 709/737–8209) is the province's largest public gallery and exhibits historical and contemporary Canadian arts and crafts with an emphasis on Newfoundland and Labrador artists and artisans. The gallery is closed Monday. The **Emma Butler Gallery** (✉ 111 George St., ☎ 709/739–7111) sells a large selection of Newfoundland art including works by David Blackwood and Christopher Pratt. **Christina Parker Fine Art** (✉ 7 Plank Rd., ☎ 709/753–0580) represents local and national artists in all media, including painting, sculpture, drawing, and fine art prints.

BOOKS

Most bookstores have a prominent section devoted to local history, fiction, and memoirs. **Word Play** (✉ 221 Duckworth St., ☎ 709/726–9193 or 800/563–9100) carries a wide selection of magazines and books of general interest to visitors.

HANDICRAFTS

St. John's has more than its fair share of fine crafts shops. **NONIA** (Newfoundland Outport Nurses Industrial Association, ✉ 286 Water St., ☎ 709/753–8062) was founded in 1920 to give Newfoundland women in the outports an opportunity to earn money to support nursing services in these remote communities. Their reputation for fierce independence was as colorful as their reputation for turning homespun wool into exquisite clothing. Today the shop continues to sell these fine homespun articles as well as lighter and more modern handmade items. **The Salt Box** (✉ 194 Duckworth St., ☎ 709/753–0622) sells local crafts and specializes in pottery. **The Cod Jigger** (✉ 245 Duckworth St., ☎ 709/726–7422) carries handmade wool sweaters, socks, and mitts as well as Newfoundland's unique Grenfell coats. **The Devon House Craft Gallery** (✉ 59 Duckworth St., ☎ 709/753–2749) is owned by the Newfoundland and Labrador Crafts Development Association and carries only juried crafts. **The Newfoundland Weavery** (✉ 177 Water St., ☎ 709/753–0496) sells rugs, prints, lamps, books, crafts, and other gifts.

MUSIC

Fred's Records (✉ 198 Duckworth St., ☎ 709/753–9191) has the best selection of local recordings, as well as other music.

Avalon Peninsula

On the southern half of the peninsula are small Irish hamlets separated by large tracts of wilderness. You can travel part of the peninsula's southern coast in one or two days, depending on how much time you have. Quaint coastal towns line the road, and the natural sites are beautiful. La Manche and Chance Cove—both now-abandoned communities turned provincial parks—attest to the bounty of natural resources of the region. At the intersection of Routes 90 and 91, in Salmonier, you need to decide whether to continue north toward Salmonier Nature Park and on to the towns on Conception Bay, or to head west and then south to Route 100 to Cape St. Mary's Ecological Reserve (☞ Route 100: The Cape Shore, *below*). Each option takes about three hours. On the former route, stop in Harbor Grace; if you plan to travel on to Bay de Verde, at the northern tip of the peninsula, and down the other side of the peninsula on Route 80 along Trinity Bay, consider turning in for the night in the Harbour Grace–Carbonear area. Otherwise turn around and follow the same route back to Route 1.

Witless Bay Ecological Reserve
❸ *29 km (18 mi) south of St. John's.*

The wildness of the peninsula's eastern coast is usually what's most striking to visitors, as evidenced at the Witless Bay Ecological Reserve

(✉ Rte. 10), a strip of water and four offshore islands between Bay Bulls and Tors Cove. Sometimes referred to as "the Serengeti of the northwest Atlantic," the reserve is the summer home of millions of seabirds—puffins, murres, kittiwakes, razorbills, and guillemots—that nest on the islands. The birds, and the humpback and minke whales that tarry here before continuing north to the summer grounds in the Arctic, feed on the billions of capelin that swarm inshore to spawn. Here, too, is an excellent place to see icebergs; the best views are from tour boats that operate in the reserve. For information, contact the **Parks and Natural Areas Division** (☎ 709/729–2421).

OUTDOOR ACTIVITIES AND SPORTS

O'Brien's Bird Island Charters (☎ 709/753–4850 or 709/334–2355, FAX 709/753–3140) offers popular two-hour excursions featuring whale-, iceberg-, and seabird-watching as well as cod jigging. **Gatherall's Puffin and Whale Watch** (☎ 709/334–2887 or 800/41WHALE) has trips for viewing wildlife in the reserve.

En Route Although a visit to many of the hamlets along the way from Witless Bay to Ferryland on **Route 10** will fulfill any search for prettiness, a few favorites are exceptional. La Manche and Brigus South have especially attractive settings and strong traditional flavors.

Ferryland

4 *43½ km (27 mi) south of Witless Bay Ecological Reserve.*

This seaside town has a long history, some of which is described in its small community museum. A major ongoing **archaeological dig** at Ferryland has uncovered the early 17th-century colony of Lord Baltimore, who abandoned the Colony of Avalon after a decade for the warmer climes of Maryland. The site includes an archaeology laboratory and exhibit center. ✉ *Rte. 10, The Pool (seasonal),* ☎ *709/432–3200.* 🎟 *Free.* ☉ *June–Oct., daily 9–8.*

En Route In springtime, between Chance Cove and Portugal Cove South, in a stretch of land about 58 km (36 mi) long, hundreds of **caribou** and their calves gather on the barrens near Route 10. Although the animals are there at other times of the year, their numbers are few and it's hard to spot them because they blend in so well with the scenery.

Salmonier Nature Park

5 *88 km (55 mi) from Ferryland, 14½ km (9 mi) north of the intersection of Rtes. 90 and 91.*

You can see many of the animal species indigenous to the province here. The park is a 3,000-acre wilderness reserve area and has an enclosed 100-acre exhibit that allows up-close viewing. ✉ *Salmonier Line, Rte. 90,* ☎ *709/729–6974.* 🎟 *Free.* ☉ *June 5–Canadian Thanksgiving (mid-Oct.), daily noon–7; other times by appointment.*

En Route From Salmonier Nature Park to Brigus, take Route 90, which passes through the scenic **Hawke Hills** before meeting up with the Trans-Canada Highway (Route 1). Turn off at the Holyrood Junction (Route 62) and follow Route 70, which skirts Conception Bay.

Brigus

6 *19 km (12 mi) off Rte. 1 and Rte. 70.*

This beautiful village on Conception Bay has a wonderful public garden, winding lanes, and a teahouse. Brigus is best known as the birthplace of Captain Bob Bartlett, the famed Arctic explorer who accompanied Admiral Peary on polar expeditions during the first decade of this century. **Hawthorne Cottage,** the home of Captain Bartlett, is one of the few surviving examples of the picturesque cottage style, with a veranda decorated with ornamental wooden fretwork. It dates from 1830 and is a National Historic Site. ⊠ *Irishtown Rd.,* ☎ *709/753–9262; in summer, 709/528–4004.* ☎ *$2.25.* ☼ *Early June–mid-Oct., daily 10–8 (shorter hours in fall; call ahead).*

Ye Old Stone Barn Museum displays photos and artifacts of the town's history, especially its connection with the fishery. ⊠ *4 Magistrate's Hill,* ☎ *709/528–3298.* ☎ *$1.* ☼ *Mid-June–Labor Day, daily 10–5; Sept.–Canadian Thanksgiving (mid-Oct.), weekends 10–5.*

Cupids
❼ *5 km (3 mi) north of Brigus.*

Cupids is the oldest English colony in Canada, founded in 1610 by John Guy, to whom the town erected a monument. In 1995 archaeologists began unearthing the long-lost site of the original colony here, and some of these artifacts are on display in the community museum, **Cupids Archaeological Site.** ⊠ *United Church Hall, Main Rd.,* ☎ *709/528–3477.* ☎ *Free.* ☼ *June–Aug., daily 9–4:30.*

Harbour Grace
❽ *21 km (13 mi) north of Cupids.*

Harbour Grace was once the headquarters of Peter Easton, a 17th-century pirate. Beginning in 1919, this town was the departure point for many attempts to fly the Atlantic. Amelia Earhart left Harbour Grace in 1932 to become the first woman to fly solo across the Atlantic. Several handsome stone churches and buildings remain as evidence of the town's pride.

Route 100: The Cape Shore

You can reach the Cape Shore on the western side of the Avalon Peninsula from Route 1, at its intersection with Route 100. The ferry from Nova Scotia docks in Argentia, near Placentia. Besides the coastal towns, a highlight of the area is the outstanding seabird colony at Cape St. Mary's.

Placentia
❾ *48 km (30 mi) south of Route 1.*

Placentia was the French capital of Newfoundland in the 1600s. Trust the French to select a beautiful place for a capital! **Castle Hill National Historic Site,** just north of town, is on what remains of the French fortifications. The visitor's center has a "life at Plaisance" exhibit that shows the life and hardships endured by early English and French settlers. ⊠ *Off Rte. 100,* ☎ *709/227–2401.* ☎ *$2.25.* ☼ *June–Labor Day, daily 8:30–8; Labor Day–May, daily 8:30–4:30.*

Ship Harbour
❿ *34 km (21 mi) north of Placentia.*

An isolated, edge-of-the-world place, Ship Harbour has historic significance. Off Route 102, amid the splendor of Placentia Bay, an unpaved road leads to a monument marking the Atlantic Charter. It was on a ship in these waters where, in 1941, Franklin Roosevelt and Winston Churchill signed the charter and formally announced the "Four Freedoms," which still shape the politics of the world's most successful democracies: freedom of speech, freedom of worship, freedom from want, and freedom from fear.

Cape St. Mary's Ecological Reserve

★ ⑪ *65 km (40 mi) south of Placentia.*

Cape St. Mary's Ecological Reserve is the most southerly nesting site in the world for gannets and common and thick-billed murres. A paved road takes you within a mile of the seabird colony. Visit the interpretation center—guides are on site during the summer—then walk to within 100 ft of the colony of nesting gannets, murres, black-billed kittiwakes, and razorbills. You'll also be able to enjoy some of the most dramatic coastal scenery in Newfoundland. For information, contact the **Parks and Natural Areas Division** (☎ 709/729–2431).

Cape St. Mary's Charters and Boat Tours (☎ 709/337–2660 or 709/337–2614) gives passengers a look at this famous gannet colony from the ocean.

Clarenville and the Bonavista Peninsula

Clarenville, about two hours northwest of St. John's via the Trans-Canada Highway (Route 1), is the departure point for two different excursions in the Bonavista Peninsula: the Discovery Trail and Terra Nova National Park.

Clarenville

⑫ *189 km (117 mi) northwest of St. John's.*

★ If history and quaint towns appeal to you, this is the starting point for Route 230A—the **Discovery Trail.** The route goes as far north as the town of Bonavista, one of John Cabot's reputed landing spots in 1497.

LODGING

$$$ 🏨 **Clarenville Inn.** This property was renovated in 1996; rooms are standard. ✉ *Rte. 1, Box 967, A0E 1J0,* ☎ *709/466–7911,* FAX *709/466–3854. 64 rooms. Restaurant, bar. AE, DC, MC, V.*

Terra Nova National Park

⑬ *24 km (15 mi) northwest of Clarenville.*

If you're interested in rugged terrain, golf, fishing, and camping, Terra Nova National Park, on the exposed coastline that adjoins Bonavista Bay, is the place to be. If you are a golfer, you can play on one of the most beautiful courses in Canada, at the Terra Nova Park Lodge in the park at Port Blandford. It's the only one where a salmon river cuts through the 18-hole course. Call 709/543–2626 for a reservation; fees run between $24 and $30 per person, depending on the season. The park also has a new Marine Interpretation Center, attractive campsites, whale-watching tours, and nature walks. ✉ *Trans-Canada Hwy., Glovertown,* ☎ *709/533–2801 or 709/533–2802,* FAX *709/533–2706.* 🎫 *Park and vehicle permit $6 daily, 4-day pass $18, seasonal pass $30 ($20 before June 22).* ☉ *June–Aug., daily 10–9; Sept.–May, weekdays 8–4:30.*

Trinity

⑭ *71 km (44 mi) northeast of Clarenville.*

Trinity is one of the jewels of Newfoundland. The village's picturesque views, winding lanes, and snug houses are the main attraction, and several homes have been turned into museums and inns. In the 1700s Trinity competed with St. John's as a center of culture and wealth. Its more contemporary claim to fame, however, is that its intricate harbor was a favorite anchorage for the British navy, and it was here that the smallpox vaccine was introduced to North America by a local rector. An information center with costumed interpreters is open daily from July through September. To get here, take Route 230 to Route 239.

The **Lester-Garland Premises** (✉ Rte. 239, ☎ 800/563–6353 at press time) is a re-creation of a fish merchant's house that was once one of the most prominent 18th-century homes in Newfoundland. The original was torn down in the 1960s, but the new house was set to open in summer 1997.

Rising Tide Theatre (☎ 709/738–3256,) conducts The New-Founde-Land Trinity Pageant walking tours (Wednesday, Saturday, and Sunday at 2) of the town that are more theater than tour, led by actors in period costumes.

THE ARTS

Rising Tide Theatre (☎ 709/738–3256) stages the **Summer in the Bight** festival. Outdoor Shakespeare productions, dinner theater, and back-porch dramas and comedies fill the bill.

WHALE-WATCHING

Ocean Contact Limited (☎ 709/464–3269) is an established specialist in whale-watching and whale research. Dr. Peter Beamish's book, *Dancing with Whales*, documents their interesting findings.

Cape Bonavista

15 *16 km (10 mi) north of Port Union.*

Cape Bonavista is a popular destination because of its association with Cabot's landing in 1497. The **Ryan Premises National Historic Site** on the waterfront, opened in 1997, depicts the almost 500-year history of the commercial cod fishery in a restored fish merchant's properties. ✉ *Off Rte. 230,* ☎ *709/772–5364.* ▣ *Free.* ☉ *Mid-June–mid-Oct., daily 10–6.*

The **lighthouse** on the point, about 1 km (½ mi) outside town, has been restored to its condition in 1870. The **Mockbeggar Property** teaches about the life of an outport merchant in the years immediately before Confederation. ✉ *Off Rte. 230,* ☎ *709/729–2460 or 709/468–7300/7444.* ▣ *Free.* ☉ *Late June–early Sept., daily 10–5:30.*

Burin Peninsula, Gander, and Notre Dame Bay

The journey down to the Burin Peninsula is a three- to four-hour drive from the intersection of Routes 230 and 1 through the craggy coastal landscapes along Route 210. The peninsula's history is tied to the rich fishing grounds of the Grand Banks, which established this area as a center for European fishery as early as the 1500s. By the early 1900s, one of the world's largest fishing fleets was based on the Burin Peninsula. Today its inhabitants hope for a recovery of the fish stocks that have sustained their economy for centuries. Marystown is the peninsula's commercial center.

Gander, in east-central Newfoundland, is famous for its airport. North of it is Notre Dame Bay, an area of rugged coastline and equally rugged islands that was once the domain of the now-extinct Beothuk tribe. Only the larger islands are now inhabited. Before English settlers moved into the area in the late 18th and early 19th centuries, it was seasonally occupied by French fishermen. Local dialects preserve centuries-old words that have vanished elsewhere. The bay is swept by the cool Labrador Current that carries icebergs south through Iceberg Alley; the coast is also a good whale-watching area.

Grand Bank

16 *53 km (33 mi) southwest of Marystown on Rte. 220.*

One of the loveliest communities in Newfoundland, Grand Bank has a fascinating history as an important fishing center. Because of trade patterns, the architecture here was influenced more by Halifax, Boston, and Bar Harbor than by the rest of Newfoundland. For details about the town's past visit the **Southern Newfoundland Seamen's Museum,** in a sail-shape building. ⊠ *Marine Dr.,* ☎ *709/832–1484.* ⊡ *Free.* ☉ *May–Oct., weekdays 9–5, weekends 2–5.*

St-Pierre and Miquelon

🕡 *55-min. ferry ride from Fortune.*

The islands of St-Pierre and Miquelon are France's only territory in North America. A ferry trip to these islands is a great idea if you crave French cuisine or a bottle of perfume. Shopping and eating are both popular pastimes. Visitors traveling to the islands should carry proof of citizenship; people from outside the United States and Canada will have to show valid visas and passports. Because of the ferry schedule, a trip to St-Pierre means an overnight stay in a modern hotel such as Hotel Robert (☎ 011–508/412419) or a pension, the French equivalent of a bed-and-breakfast. Call the St-Pierre tourist board (☎ 011–508/412222 or 800/565–5118) for information about accommodations.

A passenger ferry operated by **Lloyd G. Lake Ltd.** (☎ 709/832–2006) leaves Fortune (south of Grand Bank) daily at 2:15 PM from mid-June to late September; the crossing takes 70 minutes. The ferry leaves St-Pierre at 1 PM daily; round-trip is $55. The ferry operated by **St-Pierre Tours** (☎ 709/722–4103 or 709/832–0429) crosses daily from Fortune to St-Pierre from May through September, and weekly from October to early December. The ferry leaves Fortune at 2:45 PM, Newfoundland time, and departs St-Pierre at 1:30 PM, St-Pierre (Atlantic) time. Round-trip fare is $59.95. The trip takes 70 minutes.

Burin

🕤 *62 km (38 mi) from Grand Bank.*

Following Route 220 south and east from Grand Bank will take you around the peninsula to the old town of Burin, a community built amid intricate cliffs and coves. This was an ideal setting for pirates and privateers who used to lure ships into the rocky, dead-end areas in order to plunder them. Captain Cook was among those who watched for smugglers from "Cook's Lookout" on a hill that still bears his name.

The **Heritage House and Heritage II** museums, considered two of the best community museums in Newfoundland, give you a sense of what life was like in the past. Heritage II has a display on the 1929 tidal wave that struck Burin. ⊠ *Square off Rte. 221,* ☎ *709/891–2217.* ⊡ *Free.* ☉ *May–Oct., Mon.–Tues. 9–5, Wed.–Sun. 9–9.*

Gander

🕤 *170 km (105 mi) northwest of Goobies.*

A busy town with 12,000 people, Gander is notable for its aviation history. It also has many lodgings and makes a good base for your travels in this part of the province. During World War II, **Gander International Airport** was chosen by the Canadian and U.S. Air Forces as a major strategic air base because of its favorable weather and secure location. After the war, the airport became an international hub for civilian travel; today it is a major air traffic control center. The **Aviation Exhibition** in the airport's domestic passengers' lounge (☎ 709/256–3905 or 709/651–2656) traces Newfoundland's role in the history of air travel. It's open 24 hours, 7 days a week.

The **North Atlantic Aviation Museum,** opened in 1996, gives an expansive view of Gander's and Newfoundland's roles in aviation. In addition to viewing the expected models and photographs, you can climb into the cockpit of a real DC-3 parked outside next to a World War II Hudson bomber and a Canadian jet fighter, or take a helicopter ride in summer. ⊠ *On Rte. 1, between hospital and visitor information center,* ☎ *709/256–2923.* ⊡ *$3.* ☉ *Daily 9–5.*

DINING AND LODGING

$$ ✕⛫ **Albatross Motel.** This motel has a deserved reputation as an at-
★   tractive place to stop off for a meal. Try the cod au gratin—you won't find it this good anywhere else. Rooms are basic and clean. ⊠ *Rte. 1, Box 450, A1V 1W8,* ☎ *709/256–3956 or 800/563–4900,* FAX *709/651–2692. 103 rooms, 4 suites. Restaurant. AE, DC, MC, V.*

Boyd's Cove
⑳ *66 km (41 mi) north of Gander.*

The coastline in and near Boyd's Cove is somewhat sheltered by Twillingate Island and New World Island, and it's from this area that short causeways link the shore to the islands.

The **Boyd's Cove Beothuk Interpretation Centre** offers a fresh look at the lives of the Beothuks, an extinct aboriginal people who succumbed in the early 19th century to a combination of disease and battle with European settlers. Opened in 1995, the center uses traditional Beothuk building forms and adjoins an archaeological site that was inhabited from about 1650 to 1720, when pressure from settlers drove the Beothuk from this part of the coast. ⊠ *Rte. 340,* ☎ *709/656–3114 or 709/729–2460.* ⊡ *Free.* ☉ *Summer, daily 10–5:30.*

Twillingate
㉑ *31 km (19 mi) north of Boyd's Cove.*

The inhabitants of this scenic old fishing village make their living from the sea and have been doing so for nearly two centuries. Colorful houses, rocky waterfront cliffs, a local museum, and a nearby lighthouse add to the town's appeal. Every year on the last weekend in July, the town hosts the **Fish, Fun and Folk Festival,** where fish are cooked every kind of way. Twillingate is one of the best places on the island to see **icebergs,** and is known to the locals as "Iceberg Alley." These majestic and dangerous mountains of ice are awe-inspiring to see while they're grounded in early summer.

Twillingate Island Boat Tours (☎ 709/884–2242 or 709/882–2317) specializes in iceberg photography in the waters around Twillingate. There is an iceberg interpretation center right on the dock.

OFF THE   **CHANGE ISLANDS AND FOGO ISLAND –** You can take a ferry (☎ 709/
BEATEN PATH   627-3448) from Farewell to either Change Islands or Fogo Island. To get to Farewell, take Route 340 to Route 335, which takes you through scenic coastal communities. These islands give you the impression of a place frozen in time. Clapboard homes are precariously perched on rocks or built on small lots surrounded by vegetable gardens. As you walk the roads, watch for moose and herds of wild Newfoundland ponies who spend their summers grazing and enjoying the warm breeze off the ocean.

The Great Northern Peninsula

The Great Northern Peninsula is the most northern visible extension of the Appalachian Mountains. Its eastern side is rugged and sparsely populated. The Viking Trail—Route 430 and its side roads, and Route 510 in southern Labrador—snakes along its western coast through a national park, fjords, sand dunes, and communities that have relied on the lobster fishery for generations. At the tip of the peninsula, the Vikings established the first European settlement in North America. For thousands of years before their arrival, however, the area was home to native peoples who hunted, fished, and gathered berries and wild herbs.

Deer Lake

22 *208 km (129 mi) west of Grand Falls-Windsor.*

Deer Lake was once just another small town on the Trans-Canada Highway, but the opening of Gros Morne National Park in the early '70s and a first-class paved highway passing right through to St. Anthony changed all that. Today, with an airport and car rentals available, Deer Lake is a good starting point for a fly-drive vacation.

LODGING

$$ 🏨 **Deer Lake Motel.** The guest rooms here are clean and comfortable, and the food in the café is basic, home-cooked fare. You'll find the seafood dishes exceptionally well prepared. ⊠ *Box 820, A0K 2E0,* ☎ *709/635–2108,* FAX *709/635–3842. 54 rooms, 2 suites. Café. AE, DC, MC, V.*

OFF THE
BEATEN PATH

SIR RICHARD SQUIRES MEMORIAL PARK – From Deer Lake take Route 430 to Route 422 north to this park. Natural and unspoiled, it contains one of the most interesting salmon fishing areas in Newfoundland. This drive will also take you through Cormack, a farming region.

Gros Morne National Park

★ **23** *46 km (29 mi) north of Deer Lake on Rte. 430.*

Because of its geological uniqueness and immense splendor, this park has been named a UNESCO World Heritage Site. Among the more breathtaking visions are the expanses of wild orchids in springtime. There is an excellent **interpretation center** (☎ 709/458–2417) in Rocky Harbour, which has displays and videos about the park, plus an interactive vacation planner. Camping and hiking are popular recreations, and boat tours are available. It takes at least two days to see Gros Morne properly. Scenic **Bonne Bay,** a deep, mountainous fjord, divides the park in two. You can drive around the perimeter of the fjord on Route 430 going north.

24 In the south of the park, on Route 431, is **Woody Point,** a charming community of old houses and imported Lombardy poplars. Until it was bypassed by the now-defunct railway, the community was the commercial capital of Newfoundland's west coast. The **Tablelands,** rising behind Woody Point, are a unique rock massif that was once an ancient seabed. Its rocks, which were raised from the earth's mantle through tectonic upheaval, are toxic to most plant life, and Ice Age conditions linger in the form of persistent snow and moving rock glaciers.

25 The once-isolated small community of **Trout River** is at the western end of Route 431 on the Gulf of St. Lawrence. You pass the scenic **Trout River Pond** along the way. The **Green Gardens Trail,** a four- to five-hour hike, is also nearby, and it's one you'll remember for your lifetime, but be prepared to do a bit of climbing on your return journey. The trail passes through the Tablelands barrens and descends sharply down to a fairy-tale coastline of eroded cliffs and green meadows.

26 On the northern side of the park, along coastal Route 430, is **Rocky Harbour,** with a wide range of services and a luxurious indoor public pool—the perfect thing to soothe tired limbs after a strenuous day.

The most popular attraction in the northern portion of Gros Morne is the boat tour of **Western Brook Pond** (☞ Outdoor Activities and Sports, *below*). You park at a lot on Route 430 and take a 45-minute walk to the boat dock through an interesting mix of bog and woods. Cliffs rise 2,000 ft on both sides of the gorge, and high waterfalls tumble over ancient rocks. If you have strong legs and are in good shape, another natural attraction is the 10-mi hike up **Gros Morne Mountain,** at 2,644 ft the second-highest peak in Newfoundland. Weather permitting, your labor will be rewarded by a unique arctic landscape and spectacular views. The park's **northern coast** has an unusual mix of sand beaches, rock pools, and trails through tangled dwarf forests known locally as "tuckamore." Sunsets, seen from **Lobster Point Lighthouse,** are spectacular. Keep an eye out for whales and visit the lighthouse museum, devoted to the history of the area. ⊠ *Gros Morne National Park, via the Viking Trail (Rte. 430),* ☎ *709/458–2417.* ⌫ *Daily $3, 4 days $9.* ☉ *Summer, daily 9 AM–10 PM; winter, daily 9–4.*

LODGING

$$–$$$$ 🏨 **Sugar Hill Inn.** This small hostelry in Gros Morne National Park has quickly developed a reputation for fine wining and dining because of host Vince McCarthy's culinary talents and educated palate. You can take guided cross-country skiing and snowmobiling treks here. ⊠ *Box 100, Norris Point, A0K 3V0,* ☎ FAX *709/458–2147. 4 rooms. Hot tub, sauna. MC, V.*

OUTDOOR ACTIVITIES AND SPORTS

Gros Morne Adventure Guides (☎ 709/458–2722 or 709/686–2241) has sea kayaking up the fjords and land-locked ponds of Gros Morne National Park, as well as a variety of hikes and adventures in the area.

Bontours (☎ 709/458–2730) runs the best-known of the sightseeing trips on the west coast of Newfoundland—up Western Brook Pond in Gros Morne National Park—and another tour of Bonne Bay. **Tableland Boat Tours** (☎ 709/451–2101 or 709/451–5146) leads tours up Trout River Pond near the southern boundary of Gros Morne National Park. **Seal Island Boat Tours** (☎ 709/243–2376 or 709/243–2278) explores St. Paul's Inlet, an area of Gros Morne National Park rich in seals, terns, and other marine and shore life.

Arches Provincial Park

㉗ *20 km (12 mi) north of Gros Morne National Park.*

Arches Provincial Park is a geological curiosity where the action of undersea current millions of years ago cut a succession of caves through a bed of dolomite that was later raised above sea level by tectonic upheaval.

En Route Continuing north on Route 430, parallel to the Gulf of St. Lawrence, you'll find yourself refreshingly close to the ocean and the wave-tossed beaches: Stop to breathe the fresh sea air and listen to the breakers. The **Long Range Mountains** to your right reminded Jacques Cartier, who saw them in 1534, of the long, rectangular-shape farm buildings of his home village in France. Small villages are interspersed with rivers where salmon and trout grow to be "liar-size."

The remains of the Maritime Archaic Indians and Dorset Eskimos have been found in abundance along this coast, and **Port au Choix** has an interesting interpretation center (☎ 709/623–2608; ⌫ $1).

L'Anse aux Meadows National Historic Site

★ ㉘ 210 km (130 mi) northeast of Arches Provincial Park.

A UNESCO World Heritage Site, L'Anse aux Meadows was discovered in 1960 by a Norwegian team, Helge and Anne Stine Ingstad. Most believe the remains of the long sod houses here were built around 1000 as the site of Norseman Leif Eriksson's colony in the New World. The Canadian Parks Service has established a fine **visitor center** and has meticulously reconstructed some of the sod huts to give you a sense of centuries past. ⊠ Rte. 436, ☎ 709/623–2608. ☜ $2.50 ◷ Mid-June–Labor Day, daily 9–8.

DINING AND LODGING

$ ✕⊡ **Tickle Inn at Cape Onion.** This refurbished, century-old fisherman's house on the beach is probably the most northerly residence on the island of Newfoundland. You can relax around the Franklin stove in the parlor after a day of exploring the area meadows, hills, and coast, or taking a trip to the Viking settlement at L'Anse aux Meadows (about 45 km, or 28 mi, away). ⊠ R.R. 1, Box 62, Cape Onion, A0K 4J0, ☎ 709/452–4321 June–Sept., 709/739–5503 Oct.–May. 4 rooms share bath. Dining room. CP, MAP available. MC, V.

$ ⊡ **Valhalla Lodge Bed & Breakfast.** Comfortable and inviting, the Valhalla is 10 km (6 mi) from L'Anse aux Meadows. Note the interesting fossils in the rock fireplace in the dining room. Hot breakfasts are available, and other meals can be had on request. E. Annie Proulx, author of The Shipping News, stayed here when she was writing the novel. ⊠ Gunner's Cove, Griquet A0K 2X0, ☎ 709/623–2018 in summer, 709/896–5519 in winter. 6 rooms. V.

OUTDOOR ACTIVITIES AND SPORTS

In nearby St. Lunaire you can take a tour boat modeled after a Viking trading vessel and see the coast from the ocean. **Viking Boat Tours** (☎ 709/623–2100) visits the site at the tip of the Great Northern Peninsula where Vikings landed 1,000 years ago.

St. Anthony

㉙ 16 km (10 mi) south of L'Anse aux Meadows.

The northern part of the Great Northern Peninsula served as the model for The Shipping News, E. Annie Proulx's Pulitzer-winning novel. St. Anthony, which has a number of attractions, is built around a natural harbor on the eastern side of the Great Northern Peninsula, near its tip. Take a trip out to the **lighthouse**—you may see an iceberg or two floating by.

The **Grenfell Mission,** founded by Sir Wilfred Grenfell, a British medical missionary who established nursing stations and cooperatives and provided medical services to the scattered villages of northern Newfoundland and the south coast of Labrador in the early 1900s, remains the town's main employer. The main foyer of the **Charles S. Curtis Memorial Hospital** has a decorative tile mural that's worth a visit. **Grenfell House,** the home of Sir Wilfred and Lady Grenfell, has been restored to period condition and can be visited. ⊠ On west side of town on hill overlooking harbor, ☎ 709/454–8596. ☜ $2. ◷ June–Sept., daily 10–8; winter, by appointment.

Don't leave without visiting the **Grenfell Handicrafts** store (☎ 709/454–3576). Training villagers to become self-sufficient in a harsh environment was one of Grenfell's aims. A windproof cloth that villagers turned into well-made parkas came to be known as Grenfell cloth. Beautiful clothes fashioned out of Grenfell cloth have a unique quality and style and are available for sale here.

The West Coast

Western Newfoundland is known for the unlikely combination of world-class Atlantic salmon fishing and papermaking at two newsprint mills. This area includes Corner Brook, a major center of the west coast. To the south, the Port au Prince Peninsula west of Stephenville shows the French influence in Newfoundland; the farming valleys of the southwest were settled by Scots. A ferry from Nova Scotia docks at Port aux Basques in the far southwest corner.

Corner Brook

③⓪ *50 km (31 mi) southwest of Deer Lake.*

Corner Brook is Newfoundland's second-largest city and the hub of the west coast of the island. Mountains fringe three sides of the city, and there are beautiful views of the harbor and the Bay of Islands. Corner Brook is also home to one of the largest paper mills in the world; you may smell it. Captain James Cook, the British explorer, charted the coast in the 1760s, and a memorial to him overlooks the bay.

If you plan to explore the west coast, Corner Brook is a convenient hub and point of departure. It is only three hours from the Port aux Basques ferry from Nova Scotia and is an attractive, active city. The town enjoys more clearly defined seasons than most of the rest of the island, and in summer there are many pretty gardens. In addition, the nearby Humber River is the best-known salmon river in the province.

The north and south shores of the **Bay of Islands** have fine paved roads—Route 440 on the north shore and Route 450 on the south—and both are a scenic half-day drive from Corner Brook. On both roads, farming and fishing communities exist side by side. Take a camera with you—the scenery is breathtaking, with farms, mountains, and pockets of brilliant wildflowers.

DINING AND LODGING

$$ ✕🏨 **Best Western Mamateek Inn.** Rooms are more modern than at the
★ Glynmill Inn (☞ *below*). The dining room, which serves good New-foundland home-cooked food, is known for its exquisite view of the city. Sunsets seen from here are remarkable. ⊠ *Rte. 1, Box 787, A2H 6G7,* ☎ *709/639–8901 or 800/563–8600,* 🅵🅰🆇 *709/639–7567. 55 rooms. Restaurant. AE, MC, V.*

$$ ✕🏨 **Glynmill Inn.** This charming inn, refurbished in 1994, has the feel
★ of old England. It was once the staff house for the visiting top brass of the paper mill. Rooms are cozy and the dining room serves basic and well-prepared Newfoundland seafood, soups, and specialty desserts made with partridgeberries. There's also a popular steak house in the basement. ⊠ *1 Cobb La., Box 550, A2H 6E6,* ☎ *709/634–5181, 800/563–4400 in Canada,* 🅵🅰🆇 *709/634–5106. 57 rooms, 24 suites. 2 restaurants. AE, MC, V.*

$$ 🏨 **Comfort Inn by Journey's End Motel.** This is a comfortable, mod-ern motel with an attractive interior (the dominating colors are dusty rose and blue) and beautiful views of either the city or the Bay Islands. ⊠ *41 Maple Valley Rd., Box 1142, A2H 6T2,* ☎ *709/639–1980,* 🅵🅰🆇 *709/639–1549. 81 rooms. Restaurant. AE, DC, MC, V.*

$$ 🏨 **Holiday Inn.** There's nothing extraordinary here, aside from the con-venience of being located right in town. The outdoor pool is heated and some of the rooms have minibars. The restaurant is average, aside from good seasonal fish dishes. ⊠ *48 West St., A2H 2Z2,* ☎ *709/634–*

5381, ℻ 709/634–1723. 103 rooms. Restaurant, lobby lounge, pool.
AE, DC, MC, V.

OUTDOOR ACTIVITIES AND SPORTS

Strawberry Hill Resort (☎ 709/634–0066, ℻ 709/634–7604) in Little Rapids, 12 km (7 mi) east of Corner Brook on Route 1, was once an exclusive retreat for the owner of the Corner Brook mill. Guests here can enjoy Newfoundland's finest sport salmon fishing.

The **Marble Mountain Ski Resort** (☎ 709/637–7600), just east of the city, has the highest slopes and the most snowfall in eastern North America and is growing rapidly. There are 27 downhill runs, as well as a large day lodge, ski shop, day-care center, and restaurant at the mountain summit.

Stephenville

③ 77 km (48 mi) south of Corner Brook.

The former Harmon Air Force Base is in Stephenville, which is best known for its summer festival (☞ below). It also has a large modern paper mill. To the west of town is the Port au Port Peninsula, which was largely settled by the French, who brought their way of life and language to this small corner of Newfoundland.

THE ARTS

The **Stephenville Festival** (☎ 709/643–5756) is held mid-July to mid-August. The festival is the province's major annual summer theatrical event and presents a mix of light musicals and serious drama.

En Route As you travel down the Trans-Canada Highway toward Port aux Basques, Routes 404, 405, 406, and 407 will bring you into the small Scottish communities of the **Codroy Valley.** Nestled in the valley are some of the finest salmon rivers and most productive farms in the province, all of this against the backdrop of the Long Range Mountains and the Lewis Hills, from which gales strong enough to stop traffic hurl off the plateau and down to the coast.

Port aux Basques

③ 70 km (43 mi) south of Stephenville.

Port aux Basques was one of seven Basque ports along Newfoundland's west coast and in southern Labrador during the 1500s and early 1600s, and was given its name by the town's French successors. It is now the main ferry port connecting the island to Nova Scotia. In **J. T. Cheeseman Provincial Park** (15 km, or 9 mi) north of town on the Trans-Canada Highway and at **Grand Bay West** you can catch sight of the endangered piping plover, which nests in the sand dunes along this part of the coast.

LODGING

$$ ☒ **St. Christopher's Hotel.** This clean, comfortable hotel has quiet, air-conditioned rooms and good food. Rooms have satellite TV. ☒ Box 2049, Caribou Rd., Port aux Basques, A0M 1C0, ☎ 709/695–7034 or 800/563–4779, ℻ 709/695–9841. 54 rooms, 3 suites. Restaurant, meeting room. AE, DC, MC, V.

LABRADOR

Isolated from the rest of the continent, Labrador has remained one of the world's truly wild places, and yet its two main centers of Labrador City–Wabush and Happy Valley–Goose Bay offer all the amenities available in larger urban areas. Labrador is steeped in history, a place where the past invades the present and life evolves as it did many years ago—

a composite of natural phenomena, wilderness adventure, history, and culture. This vast landscape—293,347 square km (113,204 square mi) of land and 8,000 km (5,000 mi) of coastline—is home to 30,000 people. The small but richly diverse population has a history that in some cases stretches back thousands of years; in other cases—the mining towns of Labrador West, for example—the history goes back less than four decades.

The Straits

The Straits in southeastern Labrador were a rich hunting-and-gathering ground for the continent's earliest peoples. In the area is the oldest industrial site in the New World, the 16th-century Basque whaling station at Red Bay.

L'Anse au Clair

㉝ *5 km (3 mi) from Blanc Sablon, Québec (ferry from St. Barbe, Newfoundland, docks in Blanc Sablon).*

In L'Anse au Clair, anglers can try their luck for trout and salmon on the scenic Forteau and Pinware rivers. You can also walk the "Doctor's Path," where long ago Dr. Marcoux searched out herbs and medicinal plants in the days when hospitals and nursing stations were few and far between.

L'Anse Amour

㉞ *19 km (12 mi) east of L'Anse au Clair.*

The elaborate **Maritime Archaic Indian burial site** discovered near L'Anse Amour is 7,500 years old. A plaque marks a site that is the oldest known aboriginal funeral monument in North America. The L'Anse Amour **lighthouse** was constructed in 1857 and is the second-tallest lighthouse in Canada.

En Route   The **Labrador Straits Museum** provides a glimpse into the history and lifestyle of the area. ✉ *Rte. 510 between Forteau and L'Anse au Loup,* ☎ *709/927–5659 or 709/931–2067.* 🎫 *$1.50.* ☉ *Summer, daily.*

Red Bay

★ **㉟** *35 km (22 mi) from L'Anse Amour.*

You must drive to the very end of Route 510 to visit the area's main attraction: Red Bay, the site of a 16th-century Basque whaling station and a National Historic Site. Basque whalers began harpooning migrating whales from flimsy boats in frigid waters a few years after Cabot's discovery of the coast in 1497. Between 1550 and 1600 Red Bay was the world's whaling capital. A **visitor center** (☎ 709/920–2197) interprets the Basque heritage through film and artifact. It's open mid-June–September, Monday–Saturday 8–8 and Sunday noon–8. From June through October, a boat will take you on a five-minute journey over to the site of excavations on Saddle Island.

Coastal Labrador

This area is almost as isolated today as it was a century ago. Along the southern coast, most villages are inhabited by descendants of Europeans, while farther north they are mostly native. Over the years the European settlers have adopted native skills and survival strategies, and the natives have adopted many European technologies. In summer the ice retreats and a coastal steamer delivers goods. In winter small airplanes and snowmobiles are the only ways in and out.

You can tour central coastal Labrador aboard Marine Atlantic's car ferry from Lewisporte, Newfoundland (☞ Getting Around *in* Newfoundland and Labrador A to Z, *below*). A second vessel, a coastal freighter, travels from St. Anthony, Newfoundland, to Nain, Labrador's northernmost settlement. This trip takes two weeks to complete. Both vessels carry all sorts of food and goods for people living along the coast. On the coastal freighter you'll stop at a number of summer fishing stations and coastal communities. Reservations are required.

Battle Harbour National Historic Site
12 km (7 mi) from Mary's Harbour by boat.

This island site has the only remaining outport fishing merchant's premises that remains intact in the province. Battle Harbour was settled in the 18th century; it was the main fishing port in Labrador until the first half of the 20th century when, after fires destroyed some of the community, the people moved to nearby Mary's Harbour. The site also contains the oldest Anglican church in Labrador. ⊠ *Southern Labrador coast, accessible by boat from Mary's Harbour,* ☏ *709/921–6216, 709/497–8805 off-season.* ☉ *June–Sept.*

Happy Valley–Goose Bay
36 *525 km (326 mi) from Labrador City.*

Happy Valley–Goose Bay is the chief service center for coastal Labrador. If you've come to Labrador to fish, you'll probably pass through here. The town was founded in the 1940s as a top-secret air base used to ferry fleets of North American–manufactured aircraft to Europe. It is still used as a low-level flying training base by the British, Dutch, and German air forces.

SKIING
Ski Mount Shana (☏ 709/896–8162 or 709/896–8068), with 10 downhill runs, is between Happy Valley–Goose Bay and North West River.

North West River
37 *20 km (12 mi) northeast of Happy Valley–Goose Bay.*

North West River, which retains its frontier charm, was founded as a Hudson's Bay trading post and is the former Labrador headquarters of the International Grenfell Association.

Labrador West

Labrador West's subarctic landscape is challenging and unforgettable. Here are some of the world's best angling and wilderness adventure opportunities. The best way to see this area is to ride the **Québec North Shore and Labrador Railway** (☏ 418/968–7805 or 709/944–8205), which leaves Sept Isles, Québec, three times a week in summer and twice a week in the winter. The seven- to eight-hour trip to Schefferville takes you through nearly 600 km (372 mi) of virgin forest, spectacular waterfalls, and majestic mountains.

Wabush
38 *525 km (326 mi) west of Happy Valley–Goose Bay.*

The modern town of Wabush has all the amenities of larger centers, including accommodations, sports and recreational facilities, good shopping, live theater, and some of the finest hospitality you will find anywhere.

SKIING
The **Smokey Mountain Alpine Skiing Center** (☏ 709/944–3505), west of Wabush, is open mid-November to late April and has trails and slopes for both beginners and advanced skiers.

Labrador City

39 *525 km (326 mi) west of Happy Valley–Goose Bay.*

Labrador City has all the facilities of nearby Wabush (☞ *above*). Each
March Labrador City and Wabush play host to a 645-km (400-mi)
dogsled race, the longest such race in eastern North America.

NEWFOUNDLAND AND LABRADOR A TO Z

Arriving and Departing

By Car Ferry

Marine Atlantic (✉ Box 250, North Sydney, Nova Scotia B2A 3M3,
☎ 902/794–5700 or 709/772–7701, TTY 902/794–8109, FAX 902/564–
7480) operates a car ferry from North Sydney, Nova Scotia, to Port
aux Basques, Newfoundland (crossing time is six hours); and, from June
through October, from North Sydney to Argentia, twice a week (crossing time 12–14 hours). In all cases, reservations are required.

By Plane

The province's main airport for connections from all major North American and European destinations is in St. John's. Other airports in Newfoundland are at Stephenville, Deer Lake, St. Anthony, and Gander;
airports in Labrador are in Happy Valley–Goose Bay, Wabush, and
Churchill Falls. **Air Canada** (☎ 800/776–3000; in Canada, 800/422–
6232) flies into Newfoundland. **Royal Airlines** flies to Newfoundland
from Ireland once a week; see your travel agent. **Air Club/Air Transat**
flies from Great Britain to Newfoundland once a week (☎ 31–70–
35–88–300). The following are **regional connectors:** Air Nova (☎ 800/
776–3000; in Newfoundland, 800/563–5151); Air Atlantic (☎ 800/
426–7000); Interprovincial Airlines (☎ 709/576–1666; in Newfoundland 800/563–2800); Air Labrador (☎ 709/896–3387; in Newfoundland, 800/563–3042); Air Alliance (Québec to Wabush) (☎ 800/
363–7050).

By Train

Iron Ore Canada's Québec North Shore and Labrador Railway (☎ 418/
962–9411) has service between Sept Isles, Québec, and Labrador City
and Schefferville in Labrador.

Getting Around

In winter some highways may close during and after severe snowstorms.
For winter road conditions on the west coast and in Labrador, call the
Department of Works, Services, and Transportation (in Deer Lake,
☎ 709/635–2162; in Grand Falls–Windsor and Central Newfoundland, 709/292–4300; in Clarenville, 709/466–7953; in St. John's,
709/729–2391).

Labrador

From the island of Newfoundland, you can fly to Labrador via St. John's,
Gander, Deer Lake, or Stephenville. Route 500 links Labrador City with
Happy Valley–Goose Bay via Churchill Falls. Conditions on this 526-
km (326-mi) unpaved wilderness road are best between June and October. If you plan on doing any extensive driving in any part of Labrador,
you should contact the **Department of Tourism, Culture and Recreation**
(☎ 709/729–2830 or 800/563–6353) for advice on the best routes and
road conditions.

To explore the south coast of Labrador, catch the **ferry** at St. Barbe on Route 430 in Newfoundland to Blanc Sablon, Québec. From here you can drive to Red Bay along Route 510.

Summer travel is possible by car ferry through **Marine Atlantic** (☎ 800/341–7981; in Lewisporte, Newfoundland, ☎ 709/535–6876; in Happy Valley–Goose Bay, Labrador, 709/896–0041). The ship travels from Lewisporte in Newfoundland to Cartwright, on the coast of Labrador, and then through the Hamilton inlet to Happy Valley–Goose Bay. Reservations are required. The trip takes 33 hours one-way, and two regularly scheduled return trips are made weekly.

Newfoundland

DRL Coachlines (☎ 709/738–8088) runs a trans-island bus service. Buses leave at 8 AM from St. John's and Port aux Basques. Small buses known as outport taxis connect the major centers with surrounding communities.

Newfoundland has an excellent **highway system,** and all but a handful of secondary roads are paved. The province's roads are generally uncrowded, adding to the pleasure of driving. Travel time along the Trans-Canada Highway (Route 1) from Port aux Basques to St. John's is about 13 hours, with time out for a meal in either Gander or Grand Falls–Windsor. The trip from Corner Brook to St. Anthony at the northernmost tip of the island is about five hours. The drive from St. John's to Grand Bank on the Burin Peninsula takes about four hours.

From St. John's to the north coast of the Avalon Peninsula, take Route 30 (Logy Bay Road) to Marine Drive. If you're heading for the southern coast, pick up Route 10 just south of St. John's and follow it toward Trepassey. Locals call this trip "going up the shore," even though it looks like you're traveling down on a map.

Contacts and Resources

Emergencies

Dial **911** for medical emergencies and police.

Fishing

Seasonal and regulatory fishing information can be obtained from the **Department of Tourism, Culture and Recreation** (☎ 800/563–6353).

Guided Tours

ADVENTURE TOURS

Adventure travel in Newfoundland and Labrador is growing rapidly. Local operators offer sea kayaking, ocean diving, canoeing, wildlife viewing, mountain biking, white-water rafting, heli-hiking, and interpretive walks in summer. In winter, snowmobiling, heli-skiing, and caribou- and seal-watching expeditions are popular. Before choosing an operator it's advisable to contact the Department of Tourism, Culture and Recreation to make sure you're calling an established outfit.

Eastern Edge Outfitters (☎ 709/782–1465) leads east-coast sea-kayaking tours and gives white-water kayaking instruction. **Tuckamore Wilderness Lodge** (☎ 709/865–6361 or 709/865–4371) in Main Brook uses its luxurious lodge on the Great Northern Peninsula as a base for viewing caribou, seabird colonies, whales, and icebergs. **Labrador Scenic Ltd.** (☎ 709/497–8326) in North West River organizes tours through central and northern Labrador with an emphasis on wildlife and Labrador's spectacular coast. **Wildland Tours** (☎ 709/722–3123) in St. John's, winner of the Governor-General's Award for Conservation, has weeklong tours to view wildlife and visit historically and culturally significant sites across Newfoundland.

BUS TOURS

McCarthy's Party (☎ 709/781–2244 or 709/781–2266) in St. John's
offers guided bus tours across Newfoundland (May–October) in addition to a variety of charter services. **Fleetline Motorcoach Tours**
(☎ 709/722–2608 or 709/229–7600) in Holyrood runs island-wide
tours. Local tours are available for Port aux Basques, the Codroy Valley, Corner Brook, the Bay of Islands, Gros Morne National Park, the
Great Northern Peninsula, and St. John's.

Hospitals

St. Clare's Mercy Hospital (⊠ 154 Le Marchant Rd., St. John's, ☎ 709/
778–3111). **Grace Hospital** (⊠ 241 Le Marchant Rd., St. John's,
☎ 709/778–6222). **General Hospital** (⊠ 300 Prince Philip Dr., St. John's,
☎ 709/737–6300). **George B. Cross Hospital** (⊠ Manitoba Dr.,
Clarenville, ☎ 709/466–3411). **James Paton** (⊠ 125 Trans-Canada
Hwy., Gander, ☎ 709/651–2500). **Western Memorial** (⊠ Brookfield
Ave., Corner Brook, ☎ 709/637–5000). **Charles S. Curtis Memorial Hospital** (⊠ West St., St. Anthony, ☎ 709/454–3333). **Captain William
Jackman Hospital** (⊠ 410 Booth Ave., Labrador City, ☎ 709/944–
2632).

Visitor Information

The Department of Tourism, Culture and Recreation (⊠ Box 8730, St.
John's A1B 4K2, ☎ 709/729–2830) distributes brochures and maps
from its offices in the Confederation Building, West Block, St. John's.
The province maintains a **tourist information line** (☎ 800/563–6353),
which operates year-round, 24 hours a day.

From June until Labor Day, a network of **Visitor Information Centres,**
open daily 9–9, dots the province. These centers carry information on
events, accommodations, shopping, and crafts stores in their area.
There are in-season visitor information booths at the airports in Gander and St. John's. The city of St. John's operates an information center in a restored railway carriage next to the harbor.

15 Wilderness Canada

The Yukon, the Northwest Territories

Life above the 60th parallel in the mountainous, river-threaded Yukon and the flat, lake-dotted Northwest Territories is strange and wonderful. The landscape is austere and beautiful in ways unlike anywhere else in North America: the tundra plains that reach to the Arctic Ocean, the remote ice fields of Kluane National Park, white-water rivers snaking through mountain ranges and deep canyons. This is also the last region of North America where native peoples have managed to sustain traditional cultures relatively undisturbed.

Updated by
Tina Sebert
(The Yukon)
and Rosemary
Allerston (The
Northwest
Territories)

LET IT BE STATED AS SIMPLY AS POSSIBLE: Life in Canada's far north is strange. Strange as in weird, strange as in wonderful, strange as in uncommon. The inherent strangeness of the world north of the 60th parallel—the latitudinal line separating Canada's provinces and the Yukon and the Northwest Territories—is perceptible in empirical, practical, and mysterious ways.

Consider examples from life in the heart of strangeness:

In recent years diamond discoveries have spawned the development of remote mining camps out on the barren tundra. The people in these camps depend for survival on airplanes, as do many small communities all over the Arctic. Other residents of the far north may drive hundreds of miles to a major city to stock up on groceries. In many cases it is easier to hunt caribou or moose than it is to go shopping for vegetables.

Seasons become so overlapped in the few nonwinter months that summer wildflowers have not finished blooming by the time the foliage picks up its fall color. In winter a network of highways, built entirely of hardpacked snow over frozen lake, opens up to automotive traffic. So cold are the snow and ice that they lose their slipperiness, making areas otherwise inaccessible relatively easy to reach. Bridges over rivers are also built of ice, and northerners must learn to prepare for "break-up" and "freeze-up"—the few weeks in spring and fall when ice bridges are unstable but rivers are still too frozen for ferries to operate. Unprepared travelers will sometimes fork over several hundred dollars or more for a helicopter to sling their cars across a river. This underscores the fact that, in a region where bush pilots are held in high regard, air transport is the way to go. In a plane with pontoons an uncountable number of lakes means an uncountable number of watery runways. As the Mayor of Yellowknife once said, "We get on planes here just like a New Yorker gets in a taxi."

If a single strange element of life in the far north stands out, it is the quality of light. In mid-summer, sunrise and sunset merge, and north of the Arctic Circle, they don't occur at all. And when night does come— so belatedly in summer that it is a way of life to draw shades tightly during sunlit evenings to simulate night—there is the mystical voodoo show of the Northern Lights.

Most of the region is climatically classified as semiarid, much of it covered by the vast granite spread of the Canadian Shield. But because water evaporates and ice melts so slowly in Arctic climes, there is an abundance of water. That water is mostly in the form of lakes and ponds in the flatter Northwest Territories and in the form of rivers in the mountainous Yukon. A good deal of it, of course, remains ice; the glaciers of the St. Elias Mountains in the Yukon's Kluane National Park, topped by 19,550-ft Mt. Logan, create the largest nonpolar ice field in the world.

This is wilderness and the wildlife loves it. A migrating caribou herd exceeding 80,000 is not uncommon, and that's a number to keep in perspective: It represents the entire human census of the region. Indeed, people are profoundly outnumbered by nonhuman mammals: bears (black, grizzly, polar), Dall sheep, wolves, wolverines, moose, bison, and, of course, caribou. Humans are also outnumbered by fish and birds. Fishermen regularly throw back trout weighing 10 pounds, because a fish that size is considered in these parts to be too puny. Bald eagles are a common sight, as are the flocks of migratory waterfowl that spend their summers here.

Signs on government buildings are often inscribed in as many as eight official languages—English, French, and various native languages. One of those languages, Slavey, is so difficult to learn that it was used in coding during World War II. Native people in the far north are wielding increasing influence in governmental affairs. The main tribal groups are seven nations of Athapaskan peoples and the Inland Tlingit in the Yukon, and the Dene, Inuvialuit, and Inuit peoples of the Northwest Territories. Many of these people go about their lives much as their ancestors did centuries before them, although helped today by such 20th-century basics as electricity and motor-driven machinery. In recent years, large tracts of land have been ceded to native groups in land-claims settlements. And in 1999 the Northwest Territories will be split in two, separating the principal lands of the Dene and the Inuit. The new Inuit territory in the east is to be called *Nunavut,* or "our land." The Dene call their region *Denendeh,* which means the same thing; but there are no plans to make the name official.

A visit to the far north does not happen without commitment and preparation. Lodging under $100 a night is the exception, unless you camp, and what you get for the price is unlikely to be fancy. Having to rely on planes to get from one place to the next does not come cheaply. Guides and outfitters can be expensive, too, but their fees aren't out of line with the general cost of living in the far north, and their travel packages often end up saving you money.

Visitors must be willing to abide possible discomforts and inconveniences. Mosquitoes and blackflies rule the north during summer and early fall, and anyone without a good insect repellent is in for big trouble. Packing gloves and insulated clothing in August might seem excessive, but such are the necessities of traveling in a world where it's not uncommon for summertime temperatures to drop from above 70°F to well below freezing in a single day. And life doesn't always proceed with clockwork precision; a frontier quality still pervades much of the far north, meaning that a lot of business is conducted on an ad-hoc, by-the-bootstraps basis. Visiting the far north can be daunting, difficult, frightening, and even dangerous, but for those who prepare themselves for the commitment, it can be nothing short of exhilarating.

Pleasures and Pastimes

Dining
Cooking in the far north rarely reaches grand epicurean standards, but it can have a distinctive character, making wide use of local foods. This means that in some places and at certain times of year, a caribou steak or a moose burger may be easier to find than a fresh salad. Once outside the main cities, be prepared for limited choices; the dining room of your hotel or lodge may well be your *only* choice. But if the far north is not necessarily a gastronomic paradise, it is surprising and certainly admirable what some chefs are able to concoct given the limitations on ingredients.

CATEGORY	COST*
$$$$	over $25
$$$	$18–$25
$$	$10–$18
$	under $10

*per person, excluding drinks, service, and 7% GST

Lodging

Lodging prices in the far north are generally higher than you might find elsewhere in Canada. In many communities a lodge or hotel may be the only show in town, so if you don't like the price, you don't have much choice. In addition, the shortness of the tourism season forces lodging proprietors to try to make ends meet in two or three months of active vacation business. Although you might think you're paying a good chunk of change for pretty ordinary accommodations, consider, too, the lack of quality building materials in many areas and the prohibitive costs of construction. In months other than July and August, expect better deals—room prices reduced 50% or more—but fewer choices, because many places are closed from September through June.

Territorial, or public, campgrounds are found along all roads in the north and are open from the spring thaw until the fall freeze. Visitor Information (☞ Contacts and Resources *in* Wilderness Canada A to Z, *below*) centers throughout the region can provide information on specific campground locations and facilities as well as permits. Note: It is advisable to boil or filter all water, even water that has been designated as "drinking water" at a campground.

CATEGORY	COST*
$$$$	over $150
$$$	$120–$150
$$	$80–$120
$	under $80

All prices are for a standard double room (or equivalent, where not applicable), excluding gratuities and 7% GST.

Outdoor Activities and Sports

CROSS-COUNTRY SKIING

In a world covered by snow eight months out of the year, cross-country skiing opportunities are obviously plentiful. The best time for skiing, however, is from mid-March until the snow melts (the precise time varying according to the latitude and elevation), when days are longer and warmer. While short outings on skis are possible almost anywhere in the north, perhaps the most interesting extended excursions are in the Kluane area and the Arctic North. A number of backcountry lodges have begun opening in April and May for ski-touring enthusiasts.

DOGSLEDDING

Before there were planes and snowmobiles, dogsleds were the vital means of transportation in the far north. The Yukon Quest International Dogsled Race, along the Yukon River from Whitehorse to Fairbanks or Fairbanks to Whitehorse, takes place every year in mid-February. Destination/start points alternate annually. Top mushers compete for the $100,000 purse in this 1,600-km (1,000-mi) trek that is touted to be the "toughest dogsled race in the world." The most important race in the Northwest Territories is the Canadian Championship Dog Derby, held at Yellowknife in March.

FISHING

Fishing in wilderness Canada is a way of life, and a means of sustenance for a good many native residents. What sustains the native people of the north is also what attracts sports fishers: fish in large quantities and of considerable proportions. Farther south on the continent, an eight-pound trout might be considered a trophy fish, but in the far north it would be rejected as not much more than a sardine. Lake trout between 30 and 70 pounds are not unusual. The most common catches in the far north are Arctic char, grayling, pike, lake trout, and whitefish.

Numerous outfitters throughout the region can guide fishers on day trips or short excursions; your best bet is to check with a regional tourist office for outfitter recommendations. Day trips from Yellowknife to Great Slave Lake are especially easy to arrange. Some lakes and streams are accessible by road in the Yukon and in the Northwest Territories. However, the more typical fishing adventure in the far north involves flying to a remote lodge for several days.

HIKING

While the landscape can be spectacular, the going can be rough. Marked trails are relatively few, and sometimes the only trails to follow are those beaten down by wild animals. The four general areas that are best for hiking are Baffin Island, Kluane National Park, the Chilkoot Trail, and the mountains along the Dempster Highway.

MOUNTAINEERING

In the far north, the question is not what to climb but how to access the mountain. The major peaks of Kluane National Park, Mt. St. Elias, and particularly Canada's highest peak, Mt. Logan, are tops in the mountaineering world but can only be reached by helicopter or plane. For serious rock climbers, the Cirque of the Unclimbables, located in Nahanni National Park, presents an obvious challenge.

WATER SPORTS

Without question river travel is one of the best ways to experience the wilderness of the far north; these roads of water provide access to remote areas otherwise inaccessible. Canoes of various configurations are the preferred means of travel, although for some rivers—particularly those with considerable white water—rafts or kayaks may be used. If you decide on an unguided trip, outfitters can provide both the necessary gear as well as transportation to and from the river. The world-famous South Nahanni River in Nahanni National Park is considered a classic. The Alsek and the Tatshenshini, which run primarily through British Columbia, although they begin in the Kluane region of the Yukon are also great water sports venues. Another water-borne adventure to consider is sailing on Great Slave Lake.

Shopping

Native arts and crafts are the most compelling reason to go shopping in the far north. You may find that prices are best when buying directly from artists or craftspeople in local communities; however, buying from galleries or stores in the cities provides at least some guarantee of authenticity. Soapstone carvings, clothing, and moose- or caribou-hair tuftings (hair sewn onto velvet or hide and cut and shaped into pictures of flowers or animals) are among the most popular items to purchase. Be aware before buying, however, that some products, such as those made from hides or materials from endangered species, may not be brought into the United States. In many cases—such as a polar-bear rug—the import problem is obvious but not in all cases; for example, jewelry made of walrus ivory may be confiscated at the border.

Exploring Wilderness Canada

The Yukon and the Northwest Territories make up 3,787,800 km (1,456,375 square mi), almost three times the size of Alaska and half the size of the rest of the United States. There are cities—Whitehorse in the Yukon and Yellowknife in the Northwest Territories—but there are many more communities that are more than likely accessible only by plane. The landscape is reason enough to visit. Consider the tundra plains that reach to the Arctic Ocean, the remote ice fields of the St. Elias Mountains, white-water rivers snaking through mountain ranges and deep canyons, and the glacier-sculpted cliffs of Baffin Island.

Great Itineraries

The idea of exploring all of Canada's far north in a single trip is an absurdity. It would be comparable to trying to visit Florida, New England, and the Rocky Mountains on the same vacation, only with far fewer roads to travel. Size is only one problem; expense is another. Food, gas, and lodging are typically priced higher than in other parts of Canada, but the biggest cost is transportation, especially in those vast, roadless areas where you'll need to depend on air travel. This is not to say it is difficult to get from one place to another; in fact the number of charter plane operators and the number of expert bush pilots able to land a float plane on little more than a mud puddle make getting around easier than you might think. But the costs of traveling by small planes can be dizzying.

Thus, the best strategy for exploring the far north is to be selective. Focus on a specific area (e.g., Baffin Island, the Nahanni region, Dawson City) and/or an activity (e.g., fishing, wildlife viewing). Specific travel plans can save hundreds, even thousands, of dollars. The choices fall roughly into four categories: visiting the main cities (Dawson City, Whitehorse, Yellowknife); excursions from the main cities; adventures in the backcountry wilderness; and adventures in the Arctic north. Though there are enough activities in the Yukon and Northwest Territories to keep you occupied for months, the following itineraries are geared toward the standard short vacation traveler, for whom time is an issue.

Numbers in the text correspond to numbers in the margin and on the Yukon and Northwest Territories maps.

THE YUKON

If You Have 3 Days: Start your tour in ⊞ **Whitehorse** ①; see the S.S. *Klondike* National Historic Site, the MacBride Museum, and Miles Canyon. The next day drive down Route 2 to picturesque **Carcross** ② and on to ⊞ **Skagway** ③, Alaska, along the approximate route traversed by the Klondike Gold Rushers in 1898. You'll pass through a variety of landforms, including the Carcross Desert, the alpine tundra of the White Pass, and the coastal rain forest of the Alaskan Panhandle. On the morning of your third day, ride the historic White Pass & Yukon Route railway past blue glaciers and rushing waterfalls.

If You Have 5 Days: Start your trip as you would with the three-day itinerary, but on day three drive 8 hours, from Skagway past Whitehorse to ⊞ **Dawson City** ⑤. On your fourth day drive down Bonanza Creek Road to see **Dredge No. 4** and the original claim where the discovery of gold was made in 1896. Also highly recommended are the readings at Robert Service's cabin, the Palace Grand Theatre, and Diamond Tooth Gertie's Gambling Hall.

If You Have 10 Days: A 10-day itinerary allows travelers interested in a wilderness experience to travel the backcountry. A Klondike Gold Rush itinerary could be a hike over the **Chilkoot Trail** (three to four days) in addition to traveling to ⊞ **Skagway** ③, ⊞ **Whitehorse** ①, and ⊞ **Dawson City** ⑤. If river scenery and wildlife viewing is more of an interest, a canoe trip down the Thirty-Mile section of the Yukon River, from Whitehorse to Carmacks, might fit the bill.

Some of the planet's best hiking is possible in **Kluane National Park.** A ten-day itinerary could take you as far back as the Donjek Glacier in the heart of Kluane's ethereal wilderness. People wanting to stay on the Yukon's roadways could venture up the Dempster Highway, past

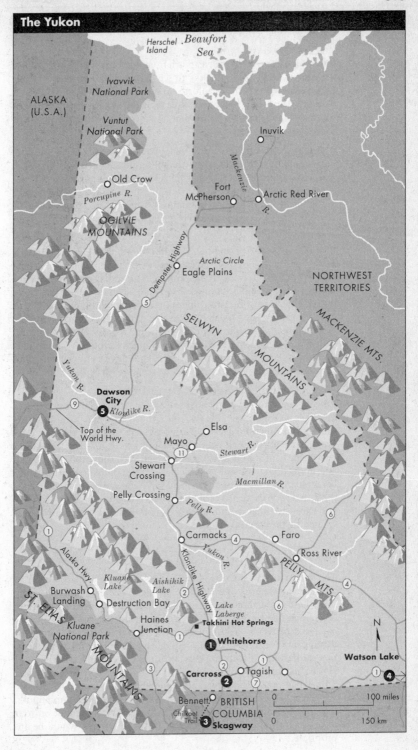

The Yukon

the Arctic Circle to ☒ **Inuvik** ⑦ in the Northwest Territories, an adventurous four-day extension to the five-day itinerary above.

THE NORTHWEST TERRITORIES

If You Have 3 Days: You can jet north from Edmonton or Calgary across the Arctic Circle to ☒ **Inuvik** ⑦ to see the amazing Mackenzie Delta, **Tuktoyaktuk** ⑧, and the Beaufort Sea. With two nights in Inuvik, you'll also have time for a flying tour over the giant estuary (where belugas romp in summer) to **Herschel Island,** which used to be the haunt of 19th-century whalers.

If You Have 5 Days: Fly up to ☒ **Yellowknife** ⑥ in late March for Caribou Carnival and the Canadian Championship Dog Derby. Bring your warmest clothes: it's still winter then, even though northerners think it's spring. But the sun's out, the ice sculptures sparkle, and everybody has loads of fun in a warm community atmosphere. You can book a dogsled ride on Great Slave Lake, go snowshoeing or ice-fishing, and cheer the dog mushers on.

If You Have 7 Days: Head for ☒ **Baffin Island,** the heart of Canada's newest political entity, Nunavut. You can fly to Iqualuit from Montréal or Edmonton, via ☒ **Yellowknife** ⑥. Depending on when you go, you can book a jaunt by dogsled or snowmobile to see icebergs up close, try sea-kayaking or hike the tundra in search of wildflowers. Fly with a regional airline to ☒ **Iqaluit,** a good base from which to access **Auyuittuq National Park**; you won't have time for a full-scale backpacking expedition, but outfitters will arrange a quick introductory tour. Baffin is the true Arctic, inhabited for thousands of years by the Inuit, and haunting relics of past cultures can be seen everywhere.

When to Tour Wilderness Canada

June through August is the high season for visiting the far north. For the other nine months of the year, many businesses and outfitters close up shop, as much for lack of business as the length of winter. However, many northerners say that March and April, when daylight lengthens, winter begins its recession, and such snow sports as skiing and dogsledding are still possible, are good months to visit. September is another choice month, when the fall colors are brilliant and ducks, geese, and animals such as caribou begin their migrations. And as harsh—and dark—as other months are, they can be prime time for visitors fascinated by the spectral displays of the Northern Lights.

THE YUKON

The stories and events surrounding the Klondike Gold Rush of 1896 attract many visitors to the Yukon. While legendary, it was relatively short-lived (though gold continues to be mined profitably by Yukon companies). At the beginning of the 20th century, mining had already entered a new era—gold miners could no longer get rich from "just digging in the ground," as they had during the gold rush. Mechanization took over, and only the large operators who could afford the expensive machinery remained. Most of the gold rushers packed up their money bags and abandoned the Klondike for good. To fully explore the places and events of that time, a visit of seven days is a minimum. If a hike over the Chilkoot Trail is part of your plan, count on four days just for that leg of your trip; a stay of two weeks would be appropriate.

If backcountry adventure is more your style, guided hiking or canoeing trips run from 6 to 14 days. The Yukon is one of the premier wilderness adventure destinations in the world. A combination of hiking, biking, canoeing, rafting, and wildlife viewing ventures could keep you occupied for months. However, backcountry travelers should be advised: the Yukon's wilderness truly remains wild. If you are an inexperienced hiker (or canoeist, or snowmobiler) you should take a guided excursion into the backcountry. Even a hike over the Chilkoot Trail, which is monitored by the U.S. and Canadian Parks Services, is extremely rigorous.

Anyone expecting to see a lot of the Yukon will need to spend a considerable amount of time in a car or a considerable amount of money on airfare. If in a car, no matter which direction you head, expect to encounter considerable bus and RV traffic during the summer; the Yukon ranks with Alaska as one of the great road-touring regions of North America.

Whitehorse

❶ *2,400 km (1,488 mi) from Vancouver.*

Whitehorse began as an encampment near the White Horse Rapids of the Yukon River. It was a logical layover for gold rushers in the late 1890s heading north along the Chilkoot Trail (☞ South of Whitehorse to Skagway, Alaska, *below*) to seek their fortune in Dawson. Today's city of 23,000 residents is the Yukon's center of commerce, communication, and transportation, and is the seat of the territorial government. Though there's enough in the city to keep one occupied for a day or two, visitors should regard Whitehorse as a base camp from which to venture out to explore other parts of the Yukon.

The **Yukon Visitor Reception Centre** is the best place to pick up information on local lodging, restaurants, shops, attractions, and special events. A free, multi-image slide show on Yukon national parks and historic sites is an excellent introduction to the history of the territory. ✉ *2nd Ave and Hanson St.,* ☎ *867/667–3084,* FAX *867/667–3546.* ☾ *Daily 8:30–4:30, mid-May–mid-Sept., extended hours in summer.*

Just west of the Yukon Visitor Reception Centre is the scenic **Waterfront Walkway,** which runs along the Yukon River. Traveling downstream (north) you'll go by the old White Pass & Yukon Route building on Main Street. One of Whitehorse's landmark buildings, it was erected in 1900. Today it marks the start or finish (depending on the year) of the Yukon Quest Dogsled race.

The **MacBride Museum** encompasses over 5,000 square ft of artifacts, natural history specimens, historic photographs, maps, and diagrams from prehistory to the present. Exhibits provide an historical overview of the Yukon, from early exploration to the present, covering the trapping era and the gold rush. The museum has the largest public collection of Yukon gold in Canada. ✉ *1st Ave. and Wood St.,* ☎ *867/667–2709,* FAX *867/633–6607.* ▣ *$3.50.* ☾ *Mid-May–Labor Day, daily 10–6; mid-Sept.–mid-May, Tues, Wed., and Thurs, noon–4.*

★ The **S.S. Klondike,** a 210-ft stern-wheeler built in 1929, was the largest boat plying the Yukon River back in the days when it was the only transportation link between Whitehorse and Dawon. Though it sank in 1936, it was rebuilt a year later, and, after successive restorations, is dry-docked in its 1930s glory. ✉ *S. Access Rd. and 2nd Ave.,* ☎ *867/667–4511.* ▣ *$3.* ☾ *May–Sept., daily 9–6:30.*

The best time to visit the **Whitehorse Rapids Dam and Fish Ladder** is August, when, during the longest Chinook (King) salmon migration in the world, between 150 and 2,100 salmon use the ladder to bypass the dam. You can watch from a viewing platform. Interpretive displays

and tanks of freshwater fish are another source of entertainment. ✉
End of Nisutlin Dr., ☎ 867/633–5965. ✆ *Free.* ☉ *Late May–June,
daily 9–5; July–Labor Day, daily 8 AM–10 PM.*

Take a two-hour cruise aboard the **M.V. Schwatka** and experience
Miles Canyon as Jack London did when he was a pilot on its turbulent waters. It was this perilous stretch of the Yukon River, since tamed
by a dam, that determined the location of Whitehorse as the place where
gold rush stampeders stopped to "wring out their socks." ✉ *Schwatka
Lake, 2 mi south of downtown Whitehorse on Miles Canyon Rd.,*
☎ 867/668–4716, ☏ 867/633–5574. ✆ *$17.* ☉ *Cruises early–mid-
June and mid-Aug.–early Sept., daily at 2; mid-June–mid-Aug., daily
at 2 and 7.*

Two km (1 mi) past Schwatka Lake, where the M.V. *Schwatka* (☞ *above*)
is moored, is picturesque **Miles Canyon** (✉ Miles Canyon Road), a public park laced with hiking trails of varying difficulty. A 20-minute trail
leads to Canyon City, where gold rush stampeders stopped before
heading through the treacherous Whitehorse Rapids. Contact the
Yukon Visitor Reception Centre (☞ *above*) for information on trails.

At the **Yukon Beringia Interpretive Centre,** the territory's newest attraction, dynamic paleontological exhibits and interactive computer
kiosks present the story of the Yukon's ice-age past. The ancient remains of woolly mammoth, giant steppe bison, 400-pound beaver,
primeval horses, giant short-faced bear, scimitar cats, and American
lions are among the centre's wonders. ✉ *Mi 915.4, Alaska Hwy.,* ☎
867/667–5340. ✆ *Free.* ☉ *Late May–mid-Sept, daily (hours had not
been determined at press time).*

The **Yukon Transportation Museum** displays artifacts and exhibits of
the Yukon's unusual transportation legacy, from snowshoes to cars,
dogsleds to airplanes. ✉ *Mi 915.4, Alaska Hwy.,* ☎ 867/668–4792.
✆ *$3.50.* ☉ *Late May–mid-Sept., daily 9–6.*

At **Takhini Hot Springs,** off the Klondike Highway, there's swimming
in the spring-warmed water (suits and towels are available for rental),
horseback riding, and areas for picnicking. ✉ *Km 9.6 on Takhini Hot
Springs Rd., 10 km (6 mi) north of Whitehorse,* ☎ 867/633–2706. ☉
Summer, daily 7 AM–10 PM; call for winter hrs.

The **Yukon Wildlife Preserve** offers a foolproof way of photographing
rarely spotted animals in a natural setting. Visitors might spot elk, caribou, mountain goats, musk oxen, bison, and mule deer, and Dall,
mountain, and Stone sheep. Two-hour tours can be arranged only
through Gray Line. ✉ *Gray Line Yukon, 208G Steele St.,* ☎ 867/668–
3225. ✆ *$21.* ☉ *Tour mid-May–mid-Sept. daily.*

Dining and Lodging

$$$$　✕ **The Cellar.** The fact that the tables have tablecloths immediately makes
this restaurant high-class in the Whitehorse dining scene. Indeed, The
Cellar, in the cellar of the Edgewater Hotel (☞ *below*), with its high-
back Victorian chairs, approaches the standards of an elegant dining
room elsewhere in the world. Alaska king crab and prime rib highlight
the menu. This may be the only restaurant in the far north where a
jacket is advised. The Gallery upstairs serves breakfast and lunch on
a much more casual basis. ✉ *101 Main St., Edgewater Hotel,* ☎ 867/
667–2572. *Reservations essential. AE, DC, MC, V.*

$$$–$$$$　✕ **Angelo's Restaurant on Top.** Angelo's has the best views of any restau-
★　　rant in town. Classic Greek and Italian cuisine is complemented by such
local delicacies as king salmon, Arctic char, Alaskan halibut, and king
crab. The calamari is especially wonderful—it's the subject of local de-

bate what the chef's secret is. Prices are a bit high, but you're certain to have a good dining experience. ⊠ *202 Strickland St.,* ☎ *867/668–6266. Reservations essential. MC, V. No lunch.*

$$ **✕ Chocolate Claim.** Besides handmade chocolates and truffles, the
★ chefs at "The Claim" produce delectable soups and baked goods that run the gamut from the exotic, like fragrant Thai soups, to homespun surprises, such as pumpkin cheesecake. The company is always interesting, the sandwiches are highly recommended, and the coffee is the best in town. It's too bad "The Claim" isn't open for dinner. ⊠ *305 Strickland St.,* ☎ *867/667–2202. V. No dinner.*

$$ **✕ No Pop Sandwich Shop.** The white-brick exterior promises all of the atmosphere of a laundromat, but inside, the dining room—with straight-edge pine furniture and walls adorned with the work of local artists—is downright cozy. A small terrace in back with a tree rising through the roof adds character to dining al fresco. People wander in and out at all hours for take-out orders, a cup of coffee, or a full sit-down dinner. Alaskan halibut and Arctic char are among the rotating dinner specials; fresh-baked pastries are good any time of day. ⊠ *312 Steele St.,* ☎ *867/668–3227. MC, V.*

$–$$ **✕ Talisman Cafe.** The pine furniture may be typical of the far north, but the menu is all over the map, from veggie burgers to Middle Eastern dishes such as tabbouleh. The dining experience here is comfortable and low-key. The take-out service provides well-prepared salads and fresh-baked goods. ⊠ *2112 2nd Ave.,* ☎ *867/667–2736. MC, V.*

$$$$ **⌂ Inconnu Lodge.** Considering most backcountry lodges in the area, Inconnu Lodge is a statement in relative luxury. This fly-in lodge on the shores of McEvoy Lake, about 300 km (186 mi) northeast of Whitehorse, provides accommodations in modern log cabins. The principal activities are fishing and heli-hiking, although the lodge also arranges canoe trips on nearby rivers. Wildlife is plentiful, as attested by the considerable taxidermy displayed in the lodge living room. The lodge also acts as a jumping-off point for canoe and climbing trips into Nahanni National Park (☞ The Northwest Territories, *below*). Rates for five-day packages, including transportation to and from Whitehorse, are about $2,600 U.S. ⊠ *Box 4730, Y1A 4N6,* ☎ FAX *867/667–4070. 5 duplex cabins. MC, V.*

$$$$ **⌂ Oldsquaw Lodge.** The original lodge was built from materials salvaged from the Canol Trail by wildlife biologists. Those beginnings point to much of what the present-day lodge is all about: a place from which to access the Canol Trail, dedicated primarily to wildlife viewing. The basic lodge program consists of daily hikes (in some cases helicopter assisted) on the open tundra in search of wildlife ranging from grizzly bears to falcons. The lodge also arranges mountain-biking trips on the Canol Trail and cross-country skiing in spring. Lodging is in six outlying cabins. Rates for weekly packages begin at $2,000 per person. ⊠ *Bag Service 2711, Y1A 4K8,* ☎ FAX *867/668–6732. 6 cabins.*

$$$ **⌂ Westmark Whitehorse Hotel.** If it weren't for all the tour-bus baggage to trip over in the hallways, this would be a fine place to stay. Rooms are attractively decorated with dark-wood furnishings and include such nice touches as coffee makers. The hotel even has its own vaudeville show, the *Frantic Follies,* a revue playing heavily on Gold Rush themes. The restaurant can get crowded. There's a gift shop and a travel agency on the premises. ⊠ *2nd Ave. and Wood St., Box 4250, Y1A 3T3,* ☎ *867/668–4700 or 800/544–0970,* FAX *867/668–2789. 181 rooms, 5 suites. Restaurant, lounge, barbershop, beauty salon. AE, DC, MC, V.*

$$ **⌂ Edgewater Hotel.** This small hotel on a quiet end of Main Street is a good alternative to the Westmark for those trying to avoid the tour-bus bustle. The lobby is small and the passageway to the rooms is a bit narrow and awkward, but the rooms are large with modern furnishings. They are also somewhat on the dark side, but when daylight stretches well into the night, this might be an asset. ⊠ *101 Main St., Y1A 2A7,* ☎ *867/667–2572,* FAX *867/668–3014. 30 rooms, 2 suites. Restaurant, lounge. AE, DC, MC, V.*

$$ 🏨 **High Country Inn.** This inn offers the budget traveler the best value in Whitehorse, without a large compromise in comfort. All of the rooms are clean, well maintained, and nicely decorated in light pastel colors. Some of the rooms are small or strangely laid out, so it's worth taking a look at what's available before you commit. The lobby, restaurant, and lounge are cozy, and the location is close to the S.S. *Klondike* and the public swimming pool. The Yukon Mining Company saloon on the outdoor deck is a favorite Friday night gathering spot. ⊠ *4051 4th Ave., Y1A 1H1,* ☎ *867/667–4471 or 800/554–4471,* FAX *867/667–5457. 100 units. Restaurant, lounge, laundry. AE, DC, MC, V.*

Golf
Mountain View Golf Course (⊠ Range Rd., Box 5883, ☎ 867/633–6020), an 18-hole, par-72 course that's open May through September, has real grass and greens.

Shopping
Native-made clothing, local artwork, and indigenous crafts ranging from moose-hair tuftings to beadwork are available at **Yukon Native Products** (⊠ 4230 4th Ave., ☎ 867/668–5955). **Murdoch's Gem Shop** (⊠ 207 Main St., ☎ 867/668–7867) is the Yukon's largest manufacturer of gold nugget. **Yukon Gallery** (⊠ 2093 2nd Ave., ☎ 867/667–2391) sells limited-edition art prints by Yukon artists. Original sculptures and paintings by local craftspeople can be found at **Arctic Memories** (⊠ 4194A 4th Ave., ☎ 867/633–2111).

South of Whitehorse to Skagway, Alaska

Route 2, which runs south out of the Yukon into British Columbia and on to Alaska, takes you through an interesting succession of geological zones. From Carcross, the first town of interest on this excursion, you'll pass through the alpine tundra of the White Pass and the coastal rain forest of the Alaskan Panhandle. By the time the road begins descending steeply into Skagway, the landscape changes dramatically to a heavily vegetated world of glacially carved fjords.

White Pass & Yukon Route
An alternative to driving from Whitehorse to Skagway is the White Pass & Yukon Route, a combined bus-and-rail trip. The train travels 1¾ hours to Fraser, British Columbia, then a bus completes the trip to Whitehorse in another 2½ hours. A three-hour round-trip is also available, starting and ending in Skagway. Nobody ever regrets a ride on this historic railway past blue glaciers and rushing waterfalls (even if they do grumble about the price before taking the trip). ⊠ *Box 435, Skagway, AK 99840,* ☎ *907/983–2217 or 800/343–7373,* FAX *907/983–2734.* 🚂 *One-way Skagway to Whitehorse, $95 U.S.; round-trip Summit Excursion $75 U.S.* ☉ *Departures mid-May–mid-Sept. daily.*

Chilkoot Trail
Another alternative to automobile travel between Whitehorse and Skagway is backpacking on the 54-km (33-mi) Chilkoot Trail, a three- to five-day historic trip through some spectacular scenery. Hikers begin their journey in Dyea on the Alaskan coast and ascend through rain forest, across alpine tundra, and into boreal forest. Along the way are

the scattered shovels and graves of gold rushers who traveled this route a century ago.

Though the trail never reaches the Yukon, it is vitally linked with Yukon history: during the Klondike Gold Rush, prospectors trekked over Chilkoot Pass to Bennett, where they built their own boats and sailed across Bennett and Tagish lakes to the headwaters of the Yukon River. The boats that weren't wrecked in Miles Canyon or the White Horse or Five Finger rapids eventually arrived in Dawson City.

Reservations are required to hike the Chilkoot Trail. For information on fees contact **Canadian Heritage, Parks Canada** (✉ Yukon National Historic Sites, Room 205, 300 Main St., Whitehorse, Yukon Territory Y1A 2B5, ☎ 867/667–3910 or 800/661–0486).

Carcross

② *74 km (46 mi) from Whitehorse.*

Originally named Caribou Crossing after the herds of caribou that passed through it, Carcross is one of the Yukon's most picturesque towns. Be sure to spend a few minutes walking along the shores of **Bennett Lake,** where thousands of gold rush stampeders landed after a rough journey on the windy waters. Near town is the **Carcross Desert,** the smallest desert in the world.

Skagway

③ *180 km (112 mi) from Whitehorse.*

Skagway is host to cruise ships traveling up the Alaskan coast. The town is known for Jefferson Randolph Smith, otherwise known as "Soapy" Smith, a notorious gold rush character. Soapy and his gang of renegades made a fine living out of fleecing gold rush stampeders. One of the tricks they used to swindle the innocent was the soap trick (hence the nickname) for which Soapy would wrap bars of soap with bills of money—there would always be a one hundred dollar bill and a couple of twenties in the box of bars. Then he would go to an establishment and ask the men to try their luck and buy a bar of soap for $5. Two of Soapy's own men would be in the crowd and would eagerly volunteer. Once Soapy's cronies received the bars wrapped in the big bucks, the rest of the poor dupes followed suit, but with less profitable results. Soapy's thieves and hand artists eventually won him control over Skagway. He was shot in July of 1898 by Frank Reid, who was also killed in the exchange of gunfire. Both of their graves can be seen in the Skagway cemetery. When you walk down Broadway today, scattered with restored buildings and historic re-creations, you'll see a scene not appreciably different from what the prospectors saw in the days of 1898.

DINING AND LODGING

$$$ ✕ **Stowaway Cafe.** This quaint building, located at the beginning of Skagway's cruise ship dock, is a great place to indulge in some local seafood and scenery. Try the Ho Chi Hilbo Dungeness crab, the Texas barbecue, or one of the fabulous soups. The view of the small boat harbor is a delight, and if you're lucky you may even spot one of the local sea otters sunning itself on the beach. ✉ *Box 189, 205 Congress Way, Skagway, AK 99840,* ☎ *907/983–3463. V, MC.*

$$–$$$ ✕▣ **Skagway Inn Bed & Breakfast.** Each room in this downtown inn
★ has a Victorian motif with antiques and cast-iron beds; some have mountain views. The building was constructed in 1897 and is thus one of Skagway's oldest. The inn's summer-only restaurant, Lorna's at the Skagway Inn, is considered by many to be Skagway's finest. Owner

and chef Lorna McDermott is a graduate of Le Cordon Bleu. ⊠ *Box 500, 7th Ave. and Broadway, Skagway, AK 99840,* ☎ *907/983–2289,* FAX *907/983–2713. 12 rooms. Restaurant. D, MC, V.*

$$ ✕🍽 **Golden North Hotel.** Alaska's most historic hotel was built in
★ 1898 in the heyday of the gold rush—golden dome and all—and has been lovingly restored to reflect that period. Pioneer Skagway families have contributed gold-rush furnishings to each of the hotel's rooms, and the stories of those families are posted on the walls of each unit. Popular choices in the Golden North Restaurant include sourdough pancakes for breakfast; soups, salads, and sandwiches for lunch; salmon or other seafood for dinner. ⊠ *Box 343, 3rd Ave. and Broadway, Skagway, AK 99840,* ☎ *907/983–2294,* FAX *907/983–2755. 32 rooms. Restaurant, lobby lounge. AE, DC, MC, V.*

Kluane National Park

160 km (99 mi) west of Whitehorse.

Kluane (pronounced kloo-AH-nee) combines with neighboring Wrangell–St. Elias National Park in Alaska and Tatshenshini Provincial Park in British Columbia to form the largest expanse of contiguous national-park land in the world. Glaciers up to 100 km (62 mi) long stretch from the huge ice fields of the interior, comprising the largest nonpolar ice mass in the world. Canada's highest mountain, Mt. Logan (19,550 ft), is another of the park's natural wonders. Few visitors, other than experienced mountaineers (climbers must receive authorization from the Park Superintendent), get a full sense of Kluane's most extraordinary terrain as neither roads nor trails lead into the interior. A helicopter or fixed-wing flight over the Kluane ice fields is well worth the price on a clear day. Expect to pay approximately $100 per person—fixed-wing flights are slightly cheaper, but they can't offer the maneuverability of a helicopter flight. Many visitors content themselves with exploring the front ranges, which have impressive mountains with abundant wildlife—Dall sheep, black bears, and grizzly bears are the most noteworthy species.

The frontcountry trail system of Kluane National Park is the most extensive in the far north, facilitating everything from half-day hikes to multiday backpacking excursions. It's possible to make a five-day backpacking trip on marked trails, with opportunities for off-trail scrambling on mountaintops affording good views of distant peaks and glaciers. Most marked hiking trails follow lake shorelines or glacially carved river basins and are relatively easy to negotiate. Be sure to pick up a tent-camping permit and free food-storage canisters at the Park Headquarters (☞ *below*); keep in mind that this is bear country, and all bear precautions—especially storing food in canisters—must be taken.

The town of Haines Junction marks the junction of the Haines and Alaska Highways and is the headquarters of the **Kluane National Park Reserve** (⊠ Box 5495, Haines Junction, ☎ 867/634–7250, FAX 867/634–7265), the most logical place to begin your excursion into the park. A free 25-minute slide presentation provides an excellent introduction to the region's geology, flora, and fauna, and the amiable staff is well-armed with valuable information concerning the condition of the many hiking trails—including any recent bear sightings. Day hikers should check in for a summer schedule of guided hikes. More ambitious hikers can backpack from the **Sheep Mountain Visitor Center** (⊠ Mi 1019, Alaska Hwy., ☎ 867/634–2251) up the Slims River valley to the toe of the Kaskawulsh Glacier, a 27-km (17-mi) jaunt. The Sheep Mountain Center, open from May through September, is an outpost of Kluane headquarters within the park's borders.

Dining and Lodging

$$$–$$$$ ✕⌺ **Raven Motel.** The Raven, Haines Junction's finest dining and lodging establishment, has crisp rooms, tastefully designed in a European style and—unbelievably—room service. Dining in the restaurant on the second floor is a treat for the eyes and appetite. Fresh local salmon and lake trout, homemade pasta, juicy steaks, and fresh herbs will gratify your taste buds as the beautiful mountain views of Kluane's front ranges delight your eyes. ⌧ *Box 5470, Alaska Hwy., Haines Junction, Y0B 1L0,* ☎ *867/634–2500,* FAX *867/634–2517. 12 rooms. CP. MC, V.*

$–$$ ✕⌺ **Cozy Corner.** The name is anything but original, yet there is a genuine coziness about this small motel. The rooms are unusually large—big enough for a bed and sofa bed—although the bathrooms are surprisingly small. Some of the rooms' small windows have fabulous views of the front ranges of Kluane National Park. ⌧ *Alaska Hwy. and Haines Rd., Box 5406, Haines Junction, Y0B 1L0,* ☎ *867/634–2511,* FAX *867/634–2119. 12 rooms. AE, MC, V.*

Outdoor Activities and Sports

Be sure to drop in on the **Kluane Park Adventure Center** (⌧ Box 5479, Haines Junction, Y0B 1L0, ☎ FAX 867/634–2313), next to the Mountain View Restaurant on the Alaska Highway. The center, which operates in summer, is a one-stop booking service for accommodations and a variety of activities, including flight-seeing, river rafting, trail rides, and nature walks, and rents canoes and bikes. Horse-packing trips in the Slims River valley can also be arranged.

Watson Lake

❹ *450 km (279 mi) east of Whitehorse.*

Gateway city for travelers heading northwest along the Alaska Highway, Watson Lake's most remarkable feature is the **Signpost Forest;** during the construction of the Alaska Highway in 1942, a homesick U.S. soldier put up a proud sign indicating the name of his hometown as well as the mileage and direction. Since then, other visitors have followed suit to the tune of more than 30,000 signs.

Lodging

$$ ⌺ **Big Horn Hotel.** Watson Lake's newest and nicest hotel is in the downtown area. Large rooms are creatively decorated with forest-theme draperies and bedspreads and wooden headboards. The whirlpool suites are especially decadent, without being prohibitively expensive. ⌧ *Box 157, Alaska Hwy., Y0A 1C0,* ☎ *867/536–2020,* FAX *867/536–2021. 29 rooms. Coin laundry. AE, MC, V.*

$–$$ ⌺ **Watson Lake Hotel.** On the western edge of Watson Lake, this hotel and its motel units provide basic services and clean, neat guest rooms at reasonable prices. Three units have kitchenettes. Log walls and exposed-stone accents add to the comfortable rustic atmosphere. ⌧ *Box 370, Y0A 1C0,* ☎ *867/536–7781,* FAX *867/536–2724. 48 units, 1 suite. Dining room, lounge, sauna, laundry. AE, DC, MC, V.*

Dawson City

❺ *536 km (332 mi) north of Whitehorse.*

Dawson City was the epicenter of gold fever at the turn of the century. Preservationists have done an admirable job of not only restoring many of the city's historic buildings but also enforcing a zoning code that requires newly built structures to adopt facades conforming to a turn-of-the-century look. If it weren't for the presence of cars and camera-toting tourists strolling along Dawson's streets in summer, you might just feel like you had entered the Gold Rush era.

The **Visitor Reception Centre** at Front and King streets (✉ Box 389, Dawson City, ☎ 867/993–5566, FAX 867/993–6415) covers everything from historical minutiae to lodging availability. Walking tours and historic presentations take place daily.

Built in 1899 the **Palace Grand Theatre** was show-time central during the Gold Rush days, staging everything from opera to vaudeville. It was restored in the 1970s by the Canadian Parks Service and today is the home of the **Palace Revue,** a musical show based on Gold Rush history. ✉ *King St. between 2nd and 3rd Aves.,* ☎ *867/993–5575.* ✉ *$15–17.* ☉ *Show mid-May–mid-Sept., nightly 8 PM except Tues.*

The construction of the **Old Post Office** in 1900 was a symbolic affirmation of Dawson's permanence as a legitimate city rather than a boomtown of opportunism. The post office today effectively captures an aura of Dawson life at the turn of the century, and philatelists may want to purchase commemorative stamps. ✉ *3rd Ave. and King St.,* ✉ *Free.* ☉ *June–Sept., daily noon–5.*

The **Dawson City Museum** chronicles the Gold Rush and includes exhibits on the material culture of the local Han native people, steam locomotives, and the paleontology of the region. The genealogical library is invaluable to visitors trying to trace relatives who traveled to Dawson during the Gold Rush. ✉ *Box 303, 5th Ave. between Mission and Turner Sts.,* ☎ *867/993–5291,* FAX *867/993–5839.* ✉ *$3.50.* ☉ *Mid-May–mid-Sept., daily 10–6.*

At **Jack London Cabin and Interpretive Center,** you can visit the cabin in which the writer entertained miners with his knowledge of the classics during the winter of 1897. Works such as *The Call of the Wild* and *White Fang* were inspired by the time he spent in the Yukon wilds. The Interpretive Center houses an exhibit of historic photographs chronicling London's life. ✉ *Jack London Interpretive Center, 8th Ave. and 1st St.,* ☎ *867/993–5575.* ✉ *Free.* ☉ *Late May–mid-Sept., daily 10–6.*

Robert Service, primarily a poet, has been dubbed "Bard of the Klondike." Originally from England, he came to the Yukon in the early 1900s, well after the Gold Rush was over. Before coming to Dawson, Service worked in Whitehorse at the Canadian Imperial Bank of Commerce. There he wrote "The Shooting of Dan McGrew," his most famous poem. The small **Robert Service Cabin** is a good representation of what a lot of Dawson cabins looked like during and after the Klondike Gold Rush. The sod roof even bears raspberries in summer. ✉ *Robert W. Service Cabin, 8th Ave. and Hanson St.,* ☎ *867/993–7228.* ✉ *$2.50.* ☉ *June–mid-Sept., daily 9–5.*

If you want a firsthand feel for river travel, board the **Yukon Queen,** the 58-ft-long twin deck vessel docked along Front Street, which makes the 173-km (107-mi) trip westward to Eagle, Alaska, in approximately five hours. One-way travelers may opt to return to Dawson by bus. Meals are included in the price of the trip. ✉ *Box 420, Dawson City,* ☎ *867/993–5599; 208G Steele St., Whitehorse,* ☎ *867/668–3225 or 800/544–2206.* ✉ *$85 one-way, $138 round-trip.* ☉ *Departures mid-May–mid-Sept. daily.*

Dawson really got its start at the gold-mining sites just east of town. Huge mounds of rock and slag along the roadside attest to the considerable amount of earth turned over in search of the precious metal.

The most famous of many mining sites is **Bonanza Creek,** 1 km (½ mi) south of Dawson City, which produced several million-dollar claims in the days when gold went for $16 an ounce. A brass plaque on Bonanza Creek Road marks the **Discovery Claim,** staked by George Carmack in August of 1896, when he and his companions, Skookum Jim and Dawson Charlie, discovered the gold that sparked the great Klondike Gold Rush. The creek is so rich in minerals that it is still being mined today.

Those who want to try their luck at gold-panning can rent the necessary gear for $5 at **Claim 33** (⊠ Mi 7, Bonanza Creek Rd., ☎ 867/993–5804). You're guaranteed some gold, but don't expect to strike it rich.

Well worth a visit is **Dredge No. 4,** 16 km (10 mi) up Bonanza Creek Road from Claim 33. During the summer, daily tours are conducted through the dredge, which was used to dig up the creek bed and sift gold from gravel during the height of Bonanza Creek's largesse. ⊠ *Mi 7.8 Bonanza Creek Rd.,* ☎ *867/993–7228.* ⊲ *$5.* ⊙ *June–mid-Sept. daily.*

Dining and Lodging

$$$ ✕ **Jack London Grill.** This restaurant in the Downtown Hotel is one of the most attractive dining rooms in Dawson. The decor evokes the urbane atmosphere of a turn-of-the-century men's club, with dark-wood siding reaching halfway up walls adorned by framed mirrors and prints. Steaks are served in three sizes. For Dawson diners looking for a touch of civility and formality, this is a good choice. ⊠ *Downtown Hotel, 2nd Ave. and Queen St.,* ☎ *867/993–5346. AE, DC, MC, V.*

$$$ ✕ **Marina's.** You'd think being so far north, you'd be inspired to order something more interesting than pizza. But the fact of the matter is, Marina's thick-crusted pizzas are first-rate and reasonably priced. There are other entrées, but it's the pizza that makes Marina's so popular. Because of the location across from the Westmark, the dining room can fill up if there's a bus tour in town (and in the summer, there usually are a few). ⊠ *5th Ave. between Princess and Harper Sts.,* ☎ *867/ 993–6800. MC, V.*

$$ ✕ **Klondike Kate's.** The line at Klondike Kate's can sometimes get a
★ little intimidating, but the food is extremely good. Mexican and Middle Eastern dishes are often on the menu, and the smoked local king salmon is a constant standout. A large, covered, outdoor deck is an airy, casual spot for a meal on a warm summer's day or evening. The main decorative statement on the deck is a large map of the world, onto which guests are invited to stick pins to mark their hometowns. ⊠ *3rd Ave. and King St.,* ☎ *867/993–6527. V.*

$$–$$$ ⊞ **Triple J Hotel.** This "hotel" does indeed come in three parts: a main hotel, a separate motel, and several outlying cabins. The motel, little more than a large mobile home, is not worth considering. The cabins, which include kitchenettes, are a nice choice; their small porches with bright flowers add comfort. But the best choice is one of the spacious, upstairs rooms of the hotel, quaintly decorated in reproduction antiques. Though these rooms may be a bit dark, this can be an asset at this latitude in summer. The kitchen is one of the better hotel kitchens; you can order your pizza to go or stay in the outdoor seating area. ⊠ *Box 359, 5th Ave. and Queen St., Y0B 1G0,* ☎ *867/993–5323, 800/661– 0405, or 800/764–3555;* ℻ *867/993–5030. 47 units. Restaurant, lounge. AE, MC, V. Closed late Oct.–mid-Apr.*

$$–$$$ ⊞ **Westmark Inn.** Though the Westmark suffers from tour-bus overload, rooms are clean, modern, and spacious. The operative concept here is to create the familiar basic-American-hotel-room comforts be-

hind a turn-of-the-century facade dictated by Dawson zoning codes. ⊠ *Box 420, 5th Ave. and Harper St., Y0B 1G0,* ☎ *867/993–5542 or 800/544–0970,* ℻ *867/993–5623. 131 rooms. Restaurant, lounge, coin laundry. AE, DC, MC, V. Closed mid-Sept.–mid-May.*

$$ ☒ **Downtown Hotel.** This hotel consists of a main building of 35 units, which is open all year, and an annex of 25 units, open only in summer, across the street from the main hotel. The rooms in the main complex are marginally better. This hotel operates an airport shuttle service, which is especially valuable as there are no taxis in Dawson. ⊠ *Box 780, 2nd Ave. and Queen St., Y0B 1G0,* ☎ *867/993–5346, 800/661–0514, or 800/765–4653;* ℻ *867/993–5076. 60 rooms. Dining room, lounge, hot tub, meeting rooms, airport shuttle. AE, DC, MC, V.*

$–$$ ☒ **Dawson City Bunkhouse.** While accommodations in the Bunkhouse are spare (no TVs or room phones), they are comfortable and clean. Some rooms have private baths; others share public washrooms. For budget-minded travelers, this is the best deal in town. ⊠ *Front and Prince Sts., Bag 4040, Y0B 1G0,* ☎ *867/993–6164,* ℻ *867/993–6051. 32 rooms. MC, V. Closed Labor Day–May.*

Nightlife and the Arts

THE ARTS

The **Dawson City Music Festival** (⊠ Dawson City Music Festival Association, Box 456, Y0B 1G0, ☎ 867/993–5584), featuring a variety of musicians from Alaska, Yukon, and the rest of Canada, is held each July. This is one of the most popular events in the north, so tickets can be extremely difficult to get. Write to the Festival Association in spring to request tickets.

NIGHTLIFE

Diamond Tooth Gertie's Gambling Hall offers a glimpse of the frolicking times of the Gold Rush. "Gertie" and her cancan dancers put on three shows nightly while grizzled miners sit at the poker table. Gamblers can enjoy real slot machines, blackjack, red dog, and roulette. Note: no minors are permitted. ⊠ *4th Ave. and Queen St.,* ☎ *867/993–5575.* ☜ *$4.75.* ☉ *Mid-May–mid-Sept., daily 7 PM–2 AM.*

Running

A Labor Day weekend event that often draws a big crowd and the enthusiastic participation of Dawson City residents is the **Great Klondike Outhouse Race** (contact the Klondike Visitors Association, ☎ 867/993–5575), in which runners pull home-built "outhouses" on wheels through the streets of Dawson.

Side Trip from Dawson City

TOP OF THE WORLD HIGHWAY

The 108-km (67-mi) trip west along the Top of the World Highway to the Yukon/Alaska border provides expansive vistas. The road partially lives up to its name, set as it is along ridge lines and high-mountain shoulders, but the dirt-and-gravel surface (which creates plenty of dust thanks to RV traffic) can hardly be called a highway. The northernmost border crossing on land between Canada and the United States is along this route; the U.S. side is in Polar Creek, Alaska—population: two.

Dempster Highway

The Dempster Highway's arctic tundra and mountain scenery is always beautiful, but in late August, it is a mind-expanding experience. Autumn comes early to the tundra and colors the landscape in searing reds and vivid yellows that can make your eyes ache. The gentle rolling hills will arouse any hiker's desire for exploration. One of the finest hikes off the Dempster is into the bizarre rock formations of the **Tombstone Mountains.**

The 766-km (475-mi) journey north to Inuvik (☞ The Arctic North *in* the Northwest Territories, *below*) on the Dempster Highway is a much more adventurous and ambitious undertaking than driving the Top of the World Highway. The only public highway in Canada to cross the **Arctic Circle,** it passes through a tundra landscape that is severe, mountainous, and ever changing.

In its southern extreme, the highway passes first by the rugged Tombstone Mountains and then into the more rounded ranges of the Ogilvie Mountains. The route crosses Eagle Plains (approximately halfway between Dawson and Inuvik and a good stopping point for gas and supplies) before reaching the Arctic Circle, marked by a sign. From here the highway passes through the Richardson Mountains and enters the flatlands surrounding the Mackenzie River Delta before reaching Inuvik. This is certainly one of *the* great wilderness drives in North America, but because there are no services for 370 km (229 mi) between the junction of the Dempster and Klondike highways and Eagle Plains, travelers should be prepared to cope with possible emergencies.

Gold City Tours (✉ Box 960, Dawson City, Y0B 1G0, ☎ 867/993–5175, ℻ 867/993–5261) has summer bus service between Dawson and Inuvik.

THE NORTHWEST TERRITORIES

Canada's vast Northwest Territories stretch across four time zones from the mountainous Yukon border to Baffin Island. Set apart from the rest of Canada by the 60th parallel, this region's northernmost boundary lies at the highest tip of Ellesmere Island, at latitude 83 degrees north, only about 400 km (248 mi) from the Geographic North Pole. Most of this huge land is uninhabited. Outside the regional centers from which travel is usually based—Yellowknife, Inuvik, Rankin Inlet, and Iqualuit—settlements are small and isolated. Wilderness and the experience of life on the frontier is the lure for most travelers. Until 1999 the Territories will remain a single political entity governed by the multicultural legislature whose elected members converge at the Yellowknife's Legislative Assembly.

Yellowknife

6 *2,595 km (1,609 mi) from Vancouver.*

Yellowknife began as a rough-and-tumble mining camp back in 1934, when gold was discovered on the North Arm of Great Slave Lake. A center of government since the 1960s, it still thrives on hard-rock mining and, lately, diamonds—Lac de Gras, 350 km (217 mi) northwest of town, is the site of the Western Hemisphere's first diamond mine. In anticipation of the success of the mine, the Northwest Territories' capital city is growing quickly, from a population of 12,000 in 1991 to an estimated 18,000 in 1997.

Downhill from downtown Yellowknife lies the **Old Town,** built around the rocky peninsula that juts into Great Slave Lake (☞ *below*). You can stroll the expanse of it along Franklin Avenue in 15 minutes or drive down, perhaps taking time to turn off and explore the winding streets of historic neighborhoods first settled in the 1930s and 1940s. One of them is called the **Woodyard.** Once a thriving fuel depot run by a pioneer businessman, it's now known for its eccentric cabins, log

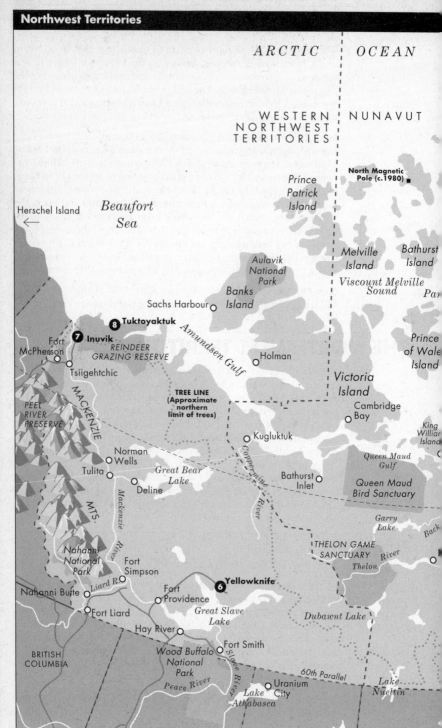

ARCTIC OCEAN

WESTERN
NORTHWEST
TERRITORIES

NUNAVUT

North Magnetic
Pole (c.1980) ■

Prince
Patrick
Island

Herschel Island
←

*Beaufort
Sea*

Melville
Island

Bathurst
Island

Aulavik
National
Park

*Viscount Melville
Sound*

Par

Banks
Island

Sachs Harbour

Prince
of Wale
Island

8 **Tuktoyaktuk**

Fort
McPherson

7 **Inuvik**

*REINDEER
GRAZING RESERVE*

Holman

Tsiigehtchic

Amundsen Gulf

Victoria
Island

Cambridge
Bay

King
Williar
Island

*PEEL
RIVER
PRESERVE*

TREE LINE
(Approximate
northern
limit of trees)

Kugluktuk

MACKENZIE

Norman
Wells

*Great Bear
Lake*

Coppermine River

Bathurst
Inlet

*Queen Maud
Gulf*

Tulita

Deline

Queen Maud
Bird Sanctuary

MTS.

Mackenzie River

*Garry
Lake*

Back

*THELON GAME
SANCTUARY*

River

*Nahanni
National
Park*

Fort
Simpson

Thelon

6 **Yellowknife**

Nahanni Butte

Liard R.

Fort
Providence

*Great Slave
Lake*

Dubawnt Lake

Fort Liard

Hay River

Fort Smith

*BRITISH
COLUMBIA*

*Wood Buffalo
National
Park*

Slave River

60th Parallel

*Lake
Nueltin*

Peace River

Uranium
City

*Lake
Athabasca*

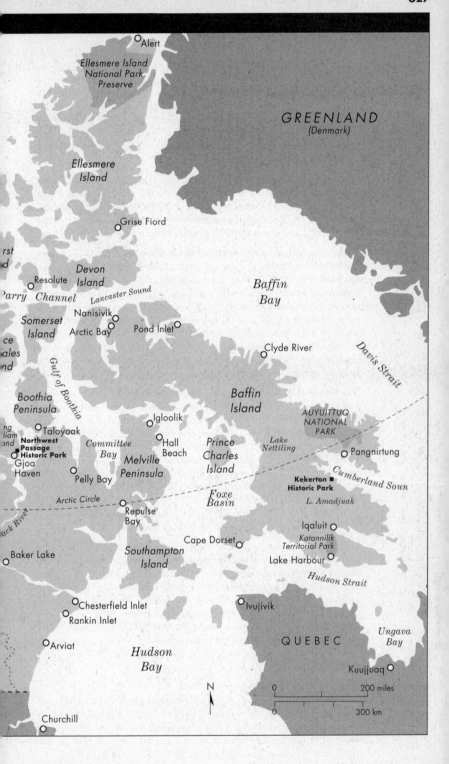

Alert

Ellesmere Island
National Park
Preserve

GREENLAND
(Denmark)

Ellesmere
Island

Grise Fiord

Devon
Island

rst
d

Resolute

Baffin
Bay

Parry Channel
Lancaster Sound

Somerset
Island

Nanisivik

ce
ales
nd

Arctic Bay

Pond Inlet

Clyde River

Davis Strait

Gulf of Boothia

Boothia
Peninsula

Baffin
Island

AUYUITTUQ
NATIONAL
PARK

ng
liam
nd

Taloyoak

Igloolik

**Northwest
Passage
■ Historic Park**

Committee
Bay

Hall
Beach

Prince
Charles
Island

Lake
Nettling

Pangnirtung

Gjoa
Haven

Melville
Peninsula

Cumberland Soun

Pelly Bay

**Kekerton ■
Historic Park**

Arctic Circle

Foxe
Basin

L. Amadjuak

ack River

Repulse
Bay

Iqaluit

Cape Dorset

Katannilik
Territorial Park

Baker Lake

Southampton
Island

Lake Harbour

Hudson Strait

Chesterfield Inlet

Ivujivik

Rankin Inlet

Ungava
Bay

Arviat

QUEBEC

Hudson
Bay

N

Kuujjuaq

Churchill

0   200 miles

0   300 km

dwellings, and Yellowknife's most famous street, Ragged Ass Road, named after hard-luck prospectors.

If you proceed north on Franklin Avenue, it becomes McDonald Drive. From McDonald Drive turn left onto Weaver Road and right onto Ingraham Drive, which travels over **The Rock,** a steep Precambrian outcropping where miners first pitched their tents 64 years ago. There are many interesting houses here, and you can't miss the stairs that climb to the Pilot's Museum, a hilltop marker built in honor of the bush flyers who opened up the north. The climb is worth it: There's an unparalleled 360° view of Great Slave Lake (☞ *below*), neighboring islands, and Yellowknife itself.

To continue exploring the Old Town, head back down to McDonald Drive and follow it around The Rock. You'll pass the **Float Plane Base,** heavy with traffic coming in and going out to mining exploration camps. You can also cross the causeway to **Latham Island,** where a handful of B&Bs and down-to-earth eateries mingle with upscale housing.

★ It's hard to overstress the beauty of **Great Slave Lake,** the sixth largest freshwater lake in North America. Clean, cold, and deep, it dwarfs Yellowknife and the few other communities along its shores. The lake's East Arm, a two- to three-day sail from Yellowknife, is prime cruise country, with dramatic cliffs rising from narrow bays. For those unsure of their navigation skills, hiring a skipper is recommended, since many of the lake's small bays are still uncharted. It's easy to arrange an excursion on the lake with any of the local operators (☞ Outdoor Activities and Sports, *below*) who provide sail and motorboat charters, cruises, and sightseeing trips.

The **Prince of Wales Northern Heritage Centre,** on the shore of Frame Lake, is just a few minutes from downtown. It houses extensive displays of such northern artifacts as caribou-hide parkas and beaded Dene clothing, and Inuit tools and stone carvings, as well as exhibits on exploration and settlement. The aviation section, documenting the north's history of flight, is especially worthwhile, as are exhibits devoted to the search for the Northwest Passage, developed over 400 years as Europeans hunted for an Arctic route to the Orient, mapping the polar islands and the coast as they did so. ✉ *Opposite City Hall,* ☎ *867/873–7551,* ℻ *867/873–0205.* 🎫 *Free.* ☉ *June–Aug., daily 10:30–5; Sept.–May, Tues.–Fri. 10:30–5, weekends noon–5.*

A few hundred meters west of the Heritage Centre, the glass-domed **Legislative Assembly of the Northwest Territories** rises from the boreal forest. The newest such building in Canada, the architecturally splendid legislature offers free guided tours in summer. You can visit the council chamber and see the translation booths that permit debates to be carried out in nine official languages. Also of interest is the ceremonial mace, a symbol of government made of Yellowknife gold, musk ox horns, and a slender narwhal tusk. ✉ *Turn left off Hwy. 3, just northwest of town.* ☎ *867/669–2200 or 800/661–0784.* ☉ *Tours weekdays 10:30, 1:30, 3:30; Sun. 1:30.*

Dining and Lodging

$$$$ ✕ **Factor's Club.** This big, airy dining room in the Explorer Hotel (☞ *below*) is highlighted by a central, circular hearth and includes on its menu such unusual northern delicacies as musk ox chops. Dinners are pricey, but lunches and Sunday brunch are bargains. ✉ *48th St. and 49th Ave.,* ☎ *867/873–3531 or 800/661–0892. AE, MC, V.*

$$$ ✕ **Bistro on Franklin.** The descent of the narrow stairs leading into the Bistro's basement setting feels vaguely ominous—more like heading down to check out the boiler room than going out to dinner. But the dining

area brings relief: Low lighting, tablecloths, and wait staff in bow ties lend a touch of formality to an otherwise casual place. Chicken and pasta dishes are excellent, including the chicken pesto pasta, a boneless breast of chicken in a pesto cream sauce, served with fettuccine; fish dishes such as Arctic char are less reliable. ⊠ *4910 Franklin Ave.,* ☎ *867/873–3991. MC, V.*

$$ ✕ **Bullock's Fish and Chips.** With its log-cabin walls and rough-hewn furniture, Bullock's has a warm, rustic atmosphere. The dining room has only five or six tables and the kitchen is effectively part of it. As for the specialty of the house, the name tells all; the fries are hand cut, and the whitefish and trout are fresh from Great Slave Lake. ⊠ *4 Lessard Dr.,* ☎ *867/873–3474. MC, V.*

$$ ✕ **Prospector Bar and Grill.** In a brand-new waterfront building not far from the famous Wildcat Cafe, this comfortable eatery features a menu of standbys: steak sandwiches, salads, and eggs Florentine. The Prospector doesn't have the Wildcat's history, but it does offer spectacular views across Back Bay, where colorful float planes boom in and out all summer long. ⊠ *3506 Wiley Rd.,* ☎ *867/920–7639,* ℻ *867/ 669–5781. MC, V.*

$$ ✕ **Wildcat Cafe.** The Wildcat is an institution as much as a restaurant, the sort of place that everybody who comes to town eventually visits. It has been around since 1937; the low-slung, log structure and split-log tables and benches inside lend to the aura of life at the frontier's edge. This is a place where strangers are expected to share tables. The food, ranging from fresh fish to vegetarian chili to caribou burgers, is excellent and modestly priced. Many people drop in at the Wildcat for coffee and desserts—mostly fresh-baked delectables. ⊠ *Doornbos La. and Wiley Rd.,* ☎ *867/873–8850. MC, V.*

$$$$ 🏨 **Bathurst Inlet Lodge.** Perhaps the most popular destination in the central Arctic, particularly for ornithologists, is this lone outpost on the tundra 49 km (30 mi) north of the Arctic Circle. Traveling by plane, boat, and foot from the lodge, guests typically spot musk oxen, Arctic foxes, wolves, falcons, and eagles. In late spring as many as a half million migrating caribou pass this way. Outings from the lodge include a hike (after a short airplane transfer) to **Wilberforce Falls,** the highest waterfall north of the Arctic Circle, where the Hood River cuts spectacularly through a series of gorges. In addition to weeklong naturalist tours, the lodge also outfits canoe or raft trips on nearby rivers and bays. Fees start at $2,400 per person for a 1-week stay, including flights to and from Yellowknife. ⊠ *Box 820 (AT7), 3618 McAvoy Rd., Yellowknife X1A 2N6,* ☎ *867/873–2595,* ℻ *867/920–4263. 15 rooms in lodge, 15 cabins. V. Closed early Aug.–late June.*

$$$$ 🏨 **Blachford Lake Lodge.** Many fishing lodges in the far north provide a minimum of services (unless patrons request otherwise) for guests seeking to keep vacation costs down. Blachford Lake Lodge is a good example of the genre. Guests are flown to and from the remote lodge (less than a half-hour flight from Yellowknife), where they stay in cabins and have the use of boats to venture out on the small lake. Guests are expected to bring and prepare their own food, as well as bring their own bedding and fishing tackle. The result is a cost that is generally under $120 per person per day (including the flights to and from the lodge), and less for groups—modest by fly-in fishing standards. The lodge is also open in winter for ice-fishing, snowmobiling, and dogsledding. ⊠ *Box 1568, X1A 2P2,* ☎ *867/873–3303,* ℻ *867/920–4013. 6 cabins sleep 14. V.*

$$$$ 🏨 **Frontier Fishing Lodge.** On the East Arm of Great Slave Lake near the Dene community of Lutsel K'e, Frontier Lodge is typical of a full-service fishing lodge. Guests are housed in outlying log cabins, in the

main lodge, and in comfortable rooms attached to the new conference and recreation building. Breakfast and dinner are served daily around a big table in the main lodge. Guides take guests to the best fishing waters on Great Slave as well as adjoining rivers and lakes, and lake trout exceeding 25 pounds are landed regularly. This is a lodge strictly dedicated to fishing; aside from reading or watching wolves feeding on dinner scraps, there is not much else to do except appreciate the lakeside wilderness setting. Packages, including flights to and from Yellowknife, begin at around $350 per day per person. ✉ *Box 32008, Edmonton, Alberta T6K 4C2,* ☎ *403/465–6843 or 403/370–3501,* FAX *867/466–3874. Shared indoor bathrooms. Capacity: 24 people. Sauna, shop, meeting facilities. Closed mid-Sept.–mid-June. MAP. No credit cards.*

$$$ **Explorer Hotel.** Atop a promontory overlooking Yellowknife, the Explorer is best recommended for its views of the city and surrounding bays of Great Slave Lake. Rooms are large and decorated with run-of-the-mill brown-veneer furniture, but they are bright and clean. ✉ *Box 7000, X1A 2R3,* ☎ *867/873–3531, 800/661–0892 in Canada,* FAX *867/873–2789. 128 rooms, 2 suites. 2 restaurants, lounge, airport shuttle. CP. AE, MC, V.*

$$$ **Yellowknife Inn.** The oldest hotel in a city where there isn't much that could be called old, the Inn has lavishly redone its lobby, which now opens into Centre Square shopping mall. Some of the older sections of the hotel complex have been demolished to make way for planned new facilities. The modern rooms are done in muted green and beige hues. The Mackenzie Lounge, with dark-wood paneling that lends it a clubby feel, is a nice place to meet for a drink before dinner. The restaurant serves bistro-style cuisine, and a complimentary continental breakfast for hotel guests. ✉ *Box 490, X1A 2N4,* ☎ *867/873–2601 or 800/661–0580,* FAX *867/873–2602. 125 rooms, 7 suites. Restaurant, lounge, shops, airport shuttle. CP. AE, DC, MC, V.*

$$ **Igloo Inn.** Don't expect much more here than a motel-style room at a decent price. Rooms are on the small side and have the basics—bed, bathroom, TV; many have kitchenettes. The Igloo is a perfectly good choice for budget-minded travelers laying over for a night before heading off to more adventurous ports of call in the territorial outback. ✉ *Box 596, 4115 Franklin Ave., X1A 2R3,* ☎ *867/873–8511,* FAX *867/873–5547. 44 rooms. Restaurant. AE, MC, V.*

$–$$ **Blue Raven.** The Blue Raven is the best of the several good bed-and-breakfast options in Yellowknife. Attractively set on a bluff at the edge of Old Town and overlooking Great Slave Lake, this is a good place for those who like their continental breakfast—served in a common room—with a view. Rooms are small, modern, clean, and quiet, set apart from one another by the home's three-story configuration. ✉ *37B Otto Dr., X1A 2T9,* ☎ *867/873–6328. 1 room with bath, 2 rooms share bath. CP. No credit cards.*

Nightlife and the Arts

Folk on the Rocks (✉ Box 326, X1A 2N3, ☎ 867/920–7806), a lakeside music festival held in mid-July, attracts musicians from throughout North America, as well as Dene and Inuit performers.

Raven Mad Daze (✉ Yellowknife Chamber of Commerce, ☎ 867/920–4944) takes place during summer solstice (the third week in June), when the sun's still out at midnight. Sidewalk sales, street vendors, concerts, and dances are part of the fun.

Boating

Sail North (✉ Box 2497, X1A 2P8, ☎ 867/873–8019) accommodates trips to Great Slave Lake with boat rentals and guided boat tours. The

M.S. Norweta (✉ N.W.T. Marine Group, 17 England Crescent, ☎ 867/ 873–2489) offers short outings, dinner cruises, and multiday cruises to the legendary East Arm of Great Slave Lake.

Shopping

CLOTHING

In a world where warm clothing is essential, parkas, mukluks, caribou-hide mittens, and the like are a fashion statement. **Polar Parkas** (✉ 5023 49th St., ☎ 867/873–3343) is the best place in Yellowknife to buy native-made parkas.

NATIVE ARTS AND CRAFTS

Northern Images (✉ Yellowknife Centre, 49th St. and 50th Ave., ☎ 867/873–5944, FAX 867/873–9224) sells a variety of native crafts and artwork, from sculpture to moose-hair tuftings to clothing, and has stores in several Canadian cities, including Whitehorse and Yellowknife. The **Arctic Art Gallery** (✉ 4801 Franklin Ave., ☎ 867/873–5666 or 800/661–0799, FAX 867/873–9155) has a selection of carvings, lithographic prints, and original paintings.

Departures from Yellowknife

Yellowknife is a transportation hub for outlying areas in the western Arctic. Sports lovers can set out from Yellowknife for backcountry lodges on the shores of Great Slave Lake or on one of the thousands of smaller lakes that, along with their barren rock underpinnings and scrub growth, are the principal geological constituents of the far north's interior. For driving excursions from Yellowknife, you can pass through Wood Buffalo National Park and Fort Smith to the south, and through Fort Liard to the west. This is not, generally speaking, a rousing scenic drive. Long stretches of road cutting through the low-lying, subarctic bush are highlighted by occasional waterfalls or the sight of wildlife near or on the highway.

Alexandra Falls

537 km (333 mi) south of Yellowknife.

Of the scenic waterfalls along the road between Yellowknife and Fort Smith, the most dramatic is Alexandra Falls, a few kilometers south of the town of Hay River, on Route 1 at the junction of Routes 1 and 2, where the Hay River drops 108 ft over limestone cliffs.

Wood Buffalo National Park

599 km (371 mi) south of Yellowknife.

The area where you're most likely to spot wildlife is Wood Buffalo National Park, straddling the Alberta/Northwest Territories border. Covering 44,807 sq km (17,026 sq mi), this is the largest national park in Canada, home, not surprisingly, to the world's largest free-roaming bison herd (about 5,000 total). It is also a summer nesting ground for many bird species, including bald eagles, peregrine falcons, and the exceedingly rare whooping crane. Much of the terrain—a flat land of bogs, swamps, salt plains, sink holes, and meandering streams and rivers— is essentially inaccessible to visitors, but a few frontcountry trails allow exploration. The park's visitor reception center in Fort Smith can provide information on interpretive programs and hikes. ✉ *Superintendent, Wood Buffalo National Park, Box 750, Fort Smith, Northwest Territories X0E 0P0,* ☎ *867/872–7900 or 867/872–7960,* FAX *867/872– 3910.*

Nahanni National Park
608 km (377 mi) west of Yellowknife.

The principal reason to head west from Yellowknife is to visit Nahanni National Park. The Mackenzie and Liard rivers, which join forces at Fort Simpson, are the region's approximate geographical dividers, separating the low-lying bush of the east and the mountains to the west. Access to Nahanni National Park is possible only by helicopter or plane; inside the park, canoes and rafts are the principal vehicles of travel. A well-maintained park campground near the falls facilitates overnight excursions. For a complete listing of air services, contact the **Nahanni National Park Reserve** (⊠ Box 348, Fort Simpson, X0E 0N0, ☎ 867/ 695–3151 or 867/695–2310, FAX 867/695–2446).

Perhaps the most impressive feature in the park is **Virginia Falls,** more than 410 ft high and about 656 ft wide—a thunderous wall of white water cascading around a central spire of rock. To get there contact Simpson Air (☞ Outdoor Activities and Sports, *below*), one of several plane and helicopter services that offer flightseeing trips to the falls.

The **Cirque of the Unclimbables** is another of Nahanni's spectacular features. This breathtaking cathedral of rock towers rising as much as 3,000 vertical ft does not entirely live up to its name, but the few who have made successful ascents here can be counted among the most proficient rock climbers in the world. Perhaps the biggest problem posed by this cirque is that it is nearly as unreachable as it is unclimbable.

It would be difficult to single out one river as *the* river to run in the far north. However, the **South Nahanni** is a logical choice. Two-week canoe trips can start from Rabbit Kettle Lake at the park's northwestern extreme, but require portage around Virginia Falls. Eight- to 12-day canoe or raft trips put in below Virginia Falls. White water along the way is minimal, so previous canoeing or rafting experience is not essential.

Outdoor Activities and Sports: Two reliable outfitters that lead guided boating trips in Nahanni National Park are **Nahanni River Adventures** (⊠ Box 4869, Whitehorse, Yukon Territory Y1A 4N6, ☎ 867/668– 3180) and **Nahanni Wilderness Adventures** (⊠ Box 4, Site 6, R.R. 1, Didsbury, Alberta T0M 0W0, ☎ 403/637–3843).

For those interested in mountaineering, **Simpson Air** (⊠ Box 260, Fort Simpson, Northwest Territories X0E 0N0, ☎ 867/695–2505, FAX 867/ 695–2925) can shuttle climbers into the Cirque of the Unclimbables from Fort Simpson.

The Arctic North

One doesn't "tour" the Arctic North in the usual sense of the word. Rather, the concept is more expeditionary: Choose a community—such as Inuvik, Rankin Inlet, Iqaluit, or Pangnirtung—as a base camp from which to make day or extended side trips. Lodging and transportation in the Arctic North tend to be expensive even by high-end northern standards, so that having a well-defined travel plan is critical to staying within a budget. Trip organizers and outfitters can be particularly helpful in tailoring a travel program to meet particular interests and budgets. Keep in mind that the prime Arctic travel season tends to be very short: Many visitor services and tour organizers operate only in July and August.

For experienced canoeists and kayakers, the Arctic's interior barren lands and coast hold a wealth of possibilities. The Coppermine River, a fairly easy-flowing river through the tundra, is a worthy destination, if for no better reason than a visit to Bloody Fall, the site of a 1771 massacre of Inuit by guides of the Northwest Passage explorer, Samuel Hearne. There is also a 16-km (10-mi) hiking trail along the river from the community of Kugluktuk (formerly Coppermine) to Bloody Fall.

Inuvik

7 *1,086 air km (673 air mi) northwest of Yellowknife.*

Inuvik overlooks the huge Mackenzie Delta where it meets the Beaufort Sea. The town's population of 3,000 mixes many major northern identities: the Gwich'in Dene, the Inuvialuit (western Inuit), and settlers from southern Canada. You can meet native people and experience their culture on guided tours to fishing and whaling camps with **Beufort Delta Tours** (✉ Box 2040, Northwest Territories X0E 0T0, ☎ 867/777–4881, FAX 867/777–4898).

DINING AND LODGING

$$$–$$$$ ✕🏨 **Finto Inn.** On the outskirts of Inuvik, at the junction of the Marine Bypass and Mackenzie Road, the Finto materializes as a two-story, square structure resembling a big box that might have been flown in by a helicopter sling and dropped on the spot. The wood siding somewhat softens the harsh edges. Elegance in accommodations is not a reason to stay at the Finto, but The Peppermill, the inn's restaurant, is generally considered Inuvik's best. The dining room overlooks green meadows and blue water; the menu features local foods, such as Arctic char and musk ox. Four of the rooms have kitchenettes; all have satellite TV. ✉ *Box 1925, Inuvik X0E 0T0,* ☎ *867/777–2647 or 800/661–0843,* FAX *867/777–3442. 44 rooms. Restaurant. AE, DC, MC, V.*

THE ARTS

The **Great Northern Arts Festival** (✉ Box 2921, X0E 0T0, ☎ 867/777–3536) in July features displays, workshops, demonstrations, and performances.

Tuktoyaktuk

8 *113 air km (70 air mi) north of Inuvik.*

Flying over Tuk Peninsula, you can see pingoes (odd conical landforms found only on the frozen borders of the Beaufort Sea), and caribou, from which the hamlet of Tuktoyaktuk derives its name, "the place where caribou cross." If you're interested in the culture of the north, Tuktoyaktuk, a small Inuvialuit (western Inuit) community a short flight north of Inuvik, is the place to experience an interesting blend of ancient culture and modern technology. Tours of Tuktoyaktuk are conducted by Arctic Tour Company (☞ Guided Tours *in* Wilderness Canada A to Z, *below*).

Banks Island

523 air km (324 air mi) northeast of Inuvik.

Banks Island, in the Mackenzie River Delta area, is best known for its large herd of musk oxen, now numbering in the thousands in **Aulavik National Park** (Parks Canada, Box 1840, Inuvik, X0E 0T0., ☎ 867/777–3248, FAX 867/777–4491). Arctic Tour Company (☞ Guided Tours *in* Wilderness Canada A to Z, *below*) conducts tours to Banks Island that include oxen and caribou watching.

Herschel Island

274 air km (170 air mi) northwest of Inuvik.

Tiny in comparison to the other islands that it shares the Beaufort Sea with, Herschel Island is an excellent base for sighting beluga and bowhead whales. It's also known for its abundant bird life, Arctic fox and polar bear dens, and wildflowers that grow from the seemingly barren tundra. Though it falls within Yukon's borders, this island is best accessed from Inuvik. Beaufort Delta Tours offers guided day-tours along the coast to Herschel, as does the Arctic Tour Company (☞ Guided Tours *in* Contacts and Resources, *below*).

Baffin Island
2,261 air km (1,402 air mi) east of Yellowknife.

Even northerners accustomed to the unique beauty of the Arctic wilderness speak of Baffin Island in tones of awe. It is a world of junctures: where mountains meet sea, where the climates of summer and winter may be experienced on the same day, where summer flowers bloom on green, tundra meadows amid ice-locked surroundings. It remains a stronghold of Inuit tradition despite the ever-increasing influences of modern culture. At least 3,000 years ago, the Thule, ancestors of the Inuit, migrated to the Canadian Arctic across the frozen Bering Sea. Later, whaling became a prime means of sustenance, both for Inuit and European hunters. A number of Baffin communities have exhibits or museums that chronicle whaling life.

Baffin tours start at the southeastern end of the island on Frobisher Bay in **Iqaluit,** which, like Inuvik and Yellowknife, is a point of reference and departure rather than a destination in itself. It is the transportation, communication, and government center of Canada's eastern Arctic, and will be the capital of Nunavut when the territorial division comes about in 1999.

From Iqaluit, visitors must choose a medium of travel: land or sea. In winter, of course, the land and sea merge under ice and snow, and April and May are the ideal months for those interested in cross-country skiing, dogsledding, or snowmobiling. Those who journey into the Baffin wilderness should have an adventurous spirit and a willingness to abide life in a world with virtually none of the trappings of civilization. While some tour organizers offer general sightseeing tours of the region, Baffin is best appreciated by those inclined (and physically fit enough) to rough it.

Sea kayaking is popular in summer in the bays and fjords of Baffin, populated by whales, narwhals, walruses, and seals. The jewel of Baffin, however, is **Auyuittuq National Park,** where rivers and glaciers have cut deep fjords and have carved out **Aksayook Pass** (formerly Pangnirtung Pass) between Cumberland Sound to the south and Davis Strait to the north. The 60-km (37-mi) pass is surrounded by jagged peaks exceeding 6,600 ft that jut up from glacial ice (glacial melt provides the water supply supporting the brief burst of summer wildflowers on the tundra lowlands). A marked trail leads through the pass, and in summer, backpacking groups regularly make the five- to seven-day journey. There are emergency shelters along the route, but this is still a trip only for those properly prepared and physically fit, given the length of the trip and the vagaries of climatic changes, even in mid-summer. All park visitors should sign up with a trip organizer and/or check in at the park headquarters in Pangnirtung for information on hiking in the park. For more information contact **Parks Canada** (✉ Eastern Arctic District, Box 1720, Iqaluit, Northwest Territories X0A 0H0, ☎ 819/979–6277). ✉ *Park headquarters, Pangnirtung NT,* ☎ *819/473–8828,* FAX *819/473–8612.* ☉ *July–Aug., weekdays 8:30–noon, 1–5, and 6–10; weekends 1–5 and 6–10; Sept.–June, weekdays 8:30–5.*

OFF THE BEATEN PATH   **ELLESMERE ISLAND NATIONAL PARK –** Even more adventurous visitors can head north from Baffin to this park, above 80° north latitude. Ellesmere, like Baffin, is intriguing as much for its climate as its landscape. Technically a "polar desert," the island, with an annual precipitation of about 2½ inches, is one of the driest places in the northern hemisphere; yet, because of the water-retaining effects of ice, parts of the island can support plant and wildlife. For more information, contact **Parks Canada** (⊠ Eastern Arctic District, Box 1720, Iqualuit, Northwest Territories X0A 0H0, ☎ 819/979–6277).

DINING AND LODGING

$$$ ✕⊞ **Discovery Lodge Hotel.** The lobby area of this hotel is brightened by skylights. An oddity here is that some rooms have trapezoidal beds, wider at the top than the bottom. The Granite Room, with its granite-slab tabletops, is perhaps the best restaurant in Iqualuit, noteworthy for its use of local ingredients, including Arctic char, Baffin Island shrimp, and scallops. ⊠ *Box 387, Iqualuit X0A 0H0,* ☎ *819/979–4433,* FAX *819/979–6591. 51 rooms, 1 suite. Dining room, lounge, laundry, airport shuttle. AE, DC, MC, V.*

$$$ ✕⊞ **Frobisher Inn.** In its brochure the inn promotes itself as being "part of an integrated, climate-controlled, indoor shopping and high-rise apartment complex." So much for the rustic charm of the far north. Rooms are boxlike and simply adorned with veneer-wood furnishings. Rooms in the front offer good views of Frobisher Bay and Iqualuit. There's no airport shuttle, but the inn will reimburse you for the taxi ride. The dining room specializes in Canadian Arctic cuisine. ⊠ *Box 610, Iqualuit X0A 0H0,* ☎ *819/979–2222,* FAX *819/979–0427. 48 rooms. Dining room, lounge, pool, sauna, laundry. AE, DC, MC, V.*

OUTDOOR ACTIVITIES AND SPORTS

Canada North Outfitting (⊠ Box 3100, 87 Mills St., Almonte, Ontario K0A 1A0, ☎ 613/256–4057, FAX 613/256–4512) leads six-day trips, supported by dogsleds, in the wilderness of Baffin Island. **Ecosummer Expeditions** (⊠ 1516 Duranleau St., Vancouver, British Columbia V6H 3S4, ☎ 800/465–8884, FAX 819/669–3244) leads guided backpacking trips on Baffin Island and Ellesmere Island.

The **Midnight Sun Marathon** (⊠ Nanisivik Mines, ☎ 819/436–7502, FAX 819/436-7435; contact Lois Sutherland or Dawn McConnell) takes place on the July 1 long weekend at Nanisivik, at the northern extreme of Baffin Island near the Inuit community of Arctic Bay. It's a series of four races ranging from 10 to 84 km (6 to 52 mi) that draws runners from Canada, the United States, Europe, and Australia.

WILDERNESS CANADA A TO Z

Arriving and Departing

By Bus

Greyhound Lines of Canada (⊠ 10324 103rd St., Edmonton, Alberta T5J 0Y9, ☎ 403/421–4211, FAX 867/425–7829) provides service from Edmonton to Hay River, Northwest Territories. Greyhound also has service from Edmonton or Vancouver to Whitehorse in the Yukon.

By Car

It hardly bears saying that getting to the Yukon or the Northwest Territories by car calls for a good deal of driving. The best route into the region is the Alaska Highway (Route 97 in British Columbia), accessible from Edmonton via Routes 43, 34, and 2 and from Vancouver via Route 1. After Fort Nelson, British Columbia, Routes 7, 1, and 3 lead to Yellowknife; the Alaska Highway (Route 1 in the Yukon) continues on to Whitehorse. The good news is that with so few roads in the region, it's difficult to make a wrong turn. Be aware that as you drive farther north, gas stations are few and gas is expensive—in some cases exceeding 70¢ a liter, or roughly U.S. $2.40 a gallon. With relatively little lodging along the way, you might want to embark on the trip in a camper or recreational vehicle.

By Plane

Whitehorse International Airport, 5 km (3 mi) from downtown Whitehorse, is the Yukon's major airport. **Yellowknife Airport,** the main facility for the Northwest Territories, is 5 km (3 mi) northwest of the city center. Many smaller settlements—notably Cambridge Bay, Inuvik, Rankin Inlet, and Iqualuit—have regular service.

Air Canada (☎ 800/776–3000, 800/387–2710 in MI and NY, 800/663–9100 in ID and WA) is one of two major air carriers with connecting service from the United States to points in the Northwest Territories and the Yukon. **NWT Air** (☎ 867/920–2500 or 800/661–0789, FAX 867/873–3272), an Air Canada affiliate, provides service within the Yukon and the Northwest Territories.

Canadian Airlines (☎ 800/426–7000) is the other major carrier with connecting service from the United States. Canadian Airlines also has a scheduling agreement with **American Airlines** (☎ 800/433–7300) for connections from the United States. Canadian Airlines affiliate, **Canadian North** (☎ 800/426–7000), is responsible for most of the connecting service throughout the far north. For the eastern Northwest Territories, **First Air** (☎ 613/839–1247 or 800/267–1247) offers extensive service from Montréal and Ottawa.

Getting Around

By Bus

Frontier Coachlines (✉ 328 Old Airport Rd., Yellowknife, Northwest Territories X1A 3T3, ☎ 867/873–4892, FAX 867/669–9197) offers service connecting Fort Smith, Fort Providence, Hay River, and Yellowknife. In the Yukon **Alaska Direct Transport and Bus Line** (✉ 4051 4th Ave., Whitehorse, Yukon Territory Y1A 1H1, ☎ 867/668–4833, FAX 867/667–7411) provides scheduled service from Whitehorse to many Alaskan communities, as well as Haines Junction, Dawson City, Burwash Landing, and Beaver Creek. **Alaskon Express** (✉ 208-G Steele St., Whitehorse, Yukon Territory Y1A 2C4, ☎ 867/668–3225, FAX 867/667–4494 or 800/544–2206) has service between Whitehorse and cities in Alaska from mid-May to mid-September. **Norline Coaches** (✉ 34 MacDonald Rd., Whitehorse, Yukon Territory Y1A 4L2, ☎ 867/633–3864, FAX 867/633–3849) provides service between Dawson City and Whitehorse.

By Car

In general, exploring by car is a more sensible idea in the Yukon than in the Northwest Territories. The only part of the Northwest Territories with any kind of highway network is the southwest, where the roads are paved from the Alberta border to Fort Providence, and again near Yellowknife. Farther north and west, they are hard-packed gravel. Many highways in the Yukon are paved, the scenery along the way considerable, and roadside services more extensive.

Anyone traveling by car in the far north should take precautions. Distances from one service area to the next typically exceed 160 km (99 mi), so make sure to monitor your fuel gauge. At least one good spare tire is essential, and many residents of the region carry more, especially when traveling long distances. Another common practice is to cover headlights, grills, and even windshields with plastic shields or wire mesh to protect against flying gravel. It is advisable to carry extra parts (air filter, fan belt, and fluids). Be sure your vehicle has good suspension, even if you plan to stick to the major highways; shifting permafrost regularly damages paved roads, and ruts and washboard occasionally appear on unpaved roads, especially after periods of bad weather.

Winter driving requires extra precautionary measures. Many a far-north resident can tell you a tale about overnighting on the road and waiting out fierce weather. Take along emergency survival gear, including ax, shovel, flashlight, plenty of matches, kindling (paper or wood) to start a fire, sleeping bag, rugged outerwear, and food. Also, you should have a properly winterized car, with light engine oil and transmission fluid, a block heater, tire chains, and good antifreeze.

In the Northwest Territories there are several river crossings without real bridges. In summer you ride a free car ferry; in winter you cross on ice bridges. However, there are the seasons known as "freeze-up" and "break-up," in fall and spring, respectively, when ice bridges aren't solid but rivers are too frozen for ferries to run. For daily ferry reports in summer (late May to late October in the south Mackenzie region, June to late October farther north), call: for Routes 1 and 3, ☎ 867/695–2018 or 800/661–0751; for the Dempster Highway, ☎ 867/979–2678 or 800/661–0752. For winter road conditions, call: for Routes 1 through 7, ☎ 867/874–2208 or 800/661–0750; for the Dempster Highway, ☎ 867/979-2678 or 800/661–0752. For Yukon Highway information, call ☎ 867/667–8215.

By Plane
Once outside the Yukon and the southwest section of the Northwest Territories, flying is pretty much the only way to get around in wilderness Canada. Canadian North, First Air, and NWT Air (☞ Arriving and Departing by Plane, *above*) have regularly scheduled service within the territories. All airlines listed below also offer charter air service, an option worth considering for groups of four or more and usually the only option for getting to and from remote wilderness areas. Check with regional tourist offices for other charter services operating locally and regionally.

THE YUKON
Alkan Air (✉ Box 4008, Whitehorse, Yukon Territory Y1A 3S9, ☎ 867/668–2107 or 800/661–0432, FAX 867/667–6117). **Air North** (✉ Box 4998, Whitehorse, Yukon Territory Y1A 4S2, ☎ 867/668–2228, FAX 867/667–6224).

THE NORTHWEST TERRITORIES
For a copy of the *Air Tourism Guide to the NWT,* call 800/661–0788.

Air Nunavut (✉ Box 1239, Iqaluit, Northwest Territories X0A 0H0, ☎ 819/979–2900, FAX 819/979–2425); **Buffalo Airways** (✉ Box 1479, Hay River, Northwest Territories X0E 0R0, ☎ 867/874–3333, FAX 867/874–3572; Box 2015, Yellowknife X1A 2R3, ☎ 867/873–6112, FAX 867/873–8393); **North-Wright Air** (✉ Bag Service 2200, Norman Wells, Northwest Territories X0E 0V0, ☎ 867/587–2288 or 800/661–0702, FAX 867/587–2962); **Ptarmigan Airways** (✉ Box 100, Yellowknife, Northwest Territories X1A 2N1, ☎ 867/873–4461 or 800/661–0808, FAX 867/873–5209).

Contacts and Resources
Car Rental
Rental agencies in both Whitehorse and Yellowknife typically rent trucks and four-wheel-drive vehicles in addition to cars. **Budget** (☎ 800/

268–8900) has locations at both the Whitehorse and Yellowknife airports. **Tilden** (☎ 800/387–4747) also has locations at both the Whitehorse and Yellowknife airports. **Avis** (☎ 800/879–2847) rents at the Yellowknife airport. **Norcan** (☎ 800/661–0445 or 800/764–1234) rents at the Whitehorse airport.

Emergencies

For emergency services in either the Yukon or the Northwest Territories, dial 0 for the operator and explain the nature of the emergency. You will then be connected with the police, fire department, or medical service, as needed. In Yellowknife the Royal Canadian Mounted Police number is 867/669–1111. You may also call a toll-free emergency number, 867/667–5555 for the Royal Canadian Mounted Police or 867/667–3333 for medical assistance, from anywhere in the Yukon. In Whitehorse dial 911 for emergencies.

It's a good idea when traveling in the far north—especially in remote wilderness areas and if unescorted by a guide or outfitter—to give a detailed itinerary to someone at home or to the police, to facilitate emergency rescue.

Guided Tours

THE YUKON

Access Yukon (✉ 212 Lambert St., Whitehorse, Yukon Territory Y1A 1Z4, ☎ 867/668–1233 or 800/661–0468, FAX 867/668–5595) offers river trips, canoe rentals, heli-hiking, camper and 4X4 rentals, trail riding, sightseeing, wilderness lodges, and transportation throughout the Yukon. **Beringia Tours** (✉ 4109 4th Ave., Suite 103, Whitehorse, Yukon, Y1A 1H6, ☎ 867/668–7391, FAX 867/668–4359) offers packaged and independent tours throughout the Yukon including the Western Arctic, northern B.C., and Alaska, and including hiking, kayaking, canoeing and other adventure excursions. **Canadian River Expeditions** (✉ #37 9571 Emerald Dr., Whistler, British Columbia V0N 1B9, ☎ 604/938–6651 or 800/898–7238, FAX 604/938–6621) offers 6- to 12-day wilderness and natural history expeditions on the Tatshenshini, Alsek, and Firth rivers. **Gray Line Yukon** (✉ 208-G Steele St., Whitehorse, Yukon Territory Y1A 2C4, ☎ 867/668–3225, FAX 867/667–4494) offers package tours to Dawson City and Alaska as well as Yukon River cruises and sightseeing tours of the Yukon Wildlife Preserve near Whitehorse. **Holland America Westours** (✉ 300 Elliott Ave. W, Seattle, WA 98119, ☎ 206/281–3535 or 888/252–7524, FAX 206/281–0631) offers bus tours through the Yukon and Alaska as well as combined cruise-ship/bus tours that link in Skagway, Alaska. In the Yukon, **Kanoe People** (✉ Box 5152, Whitehorse, Yukon Territory Y1A 4S3, ☎ 867/668–4899, FAX 867/668–4891) arranges guided and unguided canoe trips, from a half day to two weeks, for several rivers. **Rainbow Tours** (✉ 212 Lambert St., Whitehorse, Yukon Territory Y1A 1Z4, ☎ 867/668–5598 or 800/661–0468, FAX 867/668–5595) runs tours by van throughout the Yukon.

THE NORTHWEST TERRITORIES

Adventure Canada (✉ 14 Front St. S, Mississauga, Ontario L5H 2C4, ☎ 800/363–7566, FAX 905/271–5595) is particularly active in arranging trips to the Arctic North, including excursions to the North Pole. Backpacking, dogsledding, canoeing, and wildlife viewing are among the activities arranged. **Arctic Tour Company** (✉ 181 Mackenzie Rd., Box 2021, Inuvik, Northwest Territories X0E 0T0, ☎ 867/777–4100, FAX 867/777–2259) offers various Inuvik-based day and multiday trips in the area of the Mackenzie River Delta, including Tuktoyaktuk. **Beaufort Delta Tours** (✉ Box 2040, Inuvik NT X0E 0T0, ☎ 867/777–4100) arranges tours to various stops in the Mackenzie River Delta area. **Black Feather Wilderness Adventures** (✉ 1960 Scott St., Ottawa, Ontario K1Z 8L8, ☎ 613/722–9717 or 800/661–6659, FAX 613/722–0245) is one of the largest adventure-travel companies in Canada, leading backpacking trips in Auyuittuq National Park on Baffin Island, canoeing and hiking trips in Nahanni National Park, and canoe trips on rivers in the Mackenzie Mountains. They can also arrange cycling trips. **NWT Air** (☞ Arriving and Departing by Plane, *above*), in conjunction with local operators and outfitters, has an extensive tour program throughout the Northwest Territories. The **N.W.T. Marine Group** (✉ 17 England Crescent, Yellowknife, Northwest Territories X1A 3N5, ☎ FAX 867/873–2489) arranges a 1,600-km (992-mi) 10-day cruise along the Mackenzie River from Yellowknife to Inuvik aboard the **M.S. Norweta**. **Qimmiq Adventures** (✉ Box 1181, Yellowknife, Northwest Territories X1A 2N8, ☎ 867/920–7533) offers both lodge-based tours and winter-camping tours in the Yellowknife area between February and April. **Raven Tours** (✉ Box 2435, Yellowknife, Northwest Territories X1A 2P8, ☎ 867/873–4776, FAX 867/873–4856) offers a variety of tours in the Northwest Territories, including tours of Yellowknife and Northern Lights tours in winter. **Subarctic Wildlife Adventures** (✉ Box 685, Fort Smith, Northwest Territories X0E 0P0, ☎ 867/872–2467, FAX 867/872–2126) specializes primarily in wildlife-viewing tours in the Northwest Territories, but also offers canoeing, hiking, and dogsledding. **Whitewolf Adventure Expeditions** (✉ Suite 41, 1355 Citadel Dr., Port Coquitlam, British Columbia V3C 5X6, ☎ 604/944–5500) is one of several outfitters who guide trips on the Coppermine River.

Hospitals and Clinics

Limited medical services, with staff on call 24 hours a day, are available at nursing stations in all communities. **Yellowknife** (✉ Stanton Yellowknife Hospital, ☎ 867/920–4111). **Fort Smith** (✉ Fort Smith Health Care Centre, ☎ 867/872–2713). **Hay River** (✉ H. H. Williams Memorial Hospital, ☎ 867/874–6512). **Inuvik** (✉ Inuvik Regional Hospital, ☎ 867/777–2955). **Iqaluit** (✉ Baffin Regional Hospital, ☎ 819/979–5231). **Watson Lake** (✉ Watson Lake Hospital, ☎ 867/536–4444). **Whitehorse** (✉ Whitehorse General Hospital, ☎ 867/667–8700).

Late-Night Pharmacies

Pharmacies are located in major settlements of the Yukon and Northwest Territories, but late-night service is rare; after hours contact the nearest hospital or nursing station (☞ Hospitals and Clinics, *above*). If you have a preexisting medical condition requiring special medication, be sure you are well supplied; getting unusual prescriptions filled can be difficult or impossible.

Lodging Reservations Services

Inns North (✉ Arctic Cooperatives Ltd., Hotel Division, 1645 Inkster Blvd., Winnipeg, Manitoba R2X 2W1, ☎ 204/697–1625, FAX 204/697–1880) is an organization of native-operated hotels throughout the far north that may be particularly helpful to visitors planning travels in some of the region's smaller communities. The **Northern Network of Bed and Breakfasts** (✉ Box 94-T, Dawson City, Yukon Territory Y0B 1G0, ☎ FAX 867/993–5648) publishes a brochure with more than 80 listings in the Northwest Territories and the Yukon as well as Alaska and British Columbia.

RV Rentals

Ambassador Motor Home & Recreational Services Ltd. (✉ Box 4147, 37 Boswell Crescent, Whitehorse, Yukon Territory Y1A 3S9, ☎ 867/667–4130, FAX 867/633–2195. **CanaDream Inc.** (✉ 110 Copper Rd., Whitehorse, Yukon Territory Y1A 2Z6, ☎ 867/668–3610, FAX 867/668–

3795). **Klondike Recreational Rentals** (✉ Box 5156, Whitehorse, Yukon Territory Y1A 4S3, ☎ 867/668–2200 or 800/665–4755, FAX 867/668–6567). **Frontier Rentals** (✉ Box 1088-EG, Yellowknife, Northwest Territories X1A 2N7, ☎ 867/873–5413, FAX 867/873–5417).

Visitor Information

YUKON

Tourism Yukon (✉ Box 2703, Whitehorse, Yukon Territory Y1A 2C6, ☎ 867/667–5340, FAX 867/667–3546) publishes the Yukon "Vacation Guide" and is the central source of information for the entire area.

Tourism Yukon also operates six regional information centers that are open mid-May to mid-September: **Beaver Creek** (✉ Km 1,934 [Mi 1,202] on Alaska Hwy., ☎ 867/862–7321). **Carcross** (✉ Old Train Depot, ☎ 867/821–4431). **Dawson City** (✉ Front and King Sts., ☎ 867/993–5566). **Haines Junction** (✉ Kluane National Park Headquarters, ☎ 867/634–2345). **Watson Lake** (✉ Rtes. 1 and 4, ☎ 867/536–7469). **Whitehorse** (✉ 100 Hanson St. and 2nd Ave., ☎ 867/667–2915).

NORTHWEST TERRITORIES

For general information and a copy of the Northwest Territories "Explorers' Guide," contact **N.W.T. Arctic Tourism** (✉ Box 1320-EX, Yellowknife, Northwest Territories, X1A 2L9, ☎ 867/873–7200 or 800/661–0788, FAX 867/873–0294). For a complete guide to traveling in the new territory of Nunavut—including Baffin Island, the central Arctic coast and islands, Ellesmere Island, and the Keewatin—contact **Nunavut Tourism** (Box 1450, Iqualuit, Northwest Territories X0A 0H0, ☎ 800/491–7910 or 867/979–6551, FAX 867/979–1261). For more detailed information, regional tourist offices may be of further help.

For information on the Arctic coastal region, contact the **Arctic Coast Visitors Centre** (✉ Box 91, Cambridge Bay, Northwest Territories X0C 0C0, ☎ 867/983–2224, FAX 867/983–2302). For Baffin and Ellesmere islands, contact the **Baffin Regional Visitor Centre** (✉ Box 1450, Iqualuit, Northwest Territories X0A 0H0, ☎ 819/979–4636, FAX 819/979–2929). For the southwest, contact the **Big River Tourism Association** (✉ Box 185, Hay River, Northwest Territories X0E 0R0, ☎ 867/874–2422, FAX 867/874–6020). For the Keewatin region, which includes the western coast of Hudson Bay, contact **Travel Keewatin** (✉ Box 328, Rankin Inlet, Northwest Territories X0C 0G0, ☎ 819/645–2618, FAX 819/645–2320). For the Nahanni River area and the west, contact **Nahanni-Ram Tourism Association** (✉ Box 177, Fort Simpson, Northwest Territories X0E ONO, ☎ 867/695–3182 or 867/695–3307, FAX 867/695–2511). For Yellowknife and its environs, contact the **Northern Frontier Regional Visitors Association** (✉ Box 1107, 4807 49th St., Yellowknife, Northwest Territories X1A 3T5, ☎ 867/873–3131, FAX 867/873–3654). For the far northwest, contact the **Western Arctic Tourism Association** (✉ Box 2600, Inuvik, Northwest Territories X0E 0T0, ☎ 867/777–4321, FAX 867/777–2434).

INDEX

Index

NOTES

Fodor's Travel Publications

Available at bookstores everywhere, or call 1–800–533–6478, 24 hours a day.

Gold Guides

U.S.

Alaska

Arizona

Boston

California

Cape Cod, Martha's Vineyard, Nantucket

The Carolinas & Georgia

Chicago

Colorado

Florida

Hawai'i

Las Vegas, Reno, Tahoe

Los Angeles

Maine, Vermont, New Hampshire

Maui & Lāna'i

Miami & the Keys

New England

New Orleans

New York City

Pacific North Coast

Philadelphia & the Pennsylvania Dutch Country

The Rockies

San Diego

San Francisco

Santa Fe, Taos, Albuquerque

Seattle & Vancouver

The South

U.S. & British Virgin Islands

USA

Virginia & Maryland

Walt Disney World, Universal Studios and Orlando

Washington, D.C.

Foreign

Australia

Austria

The Bahamas

Belize & Guatemala

Bermuda

Canada

Cancún, Cozumel, Yucatán Peninsula

Caribbean

China

Costa Rica

Cuba

The Czech Republic & Slovakia

Eastern & Central Europe

Europe

Florence, Tuscany & Umbria

France

Germany

Great Britain

Greece

Hong Kong

India

Ireland

Israel

Italy

Japan

London

Madrid & Barcelona

Mexico

Montréal & Québec City

Moscow, St. Petersburg, Kiev

The Netherlands, Belgium & Luxembourg

New Zealand

Norway

Nova Scotia, New Brunswick, Prince Edward Island

Paris

Portugal

Provence & the Riviera

Scandinavia

Scotland

Singapore

South Africa

South America

Southeast Asia

Spain

Sweden

Switzerland

Thailand

Toronto

Turkey

Vienna & the Danube

Special-Interest Guides

Adventures to Imagine

Alaska Ports of Call

Ballpark Vacations

Caribbean Ports of Call

The Official Guide to America's National Parks

Disney Like a Pro

Europe Ports of Call

Family Adventures

Fodor's Gay Guide to the USA

Fodor's How to Pack

Great American Learning Vacations

Great American Sports & Adventure Vacations

Great American Vacations

Great American Vacations for Travelers with Disabilities

Halliday's New Orleans Food Explorer

Healthy Escapes

Kodak Guide to Shooting Great Travel Pictures

National Parks and Seashores of the East

National Parks of the West

Nights to Imagine

Rock & Roll Traveler Great Britain and Ireland

Rock & Roll Traveler USA

Sunday in San Francisco

Walt Disney World for Adults

Weekends in New York

Wendy Perrin's Secrets Every Smart Traveler Should Know

Fodor's Special Series

Fodor's Best Bed & Breakfasts

America

California

The Mid-Atlantic

New England

The Pacific Northwest

The South

The Southwest

The Upper Great Lakes

Compass American Guides

Alaska

Arizona

Boston

Chicago

Colorado

Hawaii

Idaho

Hollywood

Las Vegas

Maine

Manhattan

Minnesota

Montana

New Mexico

New Orleans

Oregon

Pacific Northwest

San Francisco

Santa Fe

South Carolina

South Dakota

Southwest

Texas

Utah

Virginia

Washington

Wine Country

Wisconsin

Wyoming

Citypacks

Amsterdam

Atlanta

Berlin

Chicago

Florence

Hong Kong

London

Los Angeles

Montréal

New York City

Paris

Prague

Rome

San Francisco

Tokyo

Venice

Washington, D.C.

Exploring Guides

Australia

Boston & New England

Britain

California

Canada

Caribbean

China

Costa Rica

Egypt

Florence & Tuscany

Florida

France

Germany

Greek Islands

Hawaii

Ireland

Israel

Italy

Japan

London

Mexico

Moscow & St. Petersburg

New York City

Paris

Prague

Provence

Rome

San Francisco

Scotland

Singapore & Malaysia

South Africa

Spain

Thailand

Turkey

Venice

Flashmaps

Boston

New York

San Francisco

Washington, D.C.

Fodor's Gay Guides

Los Angeles & Southern California

New York City

Pacific Northwest

San Francisco and the Bay Area

South Florida

USA

Pocket Guides

Acapulco

Aruba

Atlanta

Barbados

Budapest

Jamaica

London

New York City

Paris

Prague

Puerto Rico

Rome

San Francisco

Washington, D.C.

Languages for Travelers (Cassette & Phrasebook)

French

German

Italian

Spanish

Mobil Travel Guides

America's Best Hotels & Restaurants

California and the West

Major Cities

Great Lakes

Mid-Atlantic

Northeast

Northwest and Great Plains

Southeast

Southwest and South Central

Rivages Guides

Bed and Breakfasts of Character and Charm in France

Hotels and Country Inns of Character and Charm in France

Hotels and Country Inns of Character and Charm in Italy

Hotels and Country Inns of Character and Charm in Paris

Hotels and Country Inns of Character and Charm in Portugal

Hotels and Country Inns of Character and Charm in Spain

Short Escapes

Britain

France

New England

Near New York City

Fodor's Sports

Golf Digest's Places to Play

Skiing USA

USA Today The Complete Four Sport Stadium Guide

WHEREVER
YOU TRAVEL,
*H*ELP IS NEVER
FAR AWAY.

From planning your trip to providing travel assistance

along the way, American Express® Travel Service Offices

are always there to help you do more.

Canada

American Express Travel Service
Canada Trust Tower, Main Floor
421-7th Av. S.W.
Calgary
403/261-5982

American Express Travel Service
Southcentre Mall
100 Anderson Road S.E.
Calgary
403/278-0205

American Express Travel Service
Manulife Building
10180-101 Street
Edmonton
403/421-0608

American Express Travel Service
200 Graham Avenue-Level 2
Winnipeg
204/949-9349

American Express Travel Service
2000 Peel Building
1141 De Maisonneuve West
Montreal
514/284-3300

American Express Travel Service
46 Garneau
Quebec
418/692-0997

American Express Travel Service
Royal York Hotel, #133-134
100 Front Street West
Toronto
416/363-3883

American Express Travel Service
666 Burrard Street
Vancouver
604/669-2813

do more AMERICAN EXPRESS
Travel